THE OXFORD HANDBOOK OF

TERRORISM

THE OXFORD HANDBOOK OF

TERRORISM

Edited by

ERICA CHENOWETH,
RICHARD ENGLISH,
ANDREAS GOFAS,
and
STATHIS N. KALYVAS

Great Clarendon Street, Oxford, OX2 6DP,
United Kingdom

Oxford University Press is a department of the University of Oxford. It furthers the University's objective of excellence in research, scholarship, and education by publishing worldwide. Oxford is a registered trade mark of Oxford University Press in the UK and in certain other countries

First Edition published in 2019
Impression: 1

Published in the United States of America by Oxford University Press
198 Madison Avenue, New York, NY 10016, United States of America

British Library Cataloguing in Publication Data
Data available

Library of Congress Control Number: 2018949742

ISBN 978–0–19–873291–4

Printed and bound by
CPI Group (UK) Ltd, Croydon, CR0 4YY

Acknowledgments

The first iteration of this handbook's outline was drafted during the course of the 2014 Olympia Summer Academy. As is often the case with projects that involve over 60 authors, this book has been long in the making. During the process we have incurred a number of debts that we would like to acknowledge publicly.

From the outset, we made a conscious effort to be inclusive—not only by bringing together established and upcoming scholars but also by transcending various divides within the field (e.g. between pre- and post-9/11 engagement in terrorism research). We gratefully acknowledge the contributions of the authors whose commitment to the project made it possible.

Dominic Byatt at Oxford University Press has been an unfailing source of support from the early stages, while Olivia Wells provided detailed feedback that guided us to submission.

Erica Chenoweth would like to thank students, staff, and faculty at Harvard Kennedy School, the University of Denver, and the National Consortium for the Study of Terrorism and Responses to Terrorism for many stimulating discussions about terrorism and counterterrorism.

Richard English thanks colleagues and students at Queen's University Belfast and at the University of St Andrews, for their insights and discussions regarding terrorism and the study of terrorist violence.

Andreas Gofas would like to thank the Robert Schuman Centre for Advanced Studies at the European University Institute in Florence for providing a most hospitable and intellectually stimulating environment during his 2016–17 sabbatical. He, along with Stathis N. Kalyvas, would like to thank the Greek Diaspora Fellowship Program—funded by a grant from the Stavros Niarchos Foundation (SNF) to the Institute of International Education (IIE), which in collaboration with the Fulbright Foundation in Greece brought him to Greece during the summer of 2017 and allowed him to work on the handbook.

Erica Chenoweth, Cambridge, Massachusetts, USA
Richard English, Belfast, Northern Ireland, UK
Andreas Gofas, Athens, Greece
Stathis N. Kalyvas, Oxford, England, UK

Contents

PART III APPROACHES AND METHODS

PART IV CAUSES AND MOTIVATIONS

PART V TERRORISM, POLITICAL VIOLENCE, AND COLLECTIVE ACTION

PART VI ACTORS, STRATEGIES, AND MODUS OPERANDI

PART VII ISSUES AND PEDAGOGICAL CHALLENGES

PART VIII THE GEOGRAPHICAL CONTEXT OF TERRORISM

PART IX ACADEMIC AND POLICY PERSPECTIVES ON COUNTERING TERRORISM

PART X AUTOBIOGRAPHICAL REFLECTIONS ON THE EVOLUTION OF A FIELD

List of Figures

List of Tables

List of Contributors

Max Abrahms is Assistant Professor of Political Science at Northeastern University, an affiliate at the Global Resilience Institute, a term member at the Council on Foreign Relations, and a board member on the journal *Terrorism and Political Violence*. He has published extensively on terrorism with articles in *International Organization, International Security, International Studies Quarterly, Security Studies, Comparative Political Studies, Harvard Business Review, Terrorism and Political Violence, Studies in Conflict and Terrorism, Foreign Affairs, Foreign Policy*, the *New York Times*, and *Los Angeles Times*. He is also an active analyst in the media about the consequences of terrorism, its causes, and the implications for counterterrorism strategy.

Gary Ackerman is an Associate Professor in the College of Emergency Preparedness, Homeland Security, and Cybersecurity at the University at Albany (SUNY). He was previously Research Director and Director of the Special Projects Division at the National Consortium for the Study of Terrorism and Responses to Terrorism (START). His research encompasses various areas relating to terrorism and counterterrorism, including terrorist threat assessment, terrorist ideologies, the impact of emerging technologies on terrorist behavior, terrorist motivations for using chemical, biological, radiological, and nuclear (CBRN) weapons, and the modeling and simulation of terrorist behavior. Possessing an eclectic academic background, including past studies in the fields of mathematics, history, law, and international relations, he has authored multiple scholarly and popular articles on terrorism and has testified on terrorist motivations for using nuclear weapons before the Senate Committee on Homeland Security.

Eitan Azani currently serves as deputy executive director of the Institute for Counter-Terrorism (ICT) and the Head of the BA and MA Specialization in Counter-Terrorism and Homeland Security at the Lauder School of Government, Diplomacy, and Strategy at the Interdisciplinary Center (IDC) Herzliya. He is a Colonel (Res.) in the Israel Defense Forces (IDF) with operational, research, and academic experience in counterterrorism in the regional and international arenas. He is the author of *Hezbollah: The Story of the Party of God—From Revolution to Institutionalization* (Palgrave, 2009).

John Bew is Professor of History and Foreign Policy at the War Studies Department at King's College London.

Andrea Bianchi is Professor of International Law at the Graduate Institute of International and Development Studies, Geneva, since 2002. He has authored and/or edited a trilogy of books on terrorism for Hart Publishing: *Enforcing International Law Norms against Terrorism* (2004); *Counterterrorism: Democracy's Challenge* (co-edited with Alexis Keller) (2008); and *International Law and Terrorism* (co-authored with Yasmin Naqvi) (2011). His most recent books are: *International Law Theories. An Inquiry into Different Ways of Thinking* (Oxford University Press, 2016); *Interpretation in International Law* (co-edited with Dan Peat and Matt Windsor; Oxford University Press, 2015); and *Transparency in International Law* (co-edited with Anne Peters; Cambridge University Press, 2013). He has also edited *Theory and Philosophy of International Law* (Edward Elgar, 2017); and *Non-State Actors in International Law* (Ashgate, 2009).

Juliette Bird has been the head of NATO's Counter Terrorism section, within the Emerging Security Challenges Division, since September 2011. In the course of a twenty-year career in the UK foreign service she specialized in global threats including proliferation, financial crime, and, most extensively, terrorism. She served in the UK's Joint Terrorism Analysis Centre and was then seconded to NATO to set up an equivalent body for the Alliance. Her work abroad has included postings to India, Belgium, and the European Union. Her degree is from Oxford University (Corpus Christi College), in chemistry.

Lorenzo Bosi is Assistant Professor in Sociology at the Scuola Normale Superiore. He received his Ph.D. in politics from Queen's University, Belfast, in 2005 and is the past recipient of the ECRC (University of Kent), Jean Monnet and Marie Curie (EUI) post-doctorate fellowships. He is a political sociologist pursuing comparative analysis into the cross-disciplinary fields of social movements and political violence. He has directed and collaborated on a number of national and international research projects on topics relating to social movements, political violence, and political participation.

Alia Brahimi is a former Visiting Fellow at the Oxford University Changing Character of War Programme at Pembroke College. She was previously a Research Fellow at the London School of Economics (2009–13) and a Research Associate in International Relations at the University of Oxford (2007–9). Alia read for an MA in Philosophy at Edinburgh University, followed by an M.Phil. and D.Phil. in International Relations at the University of Oxford, where she also completed her post-doctoral research. She is the author of *Jihad and Just War in the War on Terror* (Oxford University Press, 2010) as well as a number of academic articles and policy briefs on jihadist ideology and strategy. Alia is co-founder of Legatus, a London-based advisory firm.

Warren C. Brown is Professor for Medieval History at the California Institute of Technology. He studies the social and political history of medieval Europe, especially the history of conflict and power. His most recent book, *Violence in Medieval Europe* (Longman, 2011), examines the social, cultural, and legal norms that governed the use of violence between 600 and 1500. He is currently exploring the instrumental use of terror in particular during this period and how understanding it might inform discussions of violence and terror in the modern world.

Daniel Byman is a Professor and Vice Dean at Georgetown University's School of Foreign Service and a Senior Fellow at the Center for Middle East Policy at the Brookings Institution. Dr. Byman has served as a Professional Staff Member with both the National Commission on Terrorist Attacks on the United States ("The 9-11

Commission") and the Joint 9/11 Inquiry Staff of the House and Senate Intelligence Committees. He has also worked as the Research Director of the Center for Middle East Public Policy at the RAND Corporation and as an analyst of the Middle East for the U.S. intelligence community. Dr. Byman has written widely on a range of topics related to terrorism, international security, and the Middle East. His publications have appeared in The New York Times, The Atlantic, The Wall Street Journal, Foreign Affairs, International Security, and numerous other scholarly, policy, and popular journals. His books include Deadly Connections: States that Sponsor Terrorism (Cambridge 2005); A High Price: The Triumphs and Failures of Israeli Counterterrorism (Oxford, 2011); Al Qaeda, the Islamic State, and the Global Jihadist Movement: What Everyone Needs to Know (Oxford, 2015); and Road Warriors: Foreign Fighters in the Armies of Jihad (Oxford, 2019). Follow @dbyman.

David B. Carter is Associate Professor of Political Science at Washington University in St Louis. His recent research addresses territoriality and conflict and how the historical legacies of boundary institutions shape patterns of conflict and cooperation among states. Ongoing projects explore topics such as how instability in the international system influences the emergence and character of territorial claims, and how the shape of secessionist groups' territorial claims affect patterns of political violence. He has published his research in a number of political science and international relations journals, including *American Political Science Review, International Organization, World Politics, American Journal of Political Science*, and *Journal of Politics*, among others.

Brahma Chellaney a geostrategist, is presently a Professor of Strategic Studies at the independent Center for Policy Research in New Delhi; a Richard von Weizsäcker Fellow of the Robert Bosch Academy in Berlin; and an affiliate with the International Centre for the Study of Radicalization at King's College London. He has served as a member of the Policy Advisory Group headed by the foreign minister of India. As a specialist on international strategic issues, he held appointments at Harvard University, the Brookings Institution, the Paul H. Nitze School of Advanced International Studies at Johns Hopkins University, and the Australian National University. He is the author of nine books, including *Water: Asia's New Battleground* (Georgetown University Press, 2011), which won the Bernard Schwartz Award. He is a Project Syndicate columnist and also writes for the *Nikkie Asian Review, Wall Street Journal, Financial Times, Le Monde, Japan Times, The Globe and Mail, South China Morning Post*, and other newspapers. He has often appeared on CNN and the BBC, among others.

Erica Chenoweth is Professor of Public Policy at Harvard Kennedy School and a Susan S. and Kenneth L. Wallach Professor at the Radcliffe Institute for Advanced Study at Harvard University. She has published numerous books and articles on political violence and its alternatives. She is co-author, most recently, of *The Politics of Terror* (Oxford University Press, 2018) with Pauline Moore.

Courtenay R. Conrad is an Associate Professor of Political Science at the University of California, Merced. Dr Conrad's research and teaching focus primarily on political violence and human rights, particularly on how repressive agents make decisions in the face of domestic and international institutional constraints. Her most recent work focuses on the effect of law on police violence in the United States and abroad; she is also interested in international organizations, with an emphasis on legislative procedure in the United Nations. Dr Conrad's research has been funded by the National Science Foundation and the Institute on Global Conflict and Cooperation; published in top journals including the *American Political Science Review*, the *American Journal of Political Science*, and the *Journal of Politics*; and referenced in media outlets including the *Washington Post* and Discovery News. Her first book (with Emily Hencken Ritter) is forthcoming with Oxford University Press.

Martha Crenshaw is a Senior Fellow at the Center for International Security and Cooperation (CISAC), Freeman Spogli Institute of International Studies, and Professor of Political Science, by courtesy, at Stanford University.

Luis De la Calle is Associate Professor of Political Science at Centro de Investigación y Docencia Económicas (CIDE) in Mexico City. His research areas are comparative politics, conflict, state capacity, and sub-state nationalism. His most recent work has been published in *Journal of Peace Research*, *Journal of Politics*, and *Conflict Management and Peace Science*. His book *Nationalist Violence in Postwar Europe* was published by Cambridge University Press in 2015.

Donatella della Porta is Professor of Political Science, Dean of the Institute for Humanities and the Social Sciences, and Director of the PD program in Political Science and Sociology at the Scuola Normale Superiore in Florence, where she also leads the Center on Social Movement Studies (Cosmos). Among the main topics of her research are social movements, political violence, terrorism, corruption, the police and protest policing. She has directed a major ERC project Mobilizing for Democracy, on civil society participation in democratization processes in Europe, the Middle East, Asia, and Latin America. In 2011, she was the recipient of the Mattei Dogan Prize for distinguished achievements in the field of political sociology. She is Honorary Doctor of the universities of Lausanne, Bucharest, and Goteborg. She is the author of 85 books, 130 journal articles, and 127 contributions in edited volumes.

Laura Dugan is a Professor in the Department of Criminology and Criminal Justice at the University of Maryland. Her research examines the predictors and consequences of terrorist violence and the efficacy of violence prevention/intervention policy and practice. Dr Dugan is a founding co-principal investigator for the Global Terrorism Database and co-principal investigator of the Government Actions in Terrorist Environments dataset. Dugan holds a doctorate in Public Policy and Management and a Masters in Statistics from Carnegie Mellon University. She has co-authored *Putting Terrorism into Context: Lessons Learned from the World's Most Comprehensive Terrorism Database* (Routledge, 2016).

Juliet U. Elu, Ph.D., is the Charles E. Merrill Professor, Division and Department Chair of Economics at Morehouse College in Atlanta, GA. An applied and policy theorist, her research has been published in a wide variety of journals such as *Journal of Third World*

Studies, *Journal of African Development*, *Review of Black Political Economy*, *American Economic Review*, *African Development Review*, and *Journal of Economic Studies*. Dr Elu earned her B.Sc. in economics and MBA/MPA from Utah State University, Logan, Utah, and completed her economics doctorate at the University of Utah, Salt Lake City, Utah.

Richard English is Professor of Politics at Queen's University Belfast, where he is also Distinguished Professorial Fellow in the Senator George J. Mitchell Institute for Global Peace, Security, and Justice. Between 2011 and 2016 he was Wardlaw Professor of Politics in the School of International Relations, and Director of the Handa Centre for the Study of Terrorism and Political Violence (CSTPV), at the University of St Andrews. He is the author of eight books, including the award-winning studies *Armed Struggle: The History of the IRA* (2003) and *Irish Freedom: The History of Nationalism in Ireland* (2006). His most recent book, *Does Terrorism Work? A History*, was published in 2016 by Oxford University Press. He is a Fellow of the British Academy, a Member of the Royal Irish Academy, a Fellow of the Royal Society of Edinburgh, a Fellow of the Royal Historical Society, an Honorary Fellow of Keble College Oxford, and an Honorary Professor at the University of St Andrews.

Jonathan Evans joined MI5, the British Security Service, from university in 1980. He worked in a variety of investigative, operational, and administrative roles in the service, specializing in counterterrorism. He was appointed Director of MI5's International Terrorism branch on September 1, 2001, ten days before 9/11. He served as Director General of MI5 from 2007 to 2013, during which time he attended the National Security Council on a regular basis and led the service's work to protect the 2012 Olympic Games. Jonathan was appointed to the House of Lords in 2014 and sits as a Crossbench Peer. He is an Honorary Professor at the Handa Centre for the Study of Terrorism and Political Violence at the University of St Andrews.

Susan Fahey is Associate Professor of Criminal Justice at Stockton University.

Megan M. Farrell is a Ph.D. Candidate in Government at the University of Texas at Austin. Her research interests include alliances among political violence groups.

Vanda Felbab-Brown is a senior fellow in the Center for 21st Century Security and Intelligence in the Foreign Policy program at Brookings. She is also the director of the Brookings project, "Improving Global Drug Policy: Comparative Perspectives Beyond UNGASS 2016," and co-director of another Brookings project, "Reconstituting Local Orders." Dr Felbab-Brown is an expert on international and internal conflicts and nontraditional security threats, including insurgency, organized crime, urban violence, and illicit economies. Her fieldwork and research have covered, among others, Afghanistan, South Asia, Burma, Indonesia, the Andean region, Mexico, Morocco, Somalia, and eastern Africa. Dr Felbab-Brown is the author of *The Extinction Market: Wildlife Trafficking and How to Counter it* (Hurst, Fall 2017); *Narco Noir: Mexico's Cartels, Cops, and Corruption* (Brookings Institution Press, 2019); *Militants, Criminals, and Outsiders: The Challenge of Local Governance in an Age of Disorder* (Brookings Institution Press, Winter 2018; co-authored with Shadi Hamid and Harold Trinkunas);

Aspiration and Ambivalence: Strategies and Realities of Counterinsurgency and State-Building in Afghanistan (Brookings Institution Press, 2013); and *Shooting Up: Counterinsurgency and the War on Drugs* (Brookings Institution Press, 2010). She is also the author of numerous policy reports, academic articles, and opinion pieces. A frequent commentator in US and international media, Dr Felbab-Brown regularly provides congressional testimony on these issues. She has also been the recipient of numerous awards in recognition of her scholarly and policy contributions. Dr Felbab-Brown received her Ph.D. in political science from MIT and her BA in government from Harvard University.

Michael G. Findley is Professor of Government at the University of Texas at Austin. His research interests include political violence and international development.

Daren G. Fisher is an Assistant Professor in the Department of Criminal Justice at The Citadel. He received his Ph.D. in Criminology and Criminal Justice from the University of Maryland, for his dissertation examining the impact of US Presidential Communications on Terrorism targeting the United States. He specializes in empirically testing the predictions of criminological theory to better inform government policies that aim to reduce terrorism using econometric methods and qualitative approaches. Dr Fisher has published articles in *Studies in Conflict and Terrorism*, the *International Journal of Law, Crime, and Justice, Police Practice and Research*, and *Critical Criminology*.

Martyn Frampton is Reader in Modern History at Queen Mary University of London.

Boaz Ganor is the Dean and the Ronald Lauder Chair for Counter-Terrorism at the Lauder School of Government, Diplomacy and Strategy, as well as the Founder and Executive Director of the International Institute for Counter-Terrorism (ICT), at the Interdisciplinary Center (IDC), Herzliya, Israel. Prof. Ganor serves as the Founding President of the International Academic Counter-Terrorism Community (ICTAC), an international association of academic institutions, experts, and researchers in fields related to the study of terrorism and counterterrorism. He is the author of *Global Alert: Modern Terrorism Rationality and the Challenge to the Democratic World* published by Columbia University Press.

Caron E. Gentry is a Senior Lecturer in the School of International Relations at the University of St Andrews. She has researched and written on women, gender, and terrorism for over fifteen years. Her publications include articles in *Terrorism and Political Violence*, the *International Feminist Journal of Politics, Millennium, Critical Studies on Terrorism*, and *Critical Studies on Security*. She has also co-authored *Beyond Mothers, Monsters, Whores: Rethinking Women's Violence in Global Politics* (Zed, 2015) with Laura Sjoberg, as well as multiple articles and chapters. Her current research focuses on the intersections of gender, race, and sexuality within terrorism studies. Her latest book stems from her other research area, feminist political theology: *This American Moment: A Feminist Christian Realist Intervention* (Oxford University Press, 2018).

Andreas Gofas is Associate Professor of International Relations at Panteion University of Athens, director of the Center for the Analysis of Terrorism and European Security

(CATES) at the European Law and Governance School, and co-director of the Olympia Summer Academy.

Jeff Goodwin is Professor of Sociology at New York University. He earned his baccalaureate and doctorate at Harvard and has taught at NYU since 1991. His writings focus on social movements, revolutions, and violence. His book *No Other Way Out: States and Revolutionary Movements, 1945–1991* (Cambridge, 2001), won the Outstanding Book Prize of the Collective Behavior and Social Movements Section of the American Sociological Association. He is the co-editor of *Passionate Politics* (Chicago, 2001), *Contention in Context* (Stanford, 2012), and *The Social Movements Reader*, 3rd edn (Wiley Blackwell, 2015). He is also the author of many articles, including "Why we were Surprised (Again) by the Arab Spring," *Swiss Political Science Review* (2011), "'The Struggle Made me a Non-Racialist': Why there was So Little Terrorism in the Anti-Apartheid Struggle," *Mobilization* (2007), and "A Theory of Categorical Terrorism," *Social Forces* (2006).

Jeffrey Haynes is Emeritus Professor of Politics at London Metropolitan University. He has research interests in several areas, including: religion and international relations; religion and politics; democracy and democratization; and the politics of development. Haynes has more than 240 publications, including 44 books. He is editor of a book series, "Routledge Studies in Religion & Politics," for the major publisher Routledge/Taylor & Francis, which publishes around four books a year; co-editor of the journal *Democratization*, published eight times a year by Taylor & Francis; and co-editor of *Democratization's* book series, "Special Issues and Virtual Special Issues," which publishes approximately three volumes a year. He serves on editorial boards of many journals, including: *Millennium: Journal of International Studies; Commonwealth and Comparative Politics; Politics, Religion and Ideology; DIALOGUE* (Italian International Relations journal*); Politics and Religion* (2012–16); *Law and Justice—Critical Law Review; Religion and Transformation in Contemporary Society; Religion, State and Society; Religion and Politics Journal* (Politology journal, Belgrade).

Charlotte Heath-Kelly is an Associate Professor of Politics and International Studies at the University of Warwick. Her research covers all areas of critical terrorism studies, including the performance of countering violent extremism in public sector organizations, and post-terrorist memorialization. She has published nearly twenty articles in leading academic journals, and her latest book is a comparative study of memorials built after terrorist attacks: *Death and Security: Memory and Mortality at the Bombsite* (Manchester University Press, 2016).

Virginia Held is Distinguished Professor of Philosophy (Emerita) at the City University of New York, Graduate School and Hunter College. Among her books are *How Terrorism is Wrong: Morality and Political Violence* (Oxford University Press, 2008); *The Ethics of Care: Personal, Political, and Global* (Oxford University Press, 2006); *Feminist Morality: Transforming Culture, Society, and Politics* (University of Chicago Press, 1993); *Rights and Goods: Justifying Social Action* (Free Press, 1984); and *The Public Interest and Individual Interests* (Basic Books, 1970); as well as the edited collections *Justice and Care: Essential Readings in Feminist Ethics* (Westview, 1995); and *Property,*

Profits, and Economic Justice (Wadsworth, 1980). In 2001–2 she was President of the Eastern Division of the American Philosophical Association. She has been a Fellow at the Center for Advanced Study in the Behavioral Sciences, has had Fulbright and Rockefeller fellowships, and been on the editorial boards of many journals.

Jennifer S. Holmes is Professor at the University of Texas at Dallas. She currently serves as Interim Dean of the School of Economic, Political and Policy Sciences. She received her AB from the University of Chicago and her Ph.D. from the University of Minnesota. Her major area of research is violence and development with an emphasis on Latin America, especially Colombia and Peru. Her ongoing research is in four areas: the landscape ecology of conflict and post-conflict, protection of critical infrastructures, urban quality of life, and the creation of real-time event data on political and social events in Latin America.

John G. Horgan is Distinguished University Professor at Georgia State University (GSU). He has a Ph.D. in psychology, and holds joint appointments at GSU's Global Studies Institute and Department of Psychology. His current research examines religious converts and terrorism, and how children are recruited to terrorist organizations. His work is widely published, with books including *The Psychology of Terrorism* (Routledge, 2005), *Divided we Stand: The Strategy and Psychology of Ireland's Dissident Terrorists* (Oxford University Press, 2013), and *Walking away from Terrorism* (Routledge, 2009). He is editor of the journal *Terrorism and Political Violence*, and serves on the editorial boards of such journals as *American Psychologist* and *Studies in Conflict and Terrorism*. He is a member of the Research Working Group of the FBI's National Center for the Analysis of Violent Crime. His research has been featured in such venues as the *New York Times*, *Foreign Affairs*, CNN, PBS, Vice News, *Rolling Stone Magazine*, *Nature*, and *Scientific American*.

Richard Jackson is the Director of the National Centre for Peace and Conflict Studies, the University of Otago, New Zealand. He is the founding editor and editor-in-chief of the journal, *Critical Studies on Terrorism*. Among many other publications on critical terrorism studies, he is the editor of *The Routledge Handbook of Critical Terrorism Studies* (Routledge, 2016).

Stathis N. Kalyvas is Gladstone Professor of Government at the University of Oxford. He is the author, among others, of *The Logic of Violence in Civil War* (Cambridge University Press, 2006).

Anastasia Koulogannes is a graduate of the University of Maryland and holds Bachelor's degrees in Government and Politics and Chinese. Her research is primarily concerned with risk in East Asia, including terrorism in China and associated foreign fighter activity, illicit finance in the Chinese financial system, and North Korean money laundering and smuggling networks.

Gary LaFree is Chair of the Department of Criminology and Criminal Justice and the Founding Director of the National Consortium for the Study of Terrorism and Responses to Terrorism (START) at the University of Maryland. His research is on the causes and consequences of violent crime and terrorism. His most recent books are *Putting Terrorism in Context* (Routledge, 2016) with Laura Dugan and Erin Miller and *Countering Terrorism* (Brookings, 2017) with Martha Crenshaw.

Brenda J. Lutz earned her Ph.D. in Politics from the University of Dundee in the United Kingdom. She is an independent scholar in Massachusetts and focuses on terrorism and international political violence as well as animal rights issues. She has co-authored four editions of *Global Terrorism* (Routledge, 2004, 2008, 2014, and 2019), *Terrorism: Origins and Evolution* (Palgrave, 2005), *Terrorism in America* (Palgrave, 2007), *Terrorism: The Basics* (Routledge, 2011), and *Globalization and the Economic Consequences of Terrorism* (Palgrave, 2017). Dr Lutz co-edited a four-volume collection of articles and chapters called *Global Terrorism* (Sage, 2008), and has authored or co-authored thirty articles or chapters dealing with animal rights, terrorism, and international political violence.

Siniša Malešević is Professor and Chair of Sociology at the University College, Dublin. He is an elected member of Royal Irish Academy and Academia Europae. His recent books include *The Rise of Organised Brutality: A Historical Sociology of Violence* (Cambridge University Press, 2017), *Nation-States and Nationalisms: Organisation, Ideology and Solidarity* (Polity, 2013), *The Sociology of War and Violence* (Cambridge University Press, 2010), and edited volumes *Empires and Nation-States: Beyond the Dichotomy* (Sage, 2017) and *Nationalism and War* (Cambridge University Press, 2013). He has also authored over 80 peer-reviewed journal articles and book chapters and his work has been translated into numerous languages.

Stefan Malthaner is a Research Fellow at the Hamburg Institute for Social Research (HIS). Previously, he was Assistant Professor at Aarhus University, Denmark, and Marie Curie Fellow at the European University Institute (EUI) in Florence, Italy. He received his Ph.D. in Sociology from Augsburg University in 2010.

Alexander Meleagrou-Hitchens is a lecturer in Terrorism and Radicalisation at King's College London and the Research Director of the Program on Extremism at George Washington University. His research focuses on the messaging and recruitment efforts of violent social movements. His book, an intellectual history of the Yemeni-American al-Qaeda ideologue, recruiter and strategist Anwar al-Awlaki will be published by Harvard University Press in 2019. His recent publications include Salafism in America: History, Evolution, Radicalization (2018) and The Travelers: American Jihadists in Syria and Iraq (2018).

Erin Miller is the Program Manager for the Global Terrorism Database at the University of Maryland.

Gregory D. Miller is Professor and Chair of the Strategy Department at the Joint Advanced Warfighting School (JAWS), National Defense University. He received his Ph.D. (2004) in Political Science from The Ohio State University. His research appears in *Security Studies, Terrorism & Political Violence, Studies in Conflict and Terrorism, The Washington Quarterly, PS: Political Science and Politics, and Small Wars Journal.* Prior to joining JAWS, Dr. Miller taught at the College of William & Mary, the University of Oklahoma, and Oklahoma State University. He was Founding Director of the Summer Workshop on Teaching about Terrorism (SWOTT), which ran from 2004 to 2008. He currently serves as Editor for the new book series "Political Violence in America" at the University of Oklahoma Press, and is an Associate Editor for the journal, Perspectives on Terrorism. Beginning in 2019, he will be in the Leadership Studies Department at the Air Command & Staff College, Air University.

Martin A. Miller is a Professor in the History Department and the Department of Slavic and Eurasian Studies at Duke University. He is the author of numerous books and articles on aspects of the intellectual history of Russia and Europe. His most recent book is *The Foundations of Modern Terrorism: State, Society and the Dynamics of Political Violence* (Cambridge University Press, 2012).

Saurabh Pant is a postdoctoral Research Fellow at the Institute for Advanced Study in Toulouse. He received his Ph.D. in Politics from Princeton University in 2018. His research interests lie at the intersection of international relations and comparative politics. He studies the political economy of conflict and militancy in divided societies Some of his research is published or forthcoming in the *Journal of Theoretical Politics and South Asia: Journal of South Asian Studies*. Support through the ANR Labex IAST is gratefully acknowledged by this author.

Evan Perkoski is an assistant professor in the Department of Political Science at the University of Connecticut. He received his Ph.D. from the University of Pennsylvania and has held fellowships at the Belfer Center for Science and International Affairs at the Harvard Kennedy school of Government as well as the Josef Korbel School of International Studies at the University of Denver. His research focuses on the dynamics of rebel, insurgent, and terrorist groups; strategies of violent and nonviolent resistance; and state operations in cyberspace.

Brian J. Phillips is a Senior Lecturer in the Department of Government at the University of Essex. His research on terrorism and other types of violence has been published in outlets such as the *Journal of Politics, Journal of Peace Research, Journal of Conflict Resolution, International Studies Quarterly, Comparative Political Studies, and Terrorism and Political Violence*. His work has been discussed in *The New York Times*, The Washington Post, and other sources.

Gregory N. Price, Ph.D. is Professor of Economics at Morehouse College. An applied econometrician and theorist, his current research interests include economic anthropometry, the economics of Historically Black Colleges/Universities, the effects of race on economic stratification, and the causes/consequences of slavery. His research has been published in a wide variety of journals such as *African Development Review, Economics and Human Biology, Review of Black Political Economy, Review of Economics and Statistics, American Economic Review,* and *Review of Development Economics.*

Ignacio Sánchez-Cuenca is Associate Professor of Political Science and Director of the Carlos III-Juan March Institute of Social Sciences at Carlos III University of Madrid.

His research areas are comparative politics, political violence, and theory of democracy. He has published articles in journals such as *Journal of Conflict Resolution, Journal of Peace Research, Terrorism and Political Violence, Studies in Conflict and Terrorism, Annual Review of Political Science, European Union Politics, Politics and Society, Party Politics,* and several others. He is also the author of several books in Spanish, including two monographs on ETA.

Ben Saul is Challis Chair of International Law at the University of Sydney, the Visiting Chair of Australian Studies at Harvard University in 2018, a barrister, and an Associate Fellow of Chatham House. Ben has published 14 books and 93 refereed articles. Significant books include *Defining Terrorism in International Law* (Oxford University Press, 2006), *Research Handbook on International Law and Terrorism* (Edward Elgar, 2014), the *Oxford Commentary on the International Covenant on Economic, Social and Cultural Rights* (Oxford University Press, 2014) (awarded a Certificate of Merit by the American Society of International Law), and *Indigenous Peoples and Human Rights* (Hart/Bloomsbury, 2016). Ben practices in international and national courts. He has advised the United Nations, governments, and NGOs, and delivered technical assistance in developing countries. Ben has served on various international and national bodies, and taught law and undertaken field missions in numerous countries. He has a doctorate from Oxford and honours degrees in Arts and Law from Sydney.

Alex P. Schmid is editor-in-chief of Perspectives on Terrorism and former co-editor of Terrorism and Political Violence. He is Director of the Terrorism Research Initiative (TRI) in Vienna and a Research Fellow at the International Centre for Counter Terrorism (ICCT) in The Hague. Previous positions included Associate Professor at the Institute of Security and Global Affairs (ISGA - Leiden University, Campus The Hague), Director of the Centre for the Study of Terrorism and Political Violence (CSTPV) at the University of St Andrews (where he also held a chair in International Relations), and Officer-in-Charge of the UN Terrorism Prevention Branch of UNODC in Vienna.

Jacob N. Shapiro is Professor of Politics and International Affairs at Princeton University. He is author of *The Terrorist's Dilemma: Managing Violent Covert Organizations* (Princeton University Press, 2013), co-author of *Foundations of the Islamic State: Management, Money, and Terror in Iraq* (RAND, 2016), and co-author of *Small Wars, Big Data: The Information Revolution in Modern Conflict* (Princeton University Press, 2018). Shapiro received the 2016 Karl Deutsch Award from ISA, given to a scholar younger than 40 or within ten years of earning a Ph.D. who has made the most significant contribution to the study of international relations.

David A. Siegel is Associate Professor of Political Science at Duke University. His research addresses the theoretical determinants of collective action in the contexts of political violence and terrorism, elections, and opinion and identity formation. He has published in journals such as the *American Political Science Review, American Journal of Political Science,* and *Journal of Politics,* and is the co-author of *A Behavioral Theory of Elections* (Princeton University Press, 2011) and *A Mathematics Course for Political and Social Research* (Princeton University Press, 2013). Prior to coming to

Duke, he was on faculty at Florida State University. He received his Ph.D. from Stanford University in 2006.

Rashmi Singh is an Associate Professor in International Relations at the Pontifical Catholic University of Minas Gerais (Brazil). She was formerly based at the Handa Centre for the Study of Terrorism and Political Violence (CSTPV), at the University of St Andrews (UK). Her primary areas of interest include the role of nationalism, culture and religion in the promulgation of terrorism in the Middle East and South Asia. She has authored numerous articles and book chapters and is also the author of, Hamas and Suicide Terrorism: A Multi-Causal and Multi-Level Approach (Routledge: March 2011) and Understanding Terrorism and Counter-Terrorism (co-authored with Jorge M. Lasmar; Routledge: forthcoming). She is an Associate Editor of Perspectives on Terrorism and part of the editorial board of the International Journal of Conflict and Violence (IJCV). She has served in numerous positions, including as a member of the Global Agenda Council of Terrorism of the World Economic Forum. Dr. Singh is the co-founder of the Terrorism, Radicalisation and Crime (TRAC) Collaborative Research Network where she currently also serves as a principal investigator. She received her PhD in International Relations from the London School of Economics and Political Science in 2008.

Jessica A. Stanton is an Associate Professor at the Humphrey School of Public Affairs at the University of Minnesota. Her research focuses on international relations, including the causes, dynamics, and resolution of civil wars; the role of international institutions and law in international relations; and criminal accountability for wartime violence and terrorism. Her book, *Violence and Restraint in Civil War: Civilian Targeting in the Shadow of International Law* (Cambridge University Press, 2016), examines why some governments and rebel groups engaged in civil war adopt strategies that involve the deliberate targeting of civilians, while other groups, in accordance with international humanitarian law, refrain from attacking civilian populations.

Harold A. Trinkunas is a senior research scholar and the deputy director of the Center for International Security and Cooperation at Stanford University. He is co-author most recently of *Militants, Criminals and Warlords: The Challenge of Local Governance in an Age of Disorder* (Brookings Institution Press, 2017).

Tim Wilson is the Director of the Handa Centre for the Study of Terrorism and Political Violence at the University of St Andrews. Trained as a modern historian, his chief research interests lie in the differing effects political violence can have across different contexts. He has worked widely on inter-communal conflict in deeply divided societies, as well as on the terrorism of both states and their opponents.

Joseph K. Young is Professor in the Schools of Public Affairs and International Service at American University. His research investigates the causes and consequences of terrorism and political violence.

CHAPTER 1

THE STUDY OF TERRORISM

achievements and challenges ahead

ERICA CHENOWETH AND ANDREAS GOFAS

Introduction

As one of the editors of this handbook has argued elsewhere: "We face two kinds of terrorist problems. One is practical, the other analytical, and our difficulties in responding to the former have been significantly exacerbated by our failings with regard to the latter" (English 2009a, ix). The practical problem is well known, highly important, and all too pressing. Terrorism and responses to terrorism continue to affect politics in deeply significant ways across much of the world. Hence, "the scholarly and analytical understanding of terrorism represents one of the grandest challenges we collectively face" (English 2016, 135).

The central goal of *The Oxford Handbook of Terrorism* is to address this analytical challenge by systematically bringing together the somewhat disjointed body of post-9/11 scholarship. In so doing it first seeks to introduce scholars and practitioners to the state of the art approaches, methods, and issues in studying this vital phenomenon. Second, it seeks to make a contribution to what is surely a large and significant process: namely, that of ensuring that our research into and understanding of, terrorism in the coming years gain strength and sharpness through honest reflection about the analytical advancements and challenges that remain since the early 1970s. It is to these achievements and analytical challenges that we presently turn as they inform the structuring rationale of the handbook.

The Evolution of a Field

Academic interest in the study of terrorism could be presented as a roller-coaster with three landmark dates. Prior to the 1970s research on terrorism was subsumed under counter-insurgency studies (Stampnitzky 2013). The rise of revolutionary terrorism in

Europe and the 1972 attack on the Munich Olympics marked a major transition for the study of terrorism on both sides of the Atlantic. Substantively, "Munich" was perceived as launching an era of internationalization of the terrorist threat (Stampnitzky 2013). Communicatively, it was equivalent to 9/11 in that it was broadcast live to a global audience. Following the Munich events, terrorism began to emerge as an autonomous, albeit marginalized, field of study. The year 1977 saw the establishment of the journal *Terrorism* (called *Studies in Conflict and Terrorism* as of 1992). The journal *Terrorism and Political Violence* was founded in 1989. A small group of dedicated scholars (two of whom—Martha Crenshaw and Alex Schmid—reflect on their personal involvement in the evolution of the field in this volume) was responsible for setting the founding agenda and conceptual apparatus for successive waves of terrorism research.

The end of the Cold War was the second major landmark. The onset of armed conflicts in the Balkans and in many post-Soviet spaces invigorated new interest in civil war and ethnic conflict. Indeed, scholarship on civil war saw its own renaissance during this time. Concurrently, a widespread misperception—captured by conspiratorially motivated books, such as Claire Sterling's 1981 *The Terror Network: The Secret War of International Terrorism*—that terrorism around the world was supported by the USSR, led to a rapid decline of funding and interest in the study of terrorism, especially in the US.

The third landmark was 9/11, whose grisly events ushered in a golden age for the study of terrorism, characterized by an unprecedented amount of terrorism-related literature, increased funding opportunities, and the recognition of terrorism studies as a distinct field. New scholarly journals on terrorism were established across many disciplines, such as *Perspectives on Terrorism, Dynamics of Asymmetric Conflict, Critical Studies on Terrorism, Behavioral Sciences of Terrorism and Political Aggression*, and the *Journal of Policing, Intelligence, and Counter Terrorism*. Moreover, articles on terrorism began to appear in more general field journals in political science, sociology, psychology, and criminology. Courses on terrorism became integrated into teaching programs at virtually every major university, and many universities adopted dedicated research centers on the topic (Ranstorp 2009; Jackson 2012). As Martha Crenshaw (2014, 556) observed, "[l]ooking back at the beginnings of academic research on terrorism just over 40 years ago, it is extraordinary to see that what was once a marginal subject for social science has developed into a full-fledged program of 'terrorism studies.'" This handbook is yet one more indicator of this massive growth.

Achievements

The expansion has had a number of positive outcomes for the field. First, despite the often cited problem of so-called parachuters with opportunistic one-off publications, the post-9/11 research wave has enriched the field with a considerable number of impressive and committed scholars (Jackson 2012, 5; Schuurman 2018). As Magnus Ranstorp (2009, 22) puts it, the "veritable avalanche of studies has usefully energized the terrorism studies field with new intellectual talents offering fresh analytical angles and contextual and cultural depth." It is, thus, no accident that a study of terrorism-related research found that post-9/11 articles amount for 63 percent of the 100 most cited articles published between 1952 and 2007 (Silke and Schmidt-Petersen 2017). In order to build on this achievement, the handbook has tried to be generationally inclusive—not only by bringing together established and upcoming colleagues but also by transcending the scholarly fault-line between those exhibiting a pre- and a post-9/11 commencement of engagement in terrorism research.

The second achievement is the rejection of poor research standards. In a 2004 review of the field, Andrew Silke notes that "terrorism literature is composed mainly of studies which rely on relatively weak research methods... There is a heavy reliance on qualitative and journalistic approaches which lack the validity and reliability generally expected within mainstream social science research" (2004, 11). The norms regarding such practices have shifted considerably with the advent of the RAND-MIPT dataset and the Global Terrorism Database—two large-scale observational data collection projects that allowed researchers to apply mainstream quantitative data analysis techniques to terrorism studies. The field of terrorism studies therefore currently reflects a robust pluralism regarding methods of inquiry (Schuurman 2018), with recent studies employing quasi-experimental designs (Huff and Kertzer 2018), quantitative analysis (e.g. LaFree and Freilich 2012), and comparative case study approaches (e.g. Crenshaw 1995). In this handbook, we attempt to reflect this methodological diversity by including chapters representing a broad range of empirical approaches.

The third achievement is that of multi-disciplinarity. Whereas forty years ago, the study of terrorism was limited to a handful of historians and political scientists, the field has expanded to include research by economists, criminologists, sociologists, psychologists, psychiatrists, and others. In this volume, we similarly attempt to reflect contributions from a wide variety of academic disciplines.

Analytical Challenges

It is often pointed out that there exists no consensus definition of terrorism and that "the problem of defining terrorism has hindered analysis since the inception of studies in the early 1970s" (Crenshaw 2000, 406). Terrorism is conceptually more contested than other forms of political violence (Sánchez-Cuenca 2014, 591), but not more contested than other pejorative terms such as fascism, populism, or imperialism (English 2016, 136).

Richard Jackson (2011, 117–18) identifies three positions to the challenge posed by the definitional quagmire. The first suggests that the term should be abandoned in academic research because its highly contested and strongly pejorative status poses barriers to unbiased scholarship and cumulative knowledge production. We think that such a position would effectively give away the analysis of the phenomenon to pundits whose sensational coverage has had a deleterious effect on how the public is informed.

Another position argues that because terrorism is a socio-historically contingent signifier that can acquire collective meaning only through a socially negotiated agreement, our research should focus on representational practices and terrorism's symbolic performance rather than the phenomenon itself. We agree that this is an important research agenda and that terrorism is not a brute fact that allows for simple observation and cataloging. Yet, "although the concepts and beliefs of actors engaged in any given social practice are integral to any understanding of that practice, they do not exhaust it" (Wight 2009, 100). That is so because although knowledge is socially constructed through language, "without a referent, the practices of discursive and linguistic articulation are meaningless" (Joseph 2009, 95). There must be something there in the first place to construct socially and attach a meaning to. Jackson himself, a key figure of critical terrorism studies, advocates a "minimal foundationalism" as the ontological basis for pursuing a definition, where the main challenge is to chart a balance "between the extremes of ontological essentialism (whilst recognizing behavioral regularities) and radical contingency (whilst accepting the importance of context to the knowledge process)" (2011, 119).

The third position to the definitional quagmire is to argue that the term terrorism can be retained only once definitional consensus is achieved and then applied consistently by all scholars. The elusive pursuit for a full consensus definition is most likely unattainable; it might even prove counterproductive, reinforcing a sense of supposed scholarly "stagnation" (Sageman 2014). Moreover, it should be noted that in addition to definitional controversy being a familiar problem within social science more generally, so too there exists much common ground between rival definitions of terrorism (English 2016, 136). Studies that have tried to evaluate the analytical ramifications of different definitions conclude that the importance of these differences may have been overstated as they do not affect key predictors and causal factors (Young and Findley 2011; Levin and Asal 2017). The crucial issue "is to be precise (what does one mean by the word in one's own work?), to adhere rigorously to one's own chosen definition, to respect the implications of others having taken a different view, and to avoid immobilization on the mere grounds of a contested term" (English 2016, 136–7).

If, as the above hints, the perennial definitional failure is a matter which should cause us comparatively little anxiety, then what are the more troublesome failures and analytical challenges? The first is cognitive fragmentation and lack of cross-fertilization between scholarship on different forms of political violence. The second is a tendency towards de-historiczation of terrorism. The third is lack of engagement between hermeneutical (i.e. qualitiative and interpretive) and nomothetic (i.e. quantitative) approaches. The fourth is lack of integration between micro- and macro-approaches. The fifth is a skewed set of research priorities that results in an over-focus on certain issues to the neglect of others, and the sixth is the tendency to avoid primary research on accused terrorists or their writings. The seventh is a lack of variation in the geo-cultural production of knowledge. Let us briefly discuss each and how the handbook attempts to address this set of problems.

Every process of institutionalizing a field of inquiry as a separate and self-contained one contains elements of disciplinary nationalism. In this context, claiming intellectual ground and drawing boundaries between the essential core of the field and cognate ones was part and parcel of the evolution of terrorism studies. The fact that this is understandable makes it no less problematic. By default, the act of establishing terrorism studies as distinct from the study of political violence is to "treat terrorism as an exceptional act, rather than as a type of political violence with some unique features" (Boyle 2012, 529). This is a problem because terrorism rarely occurs on its own. Rather, it is in a relationship of substitution and complementarity with other forms of political violence and socio-political mobilization. As Boyle aptly notes by drawing on Charles Tilly, "most actors rely on a varied repertoire of violent and non-violent tactics that they employ in different combinations in different contexts to achieve their goals. To understand terrorism is to locate the choice for that particular tactic in context with their strategic ambitions and the other tactical choices made from that repertoire" (Boyle 2012, 529). Indicative of this cognitive fragmentation is that, despite the vast literature on both terrorism and civil wars, there are only a handful of studies considering the use and role of terrorism in the context of civil wars (Kalyvas 2004; Fortna 2015).

Another unfortunate corollary of this increased specialization and fragmentation is the predominant tendency to "select on the dependent variable and focus solely on actors who have employed terrorism, while excluding actors in similar circumstances who have chosen other violent or non-violent tactics" (Boyle 2012, 529). Turning the causation question on its head by asking why terrorism did *not* occur (Brooke, 2018), or why a particular terrorist strategy, like suicide terrorism, was *not* employed (Kalyvas and Sánchez-Cuenca 2005) can provide both new analytical insights and useful policy lessons.

Furthermore, notwithstanding the important work of many historians as well as Martha Crenshaw's landmark volume *Terrorism in Context* (1995), a remaining challenge is the de-historization of terrorism as a concept. Notably, taking a naïve approach to the study of terrorism across different historical periods comes at analytical and normative costs. For instance, during times of political crisis (especially sustained political crisis), elites tend to label all dissidents as terrorists in order to distract from or undermine their claims. Rising amounts of protest may therefore correspond with rising claims of terrorism by states or their supporters. Slobodan Milosevic labeled the Otpor movement a "terrorist group" in the run-up to the Bulldozer Revolution, for instance. And certainly the US government attempted to delegitimize the Black Panther Party by labeling it a terrorist group, invoking extra constitutional powers to subvert black liberation movements through the COINTELPRO program. In other words, the pejorative classifications of groups as terrorists and events as terrorism become political weapons the state may use when it is threatened by sustained cycles of contentious mobilization. As a research program, critical terrorism studies is most explicit about these political and normative realities, as the chapter by Charlotte Heath-Kelly suggests.

Next, despite the fact that the field is methodologically pluralistic, there is little engagement across interpretivist, qualitative, quantitative, and experimental research approaches. In addition to developing substantive areas or topics of expertise, most scholars also develop methodological expertise and communicate with other scholars who employ similar research techniques. As a result, many quantitative scholars, whose primary aim is to identify general trends or conditional relationships that underlie patterns of terrorism, do not cross-reference theoretical insights produced by the voluminous body of work produced by qualitative, interpretivist, and critical scholars (Jackson et al. 2011). Likewise, some interpretivist or critical terrorism scholars neglect the insights produced by empirical terrorism studies because they reject the methodologies used to produce those insights as statist, Euro-centric, and normatively compromised (Horgan and Boyle 2008). These methodological silos contribute to the field's overall level of fragmentation, and there are certainly opportunities for greater synthesis (English 2009b).

Fourth, the field continues to suffer from a lack of integration between micro-level and macro-level approaches. While some studies focus specifically on individual-level motivations for terror, such as psychological drivers or radicalization (for example, see Merari 2010; Kruglanksi et al. 2014, respectively), others are preoccupied with structural and systemic causes of terrorism. Very few studies successfully synthesize these different levels of analysis.

The fifth failure, and associated analytical challenge, relates to the fact that the vast post-9/11 expansion of terrorism research was not accompanied by an equally vast expansion of analytical focus. Rather, what we are faced with is "a skewed set of research priorities which results in an over-focus on certain issues and the perennial neglect of others" (Jackson 2012, 9). This has to do with the event-driven character of much terrorism research. As Ranstorp (2009, 18) puts it, "current terrorism research efforts can be compared to a game of children's football where the players are rushing after the ball (the latest terrorism trends) without a strategy, rather than marking different players or utilizing different areas of the pitch." In effect, we have an ever-expanding literature on issues like Al Qaeda, ISIS, and radicalization, and a limited literature on issues like the large-scale historical evolution of terrorist violence, terrorism in areas or by groups that do not pose a direct threat to the West, and the strategic effectiveness of terrorism and counterterrorism. In this handbook, we have opted for general themes, rather than research trends, and have included a part on geographical context. Moreover, because we believe that the event-driven character of much of the current analytical focus poses challenges not only for research but also for pedagogy, we have included two chapters on pedagogical challenges.

Sixth, despite recent advances (Schuurman 2018), most scholarship in the field still does not overwhelmingly rely on primary research—interviews with accused or former terrorists, their memoirs, and/or primary documents—meaning that scholars' interpretations of data on terror are largely driven by descriptive trends gleaned from quantitative analysis, their own perspectives, or a combination of each. This means that such interpretations are largely divorced from the lived experiences and insights of those who have engaged in terrorism (or have been accused of doing so). In this handbook, we have attempted to include several chapters that draw upon primary documents to inform their analyses; however, we note that no primary field research was undertaken to produce any of the essays themselves.

Finally, and for reasons related to the post-9/11 research focus, US- and Europe-based scholars and policy priorities dominate the field of terrorism studies. This lack of geocultural variation in the field means that many voices—those in the Global South and among oppressed communities in the Global North—are missing in the field's canon. Although it is impossible for scholars from the Global North to speak for such groups and individuals, it is important to point out the existence of a major lacuna. And it is telling that, despite concerted and partially successful efforts to recruit authors from the Global South with diverse perspectives for inclusion in this handbook, the impact of Western policy and scholarly interests remain hegemonic in the field and in the chapters reflected here.

References

Boyle, Michael J. (2012) "Progress and Pitfalls in the Study of Political Violence," *Terrorism and Political Violence*, 24(4): 527–43.

Brooke, Nick (2018) *Terrorism and Nationalism in the United Kingdom: The Absence of Noise*. Basingstoke: Palgrave.

Crenshaw, Martha, ed. (1995) *Terrorism in Context*. Philadelphia: Pennsylvania State University Press.

Crenshaw, Martha (2000) "The Psychology of Terrorism: An Agenda for the 21st Century," *Political Psychology*, 21(2): 405–20.

Crenshaw, Martha (2014) "Terrorism Research: The Record," *International Interactions*, 40(4): 556–67.

English, Richard (2009a) *Terrorism: How to Respond*. Oxford: Oxford University Press.

English, Richard (2009b) "The Future of Terrorism Studies." *Critical Studies on Terrorism*, 2(2): 377–82.

English, Richard (2016) "The Future Study of Terrorism," *European Journal of International Security*, 1(2): 135–49.

Fortna, V. Page (2015) "Do Terrorists Win? The Use of Terrorism and Civil War Outcomes 1989–2009," *International Organization*, 69(3): 519–56.

Horgan, John, and Michael J. Boyle (2008) "A Case Against 'Critical Terrorism Studies,'" *Critical Studies on Terrorism*, 1(1): 51–64.

Huff, Connor, and Joshua D. Kertzer (2018) "How the Public Defines Terrorism," *American Journal of Political Science*, 62(1): 55–71.

Jackson, Richard (2011) "In Defence of 'Terrorism': Finding a Way through a Forest of Misconceptions," *Behavioral Sciences of Terrorism and Political Aggression*, 3(2): 116–30.

Jackson, Richard (2012) "The Study of Terrorism 10 Years After 9/11: Successes, Issues, Challenges," *Uluslararası İlişkiler*, 8(32): 1–16.

Jackson, Richard, Lee Jarvis, Jeroen Gunning, and Marie Breen Smyth (2011) *Terrorism: A Critical Introduction*. London: Palgrave Macmillan.

Joseph, Jonathan (2009) "Critical of What? Terrorism and its Study," *International Relations*, 23(1): 93–8.

Kalyvas, Stathis N. (2004) "The Paradox of Terrorism in Civil War," *Journal of Ethics*, 8(1): 97–138.

Kalyvas, Stathis N., and Ignacio Sánchez-Cuenca (2005) "Killing Without Dying: The Absence of Suicide Missions," in Diego Gambetta (ed.), *Making Sense of Suicide Missions*. Oxford: Oxford University Press.

Kruglanski, Arie W., Michele J. Gelfand, Jocelyn J. Bélanger, Anna Sheveland, Malkanthi Hetiarachchi, and Rohan Gunaratna (2014) "The Psychology of Radicalization and

Deradicalization: How Significance Quest Impacts Violent Extremism," *Political Psychology*, 35(S1): 69–93.

LaFree, Gary, and Joshua D. Freilich (2012) "Quantitative Approaches to the Study of Terrorism," *Journal of Quantitative Criminology*, 28: 1–5.

Levin, Rachel, and Victor Asal (2017) "Do Different Definitions of Terrorism Alter its Causal Story?," in Michael Stohl, Richard Burchill, and Scott Howard Englund (eds), *Constructions of Terrorism: An Interdisciplinary Approach to Research and Policy*. Oakland, CA: University of California Press, 151–62.

Merari, Ariel (2010) *Driven to Death: Psychological and Social Aspects of Suicide Terrorism*. New York: Oxford University Press.

Ranstorp, Magnus (2009) "Mapping Terrorism Studies After 9/11: An Academic Field of Old Problems and New Prospects," in Richard Jackson, Jeroen Gunning, and Marie Breen Smyth (eds), *Critical Terrorism Studies: A New Research Agenda*. Abingdon, Routledge, 13–33.

Sageman, Marc (2014) "The Stagnation in Terrorism Research," *Terrorism and Political Violence*, 26(4): 565–80.

Sánchez-Cuenca, Ignacio (2014) "Why do we Know So Little about Terrorism?," *International Interactions*, 40(4): 590–601.

Schuurman, Bart (2018) "Research on Terrorism, 2007–2016: A Review of Data, Methods, and Authorship," *Terrorism and Political Violence*, forthcoming.

Silke, Andrew, ed. (2004) *Research on Terrorism: Trends, Achievements, and Failures*. London: Frank Cass.

Silke, Andrew, and Jennifer Schmidt-Petersen (2017) "The Golden Age? What the 100 Most Cited Articles in Terrorism Studies Tell us," *Terrorism and Political Violence*, 29(4): 692–712.

Stampnitzky, Lisa (2013) *Disciplining Terror: How Experts and Others Invented Terrorism*. Cambridge: Cambridge University Press.

Wight, Colin (2009) "Theorising Terrorism: The State, Structure and History," *International Relations*, 23(1): 99–106.

Young, Joseph K., and Michael G. Findley (2011) "Promise and Pitfalls of Terrorism Research," *International Studies Review*, 13(3): 411–31.

PART I

CONCEPTS AND TYPOLOGIES

CHAPTER 2

THE LANDSCAPE OF POLITICAL VIOLENCE

STATHIS N. KALYVAS

INTRODUCTION

THE study of violent human conflict is fragmented across many different fields and subfields, spanning several disciplines. The phenomena studied range from violent street protests all the way up to genocide. This fragmentation represents perhaps the biggest obstacle to the development of this research field. On the one hand, the boundaries that separate the different subfields are insufficiently porous, poorly demarcated, constantly contested, and often policed with zeal by armies of experts who, nevertheless, seek to expand them at the expense of neighboring subfields. This is particularly obvious, but hardly limited to the study of terrorism, whose well-known definitional battles (Schmid 2004) have led to a considerable degree of "conceptual stretching" (Sartori 1970) and fragmentation (Sánchez-Cuenca and de la Calle 2009). It is quite common, as attested in the present handbook, to observe that the empirical study of terrorism often overlaps with the study of rebel violence against non-combatants in civil wars and other settings.

And yet, political violence is a genuinely multifaceted and varied phenomenon. A street protest entailing scuffles between demonstrators and the police, like Occupy Wall Street, and a genocide costing the life of millions, such as the Holocaust, could only be fused together at the cost of severe loss in understanding. In other words, research fragmentation reflects the underlying reality of extreme diversity in the expressions of political violence. Yet there is no denying that it is highly problematic for at least three reasons.

First, established distinctions between various types of violent human conflict are not always spelled out clearly and explicitly vis-à-vis each other. Typically, they do not result from an overarching conceptual perspective; rather they are the result of practical considerations and the often-arbitrary (and solitary) development of a given subfield.

Second, because the various types of political violence are not demarcated analytically, similar or closely overlapping phenomena are studied simultaneously from multiple conceptual angles by different teams of researchers seeking to make distinct political, legal, and normative claims. This can be the source of considerable confusion, as the same phenomenon can be studied simultaneously as an instance of a very different type of political violence. For example, the violence that targeted civilian populations in Guatemala during the early 1980s has been approached as an instance of genocide (Higonnet 2009), state terror (Sluka 2000), and the twin processes of insurgency and counter-insurgency (Stoll 1993). Conversely, empirical studies of terrorism lump together instances of transnational violence perpetrated by tiny clandestine groups or even single individuals, such as the 2017 massacres in Paris and Nice, with large-scale massacres of civilians planned and ordered by rebel groups such as the Colombian FARC in the context of civil wars.

Lastly, and perhaps most importantly from a theoretical perspective, the study of the onset of each type of political violence tends to be automatically contrasted with the absence of political violence as a whole, which is conceptualized as some kind of "peace," domestic or international. For example, the absence of civil war onset is thought to imply the presence of domestic peace, even though this might be a peace characterized by, say, high levels of state-initiated violence. As a result, researchers can be blinded to the fact that various types of political violence coexist on a broad continuum, as fundamentally non-peaceful alternatives to each other. Seen from this perspective, the absence of civil war onset might entail the presence of terrorism. More importantly perhaps, the presence of terrorism might be explained by the impossibility of launching a civil war. These problems result in findings that can be contradictory, hard to reconcile with each other, but also biased and misleading.

To tackle these problems, I introduce a typology of political violence that aims to cover the entire span of the phenomenon in a way that aims to be analytically productive. I begin by inductively identifying eleven types of political violence based on the existing research programs. I then proceed to categorize these eleven types along two key dimensions: whether the perpetrator of violence is a state or a non-state actor; and whether the target of violence is a state or a non-state entity. Finally, I discuss how these types are linked with each other, and discuss four distinct logics of connection: hierarchy, instrumentality, escalation, and substitution.

I begin with some general definitional observations about delimiting the empirical space covered by political violence; I then introduce the typology, discuss the broad characteristics of each type and key research findings, and explore how they are connected with each other. I conclude with a discussion of a future research agenda for the study of political violence.

A Typology of Political Violence

Political violence is an exceedingly broad and ill-defined term and, as such, its meaning and contents can be stretched almost infinitely. This stretching potential extends to both components of the concept. On the one hand, the political can be defined so broadly as to fit almost all human activity, as in the popular quip "the personal is political;" on the other hand, violence also can be stretched to fit almost all types of behavior; indeed "structural violence" is understood to include very broad phenomena such as poverty and inequality (Galtung 1969); likewise, "psychological violence" is often amalgamated with physical violence. However, if we are to study political violence in a meaningful way, we must somehow rein in this colossal scope.

While recognizing that violence can be an extremely varied and multidimensional concept, it can still be usefully restricted to the actual infliction of physical harm, with death being perhaps its most extreme and visible form. Likewise, we can think of the political in a more restricted way, as an action that explicitly and directly aims to impact on governance. As we will see, these narrower bounds still define a vast swath of human activity.

My aim here is to identify broad yet distinct macro-level types of political violence rather than meso-level mechanisms (as in Tilly 2003) or micro-level repertoires or patterns (as in Gutiérrez-Sanín and Wood 2017). I also use existing categories that have already generated a substantial research program and avoid neologisms. Based on a review of the literature, I identify eleven fundamental types of political violence that have been studied as distinct processes. I leave aside over-aggregated concepts that merge processes, causes, and outcomes, such as "social revolution." I relate these eleven types to each other, thus generating a "conceptual typology" (Collier et al. 2012). On an organizational dimension, we can observe at one end of the spectrum the highly organized phenomenon of interstate or international war; at the other end, we find disorganized, low-violence, contentious action, mass protest, and rebellion. In between these two poles, I identify the following phenomena: civil war, genocide, ethnic cleansing, terrorism, intercommunal violence, military coup, political assassination, state repression, and lastly the violence associated with organized crime and cartels.

As a way to reduce complexity and gain analytical tractability, I classify these eleven types of political violence on two axes. The first one defines the perpetrator of violence and the second one the target of violence. More specifically, to classify these types, I ask whether the originator of violence is a state or a non-state actor and, likewise, whether the target (direct or indirect) of violence is the state or a non-state actor. The intersection of these two axes generates four broad empirical areas allowing the placement of all eleven types of political violence in one of four separate cells, as depicted in Table 2.1.

Six caveats are in place. First, the placement of each type into the appropriate cell is based on who is the most immediate agent implementing the violence. For example, mass protests are typically a non-state activity, yet sometimes they might be instigated by rival states in the context of an interstate rivalry. Often, non-state rebel groups are abetted or even directed by a rival state. Nevertheless, even when this is the case, rival states could not have instigated the violence in the absence of these non-state actors, who are, therefore, critical in its implementation. The same holds for military coups, political assassinations, civil wars, terrorist actions, and intercommunal violence: non-state actors tend to be both immediate and critical actors for its production irrespective of the assistance they might have received. In contrast, state repression, genocide, and ethnic cleansing sometimes are perpetrated by non-state actors (such as

Table 2.1 Perpetrators and Targets of Political Violence

	Target: State	Target: Non-State
Perpetrator: State	Interstate war	State repression Genocide Ethnic cleansing
Perpetrator: Non-State	Organized crime/Cartels Mass protest/Rebellion Military coup Political assassination Civil war Terrorism	 Intercommunal violence [Political assassination]

crowds or militias), but typically these are not critical actors in the sense that the violence would have been likely implemented directly by states if these actors had not been available. The same applies for many (though not all) pro-government militias operating in the context of civil wars: they are part of the state machinery (Jentzsch et al. 2015). Second, rogue state actors might participate in, or even instigate any of the eleven forms of non-state political violence but this does not turn them into state actions. For example, military coups are organized by rogue military personnel who may also participate in anti-regime demonstrations, as was the case in Syria. Yet, through their very actions, rogue state actors lose their status as state actors. Third, an actor's status is not predicated on the outcome of the violent conflict. When successful, non-state actors ultimately accede to state status, from rag-tag opposition groups launching a street protest that may escalate into a successful social revolution to insurgents who emerge victorious out of a civil war. However, they initiated the violence as non-state actors. Fourth, the initiation of a campaign of political violence is often related to preceding (or even anticipated) activities by its target. An opposition terrorist campaign is often a response to state terror; this does not detract from the fact that it is launched by a non-state actor. As we will see, political violence is almost always interactive; mapping out this interaction, however, requires a prior distinction between types. Fifth, particularly in the context of war, civilians are often targeted by both state and non-state actors because of their presumed association with their rival; in these cases, violence directed against them is typically understood as directed against their rival, regardless of the foundation of such beliefs. Lastly one type, political assassination, can be placed simultaneously in two cells. It is typically used by non-state actors against state targets but sometimes, notably in the case of drone operations by the US in Pakistan and elsewhere, it can be also used by states against non-state actors.

With these caveats in place, it is possible to make two observations about Table 2.1. First, symmetric interactions (state versus state and non-state versus non-state) tend to produce a limited repertoire of political violence. Asymmetric interactions, on the other hand, are characterized by a much broader repertoire, with the broadest one entailing the interaction between non-state perpetrators and state targets. This pattern reflects the fact that challenging a state, by definition the monopolist of the means of legitimate violence, is inherently difficult and risky, hence necessitating a broad repertoire.

Second, this typology allows us to approach the concept of revolution, on which a vast literature exists (Goldstone 2001), in perhaps a more tractable and integrated way, as an over-aggregated type of political violence. Social revolutions have been famously defined as "rapid, basic transformations of a society's state and class structures... accompanied and in part carried through by class-based revolts from below" (Skocpol 1979, 4). As is clear, this definition merges cause, process, and outcomes. One way to simplify the concept of revolution is to see it as a process that begins as a mass protest and escalates into rebellion. In contrast, a revolutionary outcome can emerge from all kinds of political violence, including coups and civil wars—a distinction that bypasses the line that students of revolution tend to draw between revolutions and most civil wars (Goldstone 2001, 140–2).

Lastly, although all these types of political violence are conceptually distinct from each other and can be empirically observed in isolation, they are dynamically interlinked. For example, a civil war can emerge out of a military coup (as was the case in Spain, in 1937) or out of mass protests (as was the case in Syria, in 2011). Likewise, a genocide can be implemented by means of intercommunal violence (Gross 2001) and can take place within the context of an interstate war (Snyder 2010). The main strength of the typology presented here is that it offers the possibility of mapping out of these connections, as I discuss below. Before getting there, however, I briefly turn to each type of political violence.

Varieties of Political Violence

Interstate War

International or interstate war (or, simply, "war") is generally not thought of as a form of political violence, one among several others. Instead, it is generally approached as a *sui generis* human phenomenon that can only be studied in its own right (Gat 2008). Yet, it is hard to argue with Clausewitz's famous dictum about war being the continuation of politics by other means. In fact, interstate war is clearly the highest, most sophisticated manifestation of collective violence, simply because it is produced by the highest, most sophisticated form of collective human organization: the state. The military clash between rival states mobilizes enormous resources which are naturally multiplied when the number of states involved in the clash goes up. Obviously, "world wars" constitute the apex of this process, with nuclear war as its epitome.

The association between interstate war and violence is so obvious as to preclude comparisons between war and other forms of political violence. Research on the violence produced by interstate war has tended to be limited to the legal realm (related to "just war" theories or the laws of war), and violence has been often been approached as a natural and unproblematic consequence of war, worthy of less scholarly attention than more celebrated topics like war strategy or leadership. Into this mix, one must add the powerful ideological and normative dimension of interstate war. On the positive side, dying for one's country in an interstate war is a cornerstone of nationalism and is widely considered as the ultimate honor and sacrifice, while killing others at war in the name of the state is not perceived as murder. On the negative side, however, pacifist theories have attempted to relegate both war and violence to the realm of human pathology. As a result, interstate war has not been approached as one among many forms of political violence (Joas and Knöbel 2013, 1).

However, once researchers became aware of the puzzling variation in the levels of civilian victimization produced by interstate war, they began to turn their attention to the study of violence in war as something deserving of a study on its own right. In a parallel fashion, the growing attention paid to the distinction between *jus ad bellum* and *jus in bello*—or the justification a belligerent has to go to war versus its behavior within it—a process facilitated by the rise in prominence of humanitarian laws and human rights norms (Keck and Sikkink 1998; Simmons 2009), has encouraged the theoretical and empirical decoupling between war and violence (e.g. Pinker 2011). Recent work has focused on the relation between regime type and civilian victimization (Downes 2004), yet the two most striking empirical observations about interstate war constitute a paradox: as the potential destructiveness of war has risen, its incidence and actual damage have experienced a drastic decline (Pinker 2011; Goldstein 2011; Mueller 2007). As this decline has occurred in parallel with the spread of democracy, one of the most hotly debated empirical issues is the so-called "democratic peace" thesis (Russett 1993), i.e. the observation that democracies do not fight each other. One of the consequences of the decline of interstate war has been a boom in the study of civil wars. In a sense, civil wars became more visible once interstate war became scarcer (Mueller 2007).

Civil War

Civil ("internal" or "intrastate") war is primarily fought between domestic factions within a state, sometimes in the name of political and social change and sometimes to promote a secessionist agenda and the creation of a new state. Although neighboring states, regional powers, and superpowers have been consistently involved in civil wars (hence their frequent moniker of "proxy wars"), they can do so only in alliance with domestic factions, thus rendering these wars distinct from their interstate counterparts.

Unlike interstate war, civil war has been typically perceived as closely intertwined with violence, partly because of its (supposed) pronounced or even extreme victimization of civilians and partly because of its transgressive, "fratricidal" nature (Kalyvas 2006). Nevertheless, civil war remained until recently understudied, frequently thought of as a sort of second-rate war, not even really worth calling a war (Armitage 2017; Kalyvas 2007). Fortunately, such neglect is no longer the case. Indeed, four distinct trends came together during the late 1990s and early 2000s to reignite interest in the study of civil wars. First, political economists of development, some connected to the World Bank, realized they needed to better understand how conflict might have impeded development (Collier and Hoeffler 1998, 2004); second, the continuing decline of interstate war prompted a few of its students to explore whether their theoretical insights could travel to the universe of civil wars (David 1997; Posen 1993); third, the traumatic experience of the Yugoslav wars brought ethnicity back into the center of the subfield of comparative politics (Fearon and Laitin 2003); lastly, the US wars in Afghanistan and Iraq, and the ensuing "perpetual" "war on terror" generated considerable policy interest in the study of insurgency and, in particular, counter-insurgency (Berman et al. 2011).

Initially, research focused on establishing a clear set of structural, cross-national correlates, and potentially causes, of civil war onset in the post-World War II period, with the ultimate goal of developing some kind of policy prevention plan. The most robust finding out of this research program has been that poorer countries face a higher risk of civil war onset—a risk, however, that remains, overall, tiny given how rare occurrences civil wars are. Many other potential causes have been explored yet remain at best contested, most notably the role of ethnicity, which has been measured in a variety of ways, as either diversity or political exclusion (Cederman et al. 2013). State weakness has also been associated with civil war onset (Fearon and Laitin 2003), though it remains unclear whether this is epiphenomenal to poverty. Lastly, it has been argued that civil war is more likely in regimes that are neither clear democracies nor strong autocracies and in times of political change and transition (Fearon and Laitin 2003; Hegre 2001).

A sometimes-heated debate about the comparative role of opportunities versus grievances in igniting civil war also proved hard to adjudicate, only to be eventually abandoned given that grievances and opportunities are much more intertwined than initially argued. Cross-national studies have also focused on questions such as the variable duration of civil wars (Hironaka 2005), as well as their termination and third-party intervention, most notably peacekeeping (Fortna 2008). A parallel strand of research has focused on micro-level dynamics with an emphasis on subnational variation and the dynamics of violence (Balcells 2017; Kalyvas 2006). More recently, research has turned to rebel–civil relations (Arjona 2016) and to organizational dynamics within armed groups (Staniland 2014).

Civil wars experienced an upward tick in the period leading to the end of the Cold War, a process that was due less to higher levels of onset and more to the accumulation of ongoing conflicts caused by the slower rate of conflict terminations (Fearon and Laitin 2003). The end of the Cold War, however, led to a wave of negotiated settlements typically instigated and sustained by the UN, thus reducing the overall stock of civil wars, until an uptick was observed in the second decade of the 2000s, mostly driven by Islamist "jihadi" insurgencies (Kalyvas 2018; Fearon 2017).

State Repression

There is little doubt that the violence used by states against those among their own populations that, correctly or not, are suspected to oppose them, is a clear instance of political violence. State repression, violence or terror are terms used to describe this type (Sluka 2000), although a variety of terms also have been deployed, including "democide" (Rummel 1994) and "politicide" (Harff and Gurr 1988). Although state repression can be understood to include both realized and threatened coercive action by state authorities (Ritter and Conrad 2016, 86), the bulk of the research focus has been on violent repression (Poe and Tate 1994).

Usually, this type of violence is deployed by autocracies, which frequently use it in a limited way to deter opposition. It is by definition unilateral and is encountered where the opposition is either (initially) unarmed or very weak, like in Argentina, in 1974–83. In some instances, however, autocracies launch extensive campaigns of mass violence against their own unarmed citizens causing thousands and, in a few cases, millions of deaths among them. Often, this violence follows on the heels of mass contestation (for example, in Egypt following the eruption of the "Arab Spring" in 2011) or a period of political instability (e.g. in Argentina during the 1970s)—in what is sometimes referred to as "coercive responsiveness" (Davenport 2007, 7–8). In other cases, however, such violence can be deployed in a pre-emptive or entirely arbitrary way. The worst offenders in this respect were Stalin's USSR and Mao's China.

Coercive power in ways that fall short of open or deadly violence is obviously used by democracies as well, particularly when facing threats perceived to be existential—e.g. the mass internment of Japanese-Americans during World War II. Nevertheless, there is a strong association between democratic political institutions and low levels of overt state repression, a relationship that has been described as the "domestic democratic peace" (Davenport 2007, 11).

Summarizing the literature on state repression, Chenoweth et al. (2017, 1957–) describe six consensus findings. First, dissent provokes state repression; second, state repression is more likely under autocracy; third, the short- and long-term effects of repression on the opposition tend to vary so much as to be essentially indeterminate; fourth, state repression is less effective against well-organized nonviolent opposition movements; fifth, nonviolent opposition tends to provoke less intense government repression than violent dissent; and sixth, the effectiveness of repression is a function of a regime's capacity to maintain the loyalty of its security apparatus.

Approaching state repression as a form of political violence also helps address a widespread critique of the concept of terrorism that decries its exclusive focus on non-state actors (e.g. Jackson 2009). Moreover, precisely because state repression is most unambiguously observed in times of interstate peace, it is distinct from war. In contrast, so-called "one-sided" violence (e.g. violence against non-combatants) tends to occur mainly (and is best studied) in the context of civil war where combatants operate openly—hence, it is more productively approached in that context, although researchers should undertake comparisons between state repression under peace and war. Lastly, state terror is distinct from genocide, where the intention behind the use of violence is extermination rather than compliance.

Genocide

Described as "a crime of crimes" (Schabas 2009), genocide is simultaneously an empirical, moral, legal, and political concept, in other words a definitional minefield. Because of this, there is now a sustained call for positioning the study of genocide within a broader political violence framework (Straus 2012; Verdeja 2012). An important stream of thinking about genocide has stressed the fact that it is not merely an instance of politically motivated mass murder but is rather defined by its intention to achieve the complete extermination of a particular group—although how exactly this intention emerges and how it translates into action are questions that remain debated. Indeed "intentional group annihilation" is the intuition characterizing its core (Straus 2001).

Precisely because genocide is an enterprise that requires a considerable degree of planning, coordination, and organization it is typically state-led. There is a broad consensus that the basis for targeting a group is ascriptive (the targeted group is defined on the basis of characteristics determined by birth, as selected and interpreted by the perpetrator), thus pointing to the perpetrators' essentialized motivation (Straus 2001, 366). In fact, it is the emphasis on this particular feature that led some researchers to label the targeting of non-ascriptive groups as "politicide" (Harff and Gurr 1988), so as to distinguish them from genocide.

Research on genocide has focused on its causes, including the role of deep-rooted exclusivist ideologies and the impact of war, both interstate and civil (Straus 2015), but also on its microdynamics, including its geographic spread (Straus 2006), and the role of individual choices in its implementation (Finkel 2017). The "first generation" of research on genocide was driven by the study of the Holocaust and stressed "some combination of hatred, totalitarianism, and scapegoating" (Straus 2012, 546). Since then, two streams of research and interpretation have emerged. The first one, mainly located in political science, underlines the strategic rationale behind genocide with a particular emphasis on political survival during wartime, while the second one focuses on the ideology of the perpetrators which is based on some combination of exclusionary, organic nationalist, purity-seeking, and revolutionary beliefs (Straus 2012, 546–50). A parallel development has been the development of micro-level studies of genocide carefully tracing its local dynamics (Braun 2016).

Ethnic Cleansing

Ethnic cleansing, a term popularized during the Yugoslav wars of the early 1990s can be thought of as a variant of genocide (Lieberman 2010; Mann 2005). Like genocide, a group is targeted in a way that is essentialized, direct, and total, but instead of exterminating a group, the goal is instead territorial removal with the aim of creating an ethnically homogeneous state. Naimark (2001) ascribes ethnic cleansing to the most advanced stage in the development of the modern state and Man (2005) to the pressures of democratization, while Bulutgil (2016) stresses the comprehensive nature of targeting (along with the ascriptive character of the group targeted) which parallels genocide and shows that war is a key factor in its manifestation. Wartime threats, she argues, radicalize the preferences of political elites and steer them toward the targeting of minorities that are connected with neighboring rival states. As in the studies of genocide, recent research has focused on both wartime dynamics and ideological preconditions, although the exact causal mechanisms at work remain under-explored (Bulutgil 2018).

Intercommunal Volence

Communal or intercommunal violence or conflict describes situations whereby both the perpetrators and targets of violence are non-state actors. This term covers what is still widely referred to as riots and pogroms, a type of violence described by Horowitz (2000, 1) as intense, sudden (but not necessary unplanned), lethal attacks by civilian members of one ethnic group on civilian members of another ethnic group. Sundberg et al. (2012) broaden this definition by referring to non-state violence and including in it rebel groups that fight one another, supporters of political parties that take to the streets to intimidate and kill opposing party supporters, or identity groups that attack one another (like Hindus and Muslims in Gujarat). An obvious issue with this definition is that it includes intra-rebel fighting that occurs in the context of civil war and is directly connected to it. Intercommunal conflicts are typically fought over local issues: control of local government, rural land, access to mining and other resources, or urban real estate. In some cases, notably in Nigeria, Sudan, or Indonesia, intercommunal conflict can escalate in terms of organizational capacity and fatalities, thus becoming a "communal war" (Krause 2018). Some of the best studied instances of intercommunal violence focus on urban riots between Muslims and Hindus in India (Brass 1997; Varshney 2003; Wilkinson 2004) and have traced their underlying variation to either an absence of civic interaction between them or the dark machinations of political elites seeking to score electoral victories in ethnically and religiously divided societies. Indeed, an emerging theme of this fledging literature is the role of elections in triggering such violence (Dunning 2011). Unlike some of the other types of political violence which tend to be associated with autocracies, intercommunal violence is often positively associated with democratization: the "third wave" of democracy has been accompanied by a worldwide wave of opposition-initiated, election-related protests often characterized by violence (Beaulieu 2014).

A type of intercommunal violence that is attracting considerable attention is that which occurs between pastoralists or between pastoralists and sedentary farmers, a form of violence that is seen as being connected with climate change and resource stress (Meier et al. 2007), but is also sensitive to the type of existing customary institutions which can promote peace through credible nonviolent bargaining (Wig and Kromrey 2018).

Organized Crime/Cartel Violence

On its face, the violence produced by organized criminal organizations (frequently referred to as cartels) diverges widely from what we intuitively take to be political violence. Criminal organizations maximize illicit profits and even when they try to subvert governments, they do not seek to replace them. Their goal is to exercise indirect influence on state authorities so as to be able to conduct their business and continue to extract illicit profits. Furthermore, criminal organizations tend to shun high levels of violence since it generally impedes their business and attracts unwanted attention (Gambetta 1996).

Nevertheless, there are good reasons to think of organized crime as a form of political violence. First, in some instances criminal organizations produce levels of militarized violence against both civilians and the state that match those encountered in full-fledged wars, as illustrated most tellingly by the cases of Mexico, Guatemala, or Colombia (Lessing 2017, 2015; Schedler 2013). Second, some prominent theories of state formation have linked aspects of criminal activity to both state-building (Olson 1993; Tilly 1985) and political contention and rebellion (Hobsbawm 1965). Third, organized criminal groups engage in practices, such as recruitment and local rule of civilian communities, paralleling those of rebel armed groups in civil wars (Kalyvas 2015).

Like intercommunal violence, large-scale organized violence has been linked with processes of democratization and electoral competition (Trejo and Ley 2017); it is also associated with post-conflict settings, where the violent skills gained by former combatants can be put to a new use (Kaplan and Nussio 2016). Indeed, there is a significant body of research focusing precisely on how policies of combatant demobilization and reintegration can be used to minimize post-conflict criminal activity (Rozema 2008).

Military Coup

Although instigated, planned, and organized by individuals hailing from within the military, a military coup (or coup d'état) is directed against a country's government and therefore constitutes a particular instance of rebellion. More specifically, it is a particular technology of rebellion entailing the forceful seizure of executive authority and office by a dissident faction operating within the security/military apparatus, mobilizing a faction within it, and using military means (Luttwak 2016). Unlike civil wars, military coups tend to be over quickly and to produce low levels of violence, although there are some notable exceptions, with either short but intense fighting (such as the Chilean coup of 1973 or the Cyprus coup of 1974) or their transformation into civil wars (such as in Spain, in 1936). The reason for this is that their fate hangs on the ability of their organizers to convince the broader military and political apparatus that they have won, thus causing a cascade of defections (Singh 2014). Seen from this perspective, coups are fundamentally coordination games rather than military or popularity contests.

Like civil wars, there is an inverse relationship between successful coups and high levels of income; and, again like in civil wars, a coup trap might emerge, whereby coups appear to lead to a chain of countercoups (Londregan and Poole 1990). However, coups have been declining following the end of the Cold War, even in Africa where they have persisted more than everywhere else (Marinov and Goemans 2014; Clark 2007; McGowan 2003). Democratization has generally been a factor contributing to the decline of coups, and military coups have been (surprisingly perhaps) a leading pathway to democratization. Indeed, whereas the vast majority of successful coups during the Cold War period led to stable authoritarian regimes, the majority of coups after 1991 have been followed by competitive elections; the main reason behind this shift is quite straightforward and can be summarized as dependence on Western donors for development aid (Marinov and Goemans 2014). This trend has led some scholars to argue that "coups and the threat of coups can be a significant weapon in fostering democracy" (Collier 2009), a claim that has been challenged because, in spite of the rise of democratizing coups during the post-Cold War period, more coups directed against autocracies still end up ushering in new autocracies and the concomitant repression (Derpanopoulos et al. 2016). Conversely, an emerging trend during the same period is the subversion of democratic regimes via executive takeover rather than military coup, by an initially democratically elected incumbent, as illustrated by the examples of Hugo Chavez in Venezuela, Vladimir Putin in Russia, and Recep Tayyip Erdogan in Turkey (Svolik 2017).

Mass Protest/Rebellion

Also referred to as contentious collective action (Tarrow 1998), mass protest is typically a peaceful activity associated with the expression of group claims and the activity of social movements in democratic settings. Sometimes, however, mass protest escalates into low-intensity violence primarily directed against material objects. Rarely but consequentially, it might escalate into an uprising or rebellion, and rarely into a social revolution. As mentioned above, treating revolution as an extreme version of mass protest provides, a tractable way to approach the over-aggregated concept of revolution.

When mass protests erupt in democracies, the police might exceptionally over-react causing casualties and, exceptionally, fatalities. Things diverge in authoritarian settings, however. There, mass protest is either nipped in the bud through the surgical use of violence or repressed violently—part of the so-called dissent–repression nexus (Moore 1998; Pierskalla 2009). Not infrequently, however, repression fails and mass protest in authoritarian settings might lead to authoritarian breakdown and even democratization (Beissinger 2002). As already mentioned, our understanding of phenomena such as mass uprising, insurrection, rebellion, and revolution is closely connected to large-scale mass protest, either in its violent or nonviolent form. On the one hand, campaigns of nonviolent resistance in authoritarian states turn out to be more effective than armed rebellions and insurgencies—twice as effective as their violent counterparts in achieving their stated goals (Chenoweth and Stephan 2011). On the other hand, authoritarian repression may fail and backfire. Indeed, many famous revolutions, from the French to the Iranian, began with people taking to the streets and escalated to the point of regime change. This type of mass protest is often contagious, crossing national borders with remarkable speed (such as the European Revolutions of 1848, the "Velvet Revolutions" of 1989, the "Color Revolutions" of the 2000s, or the "Arab Spring" of 2011) (Mitchell 2012; Weyland 2009). Lastly, in democratizing settings, mass protest is often articulated around elections (Beaulieu 2014) and often takes the form of intercommunal violence.

Political Assassination

Among the "highest-profile acts of political violence" (Iqbal and Zorn 2008, 385), the assassination of heads of states, high government officials, and public figures for political reasons is a practice that spans history: from Julius Caesar and Abraham Lincoln to John F. Kennedy and Yitzhak Rabin (Jones and Olken 2009). This type of political violence should not be bundled under the category of terrorism, because its objective is not merely to terrorize the population at large but to produce a direct political effect. Likewise, the targeting of opposition leaders by authoritarian regimes is best subsumed under the category of state repression, unless taking place in the context of civil war. Known as "decapitation," it is launched in the (rather vain, as it turns out) hope that it could bring an end to the war (Johnson 2012; Jordan 2009; Bob and Erickson Nepstad 2007). However, the targeting of foreign rebel leaders does constitute an instance of political assassination by states against non-state actors. The use of drones by the US to target rebel leaders in Pakistan, Yemen, and elsewhere, is such a case.

Political assassination is a form of political violence whose implications are in theory more important than its limited lethality. It is more likely in unfree, fragmented, and polarized countries; in turn, it causes a further decline in democratic prospects (Perliger 2015). A key insight is that its impact depends on the institutionalization of the political regime whose leader is targeted (Havens et al. 1969). Weak, repressive leaders in non-democratic systems face the highest risk of assassination (Iqbal and Zorn 2006), but successful assassinations of political leaders in autocracies often produce sustained moves toward democracy (Jones and Olken 2009).

Terrorism

The study of terrorism has been plagued by endless definitional debates and disputes (Schmid 2004; Schmid and Jongman 1988). The hallmarks of most definitions are the non-state character of the perpetrators of violence and the use of violence as a means to intimidate a large audience beyond that of the immediate victims (e.g. Enders and Sandler, 2012). In turn, terrorist groups are defined simply by their use of terrorism.

This chapter places terrorism in the broader context of political violence by seeking to minimize conceptual overlaps with other types of violence, and hence fleshing out its distinctive character. Therefore, political assassination, and violence exercised in the context of civil wars should be distinguished from terrorism. That leaves us with a phenomenon that consists of non-state violence exercised primarily during times of peace. A distinguishing feature of terrorist groups is that they target their own state but also operate internationally, targeting foreign states: they are domestic and/or transnational rebels.

This raises the critical question of how terrorists are different from other types of rebels or what Sánchez-Cuenca and de la Calle (2009) label the "actor-sense" of terrorism as opposed to the "action-sense." According to the latter, terrorism is a type of political violence that can be carried out by very different actors as long as there is a distinction between the target of violence and the audience, and as long as the intention is to spread fear in the civilian population. However, both these features are common to many forms of coercive violence; likewise, targeting noncombatants is encountered very widely, while terrorist attacks often target security forces and combatants. In contrast, the actor-sense of terrorism focuses on insurgent actors who by virtue of being extremely weak vis-à-vis the state, are unable to control territory and deploy militarily. Unlike rebel groups in civil wars, these groups must always operate in a clandestine fashion which goes a long way toward explaining the kind of violence they engage in (Sánchez-Cuenca and de la Calle 2009, 33–5).

As Sandler (2014, 263) acknowledges, "Insofar as terrorism has myriad root causes, it is not surprising that the empirical literature has come to little consensus on the root cause of domestic and transnational terrorism." Nevertheless, many studies of terrorism have highlighted a relation to regime type that takes an inverted-U shape between domestic terrorist violence and level of democracy: highly repressive regimes and fully democratic ones are inimical to terrorist activity, resulting in a concentration of terrorist violence in semi-repressive regimes (Gates et al. 2006). However, there is also evidence that the relationship between economic development and terrorist violence by clandestine actors is concave; unlike civil wars, violence by groups that do not control territory is more likely in middle-income countries as well as democracies (de la Calle and Sánchez-Cuenca 2012). Generally, the findings of the empirical literature are highly contingent on the coding of terrorism in the first place: does the coding distinguish between domestic and transnational terrorism? Militarized rebels and clandestine ones?

Four Connecting Logics

A key theme that emerges from this brief discussion is the relation between each type of political violence and four overarching processes: war, regime type, economic development, and ethnic divisions. Some types of political violence "thrive" under war, authoritarianism, and poverty, especially in ethnically divided societies. But even if we were able to suddenly get rid of war, autocracy, poverty, and ethnic divisions, we would not be able to guarantee peace, because political violence can be observed in prosperous and peaceful democracies as well; what is more, the transition from poor autocracies to prosperous democracies also appears to open the door to violence, as some types of political violence are replaced by others. This observation calls for a discussion of how the different types of political violence are connected to each other. Typologies are analytical heuristics, useful only insofar as they allow us to derive original hypotheses and chart new research directions. The typology presented here suggests four kinds of logics linking these eleven types of political violence: hierarchical, escalation, instrumental, and substitution.

Hierarchical Logic

Some types of political violence are so transformative that they endogenously create the conditions for the emergence of other types which would have arguably not appeared otherwise. This is a logic of hierarchy, whose clearest instance is interstate war, and particularly global and total war. Interstate war has been credited with creating the conditions that make genocide and ethnic cleansing possible (Shaw 2003; Bulutgil 2016); the exploration of the precise mechanisms linking them is still ongoing and ranges from ideological radicalization to the activation of ethnic over class cleavages (Harff 2003; Straus 2012; Bulutgil 2016). Less explored is the connection between interstate and civil war. As the example of Iraq recently suggests, interstate wars often give way to civil wars in the context of occupation regimes (Edelstein 2010). World War II provides a broad range of illustrations (Kalyvas 2006). In fact, this war was clearly connected to genocide (Holocaust), widespread ethnic cleansing, both during and following its end, civil wars in several occupied countries, violently repressed mass protests, political assassinations, and terrorism by various resistance groups, state repression, and military coups in many countries. In this sense, interstate war can be thought of as the "mother of all political violence."

Civil war may also generate the conditions for the appearance of genocide, ethnic cleansing, and mass terror (Harff 2003), while it is common for processes of organized crime to emerge in its context (Andreas 2008). In turn, genocide, ethnic cleansing, and mass terror also open the door to all kinds of organized crime, especially related to the looting of the properties of the targeted populations. Lastly, intercommunal violence can emerge during mass protest, as when rival groups of government supporters and opponents clashed in the streets of Cairo in 2012.

Instrumental Logic

Unlike the hierarchical logic, the instrumental one entails the explicit deployment of a type of political violence as a tool for the implementation of another one. For example, intercommunal violence is sometimes used to implement genocide, i.e. by inciting neighbors to turn against each other in a way that might appear spontaneous yet is engineered as part of a broader, systematic plan. The Holocaust was implemented in part by such means in Nazi-occupied Poland and the Soviet Union (Snyder 2010; Gross 2001), as was the Rwandan genocide (Straus 2006) or the massacre of Indonesian communists in 1966 (Cribb 1991).

Likewise, civil war is a setting that encourages the deployment of terrorism as one among several possible military tactics used by the rebels. Several insurgent groups have relied on the use of indiscriminate attacks against soft targets, particularly in areas that are not controlled by the state (Fisher 2018; de la Calle and Sánchez-Cuenca 2012). Fortna (2015) examines the use of terrorism within civil war. She argues that it is used in spite of the fact that its disadvantages appear to outweigh its advantages: although it is a cheap way to inflict pain on one's enemy, it is useless for taking or holding territory, signals weakness rather than strength, and can undermine legitimacy among potential supporters—although it may help rebel groups to survive longer. An extensive debate has taken place about whether the Ottoman authorities used the ethnic cleansing of their Armenian population as a means toward genocide (Akçam 2012). Less obviously perhaps, civil war provides a cover for the launch of campaigns of ethnic cleansing under the pretext of counter-insurgency. The case of the Rohingya in Myanmar might be such an instance. Reasons why certain types of political violence are used as a means to accomplish others vary and may range from low cost to plausible deniability.

Escalation Logic

The logic of escalation also resembles the hierarchical logic, but instead of a broader type of political violence engendering a narrower one, it operates in the opposite direction. This is the case, for instance, when mass protests escalate into a large-scale urban uprising (or revolution) and civil war as in Iran in 1978–9, or into a civil war, as in Syria in 2011. Likewise, a political assassination can escalate into civil war, as was the case with the assassination of Jorge Eliécer Gaitán, the leader of the Liberal Party of Colombia, in 1948. Mass protests and riots ensued in Bogota and eventually, they escalated into a generalized communal war and a full-fledged civil war known as "La Violencia." The assassination of the Rwandan President Juvénal Habyarimana in 1994 is widely seen as the catalyst of the Rwandan genocide, although the exact details remain disputed. The failed military coup of General Francisco Franco in Spain, in 1936, escalated into a civil war. More generally, there is evidence of an interactive relationship between assassination and political turmoil, especially where the process of leadership succession is informal and unregulated (Iqbal and Zorn 2008). Alternatively, there is much talk of the danger that a civil war might escalate into an interstate civil war through foreign intervention, but it appears to be more common for "internationalized" civil war to act as a substitute rather than a cause of interstate war. For example, although the Second Congo War (1998–2003) saw various interstate clashes, such as Angola against Rwanda, it did not escalate into full-fledged interstate war.

Substitution Logic

The Cold War can be thought of as a period when internationalized civil wars (or "proxy wars") became substitutes for an impossibly destructive clash between the United States and the Soviet Union. Moving further into the past, Wimmer (2012) suggests a logic of substitution between interstate and civil wars that emerged as part of the replacement process of multiethnic empires by nation-states. The logic of substitution implies a strategic choice whereby one type of political violence substitutes for another one which is deemed either impossible or ineffective.

A substitution logic has been suggested for terrorism and civil war: terrorism can be understood as a substitute for (territorial) civil war, by rebels operating in the context of very strong states who prevent them from launching a full-scale insurgency; terrorism, in that framework, constitutes a non-territorial insurgency (de la Calle and Sánchez-Cuenca 2012). A substitution logic also exists between mass protest and terrorism. For example, the emergence of terrorist activities in Italy during the 1970s has been explained as a process of strategic adaptation by radical protesters unhappy with the perceived ineffectiveness of the student social movement and its protest activity (Della Porta 1988; Della Porta and Tarrow 1986). Likewise Roessler (2016) points to a substitution logic between military coups and civil wars in the ethnically divided societies of sub-Saharan Africa: African rulers face a trade-off when it comes to power-sharing. On the one hand, they face a high likelihood of being overthrown in a military coup by members of their own military-political faction who also have ties with a different ethnic group. On the other hand, however, if they exclude them from the ruling coalition, they face the danger that these individuals may mobilize their ethnic power base to launch an insurgency against them. Given this stark choice and the fact that rulers are more vulnerable to a military coup than a civil war, they are attracted by the choice of exclusion, leading them to increase the likelihood of a civil war. In this formulation, "civil war represents the consequences of a strategic choice by rulers, backed by their coethnics, to coup-proof their regimes from their ethnic rivals" (Roessler 2016, xvi).

The landscape of political violence provides many opportunities for the exploration of substitution effects. For example, it is argued that the genocide of the European Jews was launched once an alternative project of ethnic cleansing (known as the "Madagascar Plan") became impossible (Browning 1992, 18). Likewise, coup-proofing, a term describing the various methods used to deter military coups, might increase the likelihood of civil war through the military's reduced capacity to fight insurgents (Houle 2016). More broadly, it might be the case that defeating insurgents and mass protesters makes terrorism more likely or that reducing state repression raises the odds of intercommunal violence. The methodological implications of taking the logic of substitution seriously are considerable, since they point to a range of counterfactuals that tend to be ignored.

Conclusion

In this chapter I have proposed a typology of eleven types of political violence, discussed their main characteristics, and explored four distinct logics that shape the ways they are connected to each other. The discussion provides a way to think about political violence in a way that overcomes the fragmentation of the field without, however, sacrificing the distinctiveness of each type and without over-aggregating different kinds of political violence into artificial categories. Most importantly, this typology alerts us to the fact that the counterfactual to the absence of a certain kind of political violence is not necessarily peace as typically implied but, rather, a different type or types of political violence. This makes the study of political violence more complex than usually assumed, but also both more realistic and intriguing.

References

Akçam, Taner (2012) *The Young Turks' Crime Against Humanity: The Armenian Genocide and Ethnic Cleansing in the Ottoman Empire*. Princeton: Princeton University Press.

Andreas, Peter (2008) *Blue Helmets and Black Markets: The Business of Survival in the Siege of Sarajevo*. Ithaca, NY: Cornell University Press.

Arjona, Ana (2016) *Rebelocracy: Social Order in the Colombian Civil War*. New York: Cambridge University Press.

Armitage, David (2017) *Civil Wars: A History in Ideas*. New Haven: Yale University Press.

Balcells, Laia (2017) *Rivalry and Revenge: The Politics of Violence during Civil War*. New York: Cambridge University Press.

Beaulieu, Emily (2014) *Electoral Protest and Democracy in the Developing World*. New York: Cambridge University Press.

Beissinger, Mark R. (2002) *Nationalist Mobilization and the Collapse of the Soviet State*. New York: Cambridge University Press.

Berman, Eli, Joseph H. Felter, and Jacob N. Shapiro (2011) "Can Hearts and Minds be Bought? The Economics of Counterinsurgency in Iraq," *Journal of Political Economy*, 119(4): 766–819.

Bob, Clifford, and Sharon Erickson Nepstad (2007) "Kill a Leader, Murder a Movement? Leadership and Assassination in Social Movements," *American Behavioral Scientist*, 50(10): 1370–94.

Brass, Paul (1997) *Theft of an Idol: Text and Context in the Representation of Collective Violence*. Princeton: Princeton University Press.

Braun, Robert (2016) "Religious Minorities and Resistance to Genocide: The Collective Rescue of Jews in the Netherlands during the Holocaust," *American Political Science Review*, 110(1): 127–47.

Browning, Christopher R. (1992) *The Path to Genocide: Essays on Launching the Final Solution*. Cambridge: Cambridge University Press.

Bulutgil, Zeynep (2016) *The Roots of Ethnic Cleansing in Europe*. Ithaca, NY, and London: Cornell University Press.

Bulutgil, Zeynep (2018) "The State of the Field and Debates on Ethnic Cleansing," *Nationalities Papers*, 46(6): 1136-45.

Cederman, Lars-Erik, Kristian Skrede Gleditsch, and Halvard Buhaug (2013) *Inequality, Grievances, and Civil War*. New York: Cambridge University Press.

Chenoweth, Erica, and Maria Stephan (2011) *Why Civil Resistance Works: The Strategic Logic of Nonviolent Conflict*. New York: Columbia University Press.

Chenoweth, Erica, Evan Perkoski, and Sooyeon Kang (2017) "State Repression and Nonviolent Resistance," *Journal of Conflict Resolution*, 61(9): 1950–69.

Clark, John Frank (2007) "The Decline of the African Military Coup," *Journal of Democracy*, 18(3): 141–55.
Collier, David, Jody LaPorte, and Jason Seawright (2012) "Putting Typologies to Work: Concept Formation, Measurement, and Analytic Rigor," *Political Science Quarterly*, 65(1): 217–32.
Collier, Paul (2009) "In Praise of the Coup," *New Humanist*, <https://newhumanist.org.uk/articles/1997/in-praise-of-the-coup>.
Collier, Paul, and Anke Hoeffler (1998) "On Economic Causes of Civil War," *Oxford Economic Papers*, 50(4): 563–73.
Collier, Paul, and Anke Hoeffler (2004) "Greed and Grievance in Civil War," *Oxford Economic Papers*, 56(4): 563–95.
Cribb, Robert, ed. (1991) *The Indonesian Killings, 1965–1966: Studies from Java and Bali*. Monash Papers on Southeast Asia, 21.
Davenport, Christian (2007) "State Repression and Political Order," *Annual Reviews of Political Science*, 10: 1–23.
David, Steven R. (1997) "Internal War: Causes and Cures," *World Politics*, 49(4): 552–76.
De la Calle, Luis, and Ignacio Sánchez-Cuenca (2012) "Rebels without a Territory: An Analysis of Nonterritorial Conflicts in the World, 1970–1997," *Journal of Conflict Resolution*, 56(4): 580–603.
Della Porta, Donatella (1988) "Recruitment Processes in Clandestine Political Organizations: Italian Left-Wing Terrorism," *International Social Movement Research*, 1: 155–69.
Della Porta, Donatella, and Sidney Tarrow (1986) "Unwanted Children: Political Violence and the Cycle of Protest in Italy, 1966–1973," *European Journal of Political Research*, 14(5–6): 607–32.
Derpanopoulos, George, Erica Frantz, Barbara Geddes, and Joseph Wright (2016) "Are Coups Good for Democracy?" *Research and Politics*, 3(1): 1–7.
Downes, Alexander B. (2004) *Targeting Civilians in War*. Ithaca, NY, and London: Cornell University Press.
Dunning, Thad (2011) "Fighting and Voting: Violent Conflict and Electoral Politics," *Journal of Conflict Resolution*, 55(3): 327–39.
Edelstein, David M. (2010) *Occupational Hazards: Success and Failure in Military Occupation*. Ithaca, NY: Cornell University Press.
Enders, Walter, and Todd Sandler (2012) *The Political Economy of Terrorism*. Cambridge: Cambridge University Press.
Fearon, James D. (2017) "Civil War and the Current International System," *Daedalus*, 146(4): 18–32.
Fearon, James D., and David D. Laitin (2003) "Ethnicity, Insurgency, and Civil War," *American Political Science Review*, 97(1): 75–86.
Finkel, Evgeny (2017) *Ordinary Jews Choice and Survival during the Holocaust*. Princeton: Princeton University Press.
Fisher, Max (2018) "Why Attack Afghan Civilians? Creating Chaos Rewards Taliban," *New York Times*, 28 Jan., <https://www.nytimes.com/2018/01/28/world/asia/afghanistan-taliban-kabul-attacks.html>.
Fortna, Virginia Page (2008) *Does Peacekeeping Work? Shaping Belligerents' Choices After Civil War*. Princeton: Princeton University Press.
Fortna, Virginia Page (2015) "Do Terrorists Win? Rebels' Use of Terrorism and Civil War Outcomes," *International Organization*, 69(3): 519–56.
Galtung, Johan (1969) "Violence, Peace, and Peace Research," *Journal of Peace Research*, 6(3): 167–91.

Gambetta, Diego (1996) *The Sicilian Mafia: The Business of Private Protection*. Cambridge, MA: Harvard University Press.

Gat, Azar (2008) *War in Human Civilization*. Oxford: Oxford University Press.

Gates, Scott, Håvard Hegre, Mark P. Jones, and Håvard Strand (2006) "Institutional Inconsistency and Political Instability: Polity Duration, 1800–2000," *American Journal of Political Science*, 50(4): 893–908.

Goldstein, Joshua S. (2011) *Winning the War on War: The Decline of Armed Conflict Worldwide*. New York: Dutton.

Goldstone, Jack A. (2001) "Toward a Fourth Generation of Revolutionary Theory," *Annual Reviews of Political Science*, 4: 139–87.

Gross, Jan (2001) *Neighbors: The Destruction of the Jewish Community in Jedwabne, Poland*. Princeton: Princeton University Press.

Gutiérrez-Sanín, Francisco, and Elisabeth Jean Wood (2017) "What should we Mean by 'Pattern of Political Violence'? Repertoire, Targeting, Frequency, and Technique," *Perspectives on Politics*, 15(1): 20–41.

Harff, Barbara (2003) "No Lessons Learned from the Holocaust? Assessing Risks of Genocide and Political Mass Murder since 1955," *American Political Science Review*, 97(1): 57–73.

Harff, Barbara, and Ted Robert Gurr (1988) "Toward Empirical Theory of Genocides and Politicides: Identification and Measurement of Cases since 1945," *International Studies Quarterly*, 32(3): 359–71.

Havens, Murray Clark, Carl Leiden, and Karl Michael Schmitt (1969) *The Politics of Assassination*. Englewood Cliffs, NJ: Prentice Hall.

Hegre, Håvard (2001) "Toward a Democratic Civil Peace? Democracy, Political Change, and Civil War, 1816–1992," *American Political Science Review*, 95(1): 33–48.

Higonnet, Etelle, ed. (2009) *Quiet Genocide. Guatemala, 1981–1983*. New Brunswick, NJ: Transaction Publishers.

Hironaka, Ann (2005) *Neverending Wars: The International Community, and the Perpetuation of Civil War*. Cambridge, MA: Harvard University Press.

Hobsbawm, Eric (1965) *Primitive Rebels: Studies in Archaic Forms of Social Movement in the Nineteenth Century*. New York: W. W. Norton & Co.

Horowitz, Donald L. (2000) *The Deadly Ethnic Riot*. Berkeley, CA: University of California Press.

Houle, Christian (2016) "Why Class Inequality Breeds Coups But Not Civil Wars," *Journal of Peace Research*, 53(5): 680–95.

Iqbal, Zaryab, and Christopher Zorn (2006) "*Sic Semper Tyrannis*? Power, Repression, and Assassination since the Second World War," *Journal of Politics*, 68(3): 489–501.

Iqbal, Zaryab, and Christopher Zorn (2008) "The Political Consequences of Assassination," *Journal of Conflict Resolution*, 52(3): 385–400.

Jackson, Richard (2009) "The Ghosts of State Terror: Knowledge, Politics and Terrorism Studies," *Critical Studies on Terrorism*, 1(3): 377–92.

Jentzsch, Corinna, Stathis N. Kalyvas, and Livia I. Schubiger (2015) "Militias in Civil Wars: An Emerging Research Agenda," *Journal of Conflict Resolution*, 59(5): 755–69.

Joas, Hans, and Wolfgang Knöbel (2013) *War in Social Thought: Hobbes to the Present*. Princeton: Princeton University Press.

Johnson, Patrick B. (2012) "Does Decapitation Work? Assessing the Effectiveness of Leadership Targeting in Counterinsurgency Campaigns," *International Security*, 36(4): 47–79.

Jones, Benjamin F., and Benjamin A. Olken (2009) "Hit or Miss? The Effect of Assassinations on Institutions and War," *American Economic Journal: Macroeconomics*, 1(2): 55–87.

Jordan, Jenna (2009) "When Heads Roll: Assessing the Effectiveness of Leadership Decapitation," *Security Studies*, 18(4): 719–55.
Kalyvas, Stathis N. (2006) *The Logic of Violence in Civil War*. New York: Cambridge University Press.
Kalyvas, Stathis N. (2007) "Civil Wars," in Carles Boix and Susan Stokes (eds), *Handbook of Comparative Politics*. New York: Oxford University Press, 416–34.
Kalyvas, Stathis N. (2015) "How Civil Wars Help Explain Organized Crime—and How they do Not," *Journal of Conflict Resolution*, 59(8): 1517–40.
Kalyvas, Stathis N. (2018) "Jihadi Rebels in Civil War," *Daedalus*, 147(1): 36–47.
Kaplan, Oliver, and Enzo Nussio (2016) "Explaining Recidivism of Ex-Combatants in Colombia," *Journal of Conflict Resolution*, 62(1): 64–93.
Keck, Margaret E., and Kathryn Sikkink (1998) *Activists beyond Borders: Advocacy Networks in International Politics*. Ithaca, NY, and London: Cornell University Press.
Krause, Jana (2018) *Resilient Communities. Non-Violence and Civilian Agency in Communal War*. Cambridge: Cambridge University Press.
Lessing, Benjamin (2015) "Logics of Violence in Criminal War," *Journal of Conflict Resolution*, 59(8): 1486–1516.
Lessing, Benjamin (2017) *Making Peace in Drug Wars: Crackdowns and Cartels in Latin America*. New York: Cambridge University Press.
Lieberman Benjamin (2010) "'Ethnic Cleansing' versus Genocide?", in Donald Bloxham and A. Dirk Moses (eds), *The Oxford Handbook of Genocide Studies*. Oxford: Oxford University Press, 42–60.
Londregan, John B., and Keith T. Poole (1990) "Poverty, the Coup Trap, and the Seizure of Executive Power," *World Politics*, 42(2): 151–83.
Luttwak, Edward N. (2016) *Coup d'Etat: A Practical Handbook*. Cambridge, MA: Harvard University Press, rev. edn.
McGowan, Patrick J. (2003) "African Military Coups d'état, 1956–2001: Frequency, Trends and Distribution," *Journal of Modern African Studies*, 41(3): 339–70.
Mann, Michael (2005) *The Dark Side of Democracy: Explaining Ethnic Cleansing*. New York: Cambridge University Press.
Marinov, Nikolay, and Hein Goemans (2014) "Coups and Democracy," *British Journal of Political Science*, 44(4): 799–825.
Meier, Patrick, Doug Bond, and Joe Bond (2007) "Environmental Influence on Pastoral Conflict in the Horn of Africa," *Political Geography*, 26(6): 716–35.
Mitchell, Lincoln A. (2012) *The Color Revolutions*. Philadelphia: University of Pennsylvania Press.
Moore, Will H. (1998) "Repression and Dissent: Substitution, Context, and Timing," *American Journal of Political Science*, 2(3): 851–73.
Mueller, John (2007) *The Remnants of War*. Ithaca, NY, and London: Cornell University Press.
Naimark, Norman (2001) *Fires of Hatred: Ethnic Cleansing in Twentieth Century Europe*. Cambridge, MA: Harvard University Press.
Olson, Mancur (1993) "Dictatorship, Democracy, and Development," *American Political Science Review*, 87(3): 567–76.
Perliger, Arie (2015) "The Causes and Impact of Political Assassinations," *CTC Sentinel*, 8(1): 11–13.
Pierskalla, Jan Henryk (2009) "Protest, Deterrence, and Escalation: The Strategic Calculus of Government Repression," *Journal of Conflict Resolution*, 54(1): 117–45.

Pinker, Steven (2011) *The Better Angels of our Nature. The Decline of Violence in History and its Causes*. New York: Allen Lane.
Poe, Steven C., and C. Neal Tate (1994) "Repression of Human Rights to Personal Integrity in the 1980s: A Global Analysis," *American Political Science Review*, 88(4): 853–72.
Posen, Barry R. (1993) "The Security Dilemma and Ethnic Conflict," *Survival*, 35(1): 27–47.
Ritter, Emily H., and Courtney Conrad (2016) "Preventing and Responding to Dissent: The Observational Challenges of Explaining Strategic Repression," *American Political Science Review*, 110(1): 85–99.
Roessler, Philip (2016) *Ethnic Politics and State Power in Africa: The Logic of the Coup-Civil War Trap*. Cambridge: Cambridge University Press.
Rozema, Ralph (2008) "Urban DDR-Processes: Paramilitaries and Criminal Networks in Medellín, Colombia," *Journal of Latin American Studies*, 40(3): 423–52.
Rummel, Rudolph J. (1994) *Death by Government*. New Brunswick, NJ: Transaction Books.
Russett, Bruce (1993) *Grasping the Democratic Peace: Principles for a Post-Cold War World*. Princeton: Princeton University Press.
Sánchez-Cuenca, Ignacio, and Luis de la Calle (2009) "Domestic Terrorism: The Hidden Side of Political Violence," *Annual Reviews of Political Science*, 12: 31–49.
Sartori, Giovanni (1970) "Concept Misformation in Comparative Politics," *American Political Science Review*, 64(4): 1033–53.
Schabas, William (2009) *Genocide in International Law*. Cambridge: Cambridge University Press.
Schedler, Andreas (2013) "Mexico's Civil War Democracy." Paper prepared for presentation at the 109th Annual Meeting of the American Political Science Association (APSA), Chicago, Aug. 29–Sept. 1.
Schmid, Alex P. (2004) "Terrorism: The Definitional Problem," *Case Western Reserve Journal of International Law*, 36(2): 375–419.
Schmid, Alex P., and A. J. Jongman (1988) *Political Terrorism: A Research Guide to Concepts, Theories, Data Bases, and Literatures*. New Brunswick, NJ: Transaction Books.
Shaw, Martin (2003) *War and Genocide: Organised Killing in Modern Society*. Cambridge: Polity Press.
Simmons, Beth A. (2009) *Mobilizing Human Rights: International Law in Domestic Politics*. New York: Cambridge University Press.
Singh, Naunihal (2014) *Seizing Power: The Strategic Logic of Military Coups*. Baltimore: Johns Hopkins University Press.
Skocpol, Theda (1979) *States and Social Revolutions: A Comparative Analysis of France, Russia and China*. New York: Cambridge University Press.
Sluka, Jeffrey A., ed. (2000) *Death Squad: The Anthropology of State Terror*. Philadelphia: University of Pennsylvania Press.
Snyder, Timothy D. (2010) *Bloodlands: Europe between Hitler and Stalin*. New York: Basic Books.
Staniland, Paul (2014) *Networks of Rebellion: Explaining Insurgent Cohesion and Collapse*. Ithaca, NY, and London: Cornell University Press.
Stoll, David (1993) *Between Two Armies in the Ixil Towns of Guatemala*. New York: Colombia University Press.
Straus, Scott (2001) "Contested Meanings and Conflicting Imperatives: A Conceptual Analysis of Genocide," *Journal of Genocide Research*, 3(3): 349–75.

Straus, Scott (2006) *The Order of Genocide: Race, Power, and War in Rwanda*. Ithaca, NY: Cornell University Press.

Straus, Scott (2012) "'Destroy Them to Save Us': Theories of Genocide and the Logics of Political Violence," *Terrorism and Political Violence*, 24: 544–60.

Straus, Scott (2015) *Making and Unmaking Nations: War, Leadership, and Genocide in Modern Africa*. Ithaca, NY: Cornell University Press.

Sundberg, Ralph, Kristine Eck, and Joakim Kreutz (2012) "Introducing the UCDP Non-State Conflict Dataset," *Journal of Peace Research*, 49(2): 351–62.

Svolik, Milan W. (2017) "When Polarization Trumps Civic Virtue: Partisan Conflict and the Subversion of Democracy by Incumbents," Unpublished paper.

Tarrow, Sidney (1998) *Power in Movement*. New York: Cambridge University Press.

Tilly, Charles (1985) "War Making and State Making as Organized Crime," in Peter Evans, Dietrich Rueschemeyer, and Theda Skocpol (eds), *Bringing the State Back In*. Cambridge: Cambridge University Press, 169–87.

Tilly, Charles (2003) *The Politics of Collective Violence*. Cambridge: Cambridge University Press.

Trejo, Guillermo, and Sandra Ley (2017) "Why Did Drug Cartels Go to War in Mexico? Subnational Party Alternation, the Breakdown of Criminal Protection, and the Onset of Large-Scale Violence," *Comparative Political Studies*, 51(7): 900–37.

Varshney, Ashutosh (2003) *Ethnic Conflict and Civic Life: Hindus and Muslims in India*. New Haven: Yale University Press.

Verdeja, Ernesto (2012) "The Political Science of Genocide: Outlines of an Emerging Research Agenda," *Perspectives on Politics*, 10(2): 307–21.

Weyland, Kurt (2009) "The Diffusion of Revolution: '1848' in Europe and Latin America," *International Organization*, 63(3): 391–423.

Wig, Tore, and Daniela Kromrey (2018) "Which Groups Fight? Customary Institutions and Communal Conflicts in Africa," *Journal of Peace Research*, 55(4): 415–29.

Wilkinson, Steven I. (2004) *Votes and Violence: Electoral Competition and Ethnic Riots in India*. New York: Cambridge University Press.

Wimmer, Andreas (2012) *Waves of War: Nationalism, State Formation, and Ethnic Exclusion in the Modern World*. New York: Cambridge University Press.

CHAPTER 3

DEFINING TERRORISM

a conceptual minefield

BEN SAUL

Introduction

THE ordinary linguistic meaning of terrorism is reasonably simple: extreme fear. Disentangling the word from the world around it has, however, proved excruciatingly difficult. In part this is because the context of language matters: one can be terrorized by many things, whether a spider, a bad dream, a horror movie, a bank robber, or "Islamic State." The term's descriptive utility is thus immediately dissipated because of its breadth and diversity of possible applications. Scholarly attempts to define terrorism have sought to isolate a range of identifying characteristics, focusing variously on methods, targets, effects, victims, perpetrators, intention, motive, and so on. Consensus within the various epistemic communities of scholars, policy-makers, and states has proved extremely difficult, leading some to defeatism—and others to strive harder to conceptualize terrorism (Richards 2015, 9).

When the politics and geo-politics of labelling conduct as "terrorism" is added in, the challenge of distilling a useful meaning becomes more acute. The term appears to have entered into political discourse in the late eighteenth century to describe the Jacobin reign of (state) terror during the French Revolution (Saul 2006b, 1). Its usage has since vacillated between stigmatizing various kinds of state and non-state violence, depending on the disapprover's perspective.

Contestation over the meaning of terrorism is not, however, limited to rhetorical efforts to discredit one's political opponents. The struggle to define terrorism also reflects genuine normative differences (ideological, philosophical, political, religious, or moral) over when violence should be regarded as licit or illicit, justified or unjustified, or legitimate or illegitimate. Since the nineteenth century, these struggles have variously centered on causes such as revolutionary socialism, ethnic nationalism, national liberation/self-determination against colonial regimes or foreign occupation, and rebellion against authoritarian rule.

It might seem uncontroversial to say that the core of the concept of terrorism is the threat or use of instrumental or coercive violence against civilians. Yet, even that narrowest of conceptions is subject to disagreements. For some, not all civilians are innocent and some "deserve" to be attacked—whether French settlers in French Algeria or Israeli settlers in Palestine; American taxpayers (according to Al Qaeda); or those who raise funds or recruit for terrorist organizations (for the United States when targeting by aerial drones). One even still hears the view from some citizens of Western democracies that dropping atomic bombs on Japan—and exterminating Japanese civilians—was "necessary" to end that world war. Deliberately attacking civilians to intimidate an adversary is not only a tactic of weaker parties in asymmetric conflicts (as is commonly supposed), but can also appeal to the strong.

Many of the conceptual debates about what terrorism is have been shoe-horned into legal efforts to define terrorism. This chapter focuses in particular on efforts to define terrorism in international law, which has served as a kind of transnational, common language for elucidating the controversies. Lively debates about the meaning of terrorism have taken place in many other disciplines, whether psychology, literature, international relations, criminology, history, political science, security studies, and so on. This chapter cannot, and does not, attempt to skate across the universe of terrorism research. Rather, it explores the international law debates to illustrate some of the most salient conceptual issues that have arisen globally in various inter-governmental efforts to define "terrorism"—along with the narratives of resistance that have opposed state efforts to define and suppress it.

While there is a long and contested history of moral and political disapproval of "terrorism," it is only fairly recently that concepts of terrorism have taken legal form. From the mid-nineteenth century, the problem of what is often now often regarded as terrorism was framed quite differently in national law. Political violence was variously prosecuted as ordinary crime or offences against public order or state security. Highly variable national extradition laws struggled, however, to deal with political offenders who fled across borders, eventually precipitating efforts to improve transnational cooperation.

Calls to define "terrorism" as a legal concept arose in this context from the 1920s onwards, with many efforts, over eighty years to the present, to define, criminalize, and depoliticize a common global concept of "terrorism." Those efforts were largely unsuccessful and most national laws continued to avoid reference to "terrorism." At most, ordinary crimes and security offences were supplemented by the domestic implementation of transnational treaty offences (such as hijacking or hostage taking), which generally do not mention terrorism.

It was only after the terrorist attacks on the United States of September 11, 2001 ("9/11") that most states considered enacting "terrorism" offences, spurred on by the perceived threat of global religious terrorism, obligations imposed by the UN Security Council, gaps in existing criminal liabilities and police powers, and the expressive or communicative function of demarcating and stigmatizing terrorism as a special kind of violence against public interests. National laws remain, however, startlingly diverse and there is still a global divergence.

At the international level, there is certainly a basic legal consensus that terrorism is criminal violence intended to intimidate a population or coerce a government or international organization; some national laws add an ulterior intention to pursue a political, religious, or ideological cause. There remain intense moral and political disagreements, however, on whether there should be exceptions for just causes (such as liberation violence and rebellion), armed conflicts, and state violence. As a result, a conceptual impasse continues, even if international legal agreement has been edging closer. In practice, the designation of groups as "terrorist" by states and regional or international organizations is also variable, suggesting that even where there is agreement on a definition, it is applied selectively—thus perpetuating, while concealing, many of the same conceptual disagreements that have dogged attempts at definition.

Terrorism and the Law before 1945

While much contemporary discussion of terrorism presents the problem as new or unprecedented, there is a long legal history of efforts to conceptualize terrorism. Modern transnational efforts to manage "terrorism" stemmed from efforts to address gaps in national extradition laws in nineteenth-century Europe. As perpetrators of political violence fled across national borders to escape retribution or justice, victim states often demanded their surrender. Interstate tension arose where national extradition laws prohibited the extradition of suspects, typically because of the so-called "political offence exception" to extradition and the related protection of political asylum (Van den Wijngaert 1980, 191).

The most emphatic international effort to legally address "terrorism" in this period followed the assassination in France in 1934 of King Alexander of Yugoslavia and the French Foreign Minister, Louis Barthou, by a Macedonian separatist. The Italian courts refused to extradite the fugitives on the basis of the political offence exception. To avert possible conflict, from 1934 to 1937 the League of Nations drafted an international convention to repress the crime of terrorism, and another treaty establishing an international criminal court to prosecute it (Saul 2006a).

The 1937 Convention for the Prevention and Punishment of Terrorism required States to criminalize terrorist offences. Article 1(2) defined "acts of terrorism" as "criminal acts directed against a [foreign] State and intended or calculated to create a state of terror in the minds of particular persons, or a group of persons or the general public." Article 2 enumerated the physical acts which States must criminalize, including crimes against persons and property, weapons offences, and ancillary offences. Consequently, terrorism is defined by the intended aim (a state of terror), the ultimate target (a State), and the prohibited means used, but proposals to define terrorism as a means to a political end were not accepted (League of Nations 1935). "Acts of terrorism" was defined circularly by reference to "a state of terror," despite objections that the phrase was ambiguous and open to abuse.

The Convention's extradition provisions did not, however, succeed in excluding terrorism from the political offence exception. In a climate of mounting authoritarianism, many states were reluctant to confine their sovereign discretion in extradition matters, including the scope of political offences, and were at pains to protect asylum from degradation. With the coming of World War II and the demise of the League, the treaty never entered into force. As a result, the predominant approach in national laws remained that terrorist violence was generally prosecuted as ordinary or political crimes, but not as terrorism. Further, in transnational cases, extradition remained subject to varied national approaches to the political offence exception. The League definition nonetheless influenced later international legal debates.

Legal Conceptions of Terrorism between 1945 and 2001

Codification of International Crimes

After World War II, the concept of terrorism resurfaced in episodic efforts by the International Law Commission (ILC) to codify international crimes between 1954 and 1998. The emphasis was upon state-sponsored terrorism rather than violence by autonomous non-state actors. In 1954 the ILC first defined an international offence of terrorism (art. 1(5)). By 1991 the offence was as one state:

> undertaking, organizing, assisting, financing, encouraging or tolerating acts against another State directed at persons or property and of such a nature as to create a state of terror in the minds of public figures, groups of persons or the general public. (art. 24)

The revised 1995 draft added that acts must be committed "in order to compel" the victim State "to grant advantages or to act in a specific way" (ILC 1995, 58). The final ILC draft code of international crimes was approved in 1996 and no longer included an autonomous terrorism offence (ILC 1996, paras 46, 48).

The General Assembly drew the 1996 ILC Draft Code to the attention of the Preparatory Committee on the Establishment of an International Criminal Court (UNGA resolution 51/160, 1996). Ultimately, Article 5 of the 1998 Draft Rome Statute, presented to the 1998 Rome Diplomatic Conference (UN 1998, art. 5), revived autonomous "crimes of terrorism," comprising three distinct offences. The first offence was:

> Undertaking, organizing, sponsoring, ordering, facilitating, financing, encouraging or tolerating acts of violence against another State directed at persons or property and of such a nature as to create terror, fear or insecurity in the minds of public figures, groups of persons, the general public or populations, for whatever considerations and purposes of a political, philosophical, ideological, racial, ethnic, religious or such other nature that may be invoked to justify them...

This first offence resembles the 1991 ILC draft and was not limited to armed conflict (as was the 1996 ILC draft). It also shares elements of the 1937 League definition and a later 1994 General Assembly working definition of terrorism. The second offence comprised any offence in six sectoral anti-terrorism treaties (to be discussed presently). The third offence involved "the use of firearms, weapons, explosives and dangerous substances when used as a means to perpetrate indiscriminate violence involving death or serious bodily injury to persons or groups or persons or populations or serious damage to property."

At the Rome Conference, thirty-four states spoke in favor of including terrorism, including because it shocked the conscience of humanity; had grave consequences for human suffering and property damage; occurred increasingly frequently and on a larger scale; and threatened peace and security (ICC Preparatory Committee 1996, para. 66). The option of referring terrorism to the ICC was also intended to avoid jurisdictional disputes between states and empower the Security Council to addresss it.

Ultimately, terrorism was not included in the 1998 Rome Statute. A conference resolution "regretted" that "despite widespread international condemnation of terrorism, no generally acceptable definition... could be agreed upon" (UN Diplomatic Conference 1998, Resolution E). The issue of national liberation violence was contentious, and some feared terrorism would politicize the ICC (ICC Preparatory Committee 1996, para. 67; Boister 1998, 27). Pragmatically, some states felt that terrorism was better suited to national prosecution; not serious enough for international prosecution; or that investigative not legal difficulties were decisive (Arsanjani 1999, 29; Scheffer 1998). Of the twenty-three states that spoke against including terrorism, many agreed that it was a serious crime but preferred to defer its inclusion until it was defined more clearly. The omission of terrorism is significant in signaling that the international community in 1998 did not view it as an agreed international crime. As of 2019, terrorism is yet to be included in the ICC's jurisdiction.

Sectoral Counterterrorism Conventions

Transnational terrorist acts increased from the 1960s, often perpetrated by liberation movements resisting colonial powers. Because of the disagreements over the definition of terrorism, the international community responded incrementally by adopting numerous "sectoral" treaties since the 1960s addressing common methods of terrorist violence (such as hijacking, attacks on diplomats, hostage taking, endangering aviation or maritime facilities, and so on) (UN Action to Counter Terrorism, online; Saul 2014). Most of the treaties avoid referring to "terrorism," with the exception of the three most recent treaties (since 1997) on terrorist financing, terrorist bombings, and nuclear terrorism.

None of the treaties establishes a general crime of terrorism, although the Terrorist Financing Convention 1999 comes closest in providing a general definition for the limited purpose of criminalizing terrorist financing. The treaties typically require states to criminalize certain conduct, establish extraterritorial jurisdiction, and cooperate by prosecuting or extraditing suspects (the *aut dedere aut judicare* principle). A few recent treaties require states to regard the offences as non-political for the purposes of extradition, but most treaties do not.

This pragmatic approach has enabled the repression of much terrorism while side-stepping the irreconcilable problem of definition, during the post-war period of decolonization when states were unable to agree on the legitimacy of violence by liberation movements. The result has been functional transnational cooperation, even if there remain regulatory gaps because of the reactive, ad hoc nature of treaty-making. For example, some of the most common contemporary methods, such as attacks by small arms (as in the Mumbai attacks in 2008), are not prohibited by treaty law.

UN General Assembly

Some of the treaties listed were drafted under United Nations auspices. Disagreement about terrorism was particularly acrimonious in the UN General Assembly in the 1970s, following an attack by Palestinians at the Munich Olympics in 1972. In debates between 1973 and 1979, states were unable to agree on a definition of terrorism, the causes of it, or measures to address it (Saul 2006b, 199–202; Blumenau 2014, 92–103). Disagreement was particularly sharp on liberation violence and state terrorism, while socialist states also accused the Western powers of imperialistic or capitalist violence. Agreement within the UN was, however, reached on sectoral conventions against attacks on diplomats (1973) and hostage taking (1979) (Blumenau 2014, 104–90).

From the 1980s, more consensus developed, and accelerated in the 1990s after the end of the Cold War. A breakthrough came with the 1994 Declaration on Measures against International Terrorism, which condemns terrorism as "[c]riminal acts intended or calculated to provoke a state of terror in the general public, a group of persons or particular persons for political purposes" (UNGA resolution 49/60, 1994, para. 3). It adds that such acts "are in any circumstance unjustifiable, whatever the considerations of a political, philosophical, ideological, racial, ethnic, religious or any other nature that may be invoked to justify them."

Regular subsequent resolutions affirmed this attitude, although many states continued to differentiate self-determination violence from terrorism, and insist on the need for a legal definition, particularly the 118 states of the Non-Aligned Movement and the (many overlapping) fifty-six states of the Organisation of Islamic Cooperation. While the definition did not establish legal liability or the crime of terrorism, or of itself generate customary law, it indicated the international community's basic political conception of terrorism.

UN Draft Comprehensive Convention

The closest the UN has come to defining terrorism is in the ongoing negotiation of a Draft Comprehensive Terrorism Convention since 2000, based on an Indian proposal.

Agreement was reached on most of the twenty-seven articles by 2002 (UNGA Sixth Committee 2002, annex II, 7–8), spurred on by the terrorist attacks of 9/11. Negotiations stalled over outstanding issues concerning the scope of application to certain non-state and state violence in armed conflict, and the relationship to existing counterterrorism treaties. Despite regular meetings, as of 2018 agreement had still not been reached. Agreement was readily reached on the core definition of terrorist offences, although human rights concerns have been raised (Amnesty International and Human Rights Watch 2002).

Draft Article 2(1) (UNGA 2013, 6) proposes an offence if a person "unlawfully and intentionally" causes: "[d]eath or serious bodily injury to any person"; "[s]erious damage to public or private property"; or "[d]amage to property, places, facilities, or systems…resulting or likely to result in major economic loss" (UNGA Sixth Committee 2001, annex I, 16). The purpose (or motive) of such conduct, "by its nature or context," must be "to intimidate a population, or to compel a Government or an international organization to do or abstain from doing any act." There is no further requirement that acts be politically motivated (as is the case in some common law national definitions). The treaty would exclude its offences from the political offence exception to extradition.

The definition does not require proof of a political, religious, or ideological purpose, as in some common law definitions of terrorism. There is also no "democratic protest" exception as found in some national laws, which exclude acts of advocacy, protest, dissent, or industrial action, which are not intended to cause death, serious bodily harm, or serious risk to public health or safety (Canadian Criminal Code, s. 83.01(1)(E); Australian Criminal Code, s. 100.1(3); Terrorism Suppression Act 2002 (New Zealand), s. 5(5)). Such exceptions prevent criminalizing as "terrorism" minor harms (property damage or public order offences) within the tradition of direct democratic action. Like most national laws, however, the Draft Convention does not include exemptions for other just causes such as rebellion against tyrannical regimes; it is equally "terrorism" to assassinate Hitler as it is to attack the head of a rights-respecting democracy.

The key unresolved controversy in the Draft Convention concerns exceptions to its scope of application, which is really a debate about what is or is not "terrorism." First, there is disagreement whether the Convention should exclude the activities of the "parties" (as proposed by the Organization of Islamic Cooperation (OIC))—rather than the "armed forces"—during armed conflict (UNGA Sixth Committee 2004). Reference to the "parties" aims to exempt groups such as the Palestine Liberation Organization, Hamas, Islamic Jihad, and Hezbollah (von Schorlemer 2003, 272). It could preclude civilians taking part in hostilities, who are not members of non-state "armed forces," from being regarded as "terrorists." The proposal is overbroad in that it excludes attacks on civilians as "terrorism." For similar reasons, a second OIC proposal, to exclude "foreign occupation" (such as the situation in Kashmir), is also problematic (UNGA Ad Hoc Committee 2002, annex IV, 17).

International humanitarian law (IHL) already criminalizes unlawful attacks on civilians or the military in armed conflict, including during occupation. Exempting such conduct from an international crime of terrorism would not therefore confer impunity, but leave liability to the domain of war crimes law. The exclusion debate is thus partly a political struggle over labeling and the stigmatization it brings, rather than an effort to evade liability altogether. There are nonetheless real questions of liability at stake. From a law enforcement standpoint, preventive offences and special powers accompany terrorist acts but not war crimes.

A third disagreement is whether state military forces exercising their official duties are excluded from the Convention if they are merely "governed" by international law or required to be "in conformity" with it (the latter proposed by the OIC). Official duties in peacetime include, for instance, law enforcement, evacuation operations, peace operations, UN operations, or humanitarian relief. The OIC feels that the convention should cover state or state-sponsored "terrorism," notwithstanding the application of existing international laws. Again, political labeling is at stake, but also real legal consequences. Presently, state violations of international law (including human rights and state responsibility) do not always bring criminal liability, whereas non-state actors would be asymmetrically liable. "State terrorism" persists (Duncan et al. 2013) alongside non-state varieties.

Perhaps more problematic than the international debate about exclusions is the unilateral criminalization of "terrorism" in armed conflict by some national laws. Some common law states, for instance, such as the UK and Australia (and a draft Israeli law), criminalize terrorism without any exception to accommodate armed conflict and the special regime of IHL. In *R v Gul* [2013], the UK Supreme Court found that, while various counterterrorism treaties exempt aspects of armed conflict from their scope, international law does not prohibit national law from extending domestic terrorism offences to apply in armed conflict (*R v Gul (Appellant)* [2013] UKSC 64).

In consequence, every attack by non-state forces on foreign military forces can then be characterized as terrorism—namely, political violence to coerce a foreign state. This is so even if the attack solely aims at a military target, does not cause disproportionate civilian casualties, and is not perfidious or does not otherwise use prohibited means or methods of warfare (in other words, it complies with IHL). All war fighting thus becomes "terrorism," undermining incentives for non-state armed groups to comply with IHL, for there is no longer any legal difference between attacking civilians or the military.

Counterterrorism Laws of Regional Organizations

In the absence of universal agreement on a definition of terrorism, greater progress has been made at the regional level. Some regional conventions generically define terrorism, including those of the League of Arab states (1998), OIC (1999), African Union (1999), and the Shanghai Cooperation Organisation (2001) (Arab Convention on the Suppression of Terrorism 1999; OIC Convention on Combating International Terrorism 1999). While not a treaty, also relevant is the European Union's Framework Decision on

Combating Terrorism of 2002 (EU Framework Decision on Combating Terrorism 2002; Saul 2003; Murphy 2012, ch. 3), which defines "terrorist offences" to enable a common European arrest warrant and the mutual recognition of legal decisions (EU Framework Decision on the European Arrest Warrant and the Surrender Procedures between Member States 2002), and requires approximation of offences in domestic law.

The regional conventions have given rise to human rights concerns because many of their definitions of terrorism are drafted loosely and fail to satisfy the principle of legality. Some of them reclassify as terrorism ordinary crimes or public order offences (Arab Convention 1999, art. 1(2); OIC Convention 1999, art. 1(2)), or even insurrection (OAU Convention on the Prevention and Combating of Terrorism 2003, art. 1(3)). Some criminalize conduct infringing vague values such as the "stability, territorial integrity, political unity or sovereignty" of states or imperiling the "honour" or "freedoms" of individuals (OIC Convention 1999, art. 1(2)). Some safeguard against harm to ambiguous objects, such a "national resource" (Arab Convention 1999, art. 1(2); OIC Convention 1999, art. 1(2)) or "environmental or cultural heritage" (OAU Convention 2003, art. 1(3)). One intermingles terrorism with "separatism" or "extremism" (Shanghai Cooperation Organisation Convention on Combating Terrorism, Separatism and Extremism 2003, art. 1). The EU includes an ill-defined motive element of "seriously destabilising or destroying the fundamental political, constitutional, economic or social structures of a country or an international organization" (EU Framework Decision on Combating Terrorism 2002, art. 1(1)).

The elimination of the political offence exception in the context of such wide definitions of terrorism is especially problematic, since it substantially curtails the freedom of populations to resort to domestic political resistance to violent, oppressive governments. Other states in the region become legally obliged to suppress resistance, often even where such movements limit violence to IHL-compliant attacks on military objectives. At the other extreme, three conventions (OIC, Arab, and African) "carve out" acts by liberation movements in pursuit of self-determination, implying that any means may be justified for a just cause.

The War Crime of Terrorism

One of the few branches of international law that has embraced the concept of terrorism is international humanitarian law (IHL), which applies only in situations of armed conflict. Various IHL treaties prohibit terrorism (Geneva Convention IV, 1949, art. 33(1); Protocol I Additional to the Geneva Conventions, 1977, art. 51(2); Protocol II Additional to the Geneva Conventions, 1977, arts. 4(2)(d) and 13(2)), in reaction to the intimidation of civilians by the fascist powers in World War II (Saul, 2005). In 2003 the International Criminal Tribunal for the former Yugoslavia recognized, in the *Galić* case, that violations of these treaty provisions may constitute the war crime of intending to spread terror among the civilian population (*Prosecutor v Galić*, 2003, para. 138; *Prosecutor v Galić (Appeals)*, 2006). Terror was defined simply as "extreme fear" (*Prosecutor v Galić*, 2003, para. 137).

On the facts in *Galić*, the war crime of terror was found to have been committed by a campaign of sniping and shelling of civilians in the besieged city of Sarajevo, as a result of "the nature of the civilian activities targeted, the manner in which the attacks on civilians were carried out and the timing and duration of the attacks on civilians" (*Prosecutor v Galić*, 2003, paras 592, 596–7). The Special Court for Sierra Leone has also entered convictions for the war crime of terrorism (*Prosecutor v Brima* et al., 2007, paras 662, 666; *Prosecutor v Taylor*, 2012, para. 112.), committed by acts such as amputations and mutilations of civilians. The war crime of terror is distinct from the peacetime conceptions of terrorism mentioned earlier (*Prosecutor v Taylor*, 2012, paras 408–10), namely violence to compel a government or international organization to do or refrain from doing something (Saul 2006b, chs 3–4).

Concepts of Terrorism after September 11, 2001

UN Security Council Response

Prior to 9/11, the UN Security Council sporadically condemned specific terrorist acts, and in 1999 created a sanctions regime targeting particular members of Al Qaeda and the Taliban in Afghanistan. Its approach changed radically after 9/11. By resolution 1373 (2001), adopted under Chapter VII of the UN Charter, the UN Security Council directed all states to criminalize terrorism in domestic law (as well as universalizing the offences in the patchily ratified Terrorist Financing Convention).

Resolution 1373 did not define terrorism for the purpose of national criminalization, resulting in the decentralized and haphazard national implementation. Many states utilized the authority of the resolution to define terrorism to suit their own political purposes or to camouflage assaults on fundamental civil and political rights. The enactment of excessively wide national definitions of terrorism after 9/11 has raised key human rights concerns. The UN Human Rights Committee has frequently criticized the vagueness of national terrorism laws in monitoring compliance with human rights obligations, including the principle of legality and non-retrospectivity in Article 15, non-discrimination, and political freedoms (Office of the High Commissioner for Human Rights 2008, paras 20–3).

Faced with a backlash from human rights bodies and civil society, in resolution 1566 (2004) the Security Council eventually signaled its conception of terrorism as:

> criminal acts, including against civilians, committed with the intent to cause death or serious bodily injury, or taking of hostages, with the purpose to provoke a state of terror in the general public or in a group of persons or particular persons, intimidate a population or compel a government or an international organization to do or

> to abstain from doing any act, which constitute offences within the scope of and as defined in the international conventions and protocols relating to terrorism...
> (UNSC resolution 1566, 2004, para. 3)

The cumulative definition reclassifies harmful acts as "terrorism" only where they are designed to terrorize, intimidate, or compel, and already constitute a sectoral treaty offence. The UN Special Rapporteur on human rights and terrorism was satisfied that it reflects a narrow and rights-respecting concept of terrorism (UN Special Rapporteur 2005, para. 42).

This is, however, only a working definition which does not require states to conform their laws to it. By 2004, many states had already modified their laws and were not going to revise them in light of a mere recommendation by the Council, particularly one which would confine state freedom of definition. Resolution 1566 nonetheless establishes "soft" guide-posts for implementing resolution 1373, which over time may stimulate more convergence.

Terrorism as a Customary International Law Crime?

In 2011, the Appeals Chamber of the hybrid UN Special Tribunal for Lebanon, established to prosecute terrorist bombings in Lebanon in 2005, purported to identify an extant customary international crime of terrorism in peacetime, and applied it in interpreting domestic terrorism offences under Lebanese law (UN Special Tribunal for Lebanon, *Interlocutory Decision on the Applicable Law*, 2011 ("STL Decision")). The crime consists of three elements:

> (i) the perpetration of a criminal act (such as murder, kidnapping, hostage-taking, arson, and so on), or threatening such an act; (ii) the intent to spread fear among the population (which would generally entail the creation of public danger) or directly or indirectly coerce a national or international authority to take some action, or to refrain from taking it; (iii) when the act involves a transnational element.
> (STL Decision, 2011, para. 85)

The requirement of a transnational element (STL Decision 2011, para. 90) rules out purely domestic terrorism. While the Tribunal recognized only peacetime terrorism as a crime, it indicated that "a broader norm that would outlaw terrorist acts *during times of armed conflict* may also be emerging" (STL Decision 2011, paras 107–9). The generic elements of the offence are suggestive of the definition in the Terrorist Financing Convention 1999 and the UN Draft Comprehensive Convention. It is broader than the narrow, rights-respecting definition offered by the Security Council in resolution 1566. The Appeals Chamber acknowledged that a political or other motive element (as found in some common law definitions) would narrow the definition, prevent its over-expansive application, and further the principle of legality, but felt it was not yet part of the customary law definition, even if it might become so in future (STL Decision 2011, para. 106).

In reaching its conclusion, the Appeals Chamber found that the thirty-seven national terrorism laws it cited are broadly "concordant" and evince "a widespread stand on and a shared view of terrorism" (STL Decision 2011, para. 92). In particular, it was stated that "[e]lements common across national legislation defining terrorism include the use of criminal acts to terrorise or intimidate populations, to coerce government authorities, or to disrupt or destabilise social or political structures" (STL Decision 2011, para. 93).

National laws can certainly provide evidence of state practice in the formation of customary international law. However, the Appeals Chamber's conclusion is dubious. It conflates national laws addressing national and international terrorism and of varying jurisdictional reach. It conflates criminal definitions with non-criminal definitions. Further, close inspection of the national laws cited shows that many of the laws do not converge at all, but represent fundamentally different conceptions of terrorism, including ones embracing civil war and sectarian strife (Iraq), public disorder (Egypt), constitutional subversion (Peru), harm to international relations, sovereignty, or territorial integrity (Uzbekistan), or violation of honour (Sauda Arabia). Looking beyond the limited number of thirty-seven "best example" laws cited by the Appeals Chamber, it is clear that legal approaches to terrorism in the bulk of national legal systems—including the 160 states not mentioned—are even more divergent.

While the Appeals Chamber also invokes Security Council resolution 1566 (STL Decision 2011, para. 88), it does not support the Appeals Chamber's definition precisely because the resolution is narrowly pegged to sectoral treaty offences, whereas the Appeals Chamber's definition is not. The other sources relied on—including UN General Assembly resolutions, international and regional treaties, and national judicial decisions—also do not sustain the conclusion that terrorism is a customary international crime (Saul 2011). Recent authoritative national court decisions have not accepted the view that there is an agreed international definition (*R v Gul (Appellant)* [2013] UKSC 64, para. 44; *Al-Sirri v Secretary of State for the Home Department* [2013] 1 AC 745, para. 37).

Conclusion

At one level, legal concepts of terrorism may be seen as strictly unnecessary: terrorist violence can usually be prosecuted as ordinary crime. At the same time, however, a legal concept of terrorism can add further elements to ordinary offences which differentiate it and thereby signal a social community's condemnation of (for instance) instrumental political or religious violence intended to intimidate a population or coerce a government. Pragmatically, it can trigger special powers and procedures, and preventive offences and measures, all of which do not attach to ordinary offences. It can also facilitate transnational cooperation and extradition, and plug gaps in the existing ad hoc sectoral counter-terrorism treaties, although these advantages are largely dissipated where national laws define terrorism differently.

Legal concepts of terrorism bring risks too. Excessively wide or loose concepts of terrorism can seriously jeopardize internationally protected human rights. The absolutist politics of state survival and national security frequently taint the drafting and use of terrorism laws. Often the wide special powers and offences that attach to a definition, and the absence or degradation of ordinary safeguards, are even more dangerous to human rights. Terrorism laws make most sense when protecting a democracy from violent adversaries, and less sense when they shield authoritarian states from those who rightly resist them. International agreement on terrorism in a diverse community of states is so difficult for this reason. Most minimally agree that the instrumental political killing of civilians in peacetime is terrorism. Beyond that, "terrorism" remains a contested terrain of diverse political and moral opinion.

Outside of the law, which requires precision and consensus for reasons of effectiveness and fairness, unsettled disagreement is less of a problem. Different disciplines and scholars may come at terrorism from different angles, using different methods, just as many other phenomena are conceptually contested (whether nationalism, imperialism, socialism, capitalism, democracy, human rights, globalization, feminism, and so on). Some scholars have even identified over 260 definitions of terrorism (Easson and Schmid 2011, 99–200), though attempts to distill academic debates into a "consensus definition" (Schmid 2011, 39–98) have proven difficult and unwieldy. Conceptual disagreement is healthy in that it stimulates a diversity of productive insights into an acutely difficult real-world problem, even if it is sometimes frustrating or thwarts the tunnel-vision of a uniform approach.

Cases

Al-Sirri v Secretary of State for the Home Department (UNHCR intervening) [2013] 1 AC 745.

Prosecutor v Brima et al., SCSL-04-16-T, Trial Chamber, Judgment, 20 June 2007.

Prosecutor v Galić, IT-98-29-A, Appeals Chamber, Judgment, 30 November 2006.

Prosecutor v Galić, ICTY-98-29-T, Trial Chamber, Judgment, 5 December 2003.

Prosecutor v Taylor, SCSL-03-1-T, Trial Chamber, Judgment, 26 April 2012.

UN Special Tribunal for Lebanon (Appeals Chamber), Interlocutory Decision on the Applicable Law: Terrorism, Conspiracy, Homicide, Perpetration, Cumulative Charging, STL-11-01/I, 16 February 2011.

Treaties and Other Instruments

Arab Convention on the Suppression of Terrorism (adopted Apr. 22, 1998; entered into force May 7, 1999).

EU Framework Decision on Combating Terrorism (2002/475/JHA), 13 June 2002, Official Journal L164/3, 22 June 2002.

EU Framework Decision on the European Arrest Warrant and the Surrender Procedures between Member States (2002/584/JHA), 13 June 2002, Official Journal L 190/1, 18 June 2002.

Geneva Convention IV Relative to the Protection of Civilian Persons in Time of War (adopted Aug. 12, 1949, entered into force Oct. 21, 1950).
League of Nations Convention for the Prevention and Punishment of Terrorism (adopted 16 November 1937, never entered into force; (1938) League of Nations Official Journal 19).
League of Nations Convention for the Creation of an International Criminal Court (adopted 16 November 1937, never entered into force; (1938) League of Nations Official Journal 19).
Organisation of African Unity Convention on the Prevention and Combating of Terrorism (adopted 14 July 1999, entered into force 6 December 2003).
Organisation of the Islamic Conference Convention on Combating International Terrorism (adopted 1 July 1999).
Protocol I Additional to the Geneva Conventions of 12 August 1949 and Relating to the Protection of Victims of International Armed Conflicts (adopted 8 June 1977, entered into force 7 December 1978, 1125 UNTS 3).
Protocol II Additional to the Geneva Conventions of 12 August 1949 and Relating to the Protection of Victims of Non-International Armed Conflicts (adopted 8 June 1977, entered into force 7 December 1978, 1125 UNTS 609).
SAARC Additional Protocol (adopted 6 January 2004).
Shanghai Cooperation Organization Convention on Combating Terrorism, Separatism and Extremism (adopted 15 June 2001, entered into force 29 March 2003).

Legislation

Anti-terrorism Act (S.C. 2001, c. 41) (Canada).
Terrorism Suppression Act 2002 (New Zealand).

United Nations Documents

International Criminal Court Preparatory Committee, Summary of Proceedings, 25 March–12 April 1996, UN Doc A/AC.249/1 (7 May 1996).
International Law Commission, Draft Code of Offences against the Peace and Security of Mankind (Part I), in International Law Commission, Sixth Session Report (3 June–28 July 1954), UN Doc A/2693.
International Law Commission (1990) "Draft Code of Offences against the Peace and Security of Mankind 1991," *International Law Commission Year Book*, 1: 336.
International Law Commission, Report on its 47th Session (2 May–21 July 1995), UN Doc A/50/10.
International Law Commission, Report on its 48th Session (6 May–26 July 1996), UN Doc A/51/10.
Office of the High Commissioner for Human Rights (2008) Report on the Protection of Human Rights and Fundamental Freedoms while Countering Terrorism, A/HRC/8/13 (June 2).
UN, "UN Action to Counter Terrorism: International Legal Instruments," <www.un.org/en/terrorism/instruments.shtml>.
UN (1998) "Draft Rome Statute 1998," in Official Records of the UN Diplomatic Conference of Plenipotentiaries on an ICC, Rome, 15 June–17 July 1998, UN Doc A/CONF.183/13.
UN Diplomatic Conference of Plenipotentiaries on an International Criminal Court, Final Act, 17 July 1998, UN Doc A/Conf.183/10, annex, resolution E.

UN Special Rapporteur (Martin Scheinin), Report on the Promotion and Protection of Human Rights and Fundamental Freedoms while Countering Terrorism, E/CN.4/2006/98 (28 December 2005).

UNGA (56th Session) (Sixth Committee), Measures to Eliminate International Terrorism: Working Group Report, 29 October 2001, UN Doc A/C.6/56/L.9.

UNGA (57th Session) (Sixth Committee), Measures to Eliminate International Terrorism: Working Group Report, 16 October 2002, UN Doc. A/C.6/57/L.9.

UNGA, Ad Hoc Committee Report (2002), UN Doc A/57/37.

UNGA, Official Records (68th Session), Supplement No. 3: Report of the Ad Hoc Committee established by General Assembly resolution 51/210, 17 December 1996, 16th session (8–12 April 2013), UN Doc A/68/37.

UNGA resolution 49/60 (1994), annexed Declaration on Measures to Eliminate International Terrorism.

UNGA resolution 51/160 (1996).

UNGA Sixth Committee, Report of the Working Group on Measures to Eliminate International Terrorism, 8 October 2004, UN Doc. A/C.6/59/L.10.

UNSC resolution 1566 (8 October 2004).

References

Amnesty International and Human Rights Watch (2002) "Comprehensive Convention against International Terrorism," Joint Letter to Ambassadors, Jan. 28.

Arsanjani, M. (1999) "The 1998 Rome Statute of the International Criminal Court," *American Journal of International Law*, 93: 22.

Blumenau, B. (2014) *The United Nations and Terrorism: Germany, Multilateralism, and Antiterrorism Efforts in the 1970s*. Basingstoke: Palgrave Macmillan.

Boister, N. (1998) "The Exclusion of Treaty Crimes from the Jurisdiction of the Proposed International Criminal Court: Law, Pragmatism, Politics," *Journal of Armed Conflict Law*, 3: 27.

Duncan, G., O. Lynch, G. Ramsawy, and A. Watson, eds (2013) *State Terrorism and Human Rights: International Responses since the End of the Cold War*. London: Routledge.

Easson, J., and A. Schmid (2011) "Appendix 2.1: 250-Plus Academic, Governmental and Intergovernmental Definitions of Terrorism," in A. Schmid (ed.), *The Routledge Handbook of Terrorism Research*. London: Routledge, 99–157.

League of Nations (Committee on the International Repression of Terrorism), "Legislation Regarding Political Terrorist Crimes: Study by T Givenovitch," Geneva, 3 May 1935, League of Nations Doc CRT.9.

Murphy, C. (2012) *EU Counter-Terrorism Law: Pre-Emption and the Rule of Law*. Oxford: Hart.

Richards, A. (2015) *Conceptualizing Terrorism*. Oxford: Oxford University Press.

Saul, B. (2003) "International Terrorism as a European Crime: The Policy Rationale for Criminalization," *European Journal of Crime, Criminal Law and Criminal Justice* 11: 323.

Saul, B. (2005) "Crimes and Prohibitions of 'Terror' and 'Terrorism' in Armed Conflict: 1919–2005," *Journal of the International Law of Peace and Armed Conflict*, 4: 264.

Saul, B. (2006a) "The Legal Response of the League of Nations to Terrorism," *Journal of International Criminal Justice*, 4: 78.

Saul, B. (2006b) *Defining Terrorism in International Law*. Oxford: Oxford University Press.

Saul, B. (2011) "Legislating from a Radical Hague: The UN Special Tribunal for Lebanon Invents an International Crime of Transnational Terrorism," *Leiden Journal of International Law*, 24: 677.
Saul, B., ed. (2014) *Research Handbook on International Law and Terrorism*. Cheltenham: Edward Elgar.
Scheffer, D. (1998) "Developments at Rome Treaty Conference," Testimony of US Ambassador at Large for War Crimes Issues and Head of US Delegation to the Rome Conf., US Senate Foreign Relations Committee, Washington, DC, July 23.
Schmid, A. (2011) "The Definition of Terrorism," in A. Schmid (ed.), *The Routledge Handbook of Terrorism Research*. London: Routledge, 38–98.
Van den Wijngaert, C. (1980) *The Political Offence Exception to Extradition*. Boston: Kluwer.
von Schorlemer, S. (2003) "Human Rights: Substantive and Institutional Implications of the War on Terror," *European Journal of International Law*, 14: 265.

CHAPTER 4

THE EVOLUTION OF TERRORISM EVENT DATABASES

GARY LAFREE

Terrorism event databases provide systematized descriptive information about terrorist attacks, most often from the unclassified electronic and print media, where the attack is the unit of analysis. These databases generally follow the classic journalistic format of providing information on *who* is responsible for an attack, *what* happened, *where* and *when* did it happen, and *how* did it happen. Terrorism event databases are a small part of a much broader set of related databases on violent political events, including the various databases collected by the Correlates of War project (COW) and the Uppsala Conflict Data Program (UCDP 2013)/International Peace Research Institute, Oslo (PRIO) Center for the Study of Civil War's research on armed, one-sided, and non-state conflict. Terrorism event databases also resemble open source databases on terrorism that are focused instead at the group (Asal and Rethemeyer 2013) or individual (Smith et al. 2013; Chermak et al. 2013; Jensen et al. 2015) levels. While each of these databases have unique characteristics they also share similar strengths and weaknesses and are now being driven forward by some common methodological innovations.

Terrorism event databases have developed unevenly, often driven by high-profile terrorist attacks. Thus, following the Oklahoma City bombing by Timothy McVeigh and Terry Nichols on April 19, 1995, funds were made available to greatly strengthen RAND's terrorism data. Similarly, following the 9/11 attacks, funding was made available for the collection of WITS and GTD data. Thus, support for event databases on terrorism has often been reactive, based on political crisis rather than proactive efforts to establish policy priorities.

In this chapter I begin by considering why event terrorism databases have become so important. I then examine the origins of contemporary terrorism event databases and trace their evolution over the past half century. Following this brief history, I review the major strengths and limitations of event databases and examine efforts to compare them. I conclude the chapter by considering some likely future developments for terrorism event databases.

Why are Terrorism Event Databases Important?

Compared to collecting data on more traditionally studied crimes like homicide and robbery, collecting data on terrorism raises some specific challenges. In criminology, data on illegal behavior come traditionally from three sources, corresponding to the major social roles connected to criminal events: "official" data collected by legal agents, especially the police; "victimization" data collected from the general population of victims and non-victims; and "self-report" data collected from offenders (LaFree and Dugan 2004). All three of these sources are problematic when it comes to gathering data on terrorism. No worldwide official data on terrorism exist. Indeed thus far, international organizations, including the United Nations, have been unable to provide a definition of terrorism that is accepted by all member nations. Police departments in most countries do not maintain separate records for terrorism-related offenses and primary data collected by intelligence agents are often not available to researchers working in an unclassified environment. Most people convicted of behavior that would be widely regarded as terrorism are actually convicted of more common crimes like murder and weapons violations. The Uniform Crime Reports, the United States' major official source of data on crime, does not include statistics on terrorist attacks.

Victimization surveys (where random samples of individuals are polled about their experiences as crime victims) have been of little use in the study of terrorism. Despite the attention it gets in the media, terrorism is much rarer than more ordinary violent crime and thus even with extremely large sample sizes, few individuals in most countries will have been victimized by terrorists. Indeed, victims of terrorism often have no direct contact with perpetrators (e.g. in many bombings). And in too many cases, terrorism victims are killed by their attackers, leaving none to survey. Self-report data based on interviews with terrorists have provided some excellent scholarship (Post et al. 2003) but are of little use in providing national let alone worldwide trends.

For these reasons, researchers and policy-makers interested in terrorism have looked to media data sources for information on terrorist attacks. Starting in the late 1960s, the availability of satellite technology and portable video equipment made it possible for the first time in human history to send instantaneously images of conflict and violence from any one place on the planet to any other place. This development was not missed by terrorist organizations. On July 22, 1968 three armed members of the Front for the Liberation of Palestine-General Command (PLFP-GC) hijacked an El Al commercial flight scheduled to fly from Rome to Tel Aviv. The hijackers diverted the El Al plane and its forty-eight occupants to Algeria, releasing some passengers but holding five Israeli passengers and seven crew members hostage. The PFLP-GC subsequently demanded the release of Palestinian guerillas being held in Israeli prisons in exchange for these hostages. The resulting negotiations were broadcast live around the world. In many ways, this event marked the birth of worldwide terrorism event databases.

A Brief History of Terrorism Event Databases

Since the end of World War II, there have been around a dozen major attempts to construct terrorism event databases. Table 4.1 provides a summary of the most influential ones.[1] Some of these attempts (e.g. TWEED; ITERATE; GTD) were undertaken mostly for research purposes. PGIS was originally started by a for-profit company working in security risk assessment. RAND is a non-profit policy research institution that does research especially for government clients. Two of the event databases in Table 4.1 have been collected by the US government (US State Department, WITS). The GTD was originally collected mostly for researchers but has been heavily funded by US government agencies and since 2012 has supplied unclassified data to the US Department of State for a congressionally mandated annual report. Of the databases listed, ITERATE and GTD have thus far generated the most academic research. In the brief history that follows, I divide the development of terrorism event databases into two main periods of activity: the 1970s and earlier and the late 1990s and beyond.

Table 4.1 Worldwide Databases on Terrorist Attacks

	Scope	Period	Number
TWEED	Domestic (Europe)	1950–2004	11,245
ITERATE	International	1968–2008	Approx. 13,000
RAND	International	1968–1997	8,509
PGIS	Domestic & International	1970–1997	67,179
US Dept of State	International	1980–2003	10,026
RAND-MIPT/ RDWTI[a]	Domestic & International	1968–2009	40,129
GTD (Stage 1)	Domestic & International	1970–2011	104,658
WITS	Domestic & International	2004–2011[b]	79,795
GTD (Stage 2)	Domestic & International	1970–2014	141,966

[a] Funding for MIPT data collection ended in 2008 and after a relatively brief pause, RAND continued the series as the RAND Database of Worldwide Terrorism.
[b] Data reported through Mar. 31, 2011.

The Origins of Terrorism Event Databases: 1970s and Earlier

The first five databases listed in Table 4.1 originated during the 1970s and earlier. TWEED is the longest running of the major event databases, starting in 1950 and ending in 2004 (according to the website on September 11, 2015). The data have been assembled by Engene (2007) based on Keesing's Record of World Events, a source that collects news reports on a daily basis from all over the world. For each event, TWEED contains information on date of the event; name of the country where the event took place; name of acting group or organization; number of people killed or injured; type of violent means employed; government reaction; regional origins; and ideological profile. The main limitations of the TWEED database are that it is limited to terrorist attacks in eighteen Western European countries and focuses only on domestic attacks—although the database does include some attacks across borders for the countries tracked.

The International Terrorism: Attributes of Terrorist Events (ITERATE) database began coverage in 1968 and has been periodically updated through 2009 (Mickolus, 2002; Mickolus et al., 2010). ITERATE contains two different types of files: quantitatively coded data on international terrorist incidents and a qualitative description of each incident included in the quantitative files. The quantitative data are arranged into four files, containing: (1) information on the type of terrorist attack, including location, name of group taking responsibility, and number of deaths and injuries; (2) information on the fate of the terrorists or terrorist group claiming responsibility; and (3) information on terrorist attacks involving hostages and skyjackings. The ITERATE data are limited to transnational terrorist attacks, which are a small subset of all terrorist attacks.

The RAND Corporation was an early pioneer in developing terrorism event databases. With the support of the Department of State and the Defense Advanced Research Projects Agency (DARPA), in 1972, Brian Jenkins at RAND began to develop a "Chronology of International Terrorism" dating back to 1968. Like ITERATE, the original RAND data were generally limited to international attacks.[2] With varying levels of support, RAND maintained the Chronology through 1997.

Another early event database that began tracking terrorist attacks in 1970 was initiated in the mid-1970s with the support of the Pinkerton Global Intelligence Service (PGIS)—a corporate relative of the famous Scottish detective agency. PGIS trained researchers to identify and record terrorism incidents from wire services (including Reuters and the Foreign Broadcast Information Service, FBIS), US State Department reports, other US and foreign government reporting, and US and foreign newspapers (e.g. the *New York Times*, the British *Financial Times*). In the 1990s, PGIS researchers increasingly relied on the internet. Although the PGIS coding form went through three iterations, most of the items included were similar during the twenty-eight years of data collection. About two dozen persons were responsible for coding information over the years spanned by the data collection, but only two individuals were in charge of supervising data collection during the entire period. The most unique aspect of the

PGIS data is that from the beginning it included domestic as well as international terrorist attacks—the only early database to do so.

The US State Department began publishing an annual report on international terrorism in 1982 (reporting 1981 incidents), and in 1983 began calling the report "Patterns of Global Terrorism." The Patterns Report reviews international terrorist events by year, date, region, and terrorist group and includes background information on terrorist organizations, US policy on terrorism, and progress on counterterrorism. The Patterns of Global Terrorism reports were generally issued a few months after each calendar year.

Approaching the end of the 1990s, the only two terrorism event databases that included both international and domestic attacks were TWEED and PGIS, but TWEED was limited to eighteen countries in Europe and PGIS ended its data collection in 1997. Most of the early databases relied heavily on wire services and major newspapers and, as the 1990s unfolded, increasingly on the internet. As already noted, the Oklahoma City bombing of 1996 and more importantly, the coordinated attacks of September 11, 2001 focused a great deal more attention and resources on the collection of open source terrorism event data.

Terrorism Event Databases in the Late 1990s and Beyond

As shown in Table 4.1, all four of the most influential terrorism event databases that were initiated in the late 1990s or after included domestic as well as international attacks: the RAND-MIPT/RDWTI database, the Global Terrorism Database (GTD—stages 1 and 2) and the Worldwide Incidents Tracking System (WITS) data. In April 2001, the RAND corporation, which had been collecting terrorism data since 1968, received support from the National Memorial Institute for the Prevention of Terrorism (MIPT)—an organization that had been funded by the US Congress to study terrorism in the wake of the Oklahoma City bombing. With considerably more resources devoted to the database, RAND staff verified much of the earlier data and also began collecting (starting in 1998) terrorism data on domestic attacks. Funding for the RAND-MIPT data collection ended in 2008. However, shortly after, RAND received additional support and continued collecting terrorism event data, now referred to as the RAND Database of Worldwide Terrorism Incidents (RDWTI).

In 2001, a team at the University of Maryland was able to secure the original hard copies of the PGIS terrorism data—which by then contained more than 67,000 cases from 1970 to 1997.[3] With funding from the National Institute of Justice, the Maryland team completed the digitization and verification of the original PGIS data in December 2005. This marked the beginning of the Global Terrorism Database (GTD). In April 2006 the GTD team received funding from the Department of Homeland Security through the National Consortium for the Study of Terrorism and Responses to Terrorism (START) to extend the GTD beyond 1997. Primary data collection of the GTD for 1998–2011 was completed by two different research teams and then verified and compiled by the GTD team at START (LaFree et al. 2015a). This process was guided by two principles: preserving the value of the PGIS heritage data, while also making improvements in the rigor of the data collection process and the quality of the data collected. The new procedures captured more than 120 variables and unlike the original PGIS data, the process included archiving the open source texts upon which each event was based.

GTD collection during this period included researchers who were fluent in English and one or more of several other languages (especially, Arabic, French, Mandarin, Russian, and Spanish). The data collection process began by monitoring general databases such as Lexis-Nexis and Opensource.gov (previously FBIS). Data collectors were asked to review these events, to determine which qualified as terrorist attacks according to the target definition, and then to corroborate each case with at least two additional source articles. Data collectors submitted their expected cases to supervisors for review. Based on these procedures, in March 2009 START released the extended version of the GTD through 2007. Updates were subsequently released first biennially and then annually.

The next database shown in Table 4.1 is the Worldwide Incidents Tracking System data (WITS) collected by the National Counterterrorism Center (NCTC). The NCTC began collecting terrorism data in 2004 but did not provide comprehensive annual coverage until 2005. WITS originated because of congressional dissatisfaction with the quality of the State Department's Patterns of Global Terrorism report. In its 2003 Patterns Report the State Department concluded that "worldwide terrorism had dropped by 45 percent between 2001 and 2003." However, when economists Alan Krueger and David Laitin reviewed the data tables at the end of the State Department's Patterns of Global Terrorism report for 2003 they found that the numbers in the tables did not add up and that the conclusion of the report, namely that worldwide terrorism had decreased that year, was in error and that terrorism had actually increased. When they subsequently published this information in an op-ed piece in the *Washington Post* (Krueger and Laitin 2004a) and in an article in *Foreign Affairs* (Krueger and Laitin 2004b), the State Department admitted that the report was wrong and retracted it. As a result of this criticism, the name of the report was changed to "Country Reports on Terrorism," the statistical data and chronology of "significant" international terrorist events were dropped, and Congress mandated that, starting in 2004, terrorism data were to be compiled by the newly created National Counterterrorism Center (NCTC).

World-Wide Incidents Tracking System (WITS) data were collected by NCTC from open sources manually using commercial subscription news services, the US government's Open Source Center, local news websites reported in English, and as permitted by the linguistic capabilities of their employees, local news websites in foreign languages (Wigle 2010, 5). Like GTD and RAND-MIPT, WITS collected both international and domestic data. From its inception, a major goal of those administering WITS was to "cast a wider net on what may be considered terrorism" (p. 5). WITS was extremely inclusive in its coverage. From 2004 to 2011, WITS reported nearly 80,000 terrorist attacks—far more than any other events database for this time period. These numbers stand in particularly stark contrast to the earlier US State Department Patterns series, which typically reported only several hundred international terrorist attacks per year.

The final dataset included in Table 4.1 is the GTD-Stage 2. In recent years the explosive growth of online media availability is ushering in a new wave of innovation in terms of the collection of worldwide open source terrorism data. Attempts to automate the collection of open source terrorism data have been going on for several decades. For example, early efforts to collect data quickly started to rely on news aggregators like the wire service Reuters and later online aggregators like Lexis-Nexis, Factiva, and OpenSource. However, these efforts have become far more sophisticated and comprehensive over time. At present it is fair to say that none of the major open source terrorism databases rely only on manual data collection.

Starting in 2012, the GTD team at START began to increase substantially the amount of automation used to generate the data. The team still relies on primary sources including individual news outlets such as Reuters and Agence-France Presse, as well as existing media aggregators such as Lexis/Nexis and Factiva, but these are now continually evaluated in terms of which sources make the most valid contributions to the overall data collection effort. Poorly performing sources are removed and new sources are added to improve the efficiency of manual review processes. University of Maryland researchers identify GTD data collection after 2012 as "stage 2" to illustrate this transformation.

At present, data collection for the GTD begins with a universe of 2 million articles published daily worldwide in order to identify the small subset of articles that describe terrorist attacks. The team uses customized search strings to isolate an initial pool of potentially relevant articles and then relies on natural language processing techniques to automatically identify and remove duplicate source articles by measuring similarities between pairs of documents. In addition, the team has developed a machine-learning model using feedback from trained GTD staff that classifies documents identified by the initial automated processes to determine how likely they are to be relevant to terrorism. This model is continually refined using input from the research team regarding the accuracy of the classification results. To facilitate this iterative process, the team has developed a web-based interface used to provide continuous feedback to the system through the manual review of the source documents identifying both false-positives (source documents that appear to describe terrorist attacks but do not) and false-negatives (source documents that appear to not describe terrorist attacks but actually do).

The Global Terrorism Database (GTD) team reviews all the source documents that have been classified as relevant by the machine-learning model and generates database entries for individual attacks that satisfy the GTD inclusion criteria. They use script analysis tools to facilitate this process by clustering similar documents together based on key identifying features of the text. In addition, as the set of identified incidents expands they use this information to supply coders with details of already created events or related sources that are potential matches for a given attack under review. The GTD team applies automated tools, including Boolean filtering, Natural Language Processing, Named Entity Recognition, and machine-learning models to the source documents to begin the event definition process in order to identify those events most likely to qualify as terrorist attacks. At present, approximately 115,000 articles are manually reviewed to identify attacks for each month of data collection.

One of the innovations of GTD-stage 2 is to move from data coding based on area experts (e.g. Southeast Asia, Western Europe) to rely instead on domain-specific research teams organized to collect data on specific characteristics of attacks, including location, perpetrators, targets, weapons, tactics, casualties, and consequences. Each domain-specific team records information according to the ever-evolving specifications of the GTD Codebook (www.start.umd.edu/gtd/downloads/Codebook.pdf). In short, the GTD team uses automated tools to process millions of documents a day but human coders to digest the information and ensure the quality of the resulting data.

Limitations of Event Databases

Not surprisingly, event databases have serious limitations. The media may report inaccuracies and lies; there may be conflicting information or false, multiple, or no claims of responsibility. Government censorship and disinformation may also affect results. When closed societies like North Korea, Sudan, or Myanmar report extremely low terrorism rates, we can never say for sure whether it is because of actual low reporting or the ability of these societies to minimize coverage by the print or electronic media. On balance, important weaknesses of event databases include: (1) lack of a generally accepted definition of terrorism, (2) biases and inaccuracy in open source data, and (3) lack of consistency over time.

First, because there is no universally accepted definition of terrorism, individual event databases all rely on different operational definitions. As we will see in greater detail, in some cases these definitions are similar, but important differences remain. And it stands to reason that different definitions will result in different data outcomes. It is especially challenging to distinguish terrorist attacks from other violent human behavior that shares certain terrorism characteristics, notably insurrection, guerrilla warfare, hate crime, ethnic cleansing, and organized crime (for a review, see LaFree 2019).

Second, event databases also face a variety of general biases, many of which have not even been empirically explored (Dugan and Distler 2016). Because they rely on news sources, it is usually impossible to know the extent to which reported events reflect real outcomes or the freedom of the press in a particular country or region. For example, Drakos and Gofas (2006) show that the country-level distribution of press freedom strongly depends on level of democratization, especially for extreme values of the latter. In other words, for the vast majority of strongly autocratic states, the press is not free, while for strongly democratic states, it is essentially free. The authors caution that research linking the frequency of terrorist attacks to democratization levels may be biased by under-reporting of terrorist attacks in countries with low press freedom (which also tend to be more autocratic countries). Even in countries with high levels of press freedom it seems incontrovertible that news sources will be more likely to report more serious than less serious attacks.

The extent to which countries are covered by the international press also varies by region and over time. For example, Crenshaw and LaFree (2016) show that the percentage of terrorist attacks in the Global Terrorism Database where responsibility for attacks cannot be attributed to a specific group varies widely across regions of the world. While perpetrators responsible for attacks can be identified in more than 60 percent of the attacks from South America and Western Europe, responsible perpetrators are identified in less than 20 percent of attacks occurring in Russia and the states of the former Soviet Union, Eastern Europe, and Central Asia. Similarly, Fariss (2014) argues that the quality of media reporting on issues like respect for human rights may be changing over time. To the extent that media sources are more likely to identify terrorist attacks over time, open source reporting showing increases in terrorism may be picking up media change rather than increases in actual terrorist attacks.

Data collection efforts to this point have also been strongly biased toward coverage of English-language sources. GTD, RAND, and WITS all endeavor to monitor non-English sources but in each case resources limit the extent to which this is possible. Moreover, for all terrorism data collection efforts, the extensiveness of non-English coverage varies over time.

Beyond these general problems there are subtler biases related to the media itself. For example, there is a well-known tendency for news sources to fit individual stories into particular news frames so that, compared to other events, preselected themes (e.g. "improvised explosive devices" or "suicide attacks") may be more likely to receive coverage (Fishman 1980). Also, even with reliable media sources unintentional inaccuracy and intentional misinformation are constant concerns.

Finally, given the desirability of developing time series longitudinal analyses of terrorist attacks, the complexities of maintaining event databases becomes even more challenging. In substantive terms, the more time elapsed between real events and data collection the greater the chances that some data are no longer available. Thus, by the time START had computerized the original PGIS data and secured funding for new data collection on the GTD, the data collection was eight years behind real time. As the team worked to bring the data up to the current time period, it was forced to rely on sources that were older relative to the date of the event compared to the original PGIS data; but approached real time as the data collection continued. To the extent that newspaper and electronic media are not archived, availability of original sources erodes over time, increasing missing data. This is likely to be especially problematic for small, regional, and local newspapers.

Moreover, as event databases evolve, the size of the media "fire hose" supplied by news aggregators continues to increase. Thus, the media sources that the GTD relies on have moved steadily from 1 million per day to more than 2 million per day. These increases raise the possibility that longitudinal trends in attacks are being affected by increasing access to information rather than real-world escalation in attacks. They also make it increasingly difficult to identify and resolve duplicate cases (King and Lowe 2003; Schrodt and Van Brackle 2013).

Strengths of Event Databases

Despite limitations, compared to more traditional data options, or even compared to crime data in general, event databases have important advantages. In particular, because of the compelling interest that terrorist groups have in media attention, open source information may be uniquely useful in the study of terrorism. Terrorists, unlike most common criminals, actively seek media attention. Terrorism expert Brian Jenkins (1975) declared that "terrorism is theatre" and explained how terrorist attacks are often carefully choreographed to attract the attention of the electronic media and the international press. The fact that terrorists are specifically seeking attention through the media means that, compared to coverage of more common crimes, coverage of terrorism is likely to be more complete. Thus, while few researchers would suggest tracking burglary or fraud rates by studying electronic and print media, it is likely more defensible to track terrorist attacks in this way. For example, it is hard to imagine that it is possible today for an aerial hijacking or politically motivated assassination—even in remote parts of the world—to elude attention of the global media.

Event databases on terrorism also have another important advantage. One of the most serious limitations of cross-national crime research is that it has been focused overwhelmingly on a small number of highly industrialized western-style democracies. For example, reviews of cross-national research on homicide (Nivette 2011; LaFree et al. 2015b) show that most prior research had been based on fewer than forty of the world's countries. And of course these countries are not a random sample of the nations of the world but strongly over-represent Europe and North America while almost entirely excluding countries of Africa, the Middle East, and Asia. By contrast, open source terrorism databases offer at least some coverage for all countries. While it is the case that traditional media under-report news stemming from industrializing countries or highly autocratic states, the salience of terrorism as a phenomenon today makes it more likely than ever that media will report these incidents.

In sum, open source event databases have important limitations. But so do all crime databases. For example, official data sources like the Uniform Crime Reports have long been criticized for many of the same issues as those just outlined for event databases (Lynch and Addington 2007; O'Brien 1985). The bottom line is that, despite their drawbacks, there is no obvious alternative to event databases for those interested in tracking terrorism.

Comparing Event Databases

General Comparisons

One method for assessing the quality of open sources on terrorism is to do systematic comparisons across databases. But direct comparison is made difficult by the fact that the databases include differing time frames, geographical scope, and whether they include domestic terrorism data. This diversity is apparent in our earlier discussion of the history of event databases. Thus, WITS is one of the most extensive of the event databases yet it only tracks data from 2004 to 2011. TWEED goes back to 1950 but includes only domestic data from Western Europe. ITERATE does not collect domestic terrorism data at all and RAND only began collecting domestic data in 1998. Taking these limitations into account, the only years for which several of the event databases track approximately the same range and types of cases are 2004–2011 for GTD, RAND, and WITS.

Beyond these differences in coverage and scope is the even more fundamental problem that all the databases apply different terrorism definitions. Sheehan (2012) compares twelve definitional elements used in five of the databases: GTD, ITERATE, RAND, TWEED, and WITS. RAND includes nine of these elements in their definition of terrorism, ITERATE and GTD include seven, WITS includes six, and TWEED includes five. Only two elements are included in terrorism definitions for all five databases (perpetrators are sub-state groups or clandestine agents and the act is outside the context of legitimate warfare or a coup d'état). Two additional elements are included in the terrorism definitions of four of the five databases (use of violence and intended to influence or coerce an audience). The remaining eight elements are divided between different combinations of three or fewer of the five databases.

Krueger et al. (2011) undertook a partial comparison of GTD, ITERATE, RAND, and WITS, focusing mostly on trends in reporting of known perpetrators. The authors found that total events reported by the databases greatly varied. This was even true for GTD, RAND, and WITS—databases that all purported to track domestic and international terrorist attacks for the period after 2004. They also found for all four databases evidence for large increases over time in the proportion of attacks that could not be attributed to specific groups.

Sheehan (2012) examined the same four databases plus TWEED. However, his analysis of suicide attacks from GTD, RAND, and WITS showed major disparities in trends for the time period 2004–2008. In general, RAND and WITS showed higher frequencies of suicide attacks than GTD, although GTD had higher rates than RAND for part of the series (several quarters in 2007 and 2008) and higher rates than RAND or WITS at the beginning of the series in 2004.

Sheehan proposed a set of six criteria to evaluate and compare terrorism event databases: (1) conceptual clarity, (2) context and immediacy of observation, (3) citation transparency, (4) coding consistency, (5) certainty, and (6) conflict of interest. He then applied these criteria to the five databases listed. He also evaluated all of the databases in terms of accessibility and functionality. There were substantial similarities. All five databases received high marks for conceptual clarity. All five provided definitions and criteria for inclusion. All five were similar in terms of providing the context and sources used for data collection and all five depended on some combination of wire services, news articles, and other print and electronic media. He gave GTD, ITERATE, RAND, and TWEED high marks for providing detailed codebooks. He singled out GTD and WITS for providing measures of the certainty of coding decisions. For example, GTD included a field called "doubt terrorism proper" that indicated how certain the coder was that a specific incident qualifies as terrorism. And he praised GTD, ITERATE, and RAND for full disclosure on funding sources. In terms of accessibility and functionality, Sheehan noted that GTD, RAND, TWEED, and WITS were fully available online and also allowed online browsing and keyword searching. All four also offered data that can be directly downloaded with no charge.

The five databases varied considerably in terms of how discrete variables were collected. In this regard, GTD was extremely comprehensive, tracking more than 120 separate variables. By contrast, an important drawback of the WITS data was that it did not report information on perpetrators.

At present, the two databases that are most frequently analyzed by researchers are ITERATE and GTD (Krueger et al. 2011). However, because ITERATE has never included domestic terrorism cases, comparisons between these two databases have been limited. To confront this difficulty, Enders et al. (2011) developed a protocol for distinguishing international from domestic attacks in GTD and then compared international attacks in GTD and ITERATE. They found that from 1978 to 2005 the two databases provided very similar trends. However, from 1970 to mid-1977, the number of attacks in ITERATE exceeded the number of international attacks reported by GTD and, from 2005 to the present, the number of international attacks reported by GTD exceed those reported by ITERATE. LaFree et al. (2015a, ch. 8) present a new plan for distinguishing international and domestic attacks in the GTD, but this approach has not yet been systematically compared to the methods adopted by Enders and colleagues.

Comparing GTD and WITS

The two event databases that collect the most comprehensive domestic and international data on terrorist attacks are the GTD and WITS; hence comparing these two may be useful. Behlendorf and Kumar (2009) conducted a comparison of GTD and WITS country-level event counts from 2004 to 2007. They found that WITS had far more events than GTD and that the disparity varied by country. The WITS/GTD event ratio overall for these four years was 6.30 and was as high as 18.98 for Nepal, 7.75 for Iraq, and 4.68 for Thailand. For the period 2004 to the first quarter of 2007, GTD reported 9,921 terrorist attacks while WITS reported 54,944 events—about 5.5 times more events.

Rhodes (2010) randomly selected 100 cases from GTD and WITS and tried matching each with the corresponding case in the other database. Once the matching was complete, Rhodes compared variable frequencies in each database. A comparison of GTD and WITS by Rhodes (2010, 44) from April to December 2008 showed that the ratio of WITS to GTD was 2.24. Perhaps the single most important reason for the disparity between WITS and GTD was differences in the sources relied on for inclusion. From its onset WITS took a broad approach to sources relied on for data inclusion. For example,

WITS included sources like the South Asian Terrorism Portal (SATP) which does not document the print and electronic media from which its data are drawn. Given that the predecessor of WITS, the US State Department Global Patterns of Terrorism reports, was severely criticized for their narrow coverage of terrorist attacks, this is an understandable strategy. John Wigle (2010, 5), the original director of WITS noted that, from its inception, WITS collected information on "attacks that have any indication of terrorism." In other words, they erred on the side of inclusiveness. He also noted (p. 5) that, "it is very difficult and more time consuming to go back and try to retroactively collect data." This strategy no doubt explains in part the large number of events collected by WITS since 2004.

However, an extremely inclusive data collection strategy has drawbacks. Two are especially important. First, less carefully vetted sources likely increase the probability that the information contained in sources is unreliable. The Rhodes (2010) study found that WITS relied on considerably more sources than the GTD and that twenty sources that accounted for at least 1 percent of all WITS cases from 2004 to 2007 were not cited *at all* by the GTD. Further analysis revealed that most of these sources (e.g. Assam Police, Triton, Katmanduonline.com, SATP, Wikipedia) were websites and secondary media sources that the GTD excluded. As previously noted, WITS relied heavily on the South Asian Terrorism Portal (SATP); a website that did not list media sources for the events it included.

Second, a very inclusive data collection approach risks the problem of including duplicate cases. As terrorism event databases are increasingly automated, detecting and removing duplicate cases has presented a growing challenge (Schrodt 2011). By taking an extremely inclusive approach, it is likely that the threat of including duplicate cases increases. Hewitt (2010, 1) concluded that of the 60,314 WITS cases he examined from 2004 through 2009, 5,897 (9.8 percent) received multiple entries. In some cases these double entries were attempts to better capture the details of a case. So, for example, a single incident might be coded as both a "kidnapping" and a "near miss/non attack" in a case where there were different outcomes for two separate victims. In other cases, the double entries appeared to be simple duplicates. Hewitt identified (p. 2) one incident in Baghdad involving the firing of mortar rounds in the Green Zone that had been entered seven times.

More comparisons between open source databases and other official and unofficial event databases would be helpful. One way to make this task less daunting is to focus on a smaller subset of terrorist attacks. A study by Chermak et al. (2012) examined only homicides attributed to far right extremists in the United States from 1990 to 2008. Based on an examination of nine different databases, the authors found considerable variation in the number of events captured. They also reported that some sources included events that appeared to be contrary to their own inclusion criteria and that other sources excluded events that appeared to meet their criteria. Importantly, though, the authors concluded that the general attributes of victim, suspect, and incident were surprisingly similar across diverse data sources.

The Future of Terrorism Event Databases

Given continued interest in tracking terrorism around the world, event databases are likely to be with us for the foreseeable future. I make four predictions about the future of these databases. First, it is clear that, going forward, terrorism event databases will routinely include both domestic and international data. Prior research that has compared domestic and transnational terrorist attacks (Enders et al. 2011; LaFree et al. 2015a) concludes that the former outnumbers the latter by as much as seven to one. Moreover, as Falkenrath (2001, 164) points out, dividing bureaucratic responsibility and legal authority according to a domestic–international distinction is "an artifact of a simpler, less globally interconnected era." Groups such as Al Qaeda and the Islamic State of Iraq and Syria have global operations that cut across domestic and international lines. Other terrorist organizations (e.g. the Abu Nidal Organization or the Kurdistan Workers' Party) operate in multiple countries and hence engage in acts of both domestic and international terrorism. In short, excluding domestic terrorist attacks impedes a more sophisticated understanding of terrorism and may ultimately weaken counterterrorism efforts.

Second, we can expect increasingly automated data collection in the future. Schrodt and van Brakle (2013, 26) make the argument simply: "human–machine comparisons are of little practical consequence, since human coding is not an option." This is well illustrated by the current data collection of GTD which digests 2 million articles each day: in the face of an ever-growing "fire hose" of media information, a fully human coding protocol is no longer a serious option. WITS was already moving substantially toward automation before it ceased data collection in 2012. It is not entirely clear why WITS was phased out but the most likely explanation is that it was judged by government to be at once too expensive and too similar to other open source terrorism databases. Like the GTD, WITS began the data collection process by sorting through thousands of online sources. In addition, WITS used computers to validate key coding decisions made by its human contributors (Wigle 2010, 6). WITS analysts first coded the discrete parts of each potential terrorist event into a database and then used machines to analyze whether, based on the NCTC criteria, a specific case constituted terrorism and should be kept in the database. When there were disagreements between the human coder and the computer, the coders examined the reasons for the discrepancy. According to former WITS Director Wigle (2010, 6), in the vast majority of cases of disagreement, the cause was human error. Wigle claimed that this human–computer interface increasingly served a quality control function at WITS.

But at the same time, there are still important limitations to automation. A recent study by Wingenroth et al. (2016) compared the accuracy of the semi-automated data collection procedures used by the GTD to three fully automated data systems: the Global Database of Events, Language and Tone (GDELT); the Integrated Conflict Early

Warning System (ICEWS); and Phoenix.[4] To compare the databases the researchers chose as a test bed worldwide suicide bombings for January and February 2015. The authors found that the GTD was able to pick up 97 percent of the incidents identified in a "ground truth" exercise where a research team combed through sources to carefully identify actual events. By contrast, GDELT picked up 70 percent of the events, ICEWS 57 percent, and Phoenix only 10 percent. A major challenge for the fully automated databases was the presence of duplicates. Eighty-three percent of ICEWS cases, 79 percent of GDELT cases, and 65 percent of Phoenix were duplicate interpretations of the same event. Thus, while automation is likely to continually improve our ability to detect and record terrorist attacks, human validation is likely to remain as a critically important part of the process for the foreseeable future.

Third, event databases will increasingly provide geographic information system (GIS) enhancements. Before it ceased operations, WITS provided geo-coded information that permitted analysis of sub-national patterns of terrorism. All new GTD data are geo-referenced and the GTD team has geo-referenced 84 percent of the full data back to 1970. Such GIS data are critical for supporting growing research on geo-spatial patterns of terrorism (Berrebi and Lakdawalla 2007; Behlendforf et al. 2012).

And finally, future databases will increasingly be linked to other related databases, including those on counter-measures and other types of political and non-political violence and crime. For example, Eck (2012) provides the framework for integrating two of the pre-eminent armed conflict event datasets (the Uppsala Conflict Data Program's Georeferenced Event Data (UDCP-GED) and the Armed Conflict Location and Event Data Project (ACLED)). Donnay et al. (2016) are developing a dashboard that integrates the Global Terrorism Database with UCDP-GED, ACLED, and the Social Conflict Analysis Database (SCAD). Similarly, there is a dearth of social science research on how specific anti-terrorism and counterterrorism efforts impact the likelihood of terrorist attacks chronicled by event databases like the GTD. We need more information on the impact of counter- and anti-terrorism interventions and their expected impact on trajectories of terrorist activities. Such research could help us better understand what separates successful and unsuccessful counter-measures, what variables predict the counter-measures implemented by governments, and whether the same counter-measures may have different impacts when implemented in response to different groups. An illustration is provided by Dugan and Chenoweth (2012), who collected extensive counterterrorism data for Israel and used the data to compare terrorism data from the GTD to counter-measures adopted by the Israeli government.

Conclusions

The nature of terrorism makes it difficult to track through traditional criminological sources such as victimization or self-report surveys or police data. Contemporary terrorism event databases became feasible in the late 1960s, along with the availability of satellite technology and portable cameras. The scope of open source databases on terrorist attacks has greatly expanded since the early 1970s. Open source databases are generated from print and electronic media and face limitations associated with this fact. In particular, the media may report inaccuracies and falsehoods, there may be conflicting information or false, multiple, or no claims of responsibility and, despite improvements, coverage still relies more on Western than non-Western sources. It is worth pointing out that all of these problems are also frequently mentioned as drawbacks of official crime data. Certainly government censorship and disinformation affects not only media sources but official government sources. It is especially challenging to disentangle terrorism from acts of war, insurrection, or massive civil unrest. At present this is an especially difficult problem in war-torn countries such as Iraq, Afghanistan, and Syria. Even though the media now seemingly peer into every corner of the world, media coverage still varies across time and geographic space. On the other hand, event databases have the great strength of tracking a type of behavior whose success is in large part a function of its ability to be publicized. At present there is likely no other type of crime that has data as universally available for all countries of the world as terrorism.

Efforts to compare event databases have been slow to develop, hampered especially by major differences between definitions, scope, and years of coverage. However, in recent years there have been an increasing number of comparative studies of the available databases and this is likely to accelerate in the future.

Because event databases provide data on terrorism that are not available from any other source, they are likely to continue. Some of the major developments we can expect from event databases in the future include routine collection of domestic as well as international events, increased use of automated data collection and verification, geo-referencing of events, and more comprehensive linkage to other data sources.

Notes

1. This list is not exhaustive. Other efforts to develop terrorism event databases include TRITON and COBRA. However, these other databases were mostly developed by for-profit companies and thus far have not been available to researchers.
2. Although RAND did include some cases that were arguably domestic, including cases in Israel and the Palestine territories.
3. Unfortunately, PGIS lost the original 1993 data in an office move and START has never succeeded in fully restoring it.
4. The test also included the Suicide Attack Database (SAD-CPOST) collected by Pape 2005 and his colleagues. Like the GTD, SAD-CPOST relies in part on human coders but is limited to suicide attacks. Like the GTD, SAD-CPOST outperformed the fully automated data sets on both precision and percentage of cases that were duplicates.

References

Asal, Victor, and R. Karl Rethemeyer (2013) "Project Fact Sheet: Big Allied and Dangerous." <September.http://www.start.umd.edu/sites/default/files/publications/local_attachments/STARTFactSheet_BAAD.pdf>.

Behlendorf, Brandon and Sumit Kumar (2009) "Report between NCTC Worldwide Incident Tracking System (WITS) and START Global Terrorism Database (GTD) for 2004 to 2007." Unpublished manuscript, START Center, University of Maryland.

Behlendorf, Brandon, Gary LaFree, and Richard L. Legault (2012) "Predicting Microcycles of Terrorist Violence: Evidence from FMLN and ETA," *Journal of Quantitative Criminology*, 28: 49–75.

Berrebi, C., and D. Lakdawalla (2007) "How does Terrorism Risk Vary across Space and Time? An Analysis Based on the Israeli Experience," *Defence and Peace Economics*, 18: 113–31.

Chermak, Steven M., Joshua D. Freilich, William S. Parkin, and James P. Lynch (2012) "American Terrorism and Extremist Crime Data Sources and Selectivity Bias: An Investigation Focusing on Homicide Events Committed by Far-Right Extremists," *Journal of Quantitative Criminology*, 28: 191–218.

Chermak, Steven, Joshua Freilich, and Michael Suttmoeller (2013) "The Organizational Dynamics of Far-Right Hate Groups in the United States: Comparing Violent to Nonviolent Organizations," *Studies in Conflict and Terrorism*, 36(3): 193–218.

Crenshaw, Martha, and Gary LaFree (2016) *Countering Terrorism: No Simple Solutions*. Washington, DC: Brookings.

Donnay, Karsten, Eric Dunford, Erin C. McGrath, David Backer, and David E. Cunningham (2016) "MELTT: Matching Event Data by Location, Time and Type." Paper presented at the Annual Conference of the Midwest Political Science Association, Apr. 7–10, Chicago.

Drakos, Konstantinos, and Andreas Gofas (2006) "The Devil You Know But are Afraid to Face: Underreporting Bias and its Distorting Effects on the Study of Terrorism," *Journal of Conflict Resolution*, 50: 714–35.

Dugan, Laura, and Erica Chenoweth (2012) "Moving Beyond Deterrence: The Effectiveness of Raising the Expected Utility of Abstaining from Terrorism in Israel," *American Sociological Review*, 77: 597–624.

Dugan, Laura, and Michael Distler (2016) "Measuring Terrorism," in G. LaFree and J. Freilich (eds), *The Handbook of the Criminology of Terrorism*. New York: Wiley, 189–205.

Eck, Kristine (2012) "In Data We Trust? A Comparison of UCDP, GED and ACLED Conflict Events Datasets," *Cooperation and Conflict*, 47: 124–41.

Enders, Walter, Todd Sandler, and Khusrav Gaibulloev (2011) "Domestic versus Transnational Terrorism: Data, Decomposition and Dynamics," *Journal of Peace Research*, 48: 319–37.

Engene, Jan O. (2007) "Five Decades of Terrorism in Europe: The TWEED Dataset," *Journal of Peace Research*, 44: 109–21.

Falkenrath, Richard (2001) "Analytic Models and Policy Prescription: Understanding Recent Innovation in US Counterterrorism," *Journal of Conflict and Terrorism*, 24: 159–81.

Fariss, Christopher J. (2014) "Respect for Human Rights has Improved over Time: Modeling the Changing Standard of Accountability," *American Political Science Review*, 108: 297–318.

Fishman, Mark (1980) *Manufacturing the News*. Austin, TX: University of Texas Press.

Hewitt, Joseph (2010) "Data Assessment: Worldwide Incidents Tracking System (WITS), 2004–2009." Unpublished manuscript, START Center, University of Maryland.

Jenkins, Brian M. (1975) *Will Terrorists Go Nuclear?* Santa Monica, CA: RAND Corporation.

Jensen, Michael, Patrick James, and Herbert Tinsley (2015) "Profiles of Individual Radicalization in the United States: Preliminary Findings." Jan. <https://www.start.umd.edu/pubs/PIRUS%20Research%20Brief_Jan%202015.pdf>.

King, Gary, and Will Lowe (2003) "An Automated Information Extraction Tool for International Conflict Data with Performance as Good as Human Coders: A Rare Events Evaluation Design," *International Organization*, 57: 617–42.

Krueger, Alan B., and David D. Laitin (2004a) “Faulty Terror Report Card,” *Washington Post*, May 17: A21.

Krueger, Alan B., and David D. Laitin (2004b) “‘Misunderestimating’ Terrorism: The State Department’s Big Mistake,” *Foreign Affairs*, 83: 8–13.

Krueger, Alan, David Laitin, Jacob Shapiro, and Dragana Stanisic (2011) “Analysis of WITS Impact on Scholarly Work on Terrorism.” Unpublished manuscript, Princeton University.

LaFree, Gary (2019) “Conceptualizing and Measuring Terrorism: Evidence from the Global Terrorism Database,” in A. Silke (ed.), *The Handbook on Terrorism and Counter-Terrorism*. London: Routledge, 22–33.

LaFree, Gary, and Laura Dugan (2004) “How does Studying Terrorism Compare to Studying Crime?,” in Mathieu DeFlem (ed.), *Criminology and Terrorism*. Oxford: Elsevier, 53–74.

LaFree, Gary, Laura Dugan, and Erin Miller (2015a) *Putting Terrorism in Context: Lessons from the Global Terrorism*. London: Routledge.

LaFree, Gary, Karise Carrillo, and David McDowall (2015b) “How Effective are our ‘Better Angels?’ Evidence for a World-Wide Decline in Violent Crime since the 1990s,” *European Journal of Criminology*, 12: 482–504.

Lynch, James P., and Lynn A. Addington (2007) *Understanding Crime Statistics: Revisiting the Divergence of the NCVS and UCR*. Cambridge Studies in Criminology. Cambridge: Cambridge University Press.

Mickolus, Edward F. (2002) “How do we Know We’re Winning the War Against Terrorism? Issues in Measurement,” *Studies in Conflict and Terrorism*, 25: 151–60.

Mickolus, Edward F., Todd Sandler, Jean M, Murdock, and Peter Flemming (2010) *International Terrorism: Attributes of Terrorist Events (ITERATE)*. Dunn Loring, VA: Vinyard Software.

Nivette, Amy E. (2011) “Cross-National Predictors of Homicide: A Meta-Analysis,” *Homicide Studies*, 15(2): 103–31.

O’Brien, Robert (1985) *Crime and Victimization*. Beverly Hills, CA: Sage.

Pape, Robert (2005) *Dying to Win: The Strategic Logic of Suicide Terrorism*. New York: Random House.

Post, Jerrold, Ehud Sprinzak, and Laurita Denny (2003) “The Terrorists in their own Words: Interviews with 35 Incarcerated Middle Eastern Terrorists,” *Terrorism and Political Violence*, 15: 171–84.

Rhodes, Matt (2010) “Three Phase Comparison between the Global Terrorism Database and the Worldwide Incidents Tracking System.” Unpublished manuscript, START Center, University of Maryland.

Schrodt, Philip A. (2011) “Precedents, Progress and Prospects in Political Event Data.” Unpublished manuscript, Pennsylvania State University.

Schrodt, Philip A., and David Van Brakle (2013) “Automated Coding of Political Event Data,” in V. S. Subrahmanian (ed.), *Handbook of Computational Approaches to Counterterrorism*. New York: Springer, 23–48.

Sheehan, Ivan Sascha (2012) “Assessing and Comparing Data Sources for Terrorism Research,” in Cynthia Lum and Les Kennedy (eds), *Evidence-Based Counterterrorism Policy*. New York: Springer, 13–40.

Smith, Brent L., Paxton Roberts, and Kelly Damphousse (2013) “Update on Geospatial Patterns of Antecedent Behavior among Perpetrators in the American Terrorism Study (ATS),” Report to Resilient Systems Division, DHS Science and Technology Directorate. College Park, MD: START, <2013.http://start.umd.edu/pubs/START_IUSSD_Geospatial PatternsofAntecedentBehaviorAmongPerpetrators_October2013.pdf>.

UCDP/PRIO Armed Conflict Dataset Codebook (2013) *Uppsala Conflict Data Program/ International Peace Research Institute Oslo*, Version 4, 2013, accessed Aug. 23.

US Department of State (2004) *Patterns of Global Terrorism 2003*. Washington, DC: Government Printing Office.

Wigle, John (2010) "Introducing the Worldwide Incidents Tracking System (WITS)," *Perspectives on Terrorism*, 4: 3–23.

Wingenroth, B., E. Miller, M. Jensen, O. Hodwitz and K. Quinlan (2016) "Event Data and the Construction of Reality." Poster presented at the June 2016 International Conference on Social Computing, Behavioral-Cultural Modeling, and Prediction and Behavior Representation in Modeling and Simulation, Washington, DC.

CHAPTER 5

THE MORAL DIMENSIONS OF TERRORISM

VIRGINIA HELD

THERE is little doubt that terrorism is more obviously a contentious moral issue than many other uses of violence. The laws of reasonably acceptable modern states have clarified when and how a great deal of the violence that occurs—in criminal activity and in the enforcement of law—is not only legally but also morally unjustifiable, or not. Centuries of discussion of just war theory have examined the most plausible views of how and when the use of military force by states can or cannot be morally justified. And international legal documents specify some of the views on which there is agreement concerning uses of violence across borders. But terrorism is not well covered by these discussions and understandings. It is violence used for political objectives, often by those seeking to change existing political arrangements. In order to further its political aims, it tries to spread fear among a wider group than those attacked, and often succeeds in doing so. It is often carried out by non-state groups, and its agents are usually not part of an organized military force. It often deliberately targets civilians or disregards whether they will be among the victims of its violence (Hoffman 1998; Waldron 2004).

What terrorism is and how it should be understood are highly contested issues that themselves raise moral questions. Many persons and groups and states seek to attach the labels of terrorism to the actions of those they oppose, while exempting their own uses of comparable violence from similar opprobrium. As Samuel Scheffler notes, "the word 'terrorism' is in danger of becoming little more than a pejorative term used to refer to the tactics of one's enemies" (Scheffler 2006, 1). But we need not add to this danger. Reasonable definitions and discussions are possible.

Many define terrorism in such a way that it is necessarily indefensible because of the meaning of the term, but this is unhelpful in trying to understand the moral issues it raises. There are strong tendencies in the general discussion of terrorism to think of one's opponents as terrorists and those of whom one approves as the victims of terrorism who, if they use violence, are reacting to something others have initiated.

Those victimized by oppression and domination, however, may see their oppressors as maintaining a regime of terror, and those who strive to liberate them from this as fighters for freedom and justice (Honderich 2002; Richardson 2006).

Opponents of those using violence to achieve legitimate aims often strive to deflect discussion from those aims by focusing on the means used in pursuit of them. Engaging persuasively in arguments about the wrongness of terrorism as a means can deflect attention from the legitimacy of the objectives sought by those who use it. But to appropriately evaluate the moral dimensions of terrorism it is important that we consider the aims for which it is used and the alternatives open for pursuing them, as well as that we consider the characteristics and moral wrongs of terrorism (Gehring 2003; Held 2008; Primoratz 2004). We should examine what means other than violence can be effective in achieving legitimate political change, and how those in power ought to enable such means. Or, when the aims of those using terrorism are morally unjustified, we ought to consider how this can be made persuasive to potential recruits. And we should especially focus on the moral evaluation of actions that can be taken and policies that can be adopted to respond to, counter, reduce, and prevent terrorism.

Moral Evaluation

Moral evaluations of actions such as those involved in the use of terrorism, or actions engaged in to oppose it, can take various forms depending on the kinds of moral theory appealed to. The most established kinds of moral argument are utilitarian consequentialism and deontological rights-based approaches. These are illustrated by the utilitarianism of John Stuart Mill and the moral theory of Immanuel Kant.

Consequentialism holds that actions lack intrinsic moral characteristics, and that what make them right or wrong are the consequences they bring about. Utilitarianism judges these consequences in terms of the "utility"—the happiness or pleasure or preference or interest satisfaction, or, alternatively, the misery, pain, or disutility—caused by the action for all those affected. With moral approaches of this kind, a violent terrorist attack that brought about results clearly better in terms of their consequences than the pain they caused, would be justifiable. A violent act causing some bad consequences for the victims might well cause major reforms that could be judged far better for many more people such that, on balance, the act would be judged justifiable on utilitarian grounds.

Deontological, rights-based approaches hold that actions do have intrinsic moral characteristics, regardless of their consequences. These views hold that if an act is a lie, or if it breaks a promise, or if it violates someone's rights, it is, at least initially, wrong. It may have other aspects, such as that it is a lie to prevent the killing of an innocent person, or it breaks a minor promise in order to avert a major catastrophe, that need to be considered. But the action still has an important moral characteristic in itself, depending on the motive or intention with which it is performed. If a violent act violates a person's rights, this aspect of the act is inherently wrong, never mind the act's consequences.

Utilitarian arguments have often been thought to be weak foundations on which to condemn terrorism, since if a terrorist act has consequences that are on balance better than its alternatives, it will be justified. Kantian and rights-based arguments have usually been thought to offer stronger grounds on which to condemn the violence of terrorism. Terrorist acts violate the rights of their victims, rights to life and to personal security from attack.

However, rights-based approaches may not offer the firm condemnation of terrorism their proponents seek (Held 2008). In a situation in which the rights of people are already being massively violated by an existing political system or given regime, and peaceful protest and non-violent efforts to achieve respect for the rights of those deprived of it have not succeeded, or have been met with even greater violent suppression, it is not clear that a continuation of these rights violations would be morally better than a limited terrorist violation that brought about a far greater respect for rights. One set of rights violations would have to be weighed against another. It might well be thought that the continuation of the rights violations of whole populations would be morally worse than the transient rights violations of a few of those benefitting from this injustice, if the violence could be limited and effective. Some rights violations may be inevitable in any actual social system, but to achieve a more fair distribution of such violations would be a consideration of justice compatible with rights-based arguments.

In addition to utilitarianism and Kantian moral theory, the newer approach of the feminist ethics of care is becoming influential (Held 2006, 2015). It is based on the experience of caring for others and having been cared for, examining the values involved in care work, and understanding how and why they should be extended. The relevant experience really is universal, since no person can survive without having been cared for, at least in childhood. Most persons have some experience caring for others, and many persons, especially women, have enormous amounts of experience caring for children and others.

Actual care practices are often highly unsatisfactory and are embedded in morally indefensible gender hierarchies that permeate existing social structures. It is still possible to discern the values incorporated into even existing care practices and to understand how existing practices ought to be improved. We can develop more and more satisfactory appreciations of how care ought to be provided and received, and care values fostered in more and more contexts. We can distinguish actual care and *good* care, and delineate the characteristics of good care practices.

The understanding of care and its values must be developed as much from the point of view of the recipient of care as from the point of view of the provider. The initial concern some have expressed about this moral approach, that caregivers are often heavy-handed and fail to adequately respect the individuality and autonomy and rights of recipients, can effectively be answered. Contrary to the concern of these critics, providers of good care *learn* how to provide care respectfully. They engage in practices of receptivity, of listening and being open to what recipients of care are experiencing. Being sensitive to the needs and feelings of recipients is essential for good care. Care *ethics* should be built on the experience not only of providers but also of recipients of care, which includes every one of us.

In contrast with the values associated with justice—fairness, impartiality, equality—which can be seen to be especially relevant to legal and political and economic contexts, the ethics of care emphasizes the values of responsiveness to need, sensitivity, empathy, and trust. These are seen to be central not only to the more personal contexts of family and friendship but to segments of society that have had much less influence in the development of moral theory, segments such as the health care and welfare systems, and the education systems. And the insights of the ethics of care are of fundamental and transformative importance to the development of comprehensive moral approaches and to questions concerning the global issues surrounding the legal and political and economic structures of established nation states, and their opponents.

The ethics of care provides an even stronger grounding for condemning violence than do traditional moral theories. Violence is fundamentally antithetical to the values of care. But care approaches recognize that some violence is to be expected as an ordinary part of human life. Children do not become responsible adults without learning to deal with violence, their own and that of others. The ethics of care focuses on ways to reduce, deflect, curb, and prevent violence. Its approach can be seen most clearly in the contexts of family and smaller groups, but its recommendations can be extended to wider and wider contexts (Ruddick 1989). It does not encourage the illusion that massive military might should be used in a war to defeat small, weak groups using terrorism.

The ethics of care understands persons as relational, rather than as the self-sufficient individuals of traditional moral approaches, which are in many ways generalizations to the level of moral theory of views developed for the more legal and political and economic contexts of democratic, capitalist states. Care ethics values caring relations between persons, not only within families, but in wider and wider contexts. Such relations will be weaker, of course, than in personal contexts, but relations with even distant strangers can be based on non-indifference. Persons can understand others with sensitivity and respond to their needs and aspirations, fostering trust in place of hostility. They can reduce and contain violence, including terrorist violence. Caring persons can reduce the motivations of others to use violence, rather than violently destroying some violent persons while provoking more violence in others.

Terrorism and Political Reality

Among the most important moral questions concerning terrorism is whether it can ever be justifiable. This question cannot be answered by resort to definitional fiat. Terrorism is a fact of political life and needs to be understood and evaluated. How it ought to be dealt with and what policies governments and citizens ought to support in the face of it are all moral questions of great urgency.

Terrorism is not a new phenomenon, although Americans, surprised and understandably shocked by the attacks of September 11, 2001, widely assumed it to be, and responded as if nothing had been learned from earlier instances of terrorism. More knowledgeable historians recount the terrorism of the ancient world, the Middle Ages, the early modern era in Europe, and the nineteenth and twentieth centuries. As Randall Law writes, "terrorism is as old as human civilization... The weapons, methods, and goals of terrorists constantly change, but core features have remained since the earliest times" (Law 2013, 1). (On the history of terrorism see Part II of this volume.) An example is offered by the Hindu Thugs, whose organization was the longest lasting terrorist group in history, surviving from the fifth century BCE until the nineteenth century. Its members strangled their victims in service of the Goddess Kali who, they believed, demanded human blood to keep the world in balance (Bloom 2007). Some scholars argue that their primary goal in attacking travelers was actually robbery (Law 2013, 324). As is often the case, they used religion to pursue other objectives.

In his history of terrorism, Randall Law examines three aspects of terrorism: (1) the behaviors, tactics, and methods associated with terrorism; (2) "terrorism as violent theater" used to spread fear or to provoke a violent reaction and thus support for the goals of the terrorists; and (3) terrorism as cultural construct, in which the label is used "to deem another's goals or methods illegitimate" (p. 4). Terrorism has had a long history.

Mia Bloom examines the terrorism of the Jewish Zealots and Sicarri of the first century CE and the Muslim Assassins of the eleventh to thirteenth centuries as well as that of the Thugs. She points out how terrorism was a weapon of the weak. For the Assassins, "with one carefully planned attack, a small force prepared to die in the course of killing others could cripple their more powerful enemy. They realized, too, that the fear or memory of such an attack could be as paralyzing as the attack itself" (Bloom 2007, 6).

The word "terrorism" was first used to describe the terror that the revolutionary government installed after the French Revolution of 1789 inflicted on its enemies. Martin Miller, a historian, has studied the terrorism of the modern world. Focusing on the interplay between the violence of rebel movements and that of the modern state, he shows how prevalent terrorism has been from the time of the French Revolution to the present, and how it is likely to continue.

Popular conceptions of terrorism often associate it with Islamic extremism. In fact, in the United States since September 11, 2001, by mid-2015, "nearly twice as many people have been killed by white supremacists, antigovernment fanatics and non-Muslim extremists than by radical Muslims" (Shane 2015).

Historian Michael Fellman recounts the often forgotten or unacknowledged terrorism in US history. It was Christian terrorism, carried out by both the state and its opponents. Among the cases on which he focuses are the anti-slavery terrorism of the abolitionist John Brown in the mid-nineteenth century; terrorism carried out during the Civil War involving terrorizing whole populations; and white terrorism against Reconstruction during the late nineteenth century. Arguing that there are two forms of terrorism, revolutionary and reactionary, he makes clear that terrorism is an American and not only a foreign phenomenon (Fellman 2010).

While we should not overlook that there are very significant differences between, for instance, the IRA (Irish Republican Army) and ISIS (or ISIL or the Islamic State), and between the motivations that may be driving those recruited for violence by such groups, we can learn much from the terrorism of the past that can be useful in preventing and countering future instances of it. In his excellent short book on how to respond to terrorism, Richard English discusses some of these lessons. He writes that "terrorism is a very old phenomenon, and we should use this to our advantage in learning what we can" (English 2009, 119). More of a problem than current terrorism itself is that those in power often fail to learn from the past, or new politicians appeal to emotions that support positions contrary to those successful in reducing terrorism. The "most serious danger currently posed by terrorists," English suggests, "is probably their capacity to provoke ill-judged, extravagant, and counter-productive state responses" (2009, 119).

The first lesson we should learn from the long history of terrorism is, English and others argue, that we should learn to live with it. In keeping with this aim, we might hesitate to see terrorism as a kind of warfare, as some, including I, have suggested. Although doing so is helpful in conveying the political motives of terrorists, the pull of terrorists' commitments, and the vastly greater suffering and number of casualties caused by war in comparison to terrorism, we probably cannot and should not learn to live with war. At this stage of human history we ought to have figured out how to prevent and head off war. What we have learned to live with is crime, and responding to terrorist acts as to crime is often appropriate, though we should not lose sight of terrorism's political aspects. The better approach to understanding terrorism may be to see it as neither a kind of war nor a kind of crime, though it has aspects of both, but as a unique form of violence.

Other Violence

A question may arise about whether violence in the home and in the family is a kind of terrorism, as a person may terrorize a domestic partner or a child. There may be good reasons to limit the term "terrorism" to terrorizing for political purposes. Just as terrorism is not ordinary crime whose motive is profit, as in a drug cartel's killing of its rivals, or a sex trafficker's enslavement of workers, it may be advisable to distinguish terrorism as political violence from violent domination that is non-political. There are ways in which we may want to consider all uses of power to be political in a sense, captured by the slogan "the personal is political." But once the point is made that political structures uphold such social structures as gender and economic and racial hierarchies, it is often useful to identify the more specifically political, which I am attempting to do in this discussion.

Political violence, however, is by no means used primarily by opponents of given political arrangements. Max Weber's conception of the modern state as that which has a monopoly on the legitimate use of force or violence is widely accepted. But of course the justifiability of its powers to police and enforce the law, violently when it deems necessary, can always be and often is contested.

Uses of Violence

It is agreed by almost everyone that violence, which causes harm and injury and often death, should never be used for its own sake. It can be justifiable only when used for a legitimate purpose such as to enforce the just laws of a state, and used in morally acceptable ways such as those that cause no more harm than necessary to achieve their purposes. In the case of war, contemporary views and international agreements limit the justifiable use of military force by states to defense against aggression, and, more controversially, to rescue groups of persons from crimes against humanity or genocide. But it is generally thought by most citizens and by scholars studying the justifiability of war that the enormous harm caused by war, though regrettable, can nevertheless sometimes be justified (Walzer 2000; Lango 2014).

If the violence of terrorism is used for a purpose that is clearly morally wrong, such as to forcibly impose a given religion on a group of persons and to kill all who resist, such terrorism can rather obviously be seen to be morally wrong. More frequent and difficult cases are whether terrorism can justifiably be used for morally admirable objectives, such as to liberate groups of people from colonial or racial oppression. Martha Crenshaw, a scholar with decades of experience studying terrorism, has noted that terrorism has played an important role over many years in a great many successful struggles for independence from foreign domination (Crenshaw 1983). Although not all who study terrorism agree, Robert Pape, a political scientist who has studied a vast number of individual terrorist attacks, has shown that overwhelmingly they have been not the random acts of religious fanatics but part of a larger campaign to further a political objective: the self-determination of their community's homeland through compelling an enemy to withdraw. Pape argues that the primary objective of every suicide campaign from 1980 to 2001 was to coerce a foreign government that had military forces in what the terrorist group considered its homeland to withdraw those forces (Pape 2005). Sometimes such objectives may be deemed justifiable. When the aims are legitimate, and the means of opposing the organized might of oppressive states, occupying armies, or colonial domination are highly limited, it is far more difficult to condemn all terrorism on moral grounds.

Martin Miller observes that "the conditions for terrorism continue unabated, with new personnel to act out the entanglements of violence over the unresolved problems between governments and their oppositions, nationally and internationally." His conclusion is that "looking back over the last two centuries of political violence, it seems evident that political violence is not yet on the verge of demise... it may at best be managed. It is an integral part of the body politic, just as illnesses are part of our organic makeup" (Miller 2013, 244, 258).

There are strong arguments for seeking to limit and reduce political violence, rather than imagining that it can be defeated by a vastly more violent "war" against terrorism. Especially when conducted against whole populations, military campaigns increase the feelings of humiliation and desire for revenge that fuel the motivation of many to engage in terrorist actions (Held 2008; Euben 2015). A long history has shown that military over-reactions to terrorism are likely to produce more recruits for terrorism than they eliminate.

Ends and Means

Most discussions of the moral dimensions of terrorism focus on its unjustifiability. Without adequate clarity they often treat it as a means that can never be justified and that ought not be used regardless of the aims or objectives of those using it. The argument is often based on an assumption that terrorism targets or at least disregards noncombatants, and that doing so is always wrong.

As a matter of definition, it is questionable that building the targeting of civilians into the definition of terrorism is appropriate. Walter Laqueur has written that "most terrorist groups in the contemporary world have been attacking the military, the police, and the civilian population" (Laqueur 2003, 233). Attacks such as the blowing up of the Marine barracks in Lebanon in 1983, the violent attack on the US destroyer *Cole* in Yemen in 2000, and the attack on the Pentagon on September 11, 2001, on the same day and by the same group as that on the World Trade Center, are routinely considered terrorist attacks.

Terrorist groups often claim that, if they had the capacity to fight with more conventional means, they would do so. Terrorism is often the weapon of those confronting the enormous power of militarized states where, were such opposing groups to fight in conventional ways, they would simply be overwhelmingly defeated.

There is disagreement on whether the use of violence including terrorism can or cannot be effective in bringing about the social change sought by the groups that use it. Algerian terrorism was arguably successful. After provoking a war by France to defeat Algerian independence, a war that turned out to be self-defeating, Algerian terrorism led France to agree to full independence for Algeria in 1962. Randall Law summarizes these developments as "the French win the battle but lose the war" (Law 2013, 208). The cost, however, was high: a half-million to a million killed, most of them Algerian Muslims, and nearly 2,800 French civilians. Further, "the FLN, which emerged from the war as the only possible Algerian ruling party, had learned how to govern while waging a fantastically brutal campaign of terrorism. Coarsened by violence... antagonistic toward the concepts of tolerance, compromise, and the rule of law," it was not suited to its new role. "The use of terrorism," Law concludes, "is indeed poor preparation for effective, democratic governance" (Law 2013, 212).

Walter Laqueur has claimed that terrorism is counterproductive, that it has tended to bring about "violent repression and a polarization which precluded political progress" rather than the aims sought by those using it (Laqueur 1997, 233). The philosopher Albrecht Wellmer said of the terrorist violence used in Germany in the 1970s by the group called the Red Army Faction that, although it increased awareness of the injustices in the political and capitalist systems, the net effect was a more reactionary outcome. It made political repression seem legitimate and led to a defamation of the entire Left (Wellmer 1984).

A different view is that of Charles Tilly and Lewis Coser who argue that violent protest has been a near normal part of Western political progress and reform (Tilly 1969; Coser 1966). Richard Falk observes, of the bombing of the Marine barracks in Lebanon, that it seems to have been remarkably successful. It led President Ronald Reagan to remove US troops from Lebanon, thereby causing "a very strong power to accede to the demands of a very weak opponent" (Falk 1988, 35). Many argue that the threat of violence or terrorism in the background of a conflict enables non-violent activism to be successful, as Gandhi can be thought to have understood (Law, 2013, 151).

Martin Miller describes the terrorism used against Indian tribes by settlers and the US government during the US's western expansion in the nineteenth century, and the terrorism of white mobs, often with the acquiescence of government and the courts, in the long history of the lynching of African-Americans in the US. Unfortunately, this terrorism was successful in depriving Native Americans of their lands, and in delaying for many decades the progress of African-Americans (Miller 2013, ch. 6).

In his book devoted to answering the question of whether terrorism works in achieving political objectives, Richard English reaches a decidedly mixed conclusion (English 2016).

Terrorism and Justifiability

Even when the argument that terrorism is always wrong is not based on its wrongness having been built into the definition, there are difficulties with the argument. These can be illustrated by Michael Walzer's very influential book *Just and Unjust Wars* (Walzer 2000). Walzer maintains that terrorism is always wrong because of its targeting of civilians. His book argues strongly for the principle of non-combatant immunity that has traditionally been part of just war theory. However, just war theory has been developed for violent military conflict between established states with organized armed forces. Its application to the violence used by non-state groups is questionable (Goodin 2006). And, in actual war, as Stephen Nathanson writes, "both commonsense morality and standard theories of the ethics of war approve the killing of innocent people in at least some circumstances" (Nathanson 2006, 3; see also Coady 2004).

Either the exceptions made for the violence used against non-combatants by the armed forces of states whose aims are considered morally admirable must be rejected, or the claim that terrorism is always wrong is undermined. Some have tried to argue that terrorism deliberately targets civilians, while if military force kills civilians it can and should do so only unintentionally, but the distinction is too disingenuous in most cases to be persuasive.

Walzer concedes that the Allied bombing of German cities early in World War II was aimed at the civilian populations of those cities, to undermine Germany's will to fight.

Yet he considers this bombing (though not the later bombing of Dresden and Hiroshima and other cities) justified. His effort to justify it relies on the idea of the "supreme emergency" faced by the Allies, and an understanding of the great moral importance of defeating Nazi Germany. Nazism, Walzer writes, "was an ultimate threat to everything decent in our lives . . . the consequences of its [possible] victory were literally beyond calculation, immeasurably awful" (Walzer 2006, 253). But as Nathanson reflects in his discussion of Walzer's argument, "if people are subjected to brutal rule over many years and cannot lead normal, secure lives, they are likely to see their own situation as a supreme emergency for them" (2006, 22).

When attention is paid to the objectives of terrorism, it is sometimes relatively easy to conclude that the violence used is unjustified in pursuit of those objectives. No methods would be justified to establish the rule of a group such as ISIS (or ISIL or the Islamic State, depending on designation) that aims to kill all those rejecting its religious dictates, that has policies of raping and enslaving women non-believers based on its misinterpretation of the Koran (Callimachi 2015), and that destroys on religious grounds such artistic treasures as the ancient city of Palmyra and beheads the scholar protecting the site (Hubbard 2015). That this group engages widely in beheadings and is especially brutal in its operations need not be the main focus of an evaluation of its terrorism. No means would be justified to establish such a regime. However, to the extent that its vision of an Islamic caliphate to replace the failed and chaotic nation states of the region has appeal and some legitimacy, this vision needs to be evaluated and contested as a goal.

Most existing states did not come into existence by peaceful plebiscites, but neither did they originate through force and violence alone. What was required was a vision for which persons were willing to and often did die. What should be developed are the means for persons to achieve legitimate visions without having either to die or to kill.

When the objectives sought by groups using terrorism are justified, it is often very difficult to morally evaluate the means used. Where the aims are legitimate and the means of opposing the organized forces of oppressive states, occupying armies, and colonial domination are highly limited, it is unclear that all terrorism should be condemned on moral grounds.

Terrorism kills far fewer people than war, usually thought to be justified in some cases, and although terrorism causes fear and terror to achieve political advantage, the fear and terror and vast numbers of dead and wounded caused by war and its varied horrors should be better appreciated by those who see terrorism as uniquely horrendous and unjustified. World War II brought about the deaths of over 80 million people, over two-thirds of them civilians. To argue that such deaths as these were justified because the cause was just, while the terrorism that kills a very small fraction of such a number can never be justified even if its cause is just, may lack a sense of proportion.

Where the justifiability of the objectives is greater on the side of the insurgents or resisters, responsibility for avoiding violence is greater with those in power opposing these objectives. They are in a position to bring it about that peaceful protest and nonviolent actions lead to the attainment of justifiable objectives. While the stability of a political system has some value, where change is morally recommended, those resisting it with the use of violence are usually more at fault than those using it for such change. The case of South Africa is illustrative.

South Africa and Apartheid

When the aims sought by a group using violence, including terrorism, are justified, responsibility for minimizing the violence often rests especially on those in power. If they violently resist the changes needed to bring about a more just and good society, their actions are often less justifiable than those acting for the needed changes. As Nelson Mandela said, writing of the white South African government as it violently repressed efforts to end the apartheid system of white supremacy, "a government which uses force to maintain its rule teaches the oppressed to use force to oppose it" (Johns and Davis 1991, 119–20).

The case of South Africa under apartheid is a helpful one to examine. It is now almost universally agreed that the brutal system of racial apartheid in place in South Africa until 1994 was grossly unjust, a grievous violation of the human rights of non-white South Africans. The African National Congress, seeking respect for the rights of black South Africans, had engaged for many decades in non-violent protests. These were met with ever increasing repression. When Nelson Mandela and his fellow leaders of the African National Congress discussed what directions their efforts ought to take, they considered the possibilities of violent protests, using violence first against property and then, if necessary, in ways that might well harm innocent persons. As their own members were increasingly being killed by the white South African government, they concluded that if they needed to resort to terrorism to bring about a recognition of the rights of black South Africans, this would be justified. They reasoned that it would be morally better than the civil war they believed would otherwise explode between blacks and whites.

If the ANC had resorted to terrorism, it can certainly be argued that the white South African government would have been more at fault than the ANC for the wrongs of the resulting violence. In fact, the white South African government of F. W. de Klerk gradually allowed the ending of apartheid and the ascendency of the ANC. Nelson Mandela, imprisoned from 1963 to 1990 and called a terrorist until not long before his release, not only by the South African government but also by the US government, was freed and permitted to come to power through an electoral process. Black rights were recognized. Massive violence was averted.

However, if the ANC had engaged in substantial terrorism, an impartial judgment would likely conclude that the violence used by the apartheid government in attempting to suppress it was more unjustified than the violence used by the ANC. Comparisons between the struggle of black South Africans for the recognition of their rights and that of other groups, such as the Palestinians, are often appropriate.

Dealing with Terrorism

Once we recognize that terrorism is a part of history and a fact of political life, we can concentrate on questions of how best to deal with it. If we understand that political violence, used by both governments and their foreign and domestic opponents, is likely to continue to be used, we can focus on how best to limit and reduce it. We can recommend the morally most justifiable ways to reduce, contain, and prevent the wrongs involved in and the suffering caused by terrorist and other kinds of violence.

We can discuss the best ways to "respond" to terrorism, recognizing that what is original offense and what is response is often at issue. We can examine how to deflect possible new recruits to terrorist groups from joining them. We can understand how the policies of the administration of US President George W. Bush offered examples of how not to respond to terrorism. The "dangers of massive military response have been made clear again and again in history," Richard English writes (2009, 129). Especially when directed at entire civilian populations, military over-reactions tend to validate and legitimize the claims made by terrorists, and to promote recruitment by the groups targeted. While limited military force may sometimes be appropriate, especially when a terrorist group such as ISIS controls territory, the delusion that military power can defeat terrorism by being overwhelming needs to be overcome.

It has been shown repeatedly that answering terrorist attacks with large-scale war is misguided. As Louise Richardson has written, the failure of the George W. Bush administration to understand terrorism or learn from past experience with it was disastrous. To attempt to militarily overwhelm every terrorist group only generates more recruits for such groups, as has been shown over and over (Richardson 2006). The global "War on Terror" declared by the George W. Bush administration in response to the attacks of September 11, 2001, was not based on an understanding of how best to combat terrorism, but on false assumptions that military strength and an eagerness to use it can deter all challenges. Terrorism is a weapon that undermines the incomparably greater firepower of military forces.

According to Randall Law, it had been the hope of Osama bin Laden, Al Qaeda's leader, that the US would respond to Al Qaeda's attacks on the US embassies in Kenya and Tanzania with full-scale war. Only this, he thought, "would force Muslims around the world... to set aside their myriad differences and come together in a great campaign to expel U.S. forces and their allies completely from the Middle East" (Law 2013, 330). President Bill Clinton launched limited airstrikes in Sudan and Afghanistan, but not war. This aim of Al Qaeda was achieved, however, with the "War on Terror" including its invasions of Afghanistan and then Iraq launched by the administration of President George W. Bush in response to Al Qaeda's attacks on the World Trade Center in New York City and the Pentagon in Washington on September 11, 2001. It produced vast numbers of new recruits for Islamic extremism. A decade and a half later, as Al Qaeda appeared to be splintering, the Islamic State (or ISIS or ISIL depending on the designation), with its extreme and attention-getting brutality and clever use of social media, appeared to be growing successfully, though its long-term prospects are probably not unlike those of innumerable other terrorist groups.

The US's invasion of Afghanistan could at least be defended as permitted by international law because the Afghan government of the time harbored Al Qaeda, the group responsible for the 9/11 attacks. The US's invasion of Iraq was a clear violation of international law, and ineffective in reducing the chaos, violence, and further terrorism of the region (Held 2011). As Richardson argued, a war on terror or terrorism should not have been undertaken, since war involving large-scale military force cannot win against terrorism. What should be pursued instead is "the more modest and attainable goal of containing terrorist recruitment and constraining the resort to the tactic of terrorism" (Richardson 2006, xix).

Examining the Muslim terrorism used in Malabar, Aceh, and the Philippines against foreign colonial occupation in the eighteenth to twentieth centuries, Mia Bloom observed that by mid-twentieth century, Muslims "had abandoned suicidal terror. In all three areas, terrorism's end was due to the shift in the political environment in which the Muslims found themselves—one which now offered Muslims an alternative means to realizing their goals and not because of increasing coercion on the part of the colonial power" (Bloom 2007, 12).

Bloom concluded that the example of how Muslims in Asia abandoned suicide terrorism "provides an opportunity to learn from the lessons of the past. It is particularly noteworthy that the British, French, and Spanish authorities were incapable of stopping suicide terror by using more sophisticated policing tactics or punitive military actions" (12). The British and Dutch solved their terrorist problems, instead, by allowing nationalist political movements to develop that gave promise of altered political systems and of the withdrawal of colonial occupation.

Terrorists commit crimes for the sake of political objectives. They can be dealt with by the systems of criminal justice in place in existing states in ways that do not enhance the appeal of terrorists and the groups for which they engage in violence. Terrorist groups can come to understand that there are more successful ways to pursue their political goals, ways that do not alienate potential allies. Where their aims are legitimate, such groups can be enabled to pursue them in politically legitimate ways. Terrorist groups can learn that using violence is not as effective in achieving their objectives as alternative means, but those means must be made available. Groups seeking self-determination or independence or other political objectives, and the governments and other groups opposing them, should all commit themselves to bringing about or resisting change through peaceful means of organizing, protesting, demonstrating, arguing, voting in referenda, and the like, rather than through violence.

Social movements are essential components of political systems; arguably, needed reforms would not occur without them. The responsibility for allowing them to progress non-violently toward justifiable goals is not only with movement members, but even more clearly, because of their greater power, with governments.

As many who study terrorism have noted, one of the most important factors in countering it is good intelligence, and understanding ahead of time where and when threats may arise. As Richard English notes about another of the various lessons we should learn from the history of responding to terrorism, "intelligence is the most vital element in successful counter-terrorism" (2009, 131). Denouncing entire cultures or religions or groups of people, as for instance some have done in recent years concerning Muslims in general, is highly counterproductive. Yet such denunciations continue to be popular even with some at or aspiring to high levels of government.

Terrorist groups cannot survive without a steady flow of new recruits. As Bruce Hoffman reported, "the life expectancy of at least 90 per cent of terrorist organizations is less than a year" (Hoffman 1998, 170). Some groups, such as ISIS, have been clever and successful at using social media to attract new recruits from around the world. A promising way to combat it and other terrorist groups is to engage successfully in argument and persuasion to deter such recruits. Although limited military force may be necessary to prevent or end their control of territory, longer-term success in combatting such groups depends on engagement, education, argument, discussion, and persuasion.

People cannot successfully be bombed into changing their religious and ideological and even political beliefs, however misconceived. Those opposing the misguided ideologies of many groups using terrorism usually have very developed capacities to engage in education, counseling, argument, and persuasion. These have perhaps not been employed at all adequately in combatting terrorism, but they can be developed. They are not only to be far more highly recommended on moral grounds, they are likely to be more successful in the longer term.

References

Bloom, Mia (2007) *Dying to Kill: The Allure of Suicide Terror*. New York: Columbia University Press.

Callimachi, Rukmini (2015) "Enslaving Young Girls, Islamic State Builds Vast System of Rape," *New York Times*, Aug. 14: 1, 12.

Coady, Tony (2004) "Terrorism, Morality, and Supreme Emergency," *Ethics*, 114, 772–89.

Coser, Lewis A. (1966) "Some Social Functions of Violence," *Annals of the American Academy of Political and Social Science*, 364 (Mar.): 8–18.

Crenshaw, Martha (1983) "Introduction," in Martha Crenshaw (ed.), *Terrorism, Legitimacy, and Power*. Middletown, CT: Wesleyan University Press.

English, Richard (2009) *Terrorism: How to Respond*. Oxford: Oxford University Press.

English, Richard (2016) *Does Terrorism Work? A History*. Oxford: Oxford University Press.

Euben, Roxanne L. (2015) "Humiliation and the Political Mobilization of Masculinity," *Political Theory*, 43 (Aug.): 500–32.

Falk, Richard A. (1988) *Revolutionaries and Functionaries: The Dual Face of Terrorism*. New York: Dutton.

Fellman, Michael (2010) *In the Name of God and Country: Reconsidering Terrorism in American History*. New Haven: Yale University Press.

Gehring, Verna V., ed. (2003) *War After September 11*. Lanham, MD: Rowman & Littlefield.

Goodin, Robert E. (2006) *What's Wrong with Terrorism?* Malden, MA: Polity.
Held, Virginia (2006) *The Ethics of Care: Personal, Political, and Global.* New York: Oxford University Press.
Held, Virginia (2008) *How Terrorism is Wrong: Morality and Political Violence.* New York: Oxford University Press.
Held, Virginia (2011) "Morality, Care, and International Law," *Ethics and Global Politics*, 4(3): 173–94.
Held, Virginia (2015) "Gender, Care and Global Values," in Darrel Moellendorf and Heather Widdows (eds), *The Routledge Handbook of Global Ethics.* New York: Routledge, 49–60.
Hoffman, Bruce (1998) *Inside Terrorism.* New York: Columbia University Press.
Honderich, Ted (2002) *After the Terror.* Edinburgh: Edinburgh University Press.
Hubbard, Ben (2015) "Shielding Syria's Antiquities, to his Grisly Death," *New York Times*, Aug. 20: 1, 5.
Johns, Sheridan, and R. Hunt Davis, Jr., eds (1991) *Mandela, Tambo, and the African National Congress: The Struggle Against Apartheid 1948–1990. A Documentary Survey.* New York: Oxford University Press.
Lango, John W. (2014) *The Ethics of Armed Conflict: A Cosmopolitan Just War Theory.* Edinburgh: Edinburgh University Press.
Laqueur, Walter (2003) *No End to War: Terrorism in the Twenty-First Century.* New York: Continuum.
Law, Randall D. (2013) *Terrorism: A History.* Malden, MA: Polity Press.
Miller, Martin A. (2013) *The Foundations of Modern Terrorism: State, Society and the Dynamics of Political Violence.* New York: Cambridge University Press.
Nathanson, Stephen (2006) "Terrorism, Supreme Emergency, and Noncombatant Immunity," *Iyyun: The Jerusalem Philosophical Quarterly*, 55 (Jan.): 3–25.
Pape, Robert A. (2005) *Dying to Win: The Strategic Logic of Suicide Terrorism.* New York: Random House.
Primoratz, Igor, ed. (2004) *Terrorism: The Philosophical Issues.* London: Palgrave Macmillan.
Richardson, Louise (2006) *What Terrorists Want: Understanding the Enemy, Containing the Threat.* New York: Random House.
Ruddick, Sara (1989) *Maternal Thinking: Toward a Politics of Peace.* Boston: Beacon Press.
Scheffler, Samuel (2006) "Is Terrorism Morally Distinctive?," *Journal of Political Philosophy*, 14(1): 1–17.
Shane, Scott (2015) "Non-Jihadists Tied to Deadlier Toll in U.S. since 9/11," *New York Times*, June 25: 1, 15.
Tilly, Charles (1969) "Collective Violence in European Perspective," in Hugh David Graham and Ted Robert Gurr (eds), *Violence in America: Historical and Comparative Perspectives.* New York: Bantam, 4–45.
Waldron, Jeremy (2004) "Terrorism and the Uses of Terror," *Journal of Ethics*, 8: 5–35.
Walzer, Michael (2000) *Just and Unjust Wars*, 3rd edn. New York: Basic Books.
Wellmer, Albrecht (1984) "Terrorism and the Critique of Society," in Jurgen Habermas (ed.), *Observations on "The Spiritual Situation of the Age": Contemporary German Perspectives*, tr. A. Buchwalter. Cambridge, MA: MIT Press, 283–307.

PART II

THE HISTORY OF TERRORIST VIOLENCE

CHAPTER 6

THE PRE-HISTORY OF TERRORISM

WARREN C. BROWN

INTRODUCTION

LITTLE or nothing has been written on terrorism before the eighteenth century. What discussions there are usually go back to the Jewish "daggermen" or *sicarii* of the first century CE, who stabbed people to death in public, often at the cost of their own lives, to cow their fellow Jews into supporting their violent resistance to the Romans. They then jump to the so-called Assassins in the Middle East in the eleventh through the thirteenth centuries. These assassinated political and religious leaders in the Islamic world who did not agree with their particular brand of Shi'ite Islam. (See e.g. Chaliand and Blin 2007, chs 3 and 4; Richardson 2007, 23–7; Townshend 2011, 100. On the *sicarii* and Assassins see among others Brighton 2009; Lewis 2003.)

These groups wielded terror on ground that for many has come to personify terrorism: the Middle East. Terrorism as a concept and as a heuristic tool, however, is distinctly Western and in particular European. The term itself was coined during the French Revolution (*terrorisme*) to describe the so-called Reign of Terror imposed by the revolutionary government in 1793–4.[1] In this context—an effort by radical members of the French revolutionary movement to impose their views of right order on French society and to stifle dissent—it was used to describe terror wielded from the top down. Its first use in the sense that became dominant over the course of the nineteenth, twentieth, and twenty-first centuries, as a label for terror wielded from the bottom up by a small group to destabilize an existing order, came in the context of the Russian revolutionary movements of the mid- and later nineteenth century (Pomper 1995, 77). The term "terrorism," its uses, and its evolution must therefore reflect how Europeans and their Western cultural descendants understand the world, and in particular how Westerners understand order and disorder.

But Westerners have not always understood and processed the world the way they do now. Acts of violence that provoked extreme fear certainly took place in the pre-modern West; actors quite often deliberately provoked terror in order to achieve identifiable aims. But violence and terror were combined differently, understood differently, and judged according to different norms in different times and places. As we explore the pre-history of terrorism, therefore, we are not going to look simply for terrorism in the past. Instead, we will explore how people in the pre-modern heartland of the West, Europe, understood and used terror. The point is both to understand the background against which the modern idea of terrorism developed, and to explore how European societies evolved to the point that the term as it has come to be used begins to make sense. This effort will highlight the degree to which the concept "terrorism" depends on modern Western ways of viewing the world, and demonstrate possible different ways of understanding terror and its use.

Given the limitations of a handbook essay, I will be focusing on the Middle Ages, that is, the centuries from the dissolution of the Roman Empire in the West in the fifth and sixth centuries to the Protestant Reformation at the beginning of the sixteenth. These thousand years or so were the ones in which a characteristic European civilization developed. (The best introduction to this period is Rosenwein 2009. A more comprehensive and in-depth resource is *The New Cambridge Medieval History* (*NCMH*) 1995–2005.) They saw a great deal of dynamic and creative change, in which different uses and understandings of violence rose and fell, or competed with each other, in contexts shaped by often profound political, social, and economic transformations (see Brown 2011). They saw what from the modern perspective might seem like stateless societies, as well as the development of political structures that over time began to resemble the modern state. They saw changes over time in the meaning of law and its relationship to other social norms, and the development of a broad variety of legal and judicial institutions that interacted with extra-legal practices in complex ways. They saw profound changes in the available media through which political combatants could wield violence both physical and rhetorical, and influence the behavior of other political actors. In short, they present us with the material to study a uniquely broad range of attitudes toward and uses of violence and terror.

Terrorism can be understood at a basic level as the public use of violence to inspire terror, in order to influence the actions of third parties. The profusion of more narrow definitions that have emerged in the twentieth and twenty-first centuries reflect a need to create legal and moral categories that delegitimize particular uses of terror in order to justify action against them. These definitions of terrorism are fluid and unstable. They depend on who is formulating them, what their interests are, and whom they are talking about. Nevertheless, most circle around a few core ideas. (On definitions see among others Townshend 2011, 1–7; Richardson 2007, 3–23; Hoffman 2006, 1–39; Ben Saul, Ch. 2 in this volume.) They focus on such things as violence from the bottom of society directed upwards, by the weak against the strong, in order to influence or change an established political order. They focus on non-state actors attacking states. They focus in particular on violence directed at civilians or non-combatants.

They characterize terrorist actions as violations of peace; some cast them as "criminal." And some conceptually distinguish secular terrorism from that carried out for religious reasons and with religious goals.

These ideas, however, depend on analytical categories, ideas of order, and norms of behavior that for much of the Middle Ages do not apply. The state, for example: when we say that acts of terrorism are aimed at states by non-state actors, we have an idea in our heads of what a state is: a political entity, governing a fixed geographical area, that regulates the behavior of citizens, and judges and punishes criminal offenses, which it defines as actions against itself as the embodiment of the public weal. Most important, it claims a monopoly on the use of force. Although it is embedded in and tied to the economic, social, cultural, and religious organization of society, it is conceptually distinct.[2]

The Romans transmitted to medieval Europe ideas of public order and accountable office that remained present throughout the period in discourses about power and legitimate government, and to which political actors could appeal to legitimate their actions or criticize those of others. In practice, however, it is hard to find medieval states that fit this picture. To begin with, it is hard to strictly isolate "political" itself as an analytical category. For most of the period, political order was indistinguishable from social and economic order. Order was based on personal and economic relationships as much or more than it was on relationships between governing and governed. The ruling class, that is, the aristocracy, was structured by ties of kinship, friendship, fealty, and prayer; aristocrats exercised and experienced power through the norms associated with these ties. Those lower down in the hierarchy of power, that is, peasants and town or city dwellers, were bound to their lords by ties of personal and economic dependence whose gradations are often frustratingly difficult to pin down. (On this and what follows see the relevant sections of Rosenwein 2009; *NCMH* 1995–2005.)

Moreover, one cannot disassociate political order from religious order. Both theorists of power and wielders of power in the Middle Ages understood right order to be that which harmonized with the will of the Christian God. God's order was not only intimately intertwined with order in general; in a very real sense it *was* order.

Similarly, attitudes towards violence and who was entitled to use it were very different from those that prevail in the modern West. The right of the individual to use violence on his (and sometimes her) own behalf, for example to take vengeance for a wrong or an insult, or to protect his or her property and interests, was taken for granted and even legally protected. The idea of a government monopoly on the use of violent force, though approached in the early Middle Ages by strong rulers such as Charlemagne, did not take root until the later Middle Ages, and even then continued to be contested (Brown 2011, *passim*).

The term criminal is likewise problematic. In the early Middle Ages, the Latin word *crimen* meant simply an undifferentiated wrong. Wrongs were made right either by vengeance or by compensation. Though the language and ideology of a general public order survived and was occasionally deployed, in practice wrongs done to a king, either to his person, his prerogatives, or the protection he had extended to particular people or places, were treated as such: as wrongs done to the king. The king, as God's representative, was also responsible for righting wrongs done to God, his agents and followers, and his interests. Though the term is often used uncritically by medievalists, the idea of "crime" in the modern sense, as opposed to civil wrong or tort, emerged only gradually from the twelfth century onwards, and at different rates in different parts of Europe, as kings and other rulers became sufficiently powerful to successfully assert an ideology of public order, ordained by God, that the ruler was duty bound to uphold and which was injured by particular kinds of wrong (Brown 2011; Hyams 2003).

For most of the Middle Ages, Europeans did not think in terms of a strict separation between civilian and military; even their distinction between combatant and non-combatant was fluid. Among the aristocracy most males fought; by definition wielding violence was what aristocrats did. Lords were backed up by their armed followers, who were tied to them by reciprocal ties of loyalty and obligation. Only in the later Middle Ages does one begin to find what we might call civilian aristocrats, that is, those who did not fight, as opposed to military aristocrats who did. In the early Middle Ages, when larger armies were required, levies were drawn from the free landholding population. Again it was only in the later Middle Ages that the first shadows of professional armies appear, and even then it was some time before we find armies that could be called standing (Keen 1984; Allmand 1999).

Within the aristocracy, violence against women and children did draw condemnation by the community and sharp retaliation by their kin, friends, and lords or vassals. When aristocrats targeted members of the lower orders of society, however, such limits rarely applied. Armies and warbands frequently threatened or killed peasants and townspeople, including women and children; negotiations over the fate of townspeople, or of villagers who had sought refuge in a castle or church, formed an important part of ending sieges. Some clergymen tried to draw moral lines protecting the defenseless, for example, in the so-called "Peace of God" councils of the tenth and eleventh centuries that sought among other things to protect peasants, merchants, and unarmed clerics. As the last category suggests, however, it is often hard to grasp precisely who was defenseless. Members of the clergy, armed either with physical or spiritual weapons—or both—wielded violence, as did peasants and townspeople (who from the eleventh century on were increasingly armed and trained). Camp followers accompanying armies killed and plundered; women in besieged towns were known to pick up weapons and fight. Medieval theorists of just warfare tended to treat attacks on non-combatants as legitimate as long as the war their attackers were prosecuting was a righteous one (Brown 2011, 116–24; Head and Landes 1992; Russel 1975; Cox 2012).

Political and social actors in medieval Europe did use open violence to inspire terror, in order to influence the actions or behavior of third parties. But they did not understand what they were doing as terrorism; they did not single out instrumental terror as a tactic that needed its own label. The differences lie in who used terror, how they used it, why they used it, what their goals were, how its use fit in to their understandings of order, and how they and others understood and legitimated (or not) what they were doing.

THE EARLY MIDDLE AGES (C.500–1000)

Our sources from late antiquity and the early Middle Ages present the use of terror in general as top down; that is, somebody who has power uses terror to impose their power on, or maintain their power over, someone else. In his *Ten Books of Histories*, for example, the late sixth-century bishop Gregory of Tours describes the rather violent career of the first of the Frankish kings in post-Roman Gaul, Clovis. At one point, Gregory tells us that Clovis was challenged by one of his men over possession of an object that had been plundered from a church. After mustering his army on the parade ground, Clovis suddenly and without warning, and in full view of the assembled, killed the man with an axe. The rest of his men were "filled with a mighty dread." By killing the man Clovis took vengeance on a follower who had challenged his authority. By killing him spectacularly in a public setting, he inspired fear that presumably discouraged further challenges (Gregory of Tours 1967–70, i. 110–13).

Perhaps the classic example of terror as an instrument of power from this period comes in the late eighth century, in the context of the long and bitter effort by the Frankish king Charlemagne to subjugate the Saxons. According to the *Royal Frankish Annals*, in 782 Charlemagne publicly slaughtered 4,500 Saxons in an effort to cow the rest into submission. The annalist does not condemn or criticize Charlemagne's brutality. The tone of his account makes it clear that he thought the king had done what was necessary in the face of the Saxons' repeated rebellion, perfidy, and faithlessness (Rau 1987, 44–5). Charlemagne's immediate descendants used terror in a similar fashion. According to the *Annals of St Bertin*, in 841 his grandson Lothar brought "large numbers" of Saxons, Austrasians, Thuringians, and Alemans under his control, partly by terror (*terroribus*) and partly by conciliation. In 842 Lothar's younger brother Louis faced down a rebellion in Saxony; he marched throughout the region, says the annalist, and by force and terror (*terrore*) he completely crushed all who still resisted him. Having captured the ringleaders of the rebellion, he had 140 of them beheaded, hanged fourteen, and maimed many more (Rau 1969, 54–5, 58–9).

Terror also formed part of the image of divine power and Christian sainthood. Lives of early medieval saints describe God using terror, sometimes directly and sometimes through the medium of the saints, to persuade non-believers to convert, to compel Christians to behave properly, and to avenge publicly injury and insult to Himself and his followers both divine and human. To give just one example among many: in the seventh century Life of the Irish monk St Columbanus, Columbanus, while travelling in Gaul, went to the city of Tours to pray at the shrine of Tours' patron saint, St Martin. Columbanus left some of his property in a boat on the river Loire. The property was stolen. Columbanus berated the saint for not protecting his property. St Martin went into action; he tormented and tortured the thief. The miracle, says the author, struck such terror into everyone that no one dared further to touch anything belonging to Columbanus (Jonas of Bobbio 1975, 103).

The High Middle Ages (c.1000–1300)

As the Middle Ages unfold, an obvious place to look for instrumental terror is to a classic feature of medieval warfare: pillaging and wasting an enemy's lands. In wars large and small, warriors plundered and burned fields and villages, chased villagers from their homes and sometimes killed them. Churches, monasteries, and merchants suffered as well. This tactic was common throughout the Middle Ages, but it is especially easy to see in the tenth and eleventh centuries, as Charlemagne's empire dissolved and the precursors to England, France, and Germany began to emerge. Violent competition for power and resources among and between both the great and the not so great was endemic. People lost their homes and property and/or their lives; they fled to seek sanctuary whenever they could.

Nevertheless, it is hard to argue that in every case that its perpetrators were using terror instrumentally; in some cases, rather, it seems to have been a byproduct of the violence. Pillaging and wasting are cast not in terms of terror but rather in terms of vengeance, punishment, gathering supplies and plunder, or reducing an enemy's capacity to levy men and supplies. According to the English chronicler Orderic Vitalis (1075—*c.*1142), for example, the Norman duke William the Conqueror, after his conquest of the English crown in 1066, responded to a rebellion in the north of England in 1069–70 by ravaging the county of Yorkshire and other regions. He ordered his men to destroy herds, crops, villages, and everything in their path; he

> cut down many in his vengeance; destroyed the lairs of others; harried the land, and burned homes to ashes… In his anger he commanded that all crops and herds, chattels and food of every kind should be brought together and burned to ashes with consuming fire, so that the whole region north of Humber might be stripped of all means of sustenance… (Orderic Vitalis 4.230–33)

In some cases, however, warriors do seem to have intended to use terror as an instrument. Laying waste to an opponent's property and spreading terror among his people could serve to provoke him into responding to an attack or pressure him into a settlement, because doing so not only hurt him economically but also dishonored him. It demonstrated his inability to carry out one of the fundamental tasks of lordship: controlling his holdings and protecting the people who lived on them. It also displayed publicly one's willingness to engage in violence and threatened a more direct use of force. Wasting and pillaging an opponent's lands and terrorizing his people, therefore, amounted to a non-verbal but nevertheless important tool of communication and negotiation among parties in conflict. A written complaint by the castellan Hugh IV of Lusignan against Duke William V of Aquitaine, for example, composed in the early eleventh century, describes a violent back and forth for land and castles, to which the protagonists laid claim by right of vassalage, kinship, or marriage. The conflict was carried out in part by laying waste to land around castles. At the end, Hugh received a promise from William to give him what he thought he was due (Rosenwein 2006). At roughly the same time, Bishop Thietmar of the Saxon diocese of Merseburg describes a dispute between the German King Henry II and Margrave Henry of Schweinfurt, in which both sides plundered and devastated the lands of their opponents and their allies on their way to a settlement (Thietmar of Merseburg 2001, 214–15, 226–31, 237–8, 246–9).

These images of terror emerge from violence carried out between members of the aristocracy. The picture is very different when one looks at violence aimed by aristocrats at members of the lower orders. In fragmented France around the turn of the first millennium, local lords—or mounted thugs trying to be lords—used terror to cow peasants into accepting their control and to extort from them labor and supplies (see e.g. Bisson 2008, 22–83; Bisson 1998; Brown 2011, ch. 4). But peasants were not always passive victims; they could wield terror themselves, or at least be used by their betters as instruments of terror. The *Miracles of St Benedict*, written in the mid-eleventh century, describes the activities of the so-called "Peace League of Bourges" in 1038. The archbishop of Bourges imposed a peace oath on all men above the age of fifteen throughout his diocese. To enforce the oath, the archbishop created a military force composed of clerics, some members of the local nobility, but mostly peasants. The army attacked violators of the peace and destroyed their castles; "with the help of God they so terrified the rebels [i.e. the violators of the peace] that, as the coming of the faithful was proclaimed far and wide by rumor among the populace, the rebels scattered. Leaving the gates of their towns open, they sought safety in flight, harried by divinely inspired terror." The archbishop was thus able to dominate the surrounding region until one magnate finally fought back and destroyed the archbishop's army (*Miracula* 5.1–4, 192–8, excerpted and tr. in Head and Landes 1992, 339–42).

At least one divine figure used terror as a tool in what can only be called extortion, extortion that was justified, however, because (according to the author concerned) it served a divinely mandated goal. The early eleventh-century *Miracles of St Foy* tells us in a series of vignettes about miracles performed by St Foy, or St Faith, a young girl martyred by the Romans in the late third century whose relics were kept at her monastery at Conques in south central France. According to one of these stories, the monks of Conques decided that the high altar of the saint's church needed a new frontal. To make it, they needed gold. St Foy apparently agreed. According to the story's author, "this is the reason that few people are left in this whole region who have a precious ring or brooch or armbands or hairpins, or anything of this kind, because Sainte Foy, either with a simple entreaty or with bold threats, wrested away these same things for the work of the frontal." One woman from the area, knowing that the saint was requisitioning gold, decided to hide a gold ring. St Foy promptly visited the woman with a painful fever for several nights in succession until she gave it up (*Book of Sainte Foy* 1995, 82–8).

God of course worked not only through his divine representatives the saints but also through his church. Leaders of the Roman Catholic Church used, among other things, terror both spiritual and—through armed allies—physical to further what they understood to be God's aims. Here too it is not always possible to tell whether the terror was instrumental or simply a byproduct. The main spiritual tool in the clergy's arsenal was excommunication, and on a larger-scale interdict. The former prevented an individual from participating in church services and excluded him or her from the Christian community. The latter limited church services on a regional or even kingdom-wide scale. (Strayer 1985, iv, s.v. "Excommunication," 536–8 and vi, s.v. "Interdict," 493–7.) Both rested ultimately on its targets' fear of isolation and spiritual damnation. They could be used to compel an opponent of the church to negotiate or even surrender by robbing his actions of legitimacy, weakening his political support, and legitimizing rebellion or invasion. Pope Gregory VII (r. 1073–85), for example, locked in a struggle with the German Emperor Henry IV (r. 1056–1106) over control of appointments to church office, deliberately destabilized the Empire by excommunicating Henry and by freeing the German aristocracy from their oaths of allegiance. This gave cover to a rebellion in Germany and forced Henry to reconcile himself to the pope (Rosenwein 2009, 179–81; Lynch 2014, 156–70; Blumenthal 1988). At the beginning of the thirteenth century, Pope Innocent III, in a dispute with King John of England over who would be archbishop of Canterbury, placed England under an interdict. Threatened both with a loss of support at home and a French invasion under the papal banner, John surrendered and handed his kingdom over to Innocent as a fief of the papacy (Turner 1994, ch. 6, 147–74).

Papal sanction also legitimized terror as an instrument of war, inter alia in the fight against heresy. The tactic is quite visible in the Albigensian Crusade of the early thirteenth century, called by Pope Innocent III to destroy the so-called Albigensian or Cathar heretics of southern France. The crusade's military leader, Guy of Montfort, used terror to force towns in Cathar areas to surrender and hand over their heretics. In July 1209, the citizens of Béziers on the Mediterranean coast were offered peace if they would surrender the heretics in their ranks, but they refused. The crusaders captured the city and massacred the inhabitants. The leaders of the army declared that in every city that resisted them their populations would suffer the same fate. The nearby city of Narbonne promptly surrendered and offered to give up all of its known heretics; other towns and villages were abandoned as their inhabitants fled (Sumption 1999, 94). Not surprisingly, Cathars resorted to terror themselves. They occasionally assaulted or assassinated inquisitors sent out to identify and prosecute heretics. More often, they used violence to deter people from within their own ranks from defecting or betraying them (Given 1997, 117, 185).

The Later Middle Ages

It is from the twelfth, but increasingly in the thirteenth and fourteenth centuries that we can see the very first glimmerings of what we might call centralized states, that is, strong monarchies with bureaucracies and paid officials that laid claim to authority over defined areas, official accountability, and a monopoly on use of violent force. The first signs of this sort of monarchy are visible starting in the twelfth century, and their development gained steam, at different rates in different parts of Europe, in the two centuries that followed (Watts 2009; Brown 2011, parts III and IV, 165–287; Bisson 2008). The rulers of these nascent territorial states used terror to advance their interests and ward off threats, both external and internal. Paradigmatic are some of the steps taken by the French King Philip IV "the Fair" (r. 1285–1314). During a dispute with Pope Boniface VIII (r. 1294–1303) over the king's right to tax the French clergy, Philip sent a small force into Italy to attack Boniface at his residence in the central Italian town of Agnani. Boniface was captured and personally assaulted before being freed by the townspeople. The pope died, purportedly of shock, a month later (Lynch 2014, 318–20).

Philip IV also used terror in his efforts to suppress what one might call a transnational organization, the international and self-governing crusading order known as the Knights Templar. Philip was deeply in debt to the Templars; there are good reasons to suppose that his attack against them was motivated by a desire to get out from under the debt and to seize their vast assets. He presented the attack publicly, however, as his response, motivated by his duty as God's representative, to charges that the Templars were living flagrantly immoral lives. He publicized accusations against them of sexual deviance, blasphemy, and heresy in an effort to gain public support for his actions. He had members of the order arrested and tortured into confessing; he bullied Pope Clement V into ordering all of the Templars arrested. Using coerced confessions, he had dozens of Templars publicly burned at the stake in an effort to discourage those inclined to resist him. The king's tactics were successful; all resistance among the Templars themselves collapsed, and the pope disbanded the order (Barber 1994, 295–313).

When royal power broke down, the floodgates opened wide to terror wielded by what we might begin to call non-state actors. During the Hundred Years War between the English and the French of the fourteenth and fifteenth centuries (a war marked by frequent terror raids into France by English armies intended not only to gain plunder but also to force French kings to come out and fight), both sides relied heavily on mercenaries. During the truce that followed the devastating defeat of a French army at Poitiers in 1356, bands of now unemployed mercenaries from both sides came together and applied their trade to making a living until they could find legitimate employment again. These so-called "Free Companies," operating without royal sanction, terrorized the lands they were occupying to impose their power on the locals and ensure a steady flow of supplies and money. (On the Hundred Years War in general see Sumption 1990–2009; on the Companies see ii. 351–404; see also Fowler 2001.) In the Île de France in 1358, for example, one Martin Henriquez threatened villages with plunder, fire, and death if they did not make ransom agreements with his officers. The inhabitants of two villages tried to resist; after they had their barns emptied and their vines uprooted they submitted (Sumption 1990–2009, ii. 368). Members of the Free Companies were very aware of their "non-state" and therefore illegitimate status; whenever the opportunity presented itself, they were quick to sign on to the service of whatever king needed them.

The pressures and wrenching social changes brought on in the fourteenth century by decades of war, as well as by the devastating plague known as the Black Death, provoked what we would call popular revolts. These took place all over Europe, though not all at the same time. In the course of these revolts, members of the lower orders of society terrorized people from all walks of life, but especially the aristocracy. In some cases, we can see evidence of an ideology behind the terror, or at least a set of coherent aims. Prominent among them was the so-called Jacquerie that broke out in France in 1358. The Jacquerie (from the generic medieval French name for rustics: Jacques) was an uprising against the French nobility not only by the peasantry of northern France but also by city dwellers and some of the lower aristocracy of the region. It was touched off by the collapse of royal authority in the wake of the Battle of Poitiers (Sumption 1990–2009, ii. 327–36). The nobility had proven utterly incapable of protecting their subjects from the depredations and military power of the English. Free Companies were ravaging the towns and countryside; to their victims, the leaders of the Companies were essentially indistinguishable from the nobility (and were in fact often members of the nobility). In 1358 inhabitants of the region around Beauvais rebelled. Disorganized bands attacked noble manors and castles, committing what contemporary accounts portray (apparently accurately) as horrifying atrocities. They lynched the inhabitants, gang-raped women and girls, killed them in front of their husbands and fathers (or vice versa), and plundered and burned buildings.

The contemporary chronicler Jean Froissart surrounds his account of the Jacquerie with a thick fog of terror (Froissart 1978, 151–5). His perspective reflects that of his aristocratic patrons and subjects; he tells us that the Jacks deliberately created a reign of terror in the service of wiping out the aristocracy. Despite Froissart's evident biases, it appears that the Jacks did indeed want to at least overturn the established aristocratic order, if not completely wipe out the nobility. The atrocities that are reported by Froissart and others were clearly aimed at the nobility. The Jacks not only attacked the social and political hierarchy but also things that represented financial exactions, i.e. mills, property records, etc.[3] So it would appear that the terror inspired by the Jacks as a whole was in fact aimed at effecting change in the dominant order.

Once they organized themselves to crush the Jacquerie, the French aristocracy (aided by some English knights) used terror to put the Jacks back in their place. They engaged in their own excesses as they took horrible vengeance, slaughtering peasants and villagers and destroying their villages and property (Froissart 1978, 335–6).

In England, the so-called "Peasants' Revolt" broke out in 1381. Rebellions convulsed wide swaths of England. Groups of rebels killed royal officials and all who opposed them; they displayed their victims' heads on bridges and town walls for all to see. Much of the violence and terror was driven by peasants and townsmen seizing the opportunity to settle scores with their lords and improve the terms of their dependence, or simply to plunder and steal under the cover of rebellion. However, the leaders of rebellion talked about getting rid of the power of the nobility and establishing a regime based on a direct relationship between the commons and the king. They talked about abolishing serfdom, and freeing towns from oppression by their traditional lords.

Conclusion

Instrumental terror plainly formed an important part of the repertoire of power in medieval Europe. Those with power, or those who aspired to power, terrorized in order to frighten people into doing what they wanted or to discourage resistance. Others used terror as a tool of vengeance or punishment for injury or insult, to impose what were in essence protection or extortion rackets, or to intimidate or silence whistleblowers. Still others terrorized to undermine the foundations of an order, or to resist an order that was being imposed on them. However: the sources do not single out the use of terror as in any way *sui generis*. Terror appears simply as one of a number of tactics that a variety of actors could use in pursuit of their aims; it is not something that our accounts use per se to mark someone as bad or delegitimize their behavior. They simply talk about what happened, and about the goals; they blacken or praise their subjects in other terms.

Like so much else in medieval Europe, terror was theater designed to communicate. Demonstrative and public acts of violence served to send messages to individuals or communities up or down the ladder of power, or to equals with whom one was in conflict. Those who employed terror did not of course have modern means of communication or access to modern forms of mass media. Terror must, therefore, have spread beyond the realm of direct experience by word of mouth, or through travelers such as monks, merchants, pilgrims—or refugees.

Word of medieval terror reaches us through our written sources. At the time they were written, our texts, whether they were chronicles, histories, saints' lives, or documentary records, broadcast terror to those who could read or hear them. They preserved memories of terror that could continue to haunt the future and serve as warnings (i.e. to avoid resisting the king, to watch out for rebellious peasants or for unemployed mercenaries, to fear the wrath of God or his saints, etc.). They also, however, often deployed images of terror that reflected the interests or served the purposes of their authors. From this perspective, images of terror could spread fear and horror but also evoke sympathy, as when Jean Froissart regaled his aristocratic audience with tales of the terror of the Jacquerie.

The legitimacy of terror, therefore, was very much in the eye of the beholder. Accordingly, instrumental terror was often viewed, and reported, as something positive. Many of our sources do criticize it, and tell us that its victims suffered. Others, however, portray it as legitimate or necessary, or even glorious. Sources on Charlemagne valorize the terror wielded by the king to subdue his opponents. The author of the *Miracles of St Foy* casts in the glow of the miraculous the saint's use of fear to collect gold from the people living around her monastery. Churchmen regarded terror as a legitimate weapon to wield in defense of God's order as they understood it. Over all was God himself, who wielded terror either directly or through his saints, to deter immoral behavior, to spur reform, or to avenge or protect the honor and interests of God and his followers.

All such actions could be described as "terrorism" in its broadest possible sense. It is when we get into the later Middle Ages that we start to see some of the conceptual pieces that resonate with modern, more narrow definitions of terrorism. Most of what I have discussed is terror from the top down; it evokes more the terror of the French Revolution. However, it is not hard to see the terror spread by the participants in the Jacquerie or Peasants' Revolt as bottom-up terror wielded by relatively weak actors and aimed at destabilizing or overturning a dominant social and political order. The efforts by some members of the Free Companies to gain royal sanction suggests that they were aware of a quasi "state/non-state" distinction that had consequences for an action's legitimacy. I would argue that this is because both actual social and political orders and ideas about right order were changing, in ways that fit our own ideas of civilized order better and therefore make it easier to cast certain kinds of instrumental terror as "terrorism."

However, I would submit that any effort to wrestle what I have discussed here into fitting a modern category of analysis, whether plausible or not, is to miss the point. From the perspective of a historian, I would argue that "terrorism" as it is most commonly defined cannot exist without these modern assumptions about order and disorder that observers bring to the table as they try to comprehend and react to what they see. As we explore the pre-history of terrorism, therefore, we are looking as much or more at the history of worldviews, of ideas about order and power, and of the connections between fear and violence, than at an objective phenomenon that exists outside of the ways that we make sense of the world. The example of this pre-history makes it easier to see that what we understand as terrorism might be understood very differently by actors with a different idea of how the world does and ought to work.

Notes

1. *Oxford English Dictionary*, s.v. "terrorism"; Townshend 2011, 37.
2. See e.g. the *Oxford English Dictionary*, s.v. "state", III, 26a; Fukuyama 2011; Cudworth 2007. The idea that the state is fundamentally characterized by a monopoly on the use of physical force originated with Max Weber, *Politik als Beruf* (*Politics as a Vocation*), 1st publ. in 1919.
3. *Lexikon des Mittelalters*, v. Munich, 1990, s.v. "Jacquerie", cols 265–6.

References

Allmand, Christopher (1999) "War and the Non-Combatant in the Middle Ages," in Maurice Keen (ed.), *Medieval Warfare: A History*. Oxford: Oxford University Press, 253–72.

Barber, Malcom (1994) *The New Knighthood: A History of the Order of the Temple*. Cambridge: Cambridge University Press.

Bisson, Thomas N. (1998) *Tormented Voices: Power, Crisis, and Humanity in Rural Catalonia, 1140–1200*. Cambridge, MA: Harvard University Press.

Bisson, Thomas N. (2008) *The Crisis of the Twelfth Century: Power, Lordship, and the Origins of European Government*. Princeton: Princeton University Press.

Blumenthal, Uta-Renate (1988) *The Investiture Controversy: Church and Monarchy from the Ninth to the Twelfth Century*. Philadelphia: University of Pennsylvania Press.

The Book of Sainte Foy (1995) Tr. Pamela Sheingorn. Philadelphia: University of Pennsylvania Press.

Brighton, Mark A. (2009) *The Sicarii in Josephus's Judean War*. Atlanta, GA: Society of Biblical Literature.

Brown, Warren (2011) *Violence in Medieval Europe*. London and New York: Longman.

Chaliand, Gerard, and Arnaud Blin, eds (2007) *The History of Terrorism: from Antiquity to Al Qaeda*. Berkeley and Los Angeles: University of California Press.

Cox, Rory (2012) "Asymmetric Warfare and Military Conduct in the Middle Ages," *Journal of Medieval History* 38(1): 100–25.

Cudworth, Erika (2007) *The Modern State: Theories and Ideologies* (Edinburgh: Edinburgh University Press.

Fowler, Kenneth (2001) *Medieval Mercenaries*, i. *The Great Companies*. Oxford: Blackwell Publishers.

Froissart, Jean (1978) *Chronicles*, ed. and tr. Geoffrey Brereton. New York: Penguin.

Fukuyama, Francis (2011) *The Origins of Political Order: From Prehuman Times to the French Revolution*. New York: Farrar, Strauss & Giroux.

Given, James B. (1997) *Inquisition and Medieval Society: Power, Discipline, and Resistance in Languedoc*. Ithaca, NY: Cornell University Press.

Gregory of Tours (1967–70) *Zehn Bücher Geschichten*, ed. R. Buchner, 2 vols. Darmstadt: Wissenschaftliche Buchgesellschaft.

Head, Thomas, and Richard Landes (1992) *The Peace of God: Social Violence and Religious Response in France around the Year 1000*. Ithaca, NY: Cornell University Press.

Hoffman, Bruce (2006) *Inside Terrorism*, 2nd edn. New York: Columbia University Press.

Hyams, Paul R. (2003) *Rancor and Reconciliation in Medieval England*. Ithaca, NY: Cornell University Press.

Jonas of Bobbio (1975) "Life of St. Columbanus", tr. W. C. McDermott, in E. Peters (ed.), *Monks, Bishops and Pagans: Christian Culture in Gaul and Italy, 500–700*. Philadelphia: University of Pennsylvania Press.

Keen, Maurice (1984) *Chivalry*. New Haven: Yale University Press.

Lewis, Bernard (2003) *The Assassins: A Radical Sect in Islam*. New York: Basic Books, 1st publ. 1967.

Lynch, Joseph H. (2014) *The Medieval Church: A Brief History*. Abingdon: Routledge.

Miracula Sancti Benedicti (1858) Ed. E. de Certain. Paris: Jules Renouard.

The New Cambridge Medieval History (1995–2005) 7 vols. Cambridge: Cambridge University Press.

Orderic Vitalis (1969) *The Ecclesiastical History of Orderic Vitalis*, ed. Marjorie Chibnall, 6 vols. Oxford: Oxford University Press, ii.

Pomper, Philip (1995) "Russian Revolutionary Terrorism," in Martha Crenshaw (ed.), *Terrorism in Context*. University Park, PA: Pennsylvania State University Press, 63–101.

Rau, Reinhard, ed. (1969) "Jahrbücher von St. Bertin," ed. Reinhard Rau, *Quellen zur karolingischen Reichsgeschichte*, pt. 2. Darmstadt: Wissenschaftliche Buchgesellschaft.

Rau, Reinhard, ed. (1987) "Die Reichsannalen," *Quellen zur karolingischen Reichsgeschichte*, pt. 1. Darmstadt: Wissenschaftliche Buchgesellschaft.

Richardson, Louise (2007) *What Terrorists Want: Understanding the Enemy, Containing the Threat*. New York: Random House.

Rosenwein, Barbara (2006) "Agreements between Count William of the Aquitanians and Hugh of Lusignan (1028)," tr. Thomas Greene and Barbara Rosenwein, in Barbara H. Rosenwein (ed.), *Reading the Middle Ages*. Peterborough: Broadview Press, 213–19.

Rosenwein, Barbara H. (2009) *A Short History of the Middle Ages*, 3rd edn. Toronto: University of Toronto Press.

Russel, Frederick H. (1975) *The Just War in the Middle Ages*. Cambridge: Cambridge University Press.

Strayer, Joseph R. (1985) *Dictionary of the Middle Ages*. New York: Scribner.

Sumption, Jonathan (1990–2009) *The Hundred Years War*, 3 vols. Philadelphia: University of Pennsylvania Press.

Sumption, Jonathan (1999) *The Albigensian Crusade*. London: Faber & Faber.
Thietmar of Merseburg (2001) *Ottonian Germany: The Chronicon of Thietmar of Merseburg*, tr. David A. Warner. Manchester: Manchester University Press.
Townshend, Charles (2011) *Terrorism: A Very Short Introduction*. Oxford: Oxford University Press.
Turner, Ralph V. (1994) *King John*. London and New York: Longman.
Watts, John (2009) *The Making of Polities: Europe, 1300–1500*. Cambridge: Cambridge University Press.

CHAPTER 7

EUROPEAN POLITICAL VIOLENCE DURING THE LONG NINETEENTH CENTURY

MARTIN A. MILLER

SINCE the field of terrorism studies has largely been the province of scholars in political science and international relations, the sense of the term that has been dominant in the literature, certainly since the 9/11 attacks, has been insurgent-oriented. The battleground of clashing civilizations predicted by Samuel Huntington appears to have taken hold as an ever-shifting array of sub-state organizations, faux armies, and individuals attracted to the militant forces of jihadism threaten the security of established governments from Kabul to Washington.

There is, of course, a clear recognition both in government circles and in journalistic accounts that autocrats run many states and that, often, extreme tactics of violence are employed by their security services. Democracies are hardly immune from sending government forces, spies, and private contractors who, on numerous occasions, have made use also of violent tactics in accomplishing their missions. However, these efforts are invariably conducted in concert, whether openly or in secret, and are referred to as approved, defensive "counterterrorist" measures.

As conceptions globalize, definitions harden and critical thought is discouraged if not undermined by the repetition of similar justifications of "necessary" tactics which course through the vast system of electronic information that most citizens rely on and are convinced by. The civil order has come to increasingly resemble a kind of virtual battlefield for the benefit of our remote participation in the phenomenon known as the "war on terror." Security is everywhere for our protection, but levels of fear remain powerfully and persuasively channeled for maximum reception.

There are, in spite of this pervasive atmosphere, examples of new thinking about the use of violence for political goals that recognize, on the one hand, the need for a historical perspective, and, on the other, a call to recognize the role that the state has always played, and continues to, in fomenting conditions that generate dangerous components of terrorism. Colin Wight has pointed out the necessity for the adoption of "an integration of theories of the state and its development into the field [of terrorism studies]" together with "a more historically grounded understanding of terrorism as opposed to the presentism that dominates post 9/11." This is particularly relevant since the state is often responsible for encouraging and funding "freedom fighting non-state actors" (Wight 2009, 100).

Similarly, Erica Chenoweth has recently argued that it is time to turn away from the over-reliance on quantitative studies of terrorist organizations and replace that with an emphasis "on more in-depth historical and ethnographic work." Moreover, she continues, we need to "remove an ironic blind spot in research on the democracy–terrorism link: the state itself" (2013, 374). Since democratic governments present themselves as the defenders of liberty against the forces of violence, it is crucial that we question their "provocative foreign policies" that "may be indicted as well" in creating situations of terrorism (Chenoweth 2013, 375).

Taking matters further, Heinz-Gerhard Haupt and Klaus Weinhauer (2011) have made clear that attention should be directed toward the state in order to capture the core essence of the forces driving periods of high voltage political violence. Beyond reference to the generally accepted Weberian notion of the state's constant efforts to maintain its monopoly of legitimate weaponry and violence, governments often conceal their own involvement in acts of terrorism by creating "moral panics" in which declared opponents and "enemies" are delegitimized in the public mind. Moreover, the statistical evidence shows unambiguously that states are responsible for "many more deaths than the acts of so-called terrorists." Lastly, Haupt and Weinhauer point to the "close relationship between state actions and terrorist violence" by both responding to, and provoking, the harmful actions. In this way, "security forces and terrorist groups become trapped in processes of mutual escalation" in which each side claims it is reacting to its opponents' violence.

My own recent work has joined this conversation and attempted to deepen the analysis of the relationship between the state and its insurgent antagonists by emphasizing the interrelationship and mutual dependency of the two sides in making situations of terrorism possible (see Miller 2013). In this chapter, I shall present the links between the police and the insurgents more directly, with specific examples from selected clashes in modern European history. I will utilize the broad chronological framework that Eric Hobsbawm called "the long nineteenth century," from the outbreak of the French Revolution in 1789 to the advent of the Great War in 1914, as the setting for my discussion.

Prior to the modern era, the contestation between rulers and their subjects proceeded along different trajectories and involved different agents than would be the case later. In a largely decentralized Europe with territorial authorities inheriting power and sovereignty legitimized by the church, threats to kings, princes, and local barons emerged largely from competitive aristocratic cliques and families claiming the right to rule.

There were of course peasant protests periodically across the continent but these were largely economic rather than politically motivated rebellions, and none was ever successful in overthrowing a regime. Royal troops and local gendarmeries were always a part of governance but their missions were largely defined in terms of containing behavior defined as brigandage, vagabondage, smuggling, arson, theft, and harm from physical abuse when conducted in public space. Early forms of security forces were also assigned to resolve conflicts involving hostilities against minorities such as Christian heretics, Jews, and gypsies, as well as those denounced as sorcerers, witches, and Anabaptists (Raeff 1983, 167–8; Emsley 1999, 13–15).

The development of the police as a sophisticated bureaucratic branch of the governance of the state with specifically political responsibilities can be traced back to the reign of Louis XIV in France when he ordered the creation by edict in 1667 of a royal magistrate with the title of Lieutenant of Police (later changed to Lieutenant-General). The Marquis d'Argenson is credited with the formation of an elite secret police force with offices at the royal court, tasked with serving the needs of the king and the realm. He also created an army of spies (*mouchards*) who, together with their superiors, were provided with the power to enter suspicious private dwellings and the authority to arrest, interrogate, and, when apprised as necessary, torture at will. These secret agents were composed of professionals as well as domestics who regularly reported on the words and deeds deemed dangerous to the crown from their positions covering the swath of society from brothels to salons (Radzinowicz 1948, 544–5).

Thus, even before the French Revolution transformed the political situation across the continent, elements of the future clash between the police and the insurgents were set in place. Much has been written about the religious warfare in the pre-modern period that acted as a prelude to the more secular violence that lay ahead. The exclusionary aspects of the emergence of the modern state that produced its most violent moments certainly must include the destruction of the French Huguenot community at the St Bartholomew Day Massacre in 1572 in Paris, and the Gunpowder Plot led by Guy Fawkes to blow up the Houses of Parliament in London in 1605. With these two examples, we have an early modern, religiously based instance of state terror with the former, and of insurgent terror with the latter. Many others could have been selected.

There has also been much attention paid to the origins of the words "terror" and "terrorism," which were not in use in the Westphalian era of European history. We do find the term emerging in the eighteenth century during the Enlightenment. In their criticism of the church's authority as based largely upon superstition, the *philosophes* essentially mobilized their texts for a verbal war on terror.

Baron d'Holbach, one of the leading critics of all religion, conceptualized the term "terror" as the fear and trembling induced by the ecclesiastical hierarchy. By pretending to be able to answer the eternal and unknowable questions of life and death, the church cast its spell over the social order, instilling fear and "reigning by terror." His proposal for struggling against this powerful influence was to maximize the forces of "reason and philosophy." Thanks to these influences, he wrote, "calm returned to my mind; I banished from it the terrors that used to agitate it" (Schechter 2012, 38–9).

The French Revolution and its imperial aftermath altered the entire European state system dramatically, irrevocably, and comprehensively. The precedents set, while too numerous to relate here in detail, include two that contributed to the rise of modern political terrorism. The first was the creation of the continent's first secular democratic republic, which ended the political monopoly of the divine right of kings. The second was the issuing of a document, "The Declaration of the Rights of Man," adopted by the newly elected National Assembly on August 26, 1789, that empowered the state's citizens as sovereign with the right to participate in making the law.

There were few guidelines to deal with the enormous problems that soon engulfed the new regime, from grain shortages and resistance from antagonistic political factions within the territory, to the threat, and eventually the reality, of war from without. While a citizens' army with a newly created system to draft recruits (*levée en masse*) was responsible for dealing with the latter danger, internally an expanded police force was put in place to handle the former. The fears generated by these problems helped extremists to take command of the state after the execution of the king on January 21, 1793, during which time a Reign of Terror was proudly proclaimed.

"The Declaration of the Rights of Man" essentially opened the door to the notion that the nation's political solutions were theoretically now the preserve and responsibility of every citizen. The result was the proliferation of a variety of opponents to the governance of the Republic, some of whom bitterly contested the legitimacy of the elected officialdom. There were certainly realistic threats of assassination and upheaval (the Vendée) from below led by people who were willing to turn to violence to realize their own alternative fantasies of power. There were also numerous instances where the police over-reacted and misinterpreted the danger to the state, and other examples where they actually provoked the regime's opponents into acts of violence in order to silence them.

On the conservative side of the newly emerging ideological spectrum, a fierce royalist resistance to the nascent Republic was led by the Chouans, who were among the pioneers of the modern insurgent movements of the next century. Their efforts to destabilize the National Assembly's legislation were brought to the attention of the Minister of Police, Joseph Fouché, who directed a repressive campaign that has been compared to "the imposition of martial law" (Forssell 1928, 157). His agents monitored their meetings and intercepted their correspondence, which allowed him to order a massive number of arrests. Fouché also kept a large file of reports from his spies that formed a model for forensic catalogs of political criminology. His agents were to file these reports on a daily basis; "even if he knows nothing, he invents," Fouché wrote. Conspiracies can be manufactured, "conjured up," in order to defeat them (Zamoyski 2014, 122). One of the tactics he encouraged among his *mouchards* was for them to teach workers insulting, crude songs about the Bourbons to sing in public so that the police could make arrests (Zamoyski 2014, 125).

Chouan violence continued to appear throughout the years of the Republic and the Napoleonic era despite all his efforts at suppression (see Sutherland 1982). At the same time however, the terror from below on the left was even more diversely distributed. Among the most prominent groups were the Enragés, the Hebertistes, and the secret societies led by Buonarotti and Louis Blanqui, all of whom sought more radical pathways to a future society that would abolish the scourges of poverty and injustice throughout France. Fouché and his gendarmerie were equally forceful in their methods of containing and extinguishing these challenges to the state. A pattern of violent confrontation between the government and its insurgent antagonists was now firmly established in the political culture of the modern nation state, regardless of whether it adhered to monarchist or republican principles.

Following the collapse of the Napoleonic occupation of Europe, the victorious allies from London to St Petersburg set up a continental system of royalist repression at the 1815 Congress of Vienna. The nearest relative of the royal house that ruled in the countries across Europe prior to the Napoleonic occupation was "restored" to power. The major architect of this system, Klemens von Metternich, the foreign minister of the Hapsburg monarchy in Austria, acquired further agreement from Emperor Alexander I of Russia to institute a strict code of curfews, censorship, and surveillance in 1819, known as the Carlsbad Decrees.

Indeed, Metternich had been preceded by the founder of the Austrian police ministry, Count Johann von Pergen in 1793, as a response to the threat to monarchical sovereignty posed by revolutionary France. The German states set up a Central Investigations Commission in 1819 as part of the Restoration era reforms, with its headquarters situated in Mainz. It was tasked with reporting on all suspected acts of unrest and subversion. In one of the few moments of violence from below in this period, the conservative Austrian playwright (and Russian state councilor) August von Kotzebue, was assassinated on March 23, 1819. The Commission used this as a stimulus to engage in a widespread round-up of suspected sympathizers with republican and anti-royalist ideas. An atmosphere of justified pervasive fear was the order of the day as efforts to discourage any political organizations from functioning ensued.

The state's mission was to have the public fear the police while also trusting and relying on them. The police were to protect the state against political dangers and, at the same time, maintain the loyalty of society at large. Thus, an alliance between the state and the police was critical in the minds of the ministers who were ultimately responsible for the functioning of this complex set of forces. Violence was justified by "dire need" or *force majeure*. As an 1851 Zurich police instruction phrased it: "In the face of danger, all is permitted; no price is too high when the state, the fatherland, or the public weal are threatened by destruction or perdition" (Liang 1992, 16).

Perhaps Joseph de Maistre most palpably expressed the vulnerability of the ruling elite and the need for repression when he wrote: "All greatness, all power, all order, depend upon the executioner. He is the tie that binds society together. Take away this incomprehensible force and at the very moment, order is suspended by chaos, thrones fall and states disappear" (Goldstein 1983, 109).

The Italian states contributed their own version of this political police establishment with the formation of the Carabinieri in Piedmont in 1815. Similar versions soon appeared in other provinces. Though its stated purpose was to maintain law and order it was, as Clive Emsley has written, widely regarded in public "first and foremost, as an instrument of repression." Nevertheless, it formed the basis for united Italy's later national police institution, with notions of service and sacrifice for the state as its primary charge (Emsley 1999, 206–7). It would soon have many opportunities for the conduct of surveillance and arrest once intelligence focused on Giuseppe Mazzini's Young Italy societies, which began to attract recruits in the 1830s and 1840s.

It is true that every police institution is to some extent political given that it is required to enforce laws made by political actors who employ the police and provide their tactics and strategy. None perhaps fits this mold better than the Third Section of his Majesty's Chancellory in Russia, where the very raison d'être was a consciously defined political one. The Imperial Russian political police was established in 1825 after a violent confrontation between the government and two dissident secret societies, which was the most serious challenge to any European regime during the Restoration period prior to the 1848 upheavals. Indeed, one of the groups, the Southern Society, was led by Pavel Pestel, an army officer enamored by French radicalism. Pestel's plans included, after seizing power in the confusion following the death of Emperor Alexander I, nothing less than the assassination of the entire Romanov family to end the dynasty and replace it with a version of Robespierre's "republic of virtue."

The succeeding tsar, Nicholas I, accepted the memorandum composed largely by Alexander Beckendorff, who proposed the creation of a centralized, secret national police force directly responsible to the Emperor to ensure that the crown could govern safely. Not surprisingly, Nicholas appointed Beckendorff to head the new agency that effectively had cabinet status. For the next five decades, the Third Section hounded suspected critics and antagonists of the imperial government, vastly expanding the political prisoner population in the process, and inventing the network of labor camps in Siberia that would later be known by Alexander Solzhenitsyn's appellation as the Gulag Archipelago.

Long before there was an actual revolutionary underground movement seeking to actively sabotage the Romanov regime, the Third Section attacked prominent writers and editors of journals and newspapers. Russia's most renowned poet Alexander Pushkin was placed under house arrest for a time and a philosopher, Peter Chaadaev, was confined to a mental asylum because of a newspaper article he wrote that appeared in 1836 comparing Russian culture unfavorably with that of the West. These events and a series of arrests made in the 1830s led to the decision by many Russian intellectuals to leave the country and seek what they believed to be a freer existence as exiles in Western Europe (Miller 1985, ch. 1).

Transnational police cooperation intensified, since the threat to one monarchy was seen as a potential danger to the others. In particular, the Third Section developed close relations with the police in Paris and Geneva to share intelligence and, where possible, extradite exiles back to St Petersburg for punishment. Despite these efforts, Russia witnessed the rise of an insurgent movement in the 1870s that, while peaceful initially, led to the creation of the violence-oriented Party of People's Will. They succeeded in assassinating a number of state officials, simultaneously climaxing and collapsing at the moment of its most spectacular achievement on March 1, 1881, when the group successfully mortally wounded Emperor Alexander II in a bombing on the main thoroughfare in the capital. A massive arrest dragnet in the aftermath destroyed the group's functioning.

The efforts by the statesmen at the Congress of Vienna to recreate the pre-revolutionary, monarchical past were rudely shaken by the outbreak of revolts across the continent in 1848. Kings were chased from their palaces, mobs took control of urban areas, and factions united around a variety of aspirations to seek the creation of sovereign democratic republics. The contesting forces had been present throughout the Restoration period despite the forceful denial by the royal houses in power. A new generation of activist political leaders joined together with working-class organizations to help undermine the authority of the decrepit governing institutions that had denied them access to the political arena.

Within a year of violent confrontations between royalist troops and their police affiliates on the one hand, and the inexperienced defenders of the hastily convened popular assemblies, the tide had inexorably turned in favor of the former. Over the course of the next decades, the victorious rulers put into place a second Restoration, though in most countries, they permitted some form of assembly, whether elected from a narrow base of the elite ranks of society or appointed. France returned to imperial status after the successful seizure of power by Louis Napoleon and Austria dominated Central Europe under Emperor Franz Joseph.

A rising new power, Prussia, however, would soon upend this delicate balance of power as it pressed through three wars—against Denmark, Austria, and finally, France—to gain national unity in 1871. As Germany was celebrating its new status as a European nation state, Paris experienced the most violent moment of terrorism of the entire century. While the French government moved to the safer suburb of Versailles for defense against a potential Prussian invasion, its headquarters and offices in Paris at the Hŏtel de Ville were taken over by a group of militants who initially wanted to continue the battle and not surrender. Within a month, the insurgents were politicized and radicalized by their own leaders as well as by the influence of prominent socialist visitors like Karl Marx and Michael Bakunin. Calling their assembly the Commune of Paris, they soon began issuing decrees and acting increasingly like the legitimate governing body of the country.

The denouement came in June 1871, when Adolf Thiers, who presided over the government after the flight of Emperor Louis-Napoleon, ordered his troops and all available volunteers to end the Commune of Paris with all force necessary. The result was an unparalleled massacre of at least 20,000 civilians within a week (Merriman 2014). From this point on, there could be no doubt about the gradual politicization of both policing procedures and the tactics of European social movements that had become increasingly apparent.

The dominating roles played by Fouché and Metternich in the first half of the nineteenth century in state security politics were filled in the second half by German Chancellor Otto von Bismarck and his chief security official, Wilhelm Stieber. Stieber was committed to using tactics of subterfuge and violence to eliminate radical groups that he saw as immanent threats to his superiors in the court. His first major assignment was to gather intelligence on the leadership of the "International Communist League." This required a first-hand spying mission on the headquarters of the movement's many branches across Europe, which was identified as the home of Karl Marx in London.

Stieber journeyed to England and gained an interview with Marx by posing as a newspaper editor named Schmidt who was reporting on an industrial exhibit in London. While Marx was out of the room, Stieber stole several folios containing private information about the League's affiliates and their plans to sabotage the monarchical regimes in power. Stieber quoted the minutes of one of the meetings of the League where it was proclaimed that "the present rulers can only be overthrown by violent means" which included property owners who should be "liquidated" without any judicial process (Stieber 1979, 37). Ultimately, he put together a huge report in two volumes that was published under the title *The Communist Conspiracies of the Nineteenth Century* to document the insurgent threat (Steiber 1854).

This work brought him to the attention of Bismarck, who appointed him as director of the Berlin Security Division and immediately accepted his plan for a frontal assault on the targeted militants. In addition to setting up a secret spying service under his command in Vienna to counter the dangers posed by Austria, Stieber also authorized his agents to literally "incite revolutionary outbreaks among all nationalities" within the Hapsburg Empire's territory. Hungarians, Slovaks, and Czechs were mobilized by "generously paid agitators" and proclamations were posted all over Prague on Stieber's orders encouraging demonstrations and promising fulfillment of their desires "for national liberation" (Stieber 1979, 105).

All of these subversive tactics were part of Bismarck's planning for the 1866 war with Austria, to be followed by the hostilities with France four years later in the march toward national unification. Following the declaration of the newly created German Empire in 1871, Emperor Wilhelm I and Chancellor Bismarck entrusted Stieber with the formation of a special "security police force" at the national level in Berlin "to protect the ruler and safeguard the nation" In describing their duties, Stieber notes in his memorandum that his trained police regiments "were free to take any acti[on] they believed was required by the situation," even if this meant not fully obeying previous orders from superiors. (Steiber 1979, 148).

The decades leading directly to the ultimatums and declarations that plunged Europe into savage warfare in 1914 were dominated by an uptake in the hostilities between the police and a new generation of emboldened insurgents. The level of combustion was intensified because of a fusion of two separate trends. On the one hand, in Western Europe, bombings and assassinations reached previously unprecedented levels, as anarchism became the primary ideological justification for the violence, and the Great Powers declared mutual war on the movement in an effort to eradicate it completely. On the other, in Russia, the political police opened up a two-front campaign of repression against a revived insurgent threat both at home and in Europe where thousands of exiled Russian revolutionaries continued to work against the autocracy.

With regard to the European situation, the combination of the German militarism that led to national unification, and the violence of the Paris Commune remains paramount in explaining the widespread diffusion of anarchism at this critical historical juncture. The ideologies of the grand theorists of anarchism—Pierre-Joseph Proudhon, Michael Bakunin, and Peter Kropotkin—had been circulating within underground groups for some time, primarily as an antidote for socialists disillusioned by, and competing with, Marxist strategies. The shock of the Paris Commune's destruction provided a reality to what had been for many activists mainly abstract notions of state violence.

The reaction did not take long to develop. In 1878, a Russian populist, Vera Zasulich, shot the governor-general of St Petersburg in a protest against the brutalizing of a political prisoner. Against all odds, she was freed in a sensational court trial that was covered widely in the European press. Later that year, two assassination attempts were made on Emperor Wilhelm I, another on King Alfonso XII of Spain, and one more against King Umberto I of Italy. With the exception of Zasulich, each of these perpetrators justified their acts as efforts to free the repressed masses from the violence of the state in the name of anarchism.

With the increasing availability of dynamite thanks to the underground, illegal distribution of Alfred Nobel's invention, the *attentats* increased exponentially to the point where every European state leader became a target, whether an elected president or selected monarch. Major assassinations included President Sadi Carnot of France in 1894, Prime Minister Antonio Canovas del Castillo of Spain in 1897, Empress Elizabeth of Austria the following year, and King Umberto of Italy in 1900. In addition, in November 1893, an anarchist threw a bomb directly into the aristocratic audience at the Liceu Theater in Barcelona, killing at least thirty people.

In France, a wave of anarchist-inspired insurgent violence erupted in this decade. Ravachol achieved folk hero status among the poorer neighborhoods of Paris for his ability to blow up apartment buildings housing members of the detested judiciary. No less sensational was the bomb placed in the Café Terminus at the crowded Gare de Nord in Paris in 1894 where affluent wives and children were having lunch after seeing their husbands and fathers set off for work by train. The perpetrator, Emile Henry, was soon caught and brought to trial where he made a passionate defense of his act. For him, his victims were complicit with the state in the perpetuation of poverty and corruption that confined the masses to a hopeless existence. Anarchism saw no "innocents" among this privileged world (Merriman 2009).

Simultaneously, the mainstream press engaged in a campaign of fear and panic among the general public while the police increased their surveillance and arrests of suspects, driven often by "intelligence" that was frequently based on unproven rumors of alleged anarchists. While the revelations of the head of the Paris police force at this time, Louis Andrieux, are often cited in this regard, there is much more evidence to demonstrate that the police were fabricating anarchist threats and, in some instances, provoking them as undercover agents (Andrieux 1885).

Thus, both state violence and insurgent terror in Europe reached virtually epidemic proportions in these years, while becoming increasingly intertwined and interdependent with one another in terms of both tactics and strategy. Meanwhile, the efforts by the ruling authorities of Europe to contain "the anarchist peril," now regarded as a common threat, developed even further, into a larger transnational, cooperative endeavor. The police in Spain, Italy, Germany, and France were ordered by their superiors to work undercover in one another's countries, especially in the capitals, during the 1890s. Their tactics were repressive and sometimes as violent as the bombings and assassinations of their adversaries in the underground.

The Russian police, under the direction of Peter Rachkovsky, were permitted to pursue their exiled revolutionary targets, whether anarchist or Marxist, from an office in the center of Paris with the full cooperation of the French authorities. Reports emanating from the fieldwork of spies and double agents were sent not only back to St Petersburg but also were duplicated in copies to the French Prefecture of Police.

Despite many disagreements among the European ministers about how to proceed tactically in concert and how much intelligence to share with one another, they finally managed to convene an Anti-Anarchist Conference in 1898 in Rome (Jensen 2014, 131–84). Further meetings were scheduled but the Great Powers never succeeded in formulating a common agreement. In the end, the police bureaucracies of the major countries acted within a nationalist, not an internationalist, framework.

In Russia, the 1890s witnessed the spawning of the terror of the Socialist Revolutionary Party's Battle Organization and a renewed effort on the part of the state to repress its activities. Following the assassination of Tsar Alexander II in 1881, the Third Section was largely discredited for failing to prevent this tragedy. In the aftermath, the name of the national political police was changed to the Okhrana, or Security Agency. Though there were new directors in the ensuring years, the force itself maintained many of its former field operatives and tactics in its struggle against the SR Battle Organization.

According to available evidence, the number of police inquiries into subversive political activities increased exponentially in the late 1890s. Moreover, the police, under the supervision of Sergei Zubatov, established the country's first labor organizations and the most extensive police-sponsored network of workers associations anywhere on the continent. Simultaneously, his secret agents planted illegal literature and weapons in the hands of members of both the Socialist Revolutionary Party and the Russian Marxist Social Democratic Party.

Despite the close proximity in which the two sides functioned while trying to destroy each other, the police were unable to prevent a number of spectacular assassinations by the SR terrorist factions. Three prominent Ministers of Interior with jurisdiction over the police were among the victims: Dmitry Sipiagin in 1902, his successor Viachaslav Plehve two years later, and Peter Stolypin in 1911. In between, Russia underwent one of the century's most violent revolutionary periods in 1905–6 in which, though estimates vary, some 3,000 people were killed by the police and an approximately equal number by the insurgents (Daly 2006). Perhaps the most glaring example of the fusion of the police and the insurgents in this era was Evno Azev, who managed to work for both the SRs and the police. When faced with the choice of whether to assassinate his own boss in the St Petersburg police or face exposure among his revolutionary comrades if he demurred in carrying out the order, he chose the former. Cooperative terrorism had progressed to its highest stage of evolution at this point when "the counter-terrorist security police finally became itself an agency of terror" (Lauchlin 2002, 262, 265).

Conclusion

The "long nineteenth century" in many ways simply morphed into the horrors of the Great War in that the civil violence that so preoccupied both the police and the militants was unleashed with far greater brutality on the battlefields of trench warfare for four endless years. The tactical secrecy that both sides used in their internecine struggles against each other was now brought into the sunlight of legal violence as state after state proudly declared war and promised a rapid and glorious victory.

There was no victory for either side in the terrorism wars of the previous hundred years. Structurally speaking, the states continued to assert their legal right to monopolize advanced weaponry and to forcefully repress the dangers posed to their legitimacy, while their competitors for power continued to assert their own moral codes as justifications for the necessity of utilizing violence to replace those regimes. Governments protected their integrity by creating more powerful security bureaucracies with increasingly larger numbers of secret field agents, while political party organizations sought to develop their own agendas to expose the incompetence, corruption, and violence of the state and its supporters.

Both sides proved more than willing to employ imitative tactics of violence to achieve their respective political objectives as they engaged one another. They spied on each other, collected both useful and exaggerated "intelligence" on one another, lived clandestine existences that allowed them to make use of all available means of terror, and were both committed to the ultimate destruction of each other. If we count victims as a standard of evidence, the balance sheet is absurdly one-sided since the agents of states have been responsible for immeasurably more mortality and morbidity than all the insurgents combined. Perhaps we need other measures to draw conclusions before we take sides ourselves.

That said, the mirroring metaphor for the two antagonists haunts any inquiry into the nature of nineteenth-century terrorism, and nowhere has it been more clearly portrayed than in Joseph Conrad's timeless tale, *The Secret Agent*. As Inspector Heat, who heads the Special Crimes Department in London, pursues the nihilist Professor, who wears a deadly bomb device strapped to his waist, Conrad tells us that Heat believes potential terrorists can be treated like criminals because they resemble policemen so closely. "Both recognize the same conventions and have a working knowledge of each other's methods and of the routine of their respective trades." The fact that we generally consider the cops to be helpful and reliable while we regard the robbers to be dangerous and threatening has as much to do with our perceptions as it does with reality.

Though the twentieth century and beyond lie outside the chronological scope of this chapter, terrorism certainly did not wane after the Great War finally ended. On the contrary, newer weapons were fashioned by both state security forces and anti-state militants that created scenes of violence that went beyond even the imagination of their nineteenth-century predecessors. With advanced technology creating seemingly unlimited horizons for control on ground, sea, and air, the reach of both contesting forces moved into international orbits. This neo-imperialist expansionism was reinforced by nationalist impulses and utopian visions of radiant futures capable of being reached by applications of the tactics of terrorism. Even the horrors of the Paris Commune would be eclipsed by the justifications for assassinations, torture, genocides, and atomic weaponry of the twentieth century in the illusory search for collective agreement on political legitimacy, religious tolerance, and respect for the feared "other."

References

Anderson, David M., and David Killingray, eds (1991) *Policing the Empire: Government, Authority and Control, 1830–1940*. Manchester: Manchester University Press.

Andrieux, Louis (1885) *Souvenirs d'un Préfet de Police*. Paris: Mémoire du Livre.

Arnold, Eric A. (1979) *Fouché, Napoleon and the General Police*. Washington, DC: University Press of America.

Bantman, Constance (2013) *The French Anarchists in London, 1880–1914*. Liverpool: Liverpool University Press.

Bloxham, Donald, and Robert Gewarth, eds (2011) *Political Violence in Twentieth Century Europe*. Cambridge: Cambridge University Press.

Butterworth, Alex (2010) *The World that Never Was: A True Story of Dreamers, Schemers, Anarchists and Secret Agents*. New York: Pantheon Books.

Carlson, Andrew (1972) *Anarchism in Germany*, i. *The Early Movement*. Metuchen, NJ: Scareecrow Press.

Chenoweth, Erika (2013) "Terrorism and Democracy," *Annual Review of Political Science*, 16: 374.

Cobb, R. C. (1970) *The Police and the People: French Popular Protest, 1789–1820*. Oxford: Clarendon Press.

Daly, Jonathan (2006) "Police and Revolutionaries," in Dominic Lieven (ed.), *Cambridge History of Russia*, ii. *1689–1917*. New York: Cambridge University Press, 637–54.

Deflem, Mathieu (2002) *Policing World Society: Historical Foundations of International Police Cooperation*. New York: Oxford University Press.

De La Hodde, Lucien (1864) *Cradle of Rebellions: A History of the Secret Societies of France*. New York: John Bradburn.

Emerson, Donald E. (1968) *Metternich and the Political Police: Security and Subversion in the Hapburg Monarchy, 1815–1830*. The Hague: Martinus Nijhoff.

Emsley, Clive (1984) *Policing and its Context, 1750–1870*. New York: Schocken Books.

Emsley, Clive (1999) *Gendarmes and the State in Nineteenth-Century Europe*. New York: Oxford University Press.

Fitzpatrick, Matthew P. (2015) *Purging the Empire: Mass Expulsions in Germany, 1871–1914*. New York: Oxford University Press.

Forssell, Nils (1928) *Fouché: The Man Napoleon Feared*. London: George Allen Unwin.
Fouche, Joseph (1894) *Memoirs*. London: Gibbings & Co.
Galtier-Boissiere, Jean (1938) *Mysteries of the French Secret Police*. London: Stanley Paul.
Goldstein, Robert J. (1983) *Political Repression in Nineteenth Century Europe*. London: Croom Helm.
Haimson, Leopold, and Charles Tilly, eds (1989) *Strikes, Wars and Revolutions in an International Perspective*. Cambridge: Cambridge University Press.
Haupt, Heinz-Gerhard, and Klaus Weinhauer (2011) "Terrorism and the State," in Donald Bloxham and Robert Gerwarth (eds), *Political Violence in Twentieth Century Europe*. Cambridge: Cambridge University Press, 176–7.
Jensen, Richard Bach (2014) *The Battle Against Anarchist Terrorism*. Cambridge: Cambridge University Press.
Lauchlan, Iain (2002) *Russian Hide-and-Seek: The Tsarist Secret Police in St. Petersburg, 1906–1914*. Studia Historica, 67. Helsinki: SKS.FLS.
Law, Randall D. (2009) *Terrorism: A History*. Cambridge: Polity Press.
Liang, His-Huey (1992) *The Rise of the Modern Police and the European State System from Metternich to the Second World War*. Cambridge: Cambridge University Press.
Luedtke, Alf (1989) *Police and State in Prussia, 1815–1850*. Cambridge: Cambridge University Press.
Marx, Anthony W. (2003) *Faith in Nation: Exclusionary Origins of Nationalism*. New York: Oxford University Press.
Merriman, John (2006) *Police Stories: Building the French State, 1815–1851*. New York: Oxford University Press.
Merriman, John (2009) *The Dynamite Club*. New York: Houghton Mifflin Harcourt.
Merriman, John (2014) *Massacre: The Life and Death of the Paris Commune*. New York: Basic Books.
Miller, Martin A. (1985) *Origins of the Russian Revolutionary Emigration*. Baltimore: Johns Hopkins University Press.
Miller, Martin A. (2013) *The Foundations of Modern Terrorism: State, Society and the Dynamics of Political Violence*. Cambridge: Cambridge University Press.
Miller, Martin A. (2015) "Entangled Terrorisms in Late Imperial Russia," in Randall D. Law (ed.), *The Routledge History of Terrorism*. London: Routledge, 92–110.
Mladek, Klaus (2007) *Police Forces: A Cultural History of an Institution*. New York: Palgrave Macmillan.
Payne, Howard C. (1966) *The Police State of Louis Napoleon Bonaparte, 1851–1860*. Seattle: University of Washington Press.
Palmer, Stanley H. (1988) *Police and Protest in England and Ireland, 1780–1850*. New York: Cambridge University Press.
Radzinowicz, Leon (1948) "Certain Aspects of the Police of France," *A History of English Criminal Law and its Administration from 1750*. New York: Macmillan.
Raeff, Marc (1983) *The Well-Ordered Police State: Social and Institutional Change through Law in the Germanies and Russia, 1600–1800*. New Haven: Yale University Press.
Reichel, Philip, ed. (2005) *Handbook of Transnational Crime and Justice*. London: Sage Publications.
Schechter, Ronald (2012) "Conceptions of Terror in the European Enlightenment," in Michael Laffan and Max Weiss (eds), *Facing Fear: The History of an Emotion in Global Perspective*. Princeton: Princeton University Press, 38–9.

Schlieifman, Nurit (1988) *Undercovere Agents in the Russian Revolutionary Movement: The SR Party, 1902–1914*. New York: St Martin's Press.

Spencer, Elaine Glovka (1992) *Police and the Social Order in German Cities: The Dusseldort District, 1848–1914*. DeKalb, IL: Northern Illinois University Press.

Stead, Philip John (1983) *The Police of France*. New York: Macmillan.

Steiber, Wilhelm (1854) *The Communist Conspiracies of the Nineteenth Century*. Berlin: A. W. Hayn; reprinted Olms: Hildesheim, 1969, and online.

Stieber, Wilhelm (1979) *The Chancellor's Spy: The Revelations of the Chief of Bismarck's Secret Service*. New York: Grove Press.

Sutherland, Donald (1982) *The Chouans: The Social Origins of Popular Counter-Revolution in Upper Brittany, 1770–1796*. Oxford: Clarendon Press.

Tilly, Charles (2003) *The Politics of Collective Violence*. Cambridge: Cambridge University Press.

Wight, Colin (2009) "Theorizing Terrorism: The State, Structure and History," *International Relations*, 23(1): 100.

Zamoyski, Adam (2014) *Phantom Terror: The Threat of Revolution and the Repression of Liberty, 1789–1848*. London: William Collins.

Zweig, Stefan (1930) *Joseph Fouche: The Portrait of a Politician*. London: Cassell.

CHAPTER 8

THE LONG TWENTIETH CENTURY

JOHN BEW, ALEXANDER MELEAGROU-HITCHENS, AND MARTYN FRAMPTON

Introduction

Any attempt to reflect on terrorism during the twentieth century should begin with a word on the importance of perspective. This, after all, was an era which saw the deaths of tens of millions of people in two world wars, innumerable lesser conflicts, violent revolutions, civil wars, and episodes of brutal state repression. While terrorist violence was the source of much carnage and tragedy, its impact was dwarfed by the actions of governments and conventional military actors. The emergence of so-called "international terrorism" in the 1970s gave the issue greater prominence—as a shared concern for a growing number of states. Yet twentieth-century terrorism was but a prelude to the excesses that opened the twenty-first. Between 1900 and 2000, there were no terrorist attacks on the scale of what occurred on September 11, 2001; nor was there an attack that caused such a ripple effect of intended and unintended consequences. Nonetheless, in the history of terrorist violence, the twentieth century occupies a critical space. It was in this period that something identifiable as "terrorism" appeared in different contexts and continents. It was embraced by an array of groups with otherwise diametrically opposed political goals.

This chapter offers a survey of the main evolutionary leaps in terrorism during the twentieth century and a series of comments on the prevailing and recurrent characteristics of terrorist violence. That every conflict involving terrorism—or allegations of terrorism—is different is axiomatic. Nonetheless, the chapter argues that there is a unique form of violence that can be distinguished, analytically, as "terrorism"; it has been consciously and deliberately employed by a series of actors who borrowed methods and shared a mindset with one another. This is not to seek a watertight definition of "what terrorism is"—as more than one scholar has noted, a Sisyphean task, which risks consuming all the oxygen from the subject at hand. Instead, the more modest aim is to identify those characteristics and ingredients of terrorist violence that have transcended diverse historical contexts. The chapter thus emphasizes the lines of continuity in the development of terrorist methods, as well as recurring patterns of terrorist behavior. At the same time, it does not ignore those key points of rupture, when the parameters for terrorism changed.

To accomplish this, the next section offers a brief—and necessarily abridged—discussion of the various phases of terrorist violence; there then follows an attempt to embed these reflections in an analytical framework. A fundamental intellectual start-point is that terrorism, as noted by Michael Burleigh, has always been about the contest for power (Burleigh 2009). It has often occurred where the foundations of democracy are contested, or political authority has been undermined; or indeed, where the entire framework of international order is subject to challenge. Terrorist violence has been a recourse for those lacking in power, both at the political and social level. It has been harnessed to a range of ideologies, theories of historical development, and tactics of revolutionary change. But whatever their particular *causus belli*, all terrorists have sought, in some way, to contest the state. The nature of that contestation has varied: in some cases, they have challenged the existence, territorial limits, or ideological posture of the state; in others, they pointed to particular policies and injustices, whether real or perceived. Yet the underlying logic remained the same: terrorism existed "in dialogue" with the state. And for this reason, terrorist violence should be understood as an intrinsic corollary of modern state formation.

Ultimately, too, the chapter argues that terrorist violence, as practiced in the twentieth century, had both an instrumental and fanatic quality: that is, terrorism should be understood as a rational act, but that this rationality sits alongside other impulses of the human mind, such as fanaticism, rage, and millenarianism. Terrorist violence has not usually—and indeed, perhaps not ever—been the last resort of the reluctant revolutionary. Instead, it has been fueled by the assumption that murder or destruction could be a purifying or noble act. In that sense, terrorism has been not alone a condition of modernity, or an outgrowth of modern political and strategic thought, but also an appeal to something more deeply embedded in the human condition.

Twentieth-Century Terrorism: an Overview

By the turn of the twentieth century, Europe and North America—the principal focus of analysis here—had already become familiar with the concept of terrorism. Over the preceding four decades, there had been a series of high-profile assassinations and bomb attacks by those who openly declared their readiness to employ terrorist means (Laqueur 1977; Hoffman 1998). Anarchists, radical socialists, and radical nationalists had all embraced this mode of violence as the vehicle for achieving their goals. The late nineteenth century saw the crystallization of ideas such as the "propaganda of the deed" that legitimated vanguardist acts of militancy. It also saw the emergence of the first terrorist organizations like Narodnya Volya in Russia, as well as the first sustained campaigns of violence, including that of the Fenian movement against British rule in Ireland (Crenshaw 1981; Bolt et al. 2008). High-level political theatrics were deployed as a means of forcing revolutionary change and challenging the authority of the state. In the "era of the attentats," several heads of state fell victim to terrorist attacks, as did countless "ordinary" civilians. The 1901 assassination of US President McKinley by American anarchist Leon Czolgosz marked, to many, the high watermark of the so-called "Golden Age of Assassination," when anarchism and terrorism appeared symbiotic. Anti-state violence of this kind was always justified as a response to repression or illegitimate rule. Unsurprisingly, therefore, it was not restricted to comparatively liberal polities such as the United States or Western Europe; its practitioners also took aim at more obviously autocratic foes. In particular, the dysfunctional Tsarist state was subject to a wave of anarchist terrorist attacks, which fed into the broader collapse of government authority that occurred from 1905 to 1906 (Avrich 1967). Though Russian autocracy was subsequently able to reassert itself, the threat from anarchist and radical socialist terrorism endured in the years preceding the 1917 revolution. In 1908, for instance, Prime Minister Pyotr Stolypin was targeted in a crude, early form of "suicide attack." He escaped, but twenty-eight bystanders were killed; and Stolypin was himself eventually successfully assassinated in 1911. In the same period, a growing number of so-called "motiveless" terror attacks appeared to target the Russian "bourgeoisie" indiscriminately (Tokmakoff 1965; Geifman 1993).

Early twentieth-century terrorism was often seen as an outgrowth of revolutionary politics. Those who deployed terrorist methods usually did so with the stated intention of forcing the pace of historical change, rather than waiting for a moment of historically pre-conditioned triumph or deliverance. This meant that successful acts of terrorism contained within them the possibility of sparking a wider chain of events in motion. The most consequential terrorist attack of the century occurred in June 1914 with the assassination of Archduke Franz Ferdinand by Gavrilo Princip, a member of the "Young Bosnians" nationalist revolutionary society. The murder helped catalyze World War I, and as one recent account of that conflict's origins makes clear, what strikes the twenty-first-century observer is its striking modernity as a self-conscious act of terrorism (Clark 2012).

For a period thereafter, the appeal of terrorism was overtaken by the shift to total war and industrialized state violence. Against this backdrop, individualized acts of vanguard-inspired violence seemed rather passé. But the restoration of an uneasy international equilibrium after 1918—in which social disorder became a growing concern—opened up other opportunities for terrorist strategies. The United States witnessed a revived bout of terrorist violence, which was tied to labor unrest and the "red scare" of the immediate post-war period. Though short-lived, this episode also carried a distinctly modern resonance: a series of anonymous attacks, carried out in the name of a global cause, by a rather nebulous movement. The June 1919 bombings that hit a number of US cities, for instance, were accompanied only by a leaflet offering "Plain Words" about what inspired the perpetrators—thought to be followers of the anarchist Luigi Galleani. The attacks resulted in a draconian state legislative response, in which suspicion tended to focus on immigrant communities (with the passage of the Immigration and Sedition acts), and this was in turn followed by the first car bombing in history, on Wall Street in September 1920 (Murray 1955; Gage 2009; Jensen 2009).

In retrospect, these events proved to be the final act in the late nineteenth-century story of anarchist-inspired or radical socialist terrorism. Even so, others adopted terrorist methods during this period, and the phenomenon became more associated with nationalist and anti-imperialist goals. In the process of this migration, there was a degree of conscious emulation and historical learning that bespoke an underlying continuity. The British Empire, having had previous experience of "revolutionary" nationalist terrorism in both Bengal and Ireland, faced a proliferation of similar groups within its assorted imperial and neo-imperial dominions, across South Asia and the Middle East. In Egypt, for instance, terrorist "outrages" straddled the pre- and post-war period. In 1924, nationalists killed Sir Lee Stack, the British officer who commanded Egypt's army and thereby ensured the security of London's "veiled protectorate" in Cairo (Gifford 2016). In the same period, there were numerous other reminders that terrorism appealed to those wishing to challenge the imperial state (Ball 2013).

Nowhere was this more the case than in Ireland, where terrorist methods were re-embraced with a vengeance, now harnessed to a broader campaign of insurgency, as well as political agitation in favor of independence. The intensity of the "liberation war" waged by the Irish Republican Army (IRA) after 1918 was distinctive, insofar as the conflict was waged in such close proximity to the imperial metropole. Its results were far from unambiguous (the partition of the country and the creation of an Irish 'Free State' rather than the complete independence demanded). Yet the campaign waged by insurgent leaders like Michael Collins served as a template for other would-be "freedom fighters", who saw in terrorist violence a mechanism for overcoming their politico-military inferiority vis-à-vis the state. And this instinct soon became apparent in another British-controlled territory.

In 1930s Palestine, Zionist groups embraced terrorist methods as part of their struggle to achieve Jewish nationhood. Most notably, a Zionist paramilitary organization called the Irgun carried out a succession of gun and bomb attacks against British forces and the local Arab population. In 1940, the group paused its campaign in recognition of the greater threat posed by national socialism, but a splinter group, the Lehi (or Stern Gang) emerged, determined to continue the struggle (Byman 1998). Significantly, one of its leaders, Yitzhak Shamir, took the nom-de-guerre "Michael," in homage to the aforementioned IRA commander (Rynhold 2001, 35). In November 1944, Shamir and his comrades assassinated the British Minister for Middle East Affairs in Cairo, Lord Moyne (Cohen 1979). Earlier that year, the Irgun—now under the control of Menachem Begin—had opted to resume its own struggle. Begin defiantly proclaimed "the Revolt" and the intrinsic necessity of terrorist violence (Begin 1977).

More generally, the chaos and instability of World War II did appear to create opportunities for those inclined to utilize terrorist methods. In Ireland, for example, the IRA sought a partnership with Nazi Germany in 1940, offering republican support for the Germans through espionage and acts of sabotage; apparently Berlin also hoped for an insurrection in Northern Ireland. Little came of such hopes; infamously, the IRA's then chief of staff, Sean Russell, died aboard a U-boat while returning to Ireland and was buried at sea, wrapped in a swastika. After the British interned Seamus O'Donovan, a key liaison figure to the Abwehr, the fleeting relationship came to an end. Still, even without the assistance of the Germans, the IRA conducted a short-lived campaign in 1939–40, with targeted shootings and ambushes against British security forces. Attacks on the mainland included bombings in several urban centers—the worst in Coventry, where five people were killed. Overall, however, the IRA was unable to build any serious momentum—not least because of the unspoken, but firm opposition of the Irish government in Dublin, which quickly introduced internment—and as a result, their efforts were "distinctly unimpressive" (English 2004).

Elsewhere in Europe, various anti-Nazi resistance groups saw terrorism as a viable strategic option for challenging German hegemony. During the occupation of France, a rural resistance movement formed under the banner of the Maquis and, with the assistance of Britain's Special Operations Executive (SOE), pursued a guerrilla-cum-terrorist campaign against German troops and supporters of the Vichy regime (Kedward 1993; Foot 1976). This included the blowing up of rail tracks used by the German military and the use of assassination squads to target French collaborators (Ousby 2000). The effectiveness of this resistance, however, was heavily dependent on material support from the Allies, making it difficult for it "to convert daily life protest into armed struggle" (Gildea et al. 2006). While the Maquis played a significant role in providing the Allies with intelligence and assisting troops in Brittany, their use of violence never came close to seriously endangering the German occupation.

A similar story was evident in Greece. There, the Greek People's Liberation Army (Ελληνικός Λαϊκός Απελευθερωτικός Στρατός, ELAS) carried out more attacks against the Wehrmacht and Italian occupation forces than any other guerrilla organization (Mazower 1993). The group's greatest success came in late November 1942, when its fighters, in partnership with the SOE and a rival Greek guerrilla group, destroyed the Gorgopotamos railway bridge (Mazower 1993). The operation, which cut off a key German supply chain, was considered one of the most significant acts of sabotage in occupied Europe. Yet beyond this, insurgent and terrorist tactics seemed of only marginal import and limited effectiveness when set against the concrete realities of overwhelming Nazi military strength. Between March 1943 and the liberation of Greece in October 1944, 2,369 Germans were killed, as compared to 21,255 Greeks (Gildea et al. 2006). Terrorism was never more than an irritant to the Germans, who showed themselves capable of wielding devastating *force majeure* in response.

Indeed, taken as a whole, World War II seemed to confirm the eclipse and marginality of asymmetric forms of violence—in an era when more raw manifestations of state power were brought to bear on the conventional battlefield in an unprecedented manner.

However, as the tide of war ebbed, terrorist violence re-emerged as a major socio-political phenomenon—often exploiting the upheavals engendered by the war, which left the old imperial powers enfeebled and less able to corral recalcitrant populations.

In Palestine, the British faced the revived Irgun campaign. The bombing of the King David Hotel in July 1946 marked a qualitative shift in approach, with ninety-one people killed, mostly civilians. Further attacks contributed to the mounting pressure on the British authorities and formed the backdrop to the decision of the British government to abandon the Mandate (Hoffman 2016). Of course, that move flowed from the broader weakness of the British Empire in the aftermath of war, as well as the shifting international climate in favor of self-determination and US support for Zionist aims; but to many, events in Palestine again seemed to prove the efficacy of terrorist violence—and its capacity to force concessions from imperial rulers.

It was in the post-1945 period, as a number of European empires struggled to retain their territorial integrity and political authority, that other groups sought to deploy terrorist methods in an effort to replicate apparently successful insurgences in Ireland or Palestine. In several cases, while the circumstances and context were much altered, we can see the learning process at work across otherwise disparate groups. The British thus confronted another nationalist insurgency that was prepared to utilize terrorist violence in Cyprus, where the Ethniki Organosis Kyprion Agoniston (EOKA) sought unity (*enosis*) with Greece (Byford-Jones 1959; Varnavas 2001). Between 1955 and 1959, the group targeted British military bases and convoys, killing at least 105 soldiers, as well as a number of police officers and local Cypriot informants. While EOKA did not achieve its stated aim of *enosis*, the campaign was crucial in forcing the British to give up control of the island in 1959, save for two sovereign military bases (Tucker 2013).

That the old European empires bore the brunt of much of the most controversial episodes of terrorist violence reflects the late imperial setting for some of the most prominent terrorist campaigns. As much as the British, the French were challenged in various former imperial possessions—most conspicuously in Algeria, where the Front de Libération Nationale (FLN) etched its name into terrorist lore through an urban terrorism campaign. Though the French prevailed in purely military terms, the "Battle of Algiers" was a signature moment, demonstrating the capacity of terrorism to exact a serious political toll on a democratic government that retained imperial ambitions. The polarizing effects of the violence—coupled with the brutal *guerre sale*, or "dirty war," waged by the French—sapped the health of "French Algeria" and, crucially, undermined domestic political will. Eventually, the authorities in Paris felt impelled to concede independence (Gillespie 1960; Behr 1961; Horne 1977).

In places like Algeria and Palestine, of course, terrorism was merely one tactic employed by broader movements of insurgency. Yet this mode of violence seemed to energize hitherto frustrated nationalist organizations, and successfully pushed European empires towards a more rapid process of decolonization. Perhaps unsurprisingly, the effect was to cement the notion that terrorist violence was an indispensable aspect of any struggle for self-determination. Consequently, there was renewed impetus for those inclined to adopt similar methods, and the contagion spread to other nationalist causes. Yasser Arafat's Fatah movement, for example, self-consciously sought to emulate their Zionist enemies. In the mid-1960s, Arafat took over the Palestine Liberation Organization (PLO) and reoriented it towards "armed struggle," declaring this to be the sole "strategy" for achieving Palestinian statehood. In Northern Ireland, meanwhile, the Provisional IRA (PIRA) emerged to try and complete the "unfinished revolution" of complete Irish independence. Both groups explicitly took inspiration from events in Algeria and Cyprus. And yet the question of what was, and what was not, a "colonial" conflict was more open to dispute. The groups saw themselves as engaged in anti-imperialist struggles, but in each instance that claim could be (and was) challenged. In Palestine, the PLO confronted not a foreign empire, as had the Irgun, but rather the new Israeli state that viewed the terrorist threat as existential (Cobban 1984). By the same token, the "colonial" nature of the British state in Northern Ireland was complicated by the presence of over a million Protestant Unionists who remained fiercely opposed to Irish unity and independence (Loughlin 1998).

Longevity eluded many twentieth-century terrorist groups but those that operated against the backdrop of a broader national question seemed to have more staying power. Both the PLO and the PIRA waged campaigns that lasted over several decades. Simultaneously, other organizations around the world opted to embrace terrorism in the face of "internal colonialism," in an effort to realize their own nationalist goals. Hence Euskadi Ta Askatasuna (ETA) initiated an "armed struggle" against first the Francoist Spanish state, and later, its democratic successor (Bew et al. 2009). In Sri Lanka, the Liberation Tigers of Tamil Eelam (LTTE) emerged from a broad nationalist milieu to assert the Tamil right to independence from the government in Colombo. Under its authoritarian leader, Vellupilai Prabhakaran, the LTTE blended Tamil nationalism, Hindu mysticism, and Marxist-Leninism (Gunaratna 1997; Van de Voorde 2005). The latter was a common feature of most contemporary groups that were otherwise defined by their commitment to nationalist goals. The PLO, ETA, and PIRA all proclaimed their adherence to "socialist" outcomes—however vague they were as to precisely what that might mean. Such obeisance to leftist rhetoric was very much in keeping with the zeitgeist of post-1960s radicalism. As Richard Bourke has pointed out, a convenient assumption for many held that a "capitalist-imperialist" nexus stood opposed to "socialist-democratic" forces (Bourke 2003). For those committed to using violence to achieve nationalist self-fulfillment, it was a comforting framework of self-legitimation.

Various groups whose origins lay directly in the vibrant student movement and "New Left" of the late 1960s launched their own "anti-imperial" campaigns against the imagined behemoth of capitalist, authoritarian governments run by reformist left-wing parties that were perceived to have abandoned their true values. The most potent of these were in West Germany and Italy, where the Rote Armee Fraktion (RAF)—which drew direct inspiration from the PLO and events in Latin America—and the Brigate Rosse (BR) respectively carried out attacks against a variety of government targets and leaders of industry. As has been highlighted, it was no coincidence that such organizations proved most virulent in the former Axis countries (Japan, too, had its own "Red Army Faction"), where concerns about latent fascist and dictatorial tendencies carried a special resonance (Meade 1989; Pluchinsky 1993). Yet it is arresting that France and the United States, countries without recent histories of authoritarian rule, also experienced a burst of left-wing-inspired terrorism (in the forms of Action Directe and the Weather Underground, respectively), albeit limited in scale and relatively short-lived (Varon 2004).

More significant was the parallel appearance of a slew of organizations across Latin America that sought the overthrow of existing governments and mixed guerrilla and terrorist tactics in the name of radical left-communist politics. Such groups were inspired, in part, by China, where Mao Zedong's "people's war" had been triumphant (Tanham 2006). They also looked to Cuba, where Fidel Castro and Che Guevara had apparently demonstrated the capacity of rural insurgencies to overcome established state authority. The manifest social inequalities inherent in many Latin American societies, which fueled political polarization, also served to bolster the allure of revolutionary alternatives. So, too, did the fact that many governments were of a military hue and in receipt of American aid. Consequently, efforts were made to "apply" the lessons of Mao and Castro to other environments—most famously in Brazil where Carlos Marighella developed the theory of the "urban guerrilla" and declared his support for destructive—essentially terrorist—violence that might undermine the state (Marighella 1982). Marighella's Ação Libertadora Nacional (ALN) wholly failed to disrupt the country's military rulers (and Marighella himself was killed in a shootout with police in 1969), but his ideas carried an appeal that reached far beyond Brazil.

From the late 1950s, urban terrorism became an increasingly prominent part of the repertoire of revolutionary leftist movements. Some, like the Montoneros, Ejército Revolucionario del Pueblo (ERP), and Fuerzas Armadas Revolucionarias (FAR) in Argentina faced manifestly repressive regimes; but others such as the Movimiento de Izquierda Revolucionaria (MIR) in Venezuela and the Tupamaros in Uruguay launched their wars of "liberation" against democratic governments—and in the latter case, the campaign of violence furnished the military with a pretext to seize power (Gillespie 1980). By the same token, the Sendero Luminoso (Shining Path) of Peru chose to initiate "armed struggle" at precisely the moment when democracy was being restored after a period of military dictatorship, symbolically burning ballot boxes to illustrate their rejection of the electoral process (Milton 2007, 3).

Where confessional modes of politics were more pronounced, meanwhile, terrorist groups broke out of the nationalist paradigm that had defined so much of twentieth-century terrorism. In the last quarter of the twentieth century, in the Middle East and South Asia, a new form of religiously framed political violence emerged. Its origins lay in the founding of Islamist groups such as the Muslim Brotherhood in Egypt and the Jamaat-e-Islami in India during the first half of the century, which sought the restoration of Islamic power and glory in the world through the creation of avowedly Islamic states, which might then unite in a revived Caliphate (Kepel 2005). In the first instance, the enemy of such Islamists was "the West," assumed to be a pernicious politico-cultural force intent on the destruction of the Muslim world. Equally, they were deeply hostile to those local rulers and governments that—in their view—failed to uphold Islamic law (the *Shari'a*) and seemed inclined towards secularism (Mitchell 1993).

The failure of Islamists to secure power and implement their own vision led a minority to embrace the use of terrorism as an appropriate vehicle for overthrowing "apostate" governments. Radical intellectuals such as Sayyid Qutb invested this endeavour with religious value, describing it as a legitimate *jihad* against the "enemies" of Islam (Calvert 2009). It was in Egypt that the consequences of this line of thinking first became readily apparent, as the self-proclaimed heirs of Qutb (who was executed by Nasser's Arab socialist government in 1966) launched a succession of violent attacks on the state from 1974 onwards. Groups like the Islamic Liberation Organization, the Society of Muslims (Takfir wa al-Hijra) and Islamic Jihad (which included among its members one of the future founders of Al Qaeda Ayman al-Zawahiri) hoped to seize power by the targeted assassination of government officials. In 1981, Islamic Jihad successfully murdered the Egyptian President Anwar al-Sadat (Kepel 1985). In the same period, other militant groups hoped to undertake an Islamic revolution through the use of terrorist violence. In Syria, for example, the local branch of the Muslim Brotherhood launched its own "jihad" against the Ba'athist dictatorship of Hafez al-Assad in the late 1970s (Lefèvre 2013). In 1980s Lebanon, Hezbollah was formed at the aegis of the new Shi'a Islamist regime of Iran (under Ayatalloh Khomeini), in order to fight both the Israeli occupiers and American peacekeeping forces. As well as showing themselves to be proficient in more conventional forms of guerrilla warfare, the group pioneered the use of suicide terrorism in the contemporary era (Norton 2007).

Hezbollah's campaign to drive Israel out of Lebanon was unusual in this era in that it proved largely successful: the US withdrew its troops, and Israeli forces decamped to a 'security zone' along the Lebanese border. Elsewhere, most groups within this "first wave" of militant Islamism failed to bring about the revolution to which they aspired. One consequence of this was a temporary refocusing of efforts towards Afghanistan, in a conflict that was to provide the setting for the last great evolutionary leap in twentieth-century terrorism (and the consequences of which have left a lasting mark on the twenty-first). There, *jihad* had been proclaimed against the Soviet invasion of December 1979 and the subsequent occupation in support of the communist regime in Kabul. Militants from across the Arab and Muslim world flocked to the banner of the *mujahiddin*, with the more-or-less open support of their domestic governments. The ensuing conflict proved to be an important crucible for the idea (and practice) of *jihad*. And whilst the "Afghan-Arabs"—under the command of one of the key early theorists of modern *jihad* Abdullah Azzam—remained a small part of the anti-Soviet resistance, the experience proved formative for them as a cohort (Calvert 2007). As the Afghan war drew to a close by the end of the 1980s, many of those Arab veterans hoped to harness the energy unleashed by the Afghan *jihad* to launch a new bid for Islamic revolution at home.

What followed was a "second wave" of insurgency and terrorism that swept across the region in the early 1990s, as returning jihadists exploited the crisis of the post-colonial state in Egypt, Libya, and especially Algeria, in an attempt to overcome the "near enemy": secular Arab regimes. Their failure once again in this endeavor provided the impetus for another bout of reassessment, and it was in this context that Al Qaeda—a group forged as a transnational fulcrum for jihadist fighters—turned its attention to the "far enemy" (Gerges 2005). The latter, identified as the United States, was held to be the true bulwark of secular, un-Islamic regimes across the "Muslim world"; and as a result, Al Qaeda declared war on the US in 1996 (bin Laden 2005, 135). Two years later, the group carried out its first mass casualty attacks, utilizing coordinated suicide bombers to target American embassies in Tanzania and Kenya. The group also began to explore ways of striking at the US "homeland," with its attention drawn increasingly to the possibilities afforded by aviation terrorism. The stage was thus set for 9/11.

Patterns and Reflections

Looking back on the long twentieth century, David Rapoport famously described four over-arching "waves" of terrorism: anarchist, anti-colonial, New Left, and religious (Rapoport 2002, 46–9). Each wave, he averred, produced major technical developments that reflected an evolving "science" of terror (Rapoport 2002, 49). More broadly, he felt each wave was "driven by a common predominant energy" that shaped the "characteristics and mutual relationships" of multiple groups (Rapoport 2002, 47). There is much to commend in this analysis. For example, it is demonstrable that terrorist violence has proliferated by a kind of "learning process," which allows for the construction of a loose "family tree" of terrorist methodologies. The majority of organizations that have deployed terrorist violence have actively mimicked those preceding them, or their direct contemporaries. In the late nineteenth and early twentieth centuries this was reflected in the vogue for "dynamite" that swept through radical anarchist circles; more recently, it has been seen in the readiness of various groups to deploy aviation-based, or suicide terrorism. The latter, for instance, became prominent in the 1980s, with Hezbollah being the first group to use suicide attacks in a systematic manner; from there, it was taken up by other Islamist groups such as Hamas, as well as nationalist-socialist movements like the LTTE and the Partiya Karkerên Kurdistanê (PKK) in Turkey, before Al Qaeda made a strategic virtue of its use (Pape 2005). Today, it has become the defining tactic of terrorism in the twenty-first century. Rapoport was therefore right to highlight the way in which terrorism exhibits a complex, yet recognizable lineage.

However, while Rapoport's schema allows for the creation of such a lineage, it might be noted that it offers only a partial picture. Most obviously, his four waves do not include far-right terrorism, even though this has often proven lethal in various forms (Gage 2011, 89). In the United States, for instance, anti-federalist terrorism, a manifestation of the far right unique to the American experience, claimed the lives of 165 people in 1995 when Timothy McVeigh detonated a truck bomb in front of the Alfred P. Murrah Federal Building in Oklahoma City. Until the turn of the twentieth century and the September 11, 2001 attacks, it was the worst terrorist incident in American history. Similarly in Europe, neo-fascists were responsible for one of the most deadly terrorist atrocities to hit the continent with the 1980 bombing of the Bologna train station, which killed eighty-five people. In his willingness to overlook this and other right-wing attacks, Rapoport perhaps reflects the tendency of scholars to overfocus on what has been called "revolutionary terrorism" (Hutchinson 1972; Price 1977).

Beyond this, it should be noted that too rigid an adherence to the "four wave" paradigm risks over-simplification and imposing rigid chronological boundaries. In reality, nationalist organizations appeared in all four waves (Rapoport 2002, 47). In addition, the life cycle of any given terrorist organization was very much dependent on its ability to retain energy and momentum—something in turn contingent on the local conflict of which it was a part. Nevertheless, there is merit to Rapoport's contention that "the wave pattern" helps differentiate "the ethos of one generation from another" (Rapoport 2002, 48). One can see that each of the four waves took their cues from wider changes in international politics. This underlines the extent to which terrorist groups had defined themselves in opposition to the status quo—and existed in dialectic relationship with the particular state which they targeted. Indeed, it is clear that the history of any given group arose from the interplay between that group and a government. Often, for example, terrorists advanced by dint of the errors made by a state, rather than as a consequence of any intrinsic merits they possessed. This was especially true in Peru, where the growth of the Shining Path over the course of the 1980s was primarily a function of the injustices and weaknesses of successive governments. These responded to the initial campaign of violence with what Carlos Degregori bluntly called military-led "genocidal violence," which proved as ineffective as it was alienating to the bulk of the peasantry. At the same time, Peru became an economic basket-case as inflation soured to over 7,000 percent by the end of the decade. Against this background, many looked to the Shining Path as a potential alternative—until its own brutality, coupled with its crippling dependence on founding leader Presidente Gonzalo (Abimael Guzman Reynoso) and a relative improvement in the performance of the state on several indices, led to the surprisingly rapid unraveling of the Shining Path after 1992 (Palmer 1992).

Ultimately, while Rapoport's approach provides a useful template, it only tells us so much about the motives for, and nature of, terrorism. An overview of this phenomenon in the twentieth century reveals the way in which it matured, as a mode of violence, defined by several key characteristics. First, as had been the case in the nineteenth century, terrorism was defined by its symbolism. While there was an evolutionary leap in the way notions such as the "propaganda of the deed" were implemented, the basic principles remained the same. In the 1960s, for example, when Marighella spoke of the need to make "armed propaganda," he was effectively echoing his anarchist forebears (Mallin 1982, 92).

A second characteristic, again echoing the nineteenth century, was the way that terrorism was used as a means of provocation. Early anarcho-terrorist thinkers like Pyotr Kropotkin and the Italian anarchist Enrico Malatesta, focused on the idea that acts of violence could incite state oppression and thereby induce crisis (Smith 2006; Law 2009). In similar vein, Europe's New Left terrorists, in particular the RAF and the RB, used violent provocations to supposedly "unmask the fascist character of the state" (Wolin 2010).

In South America, Marighella encouraged the use of chaotic violence in the hope of inciting "brutal police and army crackdowns," which would in turn reveal the state as "a brutal fascist entity" in service to "international capital" (Law 2009, 257).

Third, terrorism underwent a process of delegitimization in the first decades of the twentieth century. Before this, some terrorists embraced the term; increasingly, it was used to stigmatize and anathematize a mode of violence. Even then, however, there were those who wore the label "terrorist" as a badge of honour. Marighella insisted that it did "not discredit," but rather provided "a focal point of attraction" (Mallin 1982, 70). More recently, some members of jihadist groups have referred to themselves as Irhabiyin, from the Arabic *irhab* or "terror," which they claim is used in the Quran to describe those who heroically "terrorised" the enemies of Islam (Zelin 2011).

Fourth, terrorist groups throughout the twentieth century were characterized by an acute sense of historical consciousness. Historical narratives—or more accurately, myths—provided ballast for nearly all of the movements under discussion. These took various forms: from long-held grievances to more recent tales of dispossession and corruption—whether as a result of external forces, internal betrayal, or social degeneracy. The best work on violent Irish nationalism, for example, all points to the way in which the different manifestations of the IRA sought to interpolate themselves into a long historical lineage (English 2007). The Cypriot group EOKA, to give another example, was led by Georgios Grivas, who assumed the nom-de-guerre Digenis in a reference to Digenis Akritas, a Byzantine leader who fought for the protection and independence of the Byzantine Empire. The EOKA mission statement also placed the group in the context of a centuries-long Greek struggle against invaders: "Cypriot brothers, looking at us from the depth of the centuries are all those who made Greek History shine, in order to preserve their freedom: the Marathon fighters, the Salamis fighters, Leonidas' Three Hundred... Let us answer them by deeds, that we shall become much better than they" (Varnavas 2001, 59).

The fifth characteristic of twentieth-century terrorism was that it invariably emerged as the violent iteration of some pre-existing socio-political movement, or claimed to embody a particular community. This was particularly evident with those groups emerging from the European radical left. In Italy, the BR declared itself the representative of millions of southern Italian migrant workers who had traveled to the north in search of work in the factories. In Germany, the RAF took on a "Third Worldist" approach, adopting the grievances and fighting on behalf of nations allegedly oppressed by Western capitalist imperialism (Gildea et al. 2011). In the same way, those groups struggling for national liberation, by definition, asserted their right to speak for their imagined nations; Islamists insisted that they alone spoke for the entire Muslim *ummah* (community).

Sixth, it is worth underlining that terrorism was frequently not, as the narrative of the reluctant revolutionary would suggest, a weapon "of last resort." Rather, it was seen as an essential mechanism for changing (adjusting, shunting along, or even reversing) the established arc of historical change. Relatedly, violence was often seen as a purifying and ennobling act. Nowhere was this sentiment expressed more clearly than in the writings of Frantz Fanon, inspired by the campaign of the FLN in Algeria. The idea, prevalent in strategic studies, that terrorism is a "tactic" fails to appreciate that the character of terrorist violence has often been more important than its rationality and instrumentality; time and again, it has been sustained by the delusion, blood lust, hatred, and egotism of the self-appointed vanguard, which holds unwavering faith in the justness of its cause.

With that said, the irreducible feature of terrorism in the twentieth century was that it was driven by the desire to obtain power—primarily through contestation of the state. Terrorist groups were therefore in constant dialogue with the state, both mirroring and taking cues from it. Absolutist government tended to produce maximalist terrorist movements (as occurred in late nineteenth-/early twentieth-century Russia), whereas liberal states gave birth to organizations perhaps more amenable, in the end, to negotiation. It is thus worth reflecting finally on the complex relationship that terrorism has enjoyed with democracy. It has flourished in open societies and itself marks the ultimate "democratization" of violence at the hands of those who lack political power in the modern world. It is in that struggle for power that terrorism has repeatedly burst forth, across the globe, as part of the ongoing contest to define social and political modernity.

References

Avrich, P. (1967) *Russian Anarchists*. Princeton: Princeton University Press.

Ball, S. (2013) "The Assassination Culture of Imperial Britain, 1909–1979," *The Historical Journal*, 56(1): 231–56.

Begin, M. (1977) *Revolt*. Los Angeles: Nash Publishing Corporation.

Behr, E. S. (1961) *The Algerian Problem*. London: Pickle Partners Publishing.

Bew, J., M. Frampton, and I. Gurruchaga (2009) *Talking to Terrorists: Making Peace in Northern Ireland and the Basque Country*. London: Hurst & Co.

bin Laden, O. (2005) *Messages to the World: The Statements of Osama Bin Laden*, ed. B. Lawrence. London: Verso.

Bolt, N., D. Betz, and J. Azari (2008) *Propaganda of the Deed 2008: Understanding the Phenomenon*. London: Royal United Services Institute for Defence and Security Studies.

Bourke, R. (2003) *Peace in Ireland: The War of Ideas*. London: Pimlico.

Burleigh, M. (2009) *Blood and Rage: A Cultural History of Terrorism*. New York: Harper Perennial.

Byford-Jones, W. (1959) *Grivas and the Story of EOKA*. London: R. Hale.

Byman, D. (1998) "The Logic of Ethnic Terrorism," *Studies in Conflict and Terrorism*, 21(2): 149–69.

Calvert, J. (2007) "The Striving Shaykh: Abdullah Azzam and the Revival of Jihad," *Journal of Religion and Society*, supplement series 2: 83–102.

Calvert, J. (2009) *Sayyid Qutb and the Origins of Radical Islamism*. Oxford: Oxford University Press.

Clark, C. M. (2012) *The Sleepwalkers: How Europe Went to War in 1914*. London: Allen Lane.

Cobban, H. (1984) *The Palestinian Liberation Organisation: People, Power and Politics*. Cambridge: Cambridge University Press.

Cohen, M. J. (1979) "The Moyne Assassination, November, 1944: A Political Analysis," *Middle Eastern Studies*, 15(3): 358–73.

Crenshaw, M. (1981) "The Causes of Terrorism," *Comparative Politics*, 13(4): 379–99.
English, R. (2004) *Armed Struggle: The History of the IRA*. Oxford: Oxford University Press.
English, R. (2007) *Irish Freedom*. London: Pan Macmillan.
Foot, M. R. D. (1976) *Resistance: An Analysis of European Resistance to Nazism, 1940–45*. London: Methuen Publishing Ltd.
Gage, B. (2009) *The Day Wall Street Exploded: A Story of America in its First Age of Terror*. Oxford: Oxford University Press.
Gage, B. (2011) "Terrorism and the American Experience: A State of the Field," *Journal of American History*, 98(1): 73–94.
Geifman, A. (1993) *Thou Shalt Kill: Revolutionary Terrorism in Russia, 1894–1917*. Princeton: Princeton University Press.
Gerges, F. A. (2005) *The Far Enemy: Why Jihad Went Global*. Cambridge: Cambridge University Press.
Gifford, J. (2016) "Extracting the Best Deal for Britain: The Assassination of Sir Lee Stack in November 1924 and the Revision of Britain's Nile Valley Policy," *Canadian Journal of History*, 48(1): 87–114.
Gildea, R., Mark, J., and Pas, N. (2011) "European Radicals and the 'Third World' Imagined Solidarities and Radical Networks, 1958–73," *Journal of the Social History Society*, 8(4): 449–71.
Gildea, R., et al. (2006) *Surviving Hitler and Mussolini: Daily Life in Occupied Europe*. London: Bloomsbury.
Gillespie, J. (1960) *Algeria: Rebellion and Revolution*. London: Ernest Benn.
Gillespie, R. (1980) "A Critique of the Urban Guerrilla: Argentina, Uruguay and Brazil," *Journal of Conflict Studies*, 1(2): 39–53.
Gunaratna, R. (1997) "Internationalisation of the Tamil Conflict (and its Implications)," *South Asia: Journal of South Asian Studies*, 20/sup001: 119–52.
Hoffman, B. (1998) *Inside Terrorism*. New York: Columbia University Press.
Hoffman, B. (2016) *Anonymous Soldiers: The Struggle for Israel, 1917–1947*. New York: Knopf Doubleday Publishing Group.
Horne, A. (1977) *A Savage War of Peace: Algeria 1954–1962*. New York: New York Review of Books.
Hutchinson, M. C. (1972) "The Concept of Revolutionary Terrorism," *Journal of Conflict Resolution*, 16(3): 383–96.
Jensen, R. B. (2009) "The International Campaign Against Anarchist Terrorism, 1880–1930s," *Terrorism and Political Violence*, 21(1): 89–109.
Kedward, H. R. (1993) *In Search of the Maquis: Rural Resistance in Southern France 1942–1944: Rural Resistance in Southern France 1942–1944*. Oxford: Clarendon Press.
Kepel, G. (1985) *Muslim Extremism in Egypt: The Prophet and Pharaoh*. Berkeley, CA: University of California Press.
Kepel, G. (2005) *The Roots of Radical Islam*. London: Saqi.
Laqueur, W. (1977) *A History of Terrorism*. Piscataway, NJ: Transaction Publishers.
Law, R. D. (2009) *Terrorism: A History*. Cambridge, MA: Polity.
Lefèvre, R. (2013) *Ashes of Hama: The Muslim Brotherhood in Syria*. Oxford: Oxford University Press.
Loughlin, J. (1998) *The Ulster Question since 1945*. Basingstoke: Macmillan.
Mallin, J. (1982) *Terror and Urban Guerillas: A Study of Tactics and Documents*. Miami, FL: University of Miami Press.
Marighella, C. (1982) "Minimanual of the Urban Guerrilla," in J. Mallin (ed.), *Terror and Urban Guerrillas: A Study of Tactics and Documents*. Coral Gables, FL: University of Miami Press, 70–115.

Mazower, M. (1993) *Inside Hitler's Greece: The Experience of Occupation, 1941–1944*. New Haven: Yale University Press.

Meade, R. C. (1989) *Red Brigades: The Story of Italian Terrorism*. New York: Springer.

Milton, C. E. (2007) "At the Edge of the Peruvian Truth Commission: Alternative Paths to Recounting the Past," *Radical History Review*, 2007(98): 3–33.

Mitchell, R. P. (1993) *The Society of the Muslim Brothers*. Oxford: Oxford University Press.

Murray, R. K. (1955) *Red Scare: A Study in National Hysteria, 1919–1920*. Minneapolis, MN: University of Minnesota Press.

Norton, A. (2007) *Hezbollah: A Short History*. Princeton: Princeton University Press.

Ousby, I. (2000) *Occupation: The Ordeal of France, 1940–1944*. New York: Cooper Square Press.

Palmer, D. S. (1992) *Shining Path of Peru*. Basingstoke: Palgrave Macmillan.

Pape, R. (2005) *Dying to Win: The Strategic Logic of Suicide Terrorism*. New York: Random House Publishing Group.

Pluchinsky, D. A. (1993) "Germany's Red Army Faction: An Obituary," *Studies in Conflict and Terrorism*, 16(2): 135–57.

Price, H. E. (1977) "The Strategy and Tactics of Revolutionary Terrorism," *Comparative Studies in Society and History*, 19(1): 52–66.

Rapoport, D., ed. (2002) *Terrorism: Critical Concepts in Political Science*. London: Routledge.

Rynhold, J. (2001) "Re-conceptualizing Israeli Approaches to 'Land for Peace' and the Palestinian Question since 1967," *Israel Studies*, 6(2): 33–52.

Smith, R. (2006) *The Utility of Force: The Art of War in the Modern World*. London: Penguin.

Tanham, G. K. (2006) *Communist Revolutionary Warfare: From the Vietminh to the Viet Cong*. Westport, CT: Greenwood Publishing Group.

Tokmakoff, G. (1965) "Stolypin's Assassin," *Slavic Review*, 24(2): 314–21.

Tucker, S. C. (2013) *Encyclopedia of Insurgency and Counterinsurgency*. Oxford: ABC-CLIO.

Varnavas, A. (2001) *A Brief History of the Liberation Struggle of EOKA, 1955–1959*. Nicosia, Cyprus: EOKA Liberation Struggle 1955–59 Foundation.

Varon, J. (2004) *Bringing the War Home: The Weather Underground, the Red Army Faction, and Revolutionary Violence in the Sixties and Seventies*. Berkeley, CA: University of California Press.

Wolin, R. (2010) *The Wind from the East: French Intellectuals, the Cultural Revolution, and the Legacy of the 1960s*. Princeton: Princeton University Press.

Zelin, A. (2011) "Jihadis and the Use of the Terms Terrorism and Terrorist," Paper delivered at 'Re-visioning Terrorism' Conference, Purdue University, September 8, 2011, available online at <https://docs.lib.purdue.edu/cgi/viewcontent.cgi?article=1005&context=revisioning>.

PART III

APPROACHES AND METHODS

CHAPTER 9

ORGANIZATIONAL AND INSTITUTIONAL APPROACHES

social movement studies perspectives on political violence

LORENZO BOSI, DONATELLA DELLA PORTA, AND STEFAN MALTHANER

Political violence by non-state actors, whether in the form of clandestine groups, riots, violent insurgencies, or civil wars, often emerges in the context of social movements, can shift back to non-violent methods of contentious collective action, and in many cases does not mark a new and separate phase of contention but proceeds in parallel with street protests, marches, boycotts, and strikes. At the same time, different forms of political violence are interlinked and are part of a continuum of repertoires of actions—rather than representing discrete and mutually exclusive types—and often occur successively or simultaneously during processes of conflict escalation (when violence increases in scale, type, and scope) or de-escalation (when violence overall decreases).

In this chapter, "political violence" is preferred to the term "terrorism" because it allows us to capture continuities and shifts between different forms of violent and non-violent contention as well as variance within violent repertoires. Moreover, "terrorism," because of its strong normative and political connotations, is much more contested, has doubtful heuristic value, and has often been used to stigmatize rather than to explain the social phenomena under examination (Tilly 2003). Political violence, in this sense, involves a heterogeneous repertoire of actions oriented at inflicting physical, psychological, and symbolic damage on individuals and/or property with the intention of influencing various audiences for affecting or resisting political, social, and/or cultural change.

While the connection between social movements and political violence has not gone unnoticed (Della Porta and Tarrow 1986; Della Porta 1990, 1995; White 1992; Wieviorka 1993; Zwerman et al. 2000), for quite some time the social movement literature was biased towards studying non-violent movements as well as movements in Western countries rather than in other parts of the world. With growing interest in the topic, what characterizes the social movement studies' approach to research on political violence is, above all, an emphasis on de-exceptionalizing violent repertoires by locating them within broader contexts and complex processes. Political violence is considered to be one among other forms of contention within a wider repertoire. Social movement studies look at how oppositional groups and movements often shift between various violent or non-violent forms of action, or use them simultaneously. They examine the choice of doing so not as predetermined by values, goals, or identities, but as emergent in processes of contention and shaped by adapting to changing environments and strategic interactions with their opponents. This perspective, therefore, contextualizes political violence also by embedding militant groups within a broader field of actors involved in the conflict, including police and state agents, counter-movements, audiences, as well as allies or competitor-groups within the same movement, which are embedded in asymmetric power balances that shape the trajectory of processes of political violence. Moreover, this perspective locates violence within broader cycles of protest, during which the development of forms of protest follows a reciprocal process of innovation and adaptation, with different actors responding to the other (Bosi and Malthaner 2015a).

In this chapter we take a closer look at organizational and institutional approaches that study political violence from a social movement studies (SMS) perspective. The first section discusses the way "classic" approaches—such as those focusing on resource mobilization theory (RMT) and political opportunity structures (POS)—have been applied to the study of political violence. In the subsequent section we present a relational approach, focusing on organizational dynamics and inter-organizational interactions, as well as suggesting mechanisms that shape processes of conflict escalation or de-escalation.[1]

Classical SMS-Perspectives

From the early 1970s, social movement scholars have criticized strain or breakdown theories which explain protest primarily as a reaction to grievances and societal friction, suggesting instead that socio-political conflicts are an integral trait of any society at every stage, without inevitably leading to collective action in general, and political violence in particular. Fundamentally, RMT considers mobilization as dependent on the capacity of social movement organizations and groups to work as "movement entrepreneurs" by strategically deploying material resources (financial resources, organizational infrastructure, etc.), utilizing and creating solidarity networks and achieving external consensus in order to convert latent discontent into potential for activism. RMT therefore challenged previous socio-psychological perspectives on "collective behaviour" as pathological and focused on rational, strategic actors and their organizational capacities and resources (McCarthy and Zald 1973, 1977; Obershall 1978; Tilly 1978). Drawing on organizational theories, social movement scholars interested in the phenomenon of political violence have studied the way armed groups emerge in the context of—and then break away from—broader non-violent social movements, particularly during phases of declining mobilization when resources decrease and internal competition increases (Della Porta and Tarrow 1986; Della Porta 1990, 1995; Zwerman et al. 2000). These splinter groups become agents for the propagation of violence. Like any political organization, armed groups struggle first of all to survive (Crenshaw 1985). Given their complete or partial underground nature, armed groups experience specific organizational and resource dilemmas that, however, differ from their non-violent counterparts in the broader social movements, as they are in constant need of resources and support to sustain both the armed struggle's maintenance and organizational reproduction but also face (usually high levels of) persecution and repression by security services and have to maintain internal cohesion and control in the face of high-risk activism (Della Porta 1990, 1995; Wieviorka 1993).

In the early 1980s, the *political opportunity structure* (POS) approach emerged within political science. Sharing with RMT the vision of social movements as strategic actors, they focused on how political and institutional context shapes repertoires of action and influences whether or not movements have successful outcomes. Arguing that the mobilization of protest reacts to—and requires—openings in the political system, this perspective stresses the importance of political opportunity structures consisting of formal political institutions as well as of informal, cultural aspects. In particular, regime shifts, periods of political instability, or changes in the composition of elites provide openings for social movements and affect the repertoires of action adopted by social movements. Moreover, POS scholars also point out that political context shapes repertoires of action in the converse way, meaning in the form of closed (or closing) political opportunities or in the form of state agents' and political elites' efforts to constrain and control social movements that challenge existing power structures. As Della Porta has suggested "centralized institutions, an exclusionary tradition, weakness of alliances, and strength of opponents are all conditions that often push toward an escalation of the forms of protest" (2003, 389). In particular, closed political opportunities motivate the escalation from non-violent to violent repertoires of action (White 1989; Della Porta 1995; Hafez 2004; Schwedler 2004). Political violence, in other words, is interpreted as an outcome of the interaction between institutional political actors and protest. Thereby, patterns of protest-policing and the more general strategies of maintaining control and societal order are particularly relevant to understanding the emergence of militant forms of protest (Della Porta and Reiter 1998), and encounters between movements and state apparatuses have been identified to produce radicalization in a wide variety of movement cases (McAdam 1982; Della Porta 1995; Tarrow 1989; Kriesi et al. 1995).

Contentious Politics: A Dynamic Approach

Resource mobilization theory and *political opportunity structure theory* have had lasting effects on the study of social movements and political violence by drawing attention to organizations as strategic and resource-dependent actors, and to the institutional environment in which they emerge and operate. Explanations based on political opportunities, in particular, have looked at the way in which contextual structures affect social movements by strongly limiting if not totally determining their extent, forms, and potential success. In addition to an emphasis on the dependency of social movement organizations upon external resources, resource mobilization scholars have also stressed strategic action, replacing behavioral explanations and downplaying normative concerns or at least considering them as exogenous to protest. Yet, they have been criticized, inter alia, for being overly structural and static.

Rather than facing stable patterns of opportunities and constraints, the *contentious politics* perspective suggests that social movements emerge and act within—and in turn reshape—a dynamic social environment. Since the turn of the century, this perspective (McAdam et al. 2001; Tilly and Tarrow 2007) has developed a more dynamic approach that analyzes organizational and institutional aspects from a fundamentally relational perspective to investigate "social movements, revolutions, strike waves, nationalism, democratization, and more" (McAdam et al. 2001, 4). Without the intention to equalize these different forms of contentious politics "this approach helps transcend the compartmentalization of different types of contentious episodes by finding similar mechanisms in each" (Buechler 2011, 196). Focusing on recurrent mechanisms, it is well suited for comparative research on violent forms of contention, as it explicitly investigates how different contexts may shape the outcomes of similar trajectories as well as how similar contexts may shape the outcomes of different trajectories (Alimi et al. 2012, 2015; Della Porta 2013; Bosi et al. 2014; McCauley and Moskalenko 2008). This final section seeks to identify within three main areas of interaction several possible mechanisms which might promote processes of conflict escalation or de-escalation: interactions between armed groups and the state; interaction between different armed groups within a movement and with counter-movements; and organizational dynamics of armed groups.

Interactions between Armed Groups and the State

Social movements and armed groups very often target states and state agents, or use them as "proxy targets." Conversely, states react to such oppositional actors with concessions, repression, co-optation, or a combination of these (Bosi and Giugni 2012; Bosi 2016b). The interactions between armed groups, states, and state agents can further promote escalation or facilitate de-escalation processes.

The *opportunities and threats mechanism* is mostly determined by the state and state agents' capacity to shape the strategic positioning of the armed group within the socio-political context and its political leverage in a purposeful way (Miller 2012). It can regard contingent changes such as the composition of the ruling coalition or structural changes such as constitutional changes. With inclusive opportunities (e.g. new political allies within the institutions) social movements are less likely to adopt violent repertoires or armed groups can opt for disengagement processes (Bosi and Della Porta 2015). On the other hand, closing opportunities and threats can induce escalation processes when certain groups favor violent repertoires over non-violent ones, as in their view there is "no other way out" (Goodwin 2001) and "the end may excuse the means" (Crenshaw 2011, 39). As Bosi writes in relation to the escalation process of the Red Brigades in Italy:

> [i]n the changed socio-political context of the early 1970s, and confronted by the threat of a neo-Gaullist restructuring of the state, leaders of the BR concluded that it was necessary to start going beyond the "armed propaganda" in the factories... But, in the face of the significant weakening of the movement strategic positioning vis-a-vis the political environment and the deepening attribution of threat that accompanied these political changes, the BR decided "to break the encirclement of the workers struggle,"[2] a break from which new strategies and goals were to follow. While shop floor confrontations could be won, the BR realized, firstly, that by staying only in the factories they were running the risk of becoming isolated and, secondly, that the "revolutionary war" could not be won there alone... Accordingly, its actions strategically started to shift from the local support of workers' struggles to more direct attacks on political targets, a shift envisioned to attain a full social dimension.
>
> (Alimi et al. 2015, 66–7)

Organizations aiming to achieve (more) political power might select violent repertoires in order to improve the position of their constituency especially when they feel non-violent means have failed. Various movement factions may view closing opportunities differently. In some cases, this development may trigger internal competition, which can, as we will see, promote escalation processes. At the same time, armed groups might themselves use violence to provoke and produce such worsening of the socio-political context, with the aim of furthering their agendas and gaining an advantage over competing armed groups, for example.

State security forces shape the armed groups' lives from early on to the end. Social movements and armed groups tend to consider state security forces' behavior an important barometer of the attitudes of the establishment toward their challengers. State security forces' interaction with social movements might escalate into violence (Della Porta 1995). High levels of repression in some cases can eliminate mobilization, whereas in other cases repression can trigger escalation processes. This variation can partly be explained by the fact that different social movement organizations react differently to repression. Some moderate factions retreat from mobilization and allow radicals to take the lead, while in other cases repression is functional in reducing armed groups' resources (Bosi 2006), which is one of the factors capable of producing intra-movement competition, as we will see.

The *policing escalation* mechanism refers to the action–counteraction dynamics in which the challengers and the security services raise the stakes of the struggle in response to each other, in a pattern of reciprocal adaptation (Della Porta 2013). Furthermore, rebel groups are not passive actors in their relationship with state security forces. Eventually many of them seek to provoke state security forces to overreact in an indiscriminate way so as to alienate the population and build key constituencies who take the side of the insurgents (Zwerman and Steinhoff 2005). In the case of the Brigate Rosse, for example, as Bosi writes,

> the strategy of the BR was to beat the system with exemplary actions and, through these actions, to train the cadres and propagate the only truly revolutionary political line—armed propaganda. The pursuit of this strategy was carried out through provocation... [t]hus, while the initial violence of the BR was justified in defensive terms, it also had an offensive plan, intended to awaken the awareness and activate the commitment to militancy of the proletariat, without which there could have been no overturn of power. By provoking the security forces' repressive measures the final aim was to marginalize its political competitors within the movement and in the broader Left, so as to obtain more resources and recruits for the BR itself.
>
> (Alimi et al. 2015: 75)

More selective repression as opposed to indiscriminate coercion is usually capable of triggering de-escalation processes (Della Porta 2013; Davenport 2014). The Italian exit from the cycle of political violence is, again, an exemplary case here (Bosi and Della Porta 2015).

States respond variously toward the mobilization of challengers. Depending on circumstances, states may respond with concessions in order to appease the challengers and impede possible processes of escalation (Bosi and Giugni 2012). However, armed groups may read concessions alone as opportunities that they seek to exploit with further violence. The *institutionalization* mechanism is a particular type of concession where the state includes some of the challengers' ideas, personnel, or entire movement and armed group strands into formal politics (Bosi 2016a). Such a mechanism tends to take place when two conditions co-occur: challengers are willing, in whole or in part, to institutionalize; and the state consents to such a path. While both conditions are necessary, they do not need to happen simultaneously (Suh 2011). In particular, states are not inclined to open up opportunities or channels of participation toward challengers (especially so in the case of armed groups) unless they feel that the costs of any other options are too high to sustain. This happens when they are confronted by overwhelming mobilizations, and when the degree of disruptiveness is very high. In these cases, they may feel threatened by the loss of their legitimacy and authority. In the Northern Ireland case, the British state has progressively co-opted the republican movement within political institutions, producing de-escalation (Bosi 2016a). Within the dissident sector, different elements within the same social movement might see the prospect of institutionalization somewhat differently, and might propose different strategies in order to achieve or avoid it. Moderate groups, in their internal competition with more radical strands within the movement, may see institutionalization as a safe way to continue their struggle for social change without antagonizing authorities and counter-movements, whereas other parts of the movement may prefer more radical repertoires of action to provoke repression. Where movements split over the issue of institutionalization, those groups that do not follow this path may distance themselves from their old allies who now operate inside formal politics. In the Northern Ireland case the institutionalization of a large part of the republican movement has not however involved the overall movement. Splinter groups, such as the Continuity IRA or the Real IRA, have tried to escalate the conflict and block the peace process through the use of political violence.

Intra-Movement and Movement–Counter-Movement Interactions

Oppositional movements are composed of networks of groups and organizations that share certain goals and collaborate in collective protest. However, these groups may also differ in their ideological and tactical preferences and compete for power and resources (Diani 1992). Within this relational field, dynamics of interaction between different groups and organizations can contribute to processes of escalation, particularly when competition triggers a mechanism in which groups try to *outbid* one another in winning attention and support by taking more radical positions or by using more militant forms of action (Bosi and Davis 2017). Thereby, competitive relations between different groups and organizations within a movement result from the fact that they depend on scarce resources, including recruits and support from constituencies and bystander publics, and struggle over who will dominate the movement's political vision and direction (Della Porta 1995; Zwerman and Steinhoff 2005).

The *Radical flank mechanism* refers to the impacts of groups that adopt more militant positions or forms of action on broader non-violent movements. It can affect political leverage and resources in positive or negative ways, either discrediting the wider movement and legitimizing repression or generating attention and resources and inducing political elites to collaborate with moderate groups (Haines 1984; Gupta 2007; McCammon et al. 2015; Chenoweth and Schock 2015).

Finally, *violent outbidding* between different armed groups that compete for recruits and support from certain constituencies has been identified as a mechanism that can raise the level of violence or lead a group to shift towards more extreme forms of violence, such as violence against civilians or suicide bombings (Della Porta 1995, 2013; Bloom 2005; Crenshaw 1985, 1995, 2001; Alimi et al. 2015). By escalating their violent campaign, some groups think they can portray themselves as the most powerful force in a field of contenders, attract new recruits, and reinforce group cohesion (Crenshaw 1985). This was the case of social-revolutionary armed groups in the Italian and German context during the 1970s (Della Porta 1995).

As indicated by this list of mechanisms, the dynamics of interaction between different (armed and non-armed) groups and organizations are closely intertwined with the broader conflict and political processes in which they take place. In particular, patterns of inter-organizational competition are shaped by cycles of protest—during which movements expand, radicalize, decline, and restabilize (Tarrow 1989, 141–150). Della Porta (1995) and Tarrow (1989) suggest that competition intensifies especially during phases of declining mobilization, when participation decreases and public attention turns elsewhere, as movement organizations now compete for a shrinking pool of recruits and increasingly scarce resources. Intra-movement competition is, however, a constant in the movement life, being present in various phases of protest cycles, even if with different effects in terms of radicalization (Bosi and Davis 2017). Movement competition can fuel escalation, but also help de-escalation instead. Indeed, the field of movement organizations is transformed during protest cycles, and phases of escalation are often accompanied by the emergence of more exclusive structures and identities that exclude multiple membership and place higher demands on their members, thus further increasing competition (della Porta 2013; Tarrow 1989; Zald and McCarthy 1979). During phases of declining mobilization and radicalization, state repression has a significant impact on intra-movement competition by (often deliberately) exacerbating internal divisions that may lead to fragmentation and by imposing higher costs on participation and thus further increasing competitive pressure (Tarrow 1989; della Porta 2013). In this situation, radical flank effects can contribute not only to delegitimizing the wider oppositional movement but also to reducing the danger that repression backfires; that is, the risk of state violence, perceived as excessive and unfair, increases public support for challengers (Chenoweth and Schock 2015).

Inter-group competition does not necessarily result in political or violent outbidding. In general, competition is strongest between organizations which pursue similar goals and target the same constituent groups, inducing differentiation in goals and tactics by which groups seek to distinguish themselves from their rivals (McCarthy and Zald 1977, 1234; Zald and McCarthy 1979). The use of more intense and brutal forms of violence might increase sympathies and recruits in radical milieux, but at the same time it risks repelling broader audiences and provoking counter-attacks against their potential constituencies. Whether competition results in an increase in violence depends on the extent of social acceptability of certain forms of violence, which often is connected to government policies targeting broader communities and escalating the overall level of violence (Bloom 2005). When the adoption of certain violent tactics is rewarded due to widespread support for militant action within a certain constituency this will push armed groups to violently outbid each other in competing for support. Absent or decreasing social acceptance, in turn, can impede or reverse violent outbidding and facilitate de-escalation (Bloom 2005; de Fazio 2014; Gupta 2014). Armed groups may, however, rely on acceptance among smaller parts of a population or a movement (core followers), which can explain the adoption of extreme forms of action despite widespread disapproval. Even when relevant target audiences reward militancy, violent outbidding may not take place due to organizational factors, particular power balances, and mutual perceptions between different groups. In particular, outbidding may not occur when militant rivals are not seen as a threat to an organization's power and support among constituencies and when its leading members oppose it (Gupta 2014). In other words, in addition to social acceptance among an organization's constituencies, attitudes among leaders and rank-and-file members—the "internal audience"—can be a factor of escalation but also of moderation, facilitating or impeding dynamics of outbidding or de-escalation.

In many cases, the state is not the only adversary for oppositional movements. Counter-movements may emerge in reaction to successful campaigns of mobilization, hostile to the agenda of a social movement and seeking to undermine its influence (Meyer and Staggenborg 1996). Ensuing interactions between movements and counter-movements significantly shape the movements' forms of action and further trajectory, as they react and adapt to their adversary's tactics and arenas of mobilization. While counter-movements always affect a movement's chances of success, militant counter-movements can play a particularly important role in processes of escalation (Alimi et al. 2012; Della Porta 1995, 2013; Della Porta and Diani 1999). They seem to be powerful especially when pre-existing social boundaries become activated, such as in episodes of ethnic contention. Hostile encounters with counter-movement activists can entail a strong animosity, reinforcing radical identities and frames of interpretation and producing escalating spirals of revenge that push activists towards violent forms of action (Della Porta 1995, 2013).

Obviously, this relational arena is closely connected to interactions between social movements and state authorities and the police. Thereby, the role of movement–counter-movement interactions can vary. They may constitute initial sequences of radicalization that trigger shifts towards militancy, to be fueled later by dynamics of repression and escalation in which the state becomes the movement's primary adversary. Or counter-movements may emerge at later stages, in reaction to ongoing militant campaigns. One important mechanism of radicalization in this pattern is *object shift*, which, with reference to Tilly, can be defined as "a change in the relations between claimants and the objects of claim, as when an additional actor enters the scene and diverts attacks to it" (Alimi et al. 2012, 11). In other words, the emergence of counter-movements changes patterns of contentious campaigns as it "opens up a new front," which often results in a movement adopting new claims directed toward the counter-movement, diverting attention (and action) away from government authorities as the main adversary. For instance, in Italy, in the late 1960s and early 1970s, as Bosi writes, "right-wing violence took on a central role in the militarization of the conflict. To counter such violence, Left-wing organizations were forced to take self-defensive measures in order to be able to protect and support the students' and workers' struggles" (Alimi et al. 2015, 94).

Organizational Dynamics of Armed Groups

Organizational compartmentalization is a mechanism that often is at play in the evolution of armed groups, particularly clandestine organizations. Armed groups tend to take inspiration from the organizational repertoires that characterize the social movement families from which they develop, adapting them to a hostile context (Clemens 1996). This produces a different balance of hierarchical and network structures, as well as different functional internal divisions. In addition, collective structures tend to reflect the organizational size in terms of members and resources. At the same time, however, there is a very similar cross-type evolution towards compartmentalized structures. Faced with rising repression and declining support, armed groups often become more hierarchical, avoiding calls for large meetings and increasing instead the (formal) power of a few leaders. Like in organized crime, however, the aspiration to effective centralization and hierarchical control meets with a reality that is more centrifugal. First of all, clandestinity reduces the roles open to sympathizers and "legal" (rather than clandestine) militants, while the various cells become increasingly independent from each other but also difficult to control from above. In this process, the very difficulty in intervening in social conflicts increases the relevance of the military over the political organizational bodies, but also produces internal splits. Factions tend in fact to form and fight each other, in a never-ending process of splitting into ever tinier units and, sometimes, bloody internal purges (Crenshaw 1995).

Action militarization is a similar mechanism. When choosing targets and forms of action, strategies are assessed instrumentally but also constrained by group norms. Frequently, a shift from violence against property to violence against people, or from wounding to killing, produces tensions within armed groups. Similarly, creating victims among people considered as "innocent" (or at least, non-committed), a further step in the escalation process, leads to internal criticism, as does violence used internally to punish withdrawal or "betrayal." Suicide missions, even if effective, tend to be used only by a few armed groups in extremely radicalized conflicts, not even entering the realm of possibility for most of them. In general, however, there is a growing detachment from action aimed at propaganda to action oriented to mere organizational survival (della Porta 2013). As repression increases organizational isolation and the internal acceptance of a military vision of the conflict, the so-called repressive apparatuses (police, army, judges, and so on) become the main targets of armed groups. The logic of action grows then increasingly military and decreasingly political. In fact, the normative constraints against the most brutal forms of action are overcome given the search for a certain type of reputation as soldiers and heroes. In a vicious circle, however, this reputation starts to damage rather than advantage armed groups. Often, territorial control means attempting to force the population into certain types of behavior, as well as extracting resources, and this in turn reduces support (Malthaner 2011). More and more isolated, the armed groups tend to target the very social and political groups they previously tried to attract. The pace of the process interacts with the degree of radicalization of existing conflicts and its cultural effects in terms of tolerance for violence; but at the same time, it influences it.

These developments also interact with still another mechanism: *ideological encapsulation* (della Porta 2013). Political violence is normatively justified, as radical beliefs are at the same time preconditions and, especially, effects of violent actions. In general, narratives promoted by armed groups describe paths from a glorious past to a long decadence, and then to a rebirth. Manichaean visions, a sense of moral superiority, and essentializing thinking all develop in action. Justification follows escalation, which is only to a certain extent strategically planned. Rather than emerging from pre-existing ideologies, ideological radicalization interacts with state repression and competition with other (violent and non-violent) movement organizations.

The narratives initially adopted by armed groups are embedded in the broader cultures of the social movements they want to address. So, for example, the Italian Left stressed resistance and revolution; the Italian Right revived the Fascist spirit; ETA built upon the Basque mythology; Islamist groups went back to specific trends in the interpretation of religious texts (della Porta 1995, 2013). All types of armed groups, however, share a path towards a narrative that becomes less and less resonant with those of the social movements they initially wanted to influence. Adapting their discourse to the organizational compartmentalization and action militarization, they change the definition of the self from (political) activists to (effective) soldiers and then (defeated) martyrs. Moreover, self-justification becomes ever more elitist, depicting an image of heroic—if not successful—fighters. And in order to justify ever more cruel forms of action, armed groups construct an image of an absolute evil, whose cognitive borders grow ever broader.

In a vicious circle, the more isolated the armed groups become, the more they withdraw from attempts at bridging their frames with those of activists in potentially sympathetic environments, developing instead a self-contained and self-referential narrative. Initially justified instrumentally, as the only way out against a powerful adversary, violence then increasingly becomes an existential response to a hostile environment. Therefore the Marxist-Leninist, neo-fascist, exclusive nationalist, or Islamist-fundamentalist ideologies—which have been available for ages—are not the direct causes of waves of political violence. Rather, they are twisted and transformed through the process. Even the language changes, becoming less and less understandable from outside, as happened for instance with the Red Brigades (Della Porta 1995).

All armed groups eventually disband (Bosi and Della Porta 2015). De-escalation tends to happen through the reversal of the mechanisms of organizational compartmentalization, action militarization, and ideological encapsulation that we have observed. Many activists in armed groups refer to their disappointment in perceiving that their group was changing from its form under the original project. There is in fact a perception of failure of the compartmentalized model. The organization's own image is transformed, while arrests make relationships with other members increasingly impersonal. In the evolution of armed groups, the increasing brutality of their actions disgust their own members. Latent tensions explode in the face of some precipitating events. So, again in Italy, former supporters of armed groups recall episodes they consider particularly cruel (such as the killing of former members who had been accused of betrayal) as critical turning points (Bosi and Della Porta 2015). Similarly, repeated experiences with the death of comrades are emotional shocks. Among the organizational developments presented as being the most difficult to justify are internal vendettas and murders.

Conclusions

In sum, SMS approaches provide important heuristic tools for understanding the use of political violence as a form of militantism. In particular, they highlight the importance of political opportunities and threats, as well as of available material and symbolic resources in influencing the escalation and de-escalation processes during social and political conflicts. By moving from causation to causal mechanisms, the contentious politics approach points at a complex process involving intense interactions. Going beyond the dilemma between structures and agencies, a relational perspective allows understanding of the (endogenous and exogenous) dynamics at play in processes of escalation, but also of de-escalation. This perspective has also the potential of bridging various streams of empirical analysis and theoretical thinking on different forms of clandestine political violence (left-wing, right-wing, nationalist, or religious) that have until now proceeded quite separately from each other (della Porta 2013; Alimi et al. 2015) and to investigate qualitative shifts and transformations in the scale and form of political violence across space and time (Bosi and Malthaner 2015b). More cross-national and cross-types analysis of escalation and de-escalation are needed in order to assess the robustness of the causal mechanisms we have discussed in this chapter. Additionally, while reflections of different forms of political violence—such as clandestine political violence, riots, or civil wars—have proceeded in parallel to each other, some more interactions would be welcome in order to further develop our knowledge.

Notes

1. For an excellent history of social movement theories, see Buechler 2011.
2. *Espresso*, "A domanda rispondono," May, 19 1974: 23–5.

References

Alimi, Eitan Y., Lorenzo Bosi, and Chares Demetriou (2012) "Relational Dynamics and Processes of Radicalization: A Comparative Framework," *Mobilization: An International Journal*, 17(1): 7–26.

Alimi, Eitan Y., Chares Demetriou, and Lorenzo Bosi (2015) *The Dynamics of Radicalization: A Relational and Comparative Approach*. Oxford: Oxford University Press.

Bloom, Mia (2005) *Dying to Kill: The Allure of Suicide Terror*. New York: Columbia University Press.

Bosi, Lorenzo (2006) "The Dynamic of Social Movement Development: Northern Ireland's Civil Rights Movement in the 1960s," *Mobilization: An International Journal*, 11(1): 81–100.

Bosi, Lorenzo (2016a) "Incorporation and Democratization: The Long Term Process of Institutionalization of the Northern Ireland Civil Rights Movement," in Lorenzo Bosi,

Marco Giugni, and Katrin Uba (eds), *The Consequences of Social Movements: People, Policies and Institutions*. Cambridge: Cambridge University Press, 338–60.

Bosi, Lorenzo (2016b) "Social Movements and Interrelated Effects: The Process of Social Change in the Post-Movement Lives of Provisional IRA Volunteers," *Revista Internacional de Sociologia*, 74(4): 1–11.

Bosi, Lorenzo, and Donagh Davis (2017) "'What is to be Done?' Agency and the Causation of Transformative Events in Ireland's 1916 Rising and 1969 Long March," *Mobilization: An International Journal*, 22(2): 223–43.

Bosi, Lorenzo, and Donatella Della Porta (2015) "Patterns of Disengagement from Political Armed Activism: A Comparative Historical Sociology Analysis of Italy and Northern Ireland," in Ioannis Tellidis and Harmonie Toros (eds), *Researching Terrorism, Peace and Conflict Studies: Interaction, Synthesis and Opposition*. Abingdon: Routledge, 81–99.

Bosi, Lorenzo, and Marco Giugni (2012) "Political Violence Outcomes: A Contentious Politics Approach," *Mobilization: An International Journal*, 18(1): 85–98.

Bosi, Lorenzo, and Stefan Malthaner (2015a) "Political Violence," in Donatella Della Porta and Mario Diani (eds), *Oxford Handbook of Social Movements*. Oxford: Oxford University Press, 439–51.

Bosi, Lorenzo, and Stefan Malthaner (2015b) "Shifting Forms of Political Violence: A Socio-Spatial Relational Approach." Unpublished paper presented at the ASA General Conference, in Chicago.

Bosi, Lorenzo, Charles Demetriou, and Stefan Malthaner, eds (2014) *Dynamics of Political Violence: A Process-Oriented Perspective on Radicalization and the Escalation of Political Conflict*. Farnham: Ashgate.

Buechler, S. M. (2011) *Understanding Social Movements: Theories from the Classical Era to the Present*. London: Paradigm Publishers.

Chenoweth, Erica, and Kurt Schock (2015) "Do Contemporaneous Armed Challenges Affect the Outcomes of Mass Nonviolent Campaigns?," *Mobilization: An International Quarterly*, 20(4): 427–51.

Clemens, Elisabeth (1996) *The People's Lobby*. Chicago: University of Chicago Press.

Crenshaw, Martha (1985) "An Organizational Approach to the Analysis of Political Terrorism," *Orbis*, 29(3): 465–89.

Crenshaw, Martha (1995) "Thoughts on Relating Terrorism to Historical Contexts," in M. Crenshaw (ed.), *Terrorism in Context*. Pennsylvania: Pennsylvania State University Press, 3–24.

Crenshaw, Martha (2001) "Theories of Terrorism: Instrumental and Organizational Approaches," in D. Rappoport (ed.), *Inside Terrorist Organizations*, 2nd edn. London: Frank Cass, 13–31.

Crenshaw, Martha (2011) *Explaining Terrorism: Causes, Processes and Consequences*. Abingdon: Routledge.

Davenport, Christian (2014) *How Social Movements Die: Repression and Demobilization of the Republic of New Africa*. Cambridge: Cambridge University Press.

De Fazio, Gianluca (2014) "Intra-Movement Competition and Political Outbidding as a Mechanism of Radicalization in Northern Ireland, 1968–1969," in L. Bosi, C. Demetriou, and S. Malthaner (eds), *Dynamics of Political Violence: A Process-Oriented Perspective on Radicalization and the Escalation of Political Conflict*. Farnham/Burlington, VT: Ashgate, 115–36.

Della Porta, Donatella (1990) *Il terrorismo di sinistra*. Bologna: Il Mulino.

Della Porta, Donatella (1995) *Political Violence and the State*. Cambridge: Cambridge University Press.

Della Porta, Donatella (2013) *Clandestine Political Violence*. Cambridge: Cambridge University Press.

Della Porta, Donatella, and Mario Diani (1999) *Social Movements: An Introduction*. Oxford: Blackwell Publishers.

Della Porta, Donatella, and Herbert Reiter (1998) *Policing Protest: Control of Mass Demonstration in Western Democracies*. Minneapolis: University of Minnesota Press.

Della Porta, Donatella, and Sidney Tarrow (1986) "Unwanted Children: Political Violence and the Cycle of Protest in Italy, 1966–1973," *European Journal of Political Research*, 14: 607–32.

Diani, Mario (1992). "The Concept of Social Movements," *Sociological Review*, 40(1): 1–25.

Goodwin, Jeff (2001) *No Other Way Out: States and Revolutionary Movements, 1945–1991*. Cambridge: Cambridge University Press.

Gupta, Devashree (2007) "Selective Engagement and its Consequences: Lessons from British Policy Northern Ireland," *Comparative Politics*, 39(3): 331–51.

Gupta, Devrashee (2014) "The Limits of Radicalization: Escalation and Restraint in the South African Liberation Movement," in L. Bosi, C. Demetriou, and S. Malthaner (eds), *Dynamics of Political Violence: A Process-Oriented Perspective on Radicalization and the Escalation of Political Conflict*. Farnham/Burlington, VT: Ashgate, 137–68.

Hafez, Mohammed M. (2004) *Why Muslims Rebel: Repression and Resistance in the Islamic World*. Boulder, CO, and London: Lynne Rienner Publishers.

Haines, Herbert H. (1984) "Black Radicalization and the Funding of Civil Rights: 1957–1970," *Social Problems*, 32(1): 31–43.

Kriesi, Hanspeter, Ruud Koopmans, Jan Willem Dyvendak, and Marco G. Giugni (1995) *New Social Movements in Western Europe: A Comparative Perspective*. Minneapolis: University of Minnesota Press.

McAdam, Doug (1982) *Political Process and the Development of Black Insurgency, 1930—1970*. Chicago and London: University of Chicago Press.

McAdam, D., S. Tarrow, and C. Tilly (2001) *Dynamics of Contention*. New York: Cambridge University Press.

McCammon, Holly J., Erin M. Bergner, and Sandra C. Arch (2015) "'Are You One of Those Women?' Within-Movement Conflict, Radical Flank Effects, and Social Movement Political Outcomes," *Mobilization: An International Quarterly*, 20(2): 157–78.

McCarthy, John D., and Mayer N. Zald (1977) "Resource Mobilization and Social Movements: A Partial Theory," *American Journal of Sociology*, 82(6): 1212–41.

McCarthy, J., and M. Zald (1973) *The Trend of Social Movements in America: Professionalization and Resource Mobilization*. Morristown, NJ: General Learning Press.

McCauley, Clark, and Sophia Moskalenko (2008) "Mechanisms of Radicalization: Pathways toward Terrorism," *Terrorism and Political Violence*, 20: 415–33.

Malthaner, Stefan (2011) *Mobilizing the Faithful: The Relationship between Militant Islamist Groups and their Constituencies*. Frankfurt/New-York: Campus.

Meyer, David S., and Suzanne Staggenborg (1996) "Movements, Countermovements, and the Structure of Political Opportunity," *American Journal of Sociology*, 101(6): 1628–60.

Miller, M. (2012) *The Foundations of Modern Terrorism: State, Society and Dynamics of Political Violence*. Cambridge: Cambridge University Press.

Oberschall, Anthony (1978) "Theories of Social Conflict," *Annual Review of Sociology*, 1: 291–315.

Schwedler, Jillian (2004) "The Islah Party in Yemen: Political Opportunities and Coalition Building in a Transitional Polity," in Q. Wiktorowicz (ed.) *Islamic Activism: A Social Movement Approach*. Bloomington, IN: Indiana University Press, 205–30

Suh, Doowon (2011) "Institutionalizing Social Movements: The Dual Strategy of the Korean Women's Movement," *Sociological Quarterly*, 52: 442–71.

Tarrow, Sidney (1989) *Democracy and Disorder*. Oxford: Clarendon Press.

Tilly, C. (1978) *From Mobilization to Revolution*. Reading, MA: Addison-Wesley.

Tilly, C. (2003) *The Politics of Collective Violence*. Cambridge: Cambridge University Press.

Tilly, C., and S. Tarrow (2007) *Contentious Politics*. Boulder, CO: Paradigm Publishers.

White, H. (1992) *Identity and Control: A Structural Theory of Social Action*. Princeton: Princeton University Press.

White, R. W. (1989) "From Peaceful Protest to Guerrilla War: Micromobilization of the Provisional Irish Republican Army," *American Journal of Sociology*, 94(6): 1277–1302.

Wieviorka, Michel (1993) *The Making of Terrorism*. Chicago: University of Chicago Press.

Wiktorowicz, Q. (2004) "Islamic Activism and Social Movement Theory," in Q. Wiktorowicz (ed.), *Islamic Activism: A Social Movement Theory Approach*. Bloomington and Indianapolis: Indiana University Press, 1–33.

Zwerman, G., and P. Steinhoff (2005) "When Activists Ask for Trouble: State–Dissident Interactions and the New Left Cycle of Resistance in the United States and Japan," in C. Davenport, H. Johnston, and C. Mueller (eds), *Repression and Mobilization*. Minneapolis: University of Minnesota Press, 85–107.

Zwerman, G., P. G. Steinhoff, and D. della Porta (2000) "Disappearing Social Movements: Clandestinity in the Cycle of New Left Protest in the US, Japan, Germany and Italy," *Mobilization*, 5: 83–100.

CHAPTER 10

FORMAL APPROACHES TO THE STUDY OF TERRORISM

JACOB N. SHAPIRO

INTRODUCTION

THIS chapter reviews a number of important areas where formal game-theoretic approaches to the study of terrorism yield important insights. Such approaches have proven quite useful for understanding the strategic logic behind complex interactions in other settings. In the case of terrorism they help scholars work through what assumptions one must make for a given set of incentives to create a given pattern of behavior. They can also illuminate whether an observed pattern of outcomes is, or is not, sufficient to establish a hypothesis about how the world works. A good example, as I will discuss, is how game-theoretic approaches have helped explain why poverty might properly be considered a root cause of individual engagement in terrorism despite the fact that most terrorists are not poor.

There have been many excellent review pieces covering the formal literature on terrorism, including: Sandler and Arce (2003) who focus on applications to thinking about defensive resource allocation; Bueno de Mesquita (2008a) who analyzes developments in the political economy literature; Sandler and Siqueira (2009) who examine a range of developments in the post-9/11 wave of formal studies of terrorism; Carter (2012) who situates empirical studies in the context of theoretical models to which they speak; and Sandler (2014) who reviews significant empirical and theoretical findings focusing on the period from 2007 to 2014. Bueno de Mesquita (2013b) provides the most thorough existing review, outlining how different theoretical perspectives yield different interpretations of the data about root causes of terrorism and its political efficacy as well as summarizing the formal literature on allocation of counterterrorism resources. As these articles make clear there has been a proliferation of work in this field.

Instead of reviewing this large literature, I will highlight a series of empirical puzzles where formal theory is helpful.[1] Citations to the more complete set of work can be found in the review articles already mentioned.

The remainder of this chapter proceeds as follows. First, I define formal approaches and define the field of study, providing a bit of background on game theory. Second, I review a series of empirical puzzles that formal approaches have helped to illuminate. I conclude by discussing next steps for the formal literature.

Definition of Formal Approaches

This chapter defines formal approaches to the study of terrorism as research employing game-theoretic models to understand terrorism. For purposes of this chapter I roughly follow Hoffman (2006) and Bueno de Mesquita (2013b) by defining terrorism as violent action(s) that are:

1. carried out by a non-state actor (which can be an individual, an informal network, or a highly structured organization);
2. in furtherance of a political objective (which could include economic policy changes, religious freedom, new social regulations, etc.); and
3. designed to influence the political preferences of an audience not directly effected by the violence (i.e. to shift the broad population's views regarding the government's legitimacy).

Note that this definition includes a broad range of political violence, including much that happens in the context of other forms of conflict (e.g. insurgent group killings of suspected informers), but excludes certain kinds of criminal violence (e.g. assassinations of criminal gangs' members by rival gangs).

So what are game-theoretic models? They are an approach to mathematically representing strategic interactions that have proven useful in a broad range of applications for modeling situations where the outcome depends not only on the actions of a single party, but on those of others whose decisions impact the consequences of the first party's actions. Game-theoretic models are a subset of rational choice models. Rational choice models require that the analyst specify a mathematical function that the actor is trying to maximize, typically called a utility function. Behavior is predicted on the basis of what would maximize subjective expected utility (SEU); that is, the expected value of the function given what the actor believes and the uncertainty of the world.

What makes game-theoretic models different is the focus on equilibrium. Equilibrium is the situation in which all players are doing the best thing they can do (what is called best responding), under the assumption that others are doing so as well. Intuitively, the logic of equilibrium is that nobody can do any better given what everyone else is doing, and that is true for everyone. The equilibrium strategy of an actor is the rule that defines how they will play in equilibrium.

This is different to simple decision-theoretic utility maximization. A simple example can help clarify how. Suppose that there is a market where firm A holds a monopoly on widgets and is selling them at price P. There is a second firm, B, that could enter the market and profitably sell widgets at $P^* < P$ so that it would make a profit by entering the market (assume the difference between P^* and P is large enough so that entering is profitable even taking account of the drop in the market-clearing price given the increased supply). In a decision-theoretic setting firm B would obviously enter. But, suppose that firm A can profitably sell widgets at $P^{**} < P^*$ and that selling at P^{**} is not profitable for firm B. Then if firm B enters the market, firm A would simply undercut its prices. In a game-theoretic setting firm B would account for that reaction by A and thus optimally choose not to enter the market.

Despite deviations from SEU maximization observed in laboratory settings, and in some real-world decision-making as is well documented in behavioral economics, game-theoretic approaches turn out to be descriptively accurate for a large range of interactions, particularly high-stakes ones that people engage in repeatedly. Professional soccer players, bridge players, and top poker players, for example, play near-perfect equilibrium strategies in their normal work lives, in their case what are called minimax strategies where the player randomizes over different moves. But members of all three populations do no better than college students at playing such strategies in unfamiliar contexts (Levitt et al., 2010).[2] In summary, game theory has been used productively to analyze a wide range of economic and political activity where it is manifestly not a descriptively accurate representation of how decisions are made, yet none the less provides important insights.

Empirical Puzzles

Formal approaches are useful for helping make sense of a complex evidence base for five interesting questions:

1. How do economic conditions affect terrorism?
2. Why do some terrorist groups keep so many records while others keep none?
3. Why does counterterrorism spending seem so oddly allocated?
4. Why do opposition groups choose terrorism when it seldom succeeds? and
5. Why is bargaining with terrorists so rarely successful in ending conflict?

This section outlines how the formal literature helps makes sense of the data on each question, or how it illustrates the deficiencies of simplistic explanations. I exclude areas where most of the work has been empirical, such as the links between democracy and terrorism, neatly summarized in Chenoweth (2013), the predictors of domestic terrorism, reviewed by Sánchez-Cuenca and de la Calle (2009), or how social welfare provision affects terrorism, ably analyzed in Burgoon (2006).

How do Economic Conditions Affect Terrorism?

The most puzzling fact about the correlation between economic conditions and terrorism is that while there is modest evidence that poorer places seem to suffer more terrorism, there is strong evidence that terrorists themselves are rarely especially poor. On the first score a range of studies using cross-national data find a negative relationship between standard measures of economic performance and terrorism (Blomberg et al. 2004; Li and Schaub 2004; Drakos and Gofas 2006). The correlation between national-level measures and locality-specific conditions is sensitive to how the data are analyzed, however, and several scholars find no relationship once other factors are controlled for or different measures of terrorism are used (Krueger and Laitin 2008; Abadie 2006). Still, the broad consensus in the policy community is that poorer places suffer more terrorism.

On the second score, however, the evidence is fairly strong that terrorists themselves are not poor. Studying the biographies of participants in loosely organized Islamist networks conducting attacks in the US and Western Europe, what he calls "the Global Salafi Jihad," Sageman (2004) finds that many were well educated and, while often underemployed compared to their degrees, they were not particularly poor. Reconstructing the biographies of terrorists in Hamas and comparing them to the average Palestinian Berrebi (2007) finds they are not particularly poor and are, in fact, better educated than the average person in their community. Krueger and Maleckova (2003) provide similar results from comparing Hezbollah fighters to the average Lebanese.[3] Lee (2011) uses data from an anti-British political movement in the Bengal province of India in the first part of the twentieth century to show that both violent and non-violent political activists are drawn from the social and economic elite, but that among activists the terrorists are lower status and lower income.[4]

How do we reconcile these findings? The answer proposed in Bueno de Mesquita (2005b) is that terrorist groups care about their operatives' skill level and so choose the best of the available operatives. The paper models a three-way interaction between a government, a terrorist group, and a potential terrorist. People with low ability are more likely to volunteer, but are screened out. In the model government crackdowns have competing effects: they can decrease the probability that terrorism succeeds, thereby reducing recruitment, but they can also create grievances and harm the economy, thereby increasing recruitment. Put analogically, terrorists skim the cream and when the economy is bad there is a larger bucket of milk from which to skim.

A second answer, proposed in Bueno de Mesquita (2008b), is that as the economy gets better extremist factions tend to break off, thereby increasing violence. Inspired by models of ideological competition in normal politics, this paper analyzes a situation where terrorist factions form endogenously and choose levels of extremism to maximize their support among a population of potential terrorists. When the economy gets better, more moderate supporters leave first, shifting the distribution of potential terrorists in the extreme direction. The group becomes more extreme in response. If levels of violence are correlated with ideological extremism, then this dynamic could lead to increased violence from improved economic conditions.

Subsequent empirical work clearly supports the screening argument but is agnostic regarding the political one. Using data on all Palestinian suicide bombers from 2000 to 2005, Benmelech and Berrebi (2007) show that operatives with more education were given targets further inside Israel, i.e. harder targets, and that holding distance constant, they were more likely to succeed. Benmelech et al. (2012) followed this paper with a more direct test, showing that increases in unemployment lead to higher-quality terrorists (as measured by education and experience), as well as increased effectiveness in attacking higher-value targets.

Why do Some Terrorist Groups Keep So Many Records?

One of the striking facts about terrorist groups as organizations is that they demonstrate tremendous heterogeneity. At one end of the scale is the "leaderless resistance" model advocated by white supremacist intellectual Louis Beam. This approach minimizes the risk of law enforcement tracking down members by making no efforts whatsoever to coordinate actions across the movement. Instead ideologues provide guidance on the need for a struggle and on what types of actions should be taken, while making no efforts to conduct operations themselves. Those are left to the individual initiative of what Beam called "independent patriots." While this approach proved useful in keeping Beam out of prison, it was a near total failure as a method of accomplishing the political goal of fomenting widespread armed resistance against the US government. At the other end of the scale is the kind of highly bureaucratized structure used by terrorist organizations operating during the Iraqi civil war, particularly Al Qaeda in Iraq (AQI) (Shapiro 2013; Johnston et al. 2016). As hundreds of declassified documents show AQI had rigid salary rules, kept detailed expense reports, and generally followed what is known as an "M-form" design in which a given set of functional bureaux at the headquarters level is replicated below (in a firm among divisions, in AQI among regional commands).

One explanation for why some terrorist groups have to go to such lengths to manage their operatives is what are known as "agency problems." Agency problems arise when three conditions exist: (1) a leader, the principal, needs to delegate certain actions or decisions to an operative, or agent: (2) the principal can neither perfectly monitor the agent's actions, nor punish him with certainty when a transgression is identified; and (3) the agent's preferences are not aligned with the those of the principal. In the case of terrorists they may want to do more violence than leaders think is politically optimal, or may want to spend money differently.

Chai (1993) was the first to apply agency theory to terrorist organizations, focusing in on the challenges of managing potential defection. Building on that work Shapiro and Siegel (2007) study why terrorist organizations often make their operatives work on a shoestring when more money is available. They model a scenario where leaders delegate financial and logistical tasks to middlemen, but security concerns make it hard to monitor these agents. This is a problem because the middlemen may prefer to keep some of the funds entrusted to them for personal use. The model has two major implications. First, there are equilibria in which terrorist leaders may choose to underfund attacks compared to what they would do if they knew their agent was completely committed to the cause. Second, restricting a group's funds may have no effect until a critical level is reached, at which point leaders' resource constraints start to matter and they will no longer tolerate graft, leading to a discontinuous drop in attacks.

Shapiro (2013) looks at a slightly different agency problem in terrorist groups, that which emerges when terrorist leaders have to pass information to their operatives about what targets should be attacked in an uncertain environment, know that operatives prefer to attack slightly different targets than they do (motivated by examples of operatives being more extreme than leaders), and pay a security cost for passing the information on. In this setting terrorist leaders only share information with their operatives when the risks of doing so are low compared to the improvement in the choice of targets from doing so. An implication of the model is that communication within groups can break down as the difference between what leaders want to attack given the political environment and what operatives would like to target gets large. When that happens, or when the group's political theory of change does not demand precise use of violence, then they will adopt looser modes of organization.

Shapiro and Siegel (2012) tie agency problems in terrorist groups directly to record keeping. They model a situation where a terrorist leader delegates an attack and can observe whether it succeeds or not, but cannot see how hard the operative tasked with the attack tried. The leader then faces a choice between retaining the operative and firing them, where the threat of being fired motivates agents to try hard. The difference between this model and standard approaches is that the pool of operatives from which the leaders can hire is limited, so firing a committed operative who fails in one period means using someone who is likely to be less committed in the next period. In extremely uncertain environments this can be inefficient, even the best employees will fail often at the hardest tasks. The authors show that being able to condition firing decisions on longer performance histories can yield gains for leaders when the environment is highly uncertain by helping leaders avoid firing good operatives who got unlucky without compromising their incentives to work hard. Paperwork, in other words, can emerge in terrorist groups as a solution to the challenge of managing a limited employee pool conducting a highly challenging production task.

As Shapiro (2013) outlines in detail, terrorist groups vary tremendously in how they are organized as a result of how intense their agency problems are. Berman (2003) and Berman (2009) help make sense of some of that heterogeneity by linking agency problems to research on the economics of religion in order to explain why certain kinds of terrorist groups are particularly deadly. They show that using religion as an organizing principle provides a number of ways to reduce agency problems, including by screening out members who are less committed to the group and by running exclusive social service organizations, i.e. clubs, whose loss creates high opportunity costs for those who inform on fellow group members. Berman and Laitin (2008) apply this logic in a model in which terrorist groups can choose to attack highly valued targets using suicide attackers or less-valued ones using other methods. Government defenders will pay more for information that can prevent suicide attacks on high-value targets, thus making defection attractive to those who have information on such attacks. In their model only groups which are good at preventing defection, religiously motivated groups for example, will attack hard targets.

Why do Government CT Efforts Often Seem Inadequate or Overly Proactive?

Formal arguments have proven useful for understanding a range of odd facts about counterterrorism policy. One puzzle is that governments often tolerate long-running, low-intensity terrorist campaigns from groups they probably could wipe out. Inspired by the history of counterterrorism aid to countries in Southeast Asia, Felter (2005) provides a simple model in which states have to decide how much effort to put into counterterrorism efforts when they receive foreign aid linked to having a terrorism problem. He shows that under minimal conditions states always put in just enough counterterrorism effort to equate the net marginal costs from terrorism and the effort to combat it with the value of the aid received because of the terrorist problem. Bapat (2011) focuses more tightly on the moral hazard problem in which states facing a terrorism problem lose their aid once terrorism is done. He shows that while aid is not likely to be effective at disarming groups it can provide sufficient incentive to prevent governments from negotiation with them.

A second puzzle is that counterterrorism efforts are often overly focused on publicly observable measures. Bueno de Mesquita (2007) explains this phenomenon with a model in which a politician chooses between tactic-specific, observable counterterrorism measures (e.g. National Guard troops in Penn Station) and general unobservable methods (e.g. signals intelligence collection by the National Security Agency). Electoral pressures arising from the fact that citizens cannot trust that government is defending adequately against terrorism if they do not see the investment lead the government to allocate more resources to observable counterterrorism efforts than it should from a pure counterterrorism perspective. This problem is worse when terrorists have more targets to choose from because this means that the returns to unobservable investments by the government are higher.

A third puzzle is that governments often respond to the threat of terrorism in ways that seem counterproductive. One superficially counterproductive response is choosing levels of counterterrorism which trigger increased grievances in the present and can lead to larger attacks in the future and in other places. Rosendorff and Sandler (2004) show such behavior can happen in a two-player model when governments fear attacks and perceive low costs to suppression. Spaniel (2018) extends this analysis in a more subtle three-player model in which government uncertainty about support for terrorist groups leads to equilibria that feature both bluffing by weak groups and over-reaction by governments unsure whether they face a strong or weak group. A second such response is reducing the rights that governments would otherwise afford their citizens. Dragu (2011) shows that when anti-terrorism agencies pay a cost for trying to suppress terrorist activities they may prefer more civil liberties restrictions to less under a broad range of threat scenarios. Dragu (2017) studies the dynamic interaction between a terrorist group and a security agency in a two-period model. When the government responds to successful attacks by curtailing free speech protections, that creates *ex ante* incentives for the terrorist group to try harder in the first period.

Why do Opposition Groups Choose Terrorism in the First Place?

One enduring puzzle in the terrorism literature is why opposition political parties use terrorism in the first place given that it so rarely seems to help groups achieve their stated objectives. Abrahms (2006) looks at the record of twenty-eight groups designated as foreign terrorist organizations by the US State Department since 2001. He finds that only 7 percent achieve their stated policy goals. In subsequent work Abrahms (2012) shows that groups which predominantly use terrorism against civilians are less likely to gain concessions than groups that mostly use guerrilla tactics against state armed forces. Neither analysis, however, compares terrorist groups to other opposition political parties that choose not to use terrorism. Terrorism could be the best of a bad set of options given the popularity of these groups' goals.

This logic is implicit in Bueno de Mesquita (2013a), who presents a model which takes seriously the notion of opposition groups choosing between tactics. In the model a rebel leader chooses irregular conflict, conventional rebellion, or withdrawal, taking account of their prospects for mobilizing members of the population. That population chooses whether to join up or not by comparing the value of doing so, which depends on their probability of success, against what they can get by remaining civilians. In the model the leader chooses terrorism when doing so offers some small chance of achieving political goals but when they are insufficiently popular to raise a full rebel army. As the economy gets better terrorism can become more likely because the rebel leader goes from being able to mobilize enough people to wage a conventional civil war to only being able to get enough to attempt to change things through terrorism. Terrorism, in other words, is endogenously chosen as the solution to a bad political hand. It might therefore be expected to fail most of the time.

Other formal work suggests that terrorism can serve a broad range of purposes beyond seeking policy concessions consistent with groups' ideologies. In an early contribution on this score Kydd and Walter (2002) study the conditions under which terrorism can be used by extremist factions to derail peace processes, showing that it is most likely to succeed in doing so when moderates are strong. Introducing the idea that rebels might choose between terrorist tactics and guerrilla warfare to hold territory in response to state force allocation decisions Carter (2015) shows that under very general conditions capable states will focus on preventing guerrilla warfare, leading rebels to employ terrorist tactics.

In one of most comprehensive assessments of varied reasons to use terrorism Kydd and Walter (2006) examine different strategic logics for the tactic. They identify five strategies of terrorism depending on (a) the target of persuasion and (b) what that target is uncertain about. The strategy of attrition fits the intuition behind the observation that terrorism rarely works. It involves convincing a target government of the power of the terrorist group, thereby inducing concessions. But other strategies follow a different logic. The logic of outbidding, for example, is about convincing the terrorist's supporting population that the group is the most motivated and powerful representative of that population. Terrorism in such settings is not about wresting concessions from a government, it is about winning the political allegiance of a population. The fact that there are clear strategic uses of terrorism independent of direct concessions means that the motivating puzzle of terrorism's seemingly dismal record as a political tool is, well, less puzzling than it might at first appear.

Finally, a more recent series of papers focuses on the use of terrorism as a way of initiating a cycle of rebellion against a disfavored government. As far back as the late 1870s, would-be revolutionaries in Russia described terrorism as a method of "awakening the masses." In the 1970s, leftist groups in Europe and South America in the 1970s posited what they called an "action–reaction cycle" in which violence by anti-government groups would trigger excessive repression by the government, thereby revealing to people the true nature of their own government. That revelation would lead to the rebellion that anti-government groups thought would inevitably follow if the people only understood how truly awful their government was.

Recent papers modeling such dynamics probe exactly what kinds of learning might motivate terrorism. Baliga and Sjöström (2012) study a model in which two factions choose actions taking account of whether their actions are strategic complements (i.e. the more violence one uses the more value violence by the other has) or strategic substitutes (the more violence one uses the higher the returns to non-violence by the other). When actions are strategic complements an extremist faction can increase the risk of conflict by sending a public message that causes hawkish behavior by the less extreme faction. Bueno de Mesquita (2010) offers a different explanation for terrorism in a model in which revolutionary entrepreneurs, a "vanguard," use violence to overcome a collective action problem. The issue is that people want to participate if they know the regime will fall but are uncertain whether enough people will turn out to avoid failure. His model highlights the fact that vanguard violence can be explained as a rational response to the situation where other citizens only join the collective action if they see vanguard violence. And Carter (2016) develops a model in which different tactics provoke different kinds of state response and provides evidence that groups effectively choose attacks that avoid strong state responses against themselves but do provoke responses that harm civilians.

These models differ in the details but share the implication that the political movement which we observe to have changed the world will not necessarily be tied to the terrorist group that actually served as the vanguard. The empirical puzzle that terrorism rarely works may thus be explained by the possibility that many terrorist groups inspire other less extreme revolutionaries who then take credit for achieving the political change.

Why Is Bargaining with Terrorists So Difficult?

A final puzzle in the empirical record on terrorism is that it seems extremely hard to end terrorist conflicts. This is odd in the sense that these conflicts often continue long after any uncertainty about the relative power of the two sides is completely clear. In standard bargaining models conflict destroys value, and thus if there is no uncertainty about relative power then there is always a compromise that makes both sides better off than fighting.

Formal models of terrorist conflicts have provided several explanations for why getting to a compromise agreement is so difficult. Drawing inspiration from models of the commitment problem in settling civil wars (see e.g. Walter 1997) two recent papers Bapat (2005) and Bueno de Mesquita (2005a) examine the conditions under which governments and terrorists can credibly commit to honor a negotiated agreement. The basic issue is that once an agreement is reached, there is nothing to stop terrorists from extending their demands and asking for more, and similarly once terrorists make themselves known to the government there is nothing to stop it from imprisoning the groups' members and then going back on the agreed-to concessions. Bapat (2006) focuses on the decision to open negotiations, arguing that insurgent groups (or terrorist groups) will do so when they have proven their ability to survive the government's initial repressive efforts, thereby clarifying uncertainty about their durability, but before they become too powerful so that they no longer want to negotiate. Bueno de Mesquita (2005a) offers a different logic, one in which terrorists who are willing to negotiate have valuable knowledge for targeting other terrorists. Once the terrorists accept concessions they can withhold that information if the government reneges. Likewise, the government can similarly ramp up enforcement against the terrorists if they do not follow through on their part of the bargain. That mutual hold-up situation makes the bargain enforceable but it also means that spoilers have a window of opportunity to stymie bargains through violence by creating uncertainty about the value of the information provided by the faction which negotiates.

What is common across these models is the idea that both sides must have something to hold over the other to sustain a bargain. An implication of that perspective is that we should expect demobilization processes to look like the drawn-out process of the Northern Ireland peace process. There, almost two decades passed between the signature of the Good Friday Agreement in April 1998 and 2005 when the Provisional Irish Republican Army completed decommissioning its weapons, let alone August 2007 when the British Army formally suspended operations in Northern Ireland.

Conclusion

Over the last twenty years a rich literature has emerged applying formal approaches to the study of terrorism. Most models necessarily focus in on particular parts aspects of terrorism. Future models should move beyond this. Terrorism is just one tool in the would-be revolutionary's arsenal. Indeed, many terrorist groups start from non-violent political movements and the decision to use violence is taken after heated debate. Once violence is chosen subsequent questions emerge about its character and intensity and those are often taken in the context of a fundamentally different set of constraints than the opposition group faced before it engaged in violence. As Laitin and Shapiro (2007) highlight, and as many others have observed, this process means that many empirical and theoretical studies are taking an incorrect approach.

On the empirical side artificially dividing events into "terrorism" versus other kinds of violence seems untenable for quantitative studies. Most terrorism occurs in settings where other kinds of conflict are ongoing, as Findley and Young (2012) demonstrate. And terrorism is but one method that opposition political groups can use. This means that analyzing how terrorism responds to changes in economic or political conditions without assessing possible substitution into or out of other kinds of violence, or non-violent political activities, can lead to erroneous conclusions. Suppose, for example, that negative economic shocks lead to increased mobilization for violence. One might see less terrorism but more attacks on security forces when the economy suffers a shock. It would be wrong to conclude that such shocks reduced contestation, but looking only at terrorism could lead one to that conclusion.

On the theory side, I see two major gaps. First, as Bueno de Mesquita (2013b) points out, many extant formal models could be applied to all manner of conflict. Few have features which are unique to terrorism. Second, and more seriously, few models account for dynamics in an empirically sound way. Once political groups begin using violence that is labeled as "terrorism," the politics of making concessions to them may fundamentally change, as may their opportunities for a role in post-conflict governance or the ability of their members to successfully demobilize. All of those changes would impact the returns to making a deal to end the conflict compared to what the returns were before terrorism was used. Developing models that allow for the endogenous choice of tactics by opposition leaders and potential opposition members under realistic assumptions about how choices of tactics today constrain opportunities tomorrow is a challenge for the next generation of formal work.

Acknowledgments

I thank Ethan Bueno de Mesquita, David Siegel, Scott Tyson, and the editorial team for tremendously helpful feedback. I have benefitted tremendously from excellent review articles written by many colleagues, in particular Daniel Arce, David Carter, Ethan Bueno de Mesquita, Todd Sandler, and David Siegel. All errors are my own.

Notes

1. I do not e.g. review the rich literature that uses game theory to highlight the tradeoffs and complications of setting counterterrorism (CT) strategy. A fascinating series of papers draws on classic attacker–defender games to study optimal decision-making for CT resources. Key insights include: that defenders optimize by putting resources to defending targets the terrorists value most, whether or not those are of great interest to the defender (Powell 2007b); that making defensive allocations public can be beneficial by shifting terrorists to less valuable targets (Bier et al. 2007); that when the government has information on the vulnerability of targets which is not public, it may risk revealing information about their vulnerability by taking defensive actions (Powell 2007a); and that defenders can benefit by making public information about vulnerabilities when doing so enhances the efficiency of protective measures more than the ability of terrorists to identify previously unknown targets (Shapiro and Siegel 2010).
2. And many violations of SEU maximization in decision-theoretic settings disappear with experience (List 2003).
3. Note the comparison should probably be to the average Lebanese Shiite, since Hezbollah has a strong sectarian identity. As the Shia in Lebanon tend to be poorer than other groups, Krueger and Malečková's results almost surely underestimate how much better off the average terrorist is than the average member of their supporting population.
4. He also effectively summarizes an earlier wave of case-based evidence showing that terrorists in the 1960s and 1970s were generally wealthier than the populations from which they were recruited.

References

Abadie, Alberto (2006) "Poverty, Political Freedom, and the Roots of Terrorism," *American Economic Review (Papers and Proceedings)*, 96(2): 50–6.

Abrahms, Max (2006) "Why Terrorism does Not Work," *International Security*, 31: 42–78.

Abrahms, Max (2012) "The Political Effectiveness of Terrorism Revisited," *Comparative Political Studies*, 45(3): 366–93.

Baliga, Sandeep, and Tomas Sjöström (2012) "The Strategy of Manipulating Conflict," *American Economic Review*, 102(6): 2897–922.

Bapat, Navin (2005) "Insurgency and the Opening of Peace Processes," *Journal of Peace Research*, 42(6): 699–717.

Bapat, Navin (2006) "State Bargaining with Transnational Terrorist Groups," *International Studies Quarterly*, 50: 213–29.

Bapat, Navin (2011) "Transnational Terrorism, US Military Aid, and the Incentive to Misrepresent," *Journal of Peace Research*, 48(3): 303–18.

Benmelech, Efraim, and Claude Berrebi (2007) "Human Capital and the Productivity of Suicide Bombers," *Journal of Economic Perspectives*, 21(3): 223–38.

Benmelech, Efraim, Claude Berrebi, and Esteban Klor (2012) "Economic Conditions and the Quality of Suicide Terrorism," *Journal of Politics*, 74(1): 113–28.

Berman, Eli (2003) *Hamas, Taliban and the Jewish Underground*. Working Paper 10004. Cambridge, MA: NBER.

Berman, Eli (2009) *Radical, Religious, and Violent: The New Economics of Terrorism*. Cambridge, MA: MIT Press.

Berman, Eli, and David D. Laitin (2008) "Religion, Terrorism, and Public Goods: Testing the Club Model," *Journal of Public Economics*, 92(10): 1942–67.
Berrebi, Claude (2007) "Evidence about the Link between Education, Poverty and Terrorism among Palestinians," *Peace Economics, Peace Science, and Public Policy*, 13(1).
Bier, Vicki, Santiago Oliveros, and Larry Samuelson (2007) "Choosing What to Protect: Strategic Defensive Allocation Against an Unknown Attacker," *Journal of Public Economic Theory*, 9(4): 563–87.
Blomberg, S. Brock, Gregory D. Hess, and Akila Weerapana (2004) "Economic Conditions and Terrorism," *European Journal of Political Economy*, 20(2): 463–78.
Bueno de Mesquita, Ethan (2005a) "Conciliation, Counterterrorism, and Patterns of Terrorist Violence," *International Organization*, 59(1): 145–76.
Bueno de Mesquita, Ethan (2005b) "The Quality of Terror," *American Journal of Political Science*, 49(3): 515–30.
Bueno de Mesquita, Ethan (2007) "Politics and the Suboptimal Provision of Counterterror," *International Organization*, 61(1): 9–36.
Bueno de Mesquita, Ethan (2008a) "The Political Economy of Terrorism: A Selective Overview of Recent Work," *Political Economist*, 10(1): 1–12.
Bueno de Mesquita, Ethan (2008b) "Terrorist Factions," *Quarterly Journal of Political Science*, 3: 399–418.
Bueno de Mesquita, Ethan (2010) "Regime Change and Revolutionary Entrepreneurs," *American Political Science Review*, 104(3): 446–66.
Bueno de Mesquita, Ethan (2013a) "Rebel Tactics," *Journal of Political Economy*, 121(2): 323–57.
Bueno de Mesquita, Ethan (2013b) "Terrorism and Counterterrorism," in Walter Carlsnaes, Thomas Risse, and Beth A. Simmons (eds), *Handbook of International Relations*, 2nd edn. London: Sage, 635–55.
Burgoon, Brian (2006) "On Welfare and Terror," *Journal of Conflict Resolution*, 50: 176–203.
Carter, David B. (2012) "Terrorist Group and Government Interaction: Progress in Empirical Research," *Perspectives on Terrorism*, 6(4–5).
Carter, David B. (2015) "When Terrorism is Evidence of State Success: Securing the State Against Territorial Groups," *Oxford Economic Papers*, 67(1): 116–32.
Carter, David B. (2016) "Provocation and the Strategy of Terrorist and Guerrilla Attacks," *International Organization*, 70(1): 133–73.
Chai, Sun-Ki (1993) "An Organizational Economics Theory of Anti-Government Violence," *Comparative Politics*, 26(1): 99–110.
Chenoweth, Erica (2013) "Terrorism and Democracy," *Annual Review of Political Science*, 16: 355–78.
Dragu, Tiberu (2011) "Is there a Tradeoff between Security and Liberty? Executive Bias, Privacy Protection, and Terrorism Prevention," *American Political Science Review*, 105(1): 64–78.
Dragu, Tiberu (2017) "The Moral Hazard of Terrorism Prevention," *Journal of Politics*, 79(1): 223–36.
Drakos, Kostas, and Andreas Gofas (2006) "In Search of the Average Transnational Terrorist Attack Venue," *Defence and Peace Economics*, 17(2): 73–93.
Felter, Joseph H. (2005) "Aligning Incentives to Combat Terrorism," in Rohan Gunaratna (ed.), *Combating Terrorism (Regionalism and Regional Security)*. Singapore: Marshall Cavendish Academic, ch. 6.

Findley, Michael G., and Joseph K. Young (2012) "Terrorism and Civil War: A Spatial and Temporal Approach to a Conceptual Problem," *Perspectives on Politics*, 10(2): 285–305.

Hoffman, Bruce (2006) *Inside Terrorism*. New York: Columbia University Press.

Johnston, Patrick B., Jacob N. Shapiro, Howard J. Shatz, Benjamin Bahney, Danielle F. Jung, Patrick Ryan, and Jonathan Wallace (2016) *Foundations of the Islamic State: Management, Money, and Terror in Iraq, 2005–2010*. Washington, DC: RAND Corporation.

Krueger, Alan B., and David Laitin (2008) "Kto Kogo? A Cross-Country Study of the Origins and Targets of Terrorism," in Philip Keefer and Norman Loayza (eds), *Terrorism, Economic Development, and Political Openness*. Cambridge: Cambridge University Press, 148–73.

Krueger, Alan B., and Jitka Maleckova (2003) "Education, Poverty, and Terrorism: Is there a Causal Connection?," *Journal of Economic Perspectives*, 17(4): 119–44.

Kydd, Andrew H., and Barbara F. Walter (2002) "Sabotaging the Peace: The Politics of Extremist Violence," *International Organization*, 56(2): 263–96.

Kydd, Andrew H., and Barbara F. Walter (2006) "The Strategies of Terrorism," *International Security*, 31(1): 49–80.

Laitin, David D., and Jacob N. Shapiro (2007) "The Sources of Terrorism: An Ecological and Organizational Perspective," in Philip Keefer and Norman Loayza (eds), *Terrorism and Economic Development*. New York: Cambridge University Press.

Lee, Alexander (2011) "Who Becomes a Terrorist?," *World Politics*, 63(2): 203–45.

Levitt, Steven D., John A. List, and David Reiley (2010) "What Happens in the Field Stays in the Field: Professionals do Not Play Minimax in Laboratory Experiments," *Econometrica*, 78(4): 1413–34.

Li, Quan, and Drew Schaub (2004) "Economic Globalization and Transnational Terrorist Incidents: A Pooled Time Series Cross Sectional Analysis," *Journal of Conflict Resolution*, 48(2): 230–58.

List, John A. (2003) "Does Market Experience Eliminate Market Anomalies?," *Quarterly Journal of Economics*, 118(1): 41–71.

Powell, Robert (2007a) "Allocating Defensive Resources with Private Information about Vulnerability," *American Political Science Review*, 101(4): 799–809.

Powell, Robert (2007b) "Defending Against Terrorist Attacks with Limited Resources," *American Political Science Review*, 101(3): 527–41.

Rosendorff, Peter, and Todd Sandler (2004) "Too Much of a Good Thing? The Proactive Response Dilemma," *Journal of Conflict Resolution*, 48(4): 657–71.

Sageman, Marc (2004) *Understanding Terror Networks*. Philadelphia: University of Pennsylvania Press.

Sánchez-Cuenca, Ignacio, and Luis de la Calle (2009) "Domestic Terrorism: The Hidden Side of Political Violence," *Annual Review of Political Science*, 12: 31–49.

Sandler, Todd (2014) "The Analytical Study of Terrorism: Taking Stock," *Journal of Peace Research*, 51(2): 257–71.

Sandler, Todd, and Daniel G. Arce M. (2003) "Terrorism and Game Theory," *Simulation and Gaming*, 3(34): 319–37.

Sandler, Todd, and Kevin Siqueira (2009) "Games and Terrorism: Recent Development," *Simulation and Gaming*, 40(2): 164–92.

Shapiro, Jacob N. (2013) *The Terrorist's Dilemma: Managing Violent Covert Organizations*. Princeton: Princeton University Press.

Shapiro, Jacob N., and David A. Siegel (2007) "Underfunding in Terrorist Organizations," *International Studies Quarterly*, 51(2): 405–29.

Shapiro, Jacob N., and David A. Siegel (2010) "Is this Paper Dangerous? Balancing Secrecy and Openness in Counterterrorism," *Security Studies*, 19(1): 66–98.
Shapiro, Jacob N., and David A. Siegel (2012) "Moral Hazard, Discipline, and the Management of Terrorist Organizations," *World Politics*, 64(1): 39–78.
Spaniel, William (2018) "Rational Overreaction to Terrorism," *Journal of Conflict Resolution*.
Walter, Barbara (1997) "The Critical Barrier to Civil War Settlement," *International Organization*, 51(3): 335–64.

CHAPTER 11

SOCIOLOGICAL AND CRIMINOLOGICAL EXPLANATIONS OF TERRORISM

DAREN G. FISHER AND LAURA DUGAN

Introduction

Theory is an integral part of the scientific exploration of terrorism as it is any phenomenon. A well-defined and articulated theory enables prejudices, superstitions, and unquestioned assumptions to be exposed and criticized, surmounting foundational barriers for scientific progress (Benton and Craib 2010). As researchers approach "everything in the light of a preconceived theory" (Popper 1970, 52), they are better able to understand the strengths and weaknesses of their ideas and ask more precise research questions. Yet, theoretical explanations of terrorism in the social sciences have been lambasted for being weak. They are criticized for being regularly based on assumptions that were never made explicit nor empirically observable, let alone testable (Lum et al. 2006a; Morris 2015). Indeed, Crenshaw (1981, 380) lamented that "even the most persuasive of statements about terrorism are not cast in the form of testable propositions." This lack of focus is attributed in part to the dominance of historical and non-systematic explorations of terrorism by scholars and within society more broadly (Gupta 2008), when, instead, the terrorism studies should be guided by theoretical reasoning that can explain many different actions across a broad range of cultural and social settings. To remedy this, attempts have recently been made across different disciplines to apply existing theories of crime and social action to terrorism.

Much of the empirical work testing the dominant theories of terrorism has been advanced to dispel the notion that terrorism is random, or merely an expression of personal "deep emotional distress" (Gupta 2008, 14). Although it has long been held that background conditions may encourage resistance to a state through acts of terrorism (Crenshaw 1981), repeatable and systematically collected evidence is required to examine whether these theories have any empirical basis to explain and predict phenomena such as terrorism (Akers and Sellers 2008). Overcoming difficulties in capturing comparable observations across nations and socio-cultural contexts (Schmid and Jongman 1988; Silke 2001), the rise of systematically collected datasets has created opportunities to empirically evaluate a number of prominent criminological and sociological theories. With the parallel rise of advanced statistical methods that are also able to better account for theoretical assumptions (Nagin and Land 1993; Anselin 1995; Dugan 2011), opportunities to test theories of terrorism across a variety of social contexts have expanded markedly over the past few decades (see LaFree and Dugan 2015).

The availability of these datasets and advanced analytic techniques has helped scholars advance and refine many theories of terrorism and dispel some of the weaker ones. Indeed, politically popular and intuitively plausible theories derived from a limited number of biographies that argued that terrorism is driven by personal narcissism and paranoia (Morf 1970; Sageman 2004) are unsupported by today's higher empirical standards (Victoroff 2005). Tests of prominent criminological and sociological theories on the other hand have provided compelling evidence that terrorism may be a function of rational decision-making or societal pressures across numerous contexts (Morris 2015). Drawing upon long-standing empirical support explaining and predicting other forms of illicit behavior, many of these theories have been adapted to study terrorism, revealing important empirical insights. This chapter presents some of the major theoretical attempts to apply criminological and sociological theories to the study of terrorism, and evaluates some of the strengths and weaknesses of these efforts.

Criminological and Sociological Influences

Understanding and predicting terrorism is now a major political issue and a growing focus across many disciplines. Indeed, LaFree and Dugan (2015) note that this increased attention on terrorism by criminologists is evidenced by major increases in federal funding for terrorism research by the Department of Justice, terrorism articles published in reputable criminological journals, and papers submitted to prominent criminological conferences. This growing volume of empirical and theoretical attention is a relatively new phenomenon however as Lum et al. (2006b) report that prior to 2001 relatively little attention was paid to terrorism in most disciplines. Further, Silke (2001, 12) equated the quality of terrorism research prior to 2001 to "fast-food"—"quick, cheap, ready-to-hand, and nutritionally dubious." Including the initial boom in articles published in 2001 and 2002, only 3 percent of all terrorism articles used empirically-based research, with approximately 96 percent being "thought pieces" (Lum et al. 2006b, 8). As more scholars across disciplines began to study terrorism, they brought their disciplinary strengths to the topic. Criminologists and sociologists brought a greater empirical commitment to testing and understanding terrorism, with approximately 60 percent of articles in criminological journals containing "statistical analysis" (Silke 2001).

Yet criminology and sociology were latecomers to terrorism research. As recently as 2004, authors in volume 5 of *Sociology of Crime, Law and Deviance* (Deflem 2004) pointed out that sociologists and criminologists have offered very little theoretical guidance to explain terrorist violence (Black 2004; Rosenfeld 2004; Deflem 2004). Documenting theoretical approaches to terrorism since these conclusions, this chapter presents some of the distinct contributions that criminology and sociology have offered to better understand terrorism and the efforts to stop it.

This chapter presents some of the major theoretical contributions to terrorism research by sociologists and criminologists. We begin by introducing theories that have sought to explain the origins and motivations for terrorism. We then turn to the theoretical underpinnings that more directly inform efforts to prevent or stop terrorism. This chapter concludes by reviewing the insights uncovered by these theoretically driven empirical studies.

Theories on Terrorism Origins and Motivations

Sociologists and criminologists have introduced many theories to explain why people engage in particular behaviors. They have been advanced in order to "transform [the] mass of raw sensory data into understanding, explanations, and recipes for appropriate action" (Pfohl 1985, 9–10), and have been developed under the assumption that it is necessary to understand the reasons for engaging in terrorism in order to influence its occurrence. This section presents three theoretical attempts by criminologists and sociologists to understand why people choose to engage in terrorism.

Theories of Rational Choice and Deterrence

Theories arguing that human behavior is a function of rational decision-making have permeated the social sciences for centuries, and can be traced back beyond the seminal works of Beccaria (1764) and Bentham (1781). Rational choice theories assume that humans are self-interested beings with free will, and who seek to maximize pleasure and minimize pain. As such, individuals will engage in crime or other socially deviant behavior when the expected utility from committing this act is positive, meaning that the expected benefits are higher than the risks (Becker 1968). Often simplified as individuals basing decisions upon the likely costs and benefits, the nature and outcomes of these decisions vary greatly across situations and offenses (Clarke and Cornish 1985; Loewenstein 1996). Further, perceptions of risks and rewards are more important than objective probabilities of punishment for actual decision-making (Nagin 1998, 2013). As such, Simon (1982) famously argues that instead of assuming pure rationality, the social sciences should investigate "bounded rationality," whereby individuals settle for solutions that appear "good enough" instead of actually maximizing their utility (Berrebi 2009: 170).

Rational choice theory and its assumptions form the basis for many criminological theories including control, opportunity, and most commonly for terrorism, deterrence. Following the assumptions of rational choice, deterrence theory argues for an inverse relationship between the certainty, severity, and celerity of punishment and crime (Beccaria 1764). Deterrence can be general by preventing would-be offenders from offending; or it can be specific by stopping perpetrators from reoffending. At this point only a handful of studies have tested the effects of general deterrence on terrorism. General deterrence is typically measured as salient threats of punishment, which are historically and politically popular responses to terrorist threats. Yet, the deterrence perspective has been theoretically criticized for its inability to anticipate the different utility structures and reactions of terrorists (Victoroff 2005), which may explain its lack of empirical support. Dugan et al. (2005) looked for empirical evidence of general deterrence through the introduction of metal detectors and security personnel at airports and found a reduced risk for transportation-motivated hijackings, but none for terrorism-motivated hijackings. Other studies found outcomes that contradict the predictions of deterrence, as policies aimed to deter terrorism were associated with subsequent increases through possible backlash effects (LaFree et al. 2009; Carson 2014). Indeed, of the six UK strategies aimed at reducing political violence in Northern Ireland from 1969 to 1992, only Operation Motorman, which deployed more than 30,000 armed service personnel, was associated with a reduced risk of terrorist violence (LaFree et al. 2009).

While these findings contradict deterrence, they would be consistent with rational choice theory if increases in the certainty, severity, and celerity of punishment are less important to some potential terrorists than the expected benefits of violence. Dugan and Chenoweth (2012) explore this further in context of the Israeli–Palestinian conflict between 1987 and 2004. They assessed whether deterring terrorism through repression or rewarding abstinence through conciliation would have stronger reductions in Palestinian terrorism. The findings showed that across political periods repressive actions by Israel were either unrelated or related to increases in subsequent terrorism; and conciliatory actions were generally related to decreases in terrorism (Dugan and Chenoweth 2012). This suggests that governments can influence terrorist decision-making through more than just the presence or absence of punishment. Further, because the findings varied across different tactical periods, this study provides evidence that other social and political contextual factors influence terrorist decisions rather than just the nature of punishment and policy.

From the perspectives of rational choice theory, if terrorists behave rationally, knowledge of their beliefs and preferences should help us understand and better predict their behavior. However, if they are irrational—as some might argue—their behavior cannot be explained through rational choice models, and no systematic trends based on these models should be observed or sought. The presence of observable trends within the studies mentioned suggests at least some rational component to terrorist decision making, however more research is needed. These findings suggest that terrorism is a strategic choice based upon social conditions and perceived consequences, yet even strict deterrence theories could still hold value and tests of specific and perceptual deterrence have yet to be pursued.

Social Disorganization

Since the work of Quetelet (1831) and Guerry (1833) in the nineteenth century, it has been well understood that crime is not randomly distributed across space. Instead, scholars turned to social disorganization theories that posit that crime, like all other behavior, is a social product as opposed to a function of differences across people (Shaw 1930). In particular, the Chicago School of Social Ecology advanced theories of social disorganization to argue that the city, and more specifically, its slums, contained criminogenic forces that lead to crime (see Park 1936). Within these areas, social forces such as ethnic heterogeneity, poverty, and rapid urban growth are seen to undermine community ties, resulting in social disorganization, which subsequently leads to crime (Shaw 1930).

Criticized as being too subjective to be generalized to other societies and potentially suffering from ecological fallacies (Clinard 1957), many updated versions of this theory have since been offered (see Kasarda and Janowitz 1974; Kornhauser 1978; Sampson et al. 1997). Social disorganization theory now asserts that variation in informal social control at the community level explains variation in crime rates across neighborhoods (Kasarda and Janowitz 1974). Acting through the inability of communities to self-regulate, realize shared values, and solve commonly experienced problems (Kornhauser 1978; Sampson et al. 1997), contemporary theories of social disorganization posit that crime should be highest in communities that are unable to coordinate in these ways.

When applied to the study of terrorism, social disorganization theories predict that more terrorism should be perpetrated by those who live in communities characterized by population heterogeneity, residential instability, and concentrated disadvantage (Sampson et al. 1997; Sampson et al. 1999). LaFree and Bersani (2014) test this using data from the US between 1990 and 2011, and find that terrorism has an identifiable geographic pattern that is consistent with some of the predictions of social disorganization theory. While this pattern is necessary, it is insufficient to confidently conclude that social disorganization predicts terrorism, as the patterns are also consistent with the predictions of opportunity theories such as routine activities (Morris 2015). As terrorists may be drawn to symbolic targets within wealthy locations (LaFree and Bersani 2014), it is important to discern whether these sites are selected because of their ineffective informal social control mechanisms (social disorganization) or because they are perceived to be attractive targets (rational choice). Consequently, without knowing the underlying mechanisms that link location to terrorism, it remains to be seen which theoretical perspective drives this relationship.

LaFree and Bersani's (2014) findings do, however, suggest that both residential mobility and population heterogeneity also predicted the location of US terrorist attacks, partially addressing this mechanism problem. Coupled with the observation that terrorist attacks were less common in counties with high levels of concentrated disadvantage, however (LaFree and Bersani 2014), it does appear that any links between social disorganization and terrorism may differ from other crime types. Although providing more robust evidence for social disorganization theories, Freilich et al. (2015) acknowledge that population heterogeneity could also support backlash theories, highlighting the difficulty in empirically distinguishing this theoretical tradition from rival theories. Examining the impact of state instability as a proxy for social disorganization Fahey and LaFree (2015) also suggest that across nations social disorganization is associated with increased terrorism. Echoing some of these arguments, however, political instability as a cause for terrorism is consistent with theories other than social disorganization; and as Fahey and LaFree (2015) note, their macro approach was unable to distinguish between social disorganization and resource mobilization theories. Concordantly, while there is a growing body of empirical evidence suggesting that social disorganization is associated with terrorism, research thus far has yet to conclusively isolate the mechanisms that could drive the impact of social disorganization on terrorism.

Terrorism as a Reaction: Frustration Aggression, Relative Deprivation, and General Strain

Across the social sciences, a number of theories have argued that terrorism is a coping mechanism for dealing with grievances. Based upon the assumption that political violence violates socialized norms and that the decision to use it is precipitated by other factors (Noricks 2009), sociological theories such as the frustration-aggression theory and relative deprivation have been offered to explain why terrorism is a reaction to previous events or conditions. Following the dictum that "violence is always a response to frustration" (Davies 1973, 251), the frustration-aggression hypothesis holds that terrorism occurs when politically motivated people "reach a point of no return" (Victoroff 2005, 19). Indeed, Pape (2003) argues that terrorism and especially suicide terrorism are high-cost and only make strategic sense when it is perceived that there are no other viable options. Yet, the rarity of terrorism in contrast to the vast majority of people who live in frustrating conditions undermines its predictive ability. Further, many terrorists come from privileged backgrounds despite expressing the frustration of the marginalized (Krueger and Malečková 2003), making it unlikely that frustration alone explains their motivation. As such, terrorism as a reaction solely to frustration appears to have little empirical support as a stand-alone theory of terrorism.

Building upon Gurr's (1970) assertion that rebellions occur when people are overwhelmed by their life circumstances, relative deprivation theories argue that economic disparities cause terrorism. This theory further argues that when this deprivation is group-based, it could lead to collective actions that overtly question socially accepted beliefs and promote prejudice toward other groups (King and Taylor 2011). Such actions are exacerbated when globalization increases awareness of others' privilege, suggesting that both relative and absolute deprivation may increase terrorism among members of oppressed underclasses (King and Taylor 2011). Like frustration-aggression theory, little empirical evidence links absolute deprivation to terrorism (Krueger and Malečková 2003), and individual socio-economic variables have been found to be unrelated to extremist sentiments (Canetti and Pedahzur 2002). Consequently, at present it remains a fundamental issue for relative deprivation theories to predict whether members of a group will engage in terrorism and under what circumstances this will occur (King and Taylor 2011).

Following a parallel theoretical tradition and beginning with the work of Merton (1938), strain theories within criminology have been among the most prominent criminological theories of the past century. Strain theories argue that crime results from being structurally precluded from achieving the culturally approved means (e.g. a job and education) to gain culturally defined aspirations (e.g. the accumulation of wealth within the US) (Merton 1938). Reformulated and expanded under the banner of General Strain Theory (GST) by Agnew in 1992, strain theories now broadly hold that individuals are pressured into crime by the strains that they experience in their lives. Rather than being a function of utilitarian calculus, Agnew (1992, 2006) suggests that individuals engage in crime in reaction to the strains experienced from the loss of positive stimuli, the experience of negative stimuli, and the inability to achieve desired goals.

Addressing the inability for these theories to predict precisely who will and will not engage in criminal or terrorist coping, Agnew (2010, 131) argues that acts of terrorism are most likely to occur when people experience "collective strains" that are: high in magnitude, with civilians affected; unjust; and inflicted by substantially more powerful others. As "a range of factors condition" the effect of these strains, Agnew (2010, 131) argues that they will not always lead to terrorism, avoiding criticisms that GST would overpredict terrorism. Although this premise allows GST to avoid criticisms of this ilk, Agnew (2010, 149) notes that most empirical tests are too simplistic to adequately test GST as "they fail to measure the key dimensions of strain, including magnitude, injustice, and the nature of the source... these tests do not examine intervening mechanisms, the subjective interpretation of strain, or conditioning variables." Concordantly, until data are collected in a reliable manner that measure all of these factors, the empirical status of General Strain Theory for predicting terrorism will remain unknown.

Theories that Inform Efforts to Prevent or Stop Terrorism

A second set of theories ignores the underlying reasons for engaging in terrorism and instead addresses ways to stop it. Following this perspective, Clarke and Newman (2006) argue that, regardless of the reasons that an individual or a group would wish to attack a government, opportunities for terror should be identified and removed so that fewer attacks will succeed. Building upon the premise that it is important to understand how crime is distributed across time, place, events, and people (see Hindelang et al. 1978), these theories have prioritized understanding the patterns of terrorism in order to better prevent it.

Opportunity Theories

Under the broad banner of opportunity theories, sociologists and criminologists have theoretically attempted to explain the distribution of crime within societies to reduce episodes of crime and violence.[1] Within this theoretical domain the notion of opportunity is crucial, as crime can only occur when motivated offenders are exposed to potential targets in the absence of capable guardians (Cohen and Felson 1979). Although opportunities for crime are ubiquitous, those such as Clarke and Cornish (1985) have sought to identify the attributes of events, places, and times that are conducive or resistant to crime. For example, Lynch (2011) notes that crime is more likely when targets are visible, attractive, and accessible, which suggests that interventions that inhibit these characteristics could reduce the prevalence and the incidence of crime (Clarke 2003). Further, when we assume that offenders are rational actors, interventions that increase the potential costs, limit the potential benefits, reduce provocations, and reduce excuses should also limit the opportunities for crime (Clarke 2003). Although some argue that such interventions would only displace crime or lead criminals to adapt, consequently nullifying any changes in the overall crime rate, a growing body of research has found that crime does not displace, while the benefits of the intervention might diffuse to surrounding areas (Barr and Pease 1990; Guerette and Bowers 2009).

A specific strategy to reduce crime is situational crime prevention (SCP), which systematically analyzes the opportunities that terrorists exploit in order to block them (Clarke and Newman 2006). Clarke and Newman (2006) offer the following three steps for SCP. First, officials should identify and reinforce potential vulnerabilities and targets that could be exploited by terrorists. Second, they should anticipate likely adaptations to attacks as perpetrators attempt to circumvent reinforcements. Finally, all SCP measures must be implemented in partnership with both public and private agencies. Justified through such reasoning, Lynch (2011) observes an abundance of counterterrorism measures that have now been implemented in order to restrict terrorism opportunities in accordance with these three principles.

Despite the widespread application of SCP, it is unclear how well opportunity theories can prospectively predict the locations in time and space for terrorism, and whether their interventions have a detectable impact on the incidence of terrorism. When we examine sites of past attacks, it appears that opportunity theories adequately predict the locations for terrorism. For example, in 2013 the Boston Marathon was clearly an attractive target that would rank highly in one or more of the criteria suggested by Clarke and Newman (2006); and indeed, it was attacked. Yet, there are hundreds of thousands of events annually that would also be identified as by Clarke and Newman as attractive targets; and are untouched by terror. Only examining known terrorist incidents from this perspective however produces a high false positive rate (Dugan and Fisher 2015). As terrorism rarely occurs in some countries, it might take years before an attractive target is attacked, making it difficult to statistically conclude that prevention efforts are worthwhile (Lynch 2011). Indeed, this may be potentially responsible for the findings that the inclusion of metal detectors and security personnel at airports had no impact on terrorist-related hijackings observed by Dugan et al. (2005). Consequently, even though widespread policies following the priorities of these theories may not show an appreciable effect on terrorism at aggregated geographic levels, the implementation of SCP may still yield counterterrorism benefits for specific vulnerable places (Morris 2015).

Diffusion of Innovations

Many of these attempts to apply criminological theories to terrorists have focused upon the similarities between other forms of crime and terrorism. Despite these similarities, the sociological theory of diffusion of innovations relies upon one important difference—terrorists seek publicity while traditional criminals go to great lengths to avoid detection. The linkage between seeking publicity and diffusion of innovations is relatively straightforward. In actively seeking attention, terrorists often strategically orchestrate strikes to draw considerable publicity and make people aware of their broader grievances. By operating in the public sphere and engaging with the government, organizations strategically operate in ways that anticipate or even incite government responses to their actions. Concordantly, organizations innovate in order to adapt to changing policy environments or to anticipate government responses.

Such innovation might account for some of recent salient terrorist behaviors, such as public beheadings. Other tactics seemed to have a broader strategic goal. For example, McCauley (2006) shows that some terrorist organizations have adopted "jujitsu" tactics in order to elicit harsh responses from the targeted government in order to sabotage its legitimacy. Further, Benjamin and Simon (2005) claim that this was Bin Laden's intent on 9/11, provoking the US government to violently strike back against Muslims, creating new enemies of the US. Jackson (2005) explains that terrorist organizations are best able to adapt and survive when their tactical repertoire is broad, enabling them to survive interventions that would otherwise nullify their capabilities. This sort of adaptive response was apparent during the Palestinian Second Intifada after Israel built a security fence with checkpoints to impede suicide bombers (Jackson et al. 2007). Anticipating subsequent government responses, the Palestinians attacked the checkpoints directly, used women as bombers, and dressed militants in Israeli Defense Forces' uniforms (Jackson et al. 2007). Further, instead of relying exclusively on penetrating the checkpoints, they also began to deploy rockets from Gaza into nearby Israeli cities, to build special ladders that avoided triggering the sensors at the top of the fence, and dug a network of tunnels in order to smuggle weapons, people, and goods in and out of the West Bank and Gaza Strip (Jackson et al. 2007).

New tactical ideas like these must come from somewhere, and the diffusion of innovations theory offers a plausible mechanism for how these ideas spread (see Horowitz 2010). Jackson (2005) explains that organizations can learn new tactics through direct experience in the field, from formal research and development units, or vicariously through the highly publicized activities of other terrorist organizations. In his famous book, *Diffusion of Innovations*, rural sociologist Everett Rogers describes hundreds of innovation studies and introduces a theory of how the adoption of innovating technologies diffuses across cultures (Rogers 1962). Rogers (1962) characterizes the diffusion of innovation process with an S-shaped curve, which demonstrates the cumulative adoption over time. The early adopters are at the bottom, followed by the early and late majority adopters, and then finally the laggards, or those who are last to adopt a new innovation.

LaFree et al. (2015) show how three terrorist tactical innovations in the late twentieth century appeared to have diffused across organizations over time. In July 1968, the Popular Front for the Liberation of Palestine (PFLP) perpetrated the first politically motivated hijacking by diverting an El Al flight from its intended route to Tel Aviv, landing it in Algiers, and successfully demanding the release of all Palestinian prisoners (Hoffman 2006). After PFLP forced Israel to negotiate and consequently meet their demands, other terrorists began to hijack airplanes, resulting in increases in terrorist motivated aerial hijackings, suggesting that the innovation of aerial hijacking had diffused. LaFree et al. (2015) reaffirm this conclusion and similar ones for suicide attacks and attacks using chemical or biological weapons by presenting the cumulative number of organizations using those tactics over time (S-shaped curves). The shapes of those figures suggest that each tactical innovation is in different stages of the diffusion process, with suicide attacks having diffused more than the others. Aerial hijacking is likely in its later stages of the process and chemical and biological weapons are likely still only used by early adopters.

Conclusions

Since the observation that sociologists and criminologists have offered very little theoretical guidance for explaining terrorist violence (Black 2004; Rosenfeld 2004), many within these fields have sought to test how well sociological and criminological theories can predict and explain terrorism. Driven by the development of more advanced analytic techniques, it is clear that the empirical standard for studying terrorism has continued to climb since the observations of Silke (2001) and Lum et al. (2006a). This growing body of research has produced a number of important insights that have helped to further dispel and refine many of the intuitively popular explanations for terrorism. However, it is evident that the current state of criminological and sociological theory falls short of effectively predicting and explaining terrorism. Instead, they need to be refined by incorporating what is known about terrorism from other disciplines in order to better measure and predict terrorists' responses to theoretically based interventions. Thus, one of the primary challenges facing the next wave of research will be to address and meet many of the more nuanced theoretical needs. Further, other prominent theories in sociology and criminology have yet to be applied to terrorism but could provide important insight into understanding terrorist behavior.

This chapter also revealed a number of difficulties associated with understanding and measuring counterterrorism success. Probably the biggest challenge comes from the observation that the absence of terrorism cannot confirm counterterrorism success (Lynch 2011). Detecting the impact of interventions remains a methodological challenge in places where terrorism is a rare occurrence. Yet, we anticipate that things will improve as methodological tools continue to be developed by social and statistical scientists that will make it more feasible to more precisely test existing theories on terrorism. Still, research over this past decade has held strongly to theoretical and empirical rigor, promising great dividends for understanding terrorism and advancing the fields of sociology and criminology more broadly.

Note

1. These theories include situational crime prevention, crime prevention through environmental design, routine activity theory, defensible space theory, opportunity-lifestyle theory, and a host of other environmental criminology theories.

References

Agnew, Robert (1992) "Foundation for a General Strain Theory of Crime and Delinquency," *Criminology*, 30(1): 47–88.

Agnew, Robert (2006) *Pressured into Crime: An Overview of General Strain Theory*. Oxford: Oxford University Press.

Agnew, Robert (2010) "A General Strain Theory of Terrorism," *Theoretical Criminology*, 14(2): 131–53.

Akers, Ronald L., and Christine S. Sellers (2008) *Criminological Theories: Introduction, Evaluation, and Application*. Oxford: Oxford University Press.

Anselin, Luc (1995) "Local Indicators of Spatial Association—LISA," *Geographical Analysis*, 27: 93–115.

Barr, Robert, and Ken Pease (1990) "Crime Placement, Displacement, and Deflection," *Crime and Justice*, 12: 277–318.

Beccaria, Cesare (1764) *On Crimes and Punishments*. Indianapolis: Hackett Publishing Co.

Becker, Gary S. (1968) "Crime and Punishment: An Economic Approach," *Journal of Political Economy*, 76: 169–217.

Benjamin, Daniel, and Steven Simon (2005) *The Next Attack: The Failure of the War on Terror and a Strategy for Getting it Right*. New York: Henry Holt & Co.

Bentham, Jeremy (1781) *The Principles of Morals and Legislation*. Oxford: Clarendon Press.

Benton, Ted, and Ian Craib (2010) *Philosophy of Social Science: The Philosophical Foundations of Social Thought*. Basingstoke: Palgrave Macmillan.

Berrebi, Claude (2009) "The Economics of Terrorism and Counterterrorism: What Matters and is Rational-Choice Theory Helpful?," in Paul K. Davis and Kim Cragin (eds), *Social Science for Counterterrorism: Putting the Pieces Together*. Santa Monica, CA: RAND Corporation 151–208.

Black, Donald (2004) "Terrorism as Social Control," in M. Deflem (ed.), *Terrorism and Counter-Terrorism*, Criminological Perspectives Sociology of Crime, Law and Deviance, 5. Oxford: Elsevier, 9–18.

Canetti, Daphna, and Ami Pedahzur (2002) "The Effects of Contextual and Psychological Variables on Extreme Right-Wing Sentiments," *Social Behavior and Personality: An International Journal*, 30(4): 317–34.

Carson, Jennifer V. (2014) "Counterterrorism and Radical Eco-Groups: A Context for Exploring the Series Hazard Model," *Journal of Quantitative Criminology*, 30: 485–504.

Clarke, Ronald V. G. (2003) "'Situational' Crime Prevention," *Crime: Critical Concepts in Sociology*, 1(136): 276–88.

Clarke, Ronald V. G., and Derek B. Cornish (1985) "Modeling Offenders' Decisions: A Framework for Research and Policy," *Crime and Justice*, 6: 147–85.

Clarke, Ronald V. G. and Graeme R. Newman (2006) *Outsmarting the Terrorists*. London: Greenwood Publishing Group.

Clinard, Marshall B. (1957) *Sociology of Deviant Behavior*. New York: Rhinehart & Co.

Cohen, Lawrence E., and Marcus Felson (1979) "Social Change and Crime Rate Trends: A Routine Activity Approach," *American Sociological Review*, 44(4): 588–608.

Crenshaw, Martha (1981) "The Causes of Terrorism," *Comparative Politics*, 13(4): 379–99.

Davies, J. C. (1973) *Aggression, Violence, Revolution, and War*. In J. N. Knutsen (ed.), *Handbook of Political Psychology*. San Francisco: Jossey-Bass, 234–60.

Deflem, Mathieu (2004) "Introduction: Towards a Criminological Sociology of Terrorism and Counter-Terrorism," in M. Deflem (ed.), *Terrorism and Counter-Terrorism*. Sociology of Crime, Law and Deviance 5. Oxford: Elsevier, 1–6.

Dugan, Laura (2011) "The Series Hazard Model: An Alternative to Time Series for Event Data," *Journal of Quantitative Criminology*, 27: 379–402.

Dugan, Laura, and Erica Chenoweth (2012) "Moving beyond Deterrence: The Effectiveness of Raising the Expected Utility of Abstaining from Terrorism in Israel," *American Sociological Review*, 77(4): 597–624.

Dugan, Laura, and Daren Fisher (2015) "Strategic Responses to the Boston Marathon Bombing," Oxford Handbooks Online. Oxford: Oxford University Press, available at: <http://www.oxfordhandbooks.com/abstract/10.1093/oxfordhb/9780199935383.001.0001/oxfordhb-9780199935383-e-99?rskey=93X7qz&result=3>.

Dugan, Laura, Gary LaFree, and Alex R. Piquero (2005) "Testing a Rational Choice Model of Airline Hijackings," *Criminology*, 43: 1031–65.

Fahey, Susan, and Gary LaFree (2015) "Does Country-Level Social Disorganization Increase Terrorist Attacks?," *Terrorism and Political Violence*, 27(1): 81–111.

Freilich, Joshua D., Amy Adamczyk, Steven M. Chermak, Katharine A. Boyd, and William S. Parkin (2015) "Investigating the Applicability of Macro-Level Criminology Theory to Terrorism: A County-Level Analysis," *Journal of Quantitative Criminology*, 31(3): 383–411.

Guerette, Rob T., and Kate J. Bowers (2009) "Assessing the Extent of Crime Displacement and Diffusion of Benefits: A Review of Situational Crime Prevention Evaluations," *Criminology*, 47(4): 1331–68.

Guerry, A. M. (1833) *Essay on the Moral Statistics of France*, tr. V. W. Reinking. Lewiston, NY: Edwin Mellen Press.

Gupta, Dipak K. (2008) *Understanding Terrorism and Political Violence: The Life Cycle of Birth, Growth, Transformation, and Demise*. London: Routledge.

Gurr, T. (1970) *Why Men Rebel*. Princeton: Princeton University Press.

Hindelang, Michael J., Michael R. Gottfredson, and James Garofalo (1978) *Victims of Personal Crime: An Empirical Foundation for a Theory of Personal Victimization*. Cambridge: Ballinger.

Hoffman, Bruce (2006) *Inside Terrorism*. New York: Columbia University Press.

Horowitz, Michael C. (2010) "Nonstate Actors and the Diffusion of Innovations: The Case of Suicide Terrorism," *International Organizations*, 64: 33–64.

Jackson, Brian A. (2005) *Aptitude for Destruction*, i. *Organizational Learning in Terrorist Groups and its Implication for Combating Terrorism*. Santa Monica, CA. Rand Corporation.

Jackson, Brian A., Peter Chalk, R. Kim Cragin, Bruce Newsome, John V. Parachini, William Rosenau, Erin M. Simpson, Melanie Sisson, and Donald Temple (2007) *Breaching the Fortress Wall Understanding Terrorist Efforts to Overcome Defensive Technologies*. Santa Monica, CA: RAND Corporation.

Kasarda, John D., and Morris Janowitz (1974) "Community Attachment in Mass Society," *American Sociological Review*, 39(3): 328–39.

King, Michael, and Donald M. Taylor (2011) "The Radicalization of Homegrown Jihadists: A Review of Theoretical Models and Social Psychological Evidence," *Terrorism and Political Violence*, 23(4): 602–22.

Kornhauser, Ruth Rosner (1978) *Social Sources of Delinquency: An Appraisal of Analytic Models*. Chicago: University of Chicago Press.

Krueger, Alan B., and Jitka Malečková (2003) "Education, Poverty and Terrorism: Is there a Causal Connection?," *Journal of Economic Perspectives*, 17(4): 119–44.

LaFree, Gary, and Bianca E. Bersani (2014) "County-Level Correlates of Terrorist Attacks in the United States," *Criminology and Public Policy*, 13(3): 455–81.

LaFree, Gary, and Laura Dugan (2015) "How has Criminology Contributed to the Study of Terrorism since 9/11?," in M. Deflem (ed.), *Terrorism and Counterterrorism Today*. Sociology of Crime, Law and Deviance, 20. Oxford: Elsevier, 1–23.

LaFree, Gary, Laura Dugan, and Raven Korte (2009) "The Impact of British Counterterrorist Strategies on Political Violence in Northern Ireland: Comparing Deterrence and Backlash Models," *Criminology*, 47: 17–45.

LaFree, Gary, Laura Dugan, and Erin Miller (2015) *Putting Terrorism in Context: Lessons from the Global Terrorism Database*. London: Routledge.

Loewenstein, George (1996) "Out of Control: Visceral Influences on Behavior," *Organizational Behavior and Human Decision Processes*, 65(3): 272–92.

Lum, Cynthia, Leslie W. Kennedy, and Alison Sherley (2006a) "Are Counter-Terrorism Strategies Effective? The Results of the Campbell Systematic Review on Counter-Terrorism Evaluation Research," *Journal of Experimental Criminology*, 2(4): 489–516.

Lum, Cynthia, Leslie W. Kennedy, and Alison Sherley (2006b) "The Effectiveness of Counter-Terrorism Strategies," *Campbell Systematic Reviews*, 2: 1–50.

Lynch, James P. (2011) "Implications of Opportunity Theory for Combating Terrorism," in B. Forst, J. Greene, and J. Lynch (eds), *Criminologists on Terrorism and Homeland Security*. Cambridge: Cambridge University Press, 151–82.

McCauley, Clark (2006) "Jujitsu Politics: Terrorism and Responses to Terrorism," in P. R. Kimmel and C. E. Stout (eds), *Collateral Damage: The Psychological Consequences of American's War on Terrorism*. Westport, CT: Praeger Publishers, 45–65.

Merton, Robert K. (1938) "Social Structure and Anomie," *American Sociological Review*, 3(5): 672–82.

Morf, Gustav (1970) *Terror in Quebec: Case Studies of the FLQ*. Toronto: Irwin.

Morris, Nancy A. (2015) "Target Suitability and Terrorism Events at Places," *Criminology and Public Policy*, 14: 417–26.

Nagin, Daniel S. (1998) "Criminal Deterrence Research at the Outset of the Twenty-First Century," *Crime and Justice*, 23: 1–42.

Nagin, Daniel S. (2013) "Deterrence: A Review of the Evidence by a Criminologist for Economists," *Annual Review of Economics*, 5(1): 83–105.

Nagin, Daniel S., and Kenneth C. Land (1993) "Age, Criminal Careers, and Population Heterogeneity: Specification and Estimation of a Nonparametric, Mixed Poisson Model," *Criminology*, 31: 327–62.

Noricks, Darcy M. E. (2009) "The Root Causes of Terrorism," in *Social Science for Counter-Terrorism: Putting the Pieces Together*. Santa Monica, CA: RAND, 11–68.

Pape, Robert A. (2003) "The Strategic Logic of Suicide Terrorism," *American Political Science Review*, 97(3): 343–61.

Park, Robert E. (1936) "Succession, an Ecological Concept," *American Sociological Review*, 1(2): 171–9.

Pfohl, Stephen J. (1985) *Images of Deviance and Social Control: A Sociological History*. New York: McGraw Hill.

Popper, Karl R. (1970) *Normal Science and its Dangers*. Cambridge: Cambridge University Press.

Quetelet, A. (1831) *Research on the Propensity for Crime at Different Ages*, tr. S. F. Sylvester. Cincinnati, OH: Anderson.

Rogers, Everett M. (2005) *Diffusion of Innovations*, 5th edn. New York: Free Press; 1st publ. 1962.

Rosenfeld, Richard (2004) "Terrorism and Criminology," in M. Deflem (ed.), *Terrorism and Counter-Terrorism*. Sociology of Crime, Law and Deviance, 5. Oxford: Elsevier, 19–32.

Sageman, Marc (2004) *Understanding Terror Networks*. Philadelphia: University of Pennsylvania Press.

Sampson, Robert J., Jeffrey D. Morenoff, and Felton Earls (1999) "Beyond Social Capital: Spatial Dynamics of Collective Efficacy for Children," *American Sociological Review*, 64(5): 633–60.

Sampson, Robert J., Stephen W. Raudenbush, and Felton Earls (1997) "Neighborhoods and Violent Crime: A Multilevel Study of Collective Efficacy," *Science*, 277(5328): 918–24.

Schmid, Alex, and Albert Jongman (1988) *Political Terrorism: A Research Guide to Concepts, Theories, Databases, and Literature*. New Brunswick, NJ: Transaction Books.

Shaw, Clifford (1930) *The Jack-Roller*. Chicago: University of Chicago Press.

Silke, Andrew (2001) "The Devil you Know: Continuing Problems with Research on Terrorism," *Terrorism and Political Violence*, 13(4): 1–14.

Simon, Herbert Alexander (1982) *Models of Bounded Rationality: Empirically Grounded Economic Reason*. Boston: MIT Press.

Victoroff, Jeff (2005) "The Mind of the Terrorist: A Review and Critique of Psychological Approaches," *Journal of Conflict Resolution*, 49(1): 3–42.

CHAPTER 12

CULTURAL AND ANTHROPOLOGICAL APPROACHES TO THE STUDY OF TERRORISM

SINIŠA MALEŠEVIĆ

INTRODUCTION

CULTURE features prominently in the common-sense understandings of terrorism. From journalistic accounts to pub discussions terrorist acts are regularly interpreted invoking such cultural parameters as "wars of religions," "clash of cultures," or "the struggle of civilizations." A more elaborate exposition of such views is present in academia too: from Spengler (1918) and Toynbee (1950) to Huntington (1996) and Juergensmeyer (2003) scholars have identified incompatible cultural values as the primary cause of violence in the world. Nevertheless, much of contemporary anthropological and sociological scholarship is deeply suspicious of such unreflective culture-centered accounts. There is an emerging consensus among the analysts of terrorism that this phenomenon is rarely if ever caused by the antagonistic worldviews and that its causes are multiple and varied (Vertigans 2011; Kalyvas 2006, 2004; Sageman 2004, 2011). However, none of this is to say that culture does not play a significant role in terrorist acts. On the contrary if one moves away from the clichéd views of violence and culture it is possible to identify how exactly cultural processes shape terrorist activities and vice versa. This chapter explores the strengths and weaknesses of the cultural and anthropological perspectives on terrorism. The first part provides a brief overview of the three dominant approaches. The second part offers an assessment of these three perspectives while the last part sketches an alternative, historically grounded, sociological interpretation of terrorism.

Three Cultural Views of Terrorism

All cultural interpretations see terrorism as a culturally mediated and socially constructed phenomenon. However, there is no agreement as to how culture shapes terrorist acts nor how this phenomenon is constructed and reproduced. Hence some emphasize the normative underpinning of social behavior, others focus on the situational logic of violence while the third group insists on the flexible and contested character of discourses and narratives that shape discussions about terrorism. Among the many culturalist perspectives on terrorism three approaches have dominated recent debates: neo-Durkhemianism, symbolic interactionism, and post-structuralism.

Neo-Durkhemianism

Contemporary neo-Durkhemianism is rooted in the classical concepts of group cohesion and solidarity associated with Emile Durkheim's distinction between mechanical and organic solidarity. In a nutshell Durkheim (1997) [1893] argued that all social orders congregate around shared values although they differ in their social structure. Hence, he associated traditional societies with the mechanical solidarity that was mostly based on simple in-group similarity. In contrast modern societies were understood to be characterized by the complex systems of interdependence, that is, organic solidarity. For Durkheim violence, including the sudden proliferation of terrorist acts, is more likely to emerge in periods when societies undergo transition from the mechanical towards the organic forms of solidarity (i.e. the temporary state of *anomie*).

This norm-centered view of social reality has been developed further by the neo-Durkhemian perspectives on organized violence and terrorism. In particular, scholars such as Jeffrey Alexander (2011, 2007, 2004a, 2004b), Philip Smith (2008, 2005), and Neil Smelser (2007) have all articulated sophisticated cultural theories of terrorism and other forms of violence. While deeply grounded in Durkhemian tradition these scholars offer more nuanced and less determinist cultural explanations of terrorism. This perspective shifts the focus from material events towards the collective understanding of such events. In other words, for the neo-Durkhemians terrorism is first and foremost a cultural event aimed at provoking, challenging, or reaffirming established normative universes. The violence generated in the terrorist act is aimed at undermining or establishing particular understandings of social reality and attaining specific collective meanings. For Alexander (2011, 2004a) and Smith (2008, 2005) terrorism does not engender social action by itself. Instead all political violence entails the presence of cultural codes and narratives that are necessary to make collective sense of the material event. Hence without the cultural framing, the violent acts are unlikely to trigger coherent and meaningful social responses. In Alexander's understanding, terrorist activities represent a form of a communication that involves perpetrators, victims, and bystanders. Hence the aftermath of any terrorist attack generates an abundance of interpretative frameworks that are intended to make a sense of the violent event. Although terrorism is now firmly associated with traumatic social situations, Alexander (2011, 2007) insists that violent terrorist events such as 9/11, the 2004 Madrid train bombings, or the 2005 London metro and bus attacks could not produce traumatic responses by themselves. In Alexander's view violence requires a degree of cultural framing and even the most devastating terrorist incidents cannot produce collective trauma without cultural mediation. In his own words: "It is the meanings that provide the sense of shock and fear, not the events in themselves." In this context Alexander (2004b, 88) departs from the traditional understandings that see terrorism as a political strategy and argues that terrorist acts represent a mode of post-political action as they indicate "the end of political possibilities." Differently stated, for the neo-Durkhemians terrorism is a performative act aimed at generating symbolic communication. For Alexander (2004b, 88) the focus here is on "thinking of its violence less in physical and instrumental terms than as a particularly gruesome kind of symbolic action in a complex performative field." Neo-Durkhemianism understands terrorism as a type of cultural and political performance that utilizes symbolic events, cultural scripts, social drama, and acts of martyrdom to reach diverse and large audiences. In this context it is central that this social drama involves clearly defined scripts with the binary representations of the main agents: "Good scripts must be agonistic, coding actors into the binaries of good and evil and narrating a plot that has beguiling beginnings, ambiguous middles and cathartic ends" (Alexander 2007, 7). For Smith (2005, 27) these binary descriptions of actors also underpin the wider narratives that distinguish rational from irrational, sacred from profane, and friend from the enemy. These narrative structures range from mundane, tragic, romantic, to apocalyptic, whereby the apocalyptic framing is identified as "the most efficient at generating and legitimising massive society-wide sacrifice." Thus, the terrorist incidents generate different dramaturgical scripts, all of which require cultural coding. For example, both 9/11 and the 2004 Madrid train bombings involved socially arbitrated framing of the key events and agents—the American and Spanish government and the mass media portrayed Al Qaeda as a morally degraded group of fanatical individuals who are irrational brutes that lack any social conscience. In contrast Al Qaeda leaders depicted American and European governments as selfish, power-hungry, and hypocritical groups that consistently break the moral norms that they advocate and, in this process, maintain injustice and inequality in the Middle East and the wider world. In Alexander's view the two conflicting performative narratives have been rather effective in producing and maintaining social cohesion among their respective publics. The apocalyptic narratives that emerge in the wake of terrorist attacks tend to generate what Alexander calls "purification after pollution." Hence rather than weakening society-wide group bonds terrorist events foster greater social cohesion: "After 9/11, the national community experienced and interpreted itself as united by feeling, marked by the loving kindness displayed among persons who once had only been friends, and by the civility and solicitude among those who once merely had been strangers" (Alexander 2004b, 100). Neil Smelser (2007) makes a similar point but focuses more on the perpetuators of violent acts. In his view terrorism is characterized by the radical visions of the present and future. He argues that terrorist narratives should be taken seriously as they provide judgments on the current state of the world, pinpoint the sources of injustices, and single out those that they deem to be responsible for existing inequality. Furthermore, these radical vistas offer visions of the better, future, world and provide justification for the use of violence to attain these radical visions. Similarly, Smelser (2007, 87–8), just as Alexander, emphasizes the mutually exclusive cultural binaries that underpin the terrorist's interpretations of the social reality involving "polarisation into systems of good and evil, deification and demonization. It is this package of beliefs that commands the moral engagement of terrorists in the cause."

Symbolic Interactionism

In contrast to the neo-Durkhemian interpretations that see culture as the master explanatory frame, symbolic interactionists understand culture through the prism of changing perceptions of social reality. Simply put, whereas neo-Durkhemians emphasize differences in shared value systems and beliefs, symbolic interactionism stands on the position that individuals create meanings through communication and interaction with others. Hence while neo-Durkhemians center their attention on shared norms, interactionists focus on the micro-world of daily interactions and changing "definitions of situation." However, symbolic interactionists are also culturalists in a sense that their explanations downplay economic, political, and military factors at the expense of ideas, symbols, and values. Thus, for interactionists terrorism is always much more of a cultural than a political or economic phenomenon. While recognizing the strategic dimensions of terrorist activity they emphasize the changing collective interpretations of reality. In this context Michael Blain (2009, 13–14) understands terrorism as "a mode of power and subjection by means of victimage ritual." More specifically he argues that terrorism entails the presence of symbolic systems that generate and perpetuate particular meanings:

> it is in the play of associated signifiers that meanings and interpretations are constituted. Symbols systems are magical because they make it possible for actors to use them to rhetorically influence, incite, and provoke others to engage in collective action. For example, the constant linking of "Islamic" and "terrorism" by a powerful figure such as a US President can provoke auditors to engage and applaud bombing actors categorized as Islamic terrorists.

In a similar way Constanza and Kilburn (2005) analyze the use of cultural resources such as "moral panic" and "symbolic security" as frames through which social reality becomes redefined. They point out that collective perceptions regularly trump material realities as security policies are shaped less by the actual terrorist threats and much more by the collective definitions of what might constitute a potential security threat.

Randall Collins (2008, 2004) has developed the most influential interactionist model of terrorism. Building on his micro-sociological theory of violence which explores violent situations as "set of pathways around confrontational tension and fear," Collins argues that terrorism necessitates the presence of unique emotional social dynamics. In his view humans are not wired for violence and, as individuals, are largely incompetent at violence. Moreover, violent acts usually engender emotional tension and anxieties. Hence to circumvent these emotional discomforts it is crucial to engage in collective action that will foster transformation of fear and tension into emotional energy. In his own words: "Successful violence battens on confrontational tension/fear as one side appropriates the emotional rhythm as dominator and the other gets caught in it as victim" (Collins 2008, 19). Hence the use of violence entails changed group dynamics. Since individuals are not good at violence they require the presence of others who all pool their individual emotional energies into the collective interactional ritual—something that Collins (2004) terms "the interactional ritual chain." In the context of terrorism this means that not everybody can be a terrorist. Instead to engage in terrorist violence one has to find a way to bypass "confrontational tension/fear" and forge new interactional rituals to justify to oneself and the wider group he involvement in violent interactions.

In Collins's view terrorism requires effective organizations but even more important is the development of distinct interactional dynamics. In this context he distinguishes between the two main types of terrorist activity: the individual, lone wolf, terrorists and the more common collective violent enterprise. The main issue for individual acts of terrorism is how to navigate the tension/fear pathways without collective interaction and support. Hence professional assassins or individual suicide bombers must develop their own rituals and practices that in some ways mimic group interaction. For example, both suicide bombers and assassins tend to engage in elaborate routine practices focused on the preparation of their violent acts. They regularly spend a considerable amount of time on very standardized and routinized practices that help them disengage from thinking about the impending violent event. By focusing on the minute details of the terrorist act an individual establishes a degree of emotional stability and also navigates the potential presence of confrontational tension/fear. According to Collins (2008) this helps explain the high representation of university graduates and other middle-class individuals among suicide bombers. Since these individuals are usually uncomfortable with the use of violence they can avoid seeing the bloody consequences of their actions by refocusing their attention on daily routine and by pretending that they are not involved in face-to-face killings. The other, more common, forms of terrorism such as kidnappings, hijackings, hostage-taking, and violent group attacks involve direct collective interactions and as such rely on established ritual interactional chains. In all these cases the group interactional dynamics and emotional solidarity of the terrorist cells are central for the success of the violent enterprise. It is through everyday group interaction that individuals overcome universal fear/tension confrontations.

Post-Structuralism

The classical representatives of post-structuralism such as Foucault, Derrida, Deleuze, Lyotard, and Baudrillard all have had a major influence on the humanities and social sciences and their impact is also visible in the anthropological and cultural studies of terrorism. This approach initially emerged as a critique of structuralism and later developed into a radical attack on all universalist paradigms within social science. Hence instead of providing an alternative explanation, the post-structuralists aim to deconstruct what they call "meta-narratives," including those articulated by social scientists. Their view is that all truth claims are contingent, provisional, and arbitrary and as such all scientific explanations require deconstruction in order to pinpoint the hegemonic and subjective practices that are already inbuilt into different narrative structures. Post-structuralists emphasize the plurality and particularity of knowledge claims and in this context aim to identify the inherent inconsistencies, incongruities, and arbitrariness of scientific and other discourses. Hence this approach tends to focus on competing discourses as well as cultural and political representations of terrorism. The concept of terrorism is challenged as being culturally constructed, politicized, and context dependent. For example, anthropologists such as Jeffrey A. Sluka (2009) and Richard Jackson (2007) show how the meaning of terrorism has changed over time and how something that traditionally referred to state violence became gradually associated with anti-state activity. Similarly, Harmonie Toros and Jeroen Gunning (2009) insist that all definitions of terrorism are subjective and as such cannot be removed from the specific discursive practices that have shaped them.

The most influential post-structuralist perspective on terrorism is represented by the scholars associated with the Copenhagen School: Barry Buzan and Ole Waever's theory of securitization. The securitization paradigm focuses on the social processes through which individuals and groups are transformed into objects of security. As Buzan and Waever (2003) explain, securitization is a phenomenon associated with state power and its capacity to frame individual and social agents as potential or actual threats to state security. The emphasis here is on the representation of the threat which rarely corresponds to the actual threat as some groups or organizations are singled out and securitized while others receive less or no attention from state apparatuses. The illustrative example is how the European Union and individual member states prioritize and securitize terrorism over road safety: "In 2005 41,600 people died in traffic accidents in the EU, while in the same year 56 people died in Western Europe from the terrorist attack. While a major political discourse is going on regarding terrorism, road safety is hardly securitized" (Zwitter and de Wilde 2014, 8). Furthermore, the securitization paradigm analyzes how, why, and when some organizations, groups, and activities become publicly framed and also popularly understood as representing an existential threat to the social order. In particular Buzan and Waever (2003) are interested in how securitization strategies succeed, in a sense that the wider public responds to and accepts claims made by security services and governments. They identify specific language and speech acts that make securitization normalized and legitimized in everyday public discourses. For example, many states deploy State of Emergency acts in order to counter the real, perceived, or imagined threats of terrorism. Under such extraordinary conditions the state apparatuses and security services are allowed to bypass some legislation and can act with impunity while deploying excessive coercion and violence against its citizens.

Post-structuralists also explore the changing discourses of terrorism. Ondrej Ditrych (2014) deploys Foucauldian discourse analysis to analyze the representations of terrorism over the last hundred years. He argues that the dominant narratives on terrorism have changed substantially over the years, but they do not follow an evolutionary logic. For example, the contemporary, post 9/11, discourses resemble in some sense the 1930s narratives on terrorism as they both operate with the order versus chaos and civilization versus barbarism dichotomy and depict the enemy as monstrous and irrational. In his own words: "as in the 1930s, a counter-construction of the civilized and ordered mankind is juxtaposed with this global threat, disciplining both the 'inside' of particular political orders and the 'outside' of the international order" (Ditrych 2014, 4). These discourses differ from the 1970s when terrorism was associated with categories that underscored innocence versus harm and regime versus people. Ditrych insists that his historical analysis shows that terrorism has no essence and is characterized by changing discourses that involve continuities and discontinuities as well as the contingent and arbitrary frames.

The Cultural Foundations of Terrorism: A Critique

Perhaps more than any other form of organized violence, terrorism is highly dependent on cultural framing. While wars, genocides, and revolutions could take place without fully developed cultural repertoires, all terrorist acts require communication, symbolism, and mediated interaction. Since terrorist activities thrive on media representation and public turmoil, they are largely envisaged as a form of political communication. Terrorism which lacks an audience has no chance of political success. If terrorism is understood as a "weapon of the weak" then the cultural narratives play a central part in its implementation. Most terrorist events involve spectacular and unexpected violent acts which are aimed at terrifying ordinary citizens. While such violent episodes usually kill a relatively small number of people they rely on the cultural coding and mass media communication to spread this massage of fear and panic to much wider audiences. Hence it is crucial for all terrorist organizations to control the message they aim to send through the use of violence. If the terrorist act goes awry and it misses its target or hits the wrong target the clandestine organization might lose support among its constituents or might be deemed ineffective or incompetent, both of which would delegitimize its existence. Therefore, the success of terrorism entails not only accomplishment of the violent act but also adequate media and public response. In this sense terrorism is a cultural phenomenon: it requires framing, communication with the target audience, justification of violence, representation in the public eye, and the display of wider narratives.

The cultural and anthropological approaches are very useful in charting and analyzing these ideational and representational aspects of terrorism. In some important respects there is no terrorism without culture. However, while culturalism is valuable in identifying the links between culture and violence it has less to offer in terms of sociological explanations. In other words, culturalists are highly persuasive in pinpointing the cultural scripting behind the terrorist acts but they cannot provide adequate explanations on the origins and the long-term social dynamics of terrorism. Instead of tracking the processual logic of terrorist violence and explaining what makes terrorism possible, the culturalist perspectives tend to focus more on the framing, labeling, and coding of terrorism. There are three pronounced pitfalls of culturalism: (a) the dominance of description over explanation; (b) the neglect of the micro-sociology of terrorism; and (c) the rampant epistemological idealism which ignores the materiality of violence.

There is no doubt that the cultural approaches provide subtle analyses of the symbols, images, and representations that accompany terrorism. However, many cultural analyses overemphasize description over explanation and rely on very slim evidence. Some anthropologists such as Sluka (2009) and Atran (2010) present high-quality analyses that draw on detailed ethnographic work involving specific case studies, such as Northern Ireland in Suka's case or Islamist terror networks in Atran's case. However, many influential culturalist studies of terrorism rely on anecdotal evidence. There is an underlining assumption, particularly pronounced among neo-Durkhemians, that the existence of specific discourses and narratives is in itself an indicator of their popular resonance. Alexander's work is full of such over-generalizing assumptions that lack strong empirical backing and that over-rely on extensive descriptions over causal or even interpretative explanations. He asserts that "After 9/11, the national community experienced and interpreted itself as united by feeling, marked by the loving kindness... and by civility and solicitude among those who once merely had been strangers" (Alexander 2004b, 100). To back up this claim Alexander mentions that there are "thousands of examples of such generalisation and abstraction [that] can be culled from the communicative media in the days, weeks, and months that followed 9/11" (2004b, 100). The issue here is not the presence or absence of mass media depictions of "national solidarity" in the aftermath of a particular terrorist incident. There is no doubt that such representations exist (although a diligent researcher should identify the frequency and timing of their spread rather than just assume that they are there). The bigger issue is taking such media representations for granted instead of providing an in-depth analysis of their popular impact. Alexander and other neo-Durkhemians as well as many post-structuralists never test audiences and rarely provide evidence on the reception of terrorist and counterterrorist narratives. For many culturalists a good metaphor is valued more than the empirical evidence. For example, Philip Smith (2005, 36) insists that "social life can be treated like a text" and that organized violence, including wars and terrorism, "is not just about culture, but it is all about culture." Nevertheless, there is much more to social life than narratives and discourse. If human beings were only culture-driven creatures there would be no place for politics, economics, biology, coercion, and so many other aspects of social life. To fully explain terrorism, one has to tackle all these elements of human sociality and not reduce everything to texts. One can deconstruct texts and hegemonic narratives but that is not the same as explaining social/violent action.

The second weakness of culturalism is its neglect of the micro-world. The neo-Durkhemians focus on shared cultural values but such explanations cannot adequately account for the sheer diversity of human action. For example, if socialization is a powerful source of cultural homogeneity it is not clear why individuals raised in the same cultural tradition often embark on different ideological trajectories, with some becoming terrorists and the majority never even contemplating this option. Similarly, there is no persuasive explanation for why and when some cultural scripts resonate with the wider public and other scripts have little or no impact. This is particularly relevant in the context of face-to-face interaction. Framing a particular terrorist event in terms of civilization versus barbarism or good versus evil will not necessarily reach the targeted audience unless it is couched in the discourses that tap into the everyday micro-level solidarities. For example, the British attempt to criminalize (P)IRA prisoners during the hunger strike in 1981 largely backfired as it was completely disconnected from the micro-level world. Consequently, the nationalist population in the Northern Ireland who traditionally did not support (P)IRA were outraged by these actions and their media representations and as a result elected several (P)IRA prisoners as MPs. Neither post-structuralists nor neo-Durkheimians provide persuasive answers to these questions. For example, when Smelser (2007, 95) deals with the micro-level analysis he invokes highly dubious characterizations stating that terrorists are "disturbed individuals with chaotic personal pasts" who are "susceptible to the meaning, comfort, and rewards the extremist groups have to offer." Nevertheless, the most up-to-date scholarship shows clearly that most individuals that embark on the terrorist careers are not only mentally sound but also come from content and stable families (Sageman 2004; McCauley 2007). Symbolic interactionists do engage much more with the micro-level dynamics of terrorism but their focus on the changing "definitions of situation" and "interactional ritual chains" does not link well with the wider macro-structures. While one can agree with Collins that terrorist acts are not easy and that their execution requires social support it is not clear how such micro-groups operate within the larger world of terrorist organizations.

The final point relates to the epistemological idealism that underpins all cultural explanations of terrorism. Although Foucault, Baudrillard, and other classical post-structuralists were adamant that their approach is epistemologically materialist in its focus on institutions and the interest of different groups, much of contemporary post-structuralism is distinctly idealist in its epistemology. This also applies to much of the post-structuralist scholarship on terrorism as it does even more so to neo-Durkheimianism and symbolic interactionism. All of these perspectives see cultural values, discourses, norms, ideas, symbols, and signification as the key drivers of collective action. The neo-Durkheimians such as Alexander and Smith are most unambiguous about this, arguing that humans are decisively shaped by the normative universes they inhabit. This idealism is also very strong among interactionists who interpret social action through the prism of shared meanings and competing "definitions of situation." Although post-structuralists refer to material factors they too focus largely on the cultural artefacts: narratives, codes, scripts, and discourses. There is no denying the importance of ideas, values, and cultural codes as they certainly confer meanings on violent acts and establish communication between the agents involved in terrorist and counter-terrorist framing of events, but terrorism cannot exist without the material factors: organizations, institutions, political and economic interests, and so on. While all terrorist acts require cultural coding and ideological articulation they are first and foremost material events involving killing, dying, destruction, and many other physical responses and events. The 2004 Beslan hostage siege or 9/11 were present in our homes through the mass media and particular discursive framing but we paid a great deal of attention to these events not because of specific cultural scripts but exclusively because these events involved huge loss of human lives. Cultural frames do make a sense of violent events, but they do not create such events.

Beyond Culturalism

Much of the mainstream research on terrorism is legitimately preoccupied with practical questions. Why and how does a person become a terrorist? Is terrorism motivated by ideological, economic, or political reasons? Which types of individuals and groups are more likely to become involved in terrorist activities? Although these are all relevant questions they tend to focus too much on agency and on a very short timespan. Nevertheless, to fully understand the social dynamics of terrorism it is paramount to engage with the broader historical contexts and the long-term structural trajectories that make terrorist action possible. While the analysis of cultural narratives certainly contributes towards understanding acts of terrorism, such analyses cannot tell us much about the long-term causal dynamics of this phenomenon. Just as the instrumentalist explanations overemphasize strategic behavior and individual rational choices so do cultural interpretations overplay the role of ideas, values, and norms. However, to understand how, when, and why values, ideas, and norms (as well as self-interest) underpin terrorism one must historically contextualize their role.

I argue that all forms of organized violence, including terrorism, necessitate a long-term historical and sociological analysis. Not only that, most forms of collective violence have a path-dependent trajectory, but they also exhibit some very similar structural properties. Hence to account for this historical dynamic it is necessary to go beyond present-centric explorations and develop a *longue durée* analysis that focuses on the three historical processes that have shaped and continue to shape terrorism and other forms of organized violence: (1) the coercive organizational capacity; (2) the ideological penetration; and (3) the envelopment of micro-solidarity (Malešević 2017, 2013, 2010). I see these three historical processes as highly interdependent and this is particularly visible in the context of terrorism which has historically been molded by the organizational, ideological, and micro-social dynamics of state power and the variety of non-state entities.

The Coercive Organizational Capacity

One of defining features of all political systems is their coercive organizational capacity. This involves the ability to administer one's territory effectively, to mobilize financial resources from society in order to implement its policies, to steer economic development, to establish symbolic legitimacy, and to monopolize the legitimate use of violence, legislation, and education on one's territory, among others (Mann 2013, Skocpol 1992). However, this conventional account requires updating as all social organizations possess a degree of "state" capacity—from business corporations, religious institutions, and NGOs to terrorist organizations. Furthermore, as I have argued before, historically this organizational capacity has experienced an upward trend and its relatively continuous expansion was largely defined by its coercive might.[1] Since many non-state actors do not control specific territories their coercive organizational capacity is visible in their ability to internally pacify and hierarchically control their social environment including their members or employees. This capacity has historically been mostly cumulative and has particularly increased with the onset of modernity and the expansion of bureaucratic modes of organization worldwide (Malešević 2017, 2013, 2010).

Hence the proliferation of terrorism is firmly linked with this historical growth of state power and the corresponding expansion of non-state entities. Terrorist organizations are no different as they too have to keep up with the greater organizational demands including more effective division of labor, transparent hierarchies, the use of ever more advanced science and technology, the adoption of reliable communication systems, and so on. Any comparison between nineteenth-century terrorist groups such as the nationalist Irish Republican Brotherhood or Russian anarchist People's Will (Narodnaya Volya) and early twenty-first-century terrorist organizations such as Al Qaeda or the Tamil Tigers would indicate an organizational supremacy of the latter over the former. The contemporary terrorist outfits resemble modern states in their complex structures, sophisticated mechanisms of hierarchy and control, elaborate disciplinary measures, long-term planning strategies, meritocratic systems of promotion, and so on. The most efficient terrorist networks aspire to establish Weberian bureaucratic models of organization: they foster professionalism, advanced division of labor, genuine expertise, meritocratic structure, rule-governed hierarchies, and loyalty towards the organization. Despite the popular perception of Islamist terrorist groups as being driven by the irrational fanaticism of charismatic leaders, most such organizations are very similar in a sense that they are highly bureaucratic and rationally organized:

> They have a clearly defined leadership—e.g. the cupola (SL), army executive (IRA), majlis shura (Islamic Jihad), council or again majlis shura (Al Qaida). They are differentiated both vertically and functionally. All terrorist organisations... have

> specialised units directly below the top leadership level. In some cases the main distinction is between a military and a support branch, in other cases various units distinguished by functions such as finance, procurement, propaganda etc. are related to the operative units in a matrix-like fashion. All terrorist organisations have furthermore a clearly circumscribed third level of operative units, the famous cells. (Mayntz 2004, 12)

Since terrorist organizations operate on the assumption that state actors are their enemies they have to emulate the state's organizational developments in order to keep up and successfully inflict damage on the state. Thus, they have to establish internally legitimate and operational organizations with a flexible structure and have to develop organizational capacities that are very similar to that of the state apparatuses: intelligence gathering, effective system of recruitment, efficient surveillance techniques, viable recruitment strategies, long-term financial planning, clandestine communication systems, technological developments, persuasive propaganda departments, and so on.

This is not to say that there are no significant differences between the sovereign states and the terrorist networks. For one thing, terrorist organizations usually do not have resources or the coercive capacity that characterizes states. Hence terrorists rely on the asymmetric violence which is geared towards sending a particular political message. To maximize the attention of their audience (the adversary governments, ordinary citizens, and their own political base) terrorist organizations tend to utilize the most visible, memorable, and thus high-impact forms of violence—suicide bombings, plane hijackings, hostage taking, or political assassinations. These violent and illegitimate acts are designed to amplify fear and trauma and thus make governments look weak and incompetent. All these actions are dangerous and involve high risks which means that the terrorist organizations differ from the states as they lack external legitimacy and have to operate underground. The clandestine character of such entities fosters more flexibility and greater organizational inventions. Hence the IRA, Italian Red Brigades, and German RAF all had to decentralize once their governments increased their coercive pressure (della Porta 2013). For example, the Provisional IRA had to develop a relatively flat system of leadership where commanders took part in armed actions (Malešević and O'Dochartaigh 2018). Nevertheless, this organizational flexibility did not mean the end of organizational hierarchy. Instead the shift underground contributed towards greater militarization and discipline, including tighter internal structure and the firmer control of the leaders. Thus, to understand the historical dynamics of terrorist organizations one has to trace their ever-increasing coercive organizational capacities.

Ideological Penetration

Terrorist networks could not exist without the substantial coercive organizational capacity. However just like any other coercive organization terrorist entities also require a degree of ideological justification. In fact since terrorist acts are generally deemed by the governments and many citizens to be illegal and illegitimate, terrorist organizations focus much of their energy on establishing political legitimacy. In this context ideology plays very significant role. Nevertheless, this is not to say that terrorism is an exclusively cultural phenomenon. Although ideological doctrines utilize cultural tropes, ideological power differs substantially from culture. In contrast to culturalist approaches that see cultural norms and values as determining social action the focus on ideological power means zooming in on the selective and strategic deployment of cultural idioms. Simply put, cultural narratives cannot do anything by themselves unless they are incorporated within the well-functioning coercive organizational entities that are capable of strategically linking these narratives with grassroots micro-universes. Thus, cultures do not determine terrorist activities. Instead terrorism relies on well-crafted ideological narratives to justify the violent acts and to mobilize a degree of popular support for their political agendas.

All social organizations legitimize their existence through ideological tropes. In modernity this means addressing one's political constituents and justifying the use of violence in terms of specific ideological vistas. Since modern citizens differ from pre-modern counterparts in terms of literacy rates, access to continuous education, and exposure to mass media (including more recently the social media), they are much more receptive to ideological messages. Hence representatives of terrorist organizations are keen to use their violent acts as a means of communication not only with their foes but also with their own political base. Since modernity creates adequate conditions for the proliferation of different ideological doctrines it is crucial that terrorist organizations maintain a degree of ideological control over their constituents. This is achieved in part through greater ideological penetration, which means that specific terrorist outfits have to tap into already existing popular narratives about grievances, injustices, and morality in order to forge a level of popular consensus on what their political struggle represents and aims to achieve. In this context the access to mass media is crucial as all terrorist acts thrive on publicity—if a particular suicide bombing is not widely reported, it is as if it did not happen at all. The spectacular violent actions galvanize mass mobilization and, in this way, reproduce ideological messages within the wider political constituencies that terrorists aim to address. In other words, greater ideological penetration allows a continuous communication and reaffirmation of the key ideological principles between and within terrorist groups and their political base. Nevertheless, ideological power cannot sustain terrorist organizations on its own. To attain political legitimacy such organizations need to achieve political success on the ground. For example, Al Qaeda attained much of its visibility and support less through ideological purity and its peculiar interpretations of Islam and much more through its violent actions. The same applies to ISIS, which quickly took over the leading role within violent Salafist movements once they achieved military success. All of this indicates that narratives, including religious doctrines, do not incite violence by themselves. Having an expert knowledge of religious texts does not make one more likely to become a terrorist. Instead such ideological resources attain social meaning only in the context of already existing political cleavages. Rather than governing violent action, ideological penetration makes it socially meaningful and acceptable for one's political base. Ideological doctrines are also useful for forging social cohesion within the terrorist movements as well as for conscripting the new membership. Thus, ideology matters a great deal but only when connected with the coercive organizational capacities and when capable of successfully tapping into networks of micro-solidarity.

Micro-Solidarity

While the presence of coercive organizational and ideological scaffolds makes terrorist networks possible it does not necessarily make them meaningful to ordinary individuals. Since most of our everyday activities involve interactions with family members, friends, neighbors, peers, and other micro-level groups, terrorist organizations cannot succeed without penetrating this micro-world. As much of recent scholarship demonstrates, an overwhelming majority of human beings derive their emotional fulfillment, comfort, and sense of ontological security from membership of very small groups (Malešević 2017, 2015, 2014; Dunbar 1998). One of the key problems for all social organizations is how to reconcile their instrumental and ideological demands with micro-level emotional attachments in order to mobilize social action. In this sense terrorist networks resemble other social organizations—they are hierarchical, bureaucratic, anonymous, and instrumentally driven. In contrast the micro-world of families, friendships, and peer groups is built on shared intimacies, familiarities, emotional bonds, communal moralities, and spontaneity. Thus, to bridge these two nominally incompatible worlds it is necessary to develop organizational and ideological mechanisms capable of projecting these deep micro-level solidarities onto large-scale organizational canvases. Hence successful terrorist networks have to penetrate the micro-world by mimicking the language and practices associated with close kinship and deep friendships. In this context all coercive social organizations regularly invoke friendship and kinship metaphors to mobilize wider support and this is also noticeable with the variety of terrorist networks. For example, nationalist-driven terrorist groups such as Tamil LTTE and Kurdish PKK would recurrently refer to "the sacred cause of the Motherland," "our Tamil/Kurdish brothers and sisters," or "our beloved comrades." The same metaphors are deployed by religiously centered terrorists such as the Nigerian Boko Haram or Pakistani Lashkar-e-Taiba who regularly refer to "our Muslim brethren" and "our brothers and sisters in Islam" (Smith 2015; Griffin 2012). Some violent organizations successfully combine nationalist and religious appeal. So, the Islamist and separatist groups in the Caucasus often utilize kinship and friendship concepts to mobilize their support base: "The Krasnodar Territory, as infidels call it, is in fact the land of our brothers, the best brothers and the best Muslims in the world. This is the land of Adygs, the land of Abazins, the land of Circassians... this is the land of our brothers... and it is our sacred duty to liberate it from infidelity" (Griffin 2012, 42).

However, micro-solidarity can have a long-term impact only when it is enveloped in organizational and ideological structures. This is particularly visible in the recruitment strategies of terrorist networks where the dynamic of micro-solidarity is central. As Atran (2010), Hassan (2011), and Sageman (2011) demonstrate, the overwhelming majority of new recruits join terrorist networks not as individuals but with their close friends and family members. They also become involved in violent activities with their friends and family and in this way ideology and coercive organizational capacities become blended with a sense of emotional and moral commitment to one's significant others.

Conclusion

Cultural and anthropological perspectives provide a very useful contribution to the study of terrorism. It is almost impossible to envisage terrorism without the articulated cultural frames, developed narratives of good and evil, and specific normative claims aimed at justifying violent actions. Since all terrorist organizations are focused on sending a particular political message, they could not operate without these cultural codes and normative scripts. Moreover, cultural representation, symbolic interaction, and communication are all indispensable ingredients of social life, including organized violent encounters. In this context culturalist approaches help us understand how terrorism and counterterrorism navigate and utilize social meanings and values in the process of violent events. Nevertheless, the cultural and anthropological approaches also suffer from several marked weaknesses including the dominance of description over explanation, the general neglect of the micro-sociology of terrorism, and the presence of staunch epistemological idealism. These weaknesses can be sidestepped by refocusing one's attention on the *longue durée* sociological analysis and by zooming in on the historical dynamics of coercive organizational capacities, ideological penetration, and the envelopment of micro-solidarity. The next step is to look for the wide-ranging empirical validation of this theoretical model.

Note

1. As I emphasize regularly, this was not a unilineal evolutionary or teleological process but something that was characterized by historical ups and downs, with some organizations expanding and others shrinking or disappearing. My point is that coercive organizational power as such has been on the increase since the establishment of pristine states, 10,000–12,000 years ago, see Malešević 2017, 2013, 2010.

References

Alexander, J. (2004a) "Toward a Theory of Cultural Trauma," in J. C. Alexander, R. Eyerman, B. Giesen, N. J. Smelser, and P. Sztompka (eds), *Cultural Trauma and Collective Identity*. Berkeley, CA: University of California Press, 1–30.

Alexander, J. (2004b) "From the Depths of Despair: Performance, Counterperformance, and 'September 11,'" *Sociological Theory*, 22(1): 88–105.

Alexander, J. (2007) *Power and Performance: War on Terror between the Sacred and Profane*. Florence: Robert Schuman Centre for Advanced Studies.

Alexander, J. (2011) *Performance and Power*. Cambridge: Polity.

Atran, S. (2010) *Talking to the Enemy*. London: Penguin.

Blain, M. (2009) *The Sociology of Terrorism: Studies in Power, Subjugation and Victimage*. Boca Raton, FL: Universal Publishers.

Buzan, B., and O. Waever (2003) *Regions and Powers: The Structure of International Security*. Cambridge: Cambridge University Press.

Collins, R. (2004) *Interaction Ritual Chains*. Princeton: Princeton University Press.

Collins, R. (2008) *Violence: Micro-Sociological Theory*. Princeton: Princeton University Press.

Constanza, S., and J. Kilburn (2005) "Symbolic Security, Moral Panic and Public Sentiment: Toward a Sociology of Counterterrorism," *Journal of Social and Ecological Boundaries*, 1(2): 106–24.

della Porta, D. (2013) *Clandestine Political Violence*. Cambridge: Cambridge University Press.

Ditrych, O. (2014) *Tracing the Discourses of Terrorism*. New York: Palgrave.

Dunbar, R. (1998) *Grooming, Gossip and the Evolution of Language*. Cambridge, MA: Harvard University Press.

Durkheim, E. (1997) *The Division of Labour in Society*. New York: Free Press.

Griffin, R. (2012) *Terrorist's Creed: Fanatical Violence and the Human Need for Meaning*. Basingstoke: Palgrave.

Hassan, R. (2011) Suicide Bombings. London: Routledge.

Huntington, S. (1996) *The Clash of Civilizations and the Remaking of the World Order*. Chicago: University of Chicago Press.

Jackson, R. (2007) "The Core Commitments of Critical Terrorism Studies," *European Political Science*, 6(3): 244–51.

Juergensmeyer, Mark (2003) *Terror in the Mind of God: The Global Rise of Religious Violence*. Berkeley, CA: University of California Press.

Kalyvas, S. (2004) "The Paradox of Terrorism in Civil War," *Journal of Ethics*, 8(1): 97–138.

Kalyvas, S. (2006) *The Logic of Violence in Civil War*. Cambridge: Cambridge University Press.

McCauley, C. (2007) "Psychological Issues in Understanding Terrorism and the Response to Terrorism," in C. Strout (ed.), *Psychology of Terrorism*. New York: Oxford University Press, 3–29.

Malešević, S. (2010) *The Sociology of War and Violence*. Cambridge: Cambridge University.

Malešević, S. (2013) *Nation-States and Nationalisms: Organization, Ideology and Solidarity*. Cambridge: Polity Press.

Malešević, S. (2014) "Is War Becoming Obsolete?," *Sociological Review*, 62(S2): 65–86.

Malešević, S. (2015) "Where Does Group Solidarity Come From? Ernest Gellner and Ibn Khaldun Revisited," *Thesis Eleven*, 128(1): 85–99.

Malešević, S. (2017) *The Rise of Organised Brutality: A Historical Sociology of Violence*. Cambridge: Cambridge University Press.

Malešević, S., and N. O'Dochartaigh (2018) "Why Combatants Fight: The Irish Republican Army and the Bosnian Serb Army Compared," *Theory and Society*, 47 (3): 293–326.

Mann, M. (2013) The Sources of Social Power III: Global Empires and Revolution 1890–1945. Cambridge: Cambridge University Press.

Mayntz, R. (2004) *Organisational Forms of Terrorism*. Cologne: Max Planck Institute for the Study of Societies.

Sageman, M. (2004) *Leaderless Jihad: Terror Networks in the Twenty-First Century*. Philadelphia: University of Pennsylvania Press.

Sageman, M. (2011) *Understanding Terror Networks*. Philadelphia: University of Pennsylvania Press.

Skocpol, T. (1992) *Protecting Soldiers and Mothers: The Political Origins of Social Policy in the United States*. Cambridge, MA: Harvard University Press.

Sluka, J. (2009) "The Contribution of Anthropology to Critical Terrorism Studies," in R. Jackson, B. Smyth, and J. Gunning (eds), *Critical Terrorism Studies*. New York: Routledge, 138–55.

Smelser, N. (2007) *The Faces of Terrorism*. Princeton: Princeton University Press.

Smith, M. (2015) *Boko Haram: Inside Nigeria's Unholy War*. London: IB Taurus.

Smith, P. (2005) *Why War? The Cultural Logic of Iraq, the Gulf War, and Suez*. Chicago: Chicago University Press.

Smith, P. (2008) *Punishment and Culture*. Chicago: Chicago University Press.

Spengler, O. (1991) [1918] *The Decline of the West*. New York: Oxford University Press.

Toros, H., and J. Gunning (2009) "Exploring a Critical Theory Approach to Terrorism Studies," in R. Jackson, B. Smyth, and J. Gunning (eds), *Critical Terrorism Studies*. New York: Routledge, 87–108.

Toynbee, A. J. (1950) *War and Civilization: Selections from A Study of History*. New York: Oxford University Press.

Vertigans, S. (2011) *The Sociology of Terrorism*. London: Routledge.

Zwitter, A., and J. De Wilde (2014) Working Paper, Securitization and the Local Level: A Prismatic Approach to Psycho-Social Mechanisms of Securitization. Groningen: University of Groningen.

CHAPTER 13

HISTORICAL APPROACHES TO TERRORISM

BRENDA J. LUTZ

THERE are many different ways to research terrorism, and the social sciences have been the source for much of the recent analyses of this topic. Historical perspectives, however, are important since they permit current analysts to put today's terrorist organizations and incidents in the appropriate contexts. As George Santanya phrased it in his famous aphorism, "Those who cannot remember the past are condemned to repeat it." Thus, knowledge of previous groups, their successes and failures, and how they ended can provide important frameworks for understanding the groups of today. Early examples of terrorism should receive much greater consideration precisely because to date they have been given less attention (Lutz and Lutz 2005: 3). Analyzing existing historical events from more modern perspectives can increase understanding. Historical perspectives can also draw upon the many classical case studies of specific groups as well as broader studies of historical currents (Gaucher 1968; Lutz and Lutz 2005; Parry 1976). Key concepts are relatively timeless, including conflict, repression, conciliation, tyranny, and terrorism. For the analysis of historical examples of terrorism that follows, a modern definition of terrorism will be used throughout to maintain continuity. Terrorism is political violence designed to achieve political objectives. There is a target audience beyond the immediate victims. An organization is behind the terrorism at some level, although there is a possibility of leaderless resistance wherein small groups or individuals undertake actions as part of a broader movement. Terrorism also involves actions by dissidents against the state or other citizens or actions by the state against its own citizens. It will not deal with actions by one state directed against another, as occurred with the Allies and the Axis states in World War II or between the United States and the Soviet Union during the Cold War.

The earliest known examples of terrorism appear more than 2,000 years ago, involving political violence in the Roman Republic and the preludes to rebellions in Judea and surrounding areas against the Seleucids and the Romans. Whilst it is known that violence in the late Republic of Rome became endemic with street brawls, intimidation, and assassinations, there have only been a few studies that analyzed this violence from the perspective of terrorism (Lutz and Lutz 2006, 2015). Different groups competing for control of the Republic and the resources of the empire engaged in terrorism in efforts to maintain or gain political power. The aristocratic groups in power, the *Optimates* were generally successful in meeting the challenges from those seeking to become part of the ruling elite, the *Populares*. Conflicts led to battles to control the streets and access to various government forums where decisions were made. Intimidation and riots were often successful in gaining passage of the desired legislation (Brunt 1966, 3–4; Millar 1998, 136). The *Optimates* were involved in the assassination of, first, Tiberius Gracchus and then his brother Gaius Gracchus. There were other assassinations, including eventually that of Julius Caesar. The violence in the streets represented planned action by the political factions in some cases and in other cases the violence was more spontaneous when groups of competing supporters clashed with each other. In the latter case, the general situation of planned violence contributed to the outbreak of spontaneous clashes.

There were a series of revolts in Judea against the incorporation of the territory into imperial states that have been analyzed as early examples of terrorism. The revolt of the Maccabees was directed against the Seleucid Greek rulers. The initial attacks against the successors of Alexander the Great involved tactics that would appear to have included terrorist tactics but the struggle quickly became one that escalated to guerrilla warfare and eventually full-scale conventional battles (Lutz and Lutz 2014, 6–8). The conflict included struggles between those who had adopted Greek cultural practices and more religious individuals who had not (Derfler 1989, 50–1). The Maccabees were ultimately successful in winning independence for Judea. The independence was relatively short-lived as Judea was incorporated into the Roman Empire which reinvigorated the struggle between those who had adapted to external influences and those who had not. The prelude to the outbreak of the Great Revolt against Roman rule that occurred in 66 CE has been analyzed as an example of terrorism (Rapoport 1984). The dissident Jews assassinated Romans in Jerusalem as well as pro-Roman Jews who were collaborating with the imperial order. The attacks were designed to neutralize the supporters of Rome by making opposition to a potential rebellion dangerous (Josephus 1981; Rapoport 1984). At one point in an action reminiscent of much more modern activities, the dissidents captured the son of the High Priest and arranged to trade him in exchange for the release of imprisoned comrades (Allegro 1972: 277). The dissident Jews were quite successful in combining terrorism and guerrilla attacks to undermine imperial authority. When a full-blown revolt did occur, the population was supportive or neutral. Rome had to mobilize significant military resources to put down the revolt. The Great Revolt of 66 CE was followed by two later revolts that drew upon many of the same discontents. The second one, which originated in Cyrenaica, spread to Egypt and Cyprus and lasted from 114 to 117 CE. The third revolt was centered in Judea from 132 to 135 CE. This revolt required another major military effort by Rome to defeat the rebels. All of these revolts shared some common characteristics. They may have been more a reflection of local opposition to the spread of foreign cultures at the expense of Judaism rather than a desire for political independence (which was a means to the end of cultural and religious autonomy). The rebels drew more heavily upon those groups that had been impoverished by the intrusion of outside forces or that had faced a loss of status as a consequence of political and social change (Chaliand and Blin 2007, 56; Lutz and Lutz 2014, 8–11; Pedahzur and Perliger 2011, 5). The rebels in the revolts targeted Greek temples and populations as part of a reaction to the intrusion of outside cultural influences (Josephus 1981, 168–9; Rapoport 1984, 669; Reich 1998, 263).

There may have been other cases where dissident groups used terrorism that have been lost in historical records. In the twelfth and thirteenth centuries, however, the Assassins appeared on the scene. They have been analyzed as a classic terrorist organization (Lutz and Lutz 2005, ch. 3; Rapoport 1984). The Assassins developed out of the unorthodox Nizari sect of Shia Islam (itself much smaller and therefore usually considered the unorthodox branch of Islam by the majority Sunni). The Nizaris faced persecution by existing states governed by more orthodox Muslim leaders. They were able to establish themselves in a period of weak states by occupying mountain strongholds in Persia and the Levant. In order to protect members of the group, the Assassins relied on the public execution of local rulers and key officials involved in the persecution of Nizaris. They were frequently successful in killing these officials despite bodyguards and other security measures. The end result was that other leaders decided out of self-interest to forgo persecuting members of the Nizari sect. The attacks of individual members of the group were especially terrifying because the assassin was inevitably either captured or killed on the spot. The chances of escape were very slim, unlike the case of Jewish dissidents before the Great Revolt who often managed to escape after killing their target. The group was quite capable of long-term planning in its activities. The sect would infiltrate members into the households of prominent political individuals so that they were well-placed in case of need as potential assassins if there were threats to the group or to those that chose to convert to the sect (Daftary 1991, 34; Rapoport 1984, 666). The Assassins as a quasi-state were able to survive for two centuries but were eventually eliminated as a political actor by the Mongols. The Assassins became well-known to Western historians as a consequence of the Crusades. Although they were responsible for the death of a number of Christian leaders, including Conrad of Montferrat who had just been chosen as king of Jerusalem, the primary targets for the Assassins were fellow Muslims (Chaliand and Blin 2007, 73; Lutz and Lutz 2005, 29). Whilst it has been suggested that the terrorism practiced by the Assassins was not successful, in fact, they survived for two centuries and provided protection for their co-religionists by successfully threatening the heads of state and instilling high levels of fear (Chaliand and Blin 2007, 77). Their political position was only undermined by an invasion from a powerful external group (the Mongols) that destroyed many other states in the region.

In the centuries after the end of the Assassins there were other instances in which terrorism appeared as a political technique. During the late Middle Ages as many have noted there was considerable violence in the Italian city-states. Conflicts between princes, aristocrats, and groups with more links to the general population were frequent in many cities. There were conventional battles that could lead to changes in the political structure of the cities, but the violence also included intimidation, street brawls, assassinations, and other types of assaults. Partisan mobs raging through the streets, the deaths of supporters, and attacks on property were often parts of organized campaigns to control political power (Day 1988, 135–7; Martines 1967–8, 80). The towers that became a major feature of many Italian cities served as refuges and bases of operations for families and their retainers in the troubled times and bases of operation for fighting for political control. These actions were undertaken by those who hoped to stay in power and those who wanted to replace them or to change the political system. Even though the violence in these city-states has been analyzed from a number of perspectives, there has only been an occasional discussion of these events in the context of analyzing terrorism (Lutz and Lutz 2005, ch. 4). It would appear that there is significant scope for analyzing such events in this period in Italy from a terrorism perspective. In many respects the techniques, including techniques that correspond to classical definitions of terrorism, were similar to those used by the different factions battling for power in the Roman Republic.

Terrorism in another form appeared in Asia in later centuries. As European powers (first the Portuguese and Spanish, then the Dutch, and finally the English) penetrated the South Asian and Southeast Asian regions opposition appeared in many forms. The local populations and their rulers were unable to defeat the Europeans through conventional warfare or guerrilla struggles; consequently, they resorted to a new tactic that was at times effective. From the seventeenth to the nineteenth centuries, in parts of India, the Philippines, and the Dutch Indies with largely Muslim populations, individuals would launch what today would be called lone-wolf attacks as a response to the occupation (Dale 1988; Andriolo 2002). When the colonial system challenged or denigrated local belief patterns, individuals would arm themselves with weapons such as knives or swords and attack European bureaucrats or colonists or members of local populations that collaborated with the colonial power until they were killed by police or soldiers. These suicide missions (known as *pagsabil* on the Malabar Coast of India and Aceh in Indonesia and *juramentado* in the Philippines) frequently were effective in prompting better treatment for the local populations from the Europeans present in these areas (Andriolo 2002, 738; Dale 1988, 48–9; Lutz and Lutz 2013, 12). The Muslim attackers were defending their communities in both a cultural and religious sense from outside influences and were at least somewhat successful in doing so. They have been specifically analyzed as a form of terrorism, providing another example from earlier time periods.

European exploration and colonialism led to a different type of terrorism in North America. The prelude to the American Revolution involved resistance to British rule in the thirteen colonies that included a limited form of violence, and these events have at least been considered within the context of an analysis of terrorism (Davis 1996; Lutz and Lutz 2007, ch. 2). In the aftermath of the French and Indian War the British crown and parliament attempted to pay for victory in war by taxing the colonists who had benefitted from the elimination of the French threat. The first effort involved the passage of the Stamp Act which required an official stamp for all kinds of legal documents and other items such as newspapers. The colonists protested against the imposition of what they saw as an illegal tax by refusing to pay the tax. The officials who were supposed to collect the tax were threatened, assaulted, or had their property destroyed. The pressure was sufficient to persuade many officials to resign their positions and others who were appointed as tax collectors never took up their posts (Morgan and Morgan 1962, ch. 8). Parliament eventually rescinded the Act, while indicating that it still had the right to levy direct taxes on the colonies. In short, terrorism by dissident Americans had been used to defeat a British policy (Davis 1996, 224). Tensions between the colonies and England continued and increased when new taxes were levied on the colonies. The reaction was similar, with tax collectors and crown supporters being assaulted including tar and feathering, assaults, and property destruction. As was the case with the Stamp Act protests, the tax collectors and other officials were intimidated into resigning or never taking up their posts. The resistance culminated with the Boston Tea Party and the destruction of tea elsewhere. With the dumping of tea in Boston harbor, king and parliament had to respond since inaction would have meant the loss of support of those loyal to the crown. These actions protesting British policies were not isolated efforts, nor were they spontaneous. They were a campaign of violent politics (Hollon 1974, 10). The closing of Boston harbor and other sanctions led to the outbreak of fighting that led to American independence. Whilst the provocative actions of the Sons of Liberty in Boston and groups elsewhere were similar to the provocative actions of the Jewish dissidents against Rome, there was one significant difference. The American dissidents challenged the authorities without inflicting any fatalities. The activities were non-lethal but effective. The dissidents "trusted to horror rather than homicide" (Scheslinger 1955, 246). The intimidation and violence were against property, and while non-lethal, were still effective in setting into motion events that led to independence as a political objective.

The Reign of Terror in France is one starting point for analysts of terrorism, especially since the period provided the name for violent activities designed to generate fear in target audiences. The use of terrorism during the turmoil in France was different in some respects from many of the earlier examples so far discussed. In this case, the violence was often undertaken with the toleration and even involvement of officials in the various governments of the revolutionary period. Wilkinson (1975, 50), in fact, has suggested that the use of terror as a means of government control originated with the Jacobins. The radicals in the government (Jacobins and Montengards) were governing groups that utilized violence to further their political objectives in some cases or at least made no attempt to prevent violence by their followers that was useful for achieving those objectives. The radicals eventually used the Parisian mobs to help them expel the more moderate Girondins from the legislature in 1793 (Rude 1959, 113). Once the moderates had been expelled, official executions were used to intimidate those who were not in agreement with the government. Those who survived the purges were cowed into silence and ceased to oppose the radicals (Parry 1976, 51). In some instances, however, violence was not directed by the radicals in government but represented popular outbreaks in which mobs attacked those targets that they blamed for economic, political, or military failures. In these cases, the attacks were beyond the control of the radical groups in government. Whether the attacks were spontaneous or at least in part linked to the radicals in government, they were effective in inducing fear in target audiences. The battles for political advantage in the various revolutionary governments were in broad outline similar to some of the confrontations in the late Republic in Rome in the sense that some of the physical violence was spontaneous and some of the violence was directed by groups contesting for power in the government that hoped to gain advantages vis-à-vis opponents (Lutz and Lutz 2006). The use of terrorism by the radicals was ultimately counterproductive, of course, since it alienated portions of the population and political elite, leading to the eventual elimination of the radicals from power.

Governmental support for the ethnic cleansing of many groups of Native Americans in the United States in the early years of the republic has been included in studies of political violence. The activities of the settler populations have been seen as ethnic cleansing which by its very nature constitutes terrorism (or even potentially genocide). The settler populations of the colonies had been involved in various conflicts with Native Americans before independence. The feeling of distrust continued after independence and eventually led to efforts by the settler population to force Indian populations to relocate from eastern areas of the country. The state of Georgia was particularly active in attempting to displace Indian populations. The state authorities were first able to pay the Creeks to abandon their title to what little land they had in Georgia. The Cherokees, however, had much more substantial holdings, leading the state authorities to use other mechanisms to convince the Cherokees to move west. The state passed laws invalidating Indian marriages, indicating that Indians had no standing in state courts—thus limiting contract rights, and overlooking settler violence against Indians. When violence broke out between Cherokees and settlers after gold was discovered on Indian lands, the state continued these actions, including prohibitions on Indians prospecting for gold. As the problems between Cherokees and miners increased, the state created a special police force to deal with the violence, but the Georgia Guard supported the miners at the expense of the Cherokees (Lutz and Lutz 2007, 27–31; Tracey 2000; Van Every 1966, 132–3). The national government eventually became involved, and national troops were sent to control the violence. President Andrew Jackson opted to support the efforts to remove the Indians. He ordered the withdrawal of federal troops, leading to a renewal of the violence, and he refused to implement Supreme Court decisions that challenged the actions of the state of Georgia (Tracey 2000, 51; Van Every 1966, 132–3). Eventually, the state triumphed as the Cherokees agreed under duress to migrate to the Indian Territory (Oklahoma). The actions of the state government in Georgia led other state governments to undertake similar actions to force Indian populations to move westward. Different state governments were actively supportive of the attempts to ethnically cleanse their territories of Indian populations through the use of violence and terrorism (Lutz and Lutz 2007, 29–31). The national government was complicit in the use of state laws, discrimination, intimidation, and violence to force Native Americans to relocate, and such government toleration of these actions is clearly support for terrorism.

The national government was later even more active with the passage of the Indian Removal Act by Congress when Andrew Jackson was in office (Lutz and Lutz 2007, 31).

Various examples of terrorism in the United States continued in the period surrounding the Civil War. In the years just before the outbreak of the war, violence in Kansas between those in favor of the extension of slavery and those opposed to slavery included a variety of terrorism incidents by both sides, although these actions are seldom discussed within the context of terrorism (Lutz and Lutz 2014). Pro-slavery groups used voter fraud and intimidation to win the initial elections. Both sides engaged in guerrilla actions against each other and used terrorism in efforts to drive out settlers aligned with the opposite side in the struggle. These actions were successful in driving out settlers affiliated with each side. The anti-slavery forces triumphed in the struggle for political control of Kansas. The terrorism by both sides largely negated the actions by the opposing forces, but the various groups involved were successful at some level in this struggle. John Brown gained the most notoriety in this regard (Fellman 2010, 18–38). One biographer noted that when he returned to Kansas and Missouri for a second time "it was his presence more than his activities, that made him a power" (Villard 1965, 230). Whether intuitively or by intention Brown hit upon one use of violence as a psychological weapon to spread fear in a target audience.

In the aftermath of the Civil War, terrorism appeared on a large scale with the creation of the Ku Klux Klan (KKK) and similar groups that represented the old white political structure in the southern states. Unlike John Brown, the KKK has always been recognized as a terrorist organization in its tactics. The KKK used armed attacks to prevent freed slaves and white Republicans from voting in elections. These attacks were successful in permitting the political dissidents to regain control of local government bodies and state governments (Davis 1996; Release 1978). Once the white population was back in control of the governing bodies, the KKK and other organizations largely disappeared from the scene. It was no longer necessary to have groups associated with white dissidents use terrorism as a mechanism for social control of black Americans. State governments were able to disenfranchise black voters and arrest individuals for real or alleged crimes and obtain convictions as necessary for purposes of social control (Lutz and Lutz 2007, 60–1). When these processes failed to keep black Americans "in their place," the state authorities would look the other way as white mobs attacked black individuals accused of crimes and murdered them. The conviction rate for white murders of black individuals was abysmal (Raper 1978). Obviously, state-tolerated terrorism and state repression were sufficient as a means of social control and have generally been recognized as such in a historical context.

At the end of the nineteenth century there were two major types of terrorism that occurred, although only the second type has been generally recognized as terrorism. The Boxer Rebellion in China involved significant elements of this kind of political violence. The Boxers were an indigenous cultural reaction to the intrusion of Western (including Japanese) economic, social, and cultural values into Chinese society, as was an earlier outbreak of violence directed against Western institutions in 1876. The Boxers and their predecessors attacked symbols of Westernization, including railroads, telegraphs, missionaries, and Chinese converts, and Westerners themselves. Initially the Boxers operated outside the government sphere, but the government tolerated their actions because the imperial court shared some of the same goals as the Boxers and wanted to use their activities to regain some freedom of action from Western powers. The Boxer attacks eventually broke out into open warfare against Western interests. Initially the government stood aside from the attacks but eventually committed imperial troops to battles against Western forces (Lutz and Lutz 2013). All of the early actions had the hallmarks of terrorism designed in this case to drive out foreign influences, much as has been seen in more recent struggles. The outcome was negative for both the Boxers and the imperial government, but the Boxers were effective in using terrorism as a means of getting support for their challenge to Western penetration of China.

The second terrorist group in the late 1800s and early 1900s was the effort of the anarchists and their successors to bring about political change in industrialized countries through the use of violence. Rapoport (2003) suggested that modern terrorism occurred in four waves, each of which lasted approximately twenty-five years. His first wave was the anarchist surge of violence in the late 1800s that carried over into the nineteenth century. His wave theory has been criticized (Parker and Sitter 2016), and it does not take into account the use of terrorism by fascists and other authoritarian groups after World War I (Rapoport 2016). The Boxer Rebellion, of course, was not part of this wave, but his theory discussed general trends and never sought to explain every outbreak of terrorist violence. Overall though, it has been a useful historical template and theoretical guide for research (Kaplan 2016; Rapoport 2016). The anarchists first tried to convince leaders and the population to open up political systems by attempts at education—propaganda of the word. When changes failed to occur, they opted for terrorist violence—propaganda of the deed. They began to assassinate political leaders, both hereditary and elected. They hoped that their actions would energize the masses to rebel, and failing that they felt that the political elites would react to the violence with massive repression that would lead to a popular uprising. Neither eventuality happened despite the fact that individual anarchists killed a number of world leaders—including the king of Italy, a Spanish prime minister, and an American president amongst others. The anarchists lacked a true international organization and were only loosely in contact with each other. They were, in effect, a very early example of leaderless resistance. They shared the same strategy and the same goals but operated independently as individuals or small groups. In Russia the major anarchist group was the People's Will that targeted government figures, including the Tsar who was assassinated in 1881 (Weinberg and Eubank 2011, 24). The People's Will was destroyed by the security forces, but it was succeeded by the Social Revolutionaries who followed a similar pattern combining assassinations with more conventional political actions such as demonstrations and strikes. They also assassinated other government officials such as cabinet ministers and local governors (Gaucher 1968, 33; Lutz and Lutz 2005, 53–4). The anarchist-inspired violence generally ended with the outbreak of World War I, but some groups reappeared after the war. Simon (2008, 211) suggests that anarchist violence in the United States after the war provides valuable lessons for current terrorism.

After World War I, there were additional examples of terrorist violence. There was continuing anarchist violence in both Europe and the United States. This violence and a fear of communism and anarchism led to the Red Scare in the United States resulting in government toleration of vigilante actions against foreign elements with radical ideas. The KKK, which was reborn in 1915, initially focused much of its attention on these foreign threats. This new version of the KKK was opposed to immigrants with dangerous ideas or representing foreign cultures and like its predecessor it has been considered a terrorist group. Closer to the outbreak of World War II the KKK also targeted blacks in the American south as its predecessor had. In Europe, the IRA was successful in winning virtual independence for the Irish Free State. Elsewhere there was also a great deal of violence and intimidation by right-wing fascist groups that used street battles, intimidation, and other types of violence as part of efforts to replace democratic governments with regimes better able to resist threats from global communism and to appropriate values from the past (Lyttelton 1982). Whilst these groups have not always been considered as terrorist organizations, there has been some recognition that terrorism was a weapon in their arsenal of activities (Wilkinson 1977, 22; Lutz and Lutz 2005, 70–3). The violence, sometimes combined with more conventional electoral practices, was successful in bringing to power the Fascists in Italy, the Nazis in Germany, and briefly the Iron Guard in Romania.

Rapoport's second wave of modern terrorism consisted of anti-colonial struggles that became prominent after the end of World War II. The struggle of the Irish for independence from Great Britain was an early precursor of this wave. It continued with the struggles in Algeria, Cyprus, Palestine, Aden, and elsewhere in Africa and Asia. This wave was followed by the third one which consisted of what Rapoport considered to be the new left. The groups involved in this wave relied on a variety of Marxist-Leninist perspectives to guide their assault on the world capitalist system. The earlier groups appeared in Latin America, protesting inequities in their countries and drawing some inspiration from Castro's victory in Cuba. Other groups then appeared in West Europe, including the Red Brigades in Italy, the Baader-Meinhoff Gang (Red Army Faction) in West Germany, and 17 November in Greece amongst others. These groups considered the US involvement in Vietnam to be part of the global capitalist scheme to exploit workers and developing countries. Most of these groups aligned themselves with the remaining national liberation struggles, including that of Palestinian groups. The fourth wave that carried into the twenty-first century consisted of terrorism based on religion. The most obvious group involved has been Al Qaeda, **ISIS**, and the associated global jihadist organizations. Terrorism rooted in religious views, of course, was not limited to Islam and included groups as different as the Christian Identity movement, Jewish extremists, the Sikh efforts to gain independence for the Punjab, groups with fundamentalist Hindu views in India, and cults like Aum Shinrikyo in Japan.

A historical perspective on terrorism that looks at early examples of the phenomenon, as with the examples above and others, demonstrates that this type of political activity has been present for many, many centuries even if many examples have not been routinely recognized as being terrorism. These cases also demonstrate that modern terrorism shares several characteristics with more ancient terrorism. Battles over political control in ancient Rome or the Italian city-states preceded similar conflicts in the Reign of Terror (which is sometimes seen as the beginning of terrorism). Dissidents in Judea kidnapped the son of a high-ranking official to successfully exchange for imprisoned rebel members. The anarchists were an early example of leaderless resistance, a technique variously associated by researchers today with global jihadists, environmental groups, or violent right-wing extremists in the United States. There have also been examples of state toleration and support of terrorism against other citizens in earlier eras as was present in the Italian city-states, the Fascist and Nazi activities after World War I, and the Boxer Rebellion. The techniques from the past have indeed become the techniques of the present and very likely the future with suitable modifications for improvements in communications and transportation as well as the fact that the weapons available to terrorist organizations can cause more and more casualties.

There is at least one important difference between the earlier examples of terrorism and more recent incidents. The outbreaks in many of the earlier times were facilitated by a lack of police to control situations. Rome in the late Republic lacked an effective police force to control the street violence, there was no effective police to deal with the dissidents in Judea, and police agencies had disappeared at the time of the French Revolution (Lutz and Lutz 2006). In the prelude to the American Revolution, the crown had to depend upon the local colonial authorities to enforce rule, regulations, and tax collection and got very little assistance in this area. The local militias were totally unreliable for dealing with attacks against loyalists, in part because the local colonial governments tolerated and even supported the dissident groups. In other cases, however, there was no lack of security forces. The Assassins reached their targets despite security precautions. The anarchists operated in a period when police forces had appeared and which attempted to deal with the threat. In yet other cases, the state provided cover for the attacks, thus neutralizing a barrier to terrorist violence. In the present times, the presence of well-organized police forces, advanced security services, and significant armed forces have not prevented the outbreak of terrorist violence. Interestingly enough, the establishment of security agencies was one historical response to political violence by dissident groups. After the collapse of the Republic, the Roman Empire established a secret police force (Africa 1971, 8–9, 12), and the nobility in Florence also established a secret police agency in an effort to better control the popular groups in the city (Hale 1977, 16). As a consequence, too much can be made of the absence of security forces in the past since it is obvious that determined dissidents can overcome the obstacles and launch their attacks. What appears to be the most important variable, both then and now, is not the level of precautions taken but the determination of such groups to challenge existing political systems and a willingness to use violence to do so when other options fail.

Ultimately, more consideration of potential terrorism in the past is necessary, and such historical analyses can be effective in informing current research. LaFree et al. (2015, 235–6) have suggested that modern terrorism is distinctly different from ancient terrorism since the potential for more death and destruction has resulted from increasingly lethal weapons and explosives and more concentrated urban populations. Whilst this conclusion is true at one level, in less recent times existing weapons were capable of inflicting death and destruction on much smaller populations and thus would be proportionately the same in their effects. For example, the death toll in Europe during World War II was extremely high as modern armies battled for control of large areas and cities, but the devastation caused by the Thirty Years War in the seventeenth century resulted in the depopulation of large portions of central Europe. As a consequence, it continues to be necessary to analyze historical contexts more deeply to determine the level of terrorism that was present in distant and not so distant times. The knowledge gained from these analyses in conjunction with analyses of more current examples can be applied to discussions of terrorism and compared in terms of the sources of the issues that led to this particular form of political violence, and may even suggest counter-strategies to deal with the conditions that lead to terrorism. Historical analyses can and do refine, reinforce, and expand upon contributions from the social sciences. Comparisons of the techniques, the role of technologies, successes and failures, and the objectives of the groups seeking change could also be quite constructive and a major contribution to the study of terrorism.

References

Africa, Thomas W. (1971) "Urban Violence in Imperial Rome," *Journal of Interdisciplinary History*, 2(1): 3–21.

Allegro, John M. (1972) *The Chosen People: A Study of Jewish History from the Time of the Exile until the Revolt of Bar Kocheba, Sixth Century B.C. to Second Century A.D.* Garden City, NY: Doubleday.

Andriolo, Karin (2002) "Murder by Suicide: Episodes from Muslim History," *American Anthropologist*, 104(3): 736–42.

Brunt, P. A. (1966) "The Roman Mob," *Past and Present*, 35: 3–27.

Chaliand, Gerard, and Arnaud Blin (2007) "Zealots and Assassins," in Gerard Chaliand and Arnaud Blin (eds), *The History of Terrorism: From Antiquity to Al Qaeda*, tr. Edward Schneider, Kathryn Pulver, and Jesse Browner (Berkeley, CA: University of California Press), 55–78.

Daftary, Farhad (1991) *The Assassin Legends: Myths of the Isma'ilis*. London: IB Taurus.

Dale, Stephen Frederic (1988) "Religious Suicide in Islamic Asia: Anticolonial Terrorism in India, Indonesia, and the Philippines," *Journal of Conflict Resolution*, 32(1): 37–59.

Davis, Paul Bradley (1996) "American Experiences and the Contemporary Perception of Terrorism," *Small Wars and Insurgencies*, 7(2): 220–42.

Day, Gerald W. (1988) *Genoa's Response to Byzantium, 1155–1204: Commercial Expansion and Factionalism in a Medieval City*. Urbana, IL: University of Illinois Press.

Derfler, Steven L. (1989) *The Hasmonean Revolt: Rebellion or Revolution*. Ancient Near Eastern Texts and Studies, 5. Lewiston, NY: Edwin Mellen Press.

Fellman, Michael (2010) *In the Name of God and Country: Reconsidering Terrorism in American History*. New Haven: Yale University Press.

Gaucher, Roland (1968) *The Terrorists: From Tsarist Russia to the O.A.S.*, tr. Paula Spurlin. London: Secker & Warburg.

Hale, J. R. (1977) *Florence and the Medici: The Pattern of Control*. London: Thames & Hudson.

Hollon, W. Eugene (1974) *Frontier Violence: Another Look*. New York: Oxford University Press.

Josephus (1981) *The Jewish War*, tr. G. A. Williamson. New York: Dorset Press.

Kaplan, Jeffrey (2016) "A Strained Criticism of Wave Theory," *Terrorism and Political Violence*, 28(2): 228–35.

LaFree, Gary, Laura Dugan, and Erin Miller (2015) *Putting Terrorism in Context: Lessons from the Global Terrorism Database*. London: Routledge).

Lutz, Brenda J., and James M. Lutz (2006) "Political Violence in the Republic of Rome: Nothing New under the Sun," *Government and Opposition*, 41(4): 491–511.

Lutz, Brenda J., and James M. Lutz (2014) "John Brown as Guerrilla and Terrorist," *Small Wars and Insurgencies*, 25(5/6): 1039–54.

Lutz, Brenda J., and James M. Lutz (2015) "Globalization, Risk Taking, and Violence: Too Much Too Soon in the Late Roman Republic and Pre-Renaissance Italian Cities," *Cambridge Review of International Affairs*, 28(2): 175–90.

Lutz, James M., and Brenda J. Lutz (2005) *Terrorism: Origins and Evolution*. New York: Palgrave.

Lutz, James M., and Brenda J. Lutz (2007) *Terrorism in America*. New York: Palgrave.

Lutz, James M., and Brenda J. Lutz (2013) "The Role of Foreign Influences in Early Terrorism: Examples and Implications for Understanding Modern Terrorism," *Perspectives on Terrorism*, 7(2): 5–22.

Lyttelton, Adrian (1982) "Fascism and Violence in Post-War Italy: Political Strategy and Social Conflict," in Wolfgang J. Mommsen and Gerhard Hirschfeld (eds), *Social Protest, Violence and Terror in Nineteenth- and Twentieth-Century Europe*. New York: St Martin's Press for the German Historical Institute, 257–74.

Martines, Lauro (1967–8) "Political Conflict in the Italian City States," *Government and Opposition*, 3(1): 69–91.

Millar, Fergus (1998) *The Crowd in the Late Roman Republic*. Thomas Spencer Jerome Lectures, 22. Ann Arbor, MI: University of Michigan Press.

Morgan, Edmund S., and Helen M. Morgan (1962) *The Stamp Act Crisis: Prologue to Revolution*, 2nd edn. New York: Collier Books.

Parker, Tom, and Nick Sitter (2016) "The Four Horsemen of Terrorism: It's Not Waves, it's Strains," *Terrorism and Political Violence*, 28(2): 197–216.

Parry, Albert (1976) *From Robespierre to Arafat*. New York: Vanguard Press.

Pedahzur, Ami, and Arie Perliger (2011) *Jewish Terrorism in Israel*. New York: Columbia University Press.

Raper, Arthur R. (1978) "The Tragedy of Lynching," in Roger Lane and John T. Turner, Jr. (eds), *Riot, Rout, and Tumult: Readings in American Social and Political Violence*. Contributions in American History, 69. Westport, CT: Greenwood Press, 292–9.

Rapoport, David (1984) "Fear and Trembling: Terrorism in Three Religious Traditions," *American Political Science Review*, 78(3): 658–77.

Rapoport, David C. (2003) "The Four Waves of Rebel Terror and September 11th," in Charles W. Kegley, Jr (ed.), *The New Global Terrorism: Characteristics, Causes, Controls*. Upper Saddle River, NJ: Prentice Hall, 36–52.

Rapoport, David C. (2016) "It is Waves, Not Strains," *Terrorism and Political Violence*, 28(2): 217–24.

Reich, Walter (1998) "Understanding Terrorist Behaviour: The Limits and Opportunities of Psychological Inquiry," in Walter Reich (ed.), *Origins of Terrorism: Psychologies, Ideologies Theologies, States of Mind*. Washington, DC: Woodrow Wilson Center Press, 261–79.

Release, Allen W. (1978) "Reconstruction: The Great Experiment," in Roger Lane and John T. Turner, Jr. (eds), *Riot, Rout, and Tumult: Readings in American Social and Political Violence*. Contributions in American History, 69. Westport, CT: Greenwood Press, 200–17.

Rude, George (1959) *The Crowd in the French Revolution*. Oxford: Clarendon Press.

Scheslinger, Arthur Meier (1955) "Political Mobs and the American Revolution, 1765–1776," *Proceedings of the American Philosophical Society*, 99(4): 244–50.

Simon, Jeffrey D. (2008) "The Forgotten Terrorists: Lessons from the History of Terrorism," *Terrorism and Political Violence*, 20(2): 195–214.

Tracey, Patricia Cleland (2000) "Cherokee Gold in Georgia and California," *Journal of the West*, 39(1): 49–55.

van Every, Dale (1966) *Disinherited: The Lost Birthright of the American Indian*. New York: William Morrow.

Villard, Oswald Garrison (1965) *John Brown, 1800–1859: A Bibliography Fifty Years After*. Gloucester, MA: Peter Smith; 1st publ. 1910.

Weinberg, Leonard, and William Eubank (2011) "Women's Involvement in Terrorism," *Gender Issues*, 28(1): 22–49.

Wilkinson, Paul (1975) *Political Terrorism*. New York: Halstead Press.

Wilkinson, Paul (1977) *Terrorism and the Liberal State*. London: Macmillan.

CHAPTER 14

PSYCHOLOGICAL APPROACHES TO THE STUDY OF TERRORISM

JOHN G. HORGAN

Introduction

In 1953 psychologist Alfred Kinsey noted the "tendency to consider anything in human behavior that is unusual, not well known, or not well understood, as neurotic, psychopathic, immature, perverse, or the expression of some other sort of psychological disturbance" (Kinsey et al. 1953, 195). Kinsey's focus was female sexual behavior, but he could just as easily have characterized terrorism in the same way. To that end, let's acknowledge a bottom line upfront: we cannot currently explain why some people engage in terrorism while others do not. After four decades of research on terrorist psychology, the unquestionable conclusion is we simply do not know. A cursory read of the psychological literature would suggest that this is unlikely to change any time soon (Horgan 2014). Whether it is realistic to expect a satisfactory answer to an inherently complex question, our inability to answer the question of why some become involved in terrorism when most do not has led some to conclude that terrorism studies per se is stagnant (Sageman 2014). Whether such characterization is fair has been addressed elsewhere. A 2014 volume of *Terrorism and Political Violence* was devoted entirely to that.

The challenge of prediction (an issue at the heart of psychological approaches to behavior) has found expression in much publicized discussions around the concept of Countering Violent Extremism (CVE). CVE is a catch-all term that encompasses a variety of formal and informal programmatic efforts to heighten education about terrorism and the dangers associated with becoming involved in it. It remains a concept as nobody really knows what CVE ought to involve, let alone whose responsibility it is to create, implement, and evaluate such programs. A common thread throughout such efforts (in the UK and US) is that in order to effectively *counter* violent extremism one should be able to identify it in its nascent stages. "Countering" is, in reality, a substitute for the more pressing focus of "Prevention." Regardless, most CVE efforts assume we ought to be able to reliably distinguish those who become involved in terrorism (or intend to) from those who do not (or do not intend to). There are instances where an individual openly declares his (or her) intent to others to engage in acts of public violence like terrorism (e.g. Gill et al., 2014) although this behavior tends to be associated with only one type of terrorism, that of so-called "lone actors." However, with most individuals who become involved in terrorism, we cannot reliably predict the precise composition of violent extremism prior to the actions taking place.

That lacuna is increasingly recognized if not necessarily accepted. It certainly has not prevented many from seizing opportunities to provide their own theories about what is causing people to become involved in terrorism. Some of these, despite launching to considerable public fanfare by suggesting a "quick fix" (Moskalenko 2013, 843), are almost always subsequently revealed, upon closer scrutiny, to be less than convincing.

What we *can* say, for which there is empirical support, is the following: Terrorism is complex and dynamic. The very *nature* of terrorism means that it will be difficult for any single parsimonious explanation to prevail. What might motivate someone to become initially involved with a terrorist group may be very different to the kinds of influences that motivate that same person to remain committed and engaged. Additionally, how a specific group attempts to attract recruits today may be different from how the same group appeals to potential future followers. Psychological research on terrorism asserts that there is no single route into terrorism, even within the same group, let alone between or across multiple groups engaged in terrorism. Further, there is no meaningful (i.e. stable) profile of who becomes a terrorist. There are people of all ages involved, young and old. Terrorists can be men, women, even children; some of whom want to become involved, others are given no choice. Some join alone, while others join because of pre-existing interest and opportunities afforded via friends, or family members. Though we can identify common themes in accounts of former terrorists (via autobiographies, interviews, and other testimony) disentangling motivation is tricky. Reconstructed accounts are easily skewed by the nuances (intentional or otherwise) of interviewer questions, biases of those doing the recall, and the simple fallibility of memory.

Potential recruits may have an inkling of what involvement might be like, while others nurture elaborate fantasies about involvement, what roles they will have or which duties they will perform. The "radicalization process" (a shorthand description to capture the process of involvement with a terrorist group as well as subsequent engagement in terrorist activity) is neither linear nor stable, and works differently for different people. The process is impacted by both the circumstances of the individual as well as the socio-political environment and organizational context in which the movement is seeking to exert pressure (Taylor and Horgan 2006). There may be a generic set of psychological risk factors associated with those who become involved, but not every factor carries the same weight for everyone, and as such the pre-involvement "symptoms" associated with one case might look a little different from one person to the next. People are drawn to extremism for different reasons, often with different expectations, and while they might share some similarities there is no consistent pattern or a neat profile that distinguishes them from each other or those who don't get involved at all. If anything, people who become involved in terrorism might tend to appear more similar only *after* they are involved in a group—as otherwise diverse people begin to "talk the talk" and "walk the walk."

Ideology is relevant, though poorly understood. Some individuals embrace an ideology before joining the group while others adopt ideology afterwards. Some espouse the group's ideology when preparing for an actual attack or because they need to justify their actions to themselves or others after the fact. Others seek out an ideology after they've decided they want to *do something*. For those who become involved in violent extremist groups (as opposed to those who act independent of accessibility to a physical group), acquiring the ideology, the language, and the mindset happens further along the path—they are just some of the acquired qualities of engagement as opposed to prerequisites for initial involvement in the first place.

Mental illness cannot explain why people are drawn to terrorism, though, of course, some individuals may be mentally ill either before or resulting from involvement in terrorism. The act of hiding, lying to friends or family, feelings of paranoia, and guilt for violence can impact the most mentally stable person. Mental illness is increasingly associated with some terrorists (notably among lone actors—e.g. Gill et al. 2014), but there is no convincing evidence that their mental condition played a role (let alone *the* major role) in predetermining their involvement.

What Does a "Psychology of Terrorism" Mean?

No matter what we do, or how well we do it, we will probably never have a simple answer to the question of who becomes involved in violent extremism and why. This is in part because of unrealistic expectations. In few areas of human activity would we expect to arrive at so elegant an answer for understanding motivation, let alone for something as dauntingly complex as terrorism. Equally, we have lingering problems with the label "terrorism." This has less to do with the perennial "definition question" but more because of its inherent categorical fuzziness—involvement in terrorism is neither limited to violence, nor does it necessarily involve one specific job or a set of discrete behaviors. Its heterogeneity is one of its defining characteristics, and even the most limited and fleeting involvement in terrorism can lead to fulfilling a variety of roles, functions, tasks (Taylor and Horgan 2006), each of which can change in type, task load, and psychological demand over time.

But it also means that we need to temper current expectations around prevention. Psychologists who study terrorism may obsess over what qualities distinguish the mere radical from the terrorist in the making. This fixation occurs at the expense of asking answerable and relevant questions that have more practical outcomes (e.g. mapping *what* terrorists actually do, and *how* they do it, versus *why* they did it).

As a consequence of all of this, the reader may be tempted to believe that psychological research on terrorism has failed—after all, surely individual-level issues seem to be the domain of the psychologist. Do these assertions confirm Sageman's thesis regarding the stagnation of terrorism research? I suggest not. Research has firmly established that the pathway to terrorism cannot be reduced to single variable theories, observations, or analogies. These assertions are not the "problem" or weakness of terrorism studies, but rather they are some of the emergent conclusions from that effort.

Even aside from this predominant question, there is progress in the development of psychological perspectives on terrorism. Psychology remains *the scientific study of behavior*. However one views terrorism (from whichever discipline, prejudice, or inherent bias) and on whatever level of analysis (e.g. individual, group, organizational, subnational, etc.) terrorism is behavior, and thus rests firmly in the sights of psychology. Given that, we have a conundrum since the field of psychology has not embraced the study of terrorism in the same way that political science or criminology have.

Though psychologists have regularly studied terrorist behavior since the early 1970s, the discipline has struggled to sustain even the most basic commentary about psychological issues related to terrorism, and has done so superficially in ways that would make most contemporary psychologists balk (Victoroff 2005; Borum 2011a, 2011b). Terrorism demands a multidisciplinary perspective, and as evidenced by this volume, this approach is now widely accepted.

However, this approach presents potentially negative consequences: in promoting cross-disciplinary engagement with considerable time and effort, we may have sacrificed intra-disciplinary development. This might explain why psychological perspectives remain bogged down in age-old debates that are less about hair-splitting and more a testament to a lack of imagination about the promise of a well-developed psychological approach. One could argue that terrorism studies remains in its infancy despite the recent growth spurts accelerated by major developments and current events, that serious psychological research on terrorism is in dire need of a lifeline.

To be fair, any critical examination of psychological research on terrorism (Silke 2003; Borum 2011a, 2011b; Victoroff 2005) identifies what we can extol, and what should be avoided. The scope of psychological research on terrorism, thus far, has addressed a litany of issues, such as:

(a) What drives/motivates someone to become involved in terrorism (Taylor 1988; Silke 2003; Victoroff 2005)?

(b) Why do some people seek to create and lead terrorist groups, while others prefer to follow (Post 1988; Reich 1990a)?

(c) Why do some people consciously withdraw from involvement in terrorism (Bjorgo and Horgan 2009)?
(d) What are the group or organizational conditions that sustain and shape involvement in terrorism (Ligon et al. 2013)?
(e) What factors cause terrorist behavior to escalate or de-escalate?
(f) What factors cause terrorist behavior to end (Barrelle 2015)?
(g) What factors cause terrorist recidivism (Horgan and Braddock 2010)?
(h) How does terrorist violence impact or affect one or more intended audiences or targets (Bongar et al. 2006)?
(i) How do terrorists psychologically equip themselves prior to engaging in acts of violence (Horgan 2014)?
(j) Does gender impact motivation (or vice versa) to engage in terrorism (Sjoberg and Gentry 2011)?
(k) How do terrorists behave during specific types of crisis (e.g. hostage-taking) (Reich 1990b)?
(l) How and why is terrorism effective as a form of psychological warfare (Hoffman 1998)?
(m) What factors affect the development of responses to terrorism (Silke 2018)?
(n) What causes some groups to use suicide bombing as a tactic (Merari 2010)?

We could easily develop this list, as there is scarcely any issue addressed by psychological research that is not in some way relevant to terrorism and terrorists. Furthermore, not all of the researchers who have "done" psychological research on terrorism are psychologists. However, the qualities of a longer list would become apparent, and a hierarchy of sorts would quickly reveal itself. Though many might consider the question of "why does someone become a terrorist?" the Holy Grail for psychologists, ironically in a recent survey of what they claim are the 100 most cited articles on terrorism research, Silke and Schmidt-Petersen (2017) found that the second and third (and then fifth and sixth) were psychological research on surveys of PTSD and stress reactions following the 9/11 attacks of 2001.

A major bottleneck in the growth of psychological approaches to terrorist behavior is a paucity of focus at the level of graduate programs; and here there is a delicate balance to be maintained. On the one hand, the field urgently requires attention from more psychologists. However, we also need a *better* psychology of terrorism, one that transcends old tropes and pseudo-science. Almost thirty years ago, Martha Crenshaw called for the "demystification of terrorism" through psychological research, and warned that if terrorism research was ignored by serious scholars, "the field will be left to simplistic rhetoric and confused assumptions" (Crenshaw 1990, 260). Yet despite the increasing interest in terrorism since the early 2000s, psychology remains aloof. As a result, the literature sees an endless parade of metaphors, analogies, and half-baked theories to fill the void.

Roberts (2015) in his review of terrorism research recommends that we "salute what has been achieved" (p. 63). Several authors have produced detailed examinations of psychological issues of terrorism that represent, in some cases, the culmination of decades of research. Some focus on particular kinds of terrorism (e.g. Atran 2010; Sageman 2008), others consider what psychology has to say about the spectrum and diversity of terrorist groups and behavior (e.g. Taylor 1988; Post 2007) while notable edited collections have encompassed the array of applications of psychology to understanding terrorism more generally (e.g. Reich 1990a; Silke 2003; Bongar et al. 2006). There are, of course, highly focused and detailed literature reviews on the individual psychology of terrorist behavior (Silke 2003; Borum 2011a, 2011b; and Victoroff 2005).

Where Have we Come From and Where are we Going?

Psychological perspectives on terrorism, for now, are in their infancy. Any psychological perspective on terrorism, Reich cautioned (1990b, 4), would be "difficult and inevitably imperfect" and, undoubtedly, each review of the literature (including those already listed) invariably spends considerable effort explaining how the field is "beset by problems that, in devious but powerful ways, limit, undermine or even vitiate it" (1990c, 261). These range from the conceptual to the theoretical to the methodological to, increasingly, limitations and narrowness of interpretation.

If we were to map this history, psychological research on terrorism corresponds to a few major waves. Mirroring the rise of mass-mediated international terrorism, it wasn't until the 1970s that psychologists and other mental health professionals (mostly psychiatrists) took an interest in exploring the terrorist mindset. From that decade into the early to mid-1980s we saw the first forays into terrorist psychology from a small group of researchers. Most produced one-off contributions, but would provide a foundation of contributions from which (and against which) subsequent generations would develop their own analysis and perspective.

Much of the early research (roughly between 1975 and 1985) could be characterized as reductionist (see especially Corrado 1981; Crenshaw, 1981) and that gave rise to a view that psychological research was fundamentally about associating terrorism with abnormality. On the one hand, terrorism is, by its very nature, a statistically and socially abnormal phenomenon. Psychological analyses (and interpretations that flowed from these) mirrored that diagnosis. For example, it was during this period that psychopathy first became associated with the terrorist (Corrado 1981; Crenshaw 1981), which would in turn serve as a focal point for the next decade of psychological research, in no small part as a reaction to those initial characterizations. But this early literature was preoccupied with what made the terrorist different, special, or abnormal in a psychological sense, whether, to paraphrase Silke (2003) in a "major" way, or a "minor" one.

From the earliest days of criminology to attempts to understand the psychology of the fanatic, efforts have been made to decipher the qualities deemed to predispose some individuals (and not others) to either form or follow violent movements. Hoffer (1951) surmised that while mass movements had much to offer the fanatic, such movements "all appeal to the same types of mind" (p. xi). Hoffer's own thesis was that: "those who fail in everyday affairs show a tendency to reach out for the impossible. It is a device to camouflage their shortcomings" (p. 76). Individual involvement in terrorism has been connected to everything from narcissism, paranoia, and many other personality disorders, to psychopathy, to the perennially curious "faulty inner-ear vestibular functioning" (Reich 1990c, 268), suicidal tendencies (Lankford 2011), as well as "barometric pressure, moon phases, alcoholism, droughts, and cranial measurements" (Reich 1990c, 268). There is scarcely an issue that has not been linked in some way to the development of extreme behavior. Though he was not specifically addressing terrorism, Hoffer himself surmised that "the decline of handicrafts in modern times" (Hoffer 1951, 34) contributed to the susceptibility of people to "violent mass movements."

Perhaps unfairly (in some cases), these types of accounts are relegated to historical curiosities. They have been explored and addressed in great detail (Silke 2003; Victoroff 2005), though not every reviewer's interpretation of the original studies is the same (Horgan 2014). In some cases, their limitations are methodological, but for the most part the problem was one of interpretation, or rather the failure to acknowledge the limitations of any one set of observations (more on this later).

Some of the most influential research from this time attempted to uncover whether specific personality traits were associated with terrorism (see Silke 2003 for detailed reviews). Furthermore, such accounts would perpetuate a tendency for psychological accounts to "ignore or blur the variety and the complexity" (Reich 1990c, 262) of both those who become involved in terrorism as well as the immense heterogeneity of roles and functions involved in even the smallest of terrorist groups (Taylor and Horgan 2006).

Some of these studies (notably those concerned with European and American left-wing terrorists) saw researchers acquiring face-to-face access with terrorist prisoners. A remarkable study, conducted in 1980–1, of over 227 West German prisoners represented one of the most ambitious studies of psychological research considered routine in any other setting. However, as Crenshaw (1990) explained, a series of methodological and ethical issues would mar the conclusions, notably because many of the "terrorists" interviewed by the mental health professionals during this time were not actually convicted of a terrorist offense—but were merely suspects, awaiting charges of involvement in groups including the Red Army Faction.

Thirty-five years later, John Monahan (2012, 2016) attempted to interview terrorist prisoners in the United States. His premise was that finding a group of terrorists in which to test many of the claims associated with psychological research (risk assessment, in this case) remained profoundly difficult. He had exasperating experiences attempting to navigate the bureaucracy associated with accessing incarcerated terrorists: "For at least six years . . . repeated attempts by me and other researchers . . . to interview terrorist prisoners have been rebuffed by the Bureau of Prisons on the grounds that obtaining the interview data required for analysis 'would pose security and workload concerns.'"

But one of the most cited assertions in terrorism studies was Martha Crenshaw's (1981) view that "the outstanding common characteristic of terrorists is their normality." Shifting the debate slightly from one of "normality versus abnormality" to appreciating the role of the "normal," i.e. the mundane and routine, social psychological dynamics would increasingly feature in attempts to understand both how people are attracted to terrorist groups as well as how, from equally mundane circumstances, extreme violence develops (Taylor 1988).

Much of that initial wave was small-scale and had a distinctly clinical tinge. But there was a gradual shift taking place. More and more researchers would come to view terrorism not as the byproduct of individual psychology, but as an inherently group process. Such a characterization would define the next twenty years of research and remains a critical feature today.

The 1980s heralded a change in focus for psychologists. Though the multi-level nature of terrorism analysis was recognized, by this point the terrorist group began to occupy a central concern. This second wave involved psychologists like Ariel Merari, Jerrold Post, Max Taylor, Clark McCauley, and others highlighting the role of social and group dynamics and how they shaped and sustained terrorist behavior. Merari, Post, and McCauley's shared emphases on group processes (echoed and amplified by Taylor), combined with Crenshaw's recurring emphasis on the role and nature of terrorist *organizations*, would provide a bedrock of conceptual thinking about terrorist psychology that persists today (crystallized in Walter Reich's 1990 seminal *Origins of Terrorism*).

Prior to 2001, there were fewer than a dozen psychologists worldwide with a sustained research interest on terrorist behavior. Over the past decade plus, we have witnessed a resurgence of interest in psychological research on terrorism. The events of September 11, 2001 would give rise to the most recent wave of terrorism research, and one in which the overwhelming majority of output would be produced for the field as a whole.

In these first few years, the knotty issue of "radicalization" would occupy center stage. The term became synonymous with psychological research on terrorism; it is virtually impossible to discuss terrorist behavior without some reference to the process of radicalization. Researchers from all disciplines and backgrounds would likewise ponder the issue. Such was the dearth of psychologists' contributions to these debates that psychological concepts would be misappropriated, confused, and incorrectly deployed as a means to support whatever cherished positions individual researchers and radicalization pundits sought to promote.

One of the most important paradigmatic shifts during this time was the move from thinking of the individual recruit as "special" or different to being largely unremarkable individuals in extraordinary circumstances (an implicit assumption of the research that emerged in the 1980s and 1990s was if they *were* "special" or different, it would only be because of what they *did* after becoming involved). Additionally, the realization that how "radicalization" worked, and the role played by individual qualities, could never be solved by looking at either individual recruits (or their *qualities*) alone.

Acknowledgement of the critical role of group and organizational dynamics in shaping terrorism had grown appreciably since the mid-1980s, but there always remained a lingering suspicion that those who became involved in terrorism were still remarkable in some way.

Missing from so much of the research was a focus on interpersonal dynamics. Recruitment implied a process of sorts, so while individual recruits may have shared a few broad psychological similarities (regardless of whether we could empirically verify their existence and subsequently measure their influence) more and more emphasis shifted to the ways in which terrorist organizations and recruiters reached out and mobilized individuals (e.g. Hegghammer 2013). Case studies of recruiters are rare, despite the clear influence and critical role played by some. Consider Djamel Beghal, responsible for the initial radicalization of Amedy Coulibaly, the Islamic State-linked militant who killed four people in a Paris supermarket in January 2015 during the Charlie Hebdo attack. Coulibaly had told French police that Beghal mentored him, and "touched me in a human way" (Birnbaum and Mekhennet 2015).

Armed with increasing insights from former terrorists willing to share their experiences with researchers, autobiographies, and court testimonies, psychologists were afforded new insights into the process of becoming involved in, remaining involved in, and disengaging from, terrorism. In the 2000s, terrorist psychology was no longer just about the "why" question, but would eventually make way for new and exciting developments that would encompass the entire "arc" of terrorism—from involvement, to engagement, to disengagement (Horgan and Taylor 2011). And even so, despite this welcome expansion, we know little about the psychological qualities of engaging in terroristic violence. Cottee and Hayward (2011) prompt us to be mindful that terrorism, "for those who practice and embrace it, can be profoundly thrilling, empowering and spiritually intoxicating, and... this particular aspect of it may inform, along with other key motivations no doubt, the decision to engage in it" (p. 965). Cottee and Hayward urge more attention be paid to the *phenomenology* of terrorism—how it *feels* like to do it.

Little is known about such interactions, as well as the ways in which individuals experience and cope with "feedback" as a result of what they do as "terrorists" (i.e. whatever range of activities they engage in as part of a terrorist group) but the psychology of such interactions is central to unlocking one of the most overlooked part of the radicalization process. Cottee and Hayward conclude: "At the moment of its inception... the central project of terrorism studies was to normalize the terrorist agent. Today, over half a century later, the more urgent task is to *humanize* him. "(2011, 980). Recruitment draws on intensely personal dynamics, and yet those continue to be ignored at the expense of incorrectly assuming the primacy of individual traits or qualities in what we assume is a knowable "closed-loop" system of motivation.

From 2005 onwards, the question of the terrorist personality, as well as whether mental illness was a key driver in terrorism, would make a comeback, and in one case (Adam Lankford's (2011) equally maligned/celebrated argument that suicide terrorists were themselves suicidal) made the pages of the *New York Times*. Lankford's findings were publicly lauded, and praised by popular scholars including Stephen Pinker and others whose endorsements filled the back cover. Yet others were not so convinced. Sophia Moskalenko (2013, 841) explains: "Lankford's thesis, stripped down to bare bones, is this: suicide terrorists are not martyrs, despite their belief and efforts to convince others that they are. What's more, suicide terrorists are deeply flawed in a weak, shameful way: they are crazy and suicidal." The reaction by terrorism scholars tended to be less than supportive of Lankford's findings, case selection for whose study excluded the Irish Hunger Strikers during the Troubles and did not include research featuring interviews with failed suicide bombers. Moskalenko's critique suggested that Lankford's thesis is replete with (p. 841):

> poor arguments, or sometimes no arguments beyond emotional appeals. In pursuit of one part of his thesis—that suicide terrorists are clinically depressed and suicidal—Lankford dismisses terrorists' own testaments, including martyrdom videos, as misleading or delusional. He also dismisses testimony of relatives and friends as the product of conspiracy or denial. What remains are the author's own interpretations of circumstances (death of brother, loneliness) that, according to psychological research, usually do not lead to suicidal thoughts.

In the new-found rush to publication, not seen since the very earliest days of terrorism studies, it would become difficult if not impossible for the novice researcher to know how to judge research without making their own minds up by returning to the original source. In a broader lament about the state of affairs, Sageman implored researchers to "get the story straight, based on reliable data before proceeding to analysis and conclusions. Too many academics make unsubstantiated claims mimicking research and cite each other, generating an echo effect of erroneous information" (2014, 618). Sageman himself in the pages of *Terrorism and Political Violence* argued,

> I simply do not see [scholarly critiques happening] in terrorism research, where publication of theoretical speculation is usually greeted with polite silence. Worse, each new terrorist incident revives the same old tired myths and polemics about terrorists in the mass media rather than scholarly debates. Indeed, it seems that many scholars are eager to appear on television right after such incidents to promote their pet speculations... One way to jump start such scholarly debates is to take each other's work seriously, break the polite silence and... ask difficult questions about unexamined assumptions and unsubstantiated assertions from other scholars.
> (2014, 617)

The history of psychological research on terrorism has demonstrated that long-term nuance is typically now sacrificed for the gratification of short-term impact. When a drama or crisis unfolds, few (whether academics or not) want to hear how complex and labyrinthine terrorist motivation is. Each terrorist crisis brings with it the unerring tendency to, as Taylor (1988) warned, reduce the complexity of terrorism to something seemingly manageable, whether it be mental illness or something else.

Towards a Scientific Study of Terrorist Behavior

Terrorism is complex but whether we yet appreciate what that means is debatable. Reich warned that it would "give pause to anyone whose aim it is to understand it" (1990c, 262). Yet in the wake of an attack, we see the first of two unerring constants: "the public [turns] to psychiatrists and psychologists... to explain this aspect of terrorist behavior; and psychiatrists and psychologists, just as regularly, have rushed to give explanations, sometimes without even being asked" (Reich 1990c, 261). The nature of these explanations suggests that acknowledging terrorism's complexity is often little more than lip service. The second constant is the issue of whether a "clear profile" exists. The pendulum has swung the other way—it is now seemingly popular to say that there is not (e.g. Plumlee 2013). While the sentiment is laudable, it's not *technically* correct (for a more detailed discussion see Horgan 2014, 39, 67, 68). There are profiles (plenty of them, in fact), but they are not very stable, nor do they amount to anything useful in the context of prevention—a key, though implicit, challenge of asking for profiles is knowing what to do with them should they ever be provided. The qualities of even the most carefully researched profiles (e.g. see Gill and Horgan's (2013) profiles of 1,240 members of the Provisional IRA) do not lend themselves to reliably answering the question of who becomes involved in terrorism. It might be more correct to suggest all any profile really gives us is a snapshot into:

> how *specific* members of *specific* groups were at *specific* times of *specific* stages in their own *specific* types of terrorist campaign. This is hardly helpful to those who have other expectations of what a terrorist profile can offer them, but perhaps helps reinforce an argument that profiles should be based on analyses of behavior, as opposed to presenting portraits of what terrorists are "like." (Horgan 2014, 67–8)

In compiling sociological and operational data on over a thousand IRA members, Gill and Horgan (2013) were more concerned with assessing role types, and how shifting profiles impacted group effectiveness, resilience, and the eventual move towards conflict de-escalation—questions that transcend the usual trappings of profile-based enquiry.

In a comprehensive assessment of the prospects of terrorist risk assessment, Monahan (2016) concludes: "in no society studied to date have personality traits been found to distinguish those who engage in terrorism from those who refrain from it." We might do better if we better articulate, from a psychological perspective, what is involved in understanding terrorist motivation, and then more generally what is involved in developing a scientific approach to motivation. Although beyond the scope of this chapter, predicting "who becomes a terrorist?" is terrorism's *Big Bang* question. Various theories, ideas, and conjectures will proliferate but until we figure out if it is actually an answerable question, our inability to provide satisfactory answers should not distract us from seeking progress. If we do not want our entire field's progress to be judged by the inability to answer one (albeit key) question, then we as psychologists need to do a better job at providing a new vision for psychological perspectives. One key issue for completing the terrorist puzzle is to first arrive at more detailed, richer answers as to what terrorists do, how they do it, and when they do it—in other words, thick description. This is not to presume that we will never return to the "why" question, but an acknowledgment that satisfactory answers to the latter may take longer to emerge. That should not be at the expense of delivering action-oriented knowledge in the short term by shifting the focus slightly onto more achievable outcomes. To that end, and with an emphasis squarely on what terrorists do, and how they do it, as opposed to being overly concerned with *why we think* they do it (after all, it is primarily what *we* think about why they do it, rather than what *they* think about why they do it), recent studies have embraced this shift in emphasis.

Gill et al. (2014) compiled open-source data on 119 lone-actor terrorists, finding that, contrary to oft-repeated myths that "we never saw it coming," detectable and observable pre-attack behaviors were associated with lone-actor terrorism. They found that, in the time preceding the commission or attempted commission of attacks, in most cases people other than the actual offender knew about the offender's intention to engage in that act. In fact, in over 60 percent of cases studied, "family and friends were aware of the individual's intent to engage in terrorism-related activities because the offender verbally told them" (p. 5). As if this wasn't striking enough, significant differences emerged between different lone-actor types. These included the observation that offenders associated with Al Qaeda were younger, more often students, and likely to have sought legitimacy prior to the attack, compared to single-issue lone actors or those lone actors affiliated in some way with extreme right-wing movements. In some obvious ways, this research reinforced Reich's (1990b) point about the "enormous diversity" of terrorism, "and those who engage in it" (p. 1), even more so given that even within the narrow category of lone-actor terrorism, we still finding striking diversity and heterogeneity of both actor and act. Even the specific category of lone actors resists being reduced to simple patterns, profiles, or definitions.

Such studies represent a departure (Gill et al. 2014, 1) from previous work in the sense that they are not weighed down by the responsibility of providing *explanations* in the traditional sense, while still illustrating a fruitful avenue for psychological enquiry. At the same time, one of the strengths of such work is in the potential for informing debates about response. That the mental illness question remains is in itself not problematic, especially given how relatively immature terrorism studies is as a field of enquiry. Those who have spent a long time researching terrorism may be bored with the focus on that, but it does not limit the curiosity of others. Less satisfactory, however, is that it should receive *such* focus given so much promise in newer areas. This may be symptomatic of a limited understanding of what psychology is, which in turn suggests that it is the absence of psychologists in these debates that allows such inaccurate, confounded, and incorrect interpretations of concepts, theories, and entire debates.

Conclusions

To paraphrase Richard Jackson, instability characterizes much "knowledge" about terrorism. Debates that were once deemed to be settled have a tendency to re-emerge. Sometimes it is because the debates were never really settled in the first place. Otherwise, it may be because a contemporary researcher has a different (not always accurate) interpretation of both the original research as well as its findings. Last but not least, the phenomenon of terrorism itself continues to morph, and we should never hesitate to abandon old ways of thinking when confronted with new challenges. Though the scientific principles underpinning human behavior do not change, there is relatively little in psychological research on *terrorism* that provides new insights into the phenomenon that is the Islamic State. We are currently better served by perspectives on mass movements than we are by studies about individual terrorists or existing terrorist groups.

Our current understanding of terrorist psychology is similarly impressionistic. Profiles, and all other simplistic explanations of terrorism, are like photographs—still captures, forever open to different reactions and interpretations. But audiences need occasional reminding that, just like photographs, they are mere snapshots in time. A challenge for academics that work in policy-relevant areas is our tendency to jump over each other in the clamor to provide simple, elegant explanations that might make us feel better in the short term (Taylor 1988), and it helps us grab people's attention. But when the dust settles, and the allure of the quick fix turns to disappointment and cynicism, our field continues to suffer. Just like terrorism itself, deciphering motivation is a hard problem. A dozen different perspectives from psychology alone provide fundamentally different (often wildly opposing) views on how to understand behavior. We can take comfort in this, but also need to realize that the inability to appreciate complexity creates an environment in which explanatory fictions, pop psychology, and easily refutable (if you know the literature) hypotheses are passed off as fact.

Hoffer (1951) said that the true believer "seems to use words as if he were ignorant of their true meaning. Hence, too, his taste for quibbling, hair-splitting and scholastic tortuousness" (p. 81). Unless we change course, and gather greater momentum as we go, psychological perspectives on terrorism run the risk of contributing little more than, at worst, a graveyard of failed ideas and at best a place where we have spent more time explaining what we do *not* know, than what we do, as well as where we could be going.

But it would be shortsighted to end on a sour note, if only because we have barely scratched the surface of what psychology has to offer the study of terrorism. The future is unquestionably bright, so let us highlight some opportunities. A broad consensus has emerged in the psychological literature on terrorism that situational, and not personal, qualities determine terrorist behavior. Mirroring research in the social sciences more broadly (McCartney 2015) that consensus is likely to remain stable. But that does not mean that there is no role for personal disposition. Rather, to echo Monahan (2012, 2016), individual qualities have thus far offered no predictive utility in who becomes a terrorist. We need to revisit just where in the terrorism process personal disposition matters, and how. We are already seeing the initial stages of exciting new applications of clinical psychology to issues of de-radicalization (e.g. see Horgan and Taylor 2011), more systematic enquiry than ever before into the role of individual traits (Merari 2010), and the welcome application of Industrial/Organizational (i.e. "workplace") psychology to issues of management in terrorist organizations, charismatic leadership, leader errors, malevolent creativity, and selection, recruitment, and retention (e.g. Ligon et al. 2013; Gill et al. 2013; Thoroughgood et al. 2011). In fact, the last five years have suggested such promise that the next wave for psychological research on terrorism will not be between psychologists and those from other disciplines, rather we will see the fruits of collaboration between different kinds of psychologists.

While I remain sympathetic to Sageman's assertions about our inability to provide answers to the "why" question, I do not accept that our progress should be determined by our inability to answer that one, lingering question. In the meantime, the aspiring student is faced with no shortage of areas deserving of enquiry. Even the most basic psychological science of terrorist behavior must aspire to understand:

(a) How does someone become involved in terrorism? What are the similarities and differences between pathways experienced by members of the same group, different groups, and between different kinds of terrorism (e.g. group-based, and truly "lone" terrorism)? Do those pathways, and the sequencing of steps inherent in the structure of those pathways, share similarities with other kinds of ideological and/or non-ideological violent phenomena (e.g. mass murderers, school shooters, and/or other militant groups)? If so, to what extent do those similarities stretch (e.g. pre-attack behaviors versus psychological pathways into violence more broadly)?

(b) How, where and when do potential recruits learn about what involvement in terrorism might bring? Why are certain people drawn to particular roles (e.g. sniper versus suicide bomber versus fundraiser)?

(c) How, why, and when do people move from one kind of role or function to another? Why is it that some people hold one role and others hold many? Are there psychological implications of task or role-load as a result?

(d) How are individuals selected by recruiters or other "gatekeepers" in terrorist groups? What makes an effective recruiter? Do recruiters evaluate fit for purpose as part of their selection process, and do recruiters (or others) assess "performance" of new recruits?

(e) What role do social media play in the radicalization process? Does problematic internet use factor into this? Can social media play a role in facilitating disengagement from terrorism, and can social media help promote self-help resources to ensure longer-term individual "de-radicalization"?

(f) What kinds of reasons or accounts do individuals give to others about their experiences of becoming involved, remaining involved, or leaving? Do those accounts differ whether provided in public (e.g. via an autobiography, or media interview) versus in private (e.g. a detailed interview with a researcher?). Do the ways in which accounts of involvement are reconstructed vary over time, across movements, within movements, etc.?

(g) How, and with what means, do individuals convince themselves of the righteousness of any act in which they are now involved?
(h) What kinds of psychological tactics do recruits engage in to make them feel better about choices they have made? How do recruits cope with uncomfortable feelings or reactions as part of their involvement?
(i) In what ways are the expectations recruits have met or challenged?
(j) How do characterizations about terrorist motivation differ depending on who does the characterizing—i.e. *us* versus *them*?
(k) Do the pathways into violent extremism share similarities with other kinds of low-volume, high-impact phenomena (e.g. mass murderers, "school shooters," etc.)?
(l) Why and how is terrorism an effective strategy of psychological warfare, and what determines the longevity of that effectiveness?
(m) How do reactions to terrorism reinforce terrorism itself and what, if anything can be done to "extinguish" terrorist behavior?

For too long, serious efforts to understand terrorism have been lumped in with the worst elements of the "terrorism industry." Not being a psychologist does not prevent anyone from offering theories and opinions about even the most minute features of the terrorist mindset (nor should it). But if psychology is to make lasting contributions with solid empirical foundations, we have to align our analyses with the rigors expected of social sciences more broadly. If we continue to do that, the future for psychological research on terrorist behavior may be a lot brighter than we think.

Acknowledgment

I am grateful to Professors Max Taylor and Mia Bloom who provided feedback on an earlier draft.

References

Atran, S. (2010) *Talking to the Enemy: Faith, Brotherhood, and the (Un)Making of Terrorists*. New York: Ecco HarperCollins.

Barrelle, K. (2015) "Pro-Integration: Disengagement from and Life After Extremism," *Behavioral Sciences of Terrorism and Political Aggression*, 7(2): 129–42.

Birnbaum, M., and S. Mekhennet (2015) "Djamel Beghal, the Charming and Chilling Mentor of Paris Jihadist Attackers," *Washington Post*, 21 May, available online at <https://www.washingtonpost.com/world/europe/the-charming-and-chilling-mentor-of-the-paris-attackers/2015/02/06/2870f13c-a7dd-11e4-a162-121d06ca77f1_story.html>.

Bjørgo, T., and J. Horgan, eds (2009) *Leaving Terrorism Behind: Individual and Collective Perspectives*. London: Routledge.

Bongar, B., L. Brown, L. Beutler, J. Breckenridge, and P. Zimbardo, eds (2006) *Psychology of Terrorism*. Oxford: Oxford University Press.

Borum, R. (2011a) "Radicalization into Violent Extremism I: A Review of Social Science Theories," *Journal of Strategic Security*, 4: 7–36.

Borum, R. (2011b) "Radicalization into Violent Extremism II: A Review of Conceptual Models and Empirical Research," *Journal of Strategic Security*, 4: 37–62.

Corrado, R. R. (1981) "A Critique of the Mental Disorder Perspective of Political Terrorism," *International Journal of Law and Psychiatry*, 4(3–4): 293–309.

Cottee, S., and K. Hayward (2011) "Terrorist (E)motives: The Existential Attractions of Terrorism," *Studies in Conflict and Terrorism*, 34: 963–86.

Crenshaw, M. (1981) "The Causes of Terrorism," *Comparative Politics*, 13: 379–99.

Crenshaw, M. (1990) "Questions to be Answered, Research to be Done, Knowledge to be Applied," In W. Reich (ed.), *Origins of Terrorism: Psychologies, Ideologies, Theologies, States of Mind*. Washington, DC: Woodrow Wilson Center Press, 247–60.

Gill, P., and J. Horgan (2013) "Who were the Volunteers? The Shifting Sociological and Operational Profile of Provisional Irish Republican Army Members," *Terrorism and Political Violence*, 25(3): 435–56.

Gill, P., J. Horgan, and P. J. Deckert (2014) "Bombing Alone: Tracing the Motivations and Antecedents of Lone-Actor Terrorists," *Journal of Forensic Sciences*, 59(2): 425–35.

Gill, P., J. Horgan, S. T. Hunter, and L. Cushenbery (2013) "Malevolent Creativity in Terrorist Organizations," *Journal of Creative Behavior*, 47: 125–51.

Hegghammer, T. (2013) "Should I Stay or Should I Go? Explaining Variation in Western Jihadists' Choice between Domestic and Foreign Fighting," *American Political Science Review*, 107(1): 1–15.

Hoffer, E. (1951) *The True Believer: Thoughts on the Nature of Mass Movements*. New York: Harper Perennial.

Hoffman, B. (1998) *Inside Terrorism*. London: Victor Gollancz.

Horgan, J. (2014) *The Psychology of Terrorism*, 2nd edn. London: Routledge.

Horgan, J. and K. Braddock (2010) "Rehabilitating the Terrorists? Challenges in Assessing the Effectiveness of De-radicalization Programs," *Terrorism and Political Violence*, 22(1): 1–25.

Horgan, J., and M. Taylor (2011) "Disengagement, De-radicalization and the Arc of Terrorism: Future Directions for Research," in R. Coolsaet (ed.), *Jihadi Terrorism and the Radicalization Challenge: European and American experiences*, 2nd edn. London: Ashgate, 173–86.

Kinsey, A. C., W. B. Pomeroy, C. B. Martin, and P. H. Gebhard (1953) *Sexual Behavior in the Human Female*. Bloomington, IN: Indiana University Press.

Lankford, A. (2011) "Could Suicide Terrorists Actually Be Suicidal?," *Studies in Conflict and Terrorism*, 34: 337–66.

Ligon, Gina Scott, Pete Simi, Mackenzie Harms, and Daniel J. Harris (2013) "Putting the 'O' in VEOs: What Makes an Organization?," *Dynamics of Asymmetric Conflict* (July): 1–25.

McCartney, C. (2015) "An Author Explains How Mass Killings Happen," Science of Us. Feb. 4, available online at <http://nymag.com/scienceofus/2015/02/author-explains-how-mass-killings-happen.html#>.

Merari, A. (2010) *Driven to Death: Psychological and Social Aspects of Suicide Terrorism*. New York: Oxford University Press.

Monahan, J. (2012) "The Individual Risk Assessment of Terrorism," *Psychology, Public Policy, and Law*, 18: 167–205.

Monahan, J. (2016) "The Individual Risk Assessment of Terrorism: Recent Developments," in G. LaFree and J. Freilich (eds), *The Handbook of the Criminology of Terrorism*. Hoboken, NJ: John Wiley & Sons, 520–34.

Moskalenko, S. (2013) Book Review: "Adam Lankford. The Myth of Martyrdom: What Really Drives Suicide Bombers, Rampage Shooters, and Other Self-Destructive Killers," *Terrorism and Political Violence*, 25(5): 840–3.

Plumlee, R. (2013) "There's No Clear Profile for Homegrown Terrorists, Experts Say," *Wichita Eagle*, Dec. 21, available online at <http://www.kansas.com/news/article1130177.html>.

Post, J. M. (2007) *The Mind of the Terrorist: The Psychology of Terrorism from the IRA to Al-Qaeda*. New York: Palgrave-Macmillan.

Reich, W., ed. (1990a) *Origins of Terrorism: Psychologies, Ideologies, Theologies, States of Mind*. Cambridge: Cambridge University Press.

Reich, W. (1990b) "Introduction," in W. Reich (ed.), *Origins of Terrorism: Psychologies, Ideologies, Theologies, States of Mind*. Washington, DC: Woodrow Wilson Center Press, 1–4.

Reich, W. (1990c) "Understanding Terrorist Behavior: The Limits and Opportunities of Psychological Enquiry," in W. Reich (ed.), *Origins of Terrorism: Psychologies, Ideologies, Theologies, States of Mind*. Washington, DC: Woodrow Wilson Center Press, 261–79.

Roberts, A. (2015) "Terrorism Research: Past, Present, and Future," *Studies in Conflict and Terrorism*, 38(1): 62–74.

Sageman, M. (2008) *Leaderless Jihad*. Philadelphia: University of Pennsylvania Press.

Sageman, M. (2014) "Low Return on Investment," *Terrorism and Political Violence*, 26(4): 614–20.

Silke, A. P. (2003) "Preface," in A. P. Silke (ed.), *Terrorists, Victims and Society: Psychological Perspectives on Terrorism and its Consequences*. Chichester: Wiley, xv–xxi.

Silke, A. P., ed. (2018) *Routledge Handbook of Terrorism and Counterterrorism*. New York: Routledge.

Silke, A., and J. Schmidt-Petersen (2017) "The Golden Age? What the 100 Most Cited Articles in Terrorism Studies Tell us," *Terrorism and Political Violence*, 29(4): 692–712.

Sjoberg, L., and C. E. Gentry, eds (2011) *Women, Gender, and Terrorism*. Athens, GA: University of Georgia Press.

Taylor, M. (1988) *The Terrorist*. London: Brassey's.

Taylor, M., and J. Horgan (2006) "A Conceptual Framework for Addressing Psychological Process in the Development of the Terrorist," *Terrorism and Political Violence*, 18(4): 585–601.

Thoroughgood, C., S. T. Hunter, and K. Sawyer (2011) "Bad Apples, Bad Barrels, and Broken Followers: An Empirical Examination of Contextual Influences on Follower Perceptions and Reactions to Aversive Leadership," *Journal of Business Ethics*, 100(4): 647–72.

Victoroff, J. (2005) "The Mind of the Terrorist: A Review and Critique of Psychological Approaches," *Journal of Conflict Resolution*, 49: 3–42.

CHAPTER 15

CRITICAL APPROACHES TO THE STUDY OF TERRORISM

CHARLOTTE HEATH-KELLY

INTRODUCTION: WHAT IS CRITIQUE?

DURING the enormous boom in terrorism studies associated with the "War on Terror," where a staggering 90 percent of *all* terrorism research has been published since the 9/11 attacks (Silke 2008), a simultaneous expansion of critical research on terrorism has also occurred—undertaken by anthropologists, sociologists, political scientists and international relations scholars. Some of this work is explicitly associated with the Critical Studies on Terrorism project,[1] while other such research is situated within the broader fields of international relations, criminology, and sociology. This chapter provides a short introduction to contemporary critical terrorism research; however it will be unable to adequately discuss the plurality of methodological approaches which constitute the field within a short word limit. Interested readers should consult one of the many excellent books on this topic to gain a fuller understanding of the application of methodologies such as discourse analysis, feminist terrorism research, and postcolonial approaches to political violence (Dixit and Stump 2015; Jackson 2016; Jackson et al. 2009, 2011; Stump and Dixit 2013).

Critical approaches have a long history across philosophy, sociology, economics, and cultural studies. They often diverge in content, offering a wide breadth of epistemological consideration. To understand what it means to study terrorism *critically*, one must first accept that there is *not one single "critical" approach*. Critical research is not a discrete methodology that can be adequately explained in a brief section of text—rather it signifies a broad array of research methods and questions which stretch across international relations, critical legal theory, sociology, criminology, the humanities, feminism, Marxism, and continental philosophy. It would be more appropriate to speak of a "critical attitude," rather than "approach," given the diversity of research undertaken beneath the critical umbrella.

But if critical research is so broadly situated, what links all these diverse endeavors under the banner of being "critical"? The nature of "criticality" signifies a skepticism regarding traditional scientific method and the presumption of objectivity. For this reason, critical research is sometimes maligned by non-critical scholars for its stubborn refusal to produce causal explanations or predictions. It doesn't accept the notion of timeless scientific truth, instead emphasizing the role of power in the constitution of knowledge (Foucault 1997; Gramsci 1975). To understand this relationship between power and the social constitution of knowledge, one could point to Thomas Kuhn's influential thesis on paradigm shifts in scientific knowledge. In 1962, Kuhn demonstrated that knowledge does not accumulate in a linear progression (as was previously assumed) and instead collects within paradigms which dictate and control understanding until they suddenly collapse and are replaced (Kuhn 2012). A truth holds for a while, as objective fact, until its operational deficiencies overcome it and it is replaced with another "timeless" truth. For example, think of the Copernican Revolution in astrophysics where, suddenly, truth changed and the Earth no longer occupied the centre of the universe as it supposedly had for hundreds of years of scientific research. Critical approaches take Kuhn's insights and explore how and why this should be. History shows us that supposedly timeless truths are replaced overnight, despite previously being assumed to be infallible, so how should we understand the world when our knowledge is constrained by the paradigms of our time?

The critical attitude explains this situation of knowledge within temporary paradigms by showing that social and political contexts consolidate to *make some things "true"* while silencing other things. Each Kuhnian paradigm is a product of its social and historical environment. Context (and thus power) creates temporary and geographically limited "truths." Knowledge is not objective but rather a product of social construction. This skeptical attitude towards the modernist, Enlightenment model of knowledge is the theme which unites critical approaches—power creates knowledge, not the other way around.

Stuart Hall, the eminent cultural theorist of race, has produced a magnificently concise pamphlet which explained the philosophical origins of the critical attitude. Hall began his philosophical tour of critical thought with Karl Marx's revelatory nineteenth-century studies of economics. Marx's prolific catalogue of research is underpinned by the argument that "men [*sic*] make history but not in conditions of their own choosing." Marx states in full:

> Man makes his own history, but he does not make it out of the whole cloth; he does not make it out of conditions chosen by himself, but out of such as he finds close to hand. The tradition of all past generations weighs like an alp upon the brain of the living. At the very time that men appear engaged in revolutionising things and themselves, in bringing about what never was before, at such very epochs of revolutionary crisis do they anxiously conjure up into their service the spirits of their past, assume their names,

> their battle cries, their costumes to enact a new historic scene in such time honoured disguise and with such borrowed language. (Marx 1852, 1)

Why is it important to realize, as Marx did, that human agency and thought is situated within social and political conditions of possibility? Because Marx's studies show (echoing Kuhn) that human societies are trapped within their own paradigms of knowledge and possibility. Marx shows that individuals could not in any true sense be the "authors" or agents of history since they can only act on the basis of the historical conditions made by others, into which they were born, and using the resources (material, ideological, and cultural) provided to them from previous generations (Hall 1992). Humans inherit the conditions which both enable and constrain their action. Subjects, then, are constituted and shaped by their environment in ways which *prevent them achieving true agency or scientific rationality*. We cannot achieve objective knowledge because we inherit constrained conditions of material possibility and intellectual landscape. We operate within historical bubbles.

Hall's portrait of critical thought then moves to explore other revolutions in epistemology, in particular: Ferdinand de Saussure's linguistic structuralism. Saussure's thought has been crucial to the development of discourse analysis as a critical methodology—something used at length to critique the field of terrorism studies, as I shall detail later.

Ferdinand De Saussure lived in the late nineteenth and early twentieth century and his thought was integral to the development of structuralism in the study of linguistics (otherwise known as semiotics) (Sanders 2004). He argued that there is no direct relationship between words and the objects they represent in the world. For example, the same object is known by different words across different languages. A cat is a chat, is a katze, is a macska, is a felis, and so on. Given this realization (and one might also think of the changing meaning of words over time: such as "gay" shifting from "happy" to "homosexual"), it becomes clear that words don't have timeless connections to the objects they represent. Words change, and there are multiple words for each object.

So what is the relationship between language and the world? The premise of structuralism rests upon the division of linguistics into categories of "signified" and "signifier" to explore this—emphasizing the lack of direct, natural, objective relationship between the two. We have *signs* to represent the world, *but these signs are not directly connected to the objects they signify*: they change, they are plural, they mutate.

As such, a word has no "objective" meaning (no timeless connection to the object it represents); instead, words give meaning to each other through their relationships in a structure. Why is this important in Hall's exploration of critical thought across history? Because Saussure's work shows that we are not the authors of the things we say and the meanings we express (Hall 1992). *Language pre-exists us*. We are subject to the possibilities of thought enabled, and prevented, by structures of language that pre-exist us—just like George Orwell's protagonist in the seminal novel *1984* and his struggles against the totalitarian invention of "newspeak" (Orwell 1949).

Like Marx's discovery of the structural conditions for agency and knowing, language both constrains and enables human expression and action. The human subject does not have access to unlimited powers of reasoning, because structures of language, culture, and history constitute and constrain our experience of the world. Recognition of this social constitution of thought and experience means that critical research does not utilize the Cartesian model of the subject: the all-knowing rational creature who can apply reason to objectively determine causes and effects.

To summarize, human subjects are the products of social, political, and historical forces. Our ability to know and to express is already conditioned and constrained within boundaries of contextual possibility. Critical research does not accept the world as it finds it, but rather inquires into the social and historical conditions of that world's construction. Knowledge is not objective; rather truth is constituted through prevalent power structures.

"Knowing" Terrorism

So, if critical research treats truth as a product of power, what does this mean for the study of terrorism?

Where traditional terrorism studies dedicates its attention to measuring terrorist phenomena and applying scientific method to understand which variables increase, or decrease, terrorist violence (Bjorgo 2005; Horgan 2005; Pape 2006; Piazza 2007), critical research approaches the subject very differently. It doesn't study the factors which increase or decrease the likelihood of terrorism occurring, rather it explores the social, historical, and cultural conditions *which have produced the concepts* of terrorism and counterterrorism. How has society come to imagine "terrorism"? Why is "terrorism" understood to be a specific sub-set of violent action, different from warfare? And if knowledge is the product of power configurations, whose interests does it serve to distinguish this particular type of illegitimate violence?

Within such a critical approach, "terrorism" is not a noun—in the sense of terrorism as an unquestionable thing in the world. Rather critical research on terrorism explores the factors involved in the constitution of "terrorism" as a concept, the connection between power and the "terrorism" label, and the consequences of counterterrorism action upon populations and societies.

As such, "terrorism" in critical terrorism research usually becomes understood as the practices of labeling something as "terrorist," and political discourses of "counter-terrorism." Given the relationship between power and knowledge, critical research asks questions about powerful actors' manipulation of language to assert that an insurgent threat exists. If something is done in the name of "countering terror" then it simultaneously contributes to the social construction of "terrorism." It makes the concept of "terrorism" appear real by connecting the signifier to an object.

But sometimes the different approach of critical research is confused with a denial of objective facts. How could terrorism be socially constructed when the brutalized evidence of terrorist attacks is there for all to see? Of course bombings happen. Critical research does not deny this. However, it deepens the study of security and politics by asking how these events are inscribed with meaning. Threats are not objectively apparent—they are socially constructed. For example, the governments, international organizations, and media agencies involved in the War on Terror would have us believe that terrorism is an important and substantial threat to the lives of civilians in the states of the Global North. Trillions of dollars have been spent on protective measures, international wars, and expansions of government capabilities. Yet this perception of threat is socially constructed and widely divergent from the reality of daily life.

John Mueller provides an excellent study of the socially constructed nature of terrorist threat in his book *Overblown* (2006). Here he deploys statistical methods to show that terrorist attacks kill fewer Americans than "accident causing deer." Even when including the numbers of deaths from 9/11, the threat of being hit by a car or dying in a household accident far outstrips the risk of terrorism. The force of Mueller's argument concerns the political construction of terrorism in the US as an extensive security threat despite its incredibly low numbers of victims. Political and media discourse portray terrorism as a terrible threat, but without any basis in casualty figures.

The impetus of this analysis is extremely critical, because it illuminates the social production of an idea of terrorist threat by powerful social institutions and organizations. Also Mueller's analysis points to something very Saussurian—the tenuous connection between the signifier (the label "terrorism") and the signified (the bombing or insurgent being referred to). "Terrorism," then, is not an objectively existing phenomenon. Indeed, in its first historical usage, "terror" signified the judicial and extra-judicial execution of opponents by a state to intimidate others (Tilly 2004, 8–9). Since that time the terms "terror" and "terrorism" have sometimes been used to describe acts of massive oppression by states (such as Stalin's purges), but a noticeable shift is evident whereby non-state actors have come to be identified as the protagonists of terror. "Terrorism" has shifted to signify non-state insurgent action.

Once we engage with the historical development of terrorism language, we see that the terms themselves ("terror," "terrorist," "terrorism") have no intrinsic, objective meaning; rather they mean *specific things at specific times and places*. This means that "terrorism" does not maintain a stable conceptual status; instead "terror," "terrorist," and "terrorism" are labels recreated for each era. Critical research inquires into the utility of these discursive processes: who do they serve? If power creates knowledge and language, then "terrorism" (the concept and category) is a construction of power which serves the interests of states, economies, and existing power structures by delegitimating certain actors.

Key Methodological Commitments in Critical Approaches to Terrorism

"Critical approaches" are a very broad family, incorporating methodologies from narrative studies, critical realism, anthropology, postcolonialism, gender studies and beyond. It is impossible to describe the methodological commitments of all such approaches in a short chapter,[2] so I have focused on commenting on the shared critical attitude (epistemology) which informs their "critique." However, many critical studies of terrorism in political science and international relations utilize a familiar and widely accepted method known as discourse analysis, which I will outline here.

Discourse analysis is a methodology which takes language, concepts, and meanings seriously. As Norman Fairclough, a key figure in the establishment of critical discourse analysis makes clear: discourse analysis does not focus on individuals or entities as the unit of research, rather it interrogates social relations (Fairclough 2013, 3). Doing this requires, but is reducible to, the systematic analysis of texts. These texts might be political speeches, newspaper articles, or academic debates. Texts are subjected to both a "content analysis," whereby the usage (and silencing) or terms and themes is noted, but also an exploration of their "ideological" nature. Terms and themes are not just counted (how many times does presidential candidate Donald Trump invoke the "Mexican"?), but the analyst then situates the discourse in its social context—exploring how language replicates assumptions about certain phenomena (how do Trump"s comments about Mexicans invoke statist readings of security and nationhood, whereby "threat" is understood to originate from outside the nation's borders?), and maintains the hegemony (Gramsci 1975) of the current political, social, and economic order by concealing alternative meanings and more radical possibilities for change.

Discourse analysis explores the use of words in books, articles, and speeches, but then situates this use of language in social relations to determine its effects. Language and concepts constitute the social world and have effects.

Discourse Analysis and the War on Terror

Discourse structures the perception of reality for both government actors and individual citizens. As Marx, De Saussure, Gramsci, and Foucault have revealed, people are not able to objectively access knowledge about the world—rather we are constrained by the limits of the linguistic, social, and political paradigms which situate us and limit our perception. Terrorism "knowledge," and languages of terrorism, are part of our contemporary "bubble."

Critical terrorism research has applied discourse analysis to the War on Terror to explore how words and concepts enable us to reflect on the political constitution of reality. The initial, and seminal, research projects within this endeavor are Stuart Croft's *Culture, Crisis and America's War on Terror* (2006) and Richard Jackson's *Writing the War on Terrorism* (2005). Both explore the multi-directional relationship between words and the practice of the War on Terror; namely that:

1. Words make war possible. Threats and crises are socially constructed, not objective realities. The practice of the War on Terror would not have been possible

without the discursive construction of terrorism as the most salient and terrible global threat.
2. War in turn makes meanings. The violence perpetrated by the coalition during the War on Terror has been functional, securing "Western" state identities as righteous and legitimate against the threat of the barbarous other.

In both points, the articulation of "terrorism" as an existential threat is functional for statecraft. It enables action (Heath-Kelly 2016).

The first point dismantles America's response to 9/11 as a natural and obvious one, as it is framed by political elites. George Bush's administration (as well as the government of Tony Blair in the UK) made prolific, repetitive use of statements and media commentaries to reinforce the perception that military intervention in Afghanistan, and later Iraq, was the only option in response to 9/11. However critical research into the War on Terror emphasizes that while America was struck by attacks on September 11, 2001, there was nothing objective, obvious, or natural about their response (Croft 2006, 2). The US could, for example, have treated the matter as a criminal act, pursuing the prosecution of those responsible in courts of law. Yet the rhetoric of the aftermath began the discursive construction of 9/11 as an act of war and as evidence of an international security crisis, legitimating the era of the War on Terror. Jackson describes this process as follows:

> The words chosen to describe these events were not simply a neutral reflection of what had happened, but actually worked to enforce a particular interpretation and meaning, most significantly that they were an "act of war". This politically constructed understanding of the events normalised the administration's response; because it was an "act of war", a "war on terrorism" appeared reasonable and logical. This war-based approach was reinforced by embedding the narrative of September 11, 2001 within larger meta-narratives about Pearl Harbour and World War II, the Cold War, civilisation versus barbarism and the advance of globalisation. In large part the purpose of the language was to prevent any interpretation that implicated American foreign policy. (Jackson 2005, 5)

Stuart Croft (2006) similarly describes this process as the social construction of 9/11 as security crisis. Social construction occurs through multiple, sequential phases: first a phase whereby "we" are identified and solidified, against which "they" are identified and demonized, and this oppositional fixing is then used to present a situation of crisis requiring a firm response. Crises are thus made, they are not objective. And they are extremely productive for political elites, enabling new potential within law-making, war- making, and power-consolidation.

On the second point, once the response to crisis is initiated it serves the consolidation of identity and meaning. Put simply, it is very useful for the practice of statecraft to identify an external bad guy. Given that constructivism broadly follows the tenets of structuralist linguistic theory, the existence of a bad guy creates your own state as the good guy through linguistic and performative juxtaposition. It reaffirms your identity as legitimate, rational, and civilized (see also Said 1978).

Discourse analysis enables critical researchers to explore the manipulation of representations and signifiers of "terrorism" to effect a performance of state identity as "legitimate." For example, the term "Islamic terrorism" has been extremely effective in justifying and naturalizing the appearance of the War on Terror invasion undertaken by the UK and US against a supposed opponent to civilization which resides outside the West. Its use across political studies of terrorism and media contributes to the manufacturing of legitimation for security measures, popular consent, and the social construction of the UK and US as defenders of the civilized, righteous West. As Jackson finds:

> One of the most important functions of the discourse of "Islamic terrorism" is to construct and maintain national identity, primarily through the articulation of a contrasting, negative "other" who defines the Western "self" through negation... as David Campbell has convincingly demonstrated, the elaboration of an external threat such as that posed by "Islamic terrorism" is crucial to maintaining internal/external, self/other boundaries and the "writing" of national identity. In fact, some have argued that Western identity is dependent on the appropriation of a backward, illiberal, violent Islamic "other" against which the West can organize a collective liberal, civilized "self" and consolidate its cultural and political norms.
>
> (Jackson 2007, 420)

States "write" themselves through their conflicts with others: they perform themselves as defenders of just causes and legitimate standard-bearers of civilization against the barbarous other. They articulate themselves through discourse as the opposite of the "terrorist," just as De Saussure explained of the oppositions within language ("cat" is not "dog") which structure comprehension. This is the functionality of generational crises such as the Cold War (Campbell 1992) and the War on Terror (Croft 2006; Jackson 2005)—they form a matrix of understanding whereby states can assert themselves as legitimate actors and find their purpose on the world stage. Authority and legitimacy are performances that rely upon the discursive construction of threatening others.

State Terrorism?

A second important strand within critical research into terrorism has involved the attempt to reclaim the "terrorism" signifier. In critical approaches, all language is political given that it has no objective connection to the object it represents (meanings of words change, shift, and are known through contrasts with other words). "Terrorism" does not naturally represent illegitimate non-state action, rather the term has become a label used to delegitimize others and to consolidate positive impressions of states by contrast. Furthermore, our contemporary discourse of "terrorism" is arbitrarily applied to non-state actors, given that the term originally emerged to describe the actions of the French government in quelling opposition. So if all language is an arbitrary representation born of social and political context, why not reappropriate the term "terrorism"?

This is what critical research into state terrorism has done to shed light on the subjugated knowledge concerning state abuses of power.

As Chomsky and Herman point out, the label of terrorism has been consistently applied to those who oppose the establish order, despite their minimal use of violence in comparison to the massive atrocities perpetrated by states against civilians, in order to intimidate them and effect change (Chomsky and Herman 1979, 85–7). This Orwellian discrepancy is directly targeted by critical terrorism researchers who apply the term "terrorism" to state violence, attempting to reappropriate the meaning of terrorism. Alexander George led this movement with his book *Western State Terrorism* which undermined the common political assumption that Western states are victims of terrorism rather than systemic perpetrators of the tactic (George 1991). In critical response to this fallacy, he sheds light on knowledge which is subjugated by the dominant paradigm—that of the US's systematic abuses of human rights for political gain in Central America and the Middle East during the Cold War. Similarly Jeffrey Sluka has argued in his edited collection *Death Squad: The Anthropology of State Terror* that if we were to interpret "terrorism" as a tactic (and not "ideologically") then terrorism studies would reveal the state as the largest purveyor of violence intended to intimidate an audience for political gain (Sluka 2000). The use of such violence by non-state actors pales in comparison.

So why do studies of terrorism focus on non-state actors? Some critical researchers argue that this discrepancy of scale implicates power structures in the production of an ideological concept ("terrorism") which silences state terror. They argue that terrorism is a corrupted concept unless it is also applied to state violence. Terrorism studies' focus on non-state violence, according to some critical researchers of state terrorism, is indicative of its implicit bias to support the agendas of powerful states in the Global North—born of a non-critical replication of state security agendas.

If terrorism is to be understood as a tactical use of violence to intimidate an audience for political gain, then it becomes interesting that academic studies predominantly explore non-state "terrorism" rather than interrogating the use of intimidatory violence by states. Richard Jackson has analyzed over one hundred mainstream books and articles within terrorism studies to explore who is understood to be a terrorist: states or non-state actors. His data demonstrate that the field of terrorism studies overwhelmingly interprets terrorism as a tactic used by non-state actors. The field silences any indication that intimidatory violence could be used by states, and that states could be terrorists. This, he concludes, sheds light on the ideological position of terrorism studies, and international relations, as academic disciplines engaged within conservative consolidations of states and international power structures (Jackson 2008). By not questioning the inherited supposition that terrorism is a non-state action, researchers within terrorism studies reify the ideological and complicit position that states are legitimate practitioners of violence and that their identities prevent them from falling into the category of terrorists.

Ruth Blakeley is another notable contemporary scholar of state terrorism who has written extensively on the use of terror tactics by Northern States to intimidate populations in the Global South for political and economic gain (2007, 2009). Powerful states in the international community have repeatedly sponsored the repression of populations in the Global South to achieve broader foreign policy objectives, often during the Cold War. However, what about the contemporary actions of Northern States within the War on Terror? In Blakeley's more recent work on the covert use of extraordinary rendition by the US, with the support of European allies, she directly shows the continuing practice of violence designed to intimidate others (terrorism) by states involved in the War on Terror. Her Rendition Project, run in collaboration with Sam Raphael, is an online resource born of collaboration between academics and human rights organizations. It collates, verifies, and publishes information about those individuals captured, detained, and "rendered" to black sites during the war on terror (http://www.therenditionproject.org.uk/index.html). The website can be used to map individual journeys of prisoners, associated rendition circuit flights, or to view the number of rendition-related flights which landed in any given country.

This is in an interesting piece of critical research because it implicitly reappropriates the discourse of terrorism to explore the behaviors of prominent "counter-terrorist" states. Does rendition, detention, and torture within the War on Terror constitute an act of terrorism in itself?

While secret rendition flights might not fit any definition of terrorism by themselves (given that their secrecy prevents the intimidation of a wider audience), the eventual depositing of the detainees in Guantanamo was a public demonstration by the United States that it would not apply the norms of international society to those who oppose it. The unconcealed existence of the detention camp and the torturous practices which occurred within, were a communicative act of violence designed to intimidate—something which approaches the tactical definition of terrorism. But what about the wider reception of this critical reappropriation of the "terrorism" signifier? Has the critical mission to reappropriate the term terrorism been successful and has it challenged the tendency for terrorism studies to only consider non-state actors?

While critical research has explored the systemic abuses of human rights associated with states and analyzed the discipline of terrorism studies, there is some debate about whether states can be terrorists. For example, the cannons of political science show that Max Weber's influential definition of the state includes its claim to possess a "monopoly on the legitimate use of force." It is, in this sense, a Hobbesian Leviathan—designed with supremacy of force in mind. Its identity within political theory supposedly entitles it to possess overwhelming means of force. Yet its claim to a monopoly of legitimate force (that no other body can use *legitimate* force) does not mean that all *its* uses of force become legitimate by definition—a state can clearly exceed the bounds of acceptability or international law (Claridge 1996). Do these oversteps qualify as terrorism? Should we reappropriate the term terrorism to describe these actions, or are they abuses of human rights? Does the Weberian definition of a state preclude the application of the label "terrorist"?

Colin Wight has responded to critical research on state terrorism stating that while the ethical intentions of such work (shedding light on state abuses of power) are honorable, the application of the term terrorism to states is analytically confused (Wight 2012). In the development of the modern state from Leviathan to contemporary governmental body, we must acknowledge that all forms of state control imply the threat of coercive punishment for the non-compliant. Indeed the modern state claims the right to legitimately deploy violence through its Weberian foundation. The justice system, for example, has historically relied upon the threat of execution to enforce social control, even if today (in Europe, at least) it threatens the violent refusal of rights through imprisonment rather than hurting the body. Importantly, these uses of violence are directly intended to affect the behaviors of a wider audience—the population of citizens. If we apply the term terrorism to state action, it becomes meaningless because all actions of governance could potentially be called terrorist. Every state policy threatens coercive punishment for the non-compliant, designed to deter others, thus applying "terrorism" to state actions would drain it of any meaning whatsoever (Wight 2012).

Furthermore, Leonard Weinberg and William Eubank respond to Jackson's indictment of terrorism studies research as ideologically complicit in its silencing of "state terrorism." They argue that terrorism studies journals rarely publish research on state terrorism not because they are attempting to silence state abuses of human rights, but because these journals have explicitly dedicated themselves to the study of insurgent groups; other forums exist for the study and discussion of state violence (Weinberg and Eubank 2008).

How does Critical Terrorism Research Respond to these Criticisms?

The dialogue between critical terrorism researchers and their positivist colleagues is, unfortunately, stalled. This is not the fault of either school of thought. Rather, dialogue is stalled because the two epistemological communities have such different ontological starting points that, in critique and response, they talk past one another.

For example, when Weinberg and Eubank highlight that terrorism studies journals are explicitly dedicated to the study of non-state insurgency (and that other journals exist for the consideration of state abuses), they draw upon and reproduce a discursive boundary: "the term terrorism is associated with non-state behavior, therefore terrorism studies journals publish articles which explore such non-state violence."

Within the positivist academic community, this makes perfect sense. Subjects and topics are divided into pockets of study and publication. However, it misses the point of the critical epistemological intervention, which is to interrogate *precisely how those discursive boundaries came about*. Critical approaches, in this case, are asking *why* it became common sense to call violence by one set of actors "terrorism" but not the violence of others (and their answer highlights the interconnection of power with language).

Different epistemological starting points lead the two schools to ask different questions about terrorism, and to study different processes.

Conclusion

In this short chapter I have outlined the "critical attitude" which informs the rejection of positivist social science methodology in critical research. I then gave a brief introduction to the popular methodology of discourse analysis before exploring its use in two constructivist analyses of the War on Terror. I showed how the work of Stuart Croft and Richard Jackson has undermined the presumption that war was a natural response to the events of 9/11, despite the discursive efforts of the Bush and Blair administrations to the contrary. Language was used to depict the threat of terrorism as existential, rather than criminal and limited, and thus a security emergency was constructed in discourse which required responsive wars. Later, these wars again intersected with language: their undertaking resulted in a prolonged political and media imagination of a barbarous other against which Western state identity could be juxtaposed as civilized and rational. The imagination of terrorist threat is thus extremely functional for legitimating political action and consolidating the identity of states as legitimate, civilized actors in comparison to the figure of the barbarous insurgent.

After exploring these early works in the critical study of terrorism, I then turned to address the state terrorism literature. Critical scholars, including Sluka, Jackson, and Blakeley, have attempted to reappropriate the term terrorism to describe state violence. The methods used in this endeavor have been two-fold. First, researchers have detailed the abuses undertaken by liberal states to rescue the subjugated knowledge of Northern States as purveyors of massive, intimidatory violence. The relationship between power and knowledge silences inconvenient facts about this history but critical research unearths histories of state oppression to correct the discursive impression that Western states are victims of terrorism and not its perpetrators. Second, other critical research within studies of state terrorism has utilized methods of discourse analysis to expose the ideological bias within terrorism studies itself, such that it reproduces the popular misconception that non-state actors are the cause of insecurity.

I have introduced these debates to explain the general attitude of critical terrorism research: it does not take the world as it finds it, but rather enquires into the social construction of "terrorism" as a concept somehow distinct from war, and usually understood to be perpetrated by non-state actors. By exploring the method of discourse analysis and its use by critical terrorism scholars, I have shown how, in their views, the concept of "terrorism" is extremely functional for statecraft.

Notes

1. The Critical Terrorism Studies movement began in 2006 with a conference ("Is it time for a Critical Terrorism Studies?") at Manchester University, before consolidating itself at Aberystwyth University's Centre for the Study of Radicalisation and Political Violence. The movement has established its own academic journal (*Critical Studies on Terrorism*) and Routledge book series, its own working group of the British International Studies

Association, and has published several textbooks and research guides, see Dixit and Stump 2015; Jackson et al. 2009; Jackson et al. 2011; Stump and Dixit 2013.

2. Interested readers should consult one of the many textbooks on critical terrorism studies methods to find out more: Dixit and Stump 2015; Jackson 2016; Jackson et al. 2009; 2011; Stump and Dixit 2013.

References

Bjorgo, Tore, ed. (2005) *The Root Causes of Terrorism*. Abingdon: Routledge.

Blakeley, Ruth (2007) "Bringing the State back into Terrorism Studies," *European Political Science*, 6(3): 228–35.

Blakeley, Ruth (2009) *State Terrorism and Neoliberalism: The North in the South*. Abingdon: Routledge.

Campbell, David (1992) *Writing Security: United States Foreign Policy and the Politics of Identity*. Minneapolis: University of Minnesota Press.

Chomsky, Noam, and Edward S. Herman (1979) *The Washington Connection and Third World Fascism*. The Political Economy of Human Rights, 1. Quebec: Black Rose.

Claridge, David (1996) "State Terrorism? Applying a Definitional Model," *Terrorism and Political Violence*, 8(3): 47–63.

Croft, Stuart (2006) *Culture, Crisis and America's War on Terror*. Cambridge: Cambridge University Press.

Dixit, Priya, and Jacob Stump, eds (2015) *Critical Methods in Terrorism Studies*. Abingdon: Routledge.

Fairclough, Norman (2013) *Critical Discourse Analysis: The Critical Study of Language*. Abingdon: Routledge.

Foucault, Michel (1997) *The Politics of Truth*, ed. Sylvere Lotringer. Los Angeles: Semiotext(e).

George, Alexander (1991) *Western State Terrorism*. Cambridge: Polity Press.

Gramsci, Antonio (1975) *Prison Notebooks, Volume 1*, ed. Joseph A. Buttigieg. New York: Columbia University Press.

Hall, Stuart (1992) "The Question of Cultural Identity," in Stuart Hall, David Held, and Anthony McGrew, *Modernity and its Futures*. Cambridge: Polity Press, 274–31.

Heath-Kelly, Charlotte (2016) "Poststructuralism and Constructivism," in Richard Jackson (ed.), *The Routledge Handbook of Critical Terrorism Studies*. Abingdon: Routledge, 60–9.

Horgan, John (2005) *The Psychology of Terrorism*. Abingdon: Routledge.

Jackson, Richard (2005) *Writing the War on Terrorism: Language, Politics and Counter-Terrorism*. Manchester: Manchester University Press.

Jackson, Richard (2007) "Constructing Enemies: 'Islamic Terrorism' in Political and Academic Discourse," *Government and Opposition*, 42(3): 394–426.

Jackson, Richard (2008) "The Ghosts of State Terror: Knowledge, Politics and Terrorism Studies," *Critical Studies on Terrorism*, 1(3): 377–92.

Jackson, Richard, ed. (2016) *The Routledge Handbook to Critical Terrorism Studies*. Abingdon: Routledge.

Jackson, Richard, Marie Breen-Smyth, and Jeroen Gunning, eds (2009) *Critical Terrorism Studies: A New Research Agenda*. Abingdon: Routledge.

Jackson, Richard, Lee Jarvis, Jeroen Gunning, and Marie Breen-Smyth (2011) *Terrorism: A Critical Introduction*. Basingstoke: Palgrave Macmillan.

Kuhn, Thomas (2012) *The Structure of Scientific Revolutions*, 50th anniversary edn. Chicago: University of Chicago Press.

Marx, Karl (1852) *The Eighteenth Brumaire of Louis Bonaparte*. New York: Cosimo.

Mueller, John (2006) *Overblown: How Politicians and the Terrorism Industry Inflate National Security Threats, and Why we Believe them*. New York: Free Press.

Orwell, George (1949) *1984*. London: Penguin.

Pape, Robert (2006) *Dying to Win: The Strategic Logic of Suicide Terrorism*. New York: Random House.

Piazza, James A. (2007) "Draining the Swamp: Democracy Promotion, State Failure, and Terrorism in 19 Middle Eastern Countries," *Studies in Conflict and Terrorism*, 30(6): 521–39.

Said, Edward (1978) *Orientalism*. New York: Pantheon Books.

Sanders, Carol, ed. (2004) *The Cambridge Companion to Saussure*. Cambridge: Cambridge University Press.

Silke, Andrew (2008) "Research on Terrorism: A Review of the Impact of 9/11 and the Global War on Terrorism," in Hsinchun Chen, Edna Reid, Joshua Sinai, Andrew Silke, and Boaz Ganor (eds), *Terrorism Informatics: Knowledge Management and Data Mining for Homeland Security*. New York: Springer, 27–50.

Sluka, Jeffrey (2000) *Death Squad: The Anthropology of State Terror*. Philadelphia: University of Pennsylvania Press.

Stump, Jacob, and Priya Dixit (2013) *Critical Terrorism Studies: An Introduction to Research Methods*. Abingdon: Routledge.

Tilly, Charles (2004) "Terror, Terrorism, Terrorists," *Sociological Theory*, 22(1): 5–13.

Weinberg, Leonard, and William Eubank (2008) "Problems with the Critical Studies Approach to the Study of Terrorism," *Critical Studies on Terrorism*, 1(2): 185–95.

Wight, Colin (2012) "State Terrorism: Who Needs it?," in Richard Jackson and Samuel Justin Sinclair (eds), *Contemporary Debates on Terrorism*. Abingdon: Routledge, 50–7.

CHAPTER 16

GEOGRAPHICAL APPROACHES IN THE STUDY OF TERRORISM

MEGAN M. FARRELL, MICHAEL G. FINDLEY, AND JOSEPH K. YOUNG

Overview

OVER the course of four days in November 2008, ten Pakistani men associated with the terrorist group Lashkar-e-Taiba carried out attacks in Mumbai, killing 164 people and injuring more than 200 others. The group used automatic weapons and grenades and targeted several highly populated areas, including hotels, a railway station, and a movie theater.[1] In the course of their investigation, Mumbai authorities found that the attackers used satellite maps from the public domain to plan the attacks and escape routes.[2] Far from indiscriminate, these attacks were planned using geographical data to inflict the maximum amount of casualties and provide the best chance of escape. What can this case and other similar events demonstrate about the relationship between geography and terrorism? Further, given the prevalence of increasingly precise geographical data, how can researchers leverage knowledge about geographical factors to better understand, predict, and prevent terrorism?

The widespread popularity of geographic information systems (GIS) in international relations research (see Gleditsch and Ward 2001; Starr 2002) has by no means bypassed the subfield of terrorism studies. Especially since 2000, there has been a wave of research taking advantage of new GIS techniques and enhanced computing power that seeks to identify trends in terrorism, with units of analysis ranging from individual streets (Kwan and Lee 2005) all the way up to cross-national studies (Findley and Young 2012b). In several instances, this research cuts across fields to include geography, criminal justice, and international relations. The precision of GIS data and its ability to provide finer-grain measurements of often-used characteristics in terrorism research such as population, ethnicity, and economic resources opens up new possibilities in the field of terrorism research.

This chapter provides an overview of the extant literature, explains the most widely used GIS techniques in the field, discusses how different research questions are best answered using specific techniques and units of analysis, explores areas of further research, and then closes with a brief discussion of the technical requirements for carrying out GIS research. While we do provide a thorough overview of the state of GIS terrorism research, we spend the majority of the chapter covering the technical and conceptual details of GIS and then exploring new avenues of research that we believe provide exciting opportunities to formulate and test hypotheses from theories of political violence and terrorism.

Extant Literature

Terrorism research that utilizes GIS data and methods can largely be divided into two types: (1) small N, country- or even city-specific studies that attempt to identify micro-level trends of terrorism attacks, and (2) large N, cross-national studies that seek to find commonalities in attacks across time and space. Although not a perfect match, this divide often mirrors the larger debate amongst comparative and international relations scholars regarding the utility of small N versus large N studies. We do not purport to provide an exhaustive examination of all studies that fit into one of these two broad categories, but use the following literature to demonstrate this conceptual divide and analyze the strengths and weaknesses of each approach.

Country-Specific Studies

The first major type of terrorism research that uses GIS data employs subnational units of analysis. That is to say, the researchers are looking at city-level, district-level, or departmental-level trends within a single country. These studies leverage the precision of GIS data to analyze patterns in terrorist attacks across time and space at the micro level, meaning trends of terrorism within a single state, district, or even city.

Since 2003, Iraq and Afghanistan have received disproportionate attention from scholars. The presence of US troops and sectarian cleavages have provided both the motive and the opportunity for a large number of terrorist attacks since 2003. Occupation has also meant, however, that because of the desire of US policy-makers to have reliable insurgency data, the reporting of terrorist events is much more widespread and well-documented than may be the case in other situations. A number of studies (Braithwaite and Johnson 2012; Johnson and Braithwaite 2009; Townsley et al. 2008; Medina et al. 2011) have examined the spatio-temporal patterns of insurgent attacks in Iraq since 2003.

Braithwaite and Johnson (2012) examine the variation from January 1, 2005 to June 30, 2005 in improvised explosive devices (IEDs) set by insurgent forces and their relationship with coalition counter-insurgency activity. They divide Iraq into 5 km × 5 km grids and code attacks by week, giving them a unit of analysis of a grid-week. Their findings include a clear spatio-temporal clustering of IED events and statistical evidence that IEDs do not tend to follow recent coalition activity. Similarly Medina et al. (2011) utilize GIS data from January 2004 to December 2009 and find that terrorist events are more likely to occur in highly populated areas but that their frequency and intensity vary widely over time. They also identify several social, political, and cultural triggers that affect the incidence of terrorist attacks, including the celebration of Islamic holy days. Though they focus only on the Iraqi case, Medina et al. argue that policy-makers can use the trends identified in their study to help combat terrorism and insurgency in other states such as Yemen and Somalia, where branches of Al Qaeda carry out terrorist attacks. They contend that Yemen and Somalia are similar enough cases to have their findings be relevant but do not go so far as to say that the trends are similar in other regions or with other terrorist groups.

Researchers have leveraged GIS data to examine terrorism in other states, as well. Given events within the United States in the past twenty years, such as 9/11 or the Oklahoma City bombing, it is unsurprising that several studies (Cothren et al. 2008; Webb and Cutter 2009; Nunn 2007) have looked at terrorism trends on American soil. Webb and Cutter (2009) and Nunn (2007) investigate spatio-temporal factors of terrorist attacks in the United States while Cothren uses geographical data to look for patterns in the *preparation* for terrorist attacks. These articles largely find that terrorism attacks cluster in geographically populated areas but that the means and targets vary according to the type of group (i.e. religious, right-wing, environmental extremists, etc.) carrying out the attack. Israel and Spain, two other states with histories of domestic terrorism, have also been the focus of research using GIS research. In the case of Israel, Berrebi and Lakdawalla (2007) use geocoded data ranging from 1949 to 2004 to examine the characteristics of the location of terrorist attacks, such as distance from international borders, proximity to centers of government administration, and ethnic homogeneity. Also studying Israel, Kliot (2006) focuses specifically on suicide terrorism and, like Berrebi and Lakdawalla, zeroes in on the importance of geography and the location of terrorist attacks relative to other important factors, such as Israeli checkpoints. Lastly, LaFree et al. examine spatio-temporal patterns of ETA terrorist attacks in Spain from 1970 to 2007 (LaFree et al. 2012). They draw from the Global Terrorism Database (GTD) and using the geographical information from the database are able to look at trends as local as district-level.

This discussion does not provide an exhaustive list of every study that uses GIS to examine terrorism trends within a single state, but instead highlights a few illustrative cases. One takeaway from these studies is that their unit of analysis is, at its largest, a state. They focus on a singular case and although some mention the possibility of drawing general lessons to be applied to terrorism studies as a whole, they typically maintain that the trends examined pertain only to their specific spatio-temporal instance. Scholars in this tradition tend to ask more focused questions, such how does a new cellphone tower lead to future terrorist attacks (Shapiro and Weidmann, 2015). By contrast, a more general question, which is more difficult to isolate a direct causal effect for a particular variable, might be: how do changes in technology lead to increases in terrorist attacks? Scholars are interested in both questions, but the first is more amenable to a clean test that can identify a causal effect. These types of studies might also have more direct albeit limited policy implications.

Cross-National Studies

Beyond more focused, local studies, GIS research on terrorism seeks to use the specificity of spatial data to parse out broader trends that transcend borders. This tool can be used to examine attacks across borders including those that cluster along borders, which was impossible in early studies of conflict. Providing more precise geographic information allows, for example, for examinations of such factors as whether a militarized dispute at a border has the same effect as the same dispute internally or at sea.

A major focus of study within this vein of research is the search for the *typical* or *average* terror venue. Part of the goal of much of this research is an attempt to identify similarities in the location of terrorist attacks across countries and across time to provide better explanations and predictions of the locations for this violence. Although the authors do not employ GIS, a good example of this is the Drakos and Gofas (2006) study of terrorist attacks from 1985 to 1998 in which they find several factors that contribute to attacks, namely low economic openness and high levels of international disputes. They also provide evidence of a regional component, meaning that terrorism seems to have a learning or diffusion quality. That is, within regions groups may learn from each other and the tactics may be adopted by socially or geographically proximate organizations. Tracking the movement of minority groups specifically, Arva and Piazza (2016) find the transnational dispersion of kin minority communities to be a robust predictor of terrorism incidents.

Using geo-referenced data from the Global Terrorism Database (GTD) and geolocated data for civil war zones, Findley and Young (2012b) find that terrorism often occurs in the context of civil war. Additionally, they show there is a strong relationship between civil conflict and terrorism, namely that terrorism is most prevalent *during* war. In their examination of six countries they find that in the post-Cold War period, post-war terrorism attacks are more likely than pre-conflict attacks, lending support for previous arguments for terrorism as a tool of spoiling the peace (Kydd and Walter 2002; Findley and Young 2015), though not necessarily for outbidding (Findley and Young 2012a).

Zeroing in on the spatial dimension, Nemeth et al. (2014) set out to identify terrorist *hotspots*, meaning areas in the world that are more prone to experiencing attacks. The authors merged a geocoded GTD dataset onto the PRIO-GRID[3] cell structure and used a hotspot analysis to see which areas are most likely to suffer from domestic terrorism.

Beyond hotspots for terrorist attacks, GIS can be further utilized to identify movement of the terrorist actors themselves. For example, Eisman et al. (2017) use geographically weighted regressions to highlight the areas most attractive to terrorists as a safe haven. From these safe havens, over one-third of attackers live and plan their activity within thirty miles of the attack location (Smith et al. 2017).

Including a temporal dimension alongside the spatial dimension, Kluch and Vauz (2016) use data on all attacks from 1970 to 2013 to analyze the levels of terrorism within over 200 countries. They find the majority of countries experience no or low-level spans of terrorism that last over long periods of time. Very few countries ever experience "elevated," long-term campaigns.

In line with much of the research just described, Nemeth et al. show that large populations and poor economic conditions make terrorism more likely, but they also show that mountainous terrain, proximity to a national capital, and population density also affect the likelihood of terrorism. The work of Findley et al. (2018) corroborates these findings. Findley and his co-authors use the ITERATE (International Terrorism: Attributes of Terrorist Events) dataset along with the PRIO-GRID dataset to show that transnational terror attacks are most likely to occur in areas of recent civil violence, locations close to capital cities and international borders, regions with low forest cover but mountainous terrain, and centers with higher populations and population densities. In sum, the cross-national GIS studies of terrorism have established a consensus that, worldwide, the areas most likely to experience terrorist attacks are heavily populated areas close to country capitals or international borders, war-affected, and have poor economic development, and mountainous terrain.

Both domestic and transnational terrorism and the diffusion therein are being analyzed using these tools, yet much work is left to do. Does domestic terrorism encourage transnational attacks? Is the reverse true? Do domestic attacks in border areas have a more profound effect than those in the capital or far from borders? These questions have clear policy implications and are far from resolved in the academic community. While we do not suggest this is the only tool to address such questions, GIS is a powerful instrument for addressing these and related questions.

Additional Applications of Geography in Terrorism Research

Much of the geographic study of terrorism fits into the two major categories described, but it bears mentioning that there are other ways in which the broader field has considered the relationship of geography and terrorism. By mapping data GTD to the subnational level, Findley and Young (2015) are able to evaluate the empirical evidence for spoiling logic in peace negotiations during civil wars. Geocoding the data within battle zones allows them to more accurately differentiate between terrorism violence and military and government violence that are a regular part of civil war.

These lines of study tap into an ongoing question in the civil conflict literature. Is terrorism different than other types of violence carried out by entities such as rebel groups, militias, or gangs? Scholars have begun to tackle this question at higher levels of a political violence typology, as evidenced by Findley and Young (2015) and studies such as Findley et al. (2012b), in which they overlay terrorist attacks in civil war zones and find a high level of overlap. However, GIS provides the technology to begin to dive into these questions with an even finer grain. For example, attack types and specific targets can be used to help differentiate among political violence types. Are attack types typically used by insurgents against military targets, such as armed assaults, different from those used indiscriminately against civilian populations, such as an IED attack? Examining the target locations of these attacks at a more micro level can illuminate these differences in attack types. For example, was the attack location a military base or a refugee camp? Overlaid with data on locations of actors and incidents known to be rebels, militias, or gangs, GIS offers promising insight into the question of political violence typologies.

Other research seeks to model the location of the terrorist groups themselves. Bennell and Corey (2007) investigate whether criminal profiling, particularly that pertaining to serial criminals, is useful in discovering the whereabouts of terrorist cells. That is, do terrorist groups, like serial criminals, engage in the sorts of behavior that would help law enforcement predict where they might be? Because of the obvious trouble with getting accurate data of terrorist locations, they are only able to examine two cases. However, they give reason to believe that criminal profiling may be useful in finding terrorist locations.

Techniques of GIS

Many scholars of political violence and terrorism are not trained in geography or GIS. To make the maps that are created and analyzed when using GIS applications, a researcher builds them through a series of spatial data layers. These individual layers generally represent different units of analysis, from continent to country to city to specific event. For example, a world map with the seven continents may be the base layer of a map, with subsequent countries, administrative levels, and cities layered on top of it to create a more comprehensive map that can be analyzed at multiple levels.

There are two main types of spatial data: raster and vector. Raster data represent continuous features as individual pixels, or cells, in a grid. The map or representation space is usually made up of a grid of square cells, but they can be rectangular as well. Each cell has a value corresponding to some spatial attribute or multiple layered attributes. Examples of raster data include slope or elevation, changes in land features, or ethnicity of a group. To represent these data visually, each cell could be a different color, depending on its slope or some other attribute which would be explained in a legend. Raster data are limited by the fact that all information inside the cell is the same. In short, a single value is attributed to all space in the cell (Longley et al. 2015). As precision in the cell size increases, this is less of an issue. Other issues, such as how to assign a value for a cell when the cell has multiple values come to the fore. For example, if the cell has to be assigned a certain ethnic group, should it be coded a 1 if that group is present in the cell? Or only if it is the dominant group?

Vector data, on the other hand, represent discrete features. These features have clearly defined names or boundaries. There are three types of vector data: points, lines, and polygons. Points represent a single pair of geographic coordinates, such as a building, or an event, such as a terrorist attack. Lines represent features that have length but not width, such as a river or a road. Polygons are areas often with boundaries that do not fit neatly into a standardized grid, such as a state, country, or lake. All points can be connected by lines. These lines build polygons rather than grid cells like the raster method.

Both raster and vector data can have associated attributes that are stored in a table linked to each feature. These attributes are non-spatial data that give further information about each feature. For example, for point data where each point represents the coordinates of a terrorist attack, each point could have further information associated with it, such as date of attack and group responsible. These attributes may come with the spatial data or they can be tables, such as an Excel file, which can be joined with an existing spatial layer, as long as a common unique identifier exists.

Vector data are frequently used in terrorism studies. Scholars such as Findley and Young (2012b) and Marineau et al. (2018) utilize point data in the form of geocoded terrorism attacks on all countries in the world; Berrebi (2008) utilize point data to analyze the spatial and temporal trends of terrorist attacks in Israel. They integrate polygon data to further analyze each point, or specific attack, in relation to line and polygon features. In looking at distance from international borders, they use line features. In looking at the relationship between point location and ethnic homogeneity, they are utilizing the attributes of a polygon (the density of a particular ethnicity within a set of boundaries). Medina et al. (2011) use point data from every geocoded terrorist attack in Iraq to perform a similar analysis. The aggregation of spatial vector data and associated attributes has proven to be a powerful tool in GIS analysis.

Chloropleth maps, in which areas are shaded in proportion to the measurement of the statistical variable being displayed on the map, such as attacks per region, are the most often used map tool in GIS applications. These maps supply a quick visual reference that allows readers to better understand existing patterns. Dot density maps are another way to convey the intensity of an attribute. These quantitative, thematic maps place dots of the same size in an area based on the proportion to a numeric attribute associated with this area, such as the number of terrorist attacks that have occurred. Findley and Young use this technique in their contribution to a forum on thinking about acts of terrorism versus terrorists (Asal et al. 2012). A dot distribution map follows the same concept, but uses one dot per area, with its size being in proportion to the numeric attribute of that area.

More nuanced techniques can be utilized in GIS analysis as well. Hotspot analysis uses density of points to analyze where clusters exist (or don't exist) and tells the user if these clusters are statistically significant. Nemeth (2014) used hotspot analysis to find local areas prone to domestic terrorism. Once these areas were defined, they analyzed attributes of each polygon to see which increased the likelihood of terrorist attacks (e.g. proximity to state capital or mountainous terrain).

Geographically weighted regression (GWR) concerns whether an estimated coefficient, fitted to the entire sample (such as every country in the world), adequately represents detailed local variations (such as individual countries). It assesses whether global models follow local regression implementations. These variations do not occur in the typical data space, however, but by moving a weighted window over the data, estimating one set of coefficient values at every chosen point (Bivand et al. 2008). Looking at patterns of terrorist attacks in Turkey, Yildirim and Calb (2013) utilize GWR to investigate the determinants of provincial terrorism and determine why most attacks occur in the south and east of Turkey. Spatial econometrics estimation methods can be used to resolve spatial dependence between observations, such as spatial autocorrelation, spillover effects, neighborhood effects, or state dependence. Spatial autocorrelation occurs when similar values are disproportionately clustered or dispersed on the map, violating the assumption of independence. Variogram tables can be created to allow users to further explore these patterns and adjust if needed.

Areas of Further Research

The fine-grain spatio-temporal characteristics of GIS data open up many exciting areas in terrorism research, of which we discuss three. Scholars could effectively bring together GIS data and quasi-experimental survey analysis. Surveys and quasi-experiments have become increasingly common in the field of international relations but a constant difficulty in these research designs is how to choose a sample. GIS data can help more accurately identify the desired sample group. For instance, if a researcher is interested in how terrorism affects public perception of the government, he or she can leverage GIS spatial data to find the hotspot areas most directly affected by attacks. This would ensure that the researcher is conducting surveys with the desired treatment group.

Another useful application of GIS would be more accurate observational matching. By establishing matching estimates, such as through propensity scores, one can look at cross-national variation to examine systematic variation in the covariates of interest across like cases. In essence, GIS data massively increase the number of possible N upon which to match because no longer would comparisons be constrained to a national level. While on the aggregate Somalia and Colombia, or Somalia and Pakistan, do not line up well for matching, it may very well be the case that certain districts *do*. Matching on a smaller observational unit can allow researchers to more precisely choose their sampling for quasi-experiments and thus provide more possible cases and look for variation across cases.

Second, GIS analysis could be used within quasi-experiments themselves. Does the presentation of how data are displayed change the actions of policy-makers? One advantage of GIS data is that it can easily be presented in visual forms, such as heat maps showing the regions, cities, or even roads with the most terrorist attacks. When mapped along with important factors like natural resources, infrastructure, or topography, these visuals can serve as powerful representations of relationships. But are these sorts of representations more impactful than a typical spreadsheet or a list of terrorist attacks? And do GIS data help to fashion more effective counterterrorism policies? In this case, GIS analysis can be useful within quasi-experiments to measure the reactions of policy-makers to different types of data representation. While some policy-makers would receive simple spreadsheets or lists of attacks, others would be given more visual representations of terrorist attacks, deaths, and means.

Lastly, researchers could use both the spatial and temporal nature of GIS data to investigate at the subnational level how terrorism affects local issues, such as regional trade, public health, or voting behavior. An attack hotspot may very well see dramatic reductions in trade, a decline in public health indices, or altered voting behavior as a result of terrorist activity, but these effects may be washed out in datasets in which the state is the smallest unit of analysis. Along these lines, terrorism's effect on local elections provides a promising avenue for future studies. Research finds that terrorism has effects on national elections (Montalvo 2011; Getmansky and Zeitzoff 2014), but research looking at subnational effects is sparse (Kibris 2011; Berrebi and Klor 2008). It may very well be that when it is localized to only a few areas of a state, terrorism has little effect on national elections but very large effects on *municipal* elections. Kibris looks at the effect of terrorism on voting in Turkish elections, but only indirectly, using the number of police deaths as a proxy for terrorist attacks. Berrebi's investigation (2008) of Israeli elections at the district level provides compelling evidence that local electorates are, indeed, sensitive to terror attacks and this sensitivity is reflected in their voting patterns. This begs the question of whether this phenomenon is specific to the Israeli case or if it can be generalized to other nation states as well. Similarly, is the magnitude of the effect on voters similar across different types of elections (federal versus local) and attacks (suicide, chemical, etc.)? GIS data allow researchers to analyze the district or municipality as the unit of analysis as opposed to the nation state and can thereby capture variation that previously went unnoticed when aggregated to the national level.

Technical Needs

The most widely used software for GIS analysis is the ArcGIS suite. This program must be run on a Windows machine (or on a Mac utilizing a virtual machine like Bootcamp or Windows Parallels). Developed by ESRI, ArcGIS is made up of several distinct applications which are integrated to allow users to aggregate data sources, build spatial models and maps, analyze them, and produce readable output. ArcCatalog, for example, provides an interface to organize and navigate data while ArcMap allows users to create, interact, and analyze features on an actual map.

A specific type of data is needed in order for ArcGIS to function. Vector spatial data (points, lines, and polygons) must have shape files. These files are available through ESRI, government websites such as census.gov or open source, such as divagis.com.

Depending on the specificity of the feature, data may need to be geocoded (recording the latitude and longitude coordinates). Points, such as specific terrorist attacks, would be an example. Geocoded data allow ArcGIS to transform information into a location on a map. Geographical coordinates (latitude, longitude) provide the most specific geo-location. However, ArcGIS has location finding services which can translate information, such as a zip code, into a general location on a map.

Attributes can be included in the base shape files that are used to build a map. If not, tables containing attributes can be joined with a shape file to supply information about each individual feature. Tables must be in .xls, .mdb, .txt, or .csv form in order to be successfully joined. The text type must match the shape files exactly, and there must be a unique identifier in order for attributes to join features (e.g. country code or date).

While it is certainly widely used, there are several alternatives to ArcGIS. R Maptools allows for the statistical program R to create simple maps. It is fundamentally different than ArcGIS because of its command line interface, in which users type commands rather than the visual interaction of pointing and clicking to select and modify features. The Rgeos and Rgdal packages of this free program can perform many of the same analytic techniques, such as geographically weighted regression and spatial interaction models, and produce maps to visualize the data. R is an integrative program, because users have more freedom and ability to edit, analyze, and visualize the data all in one interface.

The spmap, shp2dta, and mif2dta commands in Stata also allow for the use of GIS techniques. Much like ArcGIS, users merge a .shp (shape) file and a .dbf (attribute table) to visually display data. The .shp file must be an ESRI or MapInfoInterchange file. Users can create various types of maps using the command line interface of Stata, such as dot density and chloropleth, and perform spatially weighted analyses, such as spatial auto-correlation and regression.

QGIS and WorldMap are free, open source options. GeoCommons is another online program that has many features similar to ArcGIS. However, ArcGIS remains the most user friendly and comprehensive software for both building and analyzing maps.

Conclusion

The first law of geography or what is called Tobler's law suggests that, "Everything is related to everything else, but near things are more related than distant things." Judging from initial inquiries reviewed here, there appears to be considerable evidence that incidents of terrorism follow this law. We don't yet fully understand these relationships, however. While scholarly research has made significant strides in identifying and examining these effects, especially at the national level, there is much that remains to be learned about how geographic factors affect terrorism. GIS is gaining popularity in the terrorism studies field, with scholars utilizing GIS techniques to determine and explore patterns and trends in terrorism at both local and global levels, and this work is being published in some of the top outlets in the field. Whether the question is why terrorists choose targets near bus stops in a local capital or which global regions experience disproportionately high rates of terrorist attacks, GIS provides a method for investigation. The spatial and temporal analysis that GIS provides opens up a new window into the field, through which both old and new questions can be explored and answered in a more precise manner.

Acknowledgment

We thank Brian Lange for helpful contributions to the chapter.

Notes

1. *CNN* 2015.
2. *Telegraph* 2008.
3. Released by the Peace Research Institute of Oslo, the PRIO-GRID database is a spatio-temporal grid structure that divides the globe into small quadratic cells. The cells contain basic static information, such as terrain, and can be coupled with more advanced time-varying variables such as population or natural resources.

References

Arva, Bryan J., and James A. Piazza (2016) "Spatial Distribution of Minority Communities and Terrorism: Domestic Concentration versus Transnational Dispersion," *Defence and Peace Economics*, 27(1): 1–36.

Asal, Victor, Luis De la Calle, Michael Findley, and Joseph Young (2012) "Killing Civilians or Holding Territory? How to Think about Terrorism," *International Studies Review*, 14(3): 475–97.

Bennell, Craig, and Shevaun Corey (2007) "Geographic Profiling of Terrorist Attacks," in Richard Kocsis (ed.), *Criminal Profiling*. Hoboken, NJ: Springer, 189–203.

Berrebi, Claude, and Darius Lakdawalla (2007) "How Does Terrorism Risk Vary across Space and Time? An Analysis Based on the Israeli Experience," *Defence and Peace Economics*, 18(2): 113–31.

Berrebi, Claude, and Esteban F. Klor (2008) "Are Voters Sensitive to Terrorism? Direct Evidence from the Israeli Electorate." *American Political Science Review*, 102(3): 279–301.

Bivand, R. S., E. Pebesma, and V Gomez-Rubio (2008) *Applied Spatial Data Analysis with R*. New York: Springer-Verlag.

Braithwaite, Alex, and Shane D. Johnson (2012) "Space-Time Modeling of Insurgency and Counterinsurgency in Iraq," *Journal of Quantitative Criminology*, 28(1): 31–48.

CNN (2015) <http://www.cnn.com/2013/09/18/world/asia/mumbai-terror-attacks> [Accessed Aug. 2015].

Cothren, Jackson, Brent L. Smith, Paxton Roberts, and Kelly R. Damphousse (2008) "Geospatial and Temporal Patterns of Preparatory Conduct among American Terrorists," *International Journal of Comparative and Applied Criminal Justice*, 32(1): 23–41.

Drakos, Konstantinos, and Andreas Gofas (2006) "In Search of the Average Transnational Terrorist Attack Venue," *Defence and Peace Economics*, 17(2): 73–93.

Eisman, Elyktra, Jennifer Gebelein, and Thomas A. Breslin (2017) "Developing a Geographically Weighted Complex Systems Model Using Open-Source Data to Highlight Locations Vulnerable to Becoming Terrorist Safe-Havens," *Annals of GIS*, 23(4): 251–67.

Findley, Michael G., and Joseph K. Young (2012a) "More Combatant Groups, More Terror?: Empirical Tests of an Outbidding Logic," *Terrorism and Political Violence*, 24(5): 706–21.

Findley, Michael G., and Joseph K. Young (2012b) "Terrorism and Civil War: A Spatial and Temporal Approach to a Conceptual Problem," *Perspectives on Politics*, 10(02): 285–305.

Findley, Michael, and Joseph K. Young (2015) "Terrorism, Spoiling, and the Resolution of Civil Wars," *Journal of Politics*, 77(4): 1115–28.

Getmansky, Anna, and Thomas Zeitzoff (2014) "Terrorism and Voting: The Effect of Rocket Threat on Voting in Israeli Elections," *American Political Science Review*, 108(3): 588–604.

Gleditsch, Kristian S., and Michael D. Ward (2001) "Measuring Space: A Minimum-Distance Database and Applications to International Studies," *Journal of Peace Research*, 38(6): 739–58.

Johnson, Shane D., and Alex Braithwaite (2009) "Spatio-temporal Modeling of Insurgency in Iraq," in Joshua D. Freilich and Graeme R. Newman (eds), *Reducing Terrorism through Situational Crime Prevention*. Monsey, NY: Criminal Justice Press, 9–32.

Kibris, Arzu (2011) "Funerals and Elections: The Effects of Terrorism on Voting Behavior in Turkey," *Journal of Conflict Resolution*, 55(2): 220–47.

Kliot, Nurit, and Igal Charney (2006) "The Geography of Suicide Terrorism in Israel," *GeoJournal*, 66(4): 353–73.

Kluch, Sofia Pinero, and Alan Vaux (2016) "The Non-Random Nature of Terrorism: An Exploration of Where and How Global Trends of Terrorism have Developed over 40 Years," *Studies in Conflict and Terrorism*, 39(12): 1031–49.

Kwan, Mei-Po, and Jiyeong Lee (2005) "Emergency Response After 9/11: The Potential of Real-Time 3D GIS for Quick Emergency Response in Micro-Spatial Environments," *Computers, Environment and Urban Systems*, 29(2): 93–113.

Kydd, Andrew, and Barbara F. Walter (2002) "Sabotaging the Peace: The Politics of Extremist Violence," *International Organization*, 56(02): 263–96.

LaFree, Gary, Laura Dugan, Min Xie, and Piyusha Singh (2012) "Spatial and Temporal Patterns of Terrorist Attacks by ETA 1970 to 2007," *Journal of Quantitative Criminology*, 28(1): 7–29.

Longley, Paul A., Michael F. Goodchild, David J. Maguire, and David W. Rhind (2015) *Geographic Information Science and Systems*. Malden, MA: John Wiley & Sons.

Marineau, Josiah F., Henry Pascoe, Alex Braithwaite, Michael G. Findley, and Joseph K. Young (2018) "The Local Geography of Transnational Terrorist Attacks." Unpubl. manuscript, University of Texas at Austin.

Medina, Richard M., Laura K. Siebeneck, and George F. Hepner (2011) "A Geographic In formation Systems (GIS) Analysis of Spatiotemporal Patterns of Terrorist Incidents in Iraq 2004–2009," *Studies in Conflict and Terrorism*, 34(11): 862–82.

Montalvo, Jose G. (2011) "Voting After the Bombings: A Natural Experiment on the Effect of Terrorist Attacks on Democratic Elections," *Review of Economics and Statistics*, 93(4): 1146–54.

Nemeth, Stephen C., Jacob A. Mauslein, and Craig Stapley (2014) "The Primacy of the Local: Identifying Terrorist Hot Spots Using Geographic Information Systems," *Journal of Politics*, 76(2): 304–17.

Nunn, Samuel (2007) "Incidents of Terrorism in the United States, 1997–2005," *Geographical Review*, 97(1): 89–111.

Shapiro, Jacob N., and Nils B. Weidmann (2015) "Is the Phone Mightier than the Sword? Cellphones and Insurgent Violence in Iraq," *International Organization*, 69(2): 247–74.

Smith, Brent L., Paxton Roberts, and Kelly R. Damphousse (2017) "The Terrorists Planning Cycle," in Gary LaFree and Joshua Freilich (eds), *The Handbook of the Criminology of Terrorism*. Malden, MA: John Wiley & Sons, 62–76.

Starr, Harvey (2002) "Opportunity, Willingness and Geographic Information Systems (GIS): Reconceptualizing Borders in International Relations," *Political Geography*, 21(2): 243–61.

Telegraph (2008) <http://www.telegraph.co.uk/news/worldnews/asia/india/3691723/Mumbai-attacks-Indian-suit-against-Google-Earth-over-image-use-by-terrorist html> [Accessed Aug. 2015].

Townsley, Michael, Shane D. Johnson, and Jerry H. Ratcliffe (2008) "Space Time Dynamics of Insurgent Activity in Iraq," *Security Journal*, 21(3): 139–46.

Webb, Jennifer J., and Susan L. Cutter (2009) "The Geography of US terrorist Incidents, 1970–2004," *Terrorism and Political Violence*, 21(3): 428–49.

Yildirim, J., and N. Calb (2013) "Analyzing the Determinants of Terrorism in Turkey Using Geographically Weighted Regression," *Defence and Peace Economics*, 24(3): 195–209.

PART IV

CAUSES AND MOTIVATIONS

CHAPTER 17

THE CAUSES OF TERRORISM

JEFF GOODWIN

ASCERTAINING the causes of terrorism depends of course on how we define terrorism. Alas, as is well known, scholars have been unable to reach a consensus on the meaning of the word. In 1981, Martha Crenshaw, a well-known scholar of terrorism, wrote an important article titled "The Causes of Terrorism," published in the journal *Comparative Politics*. Crenshaw was interested in discovering the causes of "symbolic, low-level violence by conspiratorial organizations" (Crenshaw 1981, 379), which is one of the ways in which scholars have defined terrorism. Crenshaw had in mind violence by such groups as the Irish Republican Army, the Popular Front for the Liberation of Palestine, and the Red Army Faction in West Germany. To be sure, Crenshaw was well aware that states as well as dissident groups can employ terrorism—in some sense of the word. In fact, the first sentence of her article states, "Terrorism occurs both in the context of violent resistance to the state as well as in the service of state interests" (Crenshaw 1981, 379). But Crenshaw focused exclusively on anti-state terrorism by "conspiratorial organizations" in her article.

In this chapter, I want to consider the possible causes of terrorism defined in a rather different way, one which encompasses both state and anti-state or rebel violence. I define terrorism, like many scholars, as violence against noncombatants, usually common or ordinary people, in order to advance a political cause (cf. Richards 2014). The immediate purpose of this violence, furthermore, is not just to kill or injure people but to frighten, intimidate, provoke, or otherwise influence a larger population, among which the killed and wounded were either randomly or selectively targeted (Goodwin 2006). Terrorism thus differs from other forms of political violence, such as conventional (or guerrilla) warfare and assassination, which aim to kill soldiers (whether state or rebel troops) and political leaders, respectively.

Formally, I define terrorism as *any tactic or set of tactics used by any government, group, organization, or individual, in pursuit of a political goal (broadly defined), which is intended to kill or harm civilians or noncombatants (as opposed to soldiers or political leaders) so as to frighten, intimidate, demoralize, provoke, or pressure other civilians and/or political leaders*. A shorter, "sound bite" definition of terrorism is *the killing or harming of civilians to intimidate others*.

Terrorism, then, is *not* an ideological movement like socialism or conservatism, nor is it violence by a particular type of organization (e.g. covert or conspiratorial). Rather, terrorism refers to *tactics* that may be employed by either states or rebels, whether they are ideologically conservative, moderate, or radical. This definition encompasses (1) forms of violence or other lethal actions against noncombatants by rebel groups (i.e. "terrorism" as many if not most people tend to think of it today) but also (2) forms of violence or other lethal actions by states or allied paramilitary forces against noncombatants in conflicts with rebels. (Much counter-insurgent and indeed counterterrorist violence is itself terrorist in nature.) It also encompasses (3) violence or other lethal actions by states against noncombatants in international conflicts, and (4) violence or other lethal actions against an oppressed racial or ethnic (or other) group for purposes of controlling or intimidating that group.

"State terrorism," for its part, is important for scholars to consider for several reasons, not least because state violence against noncombatants has claimed many more victims than has anti-state violence, and because terrorism by rebel groups is sometimes a strategic response to state terrorism (see e.g. Herman and O'Sullivan 1989, chs 2–3; Gareau 2004).

My definition of terrorism entails a distinct understanding of what exactly we must explain in order to explain terrorism. What we must explain, plainly, is not why states or political groups sometimes resort to violence as such, but why they employ violence against (or otherwise seek to harm) *civilians or noncombatants* in particular, with the further goal of intimidating many others in the process. Indeed, one virtue of this definition is that it squarely focuses our attention on violations of the idea (and the ideal) of *noncombatant immunity*—the principle that noncombatants should never be targeted in wars or civil conflicts, whether by states or rebels. Noncombatant immunity is a fundamental principle of "just war" theory and international law, including the Geneva Conventions.

How, then, are we to explain terrorism defined in this way? In the remainder of this chapter I will critically review two traditional theories of terrorism, then examine at greater length the currently dominant "radicalization" perspective on terrorism, and then develop and briefly illustrate an alternative account of terrorism, which I call the "indirect-war" theory. I argue that neither the traditional theories nor the radicalization perspective tell us much at all about terrorism as I have defined it, but that the indirect-war perspective offers greater promise for the empirical analysis of a wide range of cases of terrorism.

Traditional Theories of Terrorism

How have social scientists and other analysts traditionally attempted to explain why states or rebels have sometimes used violence against, or otherwise sought to harm, civilians? Many theories have been proposed—far more than I can review here—but prior to the 9/11 attacks two hypotheses were especially influential: (1) terrorism is a product of the *weakness and/or desperation* of some rebels or states (a "weapon of the weak"), and (2) much terrorism is *a retaliatory response* to violence, including terrorism, by the perpetrators' armed enemies, whether states or rebels. After 9/11, a new theory of terrorism has become dominant. This theory holds that terrorism is the result of the "radicalization" of particular individuals or groups.

Before the radicalization perspective became dominant, perhaps the most common idea about what causes terrorism was the notion that oppositional or rebel movements turn to terrorism when they are very weak, lack popular support, and yet are desperate to redress their grievances. A similar argument has been proposed as an explanation for state terrorism, claiming that states turn to terrorism—or "civilian victimization"—when they become desperate to win wars (Downes 2008). The core idea here is that rebels and states which lack the capacity or leverage to pressure their opponents either nonviolently or through conventional or guerrilla warfare, or who fail to attain their goals when they *do* employ these strategies, will turn to terrorism as a "last resort." Disaffected elites sometimes resort to violence, according to Crenshaw's influential account (1981), because it is easier and cheaper than strategies that require mass mobilization, especially when government repression makes mass mobilization extremely difficult if not impossible.

There are, however, a number of logical and empirical problems with this "desperation" theory of terrorism, as we might call it. Most importantly, the theory seems simply to assume that desperate rebels or politicians would automatically view attacks upon civilians as beneficial instead of detrimental to their cause. But even if terrorism is cheaper and easier than many other strategies, why would one employ it at all? We need to know what beneficial consequences rebels or state officials believe their attacks on civilians, or on specific kinds of civilians, would bring about. How exactly will these attacks advance their cause? Why would officials or rebels not assume that attacks on civilians would *undermine* their popularity or otherwise *hurt* their cause?

Second, there does not in fact seem to be a particularly strong empirical relationship between the strength of states and rebel groups, on the one hand, and their use (or not) of terrorism, on the other. For example, the US government was hardly desperate when it imposed economic sanctions on Iraq during the 1990s, which may have resulted in the deaths of more than half a million children (Gordon 2010). (Although these sanctions did not entail direct violence against Iraqi civilians, they fit our definition of terrorism because they deliberately resulted in the deaths and suffering of noncombatants.) The Liberation Tigers of Tamil Eelam (LTTE) in Sri Lanka, to take another example, was a powerful rebel movement during the 1990s according to most accounts. The LTTE sometimes even waged conventional warfare against Sri Lankan government forces, and it used small aircraft in some of its attacks. Yet the LTTE, which was predominantly Tamil, also engaged in indiscriminate attacks on ethnic Sinhalese civilians, and it did so long after it had decimated rival Tamil nationalist groups (Bloom 2005, ch. 3). So its growing strength did not lead it to abandon terror tactics. The desperation theory does not tell us why.

One can also point, conversely, to relatively *weak* states and rebel movements that have largely *eschewed* terrorism. Perhaps the best example of the latter is the armed wing of the African National Congress (ANC) in South Africa. In 1961, as many of their leaders were being arrested and many others driven into exile, the ANC and the Communist Party of South Africa established an armed wing called Umkhonto weSizwe ("Spear of the Nation" or MK). The ANC explicitly adopted armed struggle as one of its main political strategies. By most accounts, however, MK failed to become an effective guerrilla force, as the South African Defense Forces were simply too strong and effective (Cherry 2011). And yet MK did *not* then embrace terror tactics against the dominant white minority, despite the fact, as Gay Seidman points out, that, "In a deeply segregated society, it would have been easy to kill random whites. Segregated white schools, segregated movie theaters, segregated shopping centers meant that if white deaths were the only goal, potential targets could be found everywhere" (Seidman 2001, 118). (I address the question of why the ANC rejected terrorism later in this chapter.)

In short, weak and desperate rebels and states do not necessarily adopt terror tactics, and strong states and rebels do not necessarily eschew such tactics. As Turk concludes, "Because any group may adopt terror tactics, it is misleading to assume either that 'terrorism is the weapon of the weak' or that terrorists are always small groups of outsiders—or at most a 'lunatic fringe'" (Turk 1982, 122). Indeed, terrorism is often and perhaps usually a weapon of the strong, and of strong states in particular.

The main insight of the desperation theory of terrorism is that states and rebel groups *do* often take up arms after they have concluded that diplomacy and nonviolent politics cannot work or that these work far too slowly or ineffectively to redress urgent grievances. But notice that this does not tell us why armed actors would employ violence against *noncombatants* in particular. Moreover, the argument that attacking "soft" targets such as unprotected civilians is easier than waging conventional or guerrilla warfare does not explain why states or rebels would *ever* wage conventional or guerrilla warfare. The argument implies that rational people would *always* prefer terrorism to these strategies, which is clearly not the case. In sum, the most we can say is that weakness and desperation may be a necessary but not sufficient cause of terrorism in some cases. But as a general theory of terrorism, this perspective is clearly inadequate.

A second traditional view of terrorism is that it is *a retaliatory response* to violence, including terrorism. Leftist and radical analysts of terrorism have often made this claim about oppositional terrorism, and it is emphasized by Herman and O'Sullivan (1989). They suggest that the "retail" terrorism of dissident groups is caused or provoked by the "wholesale" or "primary" terrorism of states, especially powerful Western states, above all the United States. The terms "wholesale" and "retail" are meant to remind readers that state terrorism has generally been much more deadly than oppositional terrorism, which is undeniable. Other scholars have rightly emphasized how state and non-state terrorism have been dynamically intertwined (e.g. English, 2016) and how, as a result, revenge often becomes a powerful motivation for terrorism (e.g. Richardson, 2006: ch. 4).

But how far does this view take us? It is certainly true that indiscriminate state violence, especially when perpetrated by relatively weak and ineffective states, has encouraged the development of violent rebel movements (Goodwin 2001). But the question is why these movements would attack and threaten *civilians* as opposed to the state's armed forces. If rebels are responding to *state* terrorism, after all, why would they not employ violence against *the state*? State terrorism, in other words, would seem more likely to induce rebels to employ guerrilla or conventional warfare than terror tactics.

Empirically, one can also point to dissident organizations that have arisen in contexts of extreme state violence which have nonetheless largely eschewed terror tactics. For example, Central American guerrilla movements of the 1970s and 1980s, including the Sandinista Front in Nicaragua and the Farabundo Martí Front for National Liberation in El Salvador, confronted states that engaged in extensive violence against noncombatants, yet neither movement engaged in much terrorism. Another example is, again, the ANC in South Africa. Interestingly, Herman and O'Sullivan's book devotes considerable attention to both South African and Israeli state terrorism (1989, ch. 2). And yet, while they note the "retail" terrorism of the Palestine Liberation Organization during the 1970s and 1980s—emphasizing that Israeli state terrorism was responsible for a great many more civilian deaths during this period—they do not discuss the oppositional terrorism in South Africa which their theory would seem to predict. In fact, as we have noted, the ANC simply did not carry out much terrorism at all. So "wholesale" state terrorism, clearly, does not *always* cause or provoke "retail" oppositional terrorism.

Having said this, it is indeed difficult to find a rebel group that has carried out extensive terrorism which has *not* arisen in a context of considerable state violence. For example, those rebels in French Algeria, the West Bank and Gaza, Sri Lanka, and Chechnya who engaged in extensive terrorism have been drawn from, and claim to act on behalf of, populations that have themselves suffered extensive and often indiscriminate state repression. The question is what to make of this correlation. Why, in these particular contexts, have rebels attacked certain civilians as well as government forces? The retaliatory theory of terrorism does not tell us.

The Radicalization Perspective

A huge literature on terrorism has appeared following the 9/11 terrorist attacks. Much of this literature is descriptive or focuses on particular aspects of terrorism, broadly conceived (e.g. recruitment, organization, ideology, etc.). Surprisingly little of this literature is concerned with proposing general causal hypotheses about the choice of terror tactics by either rebels or states. One theory of terrorism, however, has clearly risen to a position of dominance in both the journalistic and academic literature—the idea that terrorism is the result of "radicalization."

At its core, the radicalization approach to terrorism has a simple thesis: not all radicals may be terrorists, but *all terrorists are radicals*. It thus follows that *a process of ideological "radicalization" (or "violent radicalization" in some accounts) is a necessary if not sufficient cause of terrorism*. And it follows in turn that scholars need to identify the factors and processes that cause or facilitate "radicalization" if we are to explain terrorism. It also follows that individuals will be weaned away from terrorism if they can somehow be "de-radicalized."

These claims, alas, are based on a misunderstanding and misappropriation of the concept of radicalization. Indeed, there are several fundamental problems with the radicalization perspective. This approach often assumes, first of all, that terrorism is a kind of ideological movement—like socialism or conservatism, for example—which seeks out converts. The idea is that terrorists seek to radicalize people or recruit people who are already radicalized. But terror tactics have clearly been employed by groups and states with a very wide range of ideologies, not all of them "radical" in any sense of the word. In fact, the basic theoretical assumption of this approach—that only radicals engage in terrorism—is plainly wrong, unless one defines "radicalism," tautologically, as a propensity to kill civilians in order to intimidate others. It follows that the basic causal claim or hypothesis of this perspective—that radicalization is a necessary cause of political violence and terrorism—is also plainly wrong.

What does it mean, we might ask, to be a "radical"? The word has had a straightforward, uncontroversial meaning in historical and social-science discourse for many decades. According to the *Oxford English Dictionary*, "radical" means "Advocating thorough or far-reaching political or social reform... Now more generally: revolutionary, esp. left-wing" (*Oxford English Dictionary* online: <www.oed.com/view/Entry/157251#eid27277866>). A radical, in other words, is a revolutionary—usually on the left but possibly on the right. A radical desires fundamental as opposed to limited social change. Radicals differ from reformists, who desire modest or incremental socio-political changes, and from conservatives, who seek to preserve the existing order more or less as it is.

It follows from this longstanding definition that to "radicalize" means that one comes to have revolutionary or at least far-reaching goals. Historians and social scientists have always used the concept in just this sense, especially those who have written about revolutions or revolutionary movements. *The point to emphasize is that the concept of radicalization clearly speaks to ends, not means, let alone violent means.* "Radical" has never meant "violent." In fact, violence and coercion are not associated with *any* of the several definitions of "radical" which are found in the *Oxford English Dictionary*. The close association between radicalism and violence, alas, is a very recent and not particularly helpful invention of certain scholars of political violence and terrorism.

Many scholars who employ the term, to be sure, do not explicitly define "radicalization" at all (see e.g. Sageman 2008; Horgan 2008; Ranstorp 2010). And many understand "radicalization" tautologically, that is, as nothing other than the process or processes—whatever they may be—by which one becomes a terrorist. So, for example, according to two leading scholars of terrorism, "Radicalization may be understood as a process leading towards the increased use of political violence, while de-radicalization, by contrast, implies reduction in the use of political violence" (della Porta and LaFree 2012, 5). "Radicalization" and "de-radicalization" seem to have no other content or meaning for these authors. According to two other prominent scholars,

> Functionally, political radicalization is increased preparation for and commitment to intergroup conflict. Descriptively, radicalization means change in beliefs, feelings, and behaviors in directions that increasingly justify intergroup violence and demand sacrifice in defense of the ingroup... [B]ehavioral radicalization means increasing time, money, risk-taking, and violence in support of a political group.
>
> (McCauley and Moskalenko 2008, 416)

These definitions empty the words "radical" and "radicalization" of their traditional meaning. The word "radical" no longer means revolutionary, but is simply used as a synonym or placeholder for the word terrorist, and the word "radicalization" becomes a synonym for whatever process or processes might lead people to become terrorists. The underlying claim is thus entirely circular and unenlightening: Terrorism is a product of radicalization, we are told, and radicalization is the process which leads to terrorism.

It is not clear why some scholars have emptied the word "radicalization" of its traditional meaning in this way. It may be that they have done so because of the obvious fallaciousness of the basic theoretical assumption of the radicalization perspective, namely, that only revolutionaries engage in political violence or terrorism. Of course, no one would deny that revolutionaries have *sometimes* used violence and terrorism. The term terrorism, after all, was first used to describe the actions of French revolutionaries. Moreover, some scholars who write from the radicalization perspective have correctly emphasized that not *all* radicals use violence or terrorism. Indeed, some employ the concept of "violent radicalization" precisely in order to address this reality (e.g. Bartlett and Miller 2012).

But the assumption remains for most who write from this perspective that all terrorists are revolutionaries (or "extremists"). This assumption, however, is empirically wrong. There is, to begin with, what we might call conservative terrorism or what some have termed "pro-state" terrorism—in other words, non-state terrorism in defense of the status quo (e.g. Bruce 1992; White 1999). Two better-known cases of such conservative terrorist movements would be the Ku Klux Klan in the United States, which for many decades used terror tactics to reinforce white supremacy, and the Loyalist paramilitary movement in Northern Ireland, which used terrorism in order to maintain Protestant domination of those six counties as well as their union with Great Britain. It simply makes no sense to describe Klan members or Loyalists as radicals or revolutionaries who sought "fundamental socio-political changes."

The radicalization perspective fails just as clearly to explain most state terrorism, which, like conservative or pro-state terrorism, has also been mainly employed to defend the status quo. Again, state terrorism has sometimes been employed in the service of political projects aimed at radically transforming societies, as in France and Russia. But much more state violence has been used to intimidate civilians so as to maintain the existing social order or to defeat domestic rebels or foreign enemies (Downes 2008). State terrorism, indeed, is quite often *counter*-revolutionary violence in defense of the status quo.

The Indirect-War Theory of Terrorism

A causal explanation of terrorism, as we have defined it, requires us to specify why and under what conditions armed actors (state or non-state) come to regard the killing and intimidation of civilians or noncombatants as a reasonable and perhaps necessary (although not necessarily exclusive) means to attain their political ends. A causal theory should also tell us why and under what conditions armed groups consider terror tactics unnecessary and perhaps even counterproductive. Because terrorism cannot be unintended according to our (and most) definitions, the deliberate targeting of civilians—often just ordinary people—may be considered the sine qua non of terrorism.

Of course, terrorism, like other forms of violence, requires a certain infrastructure (weaponry, means of gaining proximity to targets, etc.) as well as warriors willing and able to carry out the violence. But neither of these is specific to terrorism. Conventional and guerrilla warfare as well as a strategy of assassination also require these things. The essential characteristic of terrorism is the intent to kill or harm as well as to intimidate civilians, and it is this intent which demands an explanation.

Let me now sketch what I call the indirect-war theory of terrorism, which follows in the footsteps of Charlies Tilly's "relational" approach to terrorism (Tilly 2004, 2005), so named because social relations among key actors (states, armed rebels, and civilians) carry the primary explanatory burden. The indirect-war theory is based on the idea that terrorism is an indirect way for armed groups (state or non-state) to attack their enemies. The theory proposes that an armed group will employ terror tactics against those civilians who are supporters of the group's armed enemies—provided those civilians are not also seen by the group as their own potential supporters. Terrorism arises, in other words, when one or more parties to an armed conflict seeks to harm their adversaries by harming the civilians who support those adversaries. Killing and terrorizing civilians is thus an indirect means of undermining one's armed enemies, instead of, or in addition to, directly attacking these enemies. By contrast, there is no incentive to attack civilians who are not supporters of one's armed enemies.

The indirect-war theory requires a consideration of the characteristics of the civilians or noncombatants whom states and rebels (sometimes) target for violence or harm. Why and how states and rebels come to see particular noncombatants as enemies or appropriate targets of violence is a puzzle that the aforementioned theories of terrorism, as we have seen, generally ignore. Yet states and rebels clearly do not attack just *any* civilians or noncombatants. Indeed, both states and rebels are also usually interested in winning the active support or allegiance of civilians—or at least civilians of a certain type.

So who are the "bad" or enemy civilians whom warriors choose to attack? And what good, from the warriors' perspective, might come from attacking them?

When states or rebels employ terror tactics in a civil or international conflict, they generally attack and try to intimidate civilians who in one way or another are valuable to or support their armed enemies. These are civilians upon whom enemy armed actors are dependent in different ways. Again, attacking such civilians is a way to attack indirectly one's armed opponents, and it is perfectly rational from this standpoint, despite the widespread moral condemnation of terror tactics.

The main tactical objective of and incentive for terrorism in armed conflicts is to induce the targeted civilians to stop supporting certain government or rebel policies. Terrorism, in other words, typically aims to apply such intense pressure to civilians that they will demand that their government or movement change certain policies or activities. Better yet, from the perpetrators' perspective, these civilians may even cease supporting the government or rebels altogether in order to end the violence directed at them. The perpetrators may also hope that the states or rebels they are fighting will unilaterally change or abandon certain policies or activities in order to end the killing of civilians. In either case, the government or rebels cannot be indifferent to attacks on civilians who are valuable to them.

In short, there is a general incentive for armed groups to attack and intimidate those civilians who are supporters of states or rebels with whom they are at war. But how exactly do certain civilians support armed groups? Civilians may support armed groups in two main ways—politically and economically—each of which produces a distinct incentive for armed enemies to attack them. First, terrorism is likely to be employed against noncombatants who *politically* support one's armed enemies. In this context, terror tactics are a reasonable means to weaken civilian political support (or tolerance) for violence by "their" government or rebels. For example, Al Qaeda and other "jihadist" groups have attacked civilians in the United States, the UK, France, and other Western countries in order to erode political support for their governments' policies in the Middle East. By contrast, terrorism is much less likely to be employed against civilians who do not politically support—or are substantially divided in their support for—one's armed enemies. In this case, terrorism may alienate potential allies.

Second, terrorism is likely to be employed against noncombatants who *economically* support one's armed enemies by, for example, supplying them with weapons, transportation (or the means thereof), food, and other supplies needed to employ violence. In this context, terrorism is a reasonable means to weaken civilian economic support for violence by "their" government or rebels. For example, the "terror bombing" of World War II, which resulted in hundreds of thousands and perhaps millions of civilian deaths, was undertaken primarily to destroy the industrial economies of England, Germany, and Japan (in part by eroding civilian morale), on which those countries' armed forces were dependent. Such destruction required massive civilian victimization. By contrast, terrorism is much less likely when soldiers are supplied by foreign states, for example, or through covert, black markets that involve few civilians.

Terrorism is also likely to spread and escalate in conflicts in which an armed actor has begun to attack the civilian supporters of their armed enemies. When this occurs, terrorism may become a reasonable means (other things being equal) to *deter* terrorism by armed enemies, thereby protecting one's civilian supporters, or, alternatively, to *avenge* such terrorism, thereby winning or reinforcing the political support of those civilians who feel they have been avenged.

Generally speaking, civilians who enjoy extensive civil and political rights are more likely to support their government than those who do not enjoy such rights. It follows that civilians with rights are more likely to be attacked by rebels or enemy states during times of conflict than civilians without rights, other things being equal. For example, when extensive and indiscriminate state violence appears to be supported by civilians, it is hardly surprising that rebel movements would tend to view such civilians, as well as the states perpetrating such violence, as legitimate targets of violence; the purpose of such violence is to undermine these civilians' support for their government. Extensive state ("wholesale") terrorism thus begets extensive rebel ("retail") terrorism in conflicts in which a citizenry with significant democratic rights supports the state's violence. Such a citizenry would appear to be a common if not strictly necessary precondition for extensive terrorism by rebel movements (see Pape 2005; Goodwin 2006).

The indirect-war theory also helps us to understand why rebels who are fighting autocratic or authoritarian regimes tend to eschew terror tactics. Relatively few civilians tend to support such regimes, so there is no benefit in employing terror tactics against the general civilian population, unless for economic purposes. For example, the Sandinista Front in Nicaragua carried out virtually no terror attacks during its armed conflict with the autocratic Somoza dictatorship during the late 1970s, an otherwise bloody insurgency during which some 30,000 people were killed (Booth 1983). Civilians who supported the dictatorship consisted of a small number of Somoza cronies and a loyal elite opposition, both of which were drawn mainly from Nicaragua's small bourgeoisie. Virtually all other civilians in Nicaragua, from the poorest peasant to Somoza's bourgeois opponents, were viewed by the Sandinistas as potential allies, and indeed many would become such. It obviously made no sense to attack such people. Of course, had the Somoza dictatorship been supported by broader sectors of the population—by a broader class coalition, for example, or a large ethnic group—then the Sandinistas might very well have employed terror tactics against such sectors in order to undermine their support for the dictatorship.

In summary, armed groups, whether states or rebels, are likely to attack and terrorize noncombatants who politically or economically support enemy states or rebels. This is a way to undermine indirectly one's armed enemies. By contrast, armed groups are unlikely to attack noncombatants who do not support enemy states or rebels. In such instances, attacking such noncombatants would serve no purpose and would alienate potential allies. Whether civilians are supporters of states or rebels, in other words, is the key to understanding why terror tactics are or are not likely to be employed against them in specific conflicts.

Contrasting Case Studies: Al Qaeda and the ANC

In the final section of this chapter, I want to illustrate, if only briefly, how the indirect-war theory of terrorism just outlined can help us to understand the contrasting tactics of two non-state armed groups—one that decided to employ terror tactics and one that rejected terror tactics, although not violence as such.

Al Qaeda, and armed groups affiliated with it, have carried out a number of terrorist attacks in recent years against US and certain European noncombatants (see e.g. Hoffman and Reinares 2014). Why does Al Qaeda attack such civilians? Why, in other words, has it chosen to employ terror tactics?

Al Qaeda adheres to the view that the global Muslim community, or *umma*, is currently oppressed by both "apostate" secular and "hypocritical" pseudo-Islamic regimes, from Morocco to the Philippines, as well as by the "Zionist entity" (Israel) in Palestine. And standing behind these regimes is the powerful US government and its European allies, especially the UK and France. Al Qaeda and other jihadist groups are hostile toward the United States and its allies for supporting repressive, un-Islamic regimes in Muslim countries. Al Qaeda believes that unless and until the US and its allies—the "far enemy"—can be compelled to end their support for these regimes—the "near enemy"—and withdraw their troops and other agents from Muslim countries, local struggles to overthrow these regimes cannot succeed (Gerges 2009).

Al Qaeda and other jihadist groups have attacked US military forces in the Middle East. But why have they also decided that ordinary civilians are legitimate targets of violence? After all, terrorism is rejected not only by mainstream Islamists, but also by many jihadists themselves. In fact, "when finally informed about the major attack against the United States [i.e. the 9/11 plot], most senior members of the Al Qaeda Shura Council reportedly objected on religious and strategic grounds; bin Laden overrode the majority's decision, and the attacks went forward" (Gerges 2009, 19).

Shortly after 9/11, Osama bin Laden described the rationale for the 9/11 attacks in an interview that first appeared in the Pakistani newspaper *Ausaf* on November 7, 2001:

> The United States and their allies are killing us in Palestine, Chechnya, Kashmir, Palestine and Iraq. That's why Muslims have the right to carry out revenge attacks on the U.S.... The American people should remember that they pay taxes to their government and that they voted for their president. Their government makes weapons and provides them to Israel, which they use to kill Palestinian Muslims. Given that the American Congress is a committee that represents the people, the fact that it agrees with the actions of the American government proves that America in its entirety is responsible for the atrocities that it is committing against Muslims. I demand the American people to take note of their government's policy against Muslims. They described their government's policy against Vietnam as

> wrong. They should now take the same stand that they did previously. The onus is on Americans to prevent Muslims from being killed at the hands of their government.
> (Quoted in Lawrence 2005, 140–1.)

In short, bin Laden believed that American citizens support their government and its policies in the Middle East. They have elected and pay taxes to their government, which in his view makes them responsible for its actions in Muslim countries (Wiktorowicz and Kaltner 2003, 88–9). Al Qaeda views American citizens, in other words, not as "innocents," but as economically and politically complicit in US-sponsored massacres and the oppression of Muslims. Bin Laden hoped that attacks on US citizens would lead them to reject and demand a change in the policies of their government in the Middle East. He hoped that Americans would oppose their government's actions—as they did during the Vietnam War—in order to stop it from killing more Muslims and supporting oppressive regimes (Lawrence 2005, 141). In short, Al Qaeda has attacked US citizens because they support Al Qaeda's armed enemy (the US government) both politically and economically, and the purpose of such attacks is to undermine this support. All this is consonant with the indirect-war theory of terrorism.

The indirect-war theory, as we have seen, also proposes that armed groups are *unlikely* to employ terror tactics against civilians who are not supporters—or are divided in their support—of these groups' armed enemies. An armed group is especially unlikely to employ terror tactics against a particular civilian group when some significant fraction of it has come to support that group; it would obviously make no sense for an armed group to attack a civilian population from which it draws a substantial number of supporters. Such terrorism would not only put at risk the support these warriors are receiving from those civilians, but would also make it much less likely that additional civilians would come to support these warriors.

The existence of a substantial group of "dissident civilians" of this type (i.e. civilians who support the armed enemies of "their" government or rebel group) seems largely to explain why the African National Congress—the leading anti-apartheid organization in South Africa—rejected the use of terror tactics against white South Africans. The ANC eschewed such tactics even though the apartheid regime that it sought to topple employed extensive violence, including terrorism, against its opponents. This violence, moreover, was clearly supported or tolerated by large segments of the white population. The Nationalist Party governments of the apartheid era which unleashed the security forces against the regime's enemies were elected and widely supported by the white population, which enjoyed a range of political privileges and economic benefits under apartheid.

So why did the ANC refuse to view whites as such as enemies or to employ terror tactics against them? The answer lies in the ANC's long history of "multiracialism," that is, the collaboration of whites with black South Africans in the ANC (and with South Asian and "colored" or mixed race people), both inside the ANC and in allied organizations. Especially important in this respect was the ANC's long collaboration with the South African Communist Party, which also has a long history of multiracialism. Tellingly, an important, long-time leader of the ANC's armed wing was Joe Slovo, a white Communist. (This is analogous to an Israeli Jew leading Hamas's armed wing or a Christian American directing Al Qaeda's covert operations.)

For the ANC to have indiscriminately attacked white South Africans would have soured this strategic relationship, which, among other things, was essential for securing substantial Soviet aid for the ANC. Terrorism directed at white South Africans would also have put at risk the large amount of aid that the ANC received from Western Europe during the anti-apartheid struggle. In sum, given the longstanding multiracial—including international—support for the anti-apartheid movement, the use of terrorism against white civilians made little strategic sense to ANC leaders. The ANC would have been much more likely to employ terror tactics against white South Africans if the latter (as well as Europeans) more or less exclusively supported the apartheid regime and opposed the ANC.

Conclusion

Terrorism, understood as the killing of noncombatants in order to frighten or intimidate others, has long been an important method of warfare or contention for both states and non-state armed groups. However, neither traditional theories nor the currently dominant "radicalization" perspective on terrorism help us very much in understanding why states or rebels would choose to attack and intimidate civilians as opposed to soldiers or political elites. Some armed groups undoubtedly employ terrorism out of weakness and desperation, as a "last resort," but many and probably most do not. Similarly, some warriors use terrorism as a retaliatory response to violence by others, but not always; and this claim fails to explain why warriors would retaliate against noncombatants in particular as opposed to soldiers. And the radicalization perspective, for its part, errs in assuming that all terrorists are ideologically radical and that individuals therefore become terrorists through a process of radicalization. In fact, terror tactics have been employed by rebels and states with a wide range of ideological views. Not all radicals, furthermore, employ terrorism or any other type of violent tactic for that matter.

I have argued, by contrast, that what I have called the indirect-war theory of terrorism offers a more adequate causal account of why some but not all states and armed groups have employed terror tactics. I have suggested that armed groups are likely to attack those civilians who are supporters—politically or economically—of these groups' armed enemies. The purpose of terror tactics is to undermine civilian support for armed groups—and thereby to attack the latter indirectly. On the other hand, I have suggested that armed groups are unlikely to employ terror tactics against a civilian population when such groups are themselves supported by some significant fraction of that population. I illustrated this theory with the contrasting cases of Al Qaeda, which has employed terrorism in order to undermine civilian support for US and European government policies in the Middle East, and the African National Congress, which largely rejected terror tactics in its fight against apartheid, tactics which would have undermined the support it received from white South Africans and Europeans.

References

Bartlett, J., and C. Miller (2012) "The Edge of Violence: Towards Telling the Difference between Violent and Non-Violent Radicalization," *Terrorism and Political Violence*, 24(1): 1–21.

Bloom, M. (2005) *Dying to Kill: The Allure of Suicide Terror*. New York: Columbia University Press.

Booth, J. (1983) *The End of the Beginning: The Nicaraguan Revolution*, 2nd edn. Boulder, CO: Westview Press.

Bruce, S. (1992) "The Problems of 'Pro-State' Terrorism: Loyalist Paramilitaries in Northern Ireland," *Terrorism and Political Violence*, 4(1): 67–88.

Cherry, J. (2011) *Umkhonto weSizwe*. Johannesburg: Jacana Media.

Crenshaw, M. (1981) "The Causes of Terrorism," *Comparative Politics*, 13(4): 379–99.

della Porta, D., and G. LaFree (2012) "Processes of Radicalization and De-Radicalization," *International Journal of Conflict and Violence*, 6(1): 4–10.

Downes, A. (2008) *Targeting Civilians in War*. Ithaca, NY, and London: Cornell University Press.

English, R. ed. (2016) *Illusions of Terrorism and Counter-Terrorism*. Oxford: Oxford University Press.

Gareau, F. (2004) *State Terrorism and the United States: From Counterinsurgency to the War on Terrorism*. Atlanta, GA: Clarity Press.

Gerges, F. (2009) *The Far Enemy: Why Jihad Went Global*, 2nd edn. Cambridge: Cambridge University Press.

Goodwin, J. (2001) *No Other Way Out: States and Revolutionary Movements, 1945–1991*. Cambridge: Cambridge University Press.

Goodwin, J. (2006) "A Theory of Categorical Terrorism," *Social Forces*, 84(4): 2027–46.

Gordon, J. (2010) *Invisible War: The United States and the Iraq Sanctions*. Cambridge, MA: Harvard University Press.

Herman, E., and G. O'Sullivan (1989) *The "Terrorism" Industry: The Experts and Institutions that Shape our View of Terror*. New York: Pantheon.

Hoffman, B., and F. Reinares (2014) *The Evolution of the Global Terrorist Threat: From 9/11 to Osama bin Laden's Death*. New York: Columbia University Press.

Horgan, J. (2008) "From Profiles to Pathways and Roots to Routes: Perspectives from Psychology on Radicalization into Terrorism," *Annals of the American Academy of Political and Social Science*, 618(1): 80–94.

Lawrence, B., ed. (2005) *Messages to the World: The Statements of Osama bin Laden*. London and New York: Verso.

McCauley, C., and S. Moskalenko (2008) "Mechanisms of Political Radicalization: Pathways toward Terrorism," *Terrorism and Political Violence*, 20(3): 415–33.

Pape, R. (2005) *Dying to Win: The Strategic Logic of Suicide Terrorism*. New York: Random House.

Ranstorp, M. (2010) "Introduction," in M. Ranstorp (ed.), *Understanding Violent Radicalisation: Terrorist and Jihadist Movements in Europe*. London: Routledge, 1–18.

Richards, A. (2014) "Conceptualizing Terrorism," *Studies in Conflict and Terrorism*, 37(3): 213–36.

Richardson, L. (2006) *What Terrorists Want: Understanding the Enemy, Containing the Threat*. New York: Random House.

Sageman, M. (2008) *Leaderless Jihad: Terror Networks in the Twenty-First Century*. Philadelphia: University of Pennsylvania Press.

Seidman, G. (2001) "Guerrillas in their Midst: Armed Struggle in the South African Anti-Apartheid Movement," *Mobilization: An International Quarterly*, 6(2): 111–27.

Tilly, C. (2004) "Terror, Terrorism, Terrorists," *Sociological Theory*, 22(1): 5–13.

Tilly, C. (2005) "Terrorism as Strategy and Relational Process," *International Journal of Comparative Sociology*, 46(1–2): 11–32.

Turk, A. (1982) "Social Dynamics of Terrorism," *Annals of the American Academy of Political and Social Science*, 436(1): 119–28.

White, R. (1999) "Comparing State Repression of Pro-State Vigilantes and Anti-State Insurgents: Northern Ireland, 1972–75," *Mobilization: An International Quarterly*, 4(2): 189–202.

Wiktorowicz, Q., and J. Kaltner (2003) "Killing in the Name of Islam: Al-Qaeda's Justification for September 11," *Middle East Policy*, 10(2): 76–92.

CHAPTER 18

NATIONALISM AND TERRORISM

RICHARD ENGLISH

Introduction

What is the properly understood relationship between nationalism and terrorism? The question can be considered in several main ways, each of them significant, and all of them somewhat interwoven. First, to what extent do the politics of nationalism and its associated conflicts generate non-state (and also state) terrorist violence? Second, does the nationalist legitimation of high-functioning states produce order and stability which make terrorism less likely? Third, does terrorist violence act as a means of destabilizing existing nationalist orders, whether or not it helps to usher in new ones? Fourth, does the analysis and study of terrorism vary according to rival nationalist contexts and politics?

The importance of these questions is hard to deny. That nationalism has done much to shape the modern world is beyond dispute; and its relationship to terrorist violence has frequently seemed decisive, from the 1914 assassination which triggered the First World War, through the blood-stained politics of twentieth-century decolonization, to the 9/11 wars and beyond. But the precise nature of this relationship is a complex one, and as such it deserves careful consideration.

This chapter will reflect on each of the four questions in turn. Before doing so, some issues of definition must be addressed.

Definitions

Nationalism, in the phrasing of one scholarly authority, remains "a dominant ideological narrative of the modern age", as well as "the most potent source of state legitimacy and the most reliable mechanism for mass mobilization" (Malešević 2006, 6; Ozkirimli 2010, 2). This nicely captures the dual quality of nationalism as an ideology which is simultaneously a form of embodied, social action. Moreover, a coherent definition of nationalism helps to explain its enduring ideological and practical power.

If a *nation* is a body of people considering themselves to be a distinct group with shared descent, history, and culture, and *nationality* refers to the fact of belonging to a nation, or the identity or feeling that is related to it, then the definition of *nationalism* itself lies in a particular interweaving of the politics of community, struggle, and power.

The nationalist idea of community resonates with many of humanity's deepest needs and instincts: towards survival, security, protection, and safety; towards the fulfillment of economic and other practical requirements; and towards necessary, meaningful belonging within lastingly special and distinctive groups.

For this process of belonging to work, we require shared means of durable communication between members of the group, whether these lie in the realms of shared and appealing attachment to territory, people, descent, culture, history, and ethics, or in an exclusivism which comfortingly separates us from a non-national outgroup. National communities do not require all of these features, but they do need some of them; and the emotional and practical logic within each of these elements helps to explain the existence, durability, appeal, and pervasiveness of nationalism.

Yet the process involves more than membership of self-conscious national community. Nationalism also involves struggle: collective mobilization, activity, and a programmatic striving for goals. Such goals can vary, including sovereign independence, secession from a larger political unit, the survival or rebirth of national culture, and the realization of economic advantage for the national group. Through it all, nationalist struggle involves the alluring prospect of putting right what is perceived to be wrong in the present. And here there can be both the instrumental appeal of struggle (as a means of achieving worthwhile and necessary goals) and also the attraction inherent in struggle itself (with its psychological rewards, and with its conferring upon individual and group alike of the very qualities so sought, prized, and cherished by the nationalist movement).

But nationalism involves not just community in struggle, but also the politics of power. Power is what is so frequently sought by nationalists (very often in the form of a state which matches the nation); and the deployment of power in pursuit of nationalist objectives defines and often explains the appeal of nationalist activity. It might even be suggested that, at root, nationalism is really a politics *of* legitimizing power. Nationalists tend to assume the nation to be the appropriate source of political authority and sovereignty, and therefore to seek power for their own distinctive national community. The legitimacy of national power involves the attractive prospect of those in power in your community being like yourself, coming from your own national group, and representing your own interests and values and preferences and instincts.

So community, struggle, and power offer the interwoven definition and explanation of nationalism and its extraordinary prominence in politics and history (English 2006). It is not that we cannot find other means of identifying and belonging, or of pursuing change and acquiring power. The point is rather this: that the particular interweaving of community, struggle, and power in the form of nationalism offers far grander opportunities than do these other means. The family cannot offer the scale of interaction to provide for our necessary exchange or safety; even a very powerful job will tend not to allow for access to the kind of serious, sustained power that is available through nationalism; and subnational cultural enthusiasm—whether for region, or football team, or whatever—will not allow for such large-scale, durable, all-inclusive possibilities for getting what we deeply want, as will the national.

The question of when nationalism emerged as an historical phenomenon is a complex one, and it has generated extensive scholarly debate (Kedourie 1993; Hastings 1997; Gellner 1983; Anderson 1983; Hobsbawm 1990; Smith 2000; Ozkirimli 2010). There are certainly dangers of anachronism when one applies the term nationalism to pre-French Revolution politics, I think (Kidd 1999), and my approach in this chapter will be to focus on nationalism as an essentially post-French Revolutionary phenomenon.

Despite the attractions of identifying terrorism in an earlier period, there is a compelling logic also in focusing on that phenomenon as one which emerged in the French Revolutionary era. This is when the term emerged into prominence, and so this chapter will concentrate on terrorism in the period since then.

The definition of terrorism itself is famously contentious, and among the contributors to this volume there are understandable variations of approach. My own definition is as follows:

> Terrorism involves heterogeneous violence used or threatened with a political aim; it can involve a variety of acts, of targets, and of actors; it possesses an important psychological dimension, producing terror or fear among a directly threatened group and also a wider implied audience in the hope of maximizing political communication and achievement; it embodies the exerting and implementing of power, and the attempted redressing of power relations; it represents a subspecies of warfare, and as such it can form part of a wider campaign of violent and non-violent attempts at political leverage. (English 2009, 24)

I have elsewhere explained why I think that this approach best addresses some of the problems inherent in the term (English 2009, 1–26). For the purposes of this chapter, perhaps the key point is that my definition allows for terrorism being practiced by state as well as non-state actors, and for recognition that the dynamics involved might vary greatly between and even within these different categories of actor. This, together with an acknowledgment of the often mutually shaping relationship between non-state and state violence (English 2015), represents an important foundation upon which to build answers to our four questions.

To What Extent Do the Politics of Nationalism and its Associated Conflicts Generate Non-State (and also State) Terrorist Violence?

Let's begin here with reflection on non-state terrorism. Certainly, there have been many important examples of non-state terrorist organizations whose politics have been deeply nationalist (in Israel/Palestine, the Basque Country/Spain, Ireland/UK, Chechnya, and many other settings). In each of these unique cases, the upheavals associated with nationalism have involved much terroristic expression by non-state actors. And the reason for this emerges from consideration of our definitions. If one feels that one's national territory, people, culture, and history are denied their true expression and freedom by incorporation into a state whose rulers do not reflect them; if one believes that communal-national struggle is required in order to establish an emancipating form of sovereign power; if one is convinced that a redressing of existing power relations can only or best be achieved through terrorizing violence (with its psychological, communicative, and warlike leverage); if one sees the necessity and appeal of defining or reinforcing the boundaries between one's own national community and an excluded other; if all this is the case, then it is easy to see why non-state actors have so often turned to nationalistic terrorism. The processes here vary from case to case, but they share enough family resemblances to form a recognizable community of cases (Hoffman 2015; Singh 2011; English 2006, 2012; Muro 2008).

So, if nationalism is indeed "primarily a political principle, which holds that the political and the national unit should be congruent" (Gellner 1983, 1), then terrorism has historically often been perceived by its non-state practitioners as the best way of bringing about such congruence. Scholars might judge them to have been somewhat mistaken in this perception, and to have exaggerated the extent to which terrorism is likely to bring about achievement of their central nationalist goals (English 2016a). But that does not alter the reality that nationalism and its associated conflicts have frequently generated terroristic violence in this way.

This is not to argue that the politics of nationalism inevitably has this effect. Impressive scholarship has demonstrated that there is no necessary causal relationship between nationalism and war (Malešević 2010; Laitin 2007). But where the politics of nationalist community, struggle, and power conflict with existing power structures, nationalism has frequently become a justifying ideology and an organizing collective force behind non-state terrorist violence. Moreover, the late twentieth century arguably saw not the moribundity of nationalism, but rather its revivification and re-energizing (Brubaker 1996, 2). The sought-after alignment of nation with state represented an enduring part of that process, and it is here that nationalism and terrorism have so often and so bloodily interacted even in recent decades.

The process has very long historical roots. Much of the transition to post-colonial politics in Africa happened without nationalist violence. But clearly some anti-colonial, terroristic violence did occur, and formed part of a nationalistic struggle for decolonization (in the cases of Kenya, Algeria, Angola, and Mozambique, for example). But our earlier argument about the dynamics of nationalism stressed the interweaving of nationalist politics with land, with survival, with economic necessity, with cultural identity, and so on. In the modern African case alluded to here, nationally refracted African terrorism did indeed have to do with issues such as resource access, religious (including jihadist) motivation, and personal gain of economic and other kinds. Here, as elsewhere, nationalist movements deploying terrorist violence could draw in complex ways on numerous motivating factors (Reid 2012).

The role of religion represents an important aspect of this. Relations between the world's 2.4 billion Christians, 1.6 billion Muslims, and 13 million Jews have often—and famously—involved some enmities which have been expressed through terroristic violence, and much of this has taken a nationalistic form. But it is also true that relationships between these three great religions have more often involved amity, comity, and peace (Sacks 2015, 4, 24, 90–1). It would be equally simplistic either to blame religion for terrorism, or to deny that it has had any role in generating it. And reflection on the relationship between nationalism and terrorism can help to clarify this issue. Ultimately, group-ness lies at the heart of the matter: this human instinct is one which our definition of nationalism clarified as often having had a national character. Very powerfully (from Israel/Palestine to Ireland/UK and beyond) rival nationalisms have possessed a religious flavour. And that combination (where issues of territory, people, descent, culture, history, ethics, and exclusivism become interwoven in nationalist politics and struggle) explains why we have so often seen terroristic violence with a nationalistic, but also a religious, quality (Rafferty 2016).

Yet of course not all major non-state terrorism is nationalistic. There is a global dimension to some terroristic activity, and such violence can transcend the merely national or nationalistic (Enders and Sandler 2012, 170, 200). The early twenty-first-century obsession with jihadism provides us with an important set of examples. In some ways, groups such as Al Qaeda and ISIS have been emphatically *non*-nationalistic, both movements making much of the transnational and would-be global nature of their struggle and their identity (Byman 2015; Gerges 2016). Indeed, some people hold that it is precisely their transnational challenge to a nation-based international state system that makes jihadists' threats most significant (Mendelsohn 2009). Certainly, the ISIS declaration of an Islamic Caliphate in June 2014 was explicitly transnational, being deliberately transgressive regarding national borders and identities (Cockburn 2014; Barrett 2014; Stern and Berger 2015).

And it is true that much jihadist militancy is indeed non-national or transnationalistic. The foreign fighter phenomenon reflects this, with volunteers from many nations having travelled to Syria and Iraq to join ISIS (de Guttry et al. 2016; Neumann 2016,

87–8, 189). The group has branded itself as an emphatically transnational entity, and it is in its appeal to a transnational Sunni Muslim constituency that ISIS has indeed had many of its successes (Gerges 2016). More broadly, scholarly explanations of the dynamics of causation behind jihadist violence have reinforced the idea that such terrorism is transnational (rather than national) in its nature, and that its roots lie decisively in realms other than nationalism (Gambetta and Hertog 2016).

There are, of course, subtle nuances involved here. The USA's response to 9/11 was generated in the context of an American nationalism which had been profoundly intensified in response to that terrorist assault (Croft 2006). In this anguished sequence, non-nationalistic Al Qaeda terrorism prompted a US nationalistic response which involved the Iraq invasion; in the wake of the latter, Al Qaeda in Iraq (AQI) emerged and transmogrified into ISIS (Byman 2015, 163), a movement which was deliberately non-nationalistic but at least partly terroristic. The US reaction to 9/11 also helped to bring about the dissolution and disintegration of the Iraqi national state as it had previously existed. Read through these lenses, we can see that an expressly non-nationalistic terrorist challenge had prompted a state-nationalistic reaction, which in turn helped to generate a new form of terroristic challenge in the form of ISIS (Barrett 2014; Stern and Berger 2015, 177, 238).

At a lower level of importance, perhaps, it should also be noted that ISIS's own state-building efforts have not been entirely without their nation-oriented dimensions anyway (Stern and Berger 2015, 88; Byman 2015, 170–4; McCants 2015, 125–6, 152), and that some of those who have opposed the US in Iraq and who have been involved in ISIS violence have clearly been former Iraqi or Syrian nationalists (Byman 2015, 116; McCants 2015, 10, 34, 121, 127). This should not be overstated. ISIS has been explicit about the transnational quality of its political argument and ambition. But to assume that all traces of prior nationalist attachment were removed from those who became involved with its struggle would be implausible (especially given that some such traces were clearly evident among those involved in the post-2003 resistance to the US occupation, and given the undeniable complexity of the support for ISIS's cause) (Gerges 2016, 67, 120, 125, 127–8, 165). So there are intricacies in the relationship even of seemingly non-nationalistic terrorism to nationalism.

But the jihadist world makes clear that terrorism need not have a primarily nationalistic quality to it. This point is reinforced by consideration of lone-actor terrorism too. The latter can possess a nationalistic quality, but it certainly need not do so. A figure such as Ted Kaczynski, for example, has cast his arguments in emphatically non-national mode, and in terms rather of a global challenge associated with the pernicious effects of technology and, more specifically, of what he terms "the technological world-system" (Kaczynski 2016, 55). And serious-minded scholarship on lone-actor terrorism makes clear the diversity of its origins and dynamics, many of which owe little to nationalism (Gill 2015).

In terms of non-state terrorism, therefore, the picture is a complicated one. The eye-catching nature of transnational attacks (pre-eminently but not merely that of 9/11) perhaps leads to an exaggeration of the degree to which terrorism globally has shifted away from nationalist dynamics, for the latter remains vital in many regions of the world where terrorism persists. But, as noted, the pattern even in one national or nationalist context is multifaceted rather than neatly simple. Nationalist conflicts have generated lastingly significant levels of terroristic violence in modern India, for example; but so too have leftist political ambition and religiously inflected causes, and the reasons behind each have tended to be multiple rather than single (Chenoy and Chenoy 2010). The complexity of origins behind nationalist terrorism is complemented by a complexity of later reflection. Some post-terrorist actors recall their violence with a sense of pride and celebration; others, however, revisit their former political enthusiasms and activism with deep disenchantment and stark disillusionment (O'Callaghan 2015; Flanagan 2015; English 1998, 2016a; Foster 2014).

What of state terrorism and our first question? To what extent do the politics of nationalism and its associated conflicts generate terroristic violence from the state? In many of the cases where non-state terrorism emerges from nationalistic politics, what we see is a conflict between rival nationalisms, respectively non-state and state, each of them using some violence. The definition of terrorism offered in this chapter allows us to consider both kinds of violence as potentially terroristic, and I think that this is reasonable (whether in the context of Israel/Palestine, Ireland/UK, Basque Country/Spain, Chechnya/Russia, or beyond) (English 2016a). In these instances, antagonistic nationalisms provide the context for explaining different kinds of terrorizing political violence. And it is the mutually shaping relationship between these rival nationalisms that is crucial in such conflicts (Kurtzer et al. 2013; English 2015). In such cases state responses to non-state violence often involve, at least partly, a consciousness of national interests and identity and community; indeed, the state response to terrorist challenge is often an intensely nationalistic one.

Another form of state terrorism involves the state sponsoring of non-state actors (Byman 2005). Here again national interests, and the politics of the nationalism which shapes the state, can play an important part. And very complex relationships can exist here. The Iranian state-sponsored terrorism which targeted Salman Rushdie (Rushdie 2012) is often and understandably read in terms of the relationship between a certain kind of Islamic belief and terrorist violence. But close scrutiny of Iranian politics demonstrates that it has been *nationalism* (albeit, during that period, an Islamicized nationalism) that has represented the determining and subsuming ideological element within modern Iranian politics (Ansari 2012; Malešević 2006, 96–9). Nationalism, terrorism, and religion again here interweave in significant fashion.

Nationalism can also be seen as generative of terroristic violence in a more direct form of state violence, when a nationalistic state uses deliberately terrorizing force against its own population, as with Nazi Germany. This extreme example does lie on a painful continuum, with even much less appalling nation state regimes deploying terrorism against their own (and other) populations. Our definitional location of nationalism and terrorism as phenomena emerging from the French Revolutionary crucible is fitting here, since there is something integrated about the work done by nationalism, the modern state, and terroristic method; "State terrorism is a far wider phenomenon than the paradigmatic cases of Revolutionary France, Hitler's Germany, Stalin's Soviet Union, or Mao's China" (Wilson 2013, 15). In Protean manner, nationalist states have all too frequently found it useful to threaten or to use terroristic violence in order to strengthen their own position and to deal with potential or actual enemies.

More controversially, we might consider much of what has been done by many different kinds of state during wartime to be terroristic violence anyway (English 2013). If so, and if nationalist motivations have played a part in some of those wars (which they undoubtedly have), then a strong case can be made that nationalism has had a major historical role in generating terroristic violence by many states.

Of course, this is only part of the story. The relationship between states and non-state terrorists can involve nationalism yielding *non*-terroristic state reactions too. A significant element in 1970s West German policy in response to terrorism was determined by the country's perceived need for greater national prestige; that much of this work was pursued through the multinational vehicle of the United Nations does not diminish the degree to which German nationalism and national interests were here involved in shaping eirenic counterterrorism within this important case study (Blumenau 2014).

And it is also true that the national and nationalistic interests of states have led them at times to try to pursue peaceful resolution of those conflicts which have generated non-state terrorist violence. So, while the Israeli–Palestinian conflict is one with deep roots in rival nationalisms, and with a long history of resulting terroristic violence, it is also true that the long-term efforts of the United States to try to resolve this conflict have had their own roots in explicitly US "national interest" (Kurtzer et al. 2013, 2, 5, 9, 13).

Does the Nationalist Legitimation of High-Functioning States Produce Order and Stability Which Make Terrorism Less Likely?

If the failure of nation states to offer legitimate, inclusive, stable identity has on occasions (as with ISIS) generated terrorist violence (Gerges 2016, 5, 7), then it is also true that where states involve high-functioning national communities then terrorism can be reduced. Here, where nationalism helps to legitimate coherent, stable states, then violence can be rendered less common. The mutually shared citizenship which makes some democracies less prone to terrorist violence is a phenomenon which can be, and often is, based on nationalism (Schwarzmantel 2011, 190–1).

So if the successful creation of a democratic community offers a promising means to limit political violence, then nationalism as the basis for enduring democratic state communities might indeed be seen to be inimical to the generation of terrorism, rather than causal behind it. Dealing satisfactorily with issues of social and political inclusion through democratic means, it might be argued, offers one way of limiting the degree to which exclusion generates violently expressed disaffection. If the politics of nationalist community can be resolved in ways that sustain legitimate and high-functioning power across national territory, then the seeming necessity for terroristic violence may seem less striking as a mode of struggle (English 2006; Schwarzmantel 2011).

This will prove a patchy phenomenon in practice. But there are striking examples of these dynamics. The energy behind twenty-first-century Scottish nationalism has caused a measure of destabilization within the UK state as such. But there is evidence also that the inclusive, non-ethnic nature of an intensified contemporary nationalism in Scotland has been one of the integrative means by which so many Muslims in that country have been accommodated with virtually none of the disaffected terrorist violence that has been evident in the same period in England, France, Belgium, and some other West European democracies (Bonino 2017). Here, the nationalist dynamics of community, struggle, and power have generated divisive tension between Scotland and England, but have arguably contributed to there being less violent hostility than might otherwise have emerged towards the state from within the diverse Scottish Muslim community.

Certainly, where states lack legitimacy and stability, the process often enough involves the absence of what nationalism demands: namely, the attractive prospect of those in power in your community being like yourself, coming from your own national group, and representing your own interests and values and preferences and instincts. Despite its being rebelled against in an expressly non-nationalistic form in the shape of ISIS, this is the central problem which has crippled parts of Syria and Iraq in the second decade of the twenty-first century; as such, the ISIS crisis demonstrates how a painful and destructive situation can develop without communal, state legitimacy having been established and sustained.

Does Terrorist Violence Act as a Means of Destabilizing Existing Nationalist Orders, Whether or not it Helps to Usher in New Ones?

Part of the issue here is that non-state terroristic violence can produce polarization and disorder in ways which make the subsequent creation of high-functioning and stable states more difficult to achieve. It is more certain that sustained terrorist violence will destabilize what is, than that it will produce a calmer and more cohesive alternative in the future.

In the contrasting early twenty-first-century cases of Afghanistan, Iraq, and Syria, terrorist violence not only set in train international developments which destabilized longstanding nation states, but it was also the direct means of their destabilization and fracture internally. And violence, including terroristic violence, can remain a threat even to more democratically established nations (Schwarzmantel 2011, 182). Perhaps as a result of exaggerating the threat that is actually embodied in terrorism, democratic nations have at times practiced self-damaging transgressions of their own laws, freedoms, and protections in the name of countering terrorist violence (Gearty 2013; Mueller and Stewart 2016). Of course, terroristic violence has historically played a role in helping to produce subsequently enduring democracies (Israel and Ireland among them). But its capacity to destabilize has been equally striking, not least in generating larger-scale forms of violence (insurgency, civil war) and ultimately in producing what some have termed failed states, states where there is a lack of effective legitimacy and governance across the designated territory. The latter can in turn prompt the likelihood of future violence, with there being strong evidence that failed states are prone to high levels of terrorism (Enders and Sandler 2012, 286–7).

The point here is that the lack of order in such cases can derive from the absence of exactly the kind of legitimate, coherent, high-functioning state culture which nationalisms can and do sometimes provide (Laitin 2007). Where the majority of a nation's population feel that they are emancipated through an equal share in the sovereign power embodied in their state; where the national community feels that its territory, its popular unity, its distinctive culture, and its history are protected by the national rulers; then the need for terroristic violence to bring about change—and the capacity of dissenters to do so strongly for any cause—will be diminished (English 2006).

Does the Analysis and Study of Terrorism Vary According to Rival Nationalist Contexts and Politics?

The vast majority of influential scholarship on terrorism occurs in Western nations, most of which have experienced comparatively little sustained terrorism when compared with countries such as Pakistan, Iraq, Colombia, Peru, India, and Afghanistan (the latter countries being notably under-represented in terms of the origins of scholarly debate on terrorism). This has a number of hermeneutical implications, and it surely remains one of the overriding problems in the field (English 2016b). For our purposes in this chapter, the point to consider is the degree to which nationalism as such influences these geographies of understanding and interpretation. There have certainly been divergent geographies of national-governmental *response*: the respective traditions of various nation states as they have dealt with the phenomenon have repeatedly meant that there are distinctive national ways of responding to terrorism (something which can impede international cooperation in counterterrorism) (Argomaniz 2011; Neumann 2016, p. xiv).

Behind these national habits perhaps lie national frameworks of analysis and assumption also, as anyone who has lectured in many different countries on the subject will probably confirm. This fits a wider pattern of scientific thinking, of course. Our intellectual approaches to and debates regarding many important phenomena have often reflected varied local politics, culture, religion, power dynamics, and struggles (Livingstone 2003, 2014). So too with terrorism and scholarship on terrorism. Local nationalisms have affected and partly determined the varied ways in which terrorism scholarship has been practiced among, respectively, Irish nationalists and British unionist nationalists in Belfast, or Basque nationalists as against Spanish nationalists in Spain, or Israeli nationalists as against Palestinian nationalists in the Middle East, and so forth (Whyte 1990; Watson 2007; Khalidi 2010).

This is not a mechanical process, of course. There are complexities of response, and there is no neat pattern of predictable allegiance in simple terms. But familiarity with the literatures alluded to underlines the point that I am making here. Nationalism provides lenses through which different debates on terrorism are repeatedly read. To assume a neutral scholarly terrain across nations (encompassing Pakistan as well as India, or the USA as well as Norway, or Israel as well as Colombia, or Spain as well as Ireland—not to mention nationalist divisions within some of those settings too) would be naïve. Understanding terrorism in context often means *national* context, in the sense that what we are studying involves varied and ultimately unique phenomena that are defined by local settings; it is really nationalism*s* and terrorism*s* that we are discussing. But the process is complicated further because it is often through distinctive nationalistic frameworks of assumption that we read these terrorisms and nationalisms in any case.

So particularities of time and place will have an effect on what scholars say, and the rigor of academic method needs to serve in part as a way of restraining the most vigorous excesses of this pattern. But the point relates also to the questions that we tend to ask. Post-9/11 scholarship on terrorism has been dominated by US academics, and this has generated libraries of very valuable and highly intelligent work. It has also focused very strikingly on contemporary threats to the United States of America and its national interests. This is entirely understandable. But understanding the literature on terrorism requires honest recognition of this point, and also its implications for the silences in the debate as well as the subjects which have been so admirably well-discussed.

Conclusion

There is little that is straightforward about the relationship between nationalism and terrorism. Each of these phenomena is deeply complex in itself, and the relationship between them is multiply so. What this chapter has sought has been to show some of the main ways in which the two phenomena have been intertwined historically. Some of these dynamics have tended towards violence, while others have not; and recognition of this double-facing quality to the nationalism/terrorism relationship is a crucial point.

Two other arguments might helpfully be set out in conclusion. First, consideration of the relationship between terrorism and nationalism alerts us to a central reality about terroristic violence, namely that it is less significant in itself than in what it reveals about the more major phenomena with which it is interwoven. Eric Hobsbawm was right that contemporary terrorist movements "are symptoms, not significant historic agents" (Hobsbawm 2007, 136). But this is also true of so much that has occurred throughout the history of terrorism. It is the long-term relationship between rival Spanish and Basque nationalisms that is crucial in that region of the world, rather than ETA violence or the Spanish state violence which greeted ETA. It is the politics of rival self-determination agendas in Ireland which has shaped politics there and in its relationship with the UK state; the tension between Irish and British nationalisms has generated terrorisms from numerous sources, but those terrorisms—for all of their merciless brutality and appalling human consequences—are symptoms. And so on throughout the world.

As we reflect on terrorism, therefore, we must not let its eye-catching, headline-seizing capacity delude us into thinking that terrorism itself is the main issue. It tends not to be. What lies beneath it—whether competition between religiously inflected nationalisms, tension between nation and state, the intra- or inter-religious dynamics of enmity, rivalry between those allegiant to different economic systems—is what matters most. This is why attention to the mutually shaping relationship between non-state terrorists and their state opponents is so important (English 2015). Much in the history of terrorism relates to the (often nationalistic) history and politics of the state.

Second, the question of the morality of terrorism and nationalism is hard to avoid if one wants honestly to discuss the relationship between these two phenomena. In the wake of violence, it can be understandably hard to appreciate the morality of those who have practiced the aggressive politics that have just been witnessed. But, however deluded they may be in thinking their terrorism to be effective or justified (English 2016a), those who practice non-state and state terrorism alike tend to see it as justified in causes which have something of a moral imperative to them.

More broadly, sophisticated cases can be made that there are some injustices which require violence in pursuit of their redress (Biggar 2013). In some of those instances, there will have been a nationalistic use of deliberately terrorizing violence with political purpose. I myself tend increasingly to doubt the efficacy or moral justification inherent in terrorism. But that is not the point here. The point is that if we want to explain and understand terroristic violence—whether or not it is nationalistic—then we have to face the reality that so much of it emerges from its practitioners' sense that it possesses a moral quality. This is an uncomfortable truth. But the fact that so much of that supposedly moral justification—even in the age of ISIS and Al Qaeda—lies ultimately in nationalist politics, makes the relationship between nationalism and terrorism even more significant.

REFERENCES

Anderson, B. (1983) *Imagined Communities: Reflections on the Origin and Spread of Nationalism*. London: Verso.

Ansari, A. M. (2012) *The Politics of Nationalism in Modern Iran*. Cambridge: Cambridge University Press.

Argomaniz, J. (2011) *The EU and Counter-Terrorism: Politics, Polity, and Policies after 9/11*. London: Routledge.

Barrett, R. (2014) *The Islamic State*. New York: Soufan Group.

Biggar, N. (2013) *In Defence of War*. Oxford: Oxford University Press.

Blumenau, B. (2014) *The United Nations and Terrorism: Germany, Multilateralism, and Anti-Terrorism Efforts in the 1970s*. Basingstoke: Palgrave Macmillan.

Bonino, S. (2017) *Muslims in Scotland: The Making of Community in a Post-9/11 World*. Edinburgh: Edinburgh University Press.

Brubaker, R. (1996) *Nationalism Reframed: Nationhood and the National Question in the New Europe*. Cambridge: Cambridge University Press.

Byman, D. (2005) *Deadly Connections: States that Sponsor Terrorism*. Cambridge: Cambridge University Press.

Byman, D. (2015) Al Qaeda, *the Islamic State, and the Global Jihadist Movement: What Everyone Needs to Know*. Oxford: Oxford University Press.

Chenoy, A. M., and K. A. M. Chenoy (2010) *Maoist and Other Armed Conflicts*. London: Penguin.

Cockburn, P. (2014) *The Jihadis Return: ISIS and the New Sunni Uprising*. New York: OR Books.

Croft, S. (2006) *Culture, Crisis, and America's War on Terror*. Cambridge: Cambridge University Press.

de Guttry, A., F. Capone, and C. Paulussen, eds (2016) *Foreign Fighters under International Law and beyond*. The Hague: Asser Press.

Enders, W., and T. Sandler (2012) *The Political Economy of Terrorism*. Cambridge: Cambridge University Press 1st publ. 2006.

English, R. (1998) *Ernie O'Malley: IRA Intellectual*. Oxford: Oxford University Press.

English, R. (2006) *Irish Freedom: The History of Nationalism in Ireland*. London: Pan Macmillan.

English, R. (2009) *Terrorism: How to Respond*. Oxford: Oxford University Press.

English, R. (2012) *Armed Struggle: The History of the IRA*. London: Pan Macmillan 1st publ. 2003.

English, R. (2013) *Modern War: A Very Short Introduction*. Oxford: Oxford University Press.

English, R., ed. (2015) *Illusions of Terrorism and Counter-Terrorism*. Oxford: Oxford University Press.

English, R. (2016a) *Does Terrorism Work? A History*. Oxford: Oxford University Press.

English, R. (2016b) "The Future Study of Terrorism," *European Journal of International Security*, 1(2): 1–15.

Flanagan, F. (2015) *Remembering the Revolution: Dissent, Culture, and Nationalism in the Irish Free State*. Oxford: Oxford University Press.

Foster, R. F. (2014) *Vivid Faces: The Revolutionary Generation in Ireland 1890–1923*. London: Penguin.

Gambetta, D., and S. Hertog (2016) *Engineers of Jihad: The Curious Connection between Violent Extremism and Education*. Princeton: Princeton University Press.

Gearty, C. (2013) *Liberty and Security*. Cambridge: Polity.
Gellner, E. (1983) *Nations and Nationalism*. Oxford: Basil Blackwell.
Gerges, F. A. (2016) *ISIS: A History*. Princeton: Princeton University Press.
Gill, P. (2015) *Lone-Actor Terrorists: A Behavioural Analysis*. London: Routledge.
Hastings, A. (1997) *The Construction of Nationhood: Ethnicity, Religion, and Nationalism*. Cambridge: Cambridge University Press.
Hobsbawm, E. J. (1990) *Nations and Nationalism since 1780: Programme, Myth, Reality*. Cambridge: Cambridge University Press.
Hobsbawm, E. J. (2007) *Globalization, Democracy, and Terrorism*. London: Little, Brown.
Hoffman, B. (2015) *Anonymous Soldiers: The Struggle for Israel, 1917–1947*. New York: Alfred A. Knopf.
Kaczynski, T. J. (2016) *Anti-Tech Revolution: Why and How*. Scottsdale, AZ: Fitch & Madison.
Kedourie, E. (1993) *Nationalism*. Oxford: Blackwell 1st publ. 1960.
Khalidi, R. (2010) *Palestinian Identity: The Construction of Modern National Consciousness*. New York: Columbia University Press 1st publ. 1997.
Kidd, C. (1999) *British Identities Before Nationalism: Ethnicity and Nationhood in the Atlantic World 1600–1800*. Cambridge: Cambridge University Press.
Kurtzer, D. C., S. B. Lasensky, W. B. Quandt, S. L. Spiegel, and S. Z. Telhami (2013) *The Peace Puzzle: America's Quest for Arab-Israeli Peace, 1989–2011*. Ithaca, NY: Cornell University Press.
Laitin, D. D. (2007) *Nations, States, and Violence*. Oxford: Oxford University Press.
Livingstone, D. N. (2003) *Putting Science in its Place: Geographies of Scientific Knowledge*. Chicago: University of Chicago Press.
Livingstone, D. N. (2014) *Dealing with Darwin: Place, Politics, and Rhetoric in Religious Engagements with Evolution*. Baltimore, MD: Johns Hopkins University Press.
McCants, W. (2015) *The ISIS Apocalypse: The History, Strategy, and Doomsday Vision of the Islamic State*. New York: St Martin's Press.
Malešević, S. (2006) *Identity as Ideology: Understanding Ethnicity and Nationalism*. Basingstoke: Palgrave Macmillan.
Malešević, S. (2010) *The Sociology of War and Violence*. Cambridge: Cambridge University Press.
Mendelsohn, B. (2009) *Combating Jihadism: American Hegemony and Interstate Cooperation in the War on Terrorism*. Chicago: University of Chicago Press.
Mueller, J., and M. G. Stewart (2016) *Chasing Ghosts: The Policing of Terrorism*. Oxford: Oxford University Press.
Muro, D. (2008) *Ethnicity and Violence: The Case of Radical Basque Nationalism*. London: Routledge.
Neumann, P. R. (2016) *Radicalized: New Jihadists and the Threat to the West*. London: I. B. Tauris.
O'Callaghan, S. (2015) *James Connolly: My Search for the Man, the Myth and his Legacy*. London: Century.
Ozkirimli, U. (2010) *Theories of Nationalism: A Critical Introduction*. Basingstoke: Palgrave Macmillan (1st publ. 2000).
Rafferty, O. P. (2016) *Violence, Politics, and Catholicism in Ireland*. Dublin: Four Courts Press.
Reid, R. J. (2012) *Warfare in African History*. Cambridge: Cambridge University Press.
Rushdie, S. (2012) *Joseph Anton: A Memoir*. London: Jonathan Cape.
Sacks, J. (2015) *Not in God's Name: Confronting Religious Violence*. London: Hodder & Stoughton.

Schwarzmantel, J. (2011) *Democracy and Political Violence*. Edinburgh: Edinburgh University Press.

Smith, A. D. (2000) *The Nation in History: Historiographical Debates about Ethnicity and Nationalism*. Hanover, NH: University Press of New England.

Singh, R. (2011) *Hamas and Suicide Terrorism: Multi-Causal and Multi-Level Approaches*. London: Routledge.

Stern, J., and J. M. Berger (2015) *ISIS: The State of Terror*. London: HarperCollins.

Watson, C. J. (2007) *Basque Nationalism and Political Violence: The Ideological and Intellectual Origins of ETA*. Reno: Center for Basque Studies.

Wilson, T. (2013) "State Terrorism: An Historical Overview," in G. Duncan, G. Ramsay, O. Lynch, and A. M. S. Watson (eds), State Terrorism and Human Rights: International Responses Since the End of the Cold War. London: Routledge, 14–31.

Whyte, J. (1990) *Interpreting Northern Ireland*. Oxford: Oxford University Press.

CHAPTER 19

RELIGION AND TERRORISM

JEFFREY HAYNES

Introduction

It would be impossible to single out a single event that would on its own explain all recent and current examples of religious terrorism. On the other hand, Samuel Huntington's (1993, 1996) highly influential yet very controversial argument is a good place to start, not least because it highlighted probably the most egregious example of the genre, Islamic terrorism.[1] Although Huntington was discussing what he called "clash of civilisations," this did not mean that inter-religious or inter-cultural clashes were not also in focus. Writing in the early 1990s, soon after the end of the Cold War, Huntington claimed that the (Christian) West's security—and by extension global order more generally—were now under attack from militant Islam.[2] For some, Huntington's thesis was given credence by the emergence in the 1990s of overtly anti-Western Islamic regimes in Afghanistan and Sudan, a concerted attempt to do so contemporaneously in Algeria, the tragic events of September 11, 2001 ("9/11"), when around 3,000 people were killed in the USA in Al Qaeda attacks, subsequent US-led invasions of Afghanistan (2001) and Iraq (2003), murderous bomb attacks in Madrid (2004) and London (2005), and continuing Islamist militants' responses in Somalia, Nigeria, Mali, and elsewhere.

Governments and "ordinary" people responded in broadly religious and cultural terms to both 9/11 and subsequent US retaliation against the Al Qaeda attacks. On the one hand, Western governments, including those of Britain, Italy, and Spain, strongly supported the American government and people against Al Qaeda and, more generally, Islamic terrorism. On the other hand, many "ordinary" Muslims—although not necessarily their governments—appeared to view the events rather differently. Acknowledging the undesirability of the loss of thousands of innocent people as a consequence of a terrorist outrage, for some Muslims 9/11 represented an attempt to "fight back" against what some saw as a globally destructive state: the USA (and by extension the "West" more generally) (Dolan 2005). In addition, many Muslims also regarded punitive US-led actions against both Afghanistan and Iraq as unjust, designed unfairly to "punish" fellow believers for 9/11—a tragic event over which they had no control (Shlapentokh et al. 2005).

No doubt, Al Qaeda expected Muslim reactions to the 9/11 outrage (Haynes 2005a). Al Qaeda's purpose was of course to wreak terrible destruction on the USA—but that was not all. In addition, Al Qaeda wished to create a global media spectacle, to show the mass of "downtrodden" ordinary Muslims that Osama bin Laden personally—already for some Muslims a hero following his self-proclaimed anti-Soviet exploits in Afghanistan in the late 1980s—and Al Qaeda collectively acted on *their* behalf. Thus, around the world, "ordinary" Muslims were an important target audience for the highly visual spectacle of the destruction of the Twin Towers and the contemporaneous attack on the Pentagon. For bin Laden and Al Qaeda a key goal of 9/11 was to grab the attention of ordinary (Sunni) Muslims, to encourage them to make connections between the attacks and widespread Muslim resentment against the USA. Prior to 9/11, this was already simmering as a result, inter alia, of the earlier US-led invasion of Iraq in 1990–1 and, over time, successive American governments' apparently unwavering support both for Israel's resolutely harsh treatment of the Palestinians and for many unelected and—according to Al Qaeda—"un-Islamic" rulers in the Muslim world, such as the King of Saudi Arabia.

However, even if such areas of specific concern to many Muslims were speedily resolved, it may be that associated resentment and antipathy towards the USA and by extension the (Christian) West would not necessarily dispel speedily. This is because rather than there being "only" a finite list of specific issues, potentially resolvable via negotiation and compromise, there are also less precise sources of antipathy and disquiet that go much deeper and have been in place for much longer and, as a result, are much more problematic to resolve, such as the "correct" size and territorial extent of the state of Israel. Thus, even if solutions for specific sources of complaint were quickly found, it would not necessarily deal fully with all sources of Muslim disquiet at the status quo, including an international environment which, although now challenged by the rise of non-Western states, notably China, Brazil, and India, has historically been dominated by the (Christian) West and guided by associated liberal values.

International Society and International Order

Over time, the principle of state sovereignty in international society has been sustained by two important conditions: first, the absence of transnational—that is, cross-border—ideologies that fundamentally compete with nation states for people's political loyalties; second, by the existence of a common, although not universal, set of values held by many governments that serves to engender an element of respect for other states. Recent international involvement of religious terrorist groups, such as Al Qaeda and Lashkar-e-Taiba, has seriously weakened these two essential "pillars" of the Westphalian system. This is because such challenges are bolstered by the development of new—or newly significant—transnational allegiances that challenge existing popular allegiances to the (nation) state by focusing on politically significant alternative—and often incompatible—beliefs and values, in this case militant Islamist values. As a result, they do not sit well alongside established Westphalian principles of liberal international order. This is especially the case if these beliefs and values reject and hence undermine the basic rules on which post-Westphalian international order was founded and the institutions that seek to maintain it. This is expressed in four main ways:

- Such challenges can manifest themselves in the rejection of the state as the main political unit in international relations—the rejection of the principle that leaders of states have the right and duty to deal with other leaders in international relations.
- Negation of the principle that states are the sole actors that can legitimately use force is significant, as rejection of restrictions on the use of force (e.g. in international law civilians cannot legally be targets of war; terrorists, on the other hand, explicitly target civilians as a key war-fighting technique).
- Violent non-state terrorist actors also challenge values of international society in a third way: they undermine state–society relations by weakening the ability of governments to carry out a basic governmental responsibility to their citizens: general security. It is very difficult for governments to protect citizens against random terror attacks, as seen, inter alia, on 9/11 and in the Lashkar-e-Taiba attack on the Taj Hotel, Mumbai, in November 2008.
- Violent non-state terrorists can also undermine international society by provoking an overreaction by the internationally dominant power, such as the USA, which led invasions of both Afghanistan (2001) and Iraq (2003) following 9/11. This had the effect of undermining the accepted code of conduct which decrees that state sovereignty is normally inviolable.

Globalization is the key vehicle today for projection of transnational religious terrorism. A key impact is to highlight the importance of various entities in international relations which do not share the norms and values of Western-dominated "liberal" international society, including transnational Islamist terrorist organizations, such as Al Qaeda, Lashkar-e-Taiba, and Islamic State (Haynes 2013). Such groups' activities highlight an important theoretical and practical question in international relations: are shared ideals, including "international order" and "international society," theoretically based on globally applicable norms and values, possible in today's multicultural, multi-religious, multi-national, multi-ethnic, globalized international environment? For the international relations theorist, Chris Brown (2005, 51), it makes sense to think of the idea of international society as "an occasionally idealized conceptualisation of the norms of the old, pre-1914 European states system." What he means by this is that in order to be relevant today, the notion of international society must be built on consensual—or at least very widely shared—norms and values among the members of that society. But if Brown is right, can such a consensual conception of international society be a satisfactory starting point when we bear in mind that most existing states are now *not* European or Western? The Council of Europe has forty-seven member states. The Council of Europe was established in 1949 with the goal of working towards European integration, focusing on shared regional legal standards, human rights, development of democratic rule, the rule of law, and cultural cooperation. Over three-quarters of the 192 members of the United Nations are not European countries.

Brown is also referring to the fact that the pre-1914 international order functioned relatively well—in the sense that there were no significant international conflicts between the end of the Napoleonic Wars in 1815 and World War I, a century later. Could this however have been the result of a high level of cultural homogeneity among the then members of international society, which now no longer exists? At the time, most Europeans had a common history informed not only by cultural origins in the ancient Greek and Roman civilization but also by their Christian faith. The latter did not however necessarily imply peaceful relations: historical relationships between European states were often marked by competition or conflict between, for example, followers of the (Greek) Orthodox and (Roman) Catholic churches or between Protestant and Catholic interpretations of Christianity, as in the Thirty Years War (1618–48). How much more likely is it in today's multicultural, multi-religious, multi-national, multi-ethnic, globalized international system that potential for serious conflict has increased, given that the earlier normative basis for international society appears to have been based on shared European or Western cultural underpinnings?

Religious Terrorism and International Order

Seeking to explain understand current examples of religious terrorism, it is necessary to think beyond exclusively religious motivations. Hurrell (2002, 197) notes that it "seems plausible that much [Muslim] resentment has to do with the far-reaching and corrosive encroachments of modernization, westernization and globalization." Burke (2015) contends that "if the current wave of [Islamic] militancy has its origins anywhere, it is in the religious revival across the Islamic world of the 1960s and 70s, and the urbanisation, economic development, politics and wars that prompted it." So, for both, there is something in the process of "modernization" in the Muslim world which "encourages" "Islamic terrorism."

Key to an understanding of what are sometimes called "cultural" factors in international relations (Murden 2005) are the activities of religious terrorists, especially the most eye-catching, controversial, topical, and discussed examples: Islamic terrorists. For many observers, this is new and unexpected, in two ways. First, until recently, most international relations experts believed that religion could be ignored because it appeared to be so insignificant in the mainly secular context of world politics. Second, the end of the Cold War in the late 1980s ushered in a new era of religious involvement in international terrorism, with 9/11 a prime example. The consequence of these two developments is that today most observers of international relations would probably agree that it is impossible to ignore the involvement of various "religious actors" in both domestic and international terrorism.

Following the presentation of the background to its recent emergence, the remainder of this chapter examines recent and current examples of religious terrorism, with most discussion devoted to Islamic terrorism. The aim is to explain why it has occurred and what it tells us more generally about religion's involvement in international relations in the second decade of the twenty-first century. My main argument in this chapter is that there are both specific and more general reasons for the development and spread of religious terrorism, including both domestic and international conflicts.

I need now to discuss a key term of the chapter: religious terrorism. What is it and what are its key qualities? For Martin (2007, 111),

> Religious terrorism is a type of political violence motivated by an absolute belief that an otherworldly power has sanctioned—and commanded—terrorist violence for the greater glory of the faith. Acts committed in the name of the faith will be forgiven by the otherworldly power and perhaps rewarded in an afterlife. In essence, one's religious faith legitimizes violence as long as such violence is an expression of the will of one's deity

Gregg (2014) avers that religious *terrorism* "is typically characterised as acts of unrestrained, irrational and indiscriminate violence, thus offering few if any policy options for counterterrorism measures." Juergensmeyer (2016) asserts however that

> religion may not be the problem—it does not cause violence—but it is problematic. It is problematic in two ways. One is the way that religious identities and ideologies have become aspects of a global rebellion against the European Enlightenment notion of a secular state, beginning in the last decades of the 20th century. The other is the way that certain features of religious actions and images—such as the performance of religious ritual and the awesome notion of cosmic war—are appropriated by violent actors seeking to justify their savage attempts at power and cloak them in religious garb.

For Martin, Gregg, and Juergensmeyer, religious terrorism has two key dimensions: often unconstrained political violence and an aspect of a more general rebellion against the Western liberal international order. These two dimensions highlight both the domestic and international foci of religious terrorism. How to maintain and strengthen international order is a key focus in relation to international religious terrorism, of major importance for media, policy makers, and the general public especially in the

West following 9/11. Held and McGrew (2002) contend that a key impact of globalization on international relations is to undermine the established principles and practices of international order, established after World War II and concretized in the founding of the United Nations as the key expression of global collective security. Today, however, international order is undermined by diminution of the authority of the state in various issue areas, including economic concerns, and the emergence of new realms with only limited state control (such as cyberspace and the internet), as well as "the rise of non-state actors showing signs of successfully influencing states' policies, and taking over subject areas that the state largely ignored or mishandled" (Mendelsohn 2005, 50). It is in the diminution of the state's ability to control the international environment that we see the rise of religious terrorism, representing in the case of Islamic terrorism a new and highly significant threat to international order. On the one hand, some religious transnational actors, such as the Catholic Church, accept the desirability of at least some aspects of liberal international order, characterized by, for example, improved human rights, more democracy and greater justice for the powerless and poverty-stricken. The Catholic Church is today a key component of a global coalition of forces—both religious and secular (such as Amnesty International and Transparency International)—which jointly work towards the aim of developing an international society based on liberal values (Thomas 2005; Haynes 2014).

On the other hand, challenges to liberal conceptions of international order come collectively from various Islamic terrorist groups, including Al Qaeda, Lashkar-e-Taiba, and Islamic State. Not as well-known as Al Qaeda (which we will discuss later), Lashkar-e-Taiba[3] is a Pakistan-based, transnational Islamic terrorist group responsible for a dramatic hotel bombing in Mumbai in late 2008 with the loss of hundreds of lives (Tankel 2009).

Case Study: Lashkar-e-Taiba and the Bombing of the Taj Hotel in November 2008

Attacks by Lashkar-e-Taiba on India's largest city, Mumbai, took place on 26–29 November 2008. They are known collectively as India's 9/11. The attacks involved more than ten coordinated shooting and bombing attacks. They were carried out by Islamist terrorists from Pakistan. In the attacks, over 200 people were killed and more than 300 wounded. Following a siege of the Taj hotel, where many of the Islamists were holed up, India's National Security Guards stormed the hotel, in an action officially named "Operation Black Tornado," which ended all fighting in the attacks. Ajmal Kasab, the only attacker captured alive by Indian security personnel, admitted that the attackers were members of Lashkar, a Pakistan-based Islamist militant organization, considered a terrorist entity by the governments of India, the United States, and the United Kingdom.

On January 7, 2009, after more than a month of denying the nationality of the attackers, Pakistan's Information Minister, Sherry Rehman, officially accepted Ajmal Kasab's nationality as Pakistani. On February 12, 2009, Pakistan's Interior Minister, Rehman Malik, in a televised news briefing, confirmed that parts of the attack had been planned in Pakistan and said that six people, including the alleged mastermind, were being held in connection with the attacks.

A man who identified himself as a former Lashkar militant, who now works with its charity arm, claimed in late 2009 that the organization's aim in the Mumbai attacks, as well as more generally, was to wage "war on the enemies of Islam." But who, exactly, are these "enemies of Islam?" Lashkar-e-Taiba and other (Sunni) Islamist terrorist groups have three sets of linked enemies: the "West" (in general, and the USA in particular), their own "un-Islamic" rulers in the Arab Middle East and, finally, fellow Muslims, especially Shias, who do not adhere to the militants' ideals regarding who is a "proper" Muslim. Such politically organized militant Muslims, who are prepared to use terrorism to advance their goals, are not a new phenomenon in the world of Islam. They are, instead, people who categorize themselves as having the highest moral and ethical values, the "just," involved in a struggle against the "unjust." The division between "just" and "unjust" in the promotion of social change throughout Islamic history parallels the historic tension in the West between "state" and "civil society." For many radical Islamists, the "unjust" rule the state while the "just" look in from the outside, seeking to reform the corrupt system by any means deemed necessary, including the use of terrorism. Thus their goal is to overthrow "unjust" rulers and establish a new, transnational caliphate bringing together the *umma* in a new religio-political system which moves away radically from the present state-centric system which has organized international relations for at least 200 hundred years following the French and American Revolutions of the late eighteenth century and the subsequent international emergence and development of a new, secular ideology: nationalism.

Such terrorist groups emphatically do not accept the legitimacy of the existing international order and the foundations on which international society is based. Instead, they try to advance an alternative order, based on quite different laws, norms, and values. Unlike Lashkar-e-Taiba which achieved only short-term international notoriety, Al Qaeda has been in the forefront of global attention since 9/11. For Al Qaeda, the aim of 9/11 was not simply to wreak terrible destruction but also to create a global media spectacle, a spectacular advertisement for the organization and its militant ideological goals. Al Qaeda's key target audience for the highly visual spectacle of the attacks on the Twin Towers and the Pentagon was the mass of "downtrodden ordinary Sunni Muslims." Al Qaeda used 9/11 to grab the attention of such people, inviting them to make connections between the specific attacks on the United States and the multiple resentments many Muslims felt against "America." While reasons for Muslim antipathy no doubt varied, they included: anger, especially in the Arab world, at often unwavering US support for unrepresentative rulers, US-led invasions of Iraq in 1990–1 and 2003, and Israel's continuing "harsh" treatment of the Palestinians, aided and abetted by successive US administrations. Taken together, as they often are, these issues led to widespread antipathy towards the United States in many parts of the Muslim world, repugnance not necessarily restricted to small numbers of Islamist militants who were willing to utilize terrorist tactics to try to achieve their reformist goals.

Apart from killing Americans/Westerners and their allies, Al Qaeda has four other, related goals:

- Return to a "pure and authentic" Islam as practiced by the Prophet Mohammed and his companions in seventh-century Medina, in order to bring back glory and prominence to Muslims.
- Overthrow regimes Al Qaeda deems to be "non-Islamic."
- Expel Westerners and non-Muslims from Muslim countries—particularly the holy land of Saudi Arabia, because the West is said to have subjugated the lands of Islam, while Western individualistic values are alleged to have corrupted many Muslims.
- Establish a pan-Islamic Caliphate throughout the world by working with a global network of like-minded Islamist radical organizations.

During the 1990s, Al Qaeda expanded its capacity and network, building links with various Islamist groups, including Egypt's Islamic Jihad, whose leader, Ayman al-Zawahiri, became bin Laden's deputy in 1998 and, following bin Laden's assassination by the government of the USA in 2011, Al Qaeda's leader. Other Islamist groups affiliated to Al Qaeda include the Islamic Jihad Movement (Eritrea), al-Itihaad al-Islamiya ("The Islamic Union," Somalia), al-Gama'a al-Islamiyya ("The Islamic Group," Egypt), the Islamic Movement of Uzbekistan, and Pakistan's Harakat ul-Mujahidin. Following expulsion from Afghanistan in late 2001, consequential to the US-led invasion of that country following 9/11, Al Qaeda dispersed into small, often autonomous groups in various parts of the world, a loose network of Sunni Islamic extremists. Al Qaeda developed money-making front businesses, solicited donations from like-minded supporters, especially in Saudi Arabia, and illicitly siphoned funds from donations to Muslim charitable organizations, including Islamic NGOs (Conetta 2002; Haynes 2005b).

Some argue that "Islamic fundamentalism," inextricably associated with Islamic terrorism, now poses the main existential threat facing not only the United States (Halper and Clarke 2004; Dolan 2005) but also the "West" more generally (Burke 2015). For example, Willy Claes, a former secretary-general of the North Atlantic Treaty Organization stated in the mid-1990s that

> Muslim fundamentalism is at least as dangerous as communism once was... Please do not underestimate this risk... at the conclusion of this age it is a serious threat, because it represents *terrorism, religious fanaticism and exploitation of social and economic justice*.... NATO is much more than a military alliance. It has committed itself to defending basic principles of civilisation that bind North America and Western Europe. (Emphases added; Claes quoted in *Guardian*, February 3, 1995)

Claes's contentions point to what two decades ago were of new significance in post-Cold War international relations: *cultural* factors. According to an international relations commentator, Simon Murden, the cultural dimension to international relations appears "to be reaffirmed amid the reorganization of world politics that followed the end of the cold war and the release of new waves of globalization" (Murden 2005, 539). For some Muslims, poverty and a declining faith in the development abilities of their governments led to their being receptive to fundamentalist and in some cases terrorist arguments. Poverty and an associated feeling of hopelessness may be exacerbated by a withering of community ties as people move from the countryside to the city in a search for paid employment. And when traditional communal and familial ties are seriously stretched or sundered, religion-orientated, including extremist, ones may replace them. Yet, while Islamic terrorism has taken the lion's share of attention in recent years, it is necessary to note that militant followers of several of the world religions have also resorted to terrorism in an attempt to achieve political goals. Next I briefly examine Christian, Jewish, and Hindu terrorism before returning to Islamic terrorism, the main example of religious terrorism in today's world.

Religious Terrorism and the World Faiths

Christian Terrorism

In the United States, Christian fundamentalists are often found among affluent, successful people. Clearly, it would be absurd to argue that alienation explains the existence of such people in the USA.

Christian fundamentalism, after achieving social and political prominence in the early decades of the twentieth century, re-emerged as a legitimate vehicle for political ideas in the USA from the 1970s, a period of political, social, and economic upheaval in America. Less legitimate manifestations of what purported to be religiously inspired groups, such as the Ku Klux Klan terrorists, developed from the time of the American Civil War (1861–5), but they were hardly a part of the political mainstream except in areas of the southern United States where white Protestant hostility to Jews, Catholics, and African-Americans surfaced after World War I. Instead, most Christian fundamentalists were concerned with allegedly high levels of amorality in the United States. Their success in terms of gaining recruits can be judged by the fact that, as long ago as the late 1980s, there were estimated to be around 60 million fundamentalist Christians in the USA, that is, over 20 percent of the total population. Many were political: Christian fundamentalists provided the core support for Pat Robertson's unsuccessful 1988 presidential campaign and for Pat Buchanan's in 1992, 1996, and 2000. A lapsed Catholic, Timothy McVeigh, was responsible for an egregious act of "white supremacist" terrorism: detonation of a truck bomb in front of the Alfred P. Murrah Federal Building in Oklahoma City on April 19, 1995. The attack killed 168 people and injured over 600.

In addition, over the last four decades the USA has seen terrorist activities perpetuated by fundamentalist Christians against abortion clinics and the medical personnel who work in them (http://www.religioustolerance.org/abo_viol.htm).

Jewish Terrorism

Judaism also has religious terrorists: one of them, Yigal Amir, assassinated Yitzhak Rabin, then Israeli prime minister, in November 1995. Rabin's "crime" was negotiating with the Palestine Liberation Organization (PLO) leader, the late Yassar Arafat, with the goal of allowing Palestinians a large measure of self-government, premised upon a reduction in the physical size of Israel. It was this—a proposed reduction in the size of the "God-ordained" state of Israel—which incurred the wrath of Amir and other Jewish fundamentalists. In addition, Israel has a number of Jewish terrorist groups, including the largest, Gush Emunim (Bloc of the Faithful). Such entities are characterized by rejection of negotiations with Palestinians over what the Jewish terrorist groups see as their holy land.

Gush Emunim was founded after the 1978 Camp David agreement between Israel and Egypt, which resulted in the handing back of the Sinai desert to the latter. Other terrorist groups, such as the late Rabbi Meir Kahane's organization, Kach, also now banned, also fulminated against the return of territory to Muslim-majority Egypt. The biblical entity, Eretz Israel, they argued, was significantly larger than the contemporary state of Israel. To hand back any territory to Arabs is tantamount, they maintained, to going against God's will as revealed in the Old Testament of the Christian Bible. Simmering religious opposition to the peace plan with the PLO, involving giving autonomy to the Gaza Strip and to an area around Jericho, reached tragic levels in February 1994 when a religious terrorist, Baruch Goldstein, linked with militants of two extremist groups—Kach (Thus) and Kahane Chai (Kahane Lives)—murdered twenty-nine Muslims during a dawn attack on a mosque in the occupied West Bank town of Hebron. After the massacre Israel's government banned both Kach and Kahane Chai, a sign of its commitment to crush religious extremist groups that systematically used violence to try to achieve their goals.

Hindu Terrorism

While contemporary Hindu fundamentalism (or nationalism) is rooted in cultural chauvinism it is by no means sui generis. "Mahatma" Mohandas Gandhi, the leading Indian nationalist and a committed Hindu, was assassinated by a Hindu terrorist in 1948. Gandhi's "crime" was appearing to condone the creation of a bifurcated homeland for India's Muslims, East and West Pakistan. More recently, simmering Hindu fundamentalist suspicion of India's largest religious minority—Muslims, comprising about 11 percent of India's 1.2 billion population, some 130 million people—was manifested in the destruction in 1992 of a historic mosque at Ayodhya in Uttar Pradesh. This mosque, according to militant Hindus, was built on the birthplace of the Hindu god of war, Rama. As long ago as 1950, the mosque was closed down by the Indian government, as militant Hindus sought to build a Hindu temple in place of the mosque.

In a further example of communitarian violence, the late Prime Minister, Indira Gandhi, paid with her life in 1984 by appealing to Hindu chauvinism to take on Sikh militancy in the Punjab. Later, her son, Prime Minister Rajiv Gandhi was assassinated by a Tamil Hindu terrorist in 1991—because he sent Indian troops to try to resolve the civil conflict in Sri Lanka between Hindu Tamils and Buddhist Sinhalese. After his murder, the Hindu-chauvinist Bharatiya Janata Party (BJP) became an increasingly important political player, with a leading role in government from the mid-1990s.

Islamist Terrorism

In recent years, Al Qaeda's influence among jihadists appears to have declined. Certainly, in terms of publicity and public profile most international attention is now paid to an exceptionally violent and extremist group, the newest kid on the Islamic terrorist block and unchallenged poster child: Islamic State (IS).

Islamic State is today the key regional purveyor of religious terrorism in the Middle East. IS emerged following the collapse of governance in several countries in the Middle East, especially the previously strong states of Syria and Iraq. The appeal of IS is wide-ranging. For example, over the last few years, around 700 British (Sunni) Muslims have left the UK to join IS. Overall, Reuters reported in February 2015 that 20,000 foreigners, including 3,400 from the West, have gone to join IS in Iraq and Syria (*The Times of Israel*, February 11, 2015; <http://www.timesofisrael.com/us-20000-foreigners-heading-to-syria-to-join-islamic-state>).

The last few decades have seen the Middle East emerge as a global focal point of increased political involvement of religious actors both within countries and internationally; increasingly, it appears, rivalries between Shia and Sunni are expressed via the trading of terrorist atrocities. On the one hand, religious minorities across the region are being squeezed and their security compromised, chased away from their homes by terrorism. While "Islamic fundamentalism" or "Islamism"[4] has attracted much attention in this context, we can also observe increasingly serious sectarian division and conflict across much of the Middle East and North Africa (MENA), especially in Syria, Iraq, and Yemen. The situation was exacerbated by the Arab Spring and its aftermath where state weakness or breakdown combined with the impact of politically assertive religious actors saw increasing pressure on religious minorities to convert to the dominant religious tradition or, failing that, to flee for their lives.[5]

Terrorist actors like IS thrive on sectarian division. Given the widespread diminution of state capacity in the MENA following the Arab Spring and the linked expansion of aggressive Sunni entities, such as IS, it seems highly likely that the short and medium term will feature many regional sectarian conflicts, which will cause significant friction and, in some cases, result in out and out conflict between warring sectarian groups. Tensions between Shiite Iran and the Sunni Gulf Cooperation Council (GCC) are likely to remain high in the next few years—not least because each is seen to support one sect of Islam only. However, not all Shia movements will necessarily be pro-Iranian and not every Salafi or Wahhabist Sunni movement kowtows to Saudi Arabia. Indeed, there are significant Shiite minorities in GCC countries, as well as a growing (Sunni) Salafi movement in Iran. Sectarian tensions also reflect socio-economic disparities and are likely to escalate if governments do not address these fundamental issues. For example, Bahrain and Saudi Arabia, where economic inequality between Sunni and Shia is greatest, are more likely to see tensions rise than other countries in the region. Globalization, represented by influential satellite television channels and social media, will play a growing, perhaps pivotal, role in spreading anti-government rhetoric and sectarian mistrust. In addition, over the next twenty years, we are likely to see growing tensions *within* Sunni and Shiite communities. Sunni Islam is particularly likely to become increasingly factionalized. As Salafist groups grow in prominence around the world, a backlash may emerge from moderate Sunnis. Correspondingly, Shiite Islam contains a number of internal divisions.

The countries in the Middle East that have most suffered from decades of systematic political, sectarian, and racial repression and mass killings—that is, Iraq and Syria—made possible the foundation, emergence, and development of IS. What makes these countries' situation particularly dire is the world's failure to condemn this oppression, turning a blind eye to the roots of radicalization, while failing to help deal with the existential threat that IS poses due to political considerations at home. Yet, it is no longer about a choice between countering terrorism and respecting human rights. It is impossible to win the fight against terror in this region without addressing the oppression and lack of opportunity that spawns it. Defending human rights and confronting religious extremism, working to end the discrimination against Syrian and Iraqi Sunni populations, as well as against Bedouins of Sinai, would be the necessary first steps in a long journey to deal with human rights violations in the Middle East.

In particular, tension between Sunni and Shia Islam could spread. For example, in 2012, Belgium's largest Shiite mosque was fire-bombed by hard-line Sunnis. However, while there may be an increase in such incidents, particularly in response to events in the MENA, it is unlikely that large-scale violence between the different sects will occur in Europe itself, not least because of the small number of Shias.

Today, Islamic terrorism is increasingly focused upon sectarian divisions between Shia and Sunni which are becoming globalized, often inspired by Iran–Saudi Arabia rivalry. The division is not based on theology but political conflict. Just as in the case of Christianity, the major religious differences within Islam, including the distinction between Sunni and Shia, can be traced to political conflict rather than theological debate. However, such religious differences have become real distinctions in their own right. Whether a Muslim believes in independent reasoning and the ongoing interpretation of the Quran, or believes that the gates of independent reasoning and interpretation, or *ijtihad*, have been closed, is one example of an important religious difference that may not necessarily be driven by pre-existing political orientations. Whether one believes that God continues to reveal himself by using human reason, or one believes that God has revealed himself once and for all and that a good Muslim must simply apply the Quran and Hadith without contextualization is an important theological difference of opinion. These intra-Islamic differences, like intra-Christian differences, may have political origins and political consequences, but they are essentially religious differences—differences concerning what one believes about God and how God is to be worshipped.

Conclusion

Terrorism encouraged and fueled by Islamic extremism will continue to pose a threat to US and Western interests in many parts of the world. Around the world high—and in many cases growing—levels of inequality contextualized by differences based in religion, ethnicity, and/or class, are highly likely to endure over the next twenty years. They will continue to be often serious sources of tension in many regions and will impact on the overall governance and stability of many countries, while also affecting global governance. The key focus for future research is to discover the causes of religious terrorism and seek to redress them.

It is clear that areas of considerable sectarian tension exist across the world, especially in many of the twenty or more countries that comprise the Middle East. If there was a prolonged period of escalation, perhaps underpinned by further deteriorations in political and developmental well-being, then campaigns of terrorist attacks could be carried out on a previously unseen scale, further plunging the MENA region into chaos with knock-on effects experienced in Western Europe and Sub-Saharan Africa. It is possible that attacks on such a level could cause a major power, hitherto relatively stable, such as Egypt, to descend into civil war. In addition, pre-existing religious and sectarian divides, including intra-Islamic and Islamic–Christian and/or Islamic–Jewish conflicts could come together and rapidly escalate into a transnational conflict between several components of global society. In these circumstances, it is conceivable that some countries would be drawn into a wider war, as pressure from their populations, existing treaty obligations, and allegiances force them to take sides. If the United Nations was deadlocked, weak, and hamstrung, and regional security organizations were unable to take up the challenge, then widespread killings could occur across much of the globe.

While the scenario sketched out in the previous paragraph represents an extreme outcome, it is clear that both terrorism and sectarian and inter-religious tensions and conflicts have been at the center of Western security concerns since at least 9/11 and, arguably, as far back as the late 1970s and the unexpected success of the Iranian Revolution. As we have seen in recent years in relation to the recent Arab Spring events and political developments in many countries in the Middle East more generally, governance problems are at the heart of religion's involvement in regional and transnational terrorism which directly and seriously affects Western security interests.

Notes

1. "Islamic terrorism" refers to terrorist acts committed by individuals, such as members of al Qaeda or Islamic State, who profess Islamic or Islamist motivations or goals.
2. Following Schanzer 2002, I understand Islamic militancy as "a minority outgrowth of the [Islamic] faith that exudes a bitter hatred for Western ideas, including capitalism, individualism, and consumerism."
3. Lashkar-e-Taiba is variously translated into English as "Army of the Good," "Army of the Righteous," or "Army of the Pure."
4. An "Islamist" is a Muslim who is willing to use various political means to achieve his/her faith-derived objectives.
5. Of the more than twenty countries in the Middle East and North Africa, only Tunisia underwent a post-Arab Spring transition to democracy which has so far endured.

References

Brown, C. (2005) *Sovereignty, Rights and Justice. International Political Theory Today*. Cambridge: Polity.

Burke, J. (2015) "'There is No Silver Bullet': Isis, Al Qaida and the Myths of Terrorism," *Guardian*, 20 Aug.

Conetta, C. (2002) *Dislocating Alcyoneus: How to Combat Al-Qaeda and the New Terrorism*, Project on Defense Alternatives, Briefing Memo, 23, available online at <http://www.comw.org/pda/0206dislocate.html> [Accessed Mar. 2007].

Dolan, C. (2005) *In War we Trust. The Bush Doctrine and the Pursuit of Just War*. Aldershot: Ashgate.

Gregg, H. (2014) "Defining and Distinguishing Secular and Religious Terrorism," *Perspectives on Terrorism*, 8(2), available online at <http://www.terrorismanalysts.com/pt/index.php/pot/article/view/336/html> [Accessed Aug. 2015].

Halper, S., and J. Clarke (2004) *America Alone: The Neo-Conservatives and the Global Order*, Cambridge: Cambridge University Press.

Haynes, J. (2005a) *Comparative Politics in a Globalizing World*. Cambridge, Polity.

Haynes, J. (2005b) "Review Article: Religion and International Relations After '9/11'," *Democratization*, 12(3): 398–413.

Haynes, J. (2013) *An Introduction to Religion and International Relations*, 2nd. edn. Harlow: Pearson Education.

Haynes, J. (2014) *Faith-based Organizations at the United Nations*. New York: Palgrave Macmillan.

Held, D., and A. McGrew (2002) *Globalization/Anti-Globalization*. Cambridge: Polity.

Hurrell, A. (2002) "'There are No Rules' (George W. Bush): International Order After September 11," *International Relations*, 16(2): 185–204.

Huntington, S. (1993) "The Clash of civilisations?," *Foreign Affairs*, 72(3): 22–49, at p. 26.

Huntington, S. (1996) *The Clash of Civilizations*. New York: Simon & Schuster.

Juergensmeyer, M. (2016) "Religious Terrorism in Global Politics," in J. Haynes (ed.), *Routledge Handbook of Religion and Politics*, 2nd edn. Abingdon: Routledge, 367–78.

Martin, G. (2007) *Understanding Terrorism: Challenges, Perspectives and Issues*. New York: Sage.

Mendelsohn, B. (2005) "Sovereignty under Attack: The International Society Meets the Al Qaeda Network," *Review of International Studies*, 31: 45–68.

Murden, S. (2005) "Culture in World Affairs," in J. Baylis and S. Smith (eds), *The Globalization of World Politics*, 3rd edn. Oxford: Oxford University Press, 45–62.

Rosenberg, Matthew (2009) "A Year After Mumbai Attack, Militants Thrive," *Wall Street Journal*, 24 Nov, available online at <http://online.wsj.com/article/SB125901384192861229.html> [Accessed Jan. 2010].

Schanzer, J. (2002) "At War with Whom? A Short History of Radical Islam," *Doublethink*, Spring, available online at <http://www.meforum.org/168/at-war-with-whom> [Accessed Aug. 2015].

Shlapentokh, V., J. Woods and E. Shiraev, eds (2005) *America: Sovereign Defender or Cowboy Nation*. Aldershot: Ashgate.

Tankel, S. (2009) *Lashkar-e-Taiba: From 9/11 to Mumbai*. Report prepared for the International Centre for the Study of Radicalisation and Political Violence, Kings College, London, April/May, available online at <http://www.icsr.info/publications/papers/1240835356ICSRStephenTankelReport.pdf> [Accessed Jan. 2010].

Thomas, S. (2005) *The Global Resurgence of Religion and the Transformation of International Relations: The Struggle for the Soul of the Twenty-First Century*. New York and Basingstoke: Palgrave Macmillan.

CHAPTER 20

IDEOLOGY AND TERRORISM

ALIA BRAHIMI

INTRODUCTION

THE first British man to be convicted of Syria-related terror offences was probably not a committed jihadist at all. In 2014, Mashudur Choudhury was jailed for four years, for engaging in conduct in preparation for an act of terrorism. He had traveled to Syria with a group of five young men from Portsmouth, and social media evidence indicated that he either attended a terrorist training camp or prepared to do so.

However, unlike his fellow travelers, all but one of whom were eventually killed in Syria, Choudhury returned to the UK after just seventeen days. According to the judge, the Syria trip "was not a decision made by someone who was deeply committed or indeed someone who was driven by fundamental beliefs" (Whitehead, 2014a). Rather, the decision was taken by Choudhury as a way out of the lies and failures of his personal life, including a faked cancer diagnosis, the misuse of his sister-in-law's money for "treatment" trips to Singapore on prostitutes, an invented business, multiple online personalities, and a marriage under considerable strain. When Choudhury's wife heard of his latest "barmy" fantasy to travel to Syria, she told him in a text message to "go die, I really mean it just go. I'll be relieved. At last. At last" (Whitehead, 2014b).

Mashudur Choudhury's case bears out Martha Crenshaw's (2006) observation that terrorist behavior is always determined by a combination of factors. Terrorist motivations are extremely heterogeneous. As Jeff Victoroff (2005) established, "whatever his stated goals and group of identity, every terrorist, like every person, is motivated by his own complex of psychosocial experiences and traits." In this complex picture, political belief systems play a varying part.

According to Konrad Kellen (1990), "what characterises the terrorist is the political, or pseudo political, component of their motivations, which ordinary violent people lack." This political component is usually comprised of an ideology. Although ideology has been depicted as the most elusive concept in the whole of social science (McLellan 1995), for the purposes of this chapter, ideology will be understood as an action-orientated set of political ideas. Andrew Heywood (2003) notes that all ideologies offer an account of the existing order, advance a model of a desired future, and explain how political change ought to be brought about.

Ideology can play a powerful psychological role. A compelling study in the *American Review of Psychological Affairs* (Jost et al. 2009) posited three major classes of psychological variables which comprise the motivational substructure of political ideology: epistemic motives (ideology offers certainty), existential motives (ideology offers security), and relational motives (ideology offers solidarity).[1] But, beyond the way in which it may operate on the individual's psychology, can ideology be said to drive terrorism more generally?

In recent years, ideas have been viewed as serving a causal role in terrorism born of Islamic extremism, such that *Islam*—rather than merely radical Islamist ideology—has been assumed to be the primary driver of terrorist violence. For example, the popular American author and commentator Glenn Beck (2015), who estimated that 10 percent of the world's Muslims were terrorists, argued that "Islam is at the root of everything that terrorists from ISIS, al-Qaeda, Hizballah and Hamas say and do." A self-described "Muslim atheist," Ali Rizvi wrote that "it is often religion itself, not the 'distortion,' 'hijacking,' 'misrepresentation' or 'politicisation' of religion, that is the root cause."

In *Foreign Affairs*, Ayaan Hirsi Ali (2015) suggested that Islamic scripture causes terrorism. In his riposte to this line of argumentation, William McCants (2015) observed that Islamic scripture is a constant while Muslim political behavior has varied greatly throughout history. When in 2017 Mattel released a Barbie doll modeled on the Muslim-American fencer, Ibtihaj Muhammed, who wears a hijab, the American columnist Ann Coulter tweeted to her 1.79 million followers: "JIHAD BARBIE! ISIS Ken sold separately." This focus on Islam as a faith has led, intellectually, to a confused and distracting debate on the causes of radicalization and, practically, to a narrowing of the coalition against extremism, by making it more difficult for ordinary Muslims to take part.

In any case, our focus here is radical Islamist ideology, which is explicitly connected to violent terrorist acts by their perpetrators. But even with regard to this discrete set of violent ideas, scholars differ on their causal weight. Some confidently assert that "ideology, not poverty or illiteracy is the key driver of politically motivated violence" (Gunaratna, 2005), while others focus on poor governance, economic hardship, and state failure (e.g. Joffe 2013; Howard 2014).

In privileging the examination of ideology, which serves as an important framework for reference and meaning and enables terrorist leaders to both recruit and justify what they do, this chapter does not seek to ascribe to ideology an inevitably causal role. This issue will be returned to. First, this article will examine two of the key ideas underpinning modern jihadist ideology in general, and will then turn to ISIS (Islamic State of Iraq and al-Sham) ideology in particular. Finally, it will suggest some implications for the understanding of ideology and terrorism more generally.

Jihadist Ideology

One month after the September 11 attacks, President George W. Bush stated to an audience of American troops that Al Qaeda had "no country, no ideology; they're motivated by hate." However, by 2001 Al Qaeda did possess an advanced ideological framework, which was itself an outgrowth of many of the ideas and lines of argumentation that had been around since the mid-twentieth century (see e.g. Bonney 2004; Gerges 2005; Brahimi 2010). Among the most important of these were two interconnected arguments about the individual duty of jihad (authority) and self-defense (just cause).

Jihad as an Individual Duty

Right authority is one of the most important conditions in the Islamic ethic of war, and was often viewed as the decisive test of a conflict's legitimacy. The classical jurists developed a crucial distinction in this regard, between offensive jihad and defensive jihad. While the former required the sanction of the caliph, defensive jihad did not require the authority, nor even the existence, of a central Islamic sovereign. Furthermore, whereas offensive jihad entailed a collective duty upon the Muslim community as a whole (*fard kiffayah*), defensive *jihad* imposed an *individual* duty upon all able-bodied Muslims (*fard ayn*). That is, if an element of the Muslim community is attacked anywhere, it is the duty of Muslims everywhere to come to its aid.

It is worth emphasizing that historical Islamic precedents assumed that even situations of *fard ayn* would be organized and led by publicly constituted political leaders. In declaring jihad against Israel, the 1988 Charter of Hamas drew a direct analogy with the Crusades but, as John Kelsay (2007) pointed out, Salahadin was a publicly recognized authority and, more generally, the appeal to fighting as an individual duty appears as a summons to Muslim *rulers* in neighbouring provinces to come to the aid of their co-religionists in Syro-Palestine. Nevertheless, in the second part of the twentieth century, jihadist theorists seemed to reinterpret the notion of *fard ayn* as a popular uprising by private Muslim individuals. Joining the struggle was presented as not only justified but obligatory, given that all Muslims were supposed to come forward to fight when other Muslims were attacked, whether by despotic governments or invading imperialists.

For example, the coordinator of the assassination of Egyptian president Anwar Sadat, Abd al-Salam Faraj, wrote a short pamphlet in 1981 titled *The Neglected Duty* (reprinted in Jansen 1986). Aiming to revive the duty of jihad, Faraj argued that waging war against the apostate Egyptian authorities was a personal duty for every individual Muslim who was capable of fighting. Because Egypt's leaders were "raised at the tables of imperialism, be it Crusaderism, or Communism, or Zionism," the enemy lives right in the middle of the lands of Islam and has taken hold of the reins of power. Therefore, "it is clear that today *jihad* is an individual duty for every Muslim." However, Faraj's argument was concerned with revolutionary struggle at home, and it was directed at Muslims in Egypt. Indeed, his pamphlet became something of a manual for many Egyptian jihadists in the 1980s and 1990s (Gerges 2005).

Around the same time, a Palestinian cleric based in Afghanistan, Abdullah Azzam, began to extend the argument. In 1984 he wrote *Defence of the Muslim Lands*, in which he determined that repelling the Soviet invasion of Afghanistan was an individual duty for Muslims everywhere, not just for Afghans. Utilizing his background as a professor of Islamic jurisprudence, Azzam (1987) argued that the weight of tradition was unequivocal: it was an *individual duty* for every capable Muslim to join the caravan of jihad in Afghanistan. He presented jihad as akin to one of the five pillars of the faith, and conjured the image of the individual obligation spreading in the shape of a circle until it encompassed the whole world. As Thomas Hegghammer (2010) noted, Azzam's pan-Islamist doctrine broke with the consensus of both mainstream clerics and most extremist groups at the time: "Azzam essentially advocated universal private military participation in any territorial struggle pitting Muslims versus non-Muslims."

As up to 20,000 would-be fighters responded to Azzam's call, Osama bin Laden helped to fund and organize them in Peshawar, and later established a training camp inside Afghanistan at Jaji. Some of the militants who had been attracted to Afghanistan by Azzam's *fatwa* would go on to form the nucleus of a force, led by bin Laden, dedicated to fighting causes newly defined as Islamic: Al Qaeda. For his global jihad in defense of Muslims everywhere, bin Laden (2001b) utilized Azzam's pan-Islamic argument: "I say that *jihad* is without doubt mandatory for all Muslims, to free al-Aqsa or to save the weak in Palestine, Lebanon, Iraq, and all Islamic lands." He reached out to Muslim individuals qua Muslim individuals, rather than as members of politically organized communities. This subversion of established patterns of Islamic authority is one of the most profound impacts of modern jihadism. While the classical jurists had taken great pains to arrogate the use of justified coercion exclusively to the state apparatus, radical Islamists in the late twentieth century invited private Muslim individuals, wherever they may be, to take direct action.

ISIS ideology will be discussed in more detail later, but here we must observe that, given the declaration of a caliphate, the ISIS preoccupation was with describing an individual duty for Muslims everywhere to support the fledgling "Islamic State." This appeal tended to come in two forms. First, there was the directive for individual Muslims to migrate to the Islamic State: "Therefore, rush O Muslims to your state. Yes, it is your state... O Muslims everywhere, whoever is capable of performing *hijra* to the Islamic State then let him do so, because *hijra* to the land of Islam is obligatory" (Baghdadi 2014). Second, there was the call to individual Muslims living in the West to mount attacks at home: "We will argue before Allah against any Muslim who had the ability to shed a single drop of crusader blood but does not do so, whether with an explosive device, a bullet, a knife, a car, a rock, or even a boot or a fist" (Adnani 2015).

In this regard, ISIS leaders appeared to benefit from a combination of *fard kiffayah* and *fard ayn*. From the former concept, ISIS extracted the weight of caliphal authority for waging jihad, while from the latter it took the sense of urgency inhering in defensive jihad.

Self-Defense

The claim of self-defense, in one form or another, provides the centerpiece for most, but not all,[2] terrorist ideologies. Just as the Shi'a "assassins," a radical offshoot of the Ismaili sect in the eleventh–thirteenth centuries, "made extraordinary efforts to demonstrate that they acted defensively" (Rapoport 1984), so the Tamil Tigers depicted themselves as "freedom birds" acting against the oppression of the Sinhalese majority, where "even the one carrying the child in her womb / Sends her husband to the liberation war" (from a poem by M. Icaialakan in Hellmann-Rajanayagam 2005). Even West German terrorists, particularly the radical left-wing Red Army Faction which operated in the late 1960s and 1970s, felt they were defending themselves against an aggressive and murderous world (Kellen 1990). In fact, opposition to the Vietnam War was an important aspect of the Red Army Faction's narrative, and its first terrorist operation came in response to the US Air Force's mining of North Vietnam's Haiphong harbor (Hoffman 2006). With the end of the Vietnam War, the Palestinian cause was adopted as the new framework in which to carry forward the struggle against Western imperialism.

Palestine also formed the cornerstone of Al Qaeda's case for self-defense, which was elaborated by bin Laden both before and after the 9/11 attacks. In arguing that "he who commences hostilities is the unjust one," bin Laden (2004) engaged with the Islamic modernist tradition which viewed justified war as defensive war. Referring to his men as "freedom fighters" (bin Laden 1997), bin Laden insisted, time and time again, that his was "a defensive *jihad* against the American enemy" (2003). In a letter (bin Laden 2002) addressed to the American people, he stated plainly that "as for the question why are we fighting and opposing you, the answer is very simple: because you attacked us and continue to attack us."

However, given that the US had not launched any invasion of bin Laden's country before September 11, be it Saudi Arabia, Sudan, or Afghanistan, the notion of defensive warfare was problematic. As a result, it was incumbent upon bin Laden to qualify "aggression" in two critical ways. First, he employed a religious conception of the territorial entity that was being attacked (the entire Islamic *umma*). Second, he resorted to religious idioms when defining America's aggressive actions (symbolic attacks upon the sanctity of Islam and its holy sites).

Prior to the Bush administration's "war on terror," bin Laden had little to work with in suggesting that the US had launched an unprovoked assault. Bin Laden threw together a host of international injustices framed in Islamic terms (see e.g. bin Laden 1996), which ranged from the sanctions regime against Iraq in the 1990s to Western backing for tyrannical governments which harmed Muslims. However, the occupation of Palestine was the staple feature of this narrative. Given that bin Laden was not himself Palestinian—and given, further, that his attacks were aimed at the US more than they were at Israel—he relied upon the pan-Islamic spirit of Azzam's arguments. He avoided pinning down any single act of aggression as Al Qaeda's *causus belli* and instead claimed that there was a generalized campaign against Islam: "Bush has declared in his own words 'Crusade attack'. The odd thing about this is that he has taken the words right out of our mouth" (bin Laden 2001b).[3]

In this way, bin Laden's construction of his jihad as a classic case of self-defense involved fundamental revisions to the concept of aggression, which drew upon pan-Islamic identifiers and identities. A few months prior to September 11, he told the International Conference of Deobandis that "I write these lines to you at a time when every single inch of our umma's body is being stabbed by a spear, struck by a sword, or pierced by an arrow" (bin Laden 2001a). This was surely an implicit reference to the *hadith* which describes "the believers, in their love, mutual kindness, and close ties [as] like one body; when any part complains, the whole body responds to it with wakefulness and fever."

This Ladenese theme of defending an oppressed *umma* went on to infuse the statements of ISIS. For example, despite the triumphant declaration of the Caliphate, Baghdadi (2014) used his Ramadan address to describe the tragic state of Muslims worldwide:

> Prisoners are moaning and crying for help. Orphans and widows are complaining of their plight. Women who have lost their children are weeping. Mosques are desecrated and sanctities are violated. Muslims' rights are forcibly seized in China, India, Palestine, Somalia, the Arabian Peninsula, the Caucuses, the Levant, Egypt, Iraq, Indonesia, Afghanistan, the Philippines, Ahvaz, Pakistan, Tunisia, Libya, Algeria and Morocco, in the East and in the West...And the one who commences is the more oppressive.

In Syria and Iraq, this suffering was leveraged by radical groups to attract the type of foreign fighter that is more drawn in by compassion than by bloodlust.

For example, the first British suicide bomber in Syria, Abdul Waheed Majeed, originally traveled to the north of the country in an aid convoy, explaining to his family that "Assad was not letting aid get in and people were being bombed, families torn apart" (Ramesh 2014). His brother believed that he was radicalized by what he saw and heard while in Syria. After photographic evidence emerged of the Syrian regime's torture chambers, Majeed joined the Al Qaeda linked Jabhat al Nusra and drove an explosive-laden dump truck into the gates of the notorious Aleppo central prison. Another British foreign fighter in Syria, Ifthekar Jaman, explained to the BBC that he left Portsmouth to join ISIS because "this is the duty on me...all these people are suffering. Muslims are being slaughtered" (Watson 2013). Again, therefore, we encounter the relatively new but abounding assumption that private Muslim individuals have a religious duty to defend their Sunni brethren across the seas.

ISIS Ideology

Millenarianism

The most striking aspect of ISIS ideology was its powerful eschatological component. Although many other radical Islamist belief systems have included a millenarian strain, ISIS pushed to the fore the description of violence as hastening a new millennium. In so doing, it had much in common with the terrorist groups that emerged from within a Christian or Jewish framework, as all three Abrahamic faiths suggest that a messianic deliverer will return at the end of time to fill the world with justice.

David Rapoport and Bruce Hoffman have long documented the millenarian roots of Christian and Jewish terrorist activity. Rapoport (1990) found that "Jewish and Christian terrorists (who are almost always millenarian) are antinomian, aiming at producing a catastrophic social struggle, acting as if they believed that Hell must precede Paradise." Christian terrorism tends to be related to a vision for the Second Coming as it is described in the Book of Revelation. Hoffman showed how proselytizers of Dominion theology asserted that it was incumbent upon each individual to hasten redemption by working to ensure the return of the Messiah, thus ending the burdens afflicting the American Christian white male: "the apocalypse will be followed by a thousand-year period of rule by Christians, at the end of which Christ will return to earth" (Hoffman 2006).

Centuries before, in AD 66–73 a Jewish sect known as the "Zealots-Sicarii" launched a vicious campaign of assassination and hostage-taking, which aimed at expelling the Roman occupiers from lands that comprise present-day Israel. According to Rapoport (1984), many of the actions of the Zealots-Sicarii, including the decision to burn their own food supply during the long siege of Jerusalem, are only intelligible in the context of their search for the signs of Messianic intervention, and their ultimate belief that the most profound disaster would create new hope. This same preoccupation with a divine audience is evidenced in Jewish terrorist movements that emerged in the early 1980s. These ultranationalist groups were often followers of the virulently anti-Arab Rabbi Meir Kahane, who believed that "it is precisely our refusal to deal with the Arabs according to halakhic [Jewish religious law] obligation that will bring down on our heads terrible sufferings, whereas our courage in removing them will be one of the major factors in the hurrying of the final redemption" (Hoffman 2006).

In 1984, an ultra-Zionist settler movement, Gush Emunim, plotted to blow up one of the holiest shrines in Islam, the Dome of the Rock in Jerusalem, with twenty-eight precision bombs. The aim was to provoke a war between Palestinians and Israelis which would end with the triumph of the Jews, the expulsion of Palestinians, and the return of the Messiah (Pope 2003). Thirty years later, in August 2015, the grandson of Meir Kahane, Meir Ettinger, was arrested by the Israeli authorities in response to an uptick in hate crimes, including the death of a Palestinian infant in a Molotov cocktail attack on his home. Ettinger was suspected of being a member of a shadowy youth network known as "the Revolt," which sought to bring down the Israeli state. "They want the Messiah to come, to bring back the Kingdom of Israel, like in the days of King David, to rebuild the temple and drive out all idolaters, meaning Muslims and Christians," explained one former Shin Bet officer (Kershner 2015).

The Ismaili "assassins" formed the most legendary[4] millenarian sect of Islam, and survived for two centuries. The assassins' weapon of choice was the dagger, which, beginning in 1090, their agents would plunge into the backs of the senior religious and political figures who interfered with their missionaries and obstructed their preaching. Always aiming to be captured or killed (and thereby martyred), the goal of the assassins' violence was to purify Islam in order to expedite the return of the Mahdi (Redeemer). Indeed, this concept is ingrained into the fabric of Shi'a Islam, the largest school of which believes that the last of the twelve Imams (the rightful successors of the Prophet) went into occultation in the tenth century but will eventually re-emerge.[5]

As with their cultivation of a "cult of martyrdom,"[6] radical Sunni groups have often dwelled upon the ideas of a messianic deliverer (not mentioned in the Quran) and the imminence of the end times, which are more readily associated with Shi'a Islam.[7] Though the group has moderated since its founding, the original Charter of Hamas (1988), for example, cited the "rocks and trees" *hadith*: "The Time will not come until Muslims fight the Jews and kill them, until the Jews hide behind rocks and trees, which will cry: O Muslim! There is a Jew hiding behind me, come on and kill him." The *hadith* are oral traditions which sought to record the word and deed of the Prophet Mohammed, and formed an important part of the Islamic legal system (see Guillaume 1924). Indeed, it is usually *hadith* sources—the more obscure ones, at that—which are relied upon by radical Sunni groups for their millenarian narratives. Many of these traditions did not enter the canonical collections, such as *Sahih al-Bukhari* or *Sahih Muslim*, but were instead assimilated into a body of apocalyptic literature (Cook 2005a).

Al Qaeda popularized a disputed[8] *hadith* which referred to Khurasan, the Sassanian name given to a region encompassing parts of present-day Iran, Tajikistan, Turkmenistan, Uzbekistan, and, crucially, Afghanistan: "If you see the black banners coming from Khurasan, join that army, even if you have to crawl over ice; no power will be able to stop them and they will finally reach Jerusalem, where they will erect their flags." This *hadith* was the inspiration for Al Qaeda's black flag and provided a rationale for its base in Afghanistan. These words appeared in Al Qaeda propaganda and on sympathetic web forums and, when asked by his FBI interrogator why he thought Al Qaeda would be victorious, Abu Jandal, a senior aide and bodyguard to Osama bin Laden, recited them in response (Soufan 2011). The *hadith* also recalled one messianic trend which expects the Mahdi to appear with Jesus in Khurasan before the end of time to fill the world with light.[9]

In order to bolster his moral authority to declare jihad, Osama bin Laden sought to exploit the fact that Khurasan "has powerful resonance with many Muslims because of the messianic expectations focused on that region" (Cook 2005b). However, bin Laden rarely made direct reference to the end times, the Mahdi or the apocalypse. By contrast, a hallmark of ISIS ideology was an explicit preoccupation with these messianic expectations, but with a geographic focus on its heartlands in the Levant.

One lengthy *hadith* attributed to the Prophet Mohammed references Dabiq, a town in northern Syria, where an apocalyptic battle will occur between the armies of Islam and Rome. The struggle ends with the arrival of the Redeemer, and "when the enemy of Allah sees him, he will melt as salt melts in water." ISIS propagandists named their recruitment magazine after the town and regularly employed a 2004 quotation from Abu Mus'ab al-Zarqawi: "the spark has been lit here in Iraq and its heat will continue to intensify – by Allah's permission – until it burns the Crusader armies in Dabiq." In 2014, ISIS fighters battled ferociously with other Syrian rebels to capture the strategically insignificant town, and then took to staging their beheadings of Western hostages there. "Here we are burning the first American Crusader in Dabiq, eagerly waiting for the remainder of your armies to arrive," one British executioner said to the camera (Al-Furqan Media 2014).

One article in *Dabiq* magazine (Al-Hayat Media 2014) explores a series of quotations from the founders of ISIS on signs of the Hour. "This type of certain conviction is hard for many people to comprehend," it notes. The piece includes a statement from Zarqawi's successor, Abu Hamza al-Muhajir (also known as Abu Ayyub al-Masri): "I do not doubt for a moment—and Allah knows such—that we are the army that will pass on the banner to the slave of Allah, the Mahdi." Certainly, it was under the leadership of Zarqawi and al-Masri that this millenarianism became a defining characteristic of the predecessor groups to ISIS. Towards the end of the US occupation of Iraq, they saw signs of the end times everywhere and were anticipating, within a year, the arrival of the Mahdi (Wood 2015).

When ISIS was founded, this anticipation carried over. The first official ISIS spokesman, Adnani (2015), promised that the "Crusader" armies will be defeated in Dabiq and ISIS "will then have a meeting in Jerusalem and an appointment in Rome." Here, he may well have been referring to the belief, common in ISIS circles, that after the decisive battle in Dabiq, ISIS fighters will capture Jerusalem. The Antichrist will then appear and slaughter all but 5,000 of ISIS's men, who will ultimately be rescued by Jesus, before conquering the world. Indeed, the seventh issue of *Dabiq* noted that "the sword will continue to be drawn, raised and swung until Jesus kills the Antichrist… [Thereafter] Islam and justice will prevail on the entire Earth" (Al-Hayat Media 2015a). Even the horrific practice of enslaving Yazidi women and children was directly justified with reference to the coming apocalypse. Another marginal *hadith* was invoked, which counts as one of the signs of the Hour a situation where "a slave girl gives birth to her master" (Al-Hayat Media 2014).

Nearer Enemies

Millenarianism has an important function for the ideologies of groups which do not target traditional combatants. This is because antinomianism, coupled with the focus on a divine audience, entails the celebration of violence and death. Accordingly, unlike the Nazis, for example, ISIS readily publicized its large-scale killing. This mostly took place among communities within native ISIS territories in Syria and Iraq. Indeed, the second major shift represented by ISIS ideology is the explicit focus on what might be termed the "nearer enemy."

Osama bin Laden waged war on the "far enemy" as a means of weakening the "near enemy" (Gerges 2005; Atwan 2006), but in the years after 9/11 Al Qaeda offshoots focused on the "nearer enemy": impure elements of society. While affiliates such as Al Qaeda in the Arabian Peninsula (AQAP) maintained their focus on the US and its allies, groups in Iraq, Pakistan, and elsewhere anathematized neighbors loyal to other religions and Islamic sects, employing brutal tactics for largely local ends, and often killing for killing's sake. Bin Laden (2001c) had described Al Qaeda's foundational mission as "a defensive *jihad* to protect our land and people," yet after 9/11 the victims of groups affiliated with Al Qaeda were most often Muslim civilians. Intercepted communications revealed that the group's central leadership was unable to halt this misdirected violence, which ultimately had a strategic impact (see Abdelrahman 2005; Zawahiri 2005). As bin Laden recognized, the killing of Muslims resulted in "the alienation of most of the [Islamic] nation from the mujahidin" (bin Laden 2010).

By contrast, ISIS ideology fully embraced the *jihad*'s inward turn. To begin with, its basis was unabashedly anti-Shiite. It built on the worldview elaborated by Abu Mus'ab al-Zarqawi, who described the Shi'a using genocidal language, dubbing them "the most vile people in the human race," "the prowling serpent, the crafty, evil scorpion," and "gangrene" (Zarqawi 2004). ISIS literature sought to dehumanize the Shi'a as "filthy mushrikin" (Al-Hayat Media 2015b), and regularly derided them as *rafidah* (rejecters of the truth), hypocrites, Magians, Sabeans, Safavids, Nusayriyyah (for the Alawi sect in Syria), and "the sons of al-Alqami." This latter term refers to Ibn al-Alqami, a Shi'a vizier to the caliph who was believed to have helped the Mongols sack Baghdad in the thirteenth century. The forerunners of ISIS, Al Qaeda in Iraq (AQI) and the Islamic State of Iraq, used this interpretation of Islamic history to direct the charge of *takfir* against Iraqi Shi'a as a collective, accusing them of collusion with the US-led occupation. Baghdadi's November 2014 audio address identified the Shi'a as the primary enemy and he described his fighters as "those who humiliate the *rafidah* in their strongholds and their major fortresses every day. How good you are! How good you are! We consider one of you equal to a thousand" (Baghdadi 2015).

By extension, ISIS had an aggressive posture towards religious minorities. The group's summer 2014 campaign against Iraq's Yazidis, who were ordered to convert or face death, inspired revulsion around the world and partly prompted greater Western military involvement in the region. Propaganda disseminated by ISIS boasted of reviving the institution of slavery in dealing with Yazidi women and children, portraying members of their sect as pagans: "their creed is so deviant from the truth that even cross-worshipping Christians for ages considered them devil worshippers and Satanists" (Al-Hayat Media 2014). And the grisly ultimatum given to the Yazidis was extended to Christians in Iraq and Syria.

In addition, ISIS did not try to conceal its harsh treatment of Sunnis, as part of its commitment to a brutal, puritanical application of *shari'a* law within the territory it administered, and in service to its bid for further expansion outside it. Certainly, ISIS aggressively linked jihad to the acquisition and administration of territory. This territorial project tied the group to a vision of society that made dealing with "bad Muslims" more fundamental than attacking the West, if not more urgent. Propagandists posted to the internet multiple video clips of public executions in territories under its control, including the stoning to death of women for adultery, and the hurling of "homosexuals" from rooftops. No doubt, ISIS probably killed more Sunnis than Shi'a (Soufan Group 2014). These social purges were likely also linked to the jihadist vision of the Mahdi, whose primary enemies will be those Muslims who resist his rise to power (Cook 2005a).

The official ISIS spokesman suggested that any Muslim who did not bow to Baghdadi's authority lived in sin (Adnani 2014). One IS mural in Tel Afar bore a quote from Abdullah Azzam: "if you want to liberate a land, place in your gun ten bullets. Nine for the traitors and one for the enemy" (Tamimi 2015a). To that end, ISIS waged war on other hardline Sunni groups, including Jabhat al Nusra and Jama'at Ansar al-Islam in Syria, the Abu Salim Martyr's Brigade in Libya, Ansar al-Sharia in Yemen, and other Salafi organizations in Gaza and the Palestinian refugee camps in Lebanon. It also conducted campaigns of executions against the Sunni tribes of Iraq's Anbar Province, particularly the Albu Nimr. The group even established an "Islamic Military Police" unit at its capital, Raqqa, to deal with dissenting fighters and deserters within its own ranks. After the horrific burning of a Jordanian pilot, reports emerged of the arrest in Aleppo of a Saudi cleric who had voiced his objections. ISIS executed hundreds of its own, including its spiritual leader in Deir Ezzour, Abu Abdullah al-Kuwaiti, the chief of security in Aleppo, Abu Obeida al-Maghrebi, and dozens of foreign fighters who allegedly plotted a coup.

In its search for "purity," the ISIS project was predicated on a theoretically endless process of cleavage and excommunication. The doctrine of *takfir* was deeply engrained in its ideological program. A pamphlet which laid out the ISIS creed confidently stated that "we declare *takfir* on whomsoever God and His Messenger declare to be a disbeliever. And everyone who professed something besides Islam is a disbeliever" (Tamimi 2015b). The mechanism of *takfir* seeks to differentiate between "true" and "false" Muslims and involves the declaration by one Muslim that another is not a real Muslim but an apostate. Because of its sensitivity, and the inherent danger of shedding Muslim blood, historically the practice of *takfir* was held to be the sole prerogative of the religious establishment which, for the most part, shied away from using it. In the fourteenth century, ibn Taymiyyah famously used the charge against the Mongols, arguing that it was permissible to fight them despite the Tatar dynasty's conversion to Islam, because they did not strictly apply the *shari'a*. Sayyed Qutb revived the doctrine of *takfir* during Nasser's crackdown on the Muslim Brotherhood in the 1950s, but until then it was seldom used in Islamic history and heresy trials were extremely rare. Qutb's invocation of *takfir* marked a departure from the Islamist mainstream and it became a key issue in the formation of more radical movements.

Al Takfir wa al-Hijra,[10] for example, took Qutb's theory to its logical conclusion, and pronounced *takfir* on the whole Muslim world with the exception of the group's members. In the late 1970s, these fighters were instructed to break all ties with Egyptian society, a great many of them were installed in caves in Upper Egypt, and, as a result, the short-lived group was widely viewed as a cult. During the Algerian civil war in the 1990s, the Armed Islamic Group (GIA) similarly anathematized the world around it, eventually levying the charge of *takfir* against the entire Algerian population. The Al Qaeda leadership was highly critical of this ideological move by the GIA, as well as of its ever more brutal campaign against Algerian civilians, and supported the rise of the Salafist Group for Preaching and Combat against it. Certainly, bin Laden (1995) had himself drawn upon the doctrine of *takfir* in calling for the overthrow of the House of Saud, but he never pronounced *takfir* against ordinary Muslims.

In fact, both bin Laden and Zawahiri actively courted the Muslim population at large, including members of minority sects and other faiths living among Muslims. They placed great emphasis on the integrity and unity of the *umma*. For the fanaticism of Al Qaeda affiliated groups in Iraq, bin Laden (2007) apologized. More recently, Zawahiri (2014) lamented that the expansion of the suicide attacks he once championed led to greater transgression. "We must be concerned for the sanctities and the blood that the *shari'a* made inviolable," he stressed in one interview. In *General Guidelines for Jihad*, a document released by Al Qaeda's official media foundation in 2013, Zawahiri argued that the mujahideen should remain focused on attacking the West. They should not fight "deviant sects" or "Christian, Sikh and Hindu communities living in Muslim lands." If forced to act in self-defense, only those who bear arms may be targeted—and with a proportionate response. No total war against nearer enemies, then.

For the ISIS war on impurity, these battles could not be separated. As a result, ISIS brought together different jihadist preoccupations under one umbrella: "O Jews, O Crusaders, O Rafidah, O murtaddin, O sahwat, O criminals, O enemies of Allah altogether!" (Adnani 2015). As such, ISIS sought to pose a combined threat to the West, the state, and Middle Eastern society.

Of course, ISIS was not the first modern terrorist group to anathematize large categories of people in search of purity. For example, in the 1980s Gunter Rohrmoser observed of the Red Army Faction in West Germany:

> They are fascinated by the magic of the extremes, the hard and uncompromising either/or, life or death, salvation or perdition, "pig" or man—with nothing in between. They recognize only one principle: unconditional consistency. Any compromise they do not even regard as weakness, but as treason. They are driven by their pitiless hatred for those they look upon as their enemies, a hatred fed by a disgust with what they regard as a morbid, decadent society of sly and immoral practices and mendacious hypocrisy. (Kellen 1990)

Uncompromising and destructive beliefs are not uncommon among utopian terrorist groups. For ISIS, however, these beliefs combined with both the capability and political opportunity to follow through on an unprecedented scale.

Ideology and Terrorism

The discussion in this chapter yields two implications for ideology and terrorism generally. In the first place, terrorist ideologies which integrate a nationalist aspect may enjoy greater longevity than those that do not.

ISIS ideology is underpinned by a separatist current, involving a fierce form of Sunni nationalism. This is both a cause and an effect of the politicization of sectarian affiliation in Iraq (and Syria). It was in the context of highly charged nationalism, in post-invasion Iraq, that the seeds for the transnational Caliphate were sown. ISIS and its predecessor groups emerged after the US-led military intervention, during the subsequent years of foreign occupation and (Shi'a-led) government repression.[11] Its ideology was incubated in a situation where "Washington has snatched Iraq from the hands of 'true' Islam and delivered it to 'heretical' Shias" (Nasr 2006). In fact, the ISIS strategy for seizing power was first articulated by Abu Mus'ab al-Zarqawi (2004), who sought to draw the Shi'a into battle by striking their communities and triggering their rage against the Sunni. When they retaliated, Iraqi Sunnis would be torn away from their complacency and forced into war against the Shi'a: "Our fight against the Shi'a is the way to draw the nation of Islam [Sunnis] into battle." ISIS has therefore been described as the "revenge of the Sunni" (Joffe 2015).

As a result, and despite its pronounced millenarian features and hyper-religious presentation, ISIS may well go on to support Audrey Cronin's observation that, compared to left-wing and right-wing terrorism, "terrorist groups motivated by ethnonationalist/separatist causes have had the longest average life span; their greater average longevity seems to result, at least in part, from support among the local populace of the same ethnicity for the group's political or territorial objectives" (Cronin 2006). Of course, for the case of ISIS, the characteristic shared with the local populace is more accurately described as sect. This feature of ISIS ideology may become especially useful in its quest to overtake and outlast Al Qaeda. And it goes some way to explaining how, despite losing almost all of its previously held territory in Iraq and Syria, including its capital at Raqqa in October 2017, ISIS was still estimated to have 20,000–30,000 fighters (United Nations 2018).

Second, and consequently, challenging terrorist ideology is a necessary step in combatting terrorism, but it is by no means sufficient. With its fixation upon the Redeemer, its mission of purifying the world, and its cultish characteristics, ISIS looks like an ideologically driven phenomenon par excellence. Yet its rise is inextricably linked to widespread insecurity in Iraq and Syria, the entrenchment of armed conflict, and the desperation of local populations who find no neutral or effective alternative in the official government.

Many of the foreign fighters flocking to ISIS from stable Western democracies may well have been radicalized solely by virtue of the appeal of ideas. However, while there has long been an emphasis on ideas-based radicalization, it is important to recognize that much of the radicalization that takes place outside the Western world is grievance-based (Brahimi and Mackmurdo 2015). Ideas do play a role, but grievances, many of them desperate and real, provide the critical context in which ideas take hold. Terrorism that becomes embedded in situations of conflict and mass killing is likely driven by grievances attendant to that destruction. Of course, for scholars and analysts, ideology offers an indispensable window into the moral universe of the terrorist, including the way in which he understands his actions, the wider world, and his place in it. However, contra Gunaratna, ideology may not always be the "key driver" of terrorism—particularly in the context of widespread instability.

Notes

1. Marc Sageman 2004 dwelled upon this relational element, when he argued that social bonds precede ideological commitment. His *Understanding Terror Networks* emphasised the social affiliation with *jihad* accomplished through friendship, kinship, and discipleship.
2. The Hindu Thugs, for example, who persisted for roughly 600 years and may have murdered half a million people, strangled their victims simply to please the Hindu goddess Kali.
3. Talking to reporters on the White House lawn on September 16, 2001, Bush veered off script and stated that "this Crusade, this war on terrorism is going to take a while."
4. The legend of the Assassins surrounds their reputed penchant for hashish, their fanatical commitment to their cause, and the practice of planting within the household of a target a young devotee who would dissemble for years until, at the instructed hour, he would stab his master in the back. The earliest accounts of them described pork-eating men who lived without law and practiced incest. Their deep devotion was especially noteworthy: "The bond of submission of this people to their Chief is so strong, that there is no task so arduous, difficult or dangerous that any of them would not undertake to perform it with the greatest zeal, as soon as the Chief has commanded it. If for example there be a prince who is hated or mistrusted by this people, the Chief gives a dagger to one or more of his follower. At once whoever receives the command sets out on his mission, without considering the consequences of the deed nor the possibility of escape." From a twelfth-century account by William, Archbishop of Tyre, see Lewis 1970.
5. To the consternation of outside observers and the Iranian clerical establishment alike, Mahmoud Ahmadinejad, Iran's maverick President from 2005 to 2013, claimed that "the Imam-Mahdi is in charge of the world and we see his hand directing all of the affairs of the country."
6. Navid Kermani 2002 observed after the 9/11 attacks that that the cult of martyrdom had been a Shi'a phenomenon which developed in opposition to the Islamic majority. Many of its spiritual and ritual elements are "alien to the nature of Sunni Islam, such as the idea of redemption, the need for repentance, the practice of flagellation and the idea of an imitation of suffering." As such, Al Qaeda's suicide bombers were borrowing from a past which was not even their own.
7. Crone 2005 argues that from the later Umayyad period down to the end of the Fatimid caliphate, Mahdisim had been an overwhelmingly Shi'a phenomenon. When Sunnis did put the idea to political use, "their conception of the Mahdic role comes across as strikingly different from that of the Shi'ites. None of them predicted (or was posthumously made to predict) an imminent, total, and violent transformation of the world; none of them declared the resurrection to be imminent, be it in the literal or spiritual sense; and it was not with a view to being on the right side of the coming cataclysm that any of them took to fighting."

8. The chain of transmission for this *hadith* has been called into question by many Islamic scholars who consider it to be *da'if* (weak).
9. The other asserts that he will appear in Mecca during the Hajj.
10. This was the name given to the group by the Egyptian security services; the founders had called themselves the "Society of Muslims."
11. President Nuri al-Maliki, who led Iraq from 2006 to 2014, was widely accused of promoting a sectarian agenda. When, in 2013, protesters in the Anbar province decried the government's marginalization of Sunni leaders, sweeping anti-terror laws, and endemic corruption, Maliki sent in the armed forces. At the same time, in a televised address he described the issue as part of an ancient war between the partisans of the third Shi'a Imam, Hussein, and the son of the first Umayyad ruler, Yezid, in the seventh century.

References

Abdelrahman, A. (2005) Letter to Abu Mus'ab al-Zarqawi, Dec. 11.

Adnani, A.M. al- (2014) Audio message of June 29, titled "This is the Promise of Allah."

Adnani, A.M. al- (2015) Audio message of Jan. 26, titled "Say Die in Your Rage!"

Al-Furqan Media (2014) Video titled "Although the Disbelievers Dislike it," Nov. 16.

Al-Hayat Media (2014) *Dabiq Issue 4: The Failed Crusade*, Oct.

Al-Hayat Media (2015a) *Dabiq Issue 7: From Hypocrisy to Apostasy*, Feb.

Al-Hayat Media (2015b) *Dabiq Issue 9: They Plot and Allah Plots*, May.

Ali, A. H. (2015) "A Problem from Heaven: Why the United States Should Back Islam's Reformation," *Foreign Affairs* (July/Aug.) 94(4).

Atwan, A. B. (2006) *The Secret History of Al-Qaeda*. Berkeley, CA: University of California Press.

Azzam, A. Y. (1984) *Defence of the Muslim Lands: The First Obligation After Faith*, available online at <https://archive.org/stream/Defense_of_the_Muslim_Lands/Defense_of_the_Muslim_Lands_djvu.txt> [Accessed Oct. 2004].

Azzam, A. Y. (1987) *Join the Caravan*. London: Azzam Publications.

Baghdadi, A. B. al- (2014) Audio message of 1 July, titled "A Message to the Mujahidin and the Muslim Umma in the Month of Ramadan."

Baghdadi, A. B. al- (2015) Audio message of May 14, titled "March Forth Whether Light or Heavy."

Beck, G. (2015) *It IS about Islam: Exposing the Truth about ISIS, Al-Qaeda, Iran and the Caliphate*. New York: Threshold Editions.

Bin Laden, O. (1995) *Risala Maftouha Ila Al-Malik Fahd Bimunasiba Al-Ta'dil Al-Wazari Al-Akhir*, Committee of Advice and Reform, July 11.

Bin Laden, O. (1996) Declaration of Jihad, Aug. 23.

Bin Laden, O. (1997) Interview with Peter Arnett, Mar.

Bin Laden, O. (2001a) Audiotape message to International Conference of Deobandis held in Peshawar, Apr. 9.

Bin Laden, O. (2001b) Interview with Taysir Alluni, Oct. 21.

Bin Laden, O. (2001c) Interview with Hamid Mir, Nov. 12.

Bin Laden, O. (2002) Letter to the Americans, Oct. 6.

Bin Laden, O. (2003) Audiotape address to the people of Iraq, Feb. 11.

Bin Laden, O. (2004). Television address to the peoples of Europe, Apr. 15.

Bin Laden, O. (2007) Audiotape message to our people in Iraq, Oct. 23.

Bin Laden, O. (2010) Letter addressed to Atiyeh Abdelrahman, recovered at Abbottabad compound, July–Oct. Combating Terrorism Centre, "Letters from Abbottabad: Bin Ladin Sidelined?", available online at <http://www.ctc.usma.edu/posts/letters-from-abbottabad-bin-ladin-sidelined>.

Bonney, R. (2004) *Jihad: From Qur'an to bin Laden*. New York: Palgrave Macmillan.

Brahimi, A. (2010) *Jihad and Just War in the War on Terror*. Oxford: Oxford University Press.

Brahimi, A., and C. Mackmurdo (2015) "Defining a Full-Spectrum Counter-Terrorism Strategy," International Institute for Strategic Studies, July 22, available online at <https://www.iiss.org/en/iiss%20voices/blogsections/iiss-voices-2015-dda3/july-2632/a-full-spectrum-counter-terrorism-strategy-9caf>.

Bush, G. W. (2001) "President Rallies Troops at Travis Air Force Base," Oct. 17 , available online at <https://georgewbush-whitehouse.archives.gov/news/releases/2001/10/20011017-20.html>.

Cook, D. (2005a) *Contemporary Muslim Apocalyptic Literature*. Syracuse, NY: Syracuse University Press.

Cook, D. (2005b) *Understanding Jihad*. Berkeley: University of California Press.

Crenshaw, M. (2006) "Have Motivations for Terrorism Changed?," in J. Victoroff (ed.), *Tangled Roots: Social and Psychological Factors in the Genesis of Terrorism*. Amsterdam: IOS Press, 51–60.

Crone, P. (2005) *Medieval Islamic Political Thought*. Edinburgh: Edinburgh University Press.

Cronin, A. (2006) "How Al-Qaeda Ends: The Decline and Demise of Terrorist Groups," *International Security*, 31(1): 7–48.

Gerges, F. (2005) *The Far Enemy: Why Jihad Went Global*. Cambridge: Cambridge University Press.

Guillaume, A. (1924) *The Traditions of Islam: An Introduction to the Study of the Hadith Literature*. Oxford: Clarendon Press.

Gunaratna, R. (2005) "Ideology in Terrorism and Counter Terrorism: Lessons from Combatting Al Qaeda and Al Jemaah Al Islamiyah in Southeast Asia," CSRC discussion paper 05/42 September.

Hamas (1988) "The Covenant of the Islamic Resistance Movement, 18 August 1988", available online at at <http://avalon.law.yale.edu/20th_century/hamas.asp>.

Hegghammer T. (2010) *Jihad in Saudi Arabia: Jihad and Pan-Islamism since 1979*. Cambridge: Cambridge University Press.

Hellmann-Rajanayagam, D. (2005) "And Heroes Die: Poetry of the Tamil Liberation Movement in Northern Sri Lanka," *South Asia: Journal of South Asian Studies*, 28(1): 112–53.

Heywood, A. (2003) *Political Ideologies*, 3rd edn. New York: Palgrave Macmillan.

Hoffman, B. (2006) *Inside Terrorism*. New York: Columbia University Press.

Howard, Tiffiany (2014) *Failed States and the Origins of Violence: A Comparative Analysis of State Failure as a Root Cause of Terrorism and Political Violence*. Farnham: Ashgate.

Jansen, J. (1986) *The Neglected Duty: The Creed of Sadat's Assassins and Islamic Resurgence in the Middle East*. New York: Macmillan.

Joffe, G., ed. (2013) *Islamist Radicalisation in Europe and the Middle East: Reassessing the Causes of Terrorism*. New York: I. B. Tauris & Co.

Joffe, G. (2015) "Theologies of Difference: The Takfiri Vision," Presentation delivered at All Souls College, Oxford, July 14.

Jost. J. T., C. M. Federico, and J. L. Napier (2009) "Political Ideology: Its Structure, Functions and Elective Affinities," *American Review of Psychological Affairs*, 60: 307–37.

Kellen, K. (1990) "Ideology and Rebellion: Terrorism in West Germany," In W. Reich (ed.), *Origins of Terrorism: Psychologies, Ideologies, Theologies, States of Mind*. Washington, DC: Woodrow Wilson Center Press, 43–58.

Kelsay, J. (2007) *Arguing the Just War in Islam*. Cambridge, MA: Harvard University Press.

Kermani, N. (2002) "A Dynamite of the Spirit: Why Nietzsche, Not the Koran, is the Key to Understanding the Suicide Bombers," *Times Literary Supplement*, Mar. 29.

Kershner, I. (2015) "Israel Continues Crackdown on Jewish Extremist Network in West Bank," *New York Times*, Aug. 9.

Lewis, B. (1970) *The Assassins: A Radical Sect in Islam*. London: Weidenfeld & Nicolson.

McCants, W. (2015) "Islamic Scripture is Not the Problem: And Funding Muslim Reformers is Not the Solution," *Foreign Affairs* (July/Aug.): 94(4).

McLellan, D. (1995) *Ideology: Concepts in Social Thought* (Buckingham: Open University Press).

Nasr, V. (2006) *The Shi'a Revival: How Conflicts within Islam will Shape the Future*. New York: Norton.

Pope, R. (2003) "Acts of Holy Terror? Fundamentalisms Re-examined," in R. Pope (ed.), *Honouring the Past and Shaping the Future*. Leominster: Gracewing, 213–32.

Ramesh, R. (2014) "My Brother, the Suicide Bomber: Why British Men Go to Syria," *Guardian*, July 26.

Rapoport, D. C. (1984) "Fear and Trembling: Terrorism in Three Religious Traditions," *American Political Science Review*, 78(3): 658–77.

Rapoport, D. C. (1990) "Sacred Terror: A Contemporary Example from Islam," in W. Reich (ed.), *Origins of Terrorism: Psychologies, Ideologies, Theologies, States of Mind*. Washington, DC: Woodrow Wilson Center Press, 103–30.

Rizvi, A. (2013) "An Atheist Muslim's Perspective on the 'Root Causes' of Islamist Jihadism and the Politics of Islamophobia," Huffington Post, Mar. 5.

Sageman, M. (2004) *Understanding Terror Networks*. Philadelphia: University of Pennsylvania Press.

Soufan, A. (2011) *The Black Banners: The Inside Story of 9/11 and the War Against al-Qaeda*. New York: W. W. Norton & Co.

Soufan Group (2014) "The Islamic State's Fear of History," Nov. 17.

Tamimi, A. J. al- (2015a) "The Islamic State Billboards and Murals of Tel Afar." Blog post dated Jan. 7, available online at <http://www.aymennjawad.org/2015/01/the-islamic-state-billboards-and-murals-of-tel>.

Tamimi, A. J. al- (2015b) "This is Our Aqeeda and This is Our Manhaj: Islam 101 According to the Islamic State." Blog post dated Oct. 27, available online at <http://www.aymennjawad.org/2015/10/this-is-our-aqeeda-and-this-is-our-manhaj-islam#continued>.

United Nations Security Council (2018) "Letter Dated 16 July 2018 From the Chair of the Security Council Committee Pursuant to Resolutions 1267 (1999), 1989 (2011) and 2253 (2015) Concerning Islamic State in Iraq and the Levant (Da'esh), Al-Qaida and associated individuals, groups, undertakings and entities addressed to the President of the Security Council", available online at <http://undocs.org/S/2018/705>.

Victoroff, J. (2005) "The Mind of the Terrorist: A Review and Critique of Psychological Approaches," *Journal of Conflict Resolution*, 49(1): 3–42.

Watson, R. (2013) "Briton 'Doing His Duty' by Fighting for Group Linked to al-Qaeda in Syria," *BBC News*, Nov. 21, available online at <https://www.bbc.co.uk/news/uk-2502209>.

Whitehead, T. (2014a) "Britain who Tried to Join Syrian Terror Camp may have been Rejected as Not Good Enough, Court Hears," *Daily Telegraph*, Dec. 5.

Whitehead, T. (2014b) "Man Travelled to Syrian Training Camp After Angry Wife Said 'Go Die on Battlefield,' Court Told," *Daily Telegraph*, May 7.

Wood, G. (2015) "What ISIS Really Wants," *The Atlantic*, Mar, available online at <https://www.theatlantic.com/magazine/archive/2015/03/what-isis-really-wants/384980>.

Zawahiri, A. (2005) Letter to Abu Mus'ab al-Zarqawi, Oct. 11.

Zawahiri, A. (2013) "General Guidelines for Jihad," issued by Al-Sahab Media Foundation, Sept. 13.

Zawahiri, A. (2014) Interview conducted by Al-Sahab Media Foundation, Apr. 18.

Zarqawi, A. M. (2004) Letter intercepted by Kurdish forces in Iraq, possibly to Osama bin Laden, Jan. 23.

CHAPTER 21

SINGLE-ISSUE TERRORISM

GARY ACKERMAN AND
ANASTASIA KOULOGANES

Introduction

Irrespective of how discriminate or indiscriminate their actual acts of violence might be, most terrorists with which the general public are familiar cast their grievances and calls for revolution rather broadly. It is thus not at all uncommon for terrorist groups and extremist movements of all stripes to make clarion calls for wholesale changes to entire social or political systems. Some terrorists, in contrast, seem to focus their ire around a particular issue or small set of issues, and hence direct their violence towards a narrow set of enemies and targets. Movements, groups, and individuals of this nature are often characterized using the label "single-issue terrorist." Animal rights extremists like the Animal Liberation Front and violent anti-abortion activists like the Army of God are common recipients of this label, although it can arguably be applied to a broad variety of extremists, from anti-Castro organizations like Omega-7 to the more militant members of the Straight Edge movement.

The heterogeneity across the category's constituent members might be one reason why single-issue terrorism as a class of terrorism has received relatively little attention from scholars beyond research on particular organizations and movements that fall under the general rubric. A handful of researchers have, however, written previously on the topic and some law enforcement agencies have fixed on a similar notion of "special interest terrorism." In contradistinction to these scholars and practitioners, we argue that the very concept of single-issue terrorism as a distinct category of terrorism is contestable. Instead, it is more appropriate to regard the phenomenon as an ideological attribute that can be applied to individuals, groups, and movements as part of any suitable classification scheme for terrorism.

In this chapter, we first discuss the concept of single-issue terrorism as it appears in the broader terrorism literature and formulate a working definition based on this scholarship. We then critically assess whether single-issue groups as commonly conceived of actually exist and, even if they do, whether they can persist or merely represent an ephemeral stage in the development of a terrorist group. More fundamentally, we examine the very utility of the term and suggest that our understanding of terrorism might be better served by abandoning the label altogether. Throughout, we demonstrate our ideas by reference to three ostensibly single-issue terrorist organizations.

Exemplar Special-Interest Extremists

We begin by introducing the organizations through which we will illustrate several of the features and difficulties surrounding the concept of single-issue terrorism. Two of these organizations are well-known, the third less so, and these very different groups span a range of ideological and socio-political milieus.

The Earth Liberation Front (ELF) is a radical organization that claims to act to save the environment from human exploitation (Ackerman 2003, 163). A 1992 offshoot of the broader radical environmentalist movement, the ELF was modeled on and has often collaborated with the Animal Liberation Front (ALF), yet remains ideologically distinct from the ALF in that it focuses at the macro-level on whole species and entire ecosystems (including on occasion inanimate natural objects) rather than on the treatment of individual animals. Inspired by the philosophy of Deep Ecology[1] as well as the "monkeywrenching" sabotage tactics of its predecessor Earth First!, the ELF paints "an apocalyptic vision of a natural world imperiled by corporate greed and a corrupt system" (Ackerman 2003, 146). Its adherents contend that they are the avatars of besieged ecosystems and invoke a doctrine akin to collective self-defense.[2] As one ELF communiqué claimed: "We are the burning rage of a dying Planet. We have to show the enemy that we are serious about defending what is sacred." (Quoted in Cecil-Cockwell 2008, 13). Organizationally, the ELF is diffuse and non-hierarchical, with no clear leadership and a self-selecting membership, and is made up of loosely connected or unrelated cells in a deliberate attempt to elude law enforcement. The group's attacks have been directed against a variety of enterprises that ELF members believe to be responsible for jeopardizing the environment, from ski resorts and logging operations to multinational corporations, car dealerships and apartment complexes. These so-called "direct actions" have almost exclusively abjured direct violence against human beings, mainly involving arson and various forms of sabotage (Leader and Probst 2003). Indeed, one of the ELF's main stated guidelines is "To take all necessary precautions against harming life" (North American ELF Press Office 2001, 15).[3] Despite this, the ELF in the

United States was characterized in the early 2000s by federal law enforcement agencies as a major domestic terrorist threat.[4]

Founded in 1982 on the premise of employing violence as a means to prevent abortions, the Army of God (AOG) is commonly classified as a single-issue terrorist group. During the 1980s and 1990s, there were twenty-four recorded attacks—including bombings, armed assaults, and arson—attributed to AOG, twenty two of which were directed towards targets engaging in abortion-related actions (National Consortium 2013). Michael Bray, one of the original members of AOG, was involved in ten attacks throughout the 1980s, all of which were directed at abortion-related targets (National Consortium 2013). Eric Rudolph, arguably one of the most recognized members of AOG, was responsible for several bombings, including the 1996 Centennial Olympic Park bombing in Atlanta, Georgia, which was meant to force the cancellation of the games and to "confound, anger and embarrass the Washington government in the eyes of the world for its abominable sanctioning of abortion on demand" (Rudolph n.d.). Despite several well-known individual members, comprehensive information on AOG's membership is almost nonexistent, as members largely operate individually as "ideology subscribers" rather than coordinating with others or operating within a formal organizational structure. Members are often exposed to AOG's ideologies through the internet or by other means and subsequently operate alone, making it difficult for law enforcement to develop a thorough understanding of how AOG operates. AOG's anti-abortion orientation is derived mostly from radical Christian beliefs, similar to those espoused by those affiliated with the Christian far right but focused on the notion that they are acting to save the lives and souls of the unborn from abortion providers, whom they regard as murderers. Cathy Ramey, who wrote the treatise "In Defense of Others," which is featured prominently in AOG propaganda, uses extreme religious reasoning as a means to justify the actions of AOG followers. "God has indeed given the *right of defense to the individual* even though it may result in bloodshed," she states and justifies the actions of previous AOG attackers through a doctrine of preemptive defense, declaring that they "sought to prevent future murders on the part of the serial-abortionists they shot" (Ramey n.d.).

PAGAD formed in South Africa in 1995 as a collection of local Cape Town citizens primarily concerned about the presence of crime in their city. At first only loosely structured, the group was formally organized as PAGAD—People Against Gangsterism and Drugs—about a year later. Once formally established, the group's support base spread to additional cities in the region, where communities were also grappling with high levels of criminal activity. At the time of its creation, the group was comprised of concerned citizens who had determined that government and police force activities were ineffective against the criminal presence faced by the community. It thus initially primarily took the form of an anti-crime vigilante group, a focus which it maintains to some extent today: "We are not opposed to drugs & alcohol because it [sic] is illegal; we are opposed to it because it destroys our society. We need to stop the destruction. We will oppose those who protect it, and those who benefit from it!" (PAGAD 2007b). PAGAD uses two distinct strategies to fulfill its goals: one group of members (including the leadership) works overtly to pressure the government to take action against drug dealers and other criminals, while a second group surreptitiously executes shootings and bombings targeting these criminals (Botha 2001). Since its inception, the group has been responsible for at least eleven attacks (National Consortium 2013) (and linked to a further thirty-one: Botha 2001) throughout South Africa. Although many current members are of the Muslim faith, individual adherents were originally associated with a broad array of religious and political views (Botha 2001). However, at least a portion of the organization consists of supporters of Qibla, a pro-Shi'ite fundamentalist group that promoted implementing the ideals of the Iranian revolution in South Africa in order to transform the country into a Muslim State. PAGAD has maintained an active voice in South Africa, participating in door-to-door recruiting efforts, marches against crime and drugs, and even condemning shopkeepers and other individuals on its webpage for participating in drug or gang-related activities (PAGAD 2012; Koyana 2015). As late as 2016, PAGAD was involved in a shooting against alleged gangsters (Baadjies 2016).

Definition and Usage

While the specific origin of the term single-issue terrorism is unknown, its academic popularization occurred in the 1990s following several decades of attacks attributed to groups with a seemingly narrow focus. However, literature on single-issue terrorism as a subject in and of itself is sparse, with most detailed scholarly treatments published in the 1990s and early 2000s. Indeed, some seminal works aiming to give a general overview of terrorism do not even mention single-issue terrorism, or simply afford it a short paragraph or two (see Hoffman 2006; Reich 1990; Crenshaw 1994).

Existing scholarship appears to take two stances on the term's placement within the larger array of terrorist ideological categories, characterizing single-issue terrorism as either a specific typological category itself, or a subtype within a broader class. Those who view single-issue terrorism as a unique category in and of itself include G. Davidson Smith (1998), one of the first to write authoritatively about the term, who rather nebulously defines single-issue terrorism as "Extremist militancy on the part of groups or individuals protesting a perceived grievance or wrong usually attributed to government action or inaction" (1998). This does not do much, however, to distinguish single-issue terrorists from any other kind, save perhaps for the singular indefinite article implying that there is only a single perceived grievance or wrong. Dyson (2001) more helpfully describes single-issue terror groups as those that are not interested in transforming an overall political agenda, but are instead interested in immediately influencing a specific issue—and are willing to use violence to see this through. Dyson goes further, however, and contends that not all groups supporting issues such as anti-abortion activism, environmentalism, animal rights, and other issues associated with single-issue terrorism are necessarily single-issue terrorist groups themselves. He states that anarchists, for example, often support and take part in both animal rights and environmentalist extremism, but should not be classified as single-issue terrorists (Dyson 2001, 28). The phenomenon of mutual support from and overlapping membership in groups espousing more generalized ideologies (as described by Smith) immediately raises the question of what indeed is distinct about single-issue terrorism, a topic that will be returned to later.

Monaghan (2000) also makes a strong case for single-issue terrorism to be considered as its own category, using case studies about violent animal rights activists and British militant suffragette activism in the early 1900s to demonstrate that the use of "sub-revolutionary terrorism" to describe these single-issue terror groups—as proposed by Paul Wilkinson (1977)—is too general to properly characterize the specificity of these groups' motivations. Single-issue terrorism, Monaghan argues, is the best categorization method for these groups, since it adds a level of specificity to describe their unique goals (2000). She is thus generally in agreement with Smith and Dyson, as all three seek to normalize the use of the phrase.

Other scholars take a different approach to this issue of classification, laying out the term "single-issue terrorism" as embedded within a broader category of ideological milieu. Martin discusses single-issue groups as occupying a space on the far left, stating, "The left has produced violent single-issue groups and individuals who focus on one particular issue to the exclusion of others. To them, their championed issue is the central point—arguably the political crux—for solving many of the world's problems" (Martin 2015, 446). While Martin does use a particular term to collectively describe all of these groups, he does not seem to view the term as a specific category in and of itself. Instead, he implies that "single-issue terrorism" can function as a subtype within other categories, presumably countenancing a "far left single issue terrorism" and "far right single issue terrorism", etc., as subcategories.

More operationally focused entities, such as the US Federal Bureau of Investigation (FBI), somewhat surprisingly offer more extended discussions (US Department of Justice 1999; Lewis 2005; Jarboe 2002). For example, the FBI's 1999 report on terrorism in the United States devotes several pages to discussing "special-interest terrorism," defining its practitioners as "groups [that] seek to influence specific issues, rather than effect widespread political change" (US Department of Justice 1999). This definition is somewhat more useful in that it casts this type of terrorism relative to that which seeks broader political change, but it still does not tell us much about how these "specific issues" can be identified or what kinds of influence are included.

Building on these initial explorations of the topic, we offer a working definition of "single-issue terrorism" as: *terrorist attacks perpetrated by actors whose grievances are focused on a single narrow societal domain rather than on seeking to change the structure or institutions of the society more broadly*. This attempts to capture the sense in which the term has been utilized by both scholars and law enforcement agencies, while being a little more rigorous in delimiting the scope of the label.

Satisfying the Definition

The first conceptual task that will be undertaken is to examine the extent to which real-world terrorist groups in fact satisfy this definition. We can draw on the first of the organizations described so far, the ELF, to introduce a potential difficulty that might arise with the notion of single-issue terrorism as so defined.

While the ELF and ALF possess somewhat different foci in terms of their cause and their adversaries, the two entities are close cousins ideologically, in that they both seek to protect, through illegal acts, the non-human world from a perceived uncaring and destructive society. It is thus not uncommon for individuals who were first attached to the animal rights movement to shift into radical environmentalism and vice versa, Rodney Coronado being a prominent example. Most significantly, the two groups have on several occasions jointly claimed responsibility for direct actions, which included attacks against traditional targets of both animal rights activists (such as fur breeders and animal laboratories) and environmentalists (such as forestry operations and construction).[5]

Thus, where two or more "single-issue" terrorist organizations are located near to one another in ideological space, in other words where their "single-issues" occupy the same ideological milieu, there can occur an overlap in membership, perceived adversaries, and other factors. In such cases of *cross-contamination*, the ideological, organizational, and operational lines separating the two entities can become blurred, thus undermining the notion of either group representing a single issue.

A second, more common, difficulty that is often observed in practice is the phenomenon of *ideological drift*. This occurs when, over time, the single-issue terrorists' goals begin to expand or change. In some cases, for example, a group might determine that it has accomplished its core goal and subsequently moves to another, broader, set of objectives in order to satisfy a variety of organizational and individual dynamics. In a more likely scenario, ideological drift can occur when an actor concludes that it is not making much progress towards achieving its core goal and "discovers" that a deeper and in most cases substantially broader grievance undergirds the original single issue, which thus becomes merely one manifestation of a more fundamental perceived societal malaise.

AOG is a prime example of this shift: the group started out focused on anti-abortion action, but in the mid-1990s also became associated with anti-homosexual activities, such as the bombing perpetrated by AOG member Eric Rudolph on The Otherside Lounge, a gay nightclub, in 1997 (National Consortium 2013). Rudolph's written confession—also featured on the AOG website—explains that the attack "was meant to send a powerful message in protest of Washington's continued tolerance and support for the homosexual political agenda" (Rudolph n.d.). The AOG website even includes several pages with news stories and other text condemning homosexuals, with titles such as, "Put Homosexuals to the Sword," and "Dear homosexual, what part of Leviticus 20:13 don't you understand?" (Army of God n.d.). Furthermore, AOG's rhetoric, such as "In Defense of Others" by Cathy Ramey, hovers near the cusp of a more general anti-government animus, harshly criticizing the US Supreme Court for its decision to legalize abortion, or for saying "those who kill children could walk free." The text goes on to say that the Court "tore up and threw in the trash our two-hundred-year-old imitation of God's law" (Ramey n.d.).

Ideological drift can also occur as a group's membership transforms over time. For example, when PAGAD was created in 1995, the group was comprised of a diverse collection of citizens primarily concerned with fighting rising crime and gang activity. However, PAGAD soon transformed into a group driven by radical Islamic ideas due to the influence of its Islamic fundamentalist members, and possibly due to its alleged relationship with Qibla. While the extent of Qibla's impact on PAGAD across the group's lifespan is uncertain, some suspect that the radical Islamic group's influence over PAGAD's leadership increased substantially after a rift formed in the latter organization a year after its creation (Botha 2001). A power struggle between those seeking to call the PAGAD struggle a "jihad" and those aiming to avoid such religious connections ultimately resulted in a more Islamic-oriented organization (Botha 2001). This can be seen in a 2008 guidance document, where the group outlines its Code of Conduct, membership requirements, and other group logistics. The first two lines of the document are related to the group's original—single-issue—anti-crime purpose: "No member shall under any circumstances use and deal in drugs, or associate with drug dealers and gangsters—whether for financial gain, personal favour or friendship." (PAGAD 2008). However, quotes from the Quran sandwich the flyer's content, reflecting an underlying religious motivation that appears to be driving the group's goals. On their webpage, the group also states, "The position of PAGAD is quite simple. The platform of Jumua in the Masjid must be used to guide the Muslims and encourage us to implement the laws of Allah in our daily lives." (PAGAD n.d.).

Just as tellingly, several years after the group's formation there were many attacks attributed to individuals associated with PAGAD which were not related to anti-crime activities at all. For example, PAGAD was linked to an attack in 1999, in which a bomb was thrown under a police vehicle, destroying the vehicle and injuring one person. A variety of other attacks on police, businesses, and government locations—not criminal organizations—are suspected to be linked with PAGAD (National Consortium 2013). A 2007 bulletin warned, "Shebeens, gambling and abortion are destroying our society. It kills our youth and breaks up our families", further emphasizing that these actions—including abortion—oppose the will of Allah (PAGAD 2007a). More recently, in 2015, PAGAD leader Abdus Salaam Ebrahim called for increased anti-Israel action at a public protest, and a bulletin released in 2009 had a similar emphasis, encouraging readers to avoid Coca-Cola, McDonald's, and other products that allegedly support Israel: "Ask yourselves: Will I help to finance the next shipment of bombs and bullets that will kill and maim innocent defenseless Palestinians?" (PAGAD 2009; Barnardo 2015). Thus, at least some within the umbrella of PAGAD have extended their violent behavior and messaging beyond simple anti-criminal activity in order to influence other issues—such as abortion and the Israel–Palestinian conflict—related to a possibly broadening set of core beliefs.

These examples show that, even if a terrorist group starts out strictly adhering to a single issue, this condition is often ephemeral, with the organization slowly—and perhaps inexorably—broadening the ambit of its ideology until it encompasses a far broader set of goals up to and including those that operate at the level of the entire society.

Moving from Category to Attribute

Given the varying conceptions of single-issue terrorism among scholars, as well as the observation that in practice—due to ideological cross-contamination or drift—genuinely single-issue terrorist groups might be a rare or transient phenomenon, it is reasonable to reexamine the general utility of using the label to describe a distinct category of terrorism.

Perhaps one of the reasons that the label has endured is that it has on occasion served as a convenient catch-all for terrorist groups whose ideologies might not fit neatly into traditional typologies of terrorism. Under such a scheme, it is easy to collect within a single residual category any miscellaneous extremist ideology that is sufficiently obscure as to be espoused by only a single terrorist group. Why, after all, should we go to the trouble of creating completely new ideological milieus merely to house groups like Americans for Justice, who claimed to act against high oil prices in the 1970s, or Grupo Estrella, a Puerto Rican outfit with an amorphous ideology involving revenge and protection of utility workers? Both of these organizations have been classified as single-issue terrorist groups,[6] despite the ambit of their ideologies being less than completely transparent. Whether these groups in fact qualify as "single issue" according to the definition is thus uncertain, but it appears to be the path of least resistance to place them in this category. Moreover, possessing a unique ideology is not, strictly speaking, a defensible reason for lumping such groups together under a single category. Just as linguists would never dream of combining different language families merely because their branches possessed a single member each, proper taxonomic practice demands that sufficiently distinct ideologies be given separate categories.

Yet, it is the other side of the conceptual coin that most strongly undercuts the single-issue terrorism category. The key question here is whether single-issue terrorist groups display greater ideological similarities to each other—thus justifying their inclusion in a common category—or whether they more closely resemble other ideological categories. To help answer this, we can turn again to the three exemplar groups described earlier. Beginning with the ELF, the movement as it currently stands shares many tropes with the far left, particularly its anarchist strand. For example, rather than restricting its antagonism to specific despoilers of the environment, ELF rhetoric sees the evils of capitalism as a root cause of the threats facing the environment and decry the legitimacy of the government and the current system of democracy as practiced in the United States. The group's propaganda is filled with general references to social injustices, United States imperialism, and injunctions to upend the political system (North American ELF

Press Office 2001, 4–9). As stated by Craig Rosebraugh, a former spokesperson for the North American ELF Press Office, "United States imperialism is a disease, one that continues to grow and become more powerful and dangerous. It needs to be stopped" (2002). At the same time, the primary driver behind AOG's animus against abortion is its extreme Christian beliefs, as demonstrated by the religious quotes and statements throughout its propaganda.[7] Overall, then, a strong argument can be made that just because they both possess a superficially narrow focus in their motives for acting, this is not enough to construe AOG as more similar to ELF, say, than each is to the Christian far right and anarchist far left, respectively.

If a separate category of single-issue terrorism is unjustified, what is to be done then, since it might still be useful for scholarship and counterterrorism practice to mark the fact that such groups focus their actions and propaganda on particularly narrow grievances? We propose that the concept of single-issue terrorism would be better represented as an attribute of a group or movement's ideology than as a separate ideological category. Thus, a particular terrorist group would be placed in the ideological category—say "far right" or "ethno-nationalist"—that most closely reflects its worldview, grievances, proposed solutions, and so forth (even if this is a category with only itself as a member). Separately, in any analysis of the group, one of the attributes that is applied to describe it—along with others, such as group structure, type of leadership, or experience—would be a variable describing how narrowly focused the particular manifestation of the broader ideological category is in the case of that particular group.

Not only would this avoid most of the conceptual and practical difficulties of categorization, but it would bring analytical advantages that could actually help enhance our understanding of terrorism. The first of these is that treating "single-issueness" as an attribute allows it to capture a spectrum of how narrowly focused a group's ideology is. Whereas including single-issue terrorism as its own category demands a binary choice—a group's ideology is either "single-issue" or not—regarding it as an attribute allows analysts to record the degree to which the ideology is narrowly focused. Thereby, for example, the narrowness of ideological focus could be interpreted as an ordinal variable on a ten-point scale and an analyst might rate the ELF, say, as a 6 and PAGAD as an 8, thus allowing for an investigation into whether the magnitude of such a score has any influence on various aspects of terrorist behavior. An example of how treating "single-issueness" as an attribute might provide analytical benefits is when exploring the nexus between this characteristic and a structural one like lone actor terrorism. Lone actors often seem to espouse narrow grievances, but do not necessarily do so. Viewing "single-issueness" as an attribute would allow researchers to examine the extent to which lone actors like Eric Rudolph are more likely to fixate on a narrower motivational dimension that might appeal to them for idiosyncratic reasons while controlling for the effects of ideology, something that is not possible when treating single-issue as its own, binary ideological category. Additionally, treating the degree of ideological focus as an attribute would allow one to track changes over time, which would enable an explicit recording and hence examination of the notions of ideological drift or cross-contamination discussed earlier.

Given the benefits of regarding "single-issueness" as an attribute rather than a category of terrorism, we therefore discard our earlier working definition, along with the entire effort to delineate single-issue terrorism as a separate category and replace it with an attribute that captures the notion of narrowness of ideological focus. We offer the following suggestion for a description of this attribute: *the degree to which a terrorist actor's ideology, especially its grievances and the locus of its propaganda and actions, is focused narrowly on a limited societal domain.* We leave the door open, however, for scholars and practitioners to employ terminology that best suits their purpose in describing this attribute.

Single-issue terrorism has enjoyed a relatively small amount of attention from scholars and counterterrorism practitioners, who have generally regarded it as a distinct type of terrorism. We have argued in this chapter that there is little value in treating single-issue terrorism as a separate category. This does not mean, however, that we should ignore the issue or underestimate its relevance in understanding terrorism. Studying why some extremists like ELF, AOG, and PAGAD focus their grievances and actions more narrowly than others, and how the boundaries of their ideology evolve over time and in relation to other organizational factors, might very well shed light on how terrorist ideology manifests in behavior. We thus call for more, rather than less, attention to be paid to such actors and hope that our reconceptualization of the phenomenon as an attribute might further such efforts.

Notes

1. Deep Ecology was first espoused in the 1970s by writers such as the Norwegian Arne Naess and asserts that all living things have intrinsic worth beyond their utility to human beings. See e.g. Naess 1977.
2. *Igniting the Revolution*, self-produced video by the Earth Liberation Front.
3. This attitude is not universal amongst radical environmentalists, however, evidenced in the following contribution to the Earth First! Journal: "Contributions are urgently solicited for scientific research on a species specific virus that will eliminate Homo shiticus from the planet. Only an absolutely species specific virus should be set loose. Otherwise it will be just another technological fix. Remember, Equal Rights for All Other Species" ("Gula" 1989).
4. Former FBI Director Louis Freeh referred to the ELF as one of America's leading domestic terrorism threats, *Wall Street Journal* 2001.
5. E.g. on July 3, 1998, the ELF and ALF jointly claimed responsibility for a direct action against United Vaccines in Middleton, Wisconsin, in which over 300 ferrets and minks were released. Another example of joint claims of responsibility was the destruction of USDA buildings in Olympia, Washington, in June 1998.
6. Terrorism and Extremist Violence in the United States (TEVUS) Database, Available at: <https://www.start.umd.edu/research-projects/terrorism-and-extremist-violence-united-states-tevus-database>.
7. See Army of God webpage, <http://www.armyofgod.com>.

References

Ackerman A., Gary. (2003) "Beyond Arson? A Threat Assessment of the Earth Liberation Front," *Terrorism and Political Violence*, 15(4): 143–70.

Army of God (n.d.) "The Homo News—Page 4." available online at <http://www.armyofgod.com/Leviticus4.html> [Accessed May 2016].

Baadjies, Megan (2016) "Shots Fired in Gang, Pagad Standoff," Independent Online News., Aug. 1, available online at <http://www.iol.co.za/news/crime-courts/shots-fired-in-gang-pagad-standoff-2051960>.

Bernardo, Carla (2015) "Pagad calls for more anti-Israel action." Independent Online News, Sept. 21, available online at <http://www.iol.co.za/news/politics/pagad-calls-for-more-anti-israel-action-1919297>.

Boshoff, H., A. Botha, and M. Schönteich, (2001) "The Prime Suspects? The Metamorphosis of Pagad," *Fear in the City: Urban Terrorism in South Africa*, 24. Pretoria: Institute for Security Studies.

Cecil-Cockwell, Malcolm (2008) "The Earth Liberation Front: Sabotaging a Way of Life," *Epoch Journal*, 2(3): 13.

Crenshaw, Martha (1994) *Terrorism in Context*: University Park, PA: Pennsylvania State University Press.

Dyson, William E. (2001) *Terrorism: An Investigator's Handbook*. Cincinnati, OH: Anderson.

"Gula" (1989) "Eco-Kamikazes Wanted," *Earth First! Journal*, Sept. 22: 21.

Hoffman, Bruce (2006) *Inside Terrorism*: New York: Columbia University Press.

Jarboe, James F. (2002) "The Threat of Eco-Terrorism," available online at <https://www.fbi.gov/news/testimony/the-threat-of-eco-terrorism>.

Koyana, Xolani (2015) "Pagad Marches Against Gangsterism, Drugs, and Escalating Crime," *Eyewitness News*, Oct. 17, available online at <http://ewn.co.za/2015/10/17/Pagad-marches-against-gangsterism-drugs—and-escalating-crime>.

Leader, S. H., and P. Probst (2003) "The Earth Liberation Front and Environmental Terrorism," *Terrorism and Political Violence* 15(4): 217–38.

Lewis, John E. (2005) "Addressing the Threat of Animal Rights Extremism and Eco-Terrorism," available online at <https://www.fbi.gov/news/testimony/addressing-the-threat-of-animal-rights-extremism-and-eco-terrorism>.

Martin, Gus (2015) *Understanding Terrorism: Challenges, Perspectives, and Issues*. Los Angeles: SAGE.

Monaghan, Rachel (2000) "Single-Issue Terrorism: A Neglected Phenomenon?," *Minnesota Law Review*, 23(4): 255–65.

Naess, A. (1977) "Spinoza and Ecology," *Philosophia*, 7: 45–54.

National Consortium for the Study of Terrorism and Responses to Terrorism (START) (2013). *Global Terrorism Database*: Army of God, People Against Gangsterism and Drugs, available online at <http://www.start.umd.edu/gtd>.

North American Earth Liberation Front (ELF) Press Office (2001) "Frequently Asked Questions About the Earth Liberation Front," available online at <https://archive.org/details/FrequentlyAskedQuestionsAboutTheEarthLiberationFront> [Accessed Jan. 2017].

PAGAD (n.d.) "Our View: The Sanctity of the Masjid and Jumua," available online at <http://www.pagad.co.za/our-view> [Accessed July 2015].

PAGAD (People Against Gangsterism and Drugs) (2007a) "Special Bulletin: Shebeens, Gambling, Abortion & Ebrahim Rasool..." Apr., available online at <www.pagad.co.za>.

PAGAD (2007b) "Special Bulletin: Licenced to Kill . . ," available online at <www.pagad.co.za>.

PAGAD (2008) "PAGAD Guideline: Establishing PAGAD Branches". Nov, available online at <www.pagad.co.za>.

PAGAD (2009) "Special Bulletin: While Palestine Bleeds!" 8 Jan. 8, available online at <www.pagad.co.za>.

PAGAD (2012) "Police Harass PAGAD in Manenberg." July 29, available online at <http://www.pagad.co.za/2012/police-harass-pagad-in-manenberg>.

Ramey, Cathy (n.d.) "In Defense of Others: Part 2." Army of God, available online at <http://www.armyofgod.com/InDefense2.html> [Accessed Apr. 2016].

Reich, Walter, ed. (1990) *Origins of Terrorism*. New York: Cambridge University Press.

Rosebraugh, Craig (2002) Former Spokesperson for the ELF Press Office, written testimony to the House Committee on Resources, Subcommittee on Forests and Forest Health Oversight Hearing on Eco-Terrorism and Lawlessness on the National Forests, 107th Congress, Feb. 12.

Rudolph, Eric Robert (n.d.) "Full Text of Eric Rudolph's Written Statement." Army of God, available online at <http://www.armyofgod.com/EricRudolphStatement.html> [Accessed May 2016].

Smith, G. D. (1998) *Single Issue Terrorism*. Ottawa: Canadian Security Intelligence Service, available online at <https://fas.org/irp/threat/com74e.htm> [Accessed May 2016].

US Dept. of Justice, Federal Bureau of Investigation (1999) "Terrorism in the United States." Available at: <https://www.fbi.gov/stats-services/publications/terror_99.pdf> [Accessed 2015].

Wall Street Journal (2001) "The Boy Who Cried 'ELF,'" Feb. 14: A22.

Wilkinson, Paul (1977) *Terrorism and the Liberal State*. New York: Wiley.

PART V

TERRORISM, POLITICAL VIOLENCE, AND COLLECTIVE ACTION

CHAPTER 22

STATE TERRORISM

TIM WILSON

INTRODUCTION

"TERRORISM by states remains unstudied and mostly invisible," asserts Richard Jackson (2009, 70). Taken at the face value, it seems a claim designed to lift eyebrows. As long ago as 1975, indeed, it was observed that "the three most perennially popular subjects currently to be found on the bedside tables of the reading public [are] golf, cats and the Third Reich" (Coren 1975, 1). Forty years later, something like that triptych of interests probably still holds good: at any rate, the keen postgraduate assigned a literature review on the Nazis is unlikely to find that their chief difficulty is finding books. Another piece by Jackson helpfully clarified (albeit in a footnote) that he did not actually mean "that state violence and repression has not been studied, but rather that it has not been systematically studied under the rubric of 'terrorism' or by recognised terrorism studies scholars" (Jackson 2008, 389).

Such views are clearly designed as a critique of the foundational orientation of terrorism studies towards insurgent actors. Any broad and dispassionate investigation of terrorism—broadly understood as violent intimidation for political effect—must inexorably lead into the corridors of power since "state terrorism is incontrovertibly far more prevalent and destructive than non-state or insurgent terrorism" (Jackson et al. 2010, 2). It is strongly implied in this critique that scholars of terrorism should be concentrating far more upon the state (Jackson 2008, 377). I follow that prompt, focusing here only upon states' use of domestic repression and "hard power" projection. I deliberately put the important subject of clandestine "state-sponsored terrorism" to one side, since it arguably constitutes a relatively discrete subject area in its own right (Alexander 1985; Byman 2005; Messinger 1935).

The spirited critique that I have sketched has been advanced by scholars who have recently arrayed themselves behind the banner of the "Critical Terrorism Studies" movement (George 1991; Jackson et al. 2009, 2010; Blakeley 2010, 14). Pioneering work dating back to the 1980s is duly acknowledged, but this is a critique that has gathered momentum sharply since the so-called War on Terror (Stohl and Lopez 1984). On the theoretical front, Richard Jackson and Ruth Blakeley have recently done the most sustained heavy lifting here for building the case for state terrorism as a worthy, indeed vital, subject for study (Jackson 2008; Jackson et al. 2010). Since they see the core of the phenomenon of terrorism as the instrumental use of violence (against some) to communicate (to many) they are at pains to reject an actor-centered approach to their subject in favor of an action-centered one (Jackson et al. 2010; Blakeley 2010). While non-state actors may indeed practice such tactics on a "retail" scale, states with their typically far greater resources have the luxury of doing so on a "wholesale" basis (Chomsky 1990, 26; Jackson et al. 2010, 230). Mere scales of atrocity are ultimately beside the point in this view, however. In Blakeley's words, "even if the motives, functions, and effects of terrorism by states and non-state actors are different, the act of terrorism itself is not, because the core characteristics of terrorism are the same whether the perpetrator is a state or a non-state actor" (Blakeley 2010, 13).

The proponents of this "state terrorism turn" in terrorism studies occasionally seem a little downcast that they have not made more converts (Jackson et al. 2010, 237). By their own terms of reference, this seems a little pessimistic. First, earlier and more traditionalist generations of terrorism studies scholars often acknowledged the phenomenon of state atrocity more than has been recognized (Gearty 1997; Wilkinson 2006, 1): second, this trend in emphasis continues to grow well beyond the confines of the Critical Terrorism Studies field (Schmid 2013, 48–9, 68–70, 203–6; Duncan et al. 2013). "Can the state be terrorist?" asked Peter Sproat back in 1991. If the layperson's answer was obviously "yes" back then in 1991, then it surely is all the more so now.

Yet the key question remains one of analytical utility: namely, what is gained by describing state repression as "state terrorism" rather than by some other label? Attempts to "insist upon the importance of the distinction between state terrorism and repression" on the basis of instrumentality here seem over-ambitious (Blakeley 2010, 14: also Stohl and Lopez 1984, 7–8): can we really identify a government repression that is not freighted with a wider communicative intent to terrify? It seems unlikely, even if the study of state repression has remained curiously indifferent to the question of any wider terroristic intent (Davenport and Inman 2012, 627). At any rate, we are faced with a vast expansion of the traditional subject area of terrorism.

Some would wish to widen it further. In particular, I am keen to pick up the gauntlet left by Richard Jackson in his sketch for a research agenda on state terrorism:

> we see real value in exploring the ways in which studies on state terrorism can add a value to the study of non-state terrorism. It seems clear that state and non-state terrorism are linked, and in some real-world cases, they feed off each other in violent cycles. However, a stronger case needs to be made that studying state and non-state forms of the phenomenon together is a useful way forward.
>
> (Jackson et al. 2010, 238)

Certainly, this is an important challenge: to identify the basic processes of mutual reinforcement under which state repression and anti-state political violence feed off each other voraciously. Yet an important new body of integrated comparative work has only just begun to grapple with this key dialectic: of how, in Richard English's phrasing "the mutually shaping relationship *between* non-state terrorism and state counter-terrorism continues to determine local and international experience in complex and powerful ways" (English 2015, 1: original emphasis). And here it is worth stressing that governments are as prone to miscalculation as any other actor (English 2015, 14). As a recent excellent study of the birth of the Weimar Republic concludes, "in the end, it was the fear that they would become victims of violence that led the state's political leadership and large parts of society to support unprecedented levels of warlike violence against their internal enemies, real and *imagined*" (Jones 2016, 4: added emphasis).

I

As a historian, and in line with my earlier work on the subject, I argue for the value of taking a long-term view of the general phenomenon of terrorism. If we want to understand terrorism *now*, then it might make some sense to reflect upon terrorism *past*. In other words, looking at how terrorism has developed might help us towards a deeper appreciation of our current situation. That approach might sound like common sense—to a historian, at least. But in general it is also been exactly what has *not* happened: as a rule, the academic terrorism "industry" has been conspicuously more interested in making terrorism history than making histories of terrorism.

But some consideration of the historical roots of the phenomenon is surely unavoidable. As any discussion of the origins of the term in the cauldron of the French Revolution invariably notes, "terrorism" belonged to the state long before it belonged to the counter-state (Townshend 2002; Guelke 2008, 19). State terrorism thus has roots in modernity that run both wide and deep: indeed, it constitutes one of the "elemental forces" that go to make up the contemporary world (Wilson 2013, 14).

It could hardly be otherwise, since violence is the state's core business. "The modern state is a compulsory association which organises domination," argued Max Weber in his famous 1919 lecture, "Politics as a Vocation". In this classic exposition, indeed, the *primary* business of the state is to organize violence better than anyone else: to become the Arch Terrorist on the Block and to run a successful monopoly of intimidation within its sovereign territory. Its next most important task is to disguise this foundational reality. When it is successful, the result is a type of alchemy—Bourdieu's "state magic"—by which the government's reserves of overwhelming force are converted into the liquid capital of social legitimacy: a fusion of shock and law (quoted in Thorup 2010, 51).

What, then, is to stop successful state monopolies of violence appearing blatantly terroristic? Historically, the classic European answer to that is the emergence of the *Rechtsstaat*—the commitment of state elites to perform public displays of legalistic self-restraint (Wilson 2013). A formal separation of powers between judicial, legislative, and executive functions prevents too naked a tyranny; and in doing so a merciful veil is drawn over the foundational reality that "the phenomena of government are from start to finish phenomena of force," as the American political scientist Arthur Bentley put it as long ago as 1908 (quoted in Dyson 1980, 2009, 133).

Broader populations over time may thus come to acquiesce in the "fairness" of the "Rule of Law" regardless of the uneven realities of how social and economic power actually works in practice: "it is not that anyone imagines the law to be just. Everyone knows that there is one law for the rich and another for the poor. But no one accepts the implications of this, everyone takes it for granted that the law, such as it is, will be respected, and feel a sense of outrage when it is not" (Orwell 1957, 71). More inconsistently and uncertainly, the late Ottoman Empire likewise tried to temper repression by limiting excess in line with popularly resonant Islamic values (Masters 2013). It is a model that its successor regimes have often resurrected, however flirtatiously and insincerely (Seale 1988, 328).

State terrorism is thus potentially dangerous to regime legitimacy because it unmasks the ugly potential for organized violence that always lies at the heart of modern state building. Those states and societies that have benefitted the most over the long run from such terror are often the most inclined to forget it (Tilly 1990). Thus "terror is externalized from the state (the concept of 'state terror' does not name the state but only the excessive state as terroristic, just like 'police violence' does not name the police violent but only that which exceeds the mandated violence)" (Thorup 2010, 101). Even if civilized life depends upon the very fact of its remaining hidden, state violence thus always contains the possibility of becoming mere barbarism. Social contracts can become protection rackets. Democratic regimes may hide this tension rather better than most: at least when rich and well-resourced, they allow most of their citizens most of the time to forget their intrinsic vulnerability in the face of state power. Therein lies their claim to moral superiority. But they, too, can nurture their own "deep states" (Cobain 2012, 2013; Woodworth 2001). And since domestic electorates are notoriously uninterested in foreign policy, this, too, often stinks (Hainsworth 2000; Murray 2006, 2007).

Certainly, then, one can make a logically powerful and consistent case for taking all this oppressive behavior by states and folding it together with insurgent activity into one giant omelette called "terrorism." But how do we actually sink our teeth into a dish this big? We are at some risk here of courting severe intellectual indigestion.

More fruitful, perhaps, would be to explore lower levels of analysis. We need to dig both down and sideways more in understanding violence we might loosely call "terroristic". Historians and anthropologists have much to offer here since they are avid contextualizers (see, for instance, Green 1994; Nagengast 1994). With such approaches we might usefully ask simple but still rigorously comparative questions of our case studies: why does *this* type of violence occur, but not *that*?

A striking feature of the "critical" approach to the study of terrorism here is that it proclaims a commitment to an act- rather than actor-based approach. Yet it shows little interest in the fine detail of those acts themselves. In fairness, this may simply reflect a wider tendency within international relations to study the world with stratospheric detachment. Still, it remains a key weakness to advancing understanding. From 30,000 feet all cruelty may indeed look similar. But that in itself teaches us rather little.

Any more focused attempt to dissect state terrorism might therefore usefully begin by acknowledging that different states terrorize differently. A crucial distinction drawn by the historical sociologist Michael Mann is helpful here. As ideal types, Mann distinguishes between "infrastructural" and "despotic" power (for a useful brief summary, see Thorup 2010). Despotic power refers to the exercise of overwhelming, but often temporary and localized, violence: "it is a projection of power without institutions or regularity on a territory and population not fully within the control of the state" (Thorup 2010, 47). It is worth noting in passing that lapses into despotic power may be at least semi-spontaneous: indeed, from Peterloo (1819) to Sharpeville (1960) and Marikana (2012) some of the most notorious peacetime massacres committed by modern state forces have had a highly chaotic and panicked quality to them (Marlow 1969, 1970, 137–41; Frankel 2001). By contrast, infrastructural power is relentless: "it refers to the state's ability to penetrate its territory and population, to implement and exert its dominance through institutions, legitimate practices, regularized and controlled use of force equally on all its territory" (Thorup 2010, 47–8). "Death by government" pursued by infrastructural means creates true hecatombs whose true extent fades into a "numerical haze" (Rummel 1994, p. xix). We need to try to grasp both the dynamics of despotic and infrastructural power and the areas of overlap between them.

State elites aim to create infrastructural power: for which tin-pot dictator in the "Global South" would not want to control the same density of CCTV coverage enjoyed by, say, the British state? Yet they often have to settle for far less: "despotic power may rule a territory but it does not and cannot govern it" (Thorup 2010, 48). Michael Mann's general summary of the patterns that state repression assumed after 1945 is useful here: "during the Cold War the United States mostly allied with tribal monarchies, while the Soviets allied with urban nationalists who had more progressive goals. But since they lacked mass support, these regimes turned towards despotism" (Mann, 2013, 120). Mimetic rivalry between the superpowers bred numerous Cold War Caligulas: figures such as the buffoonish Idi Amin or the priapic Colonel Gadaffi who seem to have escaped straight out of Suetonius's *Lives of the Caesars* (Cojean 2013; Kamau and Cameron 1979; Grant 1957, 1989). Such tyrants were arch-technicians of capricious violence: their courts and their harems zones of extreme turbulence.

How does despotic state terrorism function as a wider system of social control? Demonstrative atrocity is its hallmark. Travelling through northern Latvia just after the Great War one American journalist was surprised to encounter a village that reminded him of the Somme battlefield: "I mean, it was smashed to pieces, utterly flattened." This ruin lay far to the north of the battlefields of the 1914–17 fighting: it turned out to date back to the Cossacks' "punitive expeditions" of 1906 (Duranty 1935, 64–5). Across the Global South in the later twentieth century, helicopter-borne forces acted similarly. Such "aerial Cossacks" constitute a roving state reserve of highly mobile destroyers: they "came out of the helicopter firing bursts from their sub-machine guns. They fired at anything, even if it was just a leaf falling from the tree, they were already firing," recalled one Peruvian witness of the troubled 1990s (quoted in Degregori 1999). Both Iraq and El Salvador saw similar state tactics (Steele 2008, 199; McClintock 1987, 304–6).

Such despotic terrorism represents guerrilla hit-and-run tactics "from above." David Lesch has memorably described the Syrian regime's initial response to protest in 2011 as thus resembling the arcade game "whack-a-mole": "generally, wherever serious protests propped up in a particular city or region, the elite and most loyal units of the military and security forces were sent to whack them down" (Lesch 2012, 103–4). At most, despotic terrorism can seek to compensate for lack of infrastructural power through bursts of frenzied hyper-activity. But these are hard to sustain indefinitely.

II

How far, and under what circumstances, do state and anti-state terrorisms feed off each other in tightly escalating spirals? Here we have to confront the severe limits to what we know about state terrorism in general. The academic literatures are vast, but lopsided. Most specifically, the task of gaining any kind of historical overview of the development of state terrorism is not helped by a profound skewing of our knowledge base towards the most spectacular case studies.

Putting it simply, the best studied exemplars of state terrorism are also amongst the least typical: "Hitler's Germany and Stalin's Russia—for all that historians and political scientists have sought to demonstrate the apparently anarchic character of their bureaucracies—differed from most other countries in the past because of the relative orderliness, ambit, and coherence of their state machinery" (Mazower 2002, 17). The key point here was these were technologically advanced states whose huge infrastructural power became geared to social engineering through mass human destruction. In effect, these were utopian regimes that could afford to treat their masses as human playdough, to be molded or discarded as their leaders saw fit (Burleigh 2000; Kuromiya 1998; Mann 2013; Schlögel 2008, 2012). In targeting their victims, they combined spectacular state terrorism (killing within categories) with genocide or politicide (killing off a category). Strictly speaking, the latter eliminations were often more exterminatory than terroristic in intent. But the key point is the sheer size of the body counts that resulted (Bullock 1991, 1993; Geyer and Fitzpatrick 2009; Overy 2004, 2005; Snyder 2010). In their heartlands (though not always in their empires and borderlands) these states essentially achieved overwhelmingly effective monopolies of violence. Certainly, they were very little troubled by any domestic campaigns of anti-state terrorism.

Yet from a global perspective, the general point here is that most state terrorism has not been conducted by regimes enjoying the overwhelming infrastructural power of Hitler's Germany, Stalin's Russia (or, indeed, Mao's China, Suharto's Indonesia, and so on). Even in the mid-twentieth century, European colonial empires for instance still typically rested upon despotic, rather than infrastructural, power. In 1931, for instance, the vast territory of French Algeria was policed by a gendarmerie that possessed a grand total of twenty-seven automobiles and fourteen motorcycles (Thomas 2012, 96). Even before independence movements gathered momentum, memoirs of colonial officials testify repeatedly to a vertiginous sense of their own precariousness (Orwell 1957, 91–9). After

1945 European control could only be maintained by spectacular atrocity: at Sétif in 1945, Algerian insurgents killed 103 European settlers. The French backlash took perhaps 6,000 lives (Fisk 2005, 2006, 639). The profound democratization of the means of violence amongst colonial populations; exhaustion and devastation in Europe; a general revulsion at the excesses of Nazism—all these factors combined to create a highly unusual set of circumstances where time and again insurgent terrorism could not only take on colonial terrorism, but also successfully "outbid" it. After 1945, the trajectory of conflicts in Palestine, Cyprus, Kenya, and Algeria was ultimately structured by this broad dialectic, albeit severely modified by the presence or absence of "loyal" populations. State terrorism failed not because it lacked inventiveness or, in the short term, resources, but because it lacked stamina. Its "centre of gravity" (to use the Clausewitzian term) remained firmly located back in the metropolis; and to metropolitan opinion the colonial "periphery" was ultimately expendable and, indeed, largely forgettable. "Back in Britain there would be no soul-searching or public accounting for the crimes perpetrated against the hundreds of thousands of men and women in Kenya": such (lack of) reaction or remorse was typical of metropolitan populations that had the luxury of forgetting the savage wars of peace (Elkins 2005, 363).

Such mid-century liberation struggles (where colonial states caved in) contrast rather sharply with the typical outcomes of later twentieth-century "dirty wars." In these sustained auctions of intimidation waged between the rival terrorisms of authoritarian governments and their insurgent challengers, outcomes were typically clear cut. Dictatorships won hands down. Such, for instance, was the case in Syria after 1976 (Hinnebusch 2001, 2005, 93–103; Lefèvre 2013, 109–29). The final showdown at Hama in 1982 possibly cost somewhere between five and ten thousand lives (Seale 1988, 334). Although lacking such a grand climactic, the experience of Argentina in the 1970s was broadly comparable—there was an attempt to build a sustained left-wing guerrilla/terrorist campaign. But the scale of state repression simply obliterated it. The Dirty War in Argentina was very decisively won by the generals (Moyano 1995; Index on Censorship 1986).

Against the backdrop of the Cold War, superpower largesse for client governments is certainly part of the explanation for these regime triumphs. Yet it is far from being the full story. Most governments most of the time can marshal more resources than their challengers: "complete, full-blown state collapse does not happen very often" (Sorensen 2004, 134–5). Successful revolutions, too, are rather rare events. Any wavering populations forced to choose between rival terrors will seek to avoid the greater threat: and here it is a "common-sense observation that people are more likely to be terrorized by the open display of violence from heavily armed forces backed by the authority of the state than by anyone who has to hide their identity behind a mask" (Guelke 2008, 19).

Yet popular tolerance for state terrorism may have more positive drivers (Seale 1988, 328). State terrorism can indeed be *popular*—especially if disorder has persisted long enough (Moyano 1995). In the rueful judgment of one of the Argentinian guerrilla leaders, leftist armed struggle had turned out to be a "lost patrol"—overwhelmed by superior state forces and far too far out in front of public opinion (Moyano 1995). Civil society does not always choose the side of the angels: a key possibility whose significance has tended to be missed by those keen to hold the state to account. One recent study of the Chinese regime's "consultative authoritanism," indeed, concludes that "civil society might not play a role in challenging authoritarian governments, as liberal theories predict, but rather in making them more durable" (Teets 2014, 4–5).

This point can be pushed much further. Albeit with dangerously anorexic reductionism, I have sketched three broad typologies of confrontation between state and anti-state terrorism. In the first, the contest never really got going: state terror was simply unmatchable. In the second, state terror was trumped by colonial insurgency. In the third, a cycle of violence did begin, but state terror swiftly came out on top. This sketch tends to assume that state agencies are fairly clearly defined entities. But there are many other possible configurations and hybridities, since the state is itself inter-penetrated with society (Migdal 2001). Even in good times modern state apparatuses themselves are often labyrinthine in their complexity: and though we should be careful not to see states as entirely centrifugal and incoherent, we should hardly be surprised if different parts of them sometimes pull in different directions (for a possible overstatement of this case: Jarvis and Lister 2014). Indeed, deep opacity about exactly who is committing the atrocities is very often *the* defining feature of state terrorism in dirty war scenarios. This tendency demands far more explanation and historical contextualization than it typically receives. I turn to it now.

III

In a general overview of twentieth-century barbarism, Eric Hobsbawm writes that he could "find no real precedent before 1914... [for] quasi-official or tolerated strong-arm and killer squads which did the dirty work governments were not yet ready to do officially: *Freikorps*, Black-and-Tans, *squadristi*" (Hobsbawm 1999, 340). A major study of death squads similarly takes its first in-depth case study the activities of the *Freikorps* and their spin-offs in the early Weimar Republic of 1919–23 (Campbell and Brenner 2000: see also Gumbel 1922; Jones 2016). It was in exactly this period, too, that Belfast police death squads began to pioneer a distinctively new repertoire of terrorist tactics:

> They always came at night, after curfew. They left plenty of witnesses alive. Above all, they took great care to ensure no ambiguity as to whether or not they *were* the police, so that there should be no doubt as to who was giving this message of terror; thus, they introduced themselves as "police on duty"; they wore their uniforms; they mocked their victims by denying that they were the "murder gang", by reassuring them that all would be well, and by returning afterwards to offer their families fake condolences. After one killing, they chatted in the street before driving off.
>
> (Wilson 2010, 93)

In terms of the long history of the development of the modern state, then, paramilitary proliferation is a relatively *young* historical phenomenon (although one certainly more venerable than the spectacularly mistaken "New Wars" thesis allows: see Kaldor 1998, 2007, 98–9). All in all, the emergence of the death squad as the archetypal vehicle for (pro-)state terrorism seems to have something important to do with the development of the state in the period of late modernity. Most puzzlingly of all, such freelance brutality seems to have emerged in technologically advanced Europe at precisely the moment when the demands of "total war" had created the "total state": at the wartime juncture when "the state grew in size, in its multiple functions and in its authority" (Winter 2014, 2).

In a highly original—although regrettably all too brief—discussion, Brenner and Campbell begin by acknowledging the obvious attractions to modern states that are "bound by a whole range of internal and external norms that place strict limits on a state's range of options—if respected." Death squads offer the prospect of "plausible deniability." Yet as they go on to point out, this observation at best offers a partial explanation only for the rise of the phenomenon. Domestically, deniability is never fully convincing. If it were, it would cease to be authentically terroristic. Internationally, this strategy may buy time but "the charade doesn't usually last very long" (Campbell and Brenner 2000, 12–13).

They then approach the phenomenon historically. Death squads, they note, are not always mere tools of the state. They tend to draw resources from outside official circles and, to some extent, develop their own agendas: "in short, death squads cannot exist before the concept of citizenship does." Such citizen activists are the "antibodies" that spontaneously coalesce to fight infection within the body politic, at least according to their apologists (Chippendale and Harriman 1978, 14).

State elites often still deny association with them, of course. But such denials, in turn, are driven partially by "the existence of the concept of the governed, and this consent is based, among other things, on holding to the rule of law." In other words, death squads belong to the world of modern states (Brenner and Campbell 2000, 14–16). Finally, and most provocatively, they locate the appearance of death squads against a more general "crisis of the twentieth-century state" caught between centralizing and devolutionist impulses. In their view, the role of states has grown so extensive that they face being overwhelmed by the scale and variety of tasks expected of them:

> This has led to the widespread use of semistate or semi-public entities by modern states to "subcontract" important political, social, and economic tasks. Because of this, the modern state bleeds sovereignty, which is one of its defining characteristics.
>
> (Campbell and Brenner 2000, 16)

Rather than see the death squad as merely another extension of the long arm of repressive states (as others have done: see Sluka 2000, 1–36), this account presents death squads as specialized public–private partnerships that "generally involve the paradox of being secretive and covert organizations that nevertheless often act in particularly public and gruesome fashion" (Campbell and Brenner 2000, 5). A more recent study has come to a convergent conclusion: "paramilitaries challenge the typologies comparativists have traditionally relied upon in that they [are] neither entirely 'state' nor entirely 'civil society' actors. Rather they are the product of interests shared across factions of groups within both arenas" (Mazzei 2009, 217). Death squads seem to appear where the modern state is pulled between the twin imperatives of security domination and service devolution.

From a global perspective, Campbell and Brenner may underestimate the importance of state *weakness* in fostering state terrorism through death squads. Anatol Lieven comments in the context of Pakistan that this is "something that human rights groups in particular find hard to grasp, since they stem from a modern Western experience in which oppression came chiefly from over-mighty states" (Lieven 2011, 25). Death squads seem, too, to have flourished more in the under-mighty Iraqi state since 2003 than before (al-Khafaji 1991). "Seldom have death squads operated so openly" remarks Patrick Cockburn (2008, 224).

Still, Brenner and Campbell have offered a highly valuable broad account of why death squads have emerged when and where they have. One of its strengths is attention it pays to the possibility of moral hazard: that progressive change may, however unintentionally and indirectly, help structure new horrors. They write that it "is one of the many cruel ironies that crop up in connection with state violence, for it is quite likely that the increased concern for human rights has itself inadvertently been a contributing factor in the use of covert violence by governments, and in particular, in the use of death squads" (Campbell and Brenner 2000, 13). This latter point is worthy of exploration in its own right.

IV

"Today there exists," writes Pagden "even if it is only of very recent creation, an unmistakeable and universal 'human rights culture.' This is, as those from the Ayatollah Khomeini to Singapore's Lee Kuan Yew, who have opposed it in the name of theocracy or of some variant of communitarian 'Asian' values, have repeatedly insisted, the intellectual progeny of European universalism, and European universalism is the handmaiden of European imperialism" (Pagden 2015, 37). Cmiel concurs, writing in 2004 that "few political agendas have seen such a rapid and dramatic growth as that of 'human rights'" (quoted in Ron et al. 2005). Reading the academic literature on how states come to behave better, it is thus hard not to be struck by the dominance of teleological assumptions. However unevenly or slowly, the highly influential "spiral model" of human rights essentially assumes that good developments will lead to better: "while human rights progress was often uneven and our various phases occurred asynchronously in different countries over time, there was a clearly identifiable pattern of human rights progress... Over three decades from the 1960s until the 1990s, the various phases during which human rights change occurred grew progressively shorter, leading to a 'speeding up' of improvement in the overall global human rights situation" (Risse et al. 2013, 7–8). The Human Rights motorway, in this view, is a one-way street. Once joined, there may indeed be bumps and hold-ups. But there are no exit ramps. State terrorism seems here destined to wither away, like the state itself in Marxist theory.

Conversely, much of the academic community that is interested in pioneering the study of state terrorism seems little interested in evaluating the influence of human rights lobbies at all: a rather striking omission given their proclaimed, and commendable, intention to work towards "constraining state excesses and promoting genuine human and societal security" (Blakeley 2009, 19; Jackson et al. 2010, 6). There has been a notable failure to engage with important work that stresses how state repression adapts to awareness of humanitarian monitoring. Studies from James Ron and Darius Rejali are worth especial mention here.

In his important comparative study of patterns of state violence in the "semi-democracies" of Israel and Serbia, James Ron draws a basic distinction between what he calls "frontiers and ghettos" that is worth quoting at length:

> The crucial difference between frontiers and ghettos is the extent to which states control these arenas and feel a bureaucratic, moral, and political sense of responsibility for their fate. States enjoy an unrivalled level of control over the ghetto's borders and territory, suppressing challenges to their monopoly over force. Although this grants states some distinct advantages, it also implies important responsibilities. Ghetto residents are despised members of society, but both local and international rules stipulate that the state bears substantial responsibility for their welfare. Frontiers, by contrast, are perched on the edge of core states and not fully incorporated into their zone of control. States do not dominate frontiers as they do ghettos, and they are not bound by the same legal and moral obligations. (Ron 2003, 9)

Life in the ghetto is certainly not great since "the ghetto is a storage facility for the unwanted. It is incorporated, but not integrated with the polity" (Thorup 2010, 62). But life on the frontier may be even worse: states feel free to bludgeon frontiers harder than ghettos. The fate of Gaza since its "liberation" in 2005 illustrates the point with economy.

By contrast, Darius Rejali's focus on torture is much more fine-grained (although, strikingly, he, too, finds a contrast in Israeli abuse of prisoners in Lebanon and the Occupied Territories: Rejali 2007, 15). As others have usefully pointed out, torture serves as a valuable proxy marker for assessing wider practices of state terrorism. Getting prisoners to talk is only a part of the purpose of torture: getting a wider domestic constituency to "listen" to their fate is often rather more important politically (Blakeley 2007, 375; Branche 2007; Jackson et al, 2010, 4). Yet this is embarrassing internationally. How states manage the dissonance between the expectations of domestic and international audiences is the focus of Rejali's work on torture.

In this truly monumental study of torture techniques, Rejali stresses the sheer creativity of torturers in a world in which "most states perceive the advantages of at least appearing to respect human rights" (Rejali 2007, 26). His survey of torture styles and repertoires—with the central focus upon those designed to leave no lasting mark—is devastating in its wealth of accumulative detail. Democracies may indeed have tortured less. But they have also tortured "better": that is, more creatively, more cleverly, less obviously.

The techniques they have pioneered to avoid detection have led the way in teaching authoritarian types to hide their torture better: "by the late twentieth century, the clean techniques that first appeared in the main democracies can be found in countries around the world" (Rejali 2007, 4). An early pioneer was Britain. Waterboarding was standard practice in Palestine in 1936–9; Her Majesty's Torturers were at it again in Cyprus two decades later (Wilson 2013, 15–16). "When we watch interrogators, interrogators get sneaky" comments Rejali simply (2007, 9).

Rejali is careful to avoid a grand theory of cultural essentialism in his explanations of why torturers do the different things that they do: "religion and custom have little to do with the way they go about inflicting pain" (Rejali 2007, 35). But his work certainly throws much needed light on the longevity and adaptability of *sub*-cultures within "deep states": that is, those parts of the state apparatus that most shun scrutiny and accountability. If we can then talk—however broadly—of distinctive traditions of state torture, can we do the same more generally for state terrorism?

A landmark predecessor to the recent body of work produced by the Critical Terrorism Studies community was a collection of essays titled *Western State Terrorism* (George 1991). The title is a striking one in that it implies there might be a *distinctively* western way of state terrorism, perhaps parallel to a supposedly western way of war. Terminological fashion has shifted with the end of the Cold War: instead of "The West," the standard term now is the "Global North." Yet the basic comparative question remains both intriguing and strikingly under-explored. All in all, it seems that the critical terrorism tradition has largely opted to study Western state terrorism without any deep reflection upon the complex historical evolution of the Western state itself: classic studies such as Dyson's *The State Tradition in Western Europe* go conspicuously unreferenced in their bibliographies (Jackson et al. 2010). And, most strikingly of all, key conceptual distinctions between the canopy term of the *state* and specific branches of *government* simply glide by unheeded.

Crucially, too, the hegemonic power of the United States of America in the post-Cold War moment and its inglorious adventures of occupation during its "War on Terror" seem to have largely precluded explicit comparison with *other* traditions of state terrorism (Blakeley 2009). With shifts in global power towards Asia, this is surely a potential research question that will grow rather than diminish in importance: as reflected in the exponential growth of Chinese companies manufacturing "policing and security equipment" for export (Moore 2014). It is therefore encouraging here to see the focus broadening into a wider range of case studies that incorporate India and Papua New Guinea, in a recent collection (Jackson et al. 2010). But this is only a beginning.

As far as the Global North goes, there is an urgent need to contextualize its export of state violence both sociologically and historically. If the most powerful states of the Global North now go to considerable lengths to either hide or sub-contract their torture; if they would rather bomb, than occupy, "enemy" populations; and if they now choose to train more drone pilots than "pilots for fighters and bombers combined" (Crandall 2014, 464)—then, to a large extent, it is because they are authentically democratic. In other words, their executive governments are at least minimally sensitive to the broad wishes of a citizenry that has become markedly *less* militaristic than it was a hundred, or even fifty, years ago. American society would certainly not tolerate today the hundreds of military fatalities it was sustaining every week in Vietnam in the early 1970s.

Russell Crandall comments astutely that "part of the motivation behind the proliferation of drone strikes was that they could allow the U.S. military to maintain its military preponderance around the world without the long, costly, and unpopular wars and occupations that had dominated the last decade" (2014, 464). Yet the ability to kill more easily constitutes a standing temptation to kill more regularly. "Because it helps normalize the low-intensity conflicts the overall duration of the conflict could be extended and, finally, more 'lesser evils' could be committed" (Weizman 2007, 251). Drone proliferation thus forces us to recognize the resonant truth of Weber's observation that "it is *not* true that good can follow only from good and evil only from evil, but that often the opposite is true. Anyone who fails to see this is, indeed, a political infant."

Conclusion

Where, then, does this leave Richard Jackson's project of studying state and non-state terrorism together? In particular, how can we write a more integrated account of both?

Despite some recent advances, I argue that the major barrier to such a project is the naive ahistoricism that characterizes the field of terrorism studies, diverse as that field has become. We could usefully start by reflecting upon our own historical situation with regard to political violence: especially if we are scholars who happen to come from the UK or USA. Domestically, both these societies mostly had an unusually dull twentieth century. Any serious violence tended to come from outside.

It bears emphasizing how aberrational this societal experience of political violence is in global terms. If we wish to understand turmoil elsewhere better, it is worth recognizing that in many societies state violence is expected. A good place to start exploring it is therefore at its limits—to ask in other words, what is *not* expected? What does not tend to happen? What levels or types of violence are generally held to be taboo? Who sets those taboos? Are they maintained by tradition, or imposed by the international human rights community? How is violence structured accordingly? Why do limits hold or break down? Why death squads, and not full-blown genocide? Or vice versa?

Much of the study of anti-state terrorism is weakened by the tension between expansive definitions of what constitutes terrorism, and the very limited repertoire of actions and actors actually analyzed: essentially small groups conducting bombings and hostage-takings. Much of our understanding of state terrorism is distorted by a comparable over-emphasis on centralized and infrastructural mega-violence. But in between these rival foci lies another much less illuminated scene where despotic power looms larger. This seethes with overlapping anti- and pro-state activity: a dark landscape alive with lynchings, pogroms, massacres, and death squad killings.

All of this looks like political violence (at least partially) intended to spread fear. All of it therefore looks like some sort of "terrorism": and we shall not understand it better if we continue to insist on our decontextualized and ahistorical conceptualizations of what we think state/anti-state terrorism should "really" look like. If we are serious about understanding terrorism comprehensively, then, we are obliged to try to map it all in all its messy interconnectedness. We shall certainly have our work cut out.

References

Alexander, Yonah (1985) "State-Supported Terrorism," *Harvard International Review*, 7: 21–3.

Al-Khafaji, Isam (1991) "State Terror and the Degradation of Politics in Iraq," *Middle East Report*, 176: 15–21.

Blakeley, Ruth (2007) "Why Torture?," *Review of International Studies*, 33: 373–94.

Blakeley, Ruth (2009) *State Terrorism and Neoliberalism: The North in the South*. London: Routledge.

Blakeley, Ruth (2010) "State Terrorism in the Social Sciences: Theories, Methods and Concepts," in Richard Jackson, Eamon Murphy and Scott Poynting (eds), *Contemporary State Terrorism: Theory and Practice*. Abingdon: Routledge, 12–27.

Branche, Raphaëlle (2007) "Torture of Terrorists? Use of Torture in a 'War Against Terrorism': Justifications, Methods and Effects. The Case of France in Algeria, 1954–1962," *International Review of the Red Cross*, 89(867): 543–60.

Bullock, Alan (1991, 1993) *Hitler and Stalin: Parallel Lives*. London: Harper Collins.

Burleigh, Michael (2000) *The Third Reich: A New History*. London: Macmillan.

Byman, Daniel (2005) *Deadly Connections: States that Sponsor Terrorism*. Cambridge: Cambridge University Press.

Campbell, Bruce, and Arthur Brenner, eds (2000) *Death Squads in Global Perspective: Murder with Deniability*. New York: Palgrave Macmillan.

Chippendale, Peter, and Ed Harriman (1978) *Juntas United!* London: Quartet Books.

Chomsky, Noam (1990) *Pirates and Emperors: International Terrorism in the Real World*. Brattleboro, VT: Amana Books.

Cobain, Ian (2012, 2013) *Cruel Britannia: A Secret History of Torture*. London: Portobello Books.

Cockburn, Patrick (2008) *Muqtada al-Sadr and the Fall of Iraq*. London: Faber & Faber.

Cojean, Annick (2013) *Gaddafi's Harem: The Story of a Young Woman and the Abuses of Power in Libya*. London: Grove Press.

Coren, Alan (1975) *Golfing for Cats*. London: Robson Books.

Crandall, Russell (2014) *America's Dirty Wars: Irregular Warfare from 1776 to the War on Terror*. New York: Cambridge University Press.

Davenport, Christian, and Molly Inman (2012) "The State of State Repression Research since the 1990s," *Terrorism and Political Violence*, 24: 619–34.

Degregori, Carlos (1999) "Reaping the Whirlwind: The *Rondas Campesinas* and the Defeat of *Sendero Luminoso* in Ayacucho," in Kees Koonings and Dirk Kruijt (eds), *Societies of Fear: The Legacy of Civil War, Violence and Terror in Latin America*. London: Zed Books.

Duncan, Gillian, Orla Lynch, Gilbert Ramsay and Alison Watson, eds (2013) *State Terrorism and Human Rights: International Responses since the end of the Cold War*. London: Routledge.

Duranty, Walter (1935) *I Write as I Please*. London: Hamish Hamilton.

Dyson, Kenneth (1980, 2009) *The State Tradition in Western Europe: A Study of an Idea and Institution*. Colchester: ECPR.
Elkins, Caroline (2005) *Britain's Gulag: The Brutal End of Empire in Kenya*. London: Pimlico.
English, Richard, ed. (2015) *Illusions of Terrorism and Counter-Terrorism*. Oxford: Oxford University Press.
Fisk, Robert (2005, 2006) *The Great War for Civilisation: The Conquest of the Middle East*. London: Harper Perennial.
Frankel, Philip (2001) *An Ordinary Atrocity: Sharpeville and its Massacre*. Johannesburg: Witwatersrand University Press.
Gearty, Conor (1997) *Terrorism*. London: Phoenix.
George, Alexander, ed. (1991) *Western State Terrorism*. Cambridge: Polity Press.
Geyer, Michael, and Shelia Fitzpatrick, eds (2009) *Beyond Totalitarianism: Stalinism and Nazism Compared*. Cambridge: Cambridge University Press.
Grant, Michael, ed. (1957, 1989) *Suetonius: The Twelve Caesars*. London: Penguin.
Green, Linda (1994) "Fear as a Way of Life," *Cultural Anthropology*, 9(2): 227–56.
Guelke, Adrian (2008) "Great Whites, Paedophiles and Terrorists: The Need for Critical Thinking in a New Age of Fear," *Critical Studies on Terrorism*, 1(1): 17–25.
Gumbel, Emil (1922) *Vier Jahre Politischer Mord*. Berlin: Verlag der neuen Gesellschaft.
Hainsworth, Paul (2000) "New Labour, New Codes of Conduct? British Government Policy towards Indonesia and East Timor after the 1997 Election," in Paul Hainsworth and Stephen McCloskey (eds), *The East Timor Question: The Struggle for Independence from Indonesia*. London: I. B. Tauris, 95–116.
Hinnebusch, Raymond (2001, 2005) *Syria: Revolution from Above*. London: Routledge.
Hobsbawm, Eric (1999) *On History*. London: Abacus.
Index on Censorship (1986) *Nunca Mas*. London: Faber & Faber.
Jackson, Richard (2008) "The Ghosts of State Terror: Knowledge, Politics and Terrorism Studies," *Critical Studies on Terrorism*, 1(3): 377–92.
Jackson, Richard (2009) "Knowledge, Power and Politics in the Study of Political Terrorism," in Richard Jackson, Marie Breen Smyth, and Jeroen Gunning (eds), *Critical Terrorism Studies: A New Research Agenda*. Abingdon: Routledge, 66–84.
Jackson, Richard, Eamon Murphy, and Scott Poynting, eds (2010) *Contemporary State Terrorism: Theory and Practice*. Abingdon: Routledge.
Jarvis, Lee, and Michael Lister (2014) "State Terrorism Research and Critical Terrorism Studies: An Assessment," *Critical Studies in Terrorism*, 7(1): 43–61.
Jones, Mark (2016) *Founding Weimar: Violence and the German Revolution of 1918–1919*. Cambridge: Cambridge University Press.
Kaldor, Mary (1998, 2007) *New and Old Wars: Organized Violence in a Global Era*. Stanford: Stanford University Press.
Kamau, Joseph, and Andrew Cameron (1979) *Lust to Kill: The Rise and Fall of Idi Amin*. London: Corgi.
Kuromiya, Hiroaki (1998) *Freedom and Terror in the Donbas: A Ukranian–Russian Borderland, 1870s-1990s*. Cambridge: Cambridge University Press.
Lefèvre, Raphaël (2013) *Ashes of Hama: the Muslim Brotherhood in Syria*. London: Hurst & Co.
Lesch, David (2012) *Syria: The Fall of the House of Assad*. New Haven: Yale University Press.
Lieven, Anatol (2011) *Pakistan: A Hard Country*. London: Allen Lane.
McClintock, Michael (1985, 1987) *The American Connection: Volume One: State Terror and Popular Resistance in El Salvador*. London: Zed Books.

Mann, Michael (2013) *The Sources of Social Power: Volume Four: Globalizations, 1945–2011*. Cambridge: Cambridge University Press.

Marlow, Joyce (1969, 1970) *The Peterloo Massacre*. London: Rapp & Whiting.

Masters, Bruce (2013) *The Arabs of the Ottoman Empire, 1516–1918: A Social and Cultural History*. Cambridge: Cambridge University Press.

Mazower, Mark (2002) "Violence and the State in the Twentieth Century," *American Historical Review*, 107(4): 1158–78.

Mazzei, Julie (2009) *Death Squads or Self-Defence Forces? How Paramilitary Groups Emerge and Challenge Democracy in Latin America*. Chapel Hill, NC: University of North Carolina Press.

Messinger, Johann (1935) *The Death of Dollfuss: An Official History of the Revolt of July, 1934, in Austria*. London: Denis Archer.

Migdal, Joel (2001) *State in Society: Studying How States and Societies Transform and Constitute One Another*. Cambridge: Cambridge University Press.

Moore, Malcolm (2014) "China Exports its Expertise in Torture," *Daily Telegraph*, Sept. 23.

Moyano, María José (1995) *Argentina's Lost Patrol: Armed Struggle, 1969–1979*. London: Yale University Press.

Murray, Craig (2006, 2007) *Murder in Samarkand: A British Ambassador's Controversial Defiance of Tyranny in the War on Terror*. Edinburgh: Mainstream Publishing.

Nagengast, Carole (1994) "Violence, Terror, and the Crisis of the State," *Annual Review of Anthropology*, 23: 109–36.

Orwell, George (1957) *Selected Essays*. London: Penguin.

Overy, Richard (2004, 2005) *The Dictators: Hitler's Germany, Stalin's Russia*. London: Allen Lane.

Pagden, Anthony (2015) *The Burdens of Empire: 1539 to the Present*. New York: Cambridge University Press.

Rejali, Darius (2007) *Torture and Democracy*. Princeton: Princeton University Press.

Risse, Thomas, Stephen Ropp, and Kathryn Sikkink, eds (2013) *The Persistent Power of Human Rights: From Commitment to Compliance*. Cambridge: Cambridge University Press.

Ron, James (2003) *Frontiers and Ghettos: State Violence in Serbia and Israel*. Berkeley, CA: University of California Press.

Ron, James, Howard Ramos, and Kathleen Rodgers (2005) "Transnational Information Politics: NGO Human Rights Reporting, 1986–2000," *International Studies Quarterly*, 49(3): 557–87.

Rummel, R. (1994) *Death by Government*. New Brunswick: Transaction.

Schlögel, Karl (2008, 2012) *Moscow 1937*. Cambridge: Polity Press.

Schmid, Alex, ed. (2013) *The Routledge Handbook of Terrorism Research*. Abingdon: Routledge.

Seale, Patrick (1988) *Asad of Syria: The Struggle for the Middle East*. London: I. B. Tauris.

Sluka, Jeffrey (2000) *Death Squad: The Anthropology of State Terror*. Philadelphia: University of Pennsylvania Press.

Snyder, Timothy (2010) *Bloodlands: Europe between Hitler and Stalin*. London: Bodley Head.

Sorensen, Georg (2004) *The Transformation of the State: Beyond the Myth of Retreat*. Basingstoke: Palgrave Macmillan.

Sproat, Peter (1991) "Can the State be Terrorist?," *Terrorism*, 14(1): 19–29.

Steele, Jonathan (2008) *Defeat: Why they Lost Iraq*. London: I. B. Tauris.

Stohl, Michael, and George Lopez, eds (1984) *The State as Terrorist: The Dynamics of Governmental Violence and Repression*. Westport, CT: Greenwood Press.

Teets, Jessica (2014) *Civil Society under Authoritarianism: The China Model.* New York: Cambridge University Press.

Thomas, Martin (2012) *Violence and Colonial Order: Police, Workers and Protest in the European Colonial Empires, 1918–1940.* Cambridge: Cambridge University Press.

Thorup, Mikkel (2010) *An Intellectual History of Terror: War, Violence and the State.* London: Routledge.

Tilly, Charles (1990) *Coercion, Capital, and European States,* AD *990–1990.* Oxford: Basil Blackwell.

Townshend, Charles (2002) *Terrorism: A Very Short Introduction.* Oxford: Oxford University Press.

Weber, Max (1919) *Politics as a Vocation.* Munich: Duncker & Humboldt.

Weizman, Eyal (2007) *Hollow Land: Israel's Architecture of Occupation.* London: Verso.

Wilkinson, Paul (2006) *Terrorism versus Democracy: The Liberal State Response.* Abingdon: Routledge.

Wilson, Tim (2010) "'The Most Terrible Assassination that has Yet Stained the Name of Belfast': The Mcmahon Murders in Context," *Irish Historical Studies,* 37(145): 83–106.

Wilson, Tim (2013) "State Terrorism: An Historical Overview," in Gillian Duncan, Orla Lynch, Gilbert Ramsay, and Alison Watson (eds), *State Terrorism and Human Rights: International Responses since the end of the Cold War.* London: Routledge, 14–31.

Winter, Jay, ed. (2014) *The Cambridge History of the First World War,* ii. *The State.* Cambridge: Cambridge University Press.

Woodworth, Paddy (2001) *Dirty War, Clean Hands: ETA, the GAL and Spanish Democracy.* Cork: Cork University Press.

CHAPTER 23

TERRORISM, CIVIL WAR, AND INSURGENCY

JESSICA A. STANTON

MUCH of the terrorism occurring worldwide is domestic terrorism carried out by rebel groups fighting in civil wars. Rebel groups such as the Taliban in Afghanistan, Sendero Luminoso in Peru, the Tamil Tigers (LTTE) in Sri Lanka, and the Kurdistan Workers' Party (PKK) in Turkey set off bombs in train stations, on public buses, in busy marketplaces and restaurants, wounding and killing many civilians. In fact, thirty-eight of the 103 rebel groups fighting in civil wars[1] from 1989 to 2010 engaged in terrorism, measured by rebel group use of small-scale bombs to attack civilian targets (Stanton 2016). The nature of these attacks—using explosive devices to target civilians—bears similarity to attacks carried out by transnational terrorist organizations, such as Al Qaeda. And yet despite this similarity in tactics, many are reluctant to categorize domestic insurgencies—rebel groups fighting against their own governments to achieve domestic political objectives such as greater political representation or territorial autonomy—as terrorist groups or to identify the tactics used by domestic insurgencies as terrorist tactics.

Throughout this chapter, I employ what some refer to as an action-centered view of terrorism (Sánchez-Cuenca and de la Calle 2009), viewing terrorism as a distinctive form of violent behavior, and avoiding references to "terrorist groups" or "terrorist organizations." In the next section, I discuss definitional issues in greater depth, focusing on the challenges of defining terrorism in relation to civilian targeting. Through a survey of the literature, I contend that research on the dynamics of violence in civil war would benefit from a more standardized definition of the concept of terrorism as well as greater consensus on how the concept of terrorism ought to be used in relation to the concept of civilian targeting.[2] The lack of conceptual clarity in distinguishing between terrorism and civilian targeting makes it difficult to compare research findings, and thus to make progress as a field in our understanding of the causes of violence and its consequences.[3] Despite the challenges associated with drawing comparisons across studies, the second section of the chapter attempts to do precisely this, examining research on terrorism as well as research on civilian targeting to develop insights into the causes and consequences of terrorist violence employed in the context of civil war. The final section of the chapter proposes areas for future research.

The Challenges of Differentiating between Terrorism and Civilian Targeting

Conflicting Definitions of Terrorism

According to many definitions of terrorism nearly all rebel group violence against noncombatants would qualify as terrorism. The US government, for example, defines terrorism as "premeditated, politically motivated violence perpetrated against noncombatant targets by subnational groups or clandestine agents."[4] Under broad definitions such as this one, most rebel group attacks against civilians as well as against government and military forces not actively engaged in combat would qualify as terrorism. Many scholars of terrorism, however, define the term more narrowly, emphasizing that a key characteristic setting terrorism apart from other forms of violence against noncombatants is the *audience* for terrorist violence. In this view, terrorism aims to convey a message to an audience other than those targeted with violence (Hoffman 2006). Emphasizing the communicative aspects of terrorism, these scholars see terrorism as "symbolic" violence that "communicates a political message" (Crenshaw 1981, 379) to a wider audience and involves the "pursuit of publicity" (Weinberg et al. 2004, 10). In Hoffman's words, "terrorism is specifically designed to have far-reaching psychological effects beyond the immediate victim(s) or object of the terrorist attack. It is meant to instill fear within, and thereby intimidate, a wider 'target audience'" (Hoffman 2006, 40–1).

Drawing on this conceptualization of terrorism, Chenoweth explicitly contrasts terrorism with civilian targeting that takes place during civil war; in her view, "terrorism is distinguished from other forms of violence (such as civilian victimization during civil war) by its randomness and its attempt to convey a political message beyond the targets themselves" (Chenoweth 2010, 16). Kalyvas disagrees, however, arguing that much civil war violence against civilians shares a logic with terrorist violence. Civil war violence against civilians often aims both to eliminate individuals perceived as threatening—individuals believed to be aiding the opponent—as well as to influence a wider audience, seeking to deter other civilians from similar forms of enemy collaboration (Kalyvas 2004).

This lack of agreement about whether and how to distinguish between terrorism and civilian targeting is related to differences in how scholars define the audience for terrorist violence. Much of the literature on transnational and domestic terrorism conceives of the government opponent as the primary audience for terrorist violence; the aim of violence is to coerce the government into altering its policies or making political concessions (Hoffman 2006). The response of the wider civilian population is important, but only because changes in public attitudes might persuade the government to shift its policies. In Kalyvas's concept of terrorism, however, the primary audience for violence is civilians themselves. By targeting civilians who are believed to be collaborating with the opponent, armed groups seek to influence the wider civilian population, deterring them from providing material aid and intelligence to the opponent.

Kalyvas is right to point out that much wartime civilian targeting shares with terrorism the intent to influence individuals beyond the immediate targets of violence. However, distinguishing between terrorism and other forms of civilian targeting based on the primary audience for violence—the primary group whose behavior violence aims to influence—has a number of advantages for research. Such distinctions, for example, allow for analysis of whether different types of violence have different causes, how audiences might vary in their responses to violence, and the conditions under which different types of violence might aid a group in achieving its political goals.

In the remainder of this chapter, therefore, I distinguish between terrorism and civilian targeting. I define *terrorism* as "the deliberate use of violence against civilians by a nonstate actor with the aim of achieving a political objective through the intimidation or coercion of the government" (Stanton 2013, 1010). Terrorism is strategic violence in which civilians are the target for violence, but civilians are not the primary target *audience* for violence; rather, the government opponent is the primary audience for violence or target of coercion (Stanton 2013, 2016). Although some definitions of terrorism apply to both state and non-state actors, I focus on terrorism carried out by non-state actors, as this is more consistent with the literature on terrorism. I use the term *civilian targeting* as an umbrella term, referring to multiple different types of violence involving deliberate attacks on noncombatant civilians; civilian targeting thus includes terrorist violence, as well as other forms of violence against civilians, such as opportunistic violence that occurs in the context of looting, as well as strategic violence aimed at inducing civilian cooperation. Throughout the chapter, I differentiate between domestic and transnational terrorism. Domestic terrorism is violence in which "the venue, target, and perpetrators are all from the same country" (Enders et al. 2011, 321), whereas transnational terrorism involves attacks against individuals of a foreign nationality or against targets in a foreign country.

My approach views terrorism as a tactic that many different types of groups may use—groups fighting in civil wars as well as groups not actively engaged in broader military conflicts with the government. Sánchez-Cuenca and de la Calle (2009) propose an alternate, actor-based approach, focusing on differentiating types of armed actors—in particular, distinguishing guerrilla organizations from terrorist organizations—as opposed to differentiating types of behaviors. For Sánchez-Cuenca and de la Calle, guerrilla organizations possess control over territory, whereas terrorist groups are "clandestine or underground" organizations that are weak in comparison to the state and, therefore, unable to control territory.

Sánchez-Cuenca and de la Calle are right to point out the challenges action-based approaches face in specifying the boundaries of what constitutes terrorist violence.

Actor-based approaches, however, also have drawbacks—particularly when exploring questions regarding the causes and consequences of using terrorism in civil wars. First, because actor-based approaches rely, in part, on government characteristics—for example, the power of the state—to identify terrorist organizations, it is difficult then to assess the extent to which government characteristics might influence the behavior and decision-making of armed groups. Second, using an actor-based approach raises challenges for evaluating the impact of different types of political violence. If one wants to analyze the ability of groups to achieve their political objectives, confining the analysis to clandestine groups fighting against powerful governments and unable to control territory might bias the analysis toward finding that terrorism is ineffective. Finally, as Phillips (2015) points out, the action-based approach remains dominant in the literature on terrorism and insurgency.

The Advantages of a Conceptual Distinction between Terrorism and Civilian Targeting

Distinguishing between terrorism and civilian targeting has several important advantages. First, it permits greater precision in the terminology we use to describe different types of political violence that occur in the context of civil war. This precision may help to clarify the ways in which violence varies across cases of civil war or across space and time in a single civil war. The PKK in Turkey, for example, carried out terrorist attacks—setting off bombs at tourist sites, on buses, and in shopping areas—aimed at forcing the government to negotiate; but the PKK also used other forms of civilian targeting, attacking civilians in villages that organized pro-government militias.

Second, defining terrorism in the context of civil war in a way that mirrors the definitions of terrorism used in studies of transnational and domestic terrorism helps to maintain consistency across different areas of research within political science. In recent years, a number of scholars have sought to bridge the gap between studies of terrorism and studies of civil war (Abrahms and Potter 2015; Coggins 2015; Crenshaw 2017; Enders et al. 2011; Findley and Young 2012a, 2015; Fortna 2015; Polo and Gleditsch 2016; Sambanis 2008; Sánchez-Cuenca and de la Calle 2009; Stanton 2013, 2016); but more remains to be done in integrating these two bodies of research. As Findley and Young (2012a) point out, significant overlap exists between different types of political violence—and in particular, between terrorism and civil war.[5] Still, much domestic terrorism occurs outside of civil war (Findley and Young 2012a; Sambanis 2008; Sánchez-Cuenca and de la Calle 2009)—for example, the Oklahoma City bombing in the United States—suggesting the need for a definition of terrorism that can be applied both to civil war and non-civil war settings.

Third, making this conceptual distinction will also improve scholars' ability to compare the findings of different studies of violence in civil war. The present lack of clarity regarding how and whether to distinguish between terrorism and civilian targeting has made it more difficult to compare research findings. For example, a study that uses the term "terrorism" might be analyzing similar patterns of violence to a study using the term "civilian victimization" or "civilian targeting," in which case, a direct comparison of the theoretical arguments and empirical findings of these studies might be appropriate. It is also possible, however, that a study of "terrorism" is analyzing a subset of the larger category of "civilian targeting," in which case, it might not be appropriate to make direct comparisons between the theoretical claims and findings of this study and those of a study on civilian targeting. Without the ability to easily compare the findings of different studies on civil war violence, it is difficult to make progress as a field and to reach consensus regarding the dynamics of violence in civil war.

Despite these challenges in making comparisons among existing studies, the next two sections of this chapter seek to do this, by drawing on research on civilian targeting as well as research on terrorism to develop insights regarding the causes of terrorism during civil war and its consequences.

Research on the Causes of Terrorism and Civilian Targeting in Civil War

In this section, I discuss several commonly posited causes for civilian targeting and terrorism, evaluating the extent to which these factors might influence the likelihood of terrorism in civil war.

Organizational Dynamics

A number of scholars argue that the organizational characteristics of armed groups influence the likelihood of violence against civilians during civil wars. Some groups lack the organizational tools to control the use of violence among their members—for example, strong command structures or effective training—or have organizational incentives for violence. This increases the likelihood that individual group members will engage in *opportunistic violence*—violence perpetrated by individual group members that is not planned or ordered by the group's leadership (Cohen 2013, 2016; Hoover Green 2016; Manekin 2013; Salehyan et al. 2014; Weinstein 2007; E. J. Wood 2006, 2009). Often, these scholars acknowledge that strategic violence takes place alongside opportunistic violence, but do not explain variation in strategic violence, and therefore, do not address questions such as why some groups use terrorism strategically in pursuit of their political goals.

A study by Abrahms and Potter (2015), however, posits several ways in which organizational dynamics might be linked to terrorism. They contend that groups with decentralized leadership structures—in which low-level members make decisions regarding the use of violence—are more likely to use both opportunistic and strategic violence against civilians, which they term terrorism. With regard to strategic violence, Abrahms and Potter argue that low-level members lack experience and have short time horizons, making them less cognizant of the potential backlash terrorism may elicit and more concerned with securing short-term gains from civilian targeting than with pursuing the group's long-term political objectives.

Because Abrahms and Potter use a broad definition of terrorism—including all forms of civilian targeting occurring in civil wars as well as civilian targeting occurring outside of civil wars—and aggregated data on violence against civilians, it is not possible to determine whether the correlation they find between decentralized leadership structures and civilian targeting is driven primarily by opportunistic violence, primarily by strategic violence, or some combination of the two. Future research, therefore, might explore whether groups with decentralized leadership structures, indeed, are more likely to use terrorism strategically in civil wars, to elicit government concessions.

One additional aspect of organizational control arguments may be useful in understanding terrorist violence in civil war. As Wood (2009) points out, when groups use violence strategically, effective organizational control is likely to be associated with *higher* rather than lower levels of violence against civilians. Perhaps, then, among groups that are prone to using terrorism, we might expect those with effective command structures and disciplinary procedures to be capable of carrying out more violent, larger-scale attacks (Shapiro 2015).

Grievances

Several studies find that the presence of groups with strong economic and political grievances—as measured by economic discrimination (Piazza 2011), ethnic or religious tensions (Gassebner and Luechinger 2011), political exclusion (Choi and Piazza 2016), and government repression (Piazza 2017)—is associated with a greater incidence of domestic terrorism. Moreover, Gleditsch and Polo (2016) show that efforts to redress ethnic group grievances through political accommodation are associated with a *decline* in the frequency and magnitude of domestic terrorist attacks. These studies define terrorism much as this chapter does, but examine the overall incidence of domestic terrorism, including domestic terrorist incidents occurring during civil wars and domestic terrorist incidents occurring in countries not experiencing civil wars.[6] However, in an analysis of terrorism occurring *outside* of civil war, Sambanis (2008) does not find evidence linking ethnic grievances to terrorism. This suggests that civil war cases may be driving the positive relationship scholars have uncovered between grievances and terrorism. Or perhaps differences in the measurement of concepts account for divergent findings.

Arguments emphasizing the importance of grievances may be less useful for understanding why—among groups fighting in civil wars—some groups choose to use terrorism, while other groups do not. Most groups fighting in civil wars possess grievances against the government; indeed, research shows a strong link between economic and political inequality and the likelihood of civil war (Cederman et al. 2013). Thus, grievances may be more important in explaining why some *countries* experience terrorism and others do not than explaining why some *groups fighting in civil wars* use terrorism and others do not. Still, future research might examine whether the strength of grievances influences strategic choices in civil wars as well—for example, whether groups facing severe economic and political inequality are more willing to use extreme forms of violence, such as terrorist attacks against civilians.

Military Context

In their efforts to explain civil war violence, many scholars look to the dynamics of the conflict itself, arguing that the military context generates incentives to attack civilians. Kalyvas (2006) develops arguments to explain a pervasive form of violence during civil war—violence aimed at punishing suspected enemy collaborators and thereby inducing cooperation from the wider civilian population. Kalyvas contends that this form of violence escalates as contestation over territory escalates. When an armed group possesses monopoly control over territory, the group does not need to use violence to induce civilian cooperation; the group's strong presence is enough to elicit "voluntary" support from civilians. When control over territory is contested, however, armed groups lack the information needed to selectively target suspected enemy collaborators, thus increasing the likelihood of indiscriminate violence against civilians. However, as Balcells (2017) demonstrates, even when one armed group possesses monopoly control over territory, the group may still attack civilians—particularly if prewar political mobilization was high, raising concerns about civilian loyalties.

Emphasizing territorial contestation, de la Calle (2017) predicts high levels of civilian targeting aimed at inducing compliance in rural areas, where rebel groups tend to control territory. Stewart and Liou (2016) contend that rebel groups controlling *foreign* territory, where they have few political constituents, are more likely than rebel groups controlling *domestic* territory to use violence to secure civilian cooperation. Meanwhile, Weintraub (2016) argues that international development assistance to conflict areas often helps governments to extend their territorial control; thus, aid can inadvertently lead to increased insurgent violence against civilians, as insurgents attempt to regain lost territory.

Arguments regarding territorial contestation offer compelling explanations for violence whose primary objective is to elicit greater cooperation from civilians, but these explanations do not account for variation in terrorist violence whose primary objective is to force government concessions. In fact, the empirical evidence shows that groups often use these two forms of violence in conjunction with one another during civil war; the FARC in Colombia, for example, used violence to induce civilian cooperation in the interior of the country, while also carrying out terrorist attacks in major cities to pressure the Colombian government to make political concessions.

A number of scholars argue that rebel group military strength influences the use of strategic, terrorist violence against civilians. When rebel groups are weak in comparison to their government opponents—either because they have fewer troops or because they have suffered military losses—direct confrontations with government military forces are risky. To impose costs on the government, these groups instead attack soft, poorly defended targets, such as economic and civilian targets (e.g. Crenshaw 1981; Hultman 2007; Pape 2003; Polo and Gleditsch 2016). Some argue that military weakness may also lead to greater opportunistic violence against civilians, as groups resort to looting and coercive violence as a means of obtaining resources and support from civilians (R. M. Wood 2010, 2014).

These arguments regarding military weakness offer a persuasive theoretical justification for why groups are often willing to engage in forms of violence that both domestic and international audiences might find reprehensible. Most of these studies, however, use aggregated data on civilian targeting to test their claims—data that include both opportunistic violence, such as attacks that occur in the context of looting, as well as strategic violence, such as the bombing of public buses or marketplaces. Without the ability to differentiate between opportunistic and strategic violence, it is difficult to evaluate the theoretical claims: are weak groups more likely to use opportunistic violence against civilians, strategic violence against civilians, terrorist violence against civilians, or all of these? An exception is the study by Polo and Gleditsch (2016), which uses data from the Global Terrorism Database (GTD) that allows for greater differentiation among types of violence. In one of their analyses, Polo and Gleditsch use a restrictive definition of terrorist violence that requires "evidence of an intention to coerce, intimidate, or convey some other message to a larger audience" and excludes attacks against military targets. However, this analysis *does* include attacks against government and police targets, and thus, cannot shed light on whether weak groups are more likely to use terrorist violence against exclusively civilian targets.

Also emphasizing the military context, some argue that when multiple armed groups compete for support from the same constituency, groups sometimes use terrorist attacks on civilians as a means of signaling their resolve, in an effort to outbid rival groups for popular support (Bloom 2005; Chenoweth 2010; Conrad and Greene 2015; Kydd and Walter 2006). Empirical analyses of outbidding demonstrate a relationship between political competition and the incidence of transnational terrorist attacks (Chenoweth 2010), the incidence of suicide bombing (Bloom 2005), and the severity of domestic and transnational terrorist attacks (Conrad and Greene 2015).

Several studies examine outbidding in civil wars, to assess whether the presence of multiple rebel groups is associated with terrorist violence. Wood and Kathman (2015) find that in internal armed conflicts in Africa, competition among armed groups is associated with higher levels of violence against civilians (defined broadly, to include all forms of civilian targeting), arguing that rival groups use violence to coerce concessions from the government and to induce civilian cooperation. Findley and Young (2012b), however, do not find evidence that competition among armed groups fighting in internal conflicts is associated with an increased likelihood of either suicide terrorism or other forms of domestic terrorism. Using a narrower definition of terrorist violence against civilians, Stanton (2013) also does not find evidence of outbidding, showing that rebel groups in multi-party civil wars are no more likely to use terrorist violence than rebel groups in single-party civil wars. Future research, therefore, might seek to clarify these conflicting findings, specifying the conditions under which competition among groups is likely to lead to increased violence against civilians, and importantly, specifying the *types of violence* such competition is likely to produce.

Domestic Political Institutions

Many argue that the structure of domestic political institutions also shapes the strategic context within which armed groups make decisions about whether to target civilians. A number of scholars show that the likelihood of *transnational* terrorist attacks is higher in countries with democratic political institutions (e.g. Chenoweth 2010; Eubank and Weinberg 1994, 2001; Li 2005; Pape 2003; Schmid 1992), while recent studies explore whether democracies might also be more prone to *domestic* terrorism. Young and Dugan (2011), for example, argue that democratic governments are more likely to experience both transnational and domestic terrorism because greater numbers of veto players increase the likelihood of political stalemate and decrease the ability of groups to achieve their political objectives through nonviolent political participation. Meanwhile, Foster et al. (2013) demonstrate that democratic proportional representation systems lend legitimacy to small minority groups, but prevent these groups from being able to impact policy significantly, increasing the likelihood of domestic terrorism.

Not all scholars agree, however, about the relationship between democracy and terrorism. Most studies challenging the link between democracy and terrorism focus on transnational terrorism (e.g. Eyerman 1998; Kurrild-Klitgaard et al. 2006; Piazza 2008; Sandler 1995), but several include domestic terrorism in their analyses. Using data that combine incidents of transnational and domestic terrorism, both Abadie (2006) and Chenoweth (2013) find evidence of a curvilinear relationship between regime type and terrorism. Gaibulloev et al. (2017) show that this curvilinear relationship holds separately for transnational terrorist attacks as well as domestic terrorist attacks. In anocratic regimes—regimes that are neither fully democratic nor fully autocratic—grievances are sufficient to motivate violence and groups have sufficient opportunity to organize to launch attacks.

Several studies examining domestic terrorism occurring during civil war find positive associations between democracy and rebel group terrorism. Stanton (2013, 2016) argues that democratic institutions create incentives for leaders to be responsive to the domestic public, making democratic governments more vulnerable to pressure from their domestic constituents. Aware of this distinctive feature of democracies, rebel groups use terrorist attacks on the government's constituents as a means of pressuring the government to make political concessions. Media attention is crucial to the ability of rebel groups to impose costs on the government; for this reason, Polo and Gleditsch

(2016) posit, higher levels of press freedom are associated with greater numbers of terrorist attacks, even when controlling for democracy. Their analyses indicate that rebel groups fighting against democratic governments also carry out higher numbers of terrorist attacks. These findings are consistent with the findings of Eck and Hultman (2007) and Hultman (2012), showing that rebel groups fighting in civil wars against democracies are more likely to engage in civilian targeting broadly defined.

Stanton and Polo and Gleditsch argue that rebel groups are also constrained by their own constituencies of supporters. Stanton posits that rebel groups with inclusive political objectives that need support from broad civilian constituencies are likely to use lower casualty forms of terrorism, such as attacks on economic and infrastructure targets; while Polo and Gleditsch contend that groups with narrow audiences are more likely to attack "soft civilian targets" as compared with "hard and official targets" such as government, police, or transportation infrastructure. In a similar vein, Heger (2015) finds that ethno-political groups who participate in electoral politics—and thus, can be held accountable by their constituents—are less likely to use violence against civilians, broadly defined.

Despite evidence of an association between democracy and rebel group terrorism, several rebel groups have used terrorism in confrontations with autocratic opponents. Many of these cases involve rebel groups with Islamic extremist objectives—for example, al-Gama'a al-Islamiyya in Egypt and the Groupe Islamique Armé (GIA) in Algeria—raising questions about whether scholars ought to pay greater attention to the influence of ideology on rebel group violence in civil war (Crenshaw 2017; Gutiérrez Sanín and Wood 2014; Kalyvas 2018; Polo and Gleditsch 2016). As Aksoy et al. (2012) argue with regard to terrorism in general, some autocratic governments possess institutional characteristics that make terrorism attractive, whether or not a civil war is ongoing—for example, the presence of opposition political parties without institutions allowing these parties to participate in government.

International Factors

Much of the literature on terrorism and civilian targeting in civil war focuses on how group- and conflict-level variables shape incentives for violence; few consider how international-level variables might influence behavior. Among those examining international factors, a debate has emerged about how external intervention affects incentives for violence.

Weinstein (2007) posits that rebel groups with access to external sources of funding—whether from the exploitation of natural resources or from foreign governments—tend to attract low-commitment members and tend not to invest in establishing organizational discipline, leading to opportunistic violence. Salehyan et al. (2014) make a similar argument regarding external assistance and rebel group abuse of civilians, but point out that some foreign governments—democracies and countries with strong human rights movements—are more likely to try to constrain rebel group violence. Hovil and Werker (2005) also warn that external support may increase incentives for violence, but for different reasons; armed groups receiving external support, they argue, attack civilians to signal to their external sponsors that they remain active.

Other studies, however, contend that foreign support or foreign military intervention can decrease incentives for violence for the side receiving the intervention—because intervention gives armed groups access to greater resources, reducing the need to use coercive violence to obtain support from civilians (Kalyvas 2006; R. M. Wood et al. 2012). In part, this disagreement over the consequences of external aid may be related to the focus on different types of violence; Weinstein and Salehyan et al. emphasize the impact of external support on incentives for opportunistic violence, while Kalyvas and Wood et al. focus on how external involvement influences incentives to use coercive violence to induce civilian cooperation. Future research might extend these studies, examining the impact of external intervention specifically on terrorist violence. It is possible, for example, that by reducing rebel group reliance on domestic constituencies, external aid might reduce the domestic costs of terrorist violence, thus increasing groups' willingness to use this form of violence.

Also analyzing the influence of international factors on wartime dynamics, several studies explore the role of international humanitarian law, arguing that rebel groups that seek legitimacy (Fazal 2017; Jo 2015) or rebel groups that derive support from broad domestic and international constituencies (Stanton 2009, 2016) are more likely to comply with international humanitarian law prohibiting deliberate attacks on civilians. As Stanton argues, the domestic and international costs of civilian targeting—including terrorism—may be too high for groups that need to maintain a broad base of support. Researchers have yet to examine, however, whether and how other aspects of international law—for example, international anti-terrorism law—might influence the dynamics of violence in civil wars.

Do Civilian Targeting and Terrorism Share the Same Causes?

Despite a large body of research on civilian targeting and terrorism, the lack of consistency regarding definitions of civilian targeting and terrorism makes it difficult to reach conclusions about how the causes of these forms of violence compare to one another. If scholars were more precise in differentiating types of violence then it might be possible to reconcile some of the seemingly contradictory findings on civilian targeting and terrorism. Moreover, each of these literatures—the literature on terrorism and the literature on civilian targeting—has limitations in its approach to understanding violence. Studies of terrorism often overlook the overlap between terrorism and civil war, and thus, do not explore the way in which the use of terrorism might fit into the broader strategic framework of an ongoing war. Studies of civilian victimization, meanwhile, often aggregate different types of violence, precluding discussion of whether different types of violence have different causes or different impacts.

Several recent studies address these issues by distinguishing between terrorist violence and other forms of violence occurring in civil war. Carter (2016), for example, differentiates between attacks on civilian targets (terrorist attacks) and attacks on military targets (guerrilla attacks), arguing that insurgent groups use guerrilla attacks to provoke their government opponents, but do not use terrorist attacks in this way. Polo and Gleditsch (2016), meanwhile, carry out analyses using different measures of terrorism in civil war, allowing for comparison across categories of violence. Stanton (2016) focuses on violence occurring in the context of civil wars, distinguishing between three major forms of civil war violence: violence aimed at controlling civilians, violence aimed at cleansing territory of particular groups of civilians, and violence aimed at terrorism. The evidence from this research shows that, indeed, different types of violence have different determinants. When the target audience for violence is the government—as in terrorist violence—rebel groups evaluate the government's relationship with its domestic constituents to gauge how likely the government is to make concessions in response to attacks on civilians. When the target audience for violence is the wider civilian population—as in violence aimed at controlling territory—rebel groups evaluate the strength of civilian support for the government. Stanton's empirical findings thus show that, while rebel groups are more likely to use terrorist bombings against democratic opponents, government regime type is not correlated with the likelihood of other forms of violence against civilians.

Research on the Consequences of Terrorism and Civilian Targeting in Civil War

Recent studies analyze the consequences of terrorism and civilian targeting, with a robust debate emerging over the utility of intentional violence against civilians in achieving a group's political objectives.

The Consequences of Violence for Political Outcomes

Pape (2003) argues that groups use suicide terrorism because they expect that high-impact attacks on civilian targets will induce governments to make policy concessions. In a study that focuses explicitly on civil wars, Thomas (2014) makes a similar claim about the effectiveness of terrorist violence. Using data on African conflicts from 1989 to 2010, Thomas shows that groups that use terrorist tactics are more likely to participate in negotiations with the government, and receive greater numbers of political concessions than groups that do not use such forms of violence. In an examination of civilian targeting conceived broadly, Wood and Kathman (2014) demonstrate that when rebel groups target civilians, this increases the likelihood of a negotiated settlement, which they interpret as an outcome favorable to the rebel group. At very high levels, however, Wood and Kathman find civilian targeting to be counterproductive.

A number of scholars present evidence to the contrary, arguing that terrorism is not an effective strategy. Abrahms (2006, 2012) finds that among groups labeled as Foreign Terrorist Organizations by the United States, groups that primarily attack military targets are more successful in achieving their policy objectives than groups that primarily attack civilian targets. Examining the Palestinian insurgency, several studies show that terrorist attacks backfire, leading to increased public support for right-wing political parties (Berrebi and Klor 2006, 2008; Getmansky and Zeitzoff 2014). And Fortna (2015) shows that rebel groups that use terrorist violence in civil war are less likely to win a military victory and less likely to secure a negotiated settlement to the conflict. Terrorism can also spoil or interfere with peace processes, thus prolonging civil wars and sparking renewed conflict (Findley and Young 2015). These findings are also broadly consistent with research by Chenoweth and Stephan (2011) showing that nonviolent resistance movements are more successful than violent resistance movements.

As in research on the causes of violence, the lack of consensus regarding whether and how to differentiate between terrorism and civilian targeting makes it difficult to evaluate competing claims regarding conflict outcomes. Reconciling these seemingly contradictory findings requires greater attention to different types of political violence and their consequences. Abrahms and Fortna, for example, both examine terrorist violence, narrowly defined; whereas Wood and Kathman look at civilian targeting more broadly. One possible explanation for the contradictory findings in these three studies, therefore, might be that these different forms of violence against civilians influence armed group relationships with their constituents in different ways, and thus, have different consequences for conflict outcomes. Perhaps the types of civilian targeting that Kalyvas discusses—violence aimed at controlling civilians and territory—can be effective, driving Wood and Kathman's findings on civilian targeting; but perhaps terrorist violence aimed a coercing the government is less effective, explaining the findings in the studies by Abrahms and Fortna. Future research might disaggregate types of civilian targeting to explore these empirical results in greater depth, and to develop theoretical arguments for why these forms of violence might influence political outcomes in different ways.

Conclusions and Directions for Future Research

This discussion suggests at least three potentially fruitful areas for future research. First, research that bridges the divide between studies of terrorism and studies of civil war would help to improve understanding of the similarities, differences, and overlap between these two forms of political violence. Scholars might begin by examining existing theoretical arguments, asking whether these arguments can apply to other forms of political violence. For example, although the evidence suggests that political and economic grievances are associated with an increased likelihood of transnational and domestic terrorism in general, future work might examine whether the strength of political and economic grievances influences the choice of violence during civil war. To what extent do the factors influencing the likelihood of domestic and transnational terrorism also explain the likelihood of terrorism in the context of civil war?

Second, research on both the causes and consequences of civilian targeting in civil war is muddled by the lack of clarity regarding definitions of civilian targeting and terrorism, as well as a lack of precision in data sources. Scholars differ in their use of the terms "civilian targeting" and "terrorism," making it difficult to draw comparisons across studies. Perhaps even more problematic, theories of violence often do not match up well with the data employed to test these theoretical claims. For example, many scholars make predictions specifically about opportunistic violence against civilians, and do not make predictions regarding strategic violence against civilians, or vice versa. To test their claims, scholars often use the UCDP/PRIO One-Sided Violence data (Eck and Hultman 2007); these data, however, count the number of civilians killed in incidents of one-sided violence, without differentiating between civilians killed in opportunistic attacks—for example, during a looting rampage—and civilians killed in strategic attacks—for example, by a bomb exploded in a public market. This mismatch between theoretical claims and the data used to test these claims makes it difficult to evaluate and adjudicate between contending hypotheses. Future research, therefore, should be more attentive to the differences in types of violence against civilians, carefully matching theoretical claims to empirical tests.

Finally, although an extensive body of research examines the causes of civilian targeting and terrorism, few scholars have studied how audiences *respond* to different forms of political violence. Recent work analyzing civilian responses to violence shows that, indeed, civilians can influence the dynamics of armed group violence (e.g. Kaplan 2017). Future research might explore how civilian responses to violence vary across countries, contexts, or time, or in response to different forms of violence. Government responses to violence remain understudied as well, as do international responses to violence. Many have studied the effectiveness of government counter-insurgency or counterterrorism strategies, but future work might explore whether the effectiveness of these strategies depends on the character of rebel group violence. For example, are counter-insurgency strategies that emphasize winning hearts and minds equally as effective in confronting rebel groups that use terrorism as rebel groups that use other forms of violence against civilians? How might international responses to violence shape the dynamics of conflict? Research on how audiences respond to terrorism and other forms of violence against civilians would allow for more precise analyses of the *consequences* of violence—in particular, the consequences for civil war outcomes.

Notes

1. Civil wars are internal armed conflicts "between the government of a state and internal opposition groups" involving "a contested incompatibility that concerns government or territory or both where the use of armed force between two parties results in at least 25 battle-related deaths," Gleditsch et al. 2002, 618–19. Following standard definitions, I identify civil *wars* as internal armed conflicts that reach at least 1,000 cumulative battle-related deaths.
2. Phillips 2015 offers a framework for comparing definitions of terrorism and argues that lack of consensus on a common definition makes it difficult to compare research findings across studies.
3. To improve clarity in conceptualizing patterns of political violence, Gutiérrez Sanín and Wood 2017 propose focusing on four aspects of violence: repertoire, targeting, frequency, and technique.
4. See Section 140(d)(2) of the Foreign Relations Authorization Act, Fiscal Years 1988 and 1989.
5. Coggins 2015 similarly finds that severe forms of state failure—political instability and violence—are associated with an increased incidence of terrorism.
6. Gassebner and Luechinger, however, group together transnational and domestic terrorist incidents.

References

Abadie, A. (2006) "Poverty, Political Freedom, and the Roots of Terrorism," *American Economic Review*, 96(2): 50–6.

Abrahms, M. (2006) "Why Terrorism does Not Work," *International Security*, 31(2): 42–78.

Abrahms, M. (2012) "The Political Effectiveness of Terrorism Revisited," *Comparative Political Studies*, 45(3): 366–93.

Abrahms, M., and P. B. K. Potter (2015) "Explaining Terrorism: Leadership Deficits and Militant Group Tactics," *International Organization*, 69(2): 311–42.

Aksoy, D., D. B. Carter, and J. Wright (2012) "Terrorism in Dictatorships," *Journal of Politics*, 74(3): 810–26.

Balcells, L. (2017) *Rivalry and Revenge: The Politics of Violence during Civil War*. New York: Cambridge University Press.

Berrebi, C., and E. F. Klor (2006) "On Terrorism and Electoral Outcomes: Theory and Evidence from the Israeli-Palestinian Conflict," *Journal of Conflict Resolution*, 50(6): 899–925.

Berrebi, C., and E. F. Klor (2008) "Are Voters Sensitive to Terrorism? Direct Evidence from the Israeli Electorate," *American Political Science Review*, 102(3): 279–301.

Bloom, M. (2005) *Dying to Kill: The Allure of Suicide Terror*. New York: Columbia University Press.

Carter, D. B. (2016) "Provocation and the Strategy of Terrorist and Guerrilla Attacks," *International Organization*, 70(1): 133–73.

Cederman, L.-E., K. S. Gleditsch, and H. Buhaug (2013) *Inequality, Grievances, and Civil War*. New York: Cambridge University Press.

Chenoweth, E. (2010) "Democratic Competition and Terrorist Activity," *Journal of Politics*, 72(1): 16–30.

Chenoweth, E. (2013) "Terrorism and Democracy," *Annual Review of Political Science*, 16(1): 355–78.

Chenoweth, E., and M. J. Stephan (2011) *Why Civil Resistance Works: The Strategic Logic of Nonviolent Conflict*. New York: Columbia University Press.

Choi, S.-W., and J. A. Piazza (2016) "Ethnic Groups, Political Exclusion and Domestic Terrorism," *Defence and Peace Economics*, 27(1): 37–63.

Coggins, B. L. (2015) "Does State Failure Cause Terrorism? An Empirical Analysis (1999–2008)," *Journal of Conflict Resolution*, 59(3): 455–83.

Cohen, D. K. (2013) "Explaining Rape during Civil War: Cross-National Evidence (1980–2009)," *American Political Science Review*, 107(3): 461–77.

Cohen, D. K. (2016) *Rape during Civil War*. Ithaca, NY: Cornell University Press.

Conrad, J., and K. Greene (2015) "Competition, Differentiation, and the Severity of Terrorist Attacks," *Journal of Politics*, 77(2): 546–61.

Crenshaw, M. (1981) "The Causes of Terrorism," *Comparative Politics*, 13(4): 379–99.

Crenshaw, M. (2017) "Transnational Jihadism and Civil Wars," *Daedalus*, 146(4): 59–70.

de la Calle, L. (2017) "Compliance vs. Constraints: A Theory of Rebel Targeting in Civil War," *Journal of Peace Research*, 54(3): 427–41.

Eck, K., and L. Hultman (2007) "One-Sided Violence Against Civilians in War: Insights from New Fatality Data," *Journal of Peace Research*, 44(2): 233–46.

Enders, W., T. Sandler, and K. Gaibulloev (2011) "Domestic versus Transnational Terrorism: Data, Decomposition, and Dynamics," *Journal of Peace Research*, 48(3): 319–37.

Eubank, W., and L. Weinberg (1994) "Does Democracy Encourage Terrorism?," *Terrorism and Political Violence*, 6(4): 417–43.

Eubank, W., and L. Weinberg (2001) "Terrorism and Democracy: Perpetrators and Victims," *Terrorism and Political Violence*, 13(1): 155–64.

Eyerman, J. (1998) "Terrorism and Democratic States: Soft Targets or Accessible Systems," *International Interactions*, 24(2): 151–70.

Fazal, T. M. (2017) "Rebellion, War Aims and the Laws of War," *Daedalus*, 146(1): 71–82.

Findley, M. G., and J. K. Young (2012a) "Terrorism and Civil War: A Spatial and Temporal Approach to a Conceptual Problem," *Perspectives on Politics*, 10(2): 285–305.

Findley, M. G., and J. K. Young (2012b) "More Combatant Groups, More Terror? Empirical Tests of an Outbidding Logic," *Terrorism and Political Violence*, 24(5): 706–21.

Findley, M. G., and J. K. Young (2015) "Terrorism, Spoiling, and the Resolution of Civil Wars," *Journal of Politics*, 77(4): 1115–28.

Fortna, V. P. (2015) "Do Terrorists Win? Rebels' Use of Terrorism and Civil War Outcomes," *International Organization*, 69(3): 519–56.

Foster, D. M., A. Braithwaite, and D. Sobek (2013) "There Can Be No Compromise: Institutional Inclusiveness, Fractionalization and Domestic Terrorism," *British Journal of Political Science*, 43(3): 541–57.

Gaibulloev, K., J. A. Piazza, and T. Sandler (2017) "Regime Types and Terrorism," *International Organization*, 71(3): 491–522.

Gassebner, M., and S. Luechinger (2011) "Lock, Stock, and Barrel: A Comprehensive Assessment of the Determinants of Terror," *Public Choice*, 149(3): 235–61.

Getmansky, A., and T. Zeitzoff (2014) "Terrorism and Voting: The Effect of Rocket Threat on Voting in Israeli Elections," *American Political Science Review* 108(3): 588–604.

Gleditsch, K. S., and S. M. T. Polo (2016) "Ethnic Inclusion, Democracy, and Terrorism," *Public Choice*, 169(3–4): 207–29.

Gleditsch, N. P., P. Wallensteen, M. Eriksson, M. Sollenberg, and H. Strand (2002) "Armed Conflict 1946–2001: A New Dataset," *Journal of Peace Research*, 39(5): 615–37.

Gutiérrez Sanín, F., and E. J. Wood (2014) "Ideology in Civil War: Instrumental Adoption and Beyond," *Journal of Peace Research*, 51(2): 213–26.

Gutiérrez Sanín, F., and E. J. Wood (2017) "What Should We Mean by "Pattern of Political Violence"? Repertoire, Targeting, Frequency, and Technique," *Perspectives on Politics*, 15(1): 20–41.

Heger, L. L. (2015) "Votes and Violence: Pursuing Terrorism While Navigating Politics," *Journal of Peace Research*, 52(1): 32–45.

Hoffman, B. (2006) *Inside Terrorism*. New York: Columbia University Press.

Hoover Green, A. (2016) "The Commander's Dilemma: Creating and Controlling Armed Group Violence," *Journal of Peace Research*, 53(5): 619–32.

Hovil, L., and Werker, E. (2005) "Portrait of a Failed Rebellion: An Account of Rational, Sub-Optimal Violence in Western Uganda," *Rationality and Society*, 17(1): 5–34.

Hultman, L. (2007) "Battle Losses and Rebel Violence: Raising the Costs for Fighting," *Terrorism and Political Violence*, 19(2): 205–22.

Hultman, L. (2012) "Attacks on Civilians in Civil War: Targeting the Achilles Heel of Democratic Governments," *International Interactions*, 38(2): 164–81.

Jo, H. (2015) *Compliant Rebels: Rebel Groups and International Law in World Politics*. New York: Cambridge University Press.

Kalyvas, S. N. (2004) "The Paradox of Terrorism in Civil War," *Journal of Ethics*, 8(1): 97–138.

Kalyvas, S. N.(2006) *The Logic of Violence in Civil War*. New York: Cambridge University Press.

Kalyvas, S. N. (2018) "Jihadi Rebels in Civil War," *Daedalus*, 147(1): 36–47.

Kaplan, O. (2017) *Resisting War: How Communities Protect Themselves*. New York: Cambridge University Press.

Kurrild-Klitgaard, P., M. K. Justesen, and R. Klemmensen (2006) "The Political Economy of Freedom, Democracy and Transnational Terrorism," *Public Choice*, 128(1–2): 289–315.

Kydd, A. H., and B. F. Walter (2006) "The Strategies of Terrorism," *International Security*, 31(1): 49–80.

Li, Q. (2005) "Does Democracy Promote or Reduce Transnational Terrorist Incidents?," *Journal of Conflict Resolution*, 49(2): 278–97.

Manekin, D. (2013) "Violence Against Civilians in the Second Intifada: The Moderating Effect of Armed Group Structure on Opportunistic Violence," *Comparative Political Studies*, 46(10): 1273–1300.

Pape, R. A. (2003) "The Strategic Logic of Suicide Terrorism," *American Political Science Review*, 97(3): 343–61.

Phillips, B. J. (2015) "What is a Terrorist Group? Conceptual Issues and Empirical Implications," *Terrorism and Political Violence*, 27(2): 225–42.

Piazza, J. A. (2008) "Do Democracy and Free Markets Protect Us from Terrorism?," *International Politics*, 45(1): 72–91.

Piazza, J. A. (2011) "Poverty, Minority Economic Discrimination, and Domestic Terrorism," *Journal of Peace Research*, 48(3): 339–53.

Piazza, J. A. (2017) "Repression and Terrorism: A Cross-National Empirical Analysis of Types of Repression and Domestic Terrorism," *Terrorism and Political Violence*, 29(1): 102–18.

Polo, S. M., and K. S. Gleditsch (2016) "Twisting Arms and Sending Messages: Terrorist Tactics in Civil War," *Journal of Peace Research*, 53(6): 815–29.

Salehyan, I., D. Siroky, and R. M. Wood (2014). "External Rebel Sponsorship and Civilian Abuse: A Principal-Agent Analysis of Wartime Atrocities," *International Organization*, 68(3): 633–61.

Sambanis, N. (2008) "Terrorism and Civil War," In P. Keefer and N. Loayza (eds), *Terrorism, Economic Development, and Political Openness*. Cambridge: Cambridge University Press, 174–208.

Sánchez-Cuenca, I., and de la Calle, L. (2009) "Domestic Terrorism: The Hidden Side of Political Violence," *Annual Review of Political Science*, 12(1): 31–49.

Sandler, T. (1995) "On the Relationship between Democracy and Terrorism," *Terrorism and Political Violence*, 7(4): 97–122.

Schmid, A. P. (1992) "Terrorism and Democracy," *Terrorism and Political Violence*, 4(4): 14–25.

Shapiro, J. N. (2015) *The Terrorist's Dilemma: Managing Violent Covert Organizations*. Princeton: Princeton University Press.

Stanton, J. A. (2009) "Strategies of Violence and Restraint in Civil War." Ph.D. Dissertation, Columbia University, New York.

Stanton, J. A. (2013) "Terrorism in the Context of Civil War," *Journal of Politics*, 75(4): 1009–22.

Stanton, J. A. (2016) *Violence and Restraint in Civil War: Civilian Targeting in the Shadow of International Law*. New York: Cambridge University Press.

Stewart, M. A., and Liou, Y.-M. (2016) "Do Good Borders Make Good Rebels? Territorial Control and Civilian Casualties," *Journal of Politics*, 79(1): 284–301.

Thomas, J. (2014) "Rewarding Bad Behavior: How Governments Respond to Terrorism in Civil War," *American Journal of Political Science*, 58(4): 804–18.

Weinberg, L., A. Pedahzur, and S. Hirsch-Hoefler (2004) "The Challenges of Conceptualizing Terrorism," *Terrorism and Political Violence*, 16(4): 1–18.

Weinstein, J. M. (2007) *Inside Rebellion: The Politics of Insurgent Violence*. New York: Cambridge University Press.

Weintraub, M. (2016) "Do All Good Things Go Together? Development Assistance and Insurgent Violence in Civil War," *Journal of Politics*, 78(4): 989–1002.

Wood, E. J. (2006) "Variation in Sexual Violence during War," *Politics and Society*, 34(3): 307–42.

Wood, E. J. (2009) "Armed Groups and Sexual Violence: When is Wartime Rape Rare?," *Politics and Society*, 37(1): 131–61.

Wood, R. M. (2010) "Rebel Capability and Strategic Violence against Civilians," *Journal of Peace Research*, 47(5): 601–14.

Wood, R. M. (2014) "From Loss to Looting? Battlefield Costs and Rebel Incentives for Violence," *International Organization*, 68(4): 979–99.

Wood, R. M., and J. D. Kathman (2014) "Too Much of a Bad Thing? Civilian Victimization and Bargaining in Civil War," *British Journal of Political Science*, 44(3): 685–706.

Wood, R. M., and J. D. Kathman (2015) "Competing for the Crown: Inter-Rebel Competition and Civilian Targeting in Civil War," *Political Research Quarterly*, 68(1): 167–79.

Wood, R. M., J. D. Kathman, and S. E. Gent (2012) "Armed Intervention and Civilian Victimization in Intrastate Conflicts," *Journal of Peace Research*, 49(5): 647–60.

Young, J. K., and L. Dugan (2011) "Veto Players and Terror," *Journal of Peace Research*, 48(1): 19–33.

CHAPTER 24

THE CRIME–TERROR NEXUS AND ITS FALLACIES

VANDA FELBAB-BROWN

INTRODUCTION

LARGE-SCALE illicit economies and intense organized crime have received much attention from governments and international organizations since 1989. The end of Cold War brought a permissive strategic environment that allowed many states to focus on a broader menu of interests in their foreign policy agendas, such as the fight against drug trafficking and production. The reduction of Cold War aid to countries in the United States' or the Soviet Union's spheres of influence exposed the great fragility and institutional underdevelopment of many of these states, a deficiency perhaps exacerbated by globalization. At the same time, the international community turned the spotlight to criminal and belligerent actors of significant power that were previously hidden in the shadows of Cold War politics. They especially received notice when their activities were associated with the emergence of new areas of intensely violent organized crime or trafficking-related corruption.

The focus on organized crime, illicit economies, and the multiple threats they pose to states and societies only intensified after 9/11, when it became obvious that belligerent groups, such as the Taliban in Afghanistan and Pakistan and the Islamic State (IS) in Iraq and Syria, derived extensive financial profits and other benefits from participating in illicit economies, such as the drug trade. In addition to expanding the resources of terrorist and belligerent groups, the persistence and growth of illegal economies have also come to complicate post-conflict stabilization and reconstruction efforts in countries that have emerged from civil wars—be they in Cambodia or Haiti.[1]

Out of this focus emerged what has become the conventional view of the crime–terrorism nexus: namely, that since terrorists derive money from illicit economies, terrorism has merged with organized crime, and it is crucial to combat the two phenomena together. Militant groups that penetrate the drug trade and other illegal economies often derive large financial profits from it and grow powerful. Hence it is often argued that, in order to defeat the insurgents, it is necessary to take away their money by suppressing the illegal economy, such as by eradicating poppy fields.

Policy attention has focused on the escalation of violence in Central America where the intensity of organized crime has overwhelmed weak states; the emergence of drug smuggling in West Africa, which contributes to its cauldron of other illegal economies and poor governance; the deep penetration of illegal economies into the political and economic life of Afghanistan and Pakistan; massive poaching of animals in Africa and East Asia; IS illegally trading in antiquities and oil; and cybercrime around the world. After the leather-clad biker gang Night Wolves helped Russian special operations forces annex Crimea in 2014 and other criminal gang "volunteers" directed by Russian intelligence agents played a crucial role in Eastern Ukraine, the North Atlantic Treaty Organization (NATO) too has come to focus strongly on so-called hybrid threats.[2] There is no one accepted definition of hybrid threats, but they feature the "merger of different modes and means of war" (Mattis and Hoffman 2005) such as an overlap of non-state militant actors working for or with state military forces, mixtures of insurgency and criminality, and the fomenting of political, social, and economic unrest within one's opponent's territory.

The use of organized crime actors by states during conflict or for political control is, of course, nothing new. The United States forces invading Sicily during World War II relied on the mafia for intelligence provision as well as post-invasion stability; Chiang-Kai Shek depended on Du Yuesheng's Green Gang for fighting the Japanese and even made Du, the world's most accomplished drug trafficker, his minister of counternarcotics (Felbab-Brown 2009a; Martin 1996).

Yet the conventional view is often wrong-headed. Despite the fact that states often have intimate knowledge of using organized crime for their purposes and exploiting illicit economies, many policy interventions to combat organized crime and illicit economies—whether linked to violent conflict or in the absence of one—have rarely been highly effective. Not only do belligerents and illicit crop farmers find ways to adapt to the policies implemented under the siren song of eradication, but such policies are counterproductive. Eradication alienates rural populations from the government and thrusts them into the hands of the insurgents. And partnering with quasi-criminal actors has often turned out to be counterproductive with respect to other objectives, such as mitigating violent conflict, fostering good governance, and promoting human rights, and at times even counterproductive with respect to very direct objectives, such as weakening criminal groups and their linkages to terrorist organizations.

This is because although illicit economies pose multiple threats to states, their effects on societies are often highly complex. Indeed, large populations around the world in areas with inadequate or problematic state presence, great poverty, and social and political marginalization continue to be dependent on illicit economies, including the drug trade, for economic survival and the satisfaction of other socio-economic needs. For many, participation in informal economies, if not outright illegal ones, is the only way to satisfy their human security and provide any chance of their social advancement, even as they continue to live in a trap of insecurity, criminality, and marginalization.

Winning the military conflict or negotiating peace often requires the halting of suppression actions against labor-intensive illicit economies. As much as external actors may condemn tacitly or explicitly permitting illicit economies, such practices are often crucial for winning hearts and minds and ending conflict. They may also be crucial for giving belligerent groups a stake in peace. But this "narcopeace" may come at the cost of severely negative public-goods side-effects, such as extensive drug production and unrestrained environmental destruction due to logging and wildlife trafficking. Development-based policies aimed at reducing illicit drug production are crucial for avoiding such negative side-effects while maximizing the chance for peace and social justice. But they must equally focus on preventing the emergence of unrestrained logging and wildlife trafficking and other environmentally destructive replacement economies.

The Conventional View of the Crime–Terror Nexus

The conventional view of the nexus between illicit economies and armed conflicts is informed by various strands of academic literature, such as works on narcoterrorism, the "greed" literature on civil wars, works on the crime–terror nexus, the concept of the "guerre revolutionnaire" and "the cost-benefit analysis of counterinsurgency," and has been the dominant thinking in the administration of President George W. Bush.[3] This view holds that belligerent groups derive large financial profits from illegal activities. Presumably these profits critically fund increases in the military capabilities of terrorists, warlords, and insurgents and a corresponding decrease in the relative capability of government forces. Consequently, the conventional view recommends that governments focus on eliminating the belligerents' physical resources by eradicating the illicit economies on which they rely.

The conventional view also frequently maintains (or implies) that, whether or not the belligerent groups ever had any ideological goals, once they interact with the illicit economy, they lose all but pecuniary motivations and become indistinguishable from pure criminals. In many cases, they partner or merge with drug trafficking organizations. Profiting immensely from the illicit economy, they have no motivation to achieve a negotiated settlement with the government. This implication further points to aggressive law enforcement—principally through eradication of the illicit economy—as the government's preferred option.

Other versions, elaborations, or critiques of the crime–terror nexus posit that, even if terrorists and criminals continue to exist as distinct entities, they appropriate each other's methods, learn from each other, and cooperate. (See e.g. Picarelli and Shelley 2002; Williams 2008, 2001; Miklaucic and Brewer 2013; and Farah 2013.) Even if they are not the same, combatting crime and taking away organized crime money from terrorist groups is still often seen as necessary for defeating terrorists and insurgents (see e.g. Lindholm and Realuyo 2013).

In short, the conventional view is based on three key premises:

1. Belligerents make money from illicit economies.
2. The destruction of the illicit economy is both necessary and optimal for defeating the belligerents because it will critically eliminate their resources.
3. The belligerents who participate in the illicit economy must no longer be treated as different from the criminals who also participate in the illicit economy.

The Siren Song of Stopping Illicit Money

Taking money away from terrorists and insurgents by destroying an economy, including an illegal one, is actually quite difficult and rarely pans out. For that to happen, often conflict needs to have ended and government must have sufficient territorial control and state presence to alter basic economic arrangements, whether legal or illegal ones.[4] Similarly, defunding insurgent and terrorist groups is rarely successful. Like smugglers, they can adapt in various ways, including by switching to other economies. Thus when a very extensive US-sponsored eradication campaign temporarily suppressed coca production levels in Colombia in the mid-2000s, both the leftist guerrillas and the rightist paramilitaries and their descendants—the so-called *bandas criminales*—diversified their portfolios into illegal mining, logging, kidnapping, and generalized extortion. Indeed, despite the mystique of narcoterrorism, belligerents mostly merely tax goods, products, and services in areas where they have sufficient intimidation power. The Taliban in Afghanistan taxing the convoys of their opponents—i.e. the United States and NATO—is a prime example.

Nor do anti-money-laundering efforts provide the silver bullet many often hope, as Harold Trinkunas shows in Chapter 31 of this volume. There are limits to how many illicit financial flows banks can find and stop. Even with strict due diligence measures, sorting out an illegal financial transaction from a legal one amidst billions of transactions is complex (see Reuter and Truman 2004; Levi 2010). Financial interdiction rates are thus frequently in the single digits; far lower effectiveness than that of physical interdiction of smuggled goods. Financial intelligence and anti-money-laundering tools become more effective if they are directed against a particular group and supported by signal or human intelligence. But even then, illegal groups can easily move their transactions out of the banking sector into hawalas, online gaming, trade-based under- or over-invoicing, and virtual currencies—to name just a few mechanisms.

Moreover, overstrict due diligence requirements come with costs—not merely for other public goods objectives but also for counterterrorism efforts themselves. The fact that few Western banks now dare operate in Somalia has severely hampered the delivery of remittances on which some of the world's most battered people and the country overall depend. That's not merely a humanitarian problem. The employment and dislocation generated by a further suppression of an already poor economy can produce new recruits for the Shabab and various militias, further weakening the Somali government (problematic as it is), and thus stimulating instability and terrorism. When Kenya decided to shut down remittances to Somalia after the Garissa terrorist attack, Western countries, including the United States, lobbied the Kenyan government to revoke that decision since it would only further marginalize and radicalize Somalis living in Kenya. The counterterrorism payoff would be negative.

The Political Capital of Illicit Economies and Organized Armed Groups

The conventional view fails critically to recognize that belligerents derive much more than simply large financial profits from their sponsorship of illicit economies. They also obtain freedom of action and, crucially, legitimacy and support from the local population—what I call *political capital*.[5] By supporting the illicit economy, belligerents both increase their military capability and build political support. Belligerents who attempt to destroy the illicit economy suffer on both accounts.[6] As a result, the conventional narcoterrorism or crime–terror view is strikingly incomplete and leads to ineffective and even counterproductive policy recommendations.

Four factors largely determine the extent to which belligerents can benefit from their involvement with the illicit economy: the state of the overall economy; the character of the illicit economy; the presence (or absence) of criminal traffickers; and the government response to the illicit economy.

- The state of the overall economy—poor or rich—determines the availability of alternative sources of income and the number of people in a region who depend on the illicit economy for their livelihood.
- The character of the illicit economy—labor-intensive or not—determines the extent to which the illicit economy provides employment for the local population.
- The presence (or absence) of criminal traffickers.
- and the government response to the illicit economy (which can range from suppression to laissez-faire to legalization) determine the extent to which the population depends on the belligerents to preserve and regulate the illicit economy.

In a nutshell, supporting the illicit economy will generate the most political capital for belligerents when the state of the overall economy is poor, the illicit economy is labor-intensive, thuggish traffickers are active in the illicit economy, and the government has adopted a harsh strategy, such as eradication.

This does not mean that sponsorship of *non*-labor-intensive[7] illicit economies brings the anti-government belligerents or armed groups no political capital. If a non-labor-intensive illicit economy, such as drug smuggling in Sinaloa, Mexico, generates strong positive spillover effects for the overall economy in that locale, it too can be a source of important political capital. By boosting demands for durables, nondurables, and services that would otherwise be absent, such groups can indirectly provide livelihoods to and improve economic well-being of poor populations. In Sinaloa, for example, the drug trade is estimated to account for 20 percent of the state's Gross Domestic Product (GDP), and for some of Mexico's southern states, the number might be higher (Guillermo Ibara cited in Roig-Franzia 2008). Consequently, the political capital of the sponsors of the drug trade there, such as the Sinaloa cartel, is hardly negligible. Mexico's drug trafficking organizations (DTOs) also derive important political capital from their sponsorship and control of an increasing range of informal economies in Mexico (Felbab-Brown 2009b). Similarly, the ability to provide better social services and public goods than the state has allowed Brazil's drug gangs to dominate many of Brazil's poor urban areas, such as in Rio de Janeiro—at least until the adoption of the government's so-called UPP program to pacify the *favelas,* as Rio's slums are known. Criminal groups and belligerents can even provide socio-economic services, such as health clinics and trash disposal.

Moreover, both criminal groups and terrorist groups also often provide security. Although they are the source of insecurity and crime in the first place, they often regulate the level of violence and suppress street crime, such as robberies, thefts, kidnapping, and even homicides. Street crime in Latin America is very intensive, exhibiting one of the highest rates in the world. Providing public order, enforcing rules, and preventing the encroachment of oft-hated government authorities brings criminal groups important support from the community. Moreover, illicit economies themselves benefit from the reduced transaction costs, increased predictability, and lack of government interference that flow from providing security and stability.

Indeed, in many parts of Latin America, public safety has become increasingly privatized, with upper and middle classes relying on a combination of official law enforcement and legal and illegal private security entities and marginalized segments relying on organized-crime groups to establish order on the street. Organized-crime groups and belligerent actors, such as the Primero Comando da Capital in Sao Paulo's shantytowns, provide dispute resolution mechanisms and even set up unofficial courts and enforce contracts (see e.g. Desmond Arias and Davis Rodriguez 2006; Pengalese 2008). The extent to which they provide these public goods varies, of course, but it often takes place regardless of whether the non-state entities are politically motivated actors or criminal enterprises. The more they do provide such public goods, the more they become de facto proto-state governing entities.

Moreover, unlike their ideologies, which rarely motivate the wider population to support the belligerents, sponsorship of illicit economies allows belligerent groups to deliver immediate, concrete, material improvements to the lives of marginalized populations. Especially when ideological appeal wanes, the brutality of the belligerents and criminal groups threatens to alienate the general population, and other sources of support evaporate, these groups' ability to deliver material benefits to the population frequently preserves their political capital.

The ability of armed groups to provide real-time economic improvements to the lives of the population also explains why even criminal groups without a consistent ideology can garner strong political capital. This effect is especially strong when the criminal groups couple their distribution of material benefits to poor populations with the provision of otherwise-absent order and minimal security. By being able to outmaneuver the state in provision of governance, organized criminal groups can pose significant threats to states in areas or domains where the government's writ is weak and its presence limited.

Consequently, discussions of whether a group is a criminal group or a political one or whether belligerents are motivated by profit, ideology, or grievances are frequently overstated in their significance for devising policy responses (see also Sullivan 2010). Thus, criminal groups too can and do obtain political capital. Even without having an ideology or seeking to topple the state, they can have political effects if the state, out of its lack of capacity or purposeful decision, relegates some territories to their rule or if it cannot stop intense criminal violence.

The political capital theory of illicit economies has direct implications for the policy options facing governments. It suggests not only that *eradication of illicit economies*, particularly labor-intensive ones, is unlikely to weaken belligerents severely, but also that this strategy frequently is counterproductive, particularly under the conditions just outlined. Eradication will alienate the local population from the government and reduce their willingness to provide intelligence on the belligerents. Thus, eradication increases the political capital of the belligerents without accomplishing its promised goal of significantly weakening their military capabilities. *Laissez-faire*, on the other hand—tolerating the cultivation of illicit crops during conflict—will leave the belligerents' resources unaffected but will decrease their political capital. *Interdiction*—interception of illicit shipments, destruction of labs, and capture of traffickers—may be even more effective, as it can decrease both the belligerents' financial resources and their political capital (since the population's livelihood is not threatened directly and visibly). But as in the case of eradication, interdiction is extremely unlikely to bankrupt the belligerents to the point of defeating them. Finally, when feasible, *licensing* the illicit economy—India and Turkey, for example, licence opium poppy cultivation for the production of medical opiates—can both reduce the belligerents' financial resources and the political capital of the belligerents and increase the government's physical resources and political capital.

Tolerating illicit economies, such as drug production, may facilitate ending violent conflict; however, this approach can leave behind a *peace that is unstable* (see e.g. Kemp et al. 2013; Miraglia et al. 2012). International actors may disapprove of such a peace and demand a destabilizing destruction of illicit economies, perhaps once again triggering new violence. A festering illicit economy without effective extension of the state's presence, establishment and internalization of rule of law, social integration, and the provision of legal economic alternatives can generate new violent competition over the illicit economy and perpetuate unhealthy fragmentation between civilians and the state. For a narco-peace to be transformed into a lasting and socially just peace, states must implement programs emphasizing social inclusion and effective state legitimation and capacity.

The Myths of State Innocence and the Crime–Terror Monolith

A flip side of illicit economies strengthening terrorists and insurgents is that they can also weaken states. Organized crime can equally corrupt, coopt, or hollow out states; under some circumstances, the state can become fully criminalized. (See Ayittey 1999; Albanese 2011; Sullivan 2013; Miklaucic and Naím 2013; Naím 2012; Bayart et al. 1999; Chayes 2015; and Cockayne 2016.) For example, the arrival of the drug trade to West Africa[8] generated much analytical attention, with the drug trade presumably weakening states in the region and intensifying their fragility (see Cockayne and Williams 2009; O'Regan 2012; O'Regan and Thompson 2013; Carrier and Klantschnig 2012; Aning et al. 2013; Walker 2013). Thus pundits often point out that Al Qaeda in the Islamic Maghreb leader Mokhtar Belmokhtar long smuggled cigarettes and other addictive substances in West Africa and the Maghreb, and he became the poster boy of "narco-jihadism." Others frequently ascribe the collapse of the Mali military in the face of jihadi militancy and Tuareg separatism to the state's hollowing out by the drug trade.[9]

Indeed, it is a mistake to assume that illegal economies are the sole domain of insurgents and terrorists. It is a good rule of thumb that in areas of extensive illegal economies, government actors, their associates, and outside-sponsored anti-insurgent militias also make money and power through the same illegal economy. In Thailand and Vietnam during the 1950s and 1960s, anti-Communist militias extensively participated in the drug trade, as did the anti-Soviet mujahideen in Afghanistan in the 1980s, and as do many Afghan government powerbrokers today. The Burmese military is as much involved in drugs, timber, and gems, as the insurgencies it battles (see e.g. Felbab-Brown 2015). Now that the Kenya Defense Forces (KDF) in association with Jubaland president Ahmad Madobe control Somalia's port of Kismayo, no less illegal charcoal is flowing through the port than when Shabab was in charge. But instead of by Shabab, the trade is now sponsored and taxed by KDF and Madobe (Journalists for Justice 2015).

Instead of criminal elites always existing in a fully antagonistic relationship with the state, criminal organizations and the governing elites thus often develop mutually beneficial accommodations. Crime can be both a convenient excuse for elites to maintain exclusionary control over political and economic access as well as a means of accomplishing both. Crime can thus be under some circumstances—and hardly rare ones—a method of governance, sanctioned or tolerated by official political elites.

Examples abound. They include Myanmar, where the junta and Burmese state were long funded by former insurgents and drug traffickers the military had previously fought; Jamaica and Rio de Janeiro in Brazil where governments outsourced the management of poor slums to criminal gangs for decades; Mexico, where the ruling party maintained a similar corporatist relationship with drug trafficking groups as with the rest of society. (See e.g. Lintner 1998; Desmond Arias 2013; Desmond Arias and Davis Rodrigues 2006; Serrano, 2012; Felbab-Brown 2016.) For decades, in places such as Indonesia, Nepal, and India, ruling local or national elites have used criminal gangs for ruling and administering localities, intimidating and eliminating political opponents, and extracting votes and rents (Felbab-Brown 2013a, 2013b).

However, such activities do not always weaken a state. Such an accommodation between the state and elites and criminal groups is not optimal from the perspective of society and certainly undermines the rule of law and democracy. But it may well result in a sustainable internal modus operandi, at least to the extent that external actors do not threaten such an accommodation by insisting on the destruction of the illicit economy or anti-corruption measures. Such outside policy measures, while disruptive, often have only cosmetic effects. *Hybrid governance* may be deeply entrenched and highly organic to local institutional and cultural settings, making it very difficult to root out unless the outside intervener sets out to fundamentally redesign basic political arrangements and has the time, resources, and wherewithal to see such a state-remaking project through.

Nor is there always a strong social opprobrium toward the penetration of crime into politics or the appropriation of organized crime for state purposes. Sometimes, society mobilizes against such linkages, such as in Colombia when the parapolitics scandal broke out in the mid-2000s, revealing that at least a third of the Colombian congress was connected to the vicious paramilitaries and that many municipal governments were extorted or under their thumb.[10] Yet other times, having a criminal record can provide political advantages. Take the case of India, where politicians with known criminal records are regularly elected in substantial numbers into Congress. In 2014, 34 percent of elected MPs of the lower chamber of India's Congress, the Lok Sabha, disclosed indictments for murder, attempted murder, kidnapping, provoking communal disharmony, or crimes against women, up from 30 percent in 2009 (*Times of India* 2014). Such candidates also tend to perform much better than politicians with a clean record, perhaps because voters see them as more capable of getting things done and more connected to patronage resources than politicians without criminal indictments. A candidate with a criminal record had a 13 percent chance of winning in the 2014 elections whereas an MP aspirant without a criminal record had only a 5 percent chance of winning (*Times of India* 2014).

Not all organized crime groups are equally willing and capable buddies of terrorists. There is a considerable variation in the capacity of organized crime groups to penetrate new territories or domains, as Frederico Varese (2011) has shown. Few criminal groups are polycrime enterprises: smuggling cocaine is not the same as smuggling fissile material. Although it is frequently suggested that organized crime groups will easily make alliances or without restraint cooperate with terrorist and militant groups, the relationship between the two actors is often fraught and violent (see e.g. Farah 2013). Most organized crime groups are not simply blind profit maximizers, but also they weigh risks—including the risk of cooperating with militant groups and thus drawing a far different level of scrutiny and repression from law enforcement.

Conclusions and Policy Implications

For designing an effective policy response and appropriate external assistance, it is thus important to stop thinking about terrorism and organized crime solely as aberrant social activity to be suppressed, but instead think of it as competition in state-making (Felbab-Brown 2011). Moreover, a recognition that states often directly foster and use crime is equally important for designing effective global responses. In areas of state weakness and underprovision of public goods, the effective state strategy toward organized crime is thus not merely one of law enforcement suppression of crime. An appropriate response is a multifaceted state-building effort that seeks to strengthen the bonds between the state and marginalized communities dependent on or vulnerable to participation in the drug trade and other illicit economies for reasons of economic survival and physical insecurity. The goal of anti-organized crime efforts should not only be narrowly to suppress the symptoms of illegality and state-weakness, such as illicit crops or smuggling, but rather to reduce the threat that the drug trade poses from a national security concern to one of a public safety problem that does not threaten the state or society at large.

Moreover, those designing external policy assistance must develop realistic expectations about the degree to which outside policy interventions can eradicate all organized crime and illicit economies in a particular place or, for that matter, all drug trade in that place. Prioritizing policies that mitigate the most dangerous forms of criminality is important, as is designing policies closely in line with the absorptive capacity of the target state. Policy interventions to reduce organized crime and to suppress any emergent crime–terror nexus can only be effective if there is a genuine commitment and participation by recipient governments and sufficient buy-in from local communities, i.e., if they both find it in their interest to wean themselves off crime.

In the case of the suppression of illicit economies, one aspect of such a multifaceted approach that seeks to strengthen the bonds between the state and society and weaken the bonds between marginalized populations and criminal and armed actors is *the proper sequencing of suppression*, such as drug eradication, and the development of economic alternatives. For many years, the United States has emphasized suppression of illicit economies, such as forced eradication of illicit crops, above and prior to the development of legal alternatives, such as rural development or alternative livelihoods efforts. Such sequencing and emphasis have also been at odds with the lessons learned from the most successful rural development effort in the context of illicit crop cultivation, Thailand. Indeed, Thailand offers the only example where rural development succeeded in eliminating illicit crop cultivation (for details see Renard 2001; Chouvy 2009, 63–93).

Effective economic development—be it for urban or rural spaces—requires not only proper sequencing with suppression policies and security, but also a *well-funded, long-lasting, and comprehensive development approach* that centers on the creation of legal jobs—always the single hardest developmental challenge, whether in Nigeria's Delta or Rio de Janeiro's slums. Creating legal jobs is very difficult in the context of a massive youth bulge, pervasive unemployment or underemployment, taxation systems that favor capital-intensive industries, and elite capture of political and economic rule-making.

Moreover, development efforts need to address all the structural drivers of why communities participate in illegal economies—such as access to markets and their development, deficiencies in infrastructure and irrigation systems, access to microcredit, and the establishment of value-added chains—and not merely chase the replacement crop. It is critical that such social interventions are designed as sustained and comprehensive rural development or comprehensive urban planning efforts, not simply limited handouts or buyoffs.

Nor should US policy treat organized crime and terrorism as monoliths. Instead, policy should actively seek to pit the two actors against each other, while minimizing violence, and exploit the fissures, tensions, rivalries, different objectives, and trust deficiencies among two types of actors. The priority for the international community needs to be to combat the most disruptive and dangerous networks of organized crime and belligerency. Such networks are those with the greatest links or potential links to international terrorist groups with global reach. But hardly all criminal groups are such, and the purpose of law enforcement also needs to be to "make good criminals" (Felbab-Brown 2013c, 2019), including by discouraging their linkages with terrorism.

Notes

1. For a comprehensive exploration of the role of illicit economies and organized crime in conflict mitigation and post-conflict reconstruction, see Cockayne and Lupel 2011; Cockayne 2013, 10–24; Andreas 2008.
2. On the use of organized crime by Russian special operations forces, see e.g. Galeotti 2015. On Kremlin's use of cyberwarfare by an army of trolls, see e.g. Jones 2014; Chen 2015.
3. For government analyses exemplifying the convention view, see e.g. Rand Beers, Assistant Secretary for International Narcotics and Law Enforcement Affairs, "Narco-Terror: The Worldwide Connection Between Drugs and Terrorism," a hearing before the US Senate Judiciary Committee, Subcommittee on Technology, Terrorism, and Government Information," Mar. 13, 2002; <http://judiciary.senate.gov/hearing.cfm?id=196> [downloaded Apr. 2003]; and Robert Charles, US Policy and Colombia, Testimony before the House

Committee on Government Reform, June 17, 2004, <http://reform.house.gov/UploadedFiles/State%20-%20Charles%20Testimony.pdf> [downloaded June 2004]. For academic literature, see e.g. Bonnet 1958; Trinquier 1964; Wolf 1965; Ehrenfeld 2005; Davids 2002; Adams 1986; Prabhakar 2012; Wardlaw 1988; Leader and Wiencek 2000; Tarazona-Sevillano and Reuter 1990; Collier and Hoeffler 2001; Berdal and Keen 1997; Berdal and Malone 2000; Keen 1998; Dishman 2001; Farah 2004; Peters 2009; Ross 2003. Makarenko 2004; Cornell 2004; Shelley and Melzer 2008; Helfstein and Solomon 2014.

4. I explore these examples and other case studies in detail in my book *Shooting Up* (2010) and also in chapter 9 of my book *Aspiration and Ambivalence* (2013d).
5. I detail the theory of the Political Capital of Illicit Economies and test it against conventional wisdom in case studies from Asia, Latin America, and Northern Ireland in my book *Shooting Up* (2010).
6. My work draws on various academic critiques of the "hearts-and-minds" theorists of counterinsurgency and various critiques of the war on drugs and the crime–terror nexus, including Lee 1989; McClintock 1988; Clutterbuck 1995; Buscaglia and Ratliff 2001; Gutiérrez Sanín 2004; Youngers and Rosin 2005; Williams 1994; Spar 1994; Thompson 1966, 1970; Kitson 1971; Pustay 1965; Galula 1964; McCuen 1966; Scott 1976; Wolf 1969; Olson 1965; Popkin 1979; Lichbach 1994; Skocpol 1982; Wickham-Crowley 1991; and Mason and Krane 1989; O'Brien 1983; Rubenstein 1990.
7. For details on these concepts, see Felbab-Brown 2010, ch. 2.
8. See e.g. Cockayne and Williams 2009; O'Regan 2012; O'Regan and Thompson 2013; Carrier and Klantschnig 2012; Aning et al. 2013; Walker 2013.
9. For detailed analyses of the drug trade in Mali and the Sahel and at times contradictory arguments, see e.g. Tinti et al. 2014; Locher 2013; Gberie 2015.
10. For other examples of the penetration of crime into politics in Latin America, see Briscoe et al. 2014.

References

Adams, James (1986) *The Financing of Terror.* London: New English Library.

Albanese, Jay (2011) *Transnational Crime and the 21st Century: Criminal Enterprises, Corruption, and Opportunity.* Oxford: Oxford University Press.

Andreas, Peter (2008) *Blue Helmets and Black Markets.* Ithaca, NY: Cornell University Press.

Aning, Kwesi, Sampson B. Kwarkye, and John Pokoo (2013) "A Case Study of Ghana," in Camino Kavanagh (ed.), *Getting Smart and Scaling Up: The Impact of Organized Crime on Governance in Developing Countries.* New York: New York University Center for International Cooperation, June., available online at <http://cic.nyu.edu/sites/default/files/kavanagh_crime_developing_countries_ghana_study.pdf>.

Ayittey, George B. N. (1999) *Africa in Chaos.* New York: St Martin's Griffin.

Bayart, Jean-Francois, Stephen Ellis, and Beatrice Hibou (1999) *The Criminalization of the State in Africa.* London: International African Institute/James Currey.

Berdal, Mats, and David Keen (1997) "Violence and Economic Agendas in Civil Wars: Some Policy Implications," *Millennium: Journal of International Studies*, 26(3): 795–818;

Berdal, Mats, and David Malone, eds (2000) *Greed and Grievance: Economic Agendas in Civil War.* Boulder, CO: Lynne Rienner

Bonnet, Georges (1958) *Les guerres insurrectionnelles et revoluionnaires.* Paris: Payot.

Briscoe, Ivan, Catalina Perdomo, and Catalina Uribe Burcher (2014) *Illicit Networks and Politics in Latin America.* Stockholm and The Hague: International Idea, Netherlands Institute for Multiparty Democracy (NIMD), and Netherlands Institute of International Relations [Clingendael].

Buscaglia, Edgardo, and William Ratliff (2001) *War and Lack of Governance in Colombia: Narcos, Guerrillas, and U.S. Policy.* Stanford, CA: Hoover Institution on War, Revolution, and Peace.

Carrier, Neil, and Gernot Klantschnig (2012) *Africa and the War on Drugs.* London: Zed Books.

Chayes, Sarah (2015) *Thieves of States: Why Corruption Threatens Global Security.* New York: W. W. Norton.

Chen, Adrian (2015) "The Agency," *New York Times Magazine*, June 2.

Chouvy, Pierre-Arnaud (2009) *Opium: Uncovering the Politics of Poppy.* London: I. B. Taurus.

Clutterbuck, Richard (1995) *Drugs, Crime, and Corruption.* New York: New York University Press.

Cockayne, James (2013) "Chasing Shadows: Strategic Responses to Organized Crime in Conflict-Affected Situations," *RUSI Journal,* 2: 10–24.

Cockayne, James (2016) *Hidden Power: The Strategic Logic of Organized Crime.* London: Hurst.

Cockayne, James, and Adam Lupel, eds (2011) *Peace Operations and Organized Crime: Enemies or Allies.* New York: Routledge.

Cockayne, James and Phil Williams (2009) "The Invisible Tide: Towards an International Strategy to Deal with Drug Trafficking through West Africa," International Peace Institute, Oct.

Collier, Paul, and Anke Hoeffler (2001) "Greed and Grievance in Civil Wars," Oct. 21, available online at <http://econ.worldbank.org/files/12205_greedgrievance_23oct.pdf>, downloaded April 16, 2003.

Cornell, Svante (2004) "Crime Without Borders," *Axess Magazine,* 6: 18–21, available online at <http://www.silkroadstudies.org/pub/0408Axess_EN.htm> [Accessed Jan. 2005].

Davids, Douglas J. (2002) *Narco-terrorism.* Ardsley: Transnational Publishers.

Desmond Arias, Enrique (2013) "The Impact of Organized Crime on Governance: A Desk Study of Jamaica," in Camino Kavanagh (ed.), *Getting Smart and Scaling Up: The Impact of Organized Crime on Governance in Developing Countries.* New York: Center for International Cooperation, NYU, available online at <http://cic.nyu.edu/sites/default/files/kavanagh_crime_developing_countries_jamaica_study.pdf>.

Desmond Arias, Enrique, and Corrine Davis Rodrigues (2006) "The Myth of Personal Security: Criminal Gangs, Dispute Resolution, and Identity in Rio de Janeiro's Favelas," *Latin American Politics,* 48(4): 53–81.

Dishman, Chris (2001) "Terrorism, Crime, and Transformation," *Studies in Conflict and Terrorism,* 42(1): 43–58.

Ehrenfeld, Rachel (2005) *How Terrorism Is Financed and How to Stop it.* Chicago: Bonus Books.

Farah, Douglas (2004) *Blood from Stones: The Secret Financial Network of Terror.* New York: Broadway House.

Farah, Douglas (2013) "Fixers, Superfixers, and Shadow Facilitators: How Networks Connect," in Jacqueline Brewer and Michael Miklaucic, eds., *Convergence: Illicit Networks and National Security in the Age of Globalization.* Washington, DC: NDU Press, 75–96.

Felbab-Brown, Vanda (2009a) "The Political Economy of Illegal Domains in India and China," *International Lawyer,* 43(4): 1411–28.

Felbab-Brown, Vanda (2009b) *The Violent Drug Market in Mexico and Lessons from Colombia*, Foreign Policy at Brookings, Policy Paper No. 12, Mar., available online at <www.brookings.edu/~/media/Files/rc/papers/2009/03_mexico_drug_market_felbabbrown/03_mexico_drug_market_felbabbrown.pdf>.

Felbab-Brown, Vanda (2010) *Shooting Up: Counterinsurgency and the War on Drugs*. Washington, DC: Brookings Institution Press.

Felbab-Brown, Vanda (2011) *Conceptualizing Crime as Competition in State-Making and Designing an Effective Response*. Washington, DC: Brookings Institution, May, available online at <http://www.brookings.edu/research/speeches/2010/05/21-illegal-economies-felbabbrown>.

Felbab-Brown, Vanda (2013a) *Indonesia Field Report I: Crime as a Mirror of Politics: Urban Gangs in Indonesia*. Washington, DC: Brookings Institution, Feb., available online at <http://www.brookings.edu/research/reports/2013/02/06-indonesia-gangs-felbabbrown>.

Felbab-Brown, Vanda (2013b) "The Impact of Organized Crime on Governance: The Case Study of Nepal," in Camino Kavanagh, ed., *Getting Smart and Scaling Up: Impact of Organized Crime on Governance*, Center for International Cooperation, NYU, available online at <http://cic.nyu.edu/sites/default/files/kavanagh_crime_developing_countries_nepal_study.pdf>.

Felbab-Brown, Vanda (2013c) "The Purpose of Law Enforcement Is to Make Good Criminals?…or How to Effectively Respond to the Crime-Terrorism Nexus," *The Potomac Institute of Policy Studies*, Nov., available online at <http://www.brookings.edu/research/presentations/2013/11/21-how-effectively-respond-crime-terrorism-nexus-felbabbrown>.

Felbab-Brown, Vanda (2013d) *Aspiration and Ambivalence: Strategies and Realities of Counterinsurgency and State-building in Afghanistan*. Washington, DC: The Brookings Institution Press.

Felbab-Brown, Vanda (2015) *Enabling War and Peace: Drugs, Logs, Gems, and Wildlife in Thailand and Burma*. Washington, DC: Brookings Institution, Dec.

Felbab-Brown (2019) *Narco Noir: Mexico's Cartels, Corruption, and Security Strategies*. Washington, DC: Brookings Institution Press, forthcoming.

Galeotti, Mark (2015) *Spetsnaz: Russia's Special Forces*. Oxford: Osprey Publishing.

Galula, David (1964) *Counterinsurgency Warfare: Theory and Practice*. New York: Praeger.

Gberie, Lansana (2015) "Crime, Violence, and Politics: Drug Trafficking and Counternarcotics Policies in Mali and Guinea," available online at <http://www.brookings.edu/~/media/Research/Files/Papers/2015/04/global-drug-policy/Gberie—Mali-and-Guinea-final.pdf?la=en>.

Gutiérrez Sanín, Francisco (2004) "Criminal Rebels? A Discussion of Civil War and Criminality from the Colombian Experience," *Politics and Society*, 32(2): 257–85.

Helfstein, Scott, with John Solomon (2014) "Risky Business: The Global Threat Network and the Politics of Contraband," Combatting Terrorism Center, May 2014, available online at <https://www.ctc.usma.edu/v2/wp-content/uploads/2014/05/RiskyBusiness_final.pdf>.

Jones, Sam (2014) "Kremlin Alleged to Wage Cyber Warfare on Kiev," *Financial Times*, June 4.

Journalists for Justice (2015) "Black and White: Kenya's Criminal Racket in Somalia," Nairobi, Nov., available online at< http://www.jfjustice.net/userfiles/file/Research/Black%20and%20White%20Kenya's%20Criminal%20Racket%20in%20Somalia.pdf>.

Keen, David (1998) *The Economic Functions of Violence in Civil Wars*, Adelphi Paper, 320. Oxford: IISS/Oxford University Press.

Kemp, Walter, Mark Shaw, and Arthur Boutellis (2013) "The Elephant in the Room: How Can Peace Operations Deal with Organized Crime?" International Peace Institute, June, available online at <www.ipinst.org/images/pdfs/ipi_e-pub-elephant_in_the_room.pdf>.

Kitson, Frank (1971) *Low Intensity Operations*. London: Faber & Faber.

Leader, Stefan, and David Wiencek (2000) "Drug Money: The Fuel for Global Terrorism," *Jane's Intelligence Review*, Feb.: 49–54.

Lee, Rensselaer W., III (1989) *The White Labyrinth*. New Brunswick, NJ: Transaction Publishers.

Levi, Michael (2010) "Combating the Financing of Terrorism: A History and Assessment of the Control of 'Threat Finance,'" *British Journal of Criminology*, 50(4): 650–69.

Lichbach, Mark (1994) "What Makes Rational Peasants Revolutionary? Dilemma, Paradox, and Irony in Peasant Collective Action," *World Politics*, 46(2): 383–418.

Lindholm, Danielle Camner, and Celina B. Realuyo (2013) "Threat Finance: Critical Enabler for Illicit Networks," in Jacqueline Brewer and Michael Miklaucic (eds), *Convergence: Illicit Networks and National Security in the Age of Globalization*. Washington, DC: NDU Press, 111–30.

Lintner, Bertil (1998) "Drugs and Economic Growth: Ethnicity and Exports," in Robert I. Rotberg (ed.), *Burma: Prospect for a Democratic Future*. Washington, DC: Brookings Institution Press, 165–84.

Locher, Wolfram (2013) "Challenging the Myth of the Drug Terror Nexus in the Sahel," West Africa Commission on Drugs, Aug., available online at <www.wacommissionondrugs.org/…/2013/…/Challenging-the-Myth-of-the-Drug-Terror-Nexus-in-the-Sahel-2013-08-19.pdf>.

McClintock, Cynthia (1988) "The War on Drugs: The Peruvian Case," *Journal of Interamerican Studies and World Affairs*, 30(2–3): 127–42.

McCuen, John J. (1966) *The Art of Revolutionary Warfare*. London: Faber & Faber.

Makarenko, Tamara, "The Crime-Terror Continuum: Tracing the Interplay Between Transnational Crime and Terrorism," *Global Crime*, 1 (1), 2004: 129–45.

Martin, Brian (1996) *The Shanghai Green Gang: Politics and Organized Crime, 1919–1937*. Berkeley, CA: University of California Press.

Mason, T. David, and Dale A. Krane (1989) "The Political Economy of Death Squads: Toward a Theory of the Impact of State-Sanctioned Terror," *International Studies Quarterly*, 33(2): 175–98.

Mattis, James, and Frank Hoffman (2005) "Future Warfare: The Rise of Hybrid Wars," *U.S. Naval Institute Proceedings Magazine*, 132: 11/1233 (Nov.): 18–19.

Miklaucic, Michael, and Jacqueline Brewer (2013) "Introduction," in Jacqueline Brewer and Michael Miklaucic (eds), *Convergence: Illicit Networks and National Security in the Age of Globalization*. Washington, DC: NDU Press, xiii–xxi.

Miklaucic, Michael, and Moisés Naím (2013) "The Criminal State," in Michael Miklaucic and Jacqueline Brewer (eds), *Convergence: Illicit Networks and National Security in the Age of Globalization*. Washington, DC: NDU Press, 149–70.

Miraglia, Paula, Rolando Ochoa, and Ivan Brisco (2012) *Transnational Organized Crime and Fragile States*. Paris: OECD, International Center for the Prevention of Crime, and the Clingendael Institute, Oct.

Naím, Moisés (2012) "Mafia States: Organized Crime Takes Office," *Foreign Affairs*, Apr., available online at <https://www.foreignaffairs.com/articles/2012-04-20/mafia-states>.

Naylor, R. Thomas (2002) *Wages of Crime: Black Markets, Illegal Finance and the Under-world Economy*. Ithaca, NY: Cornell University Press.

O'Brien, Conor Cruise (1983) "Terrorism under Democratic Conditions," in Martha Crenshaw (ed.), *Terrorism, Legitimacy, and Power: The Consequences of Political Violence*. Middletown: Wesleyan University Press, 91–104.

Olson, Mancur (1965) *The Logic of Collective Action: Public Goods and the Theory of Groups*. Cambridge, MA: Harvard University Press.

O'Regan, Davin (2012) "Narco-States: Africa's Next Menace," *New York Times*, Mar. 12.

O'Regan, Davin and Peter Thompson (2013) *Advancing Stability and Reconciliation in Guinea-Bissau: Lessons from Africa's First Narco-State*, Africa Center for Strategic Studies Special Report, June, available online at <http://africacenter.org/wp-content/uploads/2013/06/SpecialReport-Guinea-Bissau-JUN2013-EN.pdf>;

Pengalese, Ben (2008) "The Bastard Child of the Dictatorship: The Comando Vermelho and the Birth of 'Narco-Culture' in Rio de Janeiro," *Luso-Brazilian Review*, 45(1): 118–45.

Peters, Gretchen (2009) *Seeds of Terror*. New York: St Martin's Press.

Picarelli, John, and Louise Shelley (2002) "Methods, Not Motives: Implications of the Convergence or International Organized Crime and Terrorism," *Police Practice Research: An International Journal*, 3(4) 2002: 305–18.

Popkin, Samuel L. (1979) *The Rational Peasant: The Political Economy of Rural Society in Vietnam*. Berkeley, CA: University of California Press.

Prabhakar, Hitha (2012) *Black Market Billions: How Organized Crime Funds Global Terrorists*. Upper Saddle River, NJ: FT Press.

Pustay, John S. (1965) *Counterinsurgency Warfare*. New York: Free Press.

Renard, Ronald D. (2001) *Opium Reduction in Thailand, 1970–2000: A Thirty-Year Journey*. Bangkok: UNDCP Silkworm Books.

Reuter, Peter, and Edwin Truman (2004) *Progress on Anti-Money Laundering*. Danvers, MA: Institute for International Economics.

Roig-Franzia, Manuel (2008) "Mexico's Drug Trafficking Organizations Take Barbarous Turn: Targeting Bystanders," *Washington Post*, July 30: A9.

Ross, Michael (2003) "Oil, Drugs, and Diamonds: The Varying Roles of Natural Resources in Civil War," in Karen Ballentine and Jake Sherman, *The Political Economy of Armed Conflict: Beyond Greed and Grievance* (Boulder: Lynne Rienner, 2003): 47–73.

Rubenstein, Richard E. (1990) "The Noncauses of Modern Terrorism," in Charles W. Kegley, Jr. (ed.), *International Terrorism: Characteristics, Causes, and Controls*. New York: St Martin's.

Scott, James C. (1976) *The Moral Economy Peasant*. New Haven: Yale University Press.

Serrano, Mónica (2012) "States of Violence: State–Crime Relations in Mexico," in Wil Pansters (ed.), *Violence, Coercion, and State-Making in the Twentieth-Century Mexico*. Stanford, CA: Stanford University Press, 135–58.

Shelley, Louise, and Sharon Melzer (2008) "The Nexus of Organized Crime and Terrorism: Two Case Studies in Cigarette Smuggling," *International Journal of Comparative and Applied Criminal Justice*, 32(1): 43–63.

Skocpol, Theda (1982) "What Makes Peasants Revolutionary?," *Comparative Politics*, 14(3): 351–75.

Spar, Debora (1994) *The Cooperative Edge: The Internal Politics of International Cartels*. Ithaca, NY: Cornel University Press.

Sullivan, John (2010) "Criminal Insurgency in the Americas," *Small Wars Journal*, Feb. 13, available online at <http://smallwarsjournal.com/blog/journal/docs-temp/364-sullivan.pdf>.

Sullivan, John (2013) "How Illicit Networks Impact Sovereignty," in Michael Miklaucic and Jacqueline Brewer (eds), *Convergence: Illicit Networks and National Security in the Age of Globalization*. Washington, DC: NDU Press, 173–202.

Tarazona-Sevillano, Gabriela, with John B. Reuter (1990) *Sendero Luminoso and the Threat of Narcoterrorism*. Washington, DC: Center for Strategic and International Studies.

Thompson, Robert (1966) *Defeating Communist Insurgency*. London: Chatto & Windus.

Thompson, Robert (1970) *Revolutionary War in World Strategy, 1945–1969*. London: Secker & Warburg.

Times of India (2014) "Every Third Newly-Elected MP has Criminal Background," May 18.

Tinti, Peter, et al. (2014) "Illicit Trafficking and Instability in Mali: Past, Present, and Future," The Global Initiative against Transnational Organized Crime, Jan., available online at <http://www.globalinitiative.net/download/global-initiative/Global%20Initiative%20-%20Organized%20Crime%20and%20Illicit%20Trafficking%20in%20Mali%20-%20Jan%202014.pdf>.

Trinquier, Roger (1964) *Modern Warfare.* London: Pall Mall Press.

Varese, Federico (2011) *Mafias on the Move.* Princeton: Princeton University Press.

Walker, Summer (2013) "A Desk Study of Sierra Leone," in Camino Kavanagh (ed.), *Getting Smart and Scaling Up: The Impact of Organized Crime on Governance in Developing Countries.* New York: New York University Center for International Cooperation, June, available online at <http://cic.nyu.edu/sites/default/files/kavanagh_crime_developing_countries_sierra_leone_study.pdf>.

Wardlaw, Grant (1988) "Linkages between the Illegal Drugs Traffic and Terrorism," *Conflict Quarterly*, 8(3): 5–26.

Wickham-Crowley, Timothy (1991) *Exploring Revolution: Essays on Latin American Insurgency and Revolutionary Theory.* Armonk, NY: M. E. Sharpe.

Williams, Phil (1994) "Transnational Criminal Organizations: Strategic Alliances," *Washington Quarterly*, 18(1): 57–72.

Williams, Phil (2001) "Transnational Criminal Networks," in John Arquilla and Advid Ronfeldt, *Networks and Netwars: The Future of Terror, Crime, and Militancy,* Santa Monica, CA: RAND, 61–97.

Williams, Phil (2008) "Terrorist Financing and Organized Crime: Nexus, Appropriation, or Transformation," in Thomas Biersteker and Sue Eckert (eds), *Countering the Financing of Terrorism.* New York: Routledge, 126–49.

Wolf, Jr., Charles (1965) *Insurgency and Counterinsurgency: New Myths and Old Realities,* RAND Document, No. P-3132-1. Santa Monica, CA: RAND.

Wolf, Eric (1969) *Peasant Wars of the Twentieth Century* (New York, Harper & Row.

Youngers, Coletta A., and Eileen Rosin, eds (2005) *Drugs and Democracy in Latin America.* Boulder, CO: Lynne Rienner.

PART VI

ACTORS, STRATEGIES, AND MODUS OPERANDI

CHAPTER 25

TERRORIST ORGANIZATIONAL DYNAMICS

BRIAN J. PHILLIPS

THERE are many approaches one can use to understand terrorism, including the study of individual terrorists, broad social movements, or countries where terrorists operate. However, analyzing organizations provides important leverage. Most terrorist attacks are carried out by formal organizations, and therefore most attacks are by groups with particular political goals, mobilization issues, structure, internal strain, and other characteristics. Understanding these dynamics can illuminate a great deal about the phenomenon of terrorism.

The organizational focus of terrorism studies is not new. In the 1980s, scholars presented important theoretical work on organizational dynamics of terrorism (e.g. Crenshaw 1985, 1987; Oots 1989; Post 1987). An early study of democracy and terrorism used the number of terrorist groups in a country as the outcome of interest (Eubank and Weinberg 1994). Case studies of terrorist groups have always been important topic in the field (Crenshaw 1995; Rapoport 2001). A less common, although often powerful approach, is formal theory (Bapat 2012; Lapan and Sandler 1988). A substantial development occurred around 2008, with the publication of several global datasets of terrorist organizations (Asal and Rethemeyer 2008; Cronin 2009; Jones and Libicki 2008). This has permitted scholars to explore global trends in terrorist group behavior, using the same quantitative approaches already used to study terrorism—although usually with the country or country-year as unit of analysis (Li 2005).[1]

Policy-motivated debates raise questions about which level of analysis is "best," as scholars discuss which actors pose greater threats. Formal terrorist organizations have received the most policy and scholarly attention—and for good reason. Formal groups directly carry out the vast majority of terrorist attacks, and attacks by these groups are usually far more lethal than attacks by lone actors (Alakoc 2017; Phillips 2017). Historically, organizations like the Red Brigades and the Shining Path terrorized populations, and groups such as Al Nusra Front and Boko Haram carry on the tradition.

But some analysts argue that informal networks, or "bunches of guys," are the dominant security challenge—not formal organizations (Sageman 2008). Because Al Qaeda has been weakened since the September 11, 2001, attacks, Sageman argues that small groups of individuals inspired by the group are more of a threat than the organization itself. Others maintain that lone wolf attacks are especially threatening, citing the increasing number of such attacks in Western countries (Michael 2012).

The next section discusses the definition of terrorist organization. Then, the chapter explores recent lines of research on organizational dynamics of terrorism, including outbidding, internal group dynamics, and organizational termination and longevity. The chapter concludes with suggestions for future research. A caveat is that this chapter cannot discuss every article or book written about terrorist groups. It seeks to discuss a few key lines of research, and in doing so shed light on a powerful approach to understanding terrorism.

What is a Terrorist Organization?

Terrorism is often defined as violence by subnational actors to obtain a political or social objective through the intimidation of an audience beyond the noncombatant victims (Enders and Sandler 2011, 4). The definition is of course debated, but many authors agree on core elements. However, there has been little discussion of what constitutes a "terrorist organization," despite the common use of the term. About fifteen years before this chapter was written, two separate analyses noted that there was no clear definition of "terrorist organization" (McCormick 2003, 47; Silke 2001, 3). Debating the nature of the concept is important for clarity and consistency in research. Additionally, the effects of government strategies are likely to be conditional upon the nature of the targeted group. This is what Cronin (2015) argues in an article titled, in part, "ISIS is not a terrorist group." Differences across group types help explain why leadership decapitation has distinct consequences depending on whether the targeted group is a terrorist or criminal organization (Phillips 2015b).

One conceptual dispute involves the distinction between terrorist and guerrilla groups. De la Calle and Sánchez-Cuenca (2011) argue that terrorist groups are "underground groups with no territorial control," while guerrilla groups occupy territory. The FARC and Al Qaeda in the Arabian Peninsula would not be considered terrorist groups by this standard, as they control territory. This notion is consistent with some scholars' definitions (Della Porta 1995; Cronin 2015). However, other studies use a broader understanding of terrorist organizations that includes any subnational political organizations that use terrorism (Asal 2012; Jones and Libicki 2008). Some research does not explicitly define the term, but includes organizations that hold territory or use guerrilla tactics in analyses (Asal and Rethemeyer 2008, Enders and Sandler 2011. Others use the terms interchangeably; Hoffman (2006, 35) describes Hezbollah, the FARC, and the LTTE as terrorist groups, but notes that they "are also often described as guerrilla movements."

An additional issue of contention involves blurred lines between criminal organizations and terrorist groups. For example, Shelley (2014, 113) argues that some scholars have been constrained by a "false dichotomy" of criminal groups driven by profit, and terrorists driven by political motivations. This is consistent with work suggesting convergence or hybridization of criminal and terrorist groups (Makarenko 2004). Regarding specific cases, there are debates about whether various groups are terrorist or criminal organizations. Examples include Mexican drug cartels, the Neapolitan Camorra, the FARC, and Abu Sayyaf (Flanigan 2012; Makarenko 2004; Toros and Mavelli 2013; Williams 2012)—all of whom have engaged in some degree of criminal activity while using terrorist tactics.

In spite of these debates, most studies of terrorist organizations use the term in a fairly consistent manner. After a survey of the literature, I found that most studies implicitly or explicitly used the following understanding of terrorist groups: subnational political organizations that use terrorism (Phillips 2015c, 229). They are subnational actors, although they might have connections to states. They are primarily political organizations, meaning that while groups such as the FARC and Abu Sayyaf also engage in crime, it does not seem to be their primary purpose. Groups that primarily engage in crime and only affect politics to increase their profits, such as Mexican drug cartels and Italian mafias, are thus not considered terrorist groups. This is the definition employed in this chapter. As with any concept, the appropriate conceptual boundaries likely depend on one's research question. For some purposes, it could make sense to exclude groups that primarily use other tactics, such as guerrilla warfare. Debate continues over this topic, and debate is better than the relative silence that existed for many years.

Recent Research on Terrorist Organizations

Outbidding and Competition

It has been noted that terrorism studies suffers from some shortcomings as a theoretical field, such as insufficient accumulation of knowledge over time, or a lack of rigorous hypothesis testing (e.g. Crenshaw 2014; Young and Findley 2011; Ranstorp 2006). One important exception to both of these issues, I would argue, involves the subject of outbidding. "Outbidding" generally refers to elites taking increasingly extreme positions (Sartori 1962), and it is usually used to describe ethnic or nationalist party politics (e.g. Chandra 2007; Rabushka and Shepsle 1972, 151).[2] In conflict studies, however, it has come to mean militant groups engaging in increasingly violent tactics to distinguish themselves from others.

Mia Bloom (2004, 2005) introduced outbidding to terrorism studies to explain suicide terror, joining a lively debate on the subject (Atran 2003; Crenshaw 2007;

Moghadam 2003; Pape 2003; Pedazhur 2005). Bloom argues that suicide terrorism is a tactical innovation that occurs when militant groups are competing for public support and looking for ways to stand out. Whether groups turn to, and continue to use, suicide terror depends on whether they think the public will accept or reject the tactic's use (Bloom 2005).

The idea of outbidding as violence apparently has been useful to students of terrorism, because Bloom's article and book together have been cited more than 1,500 times. In addition to suicide terror, outbidding has been applied to other violent outcomes as well. Scholars have explored how outbidding can lead to more terrorism (Nemeth 2014), new terrorist groups (Chenoweth 2010), and more "severe" attacks such as targeting civilians more than government targets (Conrad and Greene 2015). More generally, Kydd and Walter (2006) argue that outbidding is one of the principal strategies of terrorism.

Beyond terrorism studies, scholars of civil war often draw on outbidding and cite Bloom's work as they study spoiler processes, group fragmentation, and other dynamics of civil conflict (Cunningham et al. 2012; Fortna, 2015; Pearlman, 2009; Stanton 2013). The concept of outbidding seems to be one of the rare cases of a concept popularized in the terrorism literature catching on in other fields.

Scholars continue to test the outbidding hypothesis and related arguments, building on the work of those before them. Some studies find mixed or little support for the idea that competition between groups leads to suicide terror, or more terrorism (Brym and Araj 2008; Findley and Young 2012; Fortna 2015; Stanton 2013). Other results are more consistent with the outbidding hypothesis (e.g. Chenoweth 2010). Nemeth (2014) finds that the impact of competition is conditional on group ideology: competition is associated with more violence among nationalist and religious groups, but less violence among leftist groups.

Studies increasingly use the outbidding hypothesis to explain outcomes beyond terrorism rates, and have found results consistent with the argument. Chenoweth (2010) finds competition not only associated with increased terrorism, but also the emergence of new terrorist groups. Conrad and Greene (2015) show that competition leads to more shocking kinds of terrorism, such as attacking civilian instead of government targets. Competition can encourage groups to innovate and eventually survive longer than they otherwise would have (Phillips 2015a).[3] Competition is especially associated with group longevity for the "top dog" group in a country (Young and Dugan, 2014).

Research on outbidding is likely to continue, as important questions remain. The effects of competition seem to be conditional on other factors. Findley and Young (2012) note that competition leads to suicide bombing in some countries, but not others. Part of the explanation could be that the group's political goals play a role (Nemeth 2014). Useful new directions for research include questions such as: (1) What other factors condition the effects of outbidding? (2) Beyond outcomes already discussed, what are other consequences of outbidding? (3) Aside from outbidding as an independent variable, what explains outbidding? (4) Is outbidding being measured adequately? Quantitative studies often capture outbidding simply with the presence of multiple terrorist groups in a geographic area. However, future research could use more precise measures.

Internal Dynamics

A growing number of studies look comparatively at internal dynamics of terrorist organizations, as opposed to treating groups as unitary actors. Some of this research examines organizational structure, considering tradeoffs between loose networks and more hierarchical organizations. Other work looks at group mobilization issues, such as recruiting and fundraising.

Terrorist groups vary substantially in their internal organizational structure, and this can have important implications for group behavior. It has been argued that the network structure—loosely connected cells instead of a hierarchical chain of command—is increasingly common for terrorists (Arquilla and Ronfeldt 2001; Sageman 2004). As a result, a wave of research looking at so-called "dark networks" has applied social network analysis to individual terrorists (Carley 2006; Everton 2012; Raab and Milward 2003).[4] One criticism of this line of work is that focusing on networks of individual terrorists, independently of formal group membership, overlooks the importance of formal organizations and organizational processes (e.g. Helfstein 2009). Indeed, this was the source of a debate between two prominent terrorism scholars, regarding the nature of the Al Qaeda threat (Sageman and Hoffman 2008).

Many scholars are also using network or organizational studies approaches to understand dynamics within formal terrorist organizations. Understanding the structure of terrorist organizations contributes to our knowledge of group leadership, communication, and other dynamics. Some scholars consider tradeoffs between the more decentralized cell-based structures and more hierarchical structures (Enders and Su 2007, Helfstein and Wright 2011a, 2011b; Pearson et al. 2017). There is said to be a security–effectiveness tradeoff across group types, where centralized groups are more effective with their violence, but less secure from counterterrorism efforts (Kilberg 2012). Accordingly, several studies find that hierarchical terrorist groups are more lethal (Heger et al., 2012; Helfstein and Wright 2011b; Rowlands and Kilberg, 2011.[5] In spite of benefits of hierarchy, groups seem to be aware of the security–effectiveness tradeoff, as they are less likely to take a hierarchical form in states with better counterterrorism capacities (Kilberg 2012, 821).

Beyond the question of consequences of organizational structure, there are opportunities for additional research on related topics. Abrahms and Potter (2015) find that leadership deficits are associated with militant groups attacking civilians. How else do leadership types or issues affect group behavior? McCormick (2003) noted that there is a broad variety of terrorist decision-making processes, and that extant theoretical frameworks can be harnessed to help us better understand terrorist decision-making—but few scholars have taken up this challenge. Why do some groups adopt certain decision-making styles, and what are the effects of these decisions? How might internal structures of terrorist groups affect, for example, their relationships with states, including negotiation outcomes?

Mobilization, in terms of obtaining and keeping resources (such as personnel and funds), is crucial for terrorist organizations. Regarding membership, Shapiro (2013) argues that terrorist organization leaders face a fundamental challenge in trying to control their members while maintaining secrecy, in what he calls "the terrorist's dilemma." The issue of how terrorist groups find and keep recruits is an important one (Crenshaw 1987; Della Porta 1995). More recently, scholars have sought to understand why "foreign fighters" join groups in countries other than their own. Hegghammer (2011) explores the motivations of Muslim foreign fighters, and argues that their roots are in 1970s pan-Islamic thought, brought about by elite competition. He also finds that Western jihadists seem to prefer to join groups in foreign countries, and rarely return to attack in their home country (Hegghammer 2013). Once abroad, these foreign fighters play key roles in terrorist groups, such as media specialists or recruiters (Mendelsohn, 2011).

Another mobilization topic is female participation in terrorist organizations. Some studies seek to explain why groups try to recruit women, emphasizing issues such as the tendency of security forces to overlook women as suspects (Cunningham 2003). Gonzalez-Perez (2006, 2008) notes differences in female participation rates between domestic and international groups, and argues that domestic groups are especially likely to accept women, and women are relatively interested in joining these groups, given that these organizations often address perceived oppression in their own country. International organizations, on the other hand, are less likely to recruit women for more than menial roles.[6] Other research focuses on what draws women to terrorist groups. Bloom (2011) argues that revenge is one of the important factors. Less studied have been the consequences of female participation in terrorist groups. How does higher female participation affect group behavior? Are these groups more tactically or strategically effective than relatively homogeneous groups (Alakoc 2018)? Important work continues on gender dynamics of terrorism (e.g. Matfess 2017), but much remains to be understood.

There is space for more research on terrorist group recruiting and retention strategies. For example, we know that group size—in terms of members—is one of the most important factors in explaining organizational lethality, civilian targeting, and endurance (Asal and Rethemeyer 2008; Asal et al. 2009; Asal et al. 2015a; Gaibulloev and Sandler, 2014; Horowitz and Potter 2014). Some studies explore how repression affects mobilization (Bueno de Mesquita 2005b). However, we know little about why some types of group are better at drawing members than others.

Funding is also of clear importance for terrorist organizations. While terrorist attacks are famously cheap (e.g. Richardson 2003), the violence nonetheless implies non-trivial expenditures. Groups generally purchase weapons, for example, and many larger groups pay their members' salaries and even provide social services for the community they seek to represent. These dynamics are important for group discipline and, ultimately, success (Berman 2011; Shapiro 2013; Shapiro and Siegel 2007).

Many terrorist groups obtain their funds through crime such as drug trafficking (Asal et al. 2015b). This became increasingly common as Cold War-related funds dried up, and globalization made transnational black markets more feasible and lucrative (Shelley 2014). However, terrorist groups have long used criminal means to fund themselves, from kidnapping to bank robberies to drug sales (e.g. Horgan and Taylor 1999). Beyond engaging in crimes for fundraising, many terrorist organizations rely on donations—with varying degrees of coercion—from the wider community (Boylan 2015). A number of questions remain regarding terrorist group funding, including the following. Why do groups choose one funding type over another? What drives shifts from one funding type to another? What government policies, such as economic sanctions, have been effective at making terrorism funding more challenging?

Group Termination

Terrorist group termination is one of the most-studied topics of organizational dynamics of terrorism in recent years, although the line of research could be more theoretically coherent or cumulative. Attention to terrorist group termination makes sense given interest in counterterrorism, and because so many groups have come and gone in recent decades. The availability of new data sources probably also plays a role. Terrorist group termination studies have roots in the late 1980s (Crenshaw 1987, 1991; Oots 1989; Ross and Gurr 1989). Crenshaw (1991) applied her earlier work on organizational dynamics to the study of organizational decline, showing that government policies are only a small part of why some groups give up terrorism or cease to exist. She analyzed seventy-seven terrorist groups, and found that groups tended to end through government force, group disintegration, or the groups deciding to give up terrorism. Regarding giving up terrorism, Weinberg and Pedahzur's (2003) book explored relationships between terrorist groups and political parties, including when terrorists give up violence and become legal parties.[7]

Cronin (2006) provided a theoretical framework for group termination in an article, outlining seven ways that terrorist groups can end, and applying the typology to analysis of Al Qaeda. The seven ways terrorist groups end, according to the analysis, are (1) capture or killing of the leader, (2) failure to transition to the next generation, (3) achievement of the group's aims, (4) transition to a legitimate political process, (5) undermining of popular support, (6) repression, and (7) transition from terrorism to other forms of violence (Cronin 2006, 17–18). A special issue of *Dynamics of Asymmetric Conflict* looked at how criminology research can inform the study of "desistance from terrorism," analyzing why individuals and groups stop using terrorism (LaFree and Miller 2008).

Some of the first global quantitative studies on terrorist group demise were made possible by the RAND-MIPT data on terrorist organizations. Jones and Libicki's (2008) monograph analyzed 648 groups and reached a number of interesting conclusions, such as reporting that only 7 percent of groups that ended did so as a result of military force. Cronin's book (2009), following up on the earlier article, analyzed hundreds of groups, and provided rich qualitative evidence of the seven ending types. Both books applied their findings to the case of Al Qaeda.[8]

Both Jones and Libicki and Cronin draw on historical data to note the challenge that religious groups are especially durable, but they also express some optimism regarding the fact that religious terrorists rarely achieve their political goals. Jones and Libicki's

(2008, xvi–xvii) primary conclusion regarding Al Qaeda is that military force alone is unlikely to defeat the group, so they call for an end to the "war" on terror. They suggest policing and intelligence are crucial. Cronin (2009, 193–6) also argues for a more nuanced counterterrorism approach. She suggests considering negotiations with some peripheral elements of Al Qaeda to fragment it, undercutting its popular support by pointing out contradictions such as the group's civilian targeting, and avoiding overreaction to its terrorist attacks.

Scholars continue to use global data, and more sophisticated statistical analysis, to explore the question of terrorist group termination, and its flip side, group longevity (e.g. Blomberg et al. 2010; Carter 2012a; Pearson et al. 2015; Suttmoeller et al. 2015). Some of the studies seem oriented more toward introducing new independent variables, focusing on the effects of single factors such as repression (Daxecker and Hess 2013), terrorist group alliances (Phillips 2014), or state sponsorship (Carter 2012a). Others are more broadly oriented, exploring many factors to see which models seem to explain group survival best (Blomberg et al. 2011; Gaibulloev and Sandler 2013).

A puzzle regarding terrorist group termination and longevity is that meta-analysis suggests that few results are robust across multiple studies (Phillips 2018). Perhaps the most consistent result is that groups with larger memberships are more likely to survive (e.g. Blomberg et al. 2011; Jones and Libicki 2008; Phillips 2014). This is probably not surprising, but raises questions about what explains membership size. Several studies also find that inter-group relationships, cooperation, and competition, are associated with group duration (Gaibulloev and Sandler 2013; Price 2012; Phillips 2014, 2015a). Two state variables, country population and poverty, are also often related to group longevity. Population is usually included as a control variable but has not been explored in depth as a substantively and theoretically important factor. Regarding poverty, it is likely that poorer countries do not have the resources to successfully eliminate groups, and that there are grievances present that help groups recruit.

Other theoretically relevant factors—the regime type of the country in which a group operates, or whether the group is motivated by religion or nationalism—are not consistently associated with group survival. These inconsistent findings suggest scholars need to think more about factors that should affect *groups*, instead of only relying on traditional determinants of terrorism generally.

One way research on group termination could advance would be to focus on particular ending types, instead of assuming the factors that explain one ending type also explain another. The few studies to look at determinants of diverse ending types have found quite different results for each form of termination (Carter 2012a; Gaibulloev and Sandler 2014). Future research could benefit from picking one theoretically interesting type of group termination, such as elimination by the government or internal dissolution, and try to narrow down factors that robustly explain it. Additionally, beyond searching for a general explanation of terrorist group survival (or a particular termination type), scholars could simply use survival analysis as one type of outcome of interest for various questions about terrorist groups. For example, to explore consequences of leadership decapitation, group survival is a relevant dependent variable (Price 2012).

New Directions

This chapter has outlined a number of potential avenues for future research, such as analyzing outbidding with more nuance, bringing coherence to the study of terrorist group termination, and more empirical work on terrorist group funding. Here I review a few areas of organizational dynamics of terrorism that also deserve additional focus.

Because of space reasons, this chapter did not include much discussion of another aspect of organizational dynamics—groups' relationships with the state. This topic is arguably less "organizational," in that not all of it incorporates specific internal dynamics such as mobilization. However, some of the relevant work includes analysis of negotiations with groups (Bueno de Mesquita 2005a; Lapan and Sandler 1988; Zartman 2003) and state sponsorship (Bapat 2006, 2012; Byman 2005, 2008; Carter 2012a, 2015). Other relevant studies seek to understand consequences of counterterrorism policy (Asal et al. 2018; Enders and Sandler 1993), such as leadership removal (Johnston 2012; Jordan 2014; Price 2012). If one looks through the dominant terrorism journals and top field journals, rigorous analyses of policy are not as common as they could be. As more data on counterterrorism policies become available (e.g. Dugan and Chenoweth 2012; Gill et al. 2016; Smith and Walsh 2013), hopefully we will see more such analysis of these policies.

Another challenge in the literature is that empirical work does not engage sufficiently with the many important findings of the theoretical work on strategic interactions (Carter 2012b). A few scholars, such as Bapat and Sandler, combine formal theory and empirical work, but this is relatively rare. Rigorously testing implications of theoretical work on strategic interactions (e.g. Bueno de Mesquita and Dickson 2007) is an important avenue for future research.

Perhaps the broadest challenge facing terrorism studies is insufficient dialogue with research on related topics. One example is civil war studies. Studies of terrorist group longevity can learn from and inform studies of civil war duration and termination. Studies of the causes of terrorism can learn from and inform studies of civil war onset. Studies of any organizational dynamic of terrorism can learn from and inform work on rebel groups in civil wars. Terrorism and civil war are distinct phenomena, but the overlaps suggest opportunities for enhanced research.

Overall, scholars have made substantial progress toward understanding terrorism through examining organizational dynamics. As the research progresses, hopefully it can gain more conceptual clarity, contribute to important theoretical debates in terrorism studies and beyond, and overall help build a more cumulative and cohesive research program.

Notes

1. Silke, e.g. 2001 noticed that terrorism studies was unusual in the social sciences for rarely using interferential or even descriptive statistics.
2. Kaufman 1996, 109 argues that endogenous processes of outbidding, mass ethnic hostility, and security dilemma could spiral into ethnic war. However, like previous authors, he

describes outbidding as increasingly extreme nationalist positions. After Bloom, other scholars describe outbidding as escalating levels of violence, e.g. Nemeth 2014.

3. On groups innovating because of interactions with the government, instead of other terrorist groups, see Kenney 2007.
4. The term "dark networks" is principally used by public administration scholars, to indicate that they are studying covert networks, as opposed to legal organizations such as government agencies. Scholars from other disciplines use network analysis for terrorists as well, but often without using the term "dark networks," e.g. Krebs 2002; Perliger and Pedahzur 2011.
5. A somewhat related finding is that hierarchical state-sponsored militant groups are more likely to remain obedient to their sponsor, while decentralized groups are prone to breaking their commitment to their sponsoring state and attacking it, Popovic 2015.
6. Interestingly, neither ideological nor religious orientations are associated with female participation, according to one study, Dalton and Asal 2011.
7. See also Weinberg (2012).
8. Studies tend to focus on especially durable groups, but a valuable alternative approach is looking at short-lived groups to see why they failed to endure, e.g. de Graaf and Malkki 2010.

REFERENCES

Abrahms, M., and P. B. K. Potter (2015) "Explaining Terrorism: Leadership Deficits and Militant Group Tactics." *International Organization*, 69(5): 311–42.

Alakoc, B. P. (2017) "Competing to Kill: Terrorist Organizations Versus Lone Wolf Terrorists. *Terrorism and Political Violence*, 29(3): 509–532.

Alakoc, Burcu Pinar (2018) "Femme Fatale: The Lethality of Female Suicide Bombers," *Studies in Conflict & Terrorism*. Ahead of print, available online at https://doi.org/10.1080/1057610X.2018.1505685.

Arquilla, J., and D. Ronfeldt (2001) *Networks and Netwars: The Future of Terror, Crime, and Militancy*. Santa Monica, CA: Rand Corporation.

Asal, V. (2012) "John Brown, American Revolutionary War Guerrillas in the South, the Treblinka Revolt, and the Coding of Terrorist Organizations," in V. Asal (ed.), "Killing Civilians or Holding Territory? How to Think about Terrorism," forum of *International Studies Review*, 14(3): 485–90.

Asal, V., and R. K. Rethemeyer (2008) "The Nature of the Beast: Organizational Structures and the Lethality of Terrorist Attacks," *Journal of Politics*, 70(2): 437–49.

Asal, V., R. K. Rethemeyer, I. Anderson, J. Rizzo, M. M. Rozea, and A. Stein (2009) "The Softest of Targets: A Study on Terrorist Target Selection," *Journal of Applied Security Research*, 4(3): 258–78.

Asal, V., P. Gill, R. K. Rethemeyer, and J. Horgan (2015a) "Killing Range: Explaining Lethality Variance within a Terrorist Organization," *Journal of Conflict Resolution*, 59(3): 401–27.

Asal, V., H. B. Milward, and E. W. Schoon (2015b) "When Terrorists Go Bad: Analyzing Terrorist Organizations' Involvement in Drug Smuggling," *International Studies Quarterly*, 59(1): 112–23.

Asal, V., B. J. Phillips, R. K. Rethemeyer, C. Simonelli, and J. K. Young. (2018) "Carrots, Sticks, and Insurgent Targeting of Civilians." *Journal of Conflict Resolution* (OnlineFirst).

Atran, S. (2003) "Genesis of Suicide Terrorism," *Science*, 299(5612): 1534–9.

Bapat, N. A. (2006) "State Bargaining with Transnational Terrorist Groups," *International Studies Quarterly*, 50(1): 213–30.

Bapat, N. A. (2007) "The Internationalization of Terrorist Campaigns," *Conflict Management and Peace Science*, 24(4): 265–80.

Bapat, N. A. (2012) "Understanding State Sponsorship of Militant Groups," *British Journal of Political Science*, 42(1): 1–29.

Berman, E. (2011) *Radical, Religious, and Violent: The New Economics of Terrorism*. Cambridge, MA: MIT Press.

Blomberg, S. B., R. C. Engel, and R. Sawyer (2010) "On the Duration and Sustainability of Transnational Terrorist Organizations," *Journal of Conflict Resolution*, 54(2): 303–30.

Blomberg, S. B., K. Gaibulloev, and T. Sandler (2011) "Terrorist Group Survival: Ideology, Tactics, and Base of Operations," *Public Choice*, 149(3–4): 441–63.

Bloom, M. M. (2004) "Palestinian Suicide Bombing: Public Support, Market Share, and Outbidding," *Political Science Quarterly*, 119(1): 61–88.

Bloom, M. (2005) *Dying to Kill: The Allure of Suicide Terror*. New York: Columbia University Press.

Bloom, M. (2011) *Bombshell: Women and Terrorism*. Philadelphia: University of Pennsylvania Press.

Boylan, B. M. (2015) "Sponsoring Violence: A Typology of Constituent Support for Terrorist Organizations," *Studies in Conflict and Terrorism*, 38(8): 652–70.

Brym, R. J., and B. Araj (2008) "Palestinian Suicide Bombing Revisited: A Critique of the Outbidding Thesis," *Political Science Quarterly*, 123(3): 485–500.

Bueno de Mesquita, E. (2005a) "Conciliation, Counterterrorism, and Patterns of Terrorist Violence," *International Organization*, 59(1): 145–76.

Bueno de Mesquita, E. (2005b) "The Quality of Terror," *American Journal of Political Science*, 49(3): 515–30.

Bueno de Mesquita, E., and E. S. Dickson (2007) "The Propaganda of the Deed: Terrorism, Counterterrorism, and Mobilization," *American Journal of Political Science*, 51(2): 364–81.

Byman, D. (2005) *Deadly Connections: States that Sponsor Terrorism*. Cambridge: Cambridge University Press.

Byman, D. (2006) "Do Targeted Killings Work?." *Foreign Affairs*, 85(2): 95.

Byman, D. (2008) *The Changing Nature of State Sponsorship of Terrorism*. Washington, DC: Brookings Institution.

Carley, K. M. (2006) "Destabilization of Covert Networks," *Computational and Mathematical Organization Theory*, 12(1): 51–66.

Carter, D. B. (2012a) "A Blessing or a Curse? State Support for Terrorist Groups," *International Organization*, 66(1): 129–51.

Carter, D. B. (2012b) "Terrorist Group and Government Interaction: Progress in Empirical Research," *Perspectives on Terrorism*, 6(4–5): 108–24.

Carter, D. B. (2015) "The Compellence Dilemma: International Disputes with Violent Groups." *International Studies Quarterly*, 59(3): 461–76.

Chandra, K. (2007) *Why Ethnic Parties Succeed: Patronage and Ethnic Head Counts in India*. Cambridge: Cambridge University Press.

Chenoweth, E. (2010) "Democratic Competition and Terrorist Activity," *Journal of Politics*, 72(1): 16–30.

Conrad, J., and K. Greene (2015) "Competition, Differentiation, and the Severity of Terrorist Attacks," *Journal of Politics*, 77(2): 546–61.

Crenshaw, M. (1985) "An Organizational Approach to the Analysis of Political Terrorism," *Orbis: A Journal of World Affairs*, 29(3): 465–89.

Crenshaw, M. (1987) "Theories of Terrorism: Instrumental and Organizational Approaches," *Journal of Strategic Studies*, 10(4): 13–31.

Crenshaw, M. (1991) "How Terrorism Declines," *Terrorism and Political Violence*, 3(1): 69–87.

Crenshaw, M. (1995) *Terrorism in Context*. Philadelphia: Pennsylvania State University.

Crenshaw, M. (2007) "Explaining Suicide Terrorism: A Review Essay," *Security Studies*, 16(1): 133–62.

Crenshaw, M. (2014) "Terrorism Research: The Record," *International Interactions*, 40(4): 556–67.

Cronin, A. K. (2006) "How Al-Qaida Ends: The Decline and Demise of Terrorist Groups," *International Security*, 31(1): 7–48.

Cronin, A. K. (2009) *How Terrorism Ends: Understanding the Decline and Demise of Terrorist Campaigns*. Princeton: Princeton University Press.

Cronin, A. K. (2015) "ISIS is Not a Terrorist Group," *Foreign Affairs*, 94(2): 87–98.

Cunningham, K. G., K. M. Bakke, and L. J. Seymour (2012) "Shirts Today, Skins Tomorrow: Dual Contests and the Effects of Fragmentation in Self-Determination Disputes," *Journal of Conflict Resolution*, 56(1): 67–93.

Cunningham, K. J. (2003) "Cross-Regional Trends in Female Terrorism," *Studies in Conflict and Terrorism*, 26(3): 171–95.

Dalton, A., and V. Asal (2011) "Is it Ideology or Desperation: Why do Organizations Deploy Women in Violent Terrorist Attacks?," *Studies in Conflict and Terrorism*, 34(10): 802–19.

Daxecker, U. E., and M. L. Hess (2013) "Repression Hurts: Coercive Government Responses and the Demise of Terrorist Campaigns," *British Journal of Political Science*, 43(3): 559–77.

De Graaf, B., and L. Malkki (2010) "Killing it Softly? Explaining the Early Demise of Left-Wing Terrorism in the Netherlands," *Terrorism and Political Violence*, 22(4): 623–40.

De la Calle, L., and I. Sánchez-Cuenca (2011) "What we Talk about When we Talk about Terrorism," *Politics and Society*, 39(3): 451–72.

Della Porta, D. (1995) *Social Movements, Political Violence, and the State: A Comparative Analysis of Italy and Germany*. Cambridge: Cambridge University Press.

Dugan, L., and E. Chenoweth (2012) "Moving Beyond Deterrence: The Effectiveness of Raising the Expected Utility of Abstaining from Terrorism in Israel," *American Sociological Review*, 77(4): 597–624.

Enders, W., and T. Sandler (1993) "The Effectiveness of Antiterrorism Policies: A Vector-Autoregression-Intervention Analysis," *American Political Science Review*, 87(4): 829–44.

Enders, W., and T. Sandler (2011) *The Political Economy of Terrorism*. Cambridge: Cambridge University Press.

Enders, W, and X. Su (2007) "Rational Terrorists and Optimal Network Structure," *Journal of Conflict Resolution*, 51(1): 33–57.

Eubank, W. L., and L. Weinberg (1994) "Does Democracy Encourage Terrorism?," *Terrorism and Political Violence*, 6(4): 417–35.

Everton, S. F. (2012) *Disrupting Dark Networks*. Cambridge: Cambridge University Press.

Findley, M. G., and J. K. Young (2012) "More Combatant Groups, More Terror? Empirical Tests of an Outbidding Logic," *Terrorism and Political Violence*, 24(5): 706–21.

Flanigan, S. T. (2012) "Terrorists Next Door? A Comparison of Mexican Drug Cartels and Middle Eastern Terrorist Organizations," *Terrorism and Political Violence*, 24(2): 279–94.

Fortna, V. P. (2015) "Do Terrorists Win? Rebels' Use of Terrorism and Civil War Outcomes," *International Organization* 69(3): 519–56.

Gaibulloev, K., and T. Sandler (2013) "Determinants of the Demise of Terrorist Organizations," *Southern Economic Journal*, 79(4): 774–92.

Gaibulloev, K., and T. Sandler (2014) "An Empirical Analysis of Alternative Ways that Terrorist Groups End," *Public Choice*, 160(1–2): 25–44.

Gill, P., J. A. Piazza, and J. Horgan (2016) "Counterterrorism Killings and Provisional IRA Bombings, 1970–1998," *Terrorism and Political Violence*, 28(3): 473–96.

Gonzalez-Perez, M. (2006) "Guerrilleras in Latin America: Domestic and International Roles," *Journal of Peace Research*, 43(3): 313–29.

Gonzalez-Perez, M. (2008) *Women and Terrorism: Female Activity in Domestic and International Terror Groups*. London: Routledge.

Heger, L., D. Jung, and W. H. Wong. (2012) "Organizing for Resistance: How Group Structure Impacts the Character of Violence," *Terrorism and Political Violence*, 24(5): 743–68.

Hegghammer, T. (2011) *The Rise of Muslim Foreign Fighters: Islam and the Globalization of Jihad*. Cambridge, MA: MIT Press.

Hegghammer, T. (2013) "Should I Stay or Should I Go? Explaining Variation in Western Jihadists' Choice between Domestic and Foreign Fighting," *American Political Science Review*, 107(1): 1–15.

Helfstein, S. (2009) "Governance of Terror: New Institutionalism and the Evolution of Terrorist Organizations," *Public Administration Review*, 69(4): 727–39.

Helfstein, S., and D. Wright (2011a) "Covert or Convenient? Evolution of Terror Attack Networks," *Journal of Conflict Resolution*, 55(5): 785–813.

Helfstein, S., and D. Wright (2011b) "Success, Lethality, and Cell Structure across the Dimensions of Al Qaeda," *Studies in Conflict and Terrorism*, 34(5): 367–82.

Hoffman, B. (2006) *Inside Terrorism*. New York: Columbia University Press.

Horgan, J., and M. Taylor (1999) "Playing the 'Green Card': Financing the Provisional IRA: Part 1," *Terrorism and Political Violence*, 11(2): 1–38.

Horowitz, M. C., and P. B. Potter (2014) "Allying to Kill Terrorist Intergroup Cooperation and the Consequences for Lethality," *Journal of Conflict Resolution*, 58(2): 199–225.

Johnston, P. B. (2012) "Does Decapitation Work? Assessing the Effectiveness of Leadership Targeting in Counterinsurgency Campaigns," *International Security*, 36(4): 47–79.

Jones, S. G., and M. C. Libicki (2008). *How Terrorist Groups End: Lessons for Countering al Qa'ida*. Santa Monica, CA: Rand Corporation.

Jordan, J. (2014) "Attacking the Leader, Missing the Mark: Why Terrorist Groups Survive Decapitation Strikes," *International Security*, 38(4): 7–38.

Kaufman, S. J. (1996) "Spiraling to Ethnic War: Elites, Masses, and Moscow in Moldova's Civil War," *International Security*, 21(2): 108–38.

Kenney, M. (2007) *From Pablo to Osama: Trafficking and Terrorist Networks, Government Bureaucracies, and Competitive Adaptation*. Philadelphia: Penn State Press.

Kilberg, J. (2012) "'A Basic Model Explaining Terrorist Group Organizational Structure," *Studies in Conflict and Terrorism*, 35(11): 810–30.

Krause, P. (2013) "The Political Effectiveness of Non-State Violence: A Two-Level Framework to Transform a Deceptive Debate," *Security Studies*, 22(2): 259–94.

Krebs, V. E. (2002) "Mapping Networks of Terrorist Cells," *Connections*, 24(3): 43–52.

Kydd, A. H., and B. F. Walter (2006) "The Strategies of Terrorism," *International Security*, 31(1): 49–80.

LaFree, G., and E. Miller (2008) "Desistance from Terrorism: What can we Learn from Criminology?," *Dynamics of Asymmetric Conflict*, 1(3): 203–30.
Lapan, H. E., and T. Sandler (1988) "To Bargain or Not to Bargain: That is the Question," *American Economic Review*, 78(2): 16–21.
Li, Q. (2005) "Does Democracy Promote or Reduce Transnational Terrorist Incidents?," *Journal of Conflict Resolution*, 49(2): 278–97.
McCormick, G. H. (2003) "Terrorist Decision Making," *Annual Review of Political Science*, 6(1): 473–507.
Makarenko, T. (2004) "The Crime–Terror Continuum: Tracing the Interplay between Transnational Organised Crime and Terrorism," *Global Crime*, 6(1): 129–45.
Matfess, H. (2017) Women and the War on Boko Haram: Wives, Weapons, Witnesses. London: Zed Books.
Mendelsohn, B. (2011) "Foreign Fighters—Recent Trends," *Orbis*, 55(2): 189–202.
Michael, G. (2012) *Lone Wolf Terror and the Rise of Leaderless Resistance*. Nashville, TN: Vanderbilt University Press.
Moghadam, A. (2003) "Palestinian Suicide Terrorism in the Second Intifada: Motivations and Organizational Aspects," *Studies in Conflict and Terrorism*, 26(2): 65–92.
Nemeth, S. (2014) "The Effect of Competition on Terrorist Group Operations," *Journal of Conflict Resolution*, 58(2): 336–62.
Oots, K. L. (1989) "Organizational Perspectives on the Formation and Disintegration of Terrorist Groups," *Studies in Conflict and Terrorism*, 12(3): 139–52.
Pape, R. A. (2003) "The Strategic Logic of Suicide Terrorism," *American Political Science Review*, 97(3): 343–61.
Pearlman, W. (2009) "Spoiling Inside and Out: Internal Political Contestation and the Middle East Peace Process," *International Security*, 33(3): 79–109.
Pearson, F. S., I. Akbulut, and M. Olson Lounsbery (2017) "Group Structure and Intergroup Relations in Global Terror Networks: Further Explorations," *Terrorism and Political Violence*, 29(3): 550–72.
Pedahzur, A. (2005) *Suicide Terrorism*. Cambridge: Polity.
Perliger, A., and A. Pedahzur (2011) "Social Network Analysis in the Study of Terrorism and Political Violence," *PS: Political Science and Politics*, 44(1): 45–50.
Phillips, B. J. (2014) "Terrorist Group Cooperation and Longevity," *International Studies Quarterly*, 58(2): 336–47.
Phillips, B. J. (2015a) "Enemies with Benefits? Violent Rivalry and Terrorist Group Longevity," *Journal of Peace Research*, 52(1): 62–75.
Phillips, B. J. (2015b) "How does Leadership Decapitation Affect Violence? The Case of Mexico," *Journal of Politics*, 77(2): 324–36.
Phillips, B. J. (2015c) "What is a Terrorist Group? Conceptual Issues and Empirical Implications," *Terrorism and Political Violence*, 27(2): 225–42.
Phillips, B. J. (2017) "Deadlier in the US? On Lone Wolves, Terrorist Groups, and Attack Lethality." *Terrorism and Political Violence*, 29(3): 533–49.
Phillips, B. J. (2018) "Terrorist Group Survival as a Measure of Effectiveness," in Diego Muro (ed.), *When Does Terrorism Work?* London: Routledge, 52–70.
Popovic, M. (2015) "The Perils of Weak Organization: Explaining Loyalty and Defection of Militant Organizations toward Pakistan." *Studies in Conflict and Terrorism*, 38(11): 919–37.

Post, J. M. (1987) "'It's us Against them': The Group Dynamics of Political Terrorism," *Terrorism*, 10(1): 23–35.

Price, B. C. (2012) "Targeting Top Terrorists: How Leadership Decapitation Contributes to Counterterrorism," *International Security*, 36(4): 9–46.

Raab, J., and H. B. Milward (2003) "Dark Networks as Problems," *Journal of Public Administration Research and Theory*, 13(4): 413–39.

Rabushka, A., and K. A. Shepsle (1972) *Politics in Plural Societies*. Columbus, OH: Charles E. Merrill.

Ranstorp, M. (2006) *Mapping Terrorism Research: State of the Art, Gaps and Future Direction*. London: Routledge.

Rapoport, D. C. (2001) "The Fourth Wave: September 11 in the History of Terrorism," *Current History*, 100(650): 419.

Richardson, Louise (2003) Appearance for Hearing of US Senate Committee on Banking, Housing and Urban Affairs. October 22.

Ross, J. I., and T. R. Gurr (1989) "Why Terrorism Subsides: A Comparative Study of Canada and the United States," *Comparative Politics*, 21(4): 405–26.

Rowlands, D., and J. Kilberg (2011) *Organizational Structure and the Effects of Targeting Terrorist Leadership*. Centre for Security and Defence Studies Working Papers. Carleton University.

Sageman, M. (2004) *Understanding Terror Networks*. Philadelphia: University of Pennsylvania Press.

Sageman, M. (2008) *Leaderless Jihad: Terror Networks in the 21st Century*. Philadelphia: University of Pennsylvania Press.

Sageman, M., and B. Hoffman (2008) "Does Osama Still Call the Shots?," *Foreign Affairs*, 87(4): 163.

Sandler, T., and H. E. Lapan (1988) "The Calculus of Dissent: An Analysis of Terrorists' Choice of Targets," *Synthese*, 76(2): 245–61.

Sartori, G. (1962) *Democratic Theory*. Detroit, MI: Wayne State University Press.

Shapiro, J. N. (2013) *The Terrorist's Dilemma: Managing Violent Covert Organizations*. Princeton: Princeton University Press.

Shapiro, J. N., and D. A. Siegel (2007) "Underfunding in Terrorist Organizations," *International Studies Quarterly*, 51(2): 405–29.

Shelley, L. I. (2014) *Dirty Entanglements: Corruption, Crime, and Terrorism*. Cambridge: Cambridge University Press.

Silke, A. (2001) "The Devil you Know: Continuing Problems with Research on Terrorism," *Terrorism and Political Violence*, 13(4): 1–14.

Smith, M., and J. I. Walsh (2013) "Do Drone Strikes Degrade Al Qaeda? Evidence from Propaganda Output," *Terrorism and Political Violence*, 25(2): 311–27.

Stanton, J. A. (2013) "Terrorism in the Context of Civil War," *Journal of Politics*, 75(4): 1009–22.

Suttmoeller, M., S. Chermak, and J. Freilich (2015) "The Influence of External and Internal Correlates on the Organizational Death of Domestic Far-Right Extremist Groups," *Studies in Conflict and Terrorism*, 38(9): 734–58.

Toros, H., and L. Mavelli (2013) "Terrorism, Organised Crime and the Biopolitics of Violence," *Critical Studies on Terrorism*, 6(1): 73–91.

Weinberg, L. (2012) *The End of Terrorism*. London: Routledge.

Weinberg, L., and A. Pedahzur (2003) *Political Parties and Terrorist Groups*. London: Routledge.

Williams, P. (2012) "The Terrorism Debate over Mexican Drug Trafficking Violence," *Terrorism and Political Violence*, 24(2): 259–78.

Young, J. K., and L. Dugan (2014) "Survival of the Fittest: Why Terrorist Groups Endure," *Perspectives on Terrorism*, 8(2): 2–23.

Young, J. K., and M. G. Findley (2011) "Promise and Pitfalls of Terrorism Research," *International Studies Review*, 13(3): 411–31.

Zartman, I. W. (2003) "Negotiating with Terrorists," *International Negotiation*, 8(3): 443–50.

CHAPTER 26

TERRORIST TECHNOLOGICAL INNOVATION

EVAN PERKOSKI

INTRODUCTION

ARMED combat has always been intimately connected to technological developments. Throughout history, technology has acted as a limiting factor, dictating the pace at which troops are positioned, supplies delivered, communications sent, and enemies killed. Consequently, those with more advanced technology generally wield a meaningful battlefield advantage. Yet, while technological advancements in the long term shape the very nature of armed conflict, the power of innovation in the short term lies in its ability to confound and to undermine enemy preparations. As Sun Tzu notes, "Victory in war is not repetitious, but adapts its form endlessly." As a result, conflict is not only affected by technological innovation but is itself a driving force, motivating belligerents to innovate in the pursuit of victory.

This chapter examines technological innovation among terrorist organizations, focusing on their offensive capabilities. By innovation I am referring to advancements in the strategic or tactical use of force to improve upon existing capabilities. Importantly, innovation refers to technological first-movers who pioneer new advancements, whereas diffusion—often conflated with innovation—concerns the spread of these advancements across space and time (for a more detailed discussion, see Horowitz 2010b). Not surprisingly, researchers expect many of the same factors to drive both innovation and diffusion; for instance, effective counterterrorism practices and inter-group competition might motivate terrorists to seek out new tactical options to overcome defenses and achieve success. Yet, while a group might seek to develop altogether novel tactics (innovation), they might also be interested in tactics that are new to a particular theater of operations (diffusion)—both of which might provide similar benefits. The consequences of innovation, then, are often similar to those of diffusion.

The pressures to innovate are felt by states and non-state actors alike. The competition between them can be described as "cat-and-mouse game, where the cat [the state] is blocking old holes and the mouse [terrorists] always succeeds in finding new ones" (Merari 1998, 24). Yet for terrorist groups, innovation is particularly significant. Since states possess an overwhelming majority of force, the success of terrorist violence typically hinges on the element of surprise. Innovative, unforeseen methods of violence are helpful to this end. In addition, the advantages that terrorists reap from innovations are mirrored by the problems they pose to security forces: new tactics or technologies of violence undermine the state's preparations, creating conditions that are ripe for successful attacks. Understanding the factors associated with terrorist innovation therefore has important real-world consequences that extend beyond the realm of academic inquiry.

In the remainder of this chapter I survey some of the major innovations advanced by terrorist organizations around the globe. I first propose a typology of terrorist innovations that captures the underlying nature of the advancement, focusing on major and minor tactical innovations. From there I examine the drivers of innovation including the expected benefits and the characteristics that make groups or more less likely to experiment in the first place. These characteristics generally fall into one of two camps: organizational or environmental. Organizational drivers refer to characteristics of particular groups that increase or decrease their odds of innovation, while environmental drivers are aspects of the operating environment that particularly incentivize or facilitate tactical experimentation. The chapter concludes with a discussion of enduring challenges to research on terrorist innovation and possible topics for future investigation.

Forms of Terrorist Innovation

Terrorists organizations rarely, if ever, pioneer entirely new technological advances. Rather, these groups have demonstrated a remarkable ability to repurpose and recombine existing technologies to their advantage—what some have called "evolution by combination" (Arthur 2009). At a 2010 workshop at the Naval Postgraduate School, a number of leading terrorism scholars echoed this point, characterizing most terrorist innovations as "a product of a gradual, incremental synthesis of earlier innovations," and not, as some might expect, "a dramatic leap in terrorist tactics and technologies" (Rasmussen and Hafez 2010).

It is therefore relatively easy to dismiss innovations in terrorist violence. This is especially true when comparing them to innovations by state militaries—like nuclear weapons or precision-guided munitions—that can sometimes radically transform the conflict landscape. As such, scholars like Dolnik, Merari, and Hoffman point out that the "scope [of terrorist attacks] is relatively limited and remarkably unchanging. In fact when one surveys the last 50 years of terrorist operations case by case, very few incidents strike the observer as creative in any way" (Dolnik 2007, 56). This should not be all that surprising: terrorist organizations operate on resources and budgets far below national militaries and their innovations consequently tend to be more incremental and more limited in nature. Although, as some of the cases in this chapter will demonstrate, this does not mean that terrorists have been ineffective.

Of course, innovations by terrorist groups are not limited solely to their offensive, operational capabilities. Discussing this issue, Martha Crenshaw proposes a useful typology: first, strategic innovations, or "game changers," are those that alter fundamental patterns of terrorist violence. These include entirely new objectives for the use of force, "[involving] significant shifts in how groups frame their goals, and may thus require new forms of violence, target sets, or audiences to influence" (Rasmussen and Hafez 2010, 29). One oft-cited example is Al Qaeda's shift from attacking targets in the Middle East towards American targets in the continental US—moving the battle from the "near" enemy to the "far" enemy and fundamentally reshaping their overarching strategy. Second, tactical innovations are more subtle (and more frequent), encompassing developments in attack methods, operations, and targets. For instance, the IRA's switch from attacking targets in Northern Ireland to targets in mainland Britain would count, though so would their advancements in remotely detonated explosives. This would also encompass Aum Shinrikyo's sarin gas attack on the Tokyo subway—one of the most innovative nonconventional terrorist attacks to date (Dolnik 2007). Third, and finally, organizational innovations include changes to group structure and recruitment patterns. Al Qaeda's shift towards recruiting and training homegrown terrorists and away from large-scale, coordinated operations is an example (Rasmussen and Hafez 2010; Hafez and Rasmussen 2012). Although in many cases the lines between these types of innovation will be blurred, this presents a useful starting point for comparison.

While the focus of this chapter is tactical innovation, I find it is useful to disaggregate even further into two groups: major and minor. Major tactical innovations involve the creation of new methods or tactics of violence.[1] On the other hand, minor tactical innovations—or what might be called within-tactic innovation—consist of more subtle changes to operational routines and attack behaviors. These innovations either evolve or enhance existing capabilities to make them more destructive or more likely to succeed.

Major tactical innovations are relatively rare, and they do not necessarily involve new technologies. Two of the most significant tactical innovations—aerial hijackings (by the Popular Front for the Liberation of Palestine) and suicide bombings (by Hezbollah)—both utilized widely available weapons and well-known operational patterns, though they were combined in novel, innovative ways. With regards to airplane hijackings in particular, the attack is essentially an armed kidnapping at 30,000 feet. Though the method is not new, its use against a new target—the captive airline audience—is ultimately what accounts for its novelty (Potter et al. 2013). Other examples of major tactical innovation include the September 11 attacks by Al Qaeda on the United States and Aum Shinrikyo's sarin gas attacks on the Tokyo subway.

Perhaps the most well-known major tactical innovation is the development of suicide bombing during the Lebanese Civil War.[2] In October 1983, an operative from Hezbollah[3] rammed a truck laden with explosives into a US Marines compound just outside Beirut, setting off a large explosion. A second event took place about six minutes later when a separate operative drove his truck into a French military base and similarly detonated a hidden device. Two-hundred-and forty-one American and 58 French military servicemen were killed in these two attacks. But why do researchers view suicide bombing as a major tactical innovation? Although terrorist operatives were commonly killed in the course of an attack, it was never an integral part of the attack itself, designed intentionally with tactical and strategic objectives in mind. As such, the advent of suicide terrorism fundamentally altered the expectations of terrorist violence and the calculus of counterterrorist responses: when individuals are ready and willing to kill themselves in an attack, threats of force no longer carry the same deterrent potential. Ultimately, Hezbollah's decision to adopt suicide bombing over existing, conventional operations can be understood in terms of their dissatisfaction with the alternatives. As Hala Jaber notes, "Their mission was to... draw up a plan that would guarantee the maximum impact and leave no trace of the perpetrator. A human bomb was the ultimate method of attack. Not only would it bring large-scale destruction, but it would incur minimum losses and ensure that no clues were left behind" (Jaber 1997, 82). In light of prevailing defenses and offensive limitations, then, Hezbollah looked outside the box for a new approach that eventually reshaped the landscape of terrorist violence.

Minor tactical innovations are much more common. Although it is sometimes difficult to distinguish between major and minor innovations, the latter do not result in new methods of destruction or means of violence. These innovations more commonly alter existing tactics to confound the adversary, cause greater destruction, or to increase the odds of success. Consider the numerous innovations related to remote and automatic detonations of explosives by Irish republican militants (Jackson and Baker 2005). As one former member put it, "We weren't nuclear physicists, but we were good electricians." Capitalizing on these skills, groups improved bomb construction to decrease the chance of accidental explosions, to decrease the odds of detection, and to achieve particular operational goals. For instance, the mercury tilt switch devised in the late 1980s would detonate an explosive charge only when a car began moving. This enabled groups to target their victims and install devices well in advance of the eventual detonation (Drake 1991, 178; Dingley 2008). Other examples of minor innovation include new methods to bring down airplanes through onboard bombs (liquid bomb attacks like that in 2006, the infamous "Shoe Bomber" from 2001, the Bojinka plot from 1995), the Oklahoma City Bombing, the coordinated armed assaults in Mumbai in 2008, and variations on explosively formed projectiles in Iraq. With regards to these projectiles, Colonel Richard Morales of the US Army notes that "Within a week [the insurgents] would adjust to our tweaks" in operational patterns, highlighting the tit-for-tat nature of defensive and offensive innovations (Hafez and Rasmussen 2012, 16).

The recent and continuing evolution of improvised explosive devices (IEDs) in the Middle East is another useful example of ongoing minor technological innovation. To begin with, it is difficult to identify when terrorists first incorporated IEDs into their attack portfolios. Both IEDs and land mines have been used in combat for hundreds of years. Yet, the simplicity and substitutability of components for their construction is ultimately what makes them attractive to terrorists. They can also be utilized in a variety of ways, and this makes them an ideal weapon both for irregular combat and for innovation.

Although innovation in IED technology might be considered minor, it still poses substantial challenges to state forces. As Barker notes, "the clever, sustained, and adaptive use of IEDs, exploiting consumer and information technologies to maximize versatility and propaganda effect, has cheaply and effectively imposed enormous costs that present burdensome implications for American strategy, policy, and programs" (Barker 2011, 602). Examples of innovation include the use of mobile phones as remote triggers and combining explosions with both shrapnel and other chemicals to magnify their impact (Kopp 2008). Innovation is also evident among their implementation, with insurgents in Iraq and Afghanistan now detonating IEDs as part of larger coordinated attacks (Wilson 2006). This differs from more traditional operations where IEDs are deployed far in advance and detonate autonomously in response to proximity or pressure. Notably, none of these innovations alter the fundamental character of the attack itself: although they introduce significant variation that challenges their adversaries and amplifies their lethality and impact, the nature of IED attacks remains roughly consistent over time.

Existing research often fails to distinguish between different types of innovation, or it focuses solely on major innovations. Yet, there are important reasons to clearly conceptualize and to differentiate between the two. Major innovations generally require greater organizational coordination and resource endowments. And, once introduced, their influence on counterterrorism preparations can be significant, forcing states to devise new methods of detection and defense. Minor innovations are generally less resource intensive and can sometimes result from the experimentation of creative individual operatives. Although they might also stress defensive preparations to some extent, successful adaptation by state forces might only require subtle alterations to existing plans. Ultimately, innovations tend to provoke proportional responses from one's adversaries, and this remains true to terrorist violence.

The Drivers of Innovation

Capitalizing on the similarities between terrorist groups and other types of organizations, researchers have developed a keen understanding of the factors that drive innovation and experimentation. In particular, scholars commonly leverage analogies with state militaries and business firms to identify meaningful organizational characteristics (Horowitz 2010a; Shapiro 2013). These analogies also help us to understand why some organizations might be *less* likely to innovate. For instance, groups might lack the particular personnel or access to specialized equipment or materials needed to evolve new tactical abilities. For instance, facing threats to their organizational survival, some groups might favor the status quo over experimentation, embracing trusted routines over the uncertainty of new operations. Of course, there are also important differences between terrorist groups and business firms, but many of the same concepts such as competition, sunk costs, and organizational flexibility remain significant.

It is important to note that underlying this discussion of why terrorists innovate is an important assumption of group rationality. In other words, much of the extant literature assumes that the initial decision to innovate is the product of rational decision-making: groups weigh the expected costs and benefits and then decide either to innovate and seek out new tactical options, or to maintain their current trajectory with existing capabilities. Of course, whether or not a group achieves success is a different matter.

Ultimately, understanding terrorist innovation draws on two separate questions. First, what makes terrorist groups want to innovate? And second, what makes some organizations more likely to succeed? Scholars often conflate these questions though they are quite different; the former focuses on the benefits and goals that motivate the initial desire to seek out new innovations, while the latter concerns the particular conditions (both organizational and environmental) that increase the likelihood of innovation taking place. Organizations might ultimately desire to innovate, though if they lack the necessary resources they might never achieve success. Conversely, many organizations possess qualities that are ripe for tactical innovation, both major and minor, but without the desire to experiment they are unlikely to alter their operational routines.

The Benefits of Innovation

Although there are major gains to be made from innovation, these gains neither come cheaply nor easily. Comparisons to other groups suggest that uncertainty, prohibitive costs, entrenched routines, and institutional interests belie experimentation, and not all organizations are sufficiently risk- and cost-acceptant to support the initial endeavor. However, the perceived benefits of successful innovation can ultimately overcome a group's status quo tendencies, tipping the cost–benefit calculation away from complacency and towards innovation. Some of these benefits include: overcoming counterterrorist defenses, causing greater damage, and shocking and surprising their target audience.

First, terrorist organizations innovate to overcome defenses and to achieve success in what is often described as a process of competitive problem-solving vis-à-vis the state. Groups faced with some obstacle, be it a hard-to-reach target or defensive method that obstructs their operational or strategic goals, seek out new solutions through ingenuity and innovation. This view of terrorist innovation as a form of problem-solving recognizes that terrorist behavior is part of, and also driven by, their conflict with the state. As Brian Jackson aptly notes,

> Intelligence and law enforcement organizations constantly seek protection solutions to defeat current attack methods, strategies to deter attacks at sites of particular concern, and to devise new ways to counter and apprehend the terrorists. Conversely,

> the terrorist groups seek new strategies to overcome countermeasures, better tactical information to support their attacks, and methods to elude capture... These adversarial relationships place terrorist organizations within a particularly competitive ecology of learning, one in which we all have a significant stake in the outcome of the competition. (Jackson 2004, 26)

Indeed, finding a solution to a given problem or a means to counter a looming threat is one of the most common motivators of tactical and strategic innovation (Hafez and Rasmussen 2012). However, as Jackson notes, terrorist innovation does not occur in a vacuum and states are equally concerned with evolving their defenses to thwart emerging challenges. Consider the introduction of airport metal detectors following the stark rise in airline hijackings in the 1960s, and more recent advancements in body scanning technology that can detect a wider range of concealed materials. Metal detectors were only implemented in response to hijackings that predominantly used metal weapons, including guns and knives, to gain control of planes (Dugan et al. 2005). In seeking to circumvent these measures, more recent hijacking attempts have utilized sophisticated explosives and plastic weapons, forcing airports to respond in turn with millimeter wave body scanners. Terrorist and counterterrorist forces seek to remain one step ahead of their opponents and this quest for temporary supremacy is one of the most enduring causes of both defensive (counterterrorist) and offensive (terrorist) innovation.

Second, terrorist organizations will innovate to increase the lethality and destructiveness of their attacks. While the motivations behind doing so are beyond the scope of this chapter, major and minor innovations are useful to this end. While groups might seek out entirely new methods of attack to cause greater damage (as was the case with suicide bombs and sarin gas), existing tactical options can also be enhanced to produce greater lethality (e.g. adding shrapnel to explosives). Innovation is also needed to maintain and expand the lethality of tactical options since counterterrorists forces evolve in line with terrorist threats; as security forces learn to detect and thwart attacks, terrorists must in turn innovate if they are to continue causing harm.

Third, and finally, terrorist groups innovate out of concern for public relations. Innovation sends important signals to several populations: to the target of their violence and to the state, innovation showcases enduring competence and ability. It demonstrates that despite government repression, restriction, and other attempts to deny their existence, they nonetheless persevere.[4] This can be seen as a tactic of intimidation, and it also underscores their credibility and seriousness as an adversary which can be helpful in negotiations. To potential recruits and to their peers, innovation highlights a group's dedication, resolve, and ingenuity, demonstrating why it is superior to other organizations. Terrorist groups seek to outbid their peers through calculated variations in their use of violence, and innovation—just like escalation—sends strong signals about capability and determination that can help to attract recruits and win over local support (Bloom 2004; Kydd and Walter 2006). Finally, to the press, innovation is a source of sensational news that will undoubtedly attract coverage. New modes and methods of attack, and especially those that deviate from the norm and that are particularly destructive, are almost guaranteed to garner significant attention. Although major innovations are more likely to accomplish this goal, even minor tactical advances generally suffice. This is important since media coverage is a crucial element of the terrorist logic, serving to disseminate their message and transmute fear to a broader population beyond those immediately affected by their violence (Nacos 1994, 2007). Without the media, the influence of terrorist violence would be severely curtailed.

The Characteristics of Innovative Groups

The immense benefits that accompany innovation might lead one to anticipate a dizzying rate of tactical innovation among terrorist organizations. Yet, history has shown this not to be the case. If the benefits are relatively constant, then, what makes some groups more likely to experiment and tactically innovate? The factors associated with successful innovation generally fall into two camps: organizational and environmental attributes. In other words, research finds that characteristics of individual terrorist organizations as well as their operating environments strongly affect the odds that innovation eventually occurs.

To begin with, some groups are structured in ways that foster creativity and support innovation while others are not. In terms of organizational structure, many of the same factors associated with flexibility and innovation among business firms are expected to exert similar effects on terrorist groups (McAllister 2004). Strict hierarchy and bureaucracy, for instance, are often viewed as impediments to creativity, and groups structured in a more decentralized manner tend to be more effective innovators. However, decentralizing too far can also be problematic as the lack of leadership and organizational support might result in lower sophistication and a lack of direction for their creative efforts (Gill et al. 2013). Scholars find that individual leaders can be influential as well. They play a role in the innovation process by motivating their organization and guiding their efforts towards a common goal, and these skills can be brought to bear specifically on tactical advancements (Dolnik 2007).

A more obvious factor is organizational resources. Innovation is generally associated with a substantial sunk cost that groups must invest regardless of whether the process is eventually successful. Consider, for instance, how groups interested in chemical weapons, like Aum Shinrikyo and others, must first obtain and experiment with the actual chemicals, prepare them for weaponization, and then train members to carry out the attack. Together, this accounts for a sizeable initial cost in terms of both time and money. Consequently, organizations with greater resources at their disposal are less likely to view initial costs as prohibitive barriers. Of course, resources can be thought of in many ways, but with regards to tactical innovation both money and time are perhaps the two that matter most. Groups seeking out new methods of attack must devote time to design, experimentation, and training, whereas capital is often needed to purchase supplies (Ranstorp and Normark 2015). Furthermore, groups seeking to innovate might also assign their smartest operatives with specific, technical backgrounds to the task, so there is often an important human cost as well (Gill et al. 2013).

Dolnik (2007) also argues that a group's affinity to existing technologies or tactics can stymie innovation. When groups are complacent or stuck in their ways they become less likely to experiment and branch out, utilizing instead methods they know to be effective. This is similar to processes that restrict diffusion as well; Horowitz (2010a), for instance, shows how suicide bombing was more likely to transfer to younger militant groups that exhibited greater organizational flexibility. Together, this logic underscores that groups with what might be called greater organizational capital are more likely to innovate as their structures and routines are less entrenched within status quo behaviors.

Finally, the exchange of information and ideas might contribute to tactical advancement (Pedahzur and Perliger 2006; Horowitz 2010a). In particular, groups that share information are more likely to experience a greater diversity of ideas floating around, leading to innovation as they are combined in new ways. In line with this approach, some have argued that Hezbollah's links to Iran were key to their development of suicide operations since Iran had itself utilized suicide missions in its war with Iraq (Jaber 1997).

In the same way that organizational factors increase or decrease the odds of innovation and creativity, characteristics of a terrorist group's operating environment are likewise influential. Some factors raise the marginal utility of innovation (e.g. government repression) making the ultimate gains even more coveted, while others are especially conducive to creativity and experimentation (e.g. territorial safe haven).

Innovation can be viewed either as the product of necessity or the product of opportunity. In other words, groups might seek out new innovations either to overcome threats and supplant new challenges, or conversely, when more lenient conditions facilitate resources being transferred away from security towards creativity and experimentation. Both contribute to innovation in different ways: in the former, innovation is spurred by problem-solving. Groups seek out new methods of violence to retaliate against the state or overcome repressive or restrictive measures (Horowitz et al. 2018). In the latter, more lax conditions favor experimentation since time and resources can be shifted from short-term goals like survival to long-term goals like maintaining relevance and enhancing operations. Groups that were pushed to innovate include the Provisional IRA, where "The ensuing intelligence and operational cat-and-mouse game between PIRA and its enemies . . . have been matched by formidable levels of technical skills, innovation and learning curve in weapons design, bomb-making expertise and delivery of unexpected and sophisticated terrorist attacks" (Ranstorp and Brun 2013, 11). Conversely, one group that is commonly cited as an example of how leniency can support innovation is Al Qaeda in the late 1990s, where safe havens in Afghanistan under the Taliban regime allowed them to train new members, design new strategies, and tactically experiment without fear of being caught (McAllister 2004; Byman 2005; Shapiro 2013). Of course, leniency and necessity are not mutually exclusive and many innovations stem from the combination of the two—when there is both a challenge to overcome but also safe havens to provide cover.

Other factors that raise the desirability of innovation include competition from other organizations, state repression, and waning public support. Competition between groups might spur innovation as each seeks out media attention and new recruits in the resource-scarce environment (Dolnik 2007). When competition is more severe, the gains from a public relations victory are even more potent and desirable. Repression, on the other hand, might prompt a "backlash" effect whereby groups are increasingly motivated to attack the state, leading them to seek out innovative, unforeseen methods of violence. Recent research suggests this mechanism has also contributed to tactical expansion (Horowitz et al. 2018). And finally, innovation might seem like a solution to dwindling levels of public support. Groups can leverage novel attack patterns to create attention and shock the public, which might attract recruits, reinvigorate interest in the conflict, and increase support for a negotiated settlement.

Conclusion and Future Directions

It is nearly impossible to surmise operational capabilities that terrorists will wield in the future. This is especially challenging in today's environment where once exclusive technologies are now widely available, expanding the number of operational vectors that terrorists can exploit. Drones are an excellent example: at first largely confined to states, remote-controlled aircraft are now easy to obtain and relatively cheap. It is thus no surprise that groups like the Islamic State have repurposed miniature drones to conduct surveillance, deliver explosives, and attack armed forces in new ways. The internet is another factor that has shaped the potential for innovation: terrorists can now access troves of information virtually instantaneously, leading to the quick diffusion of novel tactics and practices. Internet-enabled communication via social media and mobile apps might further hasten the pace of innovation as potential collaborators can share expertise from other ends of the globe, overcoming the need for physical proximity. Finally, the internet can even serve as a new domain, providing non-state actors yet another platform on which to conduct attacks and inspire fear. The unintended consequences of globalization seemingly extend to terrorist innovation as well.

Yet, with such an extensive body of research, why is it still difficult to anticipate future terrorist innovations? First, among the factors discussed that both motivate and support tactical innovation, none are *necessary* while many are *sufficient* on their own. Although competition, state repression, and safe havens have motivated terrorists to seek out innovations in some cases, in others these factors have been entirely absent. Second, many of the variables discussed earlier have plausible theoretical links with both increased as well as decreased levels of innovation. Consider state repression, about which Zimmerman aptly notes that "there are theoretical arguments for all conceivable basic relationships between government coercion and group protest and rebellion, except for no relationship" (Zimmerman 1980, 191). Repression is theorized to escalate the drive for innovation as groups seek out more successful means of retaliating against the state. However, other research finds that repression forces groups to adopt structures and practices that are most focused on survival (Shapiro 2013). It is unclear which variables condition the effect of state repression on organizational innovation. Third, it is difficult to identify potential innovators ex ante, since many groups experience conditions that are ripe for experimentation—either through lenient home environments, competitive environmental pressures, or organizational characteristics that support creativity—but few are ever successful. This is especially true for major tactical innovations that are incredibly rare, though it is also true for minor innovations that many times require few incentives or resources to generate. Although it is relatively easy to look back and identify the factors that contributed to past cases of innovation, applying these lessons to contemporary organizations is significantly more difficult.

In future research it would be wise to distinguish between the drivers of major and minor tactical innovations. It could very well be that minor innovations are the most difficult to disrupt: since they require few resources and are often instrumented by lone, industrious individuals, states can do little to prevent them. Major innovations that are more time and resource intensive, however, might be easier to spot and to disrupt. It is also often the case that there are clues of experimentation or innovation taking place; for instance, police were initially alerted to a chorine-like smell emanating from the Aum Shinrikyo compound and although they investigated, no charges were ultimately brought. This was a missed opportunity to thwart the impending sarin gas attack on the Tokyo subway. As with the broader fight against terrorism, effective policing is a critical component of successful preventative strategies (Dolnik 2007; Perkoski and Chenoweth 2010).

Finally, it is important to remember that "no matter how innovative security personnel are, there is no guarantee that they will always outsmart the adversary" (Merari 1998, 24). With that in mind, research should be conducted on how armed forces can best respond to and maintain resilience when facing the evolution of irregular threats. Cultivating flexible force postures that can more easily adapt to new challenges, creating institutions that analyze emerging challenges as they occur, and opening channels for commanders on the ground to propose tactical and strategic initiatives can help to minimize terrorists' advantages from successful innovation. Recent efforts by the United States Army have been especially successful in this regard. They developed Information Centers to collect, synthesize, and analyze vast amounts of intel from individual soldiers on the ground, and they also streamlined the process of deploying new equipment (Wilson 2006; Flynn et al. 2010). Since the timing and the character of terrorist innovations are incredibly uncertain, research into the most effective methods of response are particularly salient.

Notes

1. I borrow part of this definition from Gill et al, though they only focus on what I call major innovations, see Gill et al. 2013, 126 Otherwise, scholars of innovation in other fields commonly distinguish between disruptive and incremental innovations. This typology is difficult to apply to terrorists, however, since few advances would fall into the disruptive category as it is most often defined.

2. There are, of course, other examples of suicide missions throughout history. Many would point to the Japanese Kamikaze attacks on Pearl Harbor as a relatively recent precursor. However, the attacks in Lebanon are generally viewed as the origin of suicide violence by violent nonstate actors to terrorize and impose a cost on their adversary.
3. The attack was initially credited to Islamic Jihad. However, later investigation revealed that Hezbollah was ultimately responsible, using the name Islamic Jihad as a front for its operation.
4. Similar to how adopting suicide terrorism sends equally meaningful signals to these same populations, e.g. Hoffman and Mccormick 2004.

References

Arthur, W. Brian (2009) *The Nature of Technology: What it is and How it Evolves*. New York: Simon & Schuster.

Barker, Alec D. (2011) "Improvised Explosive Devices in Southern Afghanistan and Western Pakistan, 2002–2009," *Studies in Conflict and Terrorism*, 34(8): 600–20.

Bloom, Mia M. (2004) "Palestinian Suicide Bombing: Public Support, Market Share, and Outbidding," *Political Science Quarterly*, 119(1): 61–88.

Byman, Daniel (2005) "Strategic Surprise and the September 11 Attacks," *Annual Review of Political Science*, 8: 145–70.

Crenshaw, Martha (1987) "Theories of Terrorism: Instrumental and Organizational Approaches," *Journal of Strategic Studies*, 10(4): 13–31.

Dingley, James (2008) *Combating Terrorism in Northern Ireland*. Abingdon: Routledge.

Dolnik, Adam (2007) *Understanding Terrorist Innovation: Technology, Tactics and Global Trends*. Abingdon: Routledge.

Drake, C. J. M. (1991) "The Provisional IRA: A Case Study," *Terrorism and Political Violence*, 3(2): 43–60.

Dugan, Laura, Gary LaFree, and Alex R. Piquero (2005) "Testing a Rational Choice Model of Airline Hijackings," in *Intelligence and Security Informatics*. Hoboken, NJ: Springer, 340–61.

Flynn, Michael T., Matthew F. Pottinger, and Paul D. Batchelo (2010) "Fixing Intel: A Blueprint for Making Intelligence Relevant in Afghanistan." DTIC Document, available online at <http://oai.dtic.mil/oai/oai?verb=getRecord&metadataPrefix=html&identifier=ADA511613>.

Gill, Paul, John Horgan, Samuel T. Hunter, and Lily D. Cushenbery (2013) "Malevolent Creativity in Terrorist Organizations," *Journal of Creative Behavior*, 47(2): 125–51.

Hafez, Mohammed M., and Maria Rasmussen (2012) "Terrorist Innovations in Weapons of Mass Effect, Phase 2." DTIC Document, available online at <http://oai.dtic.mil/oai/oai?verb=getRecord&metadataPrefix=html&identifier=ADA569725>.

Hoffman, Bruce, and Gordon H. McCormick (2004) "Terrorism, Signaling, and Suicide Attack," *Studies in Conflict and Terrorism*, 27(4): 243–81.

Horowitz, Michael C. (2010a) "Nonstate Actors and the Diffusion of Innovations: The Case of Suicide Terrorism," *International Organization*, 64(1): 33–64.

Horowitz, Michael C. (2010b) *The Diffusion of Military Power: Causes and Consequences for International Politics*. Princeton: Princeton University Press.

Horowitz, Michael, Evan Perkoski, and Philip B. K. Potter (2018) "Tactical Diversity in Militant Violence," *International Organization*, 72(1): 139–71.

Jaber, Hala (1997) *Hezbollah: Born with a Vengeance*. New York: Columbia University Press.

Jackson, Brian A. (2004) *Organizational Learning and Terrorist Groups*. Working Paper, available online at <http://www.rand.org/pubs/working_papers/WR133>.

Jackson, Brian Anthony, and John C. Baker (2005) *Aptitude for Destruction: Case Studies of Organizational Learning in Five Terrorist Groups*. PLACE: Rand Corporation.

Kopp, Carlo (2008) *Technology of Improvised Explosive Devices*. Defence Today, 4649, available online at <http://www.ausairpower.net/SP/DT-IED-1007.pdf>.

Kydd, Andrew H., and Barbara F. Walter (2006) "The Strategies of Terrorism," *International Security*, 31(1): 49–80.

McAllister, Brad (2004) "Al Qaeda and the Innovative Firm: Demythologizing the Network," *Studies in Conflict and Terrorism*, 27(4): 297–319.

Merari, Ariel (1998) "Attacks on Civil Aviation: Trends and Lessons," *Terrorism and Political Violence*, 10(3): 9–26.

Nacos, Brigitte Lebens (1994) *Terrorism and the Media: From the Iran Hostage Crisis to the World Trade Center Bombing*. New York: Columbia University Press.

Nacos, Brigitte Lebens (2007) *Mass-Mediated Terrorism: The Central Role of the Media in Terrorism and Counterterrorism*. PLACE: Rowman & Littlefield.

Pedahzur, Ami, and Arie Perliger (2006) "The Changing Nature of Suicide Attacks: A Social Network Perspective," *Social Forces*, 84(4): 1987–2008.

Perkoski, Evan, and Erica Chenoweth (2010) "The Effectiveness of Counterterrorism in Spain: A New Approach," International Studies Association Annual Meeting, New Orleans, Mar. 15–17, available online at <http://www.start.umd.edu/start/publications/Perkoski_Chenoweth_2010.pdf>.

Potter, Philip, Evan Perkoski, and Michael C. Horowitz (2013) *The Life-Cycle of Terrorist Tactics: Learning from the Case of Hijacking*. Working Paper.

Ranstorp, Magnus, and Hans Brun (2013) "Terrorism Learning and Innovation: Lessons from PIRA in Northern Ireland: A Closed Workshop Summary," available online at <http://www.diva-portal.org/smash/record.jsf?pid=diva2:684050>.

Ranstorp, Magnus, and Magnus Normark (2015) *Understanding Terrorism Innovation and Learning: Al-Qaeda and Beyond*. Abingdon: Routledge.

Rasmussen, Maria J., and Mohammed M. Hafez (2010) "Terrorist Innovations in Weapons of Mass Effect: Preconditions, Causes, and Predictive Indicators," available online at <http://calhoun.nps.edu/handle/10945/25358>.

Shapiro, Jacob N. (2013) *The Terrorist's Dilemma: Managing Violent Covert Organizations*. Princeton: Princeton University Press.

Wilson, Clay (2006) "Improvised Explosive Devices (IEDs) in Iraq and Afghanistan: Effects and Countermeasures." DTIC Document, available online at <http://oai.dtic.mil/oai/oai?verb=getRecord&metadataPrefix=html&identifier=ADA456446>.

Zimmerman, Ekkart (1980) "Macro-Comparative Research on Political Protest," in *Handbook of Political Conflict: Theory and Research* New York: The Free Press, 167–237.

CHAPTER 27

WOMEN AND TERRORISM

CARON E. GENTRY

In 2007, Laura Sjoberg and I started our book on women's violence in global politics with the question, "A woman did that?" (Sjoberg and Gentry 2007; Gentry and Sjoberg 2015). While our book focuses on violence perpetrated by women that includes terrorism as well as torture and genocide, we were trying to capture some of the astonishment we encountered from scholars, policy-makers, and students when they pondered, purportedly for the first time, the notion that women committed political violence. Yet, almost ten years later, that surprise is still evident in multiple arenas.

When Tasheen Malik open fired on a Christmas party at Inland Regional Center in San Diego, California in early December 2015, there was general surprise, and outrage, that a mother of an infant would willingly involve herself in violence. According to multiple profilers "it was highly unusual for a woman—and especially a new mother—to engage in a form of visceral, predatory violence that the clinical literature associates almost exclusively with men" (Glenza et al. 2015). Furthermore, a large amount of attention has been paid to women who are leaving the West to join ISIS in Syria. In response to this, a Brookings Institute researcher, William McCants, expressed surprise that the women IS recruited are just as "motivated as the men" (Easton 2015). Given the history and well-documented occurrences of women's involvement with terrorism and political violence, this surprise is a bit, well, surprising. It reflects the lack of general and specialized knowledge that women have been involved with the violence labeled as terrorism for over a century, at minimum.

Therefore, this chapter will begin by looking at the various theories that exist to explain women's participation in political violence. While these often differ from what is offered to explain men's involvement, this chapter will not fully engage a critique of this differentiation (see instead Gentry 2004; Sjoberg and Gentry 2007, 2008a, 2008b; Gentry and Sjoberg 2015). Instead, it will briefly discuss what approaches do exist. These include thinking about women's involvement as limited to the private sphere, thus, they act in a supporting role and have little to do with the political elements (Weinberg and Eubank 1987; Cataldo Neuburger and Valentini 1996). Another longstanding explanation is to argue that women become involved due to family and friendship ties and that element of joining is about belonging (della Porta 1992; Peteet 1991). The final, more recent, explanation is that women become involved in terrorism, particularly suicide terrorism, because they have suffered some sort of trauma, most often rape, that brings them and their family/community shame and dishonor (Bloom 2005, 2011a, 2011b; Pape 2005). Thus, they act as a way of regaining honor for self and community.

In the following section this chapter will highlight the historical involvement of women in a wide array of terrorist organizations, from Narodnaya Volya, the Liberation Tigers of Tamil Eelam, left-wing organizations across the globe in the 1960s, the multi-generational Palestinian struggle, to Al Qaeda and the Islamic State (IS). The majority of the chapter will look at the involvement of women in each of these groups or groupings to demonstrate that women's participation in terrorist violence is neither new nor distinctly different from men's.

Evaluations of Women's Participation in Terrorist Violence

When I first began researching women's participation in terrorist groups in the very early 2000s, I was somewhat shocked at the conventional wisdom. At first glance, some of the louder voices within terrorism studies indicated that women participated in political violence because they were beholden to men or completely irrational. For instance, an early piece in a policing and security journal believes that women engage in terrorist activity because they have been neglected by their fathers and society more generally. These women are not "rational" but "emotional," therefore "her violence will in all probability stem not from dedication to the particular cause . . . but from blind obedience to another more personal cause" (Anon. 1976, 245). H. H. A. Cooper's work compares them to the Gorgons of Greek mythology and describes them as "childish" imitators of men. Female terrorists are "obsessive" and "pathological" and, hence, "it is useless to inquire why women become terrorists" (Cooper 1979, 153–4). One feminist, Robin Morgan (1989), argued that female terrorists are in the "harem" of male terrorists—that the primary reason for the involvement is owed to the sexual attraction between (weak, apolitical) women and the ultimate bad-boy male terrorist. One of the commands of the West German GSG-9's, the SWAT-team-like unit created to combat the Marxist-Leninist Red Army Faction, was "shoot the women first." This stemmed from a belief that female revolutionaries were unpredictable and more prone to violence than male revolutionaries (MacDonald 1988). Yet, further investigation revealed these assumptions to be somewhat unsurprisingly superficial and, like MacDonald (1988, 11), I stopped "looking for [the women's] horns."

Some of the older explanations for women's participation reveal an outdated way of thinking about women's role in wider society: in the home and supporting the male figure. Weinburg and Eubank's earlier work on women's participation focused on left- and right-wing groups in Italy in the 1980s (1987, 1989). Of the 445 women identified as active in some form of terrorist group (out of a total number of "terrorists" identified by the Italian state as 2,512—Weinberg and Eubank 1987, 249), 91.2 percent were involved in far-left groups. For instance, one of the founders of the IRB was a woman, Mara Cagol, and over time, the leadership had a total of twelve men and seven women (Cataldo Neuburger and Valentini 1996, 3). This is different to the right wing organizations, where women made up 9.7 percent of the membership (see Weinberg and Eubank 1987, 250). Weinberg and Eubank (1987, 249, 255; see also 1989) therefore concluded that ideology shaped where women could become involved but that involvement was also tied to the relationships women had: the Marxism-Leninism of left-wing groups more naturally sought equality and right-wing conservativism and neo-fascism leant more on conservative gender roles, thereby excluding women.[1]

In this earlier research, Weinberg and Eubank (1987) initially concluded that women's roles in left-wing groups were dependent upon gender roles and gendered relationships. They became involved because their boyfriends, husbands, and/or brothers were involved, and then took care of them by feeding them and keeping their houses clean. This care-taking role is something that Cataldo Neuburger and Valentini (1996) also seized upon in their comprehensive study of the women and men of Prima Linea. After conducting interviews with members, Cataldo Neuburger and Valentini (1996, 81) determined that Prima Linea female members were living according to a "maternal-sacrifice code," a "model based on sacrifice, on caring for others, on responding to others'" needs and on "protection," which is what they found in their participation in the IRB's Prima Linea.

In Donatella della Porta's (1992) assessment of why people joined both movements and the violent elements within them, like the IRB, she concluded that close relationships were often behind joining for both men and women. This coheres with Julie Peteet's (1991) ethnographic observations of the Palestinian Resistance Movement. While one of the most comprehensive sources on how people became involved in the PRM, this text also looks in depth at women's membership. Within Peteet's framework, the PLO, Fatah, and the Popular Front for the Liberation of Palestine garner attention. Interviewing various members, she determined that friendship and family ties are some of the strongest reasons behind all people's involvement, but particularly women, because active male family members are less likely to object to a female's involvement (Peteet 1991, 119).

In the early 2000s, the second Palestinian intifada saw the widespread use of suicide bombers, a strategy that had been used in limited measure in the Middle East previously but to a larger extent by Kurds, Chechens, and the LTTE Black Tigers. Initially, women were prohibited from participating in the Palestinian suicide attacks but after Yasser Arafat gave his "Army of Roses" speech which indicated that women's participation was welcome (see Victor 2003), there was a short-lived spate of women's attacks (ten in total, primarily between 2002 and 2004, but extending until 2006: Sjoberg and Gentry 2007, 119). From this activity, several studies (Pape 2005; Bloom 2005) were published on suicide terrorism more generally but that seemed to offer some insights into female suicide terrorists more specifically. While these studies concluded that suicide terrorism is strategic because it tends to result in favorable concessions for the terrorist group, women's involvement was deemed to stem from personal reasons. For instance, Pape (2005, 209) argues that once a woman moves beyond the normative age of marriage, this may be one way to participate in her community. Mia Bloom in particular argues that women's participation in suicide terrorism is directly related to the level of rape in a conflicted society. For Bloom (2005, 2011b), a suicide attack is an inevitable outcome when a woman in these societies (Chechnya, Palestine, Sri Lanka, and heavily Muslim societies) has been raped and has therefore suffered shame and dishonor in the eyes of her community. To regain her honor, she sacrifices her body by taking other people with her.

More recent literature has focused on why women would participate in groups like Al Qaeda or the Islamic State considering their ideology is so hostile to women's independence. Again, much of the literature focuses on the women's relationships with (mainly) men in the organizations, but this time the relationships are seen as manipulative and with a significant power imbalance between women and men. Sajida Mubarak Atrous al-Rishawi attempted, alongside her husband, to commit a suicide attack on the Radisson SAS in Amman, Jordan, in 2005, although her bomb failed to detonate while his did. It was assumed that she participated because she was coerced into it (Sjoberg and Gentry 2007, 128). Similarly, when a Belgian woman detonated, again with her husband, in Iraq for Al Qaeda, there was speculation that she had been brainwashed into converting from Catholicism to Islam and further brainwashed into her violence (Gentry and Sjoberg 2015, 81).

The assumptions are similar in regard to the young women and teenagers who are leaving the US and UK for Syria to join IS; yet given how recent these examples are, most of the analysis is performed by the media and less by academics. Some parts of the media reify gendered understandings of women's involvement and are reified by scholarship. For example, the teenagers and young women who join IS are thought to be "groomed" (Erelle 2015), which is often a term associated with the method paedophiles use for drawing children into a (misplaced) trusting relationship. In this instance, it refers to IS's recruitment strategy of developing relationships with people over social media (Koerner 2016). This happens to both men and women, yet the media tend to focus on the recruitment of young women. For instance, in one *New York Times* profile of a young woman living in a rural area, she is described as naïve and lonely (Callimachi 2015). That she was raised by her grandparents after being abandoned by her alcoholic mother is used to point to her vulnerability and isolation—something the *New York Times* suggests made her a prime target for IS. Yet, the young woman never left the US, because her grandparents, who are actively involved in her life, intervened (Callimachi 2015).

That women's involvement is often attributed to emotional and personal motivation should be seen within the prism of gender. Because women are more associated with emotions and relational behavior, this influences how their actions are described. It may instead be better to think about women's (and men's) involvement as resulting from a variety of factors (see Sjoberg and Gentry 2008b). Human beings are complex and trying to reduce a person's agency and decision to join a *violent* organization to gender norms or simplistic thought processes is less than helpful.

Where the Women are: Women's Historical Engagement in Terrorist Violence

This part of the chapter will cover, very briefly, different organizations from across the globe to demonstrate how varied women's participation in political violence is. Women are ideologues; they plan violent activities; they lead; and they commit suicide attacks. Thus, women's involvement is more than just nurturing the men—their participation is active.

Narodnaya Volya (The People's Will)

Narodnaya Volya came into prominence in Russia after an era steeped in populist revolutionary discontent. After the failure of the 1848 revolutions, populist groups continued to agitate in Russia as they sought an end to Tsarist rule and to emancipate the serfs. It was driven primarily by well-educated people seeking a democratic government. It eventually inspired the Socialist Revolutionary Party, a party instrumental to the Russian Revolution. Quite interestingly, one of the founding and most prominent members of Narodnaya Volya was a woman: Vera Figner. Figner is an important figure in women's political and social thought (Carroll 2000, 233–4); she was highly articulate and seen as a significant threat to the Tsar and the state of Russia. She was inspired, however, by another revolutionary woman: Vera Zasulich.

Vera Zasulich attempted to assassinate the governor of St Petersburg, General Fedor Trepov, by shooting him twice at close range, as he met with daily petitioners (Siljak 2009). She apparently was extraordinarily calm and even directed the guards that detained her that they would have to get a woman to search her. When they acted perplexed at this, she reminded them that official midwives could be found at all police stations (Siljak 2009). When asked why she had done it, she responded, "For Bogoliubov" (Siljak 2009). Bogoluibov was a prisoner who had failed to remove his cap for Trepov; in response, Trepov had him flogged. This act of cruelty angered the revolutionaries and it led to the attempt on his life by Zasulich (Siljak 2009). Zasulich's trial was a media phenomenon. She had so much support amongst the population that she was acquitted and, apparently, carried from the courtroom on people's shoulders (Stites 1978, 308). Even though Zasulich was not a member of Narodnaya Volya, her action served as an inspiration to those who formed it.

The members of various revolutionary groups that had survived government purges eventually came together as a group first known as Zemlya i Volya (Land and Liberty); it crystallized into Narodnaya Volya in 1879 over the question of terrorism and the use of violence (Stites 1978, 145). Figner was one of the founding members and one of the best known ideologues for the group—she was treated as a hero after the 1917 February

Revolution in Russia. Born into a noble family in Russia, Figner was well educated, eventually becoming both a feminist and revolutionary. Figner was instrumental in the organization's first five years in setting out ideology and planning attacks and assassinations (Stites 1978, 146). While she regretted the violence towards the end of her life, Figner had been a major proponent of assassination, linking it in thought if not actuality to tyrannicide. When Tsar Alexander II was assassinated she is quoted as tearfully saying, "the dreadful nightmare which had suffocated young Russia before our very eyes for a whole decade was at last ended" (Stites 1978, 146). When she was eventually arrested and sent to solitary confinement for twenty months prior to trial, Tsar Alexander III was supposed to have said, "Glory to God, that horrid woman has been arrested" (Stites 1978, 146).

While it is often claimed that the women of Narodnaya Volya were more committed to violence and more willing to sacrifice themselves than the men (Bloom 2011a), this cannot be ascertained. What is important, however, is that women played a significant role in the formation and leadership of the group as well as making substantial contributions to the group's ideology. Thus, a historical examination of women's involvement in terrorism is not limited to the past two years, nor even the past fifty, but must go back at least to the latter half of the nineteenth century.

The Liberation Tigers of Tamil Eelam

The Liberation Tigers of Tamil Eelam (LTTE) were a sophisticated and nearly successful ethno-religious insurgency in Sri Lanka. The Tamils were a politically marginalized Hindu minority in Sri Lanka, where the Sinhalese, who are Buddhists, ruled (and both ethnic groups have a small Christian minority). The LTTE, led by Velupillai Prabhakaran, waged a conflict for independence from the Sri Lankan government from 1976 to 2009. It only ended when the Sri Lankan army outmaneuvered the LTTE, having driven them to the very edge of the island that is Sri Lanka, and brutally executing LTTE fighters and Tamilese civilians in an act that some have labelled genocide (Anderson 2011). The LTTE waged a fierce campaign and were known for employing suicide bombers. They were one of the first groups to engage female suicide bombers; the most well-known was Dhanu, who assassinated Indian Prime Minister Rajiv Gandhi.

In the early 2000s, LTTE membership was 8,000–10,000 strong, with 3,000–6,000 of those trained as soldiers. The LTTE was very well organized into the primary military branch and a secondary political branch (Van de Voorde 2005, 185). Beginning in the late 1980s, women were slowly recruited, but this took off in the early 1990s (Alison 2003, 39). In 2000, women comprised one-third of the LTTE and conducted between 30 to 40 percent of the suicide attacks (Van de Voorde 2005, 186). The suicide bombers were known as Black Tigers (Van de Voorde 2005, 187) and the female suicide bomber brigade were known colloquially as the Black Tigresses. Between 1987 and 2005, the Black Tigers had committed 200 attacks, aiming for high-ranked government officials and landmarks (Van de Voorde 2005, 188).

While Van de Voorde (2005, 189) argues that the rationale behind the LTTE's use of suicide bombing came from religious fanaticism, Pape (2005) and Bloom (2005) point to strategic reasons for the use of suicide attacks. As already discussed, Pape's (2005) exhaustive study of suicide attacks in democratic states (even if this democratic status was tenuous, as in the case of Sri Lanka or Russia) led to political concessions in favor of the terrorist group's aims. Additionally, Pape (2005, 17) found that those who undertook a suicide attack could not be profiled as they

> have been college educated and uneducated, married and single, men and women, isolated and socially integrated; they have ranged in age from fifteen to fifty-two. In other words, [they] come from a broad array of lifestyles.

Therefore, he did not find that religion plays, necessarily, a significant role in suicide attacks. Nor did he find that emotional or personal reasons were the main driving force.

However, when Pape and Bloom in their individual research then look at women, this rationale changes. This is particularly apparent in what they write about Dhanu. Pape (2005, 209) focuses upon the shopping trip she took on the last day of her life. Dhanu was motivated, in their individual estimations, because she was raped by Sri Lankan security forces and suffered the death of her brother in the conflict (Pape 2005, 209). Bloom (2005, 2011b) determines conclusively that shame and dishonor due to rape are one of the most significant factors in a woman's participation in suicide terrorism. This focus on sexual violence is complicated, yet again, by the scholarship and ethnographic research of Miranda Alison (2003, 2004, 2009). In her interviews with fourteen female LTTE members, she found that both political and personal oppression and suffering motivated the women to join (Alison 2003, 40–1). Thus, while Alison (2003, 43) does affirm that sexual violence was part of this suffering, a commitment to the political goals of the group as well as a desire for "emancipation and increase[ed] life opportunities" was significant. It should, therefore, be concluded that both personal and political reasons—a multi-causal process of motivation, like men—led to women's participation in the LTTE.

The Marxist-Leninist Groups of the 1960s

If people envision women's involvement in political violence, they tend to reflect upon the Marxist-Leninist groups that grew out of the student movements in the mid- to late-1960s worldwide. The best known groups included the West German Red Army Faction (RAF) and the Italian Red Brigades (IRB), but there also groups like the United States' the Weather Underground, the United Kingdom's Angry Brigade, France's Action Direct, and the Japanese Red Army. As the student movements were dominated by university students, the leadership and the membership of these groups tended to be middle class and well educated. Their main source of grievance was linked to a Marxist-Leninist critique of neo-imperialism, particularly by the United States, as seen in the

Vietnam War, but other grievances included capitalism, sexism, and racism (Gentry 2004). Due to Marxism-Leninism, many of the groups were committed to gender equality by word if not by deed. Thus, in many of the groups, women often comprised at the very least a significant minority of the membership and women were leaders in the RAF and the Weather Underground.

The most infamous of the women leaders were Ulrike Meinhof and Gudrun Enslinn of the RAF, who shared leadership with Andreas Baader. While Meinhof was older and had a successful career as a left-wing journalist in West Germany, both Meinhof and Enslinn (and Baader, too) left children in their desire to be fully committed to the RAF's cause (see Aust 1987). In their leadership capacity, Meinhof wrote a significant proportion of the ideological treatises while Enslinn planned many of the attacks and operations (Aust 1987, 142–3, 208–9). The triumvirate leadership of Meinhof, Enslinn, and Baader directed the first generation of the RAF, also known as the Baader-Meinhof Group. They were able to live underground for some time—robbing post offices and banks to keep themselves afloat. Their attacks were rarer, but some of the first generation's more famous ones include the bombing of a discotheque that American servicemen frequented and the bombing, leading to the death of a janitor, of the Springer Press Building because Springer Press was known to have conservative leanings. After the leadership was imprisoned, the second generation famously kidnapped Hanns Martin Schleyer, a business executive with former ties to the Nazi regime, in order to negotiate for their release; he was killed when the negotiations failed (Aust 1987, 239).

Group dynamics amongst the first generation were notoriously difficult. Baader despised Meinhof (Aust 1987, 132–3, 259–60, 276). Before their imprisonment, the tension forced Meinhof to leave with some of the membership to continue to plan attacks, while Baader and Enslinn (who were a couple) stayed together with still more members. During their trial, it was alleged Meinhof conducted the Springer bombing during the split and Enslinn disavowed all knowledge of it and expressed disapproval towards Meinhof. Shortly after this, Meinhof committed suicide in prison (Gentry and Sjoberg 2011, 62). Enslinn and the others, however, accused the government of killing her. Furthermore, when the second generationa's negotiation for their release failed, Enslinn and Baader, along with other members, committed suicide in prison. The RAF maintained that government killed them (Gentry and Sjoberg 2011, 63).

In the Weather Underground, Bernardine Dohrn played a key role in articulating the purpose of the group (Gentry 2004, 283–5) and Kathy Boudin, as a key member of the Weather Underground and the Black Liberation Army, robbed an armored vehicle during which one guard was killed and the other injured (Kolbert 2001). The Weather Underground activities included robbing banks and post offices to fund its activities, but also included the bombings of buildings on Wall Street, the Pentagon, and the United States Capitol Building. Group dynamics within the Weather Underground aspired to equality between all members and they aimed to get rid of bourgeois practices. In order to accomplish this, they held meetings in their collectives every evening in which they critiqued each other, which often allowed for group think to dominate.

The Weather Underground only operated for a short period of time before most of the members drifted away and the leaders went underground (Gentry 2004).

Dohrn and her partner, Bill Ayers, lived in New York City and worked as pre-school teachers and had two children of their own (and adopted Boudin's son when she was arrested and sentenced) (Kolbert 2001). When they came above ground, most of the charges against them had been dropped due to poor police procedure although Dohrn was held in contempt of court. Dohrn now works for Northwestern Law School and Ayers has worked at the University of Illinois, Chicago. (They hosted a fundraiser for Obama in their Chicago home—which was used by the Republicans to link then-presidential candidate Obama to terrorism.) Boudin was released from prison in 2003; from there she built her new career on her publications on and experience in leading groups related to education, AIDs, and prison reform.

Women's Involvement in the Palestinian Resistance

Given the long-term nature of the Israeli–Palestinian conflict, which began, roughly, with the creation of Israel in 1948, there are multiple generations of Palestinian violent resistance. Women's involvement in each of these generations has been fraught—in each, women have had to fight to participate equally. The first generation of struggle is often referred to as the Palestinian Resistance Movement. This refers broadly to the Palestinian groups that emerged after the Arab defeat in the Six-Day War of 1967 and it is mainly inclusive of the groups clustered under the Palestinian Liberation Organization (PLO) umbrella, including Fatah and the Popular Front for the Liberation of Palestine (PFLP), which has since separated. The PRM differs substantially from the groups that came to prominence in the first intifada (second generation), such as Hamas, and in the second intifada (third generation), like the Al Aqsa Martyrs' Brigade (which is closely linked to Fatah). The primary differences between the first generation and later generations are owed to the shift from a secular and/or left-wing ideology to a more religio-political ideology with the advent of Hamas.

Women's participation in the various groups is often linked to crisis. During a crisis, like the feeling of abandonment by the Arab states after their defeat in 1967, women who were normally restricted to strict gender roles were allowed to participate in various ways (Peteet 1991, 3, 32, 40). How women participate is also drawn by gender lines: for the groups that comprised the PRM, they were often limited to nursing, teaching, and secretarial work (Peteet 1991, 109–10). Nevertheless, by the end of the 1970s and mid-1980s, women were active participants in Palestinian politics (Giacaman and Johnson 1989, 159; see also Coughlin 2000, 230). With the rise of Hamas in the late 1970s and when it ascended to leadership with the first intifada, women's engagement in the public space was eroded (Schulz 1999, 71; Hammami 1990, 25–6). Participation in all of these generations, even if it conformed to gender idealizations, meant there was no going back—the women who participated would always be seen as somewhat aberrant (Peteet 1991, 69–70). There are a few women, however, who have become legends within the

Palestinian community and beyond: Leila Khaled, the first female Palestinian hijacker, and Wafa Idris, the first female Palestinian suicide martyr.

Leila Khaled was four years old during the Israeli Defense Force's shelling of Haifa (Gentry 2011, 120; Khaled 1973, 26). She remembers hiding under the stairs as the rest of her family evacuated outside, leaving that day to eventually settle in Lebanon. As a teenager, she snuck out of the house in her pyjamas to follow her older brothers and sisters to PRM meetings. In her autobiography, she recalls being impressed by the first hijackings by the PLO. She approached Fatah/PLO to join them in order to conduct hijackings of her own or to go on patrol and other operations, however Fatah tried to involve her in social work, but "social work... is not social revolution. I want[ed] to participate fully in revolution" (Khaled 1973, 106–7). Khaled then approached the PFLP, but they found her knowledge of Marxism-Leninism lacking (Khaled 1973, 110). Rebuffed again, she went to teach in Kuwait and spent her time reading Marxism and learning more about the PFLP's Marxist-Leninist platform. After two years, she reapproached them and they accepted her into their ranks (Khaled 1973, 123–4). Khaled conducted two hijackings for them: a successful one in 1969 and an unsuccessful one in 1970. In the second one, her partner was killed and she was detained in London for ten weeks until the PFLP worked to secure her release. Upon her release, Khaled found she had become so well-known that she was unable to conduct any more attacks. Instead, she has since been on the Central Committee, which plans attacks. Khaled lives relatively freely in Amman, Jordan, with her second husband and her two grown sons (see Gentry 2011).

Wafa Idris lived a very different life from Khaled. During the Nakba, Idris's parents wound up in the Am'ari Refugee Camp in the West Bank and Idris was born in 1975. She was twelve when the first intifada started in 1987 and she served on a women's committee during it, providing food assistance and other support to families. By the time the second intifada started in 2000, Idris was already married and divorced. She is also reported to have "failed" at having children. During the intifada, she volunteered for the Red Crescent and, at the time of her death, much was made of the "fact" that she was tired of picking up body parts (Bennet 2002; see Sjoberg and Gentry 2007, 122). While the second intifada introduced suicide bombing as a sustained campaign, all of the participating groups were resistant to including women. That is, until Yassir Arafat's aforementioned "Army of Roses" speech in which he indicated that women should be included as militants in the struggle against Israel. The next day, 27 January 2002, Idris detonated a 22lb bomb in Jerusalem that killed herself and one other but injured 100 people. Al Aqsa Martyrs' Brigade claimed responsibility for the attack.

It is often assumed that in a conservative society, women's actions will reflect conservative gender roles. What made the suicide campaign surprising and, indeed, Khaled's hijackings, was that these were committed by women—women whom the world had assumed were submissive and passive, content to support the men in their lives. Instead, the world was confronted with women who found it appropriate to use violence for a political cause.

Radical Islamism: Al Qaeda and the Islamic State

The beginning of this chapter uses a quote by William McCants to illustrate that people are still surprised to find women involved in terrorism. Perhaps such a surprise is owed to the general perception that terrorism seemingly began with 9/11 and the explosion of media and scholarship related to it (Silke 2009). Additionally, since 9/11, the spotlight on terrorism is focused on radical Islamism, without paying much attention to other types (Jackson 2007). So much of the Western media focuses on the misogyny within radical Islamism (Azzam 2007; Hasan 2012), particularly the religious ideology of Al Qaeda and now the Islamic State, which controls territory in Syria. Thus, it seems odd to think of women across the world as wanting to support and act for the goals of either group. Women's participation in Al Qaeda was considerably more limited than the role they are seen to be playing in IS. This is primarily because the organizations have two different aims. Al Qaeda's was a more abstract vision for the establishment of the old Islamic caliphate while it operated out of multiple bases. The Islamic State controls territory and as such needs a population to live in that territory, which is where women enter the picture. Women's participation in Islamic State is more welcome, albeit still primarily limited to conservative gender roles.

There are, like in the other groups surveyed in this chapter, several prominent women associated with Al Qaeda. One such woman is Aafia Siddiqui. While she is now serving eighty-six-years for the attempted murder of US soldiers in Afghanistan, she was never convicted on terrorism or terrorism-related charges. Yet, it is widely believed that while she was living and working in Boston, Massachusetts, she smuggled conflict diamonds to fund Al Qaeda activities and she planned an attack on United States' eastern seaboard fuel depositories (that never came to fruition). At the same time, she earned a Ph.D. from Brandeis in neuroscience (looking at learning disabilities) and had two, later three, children (see Gentry 2016). After the two women discussed in the previous section, as well as others, committed suicide bombings on behalf of Al Qaeda, there was concern in the West that more women would be mobilized. Adding to this concern was the short-lived *Al Khansa*, which was a magazine for women about how they could prepare themselves by keeping fit (see Sjoberg and Gentry 2007, 124).

In early 2015, IS demanded al-Rishawi, the woman whose bomb failed to detonate in Amman in 2005, be released in return for a Japanese hostage. It was a demand the Jordanian government ignored; she was executed after IS burned a Jordanian military pilot alive (Botelho and Ford 2015). This was perhaps the first indication that women mattered, either instrumentally or for deeper reasons, to IS. Echoing Al Qaeda, an IS document entitled "Women of the Islamic State" written by the Al Khansa Brigade, a woman-only brigade used to maintain social order within the controlled territories (Eleftheirou-Smith 2015), outlined the role that they saw women playing (see <quilliamfoundation.org>). While women's primary role was supportive, IS indicated that women could play a greater role if necessary. Most of IS's recruitment strategy towards women in the West has lauded conservative gender roles, indicating that this is both holy and the best way for women to support the strategic growth and fighting of IS. This has meant some scholars see the women as being won over by "high end appliances" (Bloom 2015), but it also speaks to the idealistic view *all recruits* have towards this political community with extremist religious beliefs.

A Cautionary Conclusion

Even if we are initially surprised that women willingly participate in political violence, it is important that, as we recognize and "see" these women and their activities, we also see their violence for what it was. To assume it stems from personal and/or emotional causes disregards that the women have observed the conflict, just as the men; that they have lost relatives, just like the men; and that they want to see change, just like the men. It is far more helpful to see both men and women as driven by both emotional and political causes—leading to a more informed and holistic assessment of terrorist violence and why it is utilized (see also Sjoberg and Gentry 2008b).

This then raises the question: what is the utility in studying "women and terrorism"? If men and women are very similarly motivated, is it helpful to analyze "women" as a distinct category? How lovely it would be if there was no need in any subject or discipline to distinguish "women" from the "norm" or the "normal," both of which are based upon a Western idealization of the white, rational, man. Indeed, it would be lovely not to distinguish "women" or any other marginalized, subordinate identity, such as those identified by race, class, or sexuality. Thus, the utility of studying "women and X" is to point out how women are treated as inherently different from men (the norm). The supposed discrepancies between men and women, or "white" and "black" individuals, or "straight" or "gay" folk, are inherently power-laden. In studying "women and terrorism," I, along with my peers, am able to highlight and point out the historical and continuing biased treatment of women. The study of women cannot end until the bias ends.

Note

1. However, that conservative groups excluded women has been complicated by more recent feminist research. Sandra McEvoy 2009 looks at women's inclusion into Loyalist and Protestant paramilitaries in Northern Ireland. She argues that their participation was either ignored or minimized historically. Instead, she reveals through her ethnographic research that these women performed highly supportive roles in hiding and smuggling people, guns, and money as well as participation in planning activities. Swati Parashar 2009, 2011 has uncovered a similar dynamic in right-wing militants in Kashmir and Sri Lanka.

References

Alison, Miranda (2003) "Cogs in the Wheel? Women in the Liberation Tigers of Tamil Eelam," *Civil Wars*, 6(4): 37–54.

Alison, Miranda (2004) "Women as Agents of Political Violence: Gendering Security," *Security Dialogue*, 35(4): 447–63.

Alison, Miranda (2009) *Women and Political Violence: Female Combatants in Ethno-National Conflict*. London: Routledge.

Anderson, Jon Lee (2011) "Death of the Tiger," *New Yorker*, Jan. 17, available online at <https://www.newyorker.com/magazine/2011/01/17/death-of-the-tiger>.

Anonymous (1976) "The Female Terrorist and her Impact on Policing," *Top Security Project No. 2 Part IV—Summary and Analysis*, 242–5.

Aust, Stefan (1987) *The Baader-Meinhof Complex*. London: Bodley Head.

Azzam, Maha (2007) "The Radicalization of Muslim Communities in Europe: Local and Global Dimensions," *Brown Journal of World Affairs*, 13(2): 123–34.

Bennet, James (2002) "Arab Woman's Path to Unlikely "Martyrdom,"" *New York Times*, Jan. 31, available online at <http://www.nytimes.com/2002/01/31/world/arab-woman-s-path-to-unlikely-martyrdom.html?pagewanted=all> [Accessed Aug. 2016].

Bloom, Mia (2005) *Dying to Kill: The Allure of Suicide Terror*. New York: University of Columbia Press.

Bloom, Mia (2011a) "Bombshells: Women and Terror," *Gender Issues*, 28(1–2): 1–21.

Bloom, Mia (2011b) *Bombshell: The Many Faces of Female Terrorists*. Toronto: Penguin Canada.

Bloom, Mia (2015) "How ISIS is Using Marriage as a Trap," Huffington Post, Mar. 2, available online at <http://www.huffingtonpost.com/mia-bloom/isis-marriage-trap_b_6773576.html> [Accessed Jan. 2016].

Botelho, Greg, and Dana Ford (2015) "Jordan Executes Prisoners After ISIS Hostage Burned Alive," CNN, Feb. 4, available online at <http://edition.cnn.com/2015/02/03/world/isis-captive> [Accessed Aug. 2016].

Callimachi, Rukmini (2015) "ISIS and the Lonely Young American," *New York Times*, June 28, available online at <http://www.nytimes.com/2015/06/28/world/americas/isis-online-recruiting-american.html> [Accessed Jan. 2016].

Carroll, Berenice A. (2000) "Vera Figner," in Hilda L. Smith and Berenice A. Carroll (eds), *Women's Political and Social Thought: An Anthology*. Bloomington, IN: Indiana University Press, 233–4.

Cataldo Neuburger, Luisella de, and Tiziana Valentini (1996) *Women and Terrorism*. London: Macmillan.

Cooper, H. H. A. (1979) "Woman as Terrorist," in Freda Adler and Rita James Simon (eds), *The Criminology of Deviant Women*. Boston: Houghton Mifflin, 150–7.

Coughlin, Kathryn M. (2000) "Women, War, and the Veil: Muslim Women in Resistance and Combat," in Gerard J. DeGroot and Corinna Peniston-Bird (eds), *A Soldier and a Woman: Sexual Integration in the Military*. London: Pearson, 223–39.

della Porta, Donatella (1992) "Introduction," in Donatella della Porta (ed.), *Social Movements and Violence: Participation in Underground Organizations*. London: JAI Press.

Easton, Nina (2015) "How ISIS is Recruiting Women—And Turning Them into Brutal Enforcers," *Fortune*, May 5, available online at <http://fortune.com/2015/05/05/isis-women-recruiting> [Accessed Mar. 2016].

Eleftheirou-Smith, Loulla-Mae (2015) "Escaped ISIS Wives Describe Life in the All-Female al-khansa Brigade Who Punish Women with 40 Lashes for Wearing Wrong Clothes," *Independent*, Apr. 20, available online at <http://www.independent.co.uk/news/world/middle-east/escaped-isis-wives-describe-life-in-the-all-female-al-khansa-brigade-who-punish-women-with-40-lashes-10190317.html> [Accessed Aug. 2016].

Erelle, Anna (2015) "Skyping with the Enemy: I went Undercover as a Jihadi Girlfriend," *Guardian*, May 26, available online at <https://www.theguardian.com/world/2015/may/26/french-journalist-poses-muslim-convert-isis-anna-erelle> [Accessed Aug. 2016].

Gentry, Caron E. (2004) "The Relationship between New Social Movement Theory and Terrorism Studies: The Role of Leadership, Membership, Ideology and Gender," *Terrorism and Political Violence*, 16(2): 274–93.

Gentry, Caron E. (2011) "The Committed Revolutionary," in Laura Sjoberg and Caron E. Gentry (eds), *Women, Gender, and Terrorism*. Athens, GA: University of Georgia Press, 120–30.

Gentry, Caron E. (2016) "The Mysterious Case of Aafia Siddiqui: Gothic Intertextual Analysis of Neo-Orientalist Narratives," *Millennium-Journal of International Studies*, 45(1), 3–24.

Gentry, Caron E., and Laura Sjoberg (2011) "The Gendering of Women's Terrorism," in Laura Sjoberg and Caron E. Gentry (eds), *Women, Gender, and Terrorism*. Athens, GA: University of Georgia Press, 57–82.

Gentry, Caron E., and Laura Sjoberg (2015) *Beyond Mothers, Monsters, Whores: Thinking about Women's Violence in Global Politics*. London: Zed Books.

Giacaman, Rita, and Penny Johnson (1989) "Palestinian Women: Building Barricades and Breaking Barriers," in Zachary Lockman and Joel Beinin (eds), *Intifada: The Palestinian Uprising Against Israeli Occupation*. Washington, DC: MERIP, 155–69.

Glenza, Jessica, Tom Dart, Andrew Gumbel, and Jon Boone (2015) "Tasheen Malik: Who was the 'Shy Housewife' Turned San Bernardino Killer?," *Guardian*, Dec. 6, available online at <http://www.theguardian.com/us-news/2015/dec/06/tashfeen-malik-who-was-the-shy-housewife-turned-san-bernardino-killer> [Accessed Jan. 2016].

Hammami, Rema (1990) "Women, the Hijab, and the Intifada," *Middle East Report*, no. 164/165: 24–8.

Hasan, Md. Mahmudul (2012) "Feminism as Islamophobia: A Review of Misogyny Charges Against Islam," *Intellectual Discourse*, 20(1): 55.

Jackson, Richard (2007) "Constructing Enemies: 'Islamic Terrorism' in Political and Academic Discourse," *Government and Opposition*, 42(3): 394–426.

Khaled, Leila (1973) *My People Shall Live: The Autobiography of a Revolutionary*. London: Hodder & Stoughton.

Koerner, Brendan I. (2016) "Why ISIS is Winning the Social Media War," Apr., available online at <https://www.wired.com/2016/03/isis-winning-social-media-war-heres-beat> [Accessed Aug. 2016].

Kolbert, Elizabeth (2001) "The Prisoner," *The New Yorker*, July 16, available online at <http://www.newyorker.com/magazine/2001/07/16/the-prisoner-3> [Accessed Aug. 2016].

MacDonald, Eileen (1988) *Shoot the Women First*. London: Arrow Books.

McEvoy, Sandra (2009) "Loyalist Women Paramilitaries in Northern Ireland: Beginning a Feminist Conversation about Conflict Resolution," *Security Studies*, 18(2): 262–86.

Morgan, Robin (1989) *The Demon Lover: The Roots of Terrorism*. New York: Washington Square Press.

Pape, Robert (2005) *Dying to Win: The Strategic Logic of Suicide Terrorism*. London: Random House.

Parashar, Swati (2009) "Feminist International Relations and Women Militants: Case Studies from Sri Lanka and Kashmir," *Cambridge Review of International Affairs*, 22(2): 235–56.

Parashar, Swati (2011) "*Aatish-e Chinar:* In Kashmir, Where Women Keep Resistance Alive," in Laura Sjoberg and Caron E. Gentry (eds), *Women, Gender, and Terrorism*. Athens, GA: University of Georgia Press, 96–119.

Peteet, Julie (1991) *Gender in Crisis: Women and the Palestinian Resistance Movement*. New York: Columbia University Press.

Schulz, Helena Linhom (1999) *The Reconstruction of Palestinian Nationalism: Between Revolution and Statehood*. Manchester: Manchester University Press.

Siljak, Ana (2009) *Angel of Vengeance: The Girl Who Shot the Governor of St Petersburg and Sparked the Age of Assassination*. New York: St Martin's Griffin.

Silke, Andrew (2009) "Contemporary Terrorism Studies: Issues in Research," in Richard Jackson, Marie Breen Smyth, and Jeroen Gunning (eds), *Critical Terrorism Studies: A New Research Agenda*. London: Routledge, 34–48.

Sjoberg, Laura, and Caron E. Gentry (2007) *Mothers, Monsters, Whores: Women's Violence in Global Politics*. London: Zed Books.

Sjoberg, Laura, and Caron E. Gentry (2008a) "Reduced to Bad Sex: Narratives of Violent Women from the Bible to the War on Terror," *International Relations*, 22(1): 5–23.

Sjoberg, Laura, and Caron E. Gentry (2008b) "Profiling Terror: Gender, Strategic Logic, and Emotion in the Study of Suicide Terrorism," *Austrian Journal of Political Science*, 37(2): 181–96.

Stites, Richard (1978) *The Women's Liberation Movement in Russia: Feminism, Nihilism, and Bolshevism, 1860–1930*. Princeton: Princeton University Press.

Van de Voorde, Cecile (2005) "Sri Lankan Terrorism: Assessing and Responding to the Threat of the Liberation Tigers of Tamil Eelam (LTTE)," *Police Practice and Research*, 6(2): 181–99.

Victor, Barbara (2003) *Army of Roses: Inside the World of Palestinian Women Suicide Bombers*. London: Robinson.

Weinberg, Leonard, and William Eubank (1987) "Italian Women Terrorists," *Terrorism*, 9(3): 241–62.

Weinberg, Leonard, and William Eubank (1989) "Leaders and Followers in Italian Terrorist Groups," *Terrorism and Political Violence*, 1(2): 156–76.

Weinberg, Leonard, and William Eubank (2011) "Women's Involvement in Terrorism," *Gender Issues*, 28(1–2): 22–49.

CHAPTER 28

SUICIDE TERRORISM

RASHMI SINGH

As a topic that falls under the broader field of terrorism studies it should come as no surprise that suicide terrorism suffers from the same sets of conceptual challenges and controversies as the discipline in general. Disagreements begin, as in terrorism studies more generally, with the most basic of questions, i.e. how should we define the concept of "suicide terrorism" followed closely by heated debates around everything from the most adequate term that best describes this phenomenon to what its key set of distinguishing features should be. The modern trend of suicide attacks began in the early 1980s with a series of bombings in Lebanon, although some would argue that the first contemporary incidences of suicide attacks can be traced to the actions of the Japanese kamikaze pilots during World War II. Nonetheless, undoubtedly the modern non-state use of the tactic originated and spread from Lebanon to locations as varied as Sri Lanka, Chechnya, and the Occupied Palestinian Territories. Suicide attacks assumed a much more transnational hue once they became part of Al Qaeda's tactical toolkit. Certainly, it was the devastatingly effective use of this tactic during the Palestinian Al Aqsa intifada and the spectacular attacks of September 11 that not only cemented public interest in suicide terrorism but also spurred academic research into this phenomenon. Since then not only have incidences of suicide attacks increased but so have the number of groups employing this method and the overall geographical spread of this tactic. However, although a number of important contributions have been made to the study of suicide terrorism there is still no real clear consensus on key issues. Consequently, the explanations remain imprecise and unevenly developed and are unable to account for the range of differences and variations in the phenomenon. Datasets also continue to remain incomplete and/or incompatible with clearly detrimental results for empirical analysis. Moreover, the "specifications of what is to be explained vary by author" and in recent years, thanks to the spike in suicide attacks, "many accounts are [simply] being overtaken by events" (Crenshaw 2007).

This chapter begins by outlining some key controversies that plague the study of suicide terrorism including the debates surrounding the use of terminology as well as key definitional issues. In many regards, these are continuing challenges that plague those dedicated to detecting the key defining characteristics of and unearthing explanations for this phenomenon. Having outlined these key controversies, this chapter then moves on to discuss some key explanations for suicide terrorism before shedding light on what is perhaps the central puzzle for scholars studying this phenomenon, i.e. the rationality underpinning a suicide attack. It concludes by offering suggestions for avenues of future research and development.

Terminology

The first challenge in the study of this concept relates to a lack of consensus around acceptable terminology. Scholars are fundamentally divided between using a normatively neutral term such as "suicide attack/mission" or "suicide bombing" and using the term "suicide terrorism" which would categorize this phenomenon as a specific form of terrorism with all its accompanying pejorative connotations. Indeed, given the absence of consensus regarding the definition of terrorism and different perspectives regarding its limits, one would have to accept that categorizing suicide terrorism as a sub-set of terrorism would also subject it to the same series of uncertainties and debates. This explains why some studies expand their interpretation of terrorism to include agents of the state, such as the Japanese kamikaze pilots, in their analyses of suicide terrorism. It also sheds light on the question whether or not "suicide attacks" can be categorized as acts of "suicide terrorism" if they avoid noncombatants and limit their targets to military personnel alone (Pape 2005; Moghadam 2006a, 2006b; Pape and Feldman 2010). Of course, there are those who deliberately choose to invoke the pejorative quality inherent in the term "suicide terrorism." Authors like Raphael Israeli (2003), for instance, insist that violence associated with Islam be referred to as terrorism, arguing that a more neutral appellation is not only weak and inaccurate but also "insufficiently condemnatory" (Crenshaw 2007). Of course, given empirical evidence, there are clear issues with associating the tactic of suicide attacks solely with Islamist groups, or indeed devoting oneself to condemning the tactic when used particularly by Islamist groups rather than consciously adopting a much more impartial and thus holistic stance.

Having said that, even scholars who opt for more the neutral lexicons of "suicide attack/mission" or "suicide bombing" disagree as to which term best describes this phenomenon. Assaf Moghadam (2006a), for instance argues that suicide bombings are essentially a technology-dependent phenomenon and as such this term does not account for other kinds of suicide attacks/missions that may not use explosives. In other words, all suicide bombings are suicide attacks but, strictly speaking, not all suicide attacks can be categorized as suicide bombings (Moghadam 2006a). The September 11, 2001 attacks are a case in point. While the 9/11 attacks were undoubtedly suicide attacks, in the absence of conventional explosive devices they cannot be categorized as suicide bombings per se. Hence, authors like Moghadam posit using the terms "suicide attack", "suicide mission," or "suicide operation" instead, in order to encompass the widest range of possible ways in which this particular type of attack may be perpetrated.

Similarly, there are scholars who argue that the terms "suicide terrorism", "suicide bombing" or "suicide attack" focus too much attention upon the individual role and death of the perpetrator and instead suggest using the term "homicide-bombing" (Ehrenfeld 2002) or "homicide-bombers" (Goldney 2014), which would shift this focus and emphasize instead the aspect of killing others. Robert Goldney further argues that lexicons incorporating the word "suicide" tend to be misleading because evidence seems to suggest that, although individual perpetrators possess a range of characteristics, in most cases they do not display suicidal tendencies. Jerrold M. Post and his colleagues (2009) corroborate this stance by illustrating not only the "normality" but also the marked absence of individual psychopathology amongst perpetrators of suicide attacks in their work. The data on suicidal tendencies amongst perpetrators are still fairly limited and it is worth noting that some degree of discrepancy exists (Merari et al. 2009). Nonetheless, there is some consensus that most perpetrators of suicide attacks tend not to display suicidal tendencies or individual psychopathology. Variations in this lexicon also exist; for instance, Anne Marie Oliver and Paul Steinberg use the term "murder-suicide" in their work on suicide attacks in the Israeli–Palestinian conflict (Oliver and Steinberg 2005). However, none of these terms enjoy widespread acceptance, potentially because they ignore critical facets of this particular type of attack, i.e. not only the fact that the death of the perpetrator is an integral part of the attack but also that it is precisely this element of self-sacrifice which elicits curiosity, concern, and interest (Merari 1998). Indeed, for some authors it is this self-sacrifice which embodies the non-negotiable prerequisite for the successful undertaking of such an attack (Ganor 2001; Schweitzer, 2001), although as will be discussed this is also a point of some contention amongst scholars.

Finally, a group of scholars argues for the use of terminology that is more culturally and socially relevant for those committing this particular type of act, i.e. "martyrdom." Most religions and societies strongly discourage, if not explicitly and strictly prohibit, suicide. Hence, the use of the term "martyrdom" (Davis 2003; Victor 2003; Singh 2011) or "sacred explosions" (Hassan 2001) to describe a suicide attack becomes a preferred option for those scholars interested in understanding the act of self-sacrifice from the perspective of the perpetrators as well as for individuals describing and justifying their own acts. Indeed, couching suicide attacks in the language of martyrdom seems to be the preferred option for those who resort to this modus operandi, irrespective of geographical location and whether they are religious or secular in their leanings. Thus, organizations as varied as the secular LTTE of Sri Lanka to the secular Fatah and the more religiously inclined Hamas in the Palestinian context, and even Salafi jihadist transnational organizations like Al Qaeda and the Islamic State, all tend use the language of martyrdom when describing suicide operations. Authors like Mohammad Hafez argue that the term "martyrdom", and its various iterations such as *shahid*, *istish'had*, etc. is not only heavily normative but also so politically charged as to distract from analyzing and explaining what is already a complex phenomenon. However, there has been recent work on understanding why multiple iterations of the same word are used in particular societies that overturns this logic. In other words, restricting our understanding to the use of the English term "martyrdom" to reference a "suicide mission" overlooks the manner in which the term has socially evolved in particular contexts, occasionally with different words used to signify different *kinds* of martyrdom, of which suicide attacks represent merely one form of self-sacrifice. For example, in the Israeli–Palestinian conflict by the second intifada, the term *istish'hadi* came to denote an active act of self-sacrifice and encompassed the actions of armed fighters and suicide bombers who died whilst actively and militarily confronting their Zionist enemies. However, the term *shahid* also continued to be used but now came to embody a passivity by signifying a noncombatant or civilian casualty at the hands of the Israeli Defence Forces (Singh 2012). Exploring these critical differences and the evolution of what these terms signify in specific contexts sheds important light on how certain groups are able to legitimize the use of this tactic under particular circumstances and may thus be a critical aspect to understanding both the rise and disappearance of suicide attacks in a given socio-cultural setting.

Overall, the most commonly used terms to describe this particular kind of attack include, in no particular order, "suicide attack/mission/or operation", "suicide terrorism," and "martyrdom attack/mission or operation." Other variations in the lexicon, although used occasionally, do not enjoy wide acceptance. It is worth noting that irrespective of which of the more commonly used terms authors choose, as with terrorism more broadly, the choice of lexicon used to describe the sub-category suicide terrorism broadly reflects the author's particular perspectives on the subject, as well as, quite often, revealing his/her own position in time and space.

Definitions

Having discussed some of the issues around terminology we can now highlight some of the most contentious issues surrounding definitions of suicide attacks. As in terrorism studies more broadly, a universally accepted definition of suicide terrorism remains elusive. Furthermore, it would not be an exaggeration to state that some of the issues raised in relation to the challenges around terminology also contribute to the fact that a more widely accepted definition of suicide attacks continues to elude scholars. Amongst a host of disagreements around the key component characteristics of a suicide attack, perhaps the most critical relates to death as a precondition in a suicide mission. There are broadly two schools of thought on this issue. According to one set of scholars (Ganor 2001; Shay 2004; Bloom 2005; Hafez 2006a; Moghadam 2008/9), the death of perpetrator is a critical precondition for a suicide mission. In other words, the very *success* of a suicide mission is dependent upon the death of the perpetrator(s) undertaking the attack. However, there are also scholars who adopt a more moderate stance. For Ami Pedahzur for instance, suicide terrorism "includes a diversity of violent actions perpetrated by people who are aware that the odds that they will return alive are close to nought" (Pedahzur 2005). Similarly, Robert Pape argues that in most cases the suicide attacker "does not expect to survive the mission and often employs a method of attack ... that requires his or her death in order to succeed" (Pape 2005). The problem with this more moderate stance is that it blurs the boundaries between what is perhaps better categorized as a high-risk mission, where the chances of survival—although minimal—still exist, and a suicide attack where death can be clearly categorized as a precondition for the attack.

Pape himself acknowledges this problem when referring to cases like Baruch Goldstein's 1994 Cave of the Patriarchs massacre in Hebron. However, he circumvents a deeper engagement with this discrepancy by calling such high-risk events "suicide *missions*" as opposed to "suicide *attacks*" (my emphasis), arguing that in such cases the perpetrator does not actively kill him/herself but expects to be executed by a third party such as the police or other defenders (Pape 2005). However, to some extent this category of high-risk attacks has, over time, come to be treated in much of the lay and scholarly literature as a somewhat different phenomenon. More recently, and especially in the South Asian context, these kinds of high-risk, potentially suicidal missions, are referred to as *fedayeen* attacks. Interestingly, *fedayeen* has its etymological roots in the term *fida'i* which carries the semantic concept of "self-sacrifice" (Johnson 1982) and was first used to reference the Palestinian revolutionary guerrilla fighters who emerged out of refugee camps in the 1960s and 1970s (Singh 2012). Today the term carries the same significance of "self-sacrifice" and "redemption" but is used specifically to reference high-risk missions. Some authors use this lexicon without much explanation (Unnithan 2014) while others clearly indicate that unlike in suicide attacks where the perpetrator intends to die, *fedayeen* attacks are high-risk attacks or "no surrender" missions where "the perpetrator intends to fight until he is either killed or captured by his adversary. There is a very small chance he is able to complete his mission and escape" (Gunaratna 2009).

There is some degree of conceptual refinement discernible here. Diego Gambetta, for instance, differentiates between suicide attacks, no-escape attacks, and high-risk missions (Gambetta 2005). In doing so, he clearly makes a distinction between suicide attacks, as requiring the death of the perpetrator; no-escape attacks, as missions where the "perpetrator's death is certain but not self-inflicted"; and high-risk attacks which are different precisely because death is neither a precondition nor does it involve "other forms of extreme self-sacrifice," such as self-immolation where perpetrators kill themselves without killing others (Gambetta 2005). However, this sort of sophisticated categorization remains fairly rare in the literature as most authors simply do not engage with the issue (see e.g. Laqueur 2005). Non-specialists, in their turn and perhaps unsurprisingly, also tend not to distinguish between suicide missions, high-risk missions, and no-escape incidents too clearly. For instance, Steve Coll of *The New Yorker*, describes the Mumbai attackers as *fedayeen* and the attacks as "suicidal" without "getaway plans or tactical exit strategies other than martyrdom." However, he also adds that these were not suicide attacks as the perpetrators did not "wire themselves up as human bombs" (Coll 2008).

The distinction between suicide attacks, no-escape attacks, and high-risk missions is somewhat difficult to discern given the character of a suicide attack. The core issue lies in the ability to detect intentionality—which raises a host of specific problems discussed later. However, for now it is worth noting that even definitions in which death is a required precondition are unable to account for cases where a mission may begin as a high-risk attack till the risk of failure transforms it into a suicide mission, thereby further muddying the waters. An excellent example of such a nuance is Hopgood's study of the LTTE's squad of suicide bombers, the Black Tigers. Hopgood argues that, in the case of the Tigers, the survival of these highly trained cadre members was preferable to death as long as the "mission objective had been secured" (Hopgood 2005). An additional problem lies in the fact that a single suicide attack may exhibit multiple levels of intentionality and voluntariness on the part of the perpetrators. Evidence from the 9/11 attacks seems to hint at this variation. According to FBI investigations conducted after the attack, it seems that eleven of the nineteen hijackers were unaware that they were on a suicide mission. Thus, it was only the eight trained pilots who left last wills and messages for their friends and families. The items found in the possession of the remaining eleven also seemed to suggest that they were preparing for incarceration as opposed to "paradise" (Rose 2001; Fenton 2001).

A further definitional complication emerges when discussing this precondition of death that relates much more directly to terminology. Thus, if the term "suicide terrorism" is used as opposed to "suicide attack" or "suicide mission," should forms of self-sacrifice such as self-immolation, in which the perpetrator dies without killing others, be included in the dataset? One could contend that if the point of terrorism is to signal commitment and spread fear beyond the immediate victim(s) for a political purpose then acts of self-immolation can fulfill these criteria even if the perpetrators kill no one else but themselves. However, such as stance is controversial and most authors view acts of self-immolation and other forms of dying without killing, not as an "extraordinary weapon of war" and terrorism but rather as "an extreme form of protest" (Biggs 2005; see also Pape 2005). In general, Crenshaw's observation holds that "authors who define their subject as suicide terrorism are typically less sensitive to the need to compare suicide attacks to other forms of terrorism or political violence" (Crenshaw, 2007). More significantly, cases of high-risk attacks or attacks where the perpetrator dies alone without killing others essentially represent what are best called "borderline cases." Borderline cases are very significant in quantitative studies primarily because they can change the analysis on the basis of which kinds of incidents are counted as suicide attacks and which are not.

Of course, as already stated, a key difficulty in all of this lies in being able to discern intentionality. This essentially leads us to a yet another point of contention, i.e. locating the intentions or voluntariness of the perpetrator, which given the character of a suicide attack can be difficult to know. A number of authors very clearly underscore the element of free will as a pre-requisite for a suicide attack to be counted as such. Gambetta argues that those who participate in suicide attacks can be neither "deceived about their prospect of survival" nor blackmailed into conducting such a mission (Gambetta 2005). Hafez and Shay, in turn, refer to a willingness to die as a critical part of their definitions (Hafez 2006a; Shay 2004), while others refer to a "readiness to die" (Merari 1998) or to a "deliberate state of awareness" (Bloom 2005). This emphasis on free will would effectively disqualify, for instance, the October 1990 IRA attack that forced a civilian cook, Patsy Gillespie, to drive an explosives-laden van into a British army checkpoint while his family were held at gunpoint. Similarly, it disqualifies Boko Haram's use of women and children as suicide bombers, a trend that skyrocketed almost immediately after the infamous Chibok kidnappings and which, UNICEF reports suggest, involves the perpetrators being forced or deceived to undertake their missions. However, this is not to say alternative views do not exist. Victor, Davis, and O'Rourke for instance, all include cases of women in their work who were duped, manipulated, or socially pressured into undertaking suicide missions (Victor 2003; Davis 2003; O'Rourke 2009). Moghadam and Alakoc make a clear reference to manipulation when they cite indoctrination as a critical organizational element in producing suicide attackers (Moghadam 2003; Alakoc 2015). Khosrokhavar also talks about the systematic manipulation undertaken by the state when he speaks of martyrdom in Iran (Khosrokhavar 2005). Strenski in his turn indirectly references social pressure and the perpetrator's sense of social responsibility when he argues that suicide attacks are a "relational reality" and tend to be undertaken because the perpetrators see themselves as "embedded in a network of social relations to which they belong or want to belong" (Strenski 2003).

A final issue that we need to deal with is the question of what counts as a suicide attack. There are two elements to this. First, should failed and foiled attempts be included, and, second, should a mission with multiple perpetrators be counted as one attack or more? Once again there is no clear consensus on these issues. Often authors lump together what are in reality multiple suicide attacks using multiple perpetrators under a single event, when strictly speaking these should be counted as separate incidents (Pape 2005; Moghadam 2006a). In some cases, this is thanks to the absence of reliable information and/or primary empirical research, which makes answering operational questions particularly difficult when it comes to suicide missions. In other cases, although obviously problematic, it is a simple methodological choice on part of the researcher. As regards unsuccessful attacks, once again there is no single approach. Hence, while some authors clearly include unsuccessful attempts (Merari 1998; Pedahzur 2006; Hafez 2007) others exclude them from their analyses, while still others simply do not shed light on their analytical and methodological choices. There are researchers who maintain a clear distinction between successful and unsuccessful attacks and code them separately (Kaplan et al. 2005) in their work, although such a nuanced engagement with this issue remains remarkably rare.

In all cases, definitional and terminological issues and choices represent more than pedantic preoccupation and pretention. As with terrorism more broadly, what we call an act of suicide terrorism and how we decide to define it not only sheds light on the particular prism of our analysis but also entirely determines our universe of cases. In turn, these choices impact our answers to a number of very fundamental questions. Questions like: what are the causes of suicide terrorism? Has there been a proportional overall increase in incidents of suicide terrorism over the last x-number of years? Can we detect contagion? Can a psychological understanding of perpetrators aid in prevention?—and so on.

Explanations for Suicide Terrorism and the Puzzle of Rationality

Over time there have been quite a number of explanations for suicide attacks and undoubtedly there has been clear progress in conceptualizing and understanding the phenomenon.[1] Quite a lot of new and very interesting research has been conducted in the area, especially post-9/11 and after the Global War on Terror. Although clearly categorized as a sub-set of terrorism, suicide terrorism elicits unmatched levels of horror and revulsion primarily because it breaks a series of normative and social taboos. Some of the dominant explanations for suicide terrorism in the field are grounded in the overall strategic effectiveness of such types of attacks. Thus, Robert Pape argues that the primary strategic function of suicide attacks is to coerce democracies to end the occupation of territories that terrorist perpetrators considered their own (Pape 2003, 2005; Pape and Feldman 2010). Similarly, authors like Shaul Mishal and Avraham Sela use the example of Hamas to illustrate how it employed campaigns of suicide terrorism for a range of strategic purposes, from "surviving" in a political landscape in which it was a relatively weak player to "spoiling" negotiations between the Palestinian Authority and the Israeli state in order to keep itself politically relevant in a post-first-intifada setting (Sela 2000). Authors like Mia Bloom further develop this logic to argue that a variety of groups use suicide attacks as a mechanism to "outbid" their political competitors in a given political context in order to garner recruits, funding, as well as social and political capital more generally and support from unaffiliated or undecided constituencies (Bloom, 2004, 2005; Gupta and Mundra 2005).

However, beyond the specifics of such particular explanations, the fundamental puzzle of suicide terrorism for scholars from the very moment it began to be studied lies the in very rationality of this act. The concept of rationality is founded upon the notion of pay-offs, i.e. in a transaction where the costs of committing any particular act are lower than the benefits accrued from doing so. This is why suicide terrorism is such an intriguing puzzle because how can the cost of giving up one's very life be less than the benefits of committing such a radical act? The attempts to engage with this puzzle have, over time, successfully produced what can be best described as a "preliminary framework of analysis," although the answers to central questions, perhaps unsurprisingly, vary (Crenshaw 2007). In the case of a handful of dedicated researchers, their answers to these central questions have also evolved with their scholarship on the subject.

Broadly speaking, early explanations of suicide attacks tried to locate its causes in individual irrationality where these were categorized as acts conducted by a handful of deranged fanatics. These early works essentially argued that it was either individual psychopathy or religious indoctrination that led to individual perpetrators engaging in such irrational acts of violence (Kramer 1998; Merari 1998; Post 1998). However, as the scholarship evolved there came to be a much clearer focus upon the multiple strategic functions of suicide operations—although works arguing for individual psychopathy continue to be produced (Kobrin 2010; Merari 2010). Much of the work addressing the strategic functions of suicide terrorism engaged with the organizational level of analysis and understood this tactic as an intrinsic part of the political and military strategy of particular organizations. Thus this work tended to "approach this phenomenon from above and assess it in terms of its kill-rates, its signalling potential, its tactical efficacy, its psychological impact on target populations, its functions in political competition and so on" (Singh 2011). In other words, suicide terrorism came to be understood as a strategic and instrumentally valuable choice made by what most scholars argued were the weaker parties in asymmetrical conflicts. As such, the choice to adopt suicide attacks as a mechanism of engaging the enemy, albeit costly, brought with it distinct strategic and tactical advantages. These ranged from the maneuvrability and flexibility of the attacks, as the perpetrator represented the epitome of the "smart bomb," to assuredly higher casualty rates, the ability to signal greater commitment to a cause, and the obvious benefit of not having to plan escape routes or worry that a captured operative could give away organizational secrets under duress (Moghadam 2003; Pape 2003, 2004; Shay 2004; Hoffman and McCormick 2004). In identifying and exploring the strategic logic and functions of suicide attacks for the organization deploying them, this scholarship marked a refreshing break from the first-generational theses that categorized suicide terrorism as acts of senseless, irrational violence. However, this second-generational literature was also limited as its nearly unmitigated focus on the organization's role in promulgating suicide attacks ensured that it ignored both the role played by the individual perpetrator as well as the factors that propelled the individual towards acts of self-sacrifice.

There is no doubt that explaining suicide terrorism from below is a much more difficult task. The rationality and motivations for the individual bomber vary widely and a range of emotions can be located in the explanations justifying their acts. These range from pride, anger, revenge, honor, and personal glory to frustration, humiliation, shame, and hopelessness (Singh 2012). However, the early scholarship that focused upon individual motivations not only tended to focus upon the psychology of individual bombers but also argued that organizational processes of coercion, recruitment, and indoctrination were instrumental in propelling the "suicide industry" or this so-called "culture of death" (Atran 2003; Berko and Erez 2005; Reuter 2006). In other words, although the focus of this research was purportedly on the individual perpetrators of suicide terrorism, the organization was still deemed as playing a much more critical role in promulgating suicide attacks than individual motivation. Even more recent work, categorized here as late second-generational literature on suicide terrorism for the sake of clarity, attempted to adopt a much more balanced approach by focusing on a range of individual motivations propelling individuals towards becoming suicide bombers (Moghadam 2003; Pape 2003; Bloom 2004, 2005). These works illustrate how the "desire for revenge, commitment to a political group, deep individual belief in nationalism or religion, and/or the desire to achieve immortality and capture material goods for the family can all motivate an individual to become a suicide bomber" (Singh 2011; see also Ganor 2001; Post et al. 2003; Kimhi and Even 2004; Bloom 2005). Now authors argued that suicide attacks fulfilled more than just strategic functions for the organization—they signaled higher levels of commitment to both the organization's own constituency and its enemies. Thus, they served as a powerful mechanism for recruiting future operatives as well as for attracting financial and moral support. The use of this tactic also served to draw international attention to the plight of a people forced to turn to such a radical tactic of confrontation. Several authors focused expressly on religion for its ability to legitimize this tactic and provide the critical tools of disengagement to individual perpetrators by successfully framing these attacks not as acts of suicide but as martyrdom and thus as a path to redemption. However, even these works tended to locate the primary impetus for suicide terrorism not with the individual perpetrator but in organizational motivations, thus continuing to subordinate individual motivations to organizational aims and ambitions. Individual choice continued to be depicted in these works as impulse, the consequence of a burst of emotion. Unfortunately, this meant that the rationality of the individual's choice of self-sacrifice remained either completely ignored or subordinated to the strategic rationality of the organization. In other words, these works implicitly accepted that either individual motivations were entirely devoid of rationality or if such a rationality existed then it was not as "means–ends" driven as that of the organization. As such, while this scholarship marked a break with first- and early second-generational literature, it still inevitably focused upon and privileged the instrumental (i.e. strategic) aspects of suicide terrorism, thereby ignoring its symbolic dimensions and functions. In sum, both early and late second-generational literature argued that organizational impetus and/or manipulation was necessary for the promulgation of suicide terrorism.

However, while certainly developing our overall understanding of suicide terrorism, this scholarship provided only a partial analysis of the phenomenon. For instance, it could not explain why suicide bombers in the Israeli–Palestinian conflict came to be either loosely affiliated or completely unaffiliated to political organizations by the time of the second intifada. Nor could these explanations account for the spike in Palestinians volunteering to participate in suicide missions and the concomitant drop in overall indoctrination and training undertaken by political groups operating in the Occupied Palestinian Territories in this period (Argo 2004, 2006). In short, these works could still neither explain the individual's drive for self-sacrifice nor what their martyrdom signified for themselves and the society they represented.

It was this gap that the third generation of suicide terrorism literature attempted to address. These works essentially focused upon unearthing the social meaning that martyrdom held for the perpetrators of suicide attacks. Hence, for the first time, suicide terrorism literature tended to ignore the role of the organization in order to focus more explicitly upon the individual perpetrator and the meaning(s) that they assigned to their self-sacrifice and martyrdom (Krueger and Maleckova 2002; Argo 2004; Khosrokhavar 2005; Hafez 2006b). In attempting to focus unambiguously on the bombers and their self-perception of their martyrdom these works fully contextualized the perpetrators of suicide terrorism in their very particular social, political, and cultural milieu. Consequently these authors not only acknowledged that the role of the organization in recruiting and indoctrinating suicide bombers may have been overstated in the previous scholarship but they also questioned if the perpetrators of these acts viewed "their actions through the same prism" as the political organizations that they were affiliated with (Singh 2011). Thus, for the first time, researchers began asking the critical question of whether or not individual perpetrators were motivated by the strategic effectiveness of martyrdom operations or if their primary motivation lay elsewhere, i.e. in nationalist, religious, or personal motivations. Thus, these scholars argued for looking "beyond instrumental rationality" (Hafez 2006b) and at the symbolic dimensions of suicide violence instead. However, in arguing that individual and organizational motivations and rationality cannot be conflated and advocating for looking "beyond rationality, into the realm of symbolic framings, to understand and explain, at least in part, why individuals become martyrs" (Hafez 2006a, 2006b), these studies simultaneously dispossessed individual motivations as well as the symbolic rationality of strategic functions (Perry and Hasisi 2015). Moreover, they tended to associate organizational motivation with instrumental rationality and individual motivations with symbolic rationality alone. In other words, they created a false dichotomy between strategic and symbolic rationality by implicitly rejecting that symbolic action could simultaneously serve an instrumental purpose, just as strategic action could be imbued with symbolic significance not only for the individual but also the organization.

It is this dichotomy that the fourth and final generation of suicide terrorism literature addresses. Although still in its formative stages, fourth-generation scholarship argues that organizational and individual rationality and motives are equally important in understanding the emergence and sustainability of suicide terrorism. Furthermore, this research refuses to disassociate individual motives from instrumental rationality and organizational motives from symbolic rationality. Instead it argues that suicide terrorism is both an act "of strategic expediency and practical reason as well as [an] act that [is] simultaneously symbolic, ritualistic and communicative" (Singh 2011, 2014). Violence when studied in purely utilitarian "means–ends" terms, not only disregards its cultural dimension but, by "inadvertently disassociating the problem of causes from that of function, also loses the wider context of violent action. In other words, a purely instrumental focus loses sight of what the practice of violence says or expresses" (Singh 2011). Simply put: why opt for a suicide attack when a remote-detonated car bomb could be wielded with equal ease and similar results? What does this choice of tactic reveal about the organization and the individual perpetrator? Violence is never totally idiosyncratic; it always says or expresses something. Hence, ignoring the ritual, symbolic, and communicative function of suicide terrorism whilst focusing solely on its strategic functions tells an incomplete story. Fourth-generation scholars thus make a case for reconceptualizing strategy "to incorporate the emotive, expressive and passionate character of political action" (Lahiri 2015). In other words, because a suicide attack is such a complex combination of symbolic and instrumental violence, this scholarship argues that it inherently incorporates within any single act not only a calculated strategic but also symbolic rationality that operates simultaneously at both the individual and organizational level of analysis (Singh 2011, 2014; Lahiri 2015).

Conclusion—Future Avenues of Research

As stated at the very beginning, although considerable scholarship has been produced around this topic, as yet we lack any real consensus on the defining elements of this concept as well as explanations for the same. What has become amply clear however is that suicide terrorism is a complex and multi-causal phenomenon that needs to be understood using multiple levels of analysis. More critically, given the differences and variations in suicide attacks, not only are general explanations insufficient but we clearly need to place the phenomenon in its very particular social, political, and cultural context(s). A key challenge lies in the absence of agreement around terminology and definition. The latter specifically results in what are essentially incompatible datasets and the resulting absence of a common standard also makes cross-case comparisons and analysis difficult. However, in addition to these broad challenges that continue to plague the study of suicide terrorism there are three clear areas which require urgent attention.

First, there is a clear recognition amongst those studying terrorism and political violence that we cannot fully understand the occurrence of violence and the conditions in which it becomes an option without understanding situations where it is patently absent (Chenoweth and Stephan 2011). This same logic needs to be extended to understanding the occurrence of suicide terrorism in any given environment. In other words, we need to understand why suicide attacks become an option in one conflict or for some groups but not others. There has been some preliminary work conducted in this area (Kalyvas and Sánchez-Cuenca 2005) but this requires more concentrated, systematic development.

Second, we know that no organization that utilizes suicide attacks uses them exclusively. Instead, suicide attacks are a part of an extensive toolkit that includes other violent, as well as often nonviolent, tactics. Consequently, we need more research that systematically compares suicide attacks to other violent and nonviolent tactics employed by the same group. Studying suicide and non-suicide attacks conducted by the same organization in a comparative manner would allow us to fully grasp when, why, and how suicide attacks become an attractive option for given groups. Furthermore, this would also allow us to determine if other violent and/or nonviolent tactics are eschewed in favor of suicide attacks by such groups over particular periods of time, as well as why this may or may not be so. Shedding light on such issues will also help us better appreciate the full range of differences and variations in the phenomenon of suicide terrorism as it exists both within groups as well as amongst different organizations that utilize this method of attack. In other words, this approach would enable us to contextualize the utility of suicide attacks in the group's overall strategy of resistance/engagement.

Third, we need concentrated study into understanding why the phenomenon of suicide terrorism disappears in particular conflicts. We have repeatedly seen in multiple cases how suicide attacks, despite being the tactic of choice for some time, still tend to disappear after a certain point. We need to better understand the causes behind this disappearance: is it founded in successful counterterrorism strategy? Is it the result of a loss of legitimacy on part of organizations utilizing this tactic? Is it because of a loss of momentum within social groups which provide volunteers for such attacks? Or is it some combination of all these factors and/or myriad other factors? More importantly, how can this understanding be exploited to better counter campaigns of suicide terrorism?

The answers to such questions are critical not only for augmenting our understanding of suicide terrorism but also because they have clear repercussions for policy. Understanding how organizations view the place and utility of suicide attacks in their overall strategy can allow governments to be better prepared to counter the threat posed by this tactic. Employing a "broad conception of the threat" (Crenshaw 2007) posed by suicide terrorism can also enable governments to respond in a more effective, resilient, and proportionate manner to what is essentially a dynamic menace. More critically, fully comprehending the lineage, longevity, as well as variations in suicide terrorism can equip governments to plan for, and better respond to, future iterations of this threat. We know that it is impossible to eradicate terrorism, and the same logic applies to incidences of suicide terrorism. Nonetheless, understanding is the first crucial step in managing a threat which, by all indications, promises to both evolve and endure for at least the immediate future.

Note

1. This section draws upon my previous work on the evolution of the literature on suicide terrorism, see Singh 2011.

References

Alakoc, B. P. (2015) "Competing to Kill: Terrorist Organisations versus Lone Wolf Terrorists," *Terrorism and Political Violence*, 29: 509–32.

Argo, N. (2004) "Understanding and Defusing Human Bombs: The Palestinian Case and the Pursuit of a Martyrdom Complex," Annual Meeting of the International Studies Association, Le Centre Sheraton Hotel, Montreal.

Argo, N. (2006) "Human Bombs: Rethinking Religion and Terror," *Audit of the Conventional Wisdom*, 1–6, available online at <https://cis.mit.edu/sites/default/files/images/Audit_Argo_HumanBombs.pdf>, 6–7.

Atran, S. (2003) "Genesis of Suicide Terrorism," *Science Magazine*, 299: 1534–9.

Berko, A., and E. Erez (2005) "Ordinary People and Death Work: Palestinian Suicide Bombers as Victimizers and Victims," *Violence and Victims*, 20: 603–23.

Biggs, M. (2005) "Dying without Killing: Self-Immolations, 1963–2002," in D. Gambetta (ed.), *Making Sense of Suicide Missions*. Oxford: Oxford University Press, 173–208.

Bloom, M. (2004) "Palestinian Suicide Bombings: Public Support, Market Share and Outbidding," *Political Science Quarterly*, 119: 61–88.

Bloom, M. (2005) *Dying to Kill: The Allure of Suicide Terror*. New York: Columbia University Press.

Chenoweth, E., and M. J. Stephan (2011) *Why Civil Resistance Works: The Strategic Logic of Non-Violent Conflict.* New York, Columbia University Press.

Coll, S. (2008) "Decoding Mumbai," *New Yorker,* Nov. 28, available online at<https://www.newyorker.com/news/steve-coll/decoding-mumbai> [Accessed Nov. 2017].

Crenshaw, M. (2007) "Explaining Suicide Terrorism: A Review Essay," *Security Studies,* 16: 133–62.

Davis, J. M. (2003) *Martyrs: Innocence, Vengeance, and Despair in the Middle East.* New York: St Martin's Griffin.

Ehrenfeld, R. (2002) "No Partner: Arafat cannot be Negotiated with," National Review Online, June 22, available online at <http://www.aish.com/jw/me/48893872.html> [Accessed Aug. 2018].

Fenton, B. (2001) "Most Hijackers 'Unaware it was a Suicide Mission,'" *Daily Telegraph,* Oct. 10, available online at <https://www.telegraph.co.uk/news/worldnews/northamerica/usa/1359040/Most-hijackers-unaware-it-was-suicide-mission.html> [Accessed Dec. 2017].

Gambetta, D., ed. (2005) *Making Sense of Suicide Missions.* New York: Oxford University Press.

Ganor, B. (2001) "Suicide Attacks in Israel," in B. Ganor (ed.), *Countering Suicide Terrorism: An International Conference.* Herzilya: The International Policy Institute for Counter-Terrorism (ICT), 134–45.

Goldney, R. D. (2014) "Time for Change: Homicide Bombers, Not Suicide Bombers," *Australian and New Zealand Journal of Psychiatry,* 48: 579–84.

Gunaratna, R. (2009) *Mumbai Investigation: The Operatives, Masterminds and Enduring Threat.* Madrid: UNISCI Discussion Papers.

Gupta, D., and K. Mundra (2005) "Suicide Bombing as a Strategic Weapon: An Empirical Investigation of Hamas and Islamic Jihad," *Terrorism and Political Violence,* 17: 573–98.

Hafez, M. (2006a) *Manufacturing Human Bombs: The Making of Palestinian Suicide Bombers.* Washington, DC, United States Institute of Peace.

Hafez, M. (2006b) "Dying to be Martyrs: The Symbolic Dimensions of Suicide Terrorism," in A. Pedahzur (ed.), *Root Causes of Suicide Terrorism: The Globalisation of Martyrdom.* London and New York: Routledge, 54–80.

Hafez, M. (2007) *Suicide Bombers in Iraq: The Strategy and Ideology of Martyrdom.* Washington, DC: USIP Press Books.

Hassan, N. (2001) "An Arsenal of Believers: Talking to the Human Bombs," *The New Yorker,* November 19, 2001.

Hoffman, B., and G. H. McCormick (2004) "Terrorism, Signalling and Suicide Attacks," *Studies in Conflict and Terrorism,* 27: 243–81.

Hopgood, S. (2005) "Tamil Tigers, 1987–2002," in D. Gambetta (ed.), *Making Sense of Suicide Missions.* Oxford: Oxford University Press, 43–76.

Israeli, R. (2003) *Islamikaze: Manifestations of Islamic Martyrology.* London: Frank Cass.

Johnson, N. (1982) *Islam and the Politics of Meaning in Palestinian Nationalism.* London: Kegan Paul International.

Kalyvas, S., and I. Sánchez-Cuenca (2005) "Killing without Dying: The Absence of Suicide Missions," in D. Gambetta (ed.), *Making Sense of Suicide Missions.* Oxford: Oxford University Press, 209–32.

Kaplan, E. H., A. Mintz, S. Mishal, and C. Samban (2005) "What Happened to Suicide Bombings in Israel? Insights from a Terror Stock Model," *Studies in Conflict and Terrorism,* 28: 225–35.

Khosrokhavar, F. (2005) *Suicide Bombers: Allah's New Martyrs.* London: Pluto Press.

Kimhi, S., and S. Even (2004) "Who are the Palestinian Suicide Bombers?," *Terrorism and Political Violence,* 16: 815–40.

Kobrin, N. H. (2010) *The Banality of Suicide Terrorism: The Naked Truth about the Psychology of Islamic Suicide Bombing.* Washington, DC: Potomac Books.

Kramer, M. (1998) "The Moral Logic of Hizballah," in W. Reich (ed.), *Origins of Terrorism: Psychologies, Ideologies, Theologies and States of Mind.* Washington, DC: Woodrow Wilson Center, 131–57.

Krueger, A. B., and J. Maleckova (2002) *Education, Poverty, Political Violence and Terrorism: Is there a Causal Link?* National Bureau of Economic Research (NBER) Working Paper Series.

Lahiri, S. (2015) "Choosing to Die: Suicide Bombing and Suicide Protest in South Asia," *Terrorism and Political Violence,* 27: 268–88.

Laqueur, W. (2005) "What Makes them Tick?," *Washington Post,* July 24, available online at<https://www.washingtonpost.com/archive/entertainment/books/2005/07/24/what-makes-them-tick/96273e25-3434-43a2-a61e-49aa4474adec/?utm_term=.cb93db578ed5> [Accessed Nov. 2017].

Merari, A. (1998) "The Readiness to Die and Kill: Suicidal Terrorism in the Middle East," in W. Reich (ed.), *Origins of Terrorism: Psychologies, Ideologies, Theologies and States of Mind.* Washington, DC: Woodrow Wilson Center, 192–207.

Merari, A. (2010) *Driven to Death: Psychological and Social Aspects of Suicide Terrorism.* Oxford: Oxford University Press.

Merari, A., et al. (2009) "Personality Characteristics of 'Self Martyrs'/'Suicide Bombers' and Organizers of Suicide Attacks," *Terrorism and Political Violence,* 22: 87–101.

Moghadam, A. (2003) "Palestinian Suicide Terrorism in the Second Intifada: Motivations and Organizational Aspects," *Studies in Conflict and Terrorism,* 26: 65–92.

Moghadam, A. (2006a) "Defining Suicide Terrorism," in A. Pedahzur (ed.), *Root Causes of Suicide Terrorism: The Globalisation of Martyrdom.* Abingdon: Routledge, 13–24.

Moghadam, A. (2006b) "Suicide Terrorism, Occupation, and the Globalization of Martyrdom: A Critique of 'Dying to Win,'" *Studies in Conflict and Terrorism,* 29: 707–29.

Moghadam, A. (2008/9) "Motives for Martyrdom: Al-Qaida, Salafi Jihad and the Spread of Suicide Attacks," *International Security,* 33: 46–78.

O'Rourke, L. A. (2009) "What's Special about Female Suicide Terrorism?," *Security Studies,* 18: 681–718.

Oliver, A. M., and P. F. Steinberg (2005) *The Road to Martyr's Square: A Journey into the World of the Suicide Bomber.* New York and Oxford: Oxford University Press.

Pape, R. A. (2003) "The Strategic Logic of Suicide Terrorism," *American Political Science Review,* 97: 343–61.

Pape, R. A. (2005) *Dying to Win: The Strategic Logic of Suicide Terrorism.* New York: Random House, Inc.

Pape, R. A., and J. K. Feldman (2010) *Cutting the Fuse: The Explosion of Global Suicide Terrorism and How to Stop it.* Chicago: University of Chicago Press.

Pedahzur, A. (2005) *Suicide Terrorism.* Cambridge: Polity Press.

Pedahzur, A., ed. (2006) *Root Causes of Suicide Terrorism: The Globalization of Martyrdom.* London: Routledge.

Perry, S., and B. Hasisi (2015) "Rational Choice Rewards and the Jihadist Suicide Bomber," *Terrorism and Political Violence,* 27: 53–80.

Post, J. M. (1998) "Terrorist Psycho-Logic: Terrorist Behaviour as a Product of Psychological Forces," in W. Reich (ed.), *Origins of Terrorism: Psychologies, Ideologies, Theologies and States of Mind.* Washington, DC: Woodrow Wilson Center, 29–40.

Post, J. M., et al. (2009) "The Psychology of Suicide Terrorism," *Psychiatry,* 72: 13–31.

Post, J. M., E. Sprinzak, and L. M. Denny (2003) "The Terrorists in their own Words: Interviews with 35 Incarcerated Middle Eastern Terrorists," *Terrorism and Political Violence*, 15: 171–84.

Reuter, C. (2006) *My Life is a Weapon: A Modern History of Suicide Bombing*. Princeton: Princeton University Press.

Rose, D. (2001) "Attackers did Not Know they were to Die," *Guardian*, Oct. 14, available online at<https://www.theguardian.com/world/2001/oct/14/terrorism.september111> [Accessed Sept. 2018].

Schweitzer, Y. (2001) "Suicide Terrorism: Development and Main Characteristics," in B. Ganor (ed.), *Countering Suicide Terrorism: An International Conference*. Herzilya: International Policy Institute for Counter-Terrorism, ICT, 75–85.

Sela, S. M. A. A. (2000) *The Palestinian Hamas: Vision, Violence and Coexistence*. New York: Columbia University Press.

Shay, S. (2004) *The Shahids: Islam and Suicide Attacks*. New Brunswick, NJ: Transaction Press.

Singh, R. (2011) *Hamas and Suicide Terrorism: Multi-Causal and Multi-Level Approaches*. London: Routledge.

Singh, R. (2012) "The Discourse and Practice of 'Heroic Resistance' in the Israeli–Palestinian Conflict: The Case of Hamas," *Politics, Religion and Ideology*, 13: 529–45.

Singh, R. (2014) "Suicide Bombers: Victims, Heroes or Martyrs?," in S. Scheipers (ed.), *Heroism and the Changing Character of War: Towards Post-Heroic Warfare?* London: Palgrave Macmillan, 251–67.

Strenski, I. (2003) "Sacrifice, Gift and the Social Logic of Muslim 'Human Bombers,'" *Terrorism and Political Violence*, 15: 1–34.

Unnithan, S. (2014) *Black Tornado: The Three Sieges of Mumbai 26/11*. New Delhi: Harper Collins.

Victor, B. (2003) *Army of Roses: Inside the World of Palestinian Women Suicide Bombers*. Pennsylvania, USA: Rodale Inc.

CHAPTER 29

THE STRATEGIC MODEL OF TERRORISM REVISITED

MAX ABRAHMS

Nobody disputes that terrorism is successful in some ways. Terrorism, by definition, captures attention and instills fear. If those are the measures of terrorist success, then the tactic has a 100 percent success rate. Terrorism is also undeniably effective at weakening economies by forcing governments to overreact and tourists to flee (Mueller 2006). It is also undisputable that terrorism can help groups to recruit among the already radicalized. Although even terrorist groups such as Islamic State have tiny membership sizes compared to nonviolent groups, terrorist violence can attract members away from organizational rivals, such as the more moderate al Nusra Front in Syria (see DeNardo 1985; Chenoweth and Stephan 2010; Abrahms 2015). The main debate is over the utility of terrorism as an instrument of coercion, that is, whether harming civilians helps non-state actors to obtain their demands by pressuring government concessions.

This debate has endured because the leading theory on terrorism has searched in vain for compelling empirical support. The conventional wisdom on terrorism is what I refer to as the Strategic Model of Terrorism (Abrahms 2008). This model posits that perpetrators of terrorism attack civilian targets because of the unmatched effectiveness in inducing government compliance (see e.g. Pape 2003, 2005; Kydd and Walter 2006; Lake 2002). Despite the prevalence of this theory within political science, empirical tests of it have rather consistently come up empty. Not only do remarkably few terrorists ever manage to achieve their political demands (Abrahms 2006), but the tactic of terrorism seems to lower the odds of achieving them (Abrahms 2012; Abrahms and Gottfried 2016). Rather than softening up governments into becoming more politically pliant, the attacks on civilians seem to empower hardliners most opposed to concessions. This disconnect between theory and practice raises what I call the puzzle of terrorism (Abrahms and Lula 2012), which is why non-state actors attack civilians given the poor political return.

The next three sections show how the strategic model of terrorism is stronger theoretically than empirically, raising new questions about why non-state actors engage in this tactic. The first section explains the intellectual origins of the strategic model and its allure as a theory for political scientists to understand terrorism. The second section examines the empirical basis of the strategic model. This section suggests that, despite the conceptual and methodological challenges of testing it, terrorism is generally an ineffective—even counterproductive—tactic for perpetrators to attain their demands. The third section explores the research implications if terrorism is indeed a suboptimal tactic for inducing government concessions contrary to the conventional wisdom.

How Terrorism Works in Theory

In theory, groups use terrorism because it helps them to achieve their demands. Nicholas Berry (1987, 7) reflects the conventional wisdom on terrorism, "If it did not produce [these] intended results... then it would cease to be a political strategy." In his 2002 best-seller, Alan Dershowitz (2002, 86) likewise contends that terrorism "works" and is thus "an entirely rational choice to achieve a political objective." David Lake (2002, 20) theorizes that terrorism is a "rational and strategic" tactic because it "enables terrorists to achieve a superior political bargain." Andrew Kydd and Barbara Walter (2006, 264) assert that terrorist groups are "surprisingly successful in their aims." Relatedly, Robert Pape (2003, 343) claims that "suicide terrorism has been rising largely because terrorists have learned that it pays," based on "reasonable assessments of the relationship between terrorists' coercive efforts and the political gains that the terrorists have achieved" (Pape and Feldman 2010, 61, 64–5). Though it is confined to suicide terrorism, his work is frequently cited as evidence that terrorism more generally is "effective in achieving a terrorist group's political aims" (see e.g. Kydd and Walter 2006, 49). These and many other prominent scholars subscribe to the strategic model of terrorism—the notion that aggrieved peoples adopt this tactic because it offers them the best chance to redress their grievances.

The strategic model is irresistible to so many political scientists not only because of its intuitive plausibility, but because it is based on bargaining theory within the field of international relations, which emphasizes how violence helps challengers to coerce concessions by lending credibility to their threats under anarchy. A product of the Cold War, bargaining theory has traditionally focused on conflict between states, not challenges to them from below. But since September 11, 2001, bargaining theorists have employed the same logic to explain the strategic value of violence for non-state actors as well.

Within bargaining theory, violence is thought to help challenger states achieve their given preferences (Byman and Waxman 2002, 10; Baldwin 2000, 104; Slantchev 2005, 533). Lake (2010) remarks: "As a general rule, the greater the violence threatened or inflicted by A (the coercer), the more likely B (the target) is to comply with A's demand. This is the dominant way in which power is conceived in international relations." Escalating with violence is believed to help challenger states coerce compliance by enhancing the credibility of their threats, in two broad ways. At their heart are Thomas Schelling's pioneering ideas on how escalation signals to the defender that the challenger is both willing and able to punish him for non-compliance.

First, bargaining theory explains how escalation adds credibility to threats by signaling that the challenger is resolved. In the 1960s, Schelling (1960, 1966) famously theorized that states possess private information about their commitment to winning a dispute. Because fighting is not cost-free, escalation separates bluffers from the truly committed. Spearheaded by Fearon (1994b, 1995) in the mid-1990s, a rich research program unlocks the strategic basis of escalation by developing stronger micro-foundations of the associated costs with waging, even threatening war. The most obvious costly signal of fighting is in blood and treasure; by depleting finite human and financial resources, warfare incurs "sunk costs" even for the triumphant. Escalation signals resolve to the extent it requires a party to sacrifice these endowments; the bigger the expected sacrifice, the greater his presumed interest in prevailing. Compared to economic sanctions, for instance, combat is registered in the literature as a more credible signal of resolve due to the elevated costs to the challenger (Morrow 1999; Powell 1987). Fighting not only inflicts human and financial tolls on challenger states, it also jeopardizes these endowments by what Schelling (1960, ch. 6) described as "leaving something to chance." Bargaining theorists have adopted this point to show how escalation adds credibility to threats by requiring states to cede control over the process and outcome of the conflict, generating an autonomous risk of ever costlier developments (see e.g. Powell 1990). Finally, an influential strain of bargaining theory expands Schelling's ideas on "audience costs" by revealing how escalation can accrue costs to challenger states from third parties independent of the defender. The relationship between escalation and costs is again positive, as Fearon (1994b, 580) explains: "The greater the escalation, the more humiliating the acquiescence, and the greater the audience's dissatisfaction." In these ways, bargaining theory highlights that there are multiple costs to challenger states for escalating, which demand resolve, enhance the credibility of their threats under anarchy, and thereby add pressure on defenders to relent.

Second, bargaining theorists highlight that escalation also lends credibility to threats by inflicting costs on the defender. Powell (1990, 7) and others demonstrate how under anarchy, "A state's punitive capability is its ability to inflict costs on an adversary." Conversely, restraint in a crisis leaves uncertain whether the challenger is capable of imposing costs on the defender for continued opposition (Walter 2009). Bargaining theory predicts that challenger states will gain coercive leverage by raising the costs of resistance; as rational actors, defenders are expected to become more pliant as their adversaries reveal heightened punishment capacity with larger amounts of pain (Lebow 1996). According to the standard rationalist narrative, coercion ultimately succeeds when the expected costs to the defender outstrip his interest in resisting the demand. As George (1991, 11) explains, "The central task of a coercive strategy is to create in the opponent the expectation of costs of sufficient magnitude to erode his motivation to continue what he is doing." Byman and Waxman (2002, 10) add: "Coercion should work when the anticipated suffering associated with a threat exceeds the anticipated gains of defiance." In sum, a key legacy of Schelling is that escalation helps to promote concessions by lending credibility to threats under anarchy with signs the challenger is both determined and able to punish for intransigence.

Since the September 11, 2001, attacks, many political scientists have applied the same bargaining framework to non-state actors, particularly those that escalate with terrorism (Berman and Laitin 2008; Kydd and Walter 2006; Lake 2002, Siegel and Young 2009). Like states, non-state actors operate in a competitive international arena of incomplete information, where they too have an incentive to overstate their threats to achieve their preferences. By escalating—in this case, against civilians—terrorists also inflict costs on themselves and the target that display their commitment and punishment capacity. In this manner, terrorists reveal the threat that they actually pose, raising pressure on targets to comply.

For non-state actors, the use of terrorism is unquestionably a credible signal of resolve based on the standard arguments in bargaining theory. Terrorist acts are certainly costly to perpetrators in blood and treasure compared to less extreme tactical options. In their historical investigation of protest, Erica Chenoweth and Maria Stephan (2010, 256–7) find: "Although nonviolent struggle is rarely casualty-free, the price of participating (and being caught) in armed struggle is often death. The likelihood of being killed while carrying out one's duties as an armed insurgent is high, whereas many lower-risk tactics are available to participants in a nonviolent resistance campaign." Indeed, scholars are nearly unanimous that compared to engaging in terrorism, nonviolent resistance invites less repression and physical dangers from the state. For this reason, violent protest is often analyzed as a collective action problem (see DeNardo 1985; Gould 1995; Weinstein 2007). Clearly, the high likelihood of expending terrorist members reveals their own commitment. Yet it also exhibits that of the larger organization from which they hail—one evidently prepared to sacrifice not only critical manpower, but the cadres whose resolve would have made them valuable in other key roles (Berman and Laitin 2008, 7). Such determined members are always in precious supply regardless of what leaders of these groups may say (DeNardo 1985). Gould (1995, 204) captures the essence of this point, "While activists might have little trouble persuading a casual acquaintance to sign a petition, they would have great difficulty convincing such a person to risk injury, death, or imprisonment." The moral repugnance of killing civilians drains the pool of potential terrorists, adding to the costs of losing even one (see Chenoweth and Stephan 2010, 255, and DeNardo 1985, 58). And naturally, the costs of utilizing terrorism include financial ones in terms of both conducting operations and bearing the response. In addition to these sunk costs for using terrorism, John Mueller's (2006) research details how adopting this tactic leaves something to chance by eliciting disproportionate government responses. The historical record is replete with aggrieved parties escalating with terrorism, knowing the additional pain to the target would boost the odds of paying a prohibitively steep price. In fact, it is often said terrorists attack not to coerce government compliance, but to provoke government overreaction (Fromkin 1975).

Such risk-taking requires undeniable commitment, as terrorists must be prepared to bear whatever form of retaliation the government metes out. Finally, non-state actors that employ terrorism are evidently willing to countenance the costs from other parties as well, namely audience costs. Perhaps more than any other tactic, terrorism offends constituencies beyond the target (Abrahms 2018). As Jeremy Weinstein (2007, 206) notes: "Undoubtedly, groups that deploy violence against noncombatants incur significant costs in consequence. Indiscriminate violence...damages the reputation of the group both within the country and outside of it." Because of all these costs to non-state actors as identified in bargaining theory, scholars agree that using terrorism enhances the credibility of their threats by revealing resolve (see e.g. Hoffman and McCormick 2004; Hultman 2005; Kydd and Walter 2006; Pape 2005; Weinstein 2007).

Terrorism also adds credibility to threats by showing that non-state challengers possess the power to hurt. Terrorism specialists acknowledge the difficulties in determining the resources of adversarial groups (Schmid and Jongman 1988, 488). For this reason, their tactics are likewise revealing. In comparison to terrorism, moderate tactics such as labor strikes, consumer boycotts, lock-downs, and sit-ins require little physical capability in terms of agility, stamina, or strength (Chenoweth and Stephan 2010, 254). Nor do such methods require arms, ammunition, explosives, or training to master them. Reliance on nonviolence therefore does not settle the crucial question under anarchy of whether the challenger poses a legitimate physical threat, whereas terrorism leaves no doubt he is capable of making the target pay (DeNardo 1985, 36). In recent years, researchers have carefully investigated the empirical relationship between organizational capabilities and terrorism. Terrorism is indeed a "weapon of the weak," but only in the sense that its practitioners are non-state actors and therefore less capable than their government foes (see Abrahms 2018). Abrahms (2006) and Gambetta (2005) show that the militant groups in their sample generally adopted terrorism when strongest. Asal and Rethemeyer (2008) reveal that membership size and other organizational resources are significant predictors of terrorist lethality. A case study on Al Qaeda illustrates this point by detailing how its production of terror peaked with organizational capacity (Eilstrup-Sangiovanni and Jones 2008). Conversely, Horowitz (2010, 37) shows that aggrieved groups sometimes want to use terrorism, but are too weak to muster attacks. In accordance with these empirics, formal models commonly use terrorism as a proxy for group capability, with greater lethality signaling additional punishment capacity (Lapan and Sandler 1993; Overgaard 1994).

When political scientists apply bargaining theory to terrorism, they naturally predict that the violence should help non-state actors to coerce government compliance. Kydd and Walter (2006, 59–60) maintain, "The greater the costs a terrorist organization is able to inflict, the more credible its threat to inflict future costs, and the more likely the target is to grant concessions." Pape (2003, 28) likewise contends that suicide terrorism "maximizes the coercive leverage." Hoffman and McCormick (2004, 250) also draw explicitly on bargaining theory, predicting that terrorist groups should gain "leverage at the bargaining table" in proportion to the lethality of their attacks. This bargaining process is frequently modeled, with governments modifying their posterior positions of whether to compromise based on the presumed resources of the perpetrators as reflected in the number of civilians killed (Lapan and Sandler 1993; Overgaard 1994). Mirroring the standard rationalist narrative applied to challenger states, defenders are expected to comply when the anticipated cost of the terrorist violence exceeds their interest in resisting the demands. As Pape (2005, 30) writes, terrorism succeeds by creating "mounting civilian costs to overwhelm the target state's interest in the issue in dispute and so to cause it to concede the terrorists' political demands." In the next section, however, I present growing empirical evidence, contra the predictions of the strategic model, that despite elevating the threats of non-state challengers, escalating against civilians tends to impede their bargaining success.

How Terrorism Fails in Practice

Empirically testing terrorism's coercive value is complicated by two broad sets of methodological challenges. The first pertains to coding the dependent variable. Historically, terrorism datasets have neglected to code the political outcomes of asymmetric campaigns, the standard unit for assessing the tactical value. Scholars testing the effectiveness of terrorism have themselves coded the political outcomes of the campaigns, inviting allegations of confirmation bias (Moghadam 2006; Rose et al. 2007; Chenoweth et al. 2009). Furthermore, scoring the extent to which terrorists accomplish their political ends is objectively difficult for reasons inherent to the complex nature of the challenger. Terrorists are notorious for issuing protean, ambiguous political demands or sometimes none at all (Schelling 1991; Stern 2003). Disagreement over terrorism's effectiveness can therefore hinge on mini-empirical disputes over whether the perpetrators accomplished their desired strategic goals. Alan Dershowitz (2002) and Robert Pape (2003), for example, maintain that terrorism works as illustrated by Palestinian political gains, whereas Max Abrahms (2006) and Assaf Moghadam (2006) score Palestinian terrorism as essentially a failure. Such dissension has likewise plagued the coding of whether Al Qaeda, its affiliates, the Irish Republican Army, its splinter groups, the Tamil Tigers, and their organizational rivals have realized their political goals, muddying assessments of terrorism's overall tactical value (Chenoweth et al. 2009; Rose et al. 2007). Adding to the confusion over coding the dependent variable is that terrorists may possess long time horizons (Lake 2002). Lashkar-e-Taiba, for example, has thus far failed in its stated mission of spreading Islamic rule throughout India. But the group may one day wrest control over Indian Kashmir. Although terrorist campaigns often persist for decades without any perceptible political return, this lengthy time frame is perhaps acceptable for those committed to the cause. Methodologically, scholars have dealt in an ad hoc way with these ongoing campaigns by excluding them from the analysis, which artificially drives up the coercion rate, or by including them in the analysis, driving down the coercion rate (see e.g. Pape 2003). Scoring political progress is also problematic if terrorists express unrealistic demands to obtain even a fraction of them. Indeed, terrorist groups tend to fall short of accomplishing their strategic demands, but may achieve some measure of progress in the form of partial government accommodation. An ordinal dependent variable can help capture such middling levels of bargaining success. Yet weighting the political outcomes inevitably introduces an element of subjectivity (Rose et al. 2007). To minimize such thorny methodological issues, economists normally use public opinion instead of policy outcomes as the dependent variable (Berrebi and Klor 2008; Gould and Klor 2010). The former is only an indirect proxy of the latter, however; when countries are terrorized, electorates may shift to the political left or right without altering policy.

The second set of methodological problems pertains to coding the independent variables, particularly terrorism versus other non-state tactics. At the conceptual level, scholars have developed a fine grained nomenclature to distinguish terrorism from other forms of resistance. European and North American scholars generally define terrorism as the use of violence by non-state actors against civilian targets in particular. When military personnel, security services, and other government officials are the ones physically harmed, the tactic is increasingly differentiated from terrorist acts as militant, guerrilla, or insurgent attacks in ascending degrees of specificity (Schmid and Jongman 1998). When nobody is physically harmed in the coercive incident, the tactic is usually differentiated as nonviolent resistance, direct action, or a failed terrorist plot in ascending degrees of extremeness (Chenoweth and Stephan 2011; Taylor 1998). Yet empirical tests of terrorism's coercive value have been far less specified and thus struggle to isolate the independent tactical effects.

Several scholars claim that terrorism helps to coerce government compliance, but proceed to highlight cases of asymmetric campaigns against military personnel that spared civilians (McCormick and Fritz 2010; Pape 2003, 2005). To substantiate their view that "terrorism often works," for example, Kydd and Walter (2006, 49) note how US Marines withdrew from Lebanon after their barracks were attacked in October 1983. The broader methodological difficulty is that non-state actors employ a hybrid of tactics, posing challenges for pinpointing their discrete effects. To exact political concessions from Israel, for instance, Fatah, Hamas, and Hezbollah have focused their violence on both the population and military, while concurrently underwriting anti-Zionist civil resistance initiatives. Teasing out the political consequences of such tactics can be difficult when employed in tandem.

Variation in their usage is also potentially problematic, however, if the tactics are not adopted at random, since that raises concerns of selection issues driving the political outcome. If non-state actors gravitate to terrorism when the prospects of victory appear dim, then its usage may be endogenous to political failure and thus epiphenomenal to the negative coercive return. Holding the strategic context fixed is the main methodological challenge of any coercion study, but is especially difficult if terrorism is a proverbial "weapon of the weak." In addition to the capabilities of non-state challengers, their strategic demands may also correlate with the use of terrorism or other tactics. Terrorism is an extremism of means, but its practitioners are also known to harbor extreme ends. Terrorists are notorious for issuing maximalist political goals that governments are loath to concede, such as for democracies to adopt communism or radical Islam as the national ideology (Abrahms 2006, 2012, 2013). Due to such confounds, researchers have struggled to isolate the independent effects of terrorism relative to tactical alternatives.

In fact, most studies on the efficacy of terrorism do not even compare the instrument to alternatives (Crenshaw 1988; Schelling 1991). Coercion studies offer limited analytical value when they do not evaluate a tactic relative to others (Baldwin 2000). Some studies compare terrorism to other methods, but to unrealistic ones. Pape (2003), for example, compares the political success rate of suicide terrorist campaigns to that of economic sanctions, even though sanctions are not a viable method for terrorist groups. Because effectiveness is intrinsically a relative concept, research on terrorism would benefit by systematically comparing the tactic to alternatives available to all perpetrators. In sum, empirically testing the coercive value of terrorism is methodologically challenging, requiring caution in both the creation and interpretation of these tests.

Perhaps for this reason, scholars have historically avoided them altogether. Crenshaw (1983, 5) has observed that "most analyses have emphasized the causes and forms rather than the consequences of terrorism." Gurr (1988, 125) added that terrorism's policy effectiveness is "a subject on which little national-level research has been done, systematically or otherwise." Across a variety of methodologies and disciplines, however, a growing body of empirical research concludes that attacking civilians is ineffective, even counterproductive, for groups to achieve their strategic demands. Terrorism may aid organizations in redressing their grievances under very specific conditions, but targeting civilians generally seems to carry substantial downside political risks. For decades, specialists have noted that terrorism rarely results in political success. In the 1970s, Laqueur (1976) published "The Futility of Terrorism" in which he claimed that practitioners seldom achieve their strategic demands. In the 1980s, Cordes, Hoffman, and Jenkins (1984, 49) observed that "terrorists have been unable to translate the consequences of terrorism into concrete political gains... In that sense terrorism has failed. It is a fundamental failure." Crenshaw (1988, 15) also pointed out how "few [terrorist] organizations actually attain the long-term ideological objectives they claim to seek, and therefore one must conclude that terrorism is objectively a failure." Schelling (1991, 20) proclaimed in the 1990s, "Terrorism almost never appears to accomplish anything politically significant." More recently, empirical studies confirm that only a handful of terrorist groups in modern history have managed to accomplish their political platforms (Abrahms 2006; Cronin 2009; Jones and Libicki 2008).

The tactic does not appear to be epiphenomenal to government intransigence. On the contrary, the latest wave of scholarship finds that escalating against civilians actually hinders non-state challengers from attaining their demands. To evaluate the political efficacy of terrorism, Abrahms (2012) exploits variation in the target selection of 125 violent non-state campaigns. Groups are significantly more likely to coerce government compliance when their violence is directed against military targets instead of civilian ones, even after controlling for the capability of the perpetrators, the nature of their demands, and other tactical confounds. Similarly, Page Fortna (2015) affirms that rebel groups lower the odds of bargaining success by attacking the population with terrorism. Anna Getmansky and Tolga Sinmazdemir (2012) find that the Israeli government in particular is significantly less likely to cede land to the Palestinians when they have perpetrated terrorism. Even in hostage settings, killing civilians lowers the chances of militant groups attaining government concessions such as financial ransoms or prisoner releases (Abrahms and Gottfried 2016).

Terrorism rarely frightens citizens of target countries into supporting more dovish politicians. Studies on public opinion find that attacks on civilians tend to raise popular support for right-wing leaders opposed to appeasing the terrorists. Berrebi and Klor (2008), for example, show that Palestinian terrorism boosts Israeli support for the Likud and other right-bloc parties. Gould and Klor (2010) reveal that the most lethal Palestinian terrorist attacks are the most likely to induce this rightward electoral shift. These trends appear to be the international norm. Chowanietz (2010) analyzes variation in public opinion within France, Germany, Spain, the United Kingdom, and the United States from 1990 to 2006. In each target country, terrorist attacks have shifted the electorate to the political right in proportion to their lethality. Related observations have been registered after Al Qaeda and its affiliates killed civilians in Britain, Canada, Egypt, Indonesia, Jordan, the Philippines, Russia, Turkey, and the United States (see e.g. Mueller 2006, 184, 587; Wilkinson 1986, 52). Controlled experiments reach similar results, further ruling out the possibility of a selection effect (Abrahms 2013). Berrebi (2009, 189) observes in a précis of the literature: "Terrorist fatalities, with few exceptions, increase support for the bloc of parties associated with a more intransigent position. Scholars may interpret this as further evidence that terrorist attacks against civilians do not help terrorist organizations achieve their stated goals." By bolstering hardliners, terrorist attacks are also among the most common ways for militant groups to end (Cronin 2009).

Research Implications

Clearly, the strategic model of terrorism is stronger theoretically than empirically. The model is intellectually rooted in bargaining theory within international relations, which posits how violence is strategic behavior by lending credibility to threats under anarchy. Although terrorism enhances the credibility of threats by non-state actors, the violence does not appear to further their political goals in terms of coercing government concessions. In fact, empirical studies on non-state actors rather consistently find that harming civilians carries substantial political risks for the perpetrators. This disconnect between terrorism in theory versus in practice invites future research exploration.

First, additional studies should investigate the effects of terrorism. The standard debate over whether terrorism works is reductive. Terrorism clearly works in some ways, but not others. Terrorist groups possess two kinds of goals—process goals and outcome goals. Process goals are intended to sustain the group by attracting media attention, scuttling organization-threatening peace processes, and boosting membership and morale, often by provoking government overreaction. The outcome goals of terrorists, by contrast, are their stated ends, such as the removal of foreign bases from Greece or the establishment of Islamism in India as the official ideology. An important difference between process goals and outcome goals is that unlike the former, the latter require the compliance of the target government. Evidence suggests that acts of terrorism are more effective in advancing process goals than outcome goals (see Abrahms 2008, 2012; Friedland and Kydd and Walter 2002; Mueller 2006), largely because countries tend to dig in their political heels in the face of terrorism. Future research should elucidate the conditions under which terrorist attacks pay, including as an instrument of coercion. Although anomalous, there are indeed salient historical cases in which terrorist attacks bucked the trend by successfully pressuring government concessions (Rose et al. 2007). These exceptions to the rule are important for understanding the rare conditions in which terrorists manage to successfully induce government compliance by attacking civilians.

Second, bargaining theorists should consider why terrorism lowers the odds of government compliance despite enhancing the credibility of non-state threats. Empirical research indicates that civilian targeting may be as politically counterproductive for governments as for non-state actors (see Downes 2007). This growing body of research suggests that bargaining theory is fundamentally flawed on the relationship between civilian escalation and compliance. Indeed, tests of bargaining theory have shown that it is not predictive (Abrahms 2013; Snyder and Diesing 1977).

Third, future research must align theories on terrorism with reality. This chapter highlights how the strategic model rests on a shaky empirical basis. The puzzle of terrorism is why groups attack civilians when doing so is generally politically counterproductive. Perhaps terrorists are irrational in the sense that they systematically overestimate the political value of civilian targeting (Abrahms and Lula 2012). Or perhaps their attacks against civilians are carried out for apolitical ends (Abrahms 2008; Abrahms and Potter 2015). Researchers must resolve why non-state actors attack civilians given the poor political return.

References

Abrahms, Max (2006) "Why Terrorism does Not Work," *International Security*, 31: 42–78.

Abrahms, Max (2008) "What Terrorists Really Want: Terrorist Motives and Counterterrorism Strategy," *International Security*, 32(4): 78–105.

Abrahms, M. (2012) "The Political Effectiveness of Terrorism Revisited," *Comparative Political Studies*, 45(3): 366–93.

Abrahms, Max (2013) "The Credibility Paradox: Violence as a Double-Edged Sword in International Politics," *International Studies Quarterly*, 57(4): 660–71.

Abrahms, Max (2015) "Why Terrorism Fails: A Discussion with Max Abrahms," Covert Contact, episode 16, available online at <http://covertcontact.com/2015/03/16/why-terrorism-fails-a-discussion-with-max-abrahms-episode-16>.

Abrahms, Max (2018) *Rules for Rebels: The Science of Victory in Militant History*. Oxford: Oxford University Press.

Abrahms, Max, and Karolina Lula (2012) "Why Terrorists Overestimate the Odds of Victory," *Perspectives on Terrorism*, 6: 4–5.

Abrahms, Max, and Matthew S. Gottfried (2016) "Does Terrorism Pay? An Empirical Analysis." *Terrorism and Political Violence*, 28(1):72–89.

Abrahms, Max, and Philip B. K. Potter (2015) "Explaining Terrorism: Leadership Deficits and Militant Group Tactics," *International Organization* 69(2): 311–42.

Asal, Victor, and R. Karl Rethemeyer (2008) "The Nature of the Beast: Organizational Structures and the Lethality of Terrorist Attacks," *Journal of Politics*, 70: 437–49.

Baldwin, David A. (2000) "The Sanctions Debate and the Logic of Choice," *International Security*, 24: 80–107.

Berman, Eli, and David D. Laitin (2008) "Religion, Terrorism and Public Goods: Testing the Club Model," *Journal of Public Economics*, 92: 1942–67.

Berrebi, Claude (2009) "The Economics of Terrorism and Counterterrorism: What Matters and is Rational-Choice Theory Helpful?," in Paul K. Davis and Kim Cragin (eds), *Social Science for Counterterrorism: Putting the Pieces Together*. Santa Monica, CA: RAND. pp. 151–208.

Berrebi, Claude, and Esteban F. Klor (2008) "Are Voters Sensitive to Terrorism: Direct Evidence from the Israeli Electorate," *American Political Science Review*, 102: 279–301.

Berry, Nicholas O. (1987) "Theories on the Efficacy of Terrorism," *Journal of Conflict Studies*, 7(1).

Byman, Daniel, and Matthew Waxman (2002) *The Dynamics of Coercion: American Foreign Policy and the Limits of Military Might*. New York: Cambridge University Press.

Chenoweth, Erica, and Maria J. Stephan (2010) "Mobilization and Resistance: A Framework for Analysis," in Erica Chenoweth and Adria Lawrence (eds), *Rethinking Violence: States and Non-State Actors in Conflict*. Cambridge, MA: MIT Press pp. 249–75.

Chenoweth, Erica, and Maria J. Stephan (2011) *Why Civil Resistance Works: The Strategic Logic of Nonviolent Conflict*. New York: Columbia Press.

Chenoweth, Erica, et al. (2009) "What Makes Terrorists Tick," *International Security*, 33(4): 180–202.

Chowanietz, Christophe (2010) "Rallying around the Flag or Railing Against the Government? Political Parties' Reactions to Terrorist Acts," *Party Politics*, 2: 111–42.

Cordes, Bonnie, Bruce Hoffman, Brian Michael Jenkins, et al. (1984) *Trends in International Terrorism, 1982 and 1983*. Santa Monica, Calif: RAND.

Crenshaw, Martha (1988) "The Logic of Terrorism: Terrorist Behavior as a Product of Strategic Choice," in Walter Reich (ed.) *Origins of Terrorism: Psychologies, Ideologies, Theologies, States of Mind*. Washington, DC: Woodrow Wilson Center Press pp. 7–24.

Crenshaw, Martha, ed. (1983) *Terrorism, Legitimacy, and Power: The Consequences of Political Violence*. Middletown, CT: Wesleyan University Press.

Cronin, Audrey Kurth (2009) *How Terrorism Ends*. Princeton: Princeton University Press.

DeNardo, James (1985) *Power in Numbers: The Political Strategy of Protest and Rebellion*. Princeton: Princeton University Press.

Dershowitz, Alan (2002) *Why Terrorism Works: Understanding the Threat, Responding to the Challenge*. New Haven, CT: Yale University Press.

Downes, Alexander B. (2007) "Draining the Sea by Filling the Graves: Investigating the Effectiveness of Indiscriminate Violence as a Counterinsurgency Strategy," *Civil Wars*, 9(4): 420–44.

Eilstrup-Sangiovanni, Mette, and Calvert Jones (2008) "Assessing the Dangers of Illicit Networks: Why Al-Qaida may be Less Threatening than Many Think," *International Security*, 33: 7–44.

Fearon, James (1995) "Rationalist Explanations for War," *International Organization*, 29: 379–414.

Fearon, James (1994b) "Domestic Political Audiences and the Escalation of International Disputes," *American Political Science Review*, 88: 577–92.

Fortna, Virginia Page (2015) "Do Terrorists Win? Rebels' Use of Terrorism and Civil War Outcomes," *International Organization*, 69(3): 519–56.

Fromkin, David (1975) "The Strategy of Terrorism," *Foreign Affairs*, 53(4): 683–98.

Gaibulloev, Khusrav, and Todd Sandler (2009) "Hostage Taking: Determinants of Terrorist Logistical and Negotiation Success," *Journal of Peace Research*, 46: 739–56.

Gambetta, Diego (2005) "Can we Make Sense of Suicide Missions?," in Diego Gambetta (ed.), *Making Sense of Suicide Missions*. Oxford: Oxford University Press, 259–99.

George, Alexander (1991) *Forceful Persuasion: Coercive Diplomacy as an Alternative to War*. Washington, DC: United States Institute of Peace.

Gould, Eric D., and Esteban F. Klor (2010) "Does Terrorism Work?," *Quarterly Journal of Economics*, 125: 1459–1510.

Gould, Roger V. (1995) *Insurgent Identities: Class, Community, and Protest in Paris from 1848 to the Commune*. Chicago: University of Chicago.

Gurr, Ted Robert (1988) "Empirical Research on Political Terrorism," in Robert O. Slater and Michael Stohl (eds), *Current Perspectives on International Terrorism*. New York: St Martin's 115–27.

Hoffman, Bruce, and Gordon H. McCormick (2004) "Terrorism, Signaling and Suicide Attack," *Studies in Conflict and Terrorism*, 27: 243–81.

Horowitz, Michael C. (2010) "Nonstate Actors and the Diffusion of Innovations: The Case of Suicide Terrorism," *International Organization*, 64: 33–64.

Horowitz, Michael, and Dan Reiter (2001) "When does Aerial Bombing Work?," *Journal of Conflict Resolution*, 45: 147–73.

Hultman, Lisa (2005) "Killing Civilians to Signal Resolve: Rebel Strategies in Intrastate Conflicts," paper presented at the annual meeting of the American Political Science Association, Sept. 3 Washington, DC.

Jones, Seth, and Martin Libicki (2008) *How Terrorist Groups End: Lessons for Countering Al-Qaeda*. Santa Monica, CA: RAND.

Kydd, Andrew, and Barbara F. Walter (2002) "Sabotaging the Peace: The Politics of Extremist Violence," *International Organization*, 56: 263–96.

Kydd, Andrew, and Barbara F. Walter (2006) "The Strategies of Terrorism," *International Security*, 31: 49–80.

Laqueur, Walter (1976) "The Futility of Terrorism," *Harper's*, 252(1510): 99–105.

Lake, David A. (2002) "Rational Extremism: Understanding Terrorism in the Twenty-First Century," *Dialogue-IO*, 1: 15–29.

Lake, David A. (2010) "Authority, Coercion, and Power in International Relations," paper presented at the Annual Meeting of the American Political Science Association, Sept. 2–5, Washington, DC.

Lapan, Harvey E., and Todd Sandler (1993) "Terrorism and Signaling," *European Journal of Political Economy*, 9: 383–97.

Lebow, Richard Ned (1996) "Thomas Schelling and Strategic Bargaining," *International Journal*, 51: 555–76.

McCormick, Gordon, and Lindsay Fritz (2010) "Is Suicide Terrorism an Effective Tactic?," *Debating Terrorism and Counterterrorism: Conflicting Perspectives on Causes, Contexts, and Responses*, 366–93.

Moghadam, Assaf (2006) "Suicide Terrorism, Occupation, and the Globalization of Martyrdom: A Critique of Dying to Win," *Studies in Conflict and Terrorism*, 29: 707–29.

Morrow, James D. (1999) "The Strategic Setting of Choices: Signaling, Commitment, and Negotiation in International Politics," in David Lake and Robert Powell (eds), *Strategic Choice in International Relations*. Princeton: Princeton University Press, 77–93.
Mueller, John (2006) *Overblown: How Politicians and the Terrorism Industry Inflate National Security Threats and Why we Believe Them*. New York: Free Press.
Overgaard, Per Baltzer (1994) "The Scale of Terrorist Attacks as a Signal of Resources," *Journal of Conflict Resolution*, 38: 452–78.
Pape, Robert A. (1996) *Bombing to Win: Air Power and Coercion in War*. Ithaca, NY: Cornell University Press.
Pape, Robert A. (2003) "The Strategic Logic of Suicide Terrorism," *American Political Science Review*, 97: 243–361.
Pape, Robert A. (2005) *Dying to Win: The Strategic Logic of Suicide Terrorism*. New York: Random House.
Pape, Robert A., and James K. Feldman (2010) *Cutting the Fuse: The Explosion of Global Suicide Terrorism and How to Stop it*. Chicago: University of Chicago Press.
Powell, Robert (1987) "Crisis Bargaining, Escalation, and MAD," *American Political Science Review*, 81: 717–35.
Powell, Robert (1990) *Nuclear Deterrence Theory: The Search for Credibility*. Cambridge: Cambridge University Press.
Rose, William, Rysia Murphy, and Max Abrahms (2007) "Correspondence: Does Terrorism Ever Work? The 2004 Madrid Train Bombings," *International Security*, 32: 185–92.
Schelling, Thomas C. (1960) *The Strategy of Conflict*. Cambridge, MA: Harvard.
Schelling, Thomas C. (1966) *Arms and Influence*. New Haven, CT: Yale University Press.
Schelling, Thomas C. (1991) "What Purposes Can International Terrorism Serve?," in Raymond Gillespie Frey and Christopher W. Morris (eds), *Violence, Terrorism, and Justice*. New York: Cambridge University Press, 32–43.
Schmid, Alex P., and Albert Jongman (1988) *Political Terrorism: A New Guide to Actors, Authors, Concepts, Data Bases, Theories and Literature*. New Brunswick, NJ: Transaction Books.
Siegel, David A., and Joseph K. Young (2009) "Simulating Terrorism: Credible Commitment, Costly Signaling, and Strategic Behavior," *PS: Political Science and Politics*, 42: 765–71.
Slantchev, Branislav L. (2005) "Military Coercion in Interstate Crises," *American Political Science Review*, 99: 533–47.
Snyder, Glenn H., and Paul Diesing (1977) *Conflict among Nations: Bargaining, Decision Making, and System Structure in International Crises*. Princeton: Princeton University Press.
Stern, Jessica (2003) "The Protean Enemy," *Foreign Affairs*, 27–40.
Taylor, Bron (1998) "Religion, Violence and Radical Environmentalism: From Earth First! to the Unabomber to the Earth Liberation Front," *Terrorism and Political Violence*, 10: 1–42.
Walter, Barbara F. (2009) "Bargaining Failures and Civil War," *Annual Review of Political Science*, 12: 243–61.
Weinstein, Jeremy (2007) *Inside Rebellion: The Politics of Insurgent Violence*. New York: Cambridge University Press.
Wilkinson, Paul (1986) *Terrorism and the Liberal State*. New York: New York University Press.

PART VII

ISSUES AND PEDAGOGICAL CHALLENGES

CHAPTER 30

THE RISE AND FALL OF TERRORISM

SUSAN FAHEY AND ERIN MILLER

Introduction

The dynamics of terrorism are a product of many inter-related mechanisms involving individual, regional, and global processes. Rather than taking place in a vacuum, patterns of terrorism are woven into broader geopolitical, social, and economic landscapes, and terrorist violence often occurs in the context of other types of conflict and violence. As a result, interpreting the rise and fall of terrorism and drawing implications for policy and theory is difficult. Here we discuss the scholarly literature that considers these mechanisms, and we examine key examples of specific contexts in which terrorism has increased and decreased in recent history. First, however, we acknowledge the challenges associated with measuring increases and decreases in terrorism.

Measuring Terrorism

Understanding the rise and fall of terrorism requires comprehensive, systematically collected data, and there are numerous challenges associated with collecting such data. Terrorism is violent. It is sometimes clandestine and difficult to classify. In some cases, terrorism is destructive to the same institutions upon which we rely to document controversial and volatile events. In sum, those seeking to comprehensively capture information about terrorism face many obstacles (LaFree et al. 2015).

Although official sources of data on terrorism do exist, certain limitations of official data have led many analysts to leverage event data derived from media sources (LaFree and Dugan 2004). Open source data collection efforts rely on attacks to be observed, reported by journalists, published by media outlets, accessed by data collectors, and determined by analysts to satisfy definitional requirements of a terrorist attack. Each of these steps introduces potential for data collection strategies or practices that may influence the resulting data and analytical inferences. As a result, any data collection effort will fail to perfectly represent the universe of terrorist attacks, and it is important for observers to be aware of the implications of measurement challenges, particularly for studying changes in terrorism over time (LaFree et al. 2015). Among the most important methodological challenges to be aware of in the context of a discussion of the rise and fall of terrorism are (1) access to source materials, (2) technology, and (3) the links between terrorism and other forms of political violence.

Access to Source Materials

The distribution and accessibility of open source media is not uniform across time or place; rather it is linked to variations in factors such as freedom of the press, government regime type, and economic development. Countries that are more open and economically developed typically have more independent media outlets than those in the developing world or those with more authoritarian governments (Stier 2015; Guseva et al. 2008). The extent to which information on global terrorism is comprehensive and complete depends on these factors. For example, the premise that information about terrorism is more thoroughly reported in more developed and more politically open countries has important implications for interpreting the relatively infrequent occurrence of recorded terrorist attacks in certain autocratic states, such as the Soviet Union and North Korea (LaFree et al. 2015). This result may reflect a real pattern—that autocratic states do experience fewer terrorist attacks than democratic states because of greater government control over the conduct of citizens (Fahey and LaFree 2015). However, it is also important to consider the possibility that this pattern is partly due to the scarcity of reliable reporting in more autocratic states due to restrictions on press freedom (Drakos and Gofas 2006).

Likewise, because greater population density allows perpetrators of terrorism to maximize harm and intimidation, it is reasonable to expect terrorist attacks to be more common in large cities than in suburban or rural areas. However, it is also plausible that disproportionate media coverage of terrorist attacks that occur in urban areas artificially exaggerates this pattern. If events that take place in urban locations are more likely to be recorded in widely accessible print media, and information about events in rural areas is less well preserved, our understanding of geography and terrorism dynamics may be distorted.

Some measurement issues are specifically relevant to the violent nature of terrorism and media coverage in especially volatile conflicts, particularly with regard to tracking attacks over time. For example, terrorist violence in countries with relatively poor coverage from international media may be subject to severe under-reporting until the conflict escalates to the point where violence against civilians captures the attention of international observers, or once locally oriented perpetrator groups evolve and become part of a broader global network of geopolitical salience.

However, the impact of violent conflict on media coverage is not straightforward. Large-scale conflicts may attract media coverage, thereby increasing the likelihood that journalists pay attention to and report terrorist attacks. On the other hand, terrorist attacks that take place in the context of violent conflict may be less likely to come to light, because it is unsafe for reporters to report from areas where fighting is particularly intense. Reporters have been targeted for imprisonment, kidnapping, and murder in certain conflict zones (Reporters Without Borders 2016), making access to reliable information on the rise and fall of terrorism scarce. For example, against the backdrop of the Syrian civil war, less than one-fifth of attacks reported in Syria between 2012 and 2015 were documented by media sources judged to be relatively independent and unbiased (according to Global Terrorism Database analysts).[1]

In countries where terrorist violence is relatively rare, attacks are more likely to be documented extensively in the media. Sources often report detailed information on fatalities and injuries, the identity and background of the perpetrator, the weapons and tactics used, and long-term outcomes. Contrast the level of detail involved in the reporting of an event like the September 11 attacks in the United States, which experiences relatively few terrorist attacks, to coverage of events in countries that sometimes experience dozens of terrorist attacks per day, such as in Iraq (National Consortium for the Study of Terrorism and Responses to Terrorism (START) 2016a). In locations that suffer a high volume of terrorist activity, attack details are typically far sparser. Media fatigue may even lead to less severe acts of violence going unreported (Gerner and Schrodt 1998).

Technology

Once the media document terrorist violence, the next obstacle is getting source documents to analysts. With the advent and growth of the internet, obtaining information on any topic has become much easier, as has processing large amounts of text for analysis. Initially, collectors of many open source databases of terrorist attacks relied on hard copies of newspaper clippings, news wires, and reports by governmental or non-governmental organizations. Analysts manually processed and organized these documents (LaFree 2007). As media companies began to publish and archive articles on the internet, efforts to find and catalog reports of terrorist attacks evolved to take into account new technologies. Access to information has expanded greatly, making it much easier to obtain information about patterns of terrorism. However, these advances presented challenges as well, particularly with respect to managing the sheer volume of potentially relevant articles (Jensen 2013).

Consider, for example, the collection of the Global Terrorism Database (GTD). The GTD is the most comprehensive event-level database on terrorism around the world, including more than 170,000 events between 1970 and 2016. The rapid growth of the internet makes it easier for information from around the globe to be aggregated and disseminated widely (LaFree et al. 2015). Automated strategies for processing source articles make it much easier to manage this large volume of content in order for analysts to identify reports of terrorist attacks. Analyzing the number of attacks over time can result in problematic inferences if one fails to consider the fact that increases and decreases reflected in terrorism data are a product of both actual changes in real-world phenomena and the evolution of the many processes by which data are produced. The issues of source document availability and the impact of technological advances are exceedingly complex and interrelated, so accounting for them is not simple.

Terrorism versus Other Types of Political Violence

There are few clear-cut boundaries between terrorism and other forms of violence, such as insurgency, genocide, civil war, and violence by states (sometimes considered "state terrorism"). For example, rebel organizations that are belligerents in civil war have been identified as perpetrators of attacks in the Global Terrorism Database (Center for Systemic Peace 2015; National Consortium 2016b). While definitions of insurgency and civil war traditionally involve attacks intended to destabilize and overthrow governments as well as targeting military and law enforcement (Forst 2009; Merari 1993), definitions of terrorism can be relatively narrow, including only attacks targeting civilians (Sandler 2015; Wigle 2010), or more broad and inclusive of attacks on combatant targets (LaFree et al. 2015).

By adopting narrower definitions of terrorism, the risk is that the universe of attacks considered does not reflect the full context of violence carried out by politically or ideologically motivated actors. Given broader definitions, analysts may conflate substantively distinct processes that lead to different types of violence, like terrorism and insurgency, for different reasons. In doing so, one might produce problematic conclusions about policy implications or, given the moral connotations of the word "terrorism," one might unfairly impugn the character of ideologically motivated actors who limit the use of violence to combatant adversaries. However, as Merari (1993) asserted, armed groups often do not exclusively choose one strategy or the other; rather, they may use several forms of political violence as circumstances dictate.

This definitional and real-world ambiguity has important implications for understanding the rise and fall of terrorism. For example, the dynamics of terrorism, including the rate of increase or decrease, the severity, and the duration of terrorist campaigns, may differ across time and place due to other types of violence taking place. Likewise, rapid decreases in reports of terrorism narrowly defined may not be indicative of national security "success" in contexts where other types of violence such as civil war, genocide, or authoritarian rule or even war crimes by state actors have supplanted terrorist violence.

Empirical Literature on the Rise and Fall of Terrorism

Rapoport (2004) hypothesized that the rise and fall of terrorism over time was governed by the rise and fall in popularity of various ideologies of political thought and terrorist organizations in the modern era. He categorized the rise and fall of different ideologies of terrorism over time from the 1880s until the current day into four waves of terrorism: the anarchist wave, the anti-colonial wave, the New Left wave, and the religious wave. He described a wave as a cycle of terrorist activity in a given time period, estimated to be about forty years, or approximately the length of an adult life. The early part of the wave is characterized by its spread and the later part of the wave is characterized by its contraction.

Rapoport further clarified that waves are international in nature, sweeping up individuals in different countries, but united by a common energy that drives the emergence of different terrorist organizations united by similar ideologies. For example, he categorized the third wave of terrorism, from the 1960s until the 1980s, as the New Left wave. This wave saw the emergence of groups around the world whose ideologies included both traditional Marxism, such as Fuerzas Armadas Revolucionarias de Colombia (FARC) in Colombia, and vaguely Marxist ideologies that were tailored by the organization to their surroundings, such as the Weather Underground's anti-imperialist, anti-corporatist, and pro-civil rights agenda in the United States. According to Rapoport (2004), waves spread via media communications from terrorist organizations and others who embrace the ideology and increasingly accessible international travel. When the wave was no longer able to inspire the formation of new terrorist organizations, it would dissipate. Rapoport (2004) predicted that if the current wave—religious terrorism—follows the pattern established in prior waves, it will die off around 2025.

Several scholars have used a statistical modeling technique known as Group-Based Trajectory Analysis (GBTA) to better understand the rise and fall of terrorism (LaFree et al. 2010; LaFree et al. 2009; Miller 2012). GBTA is a descriptive technique that allows analysts to cluster units of analysis (e.g. individuals, organizations, or countries) into discrete categories based on the similarity of their dynamics over time. For example, LaFree et al. (2010) used GBTA to examine the rise and fall of terrorism at the country level and demonstrated significant variability in the rise and fall of terrorism over time and place. Specifically, with data for more than 200 countries from 1970 to 2006 they found that country-level patterns of terrorism were best summarized by five relatively distinct trajectories of growth and decline. The most remarkable trajectory group included only ten countries, but accounted for nearly 40 percent of all attacks over the entire series. This group of countries experienced increasing or stable but high levels of terrorism throughout virtually the entire series. These locations included Colombia, France, India, Israel, Northern Ireland (analyzed separately from Great Britain), Pakistan, Russia, Spain, Sri Lanka, and Turkey.

LaFree et al. (2010) also observed a group of twenty-one countries that were characterized by a pattern of steady increase in attacks through the 1970s and 1980s, a period of elevated attacks, and a steady decline in terrorist attacks by the 2000s. This group accounted for 38 percent of attacks, and the countries in question were home to terrorist organizations that had been very active in the early years of the series but had declined in activity by the end.

In contrast, a trajectory group that included only ten countries, such as Afghanistan, Bangladesh, and Indonesia, experienced extremely low levels of terrorism from 1970 until about 1999, at which point terrorist attacks in this set of countries rapidly increased, with 60 to 160 annual attacks from 2000 until 2006. Overall, the authors observed rapidly increasing levels of terrorism in many countries in South and Southeast Asia, the Middle East, and Africa, a pattern that continued in the years to follow (National Consortium 2016a).

LaFree et al. (2009) used GBTA to examine the rise and fall of terrorist organizations over time. Specifically, they modeled the activity of fifty-three foreign terrorist organizations identified as a threat to the United States by the US Department of State. According to the GTD, the fifty-three organizations were attributed responsibility for 16,916 terrorist attacks from 1970 to 2004. Yet, only 3 percent of the 16,916 attacks targeted the United States. Furthermore, 99 percent of those attacks targeted US interests in foreign countries, such as American embassies and corporations.

For the anti-American attacks carried out by this sample of organizations, the trajectory analysis produced four separate and sequential waves of terrorist activity, with three of the four waves remaining largely limited to a particular decade. For example, the 1970s wave included 22.4 percent of the terrorist organizations, and these attacks were concentrated in the 1970s, peaking in 1974 and essentially decreasing to zero attacks by 1980. Two of the organizations best represented by this wave were Black September and the Red Brigades. The 1980s wave represented 29.3 percent of the organizations, including Dev Sol and Hezbollah, increasing rapidly in the 1980s, peaking in 1990 and ending by 1995. The 1970s and 1980s waves constituted nearly 90 percent of the attacks against US interests. The twenty-first-century wave constituted 4.3 percent of the organizations and was concentrated in the latter 1990s with a rapid increase by the end of the series in 2004. The two organizations in this wave were Al Qaeda and the Taliban. The final trajectory represented a sporadic pattern of activity, which best characterized 44 percent of the perpetrator groups and very low levels of activity throughout the entire observation period.

While LaFree et al. (2009) analyzed patterns of activity among terrorist organizations from a historical perspective, Miller (2012) examined the rise and fall of terrorist organizations over the course of their "lives." Specifically, she applied GBTA to patterns of desistance among 557 terrorist organizations whose activity spanned at least one year between 1970 and 2008. Even among the 557 organizations which lasted a year, the majority of organizations never committed terrorist attacks at a high rate. Further, she found that organizations that emerged and started attacking at a high rate quickly relative to when they started are two to three times more likely to accumulate moderate or high levels of attacks per year. Rapid onset was found to be a risk factor for an overall moderate or high rate of activity.

The majority of organizations upon reaching a peak of activity continued on to a rapid desistence. Very few organizations, only 20 percent of the sample, persisted over a lengthy time period; such organizations included the Provisional Irish Republican Army (IRA), the FARC, the National Liberation Army of Colombia (ELN), and Basque Fatherland and Freedom (ETA). Finally, high-attack-rate, high-volume organizations were more likely to persist over a long period, rather than decline rapidly.

While these statistical analyses of terrorism leverage large amounts of data to illustrate broad patterns, a great deal of research has also examined individual- and group-level mechanisms that are ultimately likely to produce such patterns. For example, scholars across disciplines have suggested that factors such as grievance and relative deprivation are important contributors to an individual's decision to engage in collective violence such as terrorism (Baumgartner 1984; Black 2004; Gurr 1970, 2011; Senechal de la Roche 1996; Smelser 1963). However, others argue that grievance alone is insufficient, and identify organizational mobilization—the capacity of an (aggrieved) group to garner resources and take action in support of a common goal—as a more salient contributor (Crenshaw 1987, 2001; Rule 1988; Tilly, 1978). Finally, scholars including Horgan (2009) and Sageman (2004) suggest that interpersonal relationships are critically important to understanding why individuals engage in and disengage from terrorism, which may in turn contribute to the rise and fall of terrorism by influencing organizational formation and decline.

Diversity of Trajectories—Country Patterns

To illustrate some of the diverse contexts in which terrorism has increased and decreased in recent history, we compare patterns of terrorist attacks and deaths resulting from terrorist attacks in the United Kingdom and Spain; Colombia, Peru, and El Salvador; and Iraq and Afghanistan. We chose these locations because they represent different within-continent comparisons, time periods, tactics, and ideological conflicts. As we will describe, these locations are also among those that have suffered the most from terrorist violence at various times in the past five decades. Bearing in mind the strengths and limitations of open source data on terrorist attacks, we leverage the GTD to present baseline statistics describing patterns of terrorism in these countries.

United Kingdom and Spain

Between 1970 and 2016 more than half (51 percent) of all terrorist attacks in Western Europe and more than two-thirds (70 percent) of all deaths resulting from terrorist attacks took place in the United Kingdom and Spain (National Consortium 2016b). As shown in Figure 30.1, terrorism in the United Kingdom and Spain during this period was most severe in the early part of the series, significantly declining by the early to mid-1990s. In both countries, the violence was largely a product of major geopolitical, nationalist conflicts: the Irish republican movement and Loyalist factions, which catalyzed a period known as "The Troubles" in the United Kingdom, and the Basque nationalist movement in Spain.

Both conflicts began long before 1970 and were rooted in lengthy conflicts in which ethnicity (in the case of the Basque region) and religion (in the case of Northern Ireland) intersect with transnational territorial claims. In particular, the Catholic republican

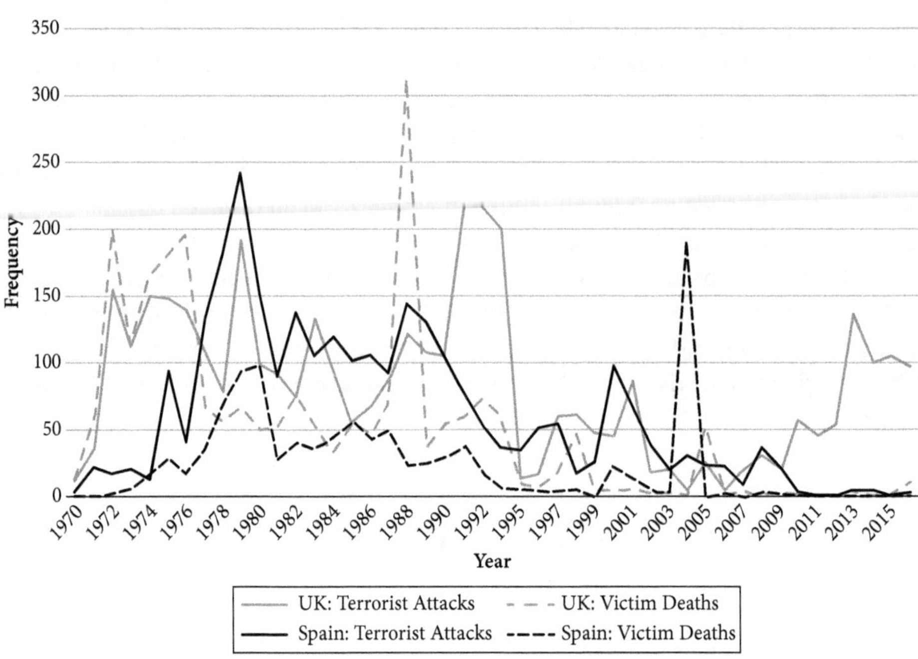

FIGURE 30.1 Terrorist attacks and deaths in the United Kingdom and Spain, 1970–2016
Source: Global Terrorism Database

movement sought to remove British control over Northern Ireland and to reunify it with the independent Republic of Ireland, while a Protestant loyalist counter-movement fought for Northern Ireland to remain unified with the United Kingdom. Likewise, the Basque nationalist-separatist movement sought to establish an independent state in the Basque region of Spain and France.

In the 1960s key organizations associated with these movements emerged and increasingly began using terrorist violence in an effort to achieve their goals. In the United Kingdom these groups most predominantly included the Provisional Irish Republican Army (PIRA), as well as various loyalist groups such as the Ulster Volunteer Force (UVF) and the Ulster Freedom Fighters (UFF), and associated rivals, factions, and offshoots on both sides of the conflict (O'Duffy, 1995). Between 1970 and 1998—during The Troubles—approximately 90 percent of terrorist attacks and deaths resulting from terrorist attacks in the United Kingdom were attributed to perpetrators engaging in this conflict (National Consortium 2016b).

Similarly, participants in the Basque nationalist-separatist conflict carried out two-thirds of terrorist attacks and were responsible for two-thirds of fatalities from terrorist attacks in Spain between 1970 and 2010. Other movements engaging in violence in Spain during this time period included the anti-fascist movement, the Catalan nationalist-separatist movement, and the Canary Islands independence movement (National Consortium 2016b).

In the United Kingdom and Spain, domestic conflicts were the primary driver of overall terrorist violence; however, international terrorist attacks impacted both countries as well.

In some cases these attacks were exceptionally deadly, such as the 1988 bombing of Pan American Flight 103 over Lockerbie, Scotland, which killed 270 people. And in 2004 and 2005, Islamist extremists carried out mass-casualty coordinated attacks against public transportation targets in Madrid and London, respectively (National Consortium 2016b).

Although patterns of terrorism in the mid-1970s and 1980s were similar in the United Kingdom and Spain, the patterns of decline in these countries were markedly different. As illustrated in Figure 30.1, the number of terrorist attacks in the United Kingdom peaked in the early 1990s, followed by a sharp decline by 1995. In contrast, the number of terrorist attacks in Spain peaked in 1979 and declined much more gradually.

By 1994 in the Northern Ireland conflict, peace talks had begun between the British government and the Irish republicans and a concomitant decrease in violence was evident in attacks by the next year with a sudden and rapid decrease in attacks observed by 1995. This depression in the level of attacks would largely continue through the adoption of the Good Friday Agreement in 1998, which is largely credited with ending active hostilities in this conflict (British Broadcasting Corporation 2017).

Although terrorism linked to the Irish republican conflict did decline rapidly at the end of the 1990s, the United Kingdom experienced a resurgence in the number, but not the lethality of terrorist attacks in the twenty-first century as violence carried out by groups like the New Irish Republican Army, Oglaigh na hEireann, and dissident republicans not affiliated with a particular organization increased (National Consortium 2016b).

In Spain, the Basque conflict declined dramatically by the mid-1990s. This was likely due to the loss of support after the killing of Miguel Angel Blanco and the resulting law enforcement operations to take out members of the organization (Aizpeolea 2017). By 2011, the organization had announced an end to its armed struggle (Goodman 2011); the level of terrorist attacks in Spain decreased to near zero by the cessation of hostilities (National Consortium 2016b).

Latin America: Colombia, Peru, and El Salvador

The story of Latin American terrorism is largely one of leftist terrorist organizations, such as the FARC, using political violence to attempt to overthrow governments with revolutionary aspirations of ruling those countries with a leftist political agenda (see Figure 30.2). In response, the governments of those countries often used violence directly against the organizations and civilians or via so-called grassroots, rightist, and government-loyal organizations, such as the Autodefensas Unidas de Colombia (AUC) in Colombia or some of the many death squads in operation during the Salvadoran civil war (National Consortium 2016b; Betancur et al. n.d.).

Columbia

In Colombia, terrorist attacks were relatively rare until the mid-1970s when there was a steady increase that continued to the series peak in 1997. Many of the attacks in the latter 1970s were attributed to the many leftist groups there, including the FARC, the National Liberation Army of Colombia (ELN), and the M-19 (Movement of April 19).

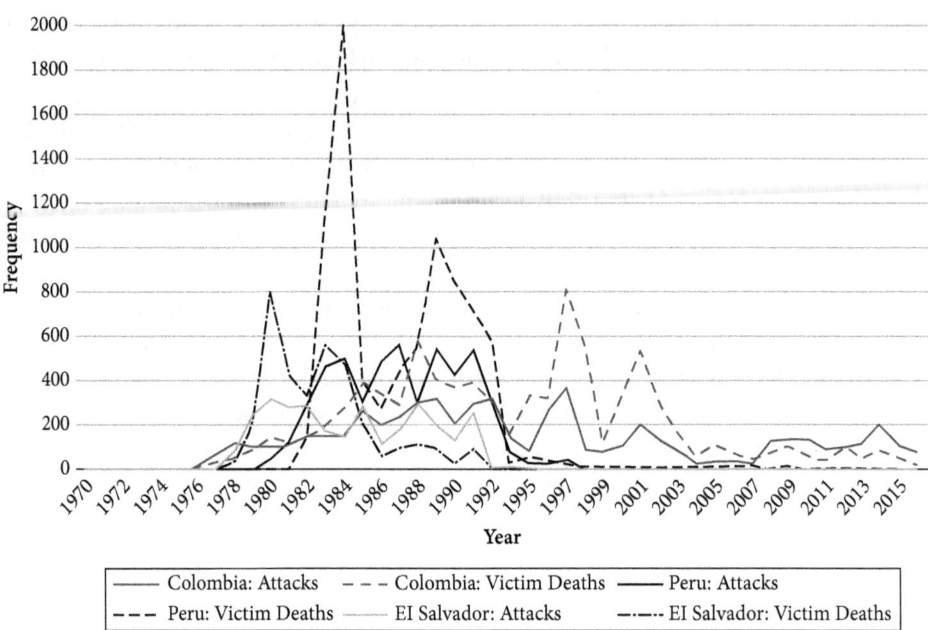

FIGURE 30.2 Terrorist attacks in Colombia, Peru, and El Salvador, 1970–2016

Source: Global Terrorism Database

These organizations, FARC most prominently, used political violence against government and civilian targets in efforts to overthrow the Colombian government and replace it with a communist regime (National Consortium 2016b).

By 1992, terrorist attacks in Colombia ranged between 300 and 500 attacks per year before a major decline in 1995, followed by another rapid increase to 600 attacks in 1997. By the following year, attacks declined and stayed at a much lower rate through the rest of the series.

In the latter years of the conflict, the chief non-government, right-wing rival to the FARC was the AUC, though they attacked in the 1990s and the 2000s at a much lower rate than FARC (National Consortium 2016b). In more recent years, the FARC have been accused of using kidnapping and drug trafficking not only to finance operations but largely as a replacement for other operations against the government. Some have questioned whether the group should even be classified as a terrorist organization any more, rather referring to them as an organized criminal network. Whether the organization continues to hold the leftist ideology upon which their name was made is an open question (Sanderson 2004). However, in 2017 the United Nations certified that over 7,000 FARC rebels had turned over their weapons in a historic peace agreement with the Colombian government (Brodzinsky 2017).

Peru

Terrorist attacks in Peru were virtually non-existent in open source reporting until about 1980 when there was a sudden, rapid increase in terrorist violence. Terrorism in

Peru remained at far elevated levels, vacillating abruptly between 175 and nearly 600 annual attacks for the next twelve years. In Peru, the main terrorist organization was a leftist group attempting to overthrow the right-wing government there, known as Sendero Luminoso or Shining Path. In fact, 4,500 of the 6,075 attacks (74 percent) reported in the GTD for Peru from 1970 to 2016 were attributed to this organization (National Consortium 2016b). A less active group with similar goals was the Tupac Amaru Revolutionary Movement (MRTA).

By 1994, attacks in Peru drastically declined and remained low, with far fewer than 100 annual attacks, until the end of 2016. The timing of this drastic decline aligns with a major strategic setback for Sendero Luminoso. In September 1992, the Peruvian police captured and imprisoned the infamous leader of the organization, Abimael Guzman, along with some other members of the organization. Although the organization does still exist and even conducted attacks as recently as 2017, it never rose above the loss of Guzman or successfully filled the power vacuum left when he was captured. Thus, terrorist activity in Peru vastly decreased and stayed low once state intervention decapitated Sendero Luminoso (National Consortium 2016b; Brooke 1992).

El Salvador

As with Peru, terrorist attacks in El Salvador were largely concentrated in time. In fact, as the UN-commissioned Truth Commission Report noted in the early 1990s (Betancur et al. n.d.), attacks quickly escalated in the early years of the Salvadoran civil war, plateaued to more moderate levels midway throughout the war, and declined rapidly by the ending of that war (National Consortium 2016b).

The civil war in El Salvador was largely between the Farabundo Marti National Liberation Front (FMLN) and the right-wing government of the country. The FMLN were a left-wing group, which formed after a violent crackdown of leftist oppositionist groups in the late 1970s. The FMLN formed a coalition of other groups in 1980 and advocated the overthrow of the government and its replacement with a communist regime.

With respect to terrorist attacks, 3,330 of 5,520 attacks (60 percent) in El Salvador from 1970 to 2014 were attributed to the FMLN. Many of the other attacks were recorded as unknown perpetrators or right-wing death squads. As documented by the Truth Commission, the government itself was responsible for the vast majority of the approximately 75,000 deaths recorded during the war. Death squads were sometimes formally affiliated with the government and wealthy land/business owners while others may have been only loosely affiliated with the government (Betancur et al. n.d.). There were also documented cases of the government—particularly the army—committing atrocities and attempting to frame the FMLN.

By 1991, the war waned, and in January 1992, the Chapultepec Peace Accord was in place, officially ending the hostilities between the FMLN and the sitting Salvadoran government. Terrorist attacks largely followed the pattern of the civil war, increasing at the creation of the FMLN and waning dramatically by the signing of the peace accords. Interestingly, FMLN would eventually become a legitimate political group and win the presidency in the twenty-first century (*The Economist* 2017).

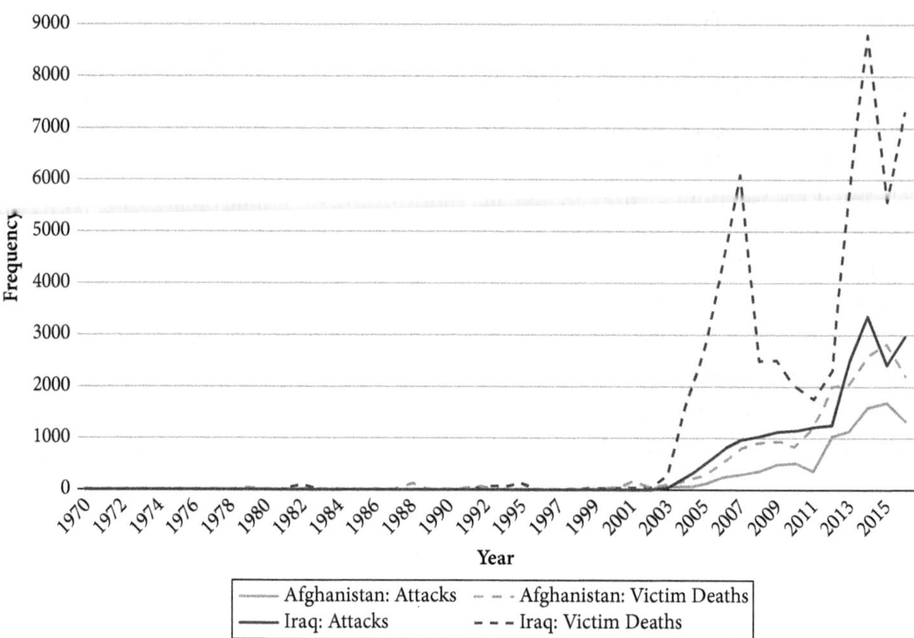

FIGURE 30.3 Terrorist attacks over time in Afghanistan via the Global Terrorism Database

Source: Global Terrorism Database

Afghanistan and Iraq

Afghanistan

Terrorism in Afghanistan follows a different trajectory over time than any of the countries discussed thus far, despite the fact that Afghanistan has suffered decades of internal conflict and civil war. Levels of terrorism remained low there until the insurgency by the Taliban and others against the occupation by the US-led coalition intensified in the mid-2000s. After this point, terrorism levels began a steady and even dramatic increase over time (National Consortium 2016b). (See Figure 30.3.)

Afghanistan in the 1970s was governed under a largely autocratic regime (Center for Systemic Peace 2016). As is typical with autocratic regimes, terrorist attacks were low during this period, likely as a combination of lack of media reports of attacks as well as actually low levels of terrorism. Following the Marxist revolution in 1978 and the Soviet invasion in 1979, terrorist attacks remained low during this period, despite an asymmetric anti-occupation struggle against the Soviet Union that included a US-backed resistance movement known as the mujahedin. This low level of terrorism during the Soviet occupation may be related as much to lack of reporting as to actually low levels of terrorism (National Consortium 2016b).

After the ousting of Soviet forces, Afghanistan devolved into a full-scale civil war. The country struggled to establish a unified and stable government until the Taliban fully eliminated challengers and took de facto control over the state in 1998. Terrorism remained low after the civil war, despite state violence against civilians. After the 9/11 attacks, the United States led a NATO intervention of Afghanistan, invading the country to topple the Taliban and eliminate Al Qaeda and its affiliates there. Terrorist attacks then began a distinct but slow increase during the initial years of the invasion. However, by 2006, terrorist attacks edged up to nearly 300 that year and continued a fairly steady rise thereafter. By 2012, attacks had increased to over nearly 1,500. This is largely demonstrative of the vigorous Taliban insurgency regaining strength and fighting with renewed vigor against civilians to destabilize the fragile Afghan government. Terrorist attacks, largely by the Taliban, continued at a high rate until the end of the series in 2016 (National Consortium 2016b).

Iraq

Terrorism in Iraq remained very low during most of the series. During the early years, this was likely a reflection of the level of control exerted by the Iraqi government, eventually formally led by the autocratic Saddam Hussein, and diminished reporting capabilities in autocratic states (Center for Systemic Peace 2016). Interestingly, terrorism remained low during the first American-led war in Iraq (Gulf War I). However, by 2004, the year after the invasion of Iraq by US-led forces, terrorist attacks began a nearly monotonic ascent, reaching greater than 1,000 annual attacks by 2007, greater than 2,500 attacks in 2013, and ending the series in 2016 with approximately 3,000 attacks (National Consortium 2016b).

The main perpetrators in the Iraq conflict have evolved. Early on in the conflict, Al Qaeda in Iraq (AQI) was a frequent perpetrator, representing the formal affiliate organization of Al Qaeda in the state of Iraq. Over time, this group came to be known as the Islamic State of Iraq (ISI). In 2013 the organization exploited state collapse in Syria due to its civil war to sweep into Iraq and conquer significant swaths of territory, rebranding itself yet again as the Islamic State of Iraq and the Levant/Syria (ISIL/ISIS). Upon the seizure of Mosul in 2014, ISIL leader Abu Bakr al Baghdadi declared a renewed Islamic Caliphate with himself as the Caliph, claiming to hold authority over all the world's Muslims (Withnall 2014).

ISIL is well-known for particularly attention-getting and violent attacks, such as the burning of a Jordanian pilot, crucifixions, stonings, and throwing members of the LGBTQ community off rooftops to kill them, and the beheadings of religious and political enemies (Perez 2017; Moore 2017a; CNN 2015). Further, ISIL has, at times, posed a realistic threat to the fragile Iraqi government, and carried out attacks in Western countries, including the deadly 2015 attacks on cultural targets in Paris and the assault on the Brussels airport in 2016 (BBC 2015; Moore 2017b). ISIL has also served as inspiration through its media outreach programs to individuals in the West who carried out violence in the name of the organization, including the mass shooters in San Bernardino, CA, and Orlando, FL, in the United States, and assailants who carried out deadly vehicle attacks in France, Germany, the United Kingdom, and the United States, among other locations (Malsin 2016; Ryan et al. 2015; Yan 2018). The United States and other states have engaged the organization in airstrikes and other activities in an attempt to decrease its territory and, ultimately, destroy it. Given its wide-reaching appeal and its territory, it is probable that terrorism by the organization—especially in Iraq—may remain high for the foreseeable future.

Conclusion

In this chapter, we illustrated that the rise and fall of terrorism is not a singular phenomenon. We discussed the ways in which data collection methodology can affect our understanding of the dynamics of terrorism by reflecting variation in access to source materials, changing technology allowing for more efficient dissemination and extraction of information, and finally, on the potential links between terrorism and other forms of political violence. We presented the literature on how terrorism varied over time, country, and organization. Finally, we analyzed how terrorism levels changed over time in several key regions: the United Kingdom and Spain; Colombia, Peru, and El Salvador; and Iraq and Afghanistan. In this analysis, we considered how the conflicts there changed over time and how those conflicts drove the rise and fall of terrorism in those states. The trends in these locations illustrate the diversity of mechanisms in which terrorism increases and decreases. However, in general, we find tentative support for Rapaport's (2004) claim that terrorism occurs in waves—and that all waves come to an end.

Note

1. This statistic comes from the Global Terrorism Database project's internal Data Management System maintained by the National Consortium for the Study of Terrorism and Responses to Terrorism (START) at the University of Maryland. More information about how the reliability of source materials impacts data collection can be found in the GTD Codebook, National Consortium 2017, 8.

References

Aizpeolea, L. R. (2017) "The Day that Basque Terror Group ETA Lost the Support of the Street," *El Pais*, July 12.

Baumgartner, M. P. (1984) "Social Control from Below," in *Toward a General Theory of Social Control*, i New York: Academic Press.

Betancur, Belisario, Reinaldo Figueredo Planchart, and Thomas Buergenthal (n.d.) *From Madness to Hope: The 12-Year War in El Salvador*. Report of the Commission on the Truth for El Salvador, available online at <https://www.usip.org/sites/default/files/file/ElSalvador-Report.pdf>.

Black, D. (2004) "Terrorism as Social Control," in M. Deflem (ed.), *Terrorism and Counter-Terrorism: Criminological Perspectives*. Amsterdam and London: JAI, 9–18.

British Broadcasting Corporation (BBC) (2015) "Paris Attacks; What Happened on the Night." Dec. 9.

British Broadcasting Corporation (BBC) (2017) "The Troubles: Thirty Years of Conflict in Northern Ireland," available online at <http://www.bbc.co.uk/history/troubles>.

Brodzinsky, S. (2017) "'Welcome to Peace': Colombia's FARC Rebels Seal Historic Disarmament," *Guardian*, June 27, available online at <https://www.theguardian.com/world/2017/jun/27/colombia-farc-weapons-war-government>.

Brooke, J. (1992) "Fugitive Leader of Maoist Rebels is Captured by the Police in Peru," *New York Times*, Sept. 14.

Center for Systemic Peace (2015) "Political Instability Task Force". [Dataset].

Center for Systemic Peace (2016) "Polity IV". [Dataset].

CNN (2015) "ISIS Video Appears to Show Beheadings of Egyptian Coptic Christians in Libya," Feb. 6, available online at <http://www.cnn.com/2015/02/15/middleeast/isis-video-beheadings-christians/index.html>.

Crenshaw, M. (1987) "Theories of Terrorism: Instrumental and Organizational Approaches," *Journal of Strategic Studies*, 10(4): 13–31.

Crenshaw, M. (2001) "Theories of Terrorism: Instrumental and Organizational Approaches," in D. C. Rapoport (ed.), *Inside Terrorist Organizations*. London and Portland, OR: F. Cass, 13–31.

Drakos, K., and A. Gofas (2006) "The Devil you Know But are Afraid to Face: Underreporting Bias and its Distorting Effects on the Study of Terrorism," *Journal of Conflict Resolution*, 50(5): 714–35.

Fahey, S., and G. LaFree (2015) "Does Country-Level Social Disorganization Increase Terrorist Attacks?," *Terrorism and Political Violence*, 27: 81–111.

Forst, B. (2009) *Terrorism, Crime and Public Policy*. New York: Cambridge University Press.

Gerner, D. J., and P. A. Schrodt (1998) "The Effects of Media Coverage on Crisis Assessment and Early Warning in the Middle East," in S. Schmeidl and H. Adelman (eds), *Early Warning and Early Response*. New York: Columbia University Press and Columbia International Affairs Online, 1–7.

Goodman, A. (2011) "Basque Group ETA Announces End to Campaign of Violence," CNN, Oct. 21.

Gurr, T. R. (1970) *Why Men Rebel*. Princeton: Princeton University Press.

Gurr, T. R. (2011) "Why Men Rebel Redux: How Valid are its Arguments 40 Years On?", available online at <http://www.e-ir.info/2011/11/17/why-men-rebel-redux-how-valid-are-its-arguments-40-years-on>.

Guseva, M., M. Nakaa, A. S. Novel, K. Pekkala, B. Souberou, and S. Stouli (2008) *Press Freedom and Development*. Paris: UNESCO, available online at <http://unesdoc.unesco.org/images/0016/001618/161825e.pdf>.

Horgan, J. (2009) *Walking Away from Terrorism: Accounts of Disengagement from Radical and Extremist Movements*. Abingdon and New York: Routledge.

Jensen, M. (2013) "Discussion Point: The Benefits and Drawbacks of Methodological Advancements in Data Collection and Coding: Insights from the Global Terrorism Database," available online at <https://www.start.umd.edu/news/discussion-point-benefits-and-drawbacks-methodological-advancements-data-collection-and-coding>.

LaFree, G. (2007) "Introducing the Global Terrorism Database," *Terrorism and Political Violence*, 19: 181–204.

LaFree, G., and L. Dugan (2004) "How does Studying Terrorism Compare to Studying Crime?," in Mathieu Deflem (ed.), *Criminology and Terrorism*, Oxford: Elsevier, 53–74.

LaFree, G., L. Dugan, and E. Miller (2015) *Putting Terrorism in Context*. New York: Routledge.

LaFree, G., N. Morris, and L. Dugan (2010) "Cross-National Patterns of Terrorism: Comparing Trajectories for Total, Attributed and Fatal Attacks, 1970–2006," *British Journal of Criminology*, 50: 622–49.

LaFree, G., S. M. Yang, and M. Crenshaw (2009) "Trajectories of Terrorism," *Criminology and Public Policy*, 8(3): 445–73.

Malsin, J. (2016) "What to Know about ISIS's Role in the Orlando Shooting," *Time*, June 13, available online at <http://time.com/4365507/orlando-shooting-isis-claims-responsibility-terror>.

Merari, A. (1993) "Terrorism as a Strategy of Insurgency," *Terrorism and Political Violence*, 4: 213–51.

Miller, E. (2012) "Patterns of Onset and Decline among Terrorist Organizations," *Journal of Quantitative Criminology*, 28: 77–101.

Moore, J. (2017a) "First LGBT Unit 'Created to Fight ISIS' in Syria. Its Name? The Queer Insurrection," *Newsweek*, July 27.

Moore, J. (2017b) "ISIS Suicide Bombers at Brussels Airport 'Targeted US Airline, Jews,'" *Newsweek*, Jan. 24.

Nagin, D. S. (2005) *Group-Based Modeling of Development*. Cambridge, MA: Harvard University Press.

National Consortium for the Study of Terrorism and Responses to Terrorism (START) (2016a). "Annex of Statistical Information". College Park, MD: START.

National Consortium for the Study of Terrorism and Responses to Terrorism. (2016b). "Global Terrorism Database" [Dataset], available online at <https://www.start.umd.edu/gtd>.

National Consortium for the Study of Terrorism and Responses to Terrorism (2017) "GTD: Codebook: Inclusion Criteria and Variables". College Park, MD: START.

O'Duffy, B. (1995) "Violence in Northern Ireland 1969–1994: Sectarian or Ethnonational?," *Ethnic and Racial Studies*, 18: 740–73.

Perez, C. (2017) "Jordanian Pilot had No Idea ISIS was about to Burn Him Alive," *New York Post*, Feb. 11.

Rapoport, D. C. (2004) "The Four Waves of Modern Terrorism," in K. Cronin and J. M. Ludes (eds), *Attacking Terrorism*. Washington, DC: Georgetown University Press, 46–73.

Reporters Without Borders (2016) "Violations of Press Freedom Barometer," available online at <https://rsf.org/en/barometre?year=2016>.

Rule, J. B. (1988) *Theories of Civil Violence*. Berkeley, CA: University of California Press.

Ryan, M., A. Goldman, A. Phillip, and J. Tate (2015) "Both San Bernadino Attackers Pledged Allegiance to the Islamic State, Officials Say," *Washington Post*, Dec. 8.

Sageman, M. (2004) *Understanding Terror Networks*. Philadelphia: University of Pennsylvania Press.

Sanderson, T. M. (2004) "Transnational Terror and Organized Crime: Blurring the Lines," *SAIS Review*, 24: 49–61.

Sandler, T. (2015) "Terrorism and Counterterrorism: An Overview," *Oxford Economic Papers*, 67(10): 1–20.

Senechal de la Roche, R. (1996) "Collective Violence as Social Control," *Sociological Forum*, 11: 97–128.

Smelser, N. (1963) *Theory of Collective Behavior*. New York: Free Press.

Stier, S. (2015) "Democracy, Autocracy and the News: The Impact of Regime Type on Media Freedom," *Democratization*, 22: 1273–95.

The Economist (2017) "Unhappy Anniversary: El Salvador Commemorates 25 Years of Peace," Jan. 21, available online at <https://www.economist.com/news/americas/21715065-country-needs-new-peace-accord-el-salvador-commemorates-25-years-peace>.

Tilly, C. (1978) *From Mobilization to Revolution*. Reading, MA: Addison-Wesley Publ. Co.

Wigle, J. (2010) "Introducing the Worldwide Incidents Tracking System (WITS)," *Perspectives on Terrorism*, 4: 3–23, available online at <http://www.terrorismanalysts.com/pt/index.php/pot/article/view/88/html>.

Withnall, A. (2014) "Iraq Crisis: ISIS Declares its Territories a New Islamic State with 'Restoration of Caliphate in Middle East,'" *Independent*, June 30.

Yan, H. (2018) "Vehicles as Weapons: Muenster Part of a Deadly Trend," *CNN*, Apr. 7, available online at <https://www.cnn.com/2017/03/22/world/vehicles-as-weapons/index.html>.

CHAPTER 31

FINANCING TERRORISM

HAROLD A. TRINKUNAS

On September 28, 2001, the United Nations Security Council, by adopting resolution 1373, took the unusual step of mandating the broad criminalization of terrorism financing by all member states under its Chapter VII authority (Rosand 2003). Since then, advocates for counterterrorism financing policies around the world have claimed broad success by pointing to the decline in the frequency of large-scale international terrorist attacks in the developed world such as those that afflicted London in 2005, Madrid in 2004, Bali in 2002, and New York and Washington in 2001. They believe that financial and material resources are the lifeblood of terrorist organizations and that interrupting these flows has the potential to degrade terrorist capabilities (Zarate 2013). This chapter provides a more tempered view, outlining how changes in the international regime to counter terrorism finance have altered incentive structures around terrorist fundraising, fund transfers, and spending, and the impact this has had on the broader phenomenon of terrorism globally.

The changes implemented post-9/11 were not the first time that shifts in global governance have affected the underlying pattern of terrorism finance. International conditions in the Cold War and post-Cold War periods also had significant impacts on the ability of terrorist organizations to raise, move, and spend money. In addition, the increasing globalization of trade and finance wrought its own effects on the relative costs and benefits of different approaches to both financing and combatting terrorism. Trends in terrorism finance and state responses suggest that policies implemented since 9/11 have affected the risk reward calculus of terrorist organizations in ways that initially displaced large-scale terrorist acts from the developed world to the developing world in places such as Syria, Iraq, Libya, Nigeria, the Philippines, and southern Thailand. The relative "hardening" of the developed world against terrorist financing and the increasing sophistication of counterterrorism financing measures in formal economies and financial networks may create incentives to shift large-scale terrorism financing towards lower risk jurisdictions. In the developed world, financiers for terrorist organizations adopted lower risk strategies, such as using small amounts of funding to avoid financial thresholds that would lead banks to alert authorities to suspicious activities, self-funding through engaging in criminal activity, or drawing on savings from formal employment. In the developing world, terrorist organizations face lower risks from state authorities and may be able to support larger scale operations. In situations of state weakness, it may create incentives for achieving territorial control, allowing terrorist organizations to draw on real economies for support as ISIS did in Syria and Iraq. Certainly, even as casualties from terrorism remain relatively low in developed countries, they have continued to grow dramatically in some parts of the developing world.[1]

Although the study of terrorism financing has gathered a good deal of empirical data of sometimes questionable reliability on the phenomenon, it remains undertheorized and largely disconnected from the broader disciplinary debates on terrorism in the social sciences. The lack of reliable data has been viewed as inhibiting systematic study, although this is true of all scholarship on illicit entities. The specific study of how terrorist organizations raise and use funds still focuses significantly on individual or comparative case studies.[2] The literature on how terrorist organizations move funds draws heavily on criminological and pragmatic studies of criminal finances, particularly money laundering.[3] Because of the role of surveillance in tracking financial transactions, a critical literature has emerged here as well that is concerned with the expansion of state power over individuals.[4] There is also a growing body of legal scholarship in reaction to the global criminalization of terrorism finance and the regulatory responses that states rely on to counter this activity, as well as the potential for human rights violations.[5] But despite some promising early efforts, the objective of making the study of terrorism financing a part of broader theoretical debates about terrorism has not yet been met (Giraldo and Trinkunas 2007; Biersteker and Eckert 2008).

This chapter outlines the existing state of the field of terrorism financing studies, identifying its main findings to date. It begins with a discussion of definitions of terrorism financing, and it then proceeds to examine the evolution of our understanding of terrorist fundraising, transfers, and spending. It considers what we have learned from the successes and failures of state responses to counter the financing of terrorism (CFT), and it concludes with a review of key theoretical and policy issues that remain to be addressed by future research.

Defining Terrorism Finance

Article 2(1) of the 1999 UN International Convention on the Suppression of Terrorism Financing (UN ICSFT) defines terrorism financing as occurring when a "person by any means, directly or indirectly, unlawfully or willfully, provides or collects funds with the intention that they should be used or in the knowledge that are to be used"[6] to carry out terrorist activities. The treaty officially entered into force in April 2002, but key provisions of the convention were earlier made binding by post-9/11 UN Security Council resolution 1373, which mandated that all member states freeze all terrorism-related assets and prohibit persons from making financial assets or services available to entities associated with terrorism. The treaty has since been signed by 187 states.[7]

Although the language of the convention is quite broad, it relies on states' nationally legislated definitions of terrorism rather than a universal definition, and there is little agreement among states about what constitutes terrorism. The 1999 convention does state that persons and their accomplices that engage in "an act intended to cause death or serious bodily injury to any person not actively involved in armed conflict in order to intimidate a population, or to compel a government or an international organization to do or abstain from doing any act"[8] are terrorists and material and financial support to such persons is terrorism financing (Pieth 2006).

Sources of Terrorism Financing

The contemporary focus of scholars of terrorism financing is on the behavior of non-state actors, but historically, this issue was frequently portrayed as an issue in which states were the dominant actors, either engaged in funding "dirty wars" against internal opponents (state terrorism), or by providing support to insurgents and/or terrorists combatting their adversaries in other states (state-sponsored terrorism). Groups such as Hezbollah in Lebanon, the Contras in Nicaragua, and Italy's Red Brigades were assumed to receive most of their funding from Iran, the United States, and the Soviet Union respectively. Countering terrorism finance was seen as a matter of putting military or diplomatic pressure on source states to reduce funding or constrain terrorist behavior, rather than directly interdicting the flows themselves.

The reality is that terrorist organizations have always attempted to diversify their sources of funding, precisely because overreliance on any one source made them vulnerable to external pressure and placed constraints on their actions (Passas 2007). The language in the 1999 UN ICSFT is a reflection of a growing consensus among states during the 1990s that the sources of financing were much broader than had traditionally been assumed, specifically that private actors played an essential role in funding terrorist efforts (Pieth 2006, 1075–6).

Popular support has always been an important source of funding, particularly for insurgent groups that employ terrorist tactics. This was the case for the Palestine Liberation Organization (PLO) in Lebanon and Palestine during the 1970s and 1980s and for the Irish Republican Army (IRA), who raised money or received in-kind assistance from Catholics across Ireland, north and south. When insurgents actually control territory, they can simply intimidate local populations into providing resources, as the Fuerzas Armadas Revolucionarias de Colombia (FARC) did in their own country in the 1990s or as the Islamic State does today in Iraq and Syria. Émigré communities have also served as sources of support for insurgents or terrorists associated with causes linked to their countries of origin. For example, Lebanese communities in West Africa and South

America provided funding to Hezbollah, and Tamil communities in Canada and Australia were important sources of support for the Liberation Tigers of Tamil Eelam operating in Sri Lanka.

However, reliance on popular support carries its own risks and limitations due to the possibility that erstwhile supporters might come to reject terrorism if the consequences of violence become too great. Where popular sentiment was particularly favorable to an organization, such as for the PLO in Palestine during the Intifada period in the 1980s, there were few risks that terrorist actions would be repudiated by the population. But as the IRA found out after the 1998 Northern Ireland Omagh bombing that killed twenty-nine and wounded 220 others, popular support could quickly turn to outrage and isolate a terrorist organization from community funding sources. (See regionally focused chapters in Giraldo and Trinkunas 2007 and in Biersteker and Eckert 2008.)

Wealthy individuals have been another important source of funding for terrorist organizations, one that is likely to place the fewest constraints on terrorist organizations if they hold extreme views. Prior to 2001, Al Qaeda benefitted from its association with wealthy individuals in the Gulf States who funneled substantial amounts of funding into its operations, including those leading to the 9/11 attacks (Gunaratna 2008). However, wealthy individuals are also particularly likely to be socially prominent and well connected to the formal economy, and as a result, they are sensitive about their reputations and their connections to terrorist organizations can be traced through the formal financial networks that hold their assets. After the United States and its allies dismantled the network of wealthy individuals associated with supporting Al Qaeda, other wealthy potential donors were strongly dissuaded from providing new financial support, even those holding extreme views (Barrett 2011).

In addition, terrorist organizations have always relied on self-funding by their members. Traditionally, illicit activities have been a way that terrorist organizations can utilize their expertise in applying violence to generate revenue. Communist terrorist organizations in Germany and Italy during the Cold War frequently engaged in bank robberies to generate funds. Groups such as the FARC in Colombia have done everything from racketeering to kidnapping to illicit drug trafficking to illegal mining and logging operations. The IRA similarly resorted to drug trafficking to generate funds as popular support dried up during the late 1990s. Hezbollah draws support from cigarette smuggling operations conducted within the United States, among other illicit activities. The 2005 Madrid bombings by Al Qaeda affiliates were funded by drug traffickers that had joined the movement after becoming radicalized while serving prison terms alongside members of Al Qaeda.[9] But it is entirely possible for individual terrorists or small cells to fund themselves through employment in the licit economy, although this would necessarily limit the resources available for attacks.

The bottom line is that terrorist financiers have always drawn from many different sources, and they share a common interest in diversification of their portfolio of funders, no matter what their cause or ideology. A diversified portfolio allows them the maximum latitude to plan attacks and sustain operations with lower risk of outside interference. It is also important to recognize that the relative weight of different funding sources in a terrorist organization's portfolio has implications for its behavior and activities. Terrorist organizations that rely on state or popular funding will always have to look over their shoulders to ensure they do not stray too far from the parameters their funding source finds acceptable. Terrorism financiers who draw on illicit activities to generate resources will always have to worry that association with crime will corrupt the organization and divert it from its focus, as well as put the group at greater risk of detection by law enforcement. Although self-funding from the legitimate economy is low profile and attracts little attention pre-attack, it is difficult for individuals or small groups to accumulate enough funding to pull off spectacular attacks, ultimately reducing their potential to inflict harm on target populations.

Movement of Terrorist Resources

The end of the Cold War and the accelerating pace of globalization also changed the nature of how terrorist organizations moved funds and resources from where they were raised to where they would be spent. The fall of the Iron Curtain in Europe and the rapid modernization and integration of China into the global market economy assured a global reach for modern financial banking networks. States and societies that had never been connected to these networks now had increasing access to modern banking, enabling sophisticated armed actors to move significant funding around the globe much more rapidly than had been possible before, as well as to collect and spend funds in territories that had once been difficult to penetrate. Globalization, here understood as the accelerating movement of people, goods, money, and ideas around the world, meant that states and societies with latent conflicts (some of which began to heat up and later erupted into open violence during the 1990s, as occurred in the former Yugoslavia, South and South East Asia, and South America) were now linked through financial networks (Clunan and Trinkunas 2010).

Financial networks maintain a traceable digital record of all transactions that cross their wires and terminals. This allows law enforcement and intelligence agencies to conduct forensic accounting in the wake of attacks. But in an effort to detect preparations before attacks, states have set increasingly strict regulatory frameworks that require financial institutions to "know their customers" (shorthand for performing due diligence on the identity of new customers and the sources of their funds) and report suspicious activity to financial intelligence units and law enforcement. In United States, for example, the 2001 USA PATRIOT Act greatly tightened rules on what types of activities were considered suspicious and should be reported by financial institutions, imposed stricter due diligence on banks that maintained correspondent accounts with foreign institutions, expanded the power of US law enforcement to subpoena records from foreign financial institutions with a US presence, and required that banks establish anti-money-laundering units.[10]

As a consequence, effective terrorist organizations (as well as other illicit actors) became increasingly sophisticated about how to evade detection using money-laundering techniques. For example, terrorism financiers could structure financing flows into many small transactions (known as "smurfing") so as to evade the algorithms used by banks to identify suspicious behavior, largely triggered by the movement of large lump sums. Routing money through multiple financial institutions, particularly through chains of transactions that passed through offshore banking havens where privacy rules hindered law enforcement intelligence efforts, also hid terrorism funding within larger flows of international capital. Each of these activities, identical to those used by money launderers, is designed to make it harder to separate the terrorism financing "signal" from the global capital flows "noise" (Gordon 2011). Thus, terrorist networks heightened the problem faced by states attempting to monitor these transactions since the movement of terrorist funds was frequently indistinguishable from either legitimate economic activity or money laundering absent other corroborating information (Levi 2010).

Terrorist organizations are similarly able to take advantage of global trade flows to shift resources from funders to the funded. At the crudest level, bulk cash can be hidden within container shipments of otherwise ordinary goods or in the trunks of cars crossing border points, much as other illicit goods have traditionally been transported: illegal drugs, precious gems, ivory, and rare woods. More sophisticated organizations can engage in the over- or under-invoicing of perfectly legal goods whereby financiers in the target country need merely overpay for items readily available at the source to move money from the destination country to the source country. To move funds in the opposite direction, financiers in the source country can sell goods at a great discount to their colleagues in the target country, which can then be resold at market prices. Either method disguises the movement of terrorist money as an ordinary economic transaction, and states have had to develop new approaches to detecting such efforts (DeKieffer 2008).

But terrorist organizations need not use formal trading and banking networks at all, as there are many informal channels through which funds can flow. In the wake of the 9/11 attacks, a good deal of attention was focused on informal value transfer systems (IVTS), particularly Hawala financial networks in South Asia and the horn of Africa. Hawaladars rely on family connections to run a trusted network of financial outlets by which immigrants to the developed world can send money home to their families. Particularly in countries that lack formal banking networks, such as Somalia, this was one of the few practical ways to send remittances. Hawala networks were perceived as particularly threatening to the international financial intelligence community because they do not generate the same electronic fingerprint in formal financial networks that allows these transactions to be traced. Instead, hawaladars in the developed world provide customers with a code which can be used by family members in their home countries to retrieve cash from their local hawaladar. The two hawaladars, typically members of an extended family, "settle up" amongst each other later through large transactions that are unconnected to any single customer (Farooqi 2010).

This type of informal financial network is not limited to South Asia and East Africa, and in fact persists today because of the advantages it provides to any individual wanting to move money across borders without generating a paper trail. For example, the black market peso dollar exchange between Colombia and the United States allows drug traffickers with dollar profits in the United States to repatriate their earnings without any cross-border financial transaction. Traffickers merely seek a Colombian entrepreneur operating in the informal economy who needs dollars to pay for imports from the United States. The entrepreneur would then wire pesos from his Colombian bank account to the trafficker's Colombian account, and the trafficker would move dollars from his account in the United States to the entrepreneur's US account. This type of transaction is very difficult to differentiate from many other kinds of financial transactions that occur in both states for entirely legitimate reasons, and moreover, no financial data crosses state borders, thus reducing the likelihood that the transaction would be detected by a financial intelligence unit (Napoleoni 2004).

Many actors, ranging from organized crime to crooked business people to corrupt politicians to terrorists, have reason to move funds in ways that minimize or evade the attention of law enforcement and intelligence agencies. While forensic accounting can use the movement of funds across financial networks to provide valuable intelligence after an attack, it is difficult to determine if pre-attack funds movements are suspicious or not without other corroborating intelligence that provides analysts with a determination of intent to commit a crime. Intelligence about financial transactions is very helpful in establishing the connections between different cells or nodes in terrorist networks, but it is not a very good substitute for information about what is going on inside the nodes of the network.

Terrorist Spending

It is important to distinguish between the day-to-day operating expenses required to maintain a terrorist organization and the funds required to execute an actual attack. To put this in perspective, the 9/11 attacks are often cited as costing approximately $500,000. Other attacks, such as those in Madrid in 2004, London in 2005, or the Charlie Hebdo attacks in Paris in 2014, cost much less, ranging from tens to hundreds of thousands of dollars. By contrast, the operating expenses of Al Qaeda were estimated by the CIA as $30 million per year in the period preceding the 9/11 attacks (Comras 2007).

The organizations with the heaviest operating expenses are typically insurgents that control territory, but also use terrorist attacks, even internationally, in support of their cause. For an organization such as ISIS in Iraq and Syria, the costs of sustaining the organization can run to hundreds of millions of dollars per year. In ISIS's case, their high operation costs were financed through smuggled oil, the sale of antiquities, illicit sales of the drug captagon, and human trafficking (Lister 2014). An organization like Hezbollah, which provides public goods such as health care and education in territories it controls, may have the largest fundraising burden of all. This helps to explain why Hezbollah relies on so many different sources of funding: state sponsorship from Iran, donations from overseas Lebanese expatriates, and participation in the licit and illicit economy in Lebanon and abroad (Levitt 2007). Territorial control enables insurgents to extract resources from populations and land under their control. It can also shelter illicit economic enterprises, such as cocaine-refining labs in Colombia or poppy cultivation in Afghanistan or along the Myanmar–China border (Felbab-Brown 2009).

Larger territorial expanses controlled by insurgents may lead to greater operating costs, not just for maintaining the organization, but because of the need to provide public goods to the inhabitants of territory they control or club goods to their supporters. Although rule by sheer terror may be possible, establishing a governance bargain with the inhabitants of controlled territory may meet an organization's goals at a lower cost by ensuring the (more or less) willing compliance of the governed. However, it is possible for terrorist organizations to control territory and provide little or no public goods, as is the case with the RUF in West Africa where the presence of high concentrations of natural resources (mining for precious metals and stones) provide wealth without governance. Such organizations are more likely to behave in a predatory fashion towards local populations (Reno 2010).

Large organizations that control territory are somewhat easier for governments to monitor because the sheer scale of resources involved makes their transactions more detectable. While gathering intelligence on hostile territory controlled by ISIS, Hezbollah (or the FARC in their heyday) is difficult, it is nevertheless a known threat whose methods of support can be studied, detected, and interdicted. However, it is the small-scale, self-funded terrorist cells that are most difficult to detect and counter before an attack is carried out. Although certain types of economic activity may attract law enforcement attention, such as the purchase of precursors for manufacturing explosives or bulk purchase of weapons, many of the day-to-day support activities for a terrorist cell—lodging, food, entertainment—appear little different from routine economic transactions.

Implications for Countering the Financing of Terrorism

Post-9/11, the United States saw an opportunity and need to greatly expand the reach of counter-financing of terrorism policies, not only in terms of the number of states brought into the fight, but also in terms of the kinds of activities that would lead to individuals or organizations being investigated and targeted. Its hegemonic role as the world's sole superpower and as a target of major terrorist attacks at that moment in time provided the leverage to overcome opposition to expanding the international regime addressing this issue. When it came to concrete policies, the United States fell back on familiar anti-money-laundering regulatory frameworks that it had long advocated when addressing other forms of illicit financing, such as organized crime.

The US role post-9/11 was quite a contrast to the 1990s, when the United States had been more ambivalent about what it defined as terrorism (the IRA frequently got a pass among Irish-Americans and Irish-American legislators, for example), and the private sector, particularly banks, had greatly resisted the implementation of anti-money laundering measures as onerous, expensive, and bad for business (Barrett 2011). In the fall of 2001, the United States and its allies worked through the UN Security Council to pass resolution 1373, which mandated the criminalization of terrorism financing by all organizations in all member states (not just Al Qaeda and the Taliban), and subsequently designated individuals and organizations as engaging in terrorism or material support to terrorism. This cut designated entities off from access to resources, savings, or the ability to use financial networks. With 9/11 still fresh in the world's collective mind, the number of states ratifying the UN ICSFT rapidly rose to over 150 and reached 187 by 2015.

Under the aegis of the G-7 sponsored Financial Action Task Force (FATF), the global implementation of anti-money-laundering measures, based on the US and UK domestic practices, received an additional impetus. FATF had already issued forty recommendations to combat money laundering in 1990, but after 9/11 it added eight (later nine) special recommendations to specifically counter the financing of terrorism. FATF had already established a practice of "naming and shaming" non-compliant countries and territories (NCCT), and with the global war on terror in full swing, the pressure to come into compliance rose sharply. The number of state financial intelligence units that were members of the Egmont Group, an umbrella organization designed to share best practices and provide technical advice on CFT, grew to over 100 by 2006. The hope was that anti-money-laundering (AML) tactics would attack terrorist networks at their weakest links, the financial operators and money launderers who were thought to be more vulnerable to international sanctions and less hardened and committed than terrorist combatants (Pieth 2006).

As the largest economy in the world and the preponderant global financial center, the United States was unusually well placed to develop financial intelligence and use sanctions to deter and punish terrorists and those providing them with material support. The International Emergency Economic Powers Act (IEEPA) provided the US President with broad authority to sanction individuals, organizations, and states that posed a national security threat to the United States. The US Treasury Office of Financial Assets Control had the authority to block the assets of anyone designated by the President under IEEPA. The US government also greatly expanded the range of activities that it would consider "material support to terrorism," including contributions to charities that were fronts for terrorism support. In the Financial Crimes Enforcement Network (FinCEN), they had an experienced financial intelligence unit to fit the pieces of the puzzle together. The objective was not only to freeze terrorist assets, but to create a chilling effect across the international financial system to deter terrorism supporters from using financial networks and thus slow or stop the movement of fresh funds to terrorist cells. Donors became much more cautious about who they provided support to and how.

International banks and financial institutions implemented "know your customer" requirements more aggressively, if only to avoid being tainted by association with the moving of funds associated with terrorism. Because the US was central to the global financial system, almost all international financial entities outside of a few pariah states (such as Iran) felt the need to comply (Reuter and Truman 2004; Zarate 2013). One of the keys to the effectiveness of the international counterterrorism financing regime created by UNSC resolution 1373 was the participation of private sector financial institutions in its enforcement.

The final piece of the puzzle was for the United States and its allies to go after IVTS operators such as hawaladars. Initially, there were attempts to shut down such networks. But once it became clear how central these systems were for the financial wellbeing of some of the poorest populations in the world, for example in Somalia and rural Pakistan, US and international authorities instead moved to regulate such operators in cases where they were not associated with other kinds of illicit activities such as tax evasion or drug trafficking. In effect IVTS operators were required to follow the best practices of formal banks, especially improved record keeping, adherence to banking regulations, and "know your customer" practices (Farooqi 2010).

However, there were costs to these policies. First, the intelligence community found that efforts to designate and freeze assets prevented them from pursuing "follow the money" strategies that allowed them to connect the dots between terrorist nodes and thus map their networks. Although the 9/11 attacks had illustrated the need for increased collaboration, interagency and international cooperation proved to be difficult because of disagreements between financial authorities, legislators, and intelligence agencies. The US government also did not fundamentally change the allocation of resources among counterterrorism activities, and CFT activities only received modest increases in budgets and personnel. Instead, the costs of implementing regulations were passed on to the private sector, which varied in its interpretation of regulation and in its capacity to implement the new measures. In addition, because banks were so nervous about the possibility that they might unwittingly be the conduit for terrorist money, they increased the number of Suspicious Activity Reports provided to government regulators, which simply injected more "noise" into the system (Clunan 2007). Eventually, this piecemeal approach was found to be insufficient and the United States decided to negotiate with the SWIFT inter-banking communications network for access to data about global financial transfers as early as 2006. SWIFT, based in Belgium, was the logical place to seek a comprehensive overview of global financial transactions, as almost all of them flow through this network. Although the US–SWIFT collaboration generated outrage when it was initially reported, the issue was eventually depoliticized and regulated by an agreement between the European Union and US authorities as part of the US Terrorism Finance Tracking Program in 2010 (Wesseling 2013).

The major push for a more comprehensive approach to CFT also met resistance internationally. First, the international and US mechanisms for designating terrorists and terrorism-affiliated organizations initially appeared to have little in the way of due process. Misdesignations of some individuals, and the difficulty in removing them from international lists once they had been placed there, generated negative publicity for the CFT agenda. The chilling effect of new regulations on charitable activities and development work, particularly in conflict zones where NGOs might come into contact with violent non-state actors, also had clear negative policy implications for important parts of the developing world where private assistance was badly needed (Levi 2010). And finally, the broad reach of CFT and AML policies caught up in its net not only terrorists, but all sorts of actors engaged in illicit activities: smugglers, corrupt politicians, tax-evading businesses, and their cognates. These actors, often politically influential in their home countries, undoubtedly resisted the full implementation of these measures (Parker 2014). Even where goodwill was available, many states lacked the capacity to effectively conduct the financial intelligence that was the basis for freezing assets or regulating the banking sector to ensure it was free of terrorist-affiliated assets.

Terrorism Financing: The Future Research Agenda

The study of terrorism financing has made progress in understanding the basic set of problems surrounding the issue of terrorism financing. It has generated insights on how different sources of funding affect terrorist behavior, and how international and national regulatory responses affect the movement of funding intended to support terrorism. We also have a better understanding of how variations in state policies and capabilities affect the incentive structures facing terrorists, their financiers, and the kinds of operations they engage in or support.

Where it has not done as well is in taking advantage of recent findings in the broader literature on terrorism to improve the study of terrorism financing. Certainly, the covert nature of the enterprise and limited availability of quantitative data are a problem for scholars. However, there are areas where theoretical debates about terrorism and about politics in general should inform the study of terrorism financing. The first area for further work is to take advantage of existing theories on the emergence, success, and failure of international regimes to better understand how states behave when making decisions on when to comply with international counterterrorism financing efforts (Sandler 2003). A research program similar to that pioneered by Enders and Sandler to apply political economy approaches to the study of terrorism could be very useful for developing better theories about terrorism financing. In particular, theories about when states choose to cooperate and take collective action, and when they choose to free-ride on the actions of powerful actors such as the United States, would seem highly applicable to the study of terrorism financing.[11]

Beyond the traditional focus on states, the study of terrorism financing should draw on insights from studies of alternative models of international governance that incorporate non-state actors in meaningful ways. Because the actual platforms over which global financial flows are transacted are frequently in the hands of private actors (banks, trading companies, and shippers), non-state financial entities are likely one of the key variables in explaining variations in terrorism financing and in the effectiveness of state efforts to counter terrorism finance. Approaches derived from the study of international regimes for global internet governance, where a multi-stakeholder model prevails, and global climate change, where both civil society and the private sector are important actors, may provide new insights into the counterterrorism financing regime (Masciandaro 1999).

At the domestic level, the literature in economics and finance on risk, regulation, and the behavior of financial actors should prove useful. In particular, we should expect private financial actors to calculate the risk–reward equation associated with compliance with financial regulations designed to counter terrorism. This includes both under-enforcement (evasion) of regulations as "bad for business" and over-enforcement (a chilling effect) in which financial actors underserve certain populations for fear of liability if they inadvertently provide material support to terrorism. This will vary with across jurisdictions and regulatory environments, providing data for comparative analyses (e.g. see Camacho et al. 2013).

With the rise (and perhaps fall) of ISIS and the existence of other similar organizations that seek and use territory, there is also reason to examine the growing literature on domestic conflict, local governance, and legitimacy. Control of territory by terrorist organizations provides access to a "real" economy on which to draw for resources, but also raises questions of governance. It is worth considering what forms of bargaining terrorist organizations will engage in with local social actors and populations in return for their compliance, instead of assuming terrorists will resort to pure coercion to control territory. Populations can be sources of recruits, intelligence, taxes, and other useful support elements (Felbab-Brown et al. 2017). As David Lake (2016) examines, local governance and legitimacy are highly intertwined and may affect the decisions by terrorist organizations bent on territorial control about what methods to employ to raise funds and what types of actions to fund given the constraints imposed by managing relations with local social actors.

There is also room for further work on what influences the behavior of individuals within groups participating in terrorism finance.[12] There has been some initial work approaching terrorism finance as a principal-agent problem, for example by Shapiro and Siegel (2007) on individual incentives within terrorist organizations, and by Byman and Kreps (2010) on relations between state sponsors and terrorist organizations. Behavioral economics may also offer insights, such as through the application of prospect theory to understanding how risk propensity in the domain of gains or losses affects financial decisions by terrorist organizations (Tversky and Kahneman 1992: 297–323). Other theories of organizations drawing on the fields of psychology and sociology may offer insights as well (Crenshaw 2000).

Serious questions also remain for policy research on terrorism financing. To the extent that terrorist attacks are increasingly self-funded in developed countries, either through participation in organized crime activities or savings from legal employment, the likelihood rises that persons and institutions operating at the local level—municipal government, law enforcement, neighborhood associations, and emergency responders—are more likely to come across behavior that may suggest pre-attack preparations. Such intelligence, in conjunction with forensic accounting, is invaluable for national intelligence agencies for preventing terrorist attacks. However, these institutions operate at an entirely different level of governance from local governments. While the United States pioneered the creation of intelligence fusion centers bringing together national, state, and local actors, the question remains as to how other states can adapt to the bureaucratic and security challenges of sharing information across different levels of government (Sullivan and Wirtz 2007).

On the other hand, when confronted by large-scale militant enterprises in developing countries or weak states, such as the Taliban, ISIS, or the FARC, then the question becomes how to go after terrorist financing without simultaneously undermining the local economy and consequently driving the local population into the arms of terrorist organizations who promise food, jobs, and protection. This is especially the case when terrorist organizations derive funding from protecting illicit economic activity that employs large numbers of persons, particularly the farming of coca and poppy to be used in the production of heroin and cocaine. As has been the case in Colombia and Afghanistan, attacking the base of terrorist financing can inadvertently generate popular support for terrorist organizations amongst those segments of the population that derive their livelihoods from farming drug-related crops, which can be quite large (Felbab-Brown 2009).

And finally, there is also a reason to question the US preference for imposing a universal anti-money-laundering regime, and whether at the domestic level anti-money-laundering regulations are an effective counterterrorism tool. The few studies that have looked at this question suggest that terrorist actors and traditional money launderers engage in similar behavior. Because they know the movement of large sums is likely to alert financial intelligence units, many terrorism financiers use money-laundering tactics to shield the movement of their funds from government scrutiny (Gordon 2011). The United States government continues to collect data through its access to the SWIFT network financial data, but it is unclear what the ratio of "ordinary" money laundering is to terrorism financing. If the ratio is quite large, pursuing money-laundering cases may not be the best use of CFT resources because of the large amount of "noise" in the system. This may be especially problematic given asymmetries among developed and developing states and between the public and private sectors in the areas of resources, access to information, and capacity (Wesseling 2013).

Notes

1. Calculations from National Consortium for the Study of Terrorism and Responses to Terrorism (START). (2016). Global Terrorism Database [Data file]. Retrieved from <https://www.start.umd.edu/gtd>.
2. For a recent example of this approach, see Freeman 2016.

3. For two recent assessments that adopt this approach, see Levi et al. 2014; and Maitland Irwin et al. 2011.
4. For a full discussion of this issue, see De Goede 2012.
5. For a sense of this debate, see Pieth 2006.
6. International Convention for the Suppression of the Financing of Terrorism, United Nations, New York, Dec. 1999. Accessed at <http://www.unodc.org/documents/treaties/Special/1999%20International%20Convention%20for%20the%20Suppression%20of%20the%20Financing%20of%20Terrorism.pdf>.
7. For status of treaty and list of signatories, see <https://treaties.un.org/Pages/ViewDetails.aspx?src=TREATY&mtdsg_no=XVIII-11&chapter=18&clang=_en>.
8. <https://treaties.un.org/Pages/ViewDetails.aspx?src=TREATY&mtdsg_no=XVIII-11&chapter=18&clang=_en>.
9. Picarelli 2006. But the crime–terrorism nexus has been frequently criticized. For a more skeptical view, see Andreas 2011.
10. "USA PATRIOT Act," FinCEN, U.S. Department of the Treasury, accessed at http://www.fincen.gov/statutes_regs/patriot/.
11. For an example of this work, see Enders and Sandler 2011. For an early effort to use a political economy approach to study terrorism finance, see Giraldo and Trinkunas 2007.
12. For some initial work in this area, see Menkhaus and Shapiro 2010.

References

Andreas, Peter (2011) "Illicit Globalization: Myths, Misconceptions, and Historical Lessons," *Political Science Quarterly*, 126(3): 403–25.

Barrett, Richard (2011) "Preventing the Financing of Terrorism," *Case Western Reserve Journal of International Law*, 44: 719.

Biersteker, Thomas J., and Sue E. Eckert, eds (2008) *Countering the Financing of Terrorism*. London and New York: Routledge.

Byman, Daniel, and Sarah E. Kreps (2010) "Agents of Destruction? Applying Principal-Agent Analysis to State-Sponsored Terrorism," *International Studies Perspectives*, 11(1): 1–18.

Camacho, Arnoldo R., et al. (2013) "Modelling the Risk Profiles of Clients in the Fight Against Money Laundering and Terrorism Financing," *International Journal of Business and Economics*, 12(2): 97–120.

Clunan, Anne L. (2007) "U.S. and International Responses to Terrorist Financing," in Jeanne K. Giraldo and Harold A. Trinkunas (eds), *Terrorism Financing and State Responses: A Comparative Perspective*. Stanford, CA: Stanford University Press, 260–81.

Clunan, Anne L., and Harold A. Trinkunas, eds (2010) *Ungoverned Spaces: Alternatives to State Authority in an Era of Softened Sovereignty*. Stanford, CA: Stanford University Press.

Comras, Victor (2007) "Al Qaeda Financing and Funding to Affiliated Groups," in Jeanne K. Giraldo and Harold A. Trinkunas (eds), *Terrorism Financing and State Responses: A Comparative Perspective*. Stanford, CA: Stanford University Press, 115–33.

Crenshaw, Martha (2000) "The Psychology of Terrorism: An Agenda for the 21st Century," *Political Psychology*, 21(2): 405–20.

De Goede, Marieke (2012) *Speculative Security: The Politics of Pursuing Terrorist Monies*. Minneapolis: University of Minnesota Press.

DeKieffer, Donald E. (2008) "Trade Diversion as a Fund Raising and Money Laundering Technique of Terrorist Organizations," in Thomas J. Biersteker and Sue E. Eckert (eds), *Countering the Financing of Terrorism*. London and New York: Routledge, 150–73.

Enders, Walter, and Todd Sandler (2011) *The Political Economy of Terrorism*. Cambridge: Cambridge University Press.

Farooqi, M. Nauman (2010) "Curbing the Use of Hawala for Money Laundering and Terrorist Financing: Global Regulatory Response and Future Challenges," *International Journal of Business Governance and Ethics*, 5(1–2): 64–75.

Felbab-Brown, Vanda (2009) *Shooting Up: Counterinsurgency and the War on Drugs*. Washington, DC: Brookings Institution.

Felbab-Brown, Vanda, Harold Trinkunas, and Shadi Hamid (2017) *Militants, Criminals, and Warlords: The Challenge of Local Governance in an Age of Disorder*. Washington, DC: Brookings Institution Press.

Freeman, Michael (2016) *Financing Terrorism: Case Studies*. Abingdon: Routledge.

Giraldo, Jeanne K., and Harold A. Trinkunas, eds (2007) *Terrorism Financing and State Responses: A Comparative Perspective*. Stanford, CA: Stanford University Press.

Gordon, Richard (2011) "Terrorism Financing Indicators for Financial Institutions in the United States," *Case Western Reserve Journal of International Law* 44: 765.

Gunaratna, Rohan (2008) "The Evolution of Al Qaeda," in Thomas J. Biersteker and Sue E. Eckert (eds), *Countering the Financing of Terrorism*. London and New York: Routledge, 47–62.

Lake, David A. (2016) *The Statebuilder's Dilemma: On the Limits of Foreign Intervention*. Ithaca, NY: Cornell University Press.

Levi, M. (2010) "Combating the Financing of Terrorism: A History and Assessment of the Control of 'Threat Finance,'" *British Journal of Criminology*, 50(4): 650–69.

Levi, Michael, Terence Halliday, and Peter Reuter (2014) "Global Surveillance of Dirty Money: Assessing Assessments of Regimes to Control Money-Laundering and Combat the Financing of Terrorism," available online at <http://orca.cf.ac.uk/88168/1/Report_Global%20Surveillance%20of%20Dirty%20Money%201.30.2014.pdf>.

Levitt, Matthew (2007) "Hezbollah Finances: Funding the Party of God," in Jeanne K. Giraldo and Harold A. Trinkunas (eds), *Terrorism Financing and State Responses: A Comparative Perspective*. Stanford, CA: Stanford University Press, 134–51.

Lister, Charles (2014) "Cutting Off ISIS' Cash Flow," Markaz blog, Brookings Institution, Oct. 24, available online at <http://www.brookings.edu/blogs/markaz/posts/2014/10/24-lister-cutting-off-isis-jabhat-al-nusra-cash-flow>.

Maitland Irwin, Angela Samantha, Kim-Kwang Raymond Choo, and Lin Liu (2011) "An Analysis of Money Laundering and Terrorism Financing Typologies," *Journal of Money Laundering Control*, 15(1): 85–111.

Masciandaro, Donato (1999) "Money Laundering: The Economics of Regulation," *European Journal of Law and Economics*, 7(3): 225–40.

Menkhaus, Ken, and Jacob N. Shapiro (2010) "Non-State Actors and Failed States: Lessons from Al Qaida's Experiences in the Horn of Africa," in Anne L. Clunan and Harold A. Trinkunas (eds), *Ungoverned Spaces: Alternatives to State Authority in an Era of Softened Sovereignty*. Stanford, CA: Stanford University Press, 77–84.

Napoleoni, Loretta (2004) "The New Economy of Terror: How Terrorism Is Financed," *Forum on Crime and Society*, 4: 31–48.

Parker, Marc (2014) "Cicero, Money and the Challenge of 'New Terrorism': Is Counter Terrorist Financing (CTF) a Critical Inhibitor? Should the Emphasis on Finance Interventions Prevail?" University of St Andrews, available online at <https://research-repository.st-andrews.ac.uk/handle/10023/4900>.

Passas, Nikos (2007) "Terrorism Financing Mechanisms and Policy Dilemmas," in Jeanne K. Giraldo and Harold A. Trinkunas (eds), *Terrorism Financing and State Responses: A Comparative Perspective*. Stanford, CA: Stanford University Press, 21–38.

Picarelli, John T. (2006) "The Turbulent Nexus of Transnational Organised Crime and Terrorism: A Theory of Malevolent International Relations," *Global Crime*, 7(1): 1–24.

Pieth, Mark (2006) "Criminalizing the Financing of Terrorism," *Journal of International Criminal Justice*, 4(5): 1074–86.

Reno, William (2010) "Persistent Insurgencies and Warlords: Who is Nasty, Who is Nice, and Why?," in Anne L. Clunan and Harold A. Trinkunas (eds), *Ungoverned Spaces: Alternatives to State Authority in an Era of Softened Sovereignty*. Stanford, CA: Stanford University Press, 57–76.

Reuter, Peter, and Edwin M. Truman (2004) *Chasing Dirty Money: The Fight Against Money Laundering*. Washington, DC: Peterson Institute for International Economics.

Rosand, Eric (2003) "Security Council Resolution 1373, the Counter-Terrorism Committee, and the Fight against Terrorism," *American Journal of International Law*, 97(2): 333–41.

Sandler, Todd (2003) "Collective Action and Transnational Terrorism," *The World Economy*, 26(6): 779–802.

Shapiro, Jacob N., and David A. Siegel (2007) "Underfunding in Terrorist Organizations," *International Studies Quarterly*, 51(2): 405–29.

Sullivan, John P., and James J. Wirtz (2007) "Terrorism Early Warning and Counterterrorism Intelligence," *International Journal of Intelligence and CounterIntelligence*, 21(1): 13–25.

Tversky, Amos, and Daniel Kahneman (1992) "Advances in Prospect Theory: Cumulative Representation of Uncertainty," *Journal of Risk and Uncertainty*, 5(4): 297–323.

Wesseling, Mara (2013) "The European Fight against Terrorism Financing." Ph.D. thesis, Amsterdam Institute for Social Science Research, available online at <http://dare.uva.nl/document/2/126131>.

Zarate, Juan Carlos (2013) *Treasury's War: The Unleashing of a New Era of Financial Warfare*, 1st edn. New York: PublicAffairs.

CHAPTER 32

TERRORISM AND STATE SPONSORSHIP IN WORLD POLITICS

DAVID B. CARTER AND SAURABH PANT

Introduction

Recent history is replete with cases of states sponsoring terrorist groups. Prominent examples include Pakistani support to groups operating in Kashmir; the Indian government's connections to the LTTE in Sri Lanka in the 1980s; Iran's role in helping create, finance, and train Hezbollah in Lebanon; and the Taliban's provision of a safe haven to Al Qaeda. State support need not be direct as in these cases, but can also take a "passive" or unintentional form. For example, the United States passively supported the Provisional Irish Republican Army (PIRA) by not taking actions to stop its citizens from donating to such groups. Although the volume of state sponsorship has declined since the Cold War (Enders and Sandler 1999; Byman 2005b), many worry its potential impact on international security could be greater given nuclear proliferation in weak states with a history of sponsorship like Pakistan (Collins 2014). Accordingly, understanding the causes, types, and consequences of state sponsorship remains an important objective for scholars and policy-makers.

Before proceeding, we define what we mean by "terrorist group." The use of the term can be misleading, as terrorism, i.e. the deliberate targeting of civilians by groups with political motivations, is just one of many tactics available to violent actors (Shapiro 2012; Bueno de Mesquita 2013; Carter 2016). Groups that use terrorism often also use guerrilla or even more conventional military tactics. We do not deeply engage with this specific issue, but rather use the term "terrorist groups" to indicate any group that uses the tactic, even though many if not most groups use a mix of tactics. Thus, non-state groups engaged in a civil war with a state government are usually terrorist groups by our definition, and groups such as the Red Brigades that were not able to escalate conflict to civil war are also terrorist groups.

The literature on state sponsorship of terrorist groups can be split into four main areas. First, scholars have tried to understand the different types of sponsorship that a state can provide. Sponsorship can come in many forms, where each option yields a different relationship between state and terrorist group. Second, scholars have tried to understand why states would want to sponsor terrorist groups. Motivations vary depending on the type of sponsorship: active, passive, or unintentional. For instance, passive or unintentional support is often not as clearly tied to specific policy goals as is active sponsorship. Third, scholars have examined the "demand" for sponsorship to explore why terrorist groups would want state sponsors. While early works emphasized the obvious benefits of sponsorship to groups, recent literature recognizes that groups face difficult trade-offs: they obtain additional resources but at costs such as giving up some autonomy. Finally, aside from the terrorist group and the sponsor, it is important to consider the state targeted by the group. How does state sponsorship complicate dealing with threatening groups? Are there any upsides to fighting groups with a state sponsor? After addressing prominent work on these four aspects of sponsorship, we propose some new avenues for research on sponsorship. Specifically, we empirically demonstrate the intimate connections between state sponsorship and other important security issues in world politics, suggesting that future research can better understand the dynamics of sponsorship by focusing on the policy issues or disputes that drive sponsors and groups together. Such a focus would also help to better connect the fast-growing literature on terrorism and political violence with the long-established literature on interstate disputes and violence.

The Types of Sponsorship

The type of state support to terrorist groups varies in complexity and depth. As Byman (2005b) describes, state support can range from simply providing ideological direction to providing a territorial sanctuary for the group. A territorial base is arguably the most significant and complicated form of support as it provides a base for operations and training, while also usually increasing the cost to directly attacking the group for the target state. The fact that the state sponsor exposes itself to potential retaliation by the target state and its allies entails real diplomatic, economic, and military risks (Byman 2005b; Salehyan 2008; Schultz 2010). Even within specific types of support, such as arms transfers or training, there is great variation in how much support different sponsors provide. Mickolus (1989) provides a somewhat different typology that focuses on the culpability of state sponsors for group actions more than the specific types of support they provide. He places regimes into different categories that range from least to most culpable in the following order: intimidated governments, ideologically supportive regimes, generally facilitative supporters, direct support in incidents by governments, and official participation. Thus, the idea here is that some states unwillingly provide sponsorship because they have no choice, i.e. "intimidated governments," while other states enthusiastically back groups and even directly help them carry out specific attacks, i.e. direct support in incidents or official participation. Both of these typologies of sponsorship have informed work on state sponsorship.

One difficulty in understanding patterns of state sponsorship is the fact that governments do not often advertise their support for terrorist groups. Scholars such as Hoffman (1997) and Pluchinsky (1997) try to directly explain why states do not often take credit for attacks. Pluchinsky (1997) even claims that, at the time of writing his article, he knew of "no state-sponsored terrorist attack that [had] been explicitly claimed by a state." The reason that these authors and others give is fairly intuitive: state sponsors want to avoid retaliation from the state targeted by the group's attacks and/or its allies. As Byman (2005b) and Carter (2012a) note, states typically sponsor a group because they have a dispute or rivalry with the state the group targets. Moreover, sponsorship is an indirect means of challenge that is also not terribly good at achieving decisive outcomes in the short or medium term. Accordingly, the states that use sponsorship tend to be states that wish to avoid direct military confrontation with their opponent. Plausible deniability is important in regard to specific attacks as sponsorship is often either highly suspected or a proven fact. For instance, most countries were almost certain that the Libyan government was highly involved and responsible in the Lockerbie airline bombing, but Gaddafi quickly and unequivocally admitting such involvement would have probably resulted in even higher costs than what actually followed.

The ties between a terrorist group and a sponsoring government are often fairly weak. A number of scholars suggest that the fact that sponsors are quite fickle reflects both the import of plausible deniability in many cases as well as the fact that the core interests of groups and sponsors are often divergent. According to McCormick and Owen (2009, 292), "the average life-span of a state-terrorist coalition is less than eight years, with a median life cycle of six years." The authors explain this structural weakness by the fact that the interests of both partners in this relationship do not completely overlap and are sometimes at odds with each other—a point also made by Byman (2005b) and Carter (2012a).

The current work on the types and nature of sponsorship has been useful and has provided interesting theoretical discussions. However, this area of the research field is still in need of further development. The typologies provide a helpful way to organize and rank the depth of sponsorship but more theoretical work needs to be done to explain the change from one type of support to another with accompanying rigorous empirical work to assess these theories. Moreover, the connection between these typologies of support and the motivations for sponsoring states (e.g. the type of policy dispute motivating its sponsorship) would clarify the conditions under which states choose more or less active forms of support for groups.

Why Sponsor Terrorism?

We anchor our discussion of the motivations for state sponsorship of terrorism by distinguishing among three broad classes of sponsorship: active, passive, and unintentional. These three classes of sponsorship vary in the amount and type of support provided by the state to the group (Byman 2005b). Accordingly, it is worthwhile considering each separately in order to better illustrate the different dynamics behind the motivations for the first two types and the necessary and sufficient conditions for the third type to exist

Active Sponsorship

The motivations for a state to actively sponsor terrorism cover a fairly wide spectrum. Byman (2005b) lists three broad categories that each motivation can be placed under: strategic concerns, ideology, and domestic politics. Even though there is some evidence (e.g. see Salehyan et al. 2011) that bonds of affinity through a shared culture, religion, or ethnicity can be the main motivation behind a state's decision to sponsor violent organizations in other countries, Byman (2005b, 32) states that "strategic motivations are the most common." In fact, even if the initial impetus for a state is non-strategic, strategic concerns eventually come to the forefront of the sponsorship question. For example, Iran might have initially supported Hezbollah out of ideological reasons to spread the Islamic revolution, but eventually strategic considerations drove Iran to use their proxy group to attack and intimidate states such as the United States, Israel, and Iraq.

State-sponsorship is thus an attractive tool as it allows a state to engage in "coercive diplomacy" against a rival in a less costly way than conventional military conflict (Bapat 2007, 2012). A state can use a terrorist group to improve their bargaining position vis-à-vis a rival while not directly engaging their opponent's military forces. This logic seems to be empirically supported. Salehyan et al. (2011) and Maoz and San-Akca (2012) show that the presence of an interstate rivalry increases the chances of cooperation between a state and non-state armed group. Similarly, Findley et al. (2012) find that interstate rivalries are positively associated with transnational terrorism. The case of Pakistan and India helps to illustrate this dynamic. Their disagreement over the status of Kashmir initially led to direct military confrontation in the early post-independence years. However, since the 1970s, Pakistan has financed and actively created and managed Kashmiri terrorist groups to put pressure on India to concede.

There can be other motivations for a state to delegate violence to a terrorist group. Byman and Kreps (2010) use a standard principal–agent framework to study why a state, the principal, would want to sponsor (i.e. delegate conflict to) a terrorist group, the agent. The authors suggest three reasons to explain this delegation. First, delegation allows states to exploit the assets of terrorist groups who are more knowledgeable about unconventional tactics. This specialization and niche skill set gives terrorist groups a comparative advantage. Second, a state might choose to delegate in order to increase the credibility of their commitment to a particular cause. Terrorist groups will have fewer incentives than states to renege on their commitment and it is also harder for a state to control their proxy's fighters than their own military forces. Finally, delegation allows a principal's preferences to be acted upon beyond the fixed tenure of a leader. A current leader thus might delegate responsibilities to a terrorist group in order to ensure that their preferred policies are still followed even after they leave their post. Salehyan (2010) also uses principal–agent theory to assess group–state alliances, noting that states are able to forego costs of direct engagement with an adversary but must also be willing to cede some foreign policy-making autonomy.

Passive Sponsorship

States might be supporting terrorist groups through their inaction as well. Byman (2005a) characterizes passive support as the situation where actors within a country (but not the government itself) aid a terrorist group, and the country chooses not to stop this support even though it has the capacity to do so. Before 9/11, citizens in Saudi Arabia financially supported Islamist terrorist groups and the Saudi government chose not to intervene to stop these transactions. In the 1970s, it was known that the Provisional Irish Republican Army (PIRA) was receiving financial support from American citizens, but the American government chose not to block these transfers.

Byman (2005a) explains how this passivity can be explained by domestic considerations. The deeply religious Saudi society and the intertwining of religion and politics at the elite level meant that any intervention could end up offending powerful actors. Groups like Al Qaeda were not considered a serious threat to the Saudi monarchy at that time, so any direct confrontation might have had little benefit and could have created the opportunity for an unwanted costly response by the group and its supporters. Similarly, in the United States, Irish Americans made up a sizeable political constituency so it would not have been electorally advantageous for many politicians to go after the funding of the PIRA at that time. Empirical evidence on passive sponsorship is relatively sparse, as it is by definition more difficult to reliably observe and measure than active sponsorship. Accordingly, empirical studies of sponsorship such as Salehyan et al. (2011) or Carter (2012a) focus on forms of active sponsorship, leaving more ambiguous passive relationships for future work.

Unintentional Sponsorship

Aside from active and passive sponsorship that is conditioned on the state having a certain level of capacity, weak states might just not be able to prevent terrorist groups from exploiting their resources. The state is not "motivated" to support terrorist groups but its weakness leaves it unable to project authority or establish legitimacy, which enables terrorist groups to operate without substantial interference. Although the link between weak states and unintentional sponsorship is theoretically plausible, additional factors might need to be considered. In other words, a weak state might be a necessary condition but not a sufficient condition to be an unintentional host for a terrorist group. Newman (2007) found that a substantial number of weak states (where weakness was measured by a country's score on certain capacity measures) are not havens for transnational terrorist groups. Newman (2007) argues that scholars should focus on finding the decisive factors that can help us better understand the link between weak states and sponsorship. Moreover, Carter (2012a) does not even consider cases in which groups are based within a weak state that cannot prevent it as indicative of sponsorship. Carter (2012a) also shows that active sponsorship has a quite distinct effect on group health relative to groups with a safe haven from a state that is not an active sponsor, i.e. an "unintentional sponsor." Specifically, safe havens in states that are not active sponsors are helpful to group survival prospects, whereas safe havens provided by active sponsors are often not helpful to groups.

Kittner (2007) potentially provides us with some additional variables by arguing that three other factors, aside from weak governance, have allowed groups to establish safe havens in other countries. First, geographic features such as rugged terrain make it difficult for a state to govern and disseminate power. Terrorist groups can thus take advantage of the inaccessibility of such an area (see also Carter et al. 2017). However, Krueger (2007) fails to find any systematic connection between terrain and patterns of terrorism, which draws this idea into question. Second, a history of corruption and violence that so often characterizes developing countries can attract terrorist groups. The ability to raise money in the illegal economy and the ease with which members can be recruited and weapons can be purchased will not only attract terrorist groups but also make it more difficult for the state to control their territory and expel such groups (Piazza 2011). Finally, poverty—which tends to be endemic in weak states—can plausibly make it easier for terrorist groups to recruit members and establish safe havens. However, it is important to note that the empirical evidence in support of the connection between poverty and terrorism is relatively weak (e.g. Piazza 2006; Krueger 2007).

Why Accept Sponsorship?

The preceding section looked at the supply side of the equation—a state choosing to sponsor a terrorist group. Here we consider the demand side of the equation, or why terrorist groups choose to accept state sponsorship. Although sponsorship can obviously bring benefits in increased funds and resources, a number of scholars point out that groups face trade-offs in accepting sponsorship (Byman 2005b; Salehyan 2010; Salehyan et al. 2011; Carter 2012a). Specifically, while groups gain essential resources, they also take on risk by giving up a degree of control to their sponsor.

Obtaining Resources to Improve Capability and Encourage Cohesion

Cronin (2009, 18) claimed that there were two ways for terrorist groups to end: target elimination or internal dissolution. State sponsorship brings resources—both material and ideological—that can help improve the capabilities and strengths of a terrorist group to help avoid elimination. Salehyan (2007) found that civil wars tended to last longer when rebels had access to external bases, so it would be intuitive to think that this dynamic works with terrorist groups as well. In fact, "many theorists have suggested that external support by governments is necessary to ensure the survival of terrorist bands, whose limited self-generated resources would otherwise cause these organizations to wither over time" (Mickolus 1989, 287). Consistent with this argument, Siqueira and Sandler (2006) show theoretically that, with state sponsorship, a terrorist group does not need to rely on popular support and that allows them to focus on their mission, which augments violence, although this argument might underemphasize the connection between popular support and group health in many cases.[1] Likewise, Byman (2008) explains how state sponsorship can help turn small terrorist groups into full-blown insurgencies. When states offer a safe haven to operate and also provide technology and training, this can hinder the ability of a target state to enact effective counterterrorism measures. Foreign sanctuaries can thus decrease the likelihood that a terrorist group's campaign ends (Bapat 2007; Carter 2012a). There is some empirical evidence to support Bapat's (2007) theoretical model, as Gaibulloev and Sandler (2014) were able to show that state sponsorship decreases the likelihood that a terrorist group ends.

Additionally, more resources can also translate into improved cohesion. Simply put, internal dissolution occurs if enough members leave to lead to the demise of the group. Members of a group usually have outside options, and in order for them to be willing to participate in terrorist activities they need to be compensated with at least as much as they would get if they left (Bueno de Mesquita 2005). As Carter (2012a) explains, given this participation constraint, increased resources through state sponsorship should help the terrorist group provide the necessary benefits to attract and keep members.[2]

Loss of Control

Leaders of terrorist groups might gain resources through finding a state sponsor but it often comes at the cost of organizational control. States are often walking a fine line when they sponsor terrorist groups. They want to inflict damage on a rival but wish to avoid costly retaliations. As a result, Byman (2008) describes how states often want to limit the scope and actions of sponsored groups and in some cases even forcefully impose such limits. Syria's tumultuous relationship with Palestinian groups, especially the PLO, illustrates this desire for control. At times Syria worked with the PLO, but at other times jailed Yasser Arafat and supported his rivals when the group behaved too independently. Terrorist groups would thus prefer to raise their finances independently rather than rely on a patron who will give them "conditional aid." On the other side, rational states should be careful in picking their partners—they want a group that is organized and that they can easily control. Corroborating this theorized calculus, Salehyan et al. (2011) find that rebel groups that are neither too weak (such that they are poorly organized) nor too rich (such that they do not need to be dependent on the state for vital resources) are more likely to receive external support. From a prospective sponsor's point of view, picking a relatively poor and desperate group might give maximum control. However, a poor group desperate for resources is also less able to inflict significant damage on the target state and is likely to exhibit more internal problems (i.e. a poor investment).

Controlling an illegal organization like a terrorist group is usually not straightforward. In Byman and Krep's (2010) principal–agent framework, the state–terrorist group relationship is fraught with problems where the autonomy of the agent (the terrorist group) allows it to sometimes act against the interest of the principal (the sponsoring state). As already explained, sponsorship is a way for a state to improve its bargaining position against rivals. However, there can be considerable trade-offs involved. The improved bargaining power comes at the potential cost that the empowered terrorist group cannot be controlled and could punish the sponsor if it negotiates an unpalatable deal. In light of this trade-off, Bapat (2012) models how states can tie their hands at the negotiating table by sponsoring such groups and corroborates these predictions with empirical evidence. Anecdotally, Pakistan's relationship with Kashmiri militant groups depicts this trade-off fairly well. Even though Pakistan had been supportive of Kashmiri militant groups in the past, this changed after the December 2001 militant attacks in India. After this attack, Pervez Musharraf (the then Pakistani leader) promised to cooperate with India in punishing those responsible, which led some militant groups to focus their violence on Musharraf's government instead.

The Target State: Impacts and Reactions

Finally, after studying the sponsoring state and the terrorist group, some of the literature has analyzed state-sponsored terror from the perspective of the target state. Aside from the examination of the impact of sponsorship on terrorist attacks in the target state, scholars have also looked into the reaction and retaliatory policies that follow such attacks. Understanding target states' incentives and behavior are of clear importance, as any theory in which a group and (potential) sponsor make decisions needs to somehow account for the anticipated reactions of the target (e.g. Carter 2012b).

Is Sponsorship Actually a Blessing?

From the preceding section, the theoretical and empirical evidence (Siqueira and Sandler 2006; Bapat 2007; Byman 2008; Gaibulloev and Sandler 2014) could lead one to logically conjecture that state sponsorship, through the mechanism of increasing the capacity of a terrorist group, is likely to lead to more frequent and more deadly attacks. Yet, such sponsorship might actually not worsen things for the target country. In fact, according to Carter (2012a), sponsorship can be a "blessing" as the sponsoring country often has incentives to strategically disclose intelligence on the terrorist group in order to avoid costly military operations. Theoretically, we would expect sponsoring states to be especially sensitive to the threat of military retaliation by the target, as the decision to sponsor (with all the noted trade-offs) rather than more directly coerce one's adversary is reflective of a strong desire to avoid military confrontation. Empirically, this logic is supported by evidence that the likelihood a terrorist group is eliminated by their target country increases when they rely on a safe haven in a sponsoring state. Furthermore, Carter (2012a) also found that sponsorship did not significantly affect whether a group ended due to internal dissolution. Thus, counterintuitively, a target state would prefer a group "to have an active sponsor with some degree of power over [the] group relative to a weak host that cannot do much about [the] group" (Carter 2012a, 149). There is additional empirical evidence to support the assertion that sponsorship might not actually be a boon for a terrorist group. Contrary to Gaibulloev and Sandler (2014), Phillips (2014) found that state sponsorship had no significant effect on the survival rate of terrorist groups, and Asal and Rethemeyer (2008) found that state sponsorship did not significantly influence the lethality of a terrorist organization.

Retaliation and its Effects

Target governments do sometimes react to terrorist activity by enacting policies—militarily and economically—aimed at punishing sponsoring states. Empirically, Maoz and San-Akca (2012) find that state–terrorist coalitions increase the likelihood of rivalry escalation. Similarly, Salehyan (2008) and Gleditsch et al. (2008) find that rebel sanctuaries and external support increase the probability of a militarized interstate dispute between the host and the target country. Schultz (2010) explains the link between sponsorship and international conflict as a form of bargaining failure between the sponsor and the target. It would be costly for both the target country and the host country if the former initiated military operations, so a mutually peaceful compromise should theoretically exist. However, if agreements cannot be monitored and enforced then military retaliation can be the best option for the target country.

Yet, the target state's retaliatory policies can actually have a harmful effect on both the sponsoring state and themselves. Although sanctions and military force can compel a host state to halt or lessen their support, the use of compellent punishments might actually end up severely weakening the host state's capabilities to control the terrorist group and could incentivize the terrorist group to be more aggressive. Carter (2015) characterizes this trade-off as the "compellence dilemma" and argues that the downstream costs of compellent punishments make them ineffective and rare. However, Carter (2015) suggests that the dilemma is less pernicious when the host state is also a sponsor, as the probability that a sponsor can effectively act against a group is significantly higher than it is for an unwilling host. This is also consistent with the findings of Carter (2012a) as safe havens from non-sponsoring states are associated with group health while safe havens from sponsors are not.

Clearly, identifying the optimal retaliatory policies across different cases of sponsorship—active, passive, or otherwise—is difficult and an area in need of much more study. In at least one successful case, an important element seemed to be having a multilateral coalition putting pressure on a sponsor. The United States enacted unilateral economic sanctions and conducted military operations against Libya in 1986. However, according to Collins (2004) and Byman (2005b), Libya only dismantled its "sponsorship" program after the 1992 UN multilateral sanctions. In a general sense, this is consistent with Lake (2002) who conjectures that multilateral responses to terrorism are relatively effective, but more theoretical and empirical work is needed on this front. Interesting cases such as the Libyan one could motivate other theoretical and empirical questions about what types of policies are best at dealing with state support for terrorism in its varying guises.

Interstate Conflict, Terrorism, and State Sponsorship

One aspect of state sponsorship in need of more analysis is the relationship between interstate disputes and patterns of sponsorship. Much of the theory that relates to why states choose to sponsor violent groups emphasizes that sponsorship is often a policy tool aimed at furthering more typical security aims (Byman 2005b; Carter 2012a). These connections have been developed empirically in some domains, as studies such as Findley et al. (2012) and Maoz and San-Akca (2012) show the relationships between terrorism and interstate rivalry (see also Boutton 2014). We suggest here that our understanding of state sponsorship can benefit from a connection to the large and well-established literature on territorial disputes.

Territorial disputes are known to be responsible for a large share of violent interstate conflict and war. A large body of work convincingly links the presence of border disputes to the outbreak of interstate war (e.g. Luard 1986; Holsti 1991; Vasquez 1993; Vasquez and Henehan 2001; Hensel 2000). Disputes over territory that escalate to war are also associated with conflicts that take longer to resolve and produce more casualties. This set of facts in conjunction with the observation that sponsors tend to be states in dispute with adversaries makes examination of connections between territorial disputes and state sponsorship of terrorist groups a worthwhile enterprise. Moreover, a number of the more prominent cases of state sponsorship are clearly tied to border disputes. For instance, the support provided by Pakistan and its intelligence agency, ISI, to Kashmiri groups targeting India is clearly tied to its longstanding dispute with India over the status of Kashmir. Syrian support for a number of Palestinian groups targeting Israel during much of the 1970s and 1980s also fits this pattern, as this behavior is not hard to link to the dispute over the Golan Heights. In short, there are numerous reasons to think that states in contentious territorial disputes might provide support to groups that carry out attacks on their territorial target.

To probe whether this dynamic is present across a large number of territorial disputes, we provide a preliminary exploration with data. To explore the connection between territorial disputes and patterns of state sponsorship, we use the most comprehensive data currently available. For territorial disputes, we use data collected by Huth (1996), and extended by Huth and Allee (2002), Huth et al. (2011), and Carter et al. (2018) to cover all border disputes globally from 1945 to 2010. For data on state sponsorship patterns, we use the recently compiled Non-State Armed Groups (NAGs) data collected by San-Akca which is used in studies such as Maoz and San-Akca (2012). While there are alternative sources of sponsorship data such as Cunningham et al. (2013) or Carter (2012a), the San-Akca data cover a broader range of groups relative to the former, which only measure patterns in civil wars identified by the UCDP-PRIO data, and have greater temporal coverage relative to the latter, which only cover post-1968 patterns in sponsorship.

The first thing we demonstrate with these data is that states in territorial disputes are also especially likely to be state sponsors of terrorism. Table 32.1 provides a simple cross-tabulation of whether a given state is embroiled in a territorial dispute or not and also whether it is a sponsor of terrorism or not. The numbers in bold are the actual cell values, meaning that out of all post-1945 country-years, the modal category is being neither in a territorial dispute nor a sponsor of terrorism, i.e. 4,691 country-years. The numbers in parentheses below the bold entries indicate the values that would be in the cells if we assume the two variables are independent of one another. About 45 percent of all country-years involve a territorial dispute, which is not overly rare, while state sponsorship is much less common, with almost 12 percent of state-years being sponsorship years. Of particular interest is the fact that there are significantly more cases of sponsorship in years where a state is embroiled in a territorial dispute than would be expected if the two variables were independent of one another. In fact, the Chi-square test statistic is very large, i.e. over 200, which indicates that these two variables are independent with a probability very close to zero. Examination of the raw numbers suggests that independence implies around 534 years of sponsorship and territorial dispute in the sample while the actual number of such years is 764, which constitutes about two-thirds of all sponsorship country-years.

Table 32.1 State Sponsorship and Territorial Disputes

	No Territorial Dispute	Territorial Dispute	Row Sum
No Sponsorship	**4,691** (4,461.3)	**3,705** (3,934.7)	**8,396**
Sponsorship	**376** (605.7)	**764** (534.3)	**1,140**
Column Sum	**5,067**	**4,469**	**9,536**

Observed values in bold, expected values in parentheses.

The idea that states in territorial disputes are especially likely to be state sponsors of terrorist groups also suggests that these states are very likely targets of sponsored groups. In other words, if the statistical association between sponsorship and territorial disputes is in fact driven by states using sponsorship to harm a territorial foe, we should also find a strong association between being the target of a sponsored terrorist group and having a border dispute. Table 32.2 shows the relationship between territorial disputes and being targeted by a state-sponsored terrorist group in a given year. The raw data suggest that there is a strong connection between being embroiled in a territorial dispute and being targeted by a sponsored group. Specifically, under an assumption of independence between the two variables we would expect around 379 country-years in which a state is both targeted by a sponsored group and embroiled in a dispute, while we actually have 575 such observations. Thus, over 70 percent of all cases in which a state is targeted by a non-state group that is sponsored by a state also involve a territorial dispute. Statistically, these two variables are easily shown highly unlikely to be independent of one another as the Chi-square test statistic again takes a value of more than 200, which implies independence with a probability arbitrarily close to zero.

Theoretically, there should be important distinctions between territorial targets and territorial challengers. Challengers in territorial disputes are the revisionist party, claiming a portion of the target state's territory. Thus, challenger states are typically the aggressors in these disputes, and both escalation to war and peaceful moves towards resolution tend to be initiated by them (Huth 1996). Accordingly, we expect territorial challengers to be more likely to choose sponsorship of a sub-state violent group that attacks its own territorial target. The target is (usually) satisfied with the territorial status quo relative to its neighbor, and thus is less aggressive absent major provocations by the challenger state. This makes target states less probable sponsors of terrorist groups relative to the challenger state.

Nicely for our purposes, the Huth territorial dispute data distinguish between territorial targets and challengers while the San-Akca data distinguish between sponsors of groups and states targeted by sponsored groups. We assess this conjecture by examining the raw data as we did in Tables 32.1–32.3, which show the cross-tabulation for whether a given state is the challenger in a territorial dispute and also the sponsor of a terrorist group. There is a significant statistical association between these two variables as there are many more instances of a territorial challenger also sponsoring a terrorist group than we would expect if these two variables were independent of one another.

Table 32.2 Targets of State-Sponsored Groups and Territorial Disputes

	No Territorial Dispute	Territorial Dispute	Row Sum
Not Targeted	**4,833** (4,637.1)	**3,894** (4,089.9)	**8,727**
Targeted	**234** (429.9)	**575** (379.1)	**809**
Column Sum	**5,067**	**4,469**	**9,536**

Observed values in bold, expected values in parentheses.

Table 32.3 State Sponsorship and Territorial Challengers

	Not Territorial Challenger	Territorial Challenger	Row Sum
No Sponsorship	**5,826** (5,726.5)	**2,570** (2,669.5)	**8,396**
Sponsorship	**678** (777.5)	**462** (362.5)	**1,140**
Column Sum	**6,504**	**3,032**	**9,536**

Observed values in bold, expected values in parentheses.

Again, the statistical association is significant as the Chi-square statistic is over 45, which implies a probability of independence close to zero.

Table 32.4 shows the cross-tabulations for targets of sponsored groups and territorial claims. Again, there are significantly more country-years in which a state is both a target of a territorial claim and also targeted by a sponsored group than we would expect if the two were independent. Specifically, we would expect around 204 cases of coincidence if the two processes were independent, while there are actually 369 such cases of coincidence. The Chi-square statistic is again statistically significant, taking a value close to 200, which implies an arbitrarily small chance that these two variables are actually independent.

To sum all of this up, these simple cross-tabulations suggest that the states embroiled in territorial disputes also tend to be disproportionately implicated in state sponsorship of terrorist groups. Moreover, while much additional analysis is needed, the basic patterns that one would expect if the relationship between border disputes and state sponsorship was systematic are borne out in the data. For instance, territorial targets also tend to be targets of state-sponsored groups, while state sponsors tend to be revisionist territorial challengers.

One of the reasons that scholars have focused so much attention on territorial disputes is because of their positive correlation with military conflict and war. A quick glance at the militarized interstate dispute (MID) incidence for states in territorial dispute and without territorial dispute confirms this pattern: the mean number of MIDs experienced in country-years with a territorial dispute is 1.19, while the mean number of MIDs is only 0.19 for country-years without a territorial dispute. This is a large difference, as MIDs are fairly rare events. A natural question to ask is whether the incidence of militarized conflict in territorial disputes is similar, lesser, or worse when state sponsorship of terrorist groups is also present.

Although we leave full assessment of the relationship between sponsorship, MID onset, and territorial disputes to future research, we provide a preliminary assessment of one of the more basic ideas suggested but not tested in the extant literature. Specifically, scholars such as Findley et al. (2012) and Carter (2012a) suggest that sponsors of terrorism that have traditional policy ends in mind, such as imposing costs on a territorial rival, tend to be in positions of military weakness relative to their opponent. The basic logic behind this idea is that states that turn to (risky) proxies to pursue major strategic goals must find the use of more direct means such as military force relatively unattractive. For example, after the unsuccessful 1973 war with Israel, the Syrian regime turned to

Table 32.4 Targets of State-Sponsored Groups and Territorial Targets

	Not Territorial Target	Territorial Target	Row Sum
Not Targeted	**6,688** (6,523.3)	**2,039** (2,203.7)	**8,727**
Targeted	**440** (604.7)	**369** (204.3)	**809**
Column Sum	**7,128**	**2,408**	**9,536**

Observed values in bold, expected values in parentheses.

funding and assisting proxies and largely refrained from any more direct military confrontations or threats. This view suggests that sponsorship is something of a substitute for disadvantaged challenger states relative to directly using their own military forces. Accordingly, while we know that territorial disputes are associated with MIDs, we might expect territorial disputes where the challenger state is a state sponsor to be associated with less interstate military violence than other territorial disputes. Given that the posited relation between interstate military conflict, territorial disputes, and sponsorship involves three variables and interactions between two of them, we explore these patterns with regression models rather than cross-tabulations.

Table 32.5 (full table shown at the end of this chapter) contains twelve regression models that explore the patterns between sponsorship, territorial dispute, and the onset of militarized interstate disputes. The unit of analysis is again country-year to facilitate comparability to the cross-tabulations in Tables 32.1–32.4. All models are logit models with a time trend and standard errors clustered by country. The key difference between models 1–6 and models 7–12 is that models 1–6 are pooled models of MID onset while models 7–12 are conditional logit models of MID onset with country-fixed effects. The country-fixed effects help us measure any time-invariant traits of each state that make them more or less prone to interstate violence and which are not captured by our key variables. Given that our dependent variable, MID onset, is binary, inclusion of fixed effects also eliminates all countries that never experience an MID onset from the sample. The logged time trend ensures that we measure any changes in MID onset activity that are correlated with time.[3] We can also include a number of other regressors that are common in such models without changing our conclusions, such as regime type or military capabilities, but we choose to keep our specification as simple as possible and to avoid losing data from missingness.

We examine three sets of variables related to sponsorship and territorial disputes and their connections to MID onset. First, in models 1 and 2, we examine the connections between being involved in any way in a sponsorship relationship, whether the target of a sponsored group or the sponsoring state, and being involved in a territorial dispute, whether the challenger state or the target state. Model 1 includes *Any Sponsorship Activity* and *Territorial Dispute* without an interaction between them, while model 2 also includes the interaction between these two variables. Second, in models 3 and 4 we explore the connections between MID onset and being a sponsor of a group and/or a

Table 32.5 Conditional Logit Models with Country-Fixed Effects: Territorial Disputes, Sponsorship, and MID Onset

	Model 1	Model 2	Model 3	Model 4	Model 5	Model 6	Model 7	Model 8	Model 9	Model 10	Model 11	Model 12
Any Sponsorship	1.180**	1.598**					0.429**	0.893**				
Activity	(0.17)	(0.26)					(0.22)	(0.30)				
Territorial Dispute	1.156**	1.285**					1.232**	1.380**				
	(0.20)	(0.22)					(0.27)	(0.28)				
Any Sponsorship		−0.618**						−0.702*				
Activity x Territorial		(0.30)						(0.39)				
Dispute												
Territorial Challenger			0.959**	1.110**					0.591*	0.778**		
			(0.20)	(0.23)					(0.31)	(0.34)		
Sponsor			1.225**	1.555**					0.459*	0.830**		
			(0.19)	(0.24)					(0.25)	(0.30)		
Territorial Challenger x				−0.770**						−0.919**		
Sponsor				(0.35)						(0.45)		
Territorial Target					1.185**	1.404**					0.752*	0.886*
					(0.22)	(0.23)					(0.46)	(0.46)
Target of Sponsorship					1.136**	1.741**					0.383	0.818**
					(0.22)	(0.27)					(0.24)	(0.33)
Territorial Target x						−1.349**						−1.157**
Target of Sponsorship						(0.36)						(0.42)
Logged Year	7.053**	7.054**	6.352**	6.379**	6.241**	6.287**	7.667**	7.670**	7.199**	7.212**	7.173**	7.174**
	(0.43)	(0.43)	(0.34)	(0.35)	(0.35)	(0.36)	(0.53)	(0.53)	(0.47)	(0.47)	(0.49)	(0.49)
Constant	−30.362**	−30.426**	−27.263**	−27.424**	−26.769**	−27.016**						
	(1.79)	(1.79)	(1.37)	(1.41)	(1.39)	(1.45)						
Country Fixed Effects	No	No	No	No	No	No	Yes	Yes	Yes	Yes	Yes	Yes
N	9,412	9,412	9,412	9,412	9,412	9,412	7,601	7,601	7,601	7,601	7,601	7,601
Psuedo R²	0.3043	0.3059	0.2821	0.2845	0.2865	0.2922	0.3983	0.3998	0.3912	0.3935	0.3914	0.3941

Standard errors clustered by state in parentheses. ** $p < 0.05$; * $p < 0.10$.

territorial challenger (the same two variables as in Table 32.3), with model 3 including these two variables without interaction and model 4 interacting with them. Finally, models 5 and 6 estimate the connections between MID onset and being a target state in a territorial dispute and the target of a non-state group that is sponsored by another state (the same variables as in Table 32.4). Model 5 includes these two variables without interaction while model 6 also includes their interaction. Exploration of these three sets of variables allows us to probe whether it seems that sponsorship and the direct use of interstate military force are substitutes for states in contentious territorial disputes. We expect similar patterns across all three sets of variables, as being involved in the onset of a MID can be the result of being targeted or being the aggressor, i.e. the territorial target or the territorial challenger. Models 7–12 contain the exact same specifications but also include country-fixed effects.

The results across all specifications suggest some initial support for the idea that state sponsorship is a substitute for the more direct use of military force. Across all three sets of variables the coefficients on the sponsorship and territorial dispute variables are positive when individually included. The coefficients are statistically significant at the 0.05 level when we include all sponsorship and territorial dispute activity regardless of who is the target or challenger (model 1), while the coefficients are significant at the 0.10 level when we include only sponsoring states and territorial challengers (model 3). In model 5, where we include the territorial target and the target of sponsorship variables, we find that being a territorial target is associated with MID onset at the 0.10 level of significance, while the target of sponsorship variable falls short of statistical significance at conventional levels. However, when we include an interaction between the sponsorship and territorial dispute variables in models 2, 4, and 6 we consistently find a negative and statistically significant relationship, while the individual variables remain positive. The positive and significant coefficients on the individual sponsorship and territorial dispute variables suggest that when a state has only a territorial dispute or only is only a state sponsor, it is more likely to experience MID onset, which is quite consistent with extant findings (e.g. Vasquez (1993) and Maoz and San-Akca (2012)).

It is well known that interaction effects from non-linear models such as a logit can be difficult to interpret from simply examining the coefficients.[4] Accordingly, we plot an interaction in Figure 32.1, which shows the interaction between being a territorial target and the target of a state-sponsored group from model 6 in Table 32.5. The plot shows the effect of being targeted in a territorial dispute on MID onset in both the absence and presence of being targeted by a state-sponsored, non-state armed group. The effect of being a target in a territorial dispute alone is unsurprisingly positive and significant, i.e. the left-hand plot in the figure. This accords with a longstanding literature on territorial disputes and interstate military conflict. In contrast, the effect of being the target in a territorial dispute becomes negative when the state in question is also targeted by a state-sponsored, non-state armed group. While the coefficient just misses the 0.05 level of significance, it easily attains significance at the 0.10 level. Whether the coefficient is considered negative and significant or insignificant, the finding is quite intriguing given the status of territorial disputes as a well-known and robust predictor of conflict (e.g. Vasquez (1993); Hensel (2000); Huth (1996)).

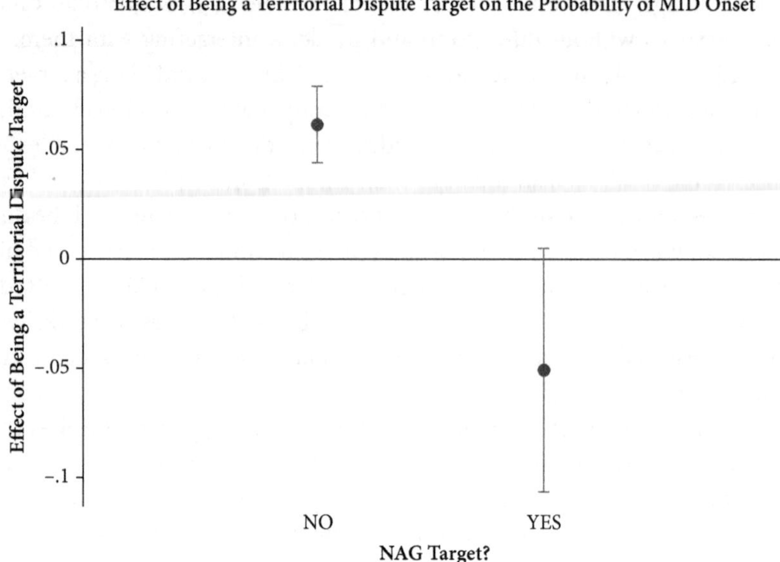

FIGURE 32.1 Plot of Interaction Effect: Territorial Targets that are Also Targeted by Sponsored Groups

The clear yet nuanced connections between state sponsorship and territorial disputes we have outlined suggest that there is much to gain from further exploration, both theoretically and empirically. Theoretically, the strategic dynamics behind the choice to empower a proxy group (i.e. to sponsor a violent non-state group) both in a contentious interstate territorial dispute as well as when there is no such dispute are in need of better specification. While the basic intuition is noted in the extant literature, the devil is often in the details and the details are not well-specified yet. Empirically, we view the cross-tabulations and regression models reported as a first-cut, as there is undoubtedly much more to uncover and learn about the connections between territorial disputes and state sponsorship. Moreover, we think empirical work will benefit from engaging with theoretical developments as theory often clarifies the particular relationships in the data that need to be explored. We hope that this chapter provides a promising start to this important area of research.

Conclusions and Suggestions for Future Research

Although the literature on state sponsorship of violent groups that use terrorist tactics is not the most well-developed of work on political violence, there are important theoretical and empirical works on most aspects of sponsorship. We survey this body of work in this chapter, highlighting connections among the different studies and frameworks and also underscoring areas in need of improvement and future work. We describe the key trade-offs theoretically for states, groups, and targets of sponsored groups to clarify the key moving parts in need of theoretical study. Finally, we suggest an area that scholars interested in state sponsorship of violent groups should think more about moving forward: the connections between sponsorship and interstate disputes over territory. We conclude here by surveying the main ideas and findings in the existing literature that we discuss in the chapter, as well as calling attention to the empirical evidence that we introduce showing the connections between sponsorship and territorial disputes.

We start the chapter by surveying the types of sponsorship available to states as well as the typical motivations for sponsorship identified in the literature. Sponsorship ranges from active, to passive, and to unintentional. While active sponsorship implies a state is directly aiding a violent group by providing resources of some type or a territorial base, passive and unintentional sponsorship are more varied and the latter category often has more to do with a lack of capacity to prevent a group from operating within one's borders than it does with using a proxy to further a policy goal. Accordingly, while it is useful to distinguish among these types of sponsorship to provide a big-picture overview of the phenomenon, future research would likely benefit from developing a distinct theory over active and passive sponsorship, as opposed to unintentional sponsorship, if the goal is to more fully specify and understand the underlying strategic dynamics. The key trade-off for state sponsors, either active or passive, is between obtaining firepower on the cheap and the possibility of blowback from one's target or losing control of a sponsored group.

The question of why groups choose to accept state help is also in need of further research. The potential benefits are fairly obvious and include gaining access to funds and weapons, training resources, and increased security from having a territorial base. It is well-known that sub-state groups usually suffer a resource imbalance relative to the states that they target (Fearon and Laitin 2003). However, there are real trade-offs to accepting sponsorship for groups, as they usually lose some control or autonomy to states that usually do not fully share their interests. Moreover, being viewed as a "tool" of a state might also cause a group to lose radical appeal among the rank and file—a problem identified by Byman (2005b) in his seminal treatment.

Target states also face a difficult set of issues in formulating a response to being targeted by violent groups supported by another state. Using force or police work to eliminate the threat from a violent group is very difficult even if the group is solely domestic. However, when the group has ties to another state, usually a rival or opponent, this often further complicates counterterrorism efforts. First, using force to retaliate becomes a much more costly option if one has to attack another state or violate another state's sovereignty. The trade-offs and uncertainties here are considerable. For example, Bapat (2007) suggests that states that host a violent non-state group can help enforce bargains, which may facilitate negotiated settlements with a group. However, hosts that are also sponsors are usually not all that interested in being helpful, and threatening to impose costs if they do not assist in dealing with a violent group is often incredible because imposition of these costs can weaken the host and empower the violent group (Carter 2015). However, as argued by Carter (2012a), active sponsors who are also hosts might have more credible levels of control over a group in addition to also having a known interest in avoiding military conflict; thus, perhaps Bapat's (2007) suggestion that host states can help target states deal with groups is correct, even if it is more conditional than originally thought. All in all, this last area is perhaps the least researched and most "ripe" in terms of the potential insights to be uncovered by future research.

We view more research on the connections between interstate disputes, such as territorial disputes, and state sponsorship to be essential in order to better understand all of these trade-offs, and think particular light will be shed on target state policy options and trade-offs. The most prominent and durable motivation for sponsoring a violent non-state group is strategic (Byman 2005b) and most scholars suggest that sponsorship is a policy instrument for states that have some kind of strategic goal in mind. While this is a point with fairly wide recognition, there has not been a lot of research into exactly what connections there are between contentious and salient interstate disputes, such as territorial disputes, and patterns in state sponsorship. We argue that territorial disputes are likely to be highly relevant for understanding state-sponsorship patterns as a large literature demonstrates them to be highly salient, prone to violence, and relatively difficult to resolve. Thus, if contentious interstate disputes are connected to sponsorship, territorial disputes seem a fruitful place to start exploring. Using the best available data, we demonstrate a strong empirical connection between territorial disputes and state sponsorship. Moreover, we demonstrate that the patterns are nuanced and consistent with theory in a way that suggests the connections go beyond "problems correlating with problems." For instance, while both state sponsorship and territorial dispute are individually associated with a greater probability of militarized dispute onset, the presence of both territorial dispute and sponsorship implies a significantly lower probability of MID onset. While the evidence is preliminary, this does suggest that states with territorial disputes that also sponsor terrorist groups are supporting proxies as a substitute for directly attacking their territorial foe. These sorts of dynamics are also likely present in other kinds of contentious interstate policy disputes. We think this set of connections, which we have shed some light on, is a very fruitful direction for future research.

Notes

1. See Bueno de Mesquita 2013 for a theory that connects the use of terrorism to building public support.
2. Carter 2012a goes on to test this hypothesis and finds no real empirical support for it.
3. Again, it does not matter for our coefficients of interest if we exclude this variable.
4. See e.g. Brambor et al. 2006.

References

Asal, Victor, and R. Karl Rethemeyer (2008) "The Nature of the Beast: Organizational Structures and the Lethality of Terrorist Attacks," *Journal of Politics*, 70(2): 437–49.

Bapat, Navin A. (2007) "The Internationalization of Terrorist Campaigns," *Conflict Management and Peace Science*, 24(4): 265–80.
Bapat, Navin A. (2012) "Understanding State Sponsorship of Militant Groups," *British Journal of Political Science*, 42(1): 1–29.
Boutton, Andrew T. (2014) "U.S. Foreign Aid, Interstate Rivalry, and Incentives for Counterterrorism Cooperation," *Journal of Peace Research* 51(6): 741–54.
Brambor, Thomas, William Roberts Clark, and Matt Golder (2006) "Understanding Interaction Models: Improving Empirical Analyses," *Political Analysis*, 14(1): 63–82.
Bueno de Mesquita, Ethan (2005) "The Quality of Terror," *American Journal of Political Science*, 49(3): 515–30.
Bueno de Mesquita, Ethan (2013) "Rebel Tactics," *Journal of Political Economy*, 121(2): 323–57.
Byman, Daniel (2005a) "Passive Sponsors of Terrorism," *Survival*, 47(4): 117–44.
Byman, Daniel (2005b) *Deadly Connections: States that Sponsor Terrorism*. Cambridge: Cambridge University Press.
Byman, Daniel (2008) "Understanding Proto-Insurgencies," *Journal of Strategic Studies*, 31(2): 165–200.
Byman, Daniel, and Sarah E. Kreps (2010) "Agents of Destruction? Applying Principal-Agent Analysis to State Sponsored Terrorism," *International Studies Perspectives*, 11(1): 1–18.
Carter, David B. (2012a) "A Blessing or a Curse? State Support for Terrorist Groups," *International Organization*, 66(1): 129–51.
Carter, David B. (2012b) "Terrorist Group and Government Interaction: Progress in Empirical Research," *Perspectives on Terrorism*, 6(4–5): 108–24.
Carter, David B. (2015) "The Compellence Dilemma: International Disputes with Violent Groups," *International Studies Quarterly*, 59(3): 461–76.
Carter, David B. (2016) "Provocation and the Strategy of Terrorist and Guerilla Attacks," *International Organization*, 70(1): 133–73.
Carter, David B., Andrew C. Shaver, and Austin L. Wright (2018) "Places to Hide: Terrain, Ethnicity, and Civil Conflict," *Journal of Politics*.
Carter, David B., Rachel Wellhausen, and Paul K. Huth (2018) "International Law, Territorial Disputes and Foreign Direct Investment." *International Studies Quarterly*.
Collins, Stephen D. (2004) "Dissuading State Support of Terrorism: Strikes or Sanctions? An Analysis of Dissuasion Measures Employed Against Libya)," *Studies in Conflict and Terrorism*, 27(1): 1–18.
Collins, Stephen D. (2014) "State Sponsored Terrorism: In Decline, Yet Still a Potent Threat," *Politics and Policy*, 42(1): 131–59.
Cronin, Audrey Kurth (2009) *How Terrorism Ends: Understanding the Decline and Demise of Terrorist Campaigns*. Princeton: Princeton University Press.
Cunningham, David E., Kristian Skrede Gleditsch, and Idean Salehyan (2013) "Non-State Actors in Civil Wars: A New Dataset," *Conflict Management and Peace Science*, 30(5): 516–31.
Enders, Walter, and Todd Sandler (1999) "Transnational Terrorism in the Post-Cold War Era," *International Studies Quarterly*, 43(1): 145–67.
Fearon, James D., and David D. Laitin (2003) "Ethnicity, Insurgency, and Civil War," *American Political Science Review*, 97(1): 75–90.
Findley, Michael G., James A. Piazza, and Joseph K. Young (2012) "Games Rivals Play: Terrorism in International Rivalries," *Journal of Politics*, 74(1): 235–48.
Gaibulloev, Khusrav, and Todd Sandler (2014) "An Empirical Analysis of Alternative Ways that Terrorist Groups End," *Public Choice*, 160(1–2): 25–44.

Gleditsch, Kristian Skrede, Idean Salehyan, and Kenneth Schultz (2008) "Fighting at Home, Fighting Abroad: How Civil Wars Lead to International Disputes," *Journal of Conflict Resolution*, 52(4): 479–506.

Hensel, Paul R. (2000) "Territory: Theory and Evidence on Geography and Conflict," in John A. Vasquez (ed.), *What do we Know about War?* Boulder, CO: Rowman & Littlefield, 57–84.

Hoffman, Bruce (1997) "Why Terrorists Don't Claim Credit," *Terrorism and Political Violence*, 9(1): 1–6.

Holsti, Kalevi Jaakko (1991) *Peace and War: Armed Conflicts and International Order, 1648–1989*. Cambridge: Cambridge University Press.

Huth, Paul K. (1996) *Standing Your Ground*. Ann Arbor, MI: University of Michigan Press.

Huth, Paul K., and Todd L. Allee (2002) *The Democratic Peace and Territorial Conflict in the Twentieth Century*. Cambridge: Cambridge University Press.

Huth, Paul K., Sarah E. Croco, and Benjamin J. Appel (2011) "Does International Law Promote the Peaceful Settlement of International Disputes? Evidence from the Study of Territorial Conflicts since 1945," *American Political Science Review*, 105(2): 415–36.

Kittner, Cristiana C. Brafman (2007) "The Role of Safe Havens in Islamist Terrorism," *Terrorism and Political Violence*, 19(3): 307–29.

Krueger, Alan B. (2007) *What Makes a Terrorist*. Princeton: Princeton University Press.

Lake, David A. (2002) "Rational Extremism: Understanding Terrorism in the Twenty-First Century," *Dialog-IO* (Spring): 15–29.

Luard, Evan (1986) *War in International Society: A Study in International Sociology*. London: I. B. Tauris.

Maoz, Zeev, and Belgin San-Akca (2012) "Rivalry and State Support of Non-State Armed Groups (NAGs), 1946–2011," *International Studies Quarterly*, 56(4): 720–34.

McCormick, Gordon H., and Guillermo Owen (2009) *Terrorists and Sponsors: An Inquiry into Trust and Double-Crossing*. Hoboken, NJ: Springer.

Mickolus, Edward F. (1989) "What Constitutes State Support to Terrorists?," *Terrorism and Political Violence*, 1(3): 287–93.

Newman, Edward (2007) "Weak States, State Failure, and Terrorism," *Terrorism and Political Violence*, 19(4): 463–88.

Phillips, Brian J. (2014) "Terrorist Group Cooperation and Longevity," *International Studies Quarterly*, 58(2): 336–47.

Piazza, James A. (2006) "Rooted in Poverty? Terrorism, Poor Economic Development and Social Cleavages," *Terrorism and Political Violence*, 18: 159–77.

Piazza, James A. (2011) "Illicit Drugs, Counternarcotics Strategies and Terrorism," *Public Choice*, 149(3–4): 297–314.

Pluchinsky, Dennis A. (1997) "The Terrorism Puzzle: Missing Pieces and No Boxcover," *Terrorism and Political Violence*, 9(1): 7–10.

Salehyan, Idean (2007) "Transnational Rebels: Neighboring States as Sanctuary for Rebel Groups," *World Politics*, 59(2): 217–42.

Salehyan, Idean (2008) "No Shelter Here: Rebel Sanctuaries and International Conflict," *Journal of Politics*, 70(1): 54–66.

Salehyan, Idean (2010) "The Delegation of War to Rebel Organizations," *Journal of Conflict Resolution*, 54(3): 493–515.

Salehyan, Idean, Kristian Skrede Gleditsch, and David E. Cunningham (2011) "Explaining External Support for Insurgent Groups," *International Organization*, 65(4): 709–44.

Schultz, Kenneth A. (2010) "The Enforcement Problem in Coercive Bargaining: Interstate Conflict over Rebel Support in Civil Wars," *International Organization*, 64(2): 281–312.

Shapiro, Jacob N. (2012) "Terrorist Decision-Making: Insights from Economics and Political Science," *Perspectives on Terrorism*, 6(4–5): 5–20.

Siqueira, Kevin, and Todd Sandler (2006) "Terrorists versus the Government: Strategic Interaction, Support, and Sponsorship," *Journal of Conflict Resolution*, 50(6): 878–98.

Vasquez, John A. (1993) *The War Puzzle*. Cambridge: Cambridge University Press.

Vasquez, John, and Marie T. Henehan (2001) "Territorial Disputes and the Probability of War, 1816–1992," *Journal of Peace Research*, 38(2): 123–38.

CHAPTER 33

TEACHING ABOUT TERRORISM

methodology and ethics

GREGORY D. MILLER

One of the biggest dilemmas facing those who teach and research on terrorism is the biases of scholars in other disciplines. Critics of the field generally believe that: (a) we are all cashing in on the US government response to 9/11, which seemingly gave money to anyone who claimed to study terrorism (Mueller 2006); or (b) since we study it we must somehow condone the act of terrorism. For the former bias, which seems to be more relevant for the terrorism researcher, we have much in common with those who studied the Soviet Union or nuclear deterrence during the Cold War. Although it is a valid criticism that some of the work after 9/11 was not particularly useful or innovative, often reinventing the wheel by ignoring the research done on terrorism prior to 9/11, government and private donor support also generated a great deal of new and innovative scholarship, that significantly advanced our understanding of terrorism. While this critique is not unique to terrorism studies, we will only mitigate it through the continued work of those who make meaningful contributions to the field both as researchers and as teachers.

For the latter bias, probably more relevant for those in the terrorism classroom, we have much in common with military historians who are often criticized for either studying mundane aspects of war (i.e. counting the number of buttons on a uniform) or for the assumption that because they study war they must be war-mongers. This bias is apparent whenever we tell someone we teach a class on terrorism, and more often than not the first question will be "is it a how-to course?" While partially intended as a joke, these biases will persist as long as there is a lack of understanding of what we do. The fact that there is no agreed-upon definition of terrorism will prolong these biases, as many have a misunderstanding of terrorism, and thus of what is taught in a terrorism course. Two ways to weaken these biases are to improve the public's understanding of terrorism through education, and to build our classes using the same pedagogical tools used by faculty offering more "mainstream" topics.

This chapter's starting point, for a discussion of ethics in the terrorism classroom, is the broad, but often cited, *Ethical Principles for College and University Teaching* (Murray et al. 1996). Although Murray and his co-authors list nine principles, the first four—content competence; pedagogical competence; dealing with sensitive topics; and student development—are particularly relevant to the topic of teaching courses on terrorism, and therefore to this chapter.[1] Many other works discuss ethics in the classroom (Rocheleau and Speck 2007; Markie 1994), but Murray et al.'s *Ethical Principles* provide the framework for this chapter's discussion because it applies to the classroom broadly, yet captures several of the challenges of teaching terrorism courses.

The main sections of the chapter focus on the first two principles—content and pedagogical competence—but the other two principles, highlighting the importance of student development while addressing a sensitive topic, arise several times throughout the chapter. According to the principle of dealing with sensitive topics, instructors should acknowledge the sensitivity of an issue, and explain why it is included in the course syllabus, as well as invite students to state their position on the issue while encouraging respect for different views. Terrorism itself is a sensitive issue, but several elements of a terrorism course—the role of religion, the intentional targeting of civilians, various counterterror methods used by states—pose particular challenges for instructors, many of which I address throughout the chapter.

The principle of student development focuses on the instructor's responsibility to design a course that facilitates learning and encourages students to think for themselves. A second purpose of this chapter, in addition to pushing forward the discussion of ethical teaching, is to highlight some of the varied methods of teaching a terrorism course, and thus help current and future instructors create courses that successfully promote student development. The discussion not only highlights some of the issues related to the sensitive topic of terrorism, but also addresses the strengths and weaknesses of the various teaching methods, primarily within the context of the terrorism classroom, with the intent of promoting greater student development. With that context in mind, let us turn to a discussion of content competence, which illustrates an ethical issue for instructors as well as administrators.

Content Competence

One of the most significant ethical issues in teaching a course on terrorism is that the instructor must have some understanding of the topic and be able to discuss what we know about terrorism as well as what we do not know about terrorism. The ethical dilemma here exists primarily on the level of the department, college, and university, but the individual instructor also has an obligation to students.

The biggest issue with terrorism courses after 9/11 was not simply the rush to create them by seemingly every college and university in the Western world. That is understandable given the demand for such courses by students and by government officials. The issue is that so few of the newly created courses were taught by people with expertise on the subject. In many cases, schools asked existing faculty members to take on terrorism courses without having the background to do so, rather than go through the effort and finances necessary to hire someone qualified to teach courses on terrorism. Too many schools allowed the business of academia to interfere with the ethics of offering a course for which no expertise existed on campus. The terrorism studies community still suffers from this because it not only led to ineffective courses, but the subsequent decisions by many schools to drop those courses hurts the ability of those in the field to find academic positions.

On the personal level, those who are unqualified to teach terrorism courses should no more volunteer to teach one than I should offer to teach an advanced statistical methods course. My lack of experience, skill, and background to teach such a course would hopefully prevent a department from asking me to do so. Even if that did not deter a department, I could not consciously subject students to a course for which I am unprepared and in which I would provide inaccurate information and be unable to answer difficult questions. Yet, too few individuals, departments, and colleges have similar restraints on their terrorism courses.

One result of misunderstanding the topic is a misuse of the term, often based on personal biases. We end up with publications and a public that not only do not understand terrorism but, much worse, equate terrorism with everything bad. Examples of how this misunderstanding makes it into the academic discourse include publications that equate terrorism with other bad acts or outcomes.[2] Publications of this sort, and professors who teach about terrorism using similar analogies, whether in a terrorism class or in other classes, hurt our ability to have a meaningful discussion, because terrorism becomes associated with everything with which we disagree or find offensive. When everything that is bad is defined as terrorism, the term becomes less meaningful.

We cannot ignore that every professor has a bias and that terrorism is a highly subjective term. It is therefore incumbent on the instructor to be clear to students how he or she defines terrorism, so that they understand what the existing biases in the course might be. It is equally necessary that the instructor make it clear that students should develop their own definition of terrorism, and more importantly be able to defend their definition. In this way, an instructor's own biases will be obvious and will clearly shape the design of the course and some of the discussion in it, but will be less likely to impede the individual student outcomes.

The solution is that terrorism courses, if they exist on a particular campus, should be taught by those who are qualified to teach such courses. The lack of terrorism studies as an accepted subfield of any discipline means that there is no set of standards to point to as an indicator of a person's qualifications. But the ability to teach in any subfield of any discipline usually requires some combination of previous coursework, publication-quality research, and recognition by peers in the field. Absent those qualifications, professors should refrain from teaching any course, but especially those covering sensitive topics like terrorism.

Pedagogical Competence

In addition to the knowledge of the relevant materials, an instructor must also be aware of the various methods of delivery, as well as which ones are most effective at helping students achieve course objectives. As with any subject, there are a variety of approaches to teaching about terrorism, each of which has its advantages and disadvantages, with respect to teaching a course on terrorism (Fox and Ronkowski 1997), but each also presents its own ethical issues in a terrorism class. I subscribe to the view that a plurality of methods is the best way to reach the widest number of students in the classroom. Lopez (1979) discussed some of the objectives for teaching about terrorism, many of which still ring true, though the materials and methods may have changed. For example, he suggests having students be able to identify the difference between the state as a terror agent and the acts of non-state terrorist groups, and applying conceptual frameworks to the study of terrorist groups. Faust and Paulson (1998) also provide several different active learning methods, ranging from simple exercises like the one-minute paper, to more complex cooperative learning strategies. Though gleaned from the natural sciences and humanities, many of them are highly applicable to the terrorism classroom.

This chapter focuses on four common methods of active learning that instructors use in a typical classroom, and that seem to be common among terrorism courses: class participation/discussion, films, case studies, and simulations. For each teaching method, I focus on the strengths and weaknesses of the approach as well as any ethical issues involved with its use on a sensitive topic like terrorism.

Passive teaching methods, like traditional lectures, and other active learning methods, like small group work and in-class writing, have their own strengths and weaknesses. I avoid a detailed discussion of the traditional lecture here, not because it lacks merit, but because scholars generally consider active learning methods to be more effective. Yet these methods come with distinct ethical issues that link to the theme of this chapter. Perhaps the most critical ethical issue related to lectures is that, if we know other teaching methods are more effective at conveying information and aiding in student learning, is it ethical to continue to lecture? I still see some value in it, regardless of the course topic, though its usefulness is not in the lecturing itself, but in its role as one of several approaches to be used in the classroom, and that when done right will complement each other.

Class Participation/Discussion

With this approach, professors engage students with questions that come from course readings, current events, or previous involvement in one of the other activities to be discussed later, i.e. watching a film or participating in a simulation (McGonigal 2005; Brookfield and Preskill 1999; Johnson and Cooper 1997). The advantages to class participation include the ability to pool ideas and experiences from a group of people who may have widely distinct backgrounds. It also provides an opportunity for everyone to participate in a more active process than occurs during a traditional lecture. Significant research suggests learning, critical thinking, and degree completion all increase when students feel more engaged with the instructor, even when it is part of a traditional lecture (Tinto 1997; Weast 1996; Kember and Gow 1994; McKeachie 1990; Smith 1977). Several works also highlight strategies for improving class participation, such as Cohen's (1991) Five-Word Game, in which students come to class with five words that describe the readings, and then justify their word choices in class (see also Pennell 2000), so this chapter will not address that particular challenge.

Unfortunately, there are several weaknesses with this method (Damron and Mott 2005), some of which can generate ethical dilemmas for the instructor. For one thing, it is often not a practical method to use in a class of more than twenty people. This may not be a problem in liberal arts colleges or in graduate courses, but is often unwieldy for undergraduate classes at a university, where even senior-level courses have thirty to fifty students. It is also easier for instructors using this method to find themselves off-track, compared to those relying exclusively on the lecture approach (which raises the specter of the ethical principle of student development). As a result, and because there is a risk of students asking questions that are only tangentially related to the intended theme of the lesson, instructors using class discussion often have to prepare even more, and be more broadly conversant on the subject, than those relying on lectures. While certainly a challenging part of this method, this may be more a strength than a weakness, because it forces the instructor to develop a more expansive understanding of the topic, enhancing his or her content competency.

The most significant ethical issue related to the discussion method has to do with the involvement of the students. Through this method, it is common for a small number of people to dominate a conversation, sometimes at the exclusion of others, who are either uncomfortable participating—due to a quieter personality or concern about weak language skills—or simply unwilling to do so and risk being challenged by the dominant voices in the room.

The potential weakness of this approach is that only a handful of students may choose to participate, either because they are the only ones who prepared for class, or because they are the only ones willing to participate in class, regardless of whether they prepared or not. To avoid this, the instructor must either tolerate only a handful of students participating, and accept that as an opportunity for the other students to still learn from each other's experiences, or the instructor can provide incentives for students to participate. One obvious way to do that is to include participation as an element of the course grade. This may compel some students to participate who otherwise might not, though it can also encourage greater participation from those who care about their grades, whether they prepared for the class discussion or not.

Another way to address this dilemma is for a professor to utilize the Socratic Method of calling on specific students to answer questions. The assumption made by those who use the Socratic Method, often used in medical and law schools, is that the fear of being called on will inspire students to do more preparation before class, and thus they will get more out of the class. The counter-argument is that students are so fearful of looking bad, that they retain less information, meaning that the Socratic Method may create less learning than a passive lecture. Research results and opinions are mixed on the pedagogical value of the Socratic Method; Dallimore (1977) gives one negative view, emphasizing the frustration it causes among students, while Jarvis (2002) provides a more positive take, when it is done correctly, and suggesting successful student participation is more a result of the teacher's style than the method used. Kerr (1999) takes a somewhat balanced look, specifically with respect to the use of the Socratic Method in law schools, while Guliuzza (1991) suggests combining the Socratic Method with debates. Ultimately, each instructor must evaluate his or her own ability to use this method effectively, either on its own or in combination with other teaching methods.

Films

There is considerable literature on the use of film in the classroom. Students retain more of what they see and hear than what they read, so visuals create the opportunity for students to learn more (Leet and Houser 2003; Weber 2001; Voller and Widdows 1993; Hannon and Marullo 1988). The obvious strength of this method, in an era when professors often feel the need to be more like entertainers than educators, is that films can raise important issues for discussion, while keeping a group's attention and providing some level of entertainment—even if it is education in disguise.

Films have some similar weaknesses as class discussion, because film use in the classroom is only as effective as the conversation that occurs afterwards. In the absence of an engaging discussion after watching a film, many students may become as passive during the movie as they would be during a lecture. This is especially possible and problematic when using popular films that students may have already seen.

Another concern is that films demonstrate an inherent bias that may distort the purpose of the intended lesson, or in the extreme cases that they portray historical inaccuracies. Butler et al. (2009) highlight some of the benefits and dangers of using popular history films. One of the best illustrations of this challenge is the book, *Terrorism in American Cinema* (Cettl 2009). While useful as an A–Z anthology of films, many of the films listed in the book are only indirectly related to terrorism, or only relate to terrorism if one takes a particular point of view. The cover illustration itself is from a film, *Taxi to the Dark Side* (2007), which focuses more on the US use of torture than it does on terrorism, illustrating the author's bias of what constitutes terrorism. While that film might be completely appropriate for a course on counterterrorism, for example to spark debate on appropriate versus inappropriate methods of counterterrorism, it is less useful in a terrorism survey course and ethically dangerous in the sense that it provides a particularly biased view of terrorism. This is an important point that relates back to content competence; the instructor must know what class he or she wants to teach. A survey course on terrorism would benefit from a very different set of films than classes on counterterrorism, the war on terror, the history of terrorism, or the psychology of terrorism.

Instructors must also accept that a tradeoff exists whenever we use films in the classroom. Films often take up an entire class period, so instructors must balance the value of the themes or issues that a film communicates, or the way in which a film conveys its message, with the lost time for lecture, discussion, or other activities (Kuzma and Haney 2001). Obvious solutions to this problem carry their own disadvantages. One solution is to assign the film outside of class, but this requires students to spend additional time watching a film. Another solution is to show only certain passages or clips, but this risks losing some of the context of the film.

There are hundreds of films—both feature films and documentaries—that one could use in the classroom, and this chapter touches on just a small sample of what is available. Each film has its own strengths and weaknesses depending on the quality, accuracy, and intended use of the film. The most common film in terrorism courses is undoubtedly *The Battle of Algiers* (1966). Despite its age, it is highly effective at identifying several aspects of modern terrorism and counterterrorism, including but not limited to: the role of women and children in terrorist groups, the use of torture as a means to gain information, the structure of terrorist groups, and the difference between counterterrorism and state terror. Other films that appear on numerous syllabi include: *The Terrorist* (1998), *Munich* (2005), and *The Siege* (1998). Each of these films represents different aspects of terrorism—the psychological preparation of the suicide bomber, the Israeli response to the Munich Olympic attack, and the tension between law enforcement and military responses to terrorism, respectively.

Engert and Spencer (2009) highlight four ways of using films in the classroom, focusing primarily on international politics classes, but these categories also apply to terrorism. First is the depiction of historical events, such as the anarchist movement in Western Europe portrayed in *The Secret Agent* (1996), or the attacks on the Israeli Olympic Athletes in *One Day in September* (1999). Second is using film to highlight a particular issue for discussion, such as the psychology of the suicide bomber portrayed in films like *The Terrorist* and *Paradise Now* (2005). This is potentially tricky, as films of this type are easily mistaken for history. While *The Terrorist* clearly draws on Tamil Tiger attacks against the Indian government, the writer and director take a fair amount of dramatic licence, and students need to be aware of that when watching those types of films. Third is using film as a cultural narrative, such as the parallels on the use of torture before and after 9/11 and the discussion of that method in the film *The Siege*. Fourth uses film to explain theory. This is probably more difficult in a terrorism course than in other types of courses, as terrorism theories are still relatively immature and there are not the same types of worldviews, or schools of thought, on terrorism as exist in international relations or comparative politics. Nevertheless, there are still some opportunities to use film to highlight theories, for instance the effectiveness of non-violent protest as an alternative to terrorism, illustrated in *Gandhi* (1982).

Case Studies

This method can provide a high level of substantive learning on a particular incident or group (Velenchik 1995; Wassermann 1994). Unfortunately, this method can have contradictory results. Students may not see the relevance of the case to their own situation or to modern politics; a case study of the Red Army Faction, though fascinating and important for understanding the history of terrorism, may not resonate with many current college students. On the other hand, a student may see too much similarity with their own beliefs, and will be unable to distance him or herself from the discussion of the case as an example of terrorism. At the extreme level, what many terrorism scholars fear is that a student will use the information in the course, or be inspired by something in the course, to engage in violent activities.

Faculty wanting to employ the case study method should be careful that the studies they use provide a wide cross-section of terrorism and do not focus on one small topic. Unless a course is specifically about a subcategory of terrorism, a course that is meant to survey the field should not rely on case studies that focus exclusively on one type of terrorism, be it Islamic, Marxist, or lone wolf terrorism. Instead, it is most effective when case studies provide students with exposure to different terrorist motivations, methods, and strategies.

The biggest challenge to using case studies, but also possibly the best learning opportunity, is the scenario in which a student does not view the subject of the case study as a terrorist group. I have had students from Lebanon that reject any reference to Hezbollah as a terrorist group. The positive is that you have a built-in opportunity to debate not only the activities of a specific group, but also the broader concepts of defining terrorism and terrorists, and how to separate the violent activities of an organization from the social services it might provide. The negative is that it is easy to get sidetracked by one student's opinion about one particular group, and the class as a whole might miss the point of the lesson. At minimum, by spending a whole class period on one group, if just one person does not agree that group commits acts of terrorism, some learning opportunities will be lost.

The related danger is the student who has a particular perspective about the most dangerous terrorists in the world. I once had a Ukrainian student who saw everything Russia did as terrorism. If the instructor's list of case studies does not cover that group or state, then at least in that student's eyes, the instructor loses some credibility. Again, there are tremendous opportunities for learning here, if nothing else to highlight how people use the term terrorism according to their own point of view. But there is also a high risk of not achieving the course objectives.

One cannot reasonably cover all possible permutations of terrorism using case studies, nor can one predict the preconceived ideas of an entire class, especially while designing a syllabus. Therefore, it is important to understand that while case studies can be a useful tool, too much emphasis on this tool can backfire.

Simulations/Role Playing

There is a significant literature on the value of simulations in the classroom (Bernstein 2008; Shellman and Turan 2006; McCarthy and Anderson 2000; Smith and Boyer 1996).

This section focuses specifically on the strengths and weaknesses of terrorism simulations, as well as the ethical problems that arise because these may be different in a terrorism class than in other classes. While the use of simulations in an introductory international relations class is relatively benign, using simulations in a terrorism course raises several ethical issues both at the personal and the professional level.

Simulations provide students with the opportunity to better appreciate other points of view by assuming new and unique roles. They also provide more opportunity than any other method to apply concepts that the instructor introduced in the course. Simulations are also a historically popular tool for training those who face terrorism on a professional level (Sloan 1981; Sloan et al. 1978). The question is whether simulations serve the same purpose in the classroom, particularly with traditional college students.

Asal (2005) discusses some of the advantages and disadvantages of using simulations to teach international relations, and develops pedagogy, much of which may be convertible to the terrorism classroom. He suggests that simulations can help clarify complex theory, encourage peer-based learning, and allow professors to observe student interaction, though they do demand more of the instructor's energy, can take up significant classroom time, and are challenging when students are uncooperative (see also Boyne 2012; Wheeler 2006). Other works detail some specific types of simulations that may be effective in the classroom. For example, Siegel and Young (2009) discuss two simulations intended to convey the strategic nature of terrorism (see also Fuller 1991). Building on the previous section, Simpson and Kaussler (2009) highlight the use of films to supplement simulations. Their discussion on how to combine teaching methods focuses on the international relations classroom, but their suggestions for combining methods are also useful in the terrorism classroom.

Simulations may not be appropriate for large groups, depending on the instructor's experience and level of administrative support. But if done correctly, they can be highly effective even in large classes. It does not resolve the problem of some students being self-conscious about their knowledge or language skills; simulations may even exacerbate those fears in some, because it is more difficult for students to hide during a simulation. On the other hand, this method can encourage some students to become more vocal and take on leadership roles that they otherwise might avoid.

There are several ethical issues involved with simulations, both for the instructor and for students. One significant question has to do with the nature of the simulation. Can you have an effective terrorism simulation in which no students play the role of the terrorists? If the goal of the course is to help students understand the mindset of a terrorist, then the best way to use a simulation is to have some students take on that role. This may mean development of a fictionalized terrorist group as well as conceiving of attacks against a government or population. This is a common type of exercise, known as a red team—in which some members of a group play the role of the adversary or competitor (Romyn and Kebbell 2014; Craig 2007). The National Strategy for Homeland Security (Office of Homeland Security 2002, 19, 33, 53) emphasized the use of red teams, which typically rely on professionals and experts to play those roles, and there is even a regular publication, *Red Team Journal*, devoted to this method. Beyond the issue of choosing which students take on the role of the terrorist, there is a larger question of whether such an exercise is ethical for a college classroom, even if it helps students understand the mindset of the terrorist. The appropriateness of college-level terrorism simulations probably requires additional research and debate, addressing all of the ethical and pedagogical points of view.

Of course, not all simulations require students to take on the role of a terrorist. Simulations in which students are all responders may be more ethical, and do convey certain lessons such as the difficulties of responding to terrorism. Yet even these can pose an ethical challenge to instructors. Even if all students play the role of decision-makers, merely responding to terrorist attacks, many instructors—especially those who are not citizens of the country in which they teach—may hesitate to use a simulation in which terrorists attack a city.

This method is perhaps the most dangerous, ethically, in terms of a student being inspired to engage in violence. Yet, there is no evidence that danger is greater in a terrorism course than the danger of a course on elections helping someone to commit election fraud, or a course on human rights leading someone to perpetrate genocide. In addition, because a simulation can put students in the position of having to make ethical decisions, it can be the most rewarding teaching method. When done correctly, simulations go beyond simply relaying substantive information, and terrorism simulations in particular can engage students in real debates over topics like the appropriate methods to defeat terrorism, the motivations of terrorists, and the treatment of terrorists in the media (Asal and Schulzke 2012).

Summary

The purpose of this chapter is to raise awareness of some of the issues involved in teaching about terrorism. Starting with the *Ethical Principles of College and University Teaching*, this chapter highlighted some of the challenges involved with addressing a sensitive topic, in a way that generates intellectual development among our students, all within the context of both content and pedagogical competence. To accomplish that, this chapter examined the strengths and weaknesses of several common teaching methods, and highlighted some ethical issues related to each, particularly as they might arise in a terrorism course.

All professors should understand their limitations and teach to their strengths, both in terms of the content of their courses and the methods they use. If someone is skilled at getting a high level of student participation without the fear associated with the Socratic Method, then he or she should use that method to generate a useful dialogue. If someone is not knowledgeable in Islam, then it is at least unprofessional, if not unethical, to offer a course on Islamic terrorism and stand in front of students intending to convey a level of expertise that does not exist.

Despite the sensitive nature of terrorism, and the potential for ethical issues to arise, the ethics of teaching a terrorism course are not significantly different from any other course. Instructors must have competency in the content of the class. If not, then they should not offer a course on the subject; instead, if colleges wish to offer terrorism courses, administrators should bring in instructors with the background and qualifications to teach the subject. Departments generally do not ask professors to teach statistics when they are not trained to do so, yet after 9/11, many universities used faculty, who had no previous experience in the subject matter, to offer terrorism courses simply because of student demand. This practice violates the first "Ethical Principle."

Beyond that, all instructors have a responsibility, regardless of the course topic, to use the most effective methods for relaying information to students and helping them to achieve the course objectives. If we do that effectively, the other principles—dealing with a sensitive topic and developing students—will largely take care of themselves.

Notes

1. The other five principles include: avoiding relationships with students; preserving student confidentiality; having respect for colleagues; making valid assessments of students; and having respect for the institution.
2. Some of this incorrect discussion of terrorism existed even before 9/11, but it was largely overlooked. Despite the national effort and energy put into researching terrorism after 9/11, similar discussions continue to exist. Rinestine 1994 equates playground harassment with terrorism, while Felix et al. 2010, conflate 9/11 with sniper shootings in assessing the ability of schools to help students recover. In a more useful approach, Schmid (2005) highlights some of the ways that the lines between terrorists and serial killers began to overlap after 9/11.

References

Asal, V. (2005) "Playing Games with International Relations," *International Studies Perspectives*, 6(3): 359–73.

Asal, V., and M. Schulzke (2012) "A Shot Not Taken: Teaching about the Ethics of Political Violence," *International Studies Perspectives*, 13(4): 408–22.

Bernstein, J. (2008) "Cultivating Civic Competence: Simulations and Skill-Building in an Introductory Government Class," *Journal of Political Science Education*, 4(1): 1–20.

Boyne, S. M. (2012) "Crisis in the Classroom: Using Simulations to Enhance Decision-Making Skills", *Journal of Legal Education*, 62(2): 311–22.

Brookfield, S., and S. Preskill (1999) *Discussion as a Way of Teaching: Tools and Techniques for Democratic Classrooms*. Ann Arbor, MI: University of Michigan Press.

Butler, A., F. Zaromb, K. Lyle, and H. Roediger (2009) "Using Popular Films to Enhance Classroom Learning: The Good, the Bad, and the Interesting," *Psychological Science*, 20(9): 1161–8.

Cettl, R. (2009) *Terrorism in American Cinema: An Analytical Filmography, 1960–2008*. Jefferson, NC: McFarland & Co., Inc.

Cohen, M. (1991) "Making Class Participation a Reality," *PS: Political Science and Politics*, 24(4): 699–703.

Craig, S. (2007) "Reflections from a Red Team Leader," *Military Review*, 87(2): 57–60.

Dallimore, S. (1977) "The Socratic Method—More Harm than Good," *Journal of Contemporary Law*, 3: 177–200.

Damron, D., and Mott, J. (2005) "Creating an Interactive Classroom: Enhancing Student Engagement and Learning in Political Science Courses," *Journal of Political Science Education*, 1(3): 367–83.

Engert, S., and A. Spencer (2009) "International Relations at the Movies: Teaching and Learning about International Politics through Film," *Perspectives: Review of International Affairs*, 17(1): 83–103.

Faust, J., and D. Paulson (1998) "Active Learning in the College Classroom," *Journal on Excellence in College Teaching*, 9(2): 3–24.

Felix, E., E. Vernberg, R. Pfefferbaum, D. Gill, J. Schorr, A. Boudreaux, R. Gurwith, S. Galea, and B. Pfefferbaum (2010) "Schools in the Shadow of Terrorism: Psychosocial Adjustment and Interest in Interventions Following Terror Attacks," *Psychology in the Schools*, 47(6): 592–605.

Fox, R., and S. Ronkowski (1997) "Learning Styles of Political Science Students," *PS: Political Science and Politics*, 30(4): 732–7.

Fuller, L. (1991) "Taking Terrorism into the Classroom," *Journal of Popular Culture*, 25(1): 93–8.

Guliuzza, F. (1991) "In-Class Debating in Public Law Classes as a Complement to the Socratic Method," *PS: Political Science and Politics*, 24(4): 703–5.

Hannon, J., and S. Marullo (1988) "Education for Survival: Using Films to Teach War as a Social Problem," *Teaching Sociology*, 16(3): 245–55.

Jarvis, P. (2002) "The Socratic Method," in P. Jarvis (ed.), *The Theory and Practice of Teaching*. London: Routledge: 90–7.

Johnson, S., and J. Cooper (1997) "Quick-Thinks: The Interactive Lecture," *The Cooperative Learning and College Teaching Newsletter*, 8(1): 2–6.

Kember, D., and L. Gow (1994) "Orientations to Teaching and their Effect on the Quality of Student Learning," *Journal of Higher Education*, 65: 58–74.

Kerr, O. (1999) "The Decline of the Socratic Method at Harvard," *Nebraska Law Review*, 78: 113–45.

Kuzma, L., and P. Haney (2001) "And... Action! Using Film to Learn about Foreign Policy," *International Studies Perspectives*, 2(1): 33–50.

Leet, D., and S. Houser (2003) "Economics Goes to Hollywood: Using Classic Films and Documentaries to Create an Undergraduate Economics Course," *Journal of Economic Education*, 34(4): 326–33.

Lopez, G. (1979) "Teaching about Terrorism: Notes on Method and Materials," *Terrorism*, 3(1–2): 131–45.

McCarthy, P., and L. Anderson (2000) "Active Learning Techniques versus Traditional Teaching Styles: Two Experiments from History and Political Science," *Innovative Higher Education*, 24(4): 279–94.

McGonigal, K. (2005) "Using Class Discussion to Meet your Teaching Goals," *Center for Teaching and Learning, Stanford University Newsletter on Teaching*, 15(1): 1–6.

McKeachie, W. (1990) "Research on College Teaching: The Historical Background," *Journal of Educational Psychology*, 82: 189–200.

Markie, P. (1994) *A Professor's Duties: Ethical Issues in College Teaching*. Lanham, MD: Rowman & Littlefield.

Mueller, J. (2006) *Overblown: How Politicians and the Terrorism Industry Inflate National Security Threats, and Why We Believe Them*. New York: Free Press.

Murray, H., E. Gillese, M. Lennon, P. Mercer, and M. Robinson (1996) "Ethical Principles for College and University Teaching," *New Directions for Teaching and Learning*, 66: 57–63.

Office of Homeland Security (2002) *National Strategy for Homeland Security*, Washington, DC: Government Printing Office.

Pennell, M. (2000) "Improving Student Participation in History Lectures: Suggestions for Successful Questioning," *Teaching History: A Journal of Methods*, 25(1): 25–35.

Rhinestine, S. (1994) "Terrorism on the Playground: What Can be Done?," *Duquesne Law Review*, 32: 799–832.

Rocheleau, J., and B. Speck (2007) *Rights and Wrongs in the College Classroom: Ethical Issues in Postsecondary Teaching*. Bolton, MA: Anker Publishing.

Romyn, D., and M. Kebbell (2014) "Terrorists' Planning of Attacks: A Simulated 'Red-Team' Investigation into Decision-Making," *Psychology, Crime and Law*, 20(5): 480–96.

Schmid, D. (2005) "Serial Killing in America after 9/11," *Journal of American Culture*, 28(1): 61–9.

Shellman, S., and K. Turan (2006) "Do Simulations Enhance Student Learning? An Empirical Evaluation of an IR Simulation," *Journal of Political Science Education*, 2(1): 19–32.

Siegel, D., and J. Young (2009) "Simulating Terrorism: Credible Commitment, Costly Signaling, and Strategic Behavior," *PS: Political Science and Politics*, 42(4): 765–71.

Simpson, A., and B. Kaussler (2009) "IR Teaching Reloaded: Using Films and Simulations in the Teaching of International Relations," *International Studies Perspectives*, 10(4): 413–27.

Sloan, S. (1981) *Simulating Terrorism*. Norman, OK: University of Oklahoma Press.

Sloan, S., R. Kearney, and C. Wise (1978) "Learning about Terrorism: Analysis, Simulations, and Future Directions," *Terrorism*, 1(3–4): 315–29.

Smith, D. (1977) "College Classroom Interactions and Critical Thinking," *Journal of Educational Psychology*, 69: 180–90.

Smith, E., and M. Boyer (1996) "Designing In-Class Simulations," *PS: Political Science and Politics*, 29(4): 690–4.

Tinto, V. (1997) "Classrooms as Communities: Exploring the Educational Character of Student Persistence," *Journal of Higher Education*, 68: 599–623.

Velenchik, A. (1995) "The Case Method as a Strategy for Teaching Policy Analysis to Undergraduates," *Journal of Economic Education*, 26(1): 29–38.

Voller, P., and S. Widdows (1993) "Feature Film as Text: A Framework for Classroom Use," *ELT Journal*, 47(4): 342–53.

Wassermann, S. (1994) *Introduction to Case Method Teaching: A Guide to the Galaxy*. New York: Teachers College Press.

Weast, D. (1996) "Alternative Teaching Strategies: The Case for Critical Thinking," *Teaching Sociology*, 24: 189–94.

Weber, C. (2001) "The Highs and Lows of Teaching IR Theory: Using Popular Films for Theoretical Critique," *International Studies Perspectives*, 2(3): 281–7.

Wheeler, S. (2006) "Role-Playing Games and Simulations for International Issues Courses," *Journal of Political Science Education*, 2(3): 331–47.

FILMS

The Battle of Algiers, 1966. Directed by Gillo Pontecorvo.

Gandhi, 1982. Directed by Richard Attenborough.

Munich, 2005. Directed by Steven Spielberg.
One Day in September, 1999. Directed by Kevin Macdonald.
Paradise Now, 2005. Directed by Hany Abu-Assad.
Taxi to the Dark Side, 2007. Directed by Alex Gibney.
The Secret Agent, 1996. Directed by Christopher Hampton.
The Siege, 1998. Directed by Edward Zwick.
The Terrorist, 1998. Directed by Santosh Sivan.

CHAPTER 34

NEW TECHNIQUES IN TEACHING TERRORISM

DAVID A. SIEGEL

TRADITIONAL teaching techniques that focus on lectures have faced mounting criticism. This criticism focuses on a simple fact: human beings are not particularly good, on average, at remembering things we are read or are told once or even a handful of times. In response to this limitation, opponents of the lecture say, students will tune out their professor, resulting in poor learning outcomes. This student response seems increasingly likely in the internet age, with an array of potentially more exciting sources of information and entertainment readily available at students' fingertips. Certainly, this argument is likely to strike a chord with anyone who has faced a sea of bored (or asleep or clearly paying attention to something else) faces.

We may be better, however, at retaining knowledge arising from our own speech and action (Stice 1987). Active-learning techniques are intended to involve the student more fully in the educational experience. They include simple role-playing exercises, in which students might speak as some other figure, perhaps a known political or historical one, and more complex simulations, in which students play out roles, interact according to some set of rules, and experience outcomes arising from their choices (Wheeler 2006). Student engagement is encouraged by placing students in positions in which they are expected to take actions that affect and are affected by those of their fellow students. This builds teamwork, critical thinking, and personal investment in understanding, theoretically improving learning outcomes (Glazier 2011; Smith and Boyer 1996).

The truth about which techniques are most effective, however, may not be so clear. Many lecture-based classes include extensive in-class discussion in which students may play a more active role in their own learning; experimental research has indicated that discussion can have similar benefits to other forms of active learning such as role play or simulation (Krain and Lantis 2006; Powner and Allendoerfer 2008). Further, it may be the case that active learning is differentially effective, helping those students who would be willing to engage with the coursework regardless the most, and already disengaged students the least (Archetti 2012). If active learning techniques are actually harmful for those in the latter group, then they would be counterproductive to adopt given their intent.

Still, there remains much evidence that, on average, the inclusion of active-learning components such as simulations or role play can be effective in boosting learning outcomes, at least in concert with more traditional techniques of lecture and discussion (Shellman and Turan 2006). This may be even truer in the context of international relations, in which students have little first-hand knowledge to draw upon (Shaw 2004; Simpson and Kaussler 2009). In this broad subject area, active-learning techniques have been used to illustrate, for example, tricky theoretical concepts (Asal 2005), two-level negotiations (Young 2006), foreign policy (Loggins 2009; Enterline and Jepsen 2009; Butcher 2012), humanitarian aid decisions (Stodden 2012), globalization and development (Pallister 2015), and, of course, terrorism (Chasek 2005; Franke 2006; Siegel and Young 2009).

It is the use of in-class simulation for teaching terrorism on which I will focus the remainder of this chapter. Aforementioned cited articles, as well as others in this vein, well describe several terrorism simulations, their intent, and their evaluation, and I will not repeat this here. Rather, I will offer my experiences on having used a pair of large-scale terrorism simulations in my own undergraduate class for the past eleven years, and suggest additional, smaller scale role-playing exercises that I've found useful in elaborating particular points.

In-Class Experiences

I have taught a class introducing undergraduate students to the study of terrorism on and off since 2006, at both Florida State and Duke Universities. The course places heavy emphasis on the strategic aspects of both terrorism and counterterrorism and includes concepts common to strategic analyses such as credible commitment, costly signaling, resource allocation, industrial organization, and incentive structures. While these ideas may be familiar to practicing political scientists and the graduate students we teach, they are often not to undergraduates, particularly the first and second year students who often take the course. Further, though it is feasible to fully work through the logic of some strategic concepts, such as the mutual defection outcome of the Prisoners' Dilemma, it is infeasible to take multiple class sessions to elaborate on the strategic underpinnings of concepts like credible commitment.

Of course, one can simply describe concepts in words. For credible commitment, one such description might go as follows: the notion of credible commitment expresses the problem of time-inconsistency. What we want at one time—say, not to negotiate with terrorists so as to avoid setting a poor precedent—might not be what we want at other times—say, to negotiate to recover a particularly valuable kidnapped citizen. Yet, while good students can grasp the concept in theory, it is quite another thing to truly understand it. Instead, students might think that the failure to stick to one's guns, so to speak, is a failure of will or personality, rather than something innate to the strategic interaction between state and terrorist group. This not only detracts from their understanding of terrorism, but also does not serve them well more broadly, as they might need to apply the concept of credible commitment in another setting.

I have found simulations to be excellent tools for helping students understand concepts like this at a deeper level. Though I tend to agree with most of the positive assessments of the simulation approach detailed in some of the articles I have referenced, it is primarily for this benefit—a deeper understanding—that I fully devote two classes a semester to in-class simulations. I find that students who participate in simulated scenarios in which they are personally forced to confront the difficult strategic decisions present in the interactions between states and terrorist groups come away not only with a better understanding of these specific interactions, but also the strategic concepts themselves, which they can then apply more widely.

Class-Long Simulations

The first full simulation I run each semester is that of a hostage crisis. It is described fully in Siegel and Young (2009), but the basics are straightforward: a group of anti-state actors has taken hostages and threatens to kill them if its demands are not met. There are many types of actor in this scenario, making it useful for even large classes. These types can be grouped into five classes of actor: (1) terrorists, (2) their hostages, (3) media outlets, (4) government officials, and (5) the public. I send terrorists and their hostages off to a different room, with a teaching assistant (TA) or other supporting individual if possible. Government officials and the public stay in the room, though separated. I typically state that the public comprises friends and family of the hostages to give them a more direct interest. I also split government actors into officials from two different states and the United Nations, all of which have competing and complementary interests. Media outlets—I usually use two, but more can be incorporated—can travel back and forth between rooms. The goal of the government is to recover the hostages safely without giving up too much, the goal of the terrorists is to achieve its demands, whatever the group decides they are, and the goal of the media is to receive the most support from the class.

Demands and counter-demands in the simulation can be done in private or in public, and can take any form to which the students' imaginations lead. In an eighty-five-minute class I can typically hold three rounds of this simulation; each free-form round ends with a brief presentation from all media outlets—the evening news. After each round I have the students vote on their favorite media outlet, update the scenario with my assessment of what has happened given students' actions thus far, and send them back to their respective rooms to start a new round if there is time remaining.

I have found the students to be highly inventive in the simulation. Over the years I have seen "terrorists" do everything from bargaining, returning a hostage's imaginary body parts, kidnapping or "killing" members of the media, to, in one memorable case, sending major state actors to the brink of nuclear war. "Government," in turn, has typically employed a combination of negotiation and force. Sometimes the two states have worked in concert, while at other times they have negotiated in secret to achieve different aims. The media is the most predictable; in an effort to increase support, media outlets almost always devolve into ever more exaggerated claims about the seriousness of the threat, a lesson in and of itself. Also echoing the real world, the government and/or the terrorist group often freeze one of the media sources out, refusing to provide it with further information. The public, from its disadvantaged position, usually attempts to play the media off the government. It is usually more aggressive than the government in advocating for its position, which is often, though not always, capitulation to obtain return of the hostages. Even the hostages themselves have been known to get into the act, attempting escape or passing along information via the media in secret.

More important, though, than the mere presence of this inventiveness is the degree to which the students internalize the core concepts of credible commitment and costly signaling over the course of the simulation. The simulation forces students to engage with these concepts, but does not require them to put the concepts into words. I use a short debriefing session to close this gap, and find a handful of questions to the class to be sufficient.

First, I ask each group what happened during the simulation. Their responses always vary somewhat, illustrating the impact of having to work through the media. Given that one of the primary definitional distinctions between terrorism and other forms of political violence is that terrorism operates by influencing audiences not directly affected by violence, that media can structure this influence in non-obvious ways is an important point in and of itself. That both government and terrorist actors in the simulation typically don't like dealing with the media drives the point home, as they can see how this dislike actually affects outcomes. The idea of underreporting (Drakos and Gofas 2006) can arise naturally in this context.

Second, with the facts clear, I ask both government and terrorist leaders to explain how they attempted to commit to their chosen courses of action and to assess how well these actions worked. In doing so, students come to realize, if they have not done so already, that many of the actions they took in the simulation were designed to "tie their hands." In other words, they deliberately took actions to limit their future options. For example, terrorists given the option to secure minor concessions only if all hostages are released unharmed might harm or kill a hostage. Similarly, government provided an opportunity to end the conflict by giving more significant concessions might inform the public that they will not capitulate, creating audience costs, or set in motion a military response that cannot easily be called back. Ideally, students would also see that more effective hand-tying would translate into more credible commitment. This is difficult to see in a single class session's simulation, though, since multiple different attempts at negotiation are needed to form a valid comparison; thus it can be helpful to make this last point directly.

Third, I ask representatives of all groups how strong or weak the terrorists and governments appeared to be, and why. In addition to providing some students an opportunity to express their frustration with the other group's intransigence, this question helps them tie particular actions each group took with perceptions of that group. Actions that entail a significant cost for groups are often associated with resolve and strength, providing a clear link to the concept of costly signaling.

In sum, I find that the main benefit of the hostage simulation is that it connects classroom discussions of strategic concepts to students' existing impulses toward signaling strength and commitment. This not only helps them to see how credible commitment and costly signaling play out in government–terrorist interactions, but also how one can translate these concepts into different settings, providing lessons beyond the substantive subject matter.

The second full simulation I run each semester, also described completely in Siegel and Young (2009), is one focused on counter-terror more broadly. It is intended to address problems of agency and organizational design and inefficiency, bringing together several class sessions on making use of the properties of terrorist groups to enhance counter-terrorism policy. Because most students have previously encountered the need to signal strength or commitment in other contexts, I leave the hostage simulation free-form, allowing these concepts to arise on their own. In contrast, comparatively few students outside of lecture have experienced first-hand the agency problems of moral hazard and adverse selection. Nor have many students had to deal with the allocation of limited resources in the context of high-cost failure. Consequently, the counterterror simulation is more structured.

I split the class into a rebel group and a government group and provide each group with a list of strategic decisions to make. The groups then have about twenty minutes to debate the merits of each. For the rebel group this involves deciding on their organizational structure, method of recruitment and fundraising, the type of operations they will attempt, the degree of control they will exert over their operatives, the level of social norms they are willing to violate in their operations, and their preferred targets. Given these multifaceted decisions, rebels can attempt everything from peaceful resistance to a WMD strike. For the government this involves deciding on overall budget allocations and allocations specific to intelligence, target defense, propaganda, and direct assaults on the rebels, as well as on policy responses to rebel actions. Together, these decisions allow everything from peaceful, conciliatory governments to aggressively brutal ones.

After the groups have turned in their decisions, I take a few minutes to evaluate the outcome. At first I did this on the fly, but I have since turned to a spreadsheet, available online, to help with this. I find that this allows me to quickly assess outcomes, allowing me to spend more time describing in detail what has happened. Students, particularly those on the "losing" side, then typically call for debriefing themselves. This provides ample opportunity to detail the trade-offs inherent in each decision, consistently allowing for two points in particular to be made: (1) opting for strategies that focus on maximizing intake for the rebel group, be it in the realm of finance or recruitment, results in trade-offs relating to agency problems that lead to diminished security; and (2) matching resource allocations to minimize damage from rebel actions is a particularly difficult strategic problem for the government.

Nearly every time I have run this simulation these lessons arose easily, usually in the context of a successful strike by a rebel group that chose to engage in terrorism. When this occurs I immediately have each student switch groups and run the simulation again, reinforcing these lessons. That said, this is not the only possible outcome of the simulation. Once, for example, I encountered a spectacularly successful government group who managed to completely decimate the rebels. Students forming the rebel group asked insistently to try again, and I let them. The same sequence of events occurred three more times before I finally refused their request. Each time the government group inferred what the rebels' new strategy would be and adjusted their own strategy to compensate, resulting in their continued victory. While this outcome required me to spell out in greater detail the trade-offs that were leading to the outcome, making the tie to agency problems less clear, I could not have asked for a better example of the merits of strategic thinking in counterterrorism.

Shorter Role-Playing Exercises

In addition to these full simulations, designed to reinforce points that arise over multiple class sessions, I have also found it useful to employ shorter simulations and role-playing exercises designed to illustrate more narrow points.

My students' first exposure to role playing, before they run through the hostage simulation, occurs in the context of studying the role of religion in terrorism. The rise of Islamist extremism has led many students to a strong necessity relationship between religion and terrorism, one that is not supported by the historical record. Of course, varied historical correlations between religion and terrorism do not imply that religion has no impact on either the prevalence or the operation of terrorism. One way to make this point clearer, and to try to divorce students' recency bias from a more objective assessment of the connection between religion and terrorism, is to break down what effect religion might have on terrorism.

One such effect arises from religion's relationship to the absolute. Religion can help to justify and to understand the context for a demand such as for control over one's ancestral land. Students may not see why arguments so often turn to absolutes, and thus not follow why religious justifications can so easily be attached to otherwise unrelated grievances. Nor may they understand why it's more difficult to resolve arguments over absolutes, leading potentially to longer-lasting religious terror groups.

To help make these points clearer, I engage in a simple role-playing exercise. I obtain two volunteers from the class. I ask one to state a grievance, and the other to reply without giving in. The only rule is that neither student is allowed to state an absolute. How long they can go without doing so varies by class and chosen grievance. Usually one or two passes back and forth are sufficient, but a grievance stated in particularly pragmatic terms might yield many passes before someone replies with a normative statement about the worth of the goal underlying the grievance. Regardless of how long the process takes, though, students—particularly the volunteers—always seem surprised by how quickly the attempted negotiation deteriorates, helping to make the point.

A second short role-playing exercise concerns recruitment into terrorist groups and outbidding between groups. Students often, quite reasonably, question how the horrific acts terrorist groups perform could be intended to garner them support from local populations. Making it even harder to see this is cross-group variation in what acts are undertaken. For example, there is substantial cross-group variation in the use of suicide attacks, in part because of variation in the degree to which populations local to each group would support suicide attacks. Actions that engender support from the population yield groups benefits in logistics, financing, recruitment, and the avoidance of counter-terror, and so are preferentially taken.

To help students see how market incentives and path dependence can lead to support for extreme options, I use an admittedly silly role-playing exercise: I split the class into groups of four or five and ask each group to come up with a new flavor of ice cream and a marketing strategy to sell it. I give them a few minutes to do this, then put each flavor on the board and have students vote on their favorites. Then I do this again, allowing them to change their flavor, marketing strategy, or both.

The outcome is fairly predictable: while some students try to improve their first idea, many switch to more extreme versions of whatever worked in the first period. And these often win, even though they can exceed the bounds of good taste (and contain entirely too much alcohol, coffee, or both for human consumption). I tie this idea to the manner in which competing dissident groups learn from each other's behavior. Groups will try different tactics, some more violent than others, and observe the response of government and the local public whose support they need. The most successful groups will not only be mimicked; other groups will attempt to outdo them.

This can lead to extreme behavior over time, but it need not do so. Whether or not it does depends on how well the tactics of each group are perceived to work. The ice cream example reveals the preferences of students in the class, preferences to which the creator of each flavor plays. Because these preferences are not known to the groups before they choose flavors, picking initial flavors involves some guesswork; more information would reduce this uncertainty. The same is true with terrorist groups. When the public makes known it supports suicide bombing, for example, groups will take note and we will observe more suicide attacks as well as competition to claim credit when an attack succeeds. We will also observe suicide attacks functioning as a recruitment mechanism, as people want to join in something that succeeds, much like sports teams acquire new fans when they're doing well. In contrast, if the public does not support such attacks, there will be less incentive for groups to compete to commit them, as well as more reluctance to claim credit for attacks. Suicide attacks also will function poorly as a recruitment mechanism in this case.

Which outcome obtains will depend on contextual factors; for example, the changing status of the peace process during the 1990s correlates with support for Hamas and credit claiming of attacks. These sorts of contextual changes are particularly likely if existing power brokers, like the PA in the case of Hamas in the 1990s, are ineffectual due to corruption, failed peace processes, or circumstances substantially out of their control, such as economic shocks. Of course, if there is no appetite for some types of attacks in the public, we would expect to see few of them regardless of context; for example, the IRA did not employ suicide bombing.

This role-playing exercise thus teaches students that divergence in groups' tactics can arise from a combination of different public preferences, search over tactics by groups, and mimicry, producing path-dependent tactic choices that vary by context.

A third exercise I run is just a revision of part of the hostage negotiation simulation, designed to reinforce its points on the role of the media. I slot this one in when discussing the media in more depth, and it consists of my taking three volunteer students outside to share with them a fabricated account of a terrorist attack. I then tell them that they run media outlets, and that the one who gets the most votes of interest for their story will win. They return to class at that point and share short news accounts. Though the outcome of this is typically the same as occurs during the hostage negotiation simulation, the point regarding the media is sufficiently important that I view this reinforcement as helpful.

Finally, a fourth exercise relates to means of terrorist financing. The popular press can often suggest that terrorism is essentially costless to commit, painting mental pictures of would-be terrorists making bombs from scrap metal and entering countries in boxes of freight. Everyone remembers attempts to detonate bombs in shoes or underwear, but people generally don't consider the infrastructure that supported the attempts. I counter this perception by discussing factual accounts of financing in class, focusing on the cost of logistics, support from the local population, secrecy, agency problems, and the like.

To help students move from this dry accounting to a deeper understanding, though, I run a role-playing exercise in which students get into groups and spend five to ten minutes coming up with their own "terrorist business plans." Their goal is innovation and effectiveness, and I have the class vote on each group's plan at the end of the exercise. I find that these votes, though meaningless, help incentivize students to put more thought into the exercise.

My goal, in contrast, is unrelated to the exact elements of their plans. Rather, I want them to think carefully about how a clandestine organization can weave together all the elements it must to secure sufficient funding for its operations without the financing operations being too much of a weak point for it. This is probably the least effective of the four role-playing exercises I run, I have to admit, as students tend to get too hung up on either: (1) covering the bases from the readings to show they've done them, or (2) coming up with outlandish financing schemes, which have over the years included everything from bake sales to organ harvesting. That said, I feel the students do get enough sense of the difficulty of the financing task—and the openings for counterterrorism to which this leads—that I keep running the role-playing exercise anyway. Plus the outlandishness is a nice break from a long semester discussing violence.

Conclusion

It is easy to tout any particular style of teaching as being optimal, drawing upon one's own experiences in the classroom. What I take from the rise of active-learning techniques, however, is that students benefit the more different ways we are able to convey the key material of our classes. By mixing lecture and discussion with simulation and role play we make our classes more accessible to students who might learn better in different ways. We also improve the likelihood that students stay engaged, diminishing the chance that they spend entire semesters as non-participants in either simulations or discussions. I have found mixing in these techniques to be particularly useful in teaching the topic of terrorism, as students benefit from more emotional investment in potentially dry strategic concepts when tearing down the popular misconceptions with which the media bombards them. It is for a similar reason that I end my class with student presentations of terrorist groups. This assignment provides them with an opportunity not only to invest emotionally in learning about a terrorist group, since they need to be able to handle a Q&A session from their peers, but also to connect the strategic concepts they've learned during the semester to the concrete goal of understanding the group.

References

Archetti, Cristina (2012) "Friend or Foe? Problem-Based Learning (PBL) in Political Communication," *European Political Science*, 11(4): 551–66.

Asal, Victor (2005) "Playing Games with International Relations," *International Studies Perspectives*, 6(3): 359–73.

Butcher, Charity (2012) "Teaching Foreign Policy Decision-Making Processes Using Role-Playing Simulations: The Case of US–Iranian Relations," *International Studies Perspectives*, 13(2): 176–94.

Chasek, Pamela S. (2005) "Power Politics, Diplomacy and Role Playing: Simulating the UN Security Council's Response to Terrorism," *International Studies Perspectives*, 6(1): 1–19.

Drakos, Konstantinos, and Andreas Gofas (2006) "The Devil you Know But are Afraid to Face: Underreporting Bias and its Distorting Effects on the Study of Terrorism," *Journal of Conflict Resolution*, 50(5): 714–35.

Enterline, Andrew J., and Eric M. Jepsen (2009) "Chinazambia and Boliviafranca: A Simulation of Domestic Politics and Foreign Policy," *International Studies Perspectives*, 10: 49–59.

Franke, Volker (2006) "The Meyerhoff Incident: Simulating Bioterrorism in a National Security Class," *PS: Political Science and Politics*, 39(1): 153–6.

Glazier, Rebecca (2011) "Running Simulations without Ruining your Life: Simple Ways to Incorporate Active Learning into your Teaching," *Journal of Political Science Education*, 7(4): 375–93.

Krain, Matthew, and Jeffrey S. Lantis (2006) "Building Knowledge? Evaluating the Effectiveness of the Global Problems Summit Simulation," *International Studies Perspectives*, 7(4): 395–407.

Loggins, Julie A. (2009) "Simulating the Foreign Policy Decision-Making Process in the Undergraduate Classroom," *PS: Political Science and Politics*, 42: 401–7.

Pallister, Kevin (2015) "Teaching Globalization and Development through a Simulation," *PS: Political Science and Politics*, 48(2): 364–7.
Powner, Leanne C., and Michelle G. Allendoerfer (2008) "Evaluating Hypotheses about Active Learning," *International Studies Perspectives*, 9(1): 75–89.
Shaw, Carolyn M. (2004) "Using Role-Play Scenarios in the IR Classroom: An Examination of Exercises on Peacekeeping Operations and Foreign Policy Decision Making," *International Studies Perspectives*, 5: 1–22.
Shellman, Stephen M., and Kürşad Turan (2006) "Do Simulations Enhance Student Learning? An Empirical Evaluation of an IR Simulation," *Journal of Political Science Education*, 2(1): 19–32.
Siegel, David A., and Joseph K. Young (2009) "Simulating Terrorism: Credible Commitment, Costly Signaling, and Strategic Behavior," *PS: Political Science and Politics*, 42(4): 765–71.
Simpson, Archie W., and Bernd Kaussler (2009) "IR Teaching Reloaded: Using Films and Simulations in the Teaching of International Relations," *International Studies Perspectives*, 10(4): 413–27.
Smith, Elizabeth, and Mark Boyer (1996) "Designing In-Class Simulations," *PS: Political Science and Politics*, 29(4): 690–4.
Stice, James E. (1987) "Using Kolb's Learning Cycle to Improve Student Learning," *Engineering Education*, 77(5): 291–6.
Stodden, William P. (2012) "Simulating Humanitarian Aid Decision Making in International Relations Classrooms," *PS: Political Science and Politics*, 45(4): 765–71.
Wheeler, Sarah M. (2006) "Role-Playing Games and Simulations for International Issues Courses," *Journal of Political Science Education*, 2(3): 331–47.
Young, Joseph K. (2006) "Simulating Two-Level Negotiations," *International Studies Perspectives*, 7(1): 77–82.

PART VIII

THE GEOGRAPHICAL CONTEXT OF TERRORISM

CHAPTER 35

TERRORISM IN WESTERN EUROPE

a homegrown trademark

LUIS DE LA CALLE AND
IGNACIO SÁNCHEZ-CUENCA

Terrorism as a European Innovation

The geography of Europe is rife with conflict and violence. International as well as civil wars have not only been a recurrent presence in the European landscape, but they have also contributed to defining its borders and institutions. After 1945, European nations settled their regional issues, but some of them still had to cope with conflicts emanating from several sources of internal contestation. The wave of violence that started in the 1960s and finished in the late 1990s covered a wide range of ideologies and political goals. Regardless of this rich variety, all took the form of terrorism: unable to liberate territory from strong states, the challengers were forced to set up clandestine cells, operate in the underground, and use the tactics usually identified with terrorism—bombings, kidnappings, and assassinations. Radicals of all persuasions resorted to terrorism to promote their aims and they did not mind carrying out lethal attacks. Europe, in a nutshell, has had the longest experience with terrorism, hosting some of the best well-known terrorist groups such as ETA (Basque Country and Freedom), IRA (Irish Republican Army), BR (Red Brigades), and RAF (Red Army Faction). There is no need to go back to Robespierre to safely claim that Europe was the cradle of terrorism.

As in most chapters in this book, we start out with a brief conceptual discussion. Second, we introduce the different terrorist trends affecting Europe in the second half of the twentieth century, with a preface on anarchist terrorism—the intellectual father of the "propaganda by the deed" theory. After sorting out data on terrorist attacks by ideology and goals, we look at the determinants of the two main terrorist currents in Europe: the revolutionary and the nationalist groups. A conclusion on future terrorist trends in Europe closes the chapter.

The Two Faces of Terrorism

We have argued somewhere else that the conundrum raised by the effort to define terrorism is largely driven by the two different, not fully overlapping understandings of the concept: the action and the actor ones (De la Calle and Sánchez-Cuenca 2011a; Sánchez-Cuenca and De la Calle 2009). Whereas the actor sense understands terrorism as a specific type of insurgency, the action sense considers terrorism a tactic. The core of terrorism lies, we claim, in underground groups (actor sense) employing coercive political violence (action sense). Although this core does not cover terrorist violence carried out by insurgencies with territorial control, it portrays quite faithfully the type of political violence that unevenly swept the Western world from the 1960s.

In the actor sense, terrorist groups are those that act underground, without controlling territory. This means that, unlike guerrillas, they cannot set up bases and rule over the local population. Territorial control is usually a defining feature of civil wars, and it is largely driven by state capacity. In underdeveloped countries, where states cannot effectively exert control over certain areas, such as jungles or mountains, guerrillas are more likely to emerge. By contrast, the greater the state capacity of the country, the more able the state will be to retain full control over their entire territory, and therefore, the more likely that insurgencies will remain underground and become terrorist (De la Calle and Sánchez-Cuenca 2012). Short on military capabilities to defeat their enemies, terrorist groups count on their power to hurt and increase the cost of the conflict as a way to achieve their goals.

In turn, the action sense of terrorism refers to some special features of violence that make it terrorist in nature. Concretely, terrorist tactics are coercive, aimed at instilling fear in an audience (Hoffman 1998, 44). And due to the high asymmetry in power that is constitutive of most terrorist attacks, the tactics that fit this form of coercive violence are explosive devices, selective killings, and hostage-taking. This is the repertoire of violence that we tend to regard as quintessentially terrorist.

We find the core of terrorism when the two senses go in the same direction. This is the case when underground groups adopt coercive tactics. Clandestine groups, because of their lack of territorial control, are only able to perpetrate violent acts that we typically consider terrorist in nature. This type of warfare does not require large investments in manpower or weaponry, allowing a low number of rebels to easily operate in urban environments. This understanding fits very well the pre-9/11 literature on terrorism, when most authors investigated the causes and dynamics of violent groups that operated clandestinely because of the extremely severe asymmetry of capabilities they faced against their enemy states.

A Brief Overview of European Terrorism

The Anarchist Precedent

The invention of modern terrorism corresponds to European anarchists. In his "Letters to a Frenchman on the Present Crisis" (1870), Mikhail Bakunin argued that deeds were the best proof of the anarchist's principles: "we must spread our principles not with words, but with deeds, for this is the most popular, the most potent, and the most irresistible form of propaganda." (Bakunin 1971, 195–6). In 1876, one of his closest associates, James Guillaume, wrote that "it is not with decrees, with words written on paper, that the Revolution will emancipate the people but with deeds" (in Bakunin 1971, 358). This doctrine was later elaborated by the Italian anarchist Errico Malatesta (Linse 1982).

In its first formulations, the "deed" was conceived in rather general terms, ranging from revolution to assassinations. However, the failure of the insurrectionary attempts in Spain in 1873 (in Alcoy), in Italy in 1874 (in Bologna), and again in 1877 (in Benevento) (Avilés 2013, ch. 3), led the anarchist movement into terrorist tactics (assassinations, bombings against the bourgeoisie). A very similar path was followed by Narodnaya Volya (People's Will) in Russia. It also tried first the purely insurrectionary way in 1874 by organizing "the pilgrimages to the people," consisting of small groups of members of the petite bourgeoisie intelligentsia that went into small villages to establish contact with the peasants (Hingley 1967, ch. 5). But as they found little echo to their revolutionary proclaims, they reacted by moving into assassinations. Independently of the European anarchist networks, People's Will came to its own formulation of the propaganda by the deed doctrine (Clutterbuck 2004).

The European anarchists oscillated between assassinations and indiscriminate attacks. In order to estimate the scope of anarchist violence, we have created a dataset of anarchist fatalities in Western European countries. According to our calculations, 138 people were killed between 1878 and 1921, among them several public officers: Sadi Carnot, the President of France, in 1894; Cánovas del Castillo, the Spanish Prime Minister, in 1897; the Empress of Austria, in 1898; and King Humbert of Italy, in 1900. Apart from assassinations, there were some purely indiscriminate attacks, such as the bombing of the Opera House in Barcelona (7 November 1893), which killed twenty-two people.

Although the death toll was not very high in comparative terms, anarchist violence generated panic and led to the first forms of transnational cooperation against terrorism (Jensen 2009). Anarchist terrorism was particularly intense in Spain, Italy, and France, being milder in Germany and Austria (in the rest of countries, it was almost non-existent). Two of these countries, Spain and Italy, would also feature much of the terrorist revolutionary violence of the 1970s and 1980s.

Anarchists were loosely organized. They worked horizontally, in networks, sometimes even carrying out attacks individually. They never developed the kind of hierarchical, underground organizations of their successors, but they nevertheless set the precedent.

The Modern Wave of Domestic Terrorism in Europe

Although anarchist terrorism had almost completely disappeared by the end of the 1920s, the idea of propaganda by the deed resurfaced in the continent in the wake of the 1960s upsurge in protest and mobilization. The late 1960s and early 1970s witnessed the emergence of ideological terrorism (both revolutionary and Fascist) as well as of territorial terrorism (Engene 2004). This great wave of armed struggle spread throughout other developed non-European countries such as the United States, Canada, and Japan.

The postwar period was quiet in terms of lethal terrorism until the 1960s—the only exception being the OAS (Organisation de l'armée secrete), a vigilante group that acted in 1961–2 to prevent the independence of Algeria from France (Engene 2004, 66). We have compiled a dataset of fatalities for the period 1965–2005, DTV (Domestic Terrorist Victims, De la Calle and Sánchez-Cuenca 2011b), which registers 4,955 killings during the period 1965–2005. Figure 35.1 provides the breakdown of annual terrorist killings in Western Europe. The peak of the activity lies in the period 1972–80. While the beginning was quite abrupt in 1970–1, the phase of decay was gradual and long.

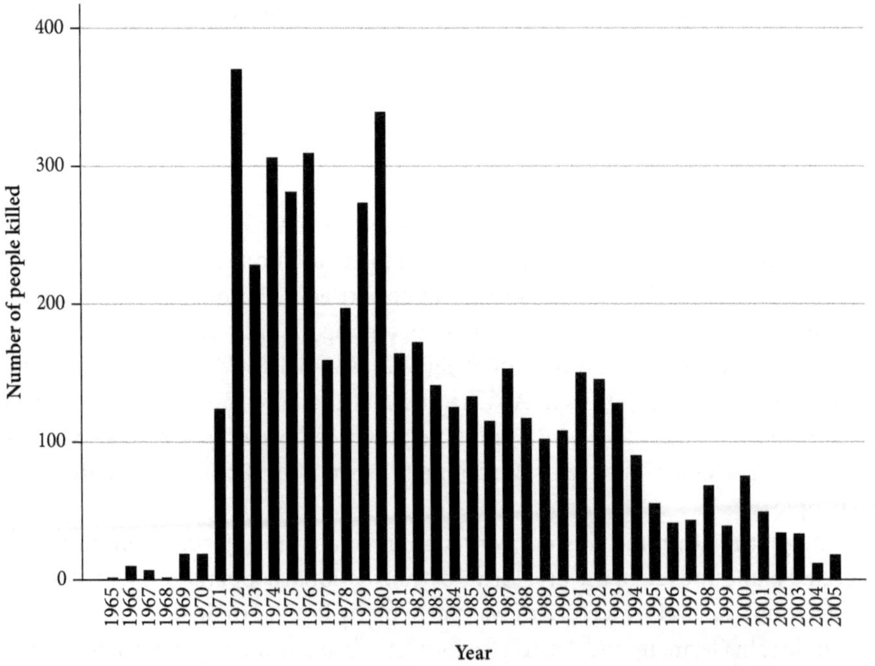

FIGURE 35.1 Number of fatalities caused by domestic terrorism in Western Europe, 1965–2005

Source: DTV

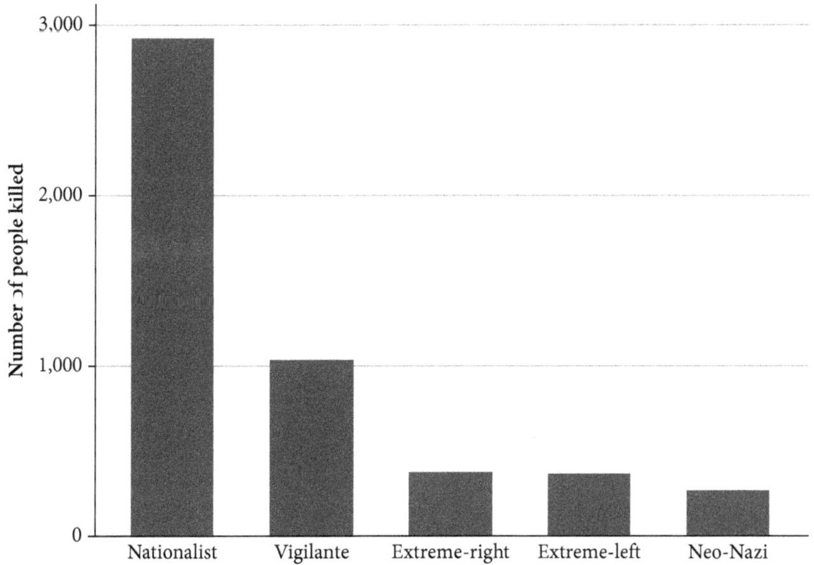

FIGURE 35.2 People killed by different types of terrorism

Source: DTV

Basic information about the ideological orientation of the killings can be found in Figure 35.2. We distinguish five types of ideology, sorted out with two coding rules. First, whether the terrorists are interested in regime change or in territory (autonomy, secession). Second, whether the terrorists fight against or for the status quo (SQ). Revolutionary and Fascist terrorism are regime-oriented and anti-SQ. Revolutionaries aim at a popular revolution against capitalism, while Fascists seek to create a situation of social panic that justifies an authoritarian regime. Nationalist terrorism aims at the autonomy or secession of a region from a state and it is clearly anti-SQ. Pro-SQ groups are usually called vigilantes. Finally, there is a residual category, that of xenophobic or neo-Nazi violence, which is a form of diffuse terrorism, very much decentralized, that targets foreigners and minority groups.

As Figure 35.2 reveals, the vast majority of killings (59 percent) are due to nationalist terrorism, followed by vigilante (21 percent), usually a response to nationalist violence. Extreme-right (Fascist) and extreme-left (revolutionary) have 7 percent each and neo-Nazi terrorism the remaining 5 percent.

Revolutionary and Fascist Terrorism

The 1960s were years of political turmoil, with big waves of strikes and demonstrations. A whole generation was socialized in radicalism and anti-system attitudes. When mobilizations waned, some among the most highly committed activists opted for armed struggle (Della Porta and Tarrow 1986). Some of these soon-to-be terrorists were strongly influenced by the experiences of the urban guerrillas in Uruguay (Tupamaros).

The aim of revolutionary groups was to overthrow the capitalist, bourgeois order. "Armed propaganda" was supposed to trigger a revolutionary movement. This radicalism, however, found little echo in the masses. With limited support, the challenge of these groups to their respective states was easily contained. In Germany, the RAF first challenged openly the postwar order by taking the momentous step of killing people (Aust 2008). But it was Italy where terrorism became the most serious concern. Not accidentally, this is the country where the 1968 protests had lasted for longer and had combined workers' and students' efforts, with an unparalleled rebound in the 1977 movement (Moss 1989; Weinberg and Eubank 1987).

Table 35.1 describes the impact of revolutionary terrorism in countries with at least one fatality. Italy and Spain are the two bloodiest countries and also the countries in which this type of terrorism was more resilient. Yet, the terrorism is very different in each case: whereas several Italian revolutionary groups enjoyed some level of support, in Spain most of the lethal activity was due to a single, highly secretive and socially isolated Maoist group called GRAPO (October First Anti-Fascist Revolutionary Groups). At a lower level, terrorist activity was also considerable in Germany, Greece, Portugal, and France.

Fascist terrorism only emerged in three countries, Italy, Spain, and Belgium, though with different peculiarities in each case. Italy concentrates most of it. Italian fascists followed the so-called strategy of tension, consisting of indiscriminate attacks against civilians that would create a climate of anxiety in which an authoritarian coup would be welcome. The first of these attacks took place on December 17, 1969, when a bomb exploded in Piazza Fontana in Milan, killing twelve and injuring more than eighty. The worst attack was the bombing of Bologna train station, which killed eighty-five people on August 2, 1980. During the *anni di piombo* (years of lead), in the 1970s and early

Table 35.1 Revolutionary Groups in Europe with at Least One Fatality

Country	Main Terrorist Groups	Fatalities	Year 1st Killing	Year Last Killing
Belgium	CCC	2	1985	1985
Denmark		1	1988	1988
France	Action Directe	15	1974	1986
Germany	RAF	39	1971	1993
Greece	17-N	25	1975	2000
Italy	Br, PI	162	1971	2003
Portugal	FP-25	21	1978	1987
Spain	GRAPO	95	1972	2000
Total		360		

Source: DTV.

CCC (Cellules Communistes Combattantes); RAF (Rote Armee Fraktion); 17-N (17-November Revolutionary Organization); Br (Brigate Rosse), PI (Prima Linea); EAAJA (East Asian Anti-Japan Armed Front); FP-25 (Forças Populares 25 de Abril); GRAPO (Grupos Revolucionarios Antifascistas Primero de Octubre).

1980s, Italy lived in a rarified context of deep political polarization with violence coming from both extremes of the ideological spectrum (Panvini 2009).

In Belgium there was a short-lived rendition of the strategy of tension: the so-called Brabant killers engaged in armed robberies in supermarkets, employing indiscriminate violence against civilians, which was hardly necessary for the robbery, killing twenty-eight of them during the years 1982–5. Although this is still surrounded by some mystery, it is usually regarded as political violence (Jenkins 1990). In Spain, Fascist terrorism was more selective, targeting mainly Basque separatists and activists from the left.

Nationalist Terrorism

Unlike revolutionary groups, nationalist movements in Europe had a few successful experiences to imitate: Cyprus, Israel, and Algeria all gained independence from imperial powers after World War II using terrorist violence. As Hoffman (2015) has documented for the British experience in Palestine, Jewish terrorism, even if not the only instrument in the toolkit for independence, had a significant role in fulfilling secessionists' goals. Although Britain and France had overwhelming military superiority, the EOKA (National Organization of Cypriot Fighters), Irgun, and FLN (National Liberation Front) were able to sustain a war of attrition that wore the colonial powers down and ultimately forced them to retreat. In a similar fashion, groups such as the ETA, IRA, and FLNC (Corsican National Liberation Front) expected they would so much increase the cost of the nationalist conflict that their respective "colonial" governments would rather give up than assume the price of occupation. After decades of violence, they failed, but in the process radical nationalists became consolidated as powerful electoral contenders.

The wave of nationalist contestation in Europe started in South Tyrol, when the BAS (Committee for the Liberation of South Tyrol) killed fourteen people in two years (1965–7). Gerrymandered within Alto Trentino, the German-speaking South Tyroleans demanded their own regional institutions. The BAS, an Austrian-financed group of right-wing radicals, planned a terrorist campaign that prompted the Italian government to open negotiations and concede wide powers to a new South Tyrol province.

In the late 1960s, Northern Ireland and the Basque Country took the lead—with the new Provisional IRA and the ETA ahead of a number of minor groups. IRA and ETA account for more than half the victims of nationalist terrorism in Europe—as Table 35.2 indicates. The largest lethality goes to the PIRA, with 1,648 victims. The so-called Provos split from the Dublin-based Official IRA in the brink of the Troubles, when Protestant mobs attacked Catholic neighborhoods in Derry and Belfast and the Officials turned a blind eye to this violence because they believed in inter-sectarian cooperation (English 2004). The Provos were involved in a three-cornered fight between British security forces, loyalist paramilitary groups, and the Republican movement. The fact that all sides committed atrocities helped in reaching a negotiated solution to the conflict. With the Good Friday Agreement, the Republicans obtained a permanent seat in the Northern Irish government, but their achievements fell short of independence.

Table 35.2 Separatist Groups in Europe with at Least One Fatality

Country	Region	Main Terrorist Groups	Fatalities	Year 1st Killing	Year Last Killing
France	Corsica	FNLC	50	1975	2001
France	Basque Country	Iparretarrak	4	1982	1987
France	Brittany	ARB	1	2000	2000
Italy	South Tyrol	BAS	14	1965	1967
Spain	Basque Country	ETA, CAA	848	1968	2010
Spain	Canary Islands	MPAIAC	1	1978	1978
Spain	Catalonia	FAC, EPOCA, TLI	6	1971	1987
Spain	Galicia	EGPGC	2		
UK	Northern Ireland	IRA, INLA	1,985	1970	2005
Total			2,911		

Source: DTV.

FNLC (Fronte di Liberazione Naziunale Corsu); ARB (Armée Républicaine Bretonne); BAS (Befreiungsausschuss Südtirol); ETA (Euskadi ta Askatasuna); CAA (Comandos Autónomos Anticapitalistas); MPAIAC (Movimiento por la Autodeterminación e Independencia del Archipiélago Canario); FAC (Front d'Alliberament Català); EPOCA (Exèrcit Popular Català); TLI (Terra Lliure); EGPGC (Exército Guerrilheiro do Povo Galego Ceive); IRA (Irish Republican Army); INLA (Irish National Liberation Army).

In comparison, the Basque conflict shows lower numbers because unionists never armed themselves to fight back. Thus, ETA did not fashion sectarian attacks and violence rarely escalated. ETA was created in 1959 to halt through violence the assimilationist drive promoted by the Franco dictatorship in the Basque provinces. Helped by bad intelligence and poor political responses, ETA survived during the last years of Francoism. In contrast, ETA took advantage of the new liberties brought by the transition to democracy to escalate its violence with a peak of 100 annual victims in 1979 and 1980. The end of the ETA's safe haven in Southern France contributed to reducing the group lethality, and by the late 1990s the group was militarily exhausted. From 1998 onwards, ETA was involved in several negotiation rounds, but it repeatedly rejected compromise agreements. After the banning of its political wing, ETA was forced to call a final unilateral end to violence in 2011.

Unlike the previous groups, the FNLC in Corsica did not overcome the stage of "propaganda war," so it never openly challenged the French state in a war of attrition. Violence broke out in 1975, but it kept a low profile until the mid-1980s, when the killing of a Corsican militant sparked a tit-for-tat terrorist campaign. Several concessions delivered by successive French governments strengthened the political side of the nationalist movement at the expense of weakening its military wing. The FLNC got involved during the 1990s in a spiral of rent-driven splintering and feuding that decimated its ranks and credibility. Today the FLNC as such remains largely inactive, although not disbanded yet.

Finally, there were minor groups operating in other regions such as Catalonia, Wales, Galicia, and Brittany. Like the FLNC, these groups were never able to attract a support constituency that sanctioned lethal operations against rivals and therefore their violence remained low. Either early attacks backfired and groups lost support, or groups never dared to trespass the symbolic limit against lethal violence imposed by many supporters. This popularity constraint is one of the main determinants of target selection, as we will discuss later.

Other Types of Terrorism

The two largest perpetrators of terrorist attacks in Europe today, neo-Nazi and homegrown jihadist militants, remained relatively unimportant until the 2000s. Both share a peculiar pattern of acting, since they tend to avoid the construction of hierarchical organizations. This makes it difficult for analysts to identify whether an attack by a single person is an act of terrorism or an ideologically disconnected crime.

With a very strict definition of terrorism, DTV reported 268 victims of neo-Nazi violence, mostly concentrated in Germany, Spain, and the UK. Because DTV stopped counting victims in 2005, homegrown jihadist terrorism does not show up in the data. More recent datasets on Islamist violence report an increase on attacks in Europe (Nesser 2014). Leaving aside the most spectacular ones—such as the ones in Madrid 2004, London 2005, and Paris 2015—it is still uncertain whether largely decentralized jihadist cells will be able to spread terror over Europe in a systematic way. In the conclusions we offer some comments on this possibility.

Target Selection

The ideological variation of terrorism in Western Europe is clearly visible in the patterns of target selection. Target selection is relevant to understand the quality of violence of the different terrorist groups We distinguish six types of targets: (i) military, (ii) police, (iii) paramilitaries, (iv) politicians and public officials, (v) entrepreneurs, and (vi) other civilians. The breakdown of the data, as shown in Table 35.3, reflects two clear camps: one composed of nationalist and revolutionary terrorism, another by Fascist, vigilante, and neo-Nazi groups. In the first family, the main targets are security forces (military and police). The generic civilian toll is higher in nationalist terrorism (36.5 percent) than in revolutionary terrorism (23.2 percent), this difference being due to a more aggressive attitude in nationalist terrorism towards people siding with the state.

The second family has a completely different pattern of target selection, with over 80 percent of killings in the category of "other civilians." The enemy was neither the state nor capitalism. For various reasons, they focused on civilians and, to a much lower extent, on paramilitaries (terrorists from opposite ideology). In the case of neo-Nazis, the targets were immigrants, people from different ethnicities, and minority groups. As for the extreme-right, the goal was to kill civilians to generate terror and anxiety in

Table 35.3 Target Selection by Ideology (Vertical Percentages)

	Nationalist	Extreme-Left	Vigilante	Extreme-Right	Neo-Nazi	Total Fatalities
Military	21.1	5.5	0.4	0.3	1.1	644
Police	33.2	47.8	1.2	7.8	2.2	1,189
Paramilitary	5.1	1.0	11.0	8.6	0.0	301
Politicians and public officials	3.2	13.3	0.2	0.8	0.4	146
Entrepreneurs	1.0	8.3	0.5	0.0	0.0	65
Other civilians	36.5	23.2	86.7	82.5	96.3	2,610

Source: DTV.

public opinion. Finally, vigilante groups acted in favor of the state and the SQ, avoiding therefore the killing of security forces.

Determinants of European Terrorism

The literature on the determinants of terrorism usually relies on the traditional country-year research design. Whereas in civil war studies the dependent variable measures whether a conflict is initiated or whether the country is undergoing a conflict, in the literature on terrorism the dependent variable is in most cases the number of annual attacks by country. There have also been some attempts to provide a unified analysis of civil war and terrorism in which the dependent variable measures the type of conflict (civil war or terrorism) rather than the number of violent incidents (De la Calle and Sanchez-Cuenca 2012; Sambanis 2008). A common assumption of large-n analyses is that there are some determinants of terrorist violence affecting all types of terrorism. These determinants are a mix of economic and political variables, such as economic development, inequality, regime type, population size, and repression. However, the findings are inconclusive. Covariates are not sufficiently robust, being sensitive to measurement decisions, different specifications, and different estimation procedures.

The analysis of European terrorism opens the way to a more nuanced approach. On the one hand, we have very accurate estimates of terrorist violence thanks to datasets such as TWEED (Engene 2004) and DTV. On the other hand, we can examine separately different types of terrorism. It is reasonable to hypothesize that different conflicts (those related to territorial claims as opposed to those related to regime change) may have different determinants. A case in point here is the analysis of Krieger and Meierrieks (2010): they test whether higher social spending led to lower terrorist violence in Western Europe. For them, social spending should produce higher satisfaction with life and therefore lower terrorism. But while this may be true of revolutionary terrorism, it is highly questionable for nationalist terrorism, for two reasons. Substantively, there is no strong correlation between nationalism and wealth (De la Calle 2015, ch. 3); and methodologically, countrywide levels of welfare spending are not the best unit of analyses to predict regional violence. It makes more sense to analyze regime-change terrorism at a country level, while territorial terrorism should be studied at the regional level. We further describe findings on each type of terrorism.

Revolutionary Terrorism

Case studies on European left-wing terrorist groups are abundant, either as monographs or chapters in edited volumes (among others, Aust 2008; Bjørgo 2005; Dartnell 1995; Kassimeris 2001; Lodge 1988). Truly comparative work is much more scarce, either small-n (Della Porta 1995; Sommier 2008; Varon 2004) or middle-n (Engene 2004; Krieger and Meierrieks 2010; Sanchez-Cuenca 2009).

Revolutionary terrorism started in the aftermath of the 1968 wave of popular mobilization (Della Porta and Tarrow 1986). However, its occurrence seems unrelated to the intensity of these mobilizations. France had large protests but very little terrorism. Likewise, Spain had very little mobilization in the late 1960s but a lot of terrorism afterwards. In Italy, by contrast, there was intense mobilization and intense political violence.

Lacking an obvious linkage between popular protest and violence, it seems natural to look for more structural variables. Revolutionary terrorism emerged in highly populated countries, a finding that is borne out in large-n studies on terrorism as well as on the civil war literature. Also, revolutionary terrorism was more likely in countries that were experiencing high economic growth in the late 1960s. A common feature of high-growth countries was higher economic inequality. Another frequent feature of countries with higher revolutionary terrorism was the presence of stronger Communist parties in the 1970s.

But perhaps the most puzzling finding is that revolutionary terrorism rose only in countries with a troubled political past (Sánchez-Cuenca 2009). More concretely, there is an almost perfect correlation between countries that experienced some authoritarian spell during the twentieth century and revolutionary terrorism. The countries that suffered more left-wing terrorism (Italy, Spain, Germany, Greece, and Portugal) all had dictatorships during the past century. The only exception is Austria, which was a dictatorship during the interwar period but never developed revolutionary violence after 1968. From the opposite angle, the only other exception is France, which can be considered a full democracy (with the short period of the Vichy regime under German occupation) and nonetheless had some low-level terrorism featured by the group Action Directe (see Table 35.1).

There are several possible interpretations of this association between past dictatorship and left-wing terrorism (Fritzsche 1989; Sanchez-Cuenca 2009). Given some of the other covariates (inequality, strong Communist parties), past dictatorship may be a symptom of countries with deep political divisions and ridden by political radicalism.

Uncompromising ways of dealing with the left–right divide would create the conditions for the emergence of ideological armed struggle.

Nationalist Terrorism

Literature on nationalist violence has focused on the most resilient cases: the IRA and the ETA; in contrast, few works have looked at truncated experiences such as Terra Lliure, the Welsh Defence Movement, and the Movimento Armato Sardo. Selection-biased research procedures have yielded partial insights. Explanations driven by the type of nationalism (ethnic versus civic) or by the relevance of previous episodes of violence do not match the empirical record, once the full universe of observations is brought into the analysis (Laitin 1995).

On the other hand, there is a growing large-n literature that looks at the determinants of ethnic violence worldwide, although without distinguishing among warfare types. It finds that states with territorially concentrated groups (i.e. nationalist), horizontally aggrieved minorities, and lack of concessions to moderates have larger chances of experiencing nationalist violence (Jenne et al. 2007; Cederman et al. 2011; Hewitt 2001).

Nationalist agitation in Western Europe started in the 1960s as a reaction against state assimilation accelerated by immigration, secularization, and the increasing reach of public institutions (De la Calle 2015). Moderate groups, such as the Flemish-language movement in Belgium and the Plaid Cymru in Wales, called for decentralization as a way to shield their regions from external influences and gain some access to power. Most nationalist movements also hosted a radical fringe willing to take up arms to extract larger concessions from the central government. The use of violence in this first stage was very limited, propagandistic, and ancillary to moderates' claims. States where governments quickly transferred powers to regional units were spared violence. In contrast, the reluctance of others to yield power weakened moderates within the nationalist movement and encouraged radicals to step up their fight. Escalation succeeded when states reacted repressively to internal challengers and the latter were able to build new support constituencies.

Two features of this stylized story are crucial: unaccounted regional elites and nationalist mobilization. The strongest terrorist groups of nationalist extraction—ETA in the Basque Country, IRA in Northern Ireland, FNLC in Corsica, and the BAS in South Tyrol—all emerged in regions where regional elites were extremely adverse to nationalist appeasement. Absent electoral incentives to cooperate with moderates, the state opted for repression, which contributed to feeding the militant wing. Additionally, radicals in these regions found fertile ground to mobilize, because many potential supporters had remained so far aloof from nationalist ranks. Indiscriminate repression just hastened the process of mobilization and cemented a strong constituency in support of nationalist violence. South Tyrol aside, the other experiences of nationalist terrorism lasted for decades, and several rounds of negotiations were necessary before bringing violence to an end.

Conclusion

Far from an anomaly, terrorism has been the trademark of political violence in Europe since World War II. Revolutionary and secessionist groups used violence to further their aims. Because the playing field was extremely biased in favor of the state, these groups operated clandestinely and carried out low-intensity campaigns of terrorist acts. With the exception of the PIRA, no terrorist group killed more than 1,000 victims, which sets a natural boundary between terrorism and civil wars around the 1,000 deaths threshold. Against the conventional wisdom, most violence focused on "hard" targets—namely, security forces and public officials. Revolutionary and nationalist groups drew on supporters to gain legitimacy, recruit militants, and raise money. Targeting was constrained by the supporters' views on the legitimacy of attacking various groups. In general, state repression uplifted these constraints, facilitating escalation and a broader focus on the strategy of attrition.

In Europe, the popular understanding of terrorism as civilian targeting corresponds to a very marginal militant current: the right-wing groups. These groups were concerned with spreading chaos to encourage the military to intervene in politics and lead authoritarian regimes. Still, this violence only accounts for less than 10 percent of the number of fatalities on the continent, and it was largely reactive in nature.

By the turn of the century, most expressions of terrorist violence in Europe were over. Revolutionary groups disbanded as a consequence of their incapacity to recruit and to counter successful state policies. Governments combined selective repression with sentence reductions for radical inmates willing to collaborate with the police. Although they were not fully under communist influence, the fall of the Soviet Union also added to the increasing discredit of these groups. Absent the threat of communism, many right-wing groups quickly vanished.

Nationalist groups also failed in their search for plain independence. But, unlike left-wing groups, they had some partial successes before disbandment (English 2016). Most groups used violence to build a support constituency that has since then been electorally mobilized. With around a quarter of votes, the inheritors of violence have strong political presence in Northern Ireland, the Basque Country, and Corsica. In other regions, the remains of radicalism converged into mainstream pro-secession parties, such as in Catalonia, the French Basque Country, Sardinia, South Tyrol, and Wales. In a sense, nationalist groups had a sweeter defeat.

Finished with the turmoil of the past, Europe was ready for a lasting internal peace. However, new terrorist challenges have emerged. Neo-Nazi groups commit a steady number of actions against immigrants and minorities, mostly in Germany, but they rarely hit the news because attacks are never claimed. As perpetrators do not seem to be coordinated, it remains to be found out whether these attacks are just hate crimes or part of an organized plan.

In contrast, homegrown jihadist militants are part of a larger plan to force Western governments out of the Middle East and mobilize supporters through "the deed"

(Lia 2008). Used to combatting hierarchically organized groups, European governments are still coping with this new internal threat. As long as local jihadist cells self-destruct after a single attack, the threat is domestically contained. But if militants can ideologically connect their isolated attacks in European countries to a larger Islamic fight, the threat grows. In this sense, jihadist terrorism strikingly mimics militant anarchism in its global reach—both in goals and operations (Gelvin 2008). But jihadists, unlike anarchists, do not need to kill presidents to impact on policy-making: their capacity to rule over large territories in the Middle East casts a more fearful shadow over European security.

References

Aust, Stefan (2008) *Baader-Meinhoff: The Inside Story of the R.A.F.* Oxford: Oxford University Press.

Avilés, Juan (2013) *La daga y la dinamita: Los anarquistas y el nacimiento del terrorismo*. Barcelona: Tusquets.

Bakunin, Mikhail (1971) *Bakunin on Anarchy: Selected Works*, ed. Sam Goldoff. New York: Vintage Books.

Bjørgo, Tore, ed. (2005) *Root Causes of Terrorism: Myths, Reality, and Ways Forward*. London: Routledge.

Cederman, Lars-Erik, Nils B. Weidmann, and Kristian Skrede Gleditsch (2011) "Horizontal Inequalities and Ethnonationalist Civil War: A Global Comparison," *American Political Science Review*, 105(3): 457–95.

Clutterbuck, Lindsay (2004) "The Progenitors of Terrorism: Russian Revolutionaries or Extreme Irish Republicans?," *Terrorism and Political Violence*, 16(1): 154–81.

Dartnell, Michael Y. (1995) *Action Directe: Ultra-Left Terrorism in France, 1979–1987*. London: Frank Cass.

De la Calle, Luis (2015) *Nationalist Violence in Postwar Europe*. New York: Cambridge University Press.

De la Calle, Luis, and Ignacio Sánchez-Cuenca (2011a) "What we Talk about When we Talk about Terrorism," *Politics and Society*, 39(3): 451–72.

De la Calle, Luis, and Ignacio Sánchez-Cuenca (2011b) "The Quantity and Quality of Terrorism: The DTV Dataset," *Journal of Peace Research*, 48(1): 49–58.

De la Calle, Luis, and Ignacio Sánchez-Cuenca (2012) "Rebels without Territory: An Analysis of Nonterritorial Conflicts in the World, 1970–1997," *Journal of Conflict Resolution*, 56(4): 580–603.

De la Calle, Luis, and Ignacio Sánchez-Cuenca (2015) "How Armed Groups Fight," *Studies in Conflict and Terrorism*, 38(10): 795–813.

Della Porta, Donatella (1995) *Social Movements, Political Violence, and the State: A Comparative Analysis of Italy and Germany*. Cambridge: Cambridge University Press.

Della Porta, Donatella, and Sidney Tarrow (1986) "Unwanted Children: Political Violence and the Cycle of Protest in Italy, 1966–1973," *European Journal of Political Research*, 14: 607–32.

Engene, Jan (2004) *Terrorism in Western Europe: Explaining the Trends since 1950*. Cheltenham: Edward Elgar Publishing.

Engene, Jan (2007) "Five Decades of Terrorism in Europe: The TWEED Dataset," *Journal of Peace Research*, 44(1): 109–21.

English, Richard (2002) *Armed Struggle: The History of the IRA*. Oxford: Oxford University Press.
English, Richard (2016) *Does Terrorism Work? A History*. Oxford: Oxford University Press.
Fritzsche, Peter (1989) "Terrorism in the Federal Republic of Germany and Italy: Legacy of the '68 Movement or 'Burden of Fascism'?," *Terrorism and Political Violence*, 1(4): 466–81.
Gelvin, James L. (2008) "Al-Qaeda and Anarchism: A Historian's Reply to Terrorology," *Terrorism and Political Violence*, 20(4): 563–81.
Hewitt, Christopher (2001) "Separatism, Irredentism and Terrorism: A Comparative Survey 1945–2000," in Alex P. Schmid (ed.), *Countering Terrorism through International Cooperation*. Milan: ISPAC, 25–37.
Hingley, Ronald (1967) *Nihilists: Russian Radicals and Revolutionaries in the Reign of Alexander II (1855–81)*. London: Weidenfeld & Nicolson.
Hoffman, Bruce (2015) *Anonymous Soldiers: The Struggle for Israel, 1917–1947*. New York: Alfred A. Knopf.
Jenne, Erin, Stephen Saideman, and Will Lowe (2007) "Separatism as a Bargaining Posture: The Role of Leverage on Minority Radicalization," *Journal of Peace Research*, 44(5): 539–58.
Jenkins, Philip (1990) "Strategy of Tension: The Belgian Terrorist Crisis 1982–1986," *Terrorism*, 13(4–5): 299–309.
Jensen, Richard Bach (2009) "The International Campaign Against Anarchist Terrorism, 1880–1930s," *Terrorism and Political Violence*, 21(1): 89–109.
Kassimeris, George (2001) *Europe's Last Red Terrorists: The Revolutionary Organization 17 November*. London: Hurst.
Krieger, Tim, and Daniel Meierrieks (2010) "Terrorism in the Worlds of Welfare Capitalism," *Journal of Conflict Resolution*, 54(6): 902–39.
Laitin, David (1995) "National Revivals and Violence." *European Journal of Sociology*, 36: 3–43.
Lia, Brynjar (2008) *Architect of Global Jihad: The Life of al-Qaida Strategist Abu Mus'ab al-Suri*. New York: Columbia University Press.
Linse, Ulrich (1982) '"Propaganda by the Deed' and 'Direct Action': Two Concepts of Anarchist Violence," in Wolfgang J. Mommsen and Gerhard Hirschfeld (eds), *Social Protest, Violence and Terror in Nineteenth- and Twentieth-century Europe*. London: Macmillan, 201–29.
Lodge, Juliett, ed. (1988) *The Threat of Terrorism*. Brighton: Wheatsheaf Books.
McCormick, Gordon H. (2003) "Terrorist Decision Making," *Annual Review of Political Science*, 6: 473–507.
Moss, David (1989) *The Politics of Left-Wing Violence in Italy, 1969–1985*. Basingstoke: Macmillan.
Nesser, Petter (2014) "Toward an Increasingly Heterogeneous Threat: A Chronology of Jihadist Terrorism in Europe 2008–2013," *Studies in Conflict and Terrorism*, 37: 440–56.
Panvini, Guido (2009) *Ordine nero, guerriglia rossa: La violenza política nell'Italia degli anni Sessanta e Settanta (1966–1975)*. Turin: Einaudi.
Sambanis, Nicholas (2008) "Terrorism and Civil War," in Philip Keefer and Norman Loayza (eds), *Terrorism, Economic Development, and Political Openness*. Cambridge: Cambridge University Press, 174–206.
Sánchez-Cuenca, Ignacio (2009) "Revolutionary Dreams and Terrorist Violence in the Developed World: Explaining Country Variation," *Journal of Peace Research*, 46(5): 687–706.
Sánchez-Cuenca, Ignacio, and Luis de la Calle (2009) "Domestic Terrorism: The Hidden Side of Political Violence," *Annual Review of Political Science*, 10: 31–49.

Sommier, Isabelle (2008) *La violence politique et son deuil: L'après 68 en France et en Italie*. Rennes: Presses Universitaires de Rennes.

Varon, Jeremy (2004) *Bringing the War Home: The Weather Underground, the Red Army Faction, and Revolutionary Violence in the Sixties and Seventies*. Berkeley, CA: University of California Press.

Weinberg, Leonard, and William L. Eubank (1987) *The Rise and Fall of Italian Terrorism*. Boulder, CO: Westview Press.

CHAPTER 36

TERRORISM IN LATIN AMERICA

JENNIFER S. HOLMES

THE state of the discipline of terrorism in Latin America is hampered by a search for cross-nationally comparable data about incidents of multiple forms of violence and state presence. The general challenge is well recognized, including Martha Crenshaw's warning that "an initial obstacle to identification of propitious circumstances for terrorism is the absence of significant empirical studies of relevant cross-national factors" (Crenshaw 1981, 381). The scope of study is large. According to the Global Terrorism Database, roughly 20 percent of the incidents recorded from 1970 to 2014 were recorded in either Central or South America. LaFree (2012, 47) lists Colombia, Peru, and El Salvador as the top three ranked countries in terms of total terrorist attacks, comprising almost 30 percent of all attacks. Latin America provides examples of many types of terrorism, including state terror, and many types of non-state terror. However, its regional importance is somewhat underappreciated since these are predominantly cases of domestic terrorism; and these groups are not ethnically[1] or religiously driven, like many of the terrorist groups in other regions. Conceptual confusion regarding the term terrorism also contributes to data concerns. The term terrorism "suffers from 'border' and 'membership' problems," and "suffers from 'stretching' and 'traveling' problems" (Weinberg et al. 2004, 778). In Latin America, conceptual confusion about terrorism is related to the relationship to other forms of political violence. Not only can groups commit violence that crosses multiple concepts, but groups also become factionalized and evolve in distinct ways that are crucial for understanding terrorist group dynamics.

LACK OF DATA

The lack of reliable, comparable data has long been recognized as a challenge to studying terrorism globally for decades. It is particularly acute in Latin America. In 1988, Ted Gurr described a "disturbing lack of good empirically-grounded research" (Gurr 1988, 115), a sentiment repeatedly echoed over time, including by Merari (1991, 89). Even after the increased attention to terrorism after 9/11: "the overriding deficiency of this state of stagnation is a dearth of empirically grounded research on terrorism" (Schultz 2004, 161). In Latin America, "the situation is slightly more dramatic… where an adequate infrastructure for empirical research is often lacking, where violence research itself is sometimes dangerous or simply impossible due to adverse circumstances… There is an urgent need to improve the kind of knowledge base on violence in different countries to get more reliable and comparative data of a longitudinal or cross-sectional type" (Imbusch et al. 2011, 133). Official statistics of terrorism are often not comparably defined by Latin American governments and may be inconsistently reported.

Quantitative data can be complemented with the extensive qualitative literature on terrorism, violence, and violent groups in the region. The region has truth commissions, which can be a rich source of evidence, especially regarding state violence. However, they are mostly retrospective and often limited in scope. They are also designed for different purposes at the end of a prolonged conflict and may not be corroborated with other available evidence. Prominent commissions include the Argentine one for documentation of state terror and the Peruvian (Peruvian Truth and Reconciliation Commission—CVR) for documentation of terrorism by both state and non-state actors. A useful resource is the United States Institute of Peace's Truth Commissions Digital Collection <http://www.usip.org/publications/truth-commission-digital-collection> (accessed December 2015). Although it is not limited to Latin America, it contains the truth commissions from Argentina, Bolivia, Chile 1990, Ecuador 1996 and 2007, El Salvador, Peru 2001, Guatemala, Haiti, Panama, Paraguay, Honduras 2010, and Uruguay. It also includes the following Commissions of Inquiry: Chile 2003, Brazil, Peru 1986, and Honduras 1993. However, a major limitation of using truth commissions as a source of data is summarized by Chapman and Ball (2001, 4): "they have very different approaches to the kind of 'truth' they are seeking. Their official mandates, the perceptions and priorities of their commissioners and key staff, the methodological orientations utilized, and the level of resources available all shape the nature of their findings and the type of report they produce." They also note limitations due to a reliance on testimony and the fact that some critical records and documentation may have been excluded by responsible actors.

Some scholars may reject statistics of violent acts that are extracted from the historical context: "The common weakness of these quantitative methods when applied to terrorism is a reflection of the fact that this form of violent subversion erupts at various times in various places as the result of an often idiosyncratic combination of factors and conditions" (Hoffman and Morrison-Taw 2000, 7). However, that claim cannot be assessed without data. Regarding contentious terms such as political violence or terrorism, it is prudent to compare multiple sources of data and closely compare their definitions and coding rules. Moreover, trends must be validated with other sources to check for under- or over-reporting that may be due to government suppression of a topic, bias, etc. Data from human rights are the best sources for validation, but other NGOs or open-sources media are also useful.

Conceptual Confusion

The well-recognized conceptual confusion contributes to the lack of comparable data. It is difficult to differentiate terrorism from other types of violence. This problem is especially acute in Latin America. For example, FARC violence has been called revolutionary, terrorist, or guerrilla. Revolutionary groups can evolve and/or switch the targets and motivation of violence, making clear differentiation very difficult. For example, the FARC attacks civilians, commits other terrorist acts, and targets conventional government forces. There are multiple manners of evolution and overlap. Peru's Shining Path, Colombia's paramilitaries, and Colombia's FARC sometimes are involved in the drug trade and other illicit economies, further complicating classification of violent acts. In Central America, many gangs and DTOs commit acts considered to be terrorist. Finally, paramilitaries and leftist guerrillas both commit acts of terror, but their positions relative to the state and their aims are diametrically opposed. Given these and other problems, it is not surprising that existing datasets or definitions do not measure the same thing and have gaps in coverage. The "problems of conceptual fuzziness... and the resulting problems with the operationalization and measurement of phenomena of violence should continue to have the highest priority" (Dollase and Ulbrich-Herrmann 2003, 1233). Separating out warlike actions from terrorist actions may be not helpful. Instead, it can be useful to tally a broader range of attacks from the same group, from armed blockades, sabotage, raids, bombings, assaults, attacks against military targets to attacks against civilians and other terrorist acts. Additionally, criminal actions should also be tallied to include extortion, drug trafficking, etc., which are excluded from existing definitions of terrorism. In summary, ontologies of violence need to be able to take into account violence from actors whose actions are not limited to one category of violence and where overlapping of categories can be accommodated later with coding rules for scholars with different purposes and with different analytic goals. A restrictive view of terrorism, narrowly defined, would omit significant activities of groups considered terrorist, including attacks on critical infrastructure, police, and soldiers, and other activities terrorist groups use for funding, such as extortion and drug trafficking. Other groups, such as the Central American and Mexican gangs, may be omitted entirely, because their ascribed motivations do not match most definitions, despite their activities being similar to terrorist acts. Even factions within groups, such as the Colombian FARC, have drastically different motivating factors, some being more ideologically oriented and others more driven by illicit markets.

Moving Forward: Creating New Subnational, Comparable Data on Violence and State Presence

Latin American countries typically vary subnationally in terms of development, violence, and state presence. There is a classic economic tradition of studying primacy (Alonso 1968; Browning 1989), or patterns of economic development, in which capital cities dominate countries, have been prevalent. Economic development continues to be unbalanced today. Politically, decentralization efforts have shifted more responsibilities to local officials, while some parts of Latin American countries have world-class state capacity in capital and major cities, whereas other regions languish with little government presence or capacity. In general, throughout the region, imbalances of political and economic development are common as are levels of violence, in addition to factors widely causally associated with violence. Subnational studies[2] offer the opportunity to clarify relationships and illuminate theorized linkages between suspected causal factors and violence.

Subnational Statistics on Violence

To more accurately measure violence, one option is to code news sources to create another estimate of terrorism, internal conflict, or other type of violence. This is not without controversy, as scholars such as Silke (2004b, 62–3), have raised concerns about accuracy and bias. However, others view this type of data as relatively reliable (Davenport and Ball 2002; King and Lowe 2003) and open to verification. Most of the existing media-based sources are created with English-language news coverage of foreign events, spanning from 1974 to 2014. Other sources can be coded; for example, Fariss et al. (2015) have machine coded over 14,000 human rights reports to create new datasets of human rights abuses.

English-language reports create the opportunity for another source of bias, driven by the type of news that main wire services cover for their English-language audiences. A new project aims to improve data collected through news coverage by extending this to Spanish-language, foreign news sources. In the near future, based on an NSF-funded RIDIR project, "Modernizing Political Event Data for Big Data Social Science Research," data on Latin America will be available. Previously, using similar methods, data on Mexican drug violence was created by Osorio (2015). In the RIDIR project, the existing CAMEO dictionaries (Schrodt 2012; Gerner et al. 2009) will be extended to include new ontologies of violence, including analysis of internal conflicts of various sorts, as opposed to solely state versus state conflict, based on Spanish-language media coverage in Latin America. These semi-automated and automated data will be geo-located, validated, and publicly available in the future.

Data generated from semi-automated and automated data need to be validated (Grimmer and Stewart 2013), and the RIDIR data (http://eventdata.utdallas.edu) will be validated using statistics from government agencies, human rights groups, other NGOs, and existing datasets. Transparency about ontologies and processes will help to meet expectations of reliability and replicability (Beieler et al. 2016). Moreover, these ontologies will be detailed and coded so that other scholars can recode events to fit other definitions of conflict, including the more narrow concepts of terrorism. These and other, existing, subnational data on violence will be key to exploring existing competing theoretical debates and empirical findings.

The Importance of State Capacity and the Need for Subnational Measures

State capacity is a key variable to understanding the presence and intensity of violence. Without a strong state it is difficult to prevent or effectively respond to violent groups. According to Mueller, "the key to the amount of... warfare in the world... is not the degree to which there is hatred, grievance, or ethnic or civilizational cleavage, but rather the degree to which governments function adequately" (Mueller 2003, 513). State capacity is a major factor in studies of civil war and insurgency (see Fearon and Laitin 2003; Humphreys 2005). Many of these studies use a measure of GDP per capita as a proxy for state capacity to understand risks of civil war onset. However, the limitation of this variable as a proxy is also widely recognized. As Fearon (2005, 502) has noted, these widely available proxies do not closely approximate state presence or capacity: "good direct measures of a state's administrative capability and integrity are lacking." Hendrix and Young (2014) also recognize the importance of state capacity in studies of terrorism (both domestic and international). In a major improvement, they operationalize state capacity in two ways: bureaucratic/administrative capacity and military capacity and find a positive relationship between military capacity and terrorist attacks, while countries with high levels of bureaucratic/administrative capacity are associated with fewer attacks. They conclude "These results point to the importance of disaggregating the concept of state capacity in studies of political violence" (Hendrix and Young 2014, 359).

Moreover, it is not just the lack of state capacity that can make a country vulnerable to conflict, but an unbalanced state. The state must also offer more than just security. Classic counter-insurgency theory counsels attention to legitimacy and citizen support and strengthening the judicial system, in addition to defense and security (O'Neill 2001, 154). In a region that provides most of the examples of *mano dura* (iron fist) traditions, a more complete conceptualization of the state is necessary to understand citizen support. The provision of security alone, without other benefits, is likely to backfire. Parts of the region, especially countries such as Peru and Colombia, have sections of the country where state presence historically was limited to taxation or sporadic (and often indiscriminately repressive) security operations.

Another aspect of the state that must be assessed is whether there are pockets of undemocratic rule, instead of looking at national-level assessments of democracy. The presence or levels of corruption, state capture, or clientelism can vary widely from city to city and region to region. Fox (1994, 106) "focuses on exclusionary political practices in 'local' politics because that is where most citizens either gain access to or find themselves excluded from the state more generally." Guillermo O'Donnell (2004, 39) described this as the dominant pattern for Latin America. "Indeed, most Latin American countries, like new democracies in other parts of the world, are cases where national-level democratic regimes coexist with undemocratic subnational regimes and serve gaps in the effectiveness of basic civil rights." Koonings and Kruijt (1999, 2007) also talk about "governance voids," especially relating to "uncivil" non-state actors.

Newman (2007, 483) calls into question the unmediated connection of state capacity and terrorism. Instead, he asks if there is complicity within the government to explain the presence or absence of terrorist groups. "Even in weak states, the complicity or acquiescence of the government or de facto powers has often been important—or even decisive—in the ability of terrorist groups to organize and operate, not a total absence of order or centralized governance." This emphasis is particularly useful when there are concerns over government complicity with death squads, concerns of complicity with paramilitary groups, or the existence of patronage networks.

To have a more complete view of state capacity, comprehensive subnational indicators are needed to reflect the provision of services and professionalism of the state. This is in contrast to most theories of concepts of the state that assume "a high degree of homogeneity in the scope, both territorial and functional, of the state and of the social order it supports" (O'Donnell 1993, 1358). This is a bad assumption for Latin America. In many countries, the capital city may dominate agenda setting and may be home to a substantial proportion of the population, all the while not being representative of the whole. "In many countries of Latin America... the reach of the legal state is limited. In many regions, not only those geographically distant from the political centers but also the peripheries of large cities, the bureaucratic state may be present in the form of buildings and officials,... but... whatever formally sanctioned law exists is applied intermittently, if at all" (O'Donnell 2004, 41). Guillermo O'Donnell (1993, 1358) presented Peru as an exemplar of extreme heterogeneity and as a country dominated by brown areas in which the state is largely absent. For example, in Peru, almost a third of the population lives in Lima. The rest of the country may experience radically different services and levels of stability. Similarly, Limeños in peripheral areas may not have access to basic state services. In Colombia, historically, the uneven depth and breadth of the state throughout the country has been long recognized as a challenge. Colombia, in the 1980s and 1990s, could be described in this way. Thoumi (2003, 274) states "the Colombian state has been extremely weak with regard to its ability to control the national territory and provide an effective policing, legal, and judiciary system to protect property rights and solve conflicts."

Gibson (2005) provides another view of the complexity of Latin American states. He wrote of "regime juxtaposition" where there is a conflict of type of regime at different levels of jurisdiction. He examines how "the study of democratization can benefit from an exploration of strategic dimensions of continuity and change in subnational authoritarianism" (Gibson 2005, 103). This concept may be essential to understanding regional and local persistence of conflict, even when national dynamics of conflict are declining. Pockets of authoritarianism at the local level can perpetuate violence directly or indirectly in some parts of the country, despite progress at the national level or in other regions of the country. Moreover, since the 1990s, most countries in the region have implemented decentralization reforms, shifting both responsibilities for the provision of basic services to local governments and municipalities, while greatly increasing the financial resources of local and regional governments.

A subnational view is essential to take into account the varying levels of state presence throughout Latin American countries. Gibson (2010, 3) noted "despite widespread agreement that subnational jurisdictions in Latin America vary considerably in the democratic character of their politics, political scientists are still largely in the dark about how to conceptualize and measure this situation, and have scant knowledge about the mechanisms that sustain and undermine it." To date, there are a few efforts to create region-wide comparable state presence indicators. Luna and Soifer (2015) use LAPOP (Latin American Public Opinion Project) data to create a new measure of state capacity, based upon survey data. They examine three components to state capacity "its *reach across territory*, its ability to impose *taxation*, and its effectiveness in *provision of property rights*" (Luna and Soifer 2015, 1). Their measure of state capacity can be created at the subnational level, "without relying on data generated by states or crude proxies, and without being limited to particular units of analysis because of data availability" (Luna and Soifer 2015, 5). Although some scholars of state capacity may prefer to operationalize things differently, this is an innovative first step to "examine the co-variation among different dimensions of statement across territory and society within the countries of the Americas" (Luna and Soifer 2015, 9). A few scholars have created other subnational state indicators. Gervasoni (2010a) created an expert survey-based measure of subnational democracy for Argentina. He uses subjective, expert assessment because "experts are most likely more reliable than secondary sources, in part because the latter lack the necessary level of detail and quality for several provinces, and in part because the subtle manner in which democracy is restricted in hybrid regimes calls for very specific pieces of information" (Gervasoni 2010a, 21). In another subnational study of Argentina, Gervasoni (2010b) ties the theme of uneven internal democratization with a fiscal consequence of decentralization. He states "differences in subnational regimes are to a large extent explained by the magnitude and origin of their fiscal resources: low levels of democracy are to be expected where subnational states enjoy plentiful central government subsidies and have a weak tax link with local citizens and businesses" (Gervasoni 2010b, 303). Federal resources have supported the survival of hybrid subnational regimes and non-democratic elites in certain parts of the country (Gervasoni 2010b, 332). Finally, Giraudy has created a province or state level dataset for Mexico and Argentina to clarify the concept of "subnational regimes" by separating the concept into "two subsets of attributes—access to and exercise of state power" (Giraudy 2013, 53).

These scholars have begun the important work of creating subnational comparative indicators of state presence that are crucial for understanding Latin American violence and its relationship to democracy.

Conclusion

The goal is to provide a cross-regional, subnational dataset of Latin American terrorism and violence that can be matched with other subnational cross-regional data. Instead of calling for a crisp concept of terrorism that doesn't overlap with other types of related political violence, future efforts will need to provide a dataset that follows Schmid's (2004, 54) advice to consider broadening the scope of collection "to include not only other acts of political violence, but also other manifestations of political conflict. Indeed, the single biggest shortcoming of current databases on terrorism is that they are generally detached from the overall political conflict situation in which the terrorist group is often only one of several actors." By contrast, collecting data to fit multiple ontologies of violence will not only allow scholars to analyze just one category of violence but also to examine the evolution of groups over time, escalation to a higher intensity conflict, or de-escalation to nonviolent action. Doing this would cover three of Schmid's five levels of analysis and move toward the goal of providing a broader view of the scope, intensity, and frequency of events. Complementing these violence data with subnational indicators of state presence will also help to contextualize these events. This approach is necessary to understand violent groups in Latin America that not only differ by front or faction, but also to examine groups that either straddle multiple categories of violence or fall in the gaps between them.

Notes

1. Despite early associations of Peru's Shining Path with indigenous groups, it was not an indigenous terrorist group, but instead a group that emerged out of rural universities.
2. This call is similar to recent research on civil wars. See Kalyvas 2012, 658.

References

Alonso, W. (1968) "Urban and Regional Imbalances in Economic Development," *Economic Development and Cultural Change*, 17(1): 1–14.

Beieler, J., P. T. Brandt, A. Halterman, P. A. Schrodt, and E. M. Simpson (2016) "Generating Political Event Data in Near Real Time: Opportunities and Challenges," in R. Michael Alvarez (ed.), *Computational Social Science*. Cambridge: Cambridge University Press, 98–120.

Browning, C. E. (1989) "Urban Primacy in Latin America," *Yearbook: Conference of Latin Americanist Geographers*, 15: 71–8.

Chapman, A. R., and P. Ball (2001) "The Truth of Truth Commissions: Comparative Lessons from Haiti, South Africa, and Guatemala," *Human Rights Quarterly*, 23(1): 1–43.

Crenshaw, M. (1981) "The Causes of Terrorism," *Comparative Politics*, 13(4): 379–99.
Davenport, C., and P. Ball. (2002) "Views to a Kill: Exploring the Implications of Source Selection in the Case of Guatemalan State Terror, 1977–1996," *Journal of Conflict Resolution*, 46(3): 427–50.
Dobbins, J, L. E. Miller, S. Pezard, C. S. Chivvis, J. E. Taylor, K. Crane, C. Trenkov-Wermuth, and T. Mengistu (2013) *Overcoming Obstacles to Peace: Local Factors in Nation-Building*. Santa Monica, CA: Rand.
Dollase, R., and M. Ulbrich–Herrmann (2003) "Strategies and Problems in Quantitative Research on Aggression and Violence," in Wilhelm Heitmeyer and John Hagen (eds), *International Handbook of Violence Research*. New York: Kluwer Academic Publishers, 1203–18.
Fariss, C. J., F. J. Linder, Z. M. Jones, C. D. Crabtree, M. A. Biek, A. M. Ross, T. Kaur, and M. Tsai (2015) "Human Rights Texts: Converting Human Rights Primary Source Documents into Data," *Plos One*, 10(9): e0138935.
Fearon, J. D. (2005) "Primary Commodity Exports and Civil War," *Journal of Conflict Resolution*, 49(4): 483–507.
Fearon, J. D., and D. Laitin (2003) "Ethnicity, Insurgency, and Civil War," *American Political Science Review*, 97(1): 75–90.
Fox, J. (1994) "Latin America's Emerging Local Politics," *Journal of Democracy*, 5(2): 105–16.
Gerner, D. J., Schrodt, P. A., and O. Yilmaz (2009) "Conflict and Mediation Event Observations (CAMEO): An Event Data Framework for a Post Cold War World," in J. Bercovitch and S. Gartner (eds), *International Conflict Mediation: New Approaches and Findings*. New York: Routledge, 287–304.
Gervasoni, C. (2010a) "Measuring Variance in Subnational Regimes: Results from an Expert-Based Operationalization of Democracy in the Argentine Provinces," *Journal of Politics in Latin America*, 2(2): 13–52.
Gervasoni, C. (2010b) "A Rentier Theory of Subnational Regimes: Fiscal Federalism, Democracy, and Authoritarianism in the Argentine Provinces," *World Politics*, 62(2): 302–40.
Gibson, E. L. (2005) "Boundary Control: Subnational Authoritarian in Democratic Countries," *World Politics*, 58(1): 101–32.
Gibson, E. L. (2010) "Politics of the Periphery: An Introduction to Subnational Authoritarianism and Democratization in Latin America," *Journal of Politics in Latin America*, 2: 3–12.
Giraudy, A. (2013) "Varieties of Subnational Undemocratic Regimes: Evidence from Argentina and Mexico," *Studies in Comparative International Development*, 48: 51–80.
Grimmer, J., and B. M. Stewart (2013) "Text as Data: The Promise and Pitfalls of Automatic Content Analysis Methods for Political Texts," *Political Analysis*, 21: 267–97.
Gurr, T. R. (1988) "Empirical Research on Political Terrorism: The State of the Art and How it Might be Improved," in R. O. Slater and M. Stohl (eds), *Current Perspectives on International Terrorism*. London: Macmillan Press, 115–54.
Hendrix, C., and J. Young (2014) "State Capacity and Terrorism: A Two-Dimensional Approach," *Security Studies*, 23: 329–63.
Hoffman, B., and J. M. Morrison-Taw (2000) "A Strategic Framework for Countering Terrorism," in F. Reinares (ed.), *European Democracies Against Terrorism: Governmental Policies and Intergovernmental Cooperation*. Adershot: Ashgate, 3–29.
Humphreys, M. (2005) "Natural Resources, Conflict, and Conflict Resolution," *Journal of Conflict Resolution*, 49(4): 508–37.
Imbusch, P., M. Misse, and F. Carrión (2011) "Violence Research in Latin America and the Caribbean: A Literature Review," *International Journal of Conflict and Violence*, 5(1): 87–154.

Kalyvas, S. N. (2012) "Micro-Level Studies of Violence in Civil War: Refining and Extending the Control-Collaboration Model," *Terrorism and Political Violence*, 24(4): 658–68.

King, G., and W. Lowe (2003) "An Automated Information Extraction Tool for International Conflict Data with Performance as Good as Human Coders: A Rare Events Evaluation Design," *International Organization*, 57(3): 617–42.

Koonings, K., and D. Kruijt, eds (1999) *Societies of Fear: The Legacy of Civil War, Violence and Terror in Latin America*. London: Zed.

Koonings, K., and D. Kruijt (2007) *Armed Actors: Organised Violence and State Failure in Latin America*. London: Zed Books.

LaFree, G. (2012) "Generating Terrorism Event Databases: Results from the Global Terrorism Database, 1970 to 2008," in C. Lum and L. W. Kennedy (eds), *Evidence-Based Counterterrorism Policy*, Springer Series on Evidence-Based Crime Policy, 3. New York: Springer, 41–64.

Luna, J. P., and H. D. Soifer (2015) *Surveying State Capacity*. AmericasBarometer Insights, 119.

Merari, A. (1991) "Academic Research and Government Policy on Terrorism," *Terrorism and Political Violence*, 3(1): 88–102.

Mueller, J. (2003) "Policing the Remnants of War," *Journal of Peace Research*, 40(5): 507–18.

Newman, E. (2007) "Weak States, State Failure, and Terrorism," *Terrorism and Political Violence*, 19(4): 463–88.

O'Donnell, G. (1993) "On the State, Democratization Conceptual Problems: A Latin American View with Glances at Some Postcommunist Countries," *World Development*, 21(8): 1355–69.

O'Donnell, G. (2004) "Why the Rule of Law Matters," *Journal of Democracy*, 15(4): 32–46.

O'Neill, B. E. (2001) *Insurgency and Terrorism: Inside Modern Revolutionary Warfare*. Washington, DC: Potomoc Books.

Osorio, J. (2015) "Contagion of Drug Violence: Spatio-Temporal Dynamics of the Mexican War on Drugs," *Journal of Conflict Resolution*, Special Issue on Mexican Drug Violence, 59(8): 1403–32.

Pécaut, D. (2001) *Guerra contra la sociedad*. Bogotá: Espasa.

Schrodt, P. A. (2012) *Conflict and Mediation Event Observations (CAMEO) Codebook*, available online at <https://eventdata.psu.edu/data.dir/cameo.html>

Schmid, A. (2004) "Statistics on Terrorism: The Challenge of Measuring Trends in Global Terrorism," *Forum on Crime and Society*, 4(1–2): 49–69.

Schulze, F. (2004) "Breaking the Cycle: Empirical Research and Postgraduate Studies on Terrorism," in A. Silke (ed.), *Research on Terrorism: Trends, Achievements and Failures*. New York: Routledge, 181–205.

Silke, A. (2004b) "The Devil you Know," in A. Silke (ed.), *Research on Terrorism: Trends, Achievements and Failures*. New York: Routledge, 57–71.

Stafford, F., and M. Palacios (2002) *Colombia Fragmented Land, Divided Society*. Oxford: Oxford University Press.

Thoumi, F. E. (2003) *Illegal Drugs, Economy, and Society in the Andes*. Baltimore, MD: Johns Hopkins University Press.

Weinberg, L., A. Pedahzur, and S. Hirsch-Hoefler (2004) "The Challenges of Conceptualizing Terrorism," *Terrorism and Political Violence*, 16(4): 777–94.

CHAPTER 37

TERRORISM IN THE MIDDLE EAST

BOAZ GANOR AND EITAN AZANI

Introduction

Terrorism is a phenomenon known to extend across countries, borders, and continents. As a method of operation that makes deliberate use of political violence against civilians in order to achieve political goals (Ganor 2010), it has been adopted by various organizations, networks, groups, and individuals around the world. Despite the fact that over the last century terrorist attacks have taken place throughout the world, it seems that the Middle East has served as fertile ground for the growth of terrorist organizations, the fundamentalist ideologies that serve as the underlying basis for local and global terrorism, and the new methods of operation that have spread from the Middle East to other regions.

The centrality of the Middle East to the development of modern terrorism around the world is the result of national and international conflicts that have taken place over the last century in this geographical region. Among the internal-national triggers that served as a catalyst for terrorist attacks in the Middle East and beyond are the following: ethnic divisions, rivalries between different groups based on ideology, religion, socio-economic gaps, the actions of autocratic, traditional, and often corrupt regimes, the formation of regions lacking effective government and security control, etc. Among the external-international triggers that have led to the execution of terrorist attacks in the Middle East are the following: European colonialism, the Cold War, and the struggle between the superpowers that was manifested in an attempt to expand their areas of control and influence in the Middle East, rivalries, competitions, and conflicts of interests between countries that led to the initiation and implementation of terrorist attacks against one another, power struggles over territory, etc. Sometimes, major events occurred in the Middle East that triggered the outbreak of waves of terrorism, such as: wars, regime changes, civil wars, etc. In other cases, international developments and events seeped into the Middle East and left their mark on the scope and characteristics of terrorism in this region, such as: the rise and fall of superpowers and ideologies (the fall of the Soviet Union) and the strengthened hegemony of an internal or external regional player (such as Iran), etc. Events such as the Israeli–Arab conflict and its various wars (Six-Day War, Yom Kippur War, Lebanon War, etc.), and specifically the Israeli–Palestinian conflict, have influenced the scope and characteristics of terrorism in the Middle East. The Gulf War (1991), the fall of Saddam Hussein (2003), the civil wars in Jordan (1970) and Lebanon (1976), and the events of the "Arab Spring" that led to government upheavals and internal struggles in Middle Eastern countries (Syria, Iraq, and Yemen), and other events were crucial factors in the development of terrorism in the Middle East and beyond, and in the transformation of the Middle East into the cradle of modern terrorism.

The 1960s and 1970s: The Growth of Secular Palestinian Terrorist Organizations

The beginning of modern terrorism in general, and in the Middle East in particular, can be traced back to the second half of the twentieth century. During this period, Palestinian nationalist terrorist organizations began to take shape at the initiative and direction of Arab states, especially Egypt and Syria.

In 1959, several Palestinian students in Egypt (some of whom were from Gaza), led by Yasser Arafat, established the Fatah organization. In an interview with "Shu'un Filastiniyya," one of the founders of Fatah, Kamal Adwan, explained that: "The birth of Fatah gave expression to fundamental meanings. It expressed the Palestinian desire to refuse the official Arab reality and to rise up against it" (Harkabi 1979, 100). Fatah made the motto of its action strategy the "armed struggle" against Israel. In the eyes of Fatah's founders, armed violence was aimed at destroying Israel's military, political, economic, financial, and cultural institutions, and at preventing any possibility of the resurrection of a new Zionist society (Harkabi 1969, 34–5). Fatah's founders, most of whom lived in Egypt, heeded the messages of Egyptian President, Gamal Abd-al-Nasser, who called for a Palestinian national organization to strengthen his struggle for hegemony in the international Arab arena (Yaari 1970, 23–4).

Fatah's action strategy was based on two fundamental principles—the independence of the Palestinian national movement from any Arab regime, and the supremacy of the armed struggle as the sole means of liberating Palestine. From the point of view of the founders, the armed struggle was meant to serve three central purposes of the Palestinian Liberation movement: to serve as an active means for bringing about the destruction of Israel, to unite the Palestinian nation and motivate it to take part in the struggle for the liberation of Palestine, and to openly declare the existence of a

Palestinian nation and the need to resolve its problems. Khaled al-Hassan explained the reasoning behind these fundamental goals and the fact that they were intertwined: "The Palestinians have no citizenship and so they have no history and no rights, duties, or sense of belonging. Without exercising those, they become nothing. Restoring [them] requires returning to the homeland, but that in turn requires force" (Yaari 1970, 91).

At the early stages of the strategic formulation of Fatah's violent activity, it seemed that the mission of obliterating the Jewish state was too heavy for the Palestinian Liberation Movement alone, which caused the Fatah leadership to declare that the armed struggle was only meant to create the conditions that would lead to a pan-Arab war against Israel. This war would lead to the realization of the Arab nations' advantages over the state of Israel (concerning manpower, in the field, and overall strength), and would translate into the destruction of Israel and the establishment of an independent Palestinian state in its place (Yaari 1970, 37–8). The Palestinian armed struggle was, therefore, supposed to serve mainly as a catalyst for a war that would lead to Israel's destruction.

On May 28, 1964 the first Palestinian National Conference convened in Jerusalem and decided to establish the "Palestinian Liberation Organization" (PLO). The conference, which was attended by 422 people, defined itself as the "Palestinian National Council" (PNC) and selected Ahmad al-Shuqeiry as its Chairman (Yaari 1970, 98). This body was supposed to operate alongside Arab states and coordinate Palestinian political and military activities. In actuality, it was a Palestinian puppet established by the leaders of Arab states, led by Egypt, in order to exploit the aspirations of the Palestinian people and strengthen the position of these countries in the Arab arena. In addition to its political activities, the PLO also entered the military realm and initiated the establishment of the "Palestinian Liberation Army" (PLA). The units of this army were formed in the framework of various Arab state armies. The recruits came from among the Palestinian population while the training and operation of the army was provided by the army of the host country. PLA units were closely and regularly monitored by the Arab governments bordering Israel, and were not allowed to carry out any military operation against Israel without their approval (Raphael 1983, 36). The establishment of the PLO was anathema to members of Fatah as it represented that which Fatah rejected—the patronage of Arab states. The PLO, led by al-Shuqeiry, and Fatah differed from one another not only in the features of their revolutionary ideologies, but also and perhaps mostly in the question of the timing of the use of armed struggle. The construction of a Palestinian power base and its prominence in the international political arena were considered by al-Shuqeiry to be the first priority, and he emphasized that a joint Palestinian–Arab battle would be waged in the future. In contrast, Fatah and the radicals maintained that from the moment a nucleus of Palestinian pioneers was formed, they should immediately begin to carry out small acts of warfare, since the Palestinian organization is of no value without the armed struggle (Harkabi 1979, 106).

Fatah reached operational capability and on January 1, 1965 (two and a half years before the Six-Day War and the occupation of the West Bank and Gaza by Israel), attempted to carry out its first terrorist attack (against the Israeli National Water Carrier) under the name "Al Asifa" ("The Storm"). The failed attack marked Fatah's transition from an unknown underground organization to one whose activities garnered extensive media coverage (Yasro 1970, 41–6). Despite expressions of dissatisfaction from Arab countries (except Syria), Fatah continued its terrorist activities until the Six-Day War (June 1967). Arab states, led by Jordan and Egypt, tried to damage Fatah through propaganda but were unsuccessful. Nasser was concerned that terrorist attacks by Fatah at that stage would cause a loss of control over the course of events and, therefore, an order was issued to Arab armies requiring that they consider themselves to be in a state of war with the Fatah (Hart 1994, 159).

Israel's victory in the Six-Day War against the Arab armies severely damaged Arab states' appeal in the eyes of the Palestinians and strengthened their resolve that the only way to achieve Palestinian national aspirations was for Palestinian organizations to carry out terrorist attacks against Israel. Against this backdrop, the PLO leadership successfully took control of PLO institutions in 1968, undermining the influence of Egypt and other Arab states on the organization's framework. They removed several senior members of the organization and replaced PLO leader, Ahmad al-Shuqeiry, with Fatah leader, Yasser Arafat. Israel's occupation of the West Bank and Gaza Strip from Jordan and Egypt during the Six-Day War, and the transfer of power over millions of Palestinians to Israel, led Fatah to try to move the main center of the armed struggle to the Occupied Territories themselves. The outcomes of the Six-Day War had other important implications that influenced the Palestinian struggle, the most important being the establishment of additional Palestinian organizations and factions that adopted the armed struggle strategy and even radicalized it. In this manner, George Habash established the Popular Front for the Liberation of Palestine in December 1967. The Popular Front was mainly composed of senior members of the "Qawmiyyin al-Arab" ("Arab Nationalists") (Yaari 1972). The new organization adopted a strict ideological stance that combined a Marxist-Leninist concept of social and economic issues with the principles of popular armed struggle in order to "liberate Palestine and eliminate imperialism and the Arab reaction." Since its establishment, the Popular Front has taken care to avoid total dependence on any country and has sought to make independent decisions on political, military, and organizational matters, but the organization soon received broad support and sponsorship from the Soviet Union. Habash's "Front" viewed Jordan as a "springboard" for the liberation of Palestine (as expressed by the emblem of the "Front," which includes an arrow passing from Jordan to Israel). Over the years, the "Front" advocated the defeat of the Hashemite Jordanian regime and its replacement with a popular regime that supports the Palestinian interest. The establishment of the Popular Front symbolized the beginning of the split in the Palestinian movement, which continued for years afterwards with the establishment of additional organizations. In October 1968, Ahmed Jibril left the Popular Front as a result of personal rivalries with the organization's leaders, George Habash and Naif Hawatmeh. In an attempt to emphasize its link to the parent organization, Jibril called his new organization "The Popular Front for the Liberation of Palestine—General Command." Jibril, who had previously served as a commander in the Syrian army, had close ties to Syria and the organization quickly received full Syrian sponsorship. The "General Command" did not adopt crystallized ideological positions on social and political issues except for its obligation to "liberate Palestine" through armed struggle. In 1968, the Syrian Ba'ath regime established another organization the "Sa'iqa." By doing so, Syria sought to strengthen its influence on the Palestinian movement without having it be considered external intervention. In contrast to most other Palestinian organizations, the majority of Sa'iqa's members were Syrian, members of the Ba'ath Party, and not of Palestinian origin. Since its establishment, Sa'iqa has essentially served as a Syrian puppet designed to promote Syrian interests in the Palestinian and regional arenas. In accordance with the ideology of the Syrian Ba'ath regime, the Sa'iqa set for itself the goal of "liberating Palestine" but the liberation was not meant to bring about the establishment of an independent state, but rather to join Palestine to the "Greater Syria." In response to the Palestinian puppets set up by Syria in April 1969, the Iraqi Ba'ath regime established the "Arab Liberation Front." However, this "Front" also did not reflect the authentic interests of the Palestinians. Rather, it was aimed, first and foremost, at promoting Iraqi interests in the Palestinian arena. As part of the Front's complete dependence on Iraq, it adopted the ideological principles of the Iraqi Ba'ath regime and so, in addition to its aspiration to the complete liberation of Palestine, the Front objected to the establishment of an independent Palestinian state. In May 1969, a faction led by Naif Hawatmeh broke off from the "Popular Front" —against the backdrop of personal disagreements with George Habash—and established the "Democratic Popular Front for the Liberation of Palestine." At first, the "Democratic Front" formulated a Communist ideological platform that was more radical than that of the "Popular Front." This platform called for a social revolution in Arab countries as a first step towards the "liberation of Palestine." Over the years, the Democratic Front toned down its revolutionary positions, became closer to Syria and Iraq, and developed a close relationship with Communist countries, especially the Soviet Union.

This period, therefore, marked the growth of secular Palestinian terrorist organizations and the increased involvement of Arab and other states in the internal Palestinian arena, as they used terrorism to fight against Israel and to promote their domestic interests in the inter-Arab framework.

The large influence of the development and activities of secular Palestinian terrorist organizations on the Arab arena could be seen in the civil wars that took place during this period, which were initiated and led by Palestinian organizations—the first in Jordan (1970) and the second in Lebanon (1976). At the end of the 1960s, most terrorist organizations concentrated their forces and operatives in Jordanian territory. Various terrorist organizations opened offices in Palestinian population centers, recruited operatives to their ranks, and even started to openly carry firearms. In addition to their activities in the Palestinian refugee camps, the terrorists also established army bases in areas next to the Israeli border. These bases helped the organizations with their terrorist activities against Israel. Terrorist cells often crossed the border into Israel to carry out terrorist attacks, to smuggle weapons, or to maintain contact with the organization's operatives in the territories. The increased activity of Palestinian organizations in Jordan posed a threat to the stability of King Hussein's rule. Friction with Jordanian rulers, which grew as a result of the increase in the number of Palestinian fighters and Israel's retaliatory acts in Jordanian territory, led King Hussein to instruct his army to attack and destroy terrorist bases in September 1970. The battle against the terrorist organizations, which was named "Black September," continued for approximately one year and led to the destruction of terrorist strongholds in Jordan. Many terrorists were killed in battle while others were jailed, and the rest were expelled or fled from Jordan.

In the years that preceded "Black September," terrorist organizations operated among the Palestinian population in Lebanon. The Lebanese government's concern over this activity led to the signing of the Cairo Agreement in November 1969, which attempted to impose restrictions on the terrorists. However, the agreement essentially sanctioned the activity of terrorist organizations and the expansion of their foothold in Lebanon. Most of the terrorists who left Jordan as a result of "Black September" made their way to Lebanon and joined the organizational infrastructure there. In this manner, Lebanon's position was solidified as the center of terrorist organizations' activities and preparations. The increased power of Palestinian organizations in Lebanon created friction with other forces in Lebanon, led by the Maronite Christians. In April 1975, these power struggles led to the outbreak of battles between Palestinian and Christian organizations in the area of Beirut. These battles were the beginning of the Lebanese civil war. The battles between the Christians and the Palestinians worsened over the coming months until early 1976 when various Lebanese movements and organizations joined the warring parties. As a result of the civil war in Lebanon, and especially after Operation Litani, Palestinian organizations came to recognize that military power and control over a separate region were essential to their existence in Lebanon, and were key to ensuring their independence. The crumbling of the central Lebanese government and, along with it, the army and police led to the actual division of Lebanon among the various players, such as West Beirut and most of the territory of southern Lebanon, which belonged to Palestinian organizations. In the territories under their control, these organizations built infrastructure that included regular military units, training camps, assistance units, militia forces, and civilian administration offices. Pretty soon, extraterritorial areas were created in which the organization controlled the traffic routes and Palestinian population centers, carried weapons openly, established checkpoints on roads, and enforced their rule (similar to the process that took place ten years earlier in Jordan). A "state within a state" was created in these semi-autonomous areas, which were controlled by the organizations' commanders in Beirut, and the Palestinian organizations, led by Fatah, managed all aspects of life there except for financial issues, which remained under the control of the state.

The process of institutionalizing army forces in organizations was reflected in the massive procurement of various weapons (mainly heavy self-propelled weapons), the establishment of military units with a quasi-regular structure and hierarchy, and the holding of training exercises and participation in military training by friendly armies. The military frameworks that were established and expanded in Lebanon enabled the employment of hundreds of thousands of Palestinians both in military roles as well as in assistance and administrative roles. Membership in the hierarchal military framework established the control of these organizations, led by Fatah, over Palestinian residents in Lebanon. Payment of salaries to members of the military forces and the administrative system made the Palestinians financially dependent on, and personally committed to, the organization. The organizations' military forces strengthened the position of Palestinians in Lebanese society and enabled the expansion of their quasi-autonomous areas to places further away and to points with geographically strategic significance. The PLO in Lebanon became a state in exile based on a combination of territorial control and international recognition (Sayigh 1997, 448). Maintaining control over the territory and the population living in it turned Fatah into a "hybrid terrorist organization"—a terrorist organization that controls both territory and population and is embedded in the civilian society. As such, some of its mechanisms were involved in initiating, directing, and executing terrorist attacks, while others were responsible for pseudo-legitimate activities such as providing services to the population (welfare, education, etc.) as well as domestic and international political activities. This model was later adopted by other organizations throughout the Middle East (such as Hamas in the Gaza Strip, and the Islamic State in Iraq and Syria).

Secular Palestinian terrorist organizations did not invent the methods of modern terrorism, in the framework of which extreme violence is used in order to draw media attention and to spread messages of fear and anxiety to target audiences in order to influence their mindset and political impact. Terrorism was used as a type of psychological warfare by non-state organizations for years long before these organizations were established.

However, Palestinian terrorist organizations in the 1970s improved and perfected known terrorism methods (taking hostages, planting bombs, etc.) and many terrorist organizations around the world chose to imitate their actions. This was demonstrated by the terrorist attacks that were carried out by Palestinian terrorist organizations against Israeli and Jewish targets and interests abroad (outside of Israel), especially the aerial attacks that were carried out by the PFLP, led by George Habash. In some of these cases, the PFLP even collaborated with foreign terrorist organizations, such as the Japanese Red Army, the Baader-Meinhof group, and the IRA, to execute these attacks. In July 1968, an EL Al plane making its way from Rome to Lod was hijacked by a terrorist cell from the Popular Front. The plane and crew were held hostage in Algeria. This attack marked the beginning of the modern international terrorism phenomenon since the main purpose of the attack was to draw media attention (Hoffman 2006, 68).

The 1980s and 1990s: The Growth and Activities of Local Islamist-Jihadist (Palestinian and Shi'ite) Terrorist Organizations

The 1980s and 1990s were marked by the growth of local Islamist-jihadist terrorist organizations, both in the Palestinian arena and in the Lebanese arena, as well as by the development of new waves of terrorism marked by the use of suicide bombers.

The strengthening of the Islamic movement in the Middle East could be attributed to developments in the Arab world, the most prominent of which was Khomeini's rise to power in Iran. After the revolution in Iran at the end of the 1970s, the Khomeini regime set for itself the central goal of "exporting the [Khomeinist] revolution" to other parts of the world. One of the most effective tools for achieving this goal was the Hezbollah movement and its members who were instructed to deploy to various parts of the world, especially to places where Shi'ite communities resided.

In the framework of the "export of the Iranian revolution," Iranian delegates worked to spread the principle of self-sacrifice and the obligation for personal jihad among members of Islamist-jihadist movements around the world through indoctrination and the annual investment of tens of millions of dollars into financial and military support for Islamist terrorist organizations, such as Hamas, the Islamic Jihad Movement in Palestine, Egyptian jihadist organizations, and others. In the framework of the military aid that Iran provided to the Islamic Jihad organizations, members of these organizations were invited to participate in instruction and training courses at military camps in Iran, which even sent Iranian instructors to the terrorist bases of these organizations in the Middle East. Iran also transferred many weapons to terrorist organizations in the Middle East, including anti-tank, anti-aircraft rockets and missiles.

The "Council of the Islamic Revolution" was established in order to coordinate the activities of pro-Iranian organizations in various countries. This council sent members to Arab states in order to recruit many young people to the framework of "Islamic Jihad." Some of the new recruits came to Iran for military training and then established additional cells in their country of origin. In the wake of local successes and the positive response from the youth in various countries, the Iranians established an additional, more senior, coordination framework in 1984 called: "The Supreme Coordinating Council between the Islamic Revolution in Iran and the Islamic Revolutionary Movements Worldwide."

The first active cells of the "Islamic Jihad" in Lebanon appeared following the outbreak of the Lebanon War (1982). Jihadist groups in the country left their bases in western Beirut and Beqaa to carry out terrorist attacks against the army forces of Western countries, the IDF, and the South Lebanon Army (SLA) that were located in Lebanon, and to kidnap Western civilians in Lebanon. These attacks were first carried out under the cover name, "The Islamic Jihad," and later responsibility for the attacks was claimed by the "Hezbollah" movement.[1] The rise and strengthening of Hezbollah (or "Party of God") in Lebanon was one of the rotten fruits of the Lebanon War. Hezbollah was established as an offshoot of Iran in the Middle East, designed to further Iranian interests in Lebanon, Syria, and other Arab countries, and to serve as the long arm of Iran in the struggle against Israel. The organization was founded by religious Shi'ites and volunteers in the training camps of the Iranian "Revolutionary Guards" in Lebanon. Over time, Hezbollah turned into a framework that incorporated several radical Shi'ite organizations. These organizations, which accepted the direct authority of Iranian leader, Ayatollah Khomeini, created a common ideological platform that included struggle until the absolute destruction of Israel and until the establishment of an

"Islamic Republic" in Lebanon. These goals were presented as a battle against "Western imperialism" and were designed to strengthen Iran's standing in Lebanon and the Arab world.

In this framework, Hezbollah's first mission was to take control over the Shi'ite population in Lebanon by defeating the Amal movement. This mission, which involved tough battles within the Shi'ite community itself in the beginning of 1980s, ended with the downfall of Amal. During the next stage, Hezbollah filled the void that was created as a result of the serious damage caused to Palestinian terrorist infrastructure following the Lebanon War (1982), and—with Iranian economic and military support as well as direct and indirect Syrian aid—the organization became the central military body carrying out terrorist attacks against foreign forces and IDF forces in Lebanon.

During the 1980s, Hezbollah shaped the policy of its terrorist attacks against IDF forces and Israel based essentially on three tiers: the execution of continuous guerrilla attacks against IDF and SLA forces in Lebanon (attacks on military posts, attacks on supply convoys, ambushes, roadside charges, laying mines, etc.), artillery fire aimed at civilian communities (in northern Israel and Lebanon), and, at the beginning of the next decade, showcase attacks as well (the bombing of the Israeli Embassies in Argentina in 1992 and the Buenos Aires Amia building in 1994). Hezbollah proved that it had high operational capability in each of these areas of operation, and Israel's many attempts to hinder Hezbollah's operational abilities and to silence the source of fire on its communities in the north (whether through extensive military operations, continuous offensive operations, or assassinations and kidnappings) were not successful. For instance, in "Operation Accountability" (June 1993), which according to various estimates cost the IDF approximately 230 million shekels,[2] the Israeli Air Force (IAF) dropped approximately 1,000 bombs on 291 targets and fired 21,000 artillery shells, while the terrorists fired 274 katyusha rockets, 142 of which fell inside Israel and 132 of which fell in the security zone.[3] In "Operation Grapes of Wrath" (April 1996), after seventeen days of battle that included thousands of IAF sorties and tens of thousands of artillery shells that cost the IDF approximately 200 million shekels,[4] Hezbollah fired over 700 katyusha rockets—approximately 500 to the Galil and approximately 200 to the security area—and continued to fire until the ceasefire, causing direct and indirect damage in the north worth an estimated 70 million shekels.[5]

Hezbollah's improved capabilities were largely the result of the quantity and quality of the military weapons that Iran sent to Hezbollah in Lebanon, and included anti-aircraft weapons, anti-tank weapons, and advanced rockets. These abilities were manifested in, among other ways, the adoption of Iranian combat doctrines that included simultaneous attacks on several posts, with artillery assistance, interoperability using explosives and assaults, the planting of explosives using sophisticated camouflage and—above all else—the use of suicide bombers to carry out terrorist attacks (the attack on US Marines in Lebanon in 1983, on the US Embassy in 1983, on the Israeli Embassy in Buenos Aires in 1992, and on the "Amia" Jewish community center in Buenos Aires in 1994). One of the methods used by Hezbollah to carry out terrorist attacks in the 1980s was the kidnapping of foreign civilians in Lebanon as a trading card for the release of Shi'ite detainees around the world and as a source of funding for the organization. In this framework, Hezbollah carried out over fifty kidnappings in Lebanon between 1984 and 1989. Aided and directed by Iran, Hezbollah also developed advanced intelligence capabilities with the help of the Shi'ite population in southern Lebanon, the operation of a network of cellphone monitoring of IDF soldiers and commanders. Hezbollah also employed active methods and means of psychological warfare against Israel and against enemies of the organization and, in doing so, became one of the first to develop a complex and effective propaganda system that included—even back in the 1980s and 1990s—radio and television stations, newspapers, internet sites, and more. Hezbollah understood the importance of psychological warfare and the use of the media.

In addition to Hezbollah and Amal, the Shi'ites operated several pro-Syrian Lebanese terrorist organizations in Lebanon during the 1980s that carried out terrorist attacks. One such Lebanese organization was the Lebanese Communist Party, which was established in 1924 in cooperation with the Syrian Communist Party and adopted a Marxist-Leninist ideology. The party was close to the Soviet Union and Communist Palestinian terrorist organizations. Another active organization was the Syrian National party, which was founded in the 1930s with the goal of establishing "Greater Syria." Most members of the party, which included several hundred military operatives, were Christian. Following the Lebanon War, party members were involved in carrying out terrorist attacks against IDF forces in southern Lebanon, including suicide attacks using car bombs. After the IDF's withdrawal from Lebanon in 2000, Hezbollah took control over all of southern Lebanon, and increased its involvement in internal Lebanese politics until it reached a position that enabled the organization to veto the existence of government coalitions. After the Second Lebanon War in 2006, the organization—armed with approximately 100,000 rockets, missiles, and other advanced weapons—acted to rehabilitate its strongholds in villages in southern Lebanon and rebuilt its operational infrastructure with hundreds of millions of dollars in Iranian assistance. After the outbreak of the civil war in Syria, most of Hezbollah's military operations were moved to Syria under Iran's instruction in order to help preserve the rule of Assad, their ally. In recent years, this has put Hezbollah in direct confrontation with rebel Islamist organizations, led by Al Nusra Front and the Islamic State.

The strengthening of the Islamic movement in the Palestinian arena can also be attributed to developments in the Arab world, most notably Khomeini's rise to power in Iran. Palestinian jihadist organizations received generous financial and military assistance from Iran (KUrz 1993, 120). The extent of Iran's impact on the development of Palestinian jihadist organizations can be seen in the book by Dr Fathi Shaqaqi, who was one of the heads of the largest faction of the Palestinian Islamic Jihad, which was titled, *Khomeini: The Islamic Solution and its Alternative*.

For years, three groups of Islamists operated in mosques in Judaea and Samaria and in East Jerusalem—Al Tahrir Al Islami, Al Jihad, and the Muslim Brotherhood. On the one hand, the members of these movements criticized Palestinian terrorist organizations that intentionally kept their platforms free of any Islamic content and opposed the establishment of a religious-Islamic Palestinian state, and on the other hand they also condemned traditional Islamic movements, which ignored the Palestinian problem, pushed the struggle for the liberation of Palestine to the backburner, and chose to focus most of their activities at that time on deepening Islamic culture and social activities in Judaea and Samaria and Gaza, with the goal of recruiting to their ranks as many young Palestinians as possible. This process of Islamization in the Palestinian arena gained momentum in the 1980s when several Islamic activists united various factions and adopted the name, “The Islamic Jihad.” The trigger for establishment of Islamic Jihad factions in the territories took place in 1985 when Israel made a prisoner exchange deal with the “Jibril Front,” and, in exchange for three of its soldiers who were being held captive by the Front in Syria, agreed to release 1,150 Palestinian terrorists from prison, most of whom were guilty of murder, and even agreed to the demand to allow these terrorists to return to live in the West Bank and Gaza Strip should they choose to do so. Some of those terrorists who embraced the teachings of the Islamic law teacher, Sheikh Assad Bayoud al-Tamimi, served as the initial group that established Palestinian Islamic Jihad factions after their release from prison (Sayigh 1997, 626).

The Palestinian jihadist groups emphasized that the Arab–Israeli conflict was not a national conflict over territory, but rather a basic religious conflict. Therefore, they maintained that they must fight for the liberation of all of “Palestine” and objected to any political agreement or diplomatic activity to resolve the problem. They maintained that the conflict with the Jews in Palestine can only be solved through violent and direct confrontation, as defined in 1990 by one of the organization’s leaders—Sheikh Tamimi—(who published a pamphlet titled, “The Destruction of Israel—a Koranic Imperative”): “The Jews must return to the countries from which they came. We will not agree to a Jewish state on our land, not even a single village.”

According to the Islamic Jihad, Israel is the spearhead of the imperialist West in the heart of the Muslim world and, therefore, the removal of this corrupt entity is the first step towards the return of all Muslims and the establishment of an Islamic state on all Muslim territory. Jihadist groups used references to Palestine from the Quran and Islamic law to support their claim that the Palestinian issue is central to the Islamic revolution.

The principles of the PIJ’s ideology were disseminated in the 1980s among members of various groups through sermons in mosques in the territories, through books and articles in newspapers, and through political indoctrination in Israeli jails. Members of jihadist organizations united in small underground cells in the territories and operated relatively independently, made contact with the group’s leadership in the territories and sometimes even with the senior leadership the resided in Jordan, and were composed mainly of the organization’s members who were expelled by Israel.

As a result of the expulsion of the leaders of the PIJ in 1988, close contact was established between Fathi Shaqaqi, and Hezbollah and Shi’ite elements in Israel, both in the military and ideological realm. The PIJ—the Sunni Palestinian organization that adopted the Iranian revolution as a role model—tried to repress the fundamental contrasts between Sunni and Shi’a, and emphasized the common interests of the Muslim Nation. During 1991–2, the PIJ and Hezbollah developed cooperation that led to the execution of several joint terrorist attacks against the IDF and SLA in the security strip.[6]

With the outbreak of the Palestinian uprising in the territories (1987), known as the "Intifada," members of Islamic jihadist organizations played an important role in initiating, directing, and executing violent protest activities and terrorist attacks in the territories. At the same time, bitter disagreements erupted between members of the Islamic Jihad, and their counterparts in the "Muslim Brotherhood" movement and members of its military wing—"Hamas." Up until 1987, the basis of the disagreement between Hamas and the Islamic Jihad could be summarized in three points: Hamas maintained that a solution to the Palestinian problem would only be possible after the establishment of an Islamic state outside of Palestine, while the Islamic Jihad maintained that the order of events must be reversed. Hamas and the Islamic Jihad also differed with regard to the importance and centrality of the Islamic revolution in Iran. However, the main disagreement between the organizations concerned the following question—"Has the time come to launch jihad against the Jews?" The outbreak of the Intifada at the end of 1987, and the rise in popularity of jihadist organizations among the Palestinian public in the territories, proved to Hamas that "sitting on the fence" was liable to seriously harm the organization.

Therefore, one outcome of the uprising in the territories was the establishment of Hamas. With the outbreak of the Intifada, the leader of Hamas—Sheikh Yassin—reached the conclusion that in order to stay relevant and to prevent many of its members from joining the ranks of the PIJ (after many years of religious-educational propaganda and welfare activities), the movement must take an active role in violent events in the territories. For this purpose, the "Muslim Brotherhood" established a military wing called "Hamas," which set for itself the goal of taking control of the Intifada through its many members in the territories and exploited the violence to harm groups and individuals that were "corrupting Palestinian society."

Hamas's ideology was based on a combination of Palestinian nationalism and the aspiration for an independent Palestinian state on all Palestinian territory under the rule of Islamic shari'a.[7] In contrast to the PIJ, Hamas was careful not to become a satellite of any Arab or Muslim country (including Iran), even though it was willing to accept any help offered to the organization by these countries. Through the use of terrorist attacks, Hamas strove to strike a harsh moral blow to Israeli society and to destabilize Israel from within in a way that would cause it to change positions and withdraw from the Gaza Strip and West Bank. By the end of the first year of the uprising, figures in Hamas estimated that the Intifada was, in fact, exhausting Israel and severely hampering its ability to expand and strengthen its hold in the territories (Kurz 1993, 182). The return to Islam, which was manifested in the establishment of Hamas and the PIJ, and in the joining of many fighters to their ranks, also left its mark on secular Palestinian organizations, which began to formulate and use propaganda in religious terms. On March 21, 1988, for example, Fatah's executive committee added the following preface to its official announcement for the first time: "In the Name of God, the Merciful and the Compassionate," and quoted several "surahs" from the Quran (Sayigh 1997, 625).

With the signing of the Oslo Accords at the beginning of the 1990s, as well as the rise of political negotiations, Hamas became a central terrorist organization operating against Israel. Hamas terrorists made use of all known methods to attack Israel and made armed resistance an alternative to the peace process between Israel and the Palestinians. In this framework, starting in 1993, Hamas and PIJ terrorists began to make use of a new type of terrorist attack that it had learnt from Hezbollah—suicide attacks.

Hezbollah had already proved in the 1980s that suicide attacks caused the largest number of casualties (the result of the ability to precisely select the time and place of the attack). By carrying out a relatively small number of suicide attacks in the early 1980s against American targets and French forces that were stationed in Lebanon, Hezbollah managed to cause the withdrawal of those forces from Lebanon. During the 1980s and 1990s, Hezbollah carried out many suicide attacks against IDF and SLA forces in Lebanon. These attacks caused many casualties among these forces but only in 2000 did they succeed in actually bringing about Israel's withdrawal from southern Lebanon.

Hamas and PIJ fighters used this method as a primary tool in their attack policies in Israel during the 1990s. By carrying out dozens of suicide attacks within Israeli territory in crowded areas, they killed hundreds of Israeli civilians and injured thousands more. The terrorists who left PA territory in the West Bank after being expelled by Israeli forces in the framework of the Oslo Accords exploited the relatively free movement from these territories to Israeli territory, Arafat's policy of turning a blind eye to their activities and organization in the territories under his control, the long border between Israel and PA territories, and the lack of a physical barrier between them. The first wave of suicide attacks from 1993 to 1997 waned at the same time as the Israeli–Palestinian peace process faded but it was renewed with even more vigor with the outbreak of the "Second Intifada" between 2000 and 2005. With the end to that outbreak of violence and following Israel's withdrawal from the Gaza Strip in the framework of the "Disengagement Plan," which was conceived by Prime Minister Ariel Sharon and completed in 2005, Hamas won the Palestinian elections and its forces took control of the Gaza Strip, which was evacuated by Israel, and used great violence to expel members of Fatah from the Strip.

The 2000s: The Growth and Activities of Global Islamist-Jihadist Organizations (Al Qaeda and the Islamic State)

The roots of the idea behind global jihad are deeply planted in the Middle East arena. They are the product of a mix of two radical Islamic ideologies: the ideology of the Muslim Brotherhood (influenced by the books of Sayyid Qutb) and the Saudi Wahabist (Salafist) ideology. This ideological mix was designed and spread in colleges and universities in Saudi Arabia in the 1960s and 1970s by members of the Muslim Brotherhood and senior Saudi ulama. The pan-Islamic Saudi policy and the availability of resources enabled this ideology to spread throughout the Muslim world on the platform of the

Saudi dawah system that was systematically established beginning in the 1960s. Advocates of the concept of global jihad and those who implement it, including Abdullah Azzam, Bin Laden, al-Zawahiri, and many other leaders of global jihadist organizations, were the instigators and graduates of this Islamic movement.

The organizational and operative roots of global jihad developed in Afghanistan during the First Afghanistan War. During this period, an organizational and ideological infrastructure was established that led to the creation of Al Qaeda, which has since served as a basis and model for global jihad organizations. Al Qaeda was established in August 1988 by Bin Laden and group of graduates of the Egyptian Islamic Jihad. A variety of documents, meeting summaries, and letters that were found in Bin Laden's hiding places shed light on the organization's establishment, leadership, objectives, policies, and organizational structure. It is widely believed that the organization was founded by Bin Laden against the backdrop of disagreements between him and Abdullah Azzam regarding how to integrate Arab volunteers in the war in Afghanistan. Bin Laden, in contrast to Abdullah Azzam, believed that an Islamic army should be established based on volunteers who came to Afghanistan: an army that would fight to protect Muslim lands from foreign occupation and corrupt regimes, and would unite Islamic fighters around the world. The declaration of the establishment of Al Qaeda in Afghanistan (the base) was the first step towards achieving this objective. The first years after the war in Afghanistan ended were characterized by the reorganization of Al Qaeda and its adjustment to the changing circumstances and arena of operation in the Middle East.

Most of Al Qaeda's operations were moved to the Middle East and Sudan. Bin Laden returned to Saudi Arabia, and then settled in Sudan from 1992 to 1996 where he worked to establish an Islamic army and to create cooperative ties with local terrorist organizations. At the same time as an Islamic army was being built in Sudan, Al Qaeda networks were operating on Saudi Arabian soil. They achieved operational maturity in 1995–6; during this time, two terrorist attacks were carried out against American military targets in Saudi Arabia, one of which was probably carried out together with Hezbollah members.

With Bin Laden's return to Afghanistan in 1996, Al Qaeda's hierarchal structure was solidified into a pyramidal system that included several sub-components under the full/partial direct control of the headquarters in Afghanistan.

The end of the Afghanistan War forced Al Qaeda to formulate its direction and to redefine its strategy. In the first years after its formulation, an internal debate still took place concerning whether to focus jihad efforts against "the near enemy" in the Middle East or against the "far enemy." In practice, an intermediate strategy was implemented that maintained that the far enemy operating on Muslim lands must be dealt with. This was also the reason that in the early 1990s, Bin Laden opposed a US presence in Saudi Arabia (against the backdrop of the First Gulf War), and called for its expulsion from Muslim lands through active fighting.

The first major declaration of war in this direction took place in September 1996. Bin Laden declared that Al Qaeda's primary goals were to expel American soldiers from the Arabian Peninsula, to overthrow the Saudi regime, to liberate Islam's holy places, and to support Islamic organizations around the world. This message was emphasized again in

November 1996 in an interview given to an American reporter with Reuters, in which Bin Laden declared his intention to wage jihad against the US and its allies unless they pull out their forces from the Persian Gulf.

In 1998, Bin Laden declared a second war. He announced the establishment of the "International Islamic Front for Jihad against the Crusaders and the Jews." By doing so, he expanded the battlefield against the US beyond the borders of the Middle East. With this declaration, which was published in *Alquds Alarabi* newspaper based in London, Bin Laden called for every American and every Jew eveywhere on Earth to be killed.

The declarations of war in 1996–8 were translated into strategic terrorist attacks (the American embassies in Kenya and Tanzania in 1998, and the USS *Cole* battleship in Yemen in 2000) against American targets in the Middle East and beyond, which peaked with the September 11, 2001 terrorist attacks. The change was primarily a move from offensive operations characterized by guerilla warfare to offensive operations characterized by terrorism, including attacks against "soft targets" using suicide bombers and simultaneous attacks. This, in Bin Laden's opinion, in combination with the establishment of a partnership system among local Islamic terrorist organizations, made it possible to leverage the success of attacks against the "far enemy" to succeed in the battle against the "near enemy."

After the 9/11 terrorist attacks and the war in Afghanistan, the freedom of operation that Al Qaeda had enjoyed uner the Taliban in Afghanistan ended, and the new reality forced the organization's leadership to go underground (some of them fled to Iran), creating a disconnect between the organization's leadership and its operatives. Many operatives, including senior members, were killed or arrested, recuitment and training camps collapsed, and the organization was forced to find alternative solutions. These constraints also motivated the organization to establish affiliates in other arenas of jihad, especially in the Middle East and Africa: 2004—Al Qaeda in Iraq (AQI), 2007—Al Qaeda in the Islamic Maghreb (AQIM), 2009—Al Qaeda in the Arabian Peninsula (AQAP). The expansion to various arenas of jihad spurred the need to establish independent Islamic entities in territories ruled by the mujahideen. The Islamic solution that was accepted was to establish Islamic emirates (territories in which the mujahideen enforce shari'a).

Meanwhile, during this period, Al Qaeda formulated and implemented its "seven step" plan regarding the stages involved in achieving the "super goal" of imposing Islamic supremacy on the world, which was supposed to be completed by 2020. The intermediate goals of this plan were: the expulsion of the US and its allies from Muslim lands (including Israel), the toppling of corrupt regimes and the establihsment of an Islamic Caliphate, and the continued war against the infidels until the attainment of Islamic supremacy across the world. The principles underlying Al Qaeda's strategy during this period can also be gleaned from harmony[8] documents. For instance, a document that was apparently written at the beginning of the second decade of the twenty-first century and posted to the CTC website in 2013 revealed Al Qaeda's main strategy and the means of implementing it.[9] The document noted that the nation was simultaneously fighting against corrupt regimes from within and against the "far enemy"—the United States.

Nevertheless, the significant threat to the nation is from the US and, therefore, efforts should be focused on actions against it. Even while battling the "near enemy," action should taken against the "far enemy" who is sitting on Muslim lands. In this case he seemed to be referring to the US which operates in Middle Eastern countries.

This period came to an end with two decisive events: the end of the Bin Laden era in Al Qaeda (May 2011) and the "Arab Spring" revolution (from 2011). These events forced Al Qaeda to create a new organizational arrangement based on: designing strategy, establishing forces in various arenas of the revolution, mobilizing the masses for jihad activities, and directing organizational activities and adapting them to the new circumstances—all while establishing al-Zawahiri's leadership as Bin Laden's successor. The selection of al-Zawahiri by Al Qaeda's leadership council and the expression of loyalty by the heads of Al Qaeda branches were the first steps in creating a functional continuity of the organization. The next essential step by al-Zawahiri was his selection of Nasir al-Wuhayshi, the leader of Al Qaeda in Yemen, as his deputy. With this move, he situated Al Qaeda's leadership in the center of events in the Middle East in an effort to reject outright any claim or criticism that the organization was removed from the field.[10]

The eruption of the revolutions in the Arab world (the Arab Spring) in 2011 changed, and is still changing, the face of the Middle East and North Africa. Its impact goes far beyond the close circle of countries in the region and is also felt in more distant locations as a result of the wave of refugees flooding the countries of the region and beyond (mainly Europe). The nation state in its old format is fading from the Middle East, and tribal and ethnic entities with extensive shared owndership and control over territories are growing in its place and dictating the agenda in these territories. One after another, the rulers of Tunisia, Libya, and Yemen fell, and Syria itself has been mired in an ongoing civil war that has claimed hundreds of thousands of lives and caused millions of refugees to abandon the country. Egypt went through two revolutions during this period of time and the regime is facing waves of violence, especially in Sinai.

Al Qaeda was surprised by the revolutions and their intensity as it had tried to generate them for years, without success. The organization's leadership, which identified an opportunity, launched a media campaign in order to define the organization's policies with regard to the revolutions and, more importantly, in order to find a way to ride the revolutionary wave to mobilize the masses and establish Islamic emirates until the conditions became ripe for the establishment of a caliphate. However, Al Qaeda (Afghanistan-Pakistan) leadership's disconnect from the scene of events in the Middle East and North Africa presented difficulties for its organizational management. In effect, this period seemed to mark the beginning of a rise in status and freedom of operation of Al Qaeda branch commanders who did not always act in accordance with al-Zawahiri's instructions. The most prominent example of this was when Abu Bakr al-Baghdadi, the leader of Al Qaeda in Iraq, rejected outright al-Zawahiri's instructions, was expelled from Al Qaeda (2014), and declared the establishment of the Islamic Caliphate in Iraq and Syria (ISIS). This move by al-Baghdadi spurred renewed debate between supporters and opponents. The line taken by Al Qaeda, and subsequently by the ideologues who support it, was that the conditions were not ripe for the establishment of a caliphate and that its establishment requires a wide consensus among global jihad leaders.[11]

The expansion of the war in the arenas of uprisings, especially in Syria, led to the creation of alternative sources of power for Al Qaeda leadership. The most prominent expression of this was the actions of Al Qaeda in Iraq, led by Abu Bakr al-Baghdadi. In 2012, al-Baghdadi identified the potential to expand beyond Syria and he established Al Nusra Front, an organization composed of jihad fighters who took part in the fighting in Iraq. At the beginning of 2013, al-Baghdadi unilaterally declared the merger of the two branches under his leadership. The leader of Al Nusra Front objected to the merger and declared his organization to be an independent branch subject to the direct authority of Al Qaeda leadership. After several months in which attempts were made to bridge the gaps, and in light of al-Baghdadi's absolute public rejection of al-Zawahiri's instructions, the latter declared the removal of the Iraq branch from the ranks of Al Qaeda in the beginning of 2014.

In the first issue of the English-language magazine, *DABIQ*, which was published by ISIS in July 2014, the five main stages of the organization's strategy were presented:

(a) Hijrah—migration to the territory of the Islamic State/Caliphate;
(b) Jama'ah—the establishment of a cohesive group that instills belief based on the Quran and the Sunnah to be responsible for propagating the "true" faith through the use of jihad;
(c) Destablilize Taghut—destabilization of dictator regimes and striving towards governmental chaos through the use of car bombings, suicide attacks, etc. in order to create conditions favorable to overthrow the regime;
(d) Tamkin—establishing itself in occupied territory;
(e) Khilafah—establishment of the Caliphate.

The components of this strategy are: topple the Arab nation states and the erase the borders between them; establish the Islamic Caliphate and defend its borders; persuade Muslims to move to the Caliphate; expand the territory of the Islamic Caliphate through the use of jihad.

In June 2014, ISIS launched a comprehensive military operation in Iraq and Syria with the goal of conquering and establishing territorial control, and establishing an Islamic Caliphate. Abu Bakr al-Baghdadi, the leader of ISIS, led the operation and was actually the person who rehabilitated the jihadist infrastructure of Al Qaeda in Iraq during 2011–13 by exploiting the weakness of the central Iraqi government, the withdrawal of US forces, and the civil war in Syria. There are many indications that former senior Iraqi army soldiers were responsible for this rehabilitation. The first stage of the military campaign—the outbreak stage (July–August 2014) was characterized by quick and significant successes in the battlefield. Central Iraqi cities, including Mosul and Tikrit, were captured by ISIS. ISIS seized control of strategic facilities such as the Mosul Dam and facilities that serve the oil refining industry. Meanwhile, ISIS began to carry out the ethnic cleansing of minority groups like the Yazidis. Even at the start of the campaign,

ISIS activities were characterized by extreme violence, which included mass executions, rapes, and beheadings. This pattern of activity continued into the next stages with the goal of influencing the psychological arena as a means of helping in the battlefield.

The success of ISIS's ground operation in Iraq and Syria, and the establishment of the Caliphate in the second half of 2014, were a magnet not only for young people in Syria and Iraq but also for the Arab and Muslim world who surged in the thousands to join the ranks of ISIS. This fact forced ISIS to build an expedited recruitment and absorption process in order to train volunteers to fight and to integrate them in various arenas of jihad. The scope of the battle, its intensity and the high price that it exacted—especially since the coalitions against ISIS were formed—made the task of recruiting and training manpower much more complicated. All of this led to the end of the conquest campaign and the operational momentum that had characterized ISIS from June to August 2014.

During 2014–15, a process of rapid growth took place with regard to manpower and means. ISIS's manpower was estimated at between 17,000 and 40,000, out of which approximately 15,000 were foreign volunteers from the Muslim Arab world and approximately 5,000 came from Western countries, especially Europe. Another fact that helped ISIS succeed was its ability to create alliances with local tribes in Syria and Iraq against the backdrop of a shared ethnic composition/territorial space/opposition to the existing regime.

ISIS's span of control in terms of territory and population (approximately one-third of Iraqi territory and over one-fourth of Syrian territory) created challenges for the organization against the backdrop of attacks carried out against domestic rivals (Kurds, Iraqi army, rival organizations) and coalition forces, and against the backdrop of the need to manage and control the population in cities and areas that were conquered. These challenges forced ISIS to establish command and control infrastructure based on the systems and mechanisms operating in those areas, and to develop the ability to maintain public order and enforce shari'a.

The leading operation strategy taken by the organization in this field is the enforcement of shari'a using brutal means, alongside the provision of basic services to civilians and encouragement for a normal life under the Caliphate. ISIS's financial capabilities—which are estimated to include over one billion dollars in the organization's coffers as well as regular sources of funding that rely on conquered state infrastructure, such as oil fields, grain reserves, banks, industrial facilities, army bases, and weapons caches—enable the organization to continue its aggressive activities and establish its dominance in the field.

ISIS's ability to wage a prolonged military battle stems from the existence of sources of manpower and weapons available to the organization. Most of the weapons are plunder from the civil war in Syria and from its conquests in Iraq during the month of June 2014. The looted weapons in Syria came from several sources: Syrian army warehouses that fell to ISIS and other rebel organizations, plunder from battles including advanced weapons that belonged to Hezbollah and Iranian Revolutionary Guards forces, weapons that were parachuted to the beleaguered Kurds but fell into ISIS hands, and plunder from weapons that were supplied to "moderate" rebels by Arab and Western countries. In the Iraqi arena, most of the weapons came from Iraqi army warehouses that were looted in Mosul and in other places, as well as from raids on security forces in central and northern Iraq. This is not enough to determine the level of professional efficiency of ISIS members in using these weapons but it should be noted that Iraqi army graduates also serve in ISIS.

The various coalitions that were put together against ISIS in Syria and Iraq—which included the US, European countries, and Arab countries on the one hand, as well as Iran and Hezbollah, which supported Assad, on the other hand—did not succeed in bringing an end to the spread of the organization in these countries during 2014–15. The entry of Russian army forces, and especially the bombings of rebel strongholds by Russian Air Force planes in Syria (including ISIS targets), led to the end of the organization's advancement and even to the loss of territories that had previously been under its control. In March 2016, Russia announced that it was withdrawing some of its forces from Syria and a ceasefire was declared between the sides, which led to a reduction in military clashes but not to their end.

Summary

For years, the Middle East has served as an incubator for the growth and establishment of many terrorist organizations, including organizations driven by secular ideological motivations (such as Marxist and Communist organizations), organizations driven by national-separatist motivations, and organizations that carry out terrorist attacks against the backdrop of a local or global religious Salafi-jihadist ideology. Over the years, terrorism bases and headquarters, as well as recruitment and training camps, were established in various territories in the Middle East, either with the knowledge and support of existing regimes or while they turned a blind eye to this activity. In some cases, the organizations managed to take control of territories and populations, and actually turned into hybrid terrorist organizations that—alongside the terrorist attacks that it carried out—provided essential services to the population under its control and violently enforced compliance.

The corruption in Arab dictatorial regimes, the interests and involvement of superpowers in the Middle East, and the Israeli–Arab conflict all served as catalysts for the growth and activity of terrorist organizations in the Middle East. In addition, the fact that this region has served as a cradle for the growth of Islamist-jihadist ideologies for over 100 years contributed to the development of terrorism in the Middle East and to its dissemination throughout the Arab and Muslim countries and the rest of the world.

The tectonic changes that began in the Middle East as a result of the "Arab Spring" uprisings, the collapse of traditional regimes, and the development of regions lacking governance served as fertile ground for the growth of terrorist organizations.[12] The Middle East is still in a cloud of tumoil whose end is not yet in sight. In any case, the Middle East is likely to continue to serve as a the center of terrorism and a platform for exporting instability, violence, and terrorism to other regions of the world.

Notes

1. For more information on Hezbollah, please see Ranstorp 1997; Azani 2009; Levitt 2013.
2. *Haaretz*, May 2, 1996.
3. *Maariv*, Aug. 2, 1993, p. 3.
4. *Maariv*, Aug. 2, 1993, p. 3.
5. *Maariv*, Apr. 21, 1996, p. 9.
6. In Mar. 1998, a US court ruled that Iran must pay $247 million in compensation to the family of Alisa Flatow, who was killed in a terrorist attack that was carried out by the Palestinian Islamic Jihad in Gush Katif in Apr. 1998. The court determined that Iran was responsible for her murder due to the support and encouragement that it provided to the PIJ to carry out terrorist attacks.
7. For further information on Hamas, please read: Mishal and Sela 2003; Levitt 2007; Gleis and Berti 2012; Ganor 2015.
8. Documents translated by the Combating Terrorism Center (CTC) at West Point.
9. <http://www.ctc.usma.edu/wp-content/uploads/2013/10/Letter-Regarding-Al-Qaida-Strategy-Translation.pdf>.
10. For a study on the evolution of Al Qaeda, please read: Hoffman and Reinares 2014.
11. From our reports on the debate over the declaration of the Caliphate.
12. For a study on the Arab Spring, please read: Roberts et al. 2016.

References

Azani, Eitan (2009) *Hezbollah: The Story of the Party of God—From Revolution to Institutionalization*. Basingstoke: Palgrave Macmillan.

Ganor, Boaz (2010) "Defining Terrorism—Is One Man's Terrorist Another Man's Freedom Fighter?," The International Institute for Counter-Terrorism (ICT), Jan. 1, available online at <https://www.ict.org.il/Article/1123/Defining-Terrorism-Is-One-Mans-Terrorist-Another-Mans-Freedom-Fighter>.

Ganor, Boaz (2015) *Global Alert: The Rationality of Modern Islamist Terrorism and the Challenge to the Liberal Democratic World*. New York: Columbia University Press.

Gleis, Joshua L., and Benedetta Berti (2012) *Hezbollah and Hamas: A Comparative Study*. Baltimore, MD: Johns Hopkins University Press.

Harkabi, Yehoshafat (1969) *Fatah in the Arab Strategy: Reflections on Yesterday and Tomorrow*. Tel Aviv: Maarachot.

Harkabi, Yehoshafat (1979) *The Palestinians: From Slumber to Awakening*. Jerusalem: The Hebrew University, The Truman Institute, Magnes.

Hart, Alan (1994) *Arafat—The Definitive Biography Written in Co-operation with Yasser Arafat*. London: Sidgwick & Jackson.

Hoffman, Bruce (2006) *Inside Terrorism*. New York: Columbia University Press.

Hoffman, Bruce, and Fernando Reinares, eds (2014) *The Evolution of Global Terrorist Threat: From 9/11 to Osama Bin Laden's Death*. New York: Columbia University Press.

Kurz, Anat (1993) *Islamic Terror and Israel—Hezbollah, Palestinian Islamic Jihad, Hamas, Papyrus*. Tel Aviv: Tel Aviv University.

Levitt, Matthew (2007) *Hamas: Politics, Charity, and Terrorism in the Service of Jihad*. New Haven: Yale University Press.

Levitt, Matthew (2013) *Hezbollah: The Global Footprint of Lebanon's Party of God*. Washington, DC: Georgetown University Press.

Mishal, Shaul, and Avraham Sela (2003) *The Palestinian Hamas: Vision, Violence and Coexistence*. New York: Columbia University Press.

Ranstorp, Magnus (1997) *Hizb'Allah in Lebanon: The Politics of the Western Hostage Crisis*. Basingstoke: Palgrave Macmillan.

Raphael, Israeli (1983) *PLO in Lebanon, Selected Documents*. London: Weidenfeld & Nicolson.

Roberts, Adam, Michael J. Willis, Rory McCarthy, and Timothy Garton Ash, eds (2016) Civil *Resistance in the Arab Spring*. Oxford: Oxford University Press.

Sayigh, Yezid (1997) *Armed Struggle and the Search for State*. Oxford: Clarendon Press.

Yaari, Ehud (1970) *Fatah*. Tel Aviv: Lewin Epstein Ltd.

Yaari, Ehud (1972) "The Short Path from Theoretical Guerilla Warfare to Murderous Terrorism," *Monthly Review*, 7 (July): 22–3.

CHAPTER 38

TERRORISM IN ASIA

a rapidly spreading scourge tests the region

BRAHMA CHELLANEY

AT a time when radicalism and extremism are threatening to spread deeper and wider in many communities across the world, Asia is firmly at the centre of the global terrorism-related challenge. A little-known fact is that Asia, not the Middle East, is the world's most terrorism-afflicted region (Mallet 2017). This scourge plagues all the Asian sub-regions, some more than the others.

Terrorism in Asia needs to be viewed against the larger Asian strategic landscape. Asia is in flux at present, with the balances between its major powers still evolving and its security architecture unclear. Still, Asia's rapid economic resurgence has come to symbolize the qualitative reordering of power in the world. In modern world history, great-power competition centred on Europe; even the Cold War was not really an East/West rivalry but a competition between two blocs over Europe. Today, it is Asia's geopolitical and resource competition—sharpened by the long shadow of history over inter-country relations there—that has a bearing on international relations and international security. Building global power equilibrium in these circumstances is a task that will be greatly influenced by Asian power dynamics. It will, in fact, likely bear a distinct Asian imprint. More fundamentally, a stable power balance in Asia has become critical to international relations at a time when Asia's own security situation, paradoxically, has become increasingly murky.

Asia has thus far prospered largely because it has enjoyed peace and stability. But the upsurge of terrorism and other extremist violence and the recrudescence of Cold War-era territorial and maritime disputes have underscored the looming dangers it faces. Various developments are highlighting the new threats to Asian peace and stability. Extremism and terrorism, for example, threaten to become Asia's defining crisis in this century, a development that would create obstacles in its path of continued rapid economic growth and exacerbate internal and external security challenges for a number of Asian states.

Defining Asia

The emergence of terrorism as a pressing problem is not a new development for the Asian continent. Rather this scourge has afflicted Asia for decades. The continent has long been wracked by insurgencies, militant movements, and terrorist attacks. In some cases, such violence has been a dangerous legacy of arbitrary, colonially drawn borders or territorial usurpation by military means. In other cases, terrorist violence has been spurred either by the growth and influence of militant ideologies or by increasing socio-economic disparities linked to a governance deficit. The role of petrodollars from the oil sheikhdoms in the Persian Gulf has been a critical factor in the spread of the jihadist ideology.

For a proper understanding of the Asian challenge, it is essential to examine the scourge of terrorism in an integrated, systematic, and comprehensive manner by analyzing the political, economic, social, religious, ideological, and other factors at play. Despite the burgeoning literature on Asia, there are few studies on terrorism in the Asian region.

One key reason is the longstanding academic challenge of how exactly to define Asia. Bound in the east by the Pacific Ocean and in the south by the Indian Ocean, Asia, in reality, extends right up to the Bosphorus and the Suez Canal and includes large parts of the Middle East and 72 per cent of the Russian Federation. Asia covers very different areas—from the subarctic, mineral-rich Siberian plains to the subtropical Indonesian archipelago; and from the oil-rich desert lands of West Asia to the fertile river valleys of southern and southeastern Asia.

The problem that scholars face in defining Asia is compounded by the fact that even the United Nations agencies differ in their approach, with some defining Asia narrowly and others identifying it more broadly. In common perception, however, Asia is seen to cover only the region extending from the Korean Peninsula and the Japanese archipelago to the Indian subcontinent.

This chapter, in keeping with the popular perception, identifies Asia less expansively in order to offer a more manageable framework for analyzing the terrorism scourge. Yet even an Asia defined in this manner is a highly varied region. It includes countries, other than city-states, with the highest and lowest population densities in the world—Bangladesh and Mongolia—as well as some of the world's wealthiest states, such as Japan and Singapore, and some of the poorest, like North Korea and Afghanistan. It has demographic titans like China, India, and Indonesia and tiny nations such as Brunei, Bhutan, and the Maldives (the flattest state in the world).

There is no book currently that presents an integrated picture of the terrorism scourge in Asia or the larger geostrategic ramifications of this problem. There is a "handbook," though, on the Asia-Pacific region (Gunaratna and Kam 2016). There is thus a conspicuous gap in the literature on the Asian region. There are, of course, books examining terrorism in the various sub-regions of Asia (see Ressa 2004, and others). Country-specific studies have also been published (one example is Solahudin 2013). In addition, there are books focused on a single theme, such as the ideology driving terror in a particular sub-region, or the role of external actors, or the dimensions of a specific terrorist strike (see US Department of Defense and US Military 2015, and others).

An Escalating Challenge

The plain fact is that Asia confronts a serious and growing terrorism-related challenge, thanks to spreading grassroots radicalization and years of complacency among policymakers in the region. The US government identifies multiple "terrorist safe havens" in Asia, including Pakistan, Afghanistan, southern Philippines (mainly Mindanao), and the Sulawesi Sea/Sulu Archipelago (US Department of State 2017a). (The US State Department defines "terrorist safe havens" as "ungoverned, under-governed, or ill-governed physical areas where terrorists are able to organize, plan, raise funds, communicate, recruit, train, transit, and operate in relative security because of inadequate governance capacity, political will, or both.") The terrorist safe havens in the Pakistan–Afghanistan belt have global implications because of the international footprint of some of the terrorist networks based there.

The unraveling of the Islamic State's caliphate in Syria-Iraq could intensify the terrorism challenge in Asia from its remnants and from its ideology. Foreign terrorist fighters have increasingly become a major source of concern for counterterrorism officials and security agencies across Asia. Those fighters that come from war-torn zones are often battle-hardened and have the operational training, skills, connections, and experience to mount major attacks in the countries they return to or target.

Most of the world's Muslims live in Asia, a reality that in the coming decades is expected to accentuate the regional challenges relating to religious bigotry and extremist violence. The Islamist ideology has been extending its influence in Asia for decades, with the support of petrodollar-financed militant groups and even governments. A study by the Washington-based Pew Research Center has projected that the aggregate Muslim population in the world by 2030 will have doubled in the period since 1990, with the largest increase being in Asia. A surging Muslim population holds wider implications.

Today, the largest Muslim populations in the world are in four Asian countries: Indonesia, Pakistan, India, and Bangladesh, in that order (Pew Forum 2011). These four nations will continue to have the world's largest concentration of Muslims in 2030. But, before 2030, Pakistan is projected to surpass Indonesia as the country with the largest Muslim population in the world. In fact, between 1998 and 2017, Pakistan's population surged dramatically by 57 percent in barely nineteen years, according to the provisional results of Pakistan's most recent census released in August 2017 (Government of Pakistan 2017). The census figures show that the country's population has reached 207.7 million, with Pakistan passing Brazil to become the fifth most populous country in the world. At Bangladesh's birth in 1971, Pakistan had about 6 million fewer people than the wing (East Pakistan) that split away. Now Pakistan has at least 44 more million people than Bangladesh. No less significant is the fact that non-Muslims in the population of the "Islamic Republic of Pakistan," as it is officially called, have declined from 23 percent at the time of its creation to barely 3 percent, underscoring what one writer has called the "drip, drip genocide" and the strengthening of the jihad culture (Ispahani 2016).

The demographic explosion in Asia, especially among Muslim communities, threatens to accentuate the stresses that are contributing to violent jihadism and thereby act as a threat multiplier. It is significant that most Muslim countries, according to United Nations figures, maintain relatively high total fertility rates (United Nations Population Division 2011). A number of them are actually caught in a vicious circle in which burgeoning populations intensify natural-resource stresses, including water scarcity, and foster growing food insecurity, rising unemployment, and greater fundamentalism and militancy. This vicious circle is a reminder that terrorism is often rooted in issues that extend beyond politics and religion. In Asia, it is not an accident that the main springboard of international terrorism—the Afghanistan–Pakistan belt—is troubled by exploding populations, a pervasive lack of jobs, high illiteracy, growing water scarcity, and fast-spreading extremism. The intersection of population and resource pressures, unemployment, political instability, popular discontent, extremism, and terrorism creates a deadly cocktail of internal disarray, spurring a cycle of unrest and violence and fostering a pervasive jihad culture.

In many cases, the terrorist groups operating are unique to each Asian country, even if they have cross-border affiliations. Yet there are some common elements that define terrorist threats across Asia, including the fact that violent Islamic extremism afflicts Asia more than the Middle East. In some cases, the threat of terrorism in Asia also emanates from across a country's frontiers, underscoring the transnational nature of the scourge. The fatal poisoning of North Korean dictator Kim Jong Un's half-brother, Kim Jong Nam, at Kuala Lumpur International Airport in February 2017 highlighted state-sponsored terrorism by a foreign government. Pyongyang was blamed for the killing of Kim Jong Nam, a reputed playboy with residences in Beijing and Macau.

An upsurge in terrorism in Asia is apparent from several developments, from the escalation of militant attacks in recent years, including in Indonesia, Malaysia, the Philippines, Thailand, India, and Afghanistan, to terrorist sieges and new armed conflicts involving jihadist groups. For example, on the southern Philippine island of Mindanao, terrorists stormed the northern city of Marawi in May 2017, capturing key government buildings and setting fire to churches and schools. The militants, who included foreign fighters, were aligned with the Islamic State, including the affiliated Maute and Abu Sayyaf jihadist groups. It took a sustained military campaign, including heavy airstrikes that reduced much of Marawi to rubble, for the armed forces to slowly regain full control of the city. The terrorist siege of Marawi, which followed rumblings of Islamist uprisings on the island for some time, lasted five months—the longest urban battle in the Philippines' modern history. In the bloody fighting, nearly

1,000 jihadists, 165 security personnel, and 87 civilians were killed, according to an official count.

The Marawi siege highlighted the serious terrorism challenge the Philippines confronts. The problem, concentrated largely in central and western Mindanao, includes kidnappings, bombings, and attacks on security forces. The jihadist outfits active include the Abu Sayyaf Group (ASG); the Maute Group, also known by its formal name, Dawlah Islamiyah Lanao (DIL); Ansar-al Khalifah Philippines; and the Bangsamoro Islamic Freedom Fighters (BIFF).

Security forces scored a major success when, during the Marawi siege, they killed ASG chief Isnilon Hapilon, who had been named by the Islamic State as its regional leader. Philippine President Rodrigo Duterte's anti-narcotics and counterterrorism operations have been accompanied by a political readiness to grant greater political and economic autonomy to Muslim-dominated areas of Mindanao so as to stem the spread of radicalization and blunt the appeal of terrorist outfits. After assuming power in 2016, Duterte also made peace overtures to the Communist Party of the Philippines (CPP) and its armed wing, the New People's Army (NPA), which he had declared a "terrorist organization" for waging guerrilla warfare in the countryside for nearly five decades—a conflict that has left some 40,000 people dead. Duterte freed several communist leaders as a gesture of good faith but later abandoned peace talks with the rebels due to escalating attacks.

The ASG is also active in Malaysia, which regards the Islamic State as a potent national-security threat and has sought to jail its supporters. For Indonesia, the 2002 Bali bombings were a wake-up call. It has since then stepped up its counterterrorism efforts in a systematic way. But continuing terrorist strikes within its borders, especially by Jemaah Ansharut Daulah (JAD), a Wahhabist, pro-Islamist State group, serve as a reminder of the serious challenge that Indonesia confronts. The attacks also underscore the imperative for Indonesian security agencies to more effectively degrade the capabilities of terrorists and their networks. As in Malaysia, Bangladesh, Pakistan, and some other Muslim states, Indonesia's terrorism-related challenge largely stems from the growing grassroots power of Islamists, who use *madrasas* (religious seminaries), social media, and private messaging to spread jihadism, raise funds, and recruit and train suicide killers. The city-state of Singapore, sandwiched between its large Muslim neighbors, Malaysia and Indonesia, views jihadist terrorism as an existential threat and, as part of a policy of zero tolerance, is quick to detain or deport Islamic radicals, including preachers and foreign workers.

In the two neighboring nations of Thailand and Myanmar, the primary terrorism-related concern centers on attacks by ethnic insurgents seeking independent homelands, although Myanmar has also confronted Rohingya jihadism since its independence. Thailand has experienced hundreds of attacks in recent years by separatist insurgents, who are active in the country's ethnic-Malay, Muslim-majority southern region. Several thousand people have perished in the jihadist campaign to create an Islamic Pattani Darrusalam encompassing Thailand's four southernmost provinces; the insurgency has ramped up since 2004 (McCargo 2015).

In Bangladesh, the brutal Dhaka café attack in July 2016 brought to light the spectre of jihadism that is haunting the world's seventh most populous nation, made up mainly of low-lying floodplains and deltas. Bangladesh's future is imperilled as much by global warming as by Islamic radicalization. The accelerating radicalization in a society with largely moderate Muslim traditions was highlighted by the fact that the slaughter of mainly foreigners in the café attack was perpetrated by educated young men who grew up in well-off families. They singled out and killed foreign patrons while sparing local Muslims who could recite verses from the Quran. Ever since her election as prime minister in late 2008 marked the restoration of democracy in Bangladesh, Sheikh Hasina has battled jihadists, including those reared previously by the country's military intelligence agency, called the Directorate General of Forces Intelligence, or DGFI, and the National Security Intelligence agency.

The Pakistan–Afghanistan belt, meanwhile, remains a critical epicentre of transnational terrorism, with significant implications for regional and international security. Several transnational terrorist groups operate out of Pakistan, including Lashkar-e-Taiba (LeT), Jaish-e-Mohammad (JeM), and the Haqqani Network (HQN). The Afghan Taliban's top leadership, as well as command and control, are also ensconced in Pakistan.

The United States has been stuck in Afghanistan in the longest and most expensive war in its history. It has tried several policies to wind down the war, but nothing has worked, in large part because the US has continued to fight the war on just one side of the Afghanistan–Pakistan divide and refused to go after the Pakistan-based sanctuaries of the Afghan Taliban and its affiliate, HQN (Gall 2015). As Gen. John Nicholson, the US military commander in Afghanistan, has acknowledged, "It is very difficult to succeed on the battlefield when your enemy enjoys external support and safe haven" (US Senate Armed Services Committee, 2017). No counterterrorism campaign has ever succeeded anywhere in the world when militants have enjoyed such cross-border havens.

Worse still, the Afghan Taliban is conspicuously missing from the US list of Foreign Terrorist Organizations, while the procreator and sponsor of that medieval militia—Pakistan—has been one of the largest recipients of American aid since 2001, when the US invasion of Afghanistan helped remove the Taliban from power. US aid to Pakistan, however, is now beginning to decline sharply, in response to rising American frustration, with most security assistance suspended in 2018. In fact, Trump's national-security strategy document, released in late 2017, stated, "The United States continues to face threats from transnational terrorists and militants operating from within Pakistan," adding: "We will insist that Pakistan take decisive action against militant and terrorist groups operating from its soil" (White House 2017). Vice President Mike Pence later said, "President Trump has put Pakistan on notice."

More than seven decades after it was created as the first Islamic republic of the post-colonial era, Pakistan is tottering on the brink of an abyss. Its internal disarray and skewed civil–military relations, which allow the powerful, meddling military and its rogue Inter-Services Intelligence (ISI) agency to remain immune to civilian oversight, have turned Pakistan into a major breeding ground of international terrorism (Fair 2014). An increasingly jihadist, cash-strapped Pakistan exemplifies how domestic factors can fuel greater extremism and violence, which, in turn, exacerbate the internal situation. Add to the picture a longstanding nexus between its military and terrorist groups that has made nuclear-armed Pakistan home to some leading terrorist figures (Byman 2007). This has raised the spectre of nuclear terrorism, prompting the US to prepare contingency plans to take out the country's "crown jewels"—nuclear weapons—in case of cataclysmic events (Windrem 2011).

In fact, the footprints of many terrorist attacks in the West have been traced to Pakistan, from the 2005 London bombings to the 2015 massacre in San Bernardino, California. In fact the main architects of the September 11, 2001, terrorist attacks in the US—Osama bin Laden and Khalid Sheik Mohammed—were found hiding in Pakistan (Ignatius 2012). It is Pakistan's neighbors, however, that have borne the brunt of its terrorism. Major terrorist attacks in South Asia, like the 2008 Mumbai strikes and the 2008 and 2011 assaults on the Indian and American embassies in Kabul, respectively, were blamed on the ISI agency, which has reared covert front organizations like LeT, JeM, and HQN for cross-border terrorism (see Fair 2015, and Mahadevan 2016). Former Pakistani military dictator Pervez Musharraf has acknowledged the state's use of such front organizations while he was in power. For the Pakistani military, waging an undeclared war against India through terrorist proxies remains a useful, low-cost option to contain a larger, more powerful adversary, as the 2016 terror attacks on several military bases in India illustrated (see e.g. Riedel 2016). But even smaller states like Afghanistan and Bangladesh accuse the ISI agency of undermining their security through terrorist surrogates. According to the US government, a number of terrorist attacks in Afghanistan were "planned and launched from safe havens in Pakistan" (US Department of State 2017a).

Consequently, terrorism has turned South Asia into a flashpoint for conflict, with the sub-region having the highest incidence of terrorist violence in Asia. Sri Lanka's prime minister, Ranil Wickremesinghe, warned that "cross-border terrorism" has imperilled the future of the regional grouping, known as the South Asian Association for Regional Cooperation, or SAARC. To be sure, South Asia is battered by other forms of terrorism as well, as highlighted by the Maoist insurgency and the Naga, Bodo, and Kashmiri separatism in India. But it is jihadist violence that is widely seen as the greatest terrorist threat across southern Asia.

Take the Maldives, a group of strategically located islands in the Indian Ocean. The rise of Islamist groups has been accompanied by anti-democratic developments there. In vandalism reminiscent of the Taliban's demolition of the monumental Buddhas of Bamyan in Afghanistan in 2001, Islamists ransacked the Maldives' main museum in Malé, the capital, on the day the country's first democratically elected president was ousted in 2012. They smashed priceless Buddhist and Hindu statues made of coral and limestone, virtually erasing all evidence of the Maldives' Buddhist past before its people converted to Islam in the twelfth century (Chellaney 2012). Since then, with a pro-Islamist government in office, "radical Maldivians have made connections to terrorist groups throughout the world and a small but steady stream of Maldivians have left the country to train and fight with these groups," including in Syria (US Department of State 2017a).

Jihadism is also the principal source of terrorism in Central Asia, a region of the five so-called "stans"—Kazakhstan, Uzbekistan, Kyrgyzstan, Tajikistan, and Turkmenistan—that is adjacent to two other "stans": Afghanistan and Pakistan. The terrorism scourge has been underscored by Salafist attacks in recent years in the five Central Asian "stans," except Turkmenistan (where the state controls mosques by appointing the clergy), as well as by the involvement of Central Asian jihadists in terror strikes elsewhere, including in Russia and Turkey (as exemplified by the 2016 Istanbul Airport attack). A number of militants from Central Asia, including about 1,000 from Tajikistan alone, have participated in jihad in Syria and Iraq. The terrorism problem is more acute in Uzbekistan and Tajikistan, which both share borders with war-torn Afghanistan. By contrast, Turkmenistan has employed draconian measures to jail extremists it classifies as "Wahhabis." It has reported no significant terrorist violence in recent years within its borders.

East Asia has experienced sporadic acts of terrorism over the decades, but the incidence of terrorist violence has been low compared to the other Asian sub-regions. In the most dramatic attack that highlighted the use of a biological weapon by a terrorist organization, the Aum Shinrikyo (AUM) group in Japan simultaneously released sarin gas on several Tokyo subway trains in 1995, killing thirteen people and causing several thousand to seek medical treatment. Subsequent police investigations found that AUM was also behind a previous sarin gas attack in the Japanese mountain resort of Matsumoto in 1994 that left seven people dead and as many as 500 injured (see Kang 2009; Murakami 2001). Four Japanese Red Army members who took refuge in North Korea after staging a 1970 plane hijacking probably still live there.

Roots of Terrorism in Asia

The roots and consequences of terrorism in Asia are extensive. In essence, the roots relate either to the continuing grievances over colonially demarcated or post-colonial frontiers or to the rise of militant ideologies that have fostered suicide bombings and other types of attacks. Some of the insurgent and terrorist organizations still active in Asia date back to the decolonization process. The territorial realignment of political frontiers happened on a large scale in Asia in the post-World War II period. With the end of World War II setting in motion the process of decolonization, the total number of nations in the world virtually doubled just between 1945 and 1960. And since 1960, the number of countries in the world has almost doubled again.

Asia's political map has changed radically since the second half of the 1940s. India, for example, was partitioned in 1947 by the departing colonialists, with Pakistan established as the first self-styled Islamic state of the post-war era, followed by Mauritania in West Africa. In fact, when the British, who elevated the strategy of "divide and rule" into an art, decided to establish two separate wings of Pakistan on either side of a partitioned India, the Rohingya in the then Burma (now Myanmar) began attempting to drive

Buddhists out of the Muslim-dominated Mayu peninsula in northern Rakhine state in what was a violent campaign of ethnic cleansing aimed at merging the region with the proposed East Pakistan. Decades earlier, the British, faced with local resistance to their rule in Burma's Arakan region (now renamed Rakhine state), had moved large numbers of the Rohingya from neighbouring East Bengal to work on rubber and tea plantations there. (Burma was administered as a province of India until 1937 before it became a separate, self-governing colony.)

It was the advance of the Imperial Japanese Army into Myanmar during World War II that first highlighted that country's Rohingya problem. Communal hatred spilled into violence as the Japanese military swept into Arakan in 1942 and the British launched a counter-offensive, with the Rohingya supporting the British and the local Buddhists largely staying neutral or siding with the Japanese. Britain recruited Rohingya Muslims into its guerrilla force—the so-called "V" Force—to ambush and kill Japanese troops. When the British eventually regained control of Arakan in 1945, they rewarded Rohingya Muslims for their loyalty by appointing them to the main posts in the local government.

Emboldened by the open British support, Rohingya militants set out to settle old scores with the local Buddhists. In July 1946, they formed the North Arakan Muslim League to seek the Muslim-dominated northern Arakan's secession from Myanmar. In the religious bloodletting that preceded and followed the partition of India, Rohingya attacks sought to drive out the Buddhists from northern Arakan as part of the militants' campaign to join East Pakistan (which became Bangladesh in 1971). Failure to achieve that goal led many of the Rohingya to take up arms in a self-declared jihad (Christie 2010).

Local *mujahedeen* began to organize attacks on government troops and seize control of territory in northern Arakan, establishing shari'a within a mainly Buddhist state. After Myanmar gained independence in 1948, martial law was declared in the region, but government forces regained territorial control there only in the early 1950s (Tinker 1961). Still, Rohingya Islamist militancy continued to thrive, with *mujahedeen* attacks occurring intermittently. In 2012, bloody clashes broke out between the Rohingya and the ethnic Rakhines, who feared becoming a minority in Rakhine state. The sectarian violence, in which rival gangs burned down villages and some 140,000 people (mostly Rohingya) were displaced, helped to transform the Rohingya militancy back into a full-blown insurgency (International Crisis Group 2016).

This is the background to the present Rohingya crisis, which has triggered an exodus of Rohingya refugees, with a three-member United Nations fact-finding panel accusing security forces of genocide. For Myanmar, however, the Rohingya militancy is just one of the insurgencies it has faced since independence. The fundamental challenge facing Myanmar is to build an inclusive national identity, or else historical tensions over identity will continue to cramp its potential (Myint-U 2001). Breaking the cycle of terror and violence that has plagued Myanmar, which is large as Britain and France combined, will require the country to address the deep-seated sectarian and ethnic tensions that, for instance, are driving the Rohingya toward jihadism. The Rohingya crisis illustrates the linkage of terrorism with the colonial legacy in some cases.

To be sure, Myanmar also serves as a good example of how insurgent and other militant violence can be sustained through cross-border support. Myanmar's Yunnan-bordering region, for example, is controlled by the China-backed Kachin Independence Army. China actually holds the key to ending decades of ethnic conflict in northern and north-eastern Myanmar, including by exercising its clout over several key insurgent leaders. But it is unclear whether Beijing, despite being invited by Myanmar's de facto leader Aung San Suu Kyi to play mediator, will genuinely aid her effort to build ethnic peace or use its role as a broker between the government and guerrilla groups to merely underpin its own leverage.

More broadly, the manner in which new political frontiers were drawn by departing colonial powers—usually with little regard for natural contours or the national-security interests of the newly emerging states—has bequeathed a troubling legacy of ethnic, sectarian, and even territorial discord and still-persisting feuds in a number of Asian nations (for an account of the arbitrary boundary making after World War I, see MacMillan 2003). Many of the borders drawn at departing colonizers' tables or produced by post-war agreements among victors created countries whose boundaries coincided neither with a division of nationalities, ethnic groups, and cultures nor with geographic features. The new borders often lumped together antagonistic ethnic groups and sects or split nationalities.

The rejigging of political borders led to festering conflicts within and between nations, giving rise to militancy, insurgencies, and terrorism. Kashmir is one such example. In some other cases, discontented ethnic and sectarian groups took up arms in a struggle against the new independent state. Artificial frontiers in a number of cases have also fostered revanchist and identity struggles.

Political boundaries have changed even after decolonization as a result of internal conflicts and other developments linked to identity and nationality issues or political and structural problems. In Asia, the breaking away of East Timor showed that political maps are not carved in stone. The current terrorism problem in Central Asia is linked with the 1991 disintegration of the Soviet Union—one of the most profound global events in modern history. The unravelling of the Soviet empire, while dramatically changing the international geopolitical landscape and spawning fifteen new nations, unleashed new ethnic and political nationalisms that continue to roil Central Asia.

Shifts in political frontiers, of course, have also resulted from military interventions and wars. For example, the terrorism problem that China confronts in Xinjiang (formerly East Turkestan) and the resistance its rule in Tibet still faces are due to its occupation of until-then autonomous regions (see Perdue 2005, and others). In more recent years, a state-sponsored influx of Han Chinese settlers that is altering the demographics of Xinjiang and Tibet has further fueled discontent and protests against Chinese rule in these vast regions, which make up more than 50 percent of China's landmass. By annexing these ethnic-minority homelands, China became the source of trans-boundary river flows to the largest number of countries in the world, extending from the Indochina Peninsula and South Asia to Kazakhstan and Russia.

Today, China views the East Turkistan Islamic Movement (ETIM), which enjoys considerable support among Xinjiang's Turkic-speaking Uighurs, as a terrorist organization, blaming it for attacks in Xinjiang and for a 2016 suicide strike on the Chinese Embassy in Bishkek, Kyrgyzstan's capital. Uighur extremists killed thirty-three people at a train station in 2014. Increasing Chinese repression in Xinjiang, meanwhile, has led thousands of Uighurs in recent years to travel for training to Syria, where some have played a key role in several battles against Syrian President Bashar Assad's forces (Associated Press 2017). Despite a chorus of international criticism, China has sustained a mass internment program that has swept up as many as one million Muslims in Xinjiang for "re-education."

Another key driver of terrorism in Asia is militant ideology that sanctifies violence. Militant ideology, to be sure, extends beyond Muslim communities. Current such examples include the militant Buddhist movements in countries as diverse as Thailand, Myanmar, and Sri Lanka and Hindu radicalism in India. Past examples include the Maoist insurrection in Nepal and the Tamil Tigers in Sri Lanka who, although Hindu, mastered the "art" of suicide attacks. Nepal's establishment of multiparty democracy within the framework of a constitutional monarchy in 1990 opened the door to a bloody Maoist insurrection. The protracted war between Maoists and government forces ended only when a peace accord in 2006 paved the way for the insurgent leaders to come to power. Sri Lanka, a self-trumpeted "island of paradise" until the early 1980s, became an island of tremendous bloodshed for more than a quarter of a century as a civil war—Asia's longest—built to a bloody crescendo in 2009. Thousands of non-combatants, according to the United Nations, were killed in the final months of the war as government forces overran the Tamil Tigers, who had established a de facto state in Sri Lanka's Tamil-majority north and east.

The single biggest ideological driver of terrorism in Asia, however, has been an ultra-conservative form of Sunni Islam known as Wahhabism, which has served as the basis for the most virulent forms of Islamist violence around the world. Wahhabism, by pushing a medieval interpretation of the Quran and rejecting modernity in all forms, has instilled the spirit of martyrdom, making a suicide killer believe in being rewarded in death, including getting seventy-two virgins in heaven (Weiss 2017). This has fueled terrorism. According to the Saudi Muslim scholar Ahmed Ali, Wahhabism advocates that non-Wahhabis (including Christians, Hindus, Jews, and Shi'ites) "be hated, be persecuted, and even be killed." Asia illustrates that the key to battling Islamist terrorism is stemming the spread of the ideology that has fostered "jihad factories."

The global offspring of Wahhabi fanaticism include Al Qaeda, the Taliban, Laskar-e-Taiba, Boko Haram, Al Shabaab and the Islamic State (also known as ISIS), all of which blend hostility towards non-Sunnis and anti-modern romanticism into nihilistic rage. The export of Wahhabism by Saudi Arabia, Qatar, and some other oil sheikhdoms is the real source of modern Islamist terror in the world. From Africa and Europe to Asia, Arab petrodollars have played a key role in fomenting militant Islamic fundamentalism that targets the West, Israel, and India as well as pro-Western governments in Muslim countries as its enemies. The effects of Wahhabism have been most pronounced in Asia since it has the world's largest concentration of Muslims.

No country, to be sure, has contributed more than Saudi Arabia to the international spread of Wahhabism, which is gradually snuffing out more liberal Islamic traditions in many Asian countries. The brand of Islam traditionally practiced in Southeast Asia, including Indonesia and Malaysia, was more moderate compared with the harsh, puritanical versions of Islam in the Gulf sheikhdoms. In South Asia, a syncretic Hindu-Muslim culture, which helped foster Sufism, defined religious diversity. But these traditions in Asia have withered or come under severe attack from the export of Wahhabism to various sub-regions. Not only are the heterodox, tolerant traditions of Islam in the East being swept away, but also Muslim terrorists have targeted religious minorities and even Sunnis who they regard as not sufficiently orthodox, including because they visit Sufi shrines. Examples of such attacks extend from the Bali bombings and church burnings in Java to strikes on Sufi shrines in several nations and the killing of the members of the Ahmadiyya sect, which has been declared non-Muslim in Pakistan.

Then US Secretary of State Hillary Clinton said in a 2009 cable released by Wikileaks that "Saudi Arabia remains a critical financial support base for Al Qaeda, the Taliban, LeT [Laskar-e-Taiba], and other terrorist groups" (*Guardian* 2010). During the 2016 US presidential campaign, Hillary Clinton deplored Saudi Arabia's support for "radical schools and mosques around the world that have set too many young people on a path towards extremism" (*Washington Post* 2016). Before he was elected president, Trump called the Saudis "the world's biggest funders of terrorism" (NBC News 2015). Yet, as if to highlight that money speaks louder than the international imperative to counter a rapidly metastasizing global jihadist threat, Trump went to Saudi Arabia on his first presidential overseas visit. The trip yielded business and investment deals for the US valued at up to almost $400 billion.

The fact is that, since the oil-price boom of the 1970s, Saudi Arabia has spent more than $200 billion on its global jihad project, including funding Wahhabi *madrasas*, mosques, clerics, and books (Weiss and Ward 2016). Add to the picture the funding from some other sheikhdoms, especially Qatar, the United Arab Emirates, and Kuwait, for the spread of the Islamist ideology. With Western support, the oil monarchies in the Gulf were able to ride out the Arab Spring; these sheikhdoms remain a cash cow for international defence, financial, energy, and manufacturing companies.

The Arab petrodollar-financed Islamist ideology has sowed the seeds of religious extremism and terrorism in Asia from the Philippines to Afghanistan. The waning of the traditionally liberal Islamic traditions has been accompanied by the rising menace of Islamist attacks. Countries like Tajikistan, Uzbekistan, and Pakistan exemplify how the spread of the Islamist ideology among their populations has led to a major upsurge of terrorist violence. Or take the case of Bangladesh: with violent jihadists gaining strength, the country has witnessed murderous attacks on liberal writers, with several of them being hacked to death in separate incidents. Hindus, Shias, and Christians have increasingly been attacked.

To be sure, several factors extending beyond foreign-backed ideological indoctrination have contributed to the growth of Islamist terrorism in Asia. The intersection of political instability, popular discontent, resource stress, population pressure, extremism, and terrorism continues to reinforce a jihad culture in many communities. In addition, a corroding state structure in some Asian countries serves as an incubator of terror, creating conditions under which transnational militant groups can thrive. Weak or dysfunctional states are more likely to host terrorist groups, especially those that carry out transnational attacks.

Still, the systematic Middle Eastern export of the obscurantist and intolerant version of Islam has created space in Asia for violent Islamist groups to become increasingly entrenched. Across Muslim communities in Asia, a proliferation of petrodollar-financed *madrasas* has helped instil religious extremism. Indeed, Wahhabi fanaticism has served as the ideological mother of Asian jihadist groups that murder, maim, and menace the innocent—from Jemaah Islamiyah in Southeast Asia to Lashkar-e-Taiba and the Taliban in the Pakistan–Afghanistan belt. Bangladesh authorities blamed the Dhaka café attack—claimed by the Islamic State terrorist organization—on a local Wahhabi-infused group, Jamaat ul-Mujahdeen, whose top two leaders were convicted and executed in 2008 for carrying out nationwide bombings in the country.

Adding to Asian security concerns is the fact that Wahhabi-indoctrinated militants from a number of countries, including Australia, the Philippines, Indonesia, Malaysia, Singapore, China, India, and Kazakhstan, have received arms training in Syria and Iraq. Singaporean Prime Minister Lee Hsien Loong has called Southeast Asia "a key recruitment centre" for the Islamic State. The jihadists returning to their homelands from Syria and Iraq could wage terror campaigns in the way the Afghan war veterans, like Osama bin Laden, came to haunt the security of Asia, the Middle East, and the West. The multinational rebels in Afghanistan, who became known as *mujahedeen* (Islamic holy warriors), were originally trained and armed by the US Central Intelligence Agency in the 1980s to help oust Soviet forces from that country (Chellaney 2001/2). US policy in the 1980s actually gave the CIA-trained insurgents battling Soviet forces in Afghanistan a veneer of religious respectability by calling them *mujahedeen*. Indeed, at a 1985 White House ceremony attended by several "mujahedeen" commanders, President Ronald Reagan gestured toward his guests and declared, "These gentlemen are the moral equivalent of America's Founding Fathers" (Chellaney 2011). Such "moral equivalent of America's Founding Fathers" later morphed into Al Qaeda, the Taliban, and other terrorist groups. "We helped to create the problem that we are now fighting," then US Secretary of State Hillary Clinton acknowledged in a July 2010 television interview (Clinton 2010).

Yet another factor that has fueled violent jihadism in Asia is state sponsorship of or collusion with terrorism. Militants, some promoted by regimes and some operating with the connivance of elements within the national military, intelligence, or government, have employed religious or ethnic causes to justify acts of cross-border terror. For example, Pakistan's use of extremist groups as an instrument of foreign policy is well documented, with the US State Department's *Country Report on Terrorism for 2015* stating that some United Nations-designated terrorist organizations continue "to operate within Pakistan, employing economic resources under their control and fundraising openly" (US State Department 2016). The Pakistani military has reared "good" terrorists for cross-border missions while battling "bad" militants that fail to toe its line. Pakistan has yet to come clean about who helped bin Laden hide for years in a military garrison town near its capital.

For states nurturing violent jihadist groups, the chickens are coming home to roost with a vengeance. While Pakistan is such a case in Asia, with the 2014 Peshawar school massacre highlighting how the vipers have turned on their keeper, the 2016 Istanbul Airport terror attack served as a reminder that Turkey has come full circle after having aided the rise of the Islamic State in Syria. Indeed, Turkey's main opposition leader Kemal Kilicdaroglu accused President Recep Tayyip Erdoğan of trapping the country in "a process of Pakistanization" by proactively "aiding and abetting terrorist organizations" and helping to turn Syria into a new Afghanistan (Millyet 2016).

Concluding Observations

The fight against terrorism in Asia is likely to prove a long and difficult one. The asymmetric weapon of terrorism is a lethal one. Dealing with such unconventional warfare remains a key challenge for many Asian governments. The murky geopolitics, however, foreshadow a difficult and protracted battle against the forces of terrorism. Asia's counterterrorism challenges are inextricably linked to the global war on terror, whose future direction remains unclear. It is important to bring back on track the US-led global war on terror, which was launched after the 9/11 attacks.

For starters, countries must refrain from politicizing the anti-terror fight. Unfortunately, US policy remains prone to injecting geopolitics into counterterrorism, a tendency that carries important implications for Asian security. For example, despite lack of credible evidence that Pyongyang was aiding international terrorism as a matter of policy, Trump reversed the US government's 2008 decision rescinding the designation of North Korea as a state sponsor of terrorism (US Department of State 2017b). Indeed, Trump's action in redesignating North Korea as a state sponsor of terrorism had little to do with the goal of combatting terrorism; it was intended to mount greater pressure on Pyongyang as part of Washington's sanctions-based approach to curb the North Korean nuclear and missile programs.

It is also important to recognize that harsh political or sectarian repression can trigger terrorism. This is exemplified by China's ruthless crackdown and high-pressure indoctrination program in the traditionally Muslim region of Xinjiang, where authorities have imposed restrictions even on growing of long beards and fasting during the Ramadan period. Indeed, China has turned Xinjiang into a "laboratory for high-tech social controls," with Urumqi, the regional capital, one of "the most closely surveilled places on earth" (Chin and Bürge 2017). Governments ought to reach out to Muslim moderates, not unite their Muslim population through provocative actions.

To be sure, salvaging the war on terror demands a sustained information campaign to discredit the ideology of radical Islam, which promotes terrorism as a sanctified tool of religion and a path to redemption. Asia's terrorism scourge, in fact, exemplifies how Wahhabi fanaticism is the root from which Islamist terrorists draw their ideological sustenance. Another important reality is that terrorism cannot be geographically confined, with the spill-over from the Afghanistan–Pakistan belt, for example, threatening Asian and international security. Significantly, terrorism not only threatens open, pluralistic societies, but also springs from the rejection of democratic and secular values. In this light, democracies located geographically close to the Muslim world tend to be more vulnerable to Islamist terrorism than those located far away.

Make no mistake: the war on terror will never be won with treacherous allies, such as jihadist rebels or Islamist rulers. Such alliances only spur greater terrorism. That is why major powers must focus on long-term goals rather than following the path of expediency. The need for caution in training militants and funnelling lethal arms to them to help overthrow any regime is highlighted by the current chaos in and refugee exodus from several conflict-torn countries where outside powers intervened. The simple fact is that what goes around comes around.

The war on terror cannot be won without closing the wellspring that feeds terrorism—Wahhabi fanaticism. As the late Singaporean leader Lee Kuan Yew said in 2003, the war on terror demands eliminating the "queen bees" (the preachers of hatred and violence) that are inspiring the "worker bees" (terrorists) to become suicide killers. It will require a concerted, sustained campaign to beat back the challenge from the forces of terror.

References

Associated Press (2017) "Uighurs Fighting in Syria Take Aim at China," *New York Times*, Dec. 22.

Byman, D. (2007) *Deadly Connections: States that Sponsor Terrorism*. Cambridge: Cambridge University Press.

Chellaney, B. (2001/2) "Fighting Terrorism in Southern Asia: The Lessons of History," *International Security*, 26(3): 94–116.

Chellaney, B. (2011) "Our Islamists," Project Syndicate, Nov. 17.

Chellaney, B. (2012) "South Asia's False Spring," Project Syndicate, 20 Feb. 20.

Chin, J., and C. Bürge (2017) "Twelve Days in Xinjiang: How China's Surveillance State Overwhelms Daily Life," *Wall Street Journal*, Dec. 19.

Christie, C. J. (2010) *A Modern History of Southeast Asia: Decolonization, Nationalism and Separatism*. London: I. B. Tauris.

Clinton, Hillary (2010) Interview with Fox News, July 10, available online at <https://www.youtube.com/watch?v=WnLvzV9xAHA> [Accessed Dec. 2017].

Coll, S. (2004) *Ghost Wars: The Secret History of the CIA, Afghanistan, and Bin Laden, from the Soviet Invasion to September 10, 2001*. New York: Penguin.

Dutta, S. (2015) *Bloodlines: The Imperial Roots of Terrorism in South Asia*. Salinas, CA: AgilePress.

Fair, C. (2014) *Fighting to the End: The Pakistan Army's Way of War*. New York: Oxford University Press.

Fair, C., and S. Ganguly (2015) "An Unworthy Ally: Time for Washington to Cut Pakistan Loose," *Foreign Affairs*. Sept./Oct.

Gall, C. (2015) *The Wrong Enemy: America in Afghanistan 2001–14*. Boston, MA: Mariner Books.

Government of Pakistan (2017) Provisional figures of Pakistan's 2017 census in table form, available online at <http://www.pbscensus.gov.pk/sites/default/files/DISTRICT_WISE_CENSUS_RESULTS_CENSUS_2017.pdf> [Accessed Dec. 2017].

Guardian (2010) "US Embassy Cables: Hillary Clinton Says Saudi Arabia 'A Critical Source of Terrorist Funding.'" Text of cable dated Dec. 30, 2009, released by Wikileaks, available online at <https://goo.gl/VoZvTA> [Accessed Oct. 2017].

Gunaratna, R., and S. Kam, eds (2016) *Handbook of Terrorism in the Asia-Pacific*. London: Imperial College Press.

Ignatius, D. (2012) "From Pakistan, Answers Needed about Osama bin Laden," *Washington Post*, Apr. 3.

International Crisis Group (2016) *Myanmar: A New Muslim Insurgency in Rakhine State*. Report 283. Brussels: International Crisis Group.

Ispahani, F. (2016) *Purifying the Land of the Pure: Pakistan's Religious Minorities*. New Delhi: HarperCollins India.

Jalal, A. (2008) *Partisans of Allah: Jihad in South Asia*. Cambridge, MA: Harvard University Press.

Kang, J. H. (2009) "1995 Tokyo Subway Attack: The Aum Shinrikyo Case," in M. Haberfeld and A. Hassell (eds), *A New Understanding of Terrorism*. New York: Springer: 219–32.

McCargo, D. (2015) *Tearing Apart the Land: Islam and Legitimacy in Southern Thailand*. Ithaca, NY: Cornell University Press.

MacMillan, M. (2003) *Paris 1919: Six Months that Changed the World*. New York: Random House.

Mahadevan, P. (2016) "Urban Counterterrorist Sieges: The 2008 Mumbai Attack and Police (In)capacity," *Central European Journal of International and Security Studies*, 10(2): 33–56.

Mallet, V. (2016) "Islamist Extremists Pose a Threat to Asian Statehood," *Financial Times*, Jan. 14.

Millyet.com.tr (2016) "Turkey is Not Governed, Kilicdaroglu Says," Feb. 21, available online at <http://www.milliyet.com.tr/turkey-is-not-governed—en-2197504/en.htm> [Accessed Nov. 2017].

Murakami, H. (2001) *Underground: The Tokyo Gas Attack and the Japanese Psyche*, tr. into English by Alfred Birnbaum and Philip Gabriel. New York: Vintage.

Myint-U, T. (2001) *The Making of Modern Burma*. Cambridge: Cambridge University Press.

NBC News (2015) "Meet the Press." Transcript. Aug. 16.

Perdue, P. (2005) *China Marches West: The Qing Conquest of Central Eurasia*. Cambridge, MA: Belknap.

Pew Forum on Religion and Public Life (2011) *The Future of the Global Muslim Population*. Washington, DC: Pew Research Center.

Rashid, A. (2012) *Descent into Chaos: How the War Against Islamic Extremism is Being Lost in Pakistan, Afghanistan and Central Asia*. New York: Penguin.

Ressa, M. (2004) *Seeds of Terror: An Eyewitness Account of Al-Qaeda's Newest Center of Operations in Southeast Asia*. New York: Free Press.

Riedel, B. (2016) "Double Game: Blame Pakistani Spy Service for Attack on Indian Air Force Base," Daily Beast, Jan. 5.

Shakya, T. (1999) *The Dragon in the Land of Snows: A History of Modern Tibet since 1947*. New York: Columbia University Press.

Smith, Jr., W. W. (1996) *Tibetan Nation: A History of Tibetan Nationalism and Sino-Tibetan Relations*. Boulder, CO: Westview Press.

Smith, P. J. (2004) *Terrorism and Violence in Southeast Asia: Transnational Challenges to States and Regional Stability*. London, Routledge.

Solahudin (2013) *The Roots of Terrorism in Indonesia: From Darul Islam to Jem'ah Islamiyah*, tr. into English by Dave McRae. Ithaca, NY: Cornell University Press.

Tinker, H. (1961) *The Union of Burma: A Study of the First Years of Independence*. Oxford: Oxford University Press.

United Nations Population Division (2011) *World Population Prospects: The 2010 Revision*. New York: United Nations.

US Department of Defense and US Military (2015) *Radical Islamic Ideology in Southeast Asia: al-Qaida, Salafi, Muslim Brotherhood, Wahhabi, Abu Sayyaf, Rajah Solaiman*. Washington, DC: Progressive Management.

US Department of State (2016) *Country Report on Terrorism for 2015*. Washington, DC: Bureau of Counterterrorism, Department of State.

US Department of State (2017a) *Country Reports on Terrorism 2016*. Washington, DC: Bureau of Counterterrorism, Department of State.

US Department of State (2017b) "State Sponsors of Terrorism," available online at <https://www.state.gov/j/ct/list/c14151.htm> [Accessed Dec. 2017].

US Senate Armed Services Committee (2017) Statement for the Record by Gen. John W. Nicholson, Commander US Forces—Afghanistan, Feb. 9, available online at <https://www.armed-services.senate.gov/imo/media/doc/Nicholson_02-09-17.pdf> [Accessed Dec. 2017].

van Walt van Praag, M. C. (1987) *The Status of Tibet: History, Rights, and Prospects in International Law*. Boulder, CO: Westview Press.

Washington Post (2016) "'Americans Need to Stand Together': Hillary Clinton's Remarks Following the Orlando Shooting," June 13.

Weiss, S. (2017) "Saudi Arabia's Influence on Indonesia's Growing Islamic Extremism," Huffington Post, Sept. 1.

Weiss, S., and Ward, T. (2016) "Five Saudi Imperial Projects The West has Slept Through," Huffington Post, Jan. 14.

White House (2017) *National Security Strategy of the United States of America*. Washington, DC: White house, available online at <Available at: https://goo.gl/CWQf1t> [Accessed Dec.].

Windrem, R. (2011) "US Prepares for Worst-Case Scenario with Pakistan Nukes," NBC News, Aug. 3, available online at <https://goo.gl/mpXimm> [Accessed Nov. 2017].

CHAPTER 39

THE CAUSES AND CONSEQUENCES OF TERRORISM IN SUB-SAHARAN AFRICA

a recapitulation

JULIET U. ELU AND GREGORY N. PRICE

Introduction

Sub-Saharan Africa has been increasingly recognized as a region warranting special counterterrorism attention (Abrahamsen 2004; Cilliers 2003). This attention is underscored by the fact that since the late 1980s, sub-state terrorist activity in countries such as Burundi, Democratic Republic of the Congo, Liberia, and Sudan have resulted in the loss of almost a million lives and significant destruction of physical property (Cilliers 2003–4). For example, between 1974 and 2008, a total of 4,993 terrorism incidents took place in Sub-Saharan Africa, of which 261 groups claimed responsibility (Elu and Price 2013). More recently, the emergence of Boko Haram in Nigeria (Akinola 2015; Maiangwa 2014), which has taken responsibility for a significant number of terrorist events in West Africa (Oyewole 2015), has further situated Sub-Saharan Africa as a significant corridor for terrorism. In this chapter, we recapitulate Elu and Price (2015) on the causes and consequences of terrorism in Sub-Saharan Africa, and consider the role of climate change as a potential catalyst for further situating Sub-Saharan Africa as a significant corridor for terrorism.

The counterterrorism policy response of governments when addressing terrorism and its economic impact on national and international security fails to consider how religion, ethnicity, colonial legacy, and rational choice interact as reasons why some individuals and groups in Africa employ terrorist acts as an approach to justify their mission and objective. Terrorism is the systematic use of violence and terror against the state, government, and those in power. There are alternative definitions of terrorism, and all emphasize use or threat of use of violence by individuals or sub-national groups to obtain political or social objectives through intimidation of a large audience beyond that of the immediate victims (Enders and Sandler 2006). In other words, terrorism is viewed as the use of terror and intimidation to gain political and social power and initiate change to achieve specific objectives. It seems a reasonable conjecture that for the median global citizen, terrorism is morally reprehensible, but for some it serves as a mechanism for change and a way to foster their political and economic agenda. Terrorism has become a bloody and robust venture around the world, which is not only a challenge for national and international policymakers, but also an issue for present and future national security.

Earlier analyses of the economics of terrorism have considered terrorism with respect to the weighted probability of success and failure. Many of the recent terrorist attacks, illustrated in Figure 39.2, are distributed approximately as follows: about 52 percent are from bombing and explosives, 23 percent from assault, 9 percent from hostage taking, 8 percent from facility/infrastructure attack and assassination respectively. Using time series and ITERATE[1] data, Enders and Sandler (2006) found that terrorist incidents such as bombings, assassinations, kidnappings, and skyjackings were reduced through intervention policies, that lower the benefit–cost ratio of terror, given the high probability of unsuccessful attempts after the implementation of such counterterrorism policies. Rational choice theory has also been applied to the airline industry using a continuous-time survival and logistic regression analysis model to determine the successful number of hijackings (Dugan et al. 2005). The studies also find that the frequency of aerial hijackings declines when the probabilities of success decrease. Other studies by Becker (1968), and Erhlich (2006), also show that the probability of apprehension, convictions, and long-term incarceration served as a deterrent for terrorist hijacking. Blomberg et al. (2002) also found that fluctuations in the business cycle affect terrorist activities and, in particular, high-income and democratic countries appear to have higher incidences of terrorism, and lower incidences of economic contractions. More recently, Brandt and Sandler (2009) find that terrorist kidnappings are sensitive to whether or not the host country of those being kidnapped makes concessions or not. Arce and Sandler (2009) find that inequality appears to increase the cost of religious fundamentalism—one prerequisite for terrorism.

In spite of the various studies on terrorism and prevention strategies, terrorism as rational choice has not been exhausted in the literature and very little of it considers Sub-Saharan Africa. The "Terrorism Knowledge Base" database indicates that the top ten terrorist groups in the world are located in Africa and South Asia.[2] In recent years, both of these regions seem to be fertile breeding and cultivating grounds for terrorist groups that want to relocate. Indeed, a recent study reveals that most of the lethal effective perpetrators groups from 2009–16 are based in Africa.[3] For example, Boko Haram, which is based in Nigeria, is responsible for approximately 80 percent of terrorist incidents. Along with the significant increase in terrorist attacks in Nigeria, Table 39.1

Table 39.1 Global Terrorism Database at START 2016

Country	2012 Per Capita GNI (US$)	2016 Per Capita GNI (US$)	2012 HDI Rank	2017 HDI Ranking	No. of Incidents (2012)	No. of Incidents (2016)	2016 Inequality Index	HDI	Multi Poverty Index	Life Expectancy
Algeria	7,418	13,533	93	83	15	9	N/A	0.745	N/A	75
Angola	4,812	6,291	148	150	0	2	0.336	0.533	N/A	52.7
Burundi	544	691	178	184	8	83	0.276	0.404	0.442	57.1
Chad	1,258	1,991	184	186	0	5	0.238	0.396	0.545	51.9
Democratic Republic of Congo	319	680	186	176	16	169	0.297	0.435	0.369	59.1
Ivory Coast (Cote d'Ivoire)	1,593	3,163	168	171	3	1	0.294	0.474	0.307	51.9
Djibouti	2,350	3,216	164	172	0	N/A	0.31	0.473	0.127	62.3
Egypt	5,401	10,064	112	111	18	365	0.491	0.691	0.016	71.3
Eritrea	531	1,490	181	179	1	N/A	N/A	0.42	N/A	64.2
Ethiopia	1,017	1,523	173	174	3	13	0.33	0.448	0.537	64.6
Kenya	1,541	2,881	145	146	41	65	0.391	0.555	0.166	62.2
Liberia	480	683	174	177	0	0	0.284	0.427	0.356	61.2
Libya	13,765	14,303	64	102	2	417	N/A	0.716	0.005	71.8
Madagascar	828	1,320	151	158	1	1	0.374	0.512	0.42	65.5
Mauritania	2,174	3,527	155	157	3	N/A	0.347	0.513	0.291	63.2
Morocco	4,384	7,195	130	123	1	N/A	0.456	0.647	0.069	74.3
Mozambique	906	1,098	185	181	0	78	0.28	0.418	0.39	55.5
Namibia	5,973	9,770	128	125	0	N/A	0.415	0.64	0.205	65.1
Niger	701	889	186	187	2	23	0.253	0.353	0.584	61.9
Nigeria	2,102	5,443	153	152	173	531	0.328	0.527	0.279	53.1
Sierra Leone	881	1,529	177	179	0	1	0.262	0.42	0.411	51.3
Somalia	N/A	N/A	N/A	N/A	184	590	N/A	N/A	N/A	N/A
South Africa	9,594	12,087	121	119	0	27	0.435	0.666	0.041	57.7
Sudan	1,848	3,846	171	165	38	173	N/A	0.49	0.29	63.7
Tunisia	8,103	10,249	94	97	3	12	0.562	0.725	0.006	75
Uganda	1,168	1,670	161	163	0	15	0.341	0.493	0.359	59.2
Zimbabwe	424	1,588	N/A	154	1	N/A	0.368	0.516	0.128	59.2

Sources: Human Development Report, 2017

reveals that Sub-Saharan countries such as Burundi, Democratic Republic of Congo, Egypt, Libya, Somalia, and Sudan have seen more than 100 percent increase in the number of attacks between 2012 and 2016.

One can consider terrorism as an existential good—terror motivated purely on political, religious, colonial, and/or other worldly grounds regardless of tangible costs and benefits—or as an economic good that can be explained within a standard rational choice model of optimizing agents. In this chapter, we consider the existing literature on the causes and consequences of terrorism in Africa. We conclude by offering policy recommendations on how to address terrorism in Africa.

Causes of Terrorism in Africa

Viewed as a conflict resolution mechanism, terrorism can be broadly viewed as a strategy deployed by individuals, either singularly or in groups to resolve disputes. The basis of such disputes could be based on distributional issues (e.g. of political power, income, wealth) or merely existential—based on religious conflict. Presumably, discriminating between these two sources can inform optimal counterterrorism policy, and if there is any value in a mode of inquiry dubbed "The Economics of Terrorism," it should inform the causes and consequences of terrorism. To date, the literature has provided substantive insight, and here we consider it—not exhaustively by any means—and offer some insight as to how it can inform the causes/consequences of terrorism in Africa.

To the extent that terrorism is caused by distributional issues such as income inequality, the analyses of Krueger and Maleckova (2003) and Krueger (2007), for example raise doubts about terrorism being caused by ignorance and poverty, as they find that terrorists are typically well-educated and typically not members of their society's poor. On the other hand, Barros et al. (2008) find that poverty in Africa is associated with terrorism, and is mediated through conditions of low political and economic freedom. As for ignorance, several analyses that appeal to rational choice models of terrorism suggest terrorists are quite rational. Two important notions or types of rationality are *present-aim* and *self-interest.*[4] Individuals in terrorist groups are present-aim oriented if they are effective and efficient in the pursuit of whatever aims that happen to hold true at the moment of their action (Parfit 1984). Under this condition, no attempt is used to assess whether the aims (terrorist act) make sense. For example, for terrorist groups that prefer self-destructive behavior, the only requirement for making a decision to engage in terror is that they behave in the most efficient and effective destructive way. In contrast, individuals in terrorist groups are self-interested oriented if the choice of terror is conditioned on trade-offs engendered by cost, benefits, and resource constraints. Given a self-interest orientation, the choice of terror must pass a tangible cost–benefit test, and under standard conditions there will exist demand and supply functions for terror that are a function of cost, benefits, and resources.

Religious organizations such as Hamas, the Taliban, Hezbollah, Al Shabaab, Al Qaeda, and other radical groups are potentially present-aim oriented as they use lethal suicide approaches as terrorism strategy. Using the club model, Berman and Laitin (2008) find that radical religious groups are more lethal and choose suicide terrorism more often when they provide benign local public goods. The motives for these terrorist groups are altruism, fidelity to principle, and a desire for justice. The desire to destroy is paramount to their cause and action. In other words, utility maximization or satisfaction comes from massive destruction to justify their cause. However, Kruglanski and Fishman (2006) support the fact that terrorism is psychological in nature, and a given means will be utilized when the expected psychological utility is higher than that of other means, and the expected utility is determined by how well a given means is seen as contributing to the desired objectives. Some studies also show that the need for political freedom and stability can result in terrorism and massive destruction as a means to protest economic and political situations in countries where political instability exists. For example, Abadie (2004) shows that terrorist risk is not significantly higher for poorer countries, and country-specific characteristics such as political freedom and countries with highly authoritarian regimes such as Iraq and Russia that are undergoing transition have a propensity to engage and sustain terrorist activities.

The benefit from terrorism under a present-aim orientation can be purely non-monetary in nature and these individuals exhibit bizarre behaviors and are content to die for their cause in some cases. Africa and South Asia have long histories of breeding terrorist groups, and these groups have high-level activities/incidents. Groups such as Al Qaeda, Abu Nidal, Algeria's Armed Islamic Group, the Lord's Resistance Army, and the Communist Party of Nepal-Maoist, housed in Afghanistan, Iraq, Libya, Syria, Algeria, Sudan, Uganda, and India, fall under this category. For these minority groups, rational behavior and utility maximization would probably be based on a present-aim standard, where non-monetary motives such as altruism, fidelity to principle, desire for justice, and political fairness would be their motive. The analyses of Kruglanski and Fishman (2006), Crenshaw (2000), and Combs (2018) suggest that terrorism is a social psychological phenomenon used by minority groups to influence economic, political, and social policies. There is a tendency for these groups to attract the powerless who seek recognition and feel that the dominant class has deprived them of what is rightfully theirs. The motivation for the minority group to become violent is based on relative deprivation theory where outcomes such as incomes experienced by individuals are inferior to those that they expect to receive or feel entitled to. Even though the theory of relative deprivation has been the dominant perception of terrorism, Bush (1996) found that this theory may no longer be considered the primary cause of collective violence, although it may serve as a significant contributing factor under some social circumstances. Davis (1999) and Crenhshaw (2000) also found that there is a positive relationship between increased repression and political and collective violence. The strategy for these groups is to choose a target that would inflect maximum harm or injuries on the majority group to demonstrate their power and existence. Their main targets are usually business-related areas with severe economic cost to the government and society. Using panel data, Greenbaum et al. (2007) found that terrorist attacks reduced the number of firms and employment in the year following an attack in Italy. The economic cost of terrorism is to deter new business formulation and expansions thereby increasing the unemployment rate in the area following terrorist attack.

The self-interest approach to terrorism on the other hand is based upon trade-offs associated with choices, when all choices are constrained by income/resources. If indeed terrorism is an optimizing choice, it can be conditioned on cost in benefits in a variety of ways. For example, terrorist activities may in some cases offer greater benefits for those with more education, and terrorist organizations (especially suicide bombers) would prefer to select those who have better education since a high level of education attainment is probably a signal of commitment, as well as ability to carry out terrorist attacks with more sophistication for higher income. Krueger and Maleckova (2003) find that there is a positive relationship between investment in human capital and suicide attacks. For example, a suicide bomber would need to be well educated and stable in order to assess and judge the trade-off and likelihood or probability of being caught or captured if poor judgment is exercised. Benmelech and Berrebi (2007) provide empirical evidence to support the theory that higher investment in human capital provides a larger marginal benefit to terrorist groups. Terrorist groups operating under self-interest are optimizing on cost/benefits, and the incentive to destroy is based on the maximum benefit that can be derived from the action considering investment in human capital.

Assume there are two types of terrorist groups with preferences defined over terror and non-terror, where for both types tastes for both terror and non-terror are exogenous. The first type is self-interested, and the second type is present-aim oriented. For the first type the indifference curves are negatively sloped, convex to the origin, and consistent in their preference ranking. This implies that terrorist groups are willing to tolerate a reduction in income in return for terrorist destruction. The indifference curves exhibit diminishing marginal utility (MRS), which indicates that the more resources the terrorist group has, the more they are willing to give up in order to obtain the successful operation of terrorist acts. Self-interested terrorists will be willing to engage in an act when their payoff is high—indicating a higher opportunity cost. The marginal rate of substitution between terror and non-terror is positive ($MRS_{T, N} > 0$) and we assume that the income and substitution effects are such that demand curves for both terror and non-terror are always downward-sloping.

For present-aim oriented terrorists, with $U = f(T, N)$, the trade-off between T and N is nonexistent or effectively zero ($MRS_{T, N} = 0$). Such a trade-off follows from the fact that as an alternative to the preferences assumed under self-interest, critical present aim theory as developed by Parfit (1984) and its modification by Savulescu (1998, 1999) makes three minimal claims about choices. (1) For a choice or act to be rational, the state of affairs promoted by that choice or act must be worth promoting. That is, it must promote some objectively valuable state such as wellbeing, achievement, knowledge, justice, and so on. (2) The state of affairs promoted must have an expected value which is good enough relative to other available alternatives. (3) An individual is not rationally required to give up a concern for one objectively valuable state which is good enough for a relevantly different state which is more valuable.

If individuals in terrorist groups are not present-aim oriented, choices are essentially "existential," and are justified not on cost relative to benefit consideration, but more on principles, representing for example idealized political goals (Savulescu 1999). In this context, seemingly irrational choices such as suicide bombings have perhaps infinitesimal afterlife and empirical benefits relative to lost empirical lives, if the act is believed by the actor to have such properties. As such, the choice of terror, if present-aim oriented, is not conditioned on tangible and/or observable costs and benefits that typically inform resource constraints in economic theory. The extent to which terrorist activity is an existential or economic good suggests that, if terrorists are self-interested, their choices should be conditioned on costs, benefits, and resource constraints. On the other hand, if terrorists are present-aim oriented, terrorism is an existential good, and it is not conditioned on cost, benefits, or resource constraints.

Is terrorism in Africa existential or economic? To get some descriptive empirical perspective on this, we consider a sample of twenty-eight terrorist groups in Africa

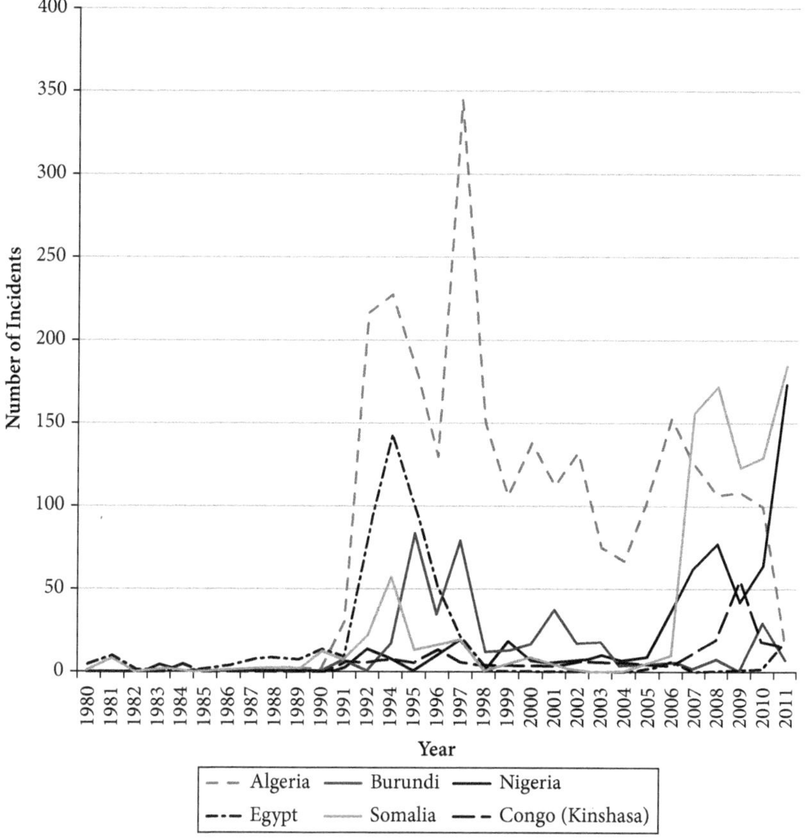

FIGURE 39.1 Trend for Countries with the most total incidents

Source: START Report, 2013

obtained from the Global Terrorism Database (GTD) that were active during 1980–2013. The GTD is an open-source database including information on terrorist events around the world since 1970 and includes systematic data on international as well as domestic terrorist incidents that have occurred during this time period and now includes almost 80,000 cases. For each GTD incident, information is available on the date and location of the incident, the weapons used and nature of the target, the number of casualties, and—when identifiable—the identity of the perpetrator. Table 39.1 reports for each African country, per capita Gross National Income (GNI), its Human Development Index (HDI) ranking, and the number of terrorists' attacks between 1980 and 2013. The six countries with the highest terrorist attacks during this period in the region are Algeria, Burundi, Nigeria, Egypt, Somalia, and Congo. Dividing the terrorist groups into two segments, one representing the "Low-end" groups who commit less than three incidents per year and the "High-end" groups that commit more than ten incidents per year, in Africa eighteen groups were classified as low-end groups compared to other parts of developing countries. These groups committed three or less attacks, and are denoted by zero incidents, therefore were excluded from the tests because they would not have an impact on the data. The "high-end groups," with ten or more incidents, were used to perform the regression analysis. The high-end groups were comprised of larger numbers of incidents, injuries, and fatalities. The sample of the high-end groups were the top six groups with ten or more incidents and both regions had ten high-end groups. Figure 39.1 depicts the trend of terrorism for select African countries. Despite the income per capita of $7,418 in 2012 and $13,533 in 2016, which is high in levels compared to other African countries, Algeria experienced the highest number of incidents from 1990 to 2011. Even Nigeria, with an increased income from $2,102 in 2012 to $5,443 in

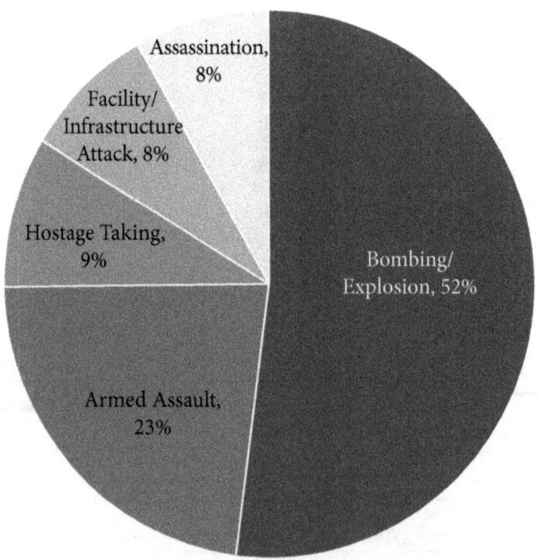

FIGURE 39.2 Tactics used in terrorist attacks worldwide, 2015

Source: National Consortium for the Study of Terrorism and Responses to Terrorism: Annex of Statistical Information 2015

2016 saw an increase in terrorist activities from 173 to 531, a 207 percent increase. This suggests a positive correlation between income and the number of terrorist incidents. Given perhaps the presence of radical Islamists organizations such as Boko Haram and Al Shabaab, Nigeria and Somalia have also seen significant increases in terrorist attacks. In general, the trend for Nigeria and Somalia is upward, underscoring perhaps the increasing radicalism of Islamic-based groups in these countries. Thus at least for the African countries considered in Table 39.1—which represent a group of countries in which the typical terrorist event takes place in Africa, the cause of terrorism appears to be existential, as the trend is dominated by the terrorist activities of radical Islamic groups in Nigeria and Somalia.

Findings emanating from the climate change literature suggest that changes in temperature and rainfall associated with climate change may also contribute to behavioral changes that incentivize violent conflict in Sub-Saharan Africa (Brown et al. 2007; Burke et al. 2009; Butler and Gates 2012; Fjelde and von Uexkull 2012; Hendrix and Salehyan 2012; Hulme et al. 2001), such as terrorism (Price and Elu 2017). In general, to the extent that shocks to rainfall and temperature induced by climate cause shocks to agricultural productivity, optimizing agents may resort to violent conflict to secure material living standards (Challinor et al. 2007; Lobell et al. 2011; O'Reilly et al. 2003) or to secure existential religious aims, made less salient by changes in temperature that lower the psychological costs of violence (Price and Elu 2017).

The results of Price and Elu (2017) provide some support for a causal nexus between climate change and Islamist terrorism in Sub-Saharan Africa—at least in Nigeria. Appealing to a model in which changes in rainfall and outdoor ambient temperature change the psychological costs of violence, they find that climate change-induced decreases in rainfall and increases in temperature are associated with increases in Islamist terrorist incidents. Such a finding provides support for the utility of a rational choice approach to terrorism in Sub-Saharan Africa, how climate change can condition the terrorist cost–benefit calculus in Sub-Saharan Africa, and for the notion that terrorism is, at least in part, a political and religious existential good.

Consequences of Terrorism in Africa

As a destructive activity that destroys property, and causes human casualties and fatalities, terrorism has obvious economic impacts and consequences for countries in general. These measurable consequences include the loss of productivity for those permanently injured and killed, the loss of productive capacity and for destroyed physical capita, reduction in Gross Domestic Product (Abadie 2004; Abadie and Gardeazabel 2008; Tavares 2004), and the loss of growth-inducing foreign direct investment (Powers and Choi 2012). Additional evidence for the adverse economic consequences of terrorism has been provided by Blomberg et al. (2004), who find that the incidence of terrorism is negatively and significantly related to GDP growth and foreign direct investment. It seems likely that terrorism has significant adverse economic consequences for Africa. However as far as we can determine, the existing economics literature provides no insight into the direct consequences of terrorism in Africa.

As for indirect insight into the consequences of terrorism in Africa, the analysis of Elu and Price (2012) is of potential significance. She reports evidence that remittances to Sub-Saharan Africa are used in part to finance terrorism. Given that remittances otherwise finance productive investments in human and physical capital (Anyanwu and Erhijakpor 2010; Fayissa and Nsiah 2010), terrorism in Sub-Saharan Africa can possibly crowd out productive investments that are important for economic growth. To the extent that terrorist activity is correlated with or complements other types of growth-reducing conflict, the analyses of Berdal (2005), Collier and Hoeffler (2004), Kaldor (2007), and Omeje (2007) suggest that the financing of terrorism in Sub-Saharan Africa is also important for the promotion, severity, and duration of wars and civil conflicts—which are associated with lower growth in Sub-Saharan Africa (Gyimah-Brempong and Corley 2005).

Last but not least, there is some evidence that terrorism in Africa may have some beneficial consequences. Wanta and Kalyango (2007) consider the impact of terrorism in Africa on media events in the US, and the extent to which it can frame US foreign policy toward Africa. In general, a key finding was that terrorist events in Africa triggered media coverage that was associated with presidential policy initiatives leading to significant inflows of foreign aid in Africa. Thus, to the extent that foreign aid is beneficial for Africa (Juselius and Moller 2014), and its elasticity with respect to growth is larger than its elasticity with respect to terrorist events, terrorism is potentially beneficial for Africa.

Conclusion

We have provided an overview and recapitulation on the causes and consequences of terrorism in Africa by considering the extent to which terrorism in Sub-Saharan Africa can be explained as rational optimizing behavior, or as a political existential good. The existing literature provides support for and against both notions for countries in general, but actual evidence for Africa is sparse, although getting increasing attention in the economics and social science literature. As such, our examination is based mostly on indirect inferences and implications. Given the lack of attention to Africa in the existing literature, more research on the causes and consequences of terrorism in Africa is clearly needed. Such research would inform the design of effective counterterrorism policy interventions, given that on average the consequences of terrorism are adverse for Africa.

Notwithstanding the sparse literature on terrorism in Africa that would inform effective counterterrorism policy, some recent results of Elu (2012) and Price and Elu (2017) are perhaps of policy significance. They find that in West Africa, regional currency integration seems to increase the cost of terrorism, which can potentially offset the effects of climate change lowering the psychological costs of terrorism, as countries sharing membership in currency unions have fewer terrorists relative to non-member countries. This suggests that regional economic integration and climate change abatement policies in Africa are policy interventions that can deliver not just higher living standards but can also affect a reduction in terrorism. Last but not least, Bolaji (2010) makes convincing arguments—but provides no empirical evidence—that improvements in Africa's governance capability/quality and security infrastructure would be an effective counterterrorism strategy. This seems a productive area for future research on terrorism in Africa—a consideration of how governance capacity/quality and security infrastructure condition the causes/consequences of terrorism.

Notes

1. ITERATE refers to the International Terrorism: Attributes of Terrorist Events. The ITERATE uses information from printed media to construct the chronology of transnational terrorist events.
2. The top ten groups in South Asia are Communist Party of Nepal, Taliban, Liberation Tigers of Tamil Ealam, Communist Party of India-Maoist, United Liberation Front of Assam, al-Gama'a al-Islamiyya, Al Qaeda, National Liberation Front of Tripura, Hizbul-Mujahideen, and PurboBanglar Communist Party.
3. From 2009 to 2012—the most lethal perpetrator groups are the Taliban, Tehrik-i-Taliban Pakistan (TTP), Boko Haram, Al Qaeda in Iraq, Communist Party of India-Maoist (CPI-Maoist), Islamic State of Iraq (IS), Al Qaeda in the Arabian Peninsula (AQAP), Al Shabaab, Lord's Resisitance Army (LRA), and Revolutionary Armed Forces of Columbia (FARC).
4. See Robert Frank, *Microeconomics and Behavior*, 2006.

References

Abadie, Alberto (2004) "Poverty, Political Freedom, and the Roots of Terrorism" National Bureau of Economic Research Working Paper 10859, Cambridge, MA.

Abadie, Alberto, and Javier Gardeazabal (2008) "Terrorism and the World Economy," *European Economic Review*, 52: 1–27.

Abrahamsen, Rita (2004) "A Breeding Ground for Terrorists? Africa and Britain's War on Terrorism," *Review of African Political Economy*, 31: 677–84.

Akinola, Olabanji (2015) "Boko Haram Insurgency in Nigeria: Between Islamic Fundamentalism, Politics and Poverty," *African Security*, 8: 1–29.

Anyanwu, John C., and Andrew E.O. Erhijakpor. (2010) "Do International Remittances Affect Poverty in Africa?," *African Development Review*, 22(1): 51–91.

Arce, Daniel G., and Todd Sandler (2003) "Terrorism and Game Theory," *Simulation and Gaming*, 34: 319–37.

Arce, Daniel G., and Todd Sandler (2009) "Fitting in: Group Effects and the Evolution of Fundamentalism," *Journal of Policy Modeling*, 31: 739–57.

Barros, Carlos Pestana, Joao Ricardo Faria, and Luis A. Gil-Alana (2008) "Terrorism Against American Citizens in Africa: Related to Poverty?." *Journal of Policy Modeling*, 30: 55–69.

Becker, S. Gary (1968) "Crime and Punishment: An Economic Approach," *Journal of Political Economy*, 76(2) (Mar.–Apr.): 169.

Berdal, Mats (2005) "Beyond Greed and Grievance and Not Too Soon," *Review of International Studies*, 31: 687–98.

Benmelech, Efraim, and Claude Berrebi (2007) "Human Capital and Productivity of Suicide Bombers," *Journal of Economics Perspectives*, 21(3): 223–38.

Berman, Eli, and David Laitin (2008) *Religion, Terrorism and Public Goods: Testing The Club Model*. Cambridge, MA: National Bureau of Economic Research.

Berrebi, Claude (2007) "Evidence about the Link between Education, Poverty and Terrorism Among Palestinians," *Peace Economics, Peace Science and Public Policy*, 13: article 2.

Blomberg, A. Brock, Gregory D. Hess, and Akila Weerapana (2002) "Terrorism from Within: An Economic Model of Terrorism." Claremont Colleges. Unpublished.

Blomberg, S. B., G. D. Hess, and A. Orphanides (2004) "The Macroeconomic Consequences of Terrorism," *Journal of Monetary Economics*, 51(5): 1007–32.

Bolaji, Kehinde A. (2010) "Preventing Terrorism in West Africa: Good Governance or Collective Security?," *Journal of Sustainable Development in Africa*, 12: 207–22.

Brandt, Patrick T., and Todd Sandler (2009) "Hostage Taking: Understanding Terrorism Event Dynamics," *Journal of Policy Modeling*, 31: 758–78.

Brown, Oli, Anne Hammil, and Robert McLeman (2007) "Climate Change as the New Security Threat: Implications for Africa," *International Affairs*, 83: 1141–54.

Brush, Stephen G. (1996) "Dynamics of Theory Change in the Social Sciences: Relative Deprivation and Collective Violence," *Journal of Conflict Resolution*, 40(4): 523–45.

Burke, Marshall B., Edward Miguel, Shanker Satyanath, John A. Dykema, and David B. Lobell (2009) "Warming Increases the Risk of Civil War in Africa," *Proceedings of the National Academy of Sciences*, 106: 20670–4.

Butler, Christopher K., and Scott Gates (2012) "African Range Wars: Climate, Conflict, and Property Rights," *Journal of Peace Research*, 49: 23–34.

Challinor, Andrew, Tim Wheeler, Chris Garforth, Peter Craufurd, and Amir Kassam (2007) "Assessing the Vulnerability of Food Crop Systems in Africa to Climate Change," *Climatic Change*, 83: 381–99.

Cilliers, Jakkie (2003–4) "Terrorism and Africa," *African Security Review*, 12: 91–103.

Collier, Paul, and Anke Hoeffler (2004) "Greed and Grievance in Civil War," *Oxford Economic Papers*, 56: 563–95.

Combs, Cindy C. (2018) *Terrorism in the Twenty-First Century*, 8th edn. New York: Routledge.

Crenshaw, Martha (2000) "The Psychology of Terrorism: An Agenda for the 21st Century," *Political Psychology*, 21: 405–20.

Davis, Gareth G. (1999) "Repression, Rationality and Relative Deprivation: A Theoretical and Empirical Examination of Cross-National Variations in Political Violence." Working Paper. 1999.04 GeorgeMasonUniversity.

Dugan, Laura, Gary LaFree, and Alex R. Piquero (2005) "Testing a Rational Choice Model of Airline Hijackings," *Criminology*, 43: 1031–65.

Ehrlich, Paul, and Jianguo Liu (2006) "Socioeconomic and Demographic Roots of Terrorism," in James J. F. Frost (ed.), *The Making of a Terrorist: Recruitment, Training and Root Causes*, 3rd edn. Westport, CT: Praeger Security International, 161–71.

Elu, Juliet U. (2012) "Terrorism In Africa and South Asia: Economic or Existential Good?," *Journal of Developing Areas*, 46: 345–58.

Elu, Juliet U., and Gregory N. Price (2012) "Remittances and the Financing of Terrorism in Sub-Saharan Africa: 1974–2006," *Peace Economics, Peace Science, and Public Policy*, 18(1), article 5.

Elu, Juliet U., and Gregory N. Price (2013) "Terrorisim and Regional Integration in Sub-Saharan Africa: The Case of the CFA Franc Zone," in D. Seck (ed.), *Regional Economic*

Integration in West Africa. Advances in African Economic, Social and Political Development. Cham: Springer, ch. 10.

Elu, Juliet U., and Gregory Price (2015) "The Causes and Consequences of Terrorism in Africa," in Celestin Monga and Justin Y. Lin (eds), *The Oxford Handbook of Africa and Economics*, vol. i. *Context and Concepts*. Oxford: Oxford University Press, 724–38.

Enders, Walter, and Todd Sandler (2006) *The Political Economy of Terrorism*. New York: Cambridge University Press.

Fayissa, Bichaka, and Christian Nsiah (2010) "The Impact of Remittances on Economic Growth and Development in Africa," *American Economist*, 55: 92–103.

Fjelde, Hanne, and Nina von Uexkull (2012) "Climate Triggers: Rainfall Anomalies, Vulnerability and Communal Conflict in Sub-Saharan Africa," *Political Geography*, 31: 444–53.

Frank, Robert (2006) *Microeconomics and Behavior*. New York: McGraw Hill.

Gold, David (2004) *Economics of Terrorism*. New York: Columbia University Press.

Greenbaum, Robert T., Laura Dugan, and Gary LaFree (2007) "The Impact of Terrorism on Italian Employment and Business Activity," *Urban Studies* 44: 1093–1108.

Gyimah-Brempong, Kwabena, and Marva E. Corley (2005) "Civil Wars and Economic Growth in Sub-Saharan Africa," *Journal of African Economies*, 14: 270–311.

Hendrix, Cullen S., and Idean Salehyan (2012) "Climate Change, Rainfall, and Social Conflict in Africa," *Journal of Peace Research*, 49: 35–50.

Hulme, Mike, Ruth Doherty, Todd Ngara, Mark New, and David Lister (2001) "African Climate Change: 1900–2100," *Climate Research*, 17: 145–68.

Juselius, Katarina, Niels Framroze Møller, and Finn Tarp (2014) "The Long-Run Impact of Foreign Aid in 36 African Countries: Insights from Multivariate Time Series Analysis," *Oxford Bulletin of Economics and Statistics*, 76: 153–84.

Kaldor, Mary (2007) *New and Old Wars: Organized Violence in a Globalized Era*, 2nd edn. Palo Alto, CA: Stanford University Press.

Kollias, Chritos, Petros Messis, Nikolaos Mylondis, and Suzanna-Maria Paleologou. (2009) "Terrorism and the Effectiveness of Security Spending in Greece: Policy Implications of Some Empirical Findings," *Journal of Policy Modeling*, 31: 788–802.

Krueger, Alan B. (2007) "What Makes a Homegrown Terrorist? Human Capital and Participation in Domestic Islamic Terrorist Groups in the USA," *Economics Letters*, 101: 293–6.

Krueger, Alan B., and Jitka Maleckova (2003) "Education, Poverty and Terrorism: Is there a Casual Connection?," *Journal of Economic Perspectives*, 17(4): 119–44.

Kruglanski, Arie W., and Shira Fishman (2006) "Terrorism between Syndrome and Tool," *Current Directions in Psychological Science*, 15: 45–8.

Lobell, David B., Marianne Bänziger, Cosmos Magorokosho, and Bindiganavile Vivek (2011) "Nonlinear Heat Effects on African Maize as Evidenced by Historical Yield Trials," *Nature Climate Change*, 1: 42–5.

Maiangwa, Benjamin (2014) "Jihadism in West Africa: Adopting a Three-Dimensional Approach to Counterterrorism," *Journal of Peacebuilding and Development*, 9: 17–32.

Omeje, Kenneth (2007) "The Diaspora and Domestic Insurgencies in Africa," *African Sociological Review*, 11: 94–107.

O'Reilly, Catherine M., Simone R. Alin, Pierre-Denis Plisnier, Andrew S. Cohen, and Brent A. McKee (2003) "Climate Change Decreases Aquatic Ecosystem Productivity of Lake Tanganyika, Africa," *Nature*, 424: 766–8.

Oyewole, Samuel (2015) "Boko Haram: Insurgency and the War Against Terrorism in the Lake Chad Region," *Strategic Analysis*, 39: 428–32.

Parfit, Derek (1984) *Reasons and Persons*. Oxford: Oxford University Press.

Powers, Matthew, and Seung-Whan Choi (2012) "Does Transnational Terrorism Reduce Foreign Direct Investment? Business-Related versus Non-Business-Related Terrorism," *Journal of Peace Research*, 49: 407–22.

Price, Gregory N., and Juliet U. Elu (2017) "Climate Change and Cross-State Islamist Terrorism in Nigeria," *Peace Economics, Peace Science and Public Policy*, 23: article 4

Sandler, Todd (2005) "Collective versus Unilateral Responses to Terrorism," in W. F. Shughart and R. D. Tollison (eds), *Policy Challenges and Political Responses*. Boston: Springer.

Savulescu, Julian (1998) "The Cost of Refusing Treatment and Equality of Outcome," *Journal of Medical Ethics*, 24: 231–6.

Savulescu, Julian (1999) "Should Doctors Do Intentionally less than the Best?," *Journal of Medical Ethics*, 25: 121–6.

Tavares, Jose. (2004) "The Open Society Assesses its Enemies: Shocks, Disasters and Terrorist Attacks," *Journal of Monetary Economics* 51: pp. 1039–70.

Wanta, Wayne, and Yusuf Kalyango (2007) "Terrorism and Africa: A Study of Agenda Building in the United States," *International Journal of Public Opinion Research*, 19: 434–50.

PART IX

ACADEMIC AND POLICY PERSPECTIVES ON COUNTERING TERRORISM

CHAPTER 40

COUNTERTERRORISM STRATEGIES

DANIEL BYMAN

COUNTERTERRORISM is under-theorized and under-researched. Although terrorism received far more attention after the 9/11 attacks, most attention focused on the militants, not on the people fighting them—and even then, work often focuses on structural variables like regime type rather than ones policymakers can more readily control (see Cronin 2009; Krause 2014; Hoffman 2006; Abrahms 2007). Yet since 9/11, scholars and policymakers in the United States and other countries have bruited about a wide range of ways to fight terrorism (Cronin and Ludes 2004). Some methods try to disrupt the group as it tries to conduct operations, while others attempt to change the overall operating environment in a way that defuses the group's anger or makes it harder for it to raise money or attract recruits. The different approaches, however, are rarely compared in a comprehensive way. In addition, some approaches complement each other, while there are inherent tradeoffs among others.

This chapter offers a comparison of eight counterterrorism strategies and instruments, many of which overlap or are pursued simultaneously: (1) crushing terrorist groups directly with massive force; (2) targeting terrorist leaders for death and arrest; (3) relying on allies to strike terrorist groups; (4) containing the terrorist group to limit its effectiveness and encourage internal divisions; (5) improving defenses against terrorism; (6) delegitimating the group's cause; (7) conciliating terrorists; and (8) going after root causes.

Although the United States has played a leading role in counterterrorism in the post-9/11 era, many of these strategies apply to other countries—some more so than the United States, in fact. A contribution of this chapter is systematizing the different counterterrorism approaches in ways that can be useful for scholars to apply to their analyses down the line. In addition, the intention is to focus on variables that policymakers can readily manipulate, an important way that scholars can influence policy (Byman and Kroenig 2016). This chapter presents the scholarly arguments for and against each one and then discusses their overall strengths, weaknesses, costs, and feasibility. The chapter concludes by suggesting several areas for future research.[1]

Strategy 1: Crushing Terrorists

The most obvious way to defeat terrorists, and one that is politically popular in many countries, is to directly target them and their supporters. Force, at times heavy force, is commonly used by democracies as well as dictatorships.[2] Authoritarian regimes in particular are often brutal to suspected terrorists, potential supporters, and indeed anyone else who crosses their paths. Torture, deportation, extra-judicial execution, indefinite detention, "disappearances," and other abuses are common.

Some scholars contend that the threat of force or its use can stop violence from spreading, while others argue that repression creates support for terrorists to transition to an insurgency and otherwise makes it easier to recruit and carry on the fight.[3] Epitomizing the view that force should be limited, the US counterinsurgency field manual notes, "the more force is used, the less effective it is."[4] One academic study found that dissidents often take advantage of "backlash mobilization," particularly when enough leaders survive and the dissident tactics adapt (Francisco 2004).[5] Another scholar finds that collective punishment can provoke additional violence from insurgents (Kalyvas 2004). And there are many cases where repression failed to work: Somoza's Nicaragua, for example, repressed on a vast scale, but the Sandinistas nevertheless overthrew the regime.

Yet for all its horrors, violence has at times prevented a population from succoring the rebels. One of the goals of the Algerian government was to "terrorize the terrorists" and instill fear among the population as well as militants, compelling cooperation (International Crisis Group 2000). As Yuri Zhukov (2012, 108) contends, Russia's long history suggests "repression works, but not in moderation." Stathis Kalyvas (2006, 158), a scholar of civil wars who is critical of indiscriminate violence, accepts that massive violence can reduce insurgent activity, a view backed up by other studies (Lyall 2009).

Effective repression could compel individuals not to support terrorists and other rebels, even if they sympathized with the anti-regime agenda (Tilly 1978, 100; Leites and Wolf 1970). Repression closes the political space, making it more difficult for terrorists to organize and raising the costs of joining. Such effects make it difficult for terrorists to gain the critical mass to sustain the fight and triumph. When repression is successful, potential supporters know there is a high probability they will suffer severe punishment. To the extent that a strong government is more important than a good government, extensive repression can prevent insurgency.[6]

Repression may make a population angry at a regime, but this effect is not consistent, and it also may turn them against the rebels if they cannot protect them from regime reprisals. (Lyall 2009). In the Syrian civil war, in some Aleppo neighborhoods the people resisted rebel attempts to move in, fearing the Syrian regime response. The population blamed the rebels more than the Assad regime for the destruction, as the population rightly believed that the regime was more likely to attack them if their neighborhood became a rebel base (Holliday 2013, 23).

There are some examples of instances where strong government campaigns have crushed terrorist groups, at least temporarily. Turkey's campaign against the once-daunting Kurdish Workers Party (PKK) is instructive. For decades after the founding of the modern Turkish state in 1923, Turkey's Kurds had repeatedly chafed at the Turkish government's efforts to assimilate them. In 1984, the PKK launched a terrorism campaign and formed a large guerrilla army. Fighting in the name of Kurdish self-determination, the PKK sparked a mini civil war, which by the time it effectively ended in 2000 had killed over 30,000 people. The Turkish government's response was a tough counterinsurgency campaign involving much of the Turkish army and intelligence service. Concurrently, Turkey also successfully pressed the PKK's two main sponsors, Iraq and Syria, to cease providing safe havens and to surrender the PKK leaders hiding in their countries, particularly the PKK's leader Abdullah Ocalan, who for years benefitted from Damascus's hostility toward Turkey.

The Turkish government's strategy illustrates how a group can at least be temporarily crushed by force applied by one government alone. After large numbers of terrorist cadres are killed or arrested, the organization is simply less able to function (Shapiro 2013). Over time, would-be members are dissuaded from joining the group out of fear that they too will be killed, arrested, or otherwise punished. Particularly important was isolating the PKK's leadership: as long as they were able to recruit, fundraise, and train new cadre in havens outside Turkey, the group was able to survive despite the government's fierce counterterrorism measures. Yet even with this optimistic reading, the renewal of Kurdish violence in Turkey in recent years has many linkages to past Turkish-Kurdish problems. Crushing the group without political follow-up proved only a temporary solution.

The requirements of such an approach are daunting, moreover, and they grow when confronting larger and more global groups like Al Qaeda. The intelligence capabilities needed are considerable. Because of Al Qaeda's and the Islamic State's global presence (to say nothing of that of its sympathizers), the United States and other countries need a massive intelligence presence in every country with a significant jihadist presence, including Pakistan, Afghanistan, Saudi Arabia, Yemen, Syria, Iraq, and Indonesia. Although the United States and Europe can improve their capacity in various countries, by themselves they usually cannot summon the necessary manpower. Militarily, the United States and NATO countries would be engaged in several Iraq-like operations and many smaller ones as well. Kashmir, Afghanistan, Iraq, Syria, the Caucasus, and Algeria would all be theaters of action, as would Indonesia, Yemen, Nigeria, and other places.

Repression also creates long-term bitterness that can contribute to conflict should repression ease or other conditions change. Russia, for example, used massive force to quell numerous insurgencies. This worked as long as the government in Moscow was strong. When the Soviet Union lost territory to the Nazis during World War II, or when it collapsed in 1991, new anti-regime insurgencies quickly arose, suggesting the bitterness that repressive policies engendered and how promoting a common political identity in the interim is likely to fail (Zhukov 2012, 4).

In addition to unwise policies, soldiers may alienate the population by committing unauthorized abuses including rape and massive theft. Indiscriminate brutality (especially if done on a more limited scale) is often counterproductive as it makes it hard for the people to appease the regime: cooperation and resistance carry the same price, so working with the rebels at least offers a chance of better conditions (Kalyvas 2006, 143–4). If the rebels already enjoy considerable support and if the regime is seen as part of a rival community, the civilian casualties inflicted by the government are likely to further reduce support for it (Lyall, Blaire, and Imai 2013).

Strategy 2: Killing Terrorist Leaders

Another approach—one that grew prominent in the Obama administration though Israel, Russia, and other countries also use this method—is the use of drones, special operations forces, and other tools to kill suspected terrorists. Killing terrorists, often referred to as "decapitation," can range from one-off strikes against top leaders, such as the killing of Hezbollah leader Abbas Musawi by Israel in 1992 to sustained campaigns directed against the middle ranks of an organization, including logisticians and recruiters, such as the US campaign against the Al Qaeda core in Pakistan.

Critics argue that terrorist organizations can survive the loss of leaders with few costs. At times they are able to use the killing to create martyrs, actually strengthening their organization. They can also easily counter killing campaigns, decentralizing their organizations, changing their tactics, and otherwise reducing the value of decapitation.[7]

Proponents contend that these claims are overstated and that, on balance, targeted killings can often weaken terrorist groups.[8] They argue that often the bar is set too high and critics focus on whether killings *alone* cause terrorist groups to be *defeated*, criteria that understate how killings might work with other means to weaken groups. Johnston, for example, argues that removing terrorist leaders makes it more likely the overall conflict will end with a government victory and reduces militant violence. Other arguments claim that targeted killings increase the mortality rate of terrorist groups and that a sustained campaign, as opposed to one-off killings and arrests, forces terrorist groups to undertake costly adaptations to survive, thus inhibiting command and control and making it harder for them to undertake attacks, especially skilled operations (Price 2012, 11; Johnston 2012, 50).

The jury is still out on many issues. As Stephanie Carvin (2012) argues, scholars use different definitions and measuring success is difficult. For many of the claims there is a dearth of evidence, making it difficult to draw firm judgments. Johnston (2012, 49) also finds a selection bias issue, as targeted killings may be more likely to succeed when a government is already more likely to win. Some scholars only focus on attacks on top leaders, while others define targeted killings more broadly. In addition, some scholars include arrests while others focus on the killing of suspected terrorists even though these approaches have profoundly different logics.

Strategy 3: Strengthening Allies to Crush Terrorists

For countries like the United States and Europe, where much (though hardly all) of the terrorism problem is external to its borders, working with other states is necessary to stop terrorism. Rather than monitor a mosque in Yemen with field agents or kill Algerian insurgents with drones, governments of European countries and the United States would often prefer to rely on the forces of allies to act in their stead. France, for example, has worked with an array of governments in Africa to fight groups that also have a presence on French soil. Foreign liaison relationships are vital for counterterrorism, particularly when confronting a foe like the Islamic State or Al Qaeda that operates in multiple countries. In 2005, a senior CIA official testified that virtually every capture or killing of a suspected terrorist outside Iraq was at least in part due to assistance from foreign intelligence services—a staggering claim (Priest 2005).

Often the local terrorist group operates primarily against the ally and only secondarily against Europe or the United States—a particular issue for Islamic State "provinces" and for Al Qaeda affiliates like Al Qaeda in Iraq or Al Qaeda of the Islamic Maghreb, which are more local and regionally focused in their efforts than global. This creates considerable local will to go after terrorist groups, and many allies have impressive capabilities to do so. Local services can draw on police and their domestic intelligence services to gather information, as they are often the "front line" of counterterrorism (Pillar 2001, 118). Their personnel in a country dwarfs the size of the contingent of US intelligence officials that might focus on a country, and these personnel are immersed in the local culture and language. For example, at the end of 2010 the US Embassy in Cairo had just under 400 employees; Egypt's domestic security services, including the police, had between 300,000 and 2 million, depending on which services are included (Zacharia 2011; *Los Angeles Times* 2011). These allies can also take advantage of the law to disrupt terrorists and recruit sources (Pillar 2001, 120). When it comes to counterinsurgency linked to counterterrorism, local forces, with more knowledge of local issues and intra-ethnic networks, are often more effective in identifying insurgents (Lyall 2010). Given these many advantages, it is not surprising that liaison services have had frequent successes in penetrating Al Qaeda and associated movements, often using their own nationals as assets while limiting their support activities. Egypt, Jordan, Morocco, Syria, and Pakistan have all reportedly penetrated Al Qaeda with human assets (Rudner 2004, 217). In some cases, certain of these countries will "run" the agent in cooperation with the United States (Warrick 2011).

The US experience illustrates how foreign liaison is so important that many counterterrorism problems can be categorized by determining how well this relationship is working. In hostile countries like Iran and the Taliban's Afghanistan in the past, there was no liaison. More ambiguous challenges come from countries like Pakistan, where the government often tolerates terrorist activity for its own purposes or Somalia, where there is no functioning government. Even when liaison works well, the services, particularly in the developing world, are often involved in corruption and repression.

When the United States relies on allies, several problems identified in the vast academic literature come to the fore beyond the specifics of counterterrorism. Allies and the United States often have different interests, different interests and capabilities. Information disparities and a lack of leverage often allow allies to draw on US aid yet pursue their own goals.[9] As a result, some scholars argue counterterrorism tends to be undersupplied (Sandler 2003). Al Qaeda and the Islamic State are hostile to almost every government in the world. Nevertheless, some allies do not see a significant threat from terrorism, while others are burdened with so many dangers they can spare few resources for counterterror efforts.

At a tactical level, allies may act in ways harmful to effective counterterrorism and counterinsurgency. Often local forces pursue their own vendettas and are corrupt, creating a spiral of revenge and frustration. At times local forces are from one privileged social group, increasing social tension and driving the disaffected into the arms of the rebels (Kalyvas 2006; Byman 2006a).

Allies, in turn, have many complaints about the United States, Europe, and other extra-regional partners. Frequent leaks of sensitive information are often cited as a reason the United States cannot be trusted. Given the unpopularity of the United States in places like Yemen and Pakistan, leaks that prove these governments' support of the drone program and of other US counterterrorism measures are deeply embarrassing for the governments. European criticism of human rights and other problems often raise hackles. Classification sensitivities inevitably cause additional issues, as the United States may not want to share what is gained from its most precious sources and methods.

Strategy 4: Containing Terrorism

An alternative to decapitating or crushing terrorist groups is to try to contain them, transforming them from a grave strategic threat to a dangerous nuisance (Porter 2009). Many of the particulars would be similar to other strategy options, the main difference would be in terms of priorities and level of effort. The struggle against jihadist groups would join the host of other foreign policy concerns, at times taking precedence but often being secondary. With Pakistan, for example, the United States would prioritize its nuclear program; with Saudi Arabia, oil price stability.

A containment strategy assumes the threat is manageable. As Philip Heymann, the former Deputy Attorney General of the United States, argues, "There will be terrorism. We can deal with it; we can discourage it; but we cannot end it completely" (Heymann 2000, 158). Indeed, according to some scholars, the threat is more than manageable—it is negligible. The scholar John Mueller notes the United States has lost relatively few people from terrorism in years after 9/11, suggesting that the threat is manageable and, indeed, the money would be better spent on other priorities (Mueller and Stewart 2012). Containment also counters the terrorists' attempt to mobilize through government repression and overreaction (Bueno de Mesquita and Dickson 2007).

Containment is thus a relatively low-cost alternative: it demands less in the way of troops and intelligence. At home, little needs to be spent on costly homeland defense measures. Even more important, it requires few policy sacrifices. Many European states, which lack robust counterterrorism apparati, often adopt containment as a default policy.

In addition to seeing the risk itself as manageable, containment has a potential strategy for long-term victory: that the adversary has internal contradictions that, given time, will discredit and divide it. For the jihadist movement, the adversary is divided on what target should receive priority, who is a true Muslim, whether it is against Western values or just US policies, and other core issues (Wiktorowicz 2006). A generation from now, these contradictions will not have destroyed the jihadist cause, but they may have weakened it dramatically.

One of the biggest problems with containment is the home front. Containment appears like weakness to audiences at home who are scared, angry, and hungry for vengeance after a terrorist attack. France, for example, felt compelled to step up bombing in Syria after the 2015 Islamic State attacks in Paris. Moreover, every government must ensure the security of its citizens in order to be credible, and the deliberate murder of civilians is a direct challenge to a government's legitimacy. It will be impossible for politicians to not respond to such provocations: You cannot take the politics out of counterterrorism (Bueno de Mesquita 2007).

Nor is it simply a matter of politics. In addition to preventing peace, terrorism can also spark a far more massive conflict. Indeed, terrorist groups often hope to provoke a larger popular struggle, seeing themselves as the vanguard, a broader movement that they can create through violence. Through the murder and intimidation of civilians—and by provoking a harsh state response—they force people to choose sides, shattering what was a peaceful accommodation. There may be few fatalities from such terrorism, but the strategic consequences are massive. Two of the world's most deadly insurgencies—Kashmir and Chechnya—grew after limited terrorism, in part a reaction to harsh government policies, that was met with overwhelming and indiscriminate repression. As a result, both conflicts quickly escalated to full-scale wars that claimed hundreds of thousands of victims. Israel, Colombia, and other parts of the world have seen terrorists derail peace talks.

Strategy 5: Defenses

If terrorists could easily enter a country and operate with impunity, the number of attacks would almost certainly increase. "Defenses" is a broad term, however. It can include emergency preparedness, domestic intelligence, better border control, port security initiatives, target-hardening, and other measures designed to make it harder for the terrorists to successfully attack.

With better defenses, the chance of finding amateurish terrorists—i.e. most terrorists—is much higher. Their shoddy passports would be inspected more carefully. Weapons dealers would be more vigilant with regard to individuals who might be terrorists, and illegal arms merchants would be under closer scrutiny.

Investigations of attacks before September 11 emphasized that warning of a particular attack may be lacking even when there is a general warning that an attack may occur. In 1985, the "Report of the Secretary of State's Advisory Panel on Overseas Security" (the "Inman Report") examined the bombings of the US Embassy and Marine Barracks in Lebanon and concluded, "If determined, well-trained and funded teams are seeking to do damage, they will eventually succeed." The inquiry into the 1996 Khobar Towers attack and that of the 1998 Embassy bombings both found strategic warning was sound even as tactical warning was lacking. Over ten years later, in 1999, the "Report of the Accountability Review Boards on the Embassy Bombings in Nairobi and Dar es Salaam" (better known as the "Crowe Commission") contended that "[W]e cannot count on having such intelligence to warn us of such attacks." (US Department of State 1999).

Yet a strategy of defense raises some rather obvious questions. First, what is to be defended? Some sites seem obvious: the White House and 10 Downing Street, for example. So too should nuclear power plants. But now it gets harder. Should state capitals be defended, or lesser government buildings? What about public transportation, which has long been a favorite target of terrorists around the world, particularly in Europe? Although difficult, choices must be made, and the broader the coverage the greater the expense (Powell 2007). Increasing airline screening since 9/11 has cost billions, and there is considerable wasteful spending (Blalock 2007; Mueller and Stewart 2011).

The primary cost of many defenses is not wasted dollars but lost time. Metal detectors for a subway, for example, would lead to massive delays and often create long lines that force people to gather in groups, making them easier targets. Moreover, they make what is supposed to be convenient transportation quite inconvenient. Delays, in turn, would create perverse effects. Less convenient subways would make more people drive, and driving is far more dangerous than taking the subway (Savage 2013).

Defenses can even backfire. Scott Sagan (2004) notes, for example, that seemingly obvious defenses like hiring more security guards create a greater risk of an "insider" attack: similar tradeoffs are inherent in most measures. Terrorist innovation is also a challenge. Israel has found that the security barrier has led Palestinian groups to shift their tactics. The barrier has contributed to a dramatic plunge in the number of Israeli deaths from Palestinian suicide attackers. But Palestinian groups like Hamas have increased their use of mortars and rockets, firing over the barrier to strike into Israel (Byman 2011).

One of the most effective forms of defense is domestic intelligence: identifying suspicious individuals and carefully monitoring their activities. But many of the biggest changes for domestic intelligence have costs in civil liberties and in the openness of our society: gaining better information on suspected terrorists at times necessitates collecting more information in general, including on many individuals who, in the end, may not be involved in terrorism. Domestic surveillance of Muslim and Arab communities, which would be the communities from which jihadist groups would recruit new members, has a risk of backfiring, alienating the community as a whole and thus increasing the risk of radicalization and decreasing willingness to cooperate with the police (Vermeulen 2014).

Strategy 6: Delegitimation

A sixth approach takes a quite different tack from the more immediate courses of action presented so far: trying to undermine support for the terrorists by delegitimating their tactics and ideas. Governments may also use moderate and respected voices in the relevant community (Muslim preachers for the jihadists, labor unions for leftists, cultural heroes for ethno-nationalist groups, and so on) to condemn the terrorists. Governments also have shone a spotlight on defectors from the group. Explaining government positions, highlighting the extreme views and brutality of the terrorist group, and otherwise employing standard political campaign tactics of making yourself look good and your opponent bad can, in theory, reduce terrorists' ability to recruit and raise money and, by winning over the populace to the government's side, increase intelligence collection (Long and Wilner 2014; Chowhundry and Krebs 2010).

Terrorism requires the deliberate killing of non-combatants. This is rarely popular. Few publics, no matter how bloodthirsty, want women and children to die.

Theologically, the terrorists are on thin ice. The vast majority of Muslim scholars reject terrorist interpretations concerning the declaration of jihad, the role of popular input into decision-making, the legitimacy of various regimes in the Muslim world, and the permissibility of deviancy from the strict codes the terrorists proclaim. Many of these clerics have views on these issues that would not comfort Western audiences, but they are far removed from those of the terrorists.[10]

One common criticism of efforts to delegitimize terrorists is that no amount of propaganda would convince someone like Ayman al-Zawahiri and his diehard followers to lay down their arms. This criticism is true, but it misses the point. Delegitimizing terrorists has little impact on those already in the organization. They are usually true believers and isolated from counter-messaging. Rather, efforts to delegitimize terrorists might have greater effects among both would-be recruits and potential financiers (Long and Wilner 2014, 162). In addition to shaping the attitudes of these more active parts of the jihadist movement, delegitimating the terrorists also shapes the public mood, which has profound effects on the ability to gather intelligence and on the long-term desirability of reform.

One of the biggest advantages of delegitimation is that it has relatively few costs. The investments are in people and changing tactics. The United States and other countries do not have to deploy troops, change allies, or otherwise shake up security to engage in delegitimation.

However, the moderates on the other side whose condemnation of terrorism is so essential are not always present. Chowdhury and Krebs (2009) argue that moderates must often be created. Moderates are often wrongly identified by their private preferences, but to be effective they must publicly present their ideas. Doing so is difficult, however, as a state embrace of a moderate position can discredit it and less state involvement makes moderates more likely to appear: state criticism and distance are often more effective.

Delegitimation also requires restraint on the part of the United States, Europe, and its allies. The essence of this strategy is to highlight the horrific violence and extreme goals of the foe. If actions like France's ban on the veil in public places take center stage instead, or high-profile measures such as invading other countries or other dramatic uses of military force, the jihadists will draw support simply by portraying themselves as defending the Muslim community: their unpopular means and ultimate goals will be lost in the din.

Strategy 7: Conciliation

Another approach is to offer terrorist groups concessions. In theory, some groups might be satisfied with half a loaf: the Provisional IRA, most famously, agreed to end its violent campaign after a series of concessions to increase the rights and political access of Catholics in Northern Ireland. It accepted the possibility, but not the likelihood, that Northern Ireland would join the Republic of Ireland, reversing itself on its core principle. Less dramatically, concessions can divide groups or weaken them as more moderate voices favor making a deal. It also makes it more likely than some radicals will disengage from the group or not join at all, weakening its recruitment and fundraising (Byman 2006b; Horgan 2009).

Some groups are maximalist, however, and will not settle for part of a loaf: they will simply use any lull in the fighting to better arm themselves and will pocket concessions and keep the violence going. Bueno de Mesquita (2005) argues that concessions can at times increase militancy: the moderates leave the group, allowing the radicals free rein. In addition, governments have a commitment problem: the terrorists are skeptical the government will make good on promises and thus are hesitant to disarm. The timing of concessions also matters. It is often done when governments are weak and cannot win through other means, but this it is more likely to fail because the group believes it is ascendant. Concessions usually work best as part of a larger package of options, with groups under pressure from more violent means having more reason to make a deal. The Provisional IRA had been devastated by a series of British intelligence successes against the group, and despite decades of struggle it had alienated the Republic of Ireland and not won over the majority of northern Catholics to its cause (Richardson 2007; Moloney 2003; Teague 2006).

Probably the biggest problem is political. Terrorism carries a normative burden, and the label is applied broadly, even to groups like Hamas that use terrorism but also run a de facto state. Negotiating with terrorism is seen as legitimating their actions and angers publics in countries where terrorists have long been (often correctly) demonized.

Strategy 8: Going after Root Causes

The 2015 National Security Strategy warns repeatedly of the danger of extremism, citing weak governance, widespread grievances, repression, and the lack of a flourishing civil society among other causes that "allow extremism to take root" (White House 2015). The Obama administration was not alone in worrying about these fundamental problems. President George W. Bush (2005) declared that it was important to fight poverty "because hope is an answer to terror" and called for democracy in the Middle East so that "the extremists will be marginalized, and the flow of violent radicalism to the rest of the world will slow, and eventually end." A study for the European Commission argued that "Wider frames of reference and customized scientific toolboxes are needed to address the specific social, economic, geopolitical and cultural circumstances surrounding jihadism." (European Commission 2016, 8).

Scholars often dismissed this relationship, finding that poverty and poor education did not correlate with involvement or support for terrorism. Indeed, some studies have found a negative correlation: many terrorists are well-educated and relatively wealthy. Terrorism, like politics in general, is seen as an activity that requires some degree of wealth (Krueger and Maleckova 2003; Benmelech and Berrebi 2007). And in places like Pakistan, poor Pakistanis are more exposed to violence and so are less supportive of militancy than are middle-class Pakistanis (Blair et al. 2013).

Yet other scholars present a contrasting view. Max Abrahms (2007) contends that democracies are less vulnerable to terrorist coercion and are superior at counterterrorism because their respect for civil liberties makes them avoid overreactions that play into terrorists' hands. One study found that the relationship between income and terrorism is non-linear. Much depends on the period studied, how the attacks are aggregated, and whether the country of origin of the perpetrators is measured or the country where the attack occurs (Enders et al. 2014). Another found that promoting education can help—but only if it is part of a broad set of development advances rather than done in isolation (Brockhoff et al. 2014). Finally, Lee argues in her examination of anticolonial activists in Bengal that if the comparison pool is "politically involved" individuals rather than the population as a whole, then lower-status and poorer individuals are more likely to use violence because they have fewer opportunity costs (Lee 2011).

The disadvantages for the more ambitious solutions largely lie in the areas of feasibility and costs. There is no recipe for making a democracy. In addition to honest elections and the protection of minority rights, common building blocks of democracy include the rule of law, a free press, civic organizations like unions and professional organizations, and a sense of trust among citizens. As the United States has discovered in Iraq and Afghanistan, it can influence the process, but much of the real work must be done by locals, many of whom are at best half-hearted democrats. And at times the impact of aggressive US diplomacy is to discredit would-be democrats in the eyes of anti-US nationalists. An additional problem with this strategy is that, for truly transformative change, the United States is often asking existing allies like the Al Saud to risk surrendering power: something most regimes are loath to do. Similarly, outside efforts to empower minorities can backfire (Kuperman 2008).

Counterterrorists should think small, in part because the problem generally involves small numbers: thousands, not millions. The focus should be on high-risk communities. Prisons, for example, are breeders of terrorists—a particular problem in Europe—and ensuring that radicals do not dominate religious instruction in prisons and that there are programs (and intelligence agents) in place to stop terrorist recruitment is vital. Particularly important is targeting what terrorism expert William McCants calls "law-abiding supporters"—those who embrace jihadist ideas on social media or are otherwise clearly at risk of joining a terrorist group but have not yet broken the law (Williams 2015).

Areas for Future Research

Given the growth in scholarship over the past two decades, scholars have an opportunity to better understand the terrorist groups themselves when they study counterterrorism as well as how governments and societies do and do not oppose them.

Variation in repression is one important question, albeit one fraught with deep normative implications. Many states repress, but the extent of repression and how it is applied often varies widely. In general, state forces also vary markedly in their skill. In addition, conciliatory measures are often ignored (Dugan and Chenoweth 2012). Often scholars leave out counterterrorism agency, assuming that level of training, information sharing, and other factors governments spend tremendous time trying to improve are ancillary to the problems being studied.

The defensive side also deserves far more attention. Groups adjust tactically but imperfectly to more defenses, but the back-and-forth dynamic has not so far received the attention it deserved. Even more important, societal resilience deserves more scrutiny. Deaths from terrorism usually are small relative to the resources expended to prevent them, and if societies are better able to combat the psychological impact of terrorism, then it will be less effective.

I urge scholars to consider non-structural variables as well as structural ones in their analysis. Policymakers in the United States, Europe, and other countries are rarely able to manipulate government type or the fundamental nature of their adversary. Instead, they have influence over the use or non-use of policy instruments and the appropriate mix, and more scholarly attention to these issues would be valuable.

Finally, counterterrorism tools need to be understood better in context rather than in isolation. Instruments and strategies that work well against a small group with little public support may fail if the group is also an insurgency, let alone if it is waging a civil war. The strategies also must be studied in combination: few of them "work" completely by themselves, but together each can combat part of the problem. Their interactions, however, may at times work against each other or otherwise create unintended effects.

Notes

1. A valuable work that looks at different ways that terrorist groups end, ranging from unsuccessful generational transitions to successful repression, is *How Terrorism Ends: Understanding the Decline and Demise of Terrorist Campaigns*. This chapter does not look at the problem of state-sponsored terrorism and how to coerce states into ending or reducing their backing of terrorists. For my thoughts on this problem, see *Deadly Connections: States that Sponsor Terrorism*.
2. Among many works, see Downes 2011; Rejali 2009; Byman 2011; Mayer 2009.
3. See e.g. Bueno de Mesquita and Dickson 2007; Braithwaite 2010; Davenport 2007; Fransisco 2004.
4. US Army 2006, I-150.
5. This study, however, focuses on unarmed dissidents and relatively small numbers of casualties. It also leaves out rural massacres and large-scale killings.
6. For a perspective that emphasizes opportunity over grievance, and thus the importance of a strong state over a benign one, see Collier and Hoeffler 2004 and Collier 2000.
7. For critical pieces, see Jordan 2009; Jordan 2014; and Cronin 2013.
8. For proponent views, see Johnston 2012; Price 2012, 9–46; Byman 2006c; and Byman, 2013.
9. For more specific works on alliance dynamics and counterterrorism, see Bensahel 2003; Byman 2006d.
10. For a contrast with the jihadist views, see Wiktorowicz and Kaltner 2003; Wiktorowicz 2006 Kelsay 2007.

References

Abrahms, M. (2007) "Why Democracies Make Superior Counterterrorists," *Security Studies*, 16(2): 223–53.

Benmelech, E., and C. Berrebi (2007) "Human Capital and the Productivity of Suicide Bombers," *Journal of Economic Perspectives*, 21: 223–38.

Bensahel, N. (2003) *The Counterterror Coalitions: Cooperation with Europe, NATO, and the European Union*. Santa Monica, CA: Rand Corporation.

Blair, G., C. Fair, N. Malhotra, and J. Shapiro (2013) "Poverty and Support for Militant Politics: Evidence from Pakistan," *American Journal of Political Science*, 57(1): 30–48.

Blalock, Garrick, Vrinda Kadiyali, and Daniel H. Simon (2007) "The Impact of Post-9/11 Airport Security Measures on the Demand for Air Travel," *Journal of Law and Economics*, 50(4) (Nov.): 731–55.

Braithwaite, A. (2010) "Resisting Infection: How State Capacity Conditions Affect Contagion," *Journal of Peace Research*, 47(3): 311–19.

Brockhoff, S., T. Krieger, and D. Meierrieks (2014) "Great Expectations and Hard Times: The (Nontrivial) Impact of Education on Domestic Terrorism," *Journal of Conflict Resolution*, 1–30.

Bueno De Mesquita, E. (2005) "Conciliation, Counterterrorism, and Patterns of Terrorist Violence," *International Organization*, 59(1): 145–76.

Bueno de Mesquita, E. (2007) "Politics and the Suboptimal Provision of Counterterror," *International Organization*, 61(1): 9–36.

Bueno de Mesquita, E., and E. Dickson (2007) "The Propaganda of the Deed: Terrorism, Counterterrorism, and Mobilization," *American Journal of Political Science*, 51(2): 364–81.

Bush, G. (2005) "President Discusses War on Terror at National Endowment for Democracy." [Speech] Oct. 6.

Byman, D. (2005) *Deadly Connections: States that Sponsor Terrorism*. New York: Cambridge University Press.

Byman, D. (2006a) "Friends like These: Counterinsurgency and the War on Terrorism," *International Security*, 31: 79–115.

Byman, D. (2006b) "The Decision to Begin Talks with Terrorists: Lessons for Policymakers," *Studies in Conflict and Terrorism*, 29(5): 403–14.

Byman, D. (2006c) "Do Targeted Killings Work?," *Foreign Affairs*, 85(2): 95–111.

Byman, D. (2006d) "Remaking Alliances for the War on Terrorism," *Journal of Strategic Studies*, 29(5): 767–811.

Byman, D. (2011) *A High Price: The Triumphs and Failures of Israeli Counterterrorism*. Oxford: Oxford University Press.

Byman, D. (2013) "Why Drones Work," *Foreign Affairs*, 92(4): 32–43.

Byman, D., and Matthew Kroenig (2016) "Reaching Beyond the Ivory Tower: A How To Manual," *Security Studies*, 25(2): 289–319.

Carvin, S. (2012) "The Trouble with Targeted Killing," *Security Studies*, 21(3): 529–55.

Chowdhury, A., and R. Krebs (2009) "Making and Mobilizing Moderates: Rhetorical Strategy, Political Networks, and Counterterrorism," *Security Studies*, 18(3): 371–99.

Chowdhury, A., and R. Krebs (2010) "Talking about Terror: Counterterrorist Campaigns and the Logic of Representation," *European Journal of International Relations*, 16(1): 125–50.

Collier, P. (2000) "Rebellion as a Quasi-Criminal Activity," *Journal of Conflict Resolution*, 44(6): 839–53.

Collier, P., and A. Hoeffler (2004) "Greed and Grievance in Civil War," *Oxford Economic Papers*, 56: 563–95.

Cronin, A. (2009) *How Terrorism Ends: Understanding the Decline and Demise of Terrorist Campaigns*. Princeton: Princeton University Press.

Cronin, A. (2013) "Why Drones Fail: When Tactics Drive Strategy," *Foreign Affairs*, 4: 44–54.

Cronin, Audrey Kurth, and James M. Ludes (2004) *Attacking Terrorism: Elements of a Grand Strategy*. Washington, DC: Georgetown University Press.

Davenport, C. (2007) "State Repression and Political Order," *Annual Review of Political Science*, 10: 1–23.

Downes, Alexander B. (2011) *Targeting Civilians in War*. Ithaca, NY: Cornell University Press.

Dugan, Laura, and Erica Chenoweth. (2012) "Moving Beyond Deterrence: The Effectiveness of Raising the Expected Utility of Abstaining from Terrorism in Israel." *American Sociological Review*, Vol 77, Issue 4, pp. 597–624.

Enders, W., G. Hoover, and T. Sandler (2014) "The Changing Nonlinear Relationship between Income and Terrorism," *Journal of Conflict Resolution*, 1–31.

European Commission (2016) *Addressing Terrorism: European Research in Social Sciences and the Humanities in Support to Policies for Inclusion and Security*. Prepared by Gilles Kepel and Bernard Rougier, available online at <*file:///Users/dlb32/Downloads/KI0216450ENN_002.pdf*>.

Francisco, R. (2004) "After the Massacre: Mobilization in the Wake of Harsh Repression," *Mobilization: An International Journal*, 9(2): 107–26.

Hawkins, D., D. Lake, D. Nielson, and M. Tierney (2005) "Delegation under Anarchy: States, International Organizations, and Principal-Agent Theory," in D. Hawkins, D. Lake, D. Nielson, and M. Tierney (eds), *Delegation and Agency in International Organizations*. Cambridge: Cambridge University Press, pp. 3–38.

Heymann, Philip B. (2000) *Terrorism and America: A Commonsense Strategy for a Democratic Society*. Cambridge, MA: MIT Press.

Hoffman, Bruce (2006) *Inside Terrorism*. New York: Columbia University Press.

Holliday, J. (2013) *The Assad Regime: From Counterinsurgency to Civil War*. Washington, DC: Institute for the Study of War.

Horgan, J. (2009) *Walking Away from Terrorism: Accounts of Disengagement from Radical and Extremist Movements*. London: Routledge.

International Crisis Group (2000) "The Algerian Crisis: Not Over Yet," Africa Report no. 24, available online at <http://www.crisisgroup.org/en/regions/middle-east-north-africa/north-africa/algeria/024-the-algerian-crisis-not-over-yet.aspx> [Accessed July 2015].

Johnston, P. (2012) "Does Decapitation Work? Assessing the Effectiveness of Leadership Targeting in Counterinsurgency Campaigns," *International Security*, 36(4): 47–79.

Jordan, J. (2009) "When Heads Roll: Assessing the Effectiveness of Leadership Decapitation," *Security Studies*, 18(4): 719–55.

Jordan, J. (2014) "Attacking the Leader, Missing the Mark: Why Terrorist Groups Survive Decapitation Strikes," *International Security*, 38(4): 7–38.

Kalyvas, S. (2004) "The Paradox of Terrorism in Civil War," *Journal of Ethics*, 8(1): 97–138.

Kalyvas, S. (2006) *The Logic of Violence in Civil Wars*. New York: Cambridge University Press.

Kelsay, J. (2007) *Arguing the Just War in Islam*. Cambridge, MA: Harvard University Press.

Krause, Peter (2014) "The Structure of Success: How the Internal Distribution of Power Drives Armed Group Behavior and National Movement Effectiveness," *International Security*, 38(3): 72–111.

Krueger, A., and J. Maleckova (2003) "Education, Poverty, and Terrorism: Is there a Causal Connection?," *Journal of Economic Perspectives*, 17(4): 119–44.

Kuperman, A. (2008) "The Moral Hazard of Humanitarian Intervention: Lessons from the Balkans," *International Studies Quarterly*, 52(1): 49–80.

Lee, A. (2011) "Who Becomes a Terrorist? Poverty, Education, and the Origins of Political Violence," *World Politics*, 63(2): 203–45.

Leites, N., and C. Wolf (1970) *Rebellion and Authority: An Analytic Essay on Insurgent Conflict*. Santa Monica, CA: RAND Corporation.

Long, J., and A. Wilner (2014) "Delegitimizing al-Qaida: Defeating an 'Army Whose Men Love Death,'" *International Security*, 39(1): 162–4.

Los Angeles Times (2011) "Egypt: U.S. Embassy Closed Indefinitely," Jan. 30.

Lyall, J. (2009) "Does Indiscriminate Violence Incite Insurgent Attacks?," *Journal of Conflict Resolution*, 53(3): 331–62.

Lyall, J. (2010) "Are Coethnics More Effective Counterinsurgents? Evidence from the Second Chechen War," *American Political Science Review*, 104(1): 1–20.

Lyall, J., G. Blaire, and K. Imai (2013) "Explaining Support for Combatants during Wartime," *American Political Science Review*, 107(4): 679–705.

Mayer, J. (2009) *The Dark Side: The Inside Story of How the War on Terror Turned into a War on American Ideals*. New York: Anchor.

Moloney, E. (2003) *A Secret History of the IRA*. New York: W. W. Norton & Co.

Mueller, John, and Mark Stewart (2011) "Balancing the Risks, Benefits and Costs of Homeland Security," *Homeland Security Affairs*, 37: 81–110, available online at <https://www.hsaj.org/articles/43>.

Mueller, John, and Mark Stewart (2012) "The Terrorism Delusion: America's Overwrought Response to 9/11," *International Security*.

National Commission on Terrorist Attacks upon the United States (2004) *The 9/11 Commission Report*. Washington, DC: GPO.

Pillar, P. (2001) *Terrorism and U.S. Foreign Policy*. Washington DC: Brookings Institution.

Porter, P. (2009) "Long Wars and Long Telegrams: Containing Al-Qaeda," *International Affairs*, 85(2): 285–305.

Powell, R. (2007) "Defending Against Terrorist Attacks with Limited Resources," *American Political Science Review*, 101(3): 527–41.

Price, B. (2012) "Targeting Top Terrorists: How Leadership Decapitation Contributes to Counterterrorism," *International Security*, 36(4): 9–46.

Priest, D. (2005) "Foreign Network at Front of CIA's Terror Fight," *Washington Post*, Nov. 18.

Rejali, Darius (2009) *Torture and Democracy*. Princeton: Princeton University Press.

Richardson, L. (2007) "Britain and the IRA," in R. Art and L. Richardson (eds), *Democracy and Counterterrorism: Lessons from the Past*. Washington, DC: USIP Press, 63–104.

Rudner, M. (2004) "Hunters and Gatherers: The Intelligence Coalition Against Islamic Terrorism," *International Journal of Intelligence and Counterintelligence*, 17(2): 193–230.

Sagan, S. (2004) "The Problem of Redundancy Problem: Why More Nuclear Security Forces May Produce Less Nuclear Security," *Risk Analysis*, 24(4): 935–46.

Sandler, Todd (2003) "Collective Action and Transnational Terrorism," *The World Economy*, 26(6): 779–802.

Savage, Ian (2013) "Comparing the Fatality Risks in United States Transportation across Modes and over Time," *Research in Transportation Economics*, 43(1): 9–22.

Shapiro, J. (2013) *The Terrorist's Dilemma: Managing Violent Covert Organizations*. Princeton: Princeton University Press.

Teague, M. (2006) "Double Blind," *The Atlantic*, 297(3): 53–62.

Tilly, C. (1978) *From Mobilization to Revolution*. Boston: Addison-Wesley.

US Army (2006) "FM 3–24 Counterinsurgency," Washington, DC: Headquarters of the Army.

US Department of State (1999) *Report of the Accountability Review Boards on the Embassy Bombings in Nairobi and Dar es Salaam on August 7, 1998*. Washington, DC: GPO.

Vermeulen, F. (2014) "Suspect Communities: Targeting Violent Extremism at the Local Level," *Terrorism and Political Violence*, 26(2): 286–306.

Warrick, J. (2011) *Triple Agent: The Mole Who Infiltrated the CIA*. New York: Doubleday.

White House (2015) *National Security Strategy*. Washington, DC: White House.

Wiktorowicz, Q. (2006) "Anatomy of the Salafi Movement," *Studies in Conflict and Terrorism*, 29(3): 207–39.

Wiktorowicz, Q., and J. Kaltner (2003) "Killing in the Name of Islam: Al-Qaeda's Justification for September 11," *Middle East Policy*, 10(2): 76–92.

Williams, J. (2015) "Countering Violent Extremism: Improving U.S. Strategy for the Future," Markaz. Posted 5 Feb, available online at <http://www.brookings.edu/blogs/markaz/posts/2015/02/06-countering-violent-extremism> [Accessed Aug. 2015].

Zacharia, J. (2011) "Egyptian President Mubarak has Never Hesitated to Use Force Against Challenge to his Rule," *Washington Post*, Jan. 29.

Zhukov, Y. (2012) "Counterinsurgency in a Non-Democratic State: The Russian Example," in I. Duyvesteyn and P. Rich (eds). *The Routledge Handbook of Insurgency and Counter Insurgency*. London: Routledge, 1–20.

CHAPTER 41

TERRORISM AND COUNTERTERRORISM

a policy perspective

JULIETTE BIRD

Introduction

Even though most of us register that terrorism-related deaths are vastly outnumbered by road traffic accidents, our fear disproportionately inflates the importance of the terrorist threat.[1] Terrorism remains an option that still makes the front page. Terrorists suppress not just reason and truth in their justifications but tradition and custom with their actions. They create abnormal situations in which governments can easily be accused of incompetence in risk management and be pushed by public opinion to "do something." Resulting counterterrorism measures can change national lifestyles in expensive and awkward ways and constant new twists to the threat (currently the Foreign Terrorist Fighter phenomenon—those travelling to support ISIL/Daesh in Iraq and Syria) mean that the process of change seems never ending. Terrorists emerge for a myriad of causes and, as a formerly "normal" part of society, exploit insider knowledge on how best to shake our comfortable existence, be it in Schengen trains or shopping malls. So what should the reaction be? What has it been to date and what, if anything, still needs to change?

"Policy" being defined as "prudent or expedient conduct or action,[2]" this chapter moves on from the overarching strategies described by Daniel Byman in Chapter 40 to look at the conduct and actions of the main players of the counterterrorism (CT) spectrum. The aim is to provide an overview of the CT context through the roles of four communities: civil society, nations, regional organizations, and international organizations. Consideration will then be given to areas where further development is likely.

Civil Society

The most immediate and visceral response to terrorism comes naturally from those individuals affected by a terrorist act. These include victims or their families, relatives of perpetrators or of group members, disgusted former members or ex-supporters of terrorist groups, or even repentant terrorists themselves. There are hundreds of thousands of small groups and individuals active against aspects of terrorism worldwide: those who resolutely continue to live their lives unchanged despite terrorist atrocities taking place around them, those who publicly air their mystification and hurt at having loved ones taken from them to ensure others will live happier lives, and committed journalists who stress that the terrorism stories they report are not normal human behavior. But effective concerted action is seldom obvious, for such individuals and lone voices are too easily overlooked. Hence the importance of community groups, charities, and other non-governmental organizations (NGOs) which can act to pull together similar stories and organize coordinated action to increase practical impact.

NGOs, due to their larger scale, often have a public profile and more visible impact. Even so their focus is usually outwards into the community rather than upwards to national bureaucracies. They are a wildly mixed bunch, differing in size, approach, and resources. There are those who use humor, art, education, or sport as a focus and tackle the views of those who feel excluded or oppressed, those who build young people's self-confidence and skills to equip them for better lives, and others who confront untruths online. Most are at grassroots level, some are effective, others are not, a few may even be fronts for something more sinister. Some remain below the radar but others are beginning to make an impact on the international stage. Examples include the Vienna-based Women without Borders/Sisters Against Violent Extremism (SAVE) which brings together women to help their communities resist terrorism and publicizes accounts of lives changed by children or husbands involved in terrorism; the Indonesian Nahdlatul Ulama and LibforAll who together spread an Islamic message of peace and justice; the German Hayat which offers a counselling service for violent extremists/would-be terrorists and their families; the Abu Dhabi-based Hedayah which is an international institution for training, dialogue, collaboration, and research to counter violent extremism and the Search for Common Ground (with headquarters in the US and Belgium) which helps communities choose dialogue over violence. These and others have spoken impressively at high-profile meetings, but few are common names and many excellent examples are not taken up as widely as they deserve to be, either in their home nation or elsewhere.

Specific mention must be made of academics and think tanks in the field of CT. Governments and international organizations would be less well equipped to act proportionately without the ability to draw on objective research and clear analysis of developments both in terrorism and in efforts to counter terrorism. Knee-jerk official reactions to specific terrorist incidents may be avoided if good records are kept and evidence of trends and precedents can be consulted. "Tribal memory" is difficult to preserve in bureaucracies, particularly as careers tend increasingly to be "portfolio" in nature rather than permitting life-long dedication to a topic. Academic accounts of recent (as well as ancient) history and discussion papers or events on esoteric sub-topics enable officials to absorb new subjects—essential when staff movements make handovers impossible. Academics are justifiably treasured for their ability to render accessible to a wider public both issues on which there is very little information (e.g. tribal dynamics within al Shabaab)—often supported by independent fieldwork—and those on which there is just too much available (e.g. the workings of the EU or the UN).

The records now kept by START (the National Consortium for the Study of Terrorism and Responses to Terrorism at Maryland University USA)[3] are an invaluable international resource and the Global Terrorism Index of the Institute for Economics and Peace makes these records accessible in a publicly digestible fashion once a year, thus providing bite-sized chunks of data to be relayed by politicians and diplomats. Shifts in public opinion on terrorism-related issues are registered through surveys, notably those of the Pew Research Center, which effectively provide a series of snapshots on issues such as support for suicide bombing, Nigeria's response to Boko Haram or national views on extremism. Likewise Eurobarometer's regular survey takes the temperature of the EU's population on security and terrorism concerns—this is interesting to compare with Europol's annual Terrorism Situation and Trends report (TESAT) which is fed by government data. Academic research is also invaluable in compiling (ideally) apolitical data and analysis. For example, the Global Centre on Cooperative Security (GCCS) has drawn together global lessons learned from early policy work on extremism (Romaniuk 2015) and is working towards an assessment of multilateral CT work for the coming decade,[4] the US Center for Strategic and International Studies (CSIS) has written impressively on the arc of instability across South Asia as part of its Transnational Threats Project[5] and RAND contributes long-term research on a range of CT-relevant issues.[6]

Lastly, academics are valued for their ability to air options for the future, both in terms of the unexpected and of possible ways ahead. There is much more liberty to think wild thoughts in a faculty than in a ministry but good bureaucracies thrive on a diet of "what ifs," "black swans," and exotic options.

Nations

Although focus is shifting towards "Human Security" and protection of the individual, nations will be the powerhouse for CT for as long as the world remains divided into (more-or-less-observed) national building blocks under domestic control. The absence of a national CT strategy provides a golden opportunity for would-be terrorists to expand their activities in that territory and yet some countries still resist putting one in place. This is counter-intuitive since each government can effectively frame terrorism for its own ends.

The principal areas for CT have remained largely unchanged over the past fifty years: laws, police, judiciary, prisons, borders, intelligence, foreign relations, the financial and travel sectors, access to weapons and explosives (both materiel and technology), with the military as a line of last resort to enforce domestic policy and project it overseas when required. In many nations, years of incremental improvements in these areas have resulted in a fairly stable legislative and practical set-up which can be tweaked slightly when required. Overall, before the appearance of ISIL/Daesh, the decline of Al Qaeda, a very low rate of successful high-profile terrorist attacks, and a more local face-to-terrorism across the world meant that a degree of satisfaction, perhaps even complacency, was creeping into all but the intelligence sector of most national governments. However, the pressure has now ratcheted up and attention is divided between dealing with an active terrorist threat, both at home and abroad, and the need to minimize the numbers of potential future terrorists appearing at home.

Nations protect their own interests from terrorist violence according to domestic priorities. The UK's former Intelligence and Security Coordinator, David Omand, writes persuasively of wise governments managing risk, providing strategic direction, promoting national resilience, and ensuring impartial justice. This instills public confidence and results in civil harmony "so that people can go about their normal business, freely and with confidence" (a quote from the UK's counterterrorism strategy CONTEST) (Omand 2010). He writes of "politically aware but impartial" input from the intelligence community and the CT-specific all-source information fusion role played by the Joint Terrorism Analysis Centre (JTAC). JTAC serves as a practical example of the domestic–external continuum required for CT as it brings together both external and internal intelligence/security services, the Home and Foreign Offices, and many other aspects of government. This inclusive approach, though deeply embedded in the UK's psyche, is alien elsewhere—some nations still look at CT as something that happens exclusively abroad, others regard it as something deeply national to be dealt with at home.

Post-9/11, the UK decided to bring together civil contingency planning and CT response at both local[7] and national[8] levels to treat consequences pragmatically, regardless of cause. This all-risks approach is furthered by mapping of critical infrastructure vulnerability, investment in resilience, and preparation. The very public CONTEST, written in 2003 and published in 2006, bears witness to the importance attached by the UK government to communication in this sensitive field where over-promising of public security is unhelpful. CONTEST successfully fired up enthusiasm across the whole of government but as Omand points out, public understanding and backing is needed for this national "Grand Strategy"—not an easy thing to achieve with a public often engrossed by minutiae. Despite careful implementation, communities can easily be alienated and stereotypes reinforced. Public reassurance that government measures are subject to authorization, to safeguards, to oversight, and to redress if they overstep the bounds of acceptable behavior, is essential. The UK has sought feedback, accepted criticism, and repeatedly amended CONTEST. Members of both Houses of Parliament have also spoken out against measures thought likely to infringe human rights and play into terrorist hands. But despite this seemingly liberal and safeguarded approach, public attitudes are mixed and controversies remain.

Some of the UK's provisions have been adopted elsewhere: JTAC is a model that has been copied or adapted across Europe and beyond, both by nations and by regional/international organizations. However, EU attempts to mirror national mapping of critical infrastructure vulnerabilities across member states have, unsurprisingly met resistance due to national security concerns. The UK is putting its experience in communicating CONTEST to wider use through the EU where it leads the Strategic Communication strand of CT and contributes significantly to work on Syria.[9] CONTEST underlines the right to a normal life and this strong attractive message can be deployed to counterbalance some of ISIL/ Daesh's state-building propaganda.

Nations do not always act alone to counter terrorism but may choose bilateral or small, trusted, multilateral formats (such as the five eyes intelligence community, G7, etc.). This brings a nation added value as a wider range of data sources can be drawn on. When the community is enlarged further (e.g. to the twenty-eight nations of the European Union or larger regional organizations) then, in addition to a difficulty with trust, consensus (and hence loss of sovereignty) becomes an issue. Despite this, national governments are expected to play in international fora to defend national interests and exploit existing expertise rather than seeking to duplicate it at home. Trusted relationships require time and shared experience to establish but, working externally with others, the CT burden can be spread and other nations' ability to shoulder it improved. "Multilateralism is used as a political tool by states to advance preferred forms of cooperation, or to resist such advances from others" (Romaniuk 2010).

Nations also act bilaterally to build capacity in partner nations. There has been much discussion of the desirability of combining national aid and development budgets with security priorities. Such a combination has traditionally been rejected as self-serving (the rules for official development aid prohibit any use of aid for financing military equipment or services) but there is growing realization that the threat of terrorism or violent extremism may adversely affect development, causing instability and poverty and prompting states to divert resources away from basic services. It is also appreciated that much aid has CT relevance (including some undesirable and unintended consequences that can assist terrorist groups). Hence, the argument that aid to police, prisons, borders, judiciary, etc. should be a valid part of development assistance (Briscoe and van Ginkel 2013; Bergin and Hately 2015). The OECD is reportedly considering "total support for development" which is likely to include security support but already in June 2014 the EU stated at the UN that "the nexus between security and development... needs to be fully agreed and mainstreamed throughout national policies."[10] This is unlikely to be easy, as witnessed by the statement by over forty US NGOs in July 2015 expressing concern over prioritization of "securitized responses over investments to address the structural causes of instability" and unwarranted coupling of two lines of effort.[11]

Finally the military aspect; this is a nation's bottom line, its insurance policy, and a way to hold foreign threats at bay. But deployed military are also a target for terrorists and a compounding factor in terrorist behavior.[12] Both the witting (attacks mounted) and unwitting (behavior in a foreign, often extremely unfamiliar, country) actions of the military during operations can prompt resentment and win recruits for terrorists. Iraq and Afghanistan illustrated the need for cultural education and language skills (or at least more effective use of interpreters) for both officers and troops to minimize adverse impact during an overseas operation and these issues are now hot topics for ministries of defense—and treasuries.

Prevention (and "CVE")

Prevention of terrorist attacks and dismantling of groups before they can act has always been the most challenging aspect of national efforts to counter terrorism. Improving responses to attacks and resilience to (and recovery from) damage is more straightforward than preventing future terrorism. However prevention is now in the spotlight of international attention, indeed even in 2010, Omand described Prevent as at "the heart" of Britain's CT strategy.

The role of intelligence as a national CT tool is not generally disputed[13] when used to expose plots before they come to fruition, but there is much concern over intelligence gathering for more extreme, "upstream" or "pre-emptive" CT. This includes concerns over the infringement of human rights, privacy issues and where to place the "red lines" of government tolerance. Dealing with the thoughts and intentions of individuals, their personal rejection of democracy and espousal of violence, does not play to government strengths and necessitates appeal to a different set of players beyond the confines of ministries and agencies, such as community, youth, and religious leaders. Relevant entities are often "new" to governments who find themselves needing to seek relationships of trust with contacts whose reputations are hard to verify. This is not a comfortable process for either side as agendas and interpretations seldom match and contact with officialdom may irrevocably damage the credibility of civil society bodies.

The field of countering violent extremism (CVE)—countering ideologies that advocate violence—has acquired a name but is, as yet, not entirely mainstream. Some nations argue that CVE is a distraction from CT, others see it as the essential accompaniment to an effective CT policy, serving as the basis for the prevention aspect, still others would wish to go further and oppose "extremism" of any sort, violent or not. The current trend, as reflected in recent UN Security Council Resolutions,[14] is towards imposing national legislation to oppose violent ideologies.

Some national approaches are easier than others to put in place: the French and Austrians have established hotlines so the public can ring in with concerns and Sweden has walk-in centers where those with ideological personal or family concerns can talk them through. UK Prime Minister Cameron stated repeatedly that his government must be "more intolerant of intolerance—taking on anyone whose views condone the extremist narrative or create the condition for it to flourish" (Cameron 2015) and a statutory duty[15] is now in force requiring UK public bodies (schools, prisons, health sector, welfare, local councils) to identify and tackle radicalization. This has not been unanimously well received as many sectors do not believe that such behavior falls within their job specification and fear it may indeed be unhelpful to their primary role. Many countries have yet to put in place a strategy to counter radicalization or recruitment of future terrorists and so watch the evolution of such measures with interest, seeking examples of how society can be used, consensually, to flag up individuals or groups of concern. The UK is to introduce a Counter-Extremism Bill[16] which will undoubtedly give rise to further argument.

It has become commonplace to hear nations speak of the need to look to the community for early warning of groups with violent ideologies or of specific individuals that may pose a risk to themselves or to society, but linking government and civil society remains a major challenge in most countries. Building trust so the public feel able to flag up concerns is a long-term project, and a light touch and more expertise are needed if future efforts are not to damage existing relations.

Regional Organizations

There are so many "regional" organizations whose membership ranges from a handful of nations to over fifty that it is hard to generalize their actions and effectiveness. The role of each is to complement and add value to the endeavors of member states. Nations have to choose which to trust and where to apply scarce national resources across a plethora of mandates and communities. The risk of duplication of effort is high and, although more nations working together should mean more leverage, national ability to control individual outcomes is low and international cooperation remains somewhat of a gamble.

Outside the United States, CT has most commonly been viewed as a primarily internal, domestic issue and hence one that is suited to the European Union (EU) whose "Area of Freedom, Security and Justice" lends itself to CT cooperation in the fields of legislation, policing, borders, etc. Although the first platform for EU CT cooperation[17] was created in 1976 and a key Council Framework Decision[18] was taken in 2002, most action has been seen in the past ten years, following the adoption of an EU CT strategy in 2005 (Coolsaet 2010). The CT strategy[19] is based on four pillars: Prevent, Protect, Pursue, and Respond.

The evolution and resulting intricacies of the EU's CT structures and relationships were rendered rational and described with magnificent clarity by Argomaniz (2011) just as the transition to the Lisbon Treaty took place. As he recounts, CT was not an established policy domain before 2001 but the terrorist attacks in USA (2001), Madrid (2004), and London (2005) each jolted the EU machinery forward a little further, e.g. post-9/11 a common list of terrorist organizations was adopted in December 2001 and a Framework Decision on combatting terrorism in 2002; post-Madrid the role of CT coordinator was created, as was the Situation Centre (producing reports based on assessed national intelligence contributions) and the Commission issued several CT-relevant Communications; post-London a CT Strategy was adopted (complementing a pre-existing action plan). Although each event stimulated action, political will to make progress died away as each shock wore off and subsequent implementation seldom reflected the initial urgency. Gilles de Kerchove, the current CT Coordinator, describes this inertia as "counter-terrorism fatigue."

The sheer range of issues covered by the EU that can contribute to countering terrorism is in its own way a brake on progress. Coordination within the EU institutions and between nations and the institutions is complicated by stove-pipes both in Brussels and in capitals. It is immensely difficult to assure a coherent approach across all CT-relevant issues even as a national government, but multiply the challenge by twenty-eight and add to the mix the, too often competing, EU institutions (the Council, the Commission, the Parliament, the External Action Service, and the agencies) and the coordination task is daunting. Coupled with nations' preference for all that is national, or in small groups, in areas that encroach on national security (from intelligence to borders or critical infrastructure), it is little wonder that the EU does more in the field of coordination than in integration. Even coordination is taxing as it requires expert knowledge of many fields and involves a myriad of committees under two EU pillars. Lubricating the impossibly complex machine are networks of helpful personal relationships but resultant coherence cannot be assumed and the CT Coordinator has deliberately not been provided with a mandate strong enough to equip him for more than a role as a collective conscience and somewhat unheeded sheepdog.

The EU's overall position was summarized in the European Agenda on Security (EU 2015) where terrorism is one of the three core priorities requiring immediate action. Whilst the EU is primarily known for its action within the EU area (e.g. police and judicial cooperation, Europol, Eurojust, a European Arrest Warrant (EAW), Joint Investigation Teams (JITs), explosives and transport security, etc.) and for pushing members to implement international obligations, it also works externally on CT cooperation (Argomaniz 2011, ch. 5). External efforts now fall to the External Action Service and the Commission (particularly DGs NEAR and DEVCO). Outreach is to individual partner countries, through dialogue, through bilateral agreements, and through technical and financial assistance projects. The EU also works with regions to ensure development and build capacity (e.g. through the External Action Service's Strategy for Security and Development in the Sahel).[20]

The effectiveness of much EU CT effort is hard for an external observer to judge, indeed a recent report claims that most of the more than 200 CT-relevant measures taken since 2001 have not been subject to democratic scrutiny or to an objective impact assessment (Hayes and Jones 2015). General impressions are that talking shops with external partners are more prevalent than action, although technical assistance is looked to as a promising way to enhance security in regions of importance to the EU (including North Africa, Pakistan, Yemen, the Sahel, and the Horn of Africa).

The EU's external CT cooperation through technical assistance is still in its infancy. The three-year STRIVE project (Strengthening Resilience to Violence and Extremism) in Pakistan until 2017 was to cost €5 million but is small compared to the combined efforts of individual nations. The CT Sahel Project (2011–14), described as the "first active intervention of the EU in the realm of CT implemented by EU Member States globally," can be reviewed online (ISS, RUSI 2014). The three-year project was implemented by a five-nation consortium under the long-term component of the EU's Instrument for Stability (IfS) and was intended to build law enforcement and security institutions in Mali, Mauritania, and Niger. The project suffered from upheaval due to the crisis in Mali and encountered other difficulties, but was deemed to have "performed well" (despite often not being attributed to the EU), reportedly holding its own against "comparable initiatives deployed by other actors." It is seen as having opened the door for other EU instruments, such as criminal justice and security sector programs or Common Security and Defense Policy missions, and the IfS[21] is recommended for use in countering trends towards violent extremism, sensitizing security institutions and communities to the risks of organized crime, working with at risk border communities within a regional perspective, and building community resilience to radicalization and extremism. The EU is still learning how it can most usefully contribute on the world CT stage. It will be interesting to monitor the use of the Union's external instruments into the future.

Of relevance to the "Prevent" pillar, Council adopted a Radicalization and Recruitment strategy in 2005 (updated in 2014). In 2011 the European Commission established the Radicalization Awareness Network (RAN) which is now beginning to deliver the hoped-for policy recommendations (e.g. on Foreign Terrorist Fighters) and practical assistance. RAN was identified in the EU Agenda on Security (EU 2015) as having further potential for the EU's external engagement. Some RAN players have responded to Horizon 2020 (the EU research budget succeeding Framework Programme 7) research calls related to Secure Societies including CT- and deradicalization-related projects (EU 2015). TACTIC[22]—a tactical approach to counterterrorism in cities—is just one example.

Of the many other regional organizations worldwide, most point to some measures they have taken against terrorism but, as these are not the organizations' main *raisons d'être*, many boil down to more words than actions and have a correspondingly low international CT profile despite genuine aspirations. For example, the African Union has a model CT law which it hopes to see implemented in its member states, it has a slowly developing Study Centre (CAERT) to provide it with advice and terrorism analyses, and the African Union's Commission now benefits from a new CT advisory group[23] which may prompt it to reach out for CT assistance in the future. The Arab League meanwhile has been prompted to move from words to action by recent developments in the Middle East but whether this will result in a coherent CT approach across its members remains to be seen.

The fifty-seven-nation Organization for Security and Cooperation in Europe (OSCE) is a higher-profile player. It adopted a Consolidated Framework for the Fight against Terrorism (in 2012) and has an Action against Terrorism Unit to assist its participating states to take "expedient and coherent action to effectively prevent and counter terrorism." The OSCE promotes cooperation and facilitates dialogue and exchange of best practice through workshops often held jointly with ODIHR (the OSCE's Office for Democratic Institutions and Human Rights) and the UN Office on Drugs and Crime (UNODC). Topics include terrorist finance and violent extremism and radicalization that lead to terrorism. OSCE cooperation with the International Civil Aviation Organization (ICAO) and Interpol improves travel document security, training is provided in border security (especially through the OSCE border college in Central Asia) and norm setting work on Internet security has begun. Useful publications include guidance on community policing (OSCE 2014) and protection of non-nuclear Critical Energy Infrastructure from terrorist attacks (OSCE 2013).

The twenty-nine-nation political-military Alliance that is the North Atlantic Treaty Organization (NATO), despite some widely held assumptions, fills a small niche in the global CT approach. Perhaps somewhat to its surprise, the only invocation of its Collective Defense article was in response to terrorism (the 9/11 terrorist attacks of 2001); until then terrorism had not been viewed as an important aspect of the threat to the Alliance (Yost 2014). CT Policy Guidelines were adopted only in 2012 but NATO now actively contributes to the UN-led global approach (Bird 2015). NATO's key strength comes from military contributions made under political guidance. This may be in the form of interventions (e.g. ISAF, Ocean Shield, etc.) or targeted support to nations. NATO assists Allies in the development of capabilities against asymmetric threats and will provide support, upon request, in the event of a terrorist crisis. Also upon request, NATO engages partners to raise awareness, build capacity, and plan for the management of crises. Practical deliverables include assistance with security sector reform, explosives and small arms management, training for CBRN first responders, education, and research. Wherever possible NATO assets, particularly its Centers of Excellence, are made available in support of UN CT capacity-building priorities. Lessons learned from operations with a CT impact are of particular importance for future interventions[24] by NATO or others.

Despite being a relative newcomer, the Global CT Forum (GCTF) is at the forefront of work to collect best practice on thematic and regional CT issues. This collection of twenty-nine nations and the EU dates from 2011 and works on civilian solutions to CT challenges, partnering closely with the UN. Its newest working group is on Foreign Terrorist Fighters and contributed substantially to the adoption of UNSCR 2178 on Foreign Fighters in 2014. Best practices are issued as memoranda, driving national work on prisons, the Sahel, community policing, violent extremism, etc. The GCTF's associated organizations, Hedayah in Abu Dhabi working on civil society, the International Institute for Justice (IIJ) in Malta, complemented by close links to the UN Center for CT, provide muscle for implementation.

It is worth noting that many regional and international organizations with budgets that in principle could be used for CT and CVE projects are ham-strung by the need to obtain members' consensus before committing funds. National contributions can sometimes be made available for specific projects. As of 2015, projects that build on GCTF principles can now also look to the new Global Community Engagement and

Resilience Fund (GCERF). This independent Swiss Foundation was established to support local, community-level initiatives aimed at strengthening resilience against violent extremist agendas. Although still in its pilot phase it has already committed an initial round of funding.

Global Approach—the United Nations

Whilst the UN has not managed a universal definition of terrorism it has achieved far more than might have been expected on such a difficult topic where political tensions are inevitable. Peter Romaniuk succinctly describes the evolution of international cooperation against terrorism from the days of the Committee for the International Repression of Terrorism (1934 at the League of Nations) to the post-9/11 situation (Romaniuk 2010). Practical international police cooperation was an early idea (the first International Criminal Police Congress took place in 1914 and the International Criminal Police Commission—which would eventually become Interpol—was set up in 1923 and dealt with anarchist terrorism) but the political aspect has always been more taxing. Constantly recurring themes include difficulties with definition and cooperation, a preference amongst nations for bilateral or "minilateral" mechanisms and a consequent lack of an overarching approach. A piecemeal approach provided the initial way forward, thus early UN instruments addressed specific acts such as hostage taking or attacks on aircraft. Although a strong camp persisted with a focus on "state terrorism," by the mid-1980s the UN General Assembly[25] had reached "unequivocal condemnation" of terrorism acts and methods as criminal. The Security Council too moved from seeing an indirect link between certain terrorist acts and a threat to the peace, to determining that terrorist acts directly amount to such a threat (Santori 2006).

The transforming effect of 9/11 was seen at work at the UN Security Council through the adoption of UNSCR 1368(2001) which made the link between the use of force in self-defense and the possibility that this might be in response to terrorism and, a few days later, UNSCR 1373 (2001) which set up a CT Committee and mandated actions against terrorism whilst allowing each nation to define terrorism domestically. The next remarkable stride forward was the General Assembly's 2006 UN Global CT strategy[26] (UNGCTS) pushed hard by the Secretary General. This now provides the key framework for international CT work and sets out guidance for nations and international/regional organizations under four pillars.[27]

Working with the UN on CT requires careful selection of an appropriately mandated body but the sheer number of CT-related bodies at the UN can be confusing. The UN CT Committee has been supported by its Executive Directorate (CTED) since 2004, the UNDOC has a longstanding Terrorism Prevention Branch (TPB since 1997) that focuses on legislation, training, and education, CT sanctions monitoring has an associated analytical support team, and the non-proliferation committee has an expert group. To these were added in 2005 the General Assembly tool, the

CT Implementation Task Force (CTITF), which now coordinates the CT-related activities of over thirty UN bodies, and in 2011 the UN Centre for CT (agreed to in 2006) which is linked to the CTITF and was launched on the back of Saudi funding.

The UN's ability to push the implementation of CT measures has always been weak. Some ten years ago Eric Rosand wrote that "unless the CT Committee is able to mobilize and coordinate effectively the assistance efforts to ensure there is comprehensive implementation of 1373, its efficacy will be questioned." (Rosand 2006). Matters are slowly improving as coordination improves. The CTITF is reaching out to group together types of organizations (e.g. centers of excellence, academic institutions, hubs of capability in crisis management, etc.) to facilitate UN work. The appointment of Jean Paul Laborde (formerly of CTITF and TPB) to head CTED was a positive factor in rendering the overall UN effort coherent.[28]

Much as nations are looking at an expanded CT remit covering extremism and radicalization, the 2014 review of the UNGCTS urged all member states to unite against violent extremism and to discuss the causes within their communities. It restated roles, especially the primary role of states, but referred also to NGOs, religious bodies, and the media.[29] Also in 2014 the UN addressed ISIL/Daesh and the Al Nusrah Front from a wide perspective in UNSCR 2170 (assets freeze, travel ban, and arms embargo) and UNSCR 2178 (national handling of foreign terrorist fighters). Both resolutions fall under Chapter VII and are therefore mandatory for nations to implement. Recommendations received from the analytical support and sanctions monitoring team on how to address the challenges of UNSCR 2170 went wider still, covering sanctions, communications strategies, an international database for information sharing, and national capacity building.[30] Nations are thus looking at new, and in many cases challenging, legislation with potentially worrying implications. Ben Emmerson, the former Special Rapporteur on the promotion and protection of human rights, cautioned that states must not overlook their obligations under international human rights law when implementing UNSCR 2178 (Emmerson 2015). Despite such controversy, the UN was expected to move to adopt a Preventing Violent Extremism program in early 2016.[31]

With these recent developments as examples, the cycle considered by this article is closed; the bottom-up reaction of individuals and small groups has reached the top-down machinery of the UN which is in turn requesting civil society communities to work with nations to prevent future terrorism.

What more is Needed? What Specifics are Missing?

CT has a long history, and terrorism an even longer one. Much experience has been gained in the fields of protecting targets, improving resilience and mitigation and responding to attacks, including the pursuit and punishment of perpetrators. Many "best practices" are identified and listed—though not all are implemented wherever they might be of help. Preventing terrorism has always been more difficult than responding to it but this aspect has now become mainstream, not only for nations but for international organizations. It is complicated still further by its extension to work against radicalization and violent extremism. So now what will happen or needs to happen?

Incremental improvements will take place in fields including explosives detection, forensics, crowd control, communication, etc. Laws, procedures, prison and police practices, etc. will continue to be refined and human rights and individual liberties will always be subject to international guidance and government protection. Across all sectors an active debate on effectiveness and cost/benefit analysis is essential and any hope that politicizing of terrorism (and counterterrorism) will cease is illusory. Wider still there are areas of urgent development and long-term effort that are necessary. Some are being addressed but others remain ideas only.

Civil Society

The CT-relevant actions of individuals and small groups are disparate and under-resourced. Little progress has been made on how up-scaling might be possible or how NGOs could work together for greater effect.

- NGOs could be encouraged to cooperate, to share lessons learned and provide advice to newcomers to the sector.
- Perhaps subsidized business management training could be made available to them?

NGOs need support, increased resources and help with outreach, however, governments and international organizations have difficulty judging which NGOs to work with. What organizations are out there? Which come with more problems than they solve? Who really represents communities? Neither side readily trusts the other so neutral assessments of potential partners are needed.

- Might the logging and assessment role be taken on by academia?
- More discussion of the goals and red lines of each side must take place—which itself is likely to improve mutual trust.
- Could guidelines be established for NGO work with governments?
- Governments might seek ways to ensure longer staff placements to avoid tensions and lack of continuity caused by (standard) staff rotation.

The academic role of bringing together disparate projects for overall review with a strong focus on evaluation and assessment is essential in the relatively new field of CVE and Prevent. Academics who go beyond the traditional role, for example by training analysts, red teaming for national exercises, identifying talent from wide range of backgrounds, can also be of enormous help to government.

Nations

Understanding the threat and acting before it is realized requires good information, effective intelligence gathering, better sharing, and the best analysis possible. This is not a trivial goal, either nationally or internationally, but an enduring priority.

- The ability to share information whilst protecting its source can be worked on if there is national will.
- Likewise the issue of oversight of special measures (surveillance, phone monitoring, etc.) must continue to be reviewed so that their use is publicly acceptable and, in the best of cases, the product can be used as evidence.

The challenge of interdepartmental coordination to ensure unity of purpose is a huge one for all governments.

- Exchange of best practice in this field, together with discussion of indicators for success and how to guarantee proportionality, will be a longstanding requirement.
- Regional trust building and government to government cooperation is essential, e.g. borders become critical if the neighbor's standards cannot be relied upon.

Evaluation of projects put in place to fulfill policies often lags behind further policy development and implementation.

- If more governments could support independent bodies such as the Institute for Strategic Dialogue, the GCCS, the international Centre for Counter Terrorism, Hedayah, etc. the cost/benefit assessment for policies under way could be produced in a timely and neutral fashion enabling more precise policy adaptation.

Governments need to improve links to NGOs.

- There is scope to help spread the NGOs' messages, provide contacts, publish successes and collect best practice. Trial projects are under way worldwide and will need urgent evaluation.

Regional Organizations

As a tool of governments, these organizations must play to their unique strengths (specific communities and expertise, e.g. legislation, police, military) and collaborate with others wherever this adds value and is politically viable. Further proliferation of such organizations is unlikely to be hugely helpful.

UN

The UN must continue its role not only as preacher of best practice and shepherd, but also as a broker of requests for help and offers of assistance. States need to continue to compare their experiences and implement the relevant findings of others. They need also to know what expertise can be called on and who might be able to fund capacity building.

As Romaniuk concluded, by now we know roughly what works (good norm and rule setting, training, technical assistance and capacity building) and what doesn't (pressure on national security reflex points of intelligence and law enforcement) and we should look to improve the efficiency of existing measures.

Just as for nations, the UN effort needs to be better organized to ensure coherence and coordination of multiple bodies. The ten-year review of UNGCTS in 2016 represents an opportunity for reform and would benefit greatly from a vigorously engaged Secretary General able to push for change. Whether the UN now proceeds to a comprehensive convention (as proposed by India in 1996) seems much less important than whether it finds a way to implement what it has already set out.

And lastly, is the swing of international attention from CT to violent extremism and radicalization merely a perishable red herring? The current fear is of citizens opting out of the mainstream and, as a worse case, leaving to join ISIL/Daesh or attacking their own nation at home. The vast majority of the world's population does not radicalize and most of those seeking refuge do so in developed countries rather than with ISIL/Daesh. However, even a small minority with violently extreme ideas is not easily accommodated and CVE comes at a high price; it requires whole populations to be aware and engaged, is difficult, controversial, and resource intensive.

Resilient government/society links require trust which is not built through contacts made only in a time of crisis but through long-term relationships, dialogue, and evidence of having listened—which takes money and time. Some individuals break off contact with ministries of interior feeling their credibility and personal safety to be endangered.

- Research is needed into how to find/create cut outs through third parties who can provide support and safe communication.

Governments can usefully establish trip wires within society to flag up potential behavioral problems when they appear to public sight (at school, prison, borders, rehab, university, unions, etc.). If handled well, this will be regarded as prudent preparation without giving rise to Big Brother accusations. Those who witness problems must know who to contact and how to flag up their concerns.

- There is a need for awareness-raising measures across society. Increasing media discussion and several terrorism study MOOCs are contributing.
- Practicalities for public communication with government have yet to be put in place in many societies.

Action to intervene with an individual thought to be at risk of moving via radicalization to violence may require several phases of one to one attention (be it psychological counseling, social welfare, financial or careers advice, or religious discussion) which comes at high cost. What are the criteria that make such an investment worthwhile?

- More studies are needed to see how, if at all, this process could be made more efficient and which aspects work best.
- Similar work is underway on effective help to members of violent groups who are seeking a way out and useful parallels may be found.

Simplistic terrorist ideologies are, in some cases, thought to win over many individuals whose general educational level may be so poor that they are incapable of absorbing more challenging counter-arguments. But even the well-educated may not able to argue effectively with the materials and ideas that target them.

- How can education coupled with training in critical thinking be guaranteed despite resource challenges in the educational sector?
- Can the strong stabilizing influence of regional, religious traditions (e.g. the Maleki school in North Africa, the Hanafi school in the Balkans, or the weak moderate Islam or even atheism in Central Asia) be supported to equip individuals to reject later, more radical, religious influences or constructs and reduce the resort to violence?[32]

How will the aid/development and security equation work out? If it becomes a mainstream approach to tie development aid to improved security, more funds should become available worldwide for the CT spectrum of work.

- Metrics will remain a challenge and international best practice must be collected.
- Languages and cultural awareness will be key skills—promoting them will be resource intensive.

Conclusion

Many players make up the CT field and still more are relevant to the CVE field. Four types of players have been considered and for all there are areas requiring more action. CVE and human security considerations complicate the "hard" security picture of CT but cannot be ignored if long-term progress against terrorism is to be made. Whilst CT can be viewed as maturing in many countries, most CVE approaches are in their infancy and their repercussions are as yet hard to predict. The biggest challenge is expected to be the building of familiarity and trust between governments and the non-governmental sector so that a "whole of society" response to violent ideas and individuals becomes possible. Such profound changes in societal balance cannot be expected to be achieved in a short time. Many experiments and trial projects are under way and sharing of their outcomes must be an urgent and continuous process if mistakes are to be avoided and best practices distilled. Problems are bound to arise due to the individual character and stance of nations, each built on individual history, ethnicity, religion, and priorities. Regional and international organizations cannot gloss over such differences but they can provide fora for their airing, thus enabling international common ground to be identified and built on as envisaged by the UN Global CT strategy.

Notes

1. Note: The views expressed here are the author's alone and do not necessarily reflect the views of NATO.
2. Oxford Dictionaries online.
3. From 1968 to 2009 this role was fulfilled by RAND's Worldwide Terrorism Incident database
4. Project description available at: <http://www.globalcenter.org/wp-content/uploads/2015/07/Global-Center_The-Next-Decade_UN-and-CT-CVE_Project-Description.pdf>.
5. <http://csis.org/program/arc-instability-militancy-across-south-asia>.
6. <http://www.rand.org/topics/terrorism-and-homeland-security.html>.
7. Under Gold-, Silver-, and Bronze-level commanders from emergency services and other agencies.
8. Through the government's Cabinet Office Briefing Room (COBRA) crisis management meetings
9. EU-Syria Strategic Communications Advisory Team (SSCAT).
10. <http://eu-un.europa.eu/articles/en/article_15165_en.htm>.
11. Press release accessible at http:/www.allianceforpeacebuilding.org/wp-content/uploads/2015/07/Statement-FINAL.pdf
12. Baitullah Mehsud of the Pakistani Taliban alleged a ten-fold rise in recruits after a drone strike.
13. Although many issues around this remain controversial, e.g. surveillance, intercept, admissibility of information as evidence, etc.
14. Particularly UNSCR 2170(2014) and UNSCR 2178(2015).
15. Through the Counter Terrorism and Security Act 2015.
16. <https://www.gov.uk/government/publications/queens-speech-2015-what-it-means-for-you/queens-speech-2015-what-it-means-for-you#extremism-bill> and <http://www.independent.co.uk/news/uk/politics/david-cameron-extremism-speech-read-the-transcript-in-full-10401948.html>.
17. TREVI—Terrorisme, Radicalisme, Extremisme et Violence Internationale.
18. 2002/475/JHA of June 13, 2002.
19. 14469/4/05 Rev 4 of 30 November 2005.
20. <http://eeas.europa.eu/africa/docs/sahel_strategy_en.pdf>.
21. Now known as the Instrument contributing to Peace and Stability (ICPS).
22. <http://www.fp7-tactics.eu>.
23. Mentioned by CAERT at Algiers international meeting July 2015.

24. ISAF commanders have remarked that the balance between technology and the human element in operations is critical and that history, culture, language, and custom cannot be ignored (e.g. De Kruif, presentation to NATO meeting 2013).
25. A/RES/40/61 of Dec. 9, 1985.
26. A/RES/60/288 of Sept. 20, 2006.
27. (1) Measures to address the conditions conducive to the spread of terrorism; (2) Measures to prevent and combat terrorism; (3) Measures to build states' capacity to prevent and combat terrorism and to strengthen the role of the United Nations system in this regard; (4) Measures to ensure respect for human rights for all and the rule of law as the fundamental basis of the fight against terrorism
28. He has since been succeeded by Michele Conincx.
29. A/RES/68/276 of June 13, 2014, para. 24.
30. S/2014/815 of Nov. 14, 2014.
31. SG Ban Ki-Moon's speech of Sept. 29, The speech is available to watch on WebTV UN.org.
32. This is now being attempted in Morocco and the region but lessons learned will be appropriate more widely.

References

Argomaniz Javier (2011) *The EU and Counter-Terrorism: Politics, Polity and Policies After 9/11*. Abingdon: Routledge.

Bergin, Anthony, and Sarah Hately (2015) "Security through Aid: Countering Violent Extremism and Terrorism with Australia's Aid Program," Strategic Insights, Australian Strategic Policy Institute, Aug., available online at <https://www.aspi.org.au/publications/security-through-aid-countering-violent-extremism-and-terrorism-with-australias-aid-program/SI95_aid_terrorism.pdf>.

Bird, Juliette (2015) "NATO's Role in Counter Terrorism," *Perspectives on Terrorism*, 9(2): 61–70.

Briscoe, Ivan, and Bibi van Ginkel (2013) "The Nexus between Development and Security: Searching for Common Ground in Countering Terrorism," ICCT Policy Brief, Mar.

Cameron, David (2015) Statement to Parliament. June 29, available online at<https://www.gov.uk/government/speeches/pm-statement-on-tunisia-and-european-council>.

Coolsaet, Rik (2010) "EU Counterterrorism Strategy: Value Added or Chimera?," *International Affairs*, 86(4): 857–73.

Emmerson, Ben (2015) A/HRC/29/51 of June 16. Report of the Special Rapporteur on the Promotion and Protection of Human Rights and Fundamental Freedoms while Countering Terrorism.

EU (2014) Statement on behalf of the EU and its Member States by Mara Marinaki, Managing Director, Global and Multilateral Issues, EEAS at the Fourth Review of the Implementation of the UN Global CT Strategy, June 12, available online at <http://eu-un.europa.eu/articles/en/article_15165_en.htm> [no longer accessible].

EU (2015) *Agenda on Security*. COM (2015) 185 final of Apr. 28. Strasbourg, available online at <http://ec.europa.eu/dgs/home-affairs/e-library/documents/basic-documents/docs/eu_agenda_on_security_en.pdf>.

Hayes, Ben, and Jones, Chris (2015) "Taking Stock: The Evolution, Adoption, Implementation and Evaluation of EU Counter-Terrorism Policy," in Fiona de Londras and Josephine

Doody (eds), *The Impact, Legitimacy and Effectiveness of EU Counter-Terrorism*. Abingdon: Routledge.

ISS/RUSI (2014) *Mid-Term Review of the CT Sahel Project: Final Report*. Praetoria and London: ISS/RUSI, available online at <http://ec.europa.eu/europeaid/documents/mid-term-review-ct-sahel-2014-final-report_en.pdf>.

Omand David (2010) *Securing the State*. London: C. Hurst & Co.

OSCE (2013) *Good Practices Guide on Non-Nuclear Critical Energy Infrastructure Protection (NNCEIP) from Terrorist Attacks Focusing on Threats Emanating from Cyberspace*. Vienna: OSCE.

OSCE (2014) *Preventing Terrorism and Countering Violent Extremism and Radicalisation that Lead to Terrorism: A Community Policing Approach*. Vienna: OSCE.

Romaniuk, Peter (2010) *Multilateral Counter-Terrorism; The Global Politics of Cooperation and Contestation*. New York and London: Routledge.

Romaniuk, Peter (2015) *Does CVE Work? Lessons Learned from the Global Effort to Counter Violent Extremism*. Goshen, IN: Global Center on Cooperative Security, Sept.

Rosand Eric (2006) "Resolution 1373 and the CTC: The Security Council's Capacity Building," in Giusepe Nesi (ed.), *International Cooperation in Counter Terrorism: The UN and Regional Organisations in the Fight Against Terrorism*. Farnham: Ashgate.

Santori, Valeria (2006) "The Security Council's (broad) Interpretation of the Notion of the Threat to Peace in Counter Terorism," in Giusepe Nesi (ed.), *International Cooperation in Counter Terrorism: The UN and Regional Organisations in the Fight Against Terrorism*. Farnham: Ashgate.

UN (2006) *The United Nations Global Counter-Terrorism. Strategy*. A/RES/60/288. Sept. 20. New York: UN.

UN (2014) *The United Nations Global Counter-Terrorism Strategy* Review. A/RES/68/276. June 29. New York: UN.

Yost, David S. (2014) *NATO's Balancing Act*. Washington, DC: United States Institute of Peace.

CHAPTER 42

COUNTERTERRORISM AND INTERNATIONAL LAW

ANDREA BIANCHI

INTRODUCTION

COUNTERTERRORISM is not a term of art with a distinct pedigree in international law. It was coined after 9/11, and was later developed to refer to the set of laws and policies adopted as a response to terrorism. In the aftermath of the 9/11 attacks, the main question for academics, decision-makers, and practitioners alike was whether international law was well equipped to tackle the threat of terrorism on such a wide scale (Bianchi 2004). Later the issue became that of evaluating whether the efficacy of the normative responses adopted to counter international terrorism as well as their legitimacy—in terms of respect for the rule of law and fundamental human rights—were satisfactory (Bianchi 2006a; Gearty 2007). As the effects of counterterrorism laws and policies unfolded over the years, it became clear that the fight against international terrorism could potentially affect the structure and functioning of the international and domestic legal systems. While it would be difficult to justify looking at "the international law of counterterrorism" as a distinct branch of international law, it can hardly be denied that counterterrorism has affected many different areas of international law and it has set in motion normative dynamics that have challenged traditional paradigms. In some instances this has brought about change in the content of the law itself. The purpose of the remarks that follow is to appreciate the overall response provided by the international community, and the main normative strategies pursued by international law in countering international terrorism.

The Normative Framework

Non-lawyers often believe in the magic power of rules—particularly those of international law—to cure the world's many diseases. Most of the time, therefore, the solution to problems is seen in the adoption of more law. In fact, international law presents no scarcity of rules dealing with international terrorism. Starting in the 1960s, when the scourge of international terrorism started manifesting itself, states had to put up with the threat of terrorism on a transnational scale (Blumenau 2014). Given the difficulties of reaching agreement on a general instrument against terrorism, at a time of deep ideological divide, the international community started concluding ad hoc treaties, proscribing specific conduct, such as acts directed against the safety of civil aviation (1963 Tokyo Convention and 1971 Montreal Convention), or maritime navigation (1988 Rome Convention). The fact that some, if not most, of the relevant treaties were adopted in the aftermath of terrorist attacks contributed to the perception that the international law response was belated and reactive, rather than preventative, and ineffective overall.

The distinctive feature of these anti-terror treaties is that they all look at acts of terrorism as criminal acts perpetrated by individuals. Such criminals must be apprehended and prosecuted, under a domestic criminal law enforcement paradigm, by states parties. In order to facilitate states in performing the task, these treaties lay down rules that expand heads of jurisdiction and enhance international judicial cooperation mechanisms. In order to ensure an effective system of prosecution states agree either to prosecute or to extradite the terrorist suspects that come under their custody. This is significant as it shows that the initial response to international terrorism by the international community was one based on criminal law enforcement and not on the laws of war. Terrorists were first and foremost criminals that had to be held accountable before states' domestic legal systems. Unfortunately, before the attacks on 9/11, the number of ratifications by states of these anti-terror treaties was scant. For instance, the United States was not a party to the 1997 UN Convention on Terrorist Bombings, which would have been applicable to the 9/11 attacks. Perhaps, if the US were a party to it and had decided to frame their response against its background, the course of events of these past fifteen years might have been dramatically different.

Regional normative instruments (see, just as an example, the 1998 Arab Convention for the Suppression of Terrorism; the 1999 Organization of African Unity Convention on the Prevention and Combating of Terrorism; the 2002 Inter-American Convention against Terrorism; the 2005 Council of Europe Convention on the Prevention of Terrorism) represent another important body of rules. The proliferation of specific normative standards at the regional level has increased in the aftermath of the 9/11 attacks, even though at times one legitimately wonders about the efficacy of treaties, which add little to existing rules and provide for no additional enforcement mechanism. Other rules of international law are applicable to international terrorism. The rules on the use of force and the responsibility of states; those that regulate the exercise of jurisdiction by states and help determine under what circumstances may a state exercise its jurisdiction over persons and activities, particularly when the latter take place outside its territory; the law of the United Nations Charter and the powers of the Security Council to maintain or restore international peace and security, and so on and so forth. Finally, it is worth noting that also soft law instruments play a very important role in counterterrorism. It suffices to think of the Financial Action Task Force (FATF) standards to fight against the financing of terrorism, recently adjusted to prevent the financing of Islamic State of Iraq and the Levant (ISIL); or of the good practices elaborated within the Global Counterterrorism Forum. If its efficacy in countering terrorism were to be judged by the number of the extant applicable rules and other normative standards, international law would no doubt pass muster.

The Definitional Quandary

Judge Baxter once said that "it is very unfortunate that the legal notion of terrorism has been imposed on us. It is imprecise, indeterminate, and, most of all, it serves no legal purpose" (Baxter 1973–4, 380). Along the same lines Rosalyn Higgins some years later maintained that "terrorism is a term without legal significance" (Higgins 1997, 28). Their marked provocative character notwithstanding, these remarks are worth pondering. They aim at downplaying the importance attached to the definitional issue that in many political and academic circles is presented as a fundamental one. I suppose that the point of the provocation was that nearly every single act that could be tagged as "terrorist" is already criminalized. In other words, the perpetrators would be liable at criminal law for murder, kidnapping, or whatever other crime they might have committed, regardless of the moral stigma that one may add by calling the act in question "terrorist." This is probably the reason why lately reference is made to "violent extremism" rather than to the "T" word.

The definitional issue has long characterized the debate in international law and politics (Schmid 2004, 2013). In fact, the widely spread conviction that international law does not provide for a general definition of terrorism is most likely inaccurate. At closer scrutiny, the definitions of terrorism abound in regional instruments, ranging from the 2002 EU Framework Decision on combating terrorism to the above-mentioned regional treaties, and national legislation. Arguably, a minimum common denominator would not be impossible to trace, if one were to look at the myriad different legal instruments that provide for a definition of terrorism. It is particularly worthy of note that since its Resolution 49/60 of 1994, the General Assembly has consistently defined international terrorism; and that even the Security Council in its Res. 1566 (2004) provided its own definition, which is very similar to the one used by the GA and laid down in other treaties and international instruments. Likewise, the "Interlocutory Decision on the Applicable Law" issued by the Special Tribunal on Lebanon in 2011 (Case No STL-11-01, Feb. 16, 2011, §83) confirmed the existence of "common themes" in the definition of international terrorism, including the criminality of the act and the intent of spreading terror or compelling a government or international organization to do or not to do something. Incidentally, even the 1937 League of Nations Convention on the Prevention and Punishment of Terrorism referred to some of these constitutive elements of the definition, emphasizing "all criminal acts directed against a State and intended or calculated to create a state of terror in the minds of particular persons or a group of persons or the general public" (Article 1). On the grounds of these similarities several commentators have expressed the view that it is perfectly possible to reconstitute a definition of terrorism in customary law that draws from this multiplicity of legal materials (Cassese 2006, 936–7).

Despite its inability to bring successfully to completion its work on the adoption of a Comprehensive Convention on Terrorism, the Ad-Hoc Committee established in 1996 by the General Assembly agreed—back in 2002—to the definition of a terrorist act (see the latest report of the Committee (2013) with the consolidated text of the draft Convention: UN/Doc. A/68/37 (May 15, 2013)). In particular, draft Article 2 provides that any person would commit an act of terrorism if that person "by any means, unlawfully and intentionally, causes (a) death or serious bodily injury to any person; or (b) serious damage to public or private property... when the purpose of the conduct, by its nature or context, is to intimidate a population, or to compel a Government or an international organization to do or to abstain from doing any act." The agreement on the definition of a terrorist act hardly hides the real bone of contention among states, namely whether or not that definition should also play out in a situation of armed conflict or foreign occupation and, if so, how. This is the real reason for which the negotiations stalled, and the draft convention could not be adopted. While it can be doubted that the adoption of the Comprehensive Convention on terrorism will ever be a landmark in the fight against terrorism in terms of efficacy, its highly symbolic value should not be underestimated (Saul 2006, 68). At the very least, its adoption would limit states' margin for maneuvering in defining unilaterally "terrorism" for domestic law purposes, and contribute to enhancing the effectiveness of international judicial cooperation, by making it easier to satisfy the requirement of "double criminality," which often represents a hurdle in terrorism-related extradition cases (Bianchi 2006b, 1048–9). Be that as it may, the definitional quandary should not be used as a pretext not to pursue a shared and comprehensive strategy to counter terrorism at the international level.

The Use of Force against Terrorist Groups

The UN Charter is unanimously regarded as the cornerstone of the international regulation of the use of force in the post-World War II legal order. In order to eliminate the scourge of war from international relations, the drafters of the UN Charter had laid down a general prohibition on the unilateral use of force (Article 2 §4). Alongside the outlawing of force, a system of collective security was set up with a view to having the Security Council maintain or restore international peace and security, according to Chapter VII of the UN Charter. The only admissible exceptions to the prohibition of the use of force should have been the enforcement action by the Security Council, or the temporary exception provided for in Article 51, the inherent right of states to individual and collective self-defense if an armed attack against a UN member occurs. As is well known the Security Council has been often unable to discharge its functions due to the veto power of its five permanent members. Only occasionally has political consensus within its ranks allowed authorizing enforcement operations involving the use of force by the member states. The first such occasion was the authorization to use force against Iraq to force Saddam Hussein to withdraw from Kuwait. In fact, Res. 678/1990 authorized the UN member states to use "all necessary means" to bring Iraq to comply with prior SC's resolutions. By that expression, the SC members clearly intended to refer to the use of force. The same clause was repeatedly invoked (sometimes in its variant, "all necessary measures") in the subsequent practice in the 1990s.

Starting from the unilateral use of force in Kosovo by NATO countries in 1999, the societal consensus on the interpretation of the rules on the use of force broke up (Bianchi 2009). The invocation of an alleged customary international law of humanitarian intervention outside the UN Charter, used as the legal grounds for legitimizing the military action, represented a major rupture with the traditional UN Charter-based justifications. Reliance on the alleged customary international law of preemptive self-defense–relied upon by the US to justify the 2003 invasion of Iraq—further contributed to the state of uncertainty about the real range of exceptions to the use of force as well as the interpretation of the notion of self-defense.

Meanwhile, the 9/11 attacks had cast a shadow on the suitability of the traditional rules on the use of force to address the new challenges posed by armed attacks carried out by non-state actors. Could self-defense be triggered by any such attack? The wide acquiescence shown by the international community to the military intervention in Afghanistan paved the way for an increasing degree of acceptance of uses of force against terrorist groups in the territory of fragile states. Ever since, practice has confirmed this trend. The Israeli campaign against Lebanon and Hezbollah in 2009, the Turkish incursions into Iraqi territory to hit PKK strongholds and militias, the frequent use of US drone strikes in Pakistan, Yemen, and Somalia against terrorist targets have not met with any particularly strong reaction by other states. The same holds true for the two raids carried out in the late 1990s by the US against Sudan and Afghanistan following the Al Qaeda attacks against the US embassies in Kenya and Tanzania.

The complexity of the legal justifications used in the air strikes campaign against Islamic State well illustrates the confusion and ambiguity surrounding the law on the use of force. A first justification is the use of force by invitation that would exclude any illegality, as the state against which territory force is used has expressly requested it (*volenti non fit iniuria*). This would apply to the strikes in Iraq carried out by a coalition of states including the US, France, and the UK, and to the Russian strikes in Syria. Alternatively, there would be an additional justification based on collective self-defense, respectively triggered by the requests of Iraq and Syria that would justify the bombings. The collective self-defense response deployed to help Iraq would also cover the bombings in the Syrian territory, as the armed attack against Iraq would be partly carried out by that swathe of Syrian territory under Islamic State's control. Finally, there have been attempts at justifying the strikes as an action in individual self-defense by France, after the Paris attacks, and by Russia, after the shooting down, allegedly by terrorist groups linked to Islamic State, of a Russian flight flying out of Egypt and bringing home to St Petersburg Russian tourists. If one sets aside the rather formalistic justification based on the consent of the territorial state (use of force by invitation), once again the common legal refrain is self-defense in its multifaceted aspects.

Indeed, short of Security Council authorization, self-defense appears as the most recurrent justification for the use of force, including against terrorist groups. Understandably so, as self-defense is the only admissible exception to the unilateral use of force by states in contemporary international law. In a world in which the unilateral use of force has been banned, there is hardly any standing for armed reprisals, that is, uses of force to punish and deter (Dinstein 2011, 244ff.). Although many of the instances of the recent uses of force against terrorist groups bear a resemblance to armed reprisals, there is no other available qualification than calling them exercises in "self-defense." The use of force against terrorist groups, particularly in the territory of failed or fragile states, seems to be largely tolerated by the international community (Tams 2009). This leads to speculation that the interpretation of the notion of self-defense may have changed. By the same token, several Western states seem happy to admit the legitimacy of preventive self-defense in case of an imminent threat (Chatham House Principles, 967–8; Leiden Policy Recommendations, §§45–8).

Resolution 2249/2015 has brought even more ambiguity into the picture. The SC has called upon the member states to take "all necessary measures," in compliance with both the Charter and international law, "to redouble and coordinate their efforts to prevent and suppress terrorist acts committed specifically by ISIL." By using the expression traditionally used for the authorization of the use of force by member states the SC most likely wanted to signal, albeit somewhat surreptitiously, its indirect support for the military action undertaken by several states. Such political endorsement was a very important factor in prompting parliamentary approval of the military action both in the United Kingdom and Germany shortly thereafter. While an ad hoc resolution modeled on the preceding ones that had authorized the use of force would have been preferable, in terms of clarity, Res. 2242 represents a first attempt to restore political consensus on the centrality of the SC on matters of international peace and security and to bring back into the framework of the UN Charter the discussion about the limits on the international legal regulation of the use of force.

The "War on Terror" and International Humanitarian Law

Shortly after 9/11 the US decided to launch a war against terror worldwide. The expression "war on terror" has come to acquire a technical legal meaning well beyond its rhetorical force. In particular, the US has claimed that this qualification would trigger the applicability of the law applicable to armed conflict. This choice, most likely prompted by the idea that the laws of war might have been less of an impediment to executive action than peacetime human rights standards, has proved to be highly controversial. First and foremost, to characterize the "war on terror" as an armed conflict is difficult under the 1949 Geneva Conventions. According to the latter, international armed conflict can only be an inter-state conflict, whereas a non-international armed conflict has to take place within the territory of one of the states parties to the Geneva Conventions. A de-localized transnational conflict of indefinite duration would not meet the requirements for an armed conflict under international humanitarian law (IHL). The US Supreme Court in the *Hamdan v Rumsfeld* case (126 S. Ct. 2749 (2006)) interpreted the scope of application of Common Article 3 (applicable to non-international armed conflicts) extremely broadly—as applying to all armed conflicts, which do not fall into the category of inter-state armed conflicts. Most likely inspired by the need to bring some minimum humanitarian guarantees to bear on the US administration war on terror, the Supreme Court's broad and bold interpretation has not met with international consensus. Its value, however, lies in having highlighted the need to interpret IHL creatively and in favor of humanitarian standards in order to overcome the rigidities of the categories created by the Geneva Conventions.

Another area in which the traditional understanding of IHL has been challenged is the legal status of terrorists. As is known, IHL provides for two types of legal status: combatants and civilians. The existence of a third category of "unlawful combatants" (Scheipers 2015), a claim put forward by some states, has been rejected by the ICRC, the ICTY, and the Israeli Supreme Court (Bianchi and Naqvi 2014: 597). The problem remains, however, of determining when civilians lose their immunity for "directly participating in the hostilities" and can therefore become the object of legitimate targeting. It is to be hoped that the ICRC *Interpretive Guidance on the Notion of Direct Participation in Hostilities* (2009) will contribute to establishing some degree of consensus among IHL actors. Indeed, the question of lawful targeting has dramatically come to the fore as regards the targeted killing of terrorist suspects (Melzer 2008). The United States has used self-defense to justify its conduct. In his 2010 Study on Targeted Killings (UN Doc A/HRC/14/24/Add. 6), the UN Special Rapporteur on extrajudicial, summary, or arbitrary executions criticized this approach, maintaining that the justification for a targeted killing cannot be provided under the rules on the use of force and that the issue of whether a specific killing is lawful depends on "whether it meets the requirements of IHL and human rights law (in the context of armed conflict) or human rights law alone (in all other contexts)" (§44). According to the Special Rapporteur, if "[o]utside the context of armed conflict, the use of drones for targeted killings is almost never likely to be legal," as it would hardly meet the human rights limitations on the use of lethal force (§85), IHL recourse to it must be appreciated against the background of strict conditions (like any other targeted killings), ranging from the need for state armed forces and agents to use all reasonably available sources (including technological ones such as intelligence and surveillance) to obtain reliable information to verify that the target is lawful, to ensuring that compliance with the IHL proportionality principle is assessed for each attack individually, and not for an overall military operation.

For persons captured as terrorist suspects during armed conflict, the determination of their status is the overriding issue, given that under IHL an individual's status determines which body of rules with regard to detention and treatment will apply (Bianchi and Naqvi 2014: 597ff.). Those terrorist suspects detained in situations where the threshold of armed conflict is unclear or outside the theaters of active hostilities, and, therefore, not appearing to benefit from protections under IHL, should retain their rights under human rights law, including the right to habeas corpus and the right to fair trial. Importantly, the US Supreme Court has repeatedly upheld the right of persons detained in relation to the so-called "war on terror" to have the legality of their detention determined by a court of law (*Boumediene v Bush*, 553 U.S. 723 (2008)).

Finally, it must be noted that terrorism and war should be clearly considered distinct phenomena. Terrorism comes under the regulation of IHL in limited circumstances, when the existence of an armed conflict can be established (Bianchi and Naqvi 2011; Duffy 2015). In particular, IHL prohibits acts of terrorism against the civilian population (Article 33 IV GC). Moreover, acts, the primary purpose of which is to spread terror among the civilian population, can be considered as war crimes (Article 51(2) I Additional Protocol to the Geneva Conventions). On these very grounds, in 2006 the ICTY condemned General Galic, the Bosnian-Serb militias' military commander in charge of the siege of Sarajevo (IT-98-29, judgment of Nov. 30, 2006). The ICTY Appeals Chamber held that the campaign of shelling and shooting civilians during the siege represented a war crime under customary international law, according to Article 3 of the ICTY Statute.

The Security Council's Normative Strategies

The UN Security Council (SC) has led the way in the international fight against terrorism as the organ in charge of the maintenance of international peace and security. Starting from Res. 1368/2001 condemning the 9/11 attacks, the SC has invariably qualified acts of international terrorism as threats to international peace and security. Such characterization triggers the UN Chapter VII sweeping powers that allow the SC's action to maintain or restore international peace and security, in particular its power to adopt decisions that are mandatory for all UN member states. Two are the normative strands of action undertaken by the SC to counter international terrorism. The first consists of acting in a quasi-legislative capacity by imposing general obligations on the UN member states—regardless of any particular situation or circumstance—and directing them about what to do to counter international terrorism (Szasz 2002). Res. 1373/2001, for example, partly took up the obligations laid down in the 1999 UN Convention for the Suppression of the Financing of Terrorism, thus making them universally applicable, and partly put forward other fairly sweeping obligations covering different aspects of terrorism prevention and repression. Res. 1373 also established a Counterterrorism Committee to supervise the proper implementation of its obligations by states. Likewise, Res. 2178/2014 on foreign terrorist fighters directs states to criminalize the conduct of their nationals who travel abroad "for the purpose of the perpetration, planning, or preparation of, or participation in terrorist acts, or the providing or receiving of terrorist training" (§5). The recruitment and providing of funds for such purposes should also be prohibited in domestic law, and considered as a serious criminal offence (§6).

Its lack of representativity, and in particular the privileged position of the five permanent members; the conspicuous absence of a "legal mindset" in the operations and practices performed; and the fact that it was originally created to maintain peace and security and not to act as a world government, have been invoked as good reasons to hold that the SC should not act in a quasi-legislative fashion (Koskenniemi 1995). In fact, the textual constraints in the Charter are tenuous, and the wide measure of discretion that the SC enjoys in deciding by what means to discharge its mission under Chapter VII, makes the argument that the SC should not undertake law-making activities as a matter of UN law rather flimsy. Moreover, whatever criticism one may raise against the SC acting as lawmaker, it is fair to acknowledge that its action under Chapter VII of the UN Charter is the only form of law-making in international law that can produce generally applicable law in a short time span (Bianchi 2006a: 8–9). Customary international law requires time to establish itself via the generality of state practice. Multilateral treaties, in turn, are difficult to negotiate and to adopt in a community of over 195 states, and can only be effective on a large scale if a significant number of states end up ratifying them. Whenever there is a perception that prompt normative action is needed at the international law level—be it to counter international terrorism, to put up with the outbreak and spread of an infectious disease, or to face the consequences of a natural catastrophe—the SC law-making process is the only one available to meet such concerns. The SC can adopt universally binding resolutions in a few hours and thus make up for the shortcomings of international law when it comes to the need for producing quickly generally applicable law. Perhaps, as highlighted by some SC members in the debate surrounding the adoption of another quasi-legislative resolution—Res. 1540/2004 on the acquisition of weapons of mass destruction by non-state actors—such law-making should be limited to cases in which no other international law rules are applicable, and when it is urgent that action is taken internationally to counter specific threats. One may add that it would also be desirable that the GA provide the SC with political backing any time the SC intends to act as general lawmaker. Widespread political consensus within the GA, possibly attested by the adoption of a resolution, would certainly help the SC's action to be perceived as more legitimate.

The other strand of action that the SC has actively pursued is the imposition of targeted sanctions on individuals and corporate entities affiliated with terrorist networks. In 1999 the SC adopted Res. 1267 to sanction the Taliban for harboring and training terrorists in the territory of Afghanistan as well as for their refusal to surrender Osama bin Laden. The resolution followed the terrorist attacks against the US embassies in Kenya and Tanzania the previous year and was meant to hit, by way of targeted sanctions, the governing elite and its economic interests. By its terms, Res. 1267/1999 imposed on the Taliban, inter alia, a ban on travel, an arms embargo, and, above all, the freezing of their assets worldwide. A Sanctions Committee was established to draw up a list of targeted individuals and entities against which the sanctions had to be applied (Ginsborg 2014). The Committee was also in charge of considering the de-listing of individuals from the "blacklist" and of reviewing the implementation reports that states must submit to the SC. SC Res. 1333 expanded the reach of the freezing measures to Osama bin Laden, Al Qaeda, and its affiliates. After the demise of the Taliban, the SC passed Res. 1390/2002 that reiterated the sanctions already enacted in Res. 1330. For the first time, however, Res. 1390 presented an open-ended character, the SC's measures not referring to any particular state. By Res. 1526, the SC created the Analytical Support and Sanctions Monitoring Team with a view to providing the Sanctions Committee with technical assistance in managing the sanctions. In 2011 the SC decided to split up the two regimes (Tladi and Taylor 2011). Res. 1989, as subsequently modified, reiterated the sanctions against Al Qaeda affiliates and envisaged the possibility for the Ombudsperson to recommend the de-listing of individuals or corporate entities from the Consolidated List. Finally, Res. 2253/2015 extended the sanctions regime to Islamic State (ISIL). Besides reasserting the assets freeze, travel ban, arms embargo, and listing criteria for ISIL, Al Qaeda, and "associated individuals, groups, undertaking and entities," the resolution reminded states of their obligation to ensure that their nationals and persons in their territory not make available economic resources to those actors—which applied to both direct and indirect trade in oil, among other natural resources. The newly renamed "1267/1989/2253 ISIL (Da'esh) and Al-Qaeda Sanctions Committee" will be in charge of listing and de-listing individuals and entities as well as of reviewing the implementation reports submitted by states, while the Al Qaeda Sanctions List would now be known as the "ISIL (Da'esh) and Al-Qaeda Sanctions List."

Targeted sanctions have proved to be highly controversial for their lack of due process guarantees. Despite the introduction of an Ombudsperson in 2009, and the subsequent expansion of its mandate and powers, the sanctions, issued by a political organ that hardly meets the requirements of an impartial and independent tribunal under human rights due process standards, still do not provide for any right to be heard, let alone a right to an effective remedy for their recipients. Although, in principle, the sanctions are temporary in character, they may nonetheless also result in a substantial (and prolonged) prejudice to the enjoyment of the right to property. Encroachment on such fundamental rights and liberties has caused legal challenges to be brought before judicial bodies, both nationally and internationally.

International and Domestic Legal Challenges

International judicial organs have expressed their preoccupation with the need to strike a fair balance between security and human rights concerns (Gearty 2013). In particular, they have stressed the need, sometimes ambiguously, not to yield to the imperatives of collective security at the price of jeopardizing fundamental human rights (Bianchi 2008). In this context, the case law of the European Union judicial organs is of particular note. Their exercise of judicial review over anti-terrorism sanctions has been very important in promoting awareness of the risks inherent in the enforcement of such sanctions. Little matters whether the basis for the exercise of such judicial review has been controversial or whether some of the arguments used were not deprived of inconsistencies and ambiguities. It suffices to think of the different approach to the *Kadi* case respectively taken by the Court of First Instance (now the General Court) and the European Court of Justice (see the judgments of the CFI of September 21, 2005 in *Kadi v Council of the EU and the Commission of the EC*, Case T-315/01, (2005) ECR II-3649; and the more recent decision by the European Court of Justice in Joined Cases C-402/05 P and C-415/05 P, *Kadi v Council of the EU and Commission of the EC*, (2008) ECR I-6351, judgment of September 3, 2008). The Court of First Instance held that—although Article 103 of the UN Charter gives priority to the obligations stemming from the Charter over other conflicting treaty obligations—the Security Council is bound to respect *jus cogens*, i.e. peremptory rules of human rights law. The European Court of Justice (ECJ) overruled the judgment of the lower court, by maintaining that, regardless of any alleged supremacy of UN law as a matter of international law, EU judicial organs must exercise full judicial review over any EU legal act against the background of the constitutive treaties, in particular Article 6 of the Treaty on European Union, providing that the European Union shall respect fundamental human rights. In the case at hand, the ECJ found that Mr Kadi's rights of defense, effective judicial protection, and property had been infringed.

What needs be underscored, however, is that the European Court of Justice clearly expressed willingness not to abdicate from its responsibility to ensure respect for fundamental rights in the name of an alleged supremacy of SC measures. This attitude has been reiterated throughout the long *Kadi* saga before the European Union's judicial organs, until the latest judgments (*Kadi v European Council & Commission*, Case T-85/09, (2010) ECR II-5177, Judgment of the General Court of September 30, 2010; and, lastly, *European Commission & the Council of the European Union v Kadi*, joined Cases C-584/10 P, C-593/10 P (2013), (2013) ECR-00000, Judgment of the Court of Justice of the European Union of July 18, 2013)). At the same time, the European Court of Human Rights has distinguished and limited the scope of the unfortunate *Behrami* doctrine (*Behrami v France* and *Saramati v France, Germany and Norway*, Grand Chamber of the ECHR, Applications nos. 71412/01 and 78166/01, Decision on Admissibility of May 2, 2007, §§148ff.), which postulated the pre-eminence of UN Charter obligations over conflicting treaty obligations including the European Convention's—to adopt a more nuanced approach, which hinges upon several interpretive strands. In *Al-Jedda v UK* (Grand Chamber of the ECtHR, Application no. 27021/08, Judgment of July 7, 2011, §102) the Court put forward the presumption of consistency of Security Council's resolutions with human rights as an interpretive principle that could avoid conflict in most cases. Furthermore, in *Nada v Switzerland* (Grand Chamber of the ECtHR, Application no. 10593/08, Judgment of September 12, 2012, §§178–80), the Court insisted on the latitude of discretion that states might still enjoy in implementing Security Council's resolutions, thus allowing for human rights protection mechanisms to apply even to cases involving the implementation of UN sanctions. Finally, in *Al-Dulimi v Switzerland* (Application no. 5809/08, Second Section of the ECtHR, Judgment of November 26, 2013), the European Court brushed up its long-neglected "equivalent protection doctrine" to state that as long as the UN does not provide its sanctions system with an adequate system of human rights protection, European Convention's Contracting Parties will have to apply the Convention's rights.

A cursory comparative overview of domestic case law in the aftermath of 9/11 confirms the judiciary's vocation to act as guarantor and arbitrator in situations of emergency, particularly vis-à-vis the executive's policies. Even if judicial decisions have to be contextualized and analyzed against the background of both the domestic legal system in which they are rendered and the particulars of underlying factual matrices, some similarities can be traced. On this basis, some room for generalization seems to be possible, particularly in terms of outcomes, and interpretive techniques used by domestic courts (Benvenisti 2008; Scobbie 2008).

The decisions rendered by the Israeli Supreme Court in its exercise of judicial review over two highly controversial practices of the Israeli Defense Forces, namely human shielding and targeted killings, are illustrative of the judicial approach to check executive action in times of emergency (*Adalah (The Legal Center for Arab Minority Rights in Israel)* et al. *v GOC Central Command, IDF* et al., Case No. HCJ 3799/02, Supreme Court of Israel Sitting as the High Court of Justice, June 23, 2005; and *Public Committee against Torture in Israel v Government of Israel*, Case No. HCJ 769/02, Supreme Court of Israel, sitting as the High Court of Justice, December 13, 2006.). In particular, in its 2006 decision the Supreme Court categorically refused the contention set forth by the executive that its acts were non-justiciable and resorted instead to balancing techniques and the principle of proportionality to evaluate the lawfulness of targeted killings. Although the judgment attracted criticism from those who would have wished the Court to condemn targeted killings *tout court*, rather than assessing their lawful character on a case by case basis in light of relevant circumstances, there is no doubt that the Israeli Supreme Court wanted to assert its role as both watchdog of the executive's conduct (even in areas clearly amenable within the executive's prerogatives) and guarantor of fundamental human rights. In doing so it drew heavily from international law arguments.

Similar considerations apply to the 2004 judgment in the *Belmarsh detainees* case (*A (FC) v Secretary of State for the Home Department*, [2004] UKHL 56), in which the then House of Lords (now the Supreme Court) held the UK legislation allowing for the indefinite detention of foreign terrorist suspects in cases where they could not be returned to their home country, to be in breach of the Human Rights Act, the UK enabling legislation for the European Convention on Human Rights. While acknowledging the executive's power to determine the existence of a state of emergency, the House of Lords proceeded to exercise its judicial review against the backdrop of Strasbourg case law. The Court eventually held the measures inconsistent with the requirements of the Human Rights Act for their lack of proportionality as regards the aim pursued and for their discriminatory character as regards the treatment of foreign nationals. The principle of proportionality seems to have provided the rule of decision also in the decision by the German *Bundesverfassungsgericht* in the case concerning the constitutionality of the legislation that allowed, in certain circumstances related to terrorist hijacking, the shooting down of civilian aircraft (1 BvR 375/05, judgment of Feb. 15, 2006). The Court found the legislation in breach of the constitutional provisions protecting human dignity and stressed that anti-terror measures must be proportionate to the aim pursued.

Also the decision by the Supreme Court of Canada in the *Charkahoui v Canada* case ([2007] S.C.C. 9, [2007] 1 SCR 350) is worth mentioning in this context. The Court ascertained the inconsistency of aliens' deportation on the basis of intelligence information with the Canadian Charter of Rights and Freedoms. In exercising its judicial review in the case at hand the Court went well beyond what it had previously said in 2002 in *Suresh v Canada* ([2002] 1 S.C.C. 3.). At closer scrutiny, however, even as regards *Suresh* the Court had set limits on the executive's conduct. While admitting in the abstract the possibility of returning an individual to a country in which she or he would risk being subjected to human rights violations, by requiring the executive to put in writing the reasons for its decision, the Court imposed a requirement which the government could not easily meet.

Finally, it is also worth noting that the US Supreme Court, less sensitive than other national high courts to external influences, has occasionally resorted, albeit *ad abundantiam*, to international law arguments in order to ascertain the unconstitutionality of some domestic law provisions. This was the case in *Hamdan v Rumsfeld* (126 S. Ct. 2749 (2006)), in which the Supreme Court, in holding military commissions established by Presidential authority unconstitutional, made reference to common Article 3 of the Geneva Conventions. In particular, the Court held that military commissions were inconsistent with the provisions of the Uniform Code of Military Justice and gave rise to a violation of the right to be tried by a "regularly constituted court" requirement of common Article 3. The acknowledgment of the Geneva Conventions standards as appropriate legal parameters for a constitutional decision is certainly a novelty for the US. Even if this argument was somewhat ancillary, as it did not provide the rule of decision, reference by the Court to international humanitarian law standards allowed the incorporation into the US legal system of normative values, the use of which remains rare in the US. The issue here is not whether the Supreme Court made a correct use of Article 3, in particular as regards its scope of application. Rather, what is relevant is that the Supreme Court for the first time made reference to international standards in assessing the lawfulness of measures taken in the context of the "war on terror."

It is stunning to realize that most of the legal measures that have turned out to encroach on human rights were adopted in a relatively short time span following the 9/11 attacks, when the prevailing feeling was fear (Bianchi 2010). Democracies' main challenge is to protect their foundational tenets not only from the exogenous threat of international terrorism, but also from the endogenous risk represented by the measures taken to counter it and by the institutional imbalances that their implementation may create. Fear cannot be the founding principle of democracies, except for short periods of time and under strict judicial control (Bianchi 2010, 191).

States of Emergency and Human Rights Constraints

In international law, the conduct of states that would like to invoke exceptional circumstances to derogate from their international obligations in times of public emergency is constrained by human rights instruments. In particular, many human rights treaties provide for the possibility of derogating from some of the rights and liberties enshrined in them at a time of public emergency (so-called "derogation clauses"), when the life of the nation is threatened. What situation may amount to a threat to the life of the nation is no easy matter to be determined once and for all, and it may well depend on countries' particular sensitivities. Human rights supervisory organs have been quite flexible in accepting states' individual determinations, and the European Court of Human Rights has acknowledged the existence of a wide measure of discretion by states in this area, applying to the interpretation of the derogation clause (Article 15) the margin of appreciation doctrine. According to the latter, states are in a better position to make an initial assessment of whether there is a state of emergency, whereas the Strasbourg court retains the final word to check whether their individual determination is compatible with the Convention's standards.

Most importantly, however, state action in states of emergency is subject to a strict proportionality test. Only those measures that are strictly required by the exigencies of the situation can be justified. This entails the burden of proving the necessity of the enacted measures, and the impossibility for states to put up with the situation that has caused the state of emergency by applying the extant legislation. States may not derogate from all rights and liberties and the various human rights instruments list a number of non-derogable rights that must be respected at all times. The lists differ from one another with a core four non-derogable rights being recognized by all of them (right not to be deprived arbitrarily of one's life; right to be free from torture and from slavery; right not to be subjected to the retroactivity of criminal law). The need to expand the list of non-derogable rights listed in human rights treaties, all of which have been adopted quite some time ago, has been a reason for the Human Rights Committee to suggest in its General Comment 29 of 2001 (U.N. Doc. CCPR/C/21/Rev.1/Add.11) that also other rights should be considered as non-derogable. The latter would include rights, such as procedural judicial guarantees, which are instrumental to ensure that substantive non-derogable rights are respected (you cannot ascertain whether someone has been tortured unless one has access to a judge to establish the legality of his or her arrest and detention), as well as rights that are considered non-derogable as peremptory norms of international law (*jus cogens*), or under specific regimes such as international humanitarian law.

States must notify international supervisory bodies of their intention to derogate, specifying by what measures and for how long. Regrettably, an overview of the Human Rights Committee's practice reveals that states frequently do not comply with notification requirements, by failing to notify internationally a state of emergency which has been internally declared; by not declaring officially a state of emergency while at the same time adopting special legislation on such grounds; by failing to repeal long-established states of emergency thus infringing on the very nature of the regime, under which restrictions must be temporary and aimed at re-establishing a state of normalcy as soon as possible; or by not disclosing full information about the derogations and by not giving a clear explanation of the reasons for their adoption (Bianchi 2004, 521).

Fairly precise legal standards for states of emergency have been laid down in treaties, and their judicial interpretation by courts and supervisory bodies has enormously contributed to their refinement. To hold that international law has no clear parameters on how to strike the balance between national security interests and human rights in such grey areas as states of emergencies, where the life of the nation is threatened by terrorist groups or otherwise, is at best an unfounded or inaccurate claim. The fact that states may disregard such standards is less evidence of the alleged inadequacy of international law than a clue that what states do by ratifying human rights treaties is often no more than indulging in a rhetorical exercise of self-complacency.

Outlook

It appears that rather than an increase of normative standards and applicable rules, international law would need a comprehensive and internationally agreed-upon strategy of implementation of the existing ones (Bianchi 2004, 525ff.). The marked unilateralism adopted by the US in the aftermath of 9/11 has no doubt jeopardized a more coordinated and effective effort to counter terrorism. Mutual trust and cooperation have long been needed, and they seem to have been only partly restored by the need to counter the threat of Islamic State. The response, however, remains primarily geared toward undermining the financing of terrorist organizations and networks, and countering the threat by security measures and the use of force. International law has been mainly used as an instrument to help implement such a strategy. Only occasionally has international law been called upon to articulate a more holistic response to international terrorism.

The main pillars of a holistic approach to fighting terrorism were laid down in the UN global strategy against terrorism, adopted by consensus by the UN General Assembly in 2006 (A/RES/60/288, September 20, 2006, reaffirmed on November 8, 2010). There for the first time the need to address the conditions conducive to terrorism, to ensure respect for human rights and the rule of law, and to enhance states' capacity building were presented as fundamental components of a comprehensive anti-terror strategy, together with the traditional policy of preventing and punishing acts of terrorism. The challenge of how effectively to implement this strategy, however, remains a daunting task. Integration of the relevant principles and norms into the action of international and domestic actors engaged in the fight against terrorism must be achieved through a set of coherent policies to be designed and implemented "on the ground." Along similar lines, the coordination among institutions involved in the fight against terrorism must be improved, as the proliferation of international bodies and UN agencies makes concerted action difficult at times.

To find concrete ways in which the coordination of norms and institutional policies can lead to the implementation of an effective holistic approach to fighting terrorism is the challenge lying ahead for the international community. The central role played in such an approach by respect for human rights and the rule of law will contribute to its legitimacy and increase its chances of efficacy and stability in the long term. Only by consolidating a narrative based on respect for human rights and the rule of law, can the international community aspire to the eradication of terrorism. In the absence of a culture based on the rule of law, there will always be the temptation for states to resort to security forces, and even to the army, in order to counter terrorist threats. The other fundamental message to convey to national and international decision-makers is that security concerns naturally underpin growth and sustainable development. Societies in which huge resources are channeled into law enforcement and military force in order to respond to security threats and social unrest stand little chance of achieving economic development. The new challenge and the real paradigm shift, particularly at times of increasing terrorist violence, lies in thinking of counterterrorism as a precondition for economic growth and sustainable development.

References

Baxter, Richard R. (1973–4) "A Skeptical Look at the Concept of Terrorism," *Akron Law Review*, 7: 380–7.

Benvenisti, Eyal (2008) "United we Stand: National Courts Reviewing Counterterrorism Measures," in Andrea Bianchi and Alexis Keller (eds), *Counterterrorism: Democracy's Challenge*. Oxford: Hart Publishing, 251–76.

Bianchi, Andrea (2004) "Enforcing International Law Norms against Terrorism: Achievements and Prospects," in Andrea Bianchi (ed.), *Enforcing International Law Norms against Terrorism*. Oxford: Hart Publishing, 491–534.

Bianchi, Andrea (2006a) "Assessing the Effectiveness of the UN Security Council's Anti-Terrorism Measures: The Quest for Legitimacy and Cohesion," *European Journal of International Law*, 17: 880–919.

Bianchi Andrea (2006b) "Security Council's Anti-Terror Resolutions and their Implementation by Member States: An Overview," *Journal of International Criminal Justice*, 4: 1044–73.

Bianchi, Andrea (2008) "International Law, Counter-terrorism and the Quest for Checks and Balances," in Andrea Bianchi and Alexis Keller (eds), *Counterterrorism: Democracy's Challenge*. Oxford: Hart Publishing, 395–424.

Bianchi, Andrea (2009) "The International Regulation of the Use of Force: The Politics of Interpretive Method," *Leiden Journal of International Law*, 22: 651–76.

Bianchi, Andrea (2010) "Fear's Legal Dimension: Counterterrorism and Human Rights," in L. Boisson de Chazournes and M. Kohen (eds), *International Law and the Quest for its Implementation: Le droit international et la quête de sa mise en oeuvre*, Liber Amicorum Vera Gowlland-Debbas. Leiden/Boston: Martinus Nijhoff, 175–92.

Bianchi, Andrea, and Yasmin Naqvi (2011) *International Humanitarian Law and Terrorism*. Oxford: Hart Publishing.

Bianchi, Andrea, and Yasmin Naqvi (2014) "Terrorism," in Andrew Clapham and Paola Gaeta (eds), *Oxford Handbook of International Law in Armed Conflict*. Oxford: Oxford University Press, 574–604.

Blumenau, Bernhard (2014) *The United Nations and Terrorism: Germany, Multilateralism and Antiterrorism Efforts in the 1970s*. Basingstoke: Palgrave Macmillan.

Cassese, Antonio (2006) "The Multifaceted Criminal Notion of Terrorism in International Law," *Journal of International Criminal Justice*, 4: 933–58.

Chatham House (2006) "Chatham House Principles of International Law on the Use of Force in Self-Defence," *International and Comparative Law Quarterly*, 55: 963–72.

Dinstein, Yoram (2011) *War, Aggression and Self-Defence*, 5th edn. Cambridge: Cambridge University Press.

Duffy, Helen (2015) *The "War on Terror" and the Framework of International Law*, 2nd edn. Cambridge: Cambridge University Press.

Gearty, Conor (2007) "Terrorism and Human Rights," *Government and Opposition*, 42: 340–62.

Gearty, Conor (2013) *Liberty and Security*. Cambridge: Polity.

Ginsborg, Lisa (2014) "The United Nations Security Council's Counter-Terrorism Al-Qaida Sanctions Regime: Resolution 1267 and the 1267 Committee," in Ben Saul (ed.), *Research Handbook of International Law and Terrorism*. Cheltenham: Edward Elgar, 608–25.

Higgins, Rosalyn (1997) "The General International Law of Terrorism," in Rosalyn Higgins and Maurice Flory (eds) *Terrorism and International Law*. London: Routledge, 13–29.

Koskenniemi, Martti (1995) "The Police in the Temple: Order, Justice and the UN: A Dialectical View," *European Journal of International Law*, 5: 325–48.

Leiden (2013) *Leiden Policy Recommendations on Counterterrorism and International Law*, published as an Annex in Larissa van den Herik and Nico Schrijver (eds), *Counterterrorism Strategies in a Fragmented International Order*. Cambridge: Cambridge University Press, 702–26.

Melzer, Nils (2008) *Targeted Killing in International Law*. Oxford: Oxford University Press.

Saul, Ben (2006) *Defining Terrorism in International Law*. Oxford: Oxford University Press.

Scheipers, Sibylle (2015) *Unlawful Combatants: A Genealogy of the Irregular Fighter*. Oxford: Oxford University Press.

Schmid, Alex P. (2004) "Terrorism and the Definitional Problem," *Case Western Reserve Journal of International Law*, 36: 375–419.

Schmid, Alex P. (2013) "The Definition of Terrorism," in Alex P. Schmid (ed.), *The Routledge Handbook of Terrorism Research*. Abingdon: Routledge, 30–99.

Scobbie, Iain (2008) "The Last Refuge of the Tyrant? Judicial Deference to Executive Actions in Time of Terror," in Andrea Bianchi and Alexis Keller (eds), *Counterterrorism: Democracy's Challenge*. Oxford: Hart Publishing, 277–312.

Szasz, Paul (2002) "The Security Council Starts Legislating," *American Journal of International Law*, 96: 901–4.

Tams, Christian (2009) "The Use of Force against Terrorists," *European Journal of International Law*, 20: 359–97.

Tladi, Dire, and Taylor, Gillian (2011) "On the Al Qaida/Taliban Sanctions Regime: Due Process and Sunsetting," *Chinese Journal of International Law*, 10: 771–89.

CHAPTER 43

TORTURE AND THE WAR ON TERRORISM

COURTENAY R. CONRAD

GOVERNMENT leaders face strong incentives to prevent terrorist attacks. In addition to its human costs, terrorism has negative economic and political implications for target states, harming their economies by decreasing foreign direct investment (FDI) (Enders and Sandler, 2006), trade (Nitsch and Schumacher 2004), and economic growth (Blomberg et al. 2004), and in democracies, influencing voting patterns and decreasing popular support for incumbent leaders (Berrebi and Klor 2006). As part of the global war on terrorism that began following the September 11, 2001 terrorist attacks on the United States, governments including Russia, China, Egypt, Malaysia, Saudi Arabia, Uzbekistan, Algeria, and Yemen have justified the use of torture to thwart terrorist threats (Amnesty International 2008). In response, international nongovernmental organizations (NGOs) like Amnesty International (AI) have repeatedly and consistently accused these governments—including democracies like the United States—of turning a blind eye to both international and domestic laws prohibiting torture.[1] In spite of this international pressure, even democratic leaders have been hesitant to promise to stop using torture as a counterterrorism strategy. In 2008, President George W. Bush defended the Central Intelligence Agency's (CIA) use of "enhanced interrogation practices," asserting the importance of giving intelligence officials "all the tools they need to stop the terrorists" (Bush 2008).

In this chapter, I review scholarly theory and empirical results concerning the relationship between terrorism and government torture. After providing working definitions of both concepts, I turn to the broader literatures on opposition dissent and state repression and argue that terrorism and torture are forms of dissent and repression, respectively. Recognizing terrorism and torture as subsets of broader conceptualizations common in the literature on political violence provides insights into the conditions under which governments respond to opposition activity with violence (and vice versa) in the context of terrorism. Following this discussion of the literature on political violence, I then present a summary of the behavioral incentives—and disincentives—that government authorities face regarding using torture as part of a counterterrorism strategy. In addition to discussing behavioral incentives to violate human rights, I also review literature about the mediating influence of domestic political institutions on the relationship between terrorism and torture, arguing that democracy does not always constrain—and sometimes incentivizes—government torture. I conclude the chapter with a discussion of unresolved challenges in the scholarly study of political violence, suggesting potential directions for future research on terrorism and torture, specifically, and dissent and repression, generally.

Conceptualizing Terrorism as Dissent and Torture as Repression

The United States Code, title 22, chapter 38, section 2656f(d) defines terrorism as the use of "premeditated, politically motivated violence against noncombatant targets by subnational groups or clandestine agents, usually intended to influence an audience."[2] Although policymakers and scholars often discuss terrorism as unique both in the extent to which terrorists wish to change government policy and in the extent to which they are willing to employ violence directed at civilians, terrorism is a form of dissent against the government. Popular dissent against the state broadly occurs when non-state actors act to collectively to (threaten to) impose costs on the incumbent government to change a particular policy or set of policies (Lichbach 1998). Terrorists engage in "a more marginalized and extreme form of violent collective action" (Daxecker 2017), but their basic goals are the same as those of non-terrorist dissidents: to convince government authorities to change status quo policies or face the costly consequences of failing to do so.

Just as terrorism is a subset of opposition dissent against the government, torture is one of many options in the state's repressive arsenal. In the last twenty years, a large scholarly literature has emerged on the causes and consequences of government repression, which includes realized or threatened coercive action undertaken by governments to control or prevent challenges to the status quo (Davenport 2007; Goldstein 1978; Lichbach 1998). This conceptualization of repression easily includes government torture, defined by the United Nations Convention against Torture and Other Cruel, Inhuman or Degrading Treatment or Punishment (CAT) as

> any act by which severe pain or suffering, whether physical or mental, is intentionally inflicted on a person for such purposes as obtaining from him or a third person information or a confession, punishing him for an act he or a third person has committed or is suspected of having committed, or intimidating or coercing him or a third person, or for any reason based on discrimination of any kind, when such pain or suffering is inflicted by or at the instigation of or with the consent or acquiescence of a public official or other person acting in an official capacity. It does not include pain or suffering arising only from, inherent in or incidental to lawful sanctions.

One of the most well-known theoretical expectations in the academic study of political violence is the positive association between opposition dissent and government repression: when governments face dissent, they almost always respond by violating human rights. The relationship between dissent and repression is so well-known that it has been referred to as the Law of Coercive Responsiveness (Davenport 2007) or Threat-Response Theory (Earl et al. 2003). Governments aiming to quell dissent with repression have many tactics at their disposal; responses to dissent can include violent repression—targeted specifically at dissenters or the general population—and non-violent restrictions on political rights and civil liberties, which are often indiscriminately applied to the general population. Scholars have shown indiscriminate violence against civilians—non-dissenters and non-terrorists—to be ineffective as a means to control dissent (Kocher et al. 2011), eliminate insurgency (Findley and Young 2007; Sullivan 2014), and reduce terrorist attacks (Dugan and Chenoweth 2012; Walsh and Piazza 2010). As such, where dissent is prevalent, governments often prefer to respond with other forms of repression: by eliminating widespread protections for human rights (Hafner-Burton and Shapiro 2010), including the freedoms of association and speech, and by violating the physical integrity rights—the rights not to be politically imprisoned, killed, tortured, or disappeared by the government (Cingranelli and Richards 1999)—of specific individuals suspected of dissident and/or terrorist activity.

Although there is general agreement that governments respond to opposition dissent with repression in theory, scholars have found mixed empirical evidence to support the relationship.[3] This lack of empirical evidence likely occurs not because repression and dissent are unrelated, but because they are endogenous: governments and potential dissidents decide how to behave—whether to dissent, whether to repress, and extent to which to engage in violence—in anticipation of one another's behavior (Pierskalla 2010; Ritter 2014; Ritter and Conrad 2015). For example, citizens who expect to face repression may choose not to dissent in the first place (Fearon and Laitin 2003; Hibbs 1973; Moore 1995). Government authorities may also engage in preventive repression prior to mobilization (Danneman and Ritter 2014; Nordås and Davenport 2013; Ritter and Conrad 2015). As such, failure to see realized repression in response to dissent (and vice versa) does not necessarily mean that no relationship exists between the two.

The relationship between terrorist activity and government torture is similarly strategic: terrorists anticipate the actions of the government when making decisions about potential attacks, and governments consider the expected behaviors of terrorists in drafting counterterrorism policies to include torture. Anecdotally, there is ample evidence suggesting that governments—from military regimes in South America (Sullivan 2014) to democracies including Great Britain and Spain (Art and Richardson 2007)—respond systematically to terrorism by violating human rights including the right not to be tortured. Because the relationship between terrorism and torture is also subject to concerns about endogeneity, however, scholars have presented mixed empirical evidence about the general relationship between terrorist attacks and subsequent torture with some scholars finding no relationship (e.g. Charters, 1994) and others showing a differential effect across physical integrity violations (e.g. Piazza and Walsh 2009).[4]

Because of the endogenous relationship and mixed empirical results between opposition dissent and government repression—and terrorism and torture—I turn to a detailed discussion of the incentives that governments face to violate human rights when they are confronted with dissent and terrorism. Although there is empirical evidence to suggest that governments respond to threats with repression (Conrad and Moore 2010; Davenport et al. 2007; Wantchekon and Healy 1999), there also exist behavioral and institutional incentives not to respond to terrorist activity by engaging in torture. In the following two sections, I examine the (dis)incentives of states to dissent with repression, generally, and to respond to terrorism with torture, specifically. I conclude the chapter by discussing several difficulties—and potential solutions for those difficulties—that will be of interest to scholars and policymakers who seek to determine the relationship between terrorism and torture.

Terrorism and Behavioral Incentives (not) to Engage in Torture

Terrorist organizations are notoriously secretive (Lake 2002). Because they are weak relative to traditional governments, lacking both the material capabilities and the popular support to engage in traditional warfare (Crenshaw 1998; Kydd and Walter 2006; Lake 2002), terrorists face incentives to behave clandestinely and misrepresent their preferences and capabilities. Although governments often attempt to negotiate with terrorist groups (Jones and Libicki 2008), the clandestine activities of terrorist organizations increase the probability of bargaining failures and make negotiations difficult. As a result, rather than only bargain and negotiate with terrorists, the counterterrorism policies of many states tend to focus on the deterrence of future threats.

Government policies to stop terrorist activities and prevent attacks are broad and far-reaching, applied equally across both terrorists and non-terrorist citizens within a given country. In the United States, for example, the 9/11 Commission Report concluded that the government severely restricted broad civil liberties following the September 11, 2001 terrorist attacks (Kean 2011). Many other governments also adopted anti-terror legislation as part of the war on terror. In Tunisia, for example, critics have pointed out that statutes to criminalize terrorism were extended to limit civil and political rights more broadly (Amnesty International 2008). Limiting widespread protections—the right to freedom of association and assembly, for example—is thought to minimize the extent to which dissidents are able to publicize their grievances and garner support for anti-government policies from among the general population (Gearty 2007; Hoffman 1998).

Indiscriminate human rights violations require less intelligence about the origin of dissident and terrorist activity and are easier to implement than targeted repression (Kalyvas 2004), but the application of widespread violence comes at a cost. By definition, indiscriminate violence victimizes even nonterrorists. These victimized individuals may consequently turn against the government following the experience of violence, and terrorist organizations often seem a good refuge for retribution against the government. Counterinsurgency operations are similarly more likely to fail when the government uses harsh repression, and particularly when that repression is directed at civilians (Joes 2006). As a result, governments face incentives to engage in targeted repression—repression directed at suspected terrorists and other key individuals who can provide information about terrorist plans and activities.

Although many forms of repression can be targeted rather than used indiscriminately, governments have historically used torture as an important component of their counterterrorism strategy. Although torture is illegal under international and most domestic law (Keith 2002), it is the most widely violated right to physical integrity protections (Cingranelli and Richards 1999); Amnesty International (AI) accuses most governments of torture in most years (Conrad et al. 2013; Conrad and Moore 2010). Although there is empirical evidence to suggest that governments respond to terrorist attacks by heightening targeted killings and disappearances and not by engaging in heightened torture (Piazza and Walsh 2009), there are at least two reasons to believe that torture is particularly appealing relative to other forms of government repression.

First, governments direct their repressive agents to use torture in an effort to generate intelligence information that may help to deter future terrorist attacks.[5] Torture techniques are used to elicit information from suspected terrorists—about plans for future attacks, motivations behind previous attacks, and the identities of terrorist group members (Dershowitz 2002; Ignatieff 2013). In addition to itself being a targeted form of violence, torture can potentially provide government authorities with information that helps them better target future violence against specific individuals involved in terrorist activity. In addition to encouraging terrorist suspects to provide additional information, torture techniques have historically been employed against detainees to establish the veracity of testimony (Rejali 2007).

Second, torture is often used to instill a sense of fear in both the individual being subjected to torture and in potential terrorist supporters and sympathizers who are made aware of the fact that torture occurred. Sullivan (2014) argues that one of the "desired results" of torture is to "create a link between disobedient behavior and pain, thereby reinforcing legal norms by associating transgression with negative sanctions." During the Algerian War, for example, the French Army is reported to have randomly tortured Algerian citizens to instill a sense of fear in the general population (DiMarco 2006).

In spite of the incentives to engage in torture following terrorist attacks, however, not all governments purport to do so. In 2007, UK Prime Minister Gordon Brown expressed such a sentiment before a meeting of the Labour Party: "We cannot win this [war on terror] militarily or by policing or intelligence alone. We need to engage people so that we can win the battle of hearts and minds" (Branigan 2007). Echoing British sentiment in the same year, the United States' military's new counterinsurgency doctrine manual highlighted the importance of respecting human rights, pointing out that failure to do so could result in grievances that would be counterproductive to counterterrorism and counterinsurgency operations (Piazza and Walsh 2010b).

Scholars are mixed as to the general effect of repression on dissent, providing no consensus as to whether the violation of human rights inhibits or exacerbates terrorist activity. Research on the general effect of government repression on opposition dissent at times supports a negative relationship (e.g. Hibbs 1973), a positive relationship (e.g. Francisco 1996), and no relationship at all (e.g. Gurr and Moore 1997). Empirical studies on the effect of human rights violations specifically on terrorism are also mixed. General restrictions on human rights have been argued to increase terrorism (e.g. Piazza and Walsh 2010a), reduce terrorism (e.g. Abrahms 2007), and to have a curvilinear effect on terrorism (e.g. Kurrild-Klitgaard et al. 2006).[6]

The government's use of torture, in particular, has similarly been argued to have mixed effects on opposition violence, with scholars arguing torture is associated with increased terrorist activity (Walsh and Piazza 2010) and a lack of reduction in insurgent violence (Sullivan 2014), but also with deterrent effects in case-study research (Lyall 2009) and under more limited conditions (Opp and Roehl 1990). In addition to the endogeneity concerns already raised, these mixed results are likely because despite the incentives that governments face to repress in response to terrorism, there are nevertheless costs associated with the violation of human rights. In what follows, I discuss concerns with the quality of intelligence garnered via torture, as well as the extent to which the government's use of torture alienates the general population in a manner that increases the likelihood of future terrorist attacks (Hafner-Burton and Shapiro 2010).

Although intelligence gathering is often cited as a reason to turn to torture in an effort to thwart terrorism, the amount—and the quality—of such intelligence has come under scrutiny. In the United States, the 2014 release of the Senate Intelligence Committee's Report reignited debate about the CIA's "enhanced interrogation" program, designed by two psychologists.[7] Partisan debate centered on whether program techniques, which were never analyzed for their effectiveness, led to actionable intelligence to thwart future terrorist attacks. The CIA argued that the interrogation of Ammar al-Baluchi—which included the use of enhanced interrogation tactics considered torture under international law—generated important intelligence information that led to the locating of courier Abu Ahmed al-Kuwaiti and the eventual capture of Osama bin Laden. Senate Democrats disagreed, claiming that more accurate intelligence was garnered without reliance on the interrogation of al-Kuwaiti. The majority of academic research on the effectiveness of coercive interrogation suggests that torture does not yield effective intelligence information (e.g. O'Mara 2015; Schiemann 2015); other research maintains that coercive interrogation techniques yield more information than non-coercive measures—both information that is true and information that is false (Johnson and Ryan 2015).

In addition to further alienating the terrorists themselves, torture has the potential to alienate three additional groups from the repressive government in power: the general population, domestic opposition groups, and the international community (Walsh and Piazza 2010). Torture can alienate citizens, inciting them to join the terrorist cause. A wealth of research in psychology and sociology shows that impressions of mistreatment and injustice contribute to individual radicalization and undermine support for authority (Huq et al. 2011; Tyler et al. 2010), and evidence that repression escalates individual violence against the government is strong. Repression can alienate members of marginalized groups, victimize citizens with no involvement in terrorism, and radicalize terrorist sympathizers (Bueno de Mesquita and Dickson 2007; Daxecker and Hess 2013; Dragu and Polborn 2014; La Free et al. 2009; Rosendorff and Sandler 2004; Walsh and Piazza 2010).

Even when they do not lead individuals to join terrorist organizations, rights violations like torture can cause citizens to withdraw support from the (counterterrorism) policies of the incumbent government. In democracies, counterinsurgency campaigns are more likely to fail when the middle class becomes alienated by the use of violence (Merom 2003). Research on civil war similarly shows that excessive violence by the government makes it more difficult for the government to get information about dissident activities because citizens are less willing to cooperate with a repressive government (Condra and Shapiro 2012; Kalyvas 2006; Kocher et al. 2011).

As citizens become increasingly dismayed with the government's repressive response to terrorism, they are more likely to sympathize with the plight of suspected terrorists. This is particularly important because terrorists rely on support from the general population to accomplish their goals: Walsh and Piazza (2010, 557) argue that the success of terrorist organizations is dependent upon "their ability to maintain the loyalty and support of some fraction of the constituent population." As a result, terrorists strategically choose targets to maximize attention to their cause (Hoffman and McCormick 2004), hoping for the government to overreact (Bueno de Mesquita and Dickson 2007; Kydd and Walter 2006). When the government responds to terrorism with repression, terrorist organizations will often publicly shame the government for violations of human rights in order to gain the sympathies of the general population (Finnemore and Sikkink 1998, 32). This is good politics on the part of the terrorists: reports of government abuse following attacks increase both the number and the quality of future terrorist recruits (Bueno de Mesquita 2005).

Governments that violate human rights are often criticized for such policies by their domestic political opposition (Walsh and Piazza 2010). In democracies, rival political parties often expose and decry violations of human rights at the hands of their opposition, and in non-democracies, dissidents often point out abuse to gain supporters and weaken the incumbent. Leaders facing the threat of losing office necessarily expend resources—time, energy, finances—on holding onto power, necessitating fewer resources for counterterrorist policies (Walsh and Piazza 2010).

Terrorism and Institutional Incentives (not) to Torture

Following the September 11, 2001 terrorist attacks on New York City and Washington, DC, popular discourse in the United States seemed to take for granted that the government had cause to limit the rights of both citizens and non-citizens to thwart future attacks on

American soil. Debate rarely focused on whether governments restrict human rights in the face of terrorism or on whether repression actually reduces the likelihood of future terrorist attacks, instead centering on the extent to which such restrictions are contrary to American ideals and should be limited by democratic institutions (Piazza and Walsh 2010b).

Government leaders differ in the extent to which they are responsive to the average citizen. In liberal democracies, leaders come to power via contested elections; as a result, they are dependent upon a large number of citizens to remain in power (e.g. Bueno de Mesquita et al. 2003). Autocratic leaders, on the other hand, are often dependent on a smaller subset of the general population to remain in power: a single ruling party or a military, for example. That democratic leaders must satisfy such a large swath of the population means that they typically provide more public goods, including general protections for citizen human rights, than their autocratic counterparts (e.g. Bueno de Mesquita et al. 2003). On average, democracies offer more protections for political rights, civil liberties, and physical integrity protections—and generally violate those rights less—than non-democracies (Davenport 2007; Moore 2010; Poe and Tate 1994; Poe et al. 1999). In addition to facing these incentives to provide protections for human rights, democracies are argued to limit repression because they typically have additional constraining institutions including elections (e.g. Cingranelli and Filippov 2010), effective judiciaries (e.g. Powell and Staton 2009), and more independent media outlets (e.g. Whitten-Woodring 2009). Each of these institutions both increases the likelihood of human rights violation allegations, as well as the likelihood of punishment for leaders and their agents who are caught repressing suspected dissidents and terrorists.

In part because they offer relatively high protections for human rights, democracies, including those that are newly transitioned (Eyerman 1998), experience more terrorist attacks than autocracies (Eubank and Weinberg 2001; Ivanova and Sandler 2006; Li and Schaub 2004; Piazza 2008; Schmid 1992; Wade and Reiter 2007). Basic government respect for citizen political rights and civil liberties, often viewed by citizens in democracies as pivotal democratic freedoms, provide openings for terrorist organizations to communicate with one another, publicize their grievances more widely, plan future attacks, and engage in the recruitment of individuals sympathetic to the cause (Eubank and Weinberg 1994; Pape 2003; Wade and Reiter 2007). Importantly, however, not all democratic institutions seem to encourage terrorist activity: Li (2005) argues that the ability to participate in the political process—via elections, for example—alleviates dissident grievances that can lead to terrorism, while constraints on the executive—separation of powers, for example—decrease the likelihood of terrorist activity.

Although threats—including terrorism—have been linked to increases in government repression (Davenport et al. 2007; Enterline and Gleditsch 2000; Poe and Tate 1994) in democracies as diverse as the United States, India, South Africa, and the Philippines (Whitaker 2007),[8] highly visible human rights violations are difficult for democracies to pursue even when they are threatened. Democratic institutions make it more difficult for governments to engage in counterterrorism strategies that broadly restrict human rights—widespread monitoring and surveillance, and broad police sweeps, for example. Clandestine violations of human rights are often more appealing. In particular, democratic leaders and their agents are reported to engage in torture—and democratic institutions are reported to constrain them less—when their governments face a threat (Conrad and Moore 2010; Davenport et al. 2007; Moore 2010).

In an effort to derive the benefits of torture already described and circumvent the costs associated with democratic institutions, democracies pioneered a new method of abuse: clean torture (Einolf 2007; Evans and Morgan 1998; Rejali 2007; Ron 1997). Clean torture does not scar the body and includes clean beating, electrocution, waterboarding, sensory deprivation, etc.[9] Rejali (2007) argues that governments prefer this type of torture when they are monitored. When they are monitored for their behavior—via domestic or international institutions—governments prefer clean torture to scarring torture because it affords the government higher levels of plausible deniability. Victim scars are difficult to deny, but clean torture creates a "he said, she said" situation when the government is accused of violating human rights. Examples of stealth torture are frequently reported in the 2014 Senate Intelligence Committee's Report about the CIA's enhanced interrogation program. Mohamed Rahim spent 140 hours shackled in a standing position. Authorities forced Khalid Sheikh Mohammed to remain awake for more than seven days. Other detainees were subjected to complete darkness and isolation, threats against themselves and their families, and several were waterboarded—forced to undergo simulated drowning.

In addition to carefully choosing clean techniques, democratic governments use additional methods to hide abuse in response to terrorism. In the United States, for example, military and police officers are often forbidden by law from sharing information on terrorist activity (Pape 2003; Schmid 1992). Reports of secretive activity by intelligence officials are also commonplace. The 2014 Senate Intelligence Committee's Report suggests that the CIA willfully misled the public, Congress, and members of the executive branch including Secretary of State Colin Powell about the use of enhanced interrogation techniques, even failing to fully brief President George W. Bush until 2006. The Agency also failed to provide an accurate count on the number of individuals in detention, with final numbers being subject to debate even after the public release of the Report. In addition to sidestepping traditional democratic institutions of accountability, clean torture tactics and other clandestine maneuvers have another potential benefit. Although scholars have previously shown "backlash" in response to torture, backlash—and the negative results of torture in response to terrorism—is only of concern if audiences know that the government has engaged in repression and/or violated human rights. When abuse is clandestine—as is the case with clean torture and torture that is hidden by other means—there is less government concern for backlash because it garners less media attention and can more easily be denied than scarring tactics (Daxecker 2017).

Even when democratic leaders fail to hide violations of human rights like torture, the public may be unconcerned about violations of human rights that do not directly affect them. When a democracy faces a threat, however, citizens who themselves feel threatened may be less likely to hold the government accountable for human rights violations

(Conrad et al. 2017a; Piazza 2014; Walzer 1973). Torture is most often directed against criminals, dissidents, and members of marginalized populations—not members of the majority (Conrad et al. 2013).

Although citizens report generally being opposed to government torture (Gronke et al. 2010), recent survey research suggests that Americans are more accepting of government torture when it is directed at individuals with Arabic names (Conrad et al. 2017a). Such a result is unsurprising in the context of psychology research suggesting that individuals experience less empathy toward persons of different racial and ethnic backgrounds (Avenanti et al. 2010) and experiments showing intolerance of outgroups (Stephan and Stephan 1996; Stephan et al. 1999). Although citizens are willing to take to the streets if their own rights are violated, these results suggest that even democracies can get away with the torture of minorities, especially in response to threats like terrorism.

Future Research on Terrorism and Torture

The relationship between terrorism and government torture has been hotly debated in recent years by citizens, policymakers, and academics. Although anecdotal evidence and popular discussion suggest that governments often respond to terrorist attacks by engaging in torture, scholars have yet to reach much of a consensus about the relationship between terror and government torture. In what follows, I consider unresolved challenges in the scholarly study of terrorism and torture, focusing on the importance of recognizing the broad literatures on dissent and repression, taking seriously endogeneity and strategic decision-making, and further disaggregating both theory and quantitative data to better isolate causal mechanisms. Within each of these discussions, I suggest directions for future research on the relationship between terrorist activity and government torture.

First, because of the nature of academia, seemingly related literatures often develop independently from one another even though they purport to be about similar topics. Such is the case with the study of political violence.[10] Although the United States government's definition of terrorism is easily subsumed by scholarly definitions of dissent, scholars interested in the study of terrorism often fail to draw from the insights of this broad literature. Similarly, work on government torture is often written without reference to the growing literature on government repression and human rights violations, writ large. Scholars interested in the causes and consequences of terrorism and torture would do well to consult scholarly work on repression and dissent as they build and test theories about political violence. Such cross-literature fertilization can also go in the other direction. Scholars interested in dissent, writ large, for example, could learn a lot about the individual incentives to mobilize against the state from the literature on suicide terrorism (e.g. Hoffman 2003; Hoffman and McCormick 2004; Pape 2005, 2003; Wade and Reiter 2007).

Second, empirical investigation of the relationship between terrorism and torture is fraught with difficulty. As many scholars have noted (Daxecker 2017; Hafner-Burton and Shapiro 2010; Piazza and Walsh 2010b; Ritter and Conrad 2015), the relationships between dissent and repression, generally, and terrorism and torture, specifically, are endogenous.[11] Do governments respond to terrorism by encouraging their agents to torture detainees? Does torture cause individuals to engage in more dissent against the state? Are both answers yes? If so, under what conditions? In addition to potentially being endogenous, the relationship between terrorism and torture is also subject to other threats to causal inference. Li (2005) argues that the relationship between terrorism and (violations of) human rights is spurious. Instead of affecting one another, he suggests that institutional constraints affect both the opposition's decision to engage in terrorism and the government's decision to respond with torture.

Previous research, including the ground-breaking quantitative studies by Piazza and Walsh (2009); Walsh and Piazza (2010), has tested hypotheses about the effect of terrorism on torture—and vice versa—using data collected at the country-year unit of observation. To deal with endogeneity and show causal relationships, they lag their main independent variables one year, suggesting that terrorism last year affects torture this year, for example. As Hafner-Burton and Shapiro (2010) point out, however, "the variables on both sides of the regression are slow-changing and strategically determined," making the use of a lagged dependent variable inappropriate.[12] Although more disaggregated data on terrorism and torture would help with determining causality, scholars can also turn to innovative research designs to better deal with endogenous political processes. For example, Hafner-Burton and Shapiro (2010) suggest a two-stage least squares model to better account for endogeneity in the relationship between terrorism and torture, but point out that instrumental variables—especially at the country-year unit of observation—may be difficult to find. This is an example of where research on dissent and repression may be able to influence work on terrorism and torture: based on arguments about voter turnout in US context, Ritter and Conrad (2015) show that rainfall can be used as a helpful instrument in disentangling the relationship between dissent and repression. In addition to using statistical tools to account for endogeneity, spurious relationships, and selection effects, scholars should also seek to exploit natural experiments: instances in which there are exogenous changes in the level of terrorism, for example, can help researchers better determine the causal effect of terrorist activity on government torture.

Third, data disaggregation is not only important for determining the causal relationship between terrorism and torture, but is also critical for being able to ask—and answer—more nuanced questions and develop more nuanced theories about political violence.[13] For example, it is impossible to use country-year data on terrorism and torture to answer research questions—and test theoretical implications—about the timing of political violence. It is also difficult to take seriously the strategic interactions between terrorists and government agents with highly aggregated data (e.g. Shellman 2006, 2009). More recent work on whether governments respond to terrorism with increased torture disaggregates the "state," suggesting that incentives to violate human rights differ across government agencies. Conrad et al. (2017b), for example, argue that because the military is responsible for defending against external enemies, transnational terrorist attacks lead to increases in torture by the military—not other government agencies. Other work suggests that disaggregation of terrorism is equally important to the disaggregation of data on government torture. Findley and Young (2007), for example, discuss in detail differences in the goals of and responses to domestic and transnational terrorism.

Conclusion

This chapter provides a call to scholars interested in the effect of terrorism on torture to better integrate their theories and empirical findings with those in the broader study of opposition dissent and government repression and to further theorize about the conditions under which behavioral and institutional (dis)incentives influence the effect of terrorism on the violation of human rights. As scholars develop additional knowledge about the conditions under which governments respond to terrorism by engaging in torture, it is important that such information not remain in the academy; careful scholarly inquiry into the causes and consequences of political violence can influence policymakers and advocates interested in the eradication of terror *and* the protection of human rights.

Acknowledgments

Thanks to Nate Monroe and Will Moore for helpful discussion on earlier drafts.

Notes

1. See e.g. <http://www.amnestyusa.org/our-work/issues/torture>.
2. Scholars have further delineated between domestic terrorism, which occurs within one country and is directed at conational targets, and transnational terrorism, which is perpetrated against foreign targets across national boundaries. While the intention of domestic terrorism is typically to generate policy change domestically, transnational attacks are generally intended to force policy change in other countries, see Young and Findley 2011.
3. For a review of the literature on this mixed empirical evidence, please see Ritter and Conrad 2015.
4. Piazza and Walsh 2009 find transnational terrorism to be associated with higher levels of government killing.
5. Even if they are not directed by principals to use torture as a tool of information acquisition, repressive agents may turn to torture on their own. For more information on agency relationships with regard to torture, please see Conrad and Moore 2010; Mitchell 2009, 2012.
6. For more on the economic roots of terrorism, see Krueger 2008.

7. The American Psychological Association (APA) has since restricted psychologist involvement in such programs, see Dizard 2015.
8. Citizens also offer their leaders more discretion over how to deal with international threats. Feaver 2009 argues that citizens provide the military with high levels of autonomy when they are expected to contend with an external threat.
9. For a complete review of the history of clean torture and examples of the practice, please see Rejali 2007.
10. For a similar argument about the need for the integration of disciplinary arguments about political violence, see English 2016.
11. Daxecker 2017 goes further to suggest that the government's choice of torture techniques "may be endogenous to its expected effect on terrorism."
12. Hafner-Burton and Shapiro 2010 also conduct a placebo test on the empirical results presented in Walsh and Piazza 2010 and show that regressing the lead of torture on terrorism leads to the same results as regressing the lag of torture on terrorism.
13. In their discussion of research on dissent and repression, Moore and Welch 2015 succinctly point out an important implication of using country-year data to test more micro-level hypotheses: "With regards to the spatial assumption, researchers that are interested in the interaction between dissent and repression that use the country-year as the unit of analysis assume that the dissent that happens in one place in the country effects the repression in another . . . with respect to time, if one is concerned with how governments and citizens react to one another's actions, it is hard to tease out any specifics when everything that happens in a year is not picked apart more scrupulously."

References

Abrahms, Max (2007) "Why Democracies Make Superior Counterterrorists," *Security Studies*, 16(2): 223–53.

Amnesty International (2008) "No Hiding Place for Torture," available online at <https://www.amnesty.org/en/documents/ACT40/008/2008/en>.

Art, Robert J., and Louise Richardson (2007) *Democracy and Counterterrorism: Lessons from the Past*. Washington, DC: US Institute of Peace Press.

Avenanti, Alessio, Angela Sirigu, and Salvatore M Aglioti (2010) "Racial Bias Reduces Empathic Sensorimotor Resonance with Other-Race Pain," *Current Biology*, 20(11): 1018–22.

Berrebi, Claude, and Esteban F Klor (2006) "On Terrorism and Electoral Outcomes Theory and Evidence from the Israeli–Palestinian Conflict," *Journal of Conflict Resolution*, 50(6): 899–925.

Blomberg, S. Brock, Gregory D. Hess, and Athanasios Orphanides (2004) "The Macroeconomic Consequences of Terrorism," *Journal of Monetary Economics*, 51(5): 1007–32.

Branigan, Tania (2007) "Brown Sets out Tougher Plans in Anti-Terror Battle," *Guardian*, June 3: 1.

Bueno de Mesquita, Ethan (2005) "Conciliation, Counterterrorism, and Patterns of Terrorist Violence," *International Organization*, 59(1): 145–76.

Bueno de Mesquita, Ethan, and Eric S Dickson (2007) "The Propaganda of the Deed: Terrorism, Counterterrorism, and Mobilization," *American Journal of Political Science*, 51(2): 364–81.

Bueno de Mesquita, Bruce, Alastair Smith, Randolph M. Siverson, and James Morrow (2003) *The Logic of Political Survival*. Cambridge, MA: MIT Press.

Bush, George W. (2008) "Text: Bush on Veto of Intelligence Bill," available online at <http://www.nytimes.com/2008/03/08/washington/08cnd-ptext.html>.

Charters, David (1994) *The Deadly Sin of Terrorism: Its Effect on Democracy and Civil Liberty in Six Countries*. Westport, CT: Greenwood Publishing Group.

Cingranelli, David L., and Mikhail Filippov (2010) "Electoral Rules and Incentives to Protect Human Rights," *Journal of Politics*, 72(1): 243–57.

Cingranelli, David L., and David L. Richards (1999) "Measuring the Level, Pattern and Sequence of Government Respect for Physical Integrity Rights," *International Studies Quarterly*, 43(2): 407–18.

Condra, Luke N., and Jacob N. Shapiro (2012) "Who Takes the Blame? The Strategic Effects of Collateral Damage," *American Journal of Political Science*, 56(1): 167–87.

Conrad, Courtenay R., and Will H. Moore (2010) "What Stops the Torture?" *American Journal of Political Science*, 54(2): 459–76.

Conrad, Courtenay R., Jillienne Haglund, and Will H. Moore (2013) "Disaggregating Torture Allegations: Introducing the Ill-Treatment and Torture (ITT) Country-Year Data," *International Studies Perspectives*, 14(2): 199–220.

Conrad, Courtenay R., Sarah E. Croco, Brad T. Gomez, and Will H. Moore (2017a) "Threat Perception and American Support for Torture," *Political Behavior* (online only).

Conrad, Courtenay R., Justin Conrad, James A. Piazza, and James Igoe Walsh (2017b) "Who Tortures the Terrorists? Transnational Terrorism and Military Torture," *Foreign Policy Analysis*, 13(4): 761–86.

Crenshaw, Martha (1998) "The Logic of Terrorism: Terrorism as the Product of Strategic Choice," in W. Reich (ed.), *Origins of Terrorism: Psychologies, Ideologies, Theologies, States of Mind*. Washington, DC: Woodrow Wilson Center Press, 7–24.

Danneman, Nathan, and Emily Hencken Ritter (2014) "Contagious Rebellion and Preemptive Repression," *Journal of Conflict Resolution*, 58(2): 254–79.

Davenport, Christian (2007) *State Repression and the Domestic Democratic Peace*. New York: Cambridge University Press.

Davenport, Christian, Will H. Moore, and David Armstrong (2007) "The Puzzle of Abu Ghraib: Are Democratic Institutions a Palliative or Panacea?" Working Paper, available online at <http://ssrn.com/abstract=1022367>.

Daxecker, Ursula (2017) "Dirty Hands: Government Torture and Terrorism," *Journal of Conflict Resolution*, 61(6): 1261–89.

Daxecker, Ursula E., and Michael L. Hess (2013) "Repression Hurts: Coercive Government Responses and the Demise of Terrorist Campaigns," *British Journal of Political Science*, 43(3): 559–77.

Dershowitz, Alan M. (2002) *Why Terrorism Works*. New Haven: Yale University Press.

DiMarco, Lou (2006) *Losing the Moral Compass: Torture and "Guerre Revolutionnaire" in the Algerian War*. Technical report. Leavenworth, KS: DTIC.

Dizard, Wilson (2015) "Psychologists Vote Not to Participate in US Torture," available online at <http://america.aljazeera.com/articles/2015/8/7/psychologists-vote-not-to-participate-in-torture.html>.

Dragu, Tiberiu, and Mattias Polborn (2014) "The Rule of Law in the Fight Against Terrorism," *American Journal of Political Science*, 58(2): 511–25.

Dugan, Laura, and Erica Chenoweth (2012) "Moving Beyond Deterrence: The Effectiveness of Raising the Expected Utility of Abstaining from Terrorism in Israel," *American Sociological Review*, 77(4): 597–624.

Earl, Jennifer, Sarah A. Soule, and John D. McCarthy (2003) "Protest Under Fire? Explaining the Policing of Protest," *American Sociological Review*, 68(4): 581–606.

Einolf, Christopher J. (2007) "The Fall and Rise of Torture: A Comparative and Historical Analysis," *Sociological Theory*, 25(2): 101–21.

Enders, Walter, and Todd Sandler (2006) *The Political Economy of Terrorism*. Cambridge: Cambridge University Press.

English, Richard (2016) *Does Terrorism Work?* Oxford: Oxford University Press.

Enterline, Andrew J., and Kristian S. Gleditsch (2000) "Threats, Opportunity, and Force: Repression and Diversion of Domestic Pressure, 1948–1982," *International Interactions*, 26(1): 21–53.

Eubank, William L., and Leonard Weinberg (1994) "Does Democracy Encourage Terrorism?," *Terrorism and Political Violence*, 6(4): 417–35.

Eubank, William L., and Leonard Weinberg (2001) "Terrorism and Democracy: Perpetrators and Victims," *Terrorism and Political Violence*, 13(1): 155–64.

Evans, Malcolm D., and Rod Morgan (1998) *Preventing Torture: A Study of the European Convention for the Prevention of Torture and Inhuman or Degrading Treatment or Punishment*. New York: Oxford University Press.

Eyerman, Joseph (1998) "Terrorism and Democratic States: Soft Targets or Accessible Systems?," *International Interactions*, 24(2): 151–70.

Fearon, James, and David Laitin (2003) "Ethnicity, Insurgency and Civil War," *American Political Science Review*, 97(1): 75–90.

Feaver, Peter D. (2009) *Armed Servants: Agency, Oversight, and Civil-Military Relations*. Cambridge, MA: Harvard University Press.

Findley, Michael G., and Joseph K. Young (2007) "Fighting Fire with Fire? How (Not) to Neutralize an Insurgency," *Civil Wars*, 9(4): 378–401.

Finnemore, Martha, and Katherine Sikkink (1998) "Norms and International Relations Theory," *International Organization*, 52(4): 887–917.

Francisco, Ronald A. (1996) "Coercion and Protest: An Empirical Test in Two Democratic States," *American Journal of Political Science*, 40(4): 1179–1204.

Gearty, Conor (2007) "Terrorism and Human Rights," *Government and Opposition*, 42(3): 340–62.

Goldstein, Robert J. (1978) *Political Repression in Modern America*. Cambridge: Schenkman Publishing Co.

Gronke, Paul, Darius Rejali, Dustin Drenguis, James Hicks, Peter Miller, and Bryan Nakayama (2010) "US Public Opinion on Torture, 2001–2009," *PS: Political Science and Politics*, 43(3): 437–44.

Gurr, Ted Robert, and Will H. Moore (1997) "Ethnopolitical Rebellion: A Cross-Sectional Analysis of the 1980's with Risk Assessment for the 1990's," *American Journal of Political Science*, 41(4): 1079–103.

Hafner-Burton, Emilie M., and Jacob N Shapiro (2010) "Tortured Relations: Human Rights Abuses and Counterterrorism Cooperation," *PS: Political Science and Politics*, 43(3): 415–19.

Hibbs, Douglas (1973) *Mass Political Violence*. New York: Wiley.

Hoffman, Bruce (1998) *Inside Terrorism*. New York: Columbia University Press.

Hoffman, Bruce (2003) "The Logic of Suicide Terrorism," *The Atlantic*, June.

Hoffman, Bruce, and Gordon H. McCormick (2004) "Terrorism, Signaling, and Suicide Attack," *Studies in Conflict and Terrorism*, 27(4): 243–81.

Huq, Aziz Z., Tom R. Tyler, and Stephen J. Schulhofer (2011) "Why does the Public Cooperate with Law Enforcement? The Influence of the Purposes and Targets of Policing," *Psychology, Public Policy, and Law*, 17(3): 419.

Ignatieff, Michael (2013) The Lesser Evil: Political Ethics in an Age of Terror. Princeton: Princeton University Press.

Ivanova, Kate, and Todd Sandler (2006) "CBRN incidents: Political Regimes, Perpetrators, and Targets," *Terrorism and Political Violence*, 18(3): 423–48.

Joes, Anthony James (2006) *Resisting Rebellion: The History and Politics of Counterinsurgency*. Lexington, KY: University Press of Kentucky.

Johnson, David Blake, and John Barry Ryan (2015) "The Interrogation Game: Using Coercion and Rewards to Elicit Information from Groups," *Journal of Peace Research*, 52(6): 822–37.

Jones, Seth G., and Martin C. Libicki (2008) *How Terrorist Groups End: Lessons for Countering al Qa'ida*. Santa Monica, CA: RAND Corporation.

Kalyvas, Stathis N. (2004) "The Paradox of Terrorism in Civil War," *Journal of Ethics*, 8(1): 97–138.

Kalyvas, Stathis N. (2006) *The Logic of Violence in Civil War*. Cambridge: Cambridge University Press.

Kean, Thomas (2011) *The 9/11 Commission Report: Final Report of the National Commission on Terrorist Attacks upon the United States*. Washington, DC: Government Printing Office.

Keith, Linda Camp (2002) "Constitutional Provisions for Individual Human Rights: Are they More than Mere Window Dressing," *Political Research Quarterly*, 55: 111–43.

Kocher, Matthew Adam, Thomas B. Pepinsky, and Stathis N. Kalyvas (2011) "Aerial Bombing and Counterinsurgency in the Vietnam War," *American Journal of Political Science*, 55(2): 201–18.

Krueger, Alan B. (2008) *What Makes a Terrorist: Economics and the Roots of Terrorism*. Princeton: Princeton University Press.

Kurrild-Klitgaard, Peter, Morgens K. Justesen, and Robert Klemmensen (2006) "The Political Economy of Freedom, Democracy and Transnational Terrorism," *Public Choice*, 128(1): 289–315.

Kydd, Andrew H., and Barbara F. Walter (2006) "The Strategies of Terrorism," *International Security*, 31(1): 49–80.

LaFree, Gary, Laura Dugan, and Raven Korte (2009) "The Impact of British Counterterrorist Strategies on Political Violence in Northern Ireland: Comparing Deterrence and Backlash Models," *Criminology*, 47(1): 17–45.

Lake, David A. (2002) "Rational Extremism: Understanding Terrorism in the Twenty-First Century," *Dialogue IO*, 1(1): 15–29.

Li, Quan (2005) "Does Democracy Promote or Reduce Transnational Terrorist Incidents?," *Journal of Conflict Resolution*, 49(2): 278–97.

Li, Quan, and Drew Schaub (2004) "Economic Globalization and Transnational Terrorism: A Pooled Time-Series Analysis," *Journal of Conflict Resolution*, 48(2): 230–58.

Lichbach, Mark Irving (1998) *The Rebel's Dilemma*. Ann Arbor, MI: University of Michigan Press.

Lyall, Jason (2009) "Does Indiscriminate Violence Incite Insurgent Attacks? Evidence from Chechnya," *Journal of Conflict Resolution*, 53(3): 331–62.

Merom, Gil (2003) *How Democracies Lose Small Wars: State, Society, and the Failures of France in Algeria, Israel in Lebanon, and the United States in Vietnam*. Cambridge: Cambridge University Press.

Mitchell, Neil J. (2009) *Agents of Atrocity: Leaders, Followers and Human Rights Violations in Civil Wars*. New York: Palgrave Macmillan.

Mitchell, Neil J. (2012) *Democracy's Blameless Leaders: From Dresden to Abu Ghraib, How Leaders Evade Accountability for Abuse, Atrocity, and Killing*. New York: New York University Press.

Moore, Will H. (1995) "Action–Reaction or Rational Expectations? Reciprocity and the Domestic–International Conflict Nexus during the 'Rhodesia Problem,'" *Journal of Conflict Resolution*, 39(1): 129–67.

Moore, Will H. (2010) "Incarceration, Interrogation, and Counterterror: Do (Liberal) Democratic Institutions Constrain Leviathan?," *PS: Political Science and Politics*, 43(3): 421–4.

Moore, Will H., and Ryan Welch (2015) "Why do Governments Violate Human Rights?," in Robert Scott and Stephan Kosslyn (eds), *Emerging Trends in the Social and Behavioral Sciences*. Chichester: John Wiley & Sons.

Nitsch, Volker, and Dieter Schumacher (2004) "Terrorism and International Trade: An Empirical Investigation," *European Journal of Political Economy*, 20(2): 423–33.

Nordås, Ragnhild, and Christian Davenport (2013) "Fight the Youth: Youth Bulges and State Repression," *American Journal of Political Science*, 57(4): 926–40.

O'Mara, Shane (2015) *Why Torture doesn't Work: The Neuroscience of Interrogation*. Cambridge, MA: Harvard University Press.

Opp, Karl-Dieter, and Wolfgang Roehl (1990) "Repression, Micromobilization, and Political Protest," *Social Forces*, 69(2): 521–47.

Pape, Robert (2005) *Dying to Win: The Strategic Logic of Suicide Terrorism*. New York: Random House.

Pape, Robert (2003) "The Strategic Logic of Suicide Terrorism," *American Political Science Review*, 97(3): 343–61.

Piazza, James A. (2008) "Incubators of Terror: Do Failed and Failing States Promote Transnational Terrorism?," *International Studies Quarterly*, 52(3): 469–88.

Piazza, James A. (2015) "Terrorist Suspect Religious Identity and Public Support for Harsh Interrogation and Detention Practices," *Political Psychology* 36(6): 667–90.

Piazza, James A., and James Igoe Walsh (2009) "Transnational Terror and Human Rights," *International Studies Quarterly*, 53(1): 125–48.

Piazza, James A., and James Igoe Walsh (2010a) "Physical Integrity Rights and Terrorism," *PS: Political Science and Politics*, 43(3): 411–14.

Piazza, James A., and James Igoe Walsh (2010b) "Terrorism and Human Rights," *PS: Political Science and Politics*, 43(3): 407–9.

Pierskalla, Jan Henryk (2010) "Protest, Deterrence, and Escalation: The Strategic Calculus of Government Repression," *Journal of Conflict Resolution*, 54(1): 117–45.

Poe, Steven, and C. Neal Tate (1994) "Repression of Personal Integrity Rights in the 1980s: A Global Analysis," *American Political Science Review*, 88: 853–72.

Poe, Steven, C. Neal Tate, and Linda Camp Keith (1999) "Repression of the Human Right to Personal Integrity Revisited: A Global, Cross-National Study Covering the Years 1976–1993," *International Studies Quarterly*, 43: 291–313.

Powell, Emilia J., and Jeffrey K. Staton (2009) "Domestic Judicial Institutions and Human Rights Treaty Violation," *International Studies Quarterly*, 53(1): 149–74.

Rejali, Darius (2007) *Torture and Democracy*. Princeton: Princeton University Press.

Ritter, Emily Hencken (2014) "Policy Disputes, Political Survival, and the Onset and Severity of State Repression," *Journal of Conflict Resolution*, 58(1): 143–68.

Ritter, Emily Hencken, and Courtenay R. Conrad (2016) "Preventing and Responding to Dissent: The Observational Challenges of Explaining Strategic Repression," *American Political Science Review*, 110(1): 85–99.

Ron, James (1997) "Varying Methods of State Violence," *International Organization*, 51(2): 275–300.

Rosendorff, B. Peter, and Todd Sandler (2004) "Too Much of a Good Thing? The Proactive Response Dilemma," *Journal of Conflict Resolution*, 48(5): 657–71.

Schiemann, John W. (2015) *Does Torture Work?* New York: Oxford University Press.

Schmid, Alex (1992) "Terrorism and Democracy," *Terrorism and Political Violence*, 4(4): 14–25.

Shellman, Stephen M. (2006) "Process Matters: Conflict and Cooperation in Sequential Government–Dissident Interactions," *Security Studies*, 15(4): 563–99.

Shellman, Stephen M. (2009) *Taking Turns: A Theory and Model of Government-Dissident Interactions*. Saarbücken: VDM Verlag.

Stephan, Walter G., and Cookie White Stephan (1996) "Predicting Prejudice," *International Journal of Intercultural Relations*, 20(3): 409–26.

Stephan, Walter G., Oscar Ybarra, and Guy Bachman (1999) "Prejudice Toward Immigrants 1," *Journal of Applied Social Psychology*, 29(11): 2221–37.

Sullivan, Christopher Michael (2014) "The (In)effectiveness of Torture for Combating Insurgency," *Journal of Peace Research*, 51(3): 388–404.

Tyler, Tom R., Stephen Schulhofer, and Aziz Z. Huq (2010) "Legitimacy and Deterrence Effects in Counterterrorism Policing: A Study of Muslim Americans," *Law and Society Review*, 44(2): 365–402.

Wade, Sara Jackson, and Dan Reiter (2007) "Does Democracy Matter? Regime Type and Suicide Terrorism," *Journal of Conflict Resolution*, 51(2): 329–48.

Walsh, James I., and James A. Piazza (2010) "Why Respecting Physical Integrity Rights Reduces Terrorism," *Comparative Political Studies*, 43(5): 551–77

Walzer, M. (1973) "Political Action: The Problem of Dirty Hands," *Philosophy and Public Affairs*, 2(2): 160–80.

Wantchekon, Leonard, and Andrew Healy (1999) "The 'Game' of Torture," *Journal of Conflict Resolution*, 43(5): 596–609.

Whitaker, Beth Elise (2007) "Exporting the Patriot Act? Democracy and the 'War on Terror' in the Third World," *Third World Quarterly*, 28(5): 1017–32.

Whitten-Woodring, Jenifer (2009) "Watchdog or Lapdog? Media Freedom, Regime Type, and Government Respect for Human Rights," *International Studies Quarterly*, 53(3): 595–625.

Young, Joseph K., and Michael G. Findley (2011) "Promise and Pitfalls of Terrorism Research," *International Studies Review*, 13(3): 411–31.

CHAPTER 44

ACADEMIC RESEARCH AND THE INTELLIGENCE COMMUNITY

some reflections

JONATHAN EVANS

As a young officer in MI5 in the 1980s I recall asking a much older and more senior colleague why the intelligence community did not consult academic experts when drawing up assessments on the geopolitical developments that were issued to Whitehall via the Joint Intelligence Committee.[1] Without pause he explained that it was because the academics did not have access to secret intelligence. So far as he was concerned that was a conclusive argument. At around the same time I attended a talk at Chatham House given by a well-known academic who spoke on the role and capabilities of the Soviet armed forces. He appeared to be remarkably familiar with the material and to have had good access to some senior Soviet military leaders. When I asked another senior colleague what he made of this he replied that it was useful for the Soviets to keep one or two tame Western academics informed as part of their propaganda activities.

In retrospect this skeptical and even suspicious attitude on the part of members of the intelligence community to the value of academic research on security matters is surprising given that the wartime success of the British intelligence community owed much to the recruitment of brilliant officers from the universities. Their contribution to, for example, the double cross system and the cracking of ENIGMA was well acknowledged. Moreover a number of the most able officers who joined MI5 in the 1970s and 1980s, including for instance Stephen Lander who subsequently became Director General, did so having had an initial career in university research. Nevertheless the 1980s were not the most outward-looking period for the agencies, and engagement with the academic world was at that point almost as limited as that with the media.

Terrorism was the phenomenon that changed all that. Following several well-known miscarriages of justice in terrorist cases in the 1970s, the need for expert and independent testimony in the courts on terrorist structures and tactics became pressing. A principal source of such expertise came from the (at that stage relatively few) academics in the field, notably the late Professor Paul Wilkinson from St Andrews University who, at some risk to himself, gave evidence in several Provisional IRA trials in the 1980s and who was also involved in training courses for the police on Irish republicanism. On a personal note I can recall, as a relatively junior official on secondment to the Home Office, having some peripheral responsibility for the security measures that were installed in Professor Wilkinson's house.

This engagement with the academic world was given a new momentum by the response to 9/11, when greatly increased funding became available for academic work on terrorism in its various manifestations. Enterprising academics responded to the opportunity by doing more work on the subject or, failing that, by repainting loosely associated work in counterterrorist colors. Departments and centers focusing on terrorism sprang up on university campuses across the country and the number of purported experts sprang up with them. To be fair the same was true in government where the sound of government purse strings being loosened brought forth all sorts of applications for security-related funding from unlikely corners of Whitehall, to such an extent that a senior Treasury high flyer had to be appointed to sift the wheat from the chaff. But though in some quarters the quality or relevance of research was questionable, the intelligence agencies and police, faced with intense pressure to understand, explain, and respond to the difficult new challenge of Al Qaeda-related terrorism, saw the value in engaging more actively with the academic community on these issues.

From a government perspective counterterrorism is a complex program that can be analyzed in different ways. The UK counterterrorist strategy CONTEST favors the well-known 4P strands of Pursue, Protect, Prevent, and Prepare. For current purposes, I think an alternative categorization is more helpful—between the policy, operational, and legal components of counterterrorism. Policy involves agreeing the aims of counterterrorist effort, finding the best interventions to bring those aims to fruition, and managing the process of delivery. Operational counterterrorism includes the intelligence, police, and, where applicable, military operations that constitute a major part of any counterterrorism strategy. The legal component comprises both devising laws that are necessary to support and implement the policy and the enforcement of those laws through the criminal justice system. Of course not all laws that contribute to counterterrorist effect are necessarily specific to counterterrorism—many terrorist acts are in themselves intrinsically criminal and I can recall a number of occasions where terrorists that we were investigating were also involved in completely unrelated criminal activity such as theft, fraud, or even sexual offences, the successful prosecution of which had the desirable side effect of disrupting their terrorist activities.

The information and training requirements of the three strands of counterterrorist effort are each very different. The starting point for policy is (or should be) a dispassionate understanding of the problem to be addressed, to serve as a basis for devising appropriate interventions, a process that should require research into what might actually work. Certain policy areas traditionally depend to a large degree on secret intelligence, particularly where the problem being addressed involves combatting opponents or outstripping rivals who have an incentive to hide their intentions. Hence the dismissive reaction of my colleague to my enquiry about intelligence assessments. But by no means all the information requirements of counterterrorism are necessarily, or best, met by secret intelligence. Intelligence, when available, is valuable for illuminating secrets but many very important matters may not be a secret at all, in which case intelligence gathering is redundant.

Take for instance some of the most important questions in UK counterterrorism policy: how someone turns to terrorism in the first place, how that process can be prevented, and how it can be reversed. Parts of this process can be illuminated by intelligence but most are not secrets and are therefore best understood through academic or other research rather than spying. In practice in the early period after the 9/11 attacks there was a strong demand from politicians and policymakers to understand the processes of radicalization but not much readily available information from any source. One influential piece of work undertaken by the Security Service at that time involved reviewing service records to find out all that was known about the histories of extremists who had been subject to Security Service surveillance and thereby to identify common patterns that might serve as indicators that an individual was susceptible to radicalization. It was hoped that this would provide evidence that could be used by policymakers who were looking for interventions to stop the radicalization process. The actual work was led by behavioral scientists working in the Security Service and the only secret element was the actual body of information on which they were working, which had in fact been gathered for operational purposes, not as a research database. Frustratingly for policymakers, particularly some ministers, the conclusion of the work was that there was no single pathway to radicalization and that "commonsense" answers like educational failure or economic deprivation did not explain very much if anything about why someone might turn to extremism. There were some interesting findings, such as indications that an individual's association with an established and charismatic radicalizer could have a disproportionate effect on the radicalization process, but the research made clear that you would search in vain for a "silver bullet" to sort out the problem.

Academic research can make a major contribution to policymaking, including on terrorism, and the range of disciplines that have been useful since 9/11 has been wide—international relations, terrorism studies, languages, sociology, behavioral sciences as well as a range of scientific and technical disciplines. In my experience insights can be particularly interesting when developed in a multidisciplinary environment. I have a clear memory of listening several years ago to an epidemiologist talking about the insights that his discipline might, by analogy, afford into how extremist views spread. It appeared to have quite a lot of explanatory power and has certainly been influential on my own thinking on the subject.

Equally there are wide areas of terrorism studies that are at best marginal so far as actual counterterrorism is concerned. I cannot remember much discussion of the definition of terrorism in the twenty-five years I spent working on counterterrorism, very little on history beyond the shortest of timescales, and virtually none at all on gender.

Operational counterterrorism benefits less obviously from academic research as its information requirements are in general quite particular, and predominantly intelligence based. Operations are mostly about who, what, where, and when, and those questions are likely to be asked about a finite number of identified or partially identified individuals who are assessed to pose a threat. They are also likely to be taking steps to avoid detection. Academic research is not the obvious way into this problem. Spying is much more promising.

Spying operations may obtain useful information but it is of a very particular nature. The corporate record on terrorist matters held by the Security Service is a good example. The main work of the service is operational and the information that it holds is principally the aggregation of many operations over a long period. It is retained either because it is judged capable of being of operational value in the future or so that the service can account for its activities to the various oversight bodies that provide supervision. Thus the information it holds is like a coral reef built up over years, rather than a consistent body of material covering whole categories of people or events. It is a bottom-up archive, not a top-down data repository. This means that the service is not necessarily well placed to answer questions like how many attacks took place in particular period and what the details were (except nowadays by a Google search). That sort of structured record for research purposes, valuable as it is in a variety of ways, is much more likely to be kept in universities or research centers.

Clearly academic research can benefit operational counterterrorism but usually at one remove. Behavioral sciences may help to improve decision-making or improve the chances that an attempt to "turn" a terrorist is successful. Technical capabilities are obviously important to operational work. Well-informed cultural and historical understanding of countries or religions may improve the ability of an organization to make appropriate operational choices and to assess risk. Research into the terrorist life cycle, that is, the way in which people are recruited into terrorism, engage in terrorism, and eventually move away from it, may likewise inform assessments and help decision-making. All of these have been valuable in practice in the last fifteen years or so since the intelligence community started to engage more actively with the academic world. The introduction of distinguished academics as science advisors, in various configurations, in the intelligence agencies, modeled on the long established practice in departments such as the Home Office and Ministry of Defence, is a demonstration of the health of this interchange.

The legal component of counterterrorism—the creation of laws and their enforcement—is in many ways the most visible to the general public and has engaged many weeks and months of impassioned debate in the media and parliament as new proposals are introduced, amended, and subsequently litigated. Academic research into terrorism is rarely central to these debates. Political, operational, and jurisprudential requirements are what generally drive the process. That said, the police did seek training and education for large numbers of their officers from academics as they faced the need to upscale their operations, both in the early days of Irish terrorism on the mainland, and after 9/11. A better informed body of police officers has been the result. It was also the police and the prosecutors who recognized the need for credible and independent voices to make sense of complex and unfamiliar material and context for juries and tribunals. Academics are an obvious source of disinterested expertise and have been in occasional demand in such circumstances over the years.

This issue of independence is seen differently in different societies. I was struck, on a recent visit to Singapore, for example, that some academic centers on terrorism there would see their role not only as the study of terrorism but as the study of terrorism in order to help government and society to counter it. That does not appear to have damaged the value of their research, presumably because the whole point is to do rigorous research that genuinely illuminates the issues in hand. This instrumental approach would, however, tend to delineate the areas of research that the center might see fit to undertake. From a personal perspective as a former practitioner, the Singaporean model has real attractions and would certainly make academic research of more immediate "real world" relevance. I recognize that there would be those who argue that it is not the role of universities to "take sides," but there does not appear to be the same reticence in seeking to use academic research capability for the public good in, for example, fighting disease or improving road safety.

The CIA has traditionally sponsored a number of "officers in residence" at academic institutions—usually, as I understand it, highly experienced officers of the agency at the end of their operational careers, who spend a period on the faculty in appropriate institutions in order to provide their insights and experience to academic colleagues. This is a model that I think has the potential to give value to the academic community and to the sponsoring agency, who will get access to relevant research, perhaps be able to dispel a few myths, and catalyze positive relationships and projects. There is potential for similar steps to be made in the UK without, in my view, any difficult ethical issues arising. Clearly a lot would depend on the caliber and character of the agency staff taking such roles, and the maturity of the institutional relationship involved, but it is a model that deserves serious consideration.

The greater involvement of the intelligence and academic communities does, however, raise some dilemmas. On the intelligence side there are the perennial issues of how far you are prepared to show your hand to those outside the intelligence world. Conversely for the academics there are risks, since they would not wish to be seen as tools of the security state and would wish to retain their integrity, independence, and ability to comment and research dispassionately in their particular areas of expertise. In practice I am not aware that either of these potential problems has actually materialized in recent years. It is quite possible for the agencies to engage with responsible academic institutions without sharing deep operational secrets with them. Equally, academics worthy of the name are probably going to be able to spot whether they are approaching a line they should not cross. Again in my experience the intelligence agencies are not seeking to engage with the academic world with sinister and hidden motives. They recognize that there is benefit in understanding what academic research tells them about the issues they care about, and they also recognize both that there is a wider public interest in academic integrity, and that they themselves derive benefit from engaging in discussion with genuinely independent integrity. Not that these concerns are new.

Paul Wilkinson was viewed with suspicion by some on the Left as at best an unwitting tool of British propaganda and at worst a willing tool who was connected to sinister American securocrats and believed conspiracy theories about covert Russian support for international terrorist groups. I have to say that having met Professor Wilkinson on a few occasions, this was not the impression I gained of him.

The dilemmas inherent in academic research into terrorism do occasionally materialize in an intensely practical form. The most obvious example is the Boston College Oral History case,[2] where the interests of disinterested academic research and those of the criminal justice system in prosecuting serious, albeit ageing, terrorist offences came into fiercely contested conflict.

Nevertheless, such dilemmas can also be successfully managed. In advance of its centenary in 2009, MI5 took the bold decision, backed by Ministers, to commission and have published a history of the Security Service written by a distinguished academic. This would be very different from the internal and private histories produced in the service from time to time before that. The author would be able to draw not only on the extensive archives of the service but also on an oral history archive that had been rather imaginatively commissioned by Sir Stephen Lander as Director General in the 1990s (perhaps a result of Lander's own previous academic career). The academic finally selected to write the Centenary history was Professor Christopher Andrew from Cambridge (Andrew 2009). The basis on which Professor Andrew agreed to take on this work was that he would have full access to the service's records, as well as the opportunity to interview some current or retired members of MI5, and that his judgments derived from the material were his own and not subject to constraint by the service or government. Nevertheless given the highly sensitive nature of some of the material, particularly recent material, it was also agreed that the service would have the right to excise any material that breached national security. As might be imagined, this process was not always straightforward but with goodwill and common sense on both sides, the outcome was beneficial for the wider public understanding of MI5's role and history, while keeping sensitive details secret and ensuring that Professor Andrew's academic integrity was maintained. It also proved to be a bestseller in the run-up to Christmas 2009, as family members throughout the UK seized on it as an alternative to giving Dad socks or wine again. How many copies were read from end to end is not known, but its critical and academic reception was almost universally positive.[3]

Of course different tribes always have suspicions and myths about each other. A cartoon that I saw at the RSIS in Singapore sums this issue up. It is headed "How Careerists View Academics." A bullet-headed American soldier is briefing the President: "...and so, Mr President, I recommend going to DEFCON FOUR, and then applying full sanctions." He is interrupted by a wild-haired, pipe-smoking academic; "Wait! You're not adhering to traditional decision making paradigms as delineated in Graham Allison's 'Essence of Decision" page 162, footnote 2.' "

Despite such caricatures, a considerably more open relationship has developed in recent years between the academic and intelligence community. This has been the result of the exceptional demands and expectations imposed by the recent Islamist terrorist threat, which occurred in parallel to a more general relaxation of the intelligence community's traditional secrecy and unwillingness to engage with outside groups. There remain plenty of issues, beyond vital technical ones such as cyber security and data analytics, where the potential insights of academics and the operational and policy concerns of counter-terrorism professionals overlap. Understanding the drivers of counter-radicalization remains a challenge. This is reinforced by the religious illiteracy that exists in both the policy world and in the media. As the Middle East disintegrates, an understanding of the historical and cultural background to the region and its multiple communities suddenly emerges from the seminar room and becomes an immediate and vital policy concern. Trying to manage or defeat the security issues arising from a globalized world starts to look increasingly impossible in the absence of a wider understanding of the overall picture.

The developing relationship between the academic and the counterterrorist worlds has been of mutual (and hopefully of public) benefit. The number of officers throughout government who have thought it worthwhile to pursue postgraduate academic qualifications in areas such as terrorism studies or international relations in parallel to their busy working lives demonstrates that there is a real interest from practitioners in what academics can teach them, and the insights of practitioners in turn provide value to the academic community. Since terrorism shows no signs of going away and remains a complex multifaceted problem, it is likely that there will be more rather than less value in such dialogue between government and the academic community on these issues in coming years.

Notes

1. The Joint Intelligence Committee is the UK interdepartmental committee that issues assessments to government based on all available information including secret intelligence.
2. Recordings of candid interviews with former loyalist and republican terrorists undertaken for research purposes were held in a library at Boston College. The recordings were subject to a lengthy court process in the US that led in 2011 to transcripts being given to the Police Service of Northern Ireland.
3. <http://www.nytimes.com/2010/01/31/books/review/MacIntyre-t.html?_r=0>.

Reference

Andrew, Christopher (2009) *The Defence of the Realm: The Authorized History of MI5*. London: Allen Lane.

PART X

AUTOBIOGRAPHICAL REFLECTIONS ON THE EVOLUTION OF A FIELD

CHAPTER 45

CONSTRUCTING THE FIELD OF TERRORISM

MARTHA CRENSHAW

This chapter reviews the evolution of my interests in and approaches to researching terrorism, a story that begins in the 1960s. The scholarly work on terrorism is now so vast that it strains my capacity to include references to all of the many excellent studies in the field, especially those that appeared in the post-9/11 burst of activity (for more traditional reviews see Crenshaw 2014, 2007, 1989). My account is thus partial and incomplete as well as personal. It proceeds in chronological as well as thematic order.

Early Developments: Before the Beginning of "Terrorism Studies"

As an undergraduate at Newcomb College, at that time the women's college of Tulane University, I majored in political science with a focus on international relations and foreign policy. I also took courses in Russian history, especially the history of the nineteenth- and twentieth-century revolutionary movements, which may be one of the original sources of my interest in terrorism. I spent my junior year studying in Paris, an experience that grounded my investigations into the Algerian War and French theories of "guerre révolutionnaire" (e.g. Trinquier 1961). My aim then was to work for government, ideally at the State Department. I chose graduate school instead largely because my professors at Newcomb kindly nominated me for a Woodrow Wilson Fellowship, which I was fortunate enough to be awarded. I still did not plan a career in academia. After graduate school I worked as an analyst for the Congressional Research Service until I decided that the world of the university was preferable to the world of government bureaucracy (although I learned a lot at CRS). At that point (1974) I accepted a position at Wesleyan University, where I taught until 2007 when I moved to Stanford.

My regular course at Wesleyan on "The Politics of Terrorism" was a testing ground for many of the ideas I pursued in my research.

My inclination to study terrorism developed as I began graduate studies in political science and international relations at the University of Virginia in 1967, during the height of the Vietnam War. As I recounted in the introduction to *Explaining Terrorism*, a 2011 selection of my previously published work, a 1962 book on guerrilla warfare that concluded by noting the absence of studies of terrorism was an inspiration (Crenshaw 2011c; Paret and Shy 1962). At the time terrorism was generally considered, if it was considered at all, as the early and preliminary stage of unconventional warfare, or internal or revolutionary war or alternatively insurgency, usually following Maoist conceptions of how conflicts proceeded (e.g. on guerrilla warfare see Taber 1965; later Laqueur 1976). There were some general histories of specific revolutionary, nationalist, or anarchist struggles in which terrorism featured (many referenced in my 1981 article on the causes of terrorism, which draws on examples from the classic anarchist, Irish, and Russian cases). And there were many contemporary primary and journalistic accounts of the ongoing Latin American insurgencies of the 1960s (Guevara 1961; Debray 1967; Marighela 1971; Guillén 1973 [original publication 1966]; Gott 1971). Some early studies of the Vietnam War were also pertinent to non-state actor terrorism (e.g. Hosmer 1970).

Although it seems inconceivable now, work specifically devoted to the subject of terrorism was rare: a 1964 chapter by Thomas P. Thornton in Harry Eckstein's edited volume *Internal War*, and a book written in 1939 by a Polish jurist on the failure of the League of Nations to deal effectively with terrorism (Thornton 1964; Waciorski 1939). The 1937 edition of the *Encyclopaedia of the Social Sciences* contained an entry on terrorism (Hardman 1937), but there was no mention in the 1968 inaugural issue of the *International Encyclopedia of the Social Sciences*.

By 1971 political theorist David Rapoport had published a collection of thoughtful essays on the distinction between simple assassination meant to eliminate a specific individual because of his or her purported transgressions and, on the other hand, terrorism meant to instill fear in an audience (Rapoport 1971). In 1974 the British scholar Paul Wilkinson authored *Political Terrorism*, a study that reflected his enduring interest in the relationship between terrorism and liberal democracy and that drew on the British experience in Northern Ireland (Wilkinson 1974). Brian Jenkins of the Rand Corporation, the original think tank "terrorism expert," produced a prescient analysis of international terrorism in 1974 (Jenkins 1974). By 1977 historian Walter Laqueur had published an influential general history of terrorism (Laqueur 1977).

My initial research effort, an article that attempted to define the concept of revolutionary terrorism as the building block of a theoretical explanation of the phenomenon, appeared in the *Journal of Conflict Resolution* in 1972 (Crenshaw 1972). It provides a basis for understanding the undeveloped state of the field at the time. It was based on a chapter of my master's thesis at the University of Virginia, which I expanded into a Ph.D. dissertation (completed in 1973). The dissertation in turn was the foundation for a 1978 book, *Revolutionary Terrorism: The FLN in Algeria, 1954–1962* (Crenshaw 1978).

I completed most of my research for the project while in France from 1970 to 1972. My inquiries included interviews with the French military expert Roger Trinquier as well as anthropologist Germaine Tillion and international relations theorist Raymond Aron.

This case study argued that terrorism was a useful strategy for the FLN as a national liberation movement combatting a determined colonial power with a vastly superior conventional army, in effect as a tool of the weaker party in an asymmetrical conflict. Terrorism functioned not only to attract worldwide attention to the cause of Algerian independence and to put pressure on the French government, but also to mobilize support among the Muslim Algerian population and widen the gap between Algerians and the European settler community. It also served to provoke French repression, which in turn attracted more media attention, turned the French public against the war, and cemented Algerian opposition to continued French rule. The events of the famous "Battle of Algiers" in 1956–7 put urban terrorism on the map (as did the subsequent film that starred the leader of the Algiers network playing himself). I also explained that the FLN used terrorism not just against the French enemy but against rivals in the overall nationalist movement and against Algerian moderates who stood for compromise.

As I pointed out in later work on the effectiveness of FLN terrorism, such violence did not always secure the outcomes that the FLN sought (Crenshaw 1995a). For example, the precipitation of severe French repression deprived the organization of important political leaders who might have led an independent Algeria after 1962 more responsibly than did those who eventually assumed power (who came largely from the military elite). Terrorism was not automatically successful even though the FLN achieved its long-term objective. In later years the issue of the effectiveness of terrorism has been taken up by political scientists and historians (e.g. Abrahms 2006, 2012; Pape 2005; Krause 2013; English 2016).

As I noted earlier, it is important to recognize the historical context in which the early questions about terrorism emerged. In the 1970s the phenomenon of terrorism became increasingly prevalent and prominent. Terrorism appeared as the main strategy of revolutionary and nationalist groups, and it targeted the industrial democracies of the West as well as authoritarian regimes and fragile states. It also developed into a transnational phenomenon, beginning with hijackings of civilian aircraft and kidnappings and assassinations of diplomats that drew media attention. As seen at the time these were shocking violations of international norms.

The Algerian War inspired imitators in other national liberation movements, and the Vietnam War shifted the ideological climate to equate anti-Americanism with anti-imperialism. The development of terrorism was partially a result of the perceived outcome of these small wars that represented the victory of insurgent revolutionaries over Western imperialism, first France and then the United States. I date the beginning of that wave of international terrorism as 1968, the date of the first Palestinian hijacking and the first diplomatic assassination in Guatemala. Latin America, Argentina, Uruguay, Brazil, El Salvador, and Chile also experienced domestic terrorism. The IRA was reconstituted in Northern Ireland as the Provisional IRA, and ETA revived in Spain. Among revolutionary groups trying to overturn the capitalist and imperialist order, the

Red Army Faction in Germany, the Red Brigades in Italy, and the Weather Underground in the United States featured in the headlines despite their small numbers and relatively low levels of violence. The 1972 attack on Israeli athletes by the Palestinian group Black September at the Munich Olympics put terrorism on the international agenda as well as on television screens worldwide. The United States established its first counterterrorism bureaucracy in the State Department. The United Nations took up the issue. The dramatic Israeli rescue of hostages at Entebbe in 1976 encouraged other states to develop a rapid reaction military response. All of these developments propelled academic research and often influenced its direction, just as later events such as the 9/11 attacks did.

In 1977–8 I received a grant from the National Endowment for the Humanities that allowed me to spend a year in London libraries reading and reflecting about terrorism, from Russian revolutionaries, European and American anarchists, and Irish Republicans in the nineteenth century to that time. As I noted earlier, narrative histories of specific historical cases comprised most of the material on terrorism. This largely historical and secondary research led me to propose an analysis that went beyond a single case study to present a comparative framework for understanding the causes of terrorism (Crenshaw 1981). I argued that three levels of analysis had to be combined. The first was society, or what we now call a meta-approach that is ecological, focusing on the conditions that might encourage or discourage terrorism. I proposed that permissive or enabling conditions are one cause but that alone this factor is insufficient to account for terrorism, especially since it is the work of a small number of people. Similarly, an environment that motivated grievances (repression, deprivation, discrimination, poverty, or inequality) was insufficient to explain the behavior of a tiny minority of those who experience it. At the other end of the spectrum of causation is the level of the individual and his or her predispositions and inclinations. There is no distinct profile of a terrorist that permits prediction (or prevention) but researchers should ask what attracts a wide variety of people to terrorism. What circumstances are similar? What catalysts drive them? What individual psychological characteristics might terrorism require? And last, we needed to understand terrorism as a group strategy and as the outcome of group dynamics. Terrorism is usually the product of group decision-making, and it can be a reasonable and calculated means to an end considering the goals and resources of the groups that resort to it and the nature of the enemy they confront as well as the audiences they seek to influence.

During that year in London, I also benefitted from a visiting fellowship at the Richardson Institute for Conflict and Peace Research, which offered me the use of a shared office. By a stroke of good luck the office was shared with Manus Midlarsky. A consequence was that we collaborated on an article published in the *International Studies Quarterly* (Midlarsky et al. 1980) that presented one of the first analyses of contagion effects in international terrorism. It was also one of the first to employ quantitative approaches to the study of terrorism (a Midlarsky skill set, not mine), using data collected in "International Terrorism: Attributes of Terrorist Events, 1968–1977" or ITERATE, a dataset whose updated form is still used by many researchers. Now many datasets of terrorist events are available, principally the more comprehensive Global

Terrorism Database, or GTD, which tracks both international and domestic terrorist attacks since 1970. Our article dealt with the spread of terrorism from what was then the "third world"—Latin America and the Middle East—to the developed West, as groups in countries like Germany deliberately imitated groups like the Tupamaros in Uruguay. We regarded this as a case of transnational diffusion of innovation.

Growth of the Field in the 1980s

In the 1980s perceptions of terrorism began to change primarily because of the establishment of Hezbollah in the context of civil war and external state intervention in Lebanon. Its appearance on the scene and its reliance on "suicide terrorism" marked the beginnings of what would come to be defined as "religious terrorism." This era was also marked by the Reagan administration's determination to take a tough stand toward state-sponsored terrorism by the Soviet Union, North Korea, Libya, Iran, and Cuba. Notable events of the decade included the 1983 bombing of the US Marine Barracks in Beirut, subsequent kidnappings of journalists, educators, and officials as well as two bombings of the American Embassy, the 1985 *Achille Lauro* affair, the TWA 847 hijacking in Beirut, the 1986 US bombing raid on Libya (a retaliation for the Libyan-instigated La Belle disco bombing in Berlin in 1985), and the midair bombing of Pan Am Flight 103 over Scotland in 1988. In other theaters, the LTTE rose to prominence in Sri Lanka, India battled Sikh extremists in the Punjab, and Action Directe entered the scene in France. The IRA and ETA persisted despite reforms and democratic transitions in Northern Ireland and Spain.

In January 1982, in honor of the sesquicentennial anniversary of its founding, Wesleyan held a conference "Terrorism: The Challenge to the State" that I organized. It resulted in an edited volume (Crenshaw 1983) that focused on the impact of terrorism on states and societies. Even then I concluded in what now seems an ironic understatement that "Like many other ill-defined and imperfectly understood problems, it has no easy solution" (p. 149).

During the 1980s the Russell Sage Foundation, the Harry Frank Guggenheim Foundation (HFG), and the Ford Foundation supported my research. Their assistance and encouragement helped me turn four strands of intellectual interest into research projects on the organizational dynamics within groups using terrorism, psychological explanations of terrorism, the decline of campaigns of terrorism, and comparative approaches to terrorism.

One line of inquiry focused on organizational theories of terrorist behavior. In a paper presented to the International Political Science Association, subsequently published in *Orbis* (Crenshaw 1985), I argued that groups using terrorism should be approached as political organizations like others that were not involved in conspiratorial violence. What we called "terrorist organizations" were not sui generis but examples of a broader category. Similar if not identical explanations could apply to their behavior.

Their coherence might depend on leaders' ability to manipulate selective incentives in order to maintain loyalty. Groups could exist simply to maintain themselves rather than achieve long-term ideological goals.

I then compared this explanation to an instrumental or strategic approach to terrorism (Crenshaw 1987, first developed in Crenshaw 1985), since I had not abandoned the understanding of terrorism as a strategic or logical means to an end, interpreted as a choice as well as the outcome of internal pressures (Crenshaw 1990). The debate over whether terrorism is internally or externally driven has continued over the years, with recent examples including the work of Robert Pape (2005), Max Abrahms (2006, 2012), and Peter Krause (2013, 2017). Scholars such as Jacob Shapiro have elaborated much more sophisticated and systematic organizational theories, in his case employing principal–agent theory to explain the contradictory pressures on terrorist undergrounds (Shapiro 2013).

During the 1980s I also developed an interest in the psychology of terrorism. In this regard I owe a debt of gratitude to Margaret Hermann, who asked me to contribute a chapter on the subject to a new handbook of political psychology that she was editing under the auspices of the International Society of Political Psychology (Crenshaw 1986). In my overview of the psychology of terrorism, a literature that I found "uneven and sparsely developed" at the time (p. 407), I added to the little I found specifically on terrorism by borrowing from other literatures such as studies of small military units under combat conditions, theories of identity formation, and social psychological analyses of small group processes.

Two pioneering studies of the psychological roots of terrorism informed my review and are still worthy of attention, especially since they were written long before terrorism became popularly stereotyped as the irrational expression of apocalyptic fantasies. One instance is the work of Jeanne Knutson (1980, 1981), who analyzed Croatian nationalist terrorism. Her work was probably the earliest case study of radicalization processes, and it also calls to mind Ehud Sprinzak's important contribution a decade later to the study of radicalization by identifying a "crisis of legitimacy" in political experience that helped motivate left-wing terrorism in the 1960s (Sprinzak 1991). Recently McCauley and Moskalenko (2011, 2017) appropriately reminded readers that the process of "radicalization" into Islamist extremism is indistinguishable from that of radicalization into any other ideology and that "radicalization" is a two-way process.

The second early contribution is a set of academic studies in sociology and psychology commissioned by the West German government to analyze the sources of left-wing terrorism in Germany (Jäger et al. 1981). It seemed conclusive to me that there is no "terrorist personality" or profile and that the influence of the group is paramount in generating cohesion, commitment, and willingness to abandon moral restraints to engage in horrifying acts of violence. Emotions matter as much as objective reasoning, and terrorism can be expressive as well as purposive. I expanded this line of thought in a series of subsequent publications (Crenshaw 1988, 1990, 1992a, 1992b, 2000a, 2000b).

Another idea that emerged in the 1980s was that we needed to understand not just the causes of terrorism, its inception or onset, but also its decline. How do campaigns of terrorism come to an end? In fact, my 1970s NEH proposal had asserted that I wanted to study both how terrorism begins and how it ends. Clearly government suppression was not an adequate answer; in fact, government over-reaction might provoke rather than discourage terrorism. Along with Ross and Gurr (1989), I suggested that processes internal to the organization might be as critical a causal mechanism in a winding down process as external constraints and pressures, particularly government use of force. Terrorist atrocities might exceed the bounds of tolerance of their constituencies, for example, or lead to disillusionment among cadres (Crenshaw 1991, 1996). Ross and Gurr called this twin phenomenon "backlash and burn-out." Leadership was clearly important as well, since my preliminary research suggested that the rank and file in an organization were likely to push for escalation, while leaders were more likely to enforce restraint and to have a clearer sense of strategic direction. This line of research has been filled out by excellent empirically grounded studies by Jones and Libicki (2008), Cronin (2009), Malkki (2010), and Weinberg (2012).

Also in the 1980s the Ford Foundation generously supported an initiative to develop a set of comparative case studies of terrorism, based on the assumption that campaigns of terrorism cannot be understood outside of their political and historical contexts. Generalization is important, but so is empirical grounding. It took a considerable amount of time as well as strenuous effort on the part of the contributors to bring the project to completion (including a major conference at Wesleyan University in 1989), but the result was *Terrorism in Context*, a volume first published in 1995 and still in print twenty years later (Crenshaw 1995b). The cases ranged from the nineteenth century to contemporary instances at the time such as Sendero Luminoso in Peru. My Wesleyan colleague, distinguished historian Philip Pomper, contributed a chapter on the Russian revolutionaries (and as a psycho-historian and biographer encouraged me to think in terms of the psychology of terrorism when I was wedded to an instrumental perspective). The edited volume of twelve case studies grew to be quite long (over 800 pages), so that finding a publisher willing to accept such a massive tome proved difficult. Fortunately Sandy Thatcher at Pennsylvania State University Press took the risk.

Responding to Terrorism

My research has also investigated various dimensions of government responses to terrorism, both national and international. My 1978 study of the Algerian War included a chapter on the French response to FLN terrorism (Crenshaw 1978). By treating terrorism as a military rather than a political problem, France eroded its own legitimacy and bolstered that of the FLN. Military elites who had been assigned the responsibility of fighting the war felt betrayed by the government and rose in rebellion. Controversy over the extensive use of torture haunted French politics for years after the war ended. It thus seems strange that the American military thought to emulate the French model of "revolutionary warfare" (see Nagl 2007).

In 2001 (before the 9/11 attacks) I published an article exploring the complexities of the American counterterrorism policy process (Crenshaw 2001). This research was the result of a project supported by the US Institute of Peace (USIP), which included an empirical survey of the extent and tone of media coverage of US counterterrorism policy from 1968 to 1998. As I had done in my work on organizational explanations of terrorism, I approached counterterrorism policy as the result of the same political processes that produced other sorts of outcomes in other policy arenas (not necessarily suboptimal but subject to the same bureaucratic pushing and pulling). I argued that bureaucracies might compete to have terrorism on their agendas, but that they might also try to avoid the problem, fearing that their performance would be found wanting usually because of budgetary constraints as well as the complexity of the challenge. Recently Frank Foley (2013) analyzed the institutional routines and norms that explain the differences between counterterrorist policies in Britain and France, democracies facing a similar threat but with divergent responses.

Before 9/11, international terrorism was far from a top tier priority for the national security agendas of most governments. In retrospect, this neglect seems somewhat surprising considering that there were significant terrorist attacks in the decade of the 1990s, such as the first bombing of the World Trade Center in 1993, the 1995 Oklahoma City bombing, and also in 1995 the Aum Shinrikyo sarin gas attacks on the Tokyo subway, as well as Al Qaeda's "war" against the United States manifested in the 1998 East Africa Embassy bombings and the 2000 bombing of the USS *Cole* in Yemen. Still neither policymakers nor academics in the fields of foreign policy and international politics were inclined to make terrorism a paramount national security threat or indeed a disturbance to international order at all (Crenshaw 2001). Although everyone recognized the existence of violent non-state actors, states remained the primary object of attention. Terrorism was only deemed to be a major threat if it should involve the use of "weapons of mass destruction," nuclear weapons in particular. Despite policymakers' fears and exhaustive academic investigations, no incident of nuclear terrorism had happened then or has happened now. (I examined the potential threat in Crenshaw 1977.) This is a classic case of a low likelihood but high consequence event. Nevertheless, the prospective use of nuclear materials by non-state actors remains a top national security concern for the United States, since the supplies of material are not completely secure, and some groups continue to express and demonstrate interest (such as Al Qaeda and more recently ISIS/ISIL, which apparently plotted an attack on a Belgian nuclear facility).

After the shock of 9/11, I expanded my research into American counterterrorism with a chapter on "Coercive Diplomacy and the Response to Terrorism" in a USIP-sponsored volume extending the seminal work of Alexander George (Crenshaw 2003). I examined Clinton and Bush administration responses primarily to Al Qaeda but also to state-supported terrorism instigated by Iran and Iraq. Unsurprisingly, I concluded that coercing non-state actors is extremely difficult; states may sometimes coerce other states, although all efforts at coercion that mixed force and diplomacy had ambiguous outcomes. The record up through the launching of the war on terror was not promising. Alexander George's argument that the coercing party can only succeed if it has superior motivation is directly applicable to countering terrorism (George 1991), and terrorists are much less risk averse than governments. Governments find it hard to identify the opponent let alone understand the opponent's motivations; gaining sufficiently precise and timely warning so as to communicate a threat and a sense of urgency is doubly difficult. These obstacles may be one reason for the shift to a preemptive strategy post-9/11, although in both cases interruption of a plot may only deflect the terrorist adversary onto another target.

I followed this work by considering the ethical implications of responding to terrorism (Crenshaw 2004a) and by analyzing the "grand strategy" (or lack thereof) of American counterterrorism, primarily under the Bush administration (Crenshaw 2004b). Here I stressed the neglect of terrorism before 9/11 and the unrealistic expectations about what the use of military force in counterterrorism could accomplish after 9/11. I argued that our policy risked setting goals that were so ambitious and so vague that no means could produce the desired end (such as the eradication of terrorism entirely). I asked whether a grand strategy was possible or, indeed, desirable.

Later I reviewed the Obama administration's counterterrorism policies and stressed the difficulties of moving away from the war on terror template established immediately after 9/11 (Crenshaw 2011a). The Obama administration tried to narrow the definition of the threat of terrorism to Al Qaeda and affiliates, shift from unilateralism and excessive claims of what could be accomplished through American action to a more modest stance, and repair relations with majority Muslim countries. Yet the Obama administration escalated the use of drones and maintained the high levels of secrecy in decision-making that characterized the Bush administration. I concluded that "the emphasis on military force as a solution to international terrorism has not been explained in terms that make it a logical means to the ends the administration has prescribed" (Crenshaw 2011a, 253). The Obama administration did not solve the problem of countering violent extremism through persuasion at home while using military force against the same enemy abroad. The Trump administration has largely followed the same strategic plan abroad as its predecessor.

The question of deterring terrorism by non-state actors became compelling to the American government after 9/11. I was a member of a National Academy of Sciences Panel on "Understanding Terrorists in Order to Deter Terrorism," the findings of which cast doubt on the likelihood of successful deterrence (National Research Council 2002). A decade later I reached a similarly pessimistic conclusion about the possibility of deterring nuclear terrorism by non-state actors through threats of retaliation, despite the fact that in 2008 the Obama administration had announced a new official policy of doing just that (Crenshaw 2012). I pointed to the barriers to accurate and timely attribution of responsibility as well as the near impossibility of threatening a non-state adversary with harm sufficient to be meaningful to them and yet involving a punishment that the United States would be willing and able to inflict. The debate over deterrence continues, with a weak consensus that deterrence by denial is possible but that threats of retaliation through military force are problematic (even though Israeli strategy is based on the assumption that military deterrence will work; see Dugan and Chenoweth 2012). Fear of drone strikes might impede terrorist operations in active battlefield theaters but it does not appear to change the fundamental calculus behind jihadist terrorism. It is hard to think how threats of retaliation might have deterred 9/11, the Madrid and London bombings in 2004 and 2005, the Boston Marathon bombing, or the Paris attacks of 2017. We should note that American drone strikes are not necessarily intended to coerce or deter but to disrupt; they appear meant to physically remove leaders and operators with valuable skills and expertise, under the assumption that the supply of such human resources is finite and that eventually the targeted organization will weaken due to lack of talent.

In the decade after 9/11 and the launching of the global war on terror, the Russell Sage Foundation sponsored a volume on the important question of the unanticipated consequences of counterterrorism, which I edited (Crenshaw 2010). Its focus was on the European democracies, Japan, and Israel. These studies stressed that, beyond their possible effectiveness in reducing or diminishing the threat of terrorism, an effectiveness that is often contested, government policies have unintended and often unwanted consequences such as undermining civil liberties or turning immigration policy into a security issue, when most immigrants are not terrorists and most terrorists are not immigrants. The volume also emphasized how hard it is to reverse course once restrictive policies have been put in place (see further Crenshaw and LaFree 2017). Whether the reason is inertia, the development of vested interests, or partisanship and politicization, the outcome is the same. The US, for example, has been unable to escape the strictures of the policies adopted in haste in the weeks and months after 9/11. The chapter by my Wesleyan Government Department colleague John Finn argued persuasively that the legal and constitutional changes provoked by terrorism have proved nearly impossible to reverse. His findings echoed those of Laura Donohue in her analysis of counterterrorism law in the United States and Great Britain (Donohue 2008).

National responses to transnational terrorism require international cooperation, and even domestic terrorism can have external ramifications (ETA militants taking refuge in France in order to organize attacks in Spain, for example). American counterterrorism policy was based on seeking the support of foreign partner states. The State Department's annual publication *Patterns of Global Terrorism* for 1999 summarized the four American policy tenets as no concessions and no deals with terrorists (a holdover from the days of hostage taking), bring terrorist suspects to justice for their crimes following the rule of law, pressure states that sponsor terrorism, and aid states that support US policy and need assistance in building counterterrorism capabilities. Bringing terrorists to justice in particular requires that other states cooperate in intelligence activities and in apprehending and extraditing or prosecuting suspects. In 1989 I argued that there were significant limits to the possibility of effective international cooperation against terrorism, in particular because of the political sensitivity of the threat (Crenshaw 1989). National interests were bound to predominate, and cooperation was often rhetorical rather than operational. Some years later in a much more thorough study Peter Romaniuk (2010) reached the similar conclusion that realism prevails in multilateral counterterrorism and that our expectations should be modest. American unilateralism predated 9/11 despite our interest in cooperation—in the 1980s frustration over the failure of even close allies to extradite or convict led to changes in American law that permitted seizure of terrorism suspects overseas (the first implementation of the law was in the Fawaz Yunis case in 1987). Most effective cooperation was bilateral or among small groups of like-minded states, and it was often at the operational level. Mendelsohn (2009) concluded that American hegemony was an important driver of post-9/11 cooperation against jihadist terrorism but that the normative principles of international society limited the extent of American dominance.

In collaboration with Gary LaFree, I tried to bring some of these threads together in a policy-oriented book *Countering Terrorism* (Crenshaw and LaFree 2017). We emphasized the attributes of terrorism itself that make it such a difficult problem for policymakers as well as for researchers. These include the fact that statistically speaking incidents of terrorism are actually rare, which makes it hard to identify trends and offer generalizations. Much interpretation of terrorism is based on attacks that produce visibly violent outcomes, rather than the many more uncompleted plots that do not result in physical consequences (introducing a selection bias, in academic terms). The actors behind terrorism are many, varied, and constantly shifting; there is no uniform monolithic "terrorist organization." This fluidity makes it hard to pin down the adversary, especially in cases of "homegrown terrorism" or "self-radicalization." Attribution of responsibility for attacks is highly problematic, which impedes punishment and deterrence of terrorism. Measuring and demonstrating the effectiveness of counterterrorism measures is notoriously difficult. Governments are still tempted to over-promise results.

The Changing Contours of Terrorism

After 9/11, studies of terrorism proliferated, some of uneven quality. "Experts" on terrorism also dominated the news media. In 2002 columnist Tom Friedman noted that his reaction to depressing Middle East news was to turn to the golf channel because "All the commentators, particularly the instructors, on the Golf Channel actually know what they're talking about, and no one on the Golf Channel is identified by the phony and meaningless title of 'Terrorism Expert' " (Friedman 2002). I tried to avoid that designation as much as possible.

One issue raised in the disputative post-9/11 debate over terrorism was whether or not the danger posed by Al Qaeda and offshoots was an entirely new phenomenon. To some, the threat was not only unprecedented but also historically exceptional in terms of apocalyptic motivations, indiscriminate ruthlessness, and decentralized organization. These arguments were often closely linked to the idea that religion is a cause of terrorism—the root of extreme ends as well as means. I argued instead that Al Qaeda was not entirely new (e.g. Crenshaw 2008, 2009, 2011b). Trends in terrorism change over time, certainly, often due to exploitation of the same modernizations in technology and communications in a setting of international interdependence that affect all actors, but there are also constants. Some assumptions about both old and new were mistaken (e.g. that terrorists of the past had reasonable goals, preferred not to kill large numbers of civilians, and were hierarchically organized—one need only recall the nineteenth-century anarchists). The constraints on policy that applied to pre-9/11 terrorism applied equally to post-9/11 terrorism. The association of religion with terrorism is hard to establish with any precision. Do religious beliefs motivate terrorism? Many if not most actors using terrorism, whether groups or individuals, have mixed motives, and it is not always easy to pinpoint the power of religious beliefs and doctrine as causes, even when the users of terrorism explicitly justify their actions in terms of religious doctrine. Nor is it clear that ideology always determines methods of violence. Suicide missions are now associated with jihadism but were not in the past (Hezbollah, for example, launched the tactic, and the Sri Lankan LTTE was an adept practitioner). The issue of the role of religion became more contentious with the rise of the Islamic State, the establishment of its self-proclaimed caliphate in Iraq and Syria, and its appeal to Western youth who became "radicalized" through social media.

A related issue concerned why the United States was targeted. I began asking why the US was targeted in 2001, arguing that the reasons lay in the spillover from a globalized civil war more than the simple assertion that "they hate our values" (Crenshaw 2001). My contention was that

> Since the late 1960s the United States has been a preferred target, the victim of approximately one-third of all international terrorist attacks over the past 30 years. In most instances Americans and American interests were attractive to the practitioners of terrorism because of United States support for unpopular local governments or regional enemies. This terrorism can thus be interpreted as a form of compellence: the use or threat of violence to compel the United States to withdraw from its external commitments. Terrorism should be seen as a strategic reaction to American power in the context of globalized civil war. (2001, 1)

More recently, Chenoweth (2013) in reviewing the literature on democracy and terrorism identified state behavior in the foreign policy realm as an explanation.

I continued this line of inquiry through participation in a post-9/11 collaborative initiative promoting serious and systematic social science research. This was the 2005 establishment of the National Consortium for the Study of Terrorism and Responses to Terrorism (START), a Center of Excellence of the Department of Homeland Security based at the University of Maryland, under the leadership of Gary LaFree, also my co-author in the book on counterterrorism alluded to earlier (2017). In one project, a group of START researchers found that most organizations using terrorism did not direct it against American interests (LaFree et al. 2009). Our analysis of fifty-three foreign organizations that had been identified by the US Department of State and subsequently the National Counterterrorism Center as especially dangerous for the United States found that local targets were much more common than foreign targets and that even the most active anti-American groups were more likely to attack at home than abroad. In fact, only slightly more than 3 percent of these organizations' attacks were directed at the United States, and only five of those were on the US homeland.

Our data for this project came from the GTD, which only includes attacks that actually occur or are very close in time to occurring, with the would-be perpetrators "out the door." Another of my collaborative research projects supported by START identified and analyzed failed and foiled plots by jihadists (Al Qaeda, ISIS, and their affiliates, associates, and sympathizers) against the homelands of the United States and its allies in NATO and the EU, as well as Australia and New Zealand (Crenshaw et al. 2017; this research is also the basis for a chapter in the 2017 Crenshaw and LaFree book). The attacks could be failed, foiled, completed, or successful. Our premise was that if we analyze only terrorist "successes" we do not get a full picture of targets, methods, and motivations. Nor can we understand how terrorist adversaries adapt (or do not) to government counter-measures. This project counted 121 attacks or attempted attacks against or in the territory of the United States in the period 1993–2017. Most were foiled by the authorities, usually through the use of surveillance and informants. The majority of these plots were not credibly associated with organizations located outside the United States, and there was no indication that externally directed plots were more likely to succeed than those only loosely connected to a jihadist cause. Among that small number, other than Al Qaeda itself and its direction of the 9/11 attacks, the group most often responsible was Al Qaeda in the Arabian Peninsula (AQAP). It is also worth noting that there were very few returned "foreign fighters" among the perpetrators or would-be perpetrators. Armed assaults were more likely to be successful than bombings.

The question of innovation in terrorism is directly relevant to understanding why we were surprised by the 9/11 attacks. In early 2001 (before 9/11) I presented a paper on terrorist innovation to a conference convened at Harvard (see Crenshaw 2010, for a revised and updated version). I distinguished between tactical, strategic, and organizational innovation. I argued that despite the widespread assumption that terrorists were not innovative—indeed that they often had no strategy at all—there were significant advances in the conceptualization of the use of violence, such as the adoption of suicide bombings in the 1980s, led by Hezbollah in Lebanon. I borrowed theories from the literature in different disciplines, analyzing innovation in the military and in social movements as well as psychological studies of creativity. These studies were similar in finding that strategic innovation in particular, which involves a reconceptualization of ends and means, is not the result of a sudden inspiration or bolt from the blue but instead represents a recombination of old methods and ideas to solve a new problem. Innovation takes time, effort, and thought as well as a catalyst for change that introduces a problem that needs solving and instigates a search for solutions. Innovation depends heavily on quality of leadership or entrepreneurship within an organization. Strategic innovation is rare and inherently unpredictable. Adam Dolnik (2007) and Assaf Moghadam (2013) have taken up the subjects of tactical or technological innovation and organizational sources of innovation. Both authors agree that we need to look more closely at the types of organizations where innovation is most likely.

In the post-9/11 years I also developed an interest in relationships among violent extremist organizations or terrorist non-state actors. It is rarely the case that governments confront a single monolithic adversary, even in Al Qaeda or ISIS. Violent oppositions typically have multiple centers, and the different groups and factions are as likely to be rivals as allies even if struggling against a common foe. Splintering is common. If governments do not understand these constantly shifting relationships as well as their causes and consequences it is impossible to formulate a sensible counterterrorist policy.

An essential first step was to map out or diagram the patterns of competition and cooperation as they changed over time in different conflict theaters. The resulting "maps" or genealogies permitted comparison of different inter-organizational trajectories. I also believed that visualizing this dynamic evolution over time would be more instructive than reading a narrative description and that such a display should be web-based. Thus with the support of a grant in 2009 from the National Science Foundation, supported by the Department of Defense Minerva Initiative, I developed the "mapping militants" project <mappingmilitants.stanford.edu>. An interactive online diagram of relationships is linked to detailed profiles of the different groups. One explanation that might be drawn from this analysis is that groups align and realign according to their changing strategic expectations about the future. These expectations are often altered by external shocks, such as military intervention by outside powers or government offers to negotiate. Interest in inter-group relationships has increased recently (see e.g. Mendelsohn 2016; Moghadam 2017; Krause 2017).

Concluding thoughts and Future Directions

Terrorism remains a challenging topic for academic analysis, never mind the extreme difficulties it poses for policymakers. Its complexities are not easy to understand or explain. Scholars in the field of terrorism studies are still struggling to answer many of the same questions that were introduced forty years ago, even though we have more comprehensive and precise data, more systematic and sophisticated methods, and deeper accumulated knowledge. Defining terrorism and distinguishing it from other forms of political violence (such as insurgency) are still problematic, as is the puzzle of determining its causes. We are still trying to arrive at a theory that represents an integrated process of causation that spans all three levels of analysis, the individual, the group, and the national and international environment, and that could apply across different contexts. In particular, post-2001 we find it hard to explain not just the "why" but the "how" of a shape-shifting yet persistent jihadist adversary with both local roots and transnational reach. Is it an organization, a social movement, or an ideology? Why has the jihadist current lasted so long? What is the relationship between transnational terrorism and civil war (Crenshaw 2017)?

A satisfactory understanding of what constitutes effective counterterrorism also escapes us. There is lack of agreement as to what national policy can accomplish to prevent or otherwise manage the threat of terrorism. Without a clear and realistic conception of goals, as well as the means that would permit their accomplishment, it is impossible to identify metrics that would produce an evaluation of effectiveness. Military force is still the centerpiece of the continuing global war on terror. Successive American presidents have promised to end it, to no avail. Surprises, such as the quick rise and expansion of the Islamic State, seem constant.

Future researchers have an ample supply of problems to analyze. A central question for a research agenda concerns the fluid interactions among violent non-state actors that I mentioned earlier. We need a better understanding of how government policy affects interactions and in turn how inter-militant relationships affect conflict trajectories and outcomes. A related question concerns the link between the dynamics of relationships among groups and the internal cohesiveness of these entities. Is an increase in number of competing groups due to splintering or to other factors, such as the formation of new groups? Are splinter groups more extreme or more moderate than their parents? We also lack a good understanding of the process of outbidding in extremism, or competitive escalation. It cannot be assumed automatically that in every conflict intergroup rivalries will produce imitation leading to increased levels of violence against a common adversary. Competition can produce differentiation among groups. Under what conditions are these different results obtained? Under what conditions are negotiated solutions possible?

Another set of puzzles concerns how beliefs, ideas, ideologies, theologies, doctrines, and cultures are related to terrorist behavior. Researchers would do well to recall the basic causal question that David Rapoport addressed in 1983: do ideas and/or cultural norms produce violence and/or shape its form? Rapoport found that in a set of classic cases doctrine prescribed some methods and proscribed others. In a modern setting, how do ideas relate to strategy? Can different belief systems or ideologies explain variation in willingness to cause civilian casualties? This question is an academic variant of a more controversial topic: the politicization of the issue as it pertains to the relationship between the religion of Islam and contemporary jihadist terrorism. What happens when the public believes that religious beliefs drive terrorism? What effect can government rhetoric or actions have on the ideas that motivate terrorism (unfortunately framed as a "battle of ideas")? What difference does it make if political leaders refer to "Islamic radicalization" as opposed to a generic "violent extremism"? Why in the United States is jihadist violence regarded as more of a threat than right-wing terrorism? Why are similar terrorist threats perceived differently?

It is also timely to revisit the question of transnational contagion processes, especially as they relate to the connection between transnational terrorism and civil war (for a recent study see LaFree et al. 2018). Researchers and policymakers are searching for plausible explanations of individual radicalization outside conflict zones, a question that depends on a refined conceptualization of what is meant by "radicalization" or "extremism." Taking a broader perspective, this question involves the relationship between the global and the local, and the individual and the environment. The question of transmission processes is complicated in the twenty-first century by the communication dominance of social media. Among many other things, the ubiquity of social media means that diffusion can be extraordinarily rapid and democratic. Anyone can be a sender, and anyone can be a receiver.

These questions are not easy to answer, but they are important, and terrorism is unlikely to fade away soon, even if the Islamic State's ambitious caliphate project in Syria and Iraq has been defeated. As we researchers have observed over the decades, terrorism is a form of violence that requires little in the way of material resources. Its appeal as a tactic of disruption is enduring.

References

Abrahms, M. (2006) "Why Terrorism does Not Work," *International Security*, 31(2): 42–78.

Abrahms, M. (2012) "The Political Effectiveness of Terrorism Revisited," *Comparative Political Studies*, 45(3): 366–93.

Chenoweth, E. (2013) "Terrorism and Democracy," *Annual Review of Political Science*, 16: 355–78.

Crenshaw [Hutchinson], M. (1972) "The Concept of Revolutionary Terrorism," *Journal of Conflict Resolution*, 16(3): 383–96.

Crenshaw [Hutchinson], M. (1977) "Defining Future Threat: Terrorists and Nuclear Proliferation," in Yonah Alexander and Seymour Maxwell Finger (eds), *Terrorism: Interdisciplinary Perspectives*. New York: John Jay Press, 298–316.

Crenshaw [Hutchinson], M. (1978) *Revolutionary Terrorism: The FLN in Algeria, 1954–1962*. Stanford, CA: Hoover Institution Press.

Crenshaw, M. (1981) "The Causes of Terrorism," *Comparative Politics*, 13(4): 379–99.

Crenshaw, M., ed. (1983) *Terrorism, Legitimacy, and Power: The Consequences of Political Violence*. Middletown, CT: Wesleyan University Press.

Crenshaw, M. (1985) "An Organizational Approach to the Analysis of Political Terrorism," *Orbis*, 29(3): 465–89.

Crenshaw, M. (1986) "The Psychology of Political Terrorism," in Margaret G. Hermann (ed.), *Political Psychology: Contemporary Problems and Issues*. San Francisco: Jossey-Bass, 379–413.

Crenshaw, M. (1987) "Theories of Terrorism: Instrumental and Organizational Approaches," *Journal of Strategic Studies* (Special Issue), 10(4): 13–31.

Crenshaw, M. (1988) "The Subjective Reality of the Terrorist," in Robert O. Slater and Michael Stohl (eds), *Current Perspectives on International Terrorism*. London: Macmillan, and New York: St. Martin's, 12–46.

Crenshaw, M. (1989) *Terrorism and International Cooperation*. New York: Institute for East–West Security Studies. Occasional Papers Series. Distributed by Westview Press.

Crenshaw, M. (1990) "The Causes of Terrorism," *Comparative Politics*, 13(4): 379–99.

Crenshaw, M. (1991) "How Terrorism Declines," *Terrorism and Political Violence*, 3(1): 69–87.

Crenshaw, M. (1992a) "How Terrorists Think: Psychological Contributions to Understanding Terrorism," in Lawrence Howard (ed.), *Terrorism: Roots, Impact, Responses*. New York: Praeger, 71–80.

Crenshaw, M. (1992b) "Decisions to Use Terrorism: Psychological Constraints on Instrumental Reasoning," in Donatella della Porta (ed.), *Social Movements and Violence: Participation in Underground Organizations*. International Social Movement Research, 4. Greenwich, CT: JAI Press Inc., 29–42.
Crenshaw, M. (1995a) "The Effectiveness of Terrorism in the Algerian War," in Martha Crenshaw (ed.), *Terrorism in Context*. University Park, PA: Pennsylvania State University Press, 473–513.
Crenshaw, M., ed. (1995b) *Terrorism in Context*. University Park, PA: Pennsylvania State University Press.
Crenshaw, M. (1996) "Why Violence is Rejected or Renounced: A Case Study of Oppositional Terrorism," in Tom Gregor (ed.), *A Natural History of Peace*. Nashville, TN: Vanderbilt University Press, 249–72.
Crenshaw, M. (2000a) "Terrorism," in *Encyclopedia of Psychology*. New York: Oxford University Press.
Crenshaw, M. (2000b) "The Psychology of Terrorism: An Agenda for the 21st Century," *Political Psychology*, 21(2): 405–20.
Crenshaw, M. (2001) "Counterterrorism Policy and the Political Process," *Studies in Conflict and Terrorism*, 24(5): 329–38.
Crenshaw, M. (2003) "Coercive Diplomacy and the Response to Terrorism," in Robert J. Art and Patrick M. Cronin (eds), *The United States and Coercive Diplomacy*. Washington, DC: United States Institute of Peace Press, 305–57.
Crenshaw, M. (2004a) "Responding to Terrorism: Ethical Implications," in Anthony F. Lang, Albert C. Pierce, and Joel H. Rosenthal (eds), *Ethics and the Future of Conflict: Lessons from the 1990s*. Upper Saddle River, NJ: Pearson/Prentice Hall.
Crenshaw, M. (2004b) "Terrorism, Strategies, and Grand Strategies," in Audrey Kurth Cronin and James M. Ludes (eds), *Attacking Terrorism: Elements of a Grand Strategy*. Washington, DC: Georgetown University Press, 74–93.
Crenshaw, M. (2007) "Explaining Suicide Terrorism: A Review Essay," *Security Studies*, 6(1): 133–62.
Crenshaw, M. (2008) "'New' vs. 'Old' Terrorism: A Critical Appraisal," in Rik Coolsaet (ed.), *Jihadi Terrorism and the Radicalisation Challenge in Europe* Aldershot and Burlington, VT: Ashgate Publishing, 25–36.
Crenshaw, M. (2009) "The Debate over 'New' vs. 'Old' Terrorism," in Ibrahim A. Karawan, Wayne McCormack, and Stephen E. Reynolds (eds), *Values and Violence: Intangible Aspects of Terrorism*. Studies in Global Justice, 4. Dordrecht: Springer Netherlands, 117–36.
Crenshaw, M., ed. (2010) *The Consequences of Counterterrorism*. New York: Russell Sage Foundation.
Crenshaw, M. (2011a) "The Obama Administration and Counterterrorism," in James Thurber (ed.), *Obama in Office: The First Two Years*. Boulder, CO: Paradigm Publishers, 243–53.
Crenshaw, M. (2011b) "The Debate over 'Old' vs 'New' Terrorism," in Rik Coolsaet (ed.), *Jihadi Terrorism and the Radicalisation Challenge: European and American Experiences*, 2nd edn. London: Ashgate, 57–67.
Crenshaw, M. (2011c) *Explaining Terrorism*. New York: Routledge.
Crenshaw, M. (2012) 'Will Threats Deter Nuclear Terrorism?,' in Andreas Wenger and Alex Wilner (eds), *Deterring Terrorism: Theory and Practice*. Stanford, CA: Stanford University Press, 136–58.

Crenshaw, M. (2014) "Terrorism Research: The Record," *International Interactions: Empirical and Theoretical Research in International Relations*, 40(4): 556–67.

Crenshaw, M. (2017) "Transnational Jihadism and Civil Wars," *Daedalus*, 146(4): 59–70.

Crenshaw, M., and LaFree, G. (2017) *Countering Terrorism*. Washington, DC: Brookings.

Crenshaw, M., E. Dahl, and M. Wilson (2017) *Comparing Failed, Foiled, Completed and Successful Terrorist Attacks: Final Report Year 5*. Report to the Office of University Programs, Science and Technology Directorate, US Department of Homeland Security. College Park, MD: START.

Cronin, A. K. (2009) *How Terrorism Ends: Understanding the Decline and Demise of Terrorist Campaigns*. Princeton: Princeton University Press.

Debray, R. (1967) *Revolution in the Revolution: Armed Struggle and Political Struggle in Latin America*. New York: Grove Press.

Dolnik, A. (2007) *Understanding Terrorist Innovation: Technologies, Tactics, and Global Trends*. London: Routledge.

Donohue, L. K. (2008) *The Cost of Counterterrorism*. New York: Cambridge University Press.

Dugan, L., and Chenoweth, E. (2012) "Moving Beyond Deterrence: The Effectiveness of Raising the Expected Utility of Abstaining from Terrorism in Israel," *American Sociological Review*, 77(4): 597–624.

English, R. (2016) *Does Terrorism Work? A History*. Oxford: Oxford University Press.

Foley, F. (2013) *Countering Terrorism in Britain and France: Institutions, Norms and the Shadow of the Past*. Cambridge: Cambridge University Press.

Friedman, T. L. (2002) "Changing the Channel," *New York Times*, Apr. 21.

George, A. (1991) *Forceful Persuasion: Coercive Diplomacy as an Alternative to War*. Washington, DC: United States Institute of Peace Press.

Gott, R. (1971) *Guerilla Movements in Latin America*. New York: Doubleday & Co. Rev. edn Chicago: University of Chicago Press, 2008.

Guevara, C. (1961) *Guerrilla Warfare*. New York: Monthly Review Press.

Guillén, A. (1973/1966) *Philosophy of the Urban Guerrilla: The Revolutionary Writings of Abraham Guillén*. New York: Wm Morrow & Co.

Hardman, J. B. S. (1937) "Terrorism," in *Encyclopaedia of the Social Sciences*. New York: Macmillan, 575–80.

Hosmer, S. (1970) *Viet Cong Repression and its Implications for the Future*. Santa Monica, CA: RAND.

Jäger, H., G. Schmidtchen, and L. Süllwold (1981) *Analysen zum Terrorismus*. Opladen: Westdeutscher Verlag.

Jenkins, B. (1974) *International Terrorism: A New Kind of Warfare*. Santa Monica, CA: RAND.

Jones, S. G., and M. C. Libicki (2008) *How Terrorist Groups End: Lessons for Countering Al Qa'ida*. Santa Monica, CA: RAND Corporation.

Knutson, J. N. (1980) "The Terrorists' Dilemmas: Some Implicit Rules of the Game," *Terrorism: An International Journal*, 4: 195–222.

Knutson, J. N. (1981) "Social and Psychodynamic Pressures toward a Negative Identity: The Case of an American Revolutionary Terrorist," in Y. Alexander and J. M. Gleason (eds), *Behavioral and Quantitative Perspectives on Terrorism* Elmsford, NY: Pergamon Press, 105–50.

Krause, P. (2013) "The Political Effectiveness of Non-State Violence: A Two-Level Framework to Transform a Deceptive Debate," *Security Studies*, 22(2): 259–94.

Krause, P. (2017) *Rebel Power: Why National Movements Compete, Fight and Win*. Ithaca, NY: Cornell University Press.

LaFree, G., M. Crenshaw, and S. M. Yang (2009) "Trajectories of Terrorism: Attack Patterns of Foreign Groups that have Targeted the United States, 1970–2004," *Criminology and Public Policy*, 8(3): 445–73.

LaFree, G., Xie, M., and Matanock, A. M. (2018) "Contagious Diffusion of World-Wide Terrorism: Is it Less Common than we Might Think?," *Studies in Conflict and Terrorism*, 41(4): 261–80.

Laqueur, W. (1976) *Guerrilla Warfare: A Historical and Critical Study*. Boston: Little, Brown.

Laqueur, W. (1977) *A History of Terrorism*. New York: Transaction Publishers.

McCauley, C., and S. Moskalenko (2011) *Friction: How Radicalization Happens to Them and Us*. New York: Oxford University Press. Revised and expanded edn 2017.

Malkki, L. (2010) "How Terrorist Campaigns End: The Campaigns of the Rode Jeugd in the Netherlands and the Symbionese Liberation Army in the United States." Unpublished Doctoral Dissertation, Faculty of Social Sciences, University of Helsinki.

Marighela, M. (1971) *For the Liberation of Brazil*. New York: Penguin Books.

Midlarsky, M. I., M. Crenshaw, and F. Yoshida (1980) "Why Violence Spreads: The Contagion of International Terrorism," and "Rejoinder to 'Observations on Why Violence Spreads,'" *International Studies Quarterly*, 24(2): 262–98, 306–10.

Moghadam, A. (2013) "How Al Qaeda Innovates," *Security Studies*, 22(3): 466–97.

Moghadam, A. (2017) *Nexus of Global Jihad: Understanding Cooperation among Terrorist Actors*. New York: Columbia University Press.

Mendelsohn, B. (2009) *Combatting Jihadism: American hegemony and Interstate Cooperation in the War on Terrorism*. Chicago: University of Chicago Press.

Mendelsohn, B. (2016) *The Al-Qaeda Franchise: The Expansion of al-Qaeda and its Consequences*. Oxford: Oxford University Press.

Nagl, J. A. (2007) "Foreword to the University of Chicago Press Edition," *Counterinsurgency Field Manual*. London and Chicago: University of Chicago Press, pp. xiii–xx.

National Research Council (2002) *Discouraging Terrorism: Some Implications of 9/11*. Panel on Understanding Terrorists in Order to Deter Terrorism, ed. Neil J. Smelser and Faith Mitchell. Washington, DC: National Academies Press.

Pape, R. (2005) *Dying to Win: The Strategic Logic of Suicide Terrorism*. New York: Random House.

Paret, P., and J. W. Shy (1962) *Guerrillas in the 1960s*. Princeton Studies in World Politics, 1. New York: Praeger.

Rapoport, D. C. (1971) *Assassination and Terrorism*. Ottawa: Canadian Broadcasting Corporation.

Rapoport, D. C. (1983) "Fear and Trembling: Terrorism in Three Religious Traditions," *American Political Science Review*, 78(3): 658–77.

Romaniuk, P. (2010) *Multilateral Counter-Terrorism: The Global Politics of Cooperation and Contestation*. New York: Routledge.

Ross, J., and T. Gurr (1989) "Why Terrorism Subsides: A Comparative Study of Canada and the United States," *Comparative Politics*, 21(4): 405–26.

Shapiro, J. N. (2013) *The Terrorist's Dilemma: Managing Violent Covert Organizations*. Princeton: Princeton University Press.

Sprinzak, E. (1991) "The Process of Delegitimation: Towards a Linkage Theory of Political Terrorism," *Terrorism and Political Violence*, 3(1): 50–68.

Taber, R. (1965) *The War of the Flea: A Study of Guerrilla Warfare Theory and Practice*. New York: Lyle Stuart.
Thornton, T. P. (1964) "Terror as a Weapon of Political Agitation," in Harry Eckstein (ed.), *Internal War: Problems and Approaches*. Princeton: Princeton University Press.
Trinquier, R. (1961) *La guerre moderne*. Paris: La Table Ronde.
Waciorski, J. (1939) *Le terrorisme politique*. Paris: A. Pedone.
Weinberg, L. (2012) *The End of Terrorism?* London and New York: Routledge.
Wilkinson. P. (1974) *Political Terrorism*. London: Macmillan Press.

CHAPTER 46

INSTITUTIONALIZING THE FIELD OF TERRORISM STUDIES

ALEX P. SCHMID

For almost forty years I have been writing and lecturing on terrorism; only a few others still active in the field have a longer record of trying to understand a phenomenon which the international community has been unable to define in a way acceptable to all member states of the United Nations. Here are some personal reflections that shed some light on how the field of terrorism studies institutionalized and my role in it.

While the field's main growth has been after 9/11 (according to one count: 17,243 books and 29,500 articles in the fourteen years following these attacks), there had already been a more modest growth before 9/11.[1] I wrote my first report "A Pilot Study on Political Terrorism" back in 1977 for the Dutch government's Advisory Group on Research into Non-Violent Conflict Resolution; my first article in 1978, and my first book in 1980[2]—all three in cooperation with Janny de Graaf, a Dutch sociologist who at that time also happened to be my wife. In those days, the study of terrorism was not institutionalized at all. The first European conference I recall took place in 1978 in Berlin and I was not invited because I was a greenhorn and nobody in the field. The convenor was, if I recall it correctly, Yonah Alexander, a Jewish-American who was the most prolific editor of conference volumes on terrorism for years to come. In 1977 he had founded the first journal in the field: *Terrorism: An International Journal.* Since the 1970s he has published and edited more than ninety-five volumes on terrorism and related subjects. With his conferences and conference volumes he probably did more to institutionalize the field than anybody else, certainly in the early years of terrorism studies, giving them a distinct American-Israeli hue. At that time, terrorism studies began to move away from counterinsurgency studies, armed conflict studies, and studies dealing with (mainly communist) state terrorism—a split that, looking back, was regrettable especially since it continues to this day.

Before the 1970s there was no continuous tradition of research on terrorism. One of the very first authors who wrote on the subject was Brian Crozier (1918–2012), an

Australian-born cosmopolitan foreign correspondent with close ties to Western intelligence communities. In 1960 he published *The Rebels* and in 1968 he founded, probably supported by the CIA (Bellamy 2012), the London-based Institute of Conflict Studies, the first think tank to study terrorism and (Communist) subversion.[3] His work, and the studies of Thomas P. Thornton and Harry Eckstein in the United States, was focused on counterinsurgency and civil war (Thornton 1964). This was the time of the Vietnam War and wars of national liberation against European colonial powers. On the European side R. Gaucher, influenced by the new type of resistance France faced in its colony Algeria, wrote *Les Terrorists* in 1965. The Algerian insurgency against the French, 1954–62, where terrorism played such a prominent role, was also the dissertation object of Martha Crenshaw (then M. Hutchinson). While she did not go to Algeria in search for primary material, she made good use of French archives, interviewing in Paris participants in the war between France and Algerian insurgents in the early 1970s. Based at the University of Virginia then, she published an article, linked to her dissertation, on "The Concept of Revolutionary Terrorism" (Crenshaw Hutchinson 1972). In this article in the *Journal of Conflict Resolution* she had defined "revolutionary terrorism" as "part of a revolutionary strategy... to seize political power from an existing government" involving "a consistent pattern of symbolic representation of the victims or objects of terrorism," with the deliberate intent to "create a psychological effect on specific groups and thereby challenge their political behavior and attitudes" (cited in Gilsinan 2005). In 1978 her seminal dissertation *Revolutionary Terrorism: The FLN in Algeria, 1954–1962* was published. Prof. Crenshaw, now at Stanford University, has been one of the few scholars who have consistently published in this field while others (including the author of this chapter) moved, by necessity or choice, in and out of the field. That consistency and independence has contributed to Martha Crenshaw's reputation as one of the most respected authorities in the field. Among those from the first hour, some—like Paul Wilkinson (1937–2011)—are no longer among us, while others, like Brian Jenkins, Martha Crenshaw, and David C. Rapoport are still dominant figures in the field of what would become a discipline—terrorism studies—of its own, partly thanks to their efforts.

David Rapoport, Professor Emeritus of the University of California, Los Angeles, has been one of the most long-lasting influences in the academic field. He taught the first course of terrorism in the United States in 1962. Despite the fact that he officially retired in 1995, he continues to be active. His influence comes partly through *Terrorism and Violence,* the scholarly journal he founded in 1989 and of which he remains the principal editor. Rapoport was the first to focus on the religious roots of terrorism. He also introduced the distinction between assassination and terrorism in 1970. The assassin, he wrote, acts against "corrupt" persons while the terrorist acts against a "corrupt" system. In his perception, "Terrorism implies a movement whose objective can only be achieved by repeated assassinations over relatively long periods of time, for fear dissipates when pressure is relaxed or exercised intermittently" (Rapoport 1970, 38; as quoted by Green 1978, 19–20). This observation let to the important distinction between the immediate victim and the ultimate target of a terrorist attack, where the victim serves as message generator to influence one or several target audiences—a theme further developed in my own work. David Rapoport has been one of a dozen truly influential thinkers in the field, authoring, inter alia, the "four waves theory" of terrorism, one of the few that deserves the name "theory" in a field that has not been too fortunate with theoretical insights (Rapoport 2004).[4]

The 1970s also saw the first efforts to create databases on terrorism. In France, Gaston Bouthoul published a "Chronique de la Violence Mondiale" from 1968 to 1970 in the journal *Guerre et Paix* which he subsequently continued in *Études Polemologiques*. Under the heading *Terrorism*, it listed kidnappings and hostage takings, including the hijacking of aircrafts as well as political assassinations, executions, and assaults against persons and objects (Schmid 1994). In the United States, Brian M. Jenkins assembled a similar chronology for the RAND corporation. It excluded domestic terrorism in the United States and focused only on "international terrorism"—probably the result of the mandate from the funders in the US government (Jenkins 1977). It contributed to the proliferation of the concept of "international terrorism" (which was eagerly linked by many to "international communism"), rather than to possible alternatives like "cross-border-terrorism" or "transnational terrorism." Jenkins described the common characteristics of the incidents he collected and studied with these words:

> International terrorism can be a single incident or a campaign of violence waged outside the presently accepted rules and procedures of international diplomacy and war; it is often designed to attract worldwide attention to the existence and cause of the terrorists and to inspire fear. Often the violence is carried out for effect. The actual victim or victim of terrorist attacks and the target audience may not be the same: the victims may be totally unrelated to the struggle.
>
> (Jenkins and Johnson 1975, 3)

In the United Kingdom, "The Troubles" in Northern Ireland stimulated the study of terrorism. Most prominent among the early academic authors was Paul Wilkinson whose studies on terrorism and the liberal state have been influential in the field. After a brief career as an education officer in the Royal Air Force Wilkinson moved into academia and began publishing while at the University of Wales in Cardiff in 1973. In the following year, his seminal volume *Political Terrorism*, the first of more than a dozen monographs from his hand on the subject, was published. In 1989 he became the first Chair in International Relations at the University of St Andrews. Contrary to the work of most other academics publishing in this field, his work was also taken seriously by the terrorists themselves: in 1990 a bomb was found hidden under the lectern table from which he was to lecture to a counterterrorism conference at the Royal Overseas League in London; luckily a sound technician who checked the working of the microphone discovered it in time.[5] Wilkinson stressed then and later that the liberal state has to adhere at all times to the rule of law and human rights while fighting terrorism, a lesson which the British government adhered to better (although not perfectly) than the American government after 9/11. At the University of St Andrews he founded, in 1994, together with Bruce Hoffman, one of the world's first academic institutes on terrorism, the Centre for the Study of Terrorism and Political Violence (CSTPV).[6] Wilkinson's middle-of-the road, pragmatic approach to countering terrorism earned him the respect of the government of the United Kingdom where he was a frequent consultant.

When I entered the field in 1977, Paul Wilkinson's *Terrorism and the Liberal State*, an expanded edition of his 1974 volume *Political Terrorism*, was published. In one of the recommendations for further research he suggested to look closer at the relationship between terrorism and the media. I took up the suggestion and wrote "Violence as Communication: Insurgent Terrorism and the Western News Media."[7] It was the first extended study on the relationship between terrorism and journalism, explaining how commercial news values play into the hands of those who stage violent pseudo-events meant to fit into the news format of mass media. The main body of this volume (part of which was co-authored by Janny de Graaf) was later published by Sage in 1982 while the Dutch case study on South Moluccan terrorism in the Netherlands was published in Dutch. In that book I recommended that editors in the media should make a distinction in their reporting between violent events that would have happened anyway even if there were no mass media, and violent "pseudo-events" which are deliberately staged with the main purpose of obtaining media coverage. In the latter case, I argued, the media should show great restraint in reporting them. My suggestion to introduce some guidelines on how media should report on staged violent pseudo-events was not well received by the media. The local newspaper *Leids Dagblad*, ran as its headline "Stupid, crazy and even dangerous—the proposals of Alex Schmid." Paul Wilkinson was also negative in his first review of the book but later, in a second review, changed to positive. While my approach was based on the terrorists' own "Propaganda by the Deed" theory of terrorism, first articulated by Carlo Pisacane in 1857,[8] it took a long time before my communication theory of terrorism became mainstream. Ten years later, in a volume co-authored and co-edited by David Paletz, *Terrorism and the Media*, my approach was well received. Another twenty or so years later the "Violence as Communication" approach to terrorism has become dominant. A bibliography compiled by Judith Tinnes in 2013 listed over 2,200 titles on Terrorism and the Media (including the internet) and was followed by a second bibliography in 2014 and a third in 2016—together more than one hundred pages listing books, book chapters, articles, and gray literature. The notion that terrorism was a combination of violence and propaganda and that fighting the propaganda was as important as countering the violence took a long time to reach center stage. I can claim credit for having pushed that perspective repeatedly over the years in a series of publications (e.g. Schmid 1981a, 1981b, 1989, 1992a, 1992b, 2005, 2006, 2010, 2014)—although the original study of 1982 is long out of print and rarely cited anymore. I regard this as my main *theoretical* contribution to the field, although I have no doubt that the field would have moved in this direction also without me. In fact, Ron Crelinsten in Canada later developed a similar theory (1987a, 1987b) that terrorism is primarily a communication strategy and so did Peter Waldmann (1998) in Germany—probably inspired by me. Later Brigitte Nacos, a journalist turned academic, became the most persuasive and prominent proponent of this perspective (1994, 2002; see also Marusitz 2013). The strength of the "Violence as Communication" theory lies in the fact that the terrorists themselves developed it in rudimentary form between the 1850s and 1880s with their "Propaganda by the Deed" concept. While there are many theories of terrorism (for an overview see McAlister and Schmid 2011), in the end the one that matters most is the one the terrorists themselves also operate with. Today, in the age of the internet, social media, and 24/7 international satellite breaking news, it matters more than ever. However, a theory of terrorism should not just be part of communication theories but also part of a larger theory of violence and, in turn, part of a theory of conflict.

But let me return to the early 1980s. I was then a contract researcher at the Center for the Study of Social Conflict (COMT) at Leiden University, without teaching obligations but also without any prospect of tenure. To feed my family, I had to do research on whatever was coming my way. Terrorism had come my way in the late 1970s because of a series of terrorist attacks by the sons of South Moluccan immigrants. They hijacked Dutch trains, and occupied a school and the seat of a provincial government in the Netherlands. At that time, regular university staff found these incidents not worth their attention as they were studying larger issues. Therefore, it fell on me as an immigrant (from Switzerland) and newcomer (to sociology—I was a historian by training) to look at what was behind these explosions of violence. My wife, a sociologist, worked then at Leiden University and soon joined me in my research, doing the interviews for the Dutch case study. When we got married, she dropped out of academia, never to return. The reason why we were given a chance to explore the South Moluccan issue had also to do with the fact that Andre Köbben, a brilliant anthropologist who changed career in mid-life and became the director of the Center for the Study of Social Conflict, was also the brother-in-law of the then Prime Minister Joop den Uyl. He was also part of a governmental Commission on Non-Violent Conflict Resolution. This helped me greatly to get work in that field, resulting also in some studies that were not directly related to terrorism.

In the years to come I almost left the nascent field of terrorism studies for good as there was no funding to be found for contract research. Occasionally a sign of appreciation for my work in this field was showing up, e.g. when Adam Roberts, Professor of International Relations at Oxford University, invited me for a lecture on terrorism as political communication strategy in his university. In the Netherlands, an unexpected but welcome sign of appreciation was an award I received for the best book in political science from the Netherlands circle of political scientists in 1985. The award was for the volume *Political Terrorism: A Research Guide to Concepts, Theories, Data Bases and Literature* (1984). While some "real" political scientists (I was only a historian cum sociologist and a contract researcher) were dismayed that the award was going to an outsider and not going to a genuine political scientist (there had been twenty-seven submissions for the award), it gave me the chance to get at least a half-time tenured position in the Department of Political Science of Leiden University where I would teach Polemology—the science of war and peace—until 1999 when I was offered a job at the United Nations in Vienna. That prize-winning volume *Political Terrorism* was the first survey of what was "on sale" in the emerging field of terrorism studies. It was praised as "the most comprehensive handbook in the field of Terrorism Studies" by Walter

Laqueur, one of the great contemporary historians. I also had the good luck that Irving L. Horowitz (1929–2012), the famous American sociologist, volunteered to write a Foreword where he praised the book as one that will "stand for many years as a quintessential effort to gather the facts theories and histories of terrorism as event and ideology." Horowitz was the editor of Transaction Books at Rutgers University in New Brunswick, NJ, and he distributed the volume in the Western Hemisphere. As a first stocktaking of what was going on in the nascent field of terrorism studies, this volume contributed to the consolidation of the field. Four years later it was followed by a new edition in which only the theory chapter was left untouched as I felt that there had not been enough progress in terms of theory. That revised, expanded, and updated new guide to "actors, authors, concepts, data bases, theories, and literature" (Schmid et al. 1988) was prepared under the auspices of the Center of International Affairs, Harvard University, which gave it added visibility in the field. It was reprinted as a paperback in 2005 and ultimately replaced in 2011 by the entirely rewritten volume, *The Routledge Handbook of Terrorism Research*.

These volumes contributed to the consolidation of the field. In them I (and some colleagues whom I had invited to co-author and, in a few cases, author some chapters, sought to separate the wheat from the chaff. There was an awful lot of ideological, ill-informed writing in the field by people who in most cases had never talked to a terrorist or even a victim of terrorism, spoke no foreign languages, and had no deeper understanding of history or other cultures. To this day there are still some scholars who believe that academic experts rather than terrorist practitioners invented "terrorism."[9]

While modern regime terrorism dates back to the Jacobin period of the French Revolution (1793–4), and the term "terrorism" was coined shortly thereafter to refer, in a distancing way, to this bloody episode epitomized by the workings of the guillotine, terrorism has its antecedents in medieval history and even in antiquity (cf. Law 2015a, 2015b; Ciment 2015; Carr 2006). For much of history, top-down regime terrorism was more prominent than bottom-up terrorism from members of society against those holding state power (Chaliand and Blin 2004; Law 2015b). In all this, practitioners rather than academic experts "invented" terrorism as a method of intimidating, coercing, or otherwise influencing many by publicly engaging in violence against a few in a demonstrative or symbolic way. Unfortunately, the term terrorism has been used in multiple ways by academics, politicians and journalists, including as a synonym for terror or the opposite of terrorism (terror referring to violence from above and terrorism referring to violence from below).

The first thing one should be able to agree on when institutionalizing a new field is that all talk about the same phenomenon. In the field of terrorism that has been a challenge. We have, on the one hand, the definitions of the terrorists themselves—those of Robespierre (1794), the Russian People's Will party (1879), up to Marighela (1971) and beyond.[10] We have national (e.g. US FBI 1984 or USSR 1989) and regional definitions (e.g. the European Union (2002) or the Organization of the Islamic Conference (1999)) and we have social science definitions (e.g. *Encyclopedia of the Social Sciences* 1936,

Richard English 2009). We had unsuccessful attempts of reaching a universal legal definition from the League of Nations (1937) to the UN's Ad Hoc Committee on Terrorism's draft definition of 2002. (See Schmid 2011.) The UN discussion on the definition of terrorism had begun in 1972 after a Palestinian terrorist attack on the Olympic Games in Munich. Twenty years later there was still no agreement. When I was a consultant to the UN Crime Prevention and Criminal Justice Branch in 1992, I proposed to the Secretariat of the UN Crime Commission to take and modify the uncontroversial existing definition of *war crimes* and extend it so that an act of terrorism would be defined as "the peacetime equivalent of a war crime," that is, attacks on civilians and non-combatants would be outlawed not only in international humanitarian law but equally in situations short of war (Schmid 1992, 8–9).

There was no significant response to my proposal in the real world of the United Nations and I therefore renewed my efforts to create more consensus at least in the academic world. In the 1980s, I had twice submitted questionnaires to scholars and counterterrorism professionals regarding the elements that should and should not go into a definition of terrorism. I reported back to those in the field of terrorism studies what the emerging consensus was, based on the responses, inviting further constructive feedback. That exercise was repeated once more in 2006 when I became director of the Centre for the Study of Terrorism and Political Violence (CSTPV) in St Andrews, following in the footsteps of Paul Wilkinson, Bruce Hoffman, and Magnus Ranstorp. Altogether, in three rounds of consultations some 200 scholars and practitioners in the field of terrorism studies provided feedback which allowed me to construct the revised academic consensus definition of terrorism consisting of twelve elements (Schmid 2011, 86–7). That definition is now widely used in academia but the sad thing is that it differs significantly from the draft legal definition developed (but not agreed upon) in the United Nations 6th (legal) Ad Hoc Committee on Terrorism.[11] The Academic Consensus Definition goes like this:

> Terrorism refers on the one hand to a *doctrine* about the presumed effectiveness of a special form or tactic of fear-generating, coercive political violence and, on the other hand, to a conspiratorial *practice* of calculated, demonstrative, direct violent action without legal or moral restraints, targeting mainly civilians and non-combatants, performed for its propagandistic and psychological effects on various audiences and conflict parties. Terrorism as a tactic is employed in three main contexts: (i) illegal state repression; (ii) propagandistic agitation by non-state actors in times of peace and outside zones of conflict and; (iii) as an illicit tactic of irregular warfare employed by state and non-state actors. (Schmid 2011, 86)

In my work, I also tried to differentiate terrorism from political violence other than terrorism and develop a typology of political action, distinguishing between persuasive, coercive and violent politics, and terrorism (see Marsden and Schmid 2011, 160–9; Schmid 2016b). That effort went back to the 1980s when I came up with a basic typology of terrorism.

To be honest, one category in the typology was missing in the one I had first developed in early 1980 (Schmid and de Graaf 1980, 60), one that I did not pick up as it was still weak—religious terrorism—which today constitutes some 70 percent of all terrorism. The year before—1979—the Iranian revolution had occurred and Russia had intervened in Afghanistan. This should have made alarm bells ring in my head and alerted me to the rise of religious terrorism—but to my shame I did not see it coming. I only added the category of religious (including millenarian) terrorism later. However, some of the other categories I developed at that time (e.g. single-issue terrorism) have, in the meantime, been accepted by the research community in the field of terrorism studies. That failure to include religious terrorism was probably the outcome of my deductive approach to typology-building, and to my mistaken belief (based on wishful thinking) that development and modernization would lead to a decline of religion in political affairs.

The importance of typology-building for the development of a field and its subfields is generally under-rated. As I wrote, together with my co-author Sarah Marsden in the chapter "Typologies of Terrorism and Political Violence" in the *Routledge Handbook of Terrorism Research*:

> in the absence of a universally accepted definition of terrorism and with the lack of a general theory of terrorism, typology construction can nevertheless be a useful instrument to advance our understanding of terrorism—provided it is embedded in a framework that looks at the conflict behavior of the opponents of the terrorists as well and takes into account additional contextual factors. Theoretical progress in the field of Terrorism Studies will have to be based on typological progress, which, in turn, is based on conceptual progress. (p. 193)

To go back to the 1980s. When I came back from Harvard University in 1987 where I had spent a sabbatical at the Center for International Affairs (CFIA) and revised *Political Terrorism*, my main activity until the late 1990s was running PIOOM, a meagerly financed research program on root causes of gross human rights violations (Schmid 1988)—a concept which overlapped to some extent with state terrorism (Schmid 1991). The study of non-state terrorism was placed on the backburner, although I occasionally manage to do some work in this area, e.g. in the form of the volume *Western Responses to Terrorism* (1993),[12] a conference volume which I edited together with Ron Crelinsten who had joined me at Leiden University. It had first been published as a Special Issue of *Terrorism and Political Violence* (vol. 4, Winter 1992/3, no. 4), the journal edited by David C. Rapoport. A lucky result of this was that David Rapoport invited me to join the Editorial Board of his journal and later, in 2006, I would become his co-editor, when Paul Wilkinson retired from that position.

The 1990s were a difficult period for researchers in the field of terrorism studies. The universities would generally not fund them and government grants declined as international terrorism declined (Silke 2004). Many scholars turned to other issues and there was little progress in institutionalizing the field of terrorism studies. Research on gross human rights violations was also difficult to get funding for at my university—human rights being considered a legal matter and I was in the social science department rather than in the law school. Therefore, I was glad to accept in 1999 a position in Vienna when an opportunity offered itself at the United Nations Office on Drugs and Crime to become Officer-in-Charge of the newly established Terrorism Prevention Branch (TPB). Yet even there funding was scarce; the original mandate of TPB was limited to narrowly defined legal issues. I therefore created a roster of experts from academia and organized conferences, making use of the great convening power of the United Nations. One result of these efforts was the conference volume *Countering Terrorism through International Cooperation* (2001)—I co-organized the conference with ISPAC, the International Scientific and Professional Advisory Council of the United Nations Crime Prevention and Criminal Justice Programme of which I had been an elected board member for a number of years. This gave me the opportunity to bring together leading researchers and experts like David Rapoport, Reuven Paz, Paul Wilkinson, Boaz Ganor, and Tore Bjorgo (whose thesis I had supervised at Leiden University). I also managed to bring scholars like Dipak Gupta and Leonard Weinberg to the UN's Terrorism Prevention Branch in Vienna for short periods of time. In addition, I introduced an internship program for promising young researchers. For some of them this was the start of their career in the field (e.g. for Stefan Malthaner, Robert Wesley, and Adam Dolnik).

Yet in many ways it was difficult to work with, and through, the United Nations. For instance, UNODC produced every year a World Drug Report and my efforts to create an equivalent World Terrorism Report were sabotaged by certain member states, as were my efforts to continue work on a UN database on terrorist incidents worldwide which I had set up.[13] When major funding became available to the United Nations in the fight against terrorism after 9/11, much of that funding would go to New York-based parts of the UN system while UNODC's work was largely confined to legal issues like the promotion of ratifications and the implementation of more than a dozen conventions and protocols dealing with sectoral aspects of countering terrorism (e. g. anti-hijacking, anti-kidnapping, anti-financing of terrorism). I left the United Nations with mixed feelings in late 2005 when I reached mandatory retirement age.

Luckily a new opportunity to work in the field of terrorism studies opened up when the position of director of the Centre for the Study of Terrorism and Political Violence (CSTPV) became vacant in early 2006. Invited by Paul Wilkinson, I moved to the University of St Andrews in Scotland. CSTPV had a great reputation as Europe's oldest academic research institute on terrorism but it had hardly any funds. Initially much of my time was taken by writing modules for a new online e-learning program which over the years became a financial success, thanks to the efforts of Max Taylor, Orla Lynch, and other members of CSTPV. In those years, I also managed to reach out to the intelligence community and strengthen exchanges between academia and intelligence and security services. This effort, however, met resistance from some academic colleagues who feared that academic independence might be endangered. However, the chance to talk "truth to power" and warn government policymakers about mistaken policies was, in my view, worth that risk. Having for much of my life been a contract researcher not enjoying the freedom of tenured colleagues, I was well aware of the dangers of rubbing shoulders with policymakers but the chance to work with primary documents unavailable to independent scholars in the end outweighed the risk.

Marc Sageman has indicated that a major cause for what he sees as "stagnation" in terrorism research stems from the separation of academic research and the intelligence community's study of terrorism. According to Sageman,"the gap between these two communities and their respective cultures is unbridgeable without any possibilities of fruitful exchange" (2014). In my rejoinder to Sageman's polemic, I tried to show that he was greatly exaggerating and that the field of terrorism studies was not stagnating at all but was showing signs of reaching maturity (Schmid 2014b).[14] Sageman's frustration was fed partly by the inability of the research community to understand and reverse the process of growing radicalization of rebellious youth, especially among Muslims in the Arab world and in Western diasporas. Yet that radicalization was to no small part due to "counter-productive counter-terrorism" (a term coined by Paul Wilkinson), in particular, due to the ill-considered overthrow of Saddam Hussein in Iraq in 2003. As a former CIA officer and subsequently as an academic, Sageman had the privilege to work with both open and secret sources of information.

Yet the divide between the academic and the intelligence community is getting smaller. In my more recent work, as Associate Professor at the Institute of Security and Global Affairs (ISGA—Campus The Hague of Leiden University) and in my position as Research Fellow of the International Centre of Counter-Terrorism (ICCT, The Hague) I find that contacts and cooperation with the intelligence community are the new normal and exchanges of researchers and analysts between universities and intelligence agencies are no longer unusual. It would be odd if it were otherwise in a situation where Salafist jihadist terrorists have declared war on the West and much of the rest of the world and where terrorism has become one of the most important security issues of our time.

Since retiring from St Andrews, I have become editor-in-chief of *Perspectives on Terrorism*, which, with the help of Prof. James Forest (University of Massachusetts, Lowell Campus), I managed to turn into the largest independent, peer-reviewed online scholarly journal in the field of terrorism studies, with 8,000 subscribers and many tens of thousands of more occasional users. Together with David Rapoport's *Terrorism and Political Violence* and Bruce Hoffman's *Studies in Terrorism and Conflict, Perspectives on Terrorism* has become one of the three leading journals in the field of terrorism studies, in terms of primary source-based research.[15] There has been a great increase in on- and offline journals since Yonah Alexander started *Terrorism: An International Journal* in 1977. There are now some 100 core and peripheral journals for terrorism research, with some thirty of them online (Tinnes 2013b).[16] There are now more than 130 institutes on terrorism worldwide (van Dongen, 2018).[17] The Terrorism Research Initiative (TRI), which, since 2007 for the first ten years was headed by Robert Wesley, James Forest, and myself, has created national and regional networks of Ph.D. thesis writers (Schmid 2015c) and TRI also issues an annual award for the best Ph.D. thesis in terrorism or counterterrorism. There are regular major conferences on terrorism, e.g. the annual

World Congress on Counter-Terrorism which has so far gathered eighteen times in Herzliya, Israel. All these are signs that the field of terrorism studies has become well institutionalized.

As I look back, I find that I myself played a role in this process since I was present at the creation of a number of these developments. Yet terrorism itself has grown faster than the field of terrorism studies. If the success of a field of studies is measured in terms of harm that could be prevented, we have not been very successful. It has been said that a problem well defined is a problem half solved. I have probably tried harder than anybody else to find common ground for a definition of terrorism. I have also pleaded for more than thirty-five years to shift the focus on countering terrorism first of all in the direction of the propaganda of the terrorists rather than focusing mainly on the violence of terrorism. While such a shift is finally under way, efforts to come up with persuasive counter-narratives and alternative narratives (Schmid 2015b) are still in their infancy (Schmid 2010, 2014a, 2015a). And so are, by and large, our efforts at successful prevention of terrorism (Schmid 2016). That is also the reason why my final major project in this field is to bring together more than thirty colleagues to produce a "Handbook of Terrorism Prevention and Preparedness"—an effort that is now under way and should see its completion in the year 2020.

Notes

1. Data compiled by Muhmmad Feyyaz, University of Management and Technology, Lahore, Dec. 2014.
2. Schmid and de Graaf 1980. Subsequently published in two volumes: Schmid and de Graaf 1982, and Schmid et al. 1982.
3. Crozier 1960. At the Institute for the Study of Conflict Studies Crozier produced the *Annual of Power and Conflict* for ten years. See Bellamy 2012.
4. Prof. Rapoport later expanded his article into a longer study for Oxford University Press.
5. Private communication. Subsequently, Prof. Wilkinson's home in Crail (Fife, Scotland) also received some extra security.
6. Now Handa Centre for the Study of Terrorism and Political Violence.
7. Schmid and de Graaf 1980. Schmid and de Graaf 1982. De Graaf's contribution was limited to the Dutch case study which in the Sage volume was only briefly summarized.
8. Pisacane 1956; cit. Law 2015b, 125.
9. Cf. Stampnitzky 2013. For a historically more accurate assessment, giving due credit to practitioners rather than academics, for the invention of modern non-state terrorism, see Dietze 2016.
10. For a sourced list and discussion of 260 definitions from M. Robespierre to Richard English and beyond, see Schmid 2011, 39–157; appendix 2.1 lists 250-plus Academic, Governmental and Intergovernmental Definitions of Terrorism, compiled by Joseph J. Easson and Alex P. Schmid.
11. The draft definition of terrorism of the UN Ad Hoc Committee goes like this:

   "*Any person* commits an offense within the meaning of this [the present] Convention if that person, by any means, unlawfully and intentionally, causes:

(a) Death or serious injury to *any person*; or
(b) Serious damage to public or private property, including a place of public use, a State or government facility, a public transportation system, an infrastructure facility or to the environment; or
(c) Damage to property, places, facilities or systems referred to in paragraph 1 (b) of this [the present] article, resulting or likely to result in major economic loss; *when the purpose of the conduct, by its nature or context, is to intimidate a population, or to compel a Government or an international organization to do or abstain from doing any act.*" [Emphasis added, APS.] Informal text of articles 2 and 2bis of the draft Comprehensive Convention, prepared by the Coordinator. Article 2. Reproduced from document A/C./6/56/L.9, annex I.B. This text represents the stage of consideration reached by the Working Group of the Sixth Committee. United Nations, Report of the Ad Hoc Committee established by the General Assembly resolution 51/210 of Dec. 17, 1996. Sixth session (January 28—February 1, 2002). General Assembly. Official Records. Supplement No. 37 (A/57/37), 6. It has remained unchanged fifteen years later as the definition issue has not been resolved in the UN General Assembly.

12. It took almost twenty-five years before someone picked up my suggestion to make a parallel volume on non-Western responses to terrorism. Such a volume on *Non-Western Responses to Terrorism*, edited by my former colleague from the University of St Andrews, Michael Boyle, is finally being published in 2018.
13. However, the template for monitoring, developed by myself at UNODC/TPB in cooperation with Wolfgang Rhomberg, would later serve as a model (among others) to be used by the Global Terrorism Database of START at the University of Maryland which later would replace the US Department of State's reporting system.
14. Schmid 2014b. For a continuation of my criticism of Marc Sageman's approach to terrorism, see my review of his latest work in *Perspectives on Terrorism*, 11(4) (Aug. 2017), 193–5: Marc Sageman. Turning to Political Violence: The Emergence of Terrorism. Philadelphia, PA: University of Pennsylvania Press, 2017, (496 pp.), reviewed by Alex P. Schmid; URL: <http://www.terrorismanalysts.com/pt/index.php/pot/article/view/630/1242>.
15. Finding from a review of the main journals in the field of terrorism studies; cf. Bart Schuurman; Research on Terrorism, 2007–2016: "A Review of Data, Methods, and Authorship. *Terrorism and Political Violence*," pp. 1–17; March 2018.; URL: https://doi.org/10.1080/09546553.2018.1439023.
16. A new list of journals in the field of Terrorism Studies has been compiled by Judith Tinnes; see: J.Tinnes, "A Resources List for Terrorism Research: Journals, Websites and Bibliographies (2018 Edition)" *Perspectives on Terrorism*, Vol. XII, Issue 4 (August 2018), pp. 115–142. URL: https://www.universiteitleiden.nl/binaries/content/assets/customsites/perspectives-on-terrorism/2018/issue-4/08-tinnes-resources-link-toevoegen.pdf.
17. An new list of research centers has been compiled by Teun van Dongen in 2017; T. van Dongen, "130+ (Counter-) Terrorism Research Centers – An Inventory," *Perspectives on Terrorism*, Vol. XII, Issue 2, (April 2018), pp.86 – 124; URL: http://www.terrorismanalysts.com/pt/index.php/pot/article/view/696/1368.

References

Bellamy, Chris (2012) "Brian Crozier: Intelligence and Security Expert Who Fought Communism and Founded his own Spy Network," *Independent*, Aug. 13, available online at

<http://www.independent.co.uk/news/obituaries/brian-crozier-intelligence-and-security-expert-who-fought-communism-and-founded-his-own-spy-network-8036652.html>.

Carr, Matthew (2006) *The Infernal Machine. A History of Terrorism*. New York: New Press.

Chaliand, Gérard, and Arnaud Blin, eds. (2004) *Histoire du Terrorism de l'Antiquité à Al Qaida*. Paris: Bayard.

Ciment, James, ed. (2015) *World Terrorism: An Encyclopedia of Political Violence from Ancient Times to the Post-9/11 Era*. 3 vols. London: Routledge.

Crelinsten, Ronald D. (1987a) "Terrorism and Political Communication: The Relationship between Controller and the Controlled," in Paul Wilkinson and A. M. Stewart (eds.), *Contemporary Research on Terrorism*. Aberdeen: University of Aberdeen Press, 3–23.

Crelinsten, Ronald D. (1987b) "Power and Meaning: Terrorism as a Struggle over Access to the Communication Structure," in Paul Wilkinson and A. M. Stewart (eds.), *Contemporary Research on Terrorism*. Aberdeen: University of Aberdeen Press, 419–50.

Crenshaw, Martha (1978) *Revolutionary Terrorism. The FLN in Algeria, 1954–1962*. Stanford, CA: Hoover Institution.

Crenshaw Hutchinson, Martha (1972) "The Concept of Revolutionary Terrorism," *Journal of Conflict Resolution*, 16(3): 383–96.

Crozier, Brian (1960) *The Rebels*. London: Chatto & Windus.

Dietze, Carola (2016) *Die Erfindung des Terrorismus in Europa, Russia und den USA 1858–1966*. Hamburg: HIS Verlagsgesellschaft.

Gaucher, R. (1965) *Les Terroristes*. Paris: Editions Albin Michels.

Gilsinan, Kathy (2005) "Today's Terrorists Want to Inspire," *The Atlantic*, Sept. 14 (including interview with Martha Crenshaw), available online at <http://www.theatlantic.com/international/archive/2015/09/history-terrorism-isis-9-11/405055>.

Green, L. C. (1978) "Aspects of Terrorism," *Terrorism*, 5(4): 19–20.

Jenkins, Brian M. (1977) *Rand's Research on Terrorism*. Santa Monica, CA: RAND, Aug.

Jenkins, Brian M., and Janera Johnson (1975) *International Terrorism: A Chronology, 1968–1974*. Santa Monica, CA: RAND.

Law, Randall D. (2015a) *Terrorism. A History*. Cambridge: Polity Press, 2nd edn, fully revised and expanded, 2016.

Law, Randall D., ed. (2015b) *The Routledge History of Terrorism*. London: Routledge,

McAlister, Bradley, and A. P. Schmid (2011) "Theories of Terrorism," in A. P. Schmid (ed.), *The Routledge Handbook of Terrorism Research*. London and New York: Routledge, 201–71.

Marsden, Sarah V., and Alex. P. Schmid (2011) "Typologies of Terrorism and Political Violence," in A. P. Schmid (ed.), *The Routledge Handbook of Terrorism Research*. London and New York: Routledge, 160–200.

Marusitz, Jonathan (2013) *Terrorism and Communication: A Critical Introduction*. Thousand Oaks, CA: Sage.

Nacos, Brigitte (1994) *Terrorism and the Media. From the Iran Hostage Crisis to the Oklahoma City Bombing*. New York: Columbia University Press.

Nacos, Brigitte (2002) *Mass-Mediated Terrorism: The Central Role of the Media in Terrorism and Counter-Terrorism*. Lanham, MD: Rowman & Littlefield.

Paletz, D. L., and A. P. Schmid, eds. (1992) *Terrorism and the Media: How Researchers, Terrorists, Governments, Press, Public and Victims View and Use the Media*. London, Sage.

Pisacane, Carlo (1956) *Saggio sulla rivoluzione*. Milan, Universale Economica.

Rapoport, David C. (1970) *Assassination and Terrorism*. Toronto: Canadian Broadcasting Corporation.

Rapoport, David C. (2004) "Modern Terror: The Four Waves," in Audrey Cronin and J. Ludes (eds.), *Attacking Terrorism: Elements of a Grand Strategy*. Washington, DC: Georgetown University Press, 46–73.

Sageman, Marc (2014) "The Stagnation in Terrorism Research," *Terrorism and Political Violence*, 26.

Schmid, A. P. (1981a) "Violence as Communication: The Case of Insurgent Terrorism," in Egbert, Jahn and Y. Sakamoto (eds.), *Elements of World Instability: Armaments, Communication, Food, International Division of Labour*. New York and Frankfurt a. M., Campus Verlag, 147–62.

Schmid, A. P. (1981b) "Terrorisme en de jacht op publiciteit" (Terrorism and the Search for Publicity), *Intermediair* (Amsterdam), 49 (Dec. 4): 1–7.

Schmid, A P. (1984) *Political Terrorism: A Research Guide to Concepts, Theories, Data Bases and Literature*. With a bibliography by the author and a world directory of "terrorist" organizations by A. J. Jongman. Amsterdam: North-Holland Publishing Co.

Schmid, A. P. (1988) *Research on Gross Human Rights Violations: A Programme*. Leiden: COMT, 2nd enlarged edn 1989.

Schmid, A. P. (1989) "Terrorism and the Media: The Ethics of Publicity," *Terrorism and Political Violence*, 1(4): 539–65.

Schmid, A. P. (1991) "Repression, State Terrorism, and Genocide: Conceptual Clarifications," in T. Bushnell et al., *State Organized Terror. The Case of Internal Repression*. Boulder, CO: Westview Press, 23–37.

Schmid, A. P. (1992a) "Editor's Perspectives," in D. Paletz and A. P. Schmid (eds.), *Terrorism and the Media. How Researchers, Terrorists, Governments, Press, Public and Victims View and Use the Media*. London: Sage, 111–36.

Schmid, A. P. (1992b) "Terrorism and the Media: Freedom of Information vs. Freedom from Intimidation," in Lawrence Howard (ed.), *Terrorism. Roots, Impact, Responses*. New York: Praeger, 95–117.

Schmid, A. P. (1992c) The Definition of Terrorism: A Study in Compliance with CTL/9/91/2207 for the U.N. Crime Prevention and Criminal Justice Branch. Leiden: PIOOM.

Schmid, A. P., ed. (2001) Countering Terrorism through International Cooperation: Proceedings of the International Conference on "Countering Terrorism Through Enhanced International Cooperation" Courmayeur, 22–4 September 2000. Milan: ISPAC.

Schmid, A. P. (2005) "Terrorism as Psychological Warfare," *Democracy and Security*, 1(2): 137–46.

Schmid, A. P. (2006) "Terrorism and the Media," in D. Rapoport (ed.), *Terrorism: Critical Concepts in Political Science*. London, Routledge, iv. 94–112.

Schmid, A. P. (2010) "The Importance of Countering Al-Qaeda's 'Single Narrative,'" in Eelco Kessels (ed.), *Countering Violent Extremist Narratives*. The Hague: NCTB, 46–57.

Schmid, A. P., (ed.) (2011) *Routledge Handbook of Terrorism Research*. London and New York: Routledge.

Schmid, A. P. (2014a) *Al-Qaeda's "Single Narrative" and Attempts to Develop Counter-Narratives: The State of Knowledge*. The Hague: International Centre for Counter-Terrorism. ICCT Research Paper, Jan, available online at <www.icct.nl>.

Schmid, A. P. (2014b) "Comments on Marc Sageman's Polemic 'The Stagnation in Terrorism Research.'" *Terrorism and Political Violence*, 26: 587–95.

Schmid, A. P. (2015a) *Challenging the Narrative of the "Islamic State."* The Hague: ICCT.

Schmid, A. P. (2015b) "The Need for Counter and Alternative Narratives for a Comprehensive Strategy to Effectively Combat ISIS Propaganda." Lecture, Oct. 27, delivered in Kuala Lumpur, available online at <http://www.gmomf.org/distinguished-lecture-by-professor-emeritus-alex-p-schmid-counter-and-alternative-narratives-as-part-of-a-comprehensive-strategy to-combat-isis>.

Schmid, A. P. (2015c) "TRI National/Regional TRI Networks (Partial) Inventory of Ph.D. Theses in the Making," *Perspectives on Terrorism*, 9(6): 170–4.

Schmid, A. P. (2016a) "Countering Terrorism Upstream: The Neglected Role of Prevention," Stockholm, EENeT Presentation.

Schmid, A. P. (2016b) "Terrorism, Political Crime and Political Justice," in Beatrice de Graaf and Alex P. Schmid, *Terrorists on Trial: A Performative Perspective*. Leiden: Leiden University Press, 23–50.

Schmid, A. P., and R. D. Crelinsten, eds. (1993) *Western Responses to Terrorism*. London: Frank Cass.

Schmid, A. P., and J. F. A. de Graaf (1977) *A Pilot Study on Political Terrorism*. The Hague: Advisory Group on Research into Non-Violent Conflict Resolution.

Schmid, A. P., and J. F. A. de Graaf (1978) "Internationaal terrorisme: Begripsbepaling, structuur en strategieën" (International Terrorism: Conceptualization, Structure and Strategies), *Intermediair* (Amsterdam), 20 (May 19): 1–11.

Schmid, A. P., and J. F. A. de Graaf (1980) *Insurgent Terrorism and the Western News Media. An Exploratory Analysis with a Dutch Case Study*. Leiden: COMT, Nov.

Schmid, A. P., and J. F. A. de Graaf (1982a) *Violence as Communication*. London, Sage.

Schmid, A. P., et al. (1982b) *Zuidmoluks terrorisme, de media en de publieke opinie* (South Moluccan Terrorism, the Media, and Public Opinion). Amsterdam: Intermediair Bibliotheek.

Schmid, A. P., Albert J. Jongman et al. (1988) *Political Terrorism: A New Guide to Actors, Authors, Concepts, Data Bases, Theories, and Literature*. Revised, expanded and updated, and prepared under the auspices of the Center for International Affairs, Harvard University. Amsterdam: North-Holland Publishing Co., and New Brunswick, NJ: Transaction Books.

Silke, Andrew, (ed.) (2004) *Research on Terrorism: Trends, Achievements and Failures*. London: Frank Cass.

Stampnitzky, Lisa (2013) *Disciplining Terror: How Experts Invented "Terrorism."* Cambridge: Cambridge University Press.

Thornton, T. P. (1964) "Terror as a Weapon of Political Agitation?," in H. Eckstein (ed.). *Internal War: Problems and Approaches*. New York: Free Press of Glencoe, 71–91.

Tinnes, Judith (2013a) "Terrorism and the Media (Including the Internet): An Extensive Bibliography," *Perspectives on Terrorism*, 7(1), available online at <http://www.terrorismanalysts.com/pt/index.php/pot/article/view/247/500>.

Tinnes, Judith (2013b) "100 Core and Peripheral Journals for Terrorism Research," *Perspectives on Terrorism*, 7(2): 95–103, available online at <http://www.terrorismanalysts.com/pt/index.php/pot/article/view/258/521>.

Tinnes, Judith (2014) "Terrorism and the Media (including the Internet: (Part 2)," *Perspectives on Terrorism*, 8(6), available online at <http://www.terrorismanalysts.com/pt/index.php/pot/article/view/392/775>.

Tinnes, Judith (2016) "Terrorism and the Media; J. Tinnes. Bibliography: Terrorism and the Media (including the Internet), Part 3," *Perspectives on Terrorism*, 10(5): 112–55. <http://www.terrorismanalysts.com/pt/index.php/pot/article/view/547/html>.

Waldmann, Peter (1998) *Terrorismus: Provokation der Macht*. Munich: Gerling Akademie Verlag.

Wilkinson, Paul (1974) *Political Terrorism*. London: Macmillan.

CHAPTER 47

REVISING THE FIELD OF TERRORISM

RICHARD JACKSON

Telling Stories

Stories, or what some scholars properly call "narratives," are everywhere. They are the necessary psycho-cultural device we need to make sense of the world, socially and scientifically. The Big Bang, particle physics, evolution, genetic predispositions, depression, post-traumatic stress syndrome, the Industrial Revolution, the civil rights movement, modernization, democracy, the Cold War, the war on terror; these are just a few of the stories society tells about how the physical world works, how the human mind works, and how society and history evolves and progresses from one era to another. The historian Hayden White (1973, 1987) explains that History as a discipline involves the construction of a plot which links characters and events into an understandable sequence with a beginning, middle, and end. Collective or national narratives are the way a diverse collection of small groups, families, and individuals come to see themselves as intrinsically linked to millions of other people in a geographically defined entity called the United States, the United Kingdom, Norway, India, New Zealand, or any one of over 200 nation states today. Benedict Anderson (1983) refers to these entities as "imagined communities," emphasizing the role that narratives play in national identity construction.

Within these larger narratives, every person has their own individual narrative—what is called an ontological narrative, which is the story of their personal origins and family history, and which in turn connects them to the larger stories of their society and their cultural world (see Baker 2006). All of these narratives provide human beings with a psychologically comforting sense of identity and belonging, and a reassurance that the world is knowable and to some degree, controllable, rather than random, chaotic, and unpredictable.

The thing we understand as "terrorism" today is currently one of our society's most important and ubiquitous narratives. It is a story with a beginning, a middle, and an end, and with archetypal characters, defining events, and moral lessons for the audience. Often, the story of terrorism begins with the Assassins, or in other cases, the French Revolution, before linking them together with the thugees, the Iscari, the anarchists, Stalin, Hitler, Palestinians, third world revolutionaries, right-wing neo-fascists, and a host of others, to create a single continuous narrative, depending on the definitions and assumptions of the author (see e.g. Laqueur 2001; Law 2009). Perhaps the most famous story in terrorism studies is David Rapoport's (2004) four wave theory, in which terrorism evolves through definable eras dominated first by characters called "anarchists," followed by anti-colonialists, leftists, and more recently, religiously inspired "jihadists." In another famous (but now discredited) version, the story of terrorism was dominated and orchestrated by the Soviet Union, and involved flamboyant characters such as Carlos the Jackal (see Sterling 1981). In more recent narrative accounts, the events of "9/11" loom large as an epoch-making moment—"the day that changed everything"—and Osama bin Laden and Al Qaeda stand out as central characters (see Jackson 2015a, 2009).

However, we can take the concept of narrative even deeper than this, because science and academia have stories too—stories about the process by which important ideas, methods of inquiry, and even entire paradigms rose and fell, expanded or contracted, mutated into other forms. The story of terrorism studies, as a field of academic research devoted to the study of one specific type of political violence, has been told in a number of different ways and from a variety of perspectives. Lisa Stampnitzky (2013), for example, tells the story of how a group of scholars and US State Department intellectuals successfully managed to separate the study of a specific violent tactic called "terrorism" from other forms of political violence by pro- or anti-state forces. Others have told the story about how the terrorism studies field came to form a central part of what could be called a "terrorism industry" (see Herman and O'Sullivan 1991; George 1991; Mueller 2006), an "invisible college" or an "epistemic community" (see Reid 1993, 1997), dominated by a number of key experts who shared the same views about what terrorism was, and how it should be controlled.

More than this, science and academia use narrative directly to understand and explain the phenomena they study. The very idea of causality itself—that a linked chain of identifiable events and actions leads to a result—is a narrativization of sequentially occurring observations. Such narrativizing is ubiquitous in the social sciences where observed correlations between sequential events require a broader causal narrative to link them together in a fashion that makes sense. Thus, for example, the dominant story today of how extremist religious ideas can, in a step-wise fashion, lead someone down the path to an act of terrorism is a causal story about the origins of contemporary terrorism (see Gunning and Jackson 2011). In many ways, the volume of which this chapter forms a part also attempts to tell the story of terrorism and terrorism studies, in that it explains who the terrorists are, what they do, where they come from, what motivates them, how states respond to them, and how the thing called "terrorism" has been studied up to now.

Critical Terrorism Studies: The Story so Far

Last year, 2015, was ten years since the publication of my first solo-authored book, *Writing the War on Terrorism* (2005), which has been by far the most successful publication of my academic career. In fact, it is probably true to say that my professional reputation as one of the main proponents of what became known as the Critical Terrorism Studies (CTS) school of terrorism research was made largely by that book, which is a little strange to me, given that it started as a side project to another book I was writing on the social construction of intrastate war—a book which remains unfinished today due to the new path my career took as a result of *Writing the War on Terrorism*. The year 2016 saw the tenth anniversary of a conference I helped to organize with Marie Breen Smyth and Jeroen Gunning entitled, "Is it time for a critical terrorism studies?" which was held at the University of Manchester where I worked at the time. It also marked ten years since the Critical Studies on Terrorism Working Group (CSTWG), a network of scholars studying terrorism from an explicitly critical perspective, was established within the British International Studies Association (BISA). The following year, 2017, was the tenth anniversary of the first issue of the journal which has become synonymous with CTS, *Critical Studies on Terrorism*.

In 2007, I also published a short article outlining what I considered to be the core intellectual commitments of what my colleagues and I had decided to call CTS (Jackson 2007). It became the basis for a volume co-edited with Jeroen Gunning and Marie Breen Smyth titled, *Critical Terrorism Studies: A New Research Agenda*, which we published in 2009. This book laid out the foundations of what we saw as a new kind of intellectual approach for the study of terrorism—a new way of narrating the story of terrorism and counterterrorism, as it were. A few years later, with Lee Jarvis now on board, we wrote a textbook, *Terrorism: A Critical Introduction* (Jackson et al. 2011). It was specifically designed to assist students and lecturers who wanted to teach terrorism studies from an explicitly critical perspective. In 2016, I published the *Routledge Handbook of Critical Terrorism Studies* (Jackson 2016). The volume attempts to evaluate ten years of CTS-inspired research, drawing out the main findings, the current state of knowledge in key areas, and the remaining gaps in our understanding.

These publications and institutional developments are all key moments in the story of how CTS began, what it aims to do to the study of terrorism, what its strengths and weaknesses are, and what kind of future challenges it faces. Elsewhere, I have tried to explain and analyze this story (see Jackson 2015b) from the perspective of what it can tell us about how "expertise" emerges in a given context, and how I see the broader CTS movement as a project akin to Bourdieu's notion of the "collective intellectual" (see Oslender 2007).

My Own Story

I don't need to tell the origin story of CTS again, at least not in its conventional form. Here, I want to tell a different story about how I, as a scholar and a person, came to see the need for a new, explicitly "critical" approach within the broader field of terrorism studies; about how I came to think differently about the dominant "terrorism" narrative and the way we conventionally view it, and importantly, how we study and teach about it in the academy. Of course, such a story cannot be easily disentangled from the broader study of CTS, or the stories of all the other people who were pivotal to its emergence. An autobiographical exercise such as this also comes with a number of dangers and challenges. There is the danger of distortion inherent to the normal psychological impulse to make oneself look good in one's own narration, and there is also the temptation to downplay the contribution of others.

More prosaically, there is the challenge of drawing out the key significant moments and events from a multitude of possibilities, and telling the tale of the past through the necessarily coloring prism of the present. How much of my personal history is relevant to this story, given that I am today the sum total of all the experiences I have had? How far back should I go? Should I start with my birth in Zambia, and the experience of growing up in a remote rural area where poverty and hunger was common? Should I mention that as a child, before I really knew or understood what I was seeing, I laughed at the local African children with their distended bellies and brown-tinged hair (Jackson 2012a)? Should I explain how my shame at this recollection later fueled my concern for social and economic justice, thereby determining the kinds of courses I chose to study when I first went to university?

Or, should I start with my direct experience of the Zimbabwean war of independence which was taking place all around me in Southern Zambia, and the ontologically destabilizing experience of facing direct personal violence without law or mercy at a road block (Jackson 2012b)? Should I include my experience of travelling around South Africa in 1984 at the height of apartheid and feeling deeply ashamed that, simply by my presence, I was contributing to the suffering of others who didn't share the color of my privileged skin (Jackson 2012a)? Is it important to explain how these events later made me question the idea that political violence could ever be used for good, or the idea that anyone, including academics, should adopt a neutral, non-political stance in the face of deep social injustice?

Or, fast-forward many years, should I talk about how I spent four and half years working in the International Politics Department of Aberystwyth University? Obviously, such sustained and direct contact with the Welsh School of critical security studies, and other key elements of critical IR theory, had a major impact on how a number of us who studied terrorism at Aberystwyth at the time articulated the ontology, epistemology, methodology, and praxis of CTS (Jackson et al. 2009). Alternately, should I include the individuals I met along the way who influenced me? Should I mention how meeting John Mueller and subsequently engaging with his work deeply influenced my understanding of the politics of fear and over-reaction to the terrorism threat in Western societies? Or how talking to Ken Booth forced me to try and understand the relevance of critical theory to security and terrorism? In truth, all of these experiences and encounters with a plethora of scholars profoundly shaped my outlook and values, and my intellectual orientation. All of them were moments along the way to where I am now, and all of them can be seen in the kind of CTS research and teaching I practice today.

In other words, any narration of how I came to write a book about how the language of terrorism and counterterrorism constructed a particular response called "war on terror," and how along with others, I came to launch a new journal, start a new scholarly network, and coalesce new writing projects about a critical approach to terrorism, will of necessity be limited, partial, subjective, distorted by time and subsequent events, and likely, contested by others involved. Nevertheless, I will attempt to tell it, albeit in a partial, disjointed form. It is best seen as a collection of moments and serendipitous encounters, revelatory and inspiring in effect, but mostly lacking in any sense of clear linearity, except that reflected through a post hoc narrativization. Together, these moments propelled me forward, launching me in a highly deliberate and determined endeavor to change the way the field of terrorism studies conceptualizes, understands, studies, and responds to—ultimately, how it narrates—the thing we currently call "terrorism."

A Moment...

It is the year 2000. I am sitting in a seminar room full of staff and graduate students at the University of Queensland. I have just given a talk on political development and violent conflict in weak states as part of a job interview process. I can't find a permanent academic post in New Zealand, so I am applying everywhere and anywhere that is advertising. This is my first interview for a permanent academic position.

I am feeling confident. I am answering questions with fluency and verve. Someone asks me what I think about the third debate inaugurated by the rise of constructivism in IR. I am concentrating hard, but I don't really understand the question. I feel a huge chasm open up beneath me. I flush with shame and mumble my way through an entirely irrelevant answer. I can see that people are embarrassed for me, which only adds to my mortification. I have not heard of constructivism; or at least, I have no real idea what it is. What is it, exactly, and is it important? You mean there's more to IR than realism and idealism?

Later, my sense of embarrassment increases as I start to investigate and discover how the field of IR has lately been convulsed by debates about the ontology and epistemology of social science, reflecting debates engendered by postmodernism in other fields. How could I not know this? How could I have studied to the level of a Ph.D. in IR and not know about constructivism? I throw myself into reading everything I can get my hands on related to the topic. I start with all the current introductory textbooks and then delve into Alexander Wendt, Nicholas Onuf, Peter Katzenstein, Emanuel Adler, David Campbell, Roxanne Doty, Jutta Weldes, and many others who write about or use constructivism in their work. I learn about critical theory and post-structuralism, ontology and epistemology, social theory and praxis. And in the process, I learn how important language is to the constitution of reality and to politics; and what social practices are; and how knowledge and power are connected; and how facts never speak for themselves but are interpreted through a pre-existing epistemic prism which shapes their meaning; and how discourses are things which produce effects and can be studied; and how political violence is as much the result of material structures as it is of social structures and discourses; and so on.

In other words, I find a whole new way of understanding the world, and a new language through which to grasp and express it. I realize that all the things which we take for granted in IR—states, war, sovereignty, anarchy, democracy, law, terrorism—are not free-standing, objectively existing, ontologically stable things; rather, they are produced in and through the way we talk about, perceive, and act towards them. They are social facts, not brute facts, even if most people, and many IR scholars, treat them as brute facts through assigning them measurable numerical values, for example, or narrating them in authoritative-sounding ways. I come to realize that "terrorism" is a social fact, which changes the entire story of terrorism I once believed in—and the story that most terrorism studies scholars believe in.

A Moment...

It is September 9, 2001. I am browsing the For Sale section of the University Bookshop in Dunedin, New Zealand, looking for anything that I might add to the small collection of books I own which I could use for class preparation. I am a teaching fellow, akin to an adjunct professor, poorly paid and working to contract. I still haven't found a permanent academic position, even though it's been two years since I finished my Ph.D. and I have had several unsuccessful job interviews. I am in the middle of a job interview process right now. After five years of being a contract teaching fellow, a permanent position has come up in the Politics Department where I work. I made the short-list, and gave a public lecture earlier today; tomorrow is the formal interview.

I spin the book stand and a title pops out at me: *Terror and Taboo: The Fables, Follies, and Faces of Terrorism* by Joseba Zulaika and William Douglass. Terrorism; it's a very important topic. It's a form of political violence, which, along with so-called "new wars," has been garnering some serious attention in the field recently. I have been rethinking the focus of my research, anyway, away from international conflict resolution where I have been focused for the past few years. My doctoral thesis involved a statistical analysis of the comparative success rates and correlational determinants of negotiation and mediation in violent international disputes since 1945. For years, I was the research assistant and mentee to Jacob Bercovitch's Correlates of Mediation project. It was widely expected after my doctorate that I would continue with empirically driven conflict-resolution research and make a name for myself as one of Jacob's acolytes.

But I've been feeling a little uneasy, in part because I can't easily reconcile the detailed, theoretically infused research I did on political development in the African state for my Masters degree, with the straightforward confidence of the conflict-resolution field of my doctorate. The kind of political violence I studied in Africa came from deep historical roots in colonialism, economic structures of exploitation, class formation processes, institutional malformation, and continuing forms of neo-colonialism, among others. Each case was highly specific to its historical, geographical, cultural, political, and economic context. It could not be reduced to categories of "ethnic conflict," "ideological conflict," "interests," "values," and so on. It could not be assigned a number and then simply correlated with a conflict-resolution method.

As a consequence, I am seriously wondering if we really do understand what causes contemporary violent conflict in the first place, and whether it is therefore advisable to recommend one conflict-resolution strategy or another before we fully understand the roots of the problem. Can we suggest a remedy before we have properly diagnosed the illness? Should I be focusing on negotiation, mediation, peacekeeping, reconciliation, and other forms of conflict resolution before I even properly understand what leads to organized violent conflict? Could it be that so much of the failure we see in international conflict-resolution efforts is due to faulty, de-contextualized conflict analysis? As a result, I have recently been much more interested in the nature and causes of violent political conflict, including intrastate wars and terrorism.

As I go to the teller and pay for my new book on terrorism, I am unaware of how the world will change in the coming days. I am also unaware of how this book will change me at the same moment when the world is changing—and how serendipitous this moment is. I have yet to realize that this book will give me a new perspective in keeping with my intellectual evolution towards constructivism, and change everything I think I already know about "terrorism" and political violence. More importantly, it will change how I understand the events of September 11, 2001 and its aftermath; it will help explain to me why the United States (and so much of the world) reacted in the way it did—because the "discourse of terrorism" was already well established, materially and epistemically, and it left little room for other kinds of responses which weren't based on counter-violence. It will also help to explain why the study of terrorism is ruled by state-centrism, an unspoken "taboo," and ritual moral condemnation, and why most "terrorism experts" have never even spoken to a "terrorist." As I took my book out the door, I didn't realize that this was in many respects, the first major "critical terrorism studies" book which had been published, and that it would be the book which would have the greatest influence on my thinking about the subject.

The Moment...

It is September 11, 2001 and I am watching the Twin Towers burn while sitting in the student union at the University of Otago. They keep showing the moment the second plane hits the tower, over and over again. My emotions are in turmoil. Last night I received a call from the chair of the appointment committee which informed me that I had come second and another candidate would be offered the position first. I was out of a job and my five years at the University of Otago would be coming to an end. At this moment, I didn't have anywhere else to go to. What would happen to me? But really, what were my problems compared to what I was watching? Thousands had obviously died and people were leaping to their certain deaths from the top of the building in their absolute desperation; I, on the other hand, might have to go on unemployment benefit. I had no right to feel upset about my life.

Later, after watching the Towers collapse and once again feeling conflicted about the way this tragedy had completely eclipsed my personal misfortune, I return to my office. I pick up Paul Roger's (2000) *Losing Control*, which I have been reading recently to better understand the emerging global security context and the seemingly reflexive Western response to threats. I remember something Rogers said about the first attack on the World Trade Center in 1993. What was it? Oh, yes:

> Take...the case of the World Trade Center bombing. If that attack had had its intended effect the results would have been calamitous, not just for the City of New York, but for the United States as a whole. But would it have resulted in any rethinking of security? Probably not. A more likely result would have been a massive and violent military reaction against any groups anywhere in the Middle East thought to have had even the slightest connection with the attack. (Rogers 2000, 118)

I make photocopies of the page and put them into every mailbox in the staffroom. I'm not entirely sure why. I just have to share it. A few weeks later, when the US starts bombing Afghanistan, it makes more sense; in 2003, I recollect it as prophesy. But that night, my wife asks me why terrorism isn't my main research focus. She thinks this attack will be world-changing, and I need to get ahead of it. I can't really disagree with her. I pick up Zulaika and Douglass's *Terror and Taboo* and start to read ...

Andrew Silke (2004) would later report on how the September 11, 2001 attacks provided the impetus for a whole generation of scholars to suddenly switch their focus to terrorism studies. Overnight, a whole new breed of "instant experts" in terrorism was born. I was one of these scholars, shocked into it through the visceral images of the day and a strong suspicion (based on Paul Rogers's assessment) of what was to come. Although, in part because I witnessed Rogers's predictions reach their fulfillment in the subsequent "war on terror," I never claimed any terrorism *expertise* for myself, and actually ended up leading a kind of "counter-expertise" movement (see Jackson 2015b).

A Moment...

It is late April 2004. The Abu Ghraib scandal has just broken and I am looking at *those* pictures. I am appalled and deeply disturbed. Those are US military personnel dragging naked men around like dogs on a lead, giving the thumbs up to corpses, piling hooded naked men on top of each other to make a grotesque human pyramid, making a man with a Klan hood stand on a box with his arms out. I realize that it shocks and disgusts me, but it also doesn't. I am appalled at the bestiality of the behavior and the profound inhumanity it is evidence of, but I totally understand the images because they exemplify—indeed, they embody—the discourse of terrorism which Zulaika and Douglass (1996) wrote so eloquently about, and which I have been studying for some time now.

Senior officials from the Bush administration, the Blair and Howard governments, the mainstream media, and a great many scholars in terrorism studies—practically everyone—have been saying that terrorists are "savages" and "animals" for years now. Well, there the terrorists are, recreated by their captors as exactly that: animals on a leash. They've been saying that terrorists are "the faceless enemies of freedom." Once again, there they are, faceless in their green hoods, squirming like parasites in a great pile of white, naked bodies. They've been saying that terrorism is a modern "scourge" which must be eradicated. Here is the naked man, covered in what looks like shit, his arms out; here is the dead terrorist, his captors smiling because one more terrorist has been eradicated from the earth.

It is at this moment that I fully understand the power of language and discourse to create and constitute the reality it purports to describe. I can literally see on the screen in front of me how a series of statements from a set of powerful actors can create the context in which the Abu Ghraib night-shift scandal becomes possible. I grasp in a much deeper way how words and language and narrative can never be neutral or objective, but how they are reality-making in their utterance. I understand that this is how "terrorism," and "counterterrorism," has been made into a real material thing in the new millennium.

I also realized that because of the way in which "terrorism" and "terrorists" have been discursively constructed in the current war on terror, and even before that, in the terrorism industry, that what happened at Abu Ghraib was predictable, if not inevitable—as was Guantanamo Bay, water-boarding, rendition, kill teams, signature strikes, mass surveillance, force-feeding, and everything else that has since come with counterterrorism. The terrorist threat and the response—the war on terror—had been constructed in a way that made all these events possible, even likely. Furthermore, my background in conflict resolution told me that this would not remain a one-sided affair for very long; in the face of such horrific violence, especially as it was directed against people who patently had nothing to do with the events of 9/11, there would be a violent reaction sooner or later. This is how violence works; while it can produce submission and acquiescence in some, more often it produces resistance and counter-violence.

At this point, I realized that we needed a kind of terrorism studies that could help us better understand how Abu Ghraib, Guantanamo Bay, torture, and Madrid, became possible. That is, we needed an approach that recognized the way in which language, discourse, and practice were intimately bound together, and that how we reached the present moment in the "war on terror" was not fixed or inevitable, but socially constructed by agents, and therefore, contingent. We needed a better "history of the present" of terrorism and counterterrorism, if we were to properly understand how it became possible to invade two countries, kill more than a million innocent people, torture thousands, render hundreds homeless, and assassinate people based on a signature profile across the world—all in response to a single, admittedly devastating, terrorist attack.

I also realized that we needed a terrorism studies which took seriously the terror unleashed by states; we needed to acknowledge that states could be terrorists too, and more often than not, were. And we needed to explore how non-state terrorism was often a weak imitation of the violence meted out by states, and often, it was a direct response to it. We needed a terrorism studies which acknowledged the dynamic relationship between state and non-state violence—between terrorism and counterterrorism.

Finally, I felt that we needed a terrorism studies firmly rooted in ethics, conflict resolution, and a more realistic understanding of the nature and effects of violence, including the "legitimate" violence used to counter the "illegitimate" violence we disapproved of. We needed to consider that counterterrorism could, and should, be conducted on an ethical basis, according to established moral and legal principles, with conflict resolution rather than "national security" as its goal, and rooted in a systematic and realistic evaluation of its effectiveness in reducing the amount of political violence in the world. We needed a terrorism studies that questioned what was wrong with the war on terror and the dominant way of responding to acts of terrorism. We needed a terrorism studies that took seriously the impossibility of separating means and ends in social action, that recognized the limits of using violence to create security, and that took seriously the efficacy of nonviolent responses to terrorism and the relevance of the guiding concept of emancipation.

The problem in 2004 was that, apart from a few lonely voices scattered across different disciplines and fields, there was no systematically articulated approach to terrorism studies which would take in these perspectives and values. For the most part, the main terrorism journals published articles which focused almost exclusively on Al Qaeda as the main continuing terrorist threat (Silke 2004); they had little to say about how "terrorism" and the "war on terror" were socially constructed, and to what ideological and material effect. Nor did they focus much on counterterrorism (except to offer helpful suggestions to state counterterrorists) and why it seemed to so regularly produce egregious human rights abuses. In general, there was very little serious questioning of the broader terrorism discourse.

As I was to discover later when I moved to Aberystwyth in 2007, there was a "critical" approach to security studies which questioned the dominant national security paradigm and its practices. But, in 2004 at least, the debates engendered by the rise of critical security studies (CSS) appeared to have largely passed the terrorism studies field by.

Fellow Travelers

One of the important contributions of constructivism in IR has been a deeper understanding of how change occurs, and how new norms arise. Integral to the rise of new normative frameworks is the role played by so-called "norm entrepreneurs"—agents who work tirelessly to introduce new concepts and language, new ways of looking at an issue, and new normative prescriptions for action. But how does one become this kind of entrepreneur; what makes someone decide to try and launch a new approach within an established field? Why did I think it was possible to articulate and then institutionalize a new approach within terrorism studies? I certainly didn't start out thinking my colleagues and I would publish a sort of manifesto for critical terrorism studies (see Jackson 2007; Jackson et al. 2009), establish a new Working Group within BISA, and launch a new journal—among others.

Obviously, all these initiatives grew out of a multitude of factors and encounters, including all those already mentioned. In part, I was able to do them because I had a naïve optimism which is part of my nature, and perhaps also, my culture. In New Zealand, we call it the can-do attitude: the notion that with the right attitude and nothing more than a piece of Number 8 wire (widely used in farming), almost anything can be fixed or achieved. You just need to "give it a go." In 2005, following a life-changing conversation with my colleague at the University of Manchester, Rorden Wilkinson, I decided to "give it a go" and challenge the existing terrorism field.

In the corridor, after a staff meeting, Rorden listened patiently to my complaints about the field of terrorism studies, and the dissatisfaction I felt at the current scholarship as published in the field's main journals. Then he told me that there were two types of scholars: those that followed the current debates in order to contribute to them, and those that led or started new debates. He said, if you don't like the existing journals, why don't you start a new one and try leading a new debate about terrorism and counterterrorism? It was a revelatory moment. I was stunned. It simply hadn't occurred to me. Why not try and lead a new debate, indeed? What was stopping me? What was the worst that could happen? I suppose the publishers could say no, and my articles could be rejected. But so what? That's normal in academia.

In the following days, with a blithe sense of optimism, I started to plan the new venture. I drew up a proposal for a new academic journal on terrorism, contacted an eminent group of terrorism scholars for the editorial board, and sent it to the top five journal publishers. I know now that it was a kind of serendipity that the new journal proposal was sent by one publisher to Marie Breen Smyth who had recently been appointed head of the Centre for the Study of Radicalisation and Contemporary Political Violence at Aberystwyth University. In short order, she and her colleague, Jeroen Gunning, contacted me as a potential fellow traveler in the world of critical approaches to the study of terrorism. They too were dissatisfied with the current state of the field and were looking for others who would join them to shake things up. Jeroen had recently established the world's first Masters degree in critical approaches to the study of terrorism.

Out of this happy coincidence, a plethora of events, activities, and developments soon occurred, all aimed at galvanizing a new approach to the study of terrorism. Having found each other, we felt hopeful that we could, at the very least, kick-start a set of debates within the field which touched on key issues of ontology, epistemology, methodology, and ethics, similar to the debates which had long been occurring within CSS.

It wasn't long before a great many other scholars and doctoral students joined with us, and CTS grew into the sort of collective project it is today.

Conclusion: Looking Forward Back

In the medium term, critical terrorism studies came out of my attempts to get to grips with the significance of constructivism, and the dawning realization that much of what we think of as fixed and hard structures are in fact, social constructions. It was given more specific form and articulation by Zulaika and Douglass's post-structural, anthropologically infused deconstruction of the American terrorism discourse and the academic field of terrorism studies of the late 1980s and early 1990s. And it was propelled into concrete entrepreneurial action by a corridor conversation in Manchester and a serendipitous meeting of fellow travelers in Aberystwyth. Of course, it also has deeper roots in my own ontological narrative, and the experiences I had growing up; my concern for human rights, social justice, nonviolence, and conflict resolution infuses pretty much everything I write on any subject.

So what's the ending of the story of CTS? Of my own story? My hope is that the story of CTS is only in its early phase and not its final stanza. As I have argued elsewhere (Jackson 2015b), I believe that the next stage of CTS will be its moving beyond the walls of academia and into the public sphere. As long as CTS remains a primarily intellectual movement which only debates with other scholars, it will be limited in its value and a disappointment to me. CTS scholars need to find ways of transmitting their research to the wider public and getting it into the public sphere where it can be used in debate, activism, and resistance to the ongoing abuses of counterterrorism. It needs to start making a concrete difference in the world.

In direct response to this imperative, and as I have detailed elsewhere (Jackson 2015c), one of my later CTS research publications was a novel entitled *Confessions of a Terrorist* (2014). This takes the idea of narratives of terrorism even further, as it attempts to share what I have learned about terrorism and political violence in a fictional narrative form for a broad, general audience. As I and others have tried to argue (see Jackson 2015c), there is real value in all kinds of stories, and terrorism studies, as with IR more generally, could benefit a lot from taking the narrative form more seriously.

References

Anderson, B. (1983) *Imagined Communities: Reflections on and Spread of Nationalism*. London: Verso.

Baker, M. (2006) *Translation and Conflict: A Narrative Account*. London: Routledge.

George, A. (1991) "The Discipline of Terrorology," in A. George (ed.), *Western State Terrorism*. Cambridge: Polity Press, 76–101.

Gunning, J., and R. Jackson (2011) "What's so 'Religious' about 'Religious Terrorism'?," *Critical Studies on Terrorism*, 4(3): 369–88.

Herman, E., and G. O'Sullivan (1991) "'Terrorism' as Ideology and Cultural Industry," in A. George (ed.), *Western State Terrorism*, Cambridge: Polity Press, 40–52.

Jackson, R. (2005) *Writing the War on Terrorism: Language, Politics and Counterterrorism*. Manchester: Manchester University Press.

Jackson, R. (2007) "The Core Commitments of Critical Terrorism Studies," *European Political Science*, 6(3): 244–51.

Jackson, R. (2009) "The 9/11 Attacks and the Social Construction of a National Narrative," in Matthew J. Morgan (ed.), *The Impact of 9–11 on the Media, Arts and Entertainment: The Day that Changed Everything?* New York: Palgrave Macmillan, 25–35.

Jackson, R. (2012a) "How I was Radicalized; or, the Effects of Opening your Eyes," available online at <https://richardjacksonterrorismblog.wordpress.com/2012/10/29/how-i-was-radicalized-or-the-effects-of-opening-your-eyes>.

Jackson, R. (2012b) "My Journey to Pacifism," available online at <https://richardjacksonterrorismblog.wordpress.com/2012/12/29/my-journey-to-pacifism>.

Jackson, R. (2014) *Confessions of a Terrorist*. London: Zed.

Jackson, R. (2015a) "Bin Laden's Ghost and the Epistemological Crisis of Counter-Terrorism," in S. Jeffords and F. al-Sumait (eds), *After bin Laden: Global Media and the Representation of Terrorism*. Urbana, IL: University of Illinois Press, 3–19.

Jackson, R. (2015b) "On How to be a Collective Intellectual—Critical Terrorism Studies (CTS) and the Countering of Hegemonic Discourse," in C. Bueger and T. Villumsen Berling (eds), *Capturing Security Expertise: Concepts, Power, Practice*. London: Routledge, 186–203.

Jackson, R. (2015c) "Terrorism, Taboo and Discursive Resistance: The Agonistic Potential of the Terrorism Novel," *International Studies Review*, 17(3): 396–413.

Jackson, R., ed. (2016) *The Routledge Handbook of Critical Terrorism Studies*. Abingdon: Routledge.

Jackson, R., M. Breen Smyth, and J. Gunning, eds. (2009) *Critical Terrorism Studies: A New Research Agenda*. Abingdon: Routledge.

Jackson, R., L. Jarvis, J. Gunning, and M. Breen Smyth (2011) *Terrorism: A Critical Introduction*. Basingstoke: Palgrave-Macmillan.

Laqueur, W. (2001) *A History of Terrorism*. New York: Transaction Publishers.

Law, R. (2009) *Terrorism: A History*, Cambridge: Polity Press.

Mueller, J. (2006) *Overblown: How Politicians and the Terrorism Industry Inflate National Security Threats and Why we Believe Them*. New York: Free Press.

Oslender, U. (2007) "The Resurfacing of the Public Intellectual: Towards the Proliferation of Public Spaces of Critical Intervention," *ACME: An International E-Journal for Critical Geographies*, 6(1): 98–123.

Rapoport, D. (2004) "The Four Waves of Modern Terrorism," in A. Cronin and J. Ludes (eds), *Attacking Terrorism: Elements of a Grand Strategy*. Washington, DC: Georgetown University Press, 46–73.

Reid, E. (1993) "Terrorism Research and the Diffusion of Ideas," *Knowledge and Policy*, 6(1): 17–37.

Reid, E. (1997) "Evolution of a Body of Knowledge: An Analysis of Terrorism Research," *Information Processing and Management*, 33(1): 91–106.

Rogers, P. (2000) *Losing Control: Global Security in the 21st Century*. London: Pluto.

Silke, A., ed. (2004) *Research on Terrorism: Trends, Achievements and Failures*. London: Frank Cass.

Stampnitzky, L. (2013) *Disciplining Terror: How Experts and Others Invented Terrorism*. Cambridge: Cambridge University Press.

Sterling, C. (1981) *The Terror Network: The Secret War of International Terrorism*. New York: Henry Holt & Co.

White, H. (1973) *Metahistory: The Historical Imagination in Nineteenth-Century Europe*. Baltimore, MD: Johns Hopkins University Press.

White, H. (1987) *The Content of the Form: Narrative Discourse and Historical Representation*. Baltimore, MD: Johns Hopkins University Press.

Zulaika, J., and W. Douglass (1996) *Terror and Taboo: The Follies, Fables, and Faces of Terrorism*. London: Routledge.

Index

Note: References to Notes will contain the letter 'n' following the Note number. Tables are indicated by an italic 't', respectively, following the page number